TEXTBOOK RENTAL SERVICE

a. For your protection,
   sign your name below.

b. DO NOT ABUSE THIS TEXTBOOK.

c. Return this textbook before
   each semester's deadline.

d. A penalty   per book
   will be charged for late
   returns.

NAME	ADDRESS & PHONE

EASTERN ILLINOIS UNIVERSITY
CHARLESTON, ILLINOIS 61920

EDUCATIONAL
RESEARCH

Fourth Edition

EDUCATIONAL RESEARCH
An Introduction

Walter R. Borg
UTAH STATE UNIVERSITY

Meredith Damien Gall
UNIVERSITY OF OREGON

Longman
New York & London

Educational Research
An Introduction

Longman Inc., 95 Church Street, White Plains, N.Y. 10601
Associated companies, branches, and representatives
throughout the world.

Developmental Editor: Nicole Benevento
Editorial and Design Supervisor: Joan Matthews
Production Supervisor: Ferne Y. Kawahara
Manufacturing Supervisor: Marion Hess
Composition: The Clarinda Company
Printing and Binding: Interstate Book Manufacturers

Library of Congress Cataloging in Publication Data

Borg, Walter R.
  Educational research.

  Includes bibliographies and index.
  1. Educational research. I. Gall, Meredith D.,
1942-   . II. Title.
LB1028.B6   1983   370'.7'8   82-20849
ISBN 0-582-28246-2

MANUFACTURED IN THE UNITED STATES OF AMERICA
Printing: 9 8 7 6 5   Year: 91 90 89 88 87 86 85

Acknowledgments

We express our appreciation to Professor Art Coladarci for his helpful comments on the third edition of *Educational Research*. His criticism was valuable to us in preparing the current edition. We thank Dean Diane Reinhard for sharing her ideas on the current state of evaluation research. We are grateful to Professor N. L. Gage for sponsoring Meredith Gall's appointment as visiting scholar at Stanford University, where part of this book was revised. We are also grateful to Dr. Joy Gall, who prepared the indexes for the book.

Contents

PART IV. RESEARCH DESIGN AND METHODOLOGY   351

To the Instructor

Educational research bears scant resemblance to the field of study that existed in 1963 when the first edition of this text was published. Since that time, the body of knowledge concerning educational research methods and the sophistication of the research process have increased greatly. One of our goals in the earlier editions was to provide the student with the essentials needed to carry through the entire research process, from identifying the problem to writing the thesis, and to introduce every research technique in common use so that the student could develop an understanding of educational research as a whole. A further goal was to present the essentials in clear, straightforward language that the average student could understand. These continue to be our goals, but we must confess that as educational research has become more complex and sophisticated, it has become much more difficult to achieve these ends. Our decision to add learning aids such as the Overview and Objectives sections to the third edition was influenced to a considerable extent by our feeling that as the field becomes more complex, the average student must be given more and more help in learning enough about educational research to plan and conduct research and to be an intelligent user of the research done by others.

Those of you who are familiar with the third edition will note that extensive revisions have been made in this fourth edition. Chapter 1 has been completely rewritten. One of our goals for chapter 1 has been to give students an insight into the excitement and satisfaction that doing educational research can bring to the investigator. We have never been satisfied with our attempts to achieve this goal, but we keep trying. Perhaps this goal can best be achieved by the instructor. Certainly, discussing the problems that the instructor has encountered in his own investigations can do much to breathe life into the research process.

Chapter 4, which deals with the ethical and legal constraints within which the educational researcher must work, has been extensively rewritten simply because considerable change has occurred in this area since the publication of the third edition.

We have also added a number of new topics to other chapters and have expanded our coverage of those areas in which there have been advances in recent years. For example, in chapter 6 we added a section on integrative research reviews and meta-analysis. We believe that a meta-analysis of an important research question can make a very valuable contribution to the field and hope to see more graduate students employ this process in their theses and dissertations. Other topics that have been added or given more thorough coverage include theory-based research, replication, deception, ways of maintaining confidentiality, the Delphi technique, the telephone interview, case study methodology, and the use of microcomputers in educational research.

Since the field of educational research has expanded to the point where it is no longer possible to cover all of the important aspects of research methodology in an introductory text, we have made a major effort to provide more annotated references that will help the student who needs additional information on some specific topic such as developing survey questionnaires, training interviewers, or conducting ethnographic research. We have tried to locate the most up-to-date sources for inclusion in the annotated reference sections, but have not hesitated to refer students to some of the older sources when we feel these provide valuable information. Similarly, we have retained some examples from the third edition when we have been unable to find a more recent example that we feel is as clear and to the point.

We have also included a great many more citations in the fourth edition. For example, in the third edition the chapter on survey research contained 23 footnotes; in the fourth edition there are 58. Many of the footnotes refer the student to recent examples of the kinds of research being discussed; others direct the student to sources that treat specific topics in much greater depth than is possible in an introductory text.

It has been a difficult problem to introduce students to the many new concepts that have become important in educational research without expanding the book into an encyclopedia. We are sure that you will find some topics in the fourth edition that you feel could have been omitted and others that you feel should have been given expanded treatment. Our past experience, however, indicates little consensus among persons who teach the research methods course concerning the amount of emphasis a given topic should receive. We note with regret that, despite our best efforts, the book has grown a bit larger. This seems an almost inevitable result of our attempt to give reasonable coverage to a rapidly expanding field of knowledge. Entire books are devoted to many of the topics that we deal with in a few pages, such as research ethics, meta-analysis, use of volunteer subjects, criterion-referenced measurement, and evaluation research—to mention but a few. We have not been satisfied to merely mention such topics in a few sentences because such cursory treatment fails to provide students with the knowledge base they need to understand the educational research process and apply it to their own research. Most students in education take only a single course in research methods, and if they do not get a good foundation in this course, it seems unlikely that they will ever become competent either in doing research or applying the research of others to their problems. Another reason we have tried to give a substantial introduction to all topics related to educational research is that many students keep this book for reference after completing the course. This is evident from the fact that few copies come onto the used book market.

The preparation of a text in educational research methods poses another problem because it is desirable to give the student a reasonable insight into statistical tools and measurement techniques as they apply to research, but to avoid covering the same ground typically dealt with in courses in statistics and educational evaluation. To deal with this problem we have followed essentially the same strategy used in previous editions. That is, we have emphasized the application of measurement and statistical techniques to problems of educational research. We have tried to give students enough information about these techniques so that they can recognize situations in which they should seek further information. Our treatment of statistical techniques continues to be as nontechnical as possible. We have tried to relate statistical techniques to the research designs with which they are commonly associated, but have avoided covering computation and formulas, which we regard as more appropriate for courses in statistics. It is our opinion that students should have at least one elementary course in statistics and one in educational measurement before taking the research methods course. However, we realize that prerequisites and degree requirements differ greatly from university to university. Therefore, we have tried to write this book so that students not having these prerequisites could still understand the book and gain a reasonable mastery of educational research methods.

The fourth edition has been reorganized to some extent and divided into five parts. The chapter concerned with opportunities in educational research has been moved up to the front of the book and is now chapter 2. We felt that this chapter, along with our new chapter 1, would give students a good orientation to the field before they start learning about the specific steps in the research process.

Beginning with chapter 3, we have organized the chapters in the same sequence that the student follows in conducting a research project, starting with the selection of a research problem and ending with preparation of the research report. Nevertheless, we believe that students should read through the entire book before attempting to plan and carry out their own research projects. Since each phase of a research project is tied very closely to every other phase, it is not possible to develop a text that permits the student to become fully competent in the initial steps of research before having gained some knowledge and insight into later steps. For example, a critical review of previous research is one of the early steps that the student must take in planning and carrying out a research project. However, the student is severely limited in the ability to evaluate previous research without some understanding of measurement, research design, and statistical analysis. In this edition we have again placed the chapter concerned with the critical review of research literature near the front of the book. We feel that it is desirable for the student to start this effort early in research training. We would suggest that the instructor assign several research articles for critical review during the course. The process of discussing articles in class and giving students feedback on their reviews will help a great deal in furthering their skills in this important area. As the student progresses through the course, the instructor's standards for the critical review assignments can be raised gradually so that a student who finishes the course will have developed sufficient skills in critical review to be prepared to review the literature for a thesis or dissertation. The authors have used this strategy in teaching their own research methods classes for several years and have found it to be effective.[1]

We have continued the pattern established in the third edition of starting each chapter with a brief overview of the chapter along with a list of specific learner objectives. A brief orientation is also provided at the beginning of each of the five parts. Because of the tremendous knowledge base that students must have before they can start functioning as educational researchers, you will find that the majority of the objectives relate to content mastery. You will also probably find that while some of these objectives are relevant to the needs and goals of your students, some are not. We would urge you to review the objectives carefully with your students, pointing out those that you regard as important and those that you feel are not important for your students. It may also be necessary for you to add objectives that we have not covered.

At the end of each chapter (except chapter 2) you will find a brief self-check test made up of ten multiple-choice questions. These few items are designed to help students check whether they understand a sampling of the material covered in the chapter, and are not intended to provide a coverage of all of the chapter objectives. You also will find a few application problems at the end of each chapter, except chapter 2. These problems give students an opportunity to apply some of what they have learned in the chapter to problems frequently encountered by educational researchers. Again, the problems are meant to cover only a sampling of the chapter objectives. Our experience with these short tests, however, indicates that they are useful in helping students determine whether they understand and can apply the concepts that they have learned.

Note that we have included a Suggestion Sheet on the back end-paper of the book (after the index). The purpose of this sheet is to obtain feedback from students that we can use in subsequent revision of the book. Each student is asked to give feedback on one chapter, although he or she is free to comment on other chapters, too. The end of each chapter contains a brief statement indicating which students are to make comments on that chapter.

Please encourage students to complete the Suggestion Sheet. It is designed so that it can be torn out and mailed as a self-stamped envelope.

---

1. An *Instructor's Manual* containing a test-item file, sample assignments, and suggestions for teaching the course is available free of charge from the publisher.

To an increasing degree educational researchers are utilizing the research methodologies that have been developed in the other behavioral sciences such as psychology, sociology, and anthropology. Therefore, although this book is aimed primarily at graduate students in the various areas of education, many of the research methods are equally relevant to students in other behavioral sciences. It is our belief that behavioral scientists are becoming more and more aware of the methodologies used by their peers in the other behavioral sciences. Although the main focus of each behavioral science will continue to be different, it seems likely that the same broad foundation of research methodology will undergird all these sciences.

We hope this new revision meets your students' needs. We have already started collecting material for our next revision and would appreciate any comments or suggestions you can give us to improve this book.

Walter R. Borg
Meredith D. Gall

To the Student

The broad goal of this book is to help you, the graduate student in education, learn the essentials needed to carry out the entire research process from identifying your research problem to writing your thesis or dissertation. Since the research methods employed in the other behavioral sciences such as psychology and sociology are often similar to those used in education, students in these disciplines will also find this book helpful.

In educational research methods classes we have found two major groups of students. The larger group includes those who plan to carry out a research project and write a thesis or dissertation. There are, however, many students who use this book who are more interested in understanding and using the results of educational research than in conducting their own research. The knowledge base to be gained from this book is sufficient for students in both groups. The student who plans to be primarily a user of research information in the future needs this knowledge base in order to evaluate critically the research of others and translate available research evidence into plans of action that can be carried out in the schools. In order to evaluate research critically the student must know a great deal about the research process, must be able to identify strengths and weaknesses in the research, and must be capable of making judgments as to how these strengths and weaknesses might have affected the findings reported by the researcher.

In the past twenty-five years educational research has become much more complex and sophisticated. This has made it possible for researchers to make increasingly valuable contributions to educational practice, but it has also made the task of the graduate student in mastering this field more difficult. We have tried to make this task easier by writing this book in clear, straightforward language. For example, although we feel it necessary to tell you something about the more advanced statistical procedures that are now being used to analyze educational research data, we have attempted to do this without using technical language, mathematical jargon, or formulas. We have also tried to keep the book down to a manageable length by including only that information we feel is essential to the student. For example, entire textbooks, some larger than this book, have been written in areas such as survey research and evaluation research. In this book, these topics are each covered in one chapter. One result of our effort to weed out unimportant information has been that the amount of important information per page is often quite high, and you will find it difficult to assimilate the information in a single reading.

Since many research concepts and techniques are difficult for the beginning researcher to understand, we have included many examples to illustrate how these techniques have been applied in specific situations.

In order to help you organize the field of educational research in your own mind, we have included an introduction to each part of the book, an overview of each chapter, and a set of objectives for each chapter. The overview is designed to give you a quick picture of what you will learn in the chapter. This will help you learn and will also help you fit each chapter into the overall research picture. While the overview is aimed at providing a general orientation, the objectives tell you the specific information you should get from the chapter. All these objectives are not of equal importance. Which are most important to you depends on the goals you wish to achieve by taking the research methods course. If you are interested primarily in becoming a competent user of research to help solve day-to-day problems, your goals will differ somewhat from the goals needed to make research a major part of your educational career. You will find that most of the objectives are concerned with content mastery. This is because you need a large foundation of knowledge before you can move on to the application of this knowledge to carrying out research projects or using the research of others.

In order to help you get feedback on how well you have mastered the content of the chapter, you will also find a brief multiple-choice self-check test at the end of each chapter. These tests do not cover all important content in the chapter, but cover a sample of this content. If you do well on the self-check test, you probably know most other information covered in the chapter. The application problems at the end of each chapter help you determine whether you can apply the concepts you have learned to practical problems and questions frequently encountered by the beginning researcher. Again, the application problems provide only a small sample of possible applications that relate to what you have learned. However, the self-check test and application problems, although brief, should be sufficient to help you decide whether you have mastered the chapter or whether you should devote more study to it.

We would recommend that you use the following strategy for studying this book:

1. Read the overviews and part introductions.

2. Read the objectives for each chapter at least twice to fix them firmly in your mind. This will focus your attention on the most important content in the chapter.

3. Read a few pages of the text each day in order to keep abreast of the instructor's presentation. As you read the text, underline or in some other manner indicate the most important points and review these points frequently as your reading carries you further into the book. You should also make marginal notes as needed and should mark for future reference information that is especially pertinent to your own research plan. Watch for the terms in **bold-face;** these are important, and you should learn their meaning. As a rule, im-

portant terms are marked only the first time they are described or defined. Try to avoid falling behind in your reading of the text. Since the information level in this text is very high, you will find it difficult to master the important concepts if you try to read too large a segment of the text at a single sitting.

4. When you finish reading the chapter, read over the list of mistakes frequently made by beginning researchers. If you are planning your own research project, mark any of these that may be relevant.

5. Next, take the self-check test and check your answers. If you miss more than two of these items it may be wise to review again the main points that you have marked in the chapter.

6. Now, work through the application problems and again check your answers against the sample answers given in the back of the text.

7. Finally, turn back to the chapter objectives, read each one, and see if you have mastered the information related to that objective.

A good way to prepare for an examination is to read over the main points only (that is, the material you have underlined) for the chapters to be tested. This procedure will take much less time than you needed to read the chapters initially. After you have done this, work with another student who is taking the course. First, ask your fellow student questions based on the material you have underlined. Then, have your study mate ask you questions on the material he or she has underlined. Try to ask questions that require an understanding of the main ideas, not just a rote learning of important facts.

Finally, we have a request to make. We want very much to get your suggestions on how to improve this book in the future. The most useful suggestions are those that are specific. For example, it is difficult for us to use comments such as "this is a good book" or "this is a terrible book" in improving the next edition. On the other hand, specific comments such as "include more examples of null hypotheses" or "add a description of a study that used cluster sampling" can be very helpful.

We would like to get your specific suggestions on the entire book. However, this would take quite a bit of your time, so we are asking for your comments on only a single chapter. Which chapter you comment on will be determined by the first three letters of your last name. This will assure us of getting suggestions for improving all 21 chapters. Of course, if you want to comment on a different chapter or on more than one chapter, we will welcome all suggestions you can give us.

The Suggestion Sheet is printed on the back end-paper of the book (after the index) and can be cut out and made into a business reply mailer.

We hope you will find this book helpful not only in completing your graduate work but in your later career as well. Good luck!

Walter R. Borg
Meredith D. Gall

Reprint Acknowledgments

The material cited below has been reprinted from other publications. We thank the authors and publishers for granting us permission to excerpt from their work.

Table 1.1 is reprinted from Herbert J. Walberg, Diane Schiller, and Geneva D. Haertel, "The Quiet Revolution in Educational Research," *Phi Delta Kappan*, 1979, 61, 179–83. By permission of the publisher.

Table 1.3 is reprinted from Eisner, Elliot, "On the Differences between Scientific and Artistic Approaches to Qualitative Research." *Educational Researcher*, vol. 10, no. 4, 1981, pp. 5–9. Copyright 1981, American Educational Research Association, Washington, D.C. By permission of the publisher and author.

The excerpts on pp. 108–110 are reprinted from Committee on Scientific and Professional Ethics and Conduct, "Ethical Principles of Psychologists," *American Psychologist* 36 (1981): 633–38. Copyright 1981 by the American Psychological Association. Reprinted by permission of the publisher and author.

Figure 5.2 and the excerpt on p. 152 are reprinted from *Psychological Abstracts* 65 (April–June 1981): 882 and 931. These citations are printed with the permission of the American Psychological Association, publishers of *Psychological Abstracts* and the Psyc-INFO Database (Copyright © by the American Psychological Association), and may not be reproduced without their prior permission.

Table 6.1 is reprinted from Cooper, Harris M., "Scientific Guidelines for Conducting Integrative Research Reviews." *Review of Educational Research*, Summer 1982, vol. 52, no. 2, pp. 291–302. Copyright 1982, American Educational Research Association, Washington D.C. By permission of the publisher and author.

The outline on pp. 220–221 is adapted from Table 1 of R. L. Rosnow and D. J. Davis, "Demand Characteristics and the Psychological Experiment," *Et Cetera* 34 (1977): 301–313. By permission of the publisher and author.

The lists on pp. 252–253 and 255 are reprinted from Robert Rosenthal and Ralph L. Rosnow, *The Volunteer Subject*, New York: John Wiley & Sons, Inc., 1975, pp. 195–196 and 198–199. By permission of the publisher and author.

Table 8.2 is reprinted from G. C. Helmstadter, PRINCIPLES OF PSYCHOLOGICAL MEASUREMENT, © 1964, p. 85. Reprinted by permission of Prentice-Hall, Inc., Englewood Cliffs, N.J.

Figure 9.1 and Table 9.1 are reprinted from *The Eighth Mental Measurements Yearbook*, edited by Oscar K. Buros, by permission of the University of Nebraska Press, © 1978.

Table 10.4 and Figure 10.2 are reprinted from Leinhardt, Gaea, Leinhardt, Samuel,

"Exploratory Data Analysis: New Tools for the Analysis of Empirical Data." *Review of Research in Education,* vol. 8, 1980, pp. 89 and 92. Copyright 1980, American Educational Research Association, Washington, D.C. By permission of the publisher and author.

The excerpts on pp. 510–511 are reprinted from Sam Leles, "Using the Critical Incidents Technique to Develop a Theory of Educational Professionalism: An Exploratory Study," *Journal of Teacher Education* 19 (Spring 1968): 59–69. By permission of the publisher.

Table 13.1 is reprinted from Jackson, Gregg, and Cosca, Cecilia, "The Inequality of Educational Opportunity in the Southwest: An Observational Study of Ethnically Mixed Classrooms." *American Educational Research Journal,* vol. 11, 1974, pp. 219–229. Copyright 1980, American Educational Research Association, Washington, D.C. By permission of the publisher and author.

The excerpts on pp. 539–540 and 542 and Tables 13.2 and 13.6 are reprinted from Ralph E. Culler and Charles J. Holahan, "Test Anxiety and Academic Performance: The Effects of Study-Related Behaviors," *Journal of Educational Psychology* 72 (1980): 16–20. Copyright 1980 by the American Psychological Association. Reprinted by permission of the publisher and author.

Table 13.5 is reprinted from Patricia B. Elmore and Ellen S. Vasu, "Relationship between Selected Variables and Statistics Achievement: Building a Theoretical Model," *Journal of Educational Psychology* 72 (1980): 457–67. Copyright 1980 by the American Psychological Association. Reprinted by permission of the publisher and the author.

Tables 14.1, 14.2, and 14.3 are reprinted from Henriette M. Lahaderne, "Attitudinal and Intellectual Correlates of Attention: A Study of Four Sixth-Grade Classrooms," *Journal of Educational Psychology* 59 (1968): 320–24. Copyright 1968 by the American Psychological Association. Reprinted by permission of the publisher and author.

Table 14.4 is reprinted from Wayne Holtzman and William F. Brown, "Evaluating the Study Habits and Attitudes of High School Students," *Journal of Educational Psychology* 59 (1968): 404–9. Copyright 1968 by the American Psychological Association. Reprinted by permission of the publisher and author.

Table 14.9 is adapted and Table 14.10 is reprinted from Brush, Donald H., and Schoenfeldt, Lyle, "Patterns of College Grades across Curricular Areas: Some Implications for GAP as a Criterion." *American Educational Research Journal,* vol. 12, 1975, pp. 313–321. Copyright 1975, American Educational Research Association, Washington, D.C. By permission of the publisher and author.

Table 14.12 is reprinted from Lawrence R. Malnig, "Anxiety and Academic Prediction," *Journal of Counseling Psychology* 11 (1964): 72–75. Copyright 1964 by the American Psychological Association. Reprinted by permission of the publisher and author.

Table 15.3 is reprinted and Table 15.4 is adapted from Reifman, B., Pascarella, E., Larson, A., and "Effects of Word-Bank Instruction of Sight Word Acquisition: An Experimental Note." *Journal of Educational Research,* vol. 74, 1981, pp. 175–178. Copyright 1981, American Educational Research Association, Washington, D.C. By permission of the publisher and author.

EDUCATIONAL RESEARCH

Part I.

EDUCATIONAL RESEARCH— THE FIELD

The field of education is a mixture of art and science. Many excellent teachers know little about educational research, and such research probably has little *direct* impact on how they teach. Yet educational researchers have learned a great deal about the processes of teaching and learning. Much of what research has discovered has gradually and *indirectly* affected virtually every aspect of education.

The chapters in part I introduce you to the field of educational research and give you a brief look at the various settings in which educational researchers carry out their work. We discuss both the contributions and the limitations of educational research. We fit educational research into the context of scientific theory and methodology, and above all, we try to help you understand why research is worth doing.

1.
THE PURPOSE OF EDUCATIONAL RESEARCH

OVERVIEW

This chapter deals primarily with the question, Why do educational research? The question is addressed by considering two types of research impact: the contributions of research to knowledge about education, and the contributions of research to the practice of education. Educational research is a form of scientific inquiry, and so the purposes and methods of science are discussed. This is followed by a description of characteristics of educational research that distinguish it from other approaches to improving education. A case study of an educational research project is presented to illustrate the personal satisfactions of doing research.

OBJECTIVES

After studying this chapter, you should be able to:

1. Describe how knowledge about education has improved as a result of research.
2. Identify at least one contribution of research to educational practice.
3. Discuss why basic research is worth supporting, even though it may not lead directly to improvement in educational practice.
4. List seven impediments to reciprocal influence between research and practice in education.
5. Explain the four purposes of science.
6. Describe the characteristics of scientific theory.
7. Differentiate between positivistic and nonpositivistic scientific methods.
8. Describe the contributions of various scientific disciplines to education.
9. Identify several bases for classifying educational research studies.
10. State six characteristics of educational research methodology.
11. Describe several sources of personal satisfaction for doing educational research.

3

INTRODUCTION

A colleague suggested to us recently that if doctors were to lose their base of medical knowledge, most of them would have to stop working. They would have no idea how to treat anything other than common ailments. A surgeon, for example, could not perform open-heart surgery if he lacked research-based knowledge about heart functions, anesthesia, the meaning of symptoms, and the likely risks of particular courses of action. If educators were to suddenly lose the body of knowledge gained through educational research, however, their work would be virtually unphased. Schools would continue to operate pretty much as they do now. It is hard to imagine a teacher who would refuse to teach students because he lacked research-based knowledge about the learning process and the effectiveness of instructional methods.

The point of our colleague's comparison of medicine and education is that research has relatively little influence on the day-to-day work of educators. Whether true or not, his assessment of educational practice raises an important question: Why do educational research? Like other researchers, we can state some of the taken-for-granted answers to this question. The major reason for educational research is to develop new knowledge about teaching and learning and administration. The new knowledge is valuable because it will lead eventually to the improvement of educational practice.

These are easy answers to the question, Why do educational research? But if you examine the question more closely, the answers do not seem satisfying. For example, what does "research" mean? A defense of educational research must depend on what is meant by this term. There are other issues, too. The matter of perspective seems important; individual researchers may be motivated to do research for one set of reasons, while society may support research for another set of reasons. Also, the relationship between research and improvement is much more complex than most people imagine. It seems unfair to dismiss research as irrelevant because a teacher does not see the application of a particular research finding to her classroom situation, or because a particular research investigation results in negative conclusions.

The purpose of this introductory chapter is to help you examine for yourself why educational research is worth supporting. The ideas presented in this chapter will help you critically examine your preconceived notions about educational research. At the least, you will develop a better understanding of why thousands of educational researchers throughout the world believe in their work and continue to refine the methodologies presented in this book. Our own belief is that research is absolutely essential to the continued development and improvement of educational practice.

RESEARCH AND THE IMPROVEMENT OF EDUCATION

Contributions of Research to Knowledge about Education

As we indicated above, the usual defense of educational research is that it develops new knowledge, which then is applied to the improvement of educational practice. In this section we consider whether research has contributed to *knowledge* about education. In the next section we consider whether this knowledge has had an impact on the *practice* of education.

Herbert Walberg, Diane Schiller, and Geneva Haertel determined the contributions of research to knowledge about education during the decade from 1969 to 1979.[1] Their method was to examine reviews of research on instructional methods and conditions. They counted the number of positive and negative results relating to a particular method or condition of instruction. A positive result was a finding that the method or condition being investigated had a positive effect[2] on an educational outcome (e.g., student academic achievement). A negative result was a finding that the method or condition had a negative effect on a desirable educational outcome. If a research project investigated several effects of the instructional method or condition, Walberg, Schiller, and Haertel counted each effect in the analysis.

Table 1.1 presents their synthesis of research contributions to knowledge about instruction.[3] Each instructional method or condition is accompanied by two pieces of information: the number of results obtained during the 1969–79 period, and the percentage of these results indicating positive effects for the method or condition. For example, there were 25 results available for the effect of instructional time on student learning. Ninety-six percent of the results demonstrated a positive effect; only 4 percent of the results demonstrated a negative effect. The consistency of results indicates that amount of instructional time reliably increases student learning: The more instructional time, the more

1. Herbert J. Walberg, Diane Schiller, and Geneva D. Haertel, "The Quiet Revolution in Educational Research," *Phi Delta Kappan* 61 (1979): 179–83.
2. The word "effect" implies cause and effect. However, many results were based on correlational rather than experimental research. Therefore, some of the results in table 1.1 may not reflect a direct causal relationship between a method/condition and an educational outcome.
3. Further information about particular methods and conditions listed in table 1.1 can be found in Walberg et al., "The Quiet Revolution."

TABLE 1.1

A Selective Summary of a Decade of Educational Research on Instruction

Research Topics	Number of Results	Percent Positive
Time on learning	25	96.0
Innovative curricula on:		
Innovative learning	45	97.8
Traditional learning	14	35.7
Smaller classes on learning:		
Pre-1954 studies	53	66.0
Pre-1954 better studies	19	84.2
Post-1954 studies	11	72.7
All comparisons	691	60.0
Behavioral instruction on: Learning	52	98.1
"Personalized Systems of Instruction" on learning	103	93.2
Mastery learning	30	96.7
Programmed instruction on learning	57	80.7
Adjunct questions on learning:		
After text on recall	38	97.4
After text on transfer	35	74.3
Before text on recall	13	76.9
Before text on transfer	17	23.5
Advance organizers on learning	32	37.5
Analytic revision of instruction on achievement	4	100.0
Direct instruction on achievement	4	100.0
Lecture versus discussion on:		
Achievement	16	68.8

TABLE 1.1—Continued

Research Topics	Number of Results	Percent Positive
Retention	7	100.0
Attitudes	8	86.0
Student-centered versus instructor-centered discussion on:		
Achievement	7	57.1
Understanding	6	83.0
Attitude	22	100.0
Student-led versus instructor-led discussion on:		
Achievement	10	100.0
Attitude	11	100.0
Factual versus conceptual questions on achievement	4	100.0
Specific teaching traits on achievement:		
Clarity	7	100.0
Flexibility	4	100.0
Enthusiasm	5	100.0
Task orientation	7	85.7
Use of student ideas	8	87.5
Indirectness	6	83.3
Structuring	3	100.0
Sparing criticism	17	70.6
Psychological incentives and engagement:		
Teacher's cues to student	10	100.0
Teacher reinforcement of student	16	87.5
Teacher engagement of class in lesson	6	100.0
Individual student engagement in lesson	15	100.0

TABLE 1.1—Continued

Research Topics	Number of Results	Percent Positive
Open versus traditional education on:		
Achievement	26	54.8
Creativity	12	100.0
Self-concept	17	88.2
Attitude toward school	25	92.0
Curiosity	6	100.0
Self-determination	7	85.7
Independence	19	94.7
Freedom from anxiety	8	37.5
Cooperation	6	100.0
Social-psychological climate and learning:		
Cohesiveness	17	85.7
Satisfaction	17	100.0
Difficulty	16	86.7
Formality	17	64.7
Goal direction	15	73.3
Democracy	14	84.6
Environment	15	85.7
Speed	14	53.8
Diversity	14	30.8
Competition	9	66.7
Friction	17	0.0
Cliqueness	13	8.3
Apathy	15	14.3
Disorganization	17	6.3
Favoritism	13	10.0
Motivation and learning	232	97.8
Social class and learning	620	97.6
Home environment on:		
Verbal achievement	30	100.0
Math achievement	22	100.0
Intelligence	20	100.0
Reading gains	6	100.0
Ability	8	100.0

students learn. The effect has been found by many researchers in many school systems.

Many other instructional effects of similar reliability are shown in table 1.1. Together they demonstrate that there was an impressive accumulation of scientific knowledge about education in a single decade. Keep in mind, too, that the focus of this research review was on instruction. The review did not include accumulation of research knowledge about school administration, basic learning processes, and other aspects of education. For example, the review did not examine the consistent results pertaining to the effects of school-level factors on student academic achievement.[4]

The empirical results shown in table 1.1 are an important type of scientific knowledge about education. Impressive gains have been made, too, in other kinds of scientific knowledge during the past decade. For example, there have been important theoretical developments in the study of moral development, artificial intelligence, brain structure, and cognitive learning processes. Important developments in research methodology have also occurred. Path analysis, multiple regression, exploratory data analysis, and ethnography are a few examples of these methodological advances. They are discussed later in the book.

Contributions of Research Knowledge to the Practice of Education

The contributions of research to educational knowledge are easy to demonstrate through reviews of the research literature. The review summarized in table 1.1 is just one of many available reviews of accumulated research knowledge. (See chapter 5 for sources of published reviews.) It is much more difficult to determine whether the accumulation of research findings has made an impact on the practice of education.

There are two major reasons for this difficulty. First, many influences act on educational practice. When a new educational practice is adopted or an old one fades, it is difficult to determine whether the change was the result of research knowledge, other factors, or both. For example, Lawrence Cremin, an historian of education, highlighted the importance of political influences on educational change. He stated that "while research can doubtless inform that enterprise, it can never replace the political process that is its essence".[5] Even when research knowledge attracts the attention of policy makers in education, they generally consider it as just one source of information to use in shaping a

4. James Sweeney, "Research Synthesis on Effective School Leadership," *Educational Leadership* 39 (1982): 346–52.
5. Lawrence A. Cremin, "Preface," in *Teacher Education in America: A Documentary History*, ed. M. L. Borrowman (New York: Teachers College Press, 1965), p. viii.

particular policy. The current interest of policy makers in evaluation research (see chapter 17) does not mean that they apply its findings literally. Policy makers may rely heavily on evaluation research results to justify unpopular decisions (e.g., cuts in funding for an education program), but they may dismiss results that go counter to their beliefs or the beliefs of powerful political constituencies.

The other difficulty in tracing the influences of research knowledge on educational practice is that the influence may vary according to the type of research. Applied research sometimes has a direct and quick impact on practice. Basic research is likely to have a more indirect, slow influence on practice, but the eventual impact may be much more profound. We discuss the distinction between basic and applied research more fully later in the chapter. For now it will suffice to say that the primary purpose of applied research is to test the effectiveness of different educational methods or programs and to gather data that will be of use in educational decision making. By contrast, the purpose of basic research is to gain an understanding of underlying processes involved in learning, schooling, and other educational phenomena.

In his presidential address to the American Educational Research Association, Fred Kerlinger took the position that there is little direct connection between research and educational practice:

> Most people assume that educational research can solve educational problems and improve educational practices. The assumption is false. And it creates expectations that cannot be fulfilled. Educational research does not lead directly to improvement in educational practice. The solution of a research problem is on a different level of discourse than the solution of an action problem.[6]

Kerlinger's position will dishearten practitioners who think that research can help them improve their work. Similarly, budding researchers will be discouraged if they are led to believe that their investigations will never be of use to students, teachers, administrators, and others.

Despite how it sounds, Kerlinger's statement is not reason for despair. First, you should realize that Kerlinger is referring primarily to *basic* research. Applied research, especially evaluation research (see chapter 17) and educational R & D (see chapter 18), is on the same level of discourse as educational practice. For this reason, applied research sometimes has relatively quick impact on practice. This point is well illustrated in medical research. The testing of new drugs and treatments by controlled experiments often leads to improve-

6. Fred N. Kerlinger, "The Influence of Research on Education Practice," *Educational Researcher* 6, no. 6 (1977): 6.

ments in medical practice. Consider the recent case of the drug propranolol.[7] This drug helps to prevent future heart attacks in patients who have already suffered at least one heart attack. An experiment with 3837 patients produced these results:

	Dead from New Attacks	Alive
Propranolol Patients	135	1781
Comparison Group	183	1738

Although the effect of propranolol on heart-attack incidence was small, the results of the experiment were considered of sufficient significance that the drug was released for use by medical doctors before clinical tests were completed. It is estimated that the lives of many thousand Americans will be saved each year because of propranolol, the benefits of which were discovered through applied research.

Similar instances of research impact on practice are harder to find in education. Yet examples can be found, especially in the field of special education. Robert Slavin offered these observations:

> The past ten years have seen a gradual but certain cumulative increase in knowledge in special education. Simple behavior modification techniques have grown in sophistication; have been applied to formerly unreachable children, such as the severely retarded and the physically disabled; have advanced into such promising new areas as cognitive behavior modification and self-instruction; and have been made easier to use and more flexible. These advances have been based exclusively on painstaking applied research.[8]

We can also point to the many functioning programs that have been validated by applied educational research. The programs are currently being disseminated by the National Diffusion Network.[9]

Another example of research impact is educational testing. Millions of standardized tests are given every year to students of all ages. These tests are usually developed through a series of applied research studies. The purpose of

7. David Perlman, "Heart Attack Drug Given a Big Boost," *San Francisco Chronicle*, 29 October 1981, pp. 1, 8. We are indebted to Professor N. L. Gage for this example.
8. Robert E. Slavin, "Basic vs. Applied Research: A Response," *Educational Researcher* 7, no. 2 (1978): 16.
9. The work of the National Diffusion Network is described in chapter 18.

these studies is to refine the validity, reliability, and other psychometric properties of the test under development. Test development also has benefited from basic research on principles of measurement. In fact, educational testing provides the strongest example to date of how research has influenced American education.

The other part of Kerlinger's statement worth noting is his contention that research does not *directly* influence educational practice. This statement leaves open the possibility that research exerts its influence *indirectly*. Geraldine Clifford, a historian of education, studied the impact of research on education practice, making special note of the current trend to promote research impact through deliberate dissemination strategies. Viewing this trend from an historical perspective, she concluded:

> However much deliberate dissemination strategies promote future research impact, the conclusion from the past is otherwise: that discrete, observable, chartable dissemination activities were far inferior in operation to the processes of *cultural diffusion*, to that obscure, ambiguous, often involuntary transaction system whereby innovations and ideas are spread widely throughout some extended subsociety or the whole culture.[10]

If Clifford's conclusion is correct, we would find it difficult to trace the influence of particular lines of research on particular practices in education.

A fascinating empirical investigation that attempted to trace the effects of research on practice was done in the field of medicine.[11] Julius Comroe and Robert Dripps started their study by identifying the 10 most important advances since the early 1940s in the treatment of cardiovascular and pulmonary diseases. (These diseases were selected because they account for more than half of all deaths in the United States each year.) The ten advances are listed in the first column of table 1.2.[12] With the assistance of 140 consultants, Comroe and Dripps identified the bodies of knowledge that needed to be developed through research before the ten clinical advances could reach their present state of achievement. A total of 137 essential bodies of knowledge were identified, such as anatomy of cardiac defects, blood typing, monitoring of blood pressure, and management of postoperative infection.

The next step in Comroe and Dripps' investigation was to identify approximately 2500 scientific reports that were important to the development of the ten clinical advances. The list of reports was subsequently reduced to 529

10. Geraldine J. Clifford, "A History of the Impact of Research on Teaching," in *Second Handbook of Research on Teaching*, ed. Robert M. W. Travers (Chicago: Rand McNally, 1973), p. 25.
11. Julius H. Comroe, Jr., and Robert D. Dripps, "Scientific Basis for the Support of Biomedical Science," *Science* 192 (1976): 105–11.
12. Table 1.2 was adapted from ibid., table 6, p. 110.

essential reports, which were then subjected to detailed analysis. Each article was classified into one of six categories:

1. Basic research unrelated to the solution of a clinical problem
2. Basic research related to the solution of a clinical problem
3. Studies not concerned with basic biological, chemical, or physical mechanisms
4. Review and critical analysis of published work and synthesis of new concepts (without new experimental data)
5. Developmental work or engineering to create, improve, or perfect apparatus or a technique for research use
6. Developmental work or engineering to create, improve, or perfect apparatus or a technique for use in diagnosis or care of patients

Table 1.2 shows the number and percentage of key reports assigned to each of the categories.

The remarkable finding in this table is the high percentage of *basic* research studies (36.8 + 24.9 = 61.7 percent) that were essential to the development of current treatment of disease. Equally remarkable is the fact that more than a third (36.8 percent) of the essential studies were not even related to the practice of cardiovascular medicine. This result suggests that research can influence practice even when this is not its intent.

The path of research influence found in Comroe and Dripps' study does not necessarily characterize education. Many scientific advances in medicine could not have been discovered in the course of everyday medical practice, whereas some research-based advances in education (e.g., mastery learning, shown in table 1.1) probably could be independently discovered by insightful practitioners without benefit of research methodology. At the same time, Comroe and Dripps' study suggests the influence that basic and applied research could have on educational practice if such research were taken seriously by practitioners. For example, it is obvious that learning occurs within the learner's head, yet teachers rarely provide instruction from this perspective. Basic research now being done on cognitive and metacognitive processes[13] is directly concerned with "inside-the-head" learning events. This basic research may eventually suggest techniques that greatly increase the effectiveness of instruction.

Impediments to Research Impact on Education

Research has contributed a substantial amount of knowledge that is relevant to education. The impact of this knowledge on practice is not easy to assess,

13. For an example, see Ann L. Brown, Joseph C. Campione, and Jeanne D. Day, "Learning to Learn: On Training Students to Learn from Texts," *Educational Researcher* 10, no. 2 (1981): 14–21.

TABLE 1.2
Types of Research Reported in 529 Key Articles

Type	Basic: Not Clinically Oriented	Basic: Clinically Oriented	Not Basic	Review and Synthesis	Development: Research	Development: Clinical	Total
Cardiac surgery	34	23	19	0	3	11	90
Vascular surgery	9	7	14	3	0	21	54
Drug treatment of hypertension	42	16	21	2	0	0	81
Medical treatment of coronary insufficiency	21	20	22	1	1	3	68
Cardiac resuscitation	16	11	9	0	0	6	42
Oral diuretics	23	13	6	1	0	0	43
Intensive care[a]	—	—	—	—	—	—	—
Chemotherapy and antibiotics	12	18	21	1	0	2	54
Diagnostic methods	49	21	5	2	17	22	116
Prevention of poliomyelitis	3	12	3	0	1	0	19
Total	209	141	120	10	22	65	567[b]
Percent of total	36.8	24.9	21.2	1.8	3.9	11.4	

[a]Because practically every key article in intensive care was also essential to other advances, these articles were assigned elsewhere.
[b]The total number of entries in the six categories (567) exceeds the total number of articles (529) because some key articles fit in more than one category.

however. The areas of special education, testing, and educational R & D provide clear examples of impact, but in other areas the influence is more uncertain.

We have identified seven reasons why research has experienced difficulty in influencing American education. These reasons constitute a set of impediments that block reciprocal influence between research and practice in education. The impediments are:

1. *Lack of funding.* Comparative research data for different disciplines are available for the year 1968.[14] Less than 2000 person-years were devoted to educational research in that year. (Person-year was used as a measure because many educational researchers work only part-time on research; two half-time researchers, for example, equals one person-year.) In the same year there were 15,000 full-time agricultural researchers and 60,000 health researchers. Even that small amount of research effort was large by historical standards. It was estimated that appropriations for educational research and development for 1966 through 1968 equaled three-fourths of all funds ever appropriated for this purpose.[15]

The funding situation has not improved substantially since then. The budget of the National Institute of Education, the principal federal agency for educational research, was only $53.3 million for the 1982 fiscal year. Increased funding of research is obviously a necessary, if not sufficient, condition for impact to occur. Assuming a constant budget for education, though, increased support for research might put the researcher and practitioner in competition with each other. Additional dollars for research will be at the expense of program operations. We hope that funding for educational research can be increased with new dollars so that practitioners do not see it as a threat to their work. If anything, practitioners should see that new research knowledge can result in better programs and more respect from the community.

2. *Isolated research studies.* Geraldine Clifford, among others, noted that "the discrete study has been the byword" in education and that "fragmented research seldom has impact."[16] Most educators never do another piece of published research after they complete the master's thesis or doctoral dissertation.[17] As a consequence, there are very few programs of educational research in which insights from one study provide direction for the next study and a surer basis

14. Gene V. Glass, "The Wisdom of Scientific Inquiry," *Journal of Research in Science Teaching* 9 (1972): 3–18.
15. U.S. Office of Education, *Educational Research and Development in the United States* (Washington, D.C.: Government Printing Office, 1969).
16. Clifford "History of the Impact of Research," p. 35.
17. M. Arlin, "One-Study Publishing Typifies Educational Inquiry," *Educational Researcher* 6, no. 9 (1977): 11–15.

for new knowledge. Isolated, poorly funded studies are less likely to achieve visibility and impact than large-scale integrated programs of basic or applied research.

3. *Inadequate R & D capability.* Many educators think that the findings of research can be translated directly into practice. Most research findings, however, require considerable development before they can be applied by practitioners. William James, the famous philosopher and psychologist, made the same point more than a half century ago:

> I say moreover that you make a great, a very great mistake, if you think that psychology, being the science of the mind's laws, is something from which you can deduce definite programs and schemes and methods of instruction for immediate schoolroom use. Psychology is a science, and teaching an art; and sciences never generate arts directly out of themselves. . . . A science only lays down lines within which the rules of the art must fall, laws which the follower of the art must not transgress; but what particular thing he shall positively do within those lines is left exclusively to his own genius.[18]

We have lacked in this country a capability for deducing "definite programs and schemes and methods of instruction" from the growing body of educational research results. The emerging field of educational R & D (see chapter 18) shows promise of being able to produce research-based programs that are responsive to the needs and circumstances of the educational practitioner. At this point, though, educational R & D capability is not nearly as well developed as R & D in such fields as medicine, engineering, and defense.

4. *Educators' lack of knowledge.* A survey of graduates from about 100 teacher-training institutions found that the graduates learned very little about research in their programs.[19] Although the survey was conducted about 15 years ago, the same situation still holds true in many training programs for teachers and other educators. You need only inspect methods books for educators-in-training to document this lack of attention to published research, research methodology, and the role of research in educational improvement. How can practitioners support, use, or participate in research if they receive so little training?

5. *Inconsistent results.* Some practitioners discount the value of educational research because it produces inconsistent results. If you examine table 1.1, you will find inconsistent results for some of the instructional methods and conditions

18. William James, *Talks to Teachers on Psychology, and to Students on Some of Life's Ideals* (London: Longman, 1925), pp. 7–8.
19. J. D. McComas and J. E. Uxer, "Graduates' Perceptions of Research," *Improving College and University Teaching* 16 (1968): 118–19.

on the list. For example, open education was superior to traditional education in promoting academic achievement in approximately half of the comparisons (54.8 percent). But this means that traditional education was superior to open education in the other half of the comparisons. Thus, no conclusions about the effectiveness of open education relative to traditional education can be reached from this review of research.

Compounding the problem is inconsistency between research reviews. The review of research on factual versus conceptual questions by Walberg and his colleagues showed perfectly consistent results in favor of factual questions (see table 1.1). However, Philip Winne also reviewed the research on the problem, and he decided that because of methodological flaws in the research, no firm conclusions could be drawn about the relative effects of factual and conceptual questions.[20] A subsequent review of much the same body of research, by Doris Redfield and Elaine Rousseau, reached the conclusion that *conceptual* questions were consistently superior to factual questions in promoting academic achievement.[21]

It may help educators to realize that few techniques in any discipline are consistently effective. Aspirin works, but not always; and in some cases it has harmful side effects. Lumber is an excellent building material, but not for all climates or all construction purposes. The fact that investigators obtain inconsistent results is not an indictment of research. It probably means that the phenomenon is not well understood. There may be interaction effects (see chapter 16 on aptitude-treatment interaction) such that an instructional method shown in table 1.1 is effective for some students but not other students. Meta-analysis (see chapter 6) is a recently developed technique for helping researchers find consistencies and inconsistencies in results across studies. Educators should make a careful study of research methodology before dismissing inconsistent results as worthless.

6. *Side effects.* Practitioners are justifiably concerned about the possibility of side effects of experimental programs and methods. For example, in table 1.1 individually paced, mastery-oriented methods of instruction ("behavioral instruction," "Personalized System of Instruction," "mastery learning," and "programmed instruction") demonstrate consistently positive effects on student academic achievement. Yet there may be negative side effects associated with these methods. For example, some of these methods place a premium on independent learning. Some students may have lowered motivation under these conditions; they need group pressure and peer support to sustain their learning

20. Philip H. Winne, "Experiments Relating Teachers' Use of Higher Cognitive Questions to Student Achievement," *Review of Educational Research* 49 (1979): 13–49.
21. Doris L. Redfield and Elaine W. Rousseau, "A Meta-Analysis of Experimental Research on Teacher Questioning Behavior," *Review of Educational Research* 51 (1981): 237–45.

efforts.[22] Also, individualized, self-paced instruction may place greater personal demands on the instructor and require additional resources. These side effects may cancel the positive, measured effects of mastery-oriented methods.

The problem of unmeasured effects is not unique to education. Factories turn out useful products for society, but scientists discovered gradually that they pollute the environment in the process. Thalidomide was validated as a tranquilizer, but later was discovered to have disastrous side effects for some pregnant women.

Practitioners need to be mindful of unmeasured side effects of programs and methods tested by researchers. As side effects are postulated, they should be measured and assessed in a continuing program of research.

7. *The is/ought problem.* Both researchers and practitioners sometimes make the mistake of prescribing changes in practice because of research results. D. C. Phillips, a philosopher of education, has cautioned educators about the problem involved in using research results prescriptively:

> Research findings take the form, roughly, of "X is Y" or "the probability of an X having the feature Y is p"; in other words, they are statements of the "is" form. On the other hand, implications for practice take the form such as, "person A ought to do Z to person B." In other words, they are statements involving an "ought" or "should" or some other locution involving the passing of a value judgment. But it is a point of logic that from statements only involving the use of "is," a conclusion involving "ought" or one of its locutions cannot validly be deduced. . . .[23]

To understand Phillips' point, we refer to a study on teacher enthusiasm discussed in more detail later in the chapter. One result of the study was that elementary students observed in the research were "on-task" approximately 75 percent of the time during instruction. This percentage is similar to results found in other research on student on-task behavior.[24] This is a finding about what "is." However, the fact that students are not attentive some of the time does not necessarily mean they "ought" to be attentive more of the time. Perhaps it is natural and desirable for students to tune out instruction periodically. Even if more time on task is associated with higher achievement, perhaps students *ought* to be free to decide when and how they will attend to classroom instruction.

22. Research demonstrating such effects is reviewed in Richard E. Snow and Penelope L. Peterson, "Recognizing Differences in Student Aptitudes," in *New Directions for Teaching and Learning: Learning, Cognition, and College Teaching,* ed. W. J. McKeachie (San Francisco: Jossey-Bass, 1980), pp. 1–24.
23. D. C. Phillips, "What Do the Researcher and the Practitioner Have to Offer Each Other?" *Educational Researcher* 9, no. 11 (1980): 19.
24. Barak V. Rosenshine, "How Time Is Spent in Elementary Classrooms," in *Time to Learn,* ed. Carolyn Denham and Ann Lieberman (Washington, D.C.: National Institute of Education, 1980), pp. 107–26.

Questions involving "is" can be answered objectively by well-designed research. Questions involving "ought" are value laden and can be resolved only through dialogue and a decision-making process that includes interested constituencies. Researchers should not expect their findings about "is" to result in educational change immediately and without critical appraisal. Practitioners who look to research for prescriptive advice are similarly unjustified. It is much more sensible to use research knowledge about what "is" to inform dialogue about what "ought" to be—a dialogue that should be informed by other considerations as well.

Early in the chapter we posed the question, Why do educational research? At this point we can say that educational research should be supported because it builds a body of knowledge that informs the practice of education. A particularly strong case can be made for applied research. Applied research helps directly to validate the effectiveness of programs, methods, and tests used in the nation's schools. The case for basic research is more uncertain, but evidence from medicine suggests that basic research has a profound effect on practice.

In the section on impediments to research impact, we examined reasons why research has not had more influence on educational practice. These reasons have much to do with the current state of ignorance about educational research and the lack of funding. The impediments do not reveal any inherent weakness in educational research or reasons for not supporting it.

The purpose of the next section is to delve more deeply into the meaning of research, science, the scientific method, and related concepts. Examination of these concepts may suggest additional reasons to you for choosing to support and conduct research on education.

SCIENCE AS AN APPROACH TO INQUIRY

The primary purpose of this section is to discuss the nature of educational research. We start, though, by considering the nature of science. The two terms are sometimes used interchangeably, but they have different connotations. A dictionary definition of **research** is: "diligent search or inquiry; scientific investigation and study to discover facts."[25] **Science** is defined as: "systematic knowledge of natural or physical phenomena; truth ascertained by observation, experiment, and induction; ordered arrangement of facts known under classes or heads; theoretical knowledge as distinguished from practical; knowledge of principles and rules of invention, construction, mechanism, etc. as distinguished from art."[26]

25. John G. Allee, comp. *Webster's Dictionary* (Baltimore, Md: Ottenheimer Publishers, 1980).
26. Ibid.

Two distinctions are apparent in these definitions of science and research. Research and science both are concerned with the discovery of facts, but in science the facts are collected to test or develop theory. Many research studies, though, involve collecting facts with no concern for theory. Market research in business and industry is an example of this type of study. The other distinction is in the nature of the facts collected. Scientific investigation implies the collection of facts about *basic* processes in nature (e.g., the nature of cellular activity, stellar motion). The term "research," however, often refers to the collection of facts that will serve a useful purpose. In other words, "science" implies a focus on basic research, whereas "research" implies a focus on applied research.

These distinctions explain why our book is titled *Educational Research: An Introduction* rather than *Educational Science: An Introduction*. Much of the research in education is atheoretical and applied in nature: for example, investigations to discover educator opinion, experiments to determine how well a new program works. There are notable exceptions, however, such as research inspired by Jean Piaget's theory of intellectual development and by Benjamin Bloom's theory of mastery learning. Also, an increasing number of theory-guided studies are appearing in educational research journals.

The Purpose of Science

The purpose of science, stated very generally, is to develop new knowledge. More specifically, science can be said to have four purposes: (1) to describe, (2) to predict, (3) to control, and (4) to explain.

Much scientific activity is concerned with the description of natural or manmade phenomena. Descriptive investigations also involve the discovery of new phenomena. Many important scientific discoveries have been made in the process of describing events or structures. For example, astronomers use their telescopes to develop descriptions of different parts of the universe. This process sometimes results in the discovery of stars and stellar events.

The descriptive function of science is heavily dependent upon instrumentation for measurement and observation. Scientists may work for many years to perfect such instruments—for example, the electron microscope, the galvanometer, standardized tests of intelligence. Once the instruments are developed, they can be used to describe phenomena of interest to the scientists.

Science could not advance without accurate identification and descriptions of structures—their size, shape, weight, brightness, color, change over time, relation to other structures, and so on. Description provides the basic knowledge that is necessary for realizing the other purposes of science. One of these purposes is prediction, which is the ability to predict phenomenon X from phenomenon Y. For example, lunar eclipses can be predicted very accurately from knowledge about the relative motion of the moon, earth, and sun. The next stage of an embryo's development can be predicted very accurately from knowledge of the embryo's current stage. A student's achievement in school can be predicted fairly accurately by an aptitude test administered a year or two earlier.

The predictive function of science often has practical applications. For example, the scientific study of climate has yielded knowledge about the conditions that predict climatic change. This knowledge has useful applications in agriculture, aviation, and other fields. The ability to predict is also an important step toward explaining phenomena. Observations of association between phenomenon X and phenomenon Y may arouse the scientist's curiosity about why the association occurred. The next step is to develop a theory or to collect further data about the phenomena.

The third purpose of science is to gain *control* over the phenomena being studied. Scientific experiments are designed to achieve this purpose. In an experiment, phenomenon X is manipulated to determine whether it exerts control over phenomenon Y. For example, a physiologist might vary the placement of implanted electrodes in a rat's brain to determine whether this factor affects a particular brain activity. If placement and activation of the electrode at a particular point in the brain (phenomenon X) leads reliably to a particular brain activity (phenomenon Y), we can say that electrode placement "controls" that brain activity.

The control purpose of science is closely related to its predictive purpose. The major difference is in whether phenomenon X is manipulated by the scientist. In predictive inquiry, the scientist studies naturally occurring associations between phenomena. In experiments, though, the scientist manipulates phenomena to determine whether he can control the condition of some other phenomenon. Experimental manipulation leads to more powerful statements about associations between phenomena than does predictive inquiry. When you study research design later in this book (chapters 10 through 16), you will learn that predictive associations between phenomena do not necessarily imply a cause-and-effect relationship between them. By contrast, experimental results do permit conclusions about cause and effect.

If experimentation is more powerful than predictive inquiry, why do the latter? The fact is that the nature of some phenomena or the state of a science's technology may not permit experimentation. For example, most of the phenomena of interest to astronomers cannot be manipulated. Astronomy is largely a science of description and prediction. Sociologists also cannot manipulate some of the phenomena of most interest to them, such as social-class structure and mob behavior. In the study of human biology, ethical considerations may preclude experiments involving certain phenomena.

The fourth purpose of science—explanation—is considered to be its ultimate goal. In a sense, explanation subsumes the other three purposes. If scientists are able to explain a set of phenomena, it means that they can describe, predict, and control the phenomena with a high level of certainty and accuracy. Scientific explanation takes the form of a theory about the phenomena being investigated. Because explanation, in the form of theory, is so important to scientific inquiry, we discuss it next in a separate section.

Scientific Theories

Many definitions of the term *theory* are available. For our purposes we will define **theory** as a system for explaining a set of phenomena by specifying constructs and the laws that relate these constructs to each other. To explain this definition, let's consider Jean Piaget's theory of intellectual development. Piaget's theory is familiar to most educators and has had a substantial influence on American curriculum and instruction.

First, note that Piaget's theory is a *system* in that it consists of a set of constructs. The system is loose in that the constructs are verbally explained through the many treatises that Piaget and his colleagues wrote over a period of many years. Other workers have attempted to pull the theory together by writing concise descriptions of it. These concise descriptions are representations of the system. The theoretical system is designed to explain a set of phenomena: the behavior of infants and children with respect to their environment. For example, Piaget would observe how children of different ages responded to a particular task. The children's responses constituted phenomena to be explained by the theory.

The theory provides an explanation of phenomena by first specifying a set of theoretical constructs. A **theoretical construct** is a concept that can be defined constitutively or operationally and that is related to the other theoretical constructs in the system. A **constitutively defined construct** is one that is defined by referring to other constructs. For example, the Piagetian construct of conservation can be defined as the ability to recognize that certain properties of an object remain unchanged when other properties of the object (e.g., substance, length, volume) undergo a transformation. Note that in this definition "conservation" is defined by referring to other constructs (e.g., "property," "transformation," "length").

An **operationally defined construct** is one that is defined by specifying the activities used to measure or manipulate it. For example, self-concept can be defined by a standardized measure such as the Coopersmith Self-Esteem Inventory, by teacher ratings, by ratings based on direct observation, and so forth. Educational programs and methods are usually defined in terms of activities. For example, the construct "reading program" could be defined operationally by referring to a particular published reading program, including its materials and activities listed in the teacher's manual. The construct "conservation" (defined constitutively above) could be defined operationally by referring to a particular task, for example, pouring a constant amount of liquid into different-sized containers and asking a child whether the amount of liquid remains the same.

The final part of our definition of *theory* states that it specifies laws relating constructs to each other. For example, Piaget theorized that there are four major stages of intellectual development: sensorimotor, preoperational, concrete operations, and formal operations. These stages are constructs defined constitutively and operationally by Piaget. Piaget proposed the law that these constructs are related to each other as an invariant sequence: The sensorimotor state is always followed by the preoperational stage; the preoperational stage is always followed by the concrete operations stage; and the concrete operations stage is always followed by the formal operations stage. Two examples of laws from other theories are: (1) A behavior (construct) will be more likely to recur if followed by a reinforcer (construct) than if not followed by a reinforcer; (2) achievement test performance (construct) will increase as a function of the amount of instruction time on content relevant to the test (construct). Each of the constructs in a well-developed theory will be connected to the other constructs by laws.

Theories serve several useful purposes. First, theoretical constructs identify commonalities in otherwise isolated phenomena. Piaget's theory, for example, pulls together many isolated infant behaviors as instances of sensorimotor intelligence. In other words, theoretical constructs identify the universals of experience so that we can make sense of experience. Second, the laws of a theory enable us to make predictions and to control phenomena. Because astronomers have a well-developed theory, they can make very accurate predictions about the occurrence of eclipses and other phenomena in the universe. Because special educators work from a well-developed theory of learning (sometimes called a "behavioral theory of learning"), they can make instructional interventions that dependably lead to positive changes in student behavior.

The constructs and laws of a theory have important heuristic functions. One heuristic function is to organize the isolated findings of research into a powerful explanatory framework. For example, consider the many positive results presented in table 1.1. These "facts" of instruction are interesting, but how do they fit together? What makes these various instructional methods and conditions effective? An instructional theorist might organize the methods and conditions into a smaller set of theoretical constructs and laws, and perhaps also integrate them with what we know about principles of learning. The result might be a powerful theoretical explanation of instruction compared with the "bag of tricks" that we currently have.

The other important heuristic function of theory is to identify areas for further research. Research results that do not fit the theory will force the scientist to revise the theory and then to collect new data to test the revised theory. Scientists can also posit theoretical constructs, even though they cannot adequately define them. For example, physical scientists have posited the existence of subatomic particles and then planned research to find them. In education, a researcher might theorize that attention plays an important role in learning from lectures, but not know quite what he means by the construct "attention." Because this construct is important to his theory, he will be motivated to conduct research to identify the relevant parameters of attention.

Theory might make a particularly important contribution to education because it emphasizes the micro-processes underlying surface phenomena. For example, we find in table 1.1 that reduction in class size generally has a positive effect on student academic achievement. But why? *Class size* is a macro-construct; it has relatively little explanatory power. Small classes probably are good because they bring into play instructional processes that are not present in large classes. Researchers could build and test theories to identify these underlying instructional processes. Knowledge about such processes might enable educators to design interventions that are more reliable and more powerful, but less expensive, than reduction in class size.

Scientists sometimes speak of "small" and "large" theories. A small theory might be developed to account for a limited set of phenomena (e.g., antecedents and consequences of teacher morale). A large theory might account for many phenomena (e.g., behavioral theory and Freud's theory). Also, a theory might "grow" as it incorporates more constructs to explain more phenomena. A researcher might start with a small theory of academic achievement. As he discovers more determinants of achievement, he can enlarge the theory to accommodate them.

The Scientific Method

The scientific method is commonly thought to include three major phases. The first step is to formulate a **hypothesis,** which is a tentative proposition about the relation between two or more theoretical constructs. (Hypothesis formulation is discussed in chapter 3.) The next step is to deduce empirical consequences of the hypothesis. Suppose the researcher's hypothesis is that teachers will be more likely to implement a new curriculum if it is consistent with their belief system than if it is not consistent. Stated more simply, the hypothesis is that consistency with personal belief system (theoretical construct A) is positively associated with (relationship) curriculum implementation (theoretical construct B). This hypothesis may grow out of the researcher's personal observations, intuition, review of previous research, existing theory of human behavior, or other source.

The next phase of the scientific method is to deduce empirical consequences of the hypothesis. Deductive reasoning in this context means the process of identifying a real-life situation or of constructing a simulation that will allow a test of the hypothesis. For example, the researcher may hear that a new curriculum program is being introduced into a school district. The researcher analyzes the program and finds that the program is based on a particular set of beliefs about student motivation for learning. The researcher would deduce that, if his hypothesis is correct, teachers whose beliefs are consistent with this particular program will be more likely to implement each of its features than those teachers whose beliefs are inconsistent.

The third phase of the scientific method is to test the hypothesis by collecting data. The researcher would administer measures of curriculum implementation and belief system to all teachers who have been asked to use the new program. One way to analyze the resulting data would be to identify teachers who score very high or very low on the belief measure. Then the mean implementation scores of the high- and low-scoring teachers would be compared. If the hypothesis is correct, the belief-consistent teachers should earn higher scores on a measure of implementation than the belief-inconsistent teachers.

According to the scientific method, the hypothesis will be either supported or rejected by this empirical test. The researcher should not overlook one other possibility, though. She may have deduced inappropriate consequences from the hypothesis (the second step of the scientific method). For example, in the research study described above, the researchers might have made an incorrect analysis of the belief system underlying this curriculum program. Or the measures might have been invalid indicators of teachers' beliefs and implementation. In this case the results of the empirical test (phase 3 of the scientific method) cannot be used to reject or support the hypothesis. Weak measures of constructs are still common in educational research. Therefore, one needs to be careful about accepting or rejecting hypotheses based on single studies.

If an hypothesis is of sufficient importance, other researchers might replicate the first researcher's test of it. Different results are sometimes obtained because of experimenter error (see chapter 15) or because different methods and measures were used. The nature of research replication is discussed in chapter 10.

The above was an account of a scientific method, but not the scientific method. B. F. Skinner, the famous behavioral psychologist, cautioned: "(I)t is a mistake to identify scientific practice with the formalized construction of statistics and scientific method. . . . They offer a method of science but not, as

is so often implied, *the* method."[27] Some scientists, for example, have proceeded atheoretically and have made important discoveries by chance.

The scientific method described above is historically recent. Centuries ago,
scientific inquiry was considered a branch of philosophy called *natural philosophy*.
Science then was intimately bound up with issues concerning the nature of
knowledge (epistemology), reality (metaphysics), and reasoning (logic). Philosophers of science still worry about such matters, but contemporary researchers
in education, especially applied researchers, tend not to dwell on the philosophic
assumptions underlying their methods of inquiry.

An exception to this statement is the continuing concern about positivistic
versus subjective methods of investigation in educational research. **Positivism**
is a system of philosophy that excludes everything from its consideration except
natural phenomena and their relations. The scientific method as described above
is part of the positivistic tradition of philosophy. Positivists even exclude cause
and effect from science because it is subjective and therefore unnecessary.[28]
For example, if we see a billiard player strike a ball with a cue stick, we are
tempted to say that the ball moved (effect) as a consequence of being struck by
the cue stick (cause). The positivist would say that the notion of cause and
effect is unnecessary to a scientific explanation of this event. It is only necessary
to say that the *movement of the ball* (constructs) *follows with perfect predictability*
(relation) the *movement of the cue stick against it* (constructs).

Most of the research methods presented in this book are positivistic in
orientation. Some educational researchers, though, have become increasingly
interested in antipositivistic, subjective methods of inquiry. Robert Stake, for
example, advocates use of the case study method in educational research:

> In American research circles most methodologists have been of positivistic
> persuasion. The more episodic, subjective procedures, common to the case
> study, have been weaker than the experimental or correlational studies
> for explaining things.
>
> When explanation, propositional knowledge, and law are the aims
> of an inquiry, the case study will often be at a disadvantage. When the
> aims are understanding, extension of experience, and increase in conviction
> in that which is known, the disadvantage disappears.[29]

The case study method (see chapters 12 and 17), ethnography (see chapter 12),
and some methods of historical research (see chapter 19) involve a strong sub-

27. B. F. Skinner, "A Case History in Scientific Method," *American Psychologist* 11 (1956): 221.
28. The problems involved in cause-and-effect explanations in science are discussed in Ernest Nagel,
    The Structure of Science (New York: Harcourt Brace Jovanovich, 1961).
29. Robert E. Stake, "The Case Study Method in Social Inquiry," *Educational Researcher* 7, no. 2
    (1978): 6.

jective element. In each method the personal framework of the researcher is a strong determinant of what he or she will discover about the phenomena under investigation. The case study researcher sacrifices generalizability—one of the hallmarks of positivistic science—for an in-depth understanding of a single instance of the phenomena under investigation.

Elliot Eisner is another educational researcher who distinguishes between positivistic and subjective approaches to scientific inquiry.[30] He characterizes the two approaches as scientific (that is, positivistic) and artistic (what we call here, *subjective*). Table 1.3 presents a list of ten differences between scientific and artistic research identified by Eisner. The case study method, ethnography, and some forms of historical investigation correspond to the artistic approach. Sampling procedures (chapter 7), measurement (chapters 8 and 9), and the major research designs (chapters 13 through 16) are features of what Eisner means by the scientific approach.

Our position is that both positivistic and subjective approaches have a contribution to make in educational research. Case studies, ethnographies, and other subjective modes of inquiry are useful for *exploratory* research. They can be employed profitably to generate observations and hypotheses in areas where little prior investigation has occurred or where more objective methods are not available. Interesting observations and hypotheses generated by this approach then can be tested using the methods of positivistic science.

The results of subjective research should not be taken as conclusive evidence. The history of science provides many examples of people's capacity for self-deception and erroneous observation. To cite just one example, observation of the rising and setting of the sun, moon, and other solar bodies led people at one time to the "common sense" conclusion that the earth was stationary. Scientists operating in a positivistic mode considered this belief a hypothesis to be supported or not supported by objectively gathered data. Accumulation of data about the motions of solar bodies led gradually to the abandonment of this commonly held belief.

Educational research conducted in a strict positivistic vein also has its problems. Many educational studies use rigorous methodology but screen out too much of the context surrounding the measured variables. The reader is often left confused about what actually happened in educational experiments. The subjects of educational research—students, teachers, and administrators—are treated as objects. We have little sense from published reports about what the experimental treatments meant to the subjects who participated in them. We also have little sense about the researcher's involvement in the experiment.

---

30. Elliot Eisner, "On the Differences Between Scientific and Artistic Approaches to Qualitative Research," *Educational Researcher* 10, no. 4 (1981): 5–9.

Information about context and research participants, collected by case study methods, would be a useful supplement to the objective data collected in a typical educational research investigation.

Both approaches—positivistic/scientific and subjective/artistic—contribute to knowledge about education. Eisner stated the point this way: "It is to the

TABLE 1.3
Differences between Scientific and Artistic Approaches to Research

Scientific Approach	Artistic Approach
1. Operationally defined laws and constructs.	Artistic, idiosyncratic forms of representation—visual, auditory, and discursive language.
2. Methods of inquiry evaluated by criteria of validity, interperson reliability, and generalizability.	Methods of inquiry evaluated by whether the researcher's personal vision informs and persuades.
3. Objective analysis of observable human behavior.	Empathic participation in the experiences of individuals.
4. Inference from a sample (collection of individuals) to a population.	Inference from an individual case to a population.
5. Standardization of reporting forms to convey objectivity.	Use of idiosyncratic forms to convey meaning; reporting style varies upon the intended audience.
6. Reporting of objective facts without bias.	Selective reporting and special emphasis (i.e., artistic license).
7. Purpose is to predict and control.	Purpose is to explicate and understand.
8. Standardized, objective methods of data collection.	Investigator's own perceptions are a major source of data.
9. Emotional neutrality.	Role of emotion in knowing is central.
10. Ultimate aim is truth, which implies singularity of vision and absolutes.	Ultimate aim is meaning, which implies diverse interpretation and relativism.

artistic to which we must turn, *not* as a rejection of the scientific, but because with both we can achieve binocular vision. Looking through one eye never did provide much depth of field."[31]

Scientific Disciplines

A **scientific discipline** is an organized field of inquiry that seeks to explain a distinctive domain of phenomena using its own theories, constructs, and methods of investigation. Anthropology, psychology, economics, and chemistry are examples of what we mean by the term *scientific discipline.*

Is educational research a scientific discipline according to this definition? The answer is no. The field of educational research has largely developed by borrowing from other scientific disciplines. In fact, many of the most important contributions to educational research have come from individuals trained in a scientific discipline. Prominent examples come to mind: Jerome Bruner (psychology), James Coleman (sociology), Margaret Mead (anthropology), Lawrence Cremin (history), Michael Scriven (philosophy), and William Labov (linguistics).

Psychology is the scientific discipline that has made the greatest impact on educational research to date. Many graduate schools of education have a separate department of educational psychology. Professional educational researchers usually have earned an advanced degree in educational psychology, although an increasing number of them have earned degrees in other disciplines, especially sociology and economics.

The following is a list of scientific disciplines and a representative contribution that each has made either to knowledge about education or to a method of inquiry that can be used in educational research:

1. Anthropology: the ethnographic method
2. Biology: the genetic basis for individual differences in intelligence
3. Computer science: the study of artificial intelligence
4. Economics: cost-benefit analysis of educational policies
5. History: the study of school reform movements
6. Linguistics: social-class differences in language patterns of children
7. Mathematics: statistical analysis of data from samples
8. Physiology: brain structures that support intellectual functions
9. Political science: political influences on school boards

---

31. Ibid., p. 9.

10. Psychology: principles of behavior modification
11. Sociology: the nature of work in schools

The list suggests the range of theories, constructs, and methods that other scientific disciplines have contributed to educational research. Researchers in education are advised to consult these other disciplines whenever it seems that their theories, constructs, or methods can illuminate the problem under investigation.

EDUCATIONAL RESEARCH

Types of Educational Research

Just as there is no *the* scientific method, there is not just one type of educational research. In fact, educational research includes many kinds of investigation. We present here several typologies for classifying educational research. The typologies are useful for analyzing published research and for thinking about the research you might undertake for your thesis or dissertation.

Topic. Educational research can be classified by the phenomena investigated. Some of the major topics investigated by educational researchers are: learning processes, cognitive abilities, classroom teaching methods, student personality and motivation, school climate, administrative leadership, school finance, programs for special groups of learners (e.g., learning disabled, gifted), teacher education, curriculum development, subject matter instruction (e.g., reading, mathematics, writing). Many education journals specialize in practice and research relating to one of these topics.

Purpose. In a sense research has only two purposes: (1) description, and (2) exploration of relationships between variables. Descriptive research seeks to characterize a sample of students, teachers, school buildings, textbooks, and so forth on one or more variables. The sample's response to one variable is not correlated with their response to another variable, though. A study to determine the favorableness of educators' attitudes toward computer-assisted instruction would be an example of descriptive research.

Relationship research goes one step further. The sample is described with respect to at least two variables and then their response to one variable is correlated with their response to another variable. The purpose of relationship research is to determine whether responses to the variables covary in a non-chance manner. An everyday example of covariation is height (variable 1) and weight (variable 2). These two variables covary in that taller people tend to weigh more and shorter people tend to weigh less.

The search for relationships subsumes the predictive, control, and explanatory purposes of scientific inquiry. Predictive research is, in fact, a search for relationships between variables measured at one point in time and variables measured at another point in time. The search for control is conducted through experiments. In experiments the researchers seek to discover relationships between a variable that is manipulated (e.g., presence versus absence of a new teaching method) and another variable (e.g., effects of the teaching method on student attitudes). Finally, explanation in science is, in its essence, a function of being able to state lawful relationships between variables.

Most research in education is concerned with inquiry about relationships between variables (see chapters 13 through 16) with description as a secondary goal. However, many useful descriptive studies have been done for the purpose of determining the current or past status of educational phenomena (see chapters 10 and 19). Another important type of descriptive research involves the development of new instruments to measure constructs (see chapters 8 and 9).

Hypothesis testing. Some research studies are exploratory in nature. These studies tend not to be guided by hypotheses, because the researcher does not have sufficient understanding of the phenomena to form conjectures about relationships between constructs. For example, the researcher may be curious about the current status of educators' attitudes toward the use of microcomputers in instruction. In this case the researcher would state her purpose as a question or objective rather than as an hypothesis. (The distinction between research questions, objectives, and hypotheses is described in chapter 3.)

Other research studies are more *confirmatory* in nature. The researcher already has a hunch based on theory, prior research, or personal observation. For example, the researcher may have reason to believe that educators' attitudes toward microcomputer education are related to their prior training in microcomputers and to their self-concept about mathematics ability. The researcher's conjectures can be stated as hypotheses and tested. The research results will support or fail to support the hypotheses.

Exploratory research tends to study many variables and their relationships in order to further understanding of the phenomena. Confirmatory research tends to be theoretically based and focused on a limited set of well-measured variables.

Basic versus applied research. We have described these types of research. Basic research focuses on fundamental structures and processes with the goal of understanding them. Applied research focuses on structures and processes as they appear in educational practice, with the goal of developing knowledge that is directly useful to practitioners. Both basic and applied research can make use of descriptive and relationship research designs. Evaluation research methodology (see chapter 17) and educational R & D (see chapter 18) are almost always used in the context of applied research.

Educational Research Methodology

Most of this book is about the methodology of educational research. Therefore, we briefly describe its main features here.

Precise measurement. Researchers measure educational constructs much more precisely than other people do. First, researchers distinguish between constructs and variables. A construct, strictly speaking, is a nonobservable inference from observed behavior. We observe the behavior of different individuals in academic situations and conclude that there is such a "thing" as *intelligence* or *self-concept.* These constructs can be defined constitutively or operationally (e.g., intelligence is that "thing" measured by the Wechsler Adult Intelligence Scale). A variable can be thought of as a quantitative expression of a construct. Variables usually take the form of scores on a measuring instrument.

Researchers take a great deal of care to develop instruments that yield reliable and valid scores on variables that relate to constructs under investigation. In contrast, persons without a research background are apt to make statements like "John is an underachiever" or "Sue is gifted" without defining their terms operationally and without basing their judgment on score data that have been checked for reliability and validity. Several chapters (e.g., chapters 3 and 12) deal with these definitional and measurement issues.

Generalizability. Researchers usually wish to generalize beyond the specific situations that they investigated. They rarely have the resources, though, to study each instance of the phenomenon. Suppose a researcher wanted to study some aspect of elementary reading instruction. More than a million teachers in this country provide instruction in this area. If the teachers' instructional behavior were the focus of study, the researcher would need to consider that each teacher might exhibit this behavior on approximately 150 to 200 days each school year. Most researchers would have resources to study only a small sample of these teachers and a small sample of their instructional behavior.

Researchers have developed many methodological tools to handle the problem of generalizing from a limited set of observations to a population. The chapter on sampling techniques (chapter 7) deals specifically with generalizability issues, but the problem is discussed in other chapters too.

Research control. Everyday observation is clouded by personal biases, selective perception, and superstitious beliefs about cause and effect. Researchers are acutely aware of these problems, and have developed a variety of methodological tools to deal with them. We have already described the researcher's use of reliable, valid measures. In the area of experimentation, different research designs have been developed to control for extraneous factors that might account for observed effects. With appropriate controls, the researcher can conclude that observed effects were due to the experimental treatment rather than extraneous factors like co-occurring events, maturation, and testing. Experimental designs are discussed in chapters 15 and 16.

Cause-and-effect relationships are much more difficult to establish in non-experimental research designs. However, research controls have been developed to increase the power of these designs to reveal causal linkages between variables and to discover whether an observed effect is multidetermined. Non-experimental research designs for detecting relationships between variables are discussed in chapters 13 and 14.

Statistical analysis. Students without a background in mathematics are often overwhelmed by the use of statistics in research. In fact, they may wrongly conclude that research is *statistics.* The truth is that statistics is a *tool* used by the researcher to increase the precision and power of the data analysis. Also, statistical tools can be used to plan the research design so that its power to yield generalizable, conclusive results is optimized.

Statistical tools, especially those used in multivariate analysis, may appear alien to the untrained student. However, keep in mind that even the most complex statistics are based on commonsense notions. Statistics are meant to help the educational researcher "depict" the phenomena of education. A good statistical analysis will illuminate, not obscure, structures and processes. Like a microscope, statistics may reveal phenomena not apparent in everyday observation. The use of statistics in educational research is introduced in chapter 10. Statistical tools used in conjunction with particular research designs are presented in chapters 13 through 16. Statistical tools used in educational measurement are described in chapter 8.

Replicability. Replication is one of the most powerful tools of science. If constructs are given clear operational definitions, other researchers can repeat the first researcher's investigation. Replication allows science to be self-correcting. If subsequent research yields the same results as the first investigation, confidence in the hypothesis is strengthened. If different results are obtained, the researchers will need to determine whether there was error in the first investigation. Another possibility is that the subsequent investigations changed the conditions of the first study. In this case the different results would indicate limits on the generalizability of the laws specified in the first researcher's hypothesis.

We encourage beginning researchers to conduct replications for their thesis or dissertation. The replication need not literally repeat the conditions of another study. The replication can duplicate critical elements and also *extend* the inquiry into new domains. The next section describes an example of what we call "replication and extension." Replication is also discussed in chapter 10.

Positivistic orientation. The methodological tools presented in this book are, for the most part, strongly positivistic. This means that the tools are intended to help the researcher minimize the impact of his subjective framework on the phenomena that he is trying to describe, predict, or control. Case study, ethnography, and history are presented as deliberate exceptions to this approach. Their strength is that they use the researcher's subjective framework as a tool for *exploring* phenomena. We emphasize the word *exploring* because we think the insights obtained by these methods should then be *confirmed* by the methods of positivistic inquiry.

This section on scientific inquiry provides another perspective for answering the question, Why do educational research? The achievement of modern science is its reliance on objective, disinterested, self-correcting methods of inquiry. These methods are needed to correct the biases, errors, and self-interest of everyday observation. Educators are all too familiar with so-called breakthroughs in programs and practices. A bandwagon effect occurs, followed by gradual disillusionment. Research is our best alternative for real progress in education.

Personal Motivation for Doing Educational Research

Thus far we have dealt with the public, institutional basis for supporting educational research. Our discussion involved such matters as the nature of scientific inquiry and the relationship between research knowledge and educational practice. Now we consider the personal reasons why researchers choose to investigate education. What satisfactions are to be derived from undertaking a research project and seeing it through to completion?

We use as an example two doctoral dissertations that were completed a few years ago.[32] The first dissertation project began when Edward Bettencourt, a doctoral student at the University of Oregon, initiated discussions with us about possible research ideas. His attention soon turned to teacher enthusiasm. During the time that he was a school principal, he observed that the teachers whom he considered effective were very enthusiastic about their work. Bettencourt believed strongly that enthusiasm was important in elementary school teaching. Together we recalled instances of principals who said that they hired teachers based on their level of enthusiasm in the interview situation.

The next step was for Bettencourt to start thinking about whether there

32. The "we" in this example refers to the second author and his two dissertation advisees. The two dissertations are: Edward M. Bettencourt, "Effects of Training Teachers in Enthusiasm on Student Achievement and Attitudes" (Ed.D. dissertation, University of Oregon, 1979); Maxwell H. Gillett, "Effects of Teacher Enthusiasm on At-Task Behavior of Students in Elementary Classes" (Ph.D. dissertation, University of Oregon, 1980).

was research evidence to support his beliefs. He decided to initiate a review of the literature to answer the question, Are enthusiastic teachers really more effective than nonenthusiastic teachers? He was helped in his search by a published review, which surveyed empirical research on teacher enthusiasm up to about 1970.[33] His post-1970 search uncovered an important dissertation study by Mary Collins. A report of this study was published in the *Journal of Teacher Education*.[34]

Collins had identified observable indicators of teacher enthusiasm and had demonstrated that her training procedure reliably increased preservice teachers' enthusiasm level. Her measure of teacher enthusiasm consisted of a five-point rating scale for each of eight enthusiasm indicators: (1) rapid uplifting, varied vocal delivery; (2) dancing, wide open eyes; (3) frequent, demonstrative questions; (4) varied, dramatic body movements; (5) varied emotive facial expressions; (6) selection of varied words, especially adjectives; (7) ready, animated acceptance of ideas and feelings; and (8) exuberant overall energy level. Ratings were made by trained observers, who studied videotapes of the teachers' classroom performance. The observers did not know whether a particular videotape was made before or after training, or whether a teacher was in the trained or untrained group. Collins' study was important because it provided a good operational definition of teacher enthusiasm and an empirically validated training program.

At this point Bettencourt was entertaining several research ideas. It happened that the author of the pre-1970 review, Barak Rosenshine, was visiting our university, and so we discussed with him the relative merits of the various research ideas. He argued that the most important problem in this area was whether teacher enthusiasm was sufficiently potent to cause students to improve their academic achievement. Previous research on this problem generally produced positive results, but most of the studies were methodologically weak. Collins' definition of teacher enthusiasm and training procedures overcame the most serious weaknesses of these studies.

As a result of this discussion, Bettencourt decided to test two hypotheses relating to teacher enthusiasm. The first hypothesis was that teachers trained in Collins' procedures would become more observably enthusiastic than teachers not so trained. The test of this hypothesis provided a replication of Collins' original findings. The second hypothesis was that students of enthusiasm-trained teachers would achieve at a higher level than students of untrained teachers.

Bettencourt planned to have the trained and untrained groups teach the same curriculum unit in order to control for academic content. The unit was to

---

33. Barak Rosenshine, "Enthusiastic Teaching: A Research Review," *School Review* 78 (1970): 499–514.
34. Mary L. Collins, "Effects of Enthusiasm Training on Preservice Elementary Teachers," *Journal of Teacher Education* 29 (1978): 53–57.

be a few weeks long so as not to disrupt the teachers' regular curriculum. Bettencourt's dissertation advisers were familiar with a suitable unit that had been developed for another research project. He contacted the director of that project and obtained his permission to use the unit's materials and achievement tests. Meanwhile Bettencourt phoned Collins and obtained her assistance in setting up the training program and the procedures for making objective ratings of teacher enthusiasm. He also obtained an agreement with the directors of the university's Resident Teacher Program (a special internship program for newly certified teachers) to incorporate the experimental training conditions as part of the internship coursework.

Before discussing Bettencourt's results, we wish to comment on a second dissertation that grew out of this study. In reviewing videotapes of Bettencourt's teachers after training, we observed that students of the trained teachers appeared more attentive and on-task during instruction. Max Gillett, another doctoral student interested in teacher enthusiasm, became intrigued by the possibility that teacher enthusiasm training might have a positive effect on student on-task behavior. He decided to conduct an experiment to test the hypothesis that students of enthusiasm-trained teachers would exhibit a higher level of on-task behavior than students of untrained teachers. He also tested Bettencourt's first hypothesis, thus providing a second replication of Collins' findings. His operational definition of on-task behavior was based on previous studies by other investigators.

The test of the first hypothesis in Bettencourt's and Gillett's studies provided a nice replication of Collins' original results. Although the trained teachers in each study started at different overall levels of enthusiasm (Collins, 1.24; Bettencourt, 1.89; Gillett, 2.43), they ended at approximately the same level (2.98, 2.65, and 2.84, respectively).[35]

Bettencourt's hypothesis about the effect of teacher enthusiasm training on student achievement was not supported by the results, which are shown in table 1.4. Gillett, however, obtained positive results for his hypothesis concerning the effect of teacher enthusiasm training on student on-task behavior. In fact, his results (shown in table 1.5) show that the students of trained teachers were more on-task both during teacher-led instruction and during seatwork.

Bettencourt's negative results were puzzling to us because other researchers had obtained positive results concerning the enthusiasm-achievement relationship. When he completed his dissertation, we had only vague ideas about why the inconsistent results occurred. When Gillett's results came in, we were even more puzzled. Gillett's results suggested that we should have found the effect we were looking for. This belief was based in part on evidence from

---

35. Overall level of enthusiasm was a composite five-point scale based on the observers' ratings of the eight individual indicators. The higher the scale score, the higher the level of enthusiasm.

TABLE 1.4

Achievement Test Results for Classes of Enthusiasm-Trained and Untrained Teachers

Achievement Test		Classes of Trained Teachers (N = 8)	Classes of Untrained Teachers (N = 9)
Preadministration	M	22.88	23.73
	SD	5.57	3.12
Postadministration	M	28.83	29.59
	SD	5.69	3.76

other research investigations that student on-task behavior has a positive effect on student achievement.[36] The reasoning ran so: If teacher enthusiasm training increases student on-task behavior (Gillett's variable), then the increase in on-task behavior should increase student academic achievement (Bettencourt's variable).

We continued to puzzle about the negative finding in Bettencourt's study as we started writing a report of both studies for publication. Rosenshine and other colleagues suggested that we might obtain useful clues by reanalyzing

TABLE 1.5

Percentage of Student On-Task Behavior for Classes of Enthusiasm-Trained and Untrained Teachers

On-Task Percentages		Classes of Trained Teachers (N = 9)	Classes of Untrained Teachers (N = 9)
Teacher-led Instruction			
Pretraining	M	76.62	75.41
	SD	12.86	6.89
Posttraining	M	87.17	76.98
	SD	8.22	12.14
Seatwork			
Pretraining	M	71.56	81.51
	SD	10.23	5.51
Posttraining	M	85.88	69.71
	SD	10.82	5.33

36. Some of this research is included in the item "time on learning" in table 1.1.

the curriculum unit and reports of previous studies. Our reanalysis led us to make two discoveries. First, the curriculum unit in Bettencourt's study relied heavily on supplementary curriculum objectives and inquiry-oriented activities. By contrast, regular mathematics instruction in elementary school emphasizes basic skills and drill-and-practice.[37] We came to the realization that the atypicality of the curriculum unit could have masked the effects of teacher enthusiasm training.

The second discovery came in rereading previous experiments involving manipulation of teacher enthusiasm level. Four of the previous experiments had demonstrated a positive effect of teacher enthusiasm on student achievement. Only one previous experiment and Bettencourt's experiment had found an absence of effect. We discovered that the few experiments with positive results have one feature in common. The comparison treatment (the no-training condition) in each study required the teacher to purposefully act in a non-enthusiastic manner. For example, in one of the comparison treatments the teacher "read an entire speech from a manuscript" and "made no gestures or direct eye contact and held vocal inflection to a minimum."[38] In the two experiments reporting no effect, however, the comparison groups of teachers were given no special instructions. They were allowed to use their natural teaching style.

This analysis suggests that the four experiments obtained positive results because an elevated level of teacher enthusiasm was compared with a depressed level of enthusiasm. Bettencourt may not have obtained positive effects because an elevated level of teacher enthusiasm was compared with a natural, nondepressed level. In other words, the difference between treatments was not sufficiently large to produce an effect on student achievement.

Our reflections on the Bettencourt and Gillett studies have led us to pose new hypotheses and questions for further research. One hypothesis is that teacher enthusiasm training would show an effect on student achievement if used with teachers with depressed affect about their work (e.g., stressed or burned-out teachers). The teachers selected for training from this group should develop elevated levels of enthusiasm relative to their nontrained, low-affect colleagues.

On another issue, we were surprised to find that the effect of enthusiasm training on students' on-task behavior was just as strong during seatwork, when teachers presumably have less opportunity to exhibit enthusiastic behavior. We would like to do further research to learn why this might be so. One line of

37. This point was documented in J. T. Fey, "Mathematics Teaching Today: Perspectives from Three National Surveys," *Mathematics Teacher* 72 (1979): 490–504.
38. W. Coats and V. Smidchens, "Audience Recall as a Function of Speaker Dynamism," *Journal of Educational Psychology* 57 (1966): 189–91.

speculation is that the nonverbal aspects of teachers' instruction convey important messages to students. If this is true, we would like to learn what messages are conveyed by teacher enthusiasm and whether the messages have the capacity to motivate student work even when the teacher is not directly communicating to all students (e.g., during seatwork). Still other issues for further research concern the duration of enthusiasm training effects and the relationship between our operational definition of enthusiasm and other possible definitions.

The experiments by Bettencourt and Gillett are completed dissertations. Also, papers describing the experiments have been presented at national conventions of the American Educational Research Association. We have received many requests for reprints of these papers. As a result, we have become acquainted with other researchers interested in investigating teacher enthusiasm phenomena.

These examples of research illustrate the factors that motivate certain individuals to pursue scientific inquiry. Our analysis suggests several factors, although other researchers undoubtedly have different reasons for pursuing their lines of investigation. First, researchers value the power of scientific inquiry to provide a check on personal belief, common sense, and ordinary observation. In our case we believed that enthusiasm is a desirable teacher trait, but we also wanted to subject this belief to a research test. Second, the researcher is motivated by curiosity. Collins demonstrated that level of teacher enthusiasm can be elevated, but we were curious about whether we could obtain the same effect. Our curiosity was also aroused by anomalies in our data: Why wasn't there an effect on student achievement? Why did students' on-task behavior during seatwork improve?

The joy of discovery is another source of motivation for doing research. We were pleased to discover that Collins' training procedure held up under two replications. We were excited, too, to discover plausible reasons why an effect on academic achievement did not occur.

The profession of educational research also has its sources of satisfaction for the individual. First, there is the satisfaction of knowing that we have contributed to knowledge about education. The Bettencourt and Gillett experiments are now part of the literature on teacher enthusiasm. Second, there is the satisfaction of thinking that our work may one day influence practice in the area of teacher education. Perhaps teacher educators will incorporate our work, along with the contributions of other researchers, in designing training in affective skills for prospective teachers. Third, there is the satisfaction of being members of the educational research community. We have been in communication with other interested researchers through their writings, personal conversations, phone calls, and professional associations. Educational researchers seldom work in isolation. If the problem is of sufficient importance, you will find other researchers working on it. There are many "invisible colleges" of researchers around the world working right now on important problems in education. Finally, professional researchers receive professional recognition for their contributions. Educators who do research are generally respected by their colleagues and by the community. If you are working in a college or university setting, research contributions are generally a major basis for awarding promotion and tenure.

The Study of Educational Research

The purpose of this chapter was to help you understand *why* educational research is worth doing. Most of the following chapters describe *how* to do educational research. However, "book knowledge" of these tools and concepts will not turn you into a competent researcher. It is essential that you acquire experience in doing research. The usual way to accomplish this goal is to apprentice yourself to an experienced researcher. We highly recommend that you seek out such opportunities. We also recommend that you read research reports in education journals as you study this book. We provide many examples of published research, but you are advised to supplement them by looking for additional examples. Finally, as you read the book, we recommend that you think about research projects you might want to undertake. Replication-and-extensions are quite feasible for the beginning researcher. Find an established line of research inquiry and build on it. The studies by Bettencourt and Gillett, described above, are examples of the replicate-and-extend model.

The next chapter describes the institutional context of educational research and professional opportunities available to the individual researcher. The remaining chapters describe procedures for planning, conducting, and reporting research studies.

ANNOTATED REFERENCES

American Educational Research Association. "Twenty-Five Years of Educational Research." *Review of Educational Research* 26, no. 3 (1956).
    This publication will be of interest to the educator who wants a historical perspective on educational research. The entire issue of the *Review* is devoted to tracing some of the major trends in educational research between 1931 and 1956. Many significant developments occurring during that time period are described. The articles cover major areas of education including school administration, curriculum, measurement, counseling, foundations of education, and research methodology.

Gage, N. L. *The Scientific Basis of the Art of Teaching*. New York: Teachers College Press, 1978.

This small book of lectures is must reading for both the beginning and advanced researcher. Gage helped initiate the modern era of educational research by editing the first *Handbook of Research on Teaching* in 1963. The book of lectures reflects his accumulated wisdom about how research has contributed to knowledge about teaching and about teacher education. The last chapter contains many substantive and methodological ideas for persons wishing to undertake research on teaching.

Kuhn, Thomas S. *The Structure of Scientific Revolutions*. Chicago: University of Chicago Press, 1962.

This classic essay changed the way people think about the progress of science. Kuhn argues that a scientific discipline progresses cumulatively within an agreed-upon paradigm until anomalies unexplained by the paradigm provoke a scientific revolution. The essay will be of great interest to educational researchers who wonder how other scientific disciplines operate.

Wolcott, Harry F. *The Man in the Principal's Office: An Ethnography*. New York: Holt, Rinehart and Winston, 1973.

This book is an important contribution to the study of education, and also a model of the case study method of research. Wolcott used a variety of techniques—participant observation, tape recordings, content analysis, questionnaire survey—to learn about the life of one elementary school principal. If you ever plan to do a case study or if you wonder what one looks like, this report by Wolcott will be highly profitable reading.

SELF-CHECK TEST

Circle the correct answer to each of the following questions. An answer key is provided on page 881.

1. Comroe and Dripps' study of medical advances demonstrated the importance of
   a. political influences on what gets researched.
   b. funding cycles for basic and applied research.
   c. basic research in bringing about improvements in medical practice.
   d. the interaction between researchers and practitioners in bringing about medical advances.
2. The impact of educational research on practice has been impeded because of
   a. inadequate R & D capability.
   b. educators' lack of knowledge about research.
   c. isolated research studies.
   d. all of the above.

3. Science can be said to "control" variable B if
   a. manipulation of variable A reliably leads to changes in variable B.
   b. measurement of variable A at one point in time leads to an accurate pre-diction of variable B at a subsequent point in time.
   c. variable B can be given an operational definition.
   d. variable B can be given a constitutive definition.
4. The statement "Aptitude will be measured by the quantitative scale of the SAT (Scholastic Aptitude Test)" is an example of a(n)
   a. theoretical law.
   b. operationally defined construct.
   c. constitutively defined construct.
   d. hypothesis.
5. Positivistic science is characterized by
   a. reliance on the researcher's subjective framework.
   b. reliance on methods for achieving objective observation.
   c. the researcher's empathic participation in the phenomena being studied.
   d. the search for cause-and-effect relationships.
6. Up to the present time educational research
   a. has ignored the methodologies of other scientific disciplines.
   b. has been influenced only by the methodology of psychology.
   c. has been influenced only by mathematical statistics.
   d. has been heavily influenced by a variety of scientific disciplines.
7. Research that focuses on fundamental, underlying structures and processes is usually described as
   a. basic.
   b. applied.
   c. exploratory.
   d. hypothesis testing.
8. Precise measurement, generalizability, and statistical analysis characterize the methodology of
   a. case studies.
   b. positivistic research.
   c. basic research.
   d. applied research.
9. The experiments on teacher enthusiasm presented in this chapter illustrate
   a. the study of a previously unexplored phenomenon in education.
   b. literal replication of previous research.
   c. replication-and-extension of previous research.
   d. research with no implications for educational practice.
10. In Bettencourt's experiment on teacher enthusiasm, the failure to find an effect of enthusiasm training on student achievement
    a. was a personal defeat for the researcher.

b. led the researcher to conclude that previous findings of positive effects were invalid.
c. motivated the researcher to discover the cause of the discrepancy between his findings and the results of other research.
d. meant that his findings could not be reported at professional meetings or in research journals.

APPLICATION PROBLEMS

The following problems are designed to give you practice in applying significant concepts and research procedures explained in chapter 1. They do not have a single correct answer. For feedback, you can compare your answers with the sample answers on page 882.

1. Suppose the federal government decides to fund a new program for training high school students in study skills. Some educators argue that all of the appropriated funds should be used to develop model programs and materials, to train teachers in summer institutes, and to hire additional school staff. Other educators argue that at least 15 percent of the appropriations should be allocated for research on study skills. What defense could you offer for this "15 percent for research" proposal?
2. Case studies and positivistic inquiry represent two contrasting traditions in educational research. Describe four major differences between these two approaches to research.

SUGGESTION SHEET

If your last name starts with letters from Aaa to Bal, please complete the Suggestion Sheet at the end of the book while this chapter is still fresh in your mind.

2.

OPPORTUNITIES IN
EDUCATIONAL RESEARCH

OVERVIEW

This chapter takes an optimistic position concerning educational research as a professional field of endeavor. There is increasing recognition that problems in education cannot be solved by common sense and trial-and-error alone. The knowledge and products yielded by research, evaluation, and R & D are also necessary. The first part of the chapter concerns sources of funding for educational research and procedures for writing a funding proposal. The second part of the chapter describes career opportunities in educational research and how to seek a position. The chapter concludes with a brief description of opportunities for financial assistance to pursue graduate study of educational research.

OBJECTIVES

After studying this chapter, you should be able to:

1. Describe the present status of financial support for educational research in this country and the problems that must be solved if support is to improve.
2. Describe the major governmental agencies and private foundations that support educational research.
3. State four criteria commonly used by funding agencies to evaluate research proposals.
4. Describe at least six types of institutional settings that employ educational researchers.
5. Name two major professional organizations for educational researchers.
6. Describe four methods for finding a position in educational research.

SOURCES OF FUNDING FOR EDUCATIONAL RESEARCH

Past and Current Status of Funding

The start of the modern era in educational research can be traced back to the Cooperative Research Act of 1954. This act authorized the then U.S. Office of Education (USOE) to fund a variety of research and development projects in universities and other educational agencies. From 1957 to 1963, USOE appropriations for educational research and development averaged $20 million or less.[1] In 1964, appropriations increased to $37 million. In the following year they increased again, to over $100 million, where they stabilized for the remainder of the decade.

David Krathwohl analyzed the progress that was made over a twenty-year period after passage of the Cooperative Research Act.[2] He identified ten areas of substantial improvement:

1. The substantially greater pool of research personnel available and their enhanced sophistication in research methods
2. The enlarged breadth of research methods—from historical, to observational, to simple quantitative, to very complex statistical methods and experimental designs
3. The multiple disciplines across the social science spectrum actively involved in research on education—especially economics, but also anthropology and political science
4. The widespread capacity to develop large-scale, field-based, empirically validated instructional materials
5. The recently increasing capacity to mount large, strong evaluative programs
6. The large number of universities that have research capacity
7. The increased proportion of deans and other administrative leaders with research credentials who were chosen both for their ability to manage R & D and for their capacity to handle the traditional responsibilities
8. The many corporate educational research units that have been formed—small and large, profit and nonprofit, freestanding and parts of large comprehensive R & D corporations
9. The expanding number of policy research centers concerned with education

1. USOE data are from U.S. Office of Education, Bureau of Research, *Educational Research and Development in the United States* (Washington, D.C.: Government Printing Office, 1969), p. 158.
2. David Krathwohl, "Improving Educational Research and Development," *Educational Researcher* 6, no. 4 (1977): 8-14.

10. The substantial group of government-initiated laboratories and research and
    development centers

Some of these developments are described in more detail elsewhere in the
chapter.

Although the field of educational research has expanded enormously since
about 1960, major problems of funding still exist. Educational research is largely
dependent upon the federal government and private foundations for funding.
Table 2.1 shows gross national product and national expenditures for education
between 1969 and 1976.[3] A total of $120 billion was spent on education in 1975,
about 8 percent of the gross national product. Federal expenditures for educational research that same year were $149 million, which is only .001 percent of
total education expenditures. Foundation support would add just slightly to
this percentage.

The lack of funding support for educational research is also apparent by
comparison with other fields. Harold Hodgkinson estimated that in the mid-
1970s agriculture spent 3.2 percent of its total expenditures on research and
development.[4] The health field spent 3.6 percent of its total expenditures on
research and development. Some businesses and industries allocated even higher
percentages of their budgets for this purpose.

These data are from some years back, but the funding situation has not
changed appreciably since then. In fact, the major federal agency for educational
research, the National Institute of Education, has seen a decline in its funding
in the early 1980s compared to the late 1970s.

Educational researchers are increasingly aware that the funding of their
work involves a political process. The task of winning political support for
educational research is difficult because, as we discussed in chapter 1, the impact
of research on the improvement of educational practice is often slow, incremental,
and unspectacular. Also, many policy makers are skeptical about the value of
educational research. Their notions about its goals and methods sometimes are
shallow and distorted.

At the present time, some R & D administrators believe that an important
part of the solution to inadequate and insecure financial support is to develop a
political coalition that includes both researchers and practitioners. David Clark

3. This table was constructed from two sources. Gross national product and education expenditure
   data are from: Social Indicators Staff (Center for Demographic Studies, Bureau of the Census),
   Social Indicators III (Washington, D.C.: Government Printing Office, 1980), p. 290. Research and
   development expenditure data are from: W. Vance Grant and Leo J. Eiden, *Digest of Education
   Statistics* (Washington, D.C.: Government Printing Office, 1981), p. 192.
4. Harold L. Hodgkinson, "Why Education R & D?" *American Education* 12 (1976): 11-13. Hodgkinson estimated that about .005 of total education expenditures were for research and development, a percentage slightly higher than our estimate derived from table 2.1.

TABLE 2.1
Expenditures for Education and for Educational Research and Development

Year	Gross National Product (in billions of dollars)	Expenditures for Education[a] (in billions of dollars)	Federal Expenditures for Educational Research and Development (in millions of dollars)
1969	935.5	70.4	154.8
1971	1,063.4	83.2	186.1
1973	1,306.6	98.5	214.2
1975	1,516.3	120.1	149.2
1976	1,692.4	131.1	—
1977	—	—	120.2
1979	—	—	146.1

[a]Includes expenditures of public and nonpublic schools at all levels of education (elementary, secondary, and higher education). Expenditures are for school year beginning in designated calendar year.

wrote about this type of solution in the mid-1970s, but his ideas still apply today. He believed that improvement in financial support for educational R & D would require

a solid coalition including diverse interests and emphases, e.g., American Educational Research Association, American Association of Colleges for Teacher Education, National Education Association, National Council of Chief State School Officers, American Federation of Teachers, Council for Educational Development and Research, Deans of Schools and Colleges of Education in State Universities and Land Grant Colleges, National School Boards Association, American Association of School Administrators, etc. Such a coalition has never existed in the past but is a must for the present and future.

The basis for this coalition will have to be built upon a reconceptualization of the role of R & D in education which will diversify the types of and sites for productivity in educational R & D. The process of inquiry will have to be brought closer to the point of effective action in education, i.e., will involve the direct participation of practitioner agencies in all the processes of educational R & D.[5]

5. David L. Clark, "Federal Policy in Educational Research and Development," *Educational Researcher* 5, no. 1 (1976): 4-8.

In brief, researchers will need to view practitioners as partners in the R & D process rather than as passive recipients of R & D products and knowledge.

The problems of financial support, the federal government's role in R & D, and the relationship between research and practice are continuing concerns of educational researchers. If you choose this field as a career, you may find yourself drawn into these problems, and you will need to work on solutions to them. Professional journals such as *Educational Researcher* and *American Psychologist* regularly have articles on developments that affect the future progress of educational research.

Now that we have a brief overview of federal funding support, let us examine the ways in which federal and other agencies sponsor various types of educational research and development. You should keep in mind that federal legislation and agency priorities are constantly shifting. Therefore, if you are interested in seeking funding support from a particular institution or agency, you should contact it directly to obtain information about its most current policies and activities.

U.S. Department of Education

The former U.S. Office of Education (USOE) was reorganized into the U.S. Department of Education (ED) in 1980 under the Carter administration. The Department of Education is by far the largest source of federal funding for education and for educational research. It administers many legislative acts designed to improve education through research and development. For example, Titles I, II, III, and IV of the famous Elementary and Secondary Education Act (ESEA) of 1965 provided funds to train educational researchers, to initiate programs to disseminate research findings, and to establish regional laboratories and R & D centers.

A distinguishing characteristic of recent federal legislation is the provision for evaluation of programs authorized by the legislation. Head Start, Follow Through, the Voucher Program, and other educational innovations have had substantial funds allocated for evaluation of their effectiveness.

Table 2.2 lists the current major organizational units ("Offices") of the Department of Education.[6] Listed directly beneath each office are the subunits (groups of programs, institutes, centers, etc.) administered by the office. Each subunit in turn administers a range of programs. We listed in the right-hand column an example of a program administered by each subunit or office. The source from which table 2.2 was constructed lists 143 such programs.

---

6. Information in table 2.2 is from *American Education* 17, no. 10 (1981): 6–30.

TABLE 2.2

Offices and Programs of the U.S. Department of Education

Offices	Sample Programs
1. Office of Elementary and Secondary Education	
Compensatory Education Programs	Education for the Disadvantaged
Educational Support Programs	Improvement in Local Educational Practices
Indian Education Programs	Indian Education—Special Programs and Projects
Migrant Education Programs	Migrant Education—High School Equivalency Program
2. Office of Special Education and Rehabilitation Services	
National Institute of Handicapped Research	Handicapped Research
Office of Special Education	Special Studies of P.L. 94–142
Rehabilitation Services Administration	Vocational Rehabilitation—Innovation and Expansion
3. Office of Vocational and Adult Education	Vocational Education—Program Improvement Projects
4. Office of Postsecondary Education	
Student Financial Assistance Programs	College Work-Study
International Education Programs	International Research and Studies
Institutional Support Programs	Fellowships for Graduate and Professional Study
Fund for the Improvement of Postsecondary Education	Mina Shaughnessy Scholars Program
5. Office of Bilingual Education and Minority Languages Affairs	Bilingual Vocational Instructional Materials, Methods, and Techniques
6. Office of Educational Research and Development	
National Center for Education Statistics	Capacity-Building Programs for Statistical Activities in State Education Agencies
National Institute of Education	Research and Development
Office of Dissemination and Professional Improvement	National Diffusion Network Program
Office of Libraries and Learning Technologies	Technology for Basic Skills Instruction

The authorizing legislation and structure of the Department of Education programs are constantly changing. For example, the Omnibus Reconciliation Act of 1981 enacted by Congress consolidated approximately 30 Department of Education programs into a block grant. The block grant programs were administered by state education agencies starting with the 1982–83 fiscal year. The journal of the Department of Education, *American Education,* is a good source of information about the current status of its programs. The annual December issue of this journal provides a comprehensive listing of Department of Education programs, authorizing legislation, contracts, and who may apply for funding.

Funds from Department of Education programs are disbursed through four mechanisms. First, the department may award funds through a **direct grant** competition. Announcements of direct grant competitions appear in the *Federal Register,* a publication issued every weekday and available in most major libraries. There are two other types of grant awards. **State formula grants** (also called "entitlement grants") are made to states based on the number of children or students to be served. In **state-administered grants,** federal funds are granted to states, which in turn award grants to individuals or organizations.

The fourth mechanism for awarding funds is contracts. A **contract** is an award of money to carry out a specific task for a federal agency. Contracts are usually more specific and restrictive about the work to be done than are grants. Notices of available contracts are published in the *Commerce Business Daily,* a publication issued every weekday and available in most major libraries. The notices are usually in the form of a **request for proposal (RFP).** Contracts are awarded to RFPs that best meet the specifications of the announced work.

Many colleges and universities maintain an office of grants and contracts to sift through the *Federal Register, Commerce Business Daily,* and other sources of funding opportunities. Pertinent opportunities are announced to faculty and students through personal contact and newsletters. We know many faculty colleagues and graduate students who have received research funding by learning about grants and contracts in their area of interest.

National Institute of Education

Although the National Institute of Education is not the largest funder of educational R & D, it probably is the most influential. The **National Institute of Education (NIE)** was established by the Education Amendments Act of 1972. Many of NIE's functions formerly were served by USOE's National Center for Educational Research and Development and, before 1969, by USOE's Bureau of Research. Both of these latter agencies have since been dissolved.

The major goals of NIE are to promote the reform and renewal of American education; to advance the practice of education as an art, science, and profession;

to strengthen the scientific and technological foundations of education; and to build an effective education R & D system. NIE policy and program priorities are set by the **National Council for Educational Research,** a panel of citizens appointed by the President and confirmed by the Senate. NIE conducts some research and development at its headquarters in Washington, D.C., but much of it is done through contracts and grants awarded through open competition.

Other Federal Agencies

Federal agencies in addition to the Department of Education and NIE have authorization to fund educational R & D projects that relate to their stated missions.

The **National Science Foundation (NSF),** authorized by the National Science Foundation Act of 1950, supports extensive research programs in all scientific fields, including areas relating to education. Some of the most important curriculum programs of the 1960s—Chemical Education Materials Study, Physical Sciences Study Committee, Biological Sciences Curriculum Study, and the School Mathematics Study Group—were sponsored by NSF. This federal agency continues to sponsor the research and development of high-quality science and mathematics curriculum at the precollege and college levels. NSF also awards grants for basic research on learning processes.

The **Office of Human Development (OHD)** supports a variety of research projects on conditions of childhood experiences that, directly or indirectly, affect schooling. Projects funded by OHD have included research on day care, adoption and foster care, early childhood, television, and single-parent families.

The **Department of Defense** supports an extensive program of research, part of which is education related. Funds are available for studies on learning and motivation, and the development of training materials, including computer-assisted instruction. The **National Foundation for the Arts and Humanities,** through the use of federal matching funds, encourages private contributions for programs which stimulate development in the arts and humanities.

These federal agencies and others often designate specific areas in which they wish research to be carried out and then invite researchers to submit proposals. Some of these agencies will also accept unsolicited research proposals relating to their stated missions. For more specific information, the researcher should contact the agency in which he is interested by submitting a proposal.

Foundations and Other Sources of Funding

In addition to federal support for educational research, research funds are also available through grants and postdoctoral fellowships from foundations, institutional research programs supported by universities, and educational research funds available in state departments of education and local school districts.

Foundations are a major source of funding support for education. The most prominent of these foundations in terms of total dollar support are the Ford Foundation, Lilly Endowment, Carnegie Corporation, Danforth Foundation, Sloan Foundation, Kellogg Foundation, Kettering Foundation, and Exxon Foundation. The researcher interested in seeking funding from these and similar sources is advised to consult *The Foundation Directory* (see Annotated References) and *Foundation News*, a bimonthly publication of The Foundation Center, 888 Seventh Avenue, New York, NY 10019.

Many universities have institutional research programs supported at least partially by the university budget. Bureaus of educational research are found at nearly all the major universities. Some universities have a centralized educational research council to consider proposals from faculty members and students. Such funds are particularly helpful to the new faculty member, as they are often made available for pilot studies and small budget studies that would be unacceptable for support under most research programs sponsored by private foundations or the federal government. Such pilot studies, if productive, however, can lead to broader and more sophisticated research proposals that can obtain support from these latter sources.

Many state departments of education include a research division, and some state departments also have research funds available to support research projects in the public schools of the state. Also, most large school districts now employ research personnel and carry out research programs on problems of special interest to the district. Even smaller districts that do not employ full-time personnel to carry out research in the district are often willing to provide released time and some financial help for teachers or administrators in the district who wish to carry out educational research.

PREPARING A RESEARCH PROPOSAL
FOR A FUNDING AGENCY

Educational researchers generally rely on government agencies or private foundations for funding of their projects. In order to obtain funding, researchers need to prepare proposals describing the proposed project, its financial requirements, and its potential contribution to education. The writing of the proposal is very important; this document is usually the sole means by which the funding agency will decide to support or reject the proposed research project. Although guidelines for preparing a proposal will vary depending upon the agency, some guidelines that are generally applicable will be described here.

Prior to the actual writing of a research proposal, you should attempt to determine which funding source is most likely to support work on your proposed research study. Federal agencies and foundations often identify a few high-priority problem areas and channel most of their funds into support of projects in these areas. Such priorities are sometimes stated in the agency's literature. News of upcoming federal requests for research proposals can be found in the *Federal Register* and *Commerce Business Daily*. Information about foundations and other agencies that support research can be found in publications described in the Annotated References at the end of this chapter. These publications are usually kept on file at a research office maintained on most university campuses. These offices provide useful services related to funding opportunities and proposal preparation.

If the priorities of the agency or foundation are not stated in their literature, they may be known to experienced researchers in the field. It is wise to check with your more experienced colleagues on the most likely source of funding for the proposed research. In selecting a funding agency, you should also note that they differ greatly in their preferences for research rigor in the proposed project. For example, the National Insitute of Education is most likely to fund proposals that attack a limited and carefully defined problem, using rigorous research procedures. On the other hand, some foundations support loosely stated, innovative attempts to deal with major educational problems.

Success in obtaining financial support often depends more upon your skill in selecting an appropriate funding source and in writing a proposal that meets its special requirements than in the intrinsic worth and research rigor of your project. Since the interest, biases, and idiosyncrasies of funding agencies shift as new problems become popular in education and new staff members administer the programs, it is important that you get as much current information as possible. "Grantsmanship" plays a significant role in many decisions on funding of research projects. Because this is the case, the researcher is wise to learn these biases so that they work for him rather than against him.

Once you have selected an appropriate funding source you should write the organization for materials that will help you prepare a proposal. Before submitting the proposal, you should make sure that it meets all the requirements set forth by the agency; otherwise, the proposal will probably be rejected even though it is well written and contains good ideas. It is particularly important that you adhere to deadlines for submitting proposals. Many funding agencies accept proposals only at certain times of the year.

The research proposal is the main document that the researcher will transmit to the funding agency. This document presents the design and budget for the proposed research project. The research proposal is usually given by the funding agency to a panel of reviewers. Since this is the only contact that the reviewers will have with the project, the proposal must contain all the pertinent information about the design of the project. The researcher should not leave anything to be assumed. In preparing the proposal, the researcher should keep in mind that proposed projects are generally evaluated in terms of four criteria:

1. Educational significance. What contribution will the proposed project make to the improvement of education?
2. Soundness of the research design.
3. Adequacy of personnel and facilities.
4. Economic efficiency. Does the proposed project achieve its objectives economically?

Before submitting a proposal, the researcher should evaluate it critically on the basis of these criteria.

There are a few general considerations to keep in mind while writing the actual proposal. First, the proposal should be written clearly, concisely, and in nontechnical language. Generally, review panels will have one or more nonspecialists on them; they will rapidly form a negative impression of the proposal if it uses terms that they do not understand. An unclear and unnecessarily long proposal can also cause panel members to form an unfavorable impression. A second general consideration is to make sure the submitted proposal is typed and neat in its appearance. If many copies of the proposal must be submitted, it is probably worth the additional expense to have them reproduced by offset press. The physical appearance of the research proposal is a small point, but it can influence some review panel members, particularly since they must rely solely on the proposal to form their impression of the researcher and the worth of his project.

The body of the proposal usually calls for four types of information. First, there is a statement of the problem and objectives. The statement of the problem should be written in such a manner as to convince the funding agency that your research project is important and likely to make a contribution to education. It is particularly important that the problem be clearly delimited. If the problem is too broadly stated, the funding agency will probably conclude that the project is unwieldy and that you have not thought through the problem deeply enough. The statement of objectives can be in the form of the research hypotheses that you wish to test or the research questions that you wish to answer. These should be stated clearly, concisely, and in simple language. This section of the proposal should also contain a review of the literature. Generally, an exhaustive review of the literature is not required. However, the review should indicate that you have a command of the research in your area, including recent research findings, if any. Also, it is advisable to discuss those studies most relevant to the proposed project. The review should be tied directly to the statement of the problem and research objectives.

The second type of information concerns the research design that will be used. It is advisable to describe the design in considerable detail. Generally, at least one review panel member will be a research methodologist who will study the proposal for flaws and weaknesses in the design. The statement of the research design includes a description of the sample, measures to be administered, and experimental treatments, if appropriate. The research design should be tied directly to the research problem and objectives. The description of the sample is particularly important, because the type of sample selected will affect the generalizability of the research findings. Funding agencies are inclined to fund projects that are likely to yield generally applicable findings rather than projects that deal only with a local problem. The researcher should also build a sound rationale for the size of the sample she has chosen, since sample size often affects the amount of funding required. Even though she may wish to study an entire defined population because it is available, the researcher should probably study a sample drawn from it in order to reduce the cost of the project. Procedures that will be used to protect the rights of subjects should be discussed, including any special procedures required by the funding agency. The researcher's plans for analyzing the data should also be described in this section. If computer services are needed to analyze the data, she should state how she plans to obtain them. Finally, she should provide a tentative time schedule for completion of the project.

The third type of information included in the body of the proposal concerns the potential relevance of the findings. The researcher must state clearly the new knowledge that may be expected to result from the study. If relevant, she should discuss how she proposes to use or build upon this knowledge when the project is completed. Also, the researcher should state how she proposes to disseminate findings resulting from the project.

Personnel and facilities constitute the fourth type of information usually asked for in a research proposal. Generally, funding agencies will want information about all personnel associated with the proposed project. The following information is usually requested: name, position, experience, responsibilities within the project, percentage of time committed to the project, and extent to which a commitment has been secured. If the researcher has identified consultants who will be used in the project, they should be identified by name. Letters from consultants stating their willingness to serve on the project are helpful and may be attached as an appendix to the proposal. Research facilities should be described, including public schools if they are to be used in the project. Funding agencies will generally want some statement of assurance that the facilities are available for the project.

The statement of the budget request is usually a separate section of the research proposal. The researcher must make careful estimates of all expenses that are likely to be incurred in carrying out the project. The budget form included in the request for a proposal (RFP) usually contains the following items:

personnel salaries, employee benefits, travel expenses, supplies and materials, communications, services (duplicating and reproduction, statistical analysis, testing), final report production, and equipment. Alternative budgets may be prepared if appropriate to the nature of the research project.

An important aspect of the budget is the statement of cost sharing to be provided by the institution with which the researcher is affiliated. Many funding agencies require that the researcher's institution, such as a school district or university, share part of the cost of the proposed project. In order to determine cost-sharing requirements, the researcher should obtain information from the funding agency and from the sponsoring institution. Generally, the institution will have a committee or person, such as a contract officer, who is responsible for making budgetary arrangements with funding agencies. In certain instances, a funding agency will pay for indirect costs. For example, most funding agencies will pay overhead to cover such costs as use of university furniture and space, and necessary bookkeeping in the project.

The research proposal may contain a number of appendixes. We have already mentioned that letters from consultants are included as an appendix. Some agencies and foundations require that the principal personnel include an appended statement describing any current research project that they are working on and the agency supporting it. If agreements with cooperating agencies, such as school districts, are involved in the project, these can be placed in the appendix.

Copies of all instruments to be used in the project (e.g., questionnaires, aptitude tests) also can be included in the appendix. If the instrument is to be developed later, sample items may be given and an outline of the proposed instrument. It is important to note that all instruments used in contract research funded by the Department of Education, if given to ten or more individuals, must be cleared by the specific sponsoring agency.[7] The purpose of the clearance is to determine whether any of the instruments represent intrusive inquiries into a person's religion, sex, politics, or morals or involve self-incriminating disclosures. Parental consent is required if any instrument is to be administered to an individual below college age. It is advisable to prepare all instruments for the clearance procedure well before you are notified whether the research proposal has been cleared for funding. If the proposal is selected for funding, then you will be able to start clearance procedures immediately.

When it is received by the funding agency, a research proposal is usually assigned an identification number and is reviewed by the staff. If it seems worthy and meets the program's requirements, the proposal may be submitted

---

7. This procedure is discussed in Launor Carter, "Federal Clearance of Educational Evaluation Instruments: Procedural Problems and Proposed Remedies," *Educational Researcher* 6, no. 6 (1977): 7-12.

to a panel of specialists for review. The panel makes a recommendation on the research proposal, and this is forwarded to the funding agency. Generally, several months elapse between receipt of the proposal and notification regarding its disposition. If the proposal is accepted for funding, a contractual arrangement will be worked out between the funding agency and the investigator and his institution of affiliation. During the course of the project, the researcher typically will need to submit progress and expenditure reports. In addition, she usually is required to submit a comprehensive final report.

The preparation of a research proposal is a complicated and difficult process. In one field competition, the National Institute of Education's Basic Skills Division funded only 38 of the 450 proposals that it received.[8] The researcher is advised, therefore, to devote much time and thought to preparing the proposal, since it is the chief basis on which funding decisions are made.

CAREER OPPORTUNITIES

A survey of persons with newly earned doctorates in education during the period 1963–72 indicated that two-thirds of them became affiliated with a university or college as their first postdoctoral employment.[9] The second largest employer of new doctorates (approximately 20 percent) was the public school system. Other new doctorates found employment in government, industry, and nonprofit organizations, or they became self-employed.

At the time of this writing, there are indications that the employment picture is changing. College student enrollment is declining, and as a consequence there are fewer employment opportunities in universities and colleges for new doctorates. Other types of institutions and agencies have a need for master's- or doctoral-level persons with expertise in educational research methods, however. You are advised to become aware of the many job areas in which educational researchers are employed in order to increase your chances of finding rewarding employment. The following sections review major employers of persons with expertise in educational research and development methods.

Universities and Colleges

For many years, large universities have placed considerable emphasis upon research productivity in the employment and promotion of faculty members,

8. Krathwohl, "Improving Educational R & D," p. 21.
9. A. Stephen Higgins, "Recent Employment Patterns of New Doctorates," *Educational Researcher* 2, no. 10 (1973): 9-12.

and this emphasis has been felt in smaller universities and colleges as well. Many university positions involve part-time research as well as part-time teaching because it has been recognized that adequate programs of graduate training in education cannot be carried out without faculty members who do research. Recent years have also seen the establishment of many new educational research bureaus at colleges and universities and the expansion of the established bureaus at the larger schools. Many university counseling centers also employ educational research workers to carry out local studies concerned with various problems related to counseling. In some universities the Dean of Students Office also employs educational researchers to carry out institutional research concerning such matters as student dropouts, educational goals, the validity of student selection procedures, and the costs/benefits of educational programs.

Regional Educational Laboratories

The **regional educational laboratories** were authorized under Title IV of ESEA in 1965. Their mission, broadly stated, is to narrow the gap between educational research and educational practice. Each laboratory serves a different region of the country, and each is governed by members of state departments of education, public and private schools, university departments of education, and industrial and cultural institutions. The governing board is responsible for determining its laboratory's program objectives, policies, personnel, and budget allocation. In effect, each laboratory functions as an independent, nonprofit corporation, funded in part by the National Institute of Education, but also free to seek financial support from other funding sources.

As a result of the manner in which they were set up, regional laboratories have evolved a diversity of R & D strategies and program emphases over the past five years. In chapter 18 we discuss the R & D strategy of one laboratory, the Far West Laboratory for Educational Research and Development. There we point out that research and development involves the construction of an educational product based on pertinent research findings and using a development-feedback-revision cycle to achieve desired objectives.

The regional laboratories typically commit their resources to large-scale programmatic efforts involving the talents of many specialists. The researcher who joins one of the laboratories is likely to be employed as a member of a research and development team rather than as an individual responsible for one or two small-scale research projects. Some of the laboratories may have internship opportunities for students interested in learning how to do educational research and development. Even if a laboratory does not have employment openings at the time you apply, laboratory staff may be able to direct you to other opportunities in the region it serves.

TABLE 2.3

Directory of Regional Educational Laboratories

Appalachia Educational Laboratory Post Office Box 1348 Charleston, WV 25325	The Network, Inc. 290 South Main Street Andover, MA 01810
CEMREL, Inc. 3120 59th Street St. Louis, MS 63139	Northwest Regional Educational Laboratory 300 S.W. Sixth Avenue Portland, OR 97204
Far West Laboratory for Educational Research and Development 1855 Folsom Street San Francisco, CA 94103	Research for Better Schools 444 North Third Street Philadelphia, PA 19123
Mid-Continent Regional Educational Laboratory 4709 Belleview Avenue Kansas City, MS 64112	Southwest Educational Development Laboratory 211 East Seventh Street Austin, TX 78701
	SWRL Educational Research and Development 4665 Lampson Avenue Los Alamitos, CA 90720

A list of the laboratories and their addresses (current as of 1982) is presented in table 2.3. You can contact a laboratory directly to determine its program emphases. Also, the Council for Educational Development and Research, of which the regional laboratories are members, publishes periodically a directory containing this information (see Annotated References).

Research and Development Centers

Since 1963, a number of **research and development centers** have been established at major universities throughout the country. The purpose of these centers is to bring together scholars from several disciplines to work on a significant educational problem. Each center may carry out a program of basic research, applied research, or product development to solve their designated problem. A list of the centers and their addresses (current as of 1982) is presented in table 2.4. The centers, together with the regional laboratories described above, are members of the Council for Educational Development and Research.

The R & D centers generally are staffed by part-time professors and a few full-time personnel. Also, they provide graduate assistantships for students in education and the behavioral sciences. These assistantships enable graduate students to receive practical training in research and development and at the same time to make substantive contributions to the center's programs. If she is

TABLE 2.4

Directory of Research and Development Centers

National Center for Research in Vocational Education Ohio State University 1960 Kenny Road Columbus, OH 43210	Research and Development Center for Teacher Education Education Annex 3.203 The University of Texas Austin, TX 78712
Center for Educational Policy and Management College of Education University of Oregon Eugene, OR 97403	Center for the Study of Evaluation UCLA Graduate School of Education 145 Moore Hall Los Angeles, CA 90024
Learning Research and Development Center University of Pittsburgh 3939 O'Hara Street Pittsburgh, PA 15260	Wisconsin Center for Education Research University of Wisconsin 1025 West Johnson Street Madison, WI 53706

Institute for Research on Educational
  Finance and Governance
CERAS Building
School of Education
Stanford University
Stanford, CA 94305

located near one of these centers, the student is well advised to explore the possibility of receiving research training there.

Public Schools

Many large- and medium-size districts employ full-time research directors who plan and carry out research projects aimed at evaluating the educational effectiveness of the district and developing and validating new curricula, teaching methods, and educational programs. Some of the very large districts have well-staffed research bureaus that carry out studies in a wide range of educational areas. Smaller districts often employ a school psychologist or pupil personnel director, part of whose time is devoted to educational research projects of particular interest to the district.

Inasmuch as considerable financial support for research and development is available through federal programs and private foundations, educational research workers are often employed to direct a specific research or development project for which the school district has received financial support. In particular, the Elementary and Secondary Act of 1965 requires school districts to conduct evaluation studies on programs instituted under Title I (funds for educationally deprived students) or Title III (innovative and exemplary programs). This requirement has led to the employment of many educational researchers qualified to perform evaluation studies. Such special projects often lead to employment of full-time research personnel by the district after the special project has been completed.

Examples of research and development that occur at the school district level can be found in *Educational Researcher*, a monthly publication of the American Educational Research Association. A regular feature of this periodical is a section entitled "R & D in Progress in the Schools."

State Departments of Education

The increased interest in educational research has been reflected in state departments of education, where research personnel are increasingly employed. Federal research support is available to state departments of education through various programs, and some of the projects currently being carried out indicate that the level of educational research in state departments has improved greatly. A few years ago, the research division in most state departments typically carried out no research but served primarily as a statistical and recordkeeping section concerned with such matters as average daily attendance and pupil cost. It is not uncommon now for state departments to coordinate large-scale research projects involving many school districts and to accumulate large data banks that can be useful in conducting research on a variety of educational problems.

Other Career Opportunities

There are many opportunities for educational research workers in federal civil service. The Department of Health and Human Services employs educational researchers to monitor research contract programs and to carry out nationwide surveys of great importance in education. One of the most famous of these was the Coleman study of educational equality in American schools. The Department of State also has a number of programs that require personnel skilled in educational research and development.

The military services employ a great many civilian research workers in education and educational psychology. Some of these personnel are employed in centralized research units, such as the Air Force Personnel and Training Research Center, the Personnel Research Branch of the Army Adjutant General's office, and the Naval Research Field Activities. Others are employed to carry out educational research and development in the many schools operated by the armed services. Because the teachers and administrators in these schools are usually military personnel with little or no professional training in education, the need for civilians skilled in educational research and development has long been recognized. Such personnel are often employed as educational consultants or in special research sections, such as the Training Analysis and Development Sections attached to many air force training facilities.

There are also a great many research agencies and corporations that employ educational research workers. These organizations carry out educational research tasks under contract with the federal government or with private companies. The American Institutes for Research at Palo Alto, California, and other locations, the Human Resources Research Office affiliated with George Washington University at Washington, D.C., the Systems Development Corporation at Santa Monica, California, and Educational Testing Service at Princeton, New Jersey, are illustrative of the various types of private research organizations that employ educational research workers.

Additional career opportunities for educational researchers are to be found in business and industry. Many large corporations hire educational researchers to organize and administer training and educational programs for their employees. Large corporations, such as Xerox and Westinghouse, have started educational divisions that employ researchers to develop new products for commercial distribution to schools. Also, in recent years the medical field has turned increasingly to educational researchers to conduct research and development on various aspects of medical and health education.

Professional Organizations

An important part of career development in educational research is to become a member of professional organizations. These organizations keep you informed about developments in the field, bring you into contact with your professional colleagues, provide publication outlets, and can be helpful in career placement. At this time, the major professional organization for educational researchers is the **American Educational Research Association,** commonly known as **AERA.** It is possible to join AERA as a graduate student member. Information can be obtained by writing: AERA, 1230 Seventeenth Street NW, Washington, DC 20036.

In addition to holding membership in AERA, one can be a member of one or more of its eight divisions: administration, curriculum and objectives, instruction and learning, measurement and research methodology, counseling and human development, history and historiography, social context of education, and school evaluation and program development. There also are a variety of special-interest groups, for example: affective education, educational R & D evaluators, military education and training, research focus on black education, and special education research. The major publications of AERA are *American Educational Research Journal, Review of Educational Research,* and *Educational Researcher.* The annual meeting of AERA is usually in March or April.

The other major national organization you may wish to join is the **American Psychological Association (APA).** Division 15 of APA is organized around the interests and concerns of educational psychologists. Information about student and regular memberships can be obtained by writing: APA, 1200 Seventeenth Street NW, Washington, DC 20036. The major publications of APA that directly relate to educational research are *Journal of Educational Psychology* and *Educational Psychologist.* The annual meeting of APA occurs in August or September.

Many other national and state professional organizations deal with general or specialized aspects of educational research and development. Your graduate advisers should be good sources of information about which of these organizations you might consider joining.

SEEKING A POSITION

The Résumé

The graduate student who plans to seek a position in educational research should prepare a résumé several months prior to completion of graduate work. The résumé should be prepared with considerable care. If possible, offset process should be used to duplicate the résumé because it provides a neater copy than either mimeograph or ditto. The employer tends to judge the applicant not only by the content of the résumé, but also by the care with which it is prepared. The résumé usually includes the following items:

1. *Biographical data.* A brief biographical sketch including name, address, age, marital status, and so on.

2. *Professional experience.* A brief chronological description of any professional experience that the student has had.

3. *Educational record.* This record should include a listing of all college and university degrees taken at both the graduate and undergraduate level.

4. *Professional affiliations.* A list of professional organizations in which the student holds membership.

5. *Publications.* The graduate student usually lists his thesis or dissertation as a publication. If he has any other publications or has read any papers

at professional meetings, they should be listed. It is also advisable to prepare one or more articles based on the research findings of one's master's thesis or doctoral dissertation as soon as possible and submit these to a professional journal for publication. Because journals publishing educational research have a publication lag, the student may have nothing to list that has actually been published. He should, however, list articles that are in preparation or have been accepted for publication, giving the title of the article and noting its status. Research publications are given a great deal of weight by most employers.

    6. *Professional references.* The résumé should contain the names and current addresses of at least three persons familiar with the student's professional training and ability. For most graduate students, these references are limited to professors. It is customary to request an individual's permission before listing his or her name as a reference. Instead of listing references by name on the résumé, some students prefer to state that "references are available upon request."

Finding Position Openings

You should register with your university placement office at least six months prior to the time that you plan to complete graduate training. Many universities and public school districts begin looking for persons in December or January to fill vacancies for the following September. The student who is tardy in preparing a résumé and making her availability known will miss many opportunities.

    Some professional placement bureaus specialize in jobs in the public schools or universities. These bureaus often advertise in the professional journals in education and may be located by checking recent issues of these journals. Before registering with a placement bureau, you should make sure that you understand the fees connected with these services.

    Placement bureaus are operated at the annual meetings of many professional organizations. Employers are present at these meetings to interview applicants. You are particularly recommended to attend the annual meeting (usually held each March or April) of the American Educational Research Association. Also, placement bureaus are often set up at the annual meetings of state educational research associations.

    You may also correspond directly with school districts, universities, or other organizations that employ educational research workers. Such inquiries are usually accompanied by a copy of the individual's résumé.

    Many positions calling for educational research workers are available in the various branches of the federal government. You should check directly with federal installations in the area in which you may wish to work. You may also correspond directly with the Civil Service Commission in Washington, D.C., and may obtain announcements of vacancies from the local post office. Many of the vacancies listed under "Research Psychologist" and "Educational Specialist" require persons with training in educational research.

FINANCIAL ASSISTANCE FOR GRADUATE STUDY

Although undergraduate scholarships are based primarily upon financial need, the emphasis in programs of financial support for graduate students is on academic accomplishment. Nevertheless, accomplishment is not enough. You need to know what aid programs are available; you need to plan sufficiently in advance so that you can obtain aid when you need it; and you must be persistent in checking the available sources until you receive the needed financial assistance.

The usual types of financial assistance include the fellowship, the teaching or research assistantship, and the student loan. In each case these forms of assistance may originate from the university's own income or may be sponsored by a private foundation, industrial organization, fraternal organization, or government agency. The amount of support available under different programs, of course, varies considerably. The fellowship usually does not require that the graduate student do any work or provide any services in return. The teaching or research assistantship requires a certain amount of work from the student, although usually this work is closely allied to his field and constitutes valuable experience. Student loans usually permit repayment over a long period and at low interest rates. Student loan programs sometimes have provisions for canceling part of the loan if the student meets certain conditions.

It is beyond the scope of this book to provide graduate students with data concerning specific fellowships or scholarships. The sources and amounts of assistance, of course, change each year so that such information would quickly become out of date. Most universities have services for helping you determine the kinds of financial assistance for which you are qualified.

ANNOTATED REFERENCES

Council for Educational Development and Research. *CEDaR Directory.* Washington, D.C.: Council for Educational Development and Research, 1982.

This directory, revised periodically, lists the names, directors, and major programs of member organizations of CEDaR. Members include regional educational laboratories and university-based research and development centers. The address of CEDaR is: 1518 K Street NW, Suite 206, Washington, DC 20005.

Directory of Federal Aid for Education: A Guide to Federal Assistance Programs for Education. Santa Monica, Calif.: Ready Reference Press, 1982.

This is a comprehensive source of information about financial and other aid available to education. Some of the opportunities for aid include funding for educational research.

Foundation Center. *The Foundation Directory.* 8th ed. New York: Foundation Center, 1981.

This directory, with its periodic supplements, includes information on more than 2500 foundations with assets over $1,000,000 or with grants of $500,000 or more annually. The directory contains an alphabetical listing of foundations by state. The directory also has an index of Fields of Interest in which the student may look up educational research, fellowships, student loans, and other topics.

Lowman, Robert P.; Holt, Virginia E.; and O'Bryant, Catherine. *American Psychological Association's Guide to Research Support.* Washington, D.C.: American Psychological Association, 1981.

This is a comprehensive handbook of federal funding for behavioral science research. Over 150 funding programs are described. For each program the handbook includes the types of research supported, funding levels, key agency staff, and directions for making an application.

Marquis Academic Media. *Annual Register of Grant Support.* 15th ed. Chicago: Marquis Who's Who, 1981.

This is a comprehensive directory, revised annually, of all existing forms of grants available for work in the humanities, social sciences (including education), and sciences. Each entry in the directory contains the name of the organization, its type of grant support, purpose, eligibility, financial data, duration, application information, deadlines, address, and special stipulations, if any. A proposal-writing guide is included.

Orlich, Donald C., and Orlich, Patricia R. *The Art of Writing Successful R & D Proposals.* New York: Hippocrene Books, 1979.

The authors share their extensive experience in preparing and reviewing federal grant proposals. Their book covers all the components (e.g., problem statement, evaluation plan, budget, dissemination procedures) that you may be required to include in your funding proposal.

Thomas, Robert C., ed. *Research Centers Directory: A Guide to University-Related and Other Non-Profit Research Organizations Established on a Permanent Basis and Carrying on Continuing Research Programs.* 7th ed. Detroit, Mich.: Gale Research Co., 1981.

This valuable reference book, and its periodic supplements, contains information about university-related and other nonprofit research centers located in the United States and Canada. Facts about each research center include name, address, director's name, source of support, composition and size of staff, dollar volume of research, publications, and activities. The current directory lists more than 400 research centers devoted to various aspects of education.

White, Virginia P. *Grants: How to Find Out About Them and What to Do Next*. New York: Plenum Press, 1975.

The author covers procedures for finding out about grants offered by governmental agencies, foundations, and industry. There are detailed sections on the process of applying for grants (including proposal writing), and on the post-application process.

SUGGESTION SHEET

If your last name starts with letters from Bam to Bor, please complete the Suggestion Sheet at the end of the book while this chapter is still fresh in your mind.

Part II.

PLANNING EDUCATIONAL RESEARCH

Planning is the most important step in any research project. The most polished procedures and sophisticated statistical analyses cannot salvage a study that is poorly planned. The first step in planning is to identify a significant problem to attack. In this section you learn how to locate a research problem and how to develop a research plan that will permit you to collect rigorous evidence related to your problem.

In planning your study you must pay careful attention to the ethics and legal rules of research. Most educational research involves the use of human subjects. Failure to follow ethical guidelines not only can cause the researcher legal problems but may do serious harm to the subjects who participate in educational research.

Research evidence is cumulative. Many researchers contribute small pieces to a puzzle until, finally, a comprehensible "picture" emerges. In order for you to plan a research project that will contribute a new piece to the "picture," you must carefully study and interpret the pieces other researchers have contributed. This process is called "reviewing the literature" and is an essential part of planning your research. Researchers who attempt to sidestep a thorough review of previous research often end up following a path that others have found to be a dead end or repeating a study that someone else has done better.

Perhaps your most difficult task in reviewing the research of others is evaluating their work and deciding, in view of its limitations, how the findings fit into the overall picture of research related to the problem you are trying to investigate. How well you can carry out this critical review is determined to a large extent by how much you know about educational research methods. Thus, although you will be able to identify a research problem, start your literature search, and develop a tentative research plan after you have read the four chapters in this part, your critical evaluation of the key studies related to your problem and your final research plan should be delayed until you have finished studying this book.

3.

THE RESEARCH PROBLEM,
RESEARCH PLAN,
AND PILOT STUDY

OVERVIEW

Chapter 3 introduces you to several important skills that are needed to write an educational research plan and to conduct the project itself. First, several approaches are suggested to help you identify possible research problems and select an appropriate problem for your own research project. Next, you are given an outline to use in developing your research plan systematically. This section deals briefly with each major part of the research plan: the problem, hypotheses, measures, subjects, research design, and data analysis.

The advantages of developing a chronological list of procedures for your research project are also discussed. Many students prepare their research plan section by section and do not give enough attention to the problem of fitting the sections together. This problem is discussed and a method for developing a related plan is illustrated. If your research plan is fairly complex, the use of a procedure such as PERT (Planned Evaluation and Review Technique) helps you better understand your research and avoid many of the errors and miscalculations often made by inexperienced researchers. This chapter introduces you to the PERT technique. You are asked to consider the advantages of conducting a pilot study prior to the main investigation in order to test and revise the research plan.

OBJECTIVES

After studying this chapter, you should be able to:

1. Describe your areas of interest in education and current research problems that are under investigation in these areas.
2. Explain the advantages and disadvantages of working on a team project.
3. Discuss the reasons for replicating significant studies.

4. Use a variety of procedures to locate unsolved research problems in a given area of education.
5. List and describe the topics that need to be included in a sound research plan.
6. Describe the advantages of a research plan.
7. Write directional hypotheses, null hypotheses, and questions that relate to a given research problem.
8. Apply four criteria to the development and evaluation of hypotheses.
9. Demonstrate the relationship among the hypotheses, measures, and analysis procedures in a research plan.
10. Describe PERT and how it can be used in research planning.
11. State at least three reasons for including a pilot study in a research project.

SELECTING A RESEARCH PROBLEM

The graduate student's research problem for his thesis or dissertation usually focuses on an educational phenomenon that he wishes to describe, an event that he has observed and will attempt to explain, or a problem for which he will try to develop a solution. The research problem often is phrased as a question such as:

1. What changes can I make in reading instruction to increase the interest of Chicano children in my class?
2. What mistakes do students make most often in solving long-division problems?
3. Some children never volunteer answers during recitation even when I am sure they know the correct answer. Why is this?

The ultimate value of a student's research project is probably determined more by the imagination and insight that goes into the research problem than by any other factor. Therefore, the selection of a research problem for the master's thesis or doctoral dissertation is a very important step for the graduate student. Often, eager to get started on research work, the student seizes upon the first research idea that comes along. A student who begins a research problem before giving the choice much careful study and thought is likely to lose many important advantages.

The very process of seeking a research problem is an important step in the professional maturation of the student. At the outset, the student usually sees no problems, or from first explorations into the research literature concludes that research has already solved all the problems in education. The student's first ideas for research are often naive; a closer check will reveal that they have already been thoroughly explored. As the student continues to search, however, insight into the literature becomes sufficiently broad so that the student can see research problems in everything he reads. This point is not reached without a considerable amount of scholarly work in the research literature, but once achieved, the student has taken a significant step.

One reason that students seize upon the first idea they encounter is that very often they go too far in their graduate program before starting to search for a suitable research problem. The student has had years of experience in taking courses and thus the classwork involved in her graduate program is a familiar experience and one that she is reasonably confident she can complete successfully. In contrast, the research aspect of the graduate program is new and different and something that she is strongly tempted to put off. Every university has a lengthy list of "allbuts" among its graduate students—those who have completed *all* work for an advanced degree *but* the thesis or dissertation. A great many such students never obtain their advanced degrees. It is usually desirable for the graduate student to gain some insight into research and to commence the search for a suitable problem as soon as possible after entering graduate work, even if she does not plan to carry out her project until she nears the end of her work.

In looking for a research problem, the student should bear in mind some of the possible outcomes of her research effort in preparing her for her profession. The review of the literature provides the student with an understanding of the work that has already taken place relating to her problem area and prepares her to carry out a project that will add to the facts and information that have been accumulated by previous research workers. Because of the extensive reading she must do in her problem area, the student will usually build up a sizable fund of knowledge. Thus, in order that this knowledge may be of significant future value, the student should attempt to develop a research problem in an area that is closely related to her professional goals. For example, a student who plans to teach elementary school will profit much more from a research project in some area such as child development or the learning of elementary school subjects than in an area involving secondary education, adolescent development, or school administration.

Another reason for the selection of a topic closely allied to the student's interest is that the research project provides an opportunity to do significant independent work in a problem area that will better prepare her for professional work and will incidentally make her a more desirable prospect for employment. Although most of them do not produce research findings of major significance, many master's theses do produce worthwhile information that makes a small but definite contribution to the field of knowledge. Because there are many significant problems in education for which we require further knowledge, the student should resist the temptation to do research that is essentially trivial or that can contribute nothing to educational knowledge. Students often rationalize carrying out a trivial study by saying that the real purpose of the master's thesis is to provide practice in independent work, and the results cannot be expected to be of any scientific value. Generally, once a significant project has been identified, it requires no more time and effort to carry out than a trivial project or one that repeats work that has already been adequately done. The difference between the trivial project and the significant project is not the amount of work required to carry it out, but the amount of thought that the student applies in selection and definition of the problem.

Another factor that should be considered by the student in selecting her problem is that she will not only gain valuable knowledge and experience in the problem area she selects, but if she carries out a worthwhile piece of research, it will be possible for her to publish the results in a professional journal. If a student publishes an article based on her thesis, this publication adds significantly to her professional status.

In defining a research problem, the student should not hesitate to entertain ideas and approaches that represent a departure from conventional educational practice. Researchers often overlook or reject promising ideas because they are strange or conflict with some of the individual's biases. B. F. Skinner provides us with an excellent example of the degree to which narrow thinking can stifle unusual ideas. During World War II, Skinner worked with a group of psychologists on a project aimed at conditioning pigeons to operate a guidance system for missiles.[1] The pigeons were conditioned to peck at a particular type of target that they viewed on a screen, such as a ship or length of coastline. If the target was not at the center of the screen, the pigeons' pecking provided a guiding signal to change the course of the missile. The device was developed to a high level of efficiency and became nearly foolproof even under unfavorable conditions. It required no materials in short supply, and once the pigeons had been conditioned the behavior persisted for long periods without reinforcement. In several demonstrations before scientific committees the conditioned pigeons performed perfectly, yet the project was abandoned because it was impossible to convince the dozen or so distinguished physical scientists on the evaluation committee that the behavior of a pigeon could be adequately controlled. To these men, who were accustomed to thinking in terms of servomotors, rheostats, and electrical circuits, the idea of using a live organism to carry out the task of missile guidance was too fantastic to be taken seriously, even when they were confronted with evidence that the pigeons could do the assigned task. Although none of us can be completely freed from the shackles of our environment, preconceptions, and prejudices, the researcher seeking a research problem should remain aware of the existence of these impediments and should make a conscious effort to avoid their influence. As Skinner points

---

1. B. F. Skinner, "Pigeons in a Pelican," *American Psychologist* 15 (1960): 28–37.

out, "One virtue in crackpot ideas is that they breed rapidly and their progeny show extraordinary mutations." Thus even the wildest idea can, if pursued, lead eventually to a unique and often practical approach to a scientific problem.

The First Step

The first step in locating a specific problem for the dissertation or thesis is for the student to identify the broad problem areas that are most closely related to his interests and professional goals. The student will find it a profitable experience to write down in as much detail as possible the type of work he wishes to do upon completion of his graduate training and the specific aspects of this work that most interest him. The process of writing down this information will help the student clarify his goals and interests. Very often he will find that these goals are somewhat less clear in his own mind than he may have supposed. Typical broad areas of interest that might be listed are high school counseling, teaching art to children in the primary grades, social problems of adolescents, remedial reading in the elementary school, relationships between teachers and principals, and intramural programs in physical education.

After one or more such areas of professional interest have been identified, the student is ready to seek out specific problems in these areas that could form the basis for his thesis.

Working on a Team Project

Twenty-five years ago almost no money was available for the support of educational research. Most research projects were small-scale studies carried out by university faculty members, and in many instances the faculty member did all the research including such tasks as administering and scoring tests used in the project. Since that time, however, money available for educational research has increased tremendously. Now most universities are receiving financial support for educational research in the form of contracts and grants from federal agencies and private foundations, and the projects being carried out are much wider in scope and often involve a team of research workers rather than a single scientist. The graduate student often has an opportunity to participate in one of these extensive research projects as a member of a team. As a rule such projects are developed by faculty members, and portions of the project are given to graduate students to complete. Completion of the allotted portion of the project then constitutes the research for the master's thesis or doctoral dissertation.

Working on team projects has both advantages and disadvantages for the graduate student. Perhaps the most important advantage for most students is that financial support is usually available for the student working on such a project. This support may cover as little as paying for test administration or providing the graduate student with needed materials or clerical assistance but in many cases also involves a scholarship or research assistantship that is sufficient to meet the student's expenses while he is completing his graduate work. The team project also offers the graduate student an opportunity to participate in a bigger and more sophisticated study than would be the case if he were working independently. These studies usually involve more complex research designs and more advanced statistical procedures, and the student thus learns more about these procedures than he would otherwise. The student also has a chance to learn something about the workings of team research, and because most major projects are now carried out by research teams this insight will be valuable in future work. He also can learn a great deal from other members of the research team. Each team member in the project brings a different background of training and experience to bear upon the research problem, and therefore the team can usually produce a more polished research effort than is the case with a single investigator.

Participation in a team research project also has disadvantages for the graduate student. Perhaps the most important of these is that he loses the opportunity to find and develop his own problem. In team research the project is usually created and designed by the faculty member who is directing it. At worst the graduate student involved in a team project is little more than a clerk who carries out various tasks involved in the research without fully understanding what he is doing or why he is doing it. Even in team projects where he does significant independent work—and this is usually the case—the student does not get firsthand experience in all aspects of developing and carrying out a research plan. Another disadvantage of taking part in a team project is that very often the problem being studied is not closely allied with the student's interest nor does it contribute as directly to his future professional work as would be the case if he designed and carried out an independent project.

Whether the student carries out a small independent project or participates in a larger team project, the experience he gains through independent scholarship and research is perhaps the most important aspect of his graduate program. A significant piece of work done at this level can add materially to the student's professional maturity, improve his employment opportunities, and start him on the path to recognition and high professional status.

A Reading Program

Perhaps the most satisfactory method of locating specific problems within the scope of the student's broad interests is through a systematic program of reading. Let us say, for example, that the student plans to teach in the elementary schools and is particularly interested in problems related to working with bright children at the elementary school level. His first step would be to check the library card catalog in order to locate current textbooks in this field. If he has selected a field in which no complete textbooks have been written, he can usually find chapters dealing with his interest area in some of the introductory textbooks used in general courses in education and psychology. He should select two or three textbooks from those available and review pertinent chapters in each. This gives the student some background of basic information about his area of interest and also gives him insight into various subtopics in the field, a knowledge of current practices, and a brief summary of recent research. This preliminary reading will help the student narrow his attention to one or more specific subtopics. For example, the student whose broad interest is in working with bright children in the elementary school may decide to develop a research problem dealing with the creative abilities of bright children or perhaps to study the social development of bright children in the primary grades. These topics are, of course, still much too broad for a specific research plan, but this narrowing permits the student to explore the selected areas in somewhat greater depth by reading additional material that deals specifically with the more narrow subject. He will also obtain valuable information by checking these topics in such sources as the *Review of Research in Education*, the *Review of Educational Research*, and the *Second Handbook of Research on Teaching*.[2]

This additional reading will usually result in the student identifying a number of tentative research problems that are sufficiently limited and specific to form a possible basis for his research. In the example given, the student interested in studying the social development of bright children in the elementary schools might develop specific research topics such as the following: (1) relationships between intelligence and sociometric choice among sixth-grade children, (2) development of interest in the opposite sex in elementary school children between grades four and six, (3) social activities of bright children as compared with those of average children in ten fifth-grade classrooms, and (4) social adjustment problems of extremely bright children in the intermediate grades.

Research Based on Theory

Perhaps the approach most likely to produce an outstanding dissertation is for the student to formulate a research problem that will test a theory related to his area of interest.

2. Bibliographic information for these references can be found in Annotated References at the end of chapter 5.

In simple terms a **theory** is an explanation of behavioral or physical events. The more "powerful" a theory is, the more events can be explained by it. Psychoanalytic theory is considered by some researchers to be powerful because it provides an explanation for a vast range of behavior from infancy to old age, from the behavior of normal persons through the continuum of mental illnesses. Theories consist of generalizations (in the physical sciences, usually called laws) and constructs. A **law** or **generalization** is a statement of a relationship between two or more events; generalizations can be used to predict events. For example, the statement that individual tutoring results in increased school achievement is a generalization. Assuming it is true, we can predict that a particular student, given tutoring, will show a gain in achievement. A **construct** is a type of concept used in scientific research to describe events that share similar elements. Motivation, achievement, learning ability, intelligence, and value are all examples of constructs. Constructs are usually defined in operational terms, that is, in terms of the "operations" needed to measure them. For example, the construct "intelligence" is usually defined in terms of scores derived from administration of an intelligence test. Motivation may be defined in terms of changes in subjects' performance after they receive "motivating" instructions. These operational measures of constructs are usually called variables because the level or degree to which different subjects display the construct varies and because values or numerals can be assigned to different levels. Theoretical research usually consists of testing a hypothesis (a speculation about the relationship between two or more variables) that is derived from a theory.

Many areas of education have virtually no theoretical foundation. In areas, however, where the problems of education cut across other behavioral sciences, such as psychology or sociology, an increasing amount of pertinent theoretical work can be found. Some of these areas of overlapping concern are learning, motivation, language development, behavioral management, attitude development, and social class. A good example of an educational research problem derived from theory in another behavioral science, psychology, is provided by a recent study of changes in school-related attitudes.[3] In this study, Robert Steiner tested a hypothesis related to attitude change derived from the theory of cognitive dissonance developed by Leon Festinger.[4] Simply stated, cognitive dissonance is a state of tension that occurs when an individual simultaneously holds two cognitions (i.e., attitudes, ideas, or beliefs) that are logically inconsistent or in conflict. According to Festinger's theory, this dis-

---

3. Robert L. Steiner, "Induced Cognitive Dissonance as a Means of Effecting Changes in School-Related Attitudes," *Journal of Research in Science Teaching* 17, no. 1 (1980): 39–45.
4. Leon Festinger, *A Theory of Cognitive Dissonance* (Stanford, Calif.: Stanford University Press, 1957).

sonance is unpleasant, and the individual experiencing it is motivated to reduce it. With regard to attitude change, Festinger's theory would indicate that
if an individual has an attitude we want to change, such as racial prejudice,
we can create cognitive dissonance by exposing him to ideas that are incompatible with his attitude or inducing him to behave in a manner contrary to his
original attitude. This in turn will create dissonance, and in order to reduce
this dissonance, the individual will shift his original attitude so that it will be
more consistent with the behavior we have induced. The theory also suggests
that the level of cognitive dissonance experienced by the individual is related
to the degree of attitude change that is likely to occur. That is, a greater degree
of dissonance will lead to greater attitude change in order to reduce the dissonance.

In Steiner's study, a measure of attitude toward science was administered
to a sample of ninth-grade science students. Steiner then divided his group
into students having high (HS) versus low (LS) attitudes toward science. These
groups in turn were randomly assigned to experimental and control treatments. Each student in the experimental treatment prepared a short videotape
extolling science and advocating that students enroll in science. According to
Festinger's theory, this behavior would cause substantial cognitive dissonance
for the LS students, whose initial attitude toward science was low. The behavior could also cause some dissonance (presumably less) among students in the
HS group if their videotape behavior was more favorable to science than their
initial attitude was. The control group was not exposed to any treatment, and
so it would be expected that their attitudes would not change. After the treatment phase, an attitude scale was again administered to all subjects, and changes
in attitudes between the pre- and post-measures were analyzed. It was found
that the attitudes of the control group remained virtually the same on the two
measures, as expected. The attitudes toward science of subjects in the experimental groups improved significantly between the pre- and post-measures.
Contrary to expectation, however, gains made by the LS and HS groups were
not significantly different. Therefore, the theory of cognitive dissonance was
partially supported in that the cognitive dissonance generated by the treatment
did result in higher scores. The theory was not fully supported because the LS
group did not change their attitudes more than the HS group did.

This study is typical of research designed to test behavioral science theory
in that it produced some relevant evidence but did not provide a definitive test
of the theory. As research of this kind slowly accumulates, the scientist gains
an increasingly better understanding of the theory, which in turn leads to changes
in the theory and eventually to its acceptance or rejection.

There are several advantages to conducting theory-based research in education. First, the theory tends to focus the direction of the research. Without
some viable theory to serve as a guide, many studies address trivial questions

or contribute nothing to the slow accumulation of knowledge needed for advancement of a science of education. Second, a theory can provide a rational basis for explaining or interpreting the results of research. Studies without a theoretical foundation often produce results that the investigator is at a loss to explain. Eventually such studies can help in the development of a theory, but their impact on our understanding of the phenomena being studied is much less clear and immediate than for theory-based research. Still another advantage of good theories is that they enable the researcher to make predictions about a wide range of situations. For example, cognitive dissonance could be employed to attempt to change a wide range of attitudes.

In summary, a valuable technique for defining a research problem is to derive a hypothesis from a theory in one of the behavioral sciences and then to test the hypothesis in a relevant educational context.

Replication

Another strategy that can be used to locate a research problem is to select a previous study for replication. In the behavioral sciences, where we are usually unable to maintain the level of experimental control that is possible in the physical sciences, important studies should always be replicated before their findings are accepted by the scientific community. Therefore, the student can often make a valuable contribution by repeating an important research project that someone else has carried out. In order to make a significant contribution, however, the student must carefully search the literature to find a study that is appropriate for replication. There is no point in replicating a trivial study or one that is so poorly designed that the results cannot be accepted with any confidence. There are, however, several valid reasons for carrying out replications, and the student should locate a study for which one of these reasons is relevant. Among the reasons for carrying out a replication are the following:

1. *To check the findings of a major or milestone study.* Occasionally a study is reported that either produces new and surprising evidence, reports findings that conflict strongly with previous research, or challenges a generally accepted theory. The replication of studies of this kind is very useful because these studies help confirm or disconfirm the validity of the new evidence. If supported by replication, such studies often open up a new area of investigation or have a major impact upon educational practice. Studies of this sort are often discussed in graduate seminars, as well as in literature reviews such as those that appear in editions of the *Handbook of Research on Teaching* or in issues of the *Review of Educational Research*. An example of a study that has had a major impact in the educational community is the work of David Wiley and Annegret

Harnischfeger.[5] Based on their reanalysis of data obtained from Coleman's sixth-grade sample in Detroit, these researchers concluded that lengthening the school year by ten days, increasing the school day to six hours, and raising the average daily attendance to 95 percent would bring about major achievement gains, including a 65 percent gain in reading comprehension and a 34 percent gain in mathematics achievement. This study dramatically illustrated the importance of time as a factor in school learning and stimulated many studies that further explored the influence of time in the schools. Considerable controversy also developed over the validity of Wiley and Harnischfeger's findings. This creates an ideal situation for replication, since their findings were both important and controversial.[6]

2. *To check the validity of research findings across different populations.* The typical research study in education is carried out with a small sample of individuals representing a single population. Without replication we are unable to determine the degree to which findings that emerge from such research apply to other populations. For example, Charles Fisher and his colleagues studied the relationship between specific teacher behaviors and the achievement of second- and fifth-grade pupils in mathematics and reading. The researchers found that teachers' use of academic monitoring was negatively related to reading achievement but positively related to mathematics achievement. They also found several teaching behaviors that were positively related to the achievement of fifth-grade students but negatively related to second-grade achievement.[7] Clearly, it is unsafe to generalize research findings on effective teaching techniques across grade levels or subject areas without first doing replication studies. Similarly, findings for male populations may or may not apply to females, and findings valid for one racial or ethnic group may or may not be valid for other groups.[8] Thus, replications provide us with a very valuable tool for determining the degree to which research findings can be generalized across populations.

3. *To check trends or change over time.* Many research results in the behavioral sciences depend in part on the environment in which the individual functions. Thus, research findings on racial attitudes that were valid twenty years

5. David E. Wiley and Annegret Harnischfeger, "Explosion of a Myth: Quantity of Schooling and Exposure to Instruction, Major Educational Vehicles," *Educational Researcher* 3, no. 4 (1974): 7–12.
6. For a recent replication of this research, see Abraham H. Daniels and Emil J. Haller, "Exposure to Instruction, Surplus Time, and Student Achievement: A Local Replication of the Harnischfeger and Wiley Research," *Educational Administration Quarterly* 17, no. 1 (1981): 48–68.
7. C. W. Fisher, N. N. Filby, R. Marleave, L. S. Cahen, M. M. Dishaw, J. E. Moore, and D. C. Berliner, *Teaching Behaviors, Academic Learning Time and Student Achievement: Final Report of Phase III-B, Beginning Teacher Evaluation Study* (San Francisco: Far West Laboratory for Educational Research and Development, 1978).
8. For an example of a cross-cultural replication, see A. C. Ramirez, R. T. Garza, and J. P. Lipton, "The Fear-Affiliation Relationship," *Journal of Cross-Cultural Psychology* 11 (1980): 173–88.

ago may be invalid today. Replication is a useful tool for checking earlier findings and identifying trends. For example, a study of curricular trends in high schools surveyed 234 principals in 1979, replicating a 1974 survey.[9] Comparisons of the 1974 and 1979 data revealed trends in 20 areas such as departmentalization, use of independent study, and moral education. These trend data give us interesting insights into where the secondary curriculum appears to be going.

If a student can locate a survey conducted several years ago that covers topics of current interest, it is fairly easy to conduct a replication that will reveal interesting trends and that will increase our understanding of the questions addressed.

4. *To check important findings using different methodology.* In any research project there is a possibility that the observed relationships are an artifact of the methodology used by the researcher and are not due to a true relationship between the phenomena being studied. A true relationship should emerge regardless of the measures and methods used as long as they are reasonably valid and appropriate. Thus, a very useful form of replication is to repeat important studies using different methodology. For example, a study by Wayne Piersel, Gene Brody, and Thomas Kratochwill found that disadvantaged minority-group children shown a videotape designed to give them a favorable experience with the test situation before being given an intelligence test earned significantly better scores than did similar children not shown the videotape.[10] This is an important finding because its application would reduce the likelihood of disadvantaged minority children being given spuriously low test scores, which psychologists suspect often happens. Leslie Raskind and Richard Nagel replicated this study but improved the research methodology by using examiners who did not know which children were in the experimental and control groups and by showing an unrelated videotape to the control group.[11] These features of experimental design, which were not present in the earlier study, reduced the likelihood of obtaining spurious results. Using the same intelligence measure (WISC-R), Raskind and Nagel found no significant IQ differences between the experimental and control groups. This suggests the results of the earlier study could have been due to deficiencies in research methodology. Since the children in the two studies were drawn from different populations, however, additional replications would be desirable before drawing any firm conclusions.

9. Mary P. Tubbs and James A. Beane, "Curricular Trends and Practices in the High School: A Second Look," *High School Journal* 64, no. 5 (1981): 203–8.
10. Wayne C. Piersel, Gene H. Brody, and Thomas R. Kratochwill, "A Further Examination of Motivational Influences on Disadvantaged Minority Group Children's Intelligence Test Performance," *Child Development* 48 (1977): 1142–45.
11. Leslie T. Raskind and Richard J. Nagel, "Modeling Effects on the Intelligence Test Performance of Test-Anxious Children," *Psychology in the Schools* 17 (1980): 351–55.

In conclusion, we have seen that replication gives us a much sounder basis for judging the validity of a research finding than is possible when only a single study is available. There has been a trend in recent years to conduct more replications of educational research. You should give this option careful thought because it offers significant advantages for thesis and dissertation studies.

Other Methods of Identifying Research Problems

If the student still has not located a problem after using the approaches just presented, a number of other approaches may be tried. One of these is to observe carefully the existing practices in his area of interest. For example, a student interested in human relations problems in the public schools may observe faculty meetings, committee activities, and other situations where such problems may arise. These observations will often provide the student with ideas and insights that can lead to a worthwhile research project. The student may observe that in faculty meetings some principals are much more effective than others in enlisting cooperation and developing enthusiasm among teachers. This observation might lead the student to a comparison of the methods of principals who are successful with those who are unsuccessful in obtaining teacher cooperation.

Another valuable source of research ideas is found in the advanced courses that the student takes in his graduate program. In graduate seminars, important research articles are often critically reviewed in class. In such discussions important research questions are raised. In many textbooks, questions are also brought up for which we have no answers. Some textbooks even go so far as to list problems that require additional research. The brief reviews of research published in the *Review of Educational Research* almost always list specific areas in which further study is needed.

When searching for a problem, the student should keep a notebook of research ideas. Whenever an interesting idea comes up in his reading or class discussions, he should make a brief note of the idea and its source. The source will be useful if he decides to probe more deeply into the idea. This approach not only produces many potential thesis and dissertation problems but also makes the student increasingly perceptive to possible problems, so that he sees many he would previously have overlooked.

The student should not hesitate to consult with professors at his college or researchers at other institutions who are working in areas related to his interests. Because they may have carried out research on a particular problem over a period of years, these people are likely to have developed a sensitivity to important unsolved problems in their field. For example, the authors have worked over the last several years on the development of training programs to improve the classroom skills of inservice teachers. As a result of this experience, we have identified a number of research problems concerning the teacher's role in the classroom. Little is known, for example, about the effect of many teacher behaviors on student performance. Does the teacher's use of higher cognitive questions in classroom discussions relate to student behavior and achievement? What is the effect of individual or small-group tutoring on student achievement? Also, little is known concerning the frequency with which certain teacher behaviors occur in the classroom, for example, how frequently teachers use tutoring, role playing, or discussion of controversial issues, and at what grade levels these techniques are most used. Another type of research problem concerns identification of variables affecting development of teaching skills. We know, for example, that the use of models facilitates skill development. However, certain variables, such as sex and status of the model, may enhance or lessen the effectiveness of modeling. By consulting with researchers in his own area of interest, the student may be able to identify problems of similar importance to the advancement of a particular field of study.

The graduate student in education has the advantage of working in an area where he has gained much experience during his years as a student. Very often the graduate student can recall problems that he encountered in his own educational experience and from one of these problems develop a worthwhile research plan. The newspapers and popular magazines are sometimes valuable sources of research ideas. These periodicals often report at length on educational problems that are currently considered of major importance and usually report the opinions of educators and other persons in public life concerning these problems. These reports usually contain assertions, suggestions, and criticisms, the merits of which can be checked by research. For example, public debate in recent years concerning the need for changes in the methods of teaching reading has stimulated many research projects aimed at trying and evaluating some of the ideas and proposals that have been put forth.

OUTLINING A RESEARCH PLAN

Purpose of the Research Plan

After having identified a specific project that appears to be satisfactory, the student should outline a research plan in as much detail as possible. The project is still tentative at this point because the student's review of the literature has yet to be completed, and this review almost always leads to some changes in the research plan. The tentative outline, however, can do much to clarify the student's thinking and will also give direction to her review of the literature and her study of educational research. In order to plan a research project, the graduate student must have tentatively identified a problem, read a substantial amount of the research and theoretical literature relevant to her problem, and have a good basic knowledge of the educational research process. Since this is only the third chapter of this text, you may wonder how you can be expected to be ready to prepare a research plan at this point. The fact is that you are probably not ready to develop a finished plan, but you should still start a preliminary plan, following the format described in the next few pages. Your preliminary plan will surely contain many blank spaces and many ideas that you will later change. The deficiencies of your plan will become apparent to you as you progress through this book. As you learn more about such topics as reviewing the literature, sampling, educational measurement and research design you can immediately apply this knowledge to the gradual refinement of your preliminary plan.

Most graduate students have two major goals in their study of the process of educational research. First, they want to develop the skills and knowledge they will need to plan and carry out their own research. Second, they must be able to apply their knowledge of the research process to the critical evaluation and interpretation of the research of others. Only by understanding the work of previous researchers can you build upon this work and move ahead, if only by a small amount, the frontiers of educational knowledge. If you keep these two broad goals in mind as you progress through this book, ideas and information presented will have much more meaning.

The tentative research plan should contain the following sections: introduction and problem description, statement of the objectives or hypotheses, listing of possible tests or measures to be used in the study, description of the proposed sample, research design, a chronological description of the procedures to be used in carrying out the project, and plans for carrying out analysis of data to be collected.

An important advantage of a research plan is that it compels one to state all one's ideas in written form so that they can be evaluated and improved upon by the researcher and others. Even a simple research project contains many elements, and it is easy to overlook some of them unless they are all written down in a systematic manner. The authors recall an instance in which a written plan helped to stop a student from making a serious error in his research project. In discussing the proposed project with the student, we found the research design satisfactory. When the research plan was read later, however, it was discovered that the student planned to have teachers try a new teaching technique with unfamiliar pupils rather than with pupils from their own classes. This procedure would confound the effect of the new teaching technique with the effect of working with unfamiliar pupils. Subsequently the student was advised to change the research design to avoid this error.

Another advantage of a detailed research plan in written form is that it can be easily submitted to several professors and consultants for their comments and suggestions. Furthermore, the final plan can be used as a guide for conducting the research project, otherwise the student will need to rely on memory and may forget important details of the project in carrying it out.

Introduction and Problem Statement

Research plans usually start with an introductory section that states the student's research problem, briefly reviews the most relevant research and theoretical literature, and states why the student believes the problem to be important and what contribution he expects to make to educational knowledge and practice.

By the time the student starts writing his research plan, he should be well along in his efforts to convert his initial research idea into a clear, specific, and manageable research problem. You will recall that the development and clarification of the research problem usually progresses as the student builds a stronger foundation of knowledge through a reading program. This program should start with books that pull together much information in a few pages, but by the time the student has selected a specific problem, should also include a review of the most relevant research articles that have appeared in recent journal issues.

Knowledge and understanding should be demonstrated through a brief review of the most important research and theoretical work that relates to his problem. Usually, a discussion of five to ten key references is sufficient to demonstrate knowledge and to help the members of the thesis committee fit the student's problem into the context of other work in this area. These few references, however, should be selected carefully and their findings should be fitted together to provide an integrated picture of the field of knowledge. If this brief review appears to be a disjointed recitation of the studies cited, as is often the case, the reader may well question the student's understanding of the problem he proposes to study.

The student is also expected to describe how his proposed study will contribute to educational knowledge. This section of the introduction usually attempts to build a bridge between his expected outcomes and major educational problems and needs. If the student has found any survey data that establish or document the importance of his problem, it should be presented.

For example, if the problem is concerned with remedial reading, surveys which report large numbers of poor readers could be cited to demonstrate the need for additional research. Quotations by experts in the field that emphasize the importance of his problem area or the need for further research can also be used to help build a justification for the student's proposed research topic.

Briefly, the introduction and problem statement should have the following characteristics:

1. It should be written in clear, nontechnical language, avoiding jargon. Try to stimulate the reader's interest.
2. The problem should be sufficiently limited in scope to be a manageable thesis or dissertation problem.
3. The problem should be carefully fitted into the broader context of current theory and relevant research. Avoid making assumptions or unsupported claims or statements.
4. The significance of the problem should be addressed; that is, does it explore an important question, meet a recognized need, or make a useful contribution to knowledge?
5. The problem should be clearly and logically related to the hypotheses that follow.

In preparing the introductory section of the research plan the student should bear in mind that the impression this section makes upon the members of the thesis committee will do much toward shaping their attitudes about him and the remainder of his plan.

Formulating Hypotheses or Objectives

In our day-to-day activities we are often faced with problems for which we must gather information and seek answers. In order to focus our information gathering we try to identify possible solutions or explanations to our problem and then gather the information needed to see if a given explanation is correct. These "educated guesses" about possible differences, relationships, or causes are called hypotheses.

For example, suppose that your car will not start. You know that there is a cause-and-effect relationship between availability of gasoline and running of the engine. Therefore, your first hypothesis may be that you are out of gas. When you note that the gauge indicates half full, you tentatively reject this hypothesis. Next, you hypothesize that you have gasoline but it is not reaching the carburetor. To test this hypothesis, you disconnect the gasoline line from the carburetor and operate the starter to see if gasoline is pumped out of the line. If so, you reject this hypothesis. Your next hypothesis may be that no electricity is reaching the spark plugs. This can be tested by removing a spark plug wire, operating the starter, and checking to see if a spark jumps from the wire to the engine. You can continue to formulate and test new hypotheses until the problem is solved.

This simple process that we use to attack our day-to-day problems is similar to the approach an investigator may use to attack a problem in educational research. First, the investigator hypothesizes a relationship between two or more variables, or a difference between two or more treatments. She then collects evidence related to her hypothesis and examines the evidence to decide whether or not to reject the hypothesis. For example, a teacher may have noted that one of her first-grade pupils appears to be making no progress in reading. Careful observation of this child plus a review of previous research in this area may suggest several possible causes for this problem. These possible causes may be stated as hypotheses. The teacher may then design and carry out a program aimed at testing each hypothesis by manipulating the possible cause and then checking the child's progress in reading.

Educational research problems tend to be more complex than "troubleshooting" your car. The first-grade pupil is infinitely more complex than an automobile engine, and consequently most educational problems are likely to have multiple causes that may interact in unexpected ways and are likely to differ from child to child. Nevertheless, formulation of a hypothesis, and gathering of relevant evidence to test the hypothesis, is usually the most productive approach to throwing light on educational problems.

Before we leave our car and take the bus, let us look a bit more closely at the process we went through in attacking the "won't start" problem. First, it is important to state our problem as precisely as possible. For example, "the car won't go" is not as good a problem statement as "the starter will turn over the engine but the engine will not start." Once we have stated our problem clearly we can formulate hypotheses, that is, possible explanations or solutions to the problem. Note, however, that you must know something about the process you are studying in order to formulate good hypotheses. For example, if you did not know that gasoline must reach the carburetor in order for the engine to run, you would not be likely to formulate the hypothesis that gasoline is not reaching the carburetor. Similarly, in educational research you will be unable to formulate good hypotheses unless you know something about the phenomenon you propose to study. Furthermore, the more you know about your topic before you conduct your research, the better will be your hypotheses and the greater will be your chances of producing useful new knowledge related to your problem. This is one reason why a careful review of relevant literature is essential to the development of a sound research plan.

Although knowledge is a crucial ingredient to the formulation of good hypotheses, imagination is equally important. The investigator who makes a real effort to look at her problem in new ways or organize relevant previous knowledge into new configurations is likely to gain perspectives and insights that other investigators have missed. When generating hypotheses the researcher must allow herself time to think through all the alternatives she can identify. Graduate students, who are typically in a great hurry to finish their research, often settle for the first promising approach or hypothesis they think of. It is always a serious mistake to hurry the planning phase of research. This is a time for careful thought, reading, and discussions with professors and fellow students. Research planning, even when done with care, requires only a small percentage of the total effort required to carry out a research project. In many cases a hastily planned project that produces nothing of value takes longer to carry out than a carefully planned project because of the mistakes, false starts, and need to repeat or replan that are an inevitable consequence of poor planning.

Since our society is highly evaluative, students often reject unique ideas that with further development would form the basis for promising hypotheses. In the initial stages of generating alternative hypotheses, the student should be noncritical. That is, she should first generate as many ideas as possible and only then should she start examining the ideas critically.

The educational researcher can often generate more imaginative hypotheses and procedures if she looks at the knowledge, ways of attacking problems and methods for gathering data that have been developed in other disciplines such as sociology, psychology, economics, history, and anthropology. For example, a number of recent studies of classrooms and school systems have generated interesting new knowledge by using procedures borrowed from anthropology.[12]

The graduate student who has formulated a well-thought-out set of hypotheses has taken a major step on the road to an effective study. Such hypotheses place clear and specific goals before the researcher and provide a basis for selecting relevant samples, dependent variables, and research procedures to meet these goals. Many studies in education fail to produce useful knowledge because the researcher plunges ahead before developing a clear and specific set of hypotheses.

Directional and Null Hypotheses

Hypotheses may be stated in two forms, directional and null. The **directional hypothesis** states a relationship between the variables being studied or a difference between experimental treatments that the researcher expects to emerge. For example, the following are directional hypotheses:

1. Pupils of low ability in ability-grouped classrooms will receive significantly higher scores on a measure of inferiority feelings than pupils of low ability in random-grouped classrooms.

---

12. See Leona M. Foerster and Dale Little Soldier, "Applying Anthropology to Educational Problems," *Journal of American Indian Education* 20, no. 3 (1981): 1–6; and John U. Ogbu, "School Ethnography: A Multilevel Approach," *Anthropology and Education Quarterly* 12, no. 1 (1981): 3–29. This topic is also discussed in chapter 12.

2. There is a positive relationship between the number of older siblings and the social maturity scores of six-year-old children.
3. Children who attend preschool will make greater gains in first-grade reading achievement than comparable children who do not attend preschool.

In contrast to the directional hypothesis, the **null hypothesis** states that no relationship exists between the variables studied or no difference will be found between the experimental treatments. For example, in null form, the aforementioned hypothesis could be stated thus: "There will be no significant difference between the scores on a measure of inferiority feelings of low ability pupils in ability-grouped classrooms and low-ability pupils in random-grouped classrooms." The null hypothesis does not necessarily reflect the scientist's expectations, but is used principally because it is better fitted to our statistical techniques, many of which are aimed at measuring the likelihood that a difference found is truly greater than zero.

Note that regardless of whether directional or null hypotheses are stated, the differences or relationships hypothesized refer to *population* differences, not *sample* differences. Stated another way, the null hypothesis, in the form usually used in education, states that no difference exists, and the statistical tools test this hypothesis by determining the probability that whatever difference is found in the research subjects is a true difference that also is present in the population from which the research samples have been drawn. The student is sometimes confused by the null hypothesis because it appears senseless to hypothesize the exact opposite of one's expectations. This is a disadvantage of the null form, because the researcher's expectations, based as they are upon considerable insight into other research and theory, often make the study clearer to the person reading the research report. Some researchers overcome this problem by using both a **working hypothesis** that reflects their expectations based on theory or previous research and a **statistical hypothesis** that is usually in the null form and is set up to make testing of the working hypothesis statistically more precise.

Directional hypotheses can also be tested as statistical hypotheses. However, your statistical hypothesis should be stated in the directional form only when there is little or no possibility that the findings will yield a difference or relationship in the opposite direction. This is because the null hypothesis and the directional hypothesis call for different statistical treatment, the first requiring what is called the two-tailed test of significance and the second requiring a one-tailed test. The two-tailed test assumes that the difference could occur in either direction—that is, either the ability-grouped or random-grouped children could have significantly greater inferiority feelings. The one-tailed test on the other hand assumes that, if a difference occurs, it can occur in only one direction. The student is referred to chapter 13 for a discussion of one-tailed and two-tailed tests.

Some investigators state their problem in the form of a question instead of stating a working hypothesis. The aforementioned hypothesis stated as a question might read: "Is there a significant difference between the scores on a measure of inferiority feelings of a group of low-ability pupils in ability-grouped classrooms as compared with low-ability pupils in random-grouped class-rooms?" The question form is often the easiest for the inexperienced research worker to use because it states specifically the question that the research will attempt to answer. In writing the research results, the student may organize his report so as to answer the questions that he has posed.

In some research carried out in education, especially descriptive studies, it is appropriate for the research worker to list objectives rather than hy-potheses. A survey, for example, aimed at determining the extent of differ-ences in the salaries of university professors in different fields of learning could test a hypothesis such as "There will be no significant differences between the mean salaries of faculty members of comparable ranks in different areas of learning." In a study of this sort, however, it is probably more desirable merely to state the objectives of the study as follows: "The objectives of this research are (1) to study the salaries paid professors of comparable academic ranks in different fields of learning and (2) if differences are found to exist, to attempt to identify the factors that appear to contribute to the observed differences."

Criteria for Good Hypotheses

If hypotheses are to be of maximum value to the researcher, they should satisfy the following four criteria:

1. *The hypothesis should state an expected relationship between two or more vari-ables.* In correlational studies, that is, those in which data on two or more variables are collected on the same individuals and correlations are computed, a direct relationship is usually stated in the hypothesis. For example, a direc-tional hypothesis for a correlational study might state: "There is a significant positive relationship between peer-group acceptance and attitude toward school of sixth-grade boys."

In experimental studies, where an experimental treatment such as a new reading program is administered to one group of subjects but not to another group, differences between the treatments are usually hypothesized. For ex-ample, a null hypothesis for an experimental study might state: "There will be no significant difference in the reading achievement of first-grade pupils trained with Experimental Program A and comparable pupils trained with Conven-tional Program B." Although this hypothesis deals with an expected difference, it also indirectly suggests a relationship. Namely, it implies a relationship be-tween characteristics of the two reading programs and reading achievement. Thus, either directly or indirectly, a good hypothesis is concerned with an ex-pected relationship between two or more variables.

In addition to stating a relationship, the hypothesis may also briefly identify the variables and the population from which the researcher plans to select
his sample. Some researchers provide a good deal of specific information about
subjects and variables in their hypotheses as in this example: "Success in engineering as measured by a composite score based on income, patents held,
and scholarly publications is positively related to freshmen scores on the Gar-
nett College Test in Engineering Science for a random sample of 100 engineers
who graduated from the University of Minnesota during 1976." As a rule,
however, researchers do not include such information in their hypotheses because it lengthens the hypothesis statement and tends to make it less clear.

2. *The researcher should have definite reasons based on either theory or evidence
for considering the hypothesis worthy of testing.* After completing the review of the
literature, the research worker will have detailed knowledge of previous work
relating to his research project. In many cases he will find conflicting research
results so that his hypothesis cannot agree with all available information. In
general, however, his hypothesis should not conflict with the preponderance
of previously reported information.

In addition to being in agreement with knowledge already established
within the field, hypotheses should be formulated in accordance with theories
in education or psychology. When this is possible, the results of the research
will contribute to the testing of the theory in question. In many areas of education so little research has been done that reasonably conclusive information
is not available. In this case educational theory may form the only basis for
developing the hypothesis. The student must always have some basis in theory
or fact for his hypotheses. Occasionally, we find a study in education that has
used the "shotgun approach." In this approach the research worker tries all
the measures he can in the hope that something he tries will yield useful results. This approach should be avoided because it uses measures for which no
hypotheses have been developed. Many dangers are involved in applying such
research results to educational practice. When we do not have some understanding of why a particular relationship exists, there is always a danger that
factors are operating that may be detrimental to the educational program.[13]

3. *A hypothesis should be testable.* Hypotheses are generally stated so as to
indicate an expected difference or an expected relationship between the variables studied in the research. The relationship or differences that are stated in
the hypotheses should be such that measurement of the variables involved can
be made and necessary statistical comparisons carried out in order to determine whether the hypothesis as stated is or is not supported by the research.
The student should not state any hypothesis that she does not have reason to
believe can be tested or evaluated by some objective means. For example, the

13. A discussion of the "shotgun approach" can be found in chapter 14.

authors recall a "hypothesis" prepared by a teacher who wished to evaluate a high school course in civics. It was "to determine whether this course will make the student a better adult citizen." Such an objective would be very difficult to test since it would require (1) waiting until pupils taking the course had become adult citizens, (2) setting up criteria to determine how good a citizen each pupil had become, (3) evaluating each adult in terms of the criteria established, and then, perhaps most difficult of all, (4) determining what aspects of the adult citizenship of the former pupils could be directly attributed to the civics course. It may be seen from this example that such hypotheses are much easier to state than they are to evaluate by objective means. The hypotheses of inexperienced research workers in education often fail to meet the criterion of testability because relationships are stated that cannot be measured using today's tests. A similar mistake often made by the graduate student is to state her hypotheses in terms that would require many years to test.

4. *The hypothesis should be as brief as possible consistent with clarity.* In stating hypotheses the simplest and most concise statement of the relationship expected is generally the best. Brief, clear hypotheses are easier for the reader to understand and also easier for the research worker to test. The question "Is a student counseling program desirable and economically feasible at the elementary school level?" reflects the sort of fuzzy thinking that handicaps many studies in education. A program can be "desirable" or "undesirable" from a very large number of different viewpoints. No specific guides are given by the question to what aspect of the guidance program is to be studied. The second part of the question dealing with the economic feasibility is determined largely by the individual school district's financial resources. In order to develop a meaningful hypothesis from this question it would be necessary to determine first the specific aspects of the elementary school counseling program that the research worker plans to study. Let us say he wished to provide counseling for three classes of sixth-grade pupils and not provide counseling for three other classes in a large elementary school and then compare his two groups on such variables as the number of behavior problems reported by the classroom teachers, the incidence of truancy, and the pupils' stated attitudes toward school. In this case perhaps three specific hypotheses would be the best approach. Stated in the null form these might be:

1. Sixth-grade pupils receiving counseling will not be significantly different in the number of behavior problems reported by the teacher from sixth-grade pupils not receiving counseling.
2. Sixth-grade pupils receiving counseling will not be significantly different in incidence of truancy from sixth-grade pupils not receiving counseling.
3. Sixth-grade pupils receiving counseling will not be significantly different in

their stated attitudes toward school from sixth-grade pupils not receiving counseling.

It will be noted in the aforementioned example that the broad general question has been changed to three specific null hypotheses, each stating a specific relationship between two variables. It is usually desirable for the student to state his hypotheses in this more precise form. The advantage of stating a hypothesis for each relationship to be studied is that this procedure is simple and clear. The testing of multiple hypotheses involving several relationships leads to some confusion because portions of the hypothesis may be supported by the research evidence and other portions may not be supported. In writing the results of the experiment, the graduate student will find it possible to present a more easily understood picture of his findings if each hypothesis has stated only a single relationship.

Possible Measures

The next step in preparing the tentative research plan is to make a listing of possible measures. Most graduate students have had courses in educational measurement that give them some background in the types of measures available and sources of information about educational measures. This topic is covered briefly in chapters 8 and 9. Very often the process of identifying possible measures will require the student to clarify further her objectives and eliminate hypotheses for which no measures are available or can be developed.

Research Subjects

The student should then describe the subjects that will be required for his study. At this point he should carefully consider the chance of obtaining the type and number of subjects he needs. If his study is concerned with a type of individual who occurs only rarely in the general population, he must be particularly careful to determine whether subjects are available to do the work he has planned. For example, studies of highly gifted children, let us say those with IQs above 160, are difficult to carry out unless the student has a very large population to draw from because children at this IQ level occur very rarely in the general population. The student's method of selecting his sample should also be considered and tentatively decided upon. Careless selection of cases is an error often found in educational studies. Considerations involved in selecting a sample of subjects are discussed in chapter 7.

Research Design

A tentative research design should be described. The student will become familiar with the various types of research designs in chapters 11 to 19. The student should be sure that the design she plans to use will permit testing her hypotheses. Students often give little thought to the design of their projects until too late.

Data Analysis

A tentative plan for analysis of the research results is very important because this plan may have a considerable bearing upon the number of subjects needed, the measures and scoring procedures used, and the methods of recording the data. Yet many students give no thought to analysis until the data are collected. Then they find that no analysis procedures fit their data very well, and often they discover that the only procedures that can be used to salvage the study are complex ones that they must then learn to use.

In no area is lack of foresight so costly and disastrous as in doing research. Careful planning saves time in the long run and results in much better research. It is emphasized that the student should complete his course in research methods prior to starting the work on his research problem, because much of the knowledge he needs to carry out even the first steps in his research problem requires an understanding of the overall field of educational research.

Procedures

After the student has spelled out her measures, subjects, design, and analysis, it is desirable to add to the research plan a chronological list of procedures that she will follow in carrying out her study. This list should be as detailed as possible. In addition to describing each activity, the researcher should give the approximate date when the activity will be completed and also estimate how many working hours will be required to carry out the activity. Making up this chronological list forces the researcher to think through the entire research process and often alerts her to problems that she might otherwise overlook. The following kinds of problems are often identified by the researcher as a result of making up a chronological list of procedures:

1. In order to start the research in October, school officials must be contacted during the summer.

2. The collection of pretest data must be speeded up or the experimental treatments will extend into the Christmas holiday.
3. Standardized tests to be administered must be ordered as soon as possible to assure their arrival by the time needed.
4. The posttests cannot be given by one person in the number of days available.
5. The research cannot be completed during the time remaining in the current school year.
6. At least three observers will be needed to collect the classroom observation data in the time allotted.
7. Some of the activities to be done by the researcher during the first month of the project must be rescheduled because they will require 200 hours and she had only 80 hours available.

Fitting the Plan Together

In their initial attempts to develop a research plan, students often focus on each section of the plan in turn, and give too little attention to relationships among the various sections. As a result, it is not uncommon to find research plans in which errors such as the following occur:

1. A hypothesis is listed that cannot be tested by the measures described later in the plan.
2. The "Measures" section of the plan includes measures that are not related to any of the hypotheses or objectives. This happens frequently in correlational studies in which the careless researcher adds a few extra measures in the hopes that something interesting will emerge, or because the schools from which he has sampled already use the measures, or for some other reason.
3. Inappropriate analysis procedures are stated. Students who do not think through their analysis often list several analysis techniques and hope that one or the other will be accepted by the thesis committee.

One way to avoid errors such as those mentioned above is to construct a table in which the hypotheses are listed in the left-hand column, the measures to be used to test each given hypothesis are described in the center column, and the method of analysis is given in the right-hand column. An example of such a table for a correlational study is given in figure 3.1. This procedure is especially useful in helping the student think through studies that have a large number of objectives or hypotheses. For example, in descriptive questionnaire surveys, items are often included in the questionnaire that do not relate to any

Hypothesis	Measures	Analysis
1. There is no relationship between overall achievement and popularity for sixth-grade boys.	1a. Achievement: total battery score on the California Achievement Tests. 1b. Popularity: a sociometric choice instrument in which each student lists names of his five best friends.	1. Product moment correlation between 1a and 1b.
2. When the effects of achievement differences are controlled, there is no relationship between popularity and self-concept of sixth-grade boys.	2a. Achievement: as in 1a. 2b. Popularity: as in 1b. 2c. Self-concept: Tennessee Self-Concept Scale.	2. Partial correlation between 2b and 2c, partialing out 2a.

Figure 3.1 Procedure for checking relationships among hypotheses, measures, and analysis. The problem of this study is to determine relationships between peer-group popularity and characteristics of sixth-grade boys.

research objective and are often stated in a form that makes analysis difficult. By matching test items with hypotheses in a table, the student is assured that all objectives are covered in his questionnaire and that no items are included that do not relate to an objective.

Using PERT in Research Planning

In the planning of research several procedures have been developed over the past twenty years. Many of these techniques were developed to improve planning for the development of complex weapons systems. They can be employed in any research or development activity, however, and are especially useful in planning large-scale projects. In educational research, **PERT (Planned Evaluation and Review Technique)** is the most widely used of these planning systems. In effect, PERT is an extension of the chronological list of procedures typically included in an educational research plan. By using PERT, the researcher can (1) clearly see the relationships among the various activities making up her research, (2) check her progress and identify activities that must be changed or speeded up in order to keep the project on schedule, and (3) focus on potential or actual problems involved in carrying out the project.

The first step involved in using PERT is to identify all goals that must be reached in the process of carrying out the project. Broad goals are first identified, and these are subsequently broken down into as many specific activities and subgoals as possible. For example, one broad goal in a study of the relationship between student attitudes and achievement could be to develop a scale to measure student attitudes toward school. This could be broken down into the activities and subgoals as shown in figure 3.2.

The researcher, having made a breakdown such as this for the entire project, can now draw a network in which the various events or subgoals are arranged in order, beginning with the first day of the project and ending with the last day. Figure 3.2 shows a PERT network for the development of the attitude scale mentioned earlier. Each circle represents one subgoal or event. The initial event, *a* in figure 3.2, is to "start scale development." The circles are connected by lines, which represent the activities that must be carried out to achieve the following subgoals. Activities that can be carried out simultaneously are drawn parallel to each other, while those that must be done in sequence are drawn end-to-end. A dashed line is called a "dummy activity" and is used mainly to connect the completion of one broad goal or event and the start of the next. In drawing the PERT network, the researcher must make decisions about the sequence of events and how she will allocate time to accomplish them. Note that each of these activities is highly specific and deals with only one small aspect of the process of developing the needed attitude scale. It is much easier for the researcher to estimate accurately how much time will be involved in achieving each specific subgoal than to estimate the work involved in achieving the broad goal without making this detailed breakdown of activities.

The next step in PERT is to make time estimates. For each subgoal the researcher makes three time estimates: optimistic *(a)*, the time that will be needed to achieve the subgoal if everything goes well; most likely *(m)*, her best estimate of time needed; and pessimistic *(b)*, the time needed if everything goes wrong that can go wrong. These estimates are usually expressed in weeks and made to the nearest tenth of a week. Figuring a five-day week, each half day equals one-tenth of a week (.1).

A researcher who has made the three estimates for a given subgoal uses the following formula to compute the expected elapsed time *(t_e)* to be spent in work planning:

$$t_e = \frac{a + 4m + b}{6}$$

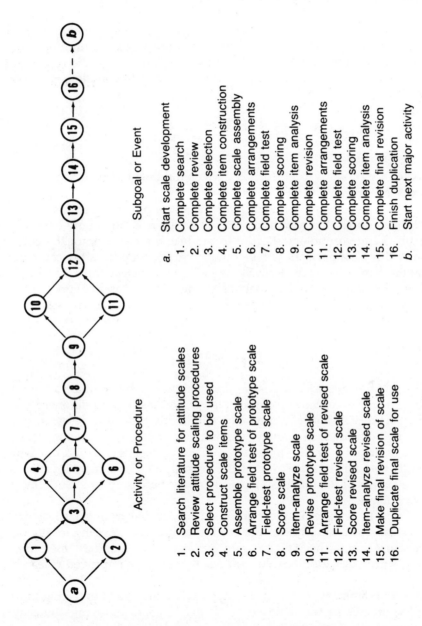

Activity or Procedure

1. Search literature for attitude scales
2. Review attitude scaling procedures
3. Select procedure to be used
4. Construct scale items
5. Assemble prototype scale
6. Arrange field test of prototype scale
7. Field-test prototype scale
8. Score scale
9. Item-analyze scale
10. Revise prototype scale
11. Arrange field test of revised scale
12. Field-test revised scale
13. Score revised scale
14. Item-analyze revised scale
15. Make final revision of scale
16. Duplicate final scale for use

Subgoal or Event

a. Start scale development
1. Complete search
2. Complete review
3. Complete selection
4. Complete item construction
5. Complete scale assembly
6. Complete arrangements
7. Complete field test
8. Complete scoring
9. Complete item analysis
10. Complete revision
11. Complete arrangements
12. Complete field test
13. Complete scoring
14. Complete item analysis
15. Complete final revision
16. Finish duplication
b. Start next major activity

Figure 3.2.   PERT network showing development of an attitude scale.

For example, for activity 6, "arrange field test of prototype scale," she may estimate that if all goes well (a) she can make the arrangements in one-half day. However, it will probably (m) take a full day by the time telephone contacts are made, appointments set up, and necessary meetings are held. If the necessary persons are difficult to contact, if appointments cannot be made on same day, and if the meetings take longer than anticipated, the researcher estimates that four and one-half days (b) will be needed to complete this task. Using the formula

$$t_e = \frac{.1 + (4 \times .2) + .9}{6} = \frac{1.8}{6} = .3$$

the researcher arrives at .3 weeks or 1.5 days as the time estimate.[14]

Figure 3.2 represents the PERT network for only one major step in a research project. In developing a network for the entire project, each major goal would be broken down; the resulting network would combine many networks such as figure 3.2 in chronological order to produce the network for the entire project. Since this final network will be quite complex even for a typical thesis or dissertation plan, it is often desirable to begin by constructing a PERT network that shows only the major goals or events. Then this network can be expanded by breaking down each broad goal, as was done in figure 3.2.

THE PILOT STUDY

A preliminary trial of research measures and techniques is essential to the development of a sound research plan. Whenever possible this preliminary trial should be enlarged into a **pilot study.** In a pilot study the entire research procedure is carried out, including analysis of the data collected, following closely the procedures planned for the main study. Pilot studies are carried out with fewer subjects than will be employed in the main study. For some pilot studies two or three subjects are sufficient, and it is rarely necessary to include more than twenty subjects.

In addition to serving all the purposes of the usual tryout, such as improving data-collecting routines, trying scoring techniques, revising locally developed measures, and checking the appropriateness of standard measures, the pilot study provides additional knowledge that leads to improved research:

1. It permits a preliminary testing of the hypotheses that leads to testing more precise hypotheses in the main study. It may lead to changing some hy-

14. Note that the formula arbitrarily gives the greatest weight to the researcher's best estimate.

potheses, dropping some, and developing new hypotheses when called for.

2. It often provides the research worker with ideas, approaches, and clues not foreseen prior to the pilot study. Such ideas and clues greatly increase the chances of obtaining clear-cut findings in the main study.

3. It permits a thorough check of the planned statistical and analytical procedures, thus allowing an appraisal of their adequacy in treating the data. Needed alterations also may be made in the data-collecting methods, so that data in the main study may be analyzed more efficiently.

4. It greatly reduces the number of treatment errors because unforeseen problems revealed in the pilot study may be overcome in redesigning the main study.

5. It may save the research worker a major expenditure of time and money on a research project that will yield nothing. Unfortunately, many research ideas that seem to show great promise are unproductive when carried out in the field or laboratory. The pilot study almost always provides enough data for the research worker to make a sound decision on the advisability of going ahead with the main study.

6. In many pilot studies it is possible to get feedback from research subjects and other persons involved that leads to important improvements in the main study. Although the pilot study should follow the main study procedures for the most part, variations such as trying alternate instruments and procedures and seeking feedback from subjects on the treatment, measures, and other aspects of the research are usually desirable. In deciding what variations are appropriate, you should remember that the pilot study is not an end in itself but is only a means by which the main study can be improved.

7. In the pilot study, the research worker may try out a number of alternative measures, and then select those that produce the best results for the main study with some tentative evidence that they would be productive. If the student plans to continue beyond the master's degree, the master's research may sometimes serve as a pilot study for later research to be carried out as part of a doctoral program. The less research experience the student has, the more he is likely to profit from the pilot study. Because of this, the student should attempt a pilot study whenever possible.

MISTAKES SOMETIMES MADE IN PLANNING RESEARCH

1. Researcher puts off selection of a problem until he has finished all or most of his courses.

2. Uncritically accepts the first research idea that he thinks of or that is suggested to him.
3. Prepares fuzzy or untestable hypotheses.
4. Hurries the planning of his research and as a result ends up with a poorly designed study that contributes nothing to educational knowledge.
5. Fails to carry out a preliminary trial of his measures and as a result makes serious mistakes when collecting data for his study.
6. Fails to conduct a pilot study and as a result, encounters many unforeseen problems that weaken his research.
7. Overlooks important steps in preparing a chronological list of procedures.

ANNOTATED REFERENCES

Carlow, C. D. "The Application of Psychological Theories to a Curriculum Development Project: An Example." *Educational Psychologist* 12 (1976): 36–48.

This article describes how the learning theories of Ausubel and the motivation theories of White and Berlyne were used as guides in the development of an elementary school mathematics curriculum. The author demonstrates how the theoretical constructs were directly applied, modified, and combined in developing the curriculum. This paper provides a good example of how theory can be applied to the development of curriculum materials, which in turn could be used in research to test the theories involved.

Davitz, Joel R., and Davitz, Lois L. *Evaluating Research Proposals in the Behavioral Sciences.* 2nd edition. New York: Teachers College Press, 1977.

This small book contains clear and simple guidelines that a student can use to evaluate a research plan. The authors pose questions that focus the student's attention on important aspects of the research plan, discuss each question briefly, and provide a reference to which the student may go for further information. There is also a chapter on the language of research that contains definitions of many terms the student will encounter in reviewing research literature.

Locke, Lawrence F., and Wyrick-Spirduso, Waneen. *Proposals That Work: A Guide for Planning Research.* New York: Teachers College Press, 1976.

This guide provides excellent guidance to the graduate student preparing a research proposal. The first two sections deal with the basic process of developing the proposal and include a diagram that takes the reader through twenty steps leading to a finished proposal. The third section contains three sample proposals, one for an experimental laboratory study, one for field-based program evaluation, and one for an historical study. The authors make extensive comments that focus the reader on weaknesses, strengths, and questions related to each proposal. Standards for judging the acceptability of a thesis or dissertation proposal are also included.

Sessions, V. S. *Directory of Data Bases in the Social and Behavioral Sciences.* New York: Science Associates/International, 1974. 23 East 26th Street, New York, NY 10010. $35.

It is often possible for students to locate data that have already been collected and to reanalyze these data to test hypotheses not studied by the original investigator. This directory describes 685 data bases, many of which are of interest to students in education. For example, the American Council on Education has a data base on about 300,000 entering college freshmen that has been collected yearly since 1965. To use the directory, first check your topic or interest area in the subject index, then read the descriptions of the data bases you have selected in the main body of the directory. These entries include enough information for you to identify data bases to check further. Information given includes name, address, and phone number of the organization having the data, major subject field, and how to gain access to the data.

Snow, Richard E. "Theory Construction for Research on Teaching." In *Second Handbook of Research on Teaching,* edited by R. M. W. Travers. Chicago: Rand McNally, 1973.

A major deficiency in education is the scarcity of educational theory that can form the basis for hypotheses. In this chapter Snow outlines the process of theory development, provides a classification for types of theories, and suggests criteria for theory evolution. Although directed primarily to research on teaching, most of this chapter is relevant to theory construction in any area of education.

PERT. The following references give recent examples of educational applications of the Planned Evaluation and Review Technique:

Colvin, George M., and Fielding, Anthony F. "A PERT Application to Curriculum Planning." *Educational Technology* 15, no. 10 (1975): 9-20.

The authors describe a modified PERT technique that can help school administrators in curriculum planning, evaluation, and decision making.

Gallagher, Stephan M. "A New Systems Tool: PER-flo." *Educational Technology* 19, no. 7 (1979): 38-40.

In the proposed system, flowcharting is combined with PERT to develop PER-flo. An example of the method is given.

Hai, D. M. "PERT in Higher Education: An Application for Doctoral Students." *Educational Technology* 17, no. 8 (1977): 33–36.

The author used the PERT procedure to plan her Ed.D. dissertation and other activities necessary for the completion of her degree program. This article provides a useful model for graduate students.

SELF-CHECK TEST

Circle the correct answer to each of the following questions. An answer key is provided on page 881.

1. For the researcher a negative aspect of working on a team project is
   a. lack of financial support for team projects.
   b. lack of opportunity to find and develop one's own project.
   c. the complexity of a team project compared to an individual project.
   d. the interaction required with the other team members.
2. Borg and Gall state that perhaps the most satisfactory method that a graduate student can use to locate specific research problems is to
   a. work in conjunction with state departments of education.
   b. initiate many action research projects.
   c. conduct a systematic reading program.
   d. maintain contacts in professional educational organizations.
3. A theory is said to be "powerful" if it
   a. is extremely accurate.
   b. provides an explanation for a large number of events.
   c. has a high degree of reliability.
   d. is valid.
4. A concept used in scientific research to describe events with similar elements is
   a. theory.
   b. generalization.
   c. construct.
   d. principle.
5. A statement of a relationship between two or more events that can be used in prediction is called a
   a. principle.
   b. developmental theory.
   c. concept.
   d. generalization.
6. Speculations about the relationship between two or more variables are called
   a. theories.
   b. hypotheses.
   c. principles.
   d. constructs.

7. When the experimenter has a reasonably high expectation concerning the relationship that exists between the variables, it is most appropriate to state the hypothesis in the _____ form.
   a. directional
   b. interrogative
   c. null
   d. objective
8. "There will be no significant difference between the scores on a measure of achievement of high- and low-anxious students" is a hypothesis written in the _____ form.
   a. directional
   b. interrogative
   c. null
   d. objective
9. Borg and Gall list several criteria of good hypotheses. Which of the criteria does the following hypothesis most violate?
   Hypothesis: The upper-division courses in civics will produce better adult citizens than the lower-division courses in civics.
   a. Hypotheses should be worthy of testing.
   b. Hypotheses should be testable within a reasonable time period.
   c. Hypotheses should be brief.
   d. All of the above are correct.
10. A pilot study is often helpful because it
   a. permits a preliminary testing of the hypotheses.
   b. provides the researcher with ideas, approaches, and clues.
   c. permits a check of procedures with the possibility of revision where needed.
   d. All of the above are correct.

APPLICATION PROBLEMS

The following problems are designed to give you practice in applying significant concepts and research procedures explained in chapter 3. Most do not have a single correct answer. For feedback, compare your answers with the sample answers on pages 882–83.

1. State three of your areas of interest in education. For each area of interest, state two problems currently being investigated by researchers. Select one of the problems and write a null hypothesis, a directional hypothesis, and an objective that fit the problem.
2. Without referring to the textbook, if possible, make a sequential list of the topics usually covered in a research plan.

3. A graduate student claims that it is not necessary to make up a research plan for a study he intends to do. He prefers to take each phase of the project as it comes; a plan would only inhibit him and keep him from improving the study as it progressed. What two advantages of a detailed written research plan could you point out to this student?

4. Consider the following statement and hypothesis:
   Several questionnaire studies of ability grouping have indicated that teachers believe such grouping to be harmful to the self-concept of students who are placed in low-ability groups. Eminent clinical psychologists have also questioned the value of ability grouping on the same grounds. However, no experimental studies have ever been done to test this view. It is the goal of our study to measure the self-concept of a group of low-ability children and then place them in ability-grouped classes and see whether their self-concepts change. *It is our hypothesis that no significant changes will take place, since we believe that any loss of self-concept occurring because of ability grouping will be offset by a gain because the students will be better able to compete in the ability-grouped class.*

   What criteria, if any, does the hypothesis fail to meet? Which, if any, does it satisfy?

5. A graduate student claims that it is not necessary for her to do a pilot study prior to conducting an experiment for her doctoral dissertation. Her experiment is primarily a replication of a previously published study, with a few modifications. What are at least three arguments in favor of doing a pilot study, even under these conditions?

SUGGESTION SHEET

If your last name starts with letters from Bos to Cam, please complete the Suggestion Sheet at the end of the book while this chapter is still fresh in your mind.

4.

ETHICS, LEGAL CONSTRAINTS, AND HUMAN RELATIONS IN EDUCATIONAL RESEARCH

OVERVIEW

In conducting an educational research project, one must never lose sight of the special requirements and problems involved in working with people. The human relations aspect of educational research is particularly important when the project is carried out in the public schools. If schoolchildren are the subjects, it is necessary to obtain the understanding and cooperation of school administrators, teachers, parents, interested community groups, and the subjects themselves. Thus the procedures section of the research plan should describe how the researcher intends to gain school cooperation, how he will deal with potential human relations problems that may arise, and what precautions he will take to ensure that the plan meets the ethical standards and legal requirements established for behavioral science research. These topics are discussed in this chapter.

OBJECTIVES

After studying this chapter, you should be able to:

1. Identify aspects of a research situation that involve ethical questions or principles.
2. State and discuss five ethical principles of research that have been developed by the American Psychological Association.
3. Describe five strategies that can be used to assure the confidentiality of research data.
4. Discuss the pros and cons of using deception in behavioral science research, and explain factors the researcher should consider before using deception.
5. Describe the legal constraints to educational research imposed by federal law.

6. Describe categories of research that are exempt from review by the Institutional Review Board.
7. State the conditions under which the Institutional Review Board can waive the requirement for informed consent.
8. Discuss the kinds of questions the researcher must answer when presenting a research plan to school officials.
9. State steps that can be taken to protect the rights of individuals who are to serve as subjects in a research project.
10. Define dehoaxing and desensitizing, identify research situations where these are required, and describe what steps should be taken to dehoax or desensitize research subjects.

ETHICAL PRINCIPLES

In recent years the ethical aspects of behavioral research have been of increasing concern to the Congress, scientists, private citizens, and institutions that support this research. In part this concern reflects the great growth of behavioral research and its impact on people's lives. Although most researchers have acted in an ethical manner, there have been occasional abuses of individuals' rights.

The American Psychological Association recently published ten ethical principles for the conduct of research activities with human participants. In planning a research project, the student should study these principles carefully:

The decision to undertake research rests upon a considered judgment by the individual psychologist about how best to contribute to psychological science and human welfare. Having made the decision to conduct research, the psychologist considers alternative directions in which research energies and resources might be invested. On the basis of this consideration, the psychologist carries out the investigation with respect and concern for the dignity and welfare of the people who participate and with cognizance of federal and state regulations and professional standards governing the conduct of research with human participants.

    a. In planning a study, the investigator has the responsibility to make a careful evaluation of its ethical acceptability. To the extent that the weighing of scientific and human values suggests a compromise of any principle, the investigator incurs a correspondingly serious obligation to seek ethical advice and to observe stringent safeguards to protect the rights of human participants.

    b. Considering whether a participant in a planned study will be a "subject at risk" or a "subject at minimal risk," according to recognized standards, is of primary ethical concern to the investigator.

c. The investigator always retains the responsibility for ensuring ethical practice in research. The investigator is also responsible for the ethical treatment of research participants by collaborators, assistants, students, and employees, all of whom, however, incur similar obligations.

d. Except in minimal-risk research, the investigator establishes a clear and fair agreement with research participants, prior to their participation, that clarifies the obligations and responsibilities of each. The investigator has the obligation to honor all promises and commitments included in that agreement. The investigator informs the participants of all aspects of the research that might reasonably be expected to influence willingness to participate and explains all other aspects of the research about which the participants inquire. Failure to make full disclosure prior to obtaining informed consent requires additional safeguards to protect the welfare and dignity of the research participants. Research with children or with participants who have impairments that would limit understanding and/ or communication requires special safeguarding procedures.

e. Methodological requirements of a study may make the use of concealment or deception necessary. Before conducting such a study, the investigator has a special responsibility to (i) determine whether the use of such techniques is justified by the study's prospective scientific, educational, or applied value; (ii) determine whether alternative procedures are available that do not use concealment or deception; and (iii) ensure that the participants are provided with sufficient explanation as soon as possible.

f. The investigator respects the individual's freedom to decline to participate in or to withdraw from the research at any time. The obligation to protect this freedom requires careful thought and consideration when the investigator is in a position of authority or influence over the participant. Such positions of authority include, but are not limited to, situations in which research participation is required as part of employment or in which the participant is a student, client, or employee of the investigator.

g. The investigator protects the participant from physical and mental discomfort, harm, and danger that may arise from research procedures. If risks of such consequences exist, the investigator informs the participant of that fact. Research procedures likely to cause serious or lasting harm to a participant are not used unless the failure to use these procedures might expose the participant to risk of greater harm, or unless the research has great potential benefit and fully informed and voluntary consent is obtained from each participant. The participant should be in-

formed of procedures for contacting the investigator within a reasonable
time period following participation should stress, potential harm, or related questions or concerns arise.

   h. After the data are collected, the investigator provides the participant with information about the nature of the study and attempts to
remove any misconceptions that may have arisen. Where scientific or hu-
mane values justify delaying or withholding this information, the investigator incurs a special responsibility to monitor the research and to ensure that there are no damaging consequences for the participant.

   i. Where research procedures result in undesirable consequences for
the individual participant, the investigator has the responsibility to detect
and remove or correct these consequences, including long-term effects.

   j. Information obtained about a research participant during the course
of an investigation is confidential unless otherwise agreed upon in advance. When the possibility exists that others may obtain access to such
information, this possibility, together with the plans for protecting confidentiality, is explained to the participant as part of the procedure for obtaining informed consent.[1]

In educational research carried out by graduate students, the principles relating
to informed consent *(d)*, deception *(e)*, debriefing subjects at the end of the
study *(h* and *i)*, and protecting confidentiality of research data *(j)* are the ones
most likely to be violated.[2]

Informed Consent

The protection of individual privacy in educational research involves two factors: the consent of the individual as to what will be disclosed to the researcher, and the confidential use of research data collected on individuals.
The researcher should obtain the individual's consent before gathering data on
him. In the case of schoolchildren, the consent of parents and appropriate school
personnel should be obtained. Ideally the student should receive some explanation of the tests and experimental procedures to be used. This explanation
must satisfy the student that participation is important and desirable and that
it is to his advantage to cooperate.

   There are occasions, however, when it would invalidate research findings

1. Committee on Scientific and Professional Ethics and Conduct, "Ethical Principles of Psychologists," *American Psychologist* 36 (1981): 633–38.
2. It is interesting that codes of ethics adopted by European psychologists are generally similar to
   the APA principles. See H. Schuler, "Ethics in Europe," in *Ethics of Human Subject Research*, ed.
   A. J. Kimmel (San Francisco: Jossey-Bass, 1981), pp. 41–48.

to tell the individual beforehand the purpose of the study and the type of information he will be expected to provide during the course of the research project. For example, in some experiments it may be necessary to give the individual false information in order to experimentally arouse or decrease his motivation. Nevertheless, even in this situation the researcher should obtain the individual's consent to be in the experiment and should tell the individual that he will be informed of the experiment's purpose *after* the study is completed.

Another way of resolving this dilemma is proposed by J. E. Atwell. He suggests that when the validity of research results would be jeopardized by informing subjects about the research, the investigator may obtain "implied consent." To do this, a sample drawn from the population to be studied is fully informed on every aspect of the proposed research. If the individuals in the sample agree by a large majority to be subjects in the study, the researcher can assume that other persons from the same population would also agree. He then selects subjects from this population, but does not seek informed consent from the actual subjects.[3]

There is clear evidence that the results of some studies can be drastically altered if research subjects are informed of all details about the research. For example, in a study by J. H. Resnick and T. Schwartz, volunteer subjects were placed in two groups. They were given cards containing a verb and the six pronouns *I, we, you, they, she, he,* and were asked to construct sentences using the verb and one pronoun.[4] During the last 80 of 100 trials, the investigator reinforced the subjects with verbal approval each time the subject constructed a sentence that began with *I* or *we*, to determine the effects of the reinforcement. The results showed that the use of "I-we" sentences increased for uninformed subjects and decreased for informed subjects. In this study, fully informing the subjects led to serious distortion of the results. But should the need to learn more about human behavior take precedence over the need to inform subjects, even in studies like this, where no conceivable harm or danger to the subjects is possible? The pros and cons raised when such studies are considered in relation to ethical standards certainly merit careful consideration.[5]

Federal regulations related to informed consent are discussed later in this chapter.

3. J. E. Atwell, "Human Rights in Human Subjects Research," in Kimmel, ed., *Ethics of Human Subject Research.*
4. J. H. Resnick and T. Schwartz, "Ethical Standards as an Independent Variable in Psychological Research," *American Psychologist* 28 (1973): 134–39.
5. For another study that clearly shows a distortion of results caused by informed consent, see Gerald T. Gardner, "Effects of Federal Human Subjects Regulations on Data Obtained in Environmental Stressor Research," *Journal of Personality and Social Psychology* 36 (1978): 628–34.

Confidentiality

Once research data have been collected, the researcher should make certain that no one has access to the data except himself and possibly a few co-investigators. Research subjects, of course, should be told at the outset who will have access to the data. Whenever possible, the names of subjects should be removed from data-collection instruments and replaced by a code. This procedure is particularly important to follow when the data are to be stored for a relatively long time. The researcher should take particular care with data that conceivably could be subpoenaed. Unfortunately, educational research data do not have privileged status (as does communication between husband and wife, lawyer and client, etc.) in most states. The confidentiality of the individual must be further protected by not using the names of individuals in any publications that result from the research project.

The student can avoid problems relating to invasion of privacy if she includes procedures in her research design for individual consent and preservation of confidentiality and if she carries out her project in an ethically responsible manner. Confidentiality of research data should be carefully guarded by either (1) collecting research data so that no one, including the researcher, can link the data to specific subjects; or (2) using some sort of linkage system, such as substituting numbers for names, so that only a person who has access to a closely guarded key can identify data for a specific subject. The first approach is regarded as ethically preferable, but it often reduces the effectiveness of the research. In many studies the researcher must retain some means of identifying the subjects. For example, in longitudinal studies where data are gathered on the same subjects over a long period of time, much valuable information is lost if the responses of specific subjects cannot be identified. Similarly, many cross-sectional studies gather data from a variety of sources. It is often necessary to link these data in order to have a clear picture of the phenomena being studied. Such linkage is difficult unless some means of identifying subjects is retained for at least a short time by the researcher.

For studies dealing with nonsensitive issues, careful linkage procedures should be set up and closely guarded. The scientific benefits usually outweigh the slight risk of a breach in confidentiality. When research deals with controversial or sensitive topics, however, confidentiality is much more important, and it may be necessary to set up very sophisticated procedures to minimize the danger of a breach.[6]

It is generally agreed among behavioral scientists that subjects should be given assurances of confidentiality by the researcher and that these assurances

6. For a detailed discussion of confidentiality, see Robert F. Boruch and Joe S. Cecil, *Assuring the Confidentiality of Social Research Data* (Philadelphia: University of Pennsylvania Press, 1979).

should be rigidly adhered to. There is evidence that an absolute assurance of confidentiality increases the number of subjects willing to cooperate in research.[7] This is especially true when sensitive topics, such as sexual intercourse or marijuana use, are involved.[8]

In recent years many strategies have been developed to assure confidentiality. Since these strategies often go beyond the needs of most graduate students, we here summarize only a few of the most widely used ones:

1. *Ask subjects to furnish information anonymously.* This strategy virtually eliminates the possibility that an individual can be linked to his responses. If it is necessary to determine who has responded (an important consideration in questionnaire surveys), the researcher can include a separate postcard with the questionnaire and can request the respondent to return the card after he has returned his questionnaire. This provides a check of who has responded, thus permitting follow-ups of nonrespondents; but because the postcard and questionnaire are mailed separately, it is not possible to link the two and identify a given respondent's questionnaire.

2. *Use an identifier that can be destroyed as soon as the individual's response is received.* This approach is often used in surveys where it is necessary to follow up on nonrespondents. In questionnaire studies, the questionnaire may be designed so that the respondent's name or code number can be torn off as soon as the questionnaire is received and before responses are tabulated.

3. *Use a third party to select the sample and collect data.* In some sensitive areas, knowledge that the individual belongs to a target population can be a breach of confidentiality regardless of the individual's responses. For example, suppose you want to study a sample of child abusers. It may be necessary to ask clinicians working with child abusers to randomly select cases from their active files, administer your measure to the selected cases, and, without identifying subjects, turn over these measures to you. This way, you do not know who is in your sample and of course cannot link names to responses.

4. *Have subjects make up their own code numbers or aliases.* When data must be collected over a period of time or when several measures must be administered to each subject, the data can be linked by having each subject make up an alias based on information not available to the researcher. The subject then puts the alias (rather than his own name) on all measures related to the research. For example, Robert Boruch and Joe Cecil recommend a number code based on the birth dates of respondents' parents.[9] Another possibility is to have the subject arrive at a four-digit "secret number," such as the odd digits in his

---

7. National Academy of Sciences, Committee on Federal Statistics, *Report of the Panel on Privacy and Confidentiality as Factors in Survey Responses* (Washington D.C.: NAS, 1979).
8. Eleanor Singer, "Informed Consent: Consequences for Response Rate and Response Quality in Social Surveys," *American Sociological Review* 43 (1978): 144–62.
9. See Annotated References at the end of this chapter.

social security number, the month and day of a friend's birth, the last four digits on his auto license, his house number from a previous residence, and so on. Since no one but the subject knows how he has arrived at his number, it would be nearly impossible to identify the subject from this number.

It is only necessary that the alias be a word or number the subject can reconstruct if he forgets it and that it be based on information that is almost certain to be different for all respondents.

5. *Data contamination or randomized response.* This approach involves introducing a random error into subject responses so that a certain number of subjects give untrue responses. For example, suppose the investigator want to estimate how many girls in a target population have had sexual intercourse before age twelve. Each subject is asked the question but is told to cast a die before answering. If the number 1 comes up, the subject is to give a false response, i.e., indicate that she has had intercourse when in fact she has not, or vice versa. The respondent is protected because the researcher has no way of knowing whether the respondent has given a true or false response. However, the researcher does know that for a large sample, one-sixth of the responses will be false; knowing this, he can estimate closely the number who have had intercourse before the age of twelve. This approach can be used in direct interviews and in telephone and mail surveys.

Various combinations of approaches that employ anonymity, a third party, aliases, and randomized responses have been proposed. If the few strategies described in this chapter do not meet the confidentiality needs of your research, Boruch and Cecil should be consulted.[10]

Deception

Many studies in the behavioral sciences could not be carried out unless the investigator withheld information or deceived the subjects. Robert Menges reviewed published reports of about 1000 psychological research studies and found that about 19 percent of them provided inaccurate information to subjects.[11] Only 3 percent gave subjects complete information. The percentage of studies giving inaccurate information varied greatly for different psychological journals. For example, 47 percent of articles in the *Journal of Personality and Social Psychology* used deception compared with only 3 percent in the *Journal of Experimental Psychology.* Clearly, different research areas require different amounts of deception. The ethical problems of using deception depend largely on the risk to subjects.

10. See Annotated References at the end of this chapter.
11. Robert J. Menges, "Openness and Honesty Versus Coercion and Deception in Psychological Research," *American Psychologist* 28 (1973): 1030–34.

There are a number of reasons why deception is used. Edward Diener and Rick Crandall classify these reasons as methodological or practical considerations, ecological validity, ethical considerations, and lack of negative effects.[12] In some studies it would be very difficult to find naturalistic situations in which the behavior being studied will occur. For example, a study of student responses to another student's cheating is much easier to observe and control if the "cheater" is a confederate.

In many studies, even though the needed data could be collected in naturalistic situations without deception, practical considerations such as limited time and money lead the researcher to use deception. Suppose, for example, you were studying teacher reactions to serious student misbehavior, such as open defiance of the teacher. Such behavior occurs rarely in most classrooms, and the cost of having observers stay in the classroom long enough to see a reasonable number of cases where student defiance occurred would be very high.[13] If student confederates are employed without the teacher's knowledge, however, open defiance can occur whenever desired by the researcher. Of course, unless the teacher is deceived, his reactions will not be natural, and the results will be of little value.

Ecological validity, which is discussed at length in chapter 15, is the degree to which the results of an experiment can be generalized from the set of environmental conditions created by the researcher to other environmental conditions. If a subject is aware that she is participating in an experiment, or if the environment of the experiment is markedly different from the natural environment to which we would like to apply our results, then the subject's responses may differ from her natural responses, and this will produce spurious results. Deception often must be practiced in order to elicit spontaneous and natural behavior so that findings may be more safely generalized to natural situations.

In some experiments it is more ethical to deceive subjects than to subject them to pain or other adverse experiences that would result if deception were not used. The classic study of obedience by S. Milgram provides a good example.[14] In this study subjects were ordered to administer increasingly severe electric shocks to another individual in the context of a learning experiment. The dependent variable was the level of shock the subject was willing to administer before refusing to continue further. Actually, the person being shocked was a confederate, and no shocks were administered. It was clearly more ethical to deceive the subjects than to allow the victim to be shocked. In Milgram's

---

12. See Annotated References at the end of this chapter.
13. Walter R. Borg and F. R. Ascione, "Classroom Management in Elementary Mainstreaming Classrooms," *Journal of Educational Psychology*, 74 (1982): 85–95.
14. S. Milgram, "Behavioral Study of Obedience," *Journal of Abnormal and Social Psychology* 67 (1963): 371–78.

initial experiment, 26 of the 40 subjects followed orders and administered what they thought was the maximum shock of 450 volts.

Most deceptions employed in behavioral research pose little or no risk to the subject. Many researchers consider such deceptions justified if the investigation promises to add to scientific knowledge. Some research indicates that most adults do not object to deception per se,[15] although a small percentage of adults surveyed found certain forms of deception objectionable.[16]

Some researchers are opposed to deception on the grounds that it is unethical and morally wrong to deceive anyone as part of a research project. Others oppose deception for more practical reasons. Probably the strongest argument against deception is that its use is widely known among such groups of potential subjects as college students. This awareness tends to make subjects suspicious and distrustful of researchers.

Sissela Bok has suggested that "the greatest harm from deception experimentation may be that to the investigators themselves, to the students trained in their professions, and to the professions as such. . . ."[17] Bok's position merits careful consideration. If researchers are perceived as liars or deceivers, or if researchers come to believe that people are objects to be manipulated or deceived, it seems inevitable that the long-term effects on science will be negative. Subjects' awareness of the practice of deception in research can lead to overt subject resistance and covert efforts to sabotage a study by giving spurious or unnatural responses. Over time, the widespread use of deception could lead to a general distrust of behavioral scientists by potential subjects.

Other arguments against deception are that it often creates as many methodological problems as it solves and that it deprives the subject of the information needed to give informed consent to participate in the research.

After a thorough review of the arguments regarding deception, Diener and Crandall recommended that researchers consider the following factors before undertaking investigations in which deception is used:

1. Researchers should decide whether research deception is ever ethically defensible and whether a particular deception could have detrimental effects on themselves or on subjects. The potential results of the study must seem important enough to justify the ethical cost of lying.
2. The research should not create negative effects in subjects outside the realm of the study itself, such as cynicism or resentment or lessened altruism in real-life situations.

15. Edwin A. Rugg, "Ethical Judgements of Social Research Involving Experimental Deception," *Dissertation Abstracts International* 36 (1975): 1976.
16. D. W. Wilson and E. Donnerstein, "Legal and Ethical Aspects of Non-Reactive Social Psychological Research: An Excursion into the Public Mind," *American Psychologist* 31 (1976): 765–73.
17. Sissela Bok, *Lying: Moral Choice in Public and Private Life* (New York: Vintage Books, 1979), p. 205.

3. Deceptions should not be practiced when they are not necessary for effective completion of the research.
4. When subjects are exposed to potential harm or surrender substantive rights, informed consent is a necessity. Deception should not undercut subjects' rights to be informed beforehand about risks.
5. Safeguards such as debriefing should be used to minimize potential negative outcomes.[18]

DEHOAXING AND DESENSITIZATION

An ethical question that is receiving increased attention in the behavioral sciences concerns the responsibilities of the researcher to debrief subjects who have participated in an experiment. Douglas Holmes points out that debriefing is of two types, *dehoaxing* and *desensitizing*.[19]

In **dehoaxing,** it is the task of the researcher to convince subjects who have been deceived as part of an experiment that they have, in fact, been deceived so that the deception can do no future harm to the subject. For example, in a study in which students were given fraudulent test scores in order to measure the effect of these scores on their aspiration level, it would be the responsibility of the researcher to convince the subjects that they had been deceived. If subjects believe that the false scores are correct, this belief could permanently damage their self-esteem and academic aspirations. Simply telling subjects that they have been deceived is often not sufficient. In this case, some form of demonstration might be needed to *convince* subjects and thus remove the undesirable effects of the experiment.

Desensitization is defined by Holmes as "the process of helping subjects deal with new information about themselves acquired as a consequence of the behaviors they exhibited during the experiment" (p. 868). For example, in a study of obedience, if subjects exhibit some behavior, such as administering electrical shocks to another person because the experimenter told them to do so, the knowledge that they did this might cause subjects grave concerns and doubts about themselves. Holmes discusses two approaches that have been used to deal with this problem. One approach is to suggest that the subjects' behavior resulted from the circumstances of the experiment and was not due to defects in the character or personality of the subjects. A second approach is to point out that the subjects' behavior is not abnormal or unusual. In effect, these approaches provide the subjects with rationalizations that make it possible for them to accept a behavior that is in conflict with their own self-percep-

---

18. Diener and Crandall (1978), p 96. See Annotated References at the end of this chapter.
19. See Annotated References at the end of this chapter.

tions or ideas of right and wrong. In studies of this sort, the experimenter may be tampering with the lives of subjects in ways that she might be unable to control and may cause damage she will be unable to correct. Before research that will require desensitization is initiated, the researcher should look very carefully into the ethical issues involved, should proceed slowly and deliberately, and should stop her work if any serious risk to the subjects appears to be developing.

LEGAL CONSTRAINTS

In recent years, laws have been enacted to place certain legal constraints on the educational researcher. For the most part these laws require the researcher to follow procedures designed to protect the research subject. Generally the procedures are in harmony with the ethical standards that behavioral scientists have developed for themselves and have observed for a number of years. Such laws have the advantage of providing a lever that can be used against the few researchers who do not follow ethical research practice. Perhaps the greatest danger of such laws is that rigid and bureaucratic interpretation can stifle many valuable research activities.

Since laws in this domain are quite recent, the process of clarification and interpretation is still under way. Also, additional legislation will almost surely be enacted within the near future. Therefore, although the following pages accurately report the status of legal constraints as they exist in 1982, the researcher should check on the most recent changes to assure that a law is not unwittingly violated or a new interpretation of one of the laws has not been made.

Family Educational Rights and Privacy Act of 1974

This act, commonly known as the **Buckley Amendment,** is designed to protect the privacy of students' educational records. One of its major provisions, which is important to educational researchers, is that in most cases data may not be made available in a personally identifiable manner from school records unless there is written consent by the parents or by the student in the case of postsecondary students or persons at least eighteen years of age. The written consent must be signed and dated by either a parent or eligible student and must include a specification of the records to be disclosed, the purpose for the disclosure, and the persons to whom the disclosure is to be made.[20]

20. See Weinberger and Michael (1977) in Annotated References at the end of this chapter.

There are several exceptions to the written consent requirement. One of these is that school personnel with "legitimate educational interest" are exempted. Thus, a graduate student who is carrying out research in his own school or district on a topic that is of interest to the district would probably be exempted from the written consent requirement. Also exempted are organizations conducting studies for local and state educational agencies for the purpose of developing, validating, or administering predictive tests, administering student-aid programs, and improving instruction. Since much educational research is concerned either directly or indirectly with improving instruction, students doing such research may be exempted from the written consent requirement. This exemption would be at the discretion of the local institution, and therefore it would be necessary for the researcher to convince local authorities that the proposed project qualifies.

If the researcher is given access to school records, he must conduct his research in such a manner that the personal identification of students and their parents by unauthorized persons would not be possible. The purposes of the research must be made known and information that identifies individuals must be destroyed when no longer needed for the purpose for which the study is conducted.

For many research projects in education the researcher does not need information that personally identifies the subject. For example, if a study were concerned with comparing the reading comprehension of pupils in fifteen first-grade classrooms who were trained with Reading Program A and pupils in fifteen other first-grade classrooms who were trained with Reading Program B, the school district could legally supply the researcher with lists of pupil scores in reading comprehension, identifying only the classrooms. Under these conditions parental consent to furnish these scores would not be required. In designing studies in which school records will be used, the researcher should try to plan the research in such a way that personally identifiable data are not needed.

Although final rules were published in June 1976 (see Annotated References), the Department of Education may publish additional regulations concerned with the Buckley Amendment as it refers explicitly to educational research.[21]

National Research Act of 1974

The *National Research Act of 1974* provides for the review by an Institutional Review Board of behavioral research (including educational research) that in-

21. Students seeking the most up-to-date information on the Buckley Amendment should contact Family Educational Rights and Privacy Office, 200 Independence Avenue SW, Room 526 E, Washington, DC 20201.

volves human subjects. At present the main function of this act is to provide a mechanism for reviewing research proposals from the standpoint of protection of human participants.[22] The concern for protecting research participants originally focused on biomedical research where risks are generally more clear-cut than in educational research.[23] In fact, very few studies in education expose subjects to any risk whatsoever. For example, a recent study of 23 evaluation research projects in several behavioral science areas failed to find any studies in which subjects were exposed to physical or mental risks.[24] **Risk** is broadly defined as exposure to the possibility of physical, psychological, or social injury as a consequence of participating as a subject in research, development, or related activity.

Most universities have established their own Institutional Review Board to conduct reviews in compliance with this act. The main function of these boards is to determine whether human participants will be placed at risk and, if so, whether the risk to the participant outweighs the importance of the information to be collected. The Institutional Review Board must also obtain assurances that the rights and welfare of participants will be adequately protected, that informed consent will be secured, and that the conduct of the research will be reviewed at timely intervals. The current definition of informed consent emphasizes the need for voluntary, uncoerced consent and for the freedom of research participants to withdraw from the research project without prejudice.

The regulations related to the National Research Act that are of most interest to educational researchers were published in the *Federal Register* on January 26, 1981, by the Department of Health and Human Services. A survey of virtually all federal agencies that conduct or fund research that involves human subjects was carried out the same year.[25] With a few minor exceptions, the survey found that all agencies substantially conform to the Health and Human Services regulations. Therefore, if you are doing research involving human subjects for any federal agency, you can safely use the HHS regulations as a guide.[26]

These regulations limit the requirement that research proposals be ap-

22. For a recent review and discussion of this topic, see Gerald Holton and Robert S. Morison, eds., *Limits of Scientific Inquiry* (New York: Norton, 1979).
23. Even in biomedical research, injury to research subjects is a very rare occurrence. For a thorough discussion of this topic, see President's Commission for the Study of Ethical Problems in Medicine and Biomedical and Behavioral Research, *Compensating for Research Injuries*, 1, *Report* (Washington D.C.: Government Printing Office, 1982).
24. Evelyn Perloff and Judith K. Perloff, "Ethics in Practice," *New Directions for Program Evaluation* 7 (1980): 77–83.
25. President's Commission for the Study of Ethical Problems in Medicine and Biomedical and Behavioral Research, *Protecting Human Subjects, Partial Preliminary Draft*, 9 October 1981.
26. See C. R. McCarthy, "The Development of Federal Regulations for Social Science Research" in Kimmel, ed., *Ethics of Human Subject Research*.

proved by an Institutional Review Board to proposals that receive funds from the Department of Health and Human Services. The regulations also name several types of research that are exempt from review because they involve "minimal risk" to human subjects. It should be noted that the Department of Health and Human Services takes the position that, although they are not legally required to, institutions should afford review and other human-subject protections regardless of source of funding. Among the categories of research that are exempt from the regulations are:

1. Research conducted in established or commonly accepted educational settings, involving normal educational practices, such as *(a)* research on regular and special education instructional strategies, or *(b)* research on the effectiveness of or the comparison among instruction techniques, curricula, or classroom management methods.
2. Research involving the use of educational tests (cognitive, diagnostic, aptitude, achievement) if information taken from these sources is recorded in such a manner that subjects cannot be identified directly or through identifiers linked to the subjects.
3. Research involving survey or interview procedures, except where all of the following conditions exist: *(a)* Responses are recorded in such a manner that the human subjects can be identified directly or through identifiers linked to the subjects; *(b)* the subject's responses, if they became known outside the research, could reasonably place the subject at risk of criminal or civil liability or be damaging to the subject's financial standing or employability; and *(c)* the research deals with sensitive aspects of the subject's own behavior, such as illegal conduct, drug use, sexual behavior, or use of alcohol. All research involving survey or interview procedures is exempt, without exception, when the respondents are elected or appointed public officials or candidates for public office.
4. Research involving the observation (including observation by participants) of public behavior, except where all of the following conditions exist: *(a)* Observations are recorded in such a manner that the human subjects can be identified directly or through identifiers linked to the subject; *(b)* the observations recorded about the individual, if they became known outside the research, could reasonably place the subject at risk of criminal or civil liability or be damaging to the subject's financial standing or employability; and *(c)* the research deals with sensitive aspects of the subject's own behavior such as illegal conduct, drug use, sexual behavior, or use of alcohol.
5. Research involving the collection or study of existing data, documents, records, pathological specimens, or diagnostic specimens if these sources are publicly available or if the information is recorded by the investigator in

such a manner that subjects cannot be identified directly or through identifiers linked to the subjects.[27]

As is the case with most federal regulations, these exempt categories are
difficult to interpret.[28] For example, nearly all educational research could be
exempt from review under the first category because it is logical to assume that
(a) and (b) are merely examples of many similar activities. Since many kinds of
tests including attitude scales, personality measures, and adjustment measures
are used in "normal educational practice," one can conclude that studies using
these measures in school settings are exempt from review. However, the second category appears to limit exemption to "cognitive, diagnostic, aptitude,
achievement" tests and then only if subjects cannot be identified.

Such inconsistencies are eventually ironed out by the bureaucracy. In the
absence of clear explanations, many researchers interpret such regulations in
whatever way best suits their purposes. Nevertheless, if you have questions
about whether your research is exempt from review, you should check with a
member of the Institutional Review Board (IRB) at your university for the latest
interpretation of the regulations.

The regulations also identify several kinds of research that can be reviewed through an "expedited review procedure" in which only one IRB member reviews the proposal. The one member may approve the proposal, but only
a vote of the entire board may disapprove. Most of the provisions for expedited
review refer to biomedical research. The following categories, however, are
relevant to behavioral science areas such as experimental psychology and physical
education:

1. Recording of data from subjects eighteen years of age or older using non-
   invasive procedures routinely employed in clinical practice. This includes
   the use of physical sensors applied either to the surface of the body or at a
   distance that do not involve input of matter (e.g., injections) or significant
   amounts of energy (e.g., electric shock) into the subject or an invasion of
   the subject's privacy. It also includes such procedures as weighing, testing
   sensory acuity, electrocardiography, electroencephalography, thermogra-
   phy, detection of naturally occurring radioactivity, diagnostic echography,
   and electroretinography. It does not include exposure to electromagnetic
   radiation outside the visible range (for example, X rays, microwaves).

27. Department of Health and Human Services, "Final Regulations Amending Basic HHS Policy
    for the Protection of Human Research Subjects," Federal Register 26, no. 16 (26 January 1981):
    8366–92.
28. For an interesting discussion of these regulations, see J. J. Thomson et al., "Regulations Gov-
    erning Research on Human Subjects—Academic Freedom and the Institutional Review Board,"
    Academe 67 (1981): 358–70.

2. Voice recordings made for research purposes, such as investigations of speech defects.
3. Moderate exercise by healthy volunteers.
4. The study of existing data, documents, records, pathological specimens, or diagnostic specimens.
5. Research on individual or group behavior or characteristics of individuals, such as studies of perception, cognition game theory, or test development, where the investigator does not manipulate subjects' behavior and the research will not involve stress to subjects.
6. Research on drugs or devices for which an investigational new drug exemption or an investigational device exemption is not required.

Informed Consent

Another requirement of the National Research Act is that investigators obtain the "informed consent" of subjects to participate in the research to be conducted. Current regulations state that the requirement for informed consent can be waived if the IRB finds either:

> (a) that the only record linking the subject and the research would be the consent document and the principal risk would be potential harm resulting from a breach of confidentiality. Each subject will be asked whether the subject wants documentation linking the subject with the research, and the subject's wishes will govern; or (b) that the research presents no more than minimal risk of harm to subjects and involves no procedures for which written consent is normally required outside the research context.

If your research involves minimum risk and uses procedures for which written consent is not normally required, it is justifiable to ask the IRB at your university to waive the informed consent requirement.

If your study is such that you must obtain informed consent, you should prepare a letter that meets the following requirements:

1. Gives the subject a reasonable opportunity to consider whether or not he wants to participate. Avoids any coercion.
2. Uses language that the subject can understand.
3. Uses no exculpatory language, i.e., language that implies release from your legal or ethical obligations to the subject.
4. Includes a reasonable explanation of the research, its purposes, procedures, and duration of participation.
5. Describes any benefits to the subject. For example, teachers involved in

research that evaluates teacher training programs are often given free tu-
ition and materials.

6. Describes appropriate alternative procedures.
7. Describes the extent to which confidentiality of records will be maintained.
8. Explains the availability of compensation and the availability of treatment
   if injury occurs. This, however, is not required for activities that involve
   minimal risk to subjects.
9. Contains instructions concerning who may be contacted for answers to
   pertinent questions.
10. States any conditions of participation, such as costs that will be incurred
    by the subjects.

A copy of the letter should be given to each subject for his/her signature and
then returned to you. These signed copies should be kept on file in case you
must later prove that consent was obtained.

For some subjects, it is preferable to give an oral presentation covering
the aforementioned points and then have subjects sign a short form. If this
approach is more appropriate for your research, check the regulations for detailed instructions.

Other informed consent provisions may be required for some studies. If
your study involves more than minimum risk to the subjects, you should study
the most recent regulations carefully and follow them in order to protect yourself from legal action.

The National Commission for the Protection of Human Subjects was created by the National Research Act and is responsible for developing guidelines,
criteria, definitions, and mechanisms required to implement the act.[29]

The Privacy Act of 1974

At present, this act is not relevant to the work of most graduate students since
its provisions are aimed primarily at protecting individuals from threats to individual privacy coming from the federal government. Nevertheless, there is
considerable sentiment for extending the act's provisions, in modified form, to
private and public institutions.

Some contractors who carry out research for the federal government are
liable under the provisions of this act. However, persons who have received
federal research grants do not currently come under the Privacy Act. Probably

---

29. Students seeking the most recent information on guidelines and regulations related to the
    National Research Act should write to National Commission for the Protection of Human Sub-
    jects, 5333 Westbard Avenue, Room 125, Bethesda, MD 20016.

the safest approach for the educational researcher is to maintain very careful control of any research evidence, such as test scores, that can be linked to individuals, following the procedures described earlier in this chapter. Under this act, federal agencies and their contractors are required to:

1. Permit an individual to determine what records related to her are collected, maintained, used, or disseminated by a given agency or organization.
2. Permit an individual to prevent records related to her that have been obtained by federal agencies for a particular purpose from being used or made available for another purpose without her consent.
3. Permit an individual to gain access to information pertaining to her in the federal records and to have a copy of such information made and to correct and amend such records.

Willful or intentional violation of an individual's rights under the Privacy Act can result in civil suits or criminal penalties. Therefore, it is advisable for the educational researcher to exercise great care in protecting the confidentiality of information and to abide by the provisions of the act in situations such as working under contract with a federal agency.

A Privacy Protection Study Commission has been established under the act. This commission has powers to study public and private data systems for the purpose of recommending legislation needed to protect the privacy of individuals. This commission has recommended that the Privacy Act be extended to include research and statistical activities in the public and private sectors alike and to pertain to federal grants as well as to contracts.

At this time it is not possible to draw very many clear conclusions about the ultimate impact of the Privacy Act upon educational research. Since the scope of this act is likely to be expanded, research activities that are not currently included may well be included within one or two years. Therefore, it is advisable for educational researchers to seek current information if they are planning work that may come under the provisions of this act.

HUMAN RELATIONS

Questions about One's Research

There are several rules that the research worker should observe if he plans to select subjects from the public schools. First he must have a thorough and detailed research design that he can explain in terms that administrators, teachers, and parents can understand. Many school administrators are doubtful of the value of educational research and are likely to be critical in their appraisal of the research design. If the student has failed to think through his design carefully, he may find himself unable to answer the questions put to him by educators, and this failure will almost certainly lead to a decision by school administrators not to participate in the study.

Before approaching parents or school administrators, the student should have thorough and convincing answers to questions that are likely to arise. Questions he must be prepared to answer include: What is the purpose of the study; what does it hope to find out? Are the findings likely to be worthwhile? Is the study important to education? If the student cannot convince school personnel that the work is worthwhile and likely to produce useful results, it is doubtful whether cooperation can be obtained. Schools generally cooperate in research projects because of a feeling of professional responsibility that exists among educators. Research projects almost always cause school personnel a certain amount of inconvenience and extra work, and unless the research worker can convince these persons that the research to be done is worth this extra effort and inconvenience, cooperation will not be obtained.

Another question that school personnel usually bring up in discussing research is: "Will the results of this research apply directly to our school?" In other words, the schools are interested in the direct returns that they may obtain from the research project. One of the direct returns, of course, will be that the research data will have greater application to the schools in which the research is done than it will to other schools. To be of significant value, of course, the research must be designed to obtain findings that can be applied beyond the situation in which the work was carried out. If research could be applied only to the isolated situation and to the specific subjects upon whom the experiment was carried out, there would be little value in doing such work. However, the fact remains that a research project will be more applicable to the specific situation in which the experiment is carried out than to similar situations in other schools.

Very often the schools are interested in other possible advantages that they may obtain from the research. These advantages differ depending upon the project, but can include such things as test scores that can be used by the school in guidance and in other of its regular activities, new curricular materials, visual aids, and improved administrative procedures. Some studies also involve the use of special measures that the school cannot afford to administer but that can be useful if administered by the research worker. These include such things as individual intelligence tests, individually administered projective measures, and depth interviews. For example, one of the authors recently carried out a research project that included administering the TAT[30] to a sam-

30. Thematic Apperception Test: a projective personality measure in which the subject is shown pictures and makes up a story around each picture.

ple of low-achieving children. Because this measure was given on an individual basis and required a clinical psychologist for administration and scoring, the cost would have been too great for most school districts. This test identified a number of children who appeared to have serious emotional disturbances. Once identified, the school district was able to arrange for help for these children. Any such possibilities of direct advantage to the schools should be pointed out by the research worker, as this is often a major consideration of school administrators in deciding whether to cooperate with the research.

Administrators will wish to know in considerable detail just what the school's role and responsibility will be in the research project. How much time will be required of the subjects? At what part of the school year must this time be scheduled? Will adjustments to the testing schedule be possible if other school activities interfere? Can subjects be tested in their classroom or will it be necessary to take subjects from their classes to another room? Will teachers be required to administer any of the tests or measures? Will it be necessary for the schools to provide pencils, answer sheets, lap boards, or other materials? Such questions should be thought through carefully by the research worker before approaching the school administrator. The price that the school generally must pay to participate in educational research is measured in the aforementioned terms, and the administrator must weigh the possible advantages to the school and to the profession against the losses in time, extra adjustments that must be made, and possible expenses to the school district.

At this point the student should be cautioned against making compromises with the administrator that weaken the research design. For example, if a random sample of subjects within the school is required for a research project and the school administrator suggests that volunteers be taken instead, the research worker should explain in detail the disadvantages of using volunteers and attempt to win the administrator over to paying the additional price in inconvenience that is required to obtain the random sample. If the administrator insists upon changes that seriously weaken the research design, it is wiser for the research worker to attempt to carry out the study elsewhere than to carry it out with disabling restrictions. In general the research worker should follow the rule that *all* concessions should be made that do not seriously weaken the scientific value of the study and *no* concessions should be made that do so compromise the research.

Another question that the administrator often will not mention but that may concern him greatly is: "Will the results of this research reflect unfavorably upon my school?" The research worker should bring this question up and discuss it objectively. As most educational research is aimed at discovering general principles and insights rather than the yielding of specific information about the participating schools and subjects, results can usually be prepared in such a way that they will not reflect unfavorably upon the schools used in the study. These results are generally reported in professional research journals, and it is customary to describe the study without identifying the specific schools involved. Such reassurance to the school administrator is especially needed when the study is such that the administrator may have some anxiety concerning the performance of pupils. Even if research findings reflect unfavorably upon participating schools, the research worker should in all his public statements emphasize that by cooperating in the research, school personnel have shown themselves to be interested in improving their service. It should be pointed out that educators who admit that their schools are not perfect and who are seeking ways to improve are more to be commended than those who are blind to their own shortcomings or those who try to hide deficiencies rather than correct them.

The school administrator will also be concerned with the specific measuring instruments that are to be used in the research. Samples of these measures should be shown to teachers and administrators in order that they may examine them carefully. The research worker should answer any questions concerning the measures and explain the specific purpose of each measure in the research. An exception to this rule occurs in some studies in which teacher or administrator knowledge of the measures can result in bias or contamination of the research results. For example, it is sometimes undesirable to allow teachers more than a brief examination of the achievement test to be used in a research project because some teachers will coach their pupils on the correct answers if they have a copy of the test available. This is usually done by teachers who are insecure and who feel that poor performance of their pupils will reflect unfavorably upon themselves.

Many psychological measures used in educational research projects are difficult for school administrators to understand. If such measures are to be used, the research worker must be prepared to explain very thoroughly the purpose of these measures and to provide evidence that the measure is a valid and useful one. In examining these measures, the administrators will often have in mind the possible response made by parents to such a measure. If the measure contains items that may cause unfavorable reactions from parents or other community groups, the research worker must have very strong justification for the use of these devices. He should also carry out careful public relations work with the groups concerned prior to the use of such measures. The research worker should avoid the use of measures that cannot be defended on the basis of appropriateness to the study and psychological significance. Prior approval for all measures to be used should be obtained from school authorities before the research is started.

In discussing a proposed research project with school personnel, it is essential that all parties understand specifically what their responsibilities are. Try to bring up and discuss any questions that may lead to future misunderstandings. Keep careful notes during planning meetings. Once you feel that all parties understand their roles in the project, make up a letter that spells out the agreement in specific terms and send this letter to the superintendent or principal involved for confirmation. On major studies it is also desirable to submit your proposal to the school board for approval.

Following Channels

When working with any administrative hierarchy, such as a school district, it is very important to follow appropriate channels of authority. If the student plans to use subjects from more than one school, it is generally necessary first to obtain approval from the district superintendent or from the assistant superintendent in charge of research. After obtaining such approval, the student must visit each school concerned and present her ideas to the principal. If the principal objects strongly to testing pupils in the school, the superintendent will usually support the principal, even though the superintendent has given tentative approval for the project. Even if the superintendent were inclined to force the principal to cooperate, such an arrangement would create a situation in which it would be very difficult to carry out effective research. The interest and cooperation of all persons concerned with the research is necessary if it is to be carried through to a successful conclusion.

After the principal and superintendent have been briefed concerning the purposes of the research and the procedures to be followed, it usually will be necessary for the research worker to meet with teachers in the schools and to obtain their interest and cooperation. Often a faculty meeting can be devoted to the research topic, and the research worker can present her plans and get the responses of the teachers at this time. Teachers and school administrators frequently will see problems or difficulties in the research plans that the research worker has not recognized. The suggestions of school personnel should be solicited and followed whenever this may be done without compromising some scientific aspect of the research.

In most studies it is also desirable that parents be informed concerning the nature of the study and given an opportunity to express their opinions. This may often be done by having the research worker present her plans at PTA meetings in the schools involved. The purposes of the study and the procedures should be discussed as frankly as possible, omitting only information that could lead to compromising the study in some way. In addition to such a presentation, it is usually necessary for the research worker to prepare a letter explaining the study. This letter is sent home to parents of all children who will participate as subjects and should provide a place where the parent may sign to signify approval of the child's participation in the research. In preparing your letter, check on the legal requirements to obtain "informed consent," given earlier in this chapter, and be sure your letter meets these requirements.

The degree of rapport that must be built up between the research worker and other community groups is dependent to a great extent upon the nature of the study. Studies dealing with areas such as achievement, which are generally regarded as a major aspect of the school's business, need a less extensive public relations program than studies involving such areas as personality and social adjustment, where the role of the school is less clear and where some of the measures to be employed might be resented or misunderstood by the parent.

It is not only necessary to establish good working relationships before starting your research; it is equally important to maintain these relationships during the time the research is carried on. If they have problems or questions that go unanswered, teachers may refuse to cooperate or may even sabotage your work by doing such things as complaining to parents that your research is interfering with class work, or taking children on field trips on days when you have scheduled testing. It is especially important to keep teachers and other persons who are involved in your project informed of your progress and alerted to coming events in the research plan. In small-scale projects, the investigator should personally keep in contact with participating teachers and administrators. In large-scale projects, periodic reports and newsletters should be sent to teachers, parents, and other interested persons. A sample letter, similar to one sent to teachers participating in a project conducted by the senior author, has been reproduced in figure 4.1.

Much research is only possible because of warm personal relationships between the educational researcher and school personnel. If you develop a sincere interest in the problems of practitioners and a respect for their ideas and points of view, you will gain insights that will improve your research plans and you will also receive a level of cooperation that makes it possible to complete your project when the going gets rough. Often you can provide help for school administrators and teachers such as helping them locate new curriculum materials, conducting a brief literature search related to a current school problem, helping prepare a research proposal for state or federal funding, or helping to analyze a test that is being considered for the district's evaluation program. The researcher who freely gives help when she can builds up a credit balance that greatly simplifies many of the problems associated with doing research in the public schools. The researcher who is regarded in the schools as a friend and colleague has a much easier time than one who is regarded as an outsider with unknown motives.

Dealing with Public Relations Problems

In spite of the efforts of the research worker to establish good rapport with concerned groups, public relations problems arise occasionally in educational field studies. A frequent problem involves protests over measures used in the

UTAH STATE UNIVERSITY · LOGAN, UTAH 84322

COLLEGE OF EDUCATION

DEPARTMENT OF
PSYCHOLOGY
UMC 28

May 20, 1982

Dear Mrs. Oliver:

With your valued assistance we have just finished collecting data for the second year of the Utah ability-grouping study. I realize that this research has caused you inconvenience and has taken time from your classes. I assure you that we are aware of the problems that such a study causes in the cooperating schools and shall continue to try to reduce these problems during the remaining two years of the study. I'm afraid that it is inevitable that progressive school districts, such as your own, that choose to support research and strive to find better ways of educating our youth must always pay for their leadership by accepting the problems that major research projects always bring.

I am pleased to tell you that we already have enough important results to indicate that this research is well worth the effort, the problems, and the inconveniences. Our work to date has yielded important new knowledge about ability grouping. The remaining two years of the study will certainly teach us more and will also give us a chance to check the results we have already obtained.

The work under way in the Utah study is the first extensive long-term evaluation of ability grouping, and I assure you that through your cooperation you are making a real and important contribution to the teaching profession.

My deepest regret as I look back on the past year's work is that I have had little opportunity to meet with the teachers cooperating in this research. I know that many of you have questions about the study that I could answer. I am also sure that you have suggestions and ideas that would help us make this research better. I plan to visit each cooperating school before we start collecting data next year and hope that you will jot down ideas and suggestions so that we may discuss them at that time.

In closing, permit me to thank you again for your patience and cooperation. I am looking forward to meeting with you and exchanging ideas during the coming year.

Sincerely,

Walter R. Borg

Walter R. Borg

Figure 4.1.   Sample of a letter sent to a participant in a field research project.

research. Such protests are usually made by small but vocal groups of citizens who are primarily interested in obtaining publicity. Often local newspapers, in the quest for more sensational news stories, will encourage such groups by giving their protests wide and sometimes biased coverage. Most of these protests can be traced back to the fact that items occur in many psychological tests, the purpose of which cannot be easily explained to the lay person. Many psychological tests in such areas as personality, mental health, social adjustment, attitudes, and interests are still in the early stages of development, and not even their strongest advocates would claim them to be highly valid measures. In many cases, however, such measures are the best available and must be used if research in a particular area is to be carried forward.

A researcher whose project is given biased coverage in news stories should make an attempt to provide reporters with his side of the story. He should particularly point out the procedures that are being used to protect individual privacy. These procedures should include obtaining prior consent and assuring confidentiality and anonymity of data.

ETHICAL AND HUMAN RELATIONS MISTAKES SOMETIMES MADE BY EDUCATIONAL RESEARCHERS

1. Fails to follow proper channels in setting up a study in the public schools.
2. Has not prepared answers for questions likely to be asked by school administrators about his research project.
3. Weakens the research design by making changes for the administrative convenience of the schools from which subjects are to be drawn.
4. Establishes good rapport and then loses it by failing to maintain communication.
5. Uses measures that cannot be defended to critics of the research.
6. Does not follow correct procedures for obtaining informed consent from parents or subjects.
7. Fails to set up adequate safeguards to ensure the confidentiality of research data.
8. Does not carry out effective debriefing of research subjects.

ANNOTATED REFERENCES

Boruch, Robert F., and Cecil, Joe S. *Assuring the Confidentiality of Social Research Data*. Philadelphia: University of Pennsylvania Press, 1979.

This is by far the most comprehensive and informative reference on confidentiality we have located. The brief section on confidentiality in this chapter is based primarily on this source. Many interesting and ingenious methods of maintaining confidentiality while gathering needed research data are discussed, and examples are given. Although focusing primarily upon the mailed questionnaire and interview, many of the strategies suggested are equally appropriate for other kinds of research.

Committee on Ethical Standards in Psychological Research. *Ethical Principles in the Conduct of Research with Human Participants.* Washington, D.C.: American Psychological Association, 1973.

This booklet lists principles that are nearly identical to those from the more recent source quoted in the text. Each principle is described in detail, incidents related to the principle are presented, and a discussion of each principle is provided. This is an excellent source for the student who needs help in weighing the pros and cons of a course of action related to any of these principles.

Department of Health, Education, and Welfare. "Privacy Rights of Parents and Students—Final Rule on Education Records." *Federal Register* 41 (1976): 24662–75.

Students who plan to use school records in their research and school administrators responsible for school records should study this publication. The sections on formulation of institutional policies and disclosure of personally identifiable information are of special interest to the researcher.

Diener, Edward, and Crandall, Rick. *Ethics in Social and Behavioral Research.* Chicago: University of Chicago Press, 1978.

In a clear, systematic manner, this excellent book deals with the ethical issues that concern behavioral scientists. For each issue, the authors explore the main ideas, arguments, and relevant research evidence and come to a conclusion. They also provide very useful guidelines for the researcher faced with an ethical problem or question.

Halpern, Andrew S. *The Impact of the Protection of Human Subjects on Research.* Working Paper no. 70. Eugene: University of Oregon, 1973. ERIC Document Reproduction Service No. ED 104 083.

The author discusses the investigator's responsibility for the protection of human subjects in research. Five general topics are explored: (1) human rights most frequently in need of protection, (2) most common threats to these rights posed by research, (3) criteria for determining risk to human subjects, (4) ways of reducing research-related risk, and (5) conditions and procedures for acceptance of risk by subjects and experimenters. The author proposes seven steps that the researcher can take to minimize risks to the subject.

Hershey, Nathan, and Miller, Robert D. *Human Experimentation and the Law.* Germantown, Md.: Aspen Systems, 1976.

The book starts with a historical perspective that describes a few important cases of abuse of human rights. Then the Institutional Review Board and its responsibilities are discussed in detail. Laws related to investigations with human subjects are reviewed. Contains much useful information, although some specifics are now out of date.

Holmes, Douglas S. "Debriefing after Psychological Experiments: I. Effectiveness of Postdeception Dehoaxing." *American Psychologist* 31 (1976): 858–67.

Holmes, Douglas S. "Debriefing after Psychological Experiments: II. Effectiveness of Postexperimental Desensitizing." *American Psychologist* 31 (1976): 868–75.

These two articles discuss the debriefing of research subjects and review research on the effectiveness of efforts to dehoax and desensitize subjects at the end of experiments. The articles will be useful to researchers planning studies that involve deception or that cause subjects to engage in behavior that may result in psychological discomfort.

Hook, S.; Durtz, P.; and Todorovich, M.; eds. *The Ethics of Teaching and Scientific Research*. Buffalo, N.Y.: Prometheus Books, 1977.

This collection of papers was presented at a conference in New York City in 1975. The first section of the book deals with objectivity and indoctrination, the second with the ethics of teaching, and the third with the ethics of research. All three sections contain thoughtful discussions of ethical questions that are of major importance to the teacher and researcher. The chapters by Horn and Kurtz on freedom of inquiry are especially recommended.

Kimmel, A. J., ed. *Ethics of Human Subject Research*. San Francisco: Jossey-Bass, 1981.

Information on codes of ethics and federal regulations related to human subject research is presented. The last five chapters, which deal with ethical problems and place ethical issues in a theoretical and philosophical context, are especially recommended.

President's Commission for the Study of Ethical Problems in Medicine and Biomedical and Behavioral Research. *Protecting Human Subjects*. Washington D.C.: Government Printing Office, 1981.

In this biennial report, the commission summarizes the results of a 1980 survey of 83 federal agencies regarding their rules governing research on human subjects. The commission found a considerable lack of uniformity and recommended that all agencies adopt the current Health and Human Services regulations. The report summarizes the current rules of all federal agencies supporting research with human subjects. The responses of federal agencies to violations of the regulations were also studied, and five case studies involving violations are discussed in some detail. Nine recommendations were made by the commission as a result of the study, and these are likely to lead to future changes in regulations related to human-subject research. This is a useful report for researchers interested in the current human-subject regulations and the operation of the commission.

Reynolds, Paul D. *Ethical Dilemmas and Social Science Research.* San Francisco: Jossey-Bass, 1979.

The author deals with three major topics: investigators' responsibilities and participants' rights, restrictions on investigators' autonomy, and social scientists' relations with society. The ethical problems of most interest to graduate students, such as informed consent, deception, and participants' rights, are analyzed. The book attempts to help the social scientist analyze moral dilemmas by emphasizing the major relevant issues. In other words, the scientist is encouraged to think through the arguments for himself rather than rely on prescriptions, which this book does not provide.

Reynolds, Paul D. *Ethics and Social Research.* Englewood Cliffs, N.J.: Prentice-Hall, 1982.

The book deals with ethical issues that arise in the conduct of social science research. Each chapter starts with an example of research and gives an example of how to analyze the research for important ethical issues. Both overt and covert research is discussed. Codes of ethics for several social science professional organizations, such as the American Psychological Association and American Sociological Association, are given along with federal guidelines and legal constraints.

Stoltz, Stephanie B. *Ethical Issues in Behavior Modification.* San Francisco: Jossey-Bass, 1978.

In 1974 the American Psychological Association set up a commission to study ethical issues in behavioral modification and to make recommendations. The commission completed its work in 1976, and this book is the result. It deals in depth with major ethical questions in a variety of settings including the schools. Students planning research that involves behavior modification should read this book carefully.

Weinberger, J. A., and Michael, J. A. "Federal Restrictions on Educational Research: A Status Report on the Privacy Act." *Educational Researcher* 6, no. 2 (1977): 5–8.

This series of articles provides a brief but excellent coverage of current federal legislation and its apparent effects upon educational research. Students interested in this topic should start with these articles, but since the situation in this field is changing rapidly, should also seek out the most recent developments.

SELF-CHECK TEST

Circle the correct answer to each of the following questions. An answer key is provided on page 881.

1. If explaining the reason for the research to subjects before data collection will invalidate the research, the experimenter should
   a. not disclose any information about the object of the research.
   b. inform them anyway, since their cooperation is vital.
   c. tell the subjects they will be informed at the completion of the research.
   d. give reasons other than the true reasons for the research.

2. Because in the school setting the researcher must have the cooperation of parents, teachers, students, and administrators, it is important that the researcher
   a. conduct as much research as possible in the laboratory setting.
   b. ask the superintendent to explain the research to all involved.
   c. devise a plan to gain school cooperation.
   d. work only in settings where immediate cooperation is available.

3. Concerning confidentiality of research data, the researcher should
   a. make certain no unauthorized individuals have access to the data.
   b. inform the subjects about the persons who will have access to the data.
   c. remove names from data-collection instruments and replace with a code.
   d. All of the above are correct.

4. If a college student agrees to participate in a research project and then, after completing part of the work, drops out,
   a. the student should be penalized in some way, such as lowering his grade in a college class.
   b. the student should be required to provide another person to substitute for him.
   c. nothing should be done since the student has the right to withdraw.
   d. the student is legally committed to complete the project and should be informed of this fact.

5. The protection of individual privacy in educational research involves two factors: consent of the individual as to what shall be disclosed to the researcher, and
   a. the length of time during which data collected are to remain confidential.
   b. confidential use of research data collected on individuals.
   c. the need for all data to be collected anonymously.
   d. disclosure based only upon significance of findings of study.

6. A graduate student is employed as a research assistant in a psychological experiment involving deception. In studying the research plan she notices that

no debriefing is planned. What should she do?

   a. Since she is not in charge of the project, she has no ethical responsibility and therefore should do nothing.
   b. If professional ethics are violated, she has a responsibility and therefore should bring up the ethical question and see that it is resolved.
   c. Although she has no ethical responsibility, she should suggest that the investigator look into the ethical question but should not pursue the matter any further.
   d. She should resign her assistantship in order to protect her ethical position.

7. Under current (1981) federal regulations, which of the following types of research is *not* exempt from review by the Institutional Review Board (IRB)?

   a. Research conducted in established or commonly accepted educational settings that involves normal educational practices.
   b. Research involving the use of educational tests if subjects cannot be identified.
   c. Research collecting voice recordings for research purposes, such as investigations of speech defects.
   d. Research involving surveys or interviews of public officials.

8. The main purpose of the Privacy Act of 1974 is

   a. to protect subjects from questions asked in research projects that might invade their privacy.
   b. to give individuals the right to refuse to participate in research projects.
   c. to protect individuals from invasion of privacy by the federal government.
   d. to require educational researchers to remove names from test answer sheets and similar materials.

9. In experiments in which subjects have been deceived, what is the ethical responsibility of the investigator?

   a. Inform subjects before the study that the experiment involves deception but do not identify what the deception is.
   b. Give subjects a written sheet at the end of the study that states that the study involved deception. The specific deception should not be described since this may damage future research.
   c. The investigator must inform the subjects in writing at the end of the study of the specific nature of the deception.
   d. The investigator must inform subjects of the deception at the end of the study and also carry out other activities such as demonstrations in order to convince subjects that they have been deceived.

10. A major provision of the "Buckley Amendment" is that

   a. in most cases data from school records cannot be released without consent of the parent (or subject if over 18).
   b. public schools cannot use data in their records for educational research.
   c. schools may not release educational records to state education agencies.

    d. all student records must be reviewed each year by the schools, and data not essential to the school operation must be destroyed.

APPLICATION PROBLEMS

The following problems are designed to give you practice in applying significant concepts and research procedures explained in chapter 4. Most of them do not have a single correct answer. For feedback, you can compare your answers with the sample answers on pages 884–85.

1. You plan to conduct a research project in which you will give tests to high school students and teachers in a particular school district. You are now meeting with the district superintendent to explain the purpose of the project. He asks you, "You plan to use students and teachers as subjects in an experiment. What steps are you taking to protect their rights as individuals?" What are two desirable steps that you could mention?

2. School people usually do not understand the nature of educational research. Therefore, the researcher only needs to inform superintendents, principals and teachers about the general purpose of his research project. They need not be informed of specifics, such as tests to be administered, number of students to be involved, how the results will be reported, etc. Is this a sound position to take? Support your answer.

3. In a study of truthfulness, you set up research conditions that make it possible to detect certain lies that could not be detected under normal conditions. At the end of the study, several subjects appear to be very upset when they discover that they have been caught in lies. As the investigator, what responsibility do you have to the subjects? Suggest steps you could take to meet this responsibility.

4. Suppose you have carried out a study in which you have given students incorrect scores on a test of algebra aptitude that they have taken (some higher and some lower than the correct scores) to see if this information would affect their responses on a vocational interest test to vocations such as engineering which require mathematics. Describe the procedure you would use to debrief the students at the completion of the study.

5. Suppose that you plan a research project designed to determine whether the use of fairly large rewards (values above $50, such as a bicycle, portable radio, record player) administered during Grade 7 can bring about significant long-term improvement in the school attitudes, attendance, and achievement of junior high school students who have a history of truancy and underachievement dating back at least three years. The school has gathered attendance and achievement data yearly for several years. You will administer an attitude mea-

sure at the end of the sixth grade to obtain a pretreatment measure of this variable. Your reward program will be carried out in Grade 7. Data on attitude, attendance, and achievement will be routinely collected each year and will be compared at the end of grades 7, 8, 9, and 10 with data collected for grades 4, 5, and 6. A comparable control group will be employed that will receive small rewards (values up to $5) such as free time for preferred activities, tickets to athletic events, magazines, and phonograph records. Students who meet the research criteria will be assigned randomly to the two treatments. List ethical and legal steps you should include in your research plan.

SUGGESTION SHEET

If your last name starts with letters from Can to Cop, please complete the Suggestion Sheet at the end of the book while this chapter is still fresh in your mind.

5.

REVIEWING THE LITERATURE

OVERVIEW

An educational researcher who would advance scientific knowledge must first identify and understand the research that has already been done in the field of interest. This chapter is designed to help you acquire the skills needed to conduct a thorough and systematic review of the research literature in your area of interest. Several reasons for conducting a review of literature are given, such as seeking to delimit the research problem and to identify new approaches. A systematic method of reviewing the educational research literature is described. Also discussed are the most important reference books and services that provide indexes and abstracts of completed research studies.

OBJECTIVES

After studying this chapter, you should be able to:

1. Describe the difference between primary and secondary sources in educational research and locate examples of each.
2. State six reasons for conducting a review of literature before starting a research project.
3. Conduct a review of the research literature on a given topic, following the three steps presented in this text.
4. Locate relevant articles in *Education Index, Psychological Abstracts, Current Index to Journals in Education,* and *Resources in Education* on a given research topic.
5. Describe at least four major preliminary sources specifically intended for use in educational research.
6. Plan a computer search of *Resources in Education, Current Index to Journals in Education,* or *Psychological Abstracts* on a given topic in educational research.
7. Read a research article and prepare a bibliographic citation and a note card that follows the models given.
8. Develop a system for coding research literature on a given topic.
9. Describe ways to obtain references not available in your university library.

INTRODUCTION

The review of the literature involves locating, reading, and evaluating reports of research as well as reports of casual observation and opinion that are related to the individual's planned research project. This review differs in a number of ways from the reading program often used to locate a tentative research project. First, such a review is much more extensive and thorough because it is aimed at obtaining a detailed knowledge of the topic being studied, while the reading program is aimed at obtaining enough general knowledge and insight to recognize problems in the selected area.

Secondary Sources

The reading program generally uses textbooks, encyclopedias, and other secondary source materials. **Secondary source** materials in education include any publications written by an author who was not a direct observer or participant in the events described. For example, most of the material found in textbooks of Roman history are secondary source materials because the author has merely compiled the reports of others and rearranged these reports into a textbook. Most of the content of textbooks in education and psychology is also secondary source material.

Let us suppose that an individual wishes to write a textbook on methods of teaching remedial reading. The prospective author does an exhaustive review of the literature in this field, noting the results of all experiments and weighing and evaluating these results in terms of various approaches to remedial reading instruction. Then, on the basis of his interpretation of the various research reports and articles he has read, he prepares his textbook. If, in the textbook, the author also reports the results of experiments that he himself has carried out, then this portion of the textbook would be considered a primary source. That portion, however, that is based on his interpretations of the work of others would be classified as a secondary source. Secondary sources are useful because they combine knowledge from many primary sources into a single publication. A good textbook, for example, combines the work of many other persons and simplifies or eliminates much of the technical material that is not of interest to the general reader, thus providing a quick and relatively easy method of obtaining a good overall understanding of the field.

Primary Sources

The **primary source** differs from the secondary source in that it is a direct description of an occurrence by an individual who actually observed or witnessed the occurrence. In educational research this generally means the description of the study by the individual who carried it out.

The principal disadvantage to the research scholar of using secondary sources is that it is never possible to be sure what changes have been made by the secondary source author. In the process of simplifying and combining the results of many studies, the author of a textbook or other secondary source report may slant her interpretation of the primary source to agree with her own views, and often she will leave out material that the person reviewing the literature needs to know. Thus a review of the literature should be based, whenever possible, upon primary sources. Most secondary sources, such as textbooks, contain a bibliography listing the sources from which the material was obtained so that the student can generally locate the primary source.

Importance of the Review

The review of the literature is an important part of the scientific approach and is carried out in all areas of scientific research, whether in the physical, natural, or social sciences. Such reviews are also the basis of most research in the humanities. In fields such as history, the review of literature not only gives the scholar an understanding of previous work that has been done, but the results of the review actually provide the data used in his research. Historical studies in education, which we will discuss in a later chapter, are based almost entirely upon a careful study of existing printed knowledge in the field.

The review of the literature in educational research provides you with the means of getting to the frontier in your particular field of knowledge. Until you have learned what others have done and what remains still to be done in your area, you cannot develop a research project that will contribute to furthering knowledge in your field. Thus the literature in any field forms the foundation upon which all future work must be built. If you fail to build this foundation of knowledge provided by the review of the literature, your work is likely to be shallow and naïve, and will often duplicate work that has already been done better by someone else. Although the importance of a thorough review of the literature is obvious to everyone, this task is more frequently slighted than any other phase of research. The research worker is always tempted to let a sketchy review of the literature suffice so that he can get started sooner on his own research project. The student, however, should make every effort to complete a thorough review before starting his research because the insights and knowledge gained by the review almost inevitably lead to a better-designed project and greatly improve the chances of obtaining important and significant results. Often the insights gained through the review will save the research worker as much time in conducting his project as the review itself required.

PURPOSES OF THE REVIEW

Although the general purpose of the review is to help the research worker develop a thorough understanding and insight into previous work and the trends that have emerged, the review can also help in reaching a number of important specific goals.

Delimiting the Research Problem

The review of the literature can help in limiting the individual's research problem and in defining it better. Many studies attempted by graduate students are doomed to failure before the student starts because she has not limited her problem to an area small enough and sufficiently specific for her to work with satisfactorily. It is far better in research to select a limited problem and treat it well than to attempt the study of a broad general problem and do it poorly. Many graduate students also commit themselves to a research problem before they have thought it out adequately. A fuzzy or poorly defined problem can sometimes result in the student's collecting data and then learning that her data cannot be applied to the problem she wishes to attack. Before she starts her review of the literature, the student should do sufficient background reading from secondary sources to permit a tentative outline of her research problem. The review of the literature will give the student the knowledge she needs to convert her tentative research problem to a detailed and concise plan of action.

Seeking New Approaches

In the process of reviewing the literature, the student should not only learn what work has been done but should also be alert to research possibilities that have been overlooked. The unique experience and background of an individual may make it possible for him to see a facet of the problem that other research workers have not seen. Such new viewpoints are likely to occur most frequently in areas where little research has been done, but even in well-researched areas, someone occasionally thinks of an approach that is unique and creative. A good example is C. E. Thompson's study of administration of the Thematic Apperception Test (TAT) to black subjects.[1] Prior to this study, many clinicians were administering the standard TAT cards to clients regardless of racial background. The persons pictured on the standard TAT cards are white,

1. C. E. Thompson, "The Thompson Modification of the Thematic Apperception Test," *Rorschach Research Exchange and Journal of Projective Techniques* 13 (1949): 469–78.

and Thompson saw that the use of these cards with Negro subjects might well lead to different responses because of racial differences. In his research he developed a comparable set of cards in which blacks were substituted for the whites in the TAT pictures and found that his hypothesis was correct. Although hundreds of research projects had been carried out prior to Thompson's work using the TAT, his special insight led to a unique and valuable contribution to our knowledge of this important instrument.

Avoiding Sterile Approaches

In reviewing the literature the student should also be on the lookout for research approaches in his area that have proved to be sterile. It is not uncommon in doing a review of the literature to encounter several very similar studies done over a period of years, all of which employ approximately the same approach and all of which fail to produce significant results. One or two repetitions of an unproductive approach can be justified on the grounds that these confirm the previous finding that the area is unproductive. Repetitions beyond this, however, serve no useful purpose and generally suggest that the persons repeating the study have not done an adequate review of the literature. In an excellent review of the literature on instructor effectiveness, Joseph Morsh and Elinore Wilder list eleven studies carried out between 1934 and 1948 in which an attempt was made to relate personality as measured by the Bernreuter Personality Inventory to instructor effectiveness.[2] None of these studies produced correlations sufficiently high to be of any value in predicting instructor effectiveness. In all likelihood additional studies following the same futile approach have been carried out since 1952, the date at which their review terminated.

Insight into Methods

The review of the literature can also give the student a great deal of insight into the methods, measures, subjects, and approaches used by other research workers and can thus lead to significant improvement of her design. A mistake made by many graduate students when reading research reports is to give little attention to anything but the results reported. Very often a study that has little to contribute by way of results can help the student a great deal by suggesting methods and useful approaches. For example, discussions of the various measures used can help the student decide which of these measures would be best

---

2. Joseph E. Morsh and Elinore W. Wilder, "Identifying the Effective Instructor: A Review of the Quantitative Studies, 1900–1952," *AFPTRC Research Bulletin TR-54-44* (Lackland Air Force Base, Tex.: October 1954).

suited for her own research. A sampling problem discussed by one research worker can help other research workers in the field avoid the same difficulties. In a study relating the degree of pupil homogeneity in the classroom to achievement, Goldberg et al. set up fifteen different classroom patterns, each having a different level of homogeneity and a different range of ability.[3] Pattern 1, which was to include classes in which all pupils were above 130 IQ, appeared the easiest to obtain because the school system had already set up classes for children at this level. Thus the research workers organized classes that were appropriate for other patterns but assumed that sufficient classes of pattern 1 would be available. On checking, however, it was found that the IQ limit had not been adhered to by schools in setting up these classes and that only one of the ten thought to be available actually met the requirements for pattern 1. Thus in a research project involving 2219 children, only 29 were included in one of the most important groups to be studied. Goldberg's study, although making many valuable contributions to our knowledge of ability grouping, would have been much stronger if the research workers had had available a larger number of pattern 1 classes. If she looks carefully at such methodological problems, the student can learn much that will help her improve her own research plan.

Recommendations for Further Research

The authors of research articles often include specific suggestions and recommendations for persons planning further research in the field. These suggestions should be considered very carefully because they represent the insights gained by the research worker after experience in the problem area. Specific research topics are often suggested that are particularly useful in helping the student delimit the research problem.

Sampling Current Opinions

Although research reports make up the most important source of information that the student covers in his review, he should also study newspaper accounts, nontechnical articles, and opinion articles related to his topic. Such articles occasionally contain unique ideas that can be tested through research and also help the research worker gain insight into those aspects of the problem area that are considered critical or controversial by educators. For example,

3. M. L. Goldberg, Joseph Justman, A. H. Passow, and Gerald Hage, *The Effects of Ability Grouping*, Interim Report (New York: Teachers College, Columbia University, Horace Mann-Lincoln Institute, 1961).

a study of opinion articles in the field of ability grouping shows that most of the disputes between educators in this field center on the possible effects of ability grouping on the child's *personality* and *social development*. On the other hand, nearly all the research reported in the field of ability grouping is concerned with the *achievement* of children in the ability-grouped situation. These studies contribute valuable knowledge but have had little effect upon the judgments of most educators. Only research that presents objective data concerning the variables that educators consider critical is likely to have any effect upon their decisions concerning whether or not they should establish or support an ability-grouping program.

SCOPE OF THE REVIEW

Perhaps the greatest frustration encountered by the graduate student in carrying out his first review of the literature centers on his attempt to determine what he should read and what he should not read. Unfortunately there are no pat formulas that can be given the student to help him make this decision. Obviously the student should read all studies that are closely related to his research problem. The decisions that cause him difficulty involve those studies that are only partially related to his research problem or perhaps only related to one phase of the problem.

Relatively new research areas usually lack an organized body of secondary source information to provide general background and thus require a fairly broad review in which even those studies that are only peripheral to the main area should be read in order to give the student the foundation of knowledge he requires.

For example, suppose a student wants to do research on the causes of "teacher burnout." Because widespread interest in teacher burnout is fairly new in education, the student should probably read most of the studies in the broad area of "burnout" even if they are not closely related to his topic. For instance, an article that discusses ways to train teachers to cope with stress, although only peripheral to the causes of teacher burnout, should be checked.[4] Also, studies that deal with the causes of burnout in other professional groups, such as nurses and social workers, should be reviewed. In new research areas, such as the causes of teacher burnout, the student may find no more than two or three studies that are very close to his topic. Thus a broader search is necessary.

In more thoroughly explored areas, where research activity has extended

4. For example, John E. Morris and Geneva W. Morris, "Stress in Student Teaching " *Action in Teacher Education* 2, no. 4 (1980): 57–62.

over a longer period of time and much of the early work is covered in secondary sources such as textbooks, the student can usually develop adequate insight into the field by reading only those studies that are reasonably close to his research topic. In these more thoroughly explored areas, much greater depth is available, and the student can cover a narrower topic range to a greater depth. In new areas little depth is available, and a broad review is therefore necessary to get sufficient insight. A study in a more thoroughly explored area might be concerned with the effectiveness of high school counseling in bringing about certain personality changes as measured by the Thematic Apperception Test. In this area the student would find some studies that relate personality changes to counseling and involve the use of various personality instruments. These should all be covered. In addition, some studies using the TAT in other related research areas should be read. For example, if studies were available involving changes in personality during psychotherapy, these studies should be read. As the TAT is a well-established instrument that has been used in a great many research projects, it would not be advisable for the student to attempt to read all research involving the use of this instrument. As of 1972 over 1500 studies dealing with the TAT had been listed in the *Mental Measurements Yearbooks*. Most of these studies would be of little value to the student carrying out the research described previously. Considerable background reading on the TAT in secondary sources, however, would be desirable.

CONDUCTING A REVIEW OF THE LITERATURE

Although a review of the literature is a preliminary step in all scientific research, the methods of conducting the review differ to some extent from field to field. The method that is described in detail in this section is one that works well in the field of education. This method has been developed over a number of years, and the student is advised to follow it closely until she has built up sufficient experience to make intelligent adaptations.

Step One—Listing Key Words

In most sciences basic reference books are available that cover most material published in the science in question. In education the most useful sources are *Resources in Education, Current Index to Journals in Education, Psychological Abstracts,* and *Education Index* (see annotated references for complete bibliographical data). These sources are organized by subject. Therefore, it is necessary that the research worker identify **key words** related to her topic so that she may look up these key words in the index to locate sources of information related to her topic. For example, let us say that you wish to search *Education Index* for studies of changes in racial attitudes that have occurred in recently desegregated public elementary schools. Your first step in reviewing the literature would be to make a list of key words that relate to this study. Your first list might include the following: attitude, attitude change, civil rights, desegregation, integration, prejudice, race relations, racial prejudice, segregation, and tolerance. This preliminary list of key words will almost certainly be incomplete and will be changed when the actual search of *Education Index* begins. It does, however, provide a starting point, and as many possible key words as the student can think of should be listed in order to reduce the likelihood of important studies being overlooked. Key words for *Resources in Education* and *Current Index to Journals in Education* are contained in the *Thesaurus of ERIC Descriptors*, which is described later in this chapter. Key words for searching *Psychological Abstracts* are listed in the *Thesaurus of Psychological Index Terms*.

Step Two—Checking Preliminary Sources

Preliminary sources are references, such as indexes and abstracts, that are intended to help one identify and locate research articles and other primary sources of information. (See Annotated References for complete bibliographic data on preliminary sources described in this section.) Many of the preliminary sources that are likely to be of help to the student in reviewing the literature in education and related fields are discussed in this section. We first discuss manual search procedures. However, some of these preliminary sources can be searched by computer. The procedure for conducting a computer search is described later in this chapter.

Education Index

Education Index provides an up-to-date listing of articles published in hundreds of education journals, books about education, and publications in related fields. Until mid-1961 *Education Index* was both an author and subject index, that is, each article was listed once under its subject and again under the name of the author. The author index was dropped for eight years, but as of mid-1969, it was reinstituted. *Education Index* is published monthly, except for July and August. It lists only the bibliographical data concerning each article or book reference. The year for *Education Index* runs from September to the following June. For the current quarter each of the monthly issues must be searched, but these monthly issues are combined quarterly, and the quarterly issues in turn are combined in a yearly volume for the immediate past year. Most reviews of the literature in education cover a minimum of ten years. For some studies it is necessary to search a longer period. In this case, *Education Index* is especially valuable since it has been published since 1929.

A systematic method of searching *Education Index* for the period of the review should be developed and followed. The author has found that preparing a checklist of key words, such as is shown in figure 5.1, is an effective method for ensuring a systematic search. After this checklist has been prepared, the student may start with the most recent issue of the *Education Index* and look up each of his key words. In looking up the key words, he should be alert for other possible key words that may be added to his list to provide more complete coverage.

To check each of these key words in a volume of *Education Index*, the student looks up the word and reads the titles of articles listed under the word. If titles are found that indicate the article deals with some phase of the student's topic, he copies the bibliographical data (author, title, and source of publication) on a 3-by-5-inch card. A separate card should be used for each article or other reference. It is often difficult to judge the contents of an article from the title, and many articles for which a student prepares bibliography cards will later be found to contain nothing pertinent to the topic being studied. In deciding whether to prepare a bibliography card and check a particular article, the student should generally follow the rule that it is better to check an article that proves of no use than to overlook an article that may be important. Thus, whenever she is in doubt, the student should prepare a bibliography card and check the article in question. After she checks the titles under a key word, the student

Education Index
Volume

Key Words	12/81	9/81	31	30		
Attitudes, elem. schl. students	N[b]	N	√[a]	√		
Attitude change	√	N	√	√		
Civil rights	N	N	N	N		
Race relations	N	√	√	√		
Race prejudice	N	N	√	N		
Segregation in educ.	N	N	√	N		
Public schools de-segregation	√	√	√	√		
Race attitudes	√	√	√	√		

[a]Indicates volume checked and bibliography cards made.
[b]Indicates volume contained no usable references under key word.

Figure 5.1. Sample of checklist used in searching the *Education Index*.

should place a check on her checklist. If, after checking several volumes of the *Education Index*, nothing pertinent to the student's topic has been found under a given key word, this key word can be dropped and not checked in the remaining volumes.

In the aforementioned example, after checking several volumes of *Education Index*, we would find that some of the original key words are satisfactory and some are unproductive and can be eliminated, and some new ones would be discovered and added. "Attitudes" would become "attitudes, elementary school students"; "desegregation" would be changed to "public schools, desegregation"; "racial prejudice" would be changed to "race prejudice"; "segregation" would be changed to "segregation in education." "Civil rights," "integration," "prejudice," and "tolerance" would be dropped, while "race attitudes" would be added. The revised list of key words is given in figure 5.1.

Psychological Abstracts

Another valuable preliminary source for research workers in education is **Psychological Abstracts.** This reference is published monthly by the American Psychological Association and contains abstracts of articles appearing in over 850 journals and other sources in psychology and related areas. Every issue of *Psychological Abstracts* has sixteen sections, each covering a different area of psychology. In addition to including abstracts, the monthly issues also include brief subject and author indexes.

The sections that are most pertinent to the research worker in education are: Developmental Psychology, which includes abstracts in areas such as Childhood Development, Developmental Stages, and Developmental Differences; and Educational Psychology, which includes such topics as Curriculum Development and Teaching Methods, Achievement, and Special Education. The coverage of these areas of psychology is very thorough. For example, many journals such as *Elementary School Journal, Harvard Educational Review,* and *Journal of Reading Behavior,* which are predominantly educational journals, are covered in *Psychological Abstracts.* In searching *Psychological Abstracts,* you should select your key words from the *Thesaurus of Psychological Index Terms,* which you will find in the reference section of the library. Although this *Thesaurus* was not developed until 1973, the terms you select will, for the most part, be satisfactory for searching earlier volumes. This is because the *Thesaurus* includes most of the 800 index terms used before 1973. The index term "bibliography" should always be looked up in *Psychological Abstracts.* Under this heading the student will find a listing of bibliographies on a wide variety of subjects. If he can locate a recent bibliography in his area of interest, it will, of course, be of great help to him in carrying out his review of the literature. We will discuss other sources of bibliographies later in this chapter.

Currently, two volumes of *Psychological Abstracts* are published each year, one including the January to June numbers and one including the July to December numbers. For each volume of abstracts, subject and author indexes are prepared in a separate volume. In using *Psychological Abstracts*, the student turns first to the subject index to check his key words. A sample page from the subject index is given in figure 5.2.[5] The index volumes of *Psychological Abstracts* do not contain complete bibliographical data such as are found in *Education Index*, but list only the subject of the article in the briefest possible terms, usually about ten to fifteen words. The student will find a number after each of these brief descriptions. This number refers to the number of the abstract. The student writes down the numbers of articles that appear to relate to his topic and then looks these up in the volume of abstracts.

For example, in the *Index* volume for January-June 1981, under *School Integration (Racial)* we find: "percentage of minority students in class and attitudes toward Whites and social class and achievement level and self esteem of Whites, prejudice, White intermediate school students, 8815." Since this article seems relevant to our research topic, we look up abstract number 8815 in volume 65 and find the following:[6]

> **8815. Rosenfield, David; Sheehan, Daniel S.; Marcus, Mary M. & Stephan, Walter G.** (Southern Methodist U) **Classroom structure and prejudice in desegregated schools.** *Journal of Educational Psychology,* 1981(Feb), Vol 73(1), 17–26. —Two experiments investigated the effect of the classroom structure and the classroom climate of desegregated schools on the prejudices of White intermediate school students in a large, southwestern school district. Cross-sectional and longitudinal analyses indicated that (a) the higher the percentage of minorities in a class, the more minority friends the White students had; (b) the more the minorities in a class displayed hostility toward Whites, the more negative were the Whites' attitudes toward minorities in general; (c) the more equal the social class and achievement levels of the Whites and minorities in a class, the more minority friends the White students had; and (d) the higher the self-esteem of the Whites in a class, the more positive their ethnic attitudes. Implications for the design of desegregation plans are also discussed. (35 ref) —*Journal abstract.*

Note that in addition to the bibliographical data needed to locate the original article, a brief but informative abstract is provided. These abstracts are very useful to the research worker because they help him make a decision as to whether or not a given article actually pertains to his problem. This decision is much easier to make on the basis of an abstract than solely on the basis of the bibliographical data found in *Education Index*. After reading the abstract, the

5. *Psychological Abstracts* 65 (April-June 1981): 882.
6. Ibid., p. 931.

short term drug therapy & psychotherapy, rapid abatement of symptoms, schizophrenics, 10776

significance of drawings of cephalopodes, understanding & representation of thought processes, schizophrenics, 1419

simultaneous lithium carbonate & neuroleptic drug therapy, drug synergism & extinction of behavioral cycle & disappearance of manifest psychosis, 62 yr old schizoaffective female hospitalized for 40 yrs, 8528

social skills training, schizophrenics, literature review, 10792

social skills training vs contingent attention, improvement of behavioral deficits, mentally retarded with vs without psychosis vs schizophrenic chronic psychiatric patients, 8500

spectral analysis method, cerebral events & visual attentional processes, schizophrenic patients, 8081

spontaneous imagery distortions, schizophrenic traits measured by MMPI, behavior therapy patients, 12925

standardized version of Luria's neuropsychological tests, discrimination between schizophrenic & brain damaged patients, 5520

stigma of mental illness as culture specific phenomenon, Orthodox Jewish family with 19 yr old schizophrenic son, 10867

structural & electrophysiological abnormalities of neuromuscular function, schizophrenic patients, implications for predisposition, 5549

structure of schizophrenia in view of "Zenonian syndrome", 3452

stuttering as side effect of phenothiazine therapy, 2 case reports of schizophrenic patients, 13332

subject relations in schizophrenic & paranoid hallucinatory syndromes, phenomenological description, 3382

sulpiride treatment, psychotic morbidity & side effects & cerebrospinal fluid levels of homovanillic acid & 4-hydroxy-3-methoxyphenylethylene glycol & 5-hydroxyindoleacetic acid, female schizophrenics, 1827

symptoms of schizophrenia & hysteria & role of self hypnosis in induction of symptoms, female patients with multiple personalities, 5540

tachistoscopically presented stimuli, iconic storage & speed of processing, subgroups of schizophrenic patients & manic controls, 10597

technique of conducting family interview & therapeutic results, schizophrenic patient & family members, 10803

theory & applications of orthomolecular medicine & megavitamin therapy, treatment of schizophrenia, 10742

theory of schizophrenia as "opting-out" of reality of life & guilt & conflict & shock as different causes, 5537

therapist personality & long vs short hospitalization, psychotherapeutic outcomes, schizophrenic & nonschizophrenic psychiatric patients, 5936

thioridazine, cognitive functioning, 11 yr old hypotonic schizophrenic male, 3830

thiothixine in active milieu setting, dysphoric responses & importance in determining dosages & side effects & therapeutic responses, newly admitted schizophrenics, 10974

tracking of sine-wave target & fixation on stationary target, occurrence of saccades, 25–37 yr old schizophrenics, 10579

trans-3-methyl-2-hexonoic acid vs other chemical effects, "back ward odor", schizophrenics, literature review, 12954

trifluoperazine vs chlorpromazine vs haloperidol, deficits in temporal information processing, medicated vs unmedicated schizophrenics vs normals, 3828

tritiated LSD binding in frontal cortex from brain samples, deceased schizophrenics, 12362

type of mental disorder & social relations & therapy outcomes & alcohol drinking patterns, cigarette smoking vs nonsmoking female psychiatric patients, 10583

unsuccessful theories of therapy, schizophrenic children, literature review, 4355

urinary acid metabolites of biogenic amines, schizophrenics, 12893

use of Trail-Making Test for differential diagnosis, schizophrenia vs brain damaged patients, 192

use of 6 alternative diagnostic systems, evidence of sex differences in age at 1st hospital admission for schizophrenia, psychiatric patients, 12929

validity of Hamburg-Wechsel Intelligence Test for adults, differentiation of neurotic vs depressive vs schizophrenic vs brain damaged patients, 11613

validity of measure of schizophrenic thought disorder, assessment of symptoms & prognosis, psychiatric patients, 4547

verbal disorders, schizophrenics & other psychotics & psychiatric patients with personality disorders, 1452

WAIS verbal/performance IQ ratio, psychodiagnosis & correlation with cerebral lateralization, schizophrenic & neurotic & alcoholic & brain damaged patients, 2513

weekly vs biweekly doses of fluspirilene, clinical evaluation, schizophrenic patients, 6051

withdrawal of depot flupentixol & clopenthixol, incidence of relapse, schizophrenics well adapted to community, implications for longer followup & periodic drug-free periods, 13303

year of birth & admission to psychiatric hospital & age at admission & season of birth, schizophrenic & manic depressive patients, 5623

Schizophrenogenic Family

family activities & games, prevention of schizophrenia, 3 yr old son of schizophrenic mother, 3390

family circumstances, schizophrenic patients, 5605

family influences in development of schizophrenia, review of early theories & empirical research, implications for family therapy, 10614

genetic & organic & familial etiological factors & schizophrenia, 20–50 yr old male schizophrenics, 8141

overview of psychodynamics of family relations, families with schizophrenic member, 10538

predisposition to schizophrenia in family & significant others as trigger for vs protection against overt illness, 12984

research on family dynamics, etiology & treatment of schizophrenia, adolescents, 5581

Schizophrenogenic Mothers

overview of psychodynamics of family relations, families with schizophrenic member, 10538

parallel between schizophrenogenic mother-child communication & communication between society & psychiatry, 10084

Scholastic Achievement [See Academic Achievement]

Scholastic Aptitude [See Academic Aptitude]

Scholastic Aptitude Test [See Coll Ent Exam Bd Scholastic Apt Test]

School Achievement [See Academic Achievement]

School Adjustment

adaptation on learning & social & personal problems behavioral dimensions, reading & mathematics achievement, elementary school students, 11179

adjustment problems, urban & semi-urban & rural secondary school students, 8819

analysis of reported problems, 10 yr olds, 5207

application of E. Kubler-Ross's model of grief stages & counselor role, problems of minority college students in cultural transition, 8878

brief system oriented family therapy, parents' & children's level of intellectual functioning & children's school adjustment & academic achievement, families, 6-mo followup, 3757

classroom social development program, role taking & problem solving & classroom adjustment, 9–10 yr olds, 13531

comprehensive treatment including medication-induced attentional increases, school adjustment & achievement, learning disabled & hyperactive children, 13178

congruence between investigative vs realistic personality orientation & academic major, academic achievement & persistence, male undergraduate engineering students, 13500

construction & validity & reliability of Academic Self-Concept Scale, college students, 8877

degree of physical disfigurement, teachers' ratings of school adjustment & impulsivity & inhibition of impulse, 10–18 yr old students with cleft palate vs cerebral palsy, 6366

demographic characteristics & parental separation & divorce, adjustment, 7–13 yr olds, 3166

development of self report measure, assessment of behavioral adjustment to school, 9–13 yr olds, 6894

developmental differences, physical maturity & peer relations & academic success & school adjustment & self concept & esteem, Mexican American vs Anglo 3rd & 8th graders, 4036

dissemination efforts & outcomes of school based Primary Mental Health Project, 8857

divorce & relationships among family members & contact with noncustodial parent, peer relations & stress & aggression & school behavior, children in divorced vs intact families, 12646

early 2 yr intervention program, school attendance & grades, urban 7th graders with adjustment problems, 11127

environment & personal coping preferences, social & school adaptations, male high school students, 4-yr longitudinal study, 10216

expressions of stress in school, children, 6374

Figure 5.2.   Sample from the Subject Index of *Psychological Abstracts.*

research worker decides whether the article is pertinent, and if it is, he records the bibliographical data on a 3-by-5-inch bibliography card so that he may read the entire article later.

When the research topic is exclusively educational, such as school lunch programs, little is gained by checking *Psychological Abstracts.* On the other hand, in areas relating to educational psychology, the student may decide to check both *Psychological Abstracts* and *Education Index* in order to be assured of getting a full coverage of the field. When both these preliminary sources are checked, the student should check *Psychological Abstracts* first because of the advantage of an abstract over bibliographical data only. A checklist such as is shown in figure 5.1 can also be used in searching *Psychological Abstracts.*

A helpful reference for the student who wishes to conduct an exhaustive long-term search of his topic is the *Cumulated Subject Index to Psychological Abstracts, 1927-1960.* This collection of several volumes makes it possible for the student to find all references on a given subject in one place, without searching thirty-four separate volumes spanning the years 1927 to 1960. If the student wishes to search all references by a given author, there is available a companion set of volumes called *Author Index to Psychological Index, 1894-1935 and Psychological Abstracts, 1927-1958.* Supplements to these two cumulative indexes are being published periodically to bring them up to date.

Educational Resources Information Center (ERIC)

ERIC, an acronym for the Educational Resources Information Center, was initiated in 1965 by the U.S. Office of Education to transmit the findings of current educational research to teachers, administrators, researchers, and the public. Two very useful preliminary sources are published by ERIC. These are **Resources in Education (RIE)** and **Current Index to Journals in Education (CIJE).** Although ERIC abstracts some of the same documents as *Education Index* and *Psychological Abstracts,* it includes many documents not abstracted by these services. For example, *RIE* provides abstracts of papers presented at education conferences, progress reports of ongoing research studies, studies sponsored by federal research programs, and final reports of projects conducted by local agencies such as school districts and Title III centers, which are not likely to appear in education journals. Thus, ERIC will be valuable to the student in providing an overview of the most current research being done in education. In contrast, many of the studies currently referenced in *Education Index* and *Psychological Abstracts* were completed several years previously because of the time lag between completion of the study, publication in a journal, and abstracting by the service.

ERIC provides a variety of services to the researcher through its central office and sixteen clearinghouses. Each clearinghouse is responsible for cataloguing, abstracting, and indexing relevant documents in its subject area. In addition, each clearinghouse publishes its own newsletters, bulletins and bibliographies. The clearinghouses also publish a variety of *Information Analysis Products* such as research reviews, knowledge syntheses, state-of-the-art studies, and interpretive reviews. These publications are very useful because they pull together a great deal of information in a brief and easily accessible form. Bibliographies that list these products are printed each year and are part of the *Resources in Education* collection. For example, a bibliography of all information analysis products for 1980 is available on *RIE* document ED-208882. The student is advised to write the clearinghouse in the area of her interest in order to obtain information that may help her in locating pertinent research literature and in planning her study. The addresses of the sixteen clearinghouses can be found in Appendix A.

The abstracts prepared by each clearinghouse appear in the monthly ERIC publications *RIE* and *CIJE*. In *RIE*, over 1000 document abstracts are included in each issue. Each abstract in *Resources in Education* is classified by subject area, author, institution, and accession number. To use *Resources in Education* the student should first select key search terms in her area of interest. To assist the user in identifying search terms, ERIC has published the *Thesaurus of ERIC Descriptors*. This volume lists all terms used to classify ERIC documents by subject; for a given subject area, it will provide synonyms, narrower terms, broader terms, and related terms. For example, the general search term "dropouts" is further analyzed into such terms as "high school dropouts," "potential dropouts," "dropout identification," and "dropout teaching."

After selecting the appropriate descriptors, the student searches the subject index in the monthly issues of *Resources in Education* for the current year and in the semiannual index volumes for previous years. When she locates a reference in the subject index that relates to her topic, she copies the ED number given at the end of the bibliographical data. She then looks up each ED number in the Document Resumes section, where she will find a description of the reference such as the sample entry shown in figure 5.3.[7] Notice in this figure that the Document Resume contains a great deal of useful information in addition to the usual brief abstract.

If she wishes to obtain the full document that is abstracted in the entry, the student can order it through the ERIC Document Reproduction Service. A Reproduction Service price is listed in the Document Resume for each document. If she needs an *RIE* document as quickly as possible, it can be ordered by computer using the ORBIT or DIALOG systems, which are available through most university libraries. See a current issue of *RIE* for detailed instructions. Whether you order by mail or computer, the document can be ordered on

7. Taken from *Resources in Education* 17, no. 4 (April 1982): viii.

ERIC Accession Number—identification number sequentially assigned to documents as they are processed.

Author(s).

Title.

Organization where document originated.

Date Published.

Contract or Grant Number.

Alternate source for obtaining document.

Language of Document.

ERIC Document Reproduction Service (EDRS) Availability "MF" means microfiche, "PC" means reproduced paper copy. When described as "Document Not Available from EDRS", alternate sources are cited above. Prices are subject to change; for latest price code schedule see section on "How to Order ERIC Documents", in the most recent issue of RIE.

Publication Type—broad categories indicating the form or organization of the document, as contrasted to its subject matter. The category name is followed by the category code.

ED 654 321   CE 123 456

Smith, John D.   *Johnson, Jane*

Career Education for Women.

Central Univ., Chicago, IL

Spons Agency—National Inst. of Education (ED), Washington, DC

Report No.—CU-2081-S

Pub Date—May 73

Contract—NIE-C-73-0001

Note—129p.; Paper presented at the National Conference on Career Education (3rd, Chicago, IL, May 15-17, 1973).

Available from—Campus Bookstore, 123 College Ave. Chicago, IL 60690 ($3.25)

Language—English, French

EDRS Price MF01/PC06 Plus Postage.

Pub Type—Dissertations/Theses (040)

Descriptors—Career Guidance, Career Planning, Careers, *Demand Occupation Employment Opportunities, Females, Labor Force, Labor Market, *Labor Needs, Occupational Aspiration, Occupations, *Working Women.

Identifier—Consortium of States, *National Occupational Competency Testing Institute, Women's Opportunities for employment will be directly related to their level of skill and experience but also to the labor market demands through the remainder of the decade. The number of workers needed for all major occupational categories is expected to increase by about one-fifth between 1980 and 1990, but the growth rate will vary by occupational group. Professional and technical workers are expected to have the highest predicted rate (39 percent), followed by service workers (35 percent) clerical workers (26 percent), sales workers (24 percent), craft workers and supervisors (20 percent), managers and administrators (15 percent), and operatives (11 percent). This publication contains a brief discussion and employment information concerning occupations for professional and technical workers, managers and administrators (15 percent) and operatives (11 percent). This publication contains a brief discussion and employment information concerning occupations for professional and technical workers, managers and administrators, skilled trades, sales workers, clerical workers, and service workers. In order for women to take advantage of increased labor market demands, employer attitudes toward working women need to change and women must: (1) receive better career planning and counseling, (2) change their career aspirations, and (3) fully utilize the sources of legal protection and assistance which are available to them. (SB)

Clearinghouse Accession Number.

Sponsoring Agency—agency responsible for initiating, funding, and managing the research project.

Report Number.

Descriptive Note (pagination first).

Descriptors—subject terms which characterize substantive content. Only the major terms, preceded by an asterisk, are printed in the subject index.

Identifiers—additional identifying terms not found in the *Thesaurus of Eric descriptors*. Only the major terms, preceded by an asterisk, are printed in the subject index.

Informative Abstract.

Abstractor's Initials.

Figure 5.3   Sample entry from *Resources in Education* and identifying characteristics.

155

microfiches, which are small sheets of microfilm, each containing up to sixty pages of text, or in hard copy form at about 70 percent of the document's original size. The advantages of microfiches are their low cost and small size. However, they require a special microfiche reader, which enlarges the image to normal page size. Most libraries now have these special readers. Also, most university libraries maintain a collection of ERIC microfiches, so it is not necessary to order them through the Reproduction Service unless the student wants a personal copy.

Since 1969 ERIC has published *CIJE*, which indexes nearly 800 education journals and journals in related fields and includes more than 1000 articles each month. Like *RIE*, *CIJE* is published monthly and cumulated semiannually. The monthly numbers contain a Subject Index, an Author Index, and a Main Entry Section. The student first selects descriptors related to her topic from the *Thesaurus of ERIC Descriptors*, and then searches the Subject Index and notes the EJ numbers of relevant references. She then looks up these EJ numbers in the Main Entry Section, which provides about the same information as is given in the document Resumes in *RIE*. Compared with *Education Index*, *CIJE* has the advantages of a more comprehensive index (based on the *Thesaurus of ERIC Descriptors*), multidisciplinary journal coverage, and abstracts of the articles indexed. *Education Index* covers a much longer time span of journal publication (1929 to date) than *CIJE* (1969 to date).

For most educational topics, the most productive strategy would probably be to search *RIE* and *CIJE* for the years from 1969 to date, search *RIE* and *Education Index* for the years 1966 to 1968, and then search *Education Index* from 1965 back as far as the student plans to extend her review.

Other Useful Preliminary Sources

Several preliminary sources are useful for locating certain kinds of information needed in some literature reviews or for searching specific subject areas. Those that are often useful to the researcher in education are described below.

The Citation Indexes

Let us suppose that in the course of your review of literature you have located two or three key references that were published several years ago. It is often very useful if you can trace the effects of these earlier works on subsequent research. Also, if your review has uncovered a controversial article, you can gain valuable insights by reading what later authors say in support or opposition. An easy way to locate later works that have cited such an article is to look up each key author in **Science Citation Index (SCI)** or **Social Science**

Citation Index (SSCI), depending on the field of study. *SCI* covers the literature of Science, Medicine, Agriculture, Technology, and the Behavioral Sciences; while *SSCI* covers literature of the Social, Behavioral, and Related Sciences. Articles in psychology are cited in both indexes, but work in education is most likely to be cited in *SSCI*.

You would start your search of *SCI* or *SSCI* with the year the key reference was published and check all volumes up to the current one. Under the name of the author of the key reference with which you are concerned you will find bibliographical data for all sources that have cited the key reference. For example, Arther R. Jensen's famous article from the 1969 *Harvard Educational Review* entitled "How Much Can We Boost I.Q. and Scholastic Achievement?" was cited in fifteen articles in the 1980 volume of *SCI*. In checking *SSCI* for 1980 we find sixty-two articles listed that have cited the Jensen article, reflecting the heavier behavioral science coverage. A review of these articles would give the student a clear picture about current thinking regarding this controversial topic.

In using these *Indexes* you should check each author's name with both given initials, only the first initial, and no initials; e.g., Jensen, A. Jensen, as well as A. R. Jensen. If an author cites the article as by A. Jensen, that is the way it will be listed in the *Index*. In compiling the *Indexes*, the A. Jensen citations are not combined with the A. R. Jensen citations, even though, since the same article is cited, they are obviously the same man. In *SSCI* for 1980, the *Harvard Educational Review* article is cited twice under "A. Jensen" and once under "Jensen." If we wanted to check all articles that had cited Jensen's 1969 article, we would, of course, have to check *SCI* back to 1969, and *SSCI* back to its beginning in 1973.

Smithsonian Science Information Exchange (SSIE)

There is a considerable lag between the time a research project is completed and the time it is indexed in the preliminary sources, such as *Psychological Abstracts*. If a researcher wants information on recently completed and ongoing research projects in his area of interst, *SSIE* is the best preliminary source available. To use *SSIE*, see the section of this chapter dealing with computer searches.

Literature Related to Measures

The *Mental Measurements Yearbooks* by O. K. Buros are very valuable to the researcher who wishes to locate articles related to published tests that he is considering for use in his research. In addition to providing bibliographies, the *Yearbooks* also print critical reviews of many of the measures listed.

Measures for Psychological Assessment contains source information on 3000 psychological measures that have been described in the research literature. These are mostly measures not published by regular test publishers, so there is little overlap between this book and the *Mental Measurements Yearbooks*. This reference contains an author index that can be used to locate articles that report application of measures already identified by the researcher and a descriptor index that will help the researcher identify measures in his field of interest. These two sources will be discussed in greater detail in a later chapter.

Abstracts and Indexes in Content Areas Related to Education

Child Development Abstracts and Bibliography covers articles in this area that are drawn from sources in medicine, psychology, biology, sociology, and education. Each issue includes abstracts under five major subject headings, as well as an author index and subject index. These are combined into annual volumes.

Sociological Abstracts is published five times each year. Each issue contains subject, author, and source indexes in addition to abstracts that are similar in format to *Psychological Abstracts*. The subject index is also similar to *Psychological Abstracts*, listing the abstract numbers for each citation after a brief description of about 10 to 15 words.

Resources in Vocational Education has been published since 1977. Essentially the same source was published from 1967 to 1976 under the name *Abstracts of Instructional and Research Materials in Vocational and Technical Education (AIM/ARM)*. Six regular issues plus an index issue are published each year. Each regular issue has four major sections: Abstracts, Subject Index, Author Index, and Institution Index. The abstracts follow the ERIC format and ERIC Descriptors are used. All documents abstracted in this source may also be found in *Resources in Education*.

Exceptional Child Education Resources (ECER) have been published quarterly since 1969 by the Council for Exceptional Children. More than 200 journals are regularly searched for material concerning exceptional children. The format is similar to that used in *Current Index to Journals in Education* since the Council operates the ERIC Clearinghouse on Handicapped and Gifted Children. However, many journals searched for *ECER* are not covered by *CIJE*. Each issue contains subject, author, and title indexes, and the final issue each year contains indexes for the entire volume.

State Education Journal Index has been published twice a year since 1963. This is a subject index that provides bibliographical data and very brief annotations on articles published in about 100 state education journals, such as *Alabama School Journal, California School Boards,* and *Oregon Education*. These journals cover a wide range of educational subjects but are probably most useful for topics of state concern such as federal aid, collective bargaining, state education agencies, and teacher certification.

Business Education Index is a combined author-subject index of articles in the field of business education published annually since 1940. Articles from about 60 periodicals are indexed along with the books and some theses relevant to business education.

Educational Administration Abstracts have been published since 1966. There are three issues a year. Approximately 100 journals containing articles related to educational administration are reviewed and abstracted. Abstracts are classified into 42 content areas. An author index and journal index is included in each issue, but no subject index is provided.

Physical Education Index has been published quarterly since 1978. It is a subject index covering about 170 periodicals, both domestic and foreign, that deal with physical education and related topics.

Bibliographies and Reviews of Research Literature

Recently, the improved procedures developed by Gene Glass and others to pull together research evidence have stimulated interest in literature reviews.[8] If a student can locate a recent review of literature related to his research topic, he can get a useful overview with little effort. The quality of such reviews varies, however, and the student should look at reviews critically before accepting the conclusions of the reviewer. J. T. Guthrie provides some useful guidelines for evaluating review articles.[9] Gregg Jackson's analysis of 36 randomly selected review articles can also be a help to students who want to know more about this topic.[10]

Bibliographic Index

An early step in searching preliminary sources is to consult *Bibliographic Index*, a subject list of bibliographies that have been published separately or as parts of books or journals. About 2200 periodicals are regularly searched for bibliographic materials. The format is similar to the *Education Index* except that only references which contain a bibliography of 50 or more citations are listed. If

---

8. See chapter 6 for a discussion of techniques for integrating research findings.
9. John T. Guthrie, "Reviews of Research," *Reading Teacher* 34 (1981): 748–51.
10. Gregg B. Jackson, "Methods for Integrative Reviews," *Review of Educational Research* 50 (1980): 438–60.

the bibliography is annotated, the abbreviation "annot" is given. If the student can locate a recent annotated bibliography on his topic, he will save much of the labor of searching the preliminary sources.

Review of Educational Research

This journal is published quarterly by the American Educational Research Association. A typical issue contains five to seven critical, integrative reviews of research literature bearing on important topics and issues. Recent issues have reviewed research on such topics as educational objectives, teacher decisions, college teaching, and student ratings of instruction. Each article includes an extensive bibliography. Graduate students should check the most recent five years of this journal to see if a review has been published in their area of interest. If so, the relevant review and bibliography will give the student an excellent start on her own search of the literature.

Review of Research in Education

The purpose of the *Review* is to present critical essays that survey and synthesize educational research in important problem areas. The first volume in this annual series was published in 1973 and contains nine essays in the areas of Learning and Instruction, School Organization, History of Education and Research Methodology. Subsequent volumes have covered such topics as Child Development and Educational Intervention, Economics of Education, Comparative Education, and Teacher Effectiveness. Essays are written by leading educational researchers and provide the reader with thorough and perceptive overviews of the areas covered.

Encyclopedia of Educational Research

The long-awaited fifth edition of this monumental work became available late in 1982. This is perhaps the best single source of information on educational research currently available. The four volumes are organized into nineteen major topics ranging from Agencies and Institutions Related to Education to Teachers and Teaching. The 317 contributors are among the nation's leading educational researchers. The student planning a review of the literature should start his work by reading relevant entries in this encyclopedia.

NSSE Yearbooks

The yearbooks of the National Society for the Study of Education contain major overviews of important educational topics. Recent yearbooks have been concerned with such topics as classroom management, adolescence, and social studies. Each yearly volume consists of two books dealing with different major areas of education. The typical book contains 10 to 12 chapters concerned with different aspects of the topic. Chapter authors, who are recognized authorities, attempt to give a clear picture of the state of knowledge in the field by focusing on a few major research and theoretical articles. Exhaustive bibliographies, such as are found in the *Review of Educational Research,* are usually not included in the yearbooks. However, if the student's area of interest has been the focus of a recent yearbook, it can provide an excellent overview of important research findings, current approaches to studying the topic, and the thinking of leaders in the field.

Second Handbook of Research on Teaching

This book contains excellent reviews of virtually every aspect of research on teaching. The 42 chapters are organized under 4 major areas. Four introductory chapters provide a historical and theoretical foundation, 13 chapters cover methods and techniques of research and development, 15 chapters review research on special problems of teaching, and 10 chapters cover research on the teaching of school subjects. The chapters are written by recognized authorities, and each includes a very comprehensive bibliography. Reading the chapters related to his topic provides an excellent introduction to the literature for any student who plans to do research on teaching.

Annual Reviews of Psychology

The *Annual Reviews* typically contain several chapters that deal with areas of psychology such as tests and measures, developmental psychology, and instructional psychology that are pertinent to many educational research topics. An annual volume usually consists of approximately 15 chapters. Each chapter deals with recent research in one area of psychology and includes an extensive bibliography covering important work in that area. Students interested in problems related to some aspect of psychology should check the most recent five volumes for reviews pertinent to their work.

Preliminary Sources Covering Theses and Dissertations

Because many theses and dissertations are never published, a check of the following is necessary for a thorough coverage of the research literature.

Dissertation Abstracts International

This is a monthly compilation of abstracts of doctoral dissertations submitted by more than 375 cooperating institutions in the United States and Canada. It has been published in various forms since 1938 when it first appeared as *Microfilm Abstracts*. At present there are two sections: Section A contains dissertations in the humanities and social sciences including education; Section B covers the sciences (including psychology) and engineering. The abstracts within each issue of Section A are organized into 32 major content areas, one of which is Education. There are 37 subtopics under the Education content area such as "adult," "art," "higher," "preschool," and "teacher training." Students interested in checking dissertations in one of these subtopics of education should check the table of contents to locate pages containing relevant abstracts.

Each monthly issue also contains a keyword title index in which the bibliographic entries are classified and arranged alphabetically by important key words contained in the title. To search a specific topic the student can check the keyword title index to locate relevant abstracts. For example, a student who is interested in the social development of preschool children could check "social," "development," and "preschool" in the keyword title index; read the titles listed under each key word; and copy the page numbers for abstracts related to her topic. She would then read each of the selected abstracts. Abstracts in education vary in length up to a full page and usually give a good coverage of the essentials of the dissertation. Any dissertation covered in **Dissertation Abstracts International** may be purchased from University Microfilms International on either microfilm or Xerox, the order number being given at the end of the abstract.

Comprehensive Dissertation Index

This reference provides a subject and author index covering virtually every doctoral dissertation accepted in U.S. and Canadian universities from 1861 through 1972, a total of nearly a half-million entries. More than 86,000 of the entries are in the area of education. Since 1972, yearly supplements have been published to keep the *Index* up to date. This index would normally be used in conjunction with *Dissertation Abstracts International*. The student should first check the subject index and note the bibliographical data on any dissertations that appear related to his topic. He will also find the volume and page of *Dissertation Abstracts International* on which the abstract of the given dissertation can be found. Once he has recorded this information on all relevant dissertations, he can read the abstracts. The final step is to obtain microfilm copies of any dissertations that are sufficiently important so that they can be studied in detail.

Master's Theses in Education

This source has been published annually since 1951. Master's theses are listed under about 40 major educational topics covered in the table of contents, such as Achievement and Progress, Adult Education, Delinquency, and Higher Education. Only the author, title, and institution are given. The coverage is quite complete, however, listing nearly all institutions in the United States and Canada that offer master's degrees in education. Earlier volumes contain an Author Index, a Subject Index, and an Institutional Index in which theses written at a given institution may be located. However, since 1980, only the Institutional Index is included. The student who locates theses that appear to be very closely related to her proposed topic may obtain them through interlibrary loan.

Master's Abstracts

Master's theses available from University Microfilms International, about 1500 per year, starting in 1962, are summarized by their authors. Entries are grouped by field of study and indexed by key words and author names.

Preliminary Sources Covering Periodicals and Newspapers

Education is a topic of wide general interest, and as a result much is written about it in popular magazines and newspapers. If your research topic is in an area that has received public attention, the following sources should be checked.

Reader's Guide to Periodical Literature. New York: H. W. Wilson Co., 1900 to date. An author and subject index similar in format to *Education Index* but covering general and nontechnical periodicals published in the United States. The magazines that are indexed change from time to time because the aim is to maintain a good subject balance and to overlook no major field rather than provide exhaustive coverage. At present more than 160 magazines are being indexed. *Reader's Guide* is an excellent source for studying the layman's views on education. Because many of the magazines covered have wide circulation, their influence upon public opinion can be significant.

Social Sciences Index. New York: H. W. Wilson Co., 1974 to date. This is an author and subject index that covers approximately 260 periodicals in the social sciences, including many foreign publications. It is a good source of references concerning how education is viewed by social scientists in fields such as anthropology, economics, environmental science, law, medical science, and sociology.

The New York Times Index. New York: The New York Times Co., 1851 to date. This preliminary source provides an index of news printed in the *New York Times.* It is primarily a subject index but is extensively cross-referenced; it is also referenced by the names of persons covered in news stories. Brief summaries of most articles are given, along with date, page, and column of the issue in which the story may be found. This index is an excellent source of current information about education and permits studying the development of educational issues and events that could not be traced as accurately through any other source. It is recommended that the student look up some current topic that interests him, such as federal aid to education, school building programs, or racial integration, in order to get some insight into the value of this index as a source of educational information.

Facts on File. New York: Facts on File, Inc., 1941 to date. This is a weekly digest of world news that is indexed twice monthly. The weekly digests are then combined into a yearbook along with an annual index. Material from newspapers, magazines, broadcasts, government reports, and so forth are processed daily to produce the weekly digest. Material is indexed by subject and names of persons appearing in the news. Date of the event, page, and location on page in the digest section of the yearbook are given. Because the yearly index and weekly digests are bound together in one volume, *Facts on File* permits the student to locate and read summaries of important educational news stories without going to another source. It is much easier to use than *The New York Times Index,* but coverage is less thorough.

Sources of Information on Educational Materials

In planning a research project the researcher is often interested in locating curriculum materials or educational products that will be useful in his research. Many graduate students carry out studies in which two groups of pupils are trained using different instructional programs and materials in order to determine which results in greater gains in pupil achievement. For example, comparisons between different first-grade reading programs or conventional versus "new" mathematics programs are often conducted and can make a useful contribution since they provide evidence that can be used by educators to help make curriculum decisions.

Since the review of literature must often be concerned with locating educational materials that can be employed in the student's research, this section briefly describes several major sources of information that index such materials. If you fail to locate needed materials in these sources, you will find other catalogs and indexes of educational materials in the reference section of your college library.

NICEM Indexes. Los Angeles: University of Southern California, revised biennially. The National Information Center for Educational Media has published a set of eleven indexes that lists audiovisual educational materials such as educational films, film strips, audiotapes, videotapes, phonograph records, overhead transparencies and multimedia programs. Each index includes a subject guide, an alphabetical guide by title, and a producer-distributor code so that the reader can determine what items are available in his area of interest and where they may be obtained. A very brief description of each entry is included in the alphabetical guide. Over 250,000 main entries are included in the eleven indexes.

Catalog of NIE Education Products, vols. 1 and 2. Washington, D.C.: National Institute of Education, 1975. These two volumes contain descriptive information on 660 educational products funded in whole or part by the National Institute of Education. Products are classified into 13 subject categories such as Aesthetic Education, Basic Skills, Early Childhood Education, Guidance and Counseling, and Teacher Education. About half of the products listed have undergone controlled tests of effectiveness. Since it is estimated that only about one percent of the 400,000 educational products currently available have undergone rigorous evaluation, these volumes are probably the best single source for validated educational products. A broad overview of each of the subject categories is given, which provides the student with a good review of the state of the art. A detailed description of each listed product is provided. There are six indexes located at the end of volume 2, which categorize the products by Subject, Use (i.e., intended users), Developer/Author, Geographical Location of Authors/Developers, Media, and Product Page. For most research uses the student will find the Subject Index useful, but she should look under all possible subject categories because products that fit more than one category are not cross-referenced.

Educational Products for the Exceptional Child: A Catalog of Products. Phoenix, Ariz.: Oryx Press, 1981. This source covers products developed in projects funded by the Bureau of Education for the Handicapped for the past 12 years. Contains a complete description, subject areas, interested users, goals, and contact address for every product listed.

Contemporary Education: A Journal of Reviews. This journal publishes reviews of books, instructional materials, media, and nonprint educational products judged to have a significant impact on education. It is very useful in helping the student locate products for use in thesis or dissertation studies.

Audiovisual Market Place. New York: R. R. Bowker, published annually. This source covers about 5000 producers of audiovisual learning materials. Entries include name of organization, address, phone number, name of one or more executives, and list of products, services or interests. There is an alphabetical index.

Educators Guide to Free Films (and others as listed below). Randolph, Wisconsin: Educators Progress Service, published annually. This is a series of guides to free films, filmstrips, guidance materials, science materials, social studies materials, teaching aids, audio and video materials, and health, physical education, and recreation materials. They are revised annually, and since a large percentage of the items listed change from year to year, it is necessary to refer to the latest edition. The guides usually include brief descriptions and are indexed by title, subject, and source. A related source is the *Educators Index of Free Materials* from the same publisher.

Educational Product Reports, Published by Educational Products Information Exchange Institute (EPIE), 463 West Street, New York, NY 10014. The institute is a nonprofit organization established to provide independent evaluations of educational products. The *Reports* contain evaluations of educational materials. There are six issues per year. The institute also publishes *EPIEgram: The Educational Consumer's Newsletter* and occasional special reports. A good source of objective information on educational products and materials.

Many indexes and guides to educational materials are listed in the Guide to American Educational Directories.[11] The latest edition to this guide should be checked for new sources of educational materials and for specialized sources not described in this chapter.

Conducting a Computer Search

In a comprehensive review of the literature a computer search can be used to accomplish step 2 of the manual search process, that is, checking preliminary sources. The student must still read the references that she selects from the computer search, and should make notes following essentially the same procedures described in this chapter. This work, however, is made easier because computer searches often provide printouts of abstracts; these belong to the student and can be used to reject references that are not close enough to her topic to be read. If the student receives a computer printout of her search, the bibliographical data and abstracts of articles she plans to read can be cut out and pasted onto note cards, thereby saving the effort of copying this information from a preliminary source such as *Resources in Education*. In many cases

---

11. See Annotated References at the end of this chapter.

she will have to make additional notes when she reads the reference to supplement the abstract obtained in the computer search, but the savings in time will still be significant.

A manual search of preliminary sources is a dull, time-consuming activity that the computer can carry out in a matter of minutes at low cost. Most of the computer search services described in this chapter mail the computer printouts shortly after the on-line search is completed so the student usually receives them within ten days or less. For searches that involve only a few references, a printout may be obtained immediately from the terminal at which the student is conducting the search. This procedure, however, becomes expensive for long searches since it greatly increases the time that the terminal is connected to the computer, that is, on-line time.

Manual searches are difficult to conduct for problems that involve several concepts that must all be present in a reference in order to fit the researcher's needs. For example, a problem such as "the effects of television violence on the aggressive behavior of preschool children" involves four major concepts: *television, violence, aggression,* and *preschool children.* In a manual search, the student would have to search at least one of these concepts (e.g., television) very thoroughly and then read the abstracts or the articles themselves to find references in which the other three concepts are also present. The computer can search designated preliminary sources in a matter of seconds to locate references in which all four concept terms are present.

Where Can You Have a Computer Search Conducted?

Many universities have terminals that link them to one of the information retrieval systems such as the Lockheed **DIALOG** system, or the SDC/ORBIT system. You should visit the reference section of your library and see if a terminal is available. If not, many organizations provide computer searches of ERIC, which includes *RIE* and *CIJE* and is probably the most useful single data base for researchers in education. Having an on-line terminal available speeds up the computer search process, permits the researcher to check the number of relevant references and to get other information that will usually result in a better search. If an on-line terminal is not available, commercial information retrieval services provide order forms on which the researcher can list his problem, descriptors, and other information. These forms are then mailed to the service center where the information is fed into the computer and the search is carried out.

The cost of a computer search varies with the service used, the data base searched, and the length of the search. On-line computer time ranges from about $25 to $120 per hour, while the cost of printouts of the selected citations ranges from $.05 to $.35 for each citation. Careful planning of the search is essential in order to keep on-line computer time to a minimum. It is usually advisable for the student to go over his search strategy with the person who operates the terminal before going on-line. A typical ERIC search on the Lockheed DIALOG system including a printout of 200 abstracts that is mailed to the student will cost about $30.

In addition to ERIC, many other data bases can be very useful for reviewing literature on research problems. For example, there are currently more than 140 data bases available in the DIALOG system. A few of those most relevant to behavioral science research are listed below.[12]

Exceptional Child Education Resources (1966 to present) focus on the education of handicapped and gifted children. References are indexed using ERIC descriptors. This data base covers published and unpublished literature and is a valuable supplement to ERIC since only about one-fourth of the *ECER* citations are duplicated in ERIC. Information can be obtained from the Council for Exceptional Children, 1920 Association Drive, Reston, VA 22091.

PSYCINFO (1967 to present) is essentially the computer form of *Psychological Abstracts*. The data base covers the world literature in psychology and related behavioral sciences. References are indexed using the *Thesaurus of Psychological Index Terms*. Many of the descriptors in this thesaurus differ from the ERIC descriptors. The student should check to see which descriptors best fit his problem. It may be desirable to search both data bases. For further information contact the American Psychological Association, 1200 Seventeenth Street NW, Washington, DC 20036.

Comprehensive Dissertation Index (1861 to present) is based on material from *Dissertation Abstracts International* and *American Doctoral Dissertations*. It is a definitive subject, title, and author guide to virtually every American dissertation, thousands of Canadian dissertations, and many from institutions abroad. The student may search this source using DIALOG or may use the DATRIX system by obtaining an order form from University Microfilms, 300 North Zeeb Road, Ann Arbor, MI 48106. The student lists key words and other information about his topic, mails his order form, and receives a printout giving the title, author, degree date, and university for each reference. The issue and page reference in *Dissertation Abstracts International* (DAI) is also given if the dissertation has been abstracted. The student must then locate the abstracts he wants to read in *DAI*.

SSIE Current Research (Smithsonian Science Information Exchange) gathers information on ongoing and recently completed research projects in all fields, including about 1800 per year in the behavioral sciences. Several services are offered including research information packages on major topics, custom

---

12. For a complete list of data bases available in DIALOG, check the most recent *Database Catalog* published by DIALOG Information Services. Information on this service can also be obtained by phoning (800) 227-1960. In California phone (800) 982-5838.

searches, and computer searches. All searches are based on the *Notice of Research Project*, a form that contains the project title, funding organization, performing organization, names of investigators, period covered, funding level, and a 200-word technical summary of the work to be performed. This information can be useful in avoiding duplication of research effort, learning about current work, and locating possible funding sources for similar work. For further information contact SSIE, Room 300, 1730 M Street NW, Washington, DC 20036.

In addition to the aforementioned, there are many data bases in the DIALOG system that are occasionally useful to researchers in the behavioral sciences. Among these are:

Magazine Index (1976 to present) provides a very broad coverage of general magazines. Over 370 popular magazines are covered.

National Newspaper Index (1979 to present) indexes virtually everything printed in the *Christian Science Monitor*, the *New York Times*, and the *Wall Street Journal*.

Child Abuse and Neglect (1965 to present) contains more than 10,000 citations related to this topic.

Mental Health Abstracts (1969 to present) covers worldwide information related to mental health. Sources include over 12,000 journals from 41 countries.

SOCIAL SCISEARCH (1972 to present) indexes every significant item from the 1000 most important social science journals throughout the world plus selected items from 2200 additional journals. Based on *Social Science Citation Index*.

Sociological Abstracts (1963 to present) covers the world's literature in sociology and related disciplines. Covers more than 1200 journals and other sources.

NICEM (1979 edition) gives a comprehensive coverage of nonprint educational material such as films, filmstrips, audio tapes, and phonograph records. This source is revised biennially.

NICSEM/NIMIS (1978 edition) contains descriptions of media and devices for use with handicapped children.

Special Education Materials (1977 to present) provides comprehensive coverage of printed and audiovisual materials related to the education and care of handicapped learners.

U.S. Public School Directory (updated annually) provides a variety of information on public schools throughout the United States including a listing of all public schools. For each school, name and address are given. This source can be very useful in selecting samples of schools for research.

Steps in Conducting an On-Line Computer Search

The following steps have been carried out using the Lockheed DIALOG system as an example. This system contains the data bases that are usually the most important for educational research problems. The same procedure can be used, with some adaptation, for conducting on-line searches with other systems.

1. *Define research problem.* To conduct a successful search you must write a short but precise statement of your research problem. If your description is too general your search will probably produce a great many items that are not closely related to your problem and that will increase the cost. A statement such as "the academic self-concept of handicapped children in the elementary school" describes the researcher's interest in a few words and is written in terms that will help focus the search, such as *handicapped, self-concept, elementary.* In contrast a statement such as "the self-concept of schoolchildren" is not precise enough to describe the problem.

2. *State specific purpose of search.* Literature searches are conducted for several reasons. You should think through the precise purpose of your search since you will use different approaches for different kinds of searches.

Most searches are conducted as part of an exhaustive review of literature to be included as part of the student's thesis or dissertation. This kind of review must be very sharply focused but usually should include all relevant references for the past ten years. All relevant narrow descriptors are chosen when possible, and the computer is instructed to locate references that contain combinations of descriptors, which further narrows the search. How narrow your search should be is determined partially by your topic, as discussed earlier in this chapter.

The computer can also be useful in assisting in a preliminary review of literature that the researcher may conduct to locate possible research problems. A computer search can locate recent references in the researcher's area of interest; these in turn can assist in limiting and better defining the problem. Usually such searches use broader descriptors and fewer combinations of descriptors since the researcher has not yet settled on a narrow problem. To avoid getting very large numbers of references, it is advisable to instruct the computer to select only the 10 to 30 most recent references for each descriptor or descriptor combination.

Computer searches can also be helpful in updating a review of literature. It is not uncommon for a graduate student to take two or three years after completing the review of literature to complete his research project and write his thesis or dissertation. By this time the review will be somewhat out of date. Using the same descriptors he employed in his initial search, he can update his review by instructing the computer to select only those references published since his initial computer search was conducted.

3. *Select data base.* The next step is to select one or more data bases that are most relevant to the research problem. For most educational studies a search of the ERIC data base will produce most of the relevant literature. For the self-concept problem given as an example above, a search of *Exceptional Child Education Resources* and *Psychological Abstracts,* both of which are also available in

the DIALOG system, could be added to ERIC to give a more complete coverage or could be used instead of ERIC.

4. *Select descriptors.* Using the procedures prescribed for your data bank, select the descriptors, index terms, or key words (all synonymous terms) that best describe your problem in terms the computer will accept. Remember that the *exact* terms used in indexing the materials into the system must be used. If you spell a descriptor incorrectly or make some similar error such as adding an *s*, the computer will not recognize the descriptor and will report no references.

Using the *Thesaurus of ERIC Descriptors* we would locate the descriptors that would fit our study of "the academic self-concept of handicapped children in the elementary school." First we would find that there is no descriptor for academic self-concept. Instead, we find *self-concept* and *self-esteem*, both of which seem to fit our topic. Since there is no source available that gives precise definitions of the ERIC descriptors, we have no way of knowing how a reviewer decides to use one of these descriptors or the other. In this case it is best to include both in our search and to instruct the computer to select articles that use either. We also find two broad descriptors that can be used for handicapped schoolchildren. These are *handicapped children* and *handicapped students*. Our final descriptor is *elementary school students*.

If we decided to use the *Psychological Abstracts* data base instead of ERIC, we would find the following in the *Thesaurus of Psychological Index Terms*: *self-concept, self-perception, self-esteem, handicapped*, and *elementary school students*. Note that, although similar, these index terms are not identical to our ERIC descriptors.

5. *Plan the computer search.* In planning your search it is usually best to start with combinations of descriptors that produce references that precisely fit your needs. Descriptors may be combined using *and* and *or*. For example, using the five ERIC descriptors: (1) *self-concept*, (2) *self-esteem*, (3) *handicapped children*, (4) *handicapped students*, and (5) *elementary school students* we can instruct the computer to select references having the following combination of descriptors:

(1) self-concept

or

(2) self-esteem

and

(3) handicapped children

or

(4) handicapped students

and (5) elementary school students

For the computer, we would print this combination as (1 or 2) and (3 or 4) and (5). This asks the computer for any reference that includes a combination of either *self-concept* or *self-perception* and either *handicapped children* or *handicapped students* and *elementary school students*. Notice that *or* connections tend to increase the number of references selected since there are more references that have one descriptor or the other than have either by itself. But *and* connections tend to reduce the number of selections since only references that have all the descriptors connected by *and* would be selected. We have limited the three sample searches described below to a few descriptors. A far more complete search is achieved if more descriptors are selected and sets of related descriptors are connected with *or*. This procedure is described below in the section on using "or" connectors.

Our search of the above combination produced only one reference, which indicates that our search was too narrow. When three or more descriptors are connected with *and,* the search usually will produce very few references, although the few produced will be on target.

You will recall that for research topics on which much work has been done a narrow search is called for, whereas for topics on which little has been done the search must cover a broader area. In our example, since our initial search was too narrow, we can broaden it by removing the grade-level descriptor, that is, *elementary school students.* When we ask the computer for references having (1 or 2) and (3 or 4), we find that there are 41 references.

In order to provide more insight on how the various data bases are related, we then carried out the same search using the *Exceptional Child Education Resources* data base. This search located 31 references, of which 15 duplicated those found in the ERIC search.

We then carried out a third search using the *Psychological Abstracts* data base. The index terms selected were (1) *handicapped,* (2) *self-concept,* (3) *self-perception,* (4) *self-esteem,* and (5) *elementary school students.* We first asked for (1) and (2 or 3 or 4) and (5). This produced 4 references. When we dropped the *elementary school students* descriptor and asked for (1) and (2 or 3 or 4), we located 92 references, none of which were duplicated in either the ERIC or *Exceptional Child Education Resources* searches. These results suggest that in order to obtain a complete search it is advisable to check all relevant data bases.

The importance of using combinations of descriptors is illustrated by the fact that the ERIC search produced 2277 references with the *handicapped children* descriptor and 4433 references with the *self-concept* descriptor. Obviously, using a single descriptor will usually result in a very broad search and will produce many references that are of no importance to the researcher.

6. *Using "or" connectors.* One of the rules for assigning ERIC descriptors requires that a document be indexed to the specific level of subject matter covered. This means that an article dealing with *deaf children* would not be given the additional descriptor *handicapped children* unless it deals with *both* handicapped children in general and also with deaf children. This often confuses the researcher, who is likely to assume that a general term such as *teaching* would also be assigned to all the narrow terms under teaching such as *diagnostic teach-*

ing, creative teaching, and *peer teaching.* In terms of planning a search, this rule means that in order to get the most complete coverage, the researcher must include both the broad descriptors and narrow descriptors that are directly related to her research problem. For example, in our search of "the academic self-concept of handicapped children in the elementary school" let us suppose that the four specific groups of (1) *handicapped children* with which the researcher was most concerned were (2) *mentally handicapped,* (3) *academically handicapped,* (4) *children with learning disabilities,* and (5) *emotionally disturbed children.* He could link these descriptors with (6) *self-concept* and (7) *self-esteem* as follows: (1 or 2 or 3 or 4 or 5) and (6 or 7). This search of the ERIC data base produced 214 references as compared with 41 when only the broad descriptor *handicapped children* was used.

In addition to descriptors, ERIC reports are also classified by *author,* by *institution,* and by *identifier.* For most computer searches these classifications are of little value. However, if the researcher knows that much important work in her area of interest has been conducted by a specific author or at a specific institution, she can search these classifications. Identifiers include terms such as *geographical locations, trade names, equipment names, specific theories, tests,* and *testing programs.* Although they may be useful in some searches, the authors have found them of little value in the kinds of computer searches usually conducted by graduate students.

7. *Conduct the search.* Once you are on-line, the first step is to enter your descriptors and determine how many references are available under each descriptor. For example, in the ERIC search on self-concept of handicapped children we found the following frequencies: handicapped children 277, handicapped students 450, self-concept 4433, self-esteem 894, and elementary school students 5031.

The next step is to enter each of your planned combinations of descriptors into the computer and ask how many references are available for each combination. Next, you may decide to have the computer print the bibliographical data on five to ten of the references in a given combination to see what sort of references have been selected.

You would then select the combination of descriptors that will produce from 50 to 200 items and instruct the computer to send you a printout. For some data bases, such as ERIC, you can request bibliographical data only, or you can request that abstracts also be provided. When available, the abstracts are usually worth the additional cost; for a DIALOG search of ERIC, the cost is five cents per citation for bibliographic data only, and ten cents for bibliographic data plus abstract.

8. *Review the printout.* Once the student has received the printout of the references located in his computer search, he should study the abstracts and proceed with the rest of his literature review using the procedures described in this chapter. If, in checking the bibliographies of articles he reads, he locates

important references that were not found in his computer search, he should study these carefully and try to determine why they were missed. Unless the student is very thorough in planning his computer search, he may miss a great many important references. Therefore, it is often desirable for the student to conduct a second computer search after he has become more familiar with his field of study.

Full Text Searching

Full text searching is a procedure for searching the citations entered in the data base for specific words or phrases. This technique is very useful (1) when you want to search a very narrow and sharply defined topic or (2) when there are no descriptor terms that really fit your topic.

Full text searching may be carried out with any of the DIALOG data bases, although the coverage may differ from one data base to another. The search may be carried out for single words, phrases, or for two or more words that appear in close proximity in the material searched. These words do not have to be descriptor terms; any combination of words can be used.

It is also possible to conduct a full text search on terms that have been truncated so that only the root term remains. For example, a search of the root term *librar* would locate references containing any variation of the root term, such as *library, libraries, librarians*, thus providing a broader coverage of relevant citations.

For ERIC, the material searched for each reference includes the title, descriptions, identifiers, and abstract. For example, suppose the researcher were interested in studies dealing with forced busing. Some ERIC descriptors that relate to this topic are *bus transportation* (521 references), *school buses* (121 refer ences), or *bus transportation* combined with *integration* (273 references). Using these descriptors would probably produce most references related to forced busing but would also require the researcher to review hundreds of citations in order to find those that were relevant. The researcher will obtain much more sharply focused citations if she carries out a full text search using the words "forced busing." In conducting a full text search, different instructions can be given to the computer so that different criteria will be met before a citation is selected. For example, if the "W-limiter" is used, one of the selected words *(busing)* must directly follow the other *(forced)* in order for the reference to be selected. If the "F-limiter" is used, both words must appear in the same field (for example, both words must be somewhere in the title). If the "C-limiter" is used, the selected words need only appear someplace in the citation. Thus the limiters can be used to broaden or narrow the search as desired.

When we searched forced (W) busing, we located three references. A search of forced (F) busing produced eight citations, while forced (C) busing produced nine citations. These few citations were all "on target," thus saving much of the labor that would have been required if a search of descriptors had been conducted.

For most educational topics a search of relevant descriptors is the best choice. The full text search, however, is a very useful tool when a problem arises where its special characteristics are needed.

Step Three—Reading and Noting Selected References

Bibliography Card

During his search of the preliminary sources, the student should prepare a bibliography card for each book or article that he believes might contain material pertinent to the review. Although information included in the bibliographical data for a given citation is always about the same, these data can be recorded in many different formats. Before starting his review of the literature, the graduate student should check the rules in effect at his college concerning acceptable format for the bibliography section of the thesis or dissertation. Some schools permit the student to use any format that is generally acceptable in his field of study. Other schools have a specific format that must be followed by all graduate students. If your school permits the use of any form that is acceptable in your field, the easiest approach will be for you to use the format of the preliminary source from which you expect to obtain most of your references. *Current Index to Journals in Education* is the most productive source for most students working in education, and therefore its format is advantageous to use when permitted. Most of the references will come from the subject index of *CIJE*, and articles listed by subject give the title of the book or article before the author's name. For your bibliography card, the author's name (last name first) should be listed before the title. This change is necessary because it is much more convenient for you to maintain your note-card file in alphabetical order by author, and the bibliography as prepared for your thesis normally will be listed in this order. It is advisable to print the author's name; misspelled names are a common source of errors and are difficult to detect when proofreading.

Figure 5.4 shows a bibliography card in the *CIJE* format. If this format is chosen, the bibliographic data from articles found in other sources, such as *Education Index* and *Psychological Abstracts*, should be converted to the *CIJE* format. Let us compare bibliographical data for an article as it appears in *CIJE*, *Education Index*, and *Psychological Abstracts*:

Current Index to Journals in Education:
Battista, Michael   The Interaction between Two Instructional Treatments

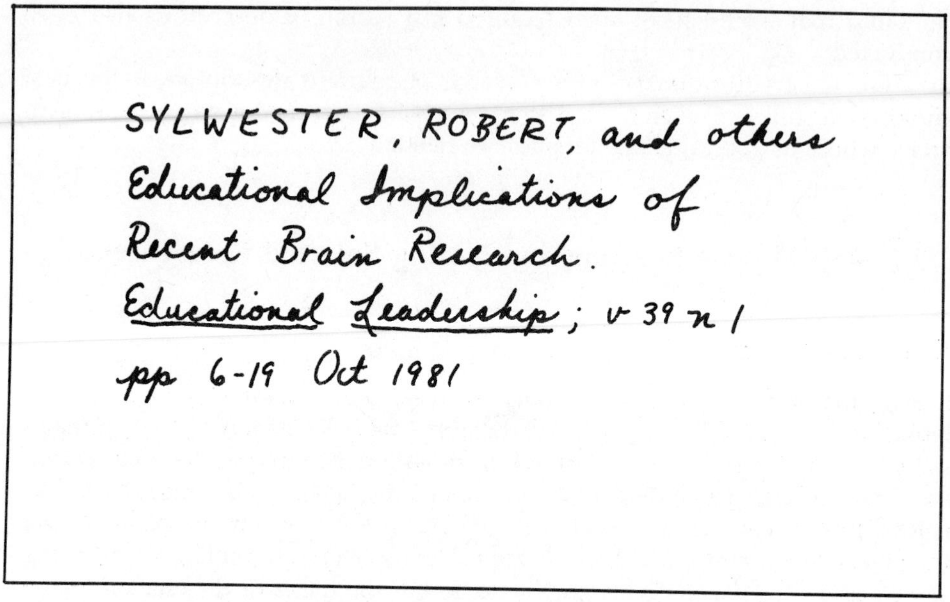
SYLWESTER, ROBERT, and others
Educational Implications of
Recent Brain Research.
Educational Leadership; v 39 n 1
pp 6-19 Oct 1981

Figure 5.4. Sample bibliography card in *CIJE* format.

of Algebraic Structures and Spatial-Visualization Ability. *Journal of Educational Research;* v74 n5 p337–41 May-Jun 1981 (Reprint: UMI)

Education Index:
BATTISTA, Michael Interaction between two instructional treatments of algebraic structures and spatial-visualization ability. J Educ Res 74:337–41 My/Je'81

Psychological Abstracts:
Battista, Michael. (Purdue U) The interaction between two instructional treatments of algebraic structures and spatial-visualization ability. *Journal of Educational Research,* 1981 (May-Jun), Vol 74 (5), 337–341.

Although these forms are similar, note that the *Journal of Educational Research* is abbreviated in *Education Index* and not in the other two sources and that the volume number, pages, and year are given in different format. Note also that all main words in the title are capitalized in *CIJE* while only the first word is capitalized in the other sources. Finally, note that *Education Index* format omits "The" when this is the first word in the title. Obviously, many errors and inconsistencies can be avoided if the student selects one format and converts all references to that format when making up bibliography cards. Students reviewing the literature in one of the areas of educational psychology will normally obtain the majority of their references from *Psychological Abstracts,* and in this case, the *Psychological Abstracts* format may be preferred.

If your college has specified a format for the thesis bibliography that differs from the one used by your preliminary sources, the easiest procedure is to copy the bibliographic data from the preliminary sources in whatever form it is found. Then, when checking the reference in order to determine whether it contains anything pertinent to your review of the literature, you may recopy the bibliographic data in the required school format at the bottom of your bibliography card. You need copy this only for studies that contain pertinent information. Usually, only one out of every three or four references for which the student has prepared bibliography cards will contain material that he wishes to use in his review of the literature.

Accuracy is extremely important in preparing bibliography cards. A mistake made in copying the bibliographic data can often cause the student a great deal of extra work. For example, if he incorrectly copies the name of the journal, date, volume number, or pages, the student will fail to find the article when checking out the source. On failing to find the article, he is faced with the problem of trying to determine which portion of his bibliographic material is incorrect. Unless the student takes special care, it is easy to make any of these mistakes. After it has been made, the student must usually go back to the preliminary sources in order to find the mistake. As he may well have covered a number of preliminary sources, this search can take much longer than it would have taken to use more care initially. Even if the student makes an error in some portion of the bibliographic data that will not interfere with his finding the material, such as misspelling the author's name, the mistake is still serious because it will probably be repeated in his thesis. Nothing reflects more unfavorably upon the scholarship of the research worker than frequent errors in bibliographic data.

Using the Library

Now that you have completed your search of the preliminary sources in your field and have assembled a set of bibliography cards, it is time to start checking these references in the library. The majority of your references will probably be in professional journals, because this is the principal outlet for primary source research articles.

In using the library to obtain these materials, a great deal of time may be wasted. The student, therefore, is advised to obtain a stack permit and examine the layout of the library to determine what method of obtaining her materials will require the least amount of time. In a library where periodicals in a given field are all shelved in a central location and where study space is available in the stacks, it is usually desirable for the student to work in the stacks. Some libraries, however, do not permit students to enter the stacks, and some, because of space limitations, have journals shelved in such a way that they are difficult to find and cannot be used in the immediate area in which they are shelved. In this case the student can usually save time by making out call slips for about ten periodicals. While waiting for the library clerk to return with these periodicals, the student can make out call slips for her next ten references. The clerk can then look for the second ten references while the student is scanning and making notes on whatever she has received from the first ten call slips. Because a certain percentage of the references that the student wants will be lost, checked out, or in the bindery, it is always advisable to submit call slips for ten or more at a time.

Many professional journals are now available on microfilm. Libraries are making increasing use of this format because it is less expensive and requires less space. You should check the room in your library where microfilms and microfiche are stored. Most university libraries have equipment available for copying microfilm onto regular-sized sheets of paper. This is a useful service if you need a copy of an article or report for later reference.

Spending a few minutes to determine the most efficient way of obtaining references in her college library will, in the long run, save the student a great deal of time and effort.

Obtaining Materials Not Locally Available

The student will almost certainly find that some of the materials he wishes to examine are not available in his college library. There are several ways to obtain these materials, and the student should not give up merely because a source is not available locally. With respect to articles published in professional journals, the quickest and easiest way to obtain those not locally available is to write directly to the author and ask for a reprint of the article. Authors usually receive reprints of their articles and usually are willing to send a reprint to anyone requesting it. It is advisable to send a stamped, self-addressed envelope with your request. Reprints thus received are the student's personal property and should be kept in his file so that he may recheck the article if necessary. The main problem encountered by students in writing for reprints is obtaining the address of the author. If the source has been located in *Psychological Abstracts*, the address is usually given. This information is not available in *Education Index*, however. A great many authors may be located by checking the various professional directories that are available, such as *Who's Who In American Education*, *Biographical Directory of the American Psychological Association*, and

American Educational Research Association Directory of Members. The reference librarian can usually suggest other directories if an individual is not listed in any of the aforementioned.

If the student is unable to obtain a reprint of the article from the author, the next step is to see if the needed journal is available in other libraries in the student's vicinity. In large population centers, where several colleges or universities are located within a small geographical area, the student can usually find the materials he needs at one of the libraries available. In areas where other libraries are not locally available, the student may obtain materials he needs through interlibrary loan. The student should check the policies of his local library regarding interlibrary loan. Many libraries place restrictions upon graduate students in the use of this service because it is rather expensive.

Very often the student wishes to examine several theses and dissertations that are available only in the school library where the work was done. These may be obtained through interlibrary loan, or microfilm copies of most dissertations may be obtained from University Microfilms, Inc., Ann Arbor, Michigan. Microfilm copies of a dissertation often can be obtained at less expense than borrowing the dissertation through interlibrary loan. Even when more expensive, the microfilm copy is often preferable as it need not be returned and is available for future reference.

The student may usually obtain microfilm or photostatic copies of any reference not locally available. The librarian in his local library will locate needed materials and arrange for their reproduction, but the cost of reproduction and shipping must usually be borne by the student. This cost varies considerably, usually from fifteen to thirty-five cents per page. This method is often practical for short articles but expensive for books or lengthy documents. If, however, the needed reference appears to be of major importance, the student should obtain it by some means. The satisfaction of knowing you have done a thorough and scholarly review of the literature will more than compensate for the expense.

Taking Notes on Research Articles

It is advisable for the student to check through her bibliography cards and identify those covering studies that appear most important to her review of the literature. The student should then start her review by checking the most recent of these important studies. The reason for starting with the most recent studies is that these, having the earlier research as a foundation, are likely to be more valuable. By reading the most important articles first, the student quickly builds up a reasonably deep understanding of her problem, and this makes it possible for her to profit more from the subsequent study of articles that are only peripherally related to her topic. After gaining this insight, it is much easier for her to fit these less important studies into the overall picture that she builds of her field through a review of the literature.

When she finally opens the journal to an article she wishes to check, the student should first read the abstract. Most research articles start with a brief abstract or end with a summary. By reading this the student can usually determine whether the article contains any information that would justify reading the entire article. After reading the abstract or summary, if she decides the article is sufficiently pertinent, the student should first check the accuracy of the data on her bibliography card, because the source where she obtained these data could have been in error. She should then record the same bibliographic data on the top of a 5-by-8-inch note card and take notes on the article as she reads it. In order to save time, the bibliographic data can be abbreviated on the note card.

In a research article, the writer attempts to present the essential materials in as brief a form as possible. The student will find that the average research article is only five or six pages in length and thus takes little time to read. The student will also find that the majority of research articles follow a standard pattern that further reduces the time needed to review them. This format usually includes (1) a brief introduction; (2) the hypotheses to be tested; (3) a statement of the procedure including a description of subjects, measures used, and research design; (4) a section giving the findings; and (5) a summary and conclusions. In taking notes the student should be as brief as possible but should not omit anything that she feels she will later use in the design of her study or in the preparation of her research report. A brief outline of the reference using short sentences or phrases with headings for the problem or hypotheses, procedure, findings, and conclusions will usually be sufficient.

The procedures and findings usually require the most detailed notetaking. In order to make comparisons among related studies later on, the student should record the number of subjects, sampling methods, treatments (independent variable), measures employed (dependent variable), research design, and any other procedure worthy of attention.

Findings should also be reported in some detail, especially for studies that are very relevant to the student's problem. Both significant and nonsignificant findings should be recorded, along with levels of significance for the former. In order to combine studies and draw an overall picture of the findings, it is useful to categorize studies as significant ($+$), nonsignificant ($+$), nonsignificant ($-$), and significant ($-$). The meta-analysis technique developed by Gene Glass and his associates provides a more sophisticated method of combining the results of related studies. If the student plans to use this method, he should record the means and standard deviations of the experimental and control groups in experimental and quasi-experimental studies and the product-moment correlations in correlational studies.[13]

It is also desirable for the student to record her own evaluation of the study and to note how it may relate to her research while the article is still fresh in her mind. In addition to her outline of the study, it is often profitable to record promising or unusual techniques employed in the study, new measures that may be of use, interesting theoretical points, and a critical evaluation including apparent weaknesses that make the results questionable. This critical evaluation of the research is important because the student will often find several research reports that test similar hypotheses but yield different results. Unless the student can make a critical evaluation of the research, it is difficult to determine which of the conflicting results is more likely to be correct. Chapter 6 presents a detailed discussion of methods for critically evaluating research articles (see figure 5.5 for a sample note card).

Taking Notes on Opinion Articles

In education many of the articles that the student encounters will not be reports of research projects, but will state the experiences or opinions of the author concerning some educational topic. Opinion articles do not follow the research article format and usually do not contain a summary. When checking the opinion article, the student should first scan the article to get some idea of its content. One method of scanning is to read only the first sentence in each paragraph. After scanning, the student should decide whether the article contains material of importance, in which case he should read the entire article. An abstract of the opinion article can usually be prepared most quickly using a sentence outline approach.

Quotations

When reading articles the student should be alert for quotations that might be useful in preparing the review of the literature for his thesis or dissertation. If the student finds material he may wish to quote, the material to be quoted should be copied very carefully on the note card, enclosed in quotation marks, and the page from which the quote was taken noted. Most systems of referencing require that the page be given for direct quotations, and this also facilitates checking the quotation if necessary.

Students often use far too many quotations in their reviews. A good rule to follow is to copy for possible quotations only materials that are stated very

---

13. See chapter 6 for a discussion of meta-analysis.

OLETNIK, S.F. and DOEYAN, J.D. Soliciting teacher participants for classroom research. *Journal of Educational Research*, 1982, 75(3), 165-168.

<u>Problem</u>. Effects on teacher interest to participate in a res. proj. of the following 3 variables: (1) nature of the res.; i.e., exp. vs. non-exp. (in exp.) teachers randomly assigned to treatment; in non-exp. could choose treatment); (2) monetary reward vs. no reward; (3) time required to participate i.e. 1-4 hours vs. 4-12 hours over 2-week period.

<u>Procedure</u>. Subj. were 58 teachers, gr. 2-8. 15 teachers gr. K, 1 & special subject dropped after data collected. Randomly assigned to 8 treatments, N per cell 5-11. Each tr. contained desc. of 5 proposed studies. Desc. identical except that the 3 ind. variables were manipulated.

<u>Findings</u>. ANOVA gave sig. higher interest for groups getting honorarium (10% level); NSD exp vs non-exp., NSD time, no interactions were sig.

<u>Conclusions</u>. Financial incentive sig. increased teacher interest in participating.

<u>Comments</u>. Request for teacher commitment instead of interest would be more realistic. Cell sizes small. Dropping K, 1, & spec. teachers indicates poor planning.

Figure 5.5   Sample note card.

skillfully, or in very concise terms, or are typical and clear reflections of a particular point of view the student wishes to illustrate in his thesis. After copying a quotation, the student should recheck to be sure that he has copied it exactly. Inaccurate quotations are a serious reflection on the scholarship of the writer, and it is almost certain that some of the quotations will be checked for accuracy by the faculty members who read the thesis.

Classifying Articles You Read

In reading articles for your review of the literature, you should keep constantly in mind the objective of your research and should attempt to relate the material you read to your research plan. Do not restrict yourself to the narrow study of only that research that is closely related to the work you are planning. Very often studies that are only partially related to your work will give you new theoretical viewpoints and acquaint you with new tools and methods that can be profitably applied to your research plan.

In doing her review of the literature, the student usually finds that the articles she reads can be classified into several categories. For example, in doing a review of literature in the field of ability grouping, one of the authors found some articles that compared the achievement of students in ability-grouping and random-grouping systems, some articles that made comparisons of sociometric scores and social status measures between the two systems, some that discussed methods of grouping, and so on. In carrying out her review, the student should be alert for such natural subdivisions because they form a basis for classifying note cards.

A Coding System

As some such pattern for his review emerges, the student should develop a system of coding that will permit him to indicate what type of material is contained on a given note card. The coding system adopted by the research worker will be different for each review of the literature. An example of a coding system used by one of the authors in a review of the literature in ability grouping may be helpful to the student in developing his own coding. These codes are generally placed in the upper-right-hand corner of the note card.

+ An important study
S Studies dealing with social interaction
A Studies dealing with achievement of pupils in different grouping systems
G Studies describing grouping systems and studies discussing problems involved in grouping, such as individual variability, and so forth
B Studies relating grouping to behavior problems

P   Studies relating grouping to personality adjustment, personality variables, and self-concept

Using such a code is helpful to the student in several ways. It makes him actively aware of the major areas of concentration in his topic. It makes it possible for him to check quickly his notes on a specific portion of the literature, and it makes the job of writing up his review of the literature much easier. The more extensive studies, of course, may contain material relating to two or three subtopics. These are recorded by indicating all the codes for subtopics.

MISTAKES SOMETIMES MADE IN REVIEWING RESEARCH LITERATURE

1. Student carries out a hurried review of the literature to get started on the research project. This usually results in overlooking previous studies containing ideas that would have improved the student's project.
2. Relies too heavily upon secondary sources.
3. Concentrates on research findings when reading research articles, thus overlooking valuable information on methods, measures, and so forth.
4. Overlooks sources other than education journals, such as newspapers and popular magazines, which often contain articles on educational topics.
5. Fails to define satisfactorily the topic limits of his review of the literature. Searching too broad an area often leads to the student's becoming discouraged or doing a slipshod job. Searching too narrow an area causes him to overlook many articles that are peripheral to his research topic but contain information that would help him design a better study.
6. Copies bibliographic data incorrectly and is then unable to locate the reference needed.
7. Copies far too much material onto note cards. This often indicates that the student does not have a clear understanding of her project and thus cannot separate important from unimportant information.
8. Fails to use all relevant narrow descriptors when conducting a computer search.

ANNOTATED REFERENCES

Jackson, Gregg B. "Methods for Integrative Reviews." *Review of Educational Research* 50 (1980): 438–60.
The author critically analyzes procedures used by reviewers of the edu-

cational research literature. Since your thesis or dissertation will include a literature review, you can learn much from studying this article. The study analyzes 36 randomly sampled review articles and relates the findings to 6 basic tasks involved in conducting an integrative review: (1) selecting questions or hypotheses for the review, (2) sampling research articles to be reviewed, (3) describing the characteristics of the studies, (4) analyzing the findings, (5) interpreting the results, and (6) reporting the review. Jackson's work identifies many deficiencies frequently found in literature reviews and suggests effective ways to overcome these deficiencies. A brief but informative discussion of meta-analysis is also included.

Pugh, Elizabeth. *Directory of ERIC Search Services*, Washington, D.C.: National Institute of Education. Published biennially in even years.

This source currently lists about 340 organizations that provide ERIC computer searches. Entries include name and address of organizations, population served, data bases available, cost, and other information. Available free of charge from ERIC Facility, 4833 Rugby Avenue, Bethesda, MD 20014.

Woodbury, Marda L. *A Guide to Sources of Educational Information*. Washington, D.C.: Information Resources Press, 1976.

This is a comprehensive guide to virtually every type of information related to education. It contains detailed descriptions of more than 700 sources, plus backup chapters on how to locate them and how to use them. Among the kinds of sources included are dictionaries, encyclopedias, bibliographies, abstracting and indexing services, instructional materials, tests and assessment instruments, and many more.

Yarborough, J. *How to Prepare a Computer Search of ERIC: A Non-technical Approach*. Stanford, Calif.: ERIC Clearinghouse on Information Resources, September 1975 (ED 110096).

This booklet provides a brief description of the ERIC system, describes data bases of interest to educators, and gives the reader a step-by-step process for preparing an ERIC computer search. Also included is a glossary of terms used in information retrieval systems and an annotated bibliography.

Abstracting and Indexing Sources

The following sources are useful in locating research articles that have been published in psychology, education, and related fields.

Author Index to Psychological Index, 1894-1935 and Psychological Abstracts, 1927-1958. Boston: Hall, 1960.

Bibliographic Index. New York: H. W. Wilson, 1938 to date.

Buros, Oscar K., ed. *The Eighth Mental Measurements Yearbook*. Highland Park, N.J.: Gryphon Press, 1978.

Business Education Index. New York: Delta Pi Epsilon Fraternity through Gregg Division, McGraw-Hill, 1940 to date.

Child Development Abstracts and Bibliography. Washington, D.C.: Society for Research in Child Development, 1927 to date.

Comprehensive Dissertation Index. Ann Arbor, Mich.: University Microfilms International. Covers dissertations 1861 to date.

Cumulated Subject Index to the Psychological Abstracts, 1927-1960. Boston: Hall, 1966.

Cumulative Author Index to Psychological Abstracts Second Supplement 1964-1968. 2 vols. Boston: Hall, 1970.

Current Index to Journals in Education. New York: Macmillan Information, 1969 to date.

Dissertation Abstracts International. Ann Arbor, Mich.: University Microfilms International, 1938 to date.

Education Index. New York: H. W. Wilson, 1929 to date.

Educational Administration Abstracts. Columbus, Ohio: University Council for Educational Administration, 1966 to date.

Exceptional Child Education Resources. Reston, Va.: Council for Exceptional Children, 1969 to date.

First Supplement to the Cumulative Author Index to Psychological Abstracts, 1959-1963. Boston: Hall, 1965.

Psychological Abstracts. Washington, D.C.: American Psychological Association, 1927 to date.

Resources in Education. Washington, D.C.: National Institute of Education, 1966 to date.

Resources in Vocational Education. Columbus, Ohio: Ohio State University, 1967 to date.

Science Citation Index. Philadelphia: Institute for Scientific Information, 1961 to date.

Social Science Citation Index. Philadelphia: Institute for Scientific Information, 1973 to date.

Sociological Abstracts. New York: Sociological Abstracts Inc., 1954 to date.

State Education Journal Index. Westminster, Colo.: L. S. Ratliff, 1963 to date.

Reviews of Research Literature

The following sources are helpful to the student in gaining a quick overview of research in education or psychology.

Annual Review of Psychology. Palo Alto, Calif.: Annual Reviews, 1950 to date.

Review of Educational Research. Washington, D.C.: American Educational Research Association, 1931 to date. Published five times a year.

Review of Research in Education. Itasca, Ill.: F. E. Peacock (a publication of the American Educational Research Association), 1973 to date. Annual volumes.

Travers, R. M. W., ed. *Second Handbook of Research on Teaching.* Chicago: Rand McNally, 1973.

Yearbook of the National Society for the Study of Education. Chicago: University of Chicago Press, 1902 to date. Published annually.

Directories

The following directories will help the student locate the addresses of professional workers in education and psychology. This information is needed in order to obtain reprints of articles not available in the local library. If the following directories do not produce the needed information, check under "Directories" in recent issues of *Education Index, Guide to American Educational Directories,* or *Guide to American Directories* for additional sources. If your library does not have a directory you need, check with faculty members or local educators who may be members of the association publishing the directory.

American Educational Research Association: Directory of Members. Washington, D.C.: American Educational Research Association. Published biannually.

This is a complete roster of over 10,000 members with titles and addresses.

Directory of the American Psychological Association. Washington, D.C.: American Psychological Association. Published triennially.

The 1981 edition of this directory provides a biographical listing of over 52,000 members.

Ethridge, James M., ed. *The Directory of Directories.* 1st ed. Detroit, Mich.: Information Enterprises, 1980.

This source organizes directories into 15 subject areas, one of which is education. A revised edition will be published every two years with supplementary issues between editions. A subject index and title index are provided. Students will find it well worth their while to scan the 27 pages in the education section. The information provided for each directory includes address and phone number of publisher, persons or institutions covered, information included in entry, how directory is arranged (e.g., alphabetical), and what indexes are provided.

Klein, Barry T., ed. *Guide to American Educational Directories.* 5th ed. Rye, N.Y.: Todd Publications, 1980.

Many sources of educational materials may be found in this guide under "Curriculum Aids" and also under specific subject headings such as Art, Biology, Geography, and Mathematics. The coverage in education appears to be about the same as in the *Guide to American Directories*, but is easier to use since directories are arranged by subtopic rather than alphabetically.

Klein, Bernard, ed. *Guide to American Directories.* 10th ed. Coral Springs, Fla.: B. Klein Publication, 1978.

This guide lists directories in a great many subject areas including a very thorough coverage of membership directories in education. Directories in psychology, social science, and science are also included.

The National Faculty Directory 1982. Detroit, Mich.: Gale Research Co. Published annually since 1970.

This is an alphabetical list, with departments and full institutional addresses, of about 450,000 members of teaching faculties at junior colleges, colleges, and universities in the U.S. and some Canadian institutions. Since much educational research is conducted by faculty members, this source is very useful in locating current addresses of researchers.

SELF-CHECK TEST

Circle the correct answer to each of the following questions. An answer key is provided on page 881.

1. The general term applied to publications that contain descriptions of educational research by an author who was not a direct observer or participant is " —— source."

    a. secondary

    b. primary

    c. preliminary

    d. review

2. If an author of a textbook reports results of his own experiments, that portion of the text would be considered a —— source.

    a. review

    b. primary

    c. secondary

    d. preliminary

3. A good rule to follow is to develop a reading program based on —— sources to locate a tentative research problem followed by a review of the literature based on —— sources.

    a. primary/secondary

    b. secondary/primary

    c. secondary/preliminary

    d. preliminary/secondary

4. The initial step in reviewing the literature is to

    a. make a list of key words related to the study.

    b. take notes on research articles.

    c. check the preliminary sources.

    d. study opinion articles to gain insight into the problems related to the study.

5. *Education Index, Psychological Abstracts,* and *Resources in Education* are all examples of —— sources.

    a. preliminary

    b. primary

    c. reference

    d. secondary

6. Unlike *Education Index* and *Psychological Abstracts,* the ERIC system includes abstracts of

    a. conference papers.

    b. final reports of school district studies.

    c. progress reports of educational research studies.

    d. All of the above are correct.

7. The purpose of the *Review of Educational Research* is to

    a. provide bibliographies of research completed in each calendar year.

    b. summarize the research literature on a variety of educational topics.

    c. produce a current index to the major preliminary sources in education.

    d. All of the above are correct.

8. The best source of bibliographies of research on particular tests is

    a. *Mental Measurements Yearbooks.*

    b. *Review of Educational Research.*

    c. *Bibliographic Index.*
    d. *Dissertation Abstracts.*

9. The purpose of DATRIX is to help the researcher by
    a. preparing article abstracts that contain sample size, research design, and statistical techniques used.
    b. selecting ERIC documents on a given topic.
    c. selecting doctoral dissertations on a given topic.
    d. providing names of other researchers doing current studies on a given topic.

10. Probably the most often used preliminary source covering popular periodicals and newspapers is
    a. *The New York Times Index.*
    b. *Sociological Abstracts.*
    c. *Reader's Guide to Periodical Literature.*
    d. *Facts on File.*

APPLICATION PROBLEMS

The following problems are designed to give you practice in applying significant concepts and research procedures explained in chapter 5. Most of them do not have a single correct answer. For feedback, you can compare your answers with the sample answers on pages 885–87.

1. Select a research topic in which you are interested and locate a primary and secondary source related to it. Enter the bibliographic data on the two sources and explain why each is a primary or secondary source.

2. Suppose you wanted to conduct a manual search of research literature related to the effect of praise on the sharing behavior of young children.
    a. Check the *Thesaurus of Psychological Index Terms* and list key index terms related to praise and sharing that you could check in *Psychological Abstracts.*
    b. Check the *Thesaurus of ERIC Descriptors* and list key descriptors you could use in checking *RIE* and *CIJE.*
    c. Check *Psychological Abstracts* and locate one article that appears relevant to this topic. Make up a bibliography card.

3. Graduate students often find it helpful to learn something about the research work of faculty members with whom they are working. Select one member of your graduate committee or a faculty member in your major department and collect the following information:
    a. List articles published by the faculty member over the past five years and make up bibliography cards.
    b. Check how many times each article has been cited by other authors over the past two years.

    c. Read the article cited most frequently and prepare a note card.
4. Locate an article on experimental procedures published in 1976 by Harold W. Richey.
    a. Prepare a bibliography card.
    b. Prepare a note card on this article.
5. Suppose that a researcher wanted to carry out a computer search of the ERIC data base in order to locate references related to the question "What teaching techniques make a difference in learner achievement?" Following the procedures in this chapter, make up a search plan using all relevant descriptors in *and/or* relationships such as the example given on pages 886–87.

SUGGESTION SHEET

If your last name starts with letters from Cor to Doc, please complete the Suggestion Sheet at the end of the book while this chapter is still fresh in your mind.

6.

CRITICAL EVALUATION
OF RESEARCH

OVERVIEW

This chapter introduces you to techniques for critically evaluating research reports and combining your findings into an integrated picture of knowledge related to your topic. Since your own research must build upon the previous work in your field, it is essential that you be able to interpret this work. Often you will find two studies in the literature that report conflicting results. When this occurs, you must be able to analyze the articles and interpret the findings in light of the strengths and weaknesses of the two studies. Particularly, you should estimate how design flaws and research biases could have affected the results of each study. This chapter provides techniques to analyze research reports for evidence of (1) deliberate bias or distortion, (2) nondeliberate bias, (3) sampling bias, (4) failure to consider important variables, (5) use of weak or inappropriate measurement procedures, (6) observer bias, (7) the Hawthorne and John Henry effects, (8) contamination, and (9) demand characteristics that could distort the research results.

OBJECTIVES

After studying this chapter, you should be able to:

1. Identify sections of research reports and aspects of research design that indicate possible bias or contamination.
2. Describe three procedures for combining and interpreting research evidence related to your topic.
3. Describe aspects of a research report that may indicate deliberate bias.
4. Describe ways in which a researcher can unintentionally bias his results.
5. Describe four types of situations that indicate sampling bias.
6. State the four questions that one should ask when evaluating measurement tools used in research projects.

7. Explain the Hawthorne Effect, the John Henry Effect, and demand characteristics; and identify research situations in which these effects may occur.
8. Explain the function of placebos in research.
9. Explain the concepts of statistical and practical significance, and use them to evaluate the significance of findings reported in research.
10. Describe sources of bias that can influence the results of interview and observational data.

INTRODUCTION

The research worker must build the research upon the knowledge accumulated by previous researchers, and a major goal of the review of the literature is to establish this foundation. Nevertheless, soon after starting a first review of the literature, the graduate student will discover that instead of a solid foundation, the previous research appears to provide a foundation of shifting sands. The findings of similar studies will often be contradictory, leaving the student at a loss to decide which, if any, to accept. This problem must usually be resolved through a critical evaluation of the previous research in which the strengths and weaknesses of each study are carefully weighed.

Research Quality

Although the quality of educational research is improving, evidence still indicates that much of the research published has important weaknesses that should be considered by the reviewer in weighing research results. Perhaps the most extensive study on the quality of educational research is the work of Caroline Persell.[1] Her study included all articles published in a single year in American behavioral science and education journals plus all papers presented at an annual meeting of the American Educational Research Association. This provided a total of 1100 papers from which a sample of 390 papers was selected. A national panel of 39 outstanding researchers each evaluated 11 papers, the eleventh paper for each researcher being one that was evaluated by several other researchers in order to obtain estimates of the reliability of the ratings. Each paper was rated on a 5-point scale on a number of variables. A total of 43 percent of the papers were rated below average or incompetent in terms of their contribution to theory; 35 percent were rated at this level on their contri-

1. Caroline H. Persell, *Quality, Careers and Training in Educational and Social Research* (Bayside, N.Y.: General Hall, 1976).

bution to practice; and 39 percent on their use of research methods. These results are generally in agreement with an earlier study by E. Wandt[2] of 125 articles; and a study by N. E. W. Ward, B. W. Hall, and C. F. Schramm that evaluated a sample of 121 articles published in 44 journals.[3] Even if we discount some of these findings on the grounds that experienced researchers have high standards and tend to be critical, the conclusion remains that a substantial percentage of studies published in education have serious deficiencies.

In Persell's study the judges indicated reasons for their ratings of below average or incompetent. Of the 178 papers that received poor ratings on theory or practice, the judges thought that 59 percent dealt with an important problem but contributed little to its understanding, while 25 percent dealt with unimportant problems. For papers that received low ratings on methodology, the most frequently cited reasons were poor data analysis (25 percent), poor research design (24 percent), and poor data collection (15 percent). Other reasons for low ratings included poor reporting, poor interpretation, and inadequate analysis. Correlations between ratings in the three rating areas were high, ranging from .68 to .91. This suggests that papers that are weak in one area tend to be weak in the others. Or, put another way, a substantial number of papers were generally weak across the rating areas.

The most frequent shortcomings cited by judges in the Ward, Hall, and Schramm study were: specific weaknesses in the research design (27 percent), inappropriate research designs (23 percent), inadequate data on reliability and validity (22 percent), and conclusions not supported by the evidence (22 percent). Other analyses of educational research, such as the work of R. Haney and his associates[4] and J. J. Gallagher,[5] have found similar deficiencies.

Although many weak research articles are still being published in education, a comparison by Ward, Hall, and Schramm of articles published in 1962 and 1971 shows several areas of improvement. For example, the percentage of articles that the judges believed should have been rejected dropped from 40 percent in 1962 to 27 percent in 1971.

Analyses of educational research tend to give most of their attention to weaknesses rather than strengths and therefore obscure the fact that many good studies are being conducted. This emphasis on the weaknesses of educational research is continued in many research methods courses in which the

2. Edwin Wandt, ed., *A Cross-section of Educational Research* (New York: David McKay, 1965).
3. N. E. W. Ward, B. W. Hall, and C. F. Schramm, "Evaluation of Published Educational Research: A National Survey," *American Educational Research Journal* 12 (1975): 109–28.
4. R. Haney et al., *A Summary of Research in Science Education for the Years 1965-1967, Elementary School Level* (Columbus: ERIC Information Analysis Center for Science and Mathematics Education, 1969, ED038554).
5. James J. Gallagher, "A Summary of Research in Science Education for the Years 1968-1969: Elementary School Level," *Journal of Research in Science Teaching* 9, no. 1 (1972): 19–46.

student is often asked to evaluate poor articles critically. One reason that instructors select weak articles for students to evaluate is probably to emphasize the danger of accepting research findings uncritically, which can, of course, lead to misinterpretations and unsound decisions. Also, during the time graduate students are learning about research methods, they can more easily detect the obvious weaknesses found in poor articles than the more subtle weaknesses found in better articles. Since both good and poor research is reported in the educational literature, the real task of the graduate student is to evaluate the articles that are relevant to his problem, give more weight to the better research, and estimate how the results of a given study might have been altered due to weaknesses in the research process. He can then combine the results into an accurate composite picture of the state of knowledge in his area of interest.

Mistakes, oversights, and biases may occur at any stage of the research process, from the initial steps taken in problem definition to the final phases of statistical analysis. The research worker's effectiveness in detecting these errors is dependent for the most part upon two factors: knowledge and understanding of the total research process in education, and knowledge in the specific field of his review. Thus, this chapter should properly be studied after one has mastered the next thirteen chapters, which cover the entire research process. Because the chapters are arranged sequentially in terms of the skills required at each step of the research process, however, it is placed here. Skill in critical evaluation of research is needed early in the research process so that the student can determine the strengths and weaknesses of previous research in his area of interest. The student who cannot properly evaluate the weaknesses of previous research may well repeat them in his own research project. In contrast, the student who can avoid these weaknesses stands a good chance of making a substantial contribution to his area of interest.

Each topic discussed here is covered more fully in a later chapter. Therefore, a student who cannot understand a particular topic is advised to look it up in the index and read ahead in the appropriate chapter. Also, the student may profit by supplementing his reading of this chapter with study of the research evaluation checklist presented in Appendix B.

Systematic Literature Analysis

One of the most imporant and difficult tasks that a student must complete before starting her research is to pull together the research findings that are relevant to her topic, extract useful knowledge, and draw some general conclusions. Many procedures can be used to combine research findings of related studies and estimate the overall significance of the combined results.[6] We will discuss three procedures that differ in difficulty and information required. It should be emphasized that all these methods assume either an exhaustive review of literature or the selection of a representative sample of studies related to a given topic or hypothesis. If a biased sample of studies is selected, then the combined results of the studies will also be biased.

Vote Counting

The first approach and by far the easiest to use was recommended by Gregg Jackson.[7] This method involves classifying all studies into four categories: (1) significant $(+)$, (2) nonsignificant $(+)$, (3) nonsignificant $(-)$, and (4) significant $(-)$. In addition to being easy to use, this method permits the classification of virtually all studies. More precise methods of combining research findings require additional information, and studies not reporting this information cannot be classified. Either the sign test or chi-square can be used to determine the statistical significance of the combined data.[8]

The Chi-Square Method

An approach advocated by N. L. Gage takes into account the size of the sample and the magnitude of the relationship or difference reported in each study.[9] The model is based on the fact that any p value can be transformed into a chi-square with two degrees of freedom. This method involves first converting whatever inferential statistics are reported in each study (e.g., t, F, r) into exact probability (p) values by checking the appropriate statistical tables.[10] The probability values are next converted to chi-square values.[11] Because chi-square values and degrees of freedom (df) are additive, the chi-squares and dfs for all studies are then summed. To determine the overall level of significance of the

6. See Rosenthal in Annotated References at the end of this chapter.
7. See Annotated References at the end of chapter 5.
8. Although simple to use, the vote-counting procedure can produce misleading results, failing to detect an effect even when a fairly large effect size is present. See Larry V. Hedges and Ingram Olkin, "Vote Counting Methods in Research Analysis," *Psychological Bulletin* 88 (1980): 359–69.
9. See N. L. Gage, *The Scientific Basis of the Art of Teaching* (New York: Teachers College Press, 1978), chap. 1.
10. There are also computer programs available that convert a given statistical finding into an exact probability value.
11. The formulas for converting p to chi-square are given in Lyle V. Jones and Donald W. Fiske, "Models for Testing the Significance of Combined Results," *Psychological Bulletin* 50, no. 5 (1953): 375–82. A table for converting p to chi-square may be found in Mordecai H. Gordon, Edward H. Loveland, and Edward E. Cureton, "An Extended Table of Chi-Square for Two Degrees of Freedom for Use in Combining Probabilities From Independent Samples," *Psychometrika* 17, (1952): 311–16.

studies being combined, it is only necessary to check in a regular chi-square probability table for the summed values of chi-square and degrees of freedom.

The main limitation of the chi-square method is that it is based on the assumption that the studies being combined are independent of one another. In many studies, several significance tests are carried out on the same subjects. These tests are not independent, so the investigator must include only one probability value for each study. Gage suggests that the least significant result from each study be used, since this will lead to the most conservative conclusion. Another option would be to compute the probability value for the finding in each study that is most relevant to the student's problem.

Meta-Analysis

In recent years, the meta-analysis approach developed by Gene Glass and his colleagues (see Annotated References) has been widely adopted by researchers. This method involves converting the findings of each study to an *effect size* (Δ). For studies that compare an experimental and control group, the effect size is computed by subtracting the mean score of the control group on the dependent variable from the experimental group mean and dividing by the control group standard deviation.[12] Similar formulas have been developed to convert most inferential statistics, such as *t*-ratios, *F*-ratios, percentages, and correlation coefficients to an effect size. The mean of the effect sizes for all studies included in the research review is then calculated to estimate the typical effect of the phenomenon under study. For example, a meta-analysis of the effects of psychotherapy on alcoholism combined the results of twenty experiments in which control groups were employed.[13] The dependent variable in this analysis was "success rate," which was usually defined as abstinence or near abstinence. Success rates for experimental and control groups in each study were compared to estimate the effect of treatment. The average success rate for experimental groups was 51 percent versus 33 percent for control groups. This represents a difference of .96 standard deviation. These results suggest that the overall effect of psychotherapy is positive. A correlation of .49 was found between the hours of therapy provided in each experiment and the success rate. The reviewers also examined kinds of therapy and duration of the effect. Certainly the methods of quantification used in this meta-analysis give the reviewer a better understanding of the effects of psychotherapy than would emerge from less sophisticated methods of data integration, such as vote counting.

12. $\Delta = \dfrac{\overline{X}_{Exp} - \overline{X}_{Con}}{SD_{Con}}$

13. H. J. Schlesinger, E. Mumford, and G. V Glass, "A Critical Review and Indexed Bibliography of the Literature to 1978 on the Effects of Psychotherapy on Medical Utilization" (Department of Psychiatry, University of Colorado Medical Center, Denver, Colo., 1978).

Compared with other methods of integrating research data, the meta-analysis technique has advantages and disadvantages. Jackson (see Annotated References at end of chapter 5) described several limitations of this procedure that should be considered by anyone who plans to conduct a meta-analysis. Glass and his associates devoted a chapter in their book to the most common criticisms of their procedure and give well-thought-out arguments to counter them. Despite the limitations of meta-analysis, it is currently the best available method for cumulating and integrating the results of research.

Perhaps the most persistent criticism of meta-analysis is the inclusion of data from poor studies. In meta-analysis all studies that provide evidence related to the question under investigation are included, regardless of quality. Glass justifies this approach by pointing out that methodologically weak studies often report results similar to those found in stronger studies; by combining the results of all studies, these results can be accepted with more confidence. Even when the results of strong and weak studies do not agree, Glass argues that including all results will give the reviewer a better understanding of the phenomenon under investigation than if weaker studies are eliminated at the offset.

This argument is valid under the condition that the investigator looks at the results of his meta-analysis in depth. If a mean effect size is computed without giving close attention to the findings of specific studies, serious misinterpretations of the data could result. For example, one of the authors once did an exhaustive review of research literature related to ability grouping. Most of the studies located were one-year studies in which ability grouping was the "new innovation," while conventional grouping was the control condition. These one-year studies generally found that ability grouping resulted in higher student achievement. However, these studies were probably biased by the Hawthorne Effect. A few methodologically superior studies extended over several years and were, therefore, less subject to the Hawthorne Effect. These studies generally found no significant differences in achievement between the two grouping systems. If a meta-analysis of all studies had been done, the large number of weak studies would have produced a spurious effect favoring ability grouping.

Literature Analysis as Research

In recent years an increasing number of students have reported a literature analysis (mostly meta-analyses) for their thesis or dissertation, instead of conducting primary research. The conduct of a rigorous literature analysis makes a significant contribution to our understanding of research on a particular problem. Also, because of the huge number of research reports now available, integrative research reviews such as meta-analyses are very useful in helping researchers keep up with the current state of knowledge in their interest areas.

For the student who is considering doing an extensive analysis of research literature, Harris Cooper (see Annotated References) provides a very useful set of guidelines. He conceptualizes the research review as a scientific inquiry involving five stages that parallel those in primary research: problem formulation, data collection, data evaluation, analysis and interpretation, and public presentation. He then describes threats to validity that can occur at each stage. For example, in discussing data collection he identifies two potential sources of invalidity, both dealing with sampling. First, the reviewer may select a sample of research studies that is not representative of the total set of studies conducted on his research problem. Second, the individuals used in the selected studies may not be representative of the population to which results are to be generalized. Some characteristics of the population may be missing, while others may be overrepresented. Cooper also suggests ways of protecting the validity of the literature analysis at each stage.

Cooper's guidelines for conducting an integrative review are summarized in table 6.1.[14] In planning a review, the student should read Cooper's article and refer to this table. For example, suppose the student has developed a tentative literature review plan and wants to evaluate its soundness. Using Cooper's procedure, the student would analyze four main aspects of the plan (the four stage characteristics of the first column of table 6.1). Consider one such aspect, "Research question asked." The student would check the soundness of his research question formulation by answering the five questions across the top row of the table. If the student's plan deals adequately with all the questions and procedures listed in this table, he may feel confident that he will produce a thorough and valid integrative review of the findings relating to his research question.

FACTORS TO CONSIDER IN EVALUATING RESEARCH

Formulation of the Research Hypothesis or Objective

The first aspect of a research study that should be critically evaluated is the researcher's statement of her hypothesis or objective. Gerald Smith found that weaknesses in this area are a major reason why an average of 70 percent of research proposals submitted to the Cooperative Research Program (see chapter 2) were not recommend for funding.[15] Smith provides as an illustration a

---

14. See Cooper (1982) in Annotated References at the end of this chapter.
15. Gerald R. Smith. "A Critique of Proposals Submitted to the Cooperative Research Program," in *Educational Research: New Perspectives*, ed. Jack A. Culbertson and Stephan P. Hencley (Danville, Ill.: Interstate, 1963), pp. 277–87.

TABLE 6.1

The Integrative Review Conceptualized as a Research Project

Stage Characteristics	Stage of Research				
	Problem Formulation	Data Collection	Data Evaluation	Analysis and Interpretation	Public Presentation
Research question asked	What evidence should be included in the review?	What procedure should be used to find relevant evidence?	What retrieved evidence should be included in the review?	What procedures should be used to make inferences about the literature as a whole?	What information should be included in the review report?
Primary function in review	Constructing definitions that distinguish relevant from irrelevant studies.	Determining which potentially relevant studies to examine.	Applying criteria to separate "valid" from "invalid" studies.	Synthesizing valid retrieved studies.	Applying editorial criteria to separate important from unimportant information.
Procedural differences that create variation in review conclusions	1. Differences in abstractness of definition. 2. Differences in operational detail.	Differences in the research contained in sources of information.	1. Differences in quality criteria. 2. Differences in the influence of nonquality criteria.	Differences in rules of inference.	Differences in guidelines for editorial judgment.
Sources of potential invalidity in review conclusions	1. Narrow concepts may make review conclusions less general. 2. Superficial operational detail may obscure interacting variables.	1. Accessed studies may be qualitatively different from the target population of studies. 2. People sampled in accessible studies may be different from the target population.	1. Nonquality factors may cause improper weighting of study information. 2. Omissions in study reports may make conclusions unreliable.	1. Rules for distinguishing patterns from noise may be inappropriate. 2. Review-based evidence may be used to infer causality.	1. Omission of review procedures may make conclusions irreproducible. 2. Omission of review findings and study procedures may make conclusions obsolete.

proposal for an intended study of the role of the high school guidance counselor. This problem in itself is not trivial. However, the researcher's specific objective was to determine how counselors distribute their time between counseling, group procedures, and student appraisal. Not only do they overlap, but also these categories grossly oversimplify the role of the high school counselor. No matter how well executed such a study may be, the findings are likely to be of little significance.

In critically evaluating a research project, the student should also determine whether the research hypothesis or objective is specific and clearly stated. An ambiguous, broadly stated hypothesis is a sign that the researcher has not analyzed the problem in sufficient detail. Suppose the only statement of the researcher's hypothesis is that use of audiovisual materials in lectures will result in gains in student achievement. This hypothesis leaves many important questions unanswered. What types of lectures? What types of student achievement? What is the rationale or theoretical basis for the hypothesis? The unfortunate consequence of ambiguous, broadly stated hypotheses is that they yield only ambiguous, broadly stated conclusions when the study is completed. Suppose the hypothesis were not confirmed. What can one conclude about the value of audiovisual materials in lectures? Very little, since the hypothesis as stated provided little basis for expecting either positive or negative results. Therefore, as a first step in evaluating a research project, the student is advised to examine critically whether the researcher's hypothesis or objective was developed specifically from theory and previous research findings, and whether it meets the criteria presented in chapter 3.

Deliberate Bias or Distortion

The goal of research must be the discovery of scientific truth. Unfortunately, a few persons who carry out educational research are more interested in obtaining evidence to support a particular viewpoint than in discovering truth. Whenever the researcher has reasons for wanting her research to support a particular viewpoint, the likelihood of bias is greatly increased. Occasionally the individual will be so emotionally involved with her topic that she deliberately slants her findings or even structures her design to produce a predetermined result.[16] Such cases of deliberate bias are usually easy to detect because the same emotional involvement that motivates the individual to bias her work is usually reflected in her research report. Studies that are introduced with "this study was conducted to prove" must be considered suspect. The scientist does not carry out his work to prove a point, but to get an anwer.

16. P. Evans, "The Burt Affair—Sleuthing in Science," *APA Monitor*, no. 12 (1976): 1, 4.

The use of emotionally charged words, or slanted or intemperate language is the most obvious indicator of a biased viewpoint. For example, in reviewing the literature on aptitude testing, the authors found an article entitled "The Reign of ETS" (Educational Testing Service).[17] Since the word "reign" in this context appeared slanted, we were not surprised to find that article was highly critical of ETS and aptitude testing. Only quotations and studies illustrating the weaknesses of testing were cited. An unbiased article would have reviewed research on both sides of the issue in order that the reader could weigh the pros and cons and come to his own conclusions.

Occasionally, one encounters an article in which the investigator appears to be deliberately trying to mislead the reader. For example, misleading statistics are sometimes found in reports of survey research in which results are reported in percentages. In reviewing survey studies, the student should pay close attention to the number of cases upon which the percentages are based. If the number of cases is not reported, the reader should view the results with suspicion because they may be based on very few cases. To illustrate, David Martin discussed some misleading statistics published by the Children's Defense Fund in a report entitled *Children Out of School in America*.[18] The report stated that of all the secondary students who had been suspended more than once in census tract 22 in Columbia, South Carolina, 33 percent had been suspended two times and 67 percent had been suspended three or more times. Actually, the survey had found only three children in the entire census tract who had been suspended more than once. One of these children had been suspended twice and the other two children three or more times. Another part of the report stated that 25 percent of the sixteen- and seventeen-year-olds in a housing project in Portland, Maine, were out of school. The fact is that only eight children were surveyed, and two of them were found to be out of school. It may be seen from this example that very impressive percentages reported in survey research may be virtually meaningless if they are based on only a few cases. Such percentage data are especially suspect if published by an organization that is attempting to prove a point or build a case supporting a particular point of view.

The reader may also be misled by studies that report research results to several decimal places, thus creating the illusion that these results are highly accurate. W. P. Dickson attributes this tendency to the fact that many computer programs print the results of statisical analyses to several decimals.[19]

17. Allan Naire et al., "The Reign of ETS," *Today's Education* 69 (1980): 58–64.
18. David L. Martin, "Firsthand Report: How Flawed Statistics Can Make an Ugly Picture Look Even Worse," *American School Board Journal* 162, no. 3 (1975): 57–59.
19. W. P. Dickson, "Insignificant Figures, Statistical Insignificance, and Misconclusions," *Journal of Research in Science Teaching* 10, no. 2 (1973): 183–85.

Few, if any, measures employed in education are sufficiently accurate to justify reporting results to more than two decimal places.

Another form of deliberate bias occurs when researchers focus on surprising or newsworthy findings, while minimizing weaknesses in the research that reduce the validity or generalizability of the findings. Often the complete research report clearly states the limitations of the research, but these are omitted in speeches, shorter articles for "popular consumption," or news interviews. As a result, the researcher gets a good deal of publicity and the public is misled. Other researchers invariably challenge such biased reporting, but these challenges, however valid, are rarely reported in mass media.[20]

Even when a scientist attempts to report his findings objectively, they will usually be distorted by mass media in order to make them brief, interesting, and "more newsworthy." Thus the student is well advised to believe nothing about scientific research that he reads in the newspapers until he has checked the facts in the original research report.

Nondeliberate Bias

The student should remember that we are all products of an environment that subtly shapes and distorts our perceptions in innumerable ways. As a result, biases can influence the work of even the most competent scientists without their awareness of what is happening. Sir Francis Galton, for example, argued in his treatise *Hereditary Genius* that the English were superior intellectually to Africans because in almost every instance of conflict between the two, the English won. He overlooked the fact that the English had guns and the Africans had spears. To a less biased observer, differences in weaponry rather than differences in intelligence would be a more tenable explanation of the English victories.[21]

The researcher who has an emotional stake in the outcome of the research is especially susceptible to bias. Many persons who are emotionally involved with the topic of their research will not deliberately bias their research. Nevertheless, a strong likelihood of bias exists because the person may unconsciously slant his work in a hundred different ways. He may make certain systematic "errors" in sampling, in selecting measures, in scoring the responses of his subjects, in the way he treats his subjects, in his observations

---

20. See Russell H. Weigal and Jeffrey J. Pappas, "Social Science and the Press, A Case Study and Its Implications," *American Psychologist* 36 (1981): 480–87, for an interesting report of this form of bias and the contribution to it by the news media.
21. See Frank P. Besag, "Social Darwinism, Race, and Research," *Educational Evaluation and Policy Analysis* 3 (1981): 55–69, for a discussion of racism as an influence in educational research.

of performance, in recording of research data, and in analyzing and interpreting his results, all of which tend to favor the outcome he wants.

Objectivity is always difficult to attain in research in the behavioral sciences and is probably impossible when the researcher is emotionally involved with his topic. The researcher should avoid working in such areas whenever possible. If his position is such that he must do research in an area where he is involved emotionally, he should have his design checked by several other researchers for omissions or unconscious biases. One of the authors was once directed to conduct a study comparing the effectiveness of air force second lieutenants who had received commissions through the Officer Candidate School (OCS) of the U.S. Air Force with those who had received commissions through the ROTC. Realizing some bias in favor of the OCS graduate, he had the design carefully checked by other psychologists. One phase of the experiment called for a comparative rating of the effectiveness of officers from the two groups in drilling a company of basic trainees. Officers to be evaluated were to be instructed to report to the drill field in khaki uniform. Raters were not to be told the source of commission of officers being rated. One psychologist, upon reviewing these plans, pointed out that the officers who had graduated from OCS would be immediately recognized as they were required to have their khaki shirts tailored to a close fit, while the ROTC officers wore loose-fitting shirts, which they purchased from the post exchange. Although trying, at least on the conscious level, to avoid bias in this research, the author had "forgotten" this difference in uniforms when designing the research. This clue to source of commission would have permitted the raters to have reflected their biases in their ratings. In summary, the student should look for the following clues when attempting to locate possible biases of the research worker in a research report:

1. Does the phraseology used suggest that the research worker is inclined to favor one side of the question?
2. Is emotional or intemperate language of either a favorable or unfavorable nature employed?
3. Does the person hold a theoretical position or have a stake in a particular point of view, or does he belong to a group (racial, vocational, religious, political, ethnic, etc.) that would predispose him in a given direction about the subject of his research?

Sampling Bias

All the points that must be remembered in setting up the procedures for selecting a sample for your own research should be applied to evaluating the sampling techniques used by other researchers. Sampling bias in one form or another probably weakens more educational studies than any other factors. (Sampling techniques are discussed in chapter 7.) Let us review some forms of sampling bias that should be looked for in evaluating the research of others.

1. *Did the study use volunteers?* Volunteer groups are rarely representative, differing at least in motivation level from nonvolunteers. Motivation is, of course, an extremely important variable in most educational research. A basic weakness of most questionnaire studies is that the persons responding are essentially "volunteers," who may differ greatly from the nonresponding subjects. The results of studies using volunteer groups can probably be safely applied to other volunteer groups, but not to the population from which the volunteers were drawn. In many field studies, however, such as research on teaching effectiveness, the results will probably be applied to volunteers in other teaching situations, so the use of volunteers is appropriate.

Because of the legal and ethical constraints discussed in chapter 4, many studies cannot be carried out with human subjects unless the informed consent of the subjects (or their parents in the case of minors) has been obtained. It is therefore pointless to reject all research that employs volunteers, since in most instances the choice is either to use volunteers or not do the research. Instead, the reviewer should review the characteristics of the volunteer sample reported by the researcher.

These characteristics, along with the information given in chapter 7 on frequently found characteristics of volunteer samples, should be considered by the reviewer. This will permit drawing tentative conclusions about the population from which the volunteers were obtained. In effect the reviewer can ask: "In what ways have the results of this study probably been altered because of the use of volunteers?" The reviewer can then reassess the results so as to determine their probable relevance to the population. Such adjustments, of course, will be crude approximations, but they still give the reviewer useful insights about the population. For example, in a study of the vocational aspirations of young adults, a volunteer sample might be expected to have higher aspirations than the population because volunteers are likely to be better educated, of higher social-class status, more intelligent, and higher in need for achievement.[22] Of course, these would not be characteristics of all volunteer samples, and the reviewer's interpretation of the results should also reflect information provided by the researcher about the specific volunteer sample.

2. *Have subjects been lost?* Studies reporting large losses of subjects in one or more of the groups involved can usually be expected to have sampling bias. The reason for this bias is that subjects are not lost on a random basis. The subjects lost will generally be different from the ones who remain with the

22. See R. Rosenthal and R. L. Rosnow (1975) in Annotated References at the end of this chapter.

study until its completion. The nature and magnitude of these differences, and therefore their effect upon the research results, are difficult to estimate. Another source of bias when subjects are lost in experimental studies is that different levels of attrition occur in experimental and control groups. For example, subjects in the experimental group are often required to complete a time-consuming treatment such as participating in a remedial writing program, while no special demands are made on the control group. Under these conditions the rate of attrition often will be much higher for the experimental group. Thus, even if the two groups were closely comparable at the outset, they may differ considerably at the end of the study because of this difference in attrition.

3. *In an effort to get subjects who differ in the variable being studied, have groups been selected that also differ in other important respects?* Causal-comparative studies often suffer from this form of sampling bias. Some of the early studies of relationships between cigarette smoking and lung cancer illustrate such bias. The "heavy smoker" samples were obtained in large cities, the "nonsmoker" samples came from rural areas. These two groups were vastly different in many factors other than smoking, such as living habits, amounts of impurities in the air breathed, and pressures of daily life. With sampling biases of this magnitude, it would be difficult for such studies to link lung cancer to smoking with any degree of confidence.

4. *Are subjects extremely nonrepresentative of the population?* Few educational studies are able to employ truly random or representative samples of national populations. Yet, unless samples are extremely biased, the results often have important implications for the population. For example, although no one would assert that a sample of poor readers taken from the different school districts in Los Angeles County is representative of the nation as a whole, a study involving this sample may well have national implications. This is because most American public schools have much in common, and pupils in a large heterogeneous area such as Los Angeles County who are having reading problems are probably quite similar to pupils in other areas of the country. As the sample becomes less heterogeneous and less representative, however, the general significance of the findings diminishes. Subjects from a single district may lead to a less useful study because of unique district policies concerning reading instruction. On the other hand, a study using subjects from an obviously nontypical school district, such as one in which 80 percent of the students are Chicano, may have no general implications because of the nonrepresentative nature of the group and the relationship between bilingualism and reading difficulties. Similarly, a study of attitudes toward blacks using a sample from New Orleans, or a study of attitudes toward smoking using a sample from Salt Lake City, would produce little information of general significance, although such studies might throw much light on the situation in the area sampled. Since most studies are unable to employ broad representative samples, the

investigator can help the reader interpret the findings by describing the sample in detail with emphasis upon the characteristics of the sample that are probably different than the broad population.

In some studies much more care is devoted to obtaining a representative experimental group than a representative control group. This difference probably stems from the erroneous notion of inexperienced researchers that the experimental group is far more important and that any subjects will serve for the control group. This form of bias often occurs in experimental studies of some types of exceptional children, such as the severely retarded, who occur rarely in the general population. In this case the investigator uses all the available exceptional children in his experimental group and then draws his control group from the normal population. All subjects in an experimental study should be drawn from the same population. Because the performance of the experimental group must be weighed against the control group, a biased control group can obviously lead to erroneous results. Thus, careless selection of the control group should be watched for. In reviewing the research of others, one must remember that nonrepresentative samples do not produce data of general significance; rather, they often yield results that are misleading and can lead to serious blunders if applied to the general population. When such a study is read, the findings must be interpreted with the sampling bias in mind.

Have Important Variables Been Overlooked?

The environments in which most educational studies are carried out are extremely complex, and as a result the investigator cannot control, and for that matter is usually not aware of, all the variables in the situation that might affect her results. Nevertheless, the researcher should be able to identify and should attempt to control the most important variables that relate to her research. Many studies are found in education that have overlooked or failed to control important variables. Such studies usually produce misleading results because the influence of the uncontrolled variable upon the dependent variable cannot be assessed. For example, many early studies comparing the effectiveness of televised instruction with conventional classroom instruction failed to control preparation time and teaching ability. The usual procedure was to select the best teacher available and give this person the full day to prepare a TV lesson. Progress of TV pupils was then compared with progress of pupils in conventional classrooms having average teachers who taught the usual four to six classes daily. The results, which were loudly hailed as proof that television had some intrinsic merit that greatly increased learning, were in fact nothing more than a demonstration that better teachers who have more preparation time do a better job. Better-controlled studies concerned with TV instruction showed little or no difference compared with conventional classroom instruction.

A study by C. R. Atherton attempted to compare the achievement of three groups of college students who had been exposed to the same content with lecture, discussion, and independent study methods.[23] Students in the lecture and discussion treatments were exposed to the material for three 50-minute periods. But students in the independent study treatment were given the material and *told* to study it for three hours during the week. There was no real control on how much time they devoted to study or when they studied. Therefore, students in this group could have studied more than three hours or not at all and could have studied immediately before their achievement was measured or immediately after they received the materials. This failure to control study time makes any comparison of the effectiveness of the three treatments meaningless.

David Warden describes several cases in which studies of children's language have provided conflicting results.[24] For example, a study by E. Clark found that two- to five-year-old children were deficient in their comprehension of the prepositions *in, on,* and *under* when they were required to place objects at locations specified by the prepositions (e.g., *on* the table or *under* the cot).[25] Clark had overlooked the fact that his procedure not only required comprehension of the prepositions but also involved the additional task of manipulating the objects. When R. Grieve and his associates separated comprehension from manipulation of the objects, they were able to demonstrate that two- and three-year-olds did comprehend these prepositions.[26]

Inasmuch as each of us brings a different background of perception and experience to focus upon a given problem, it is not surprising that one person may overlook the importance of a variable that is immediately apparent to another. The best way to avoid overlooking important variables in your own research is to have your design studied and criticized by several other researchers before starting to collect data. The previous research that the researcher reviews also exposes her to a number of different viewpoints about her research area and reduces her chances of overlooking or failing to control an important variable. Many such oversights can be traced to a careless and inadequate review of the literature.

23. C. R. Atherton, "Lecture, Discussion, and Independent Study Instructional Methods Revisited," *Journal of Experimental Education* 40 (1972): 24–28.
24. David A. Warden, "Experimenting With Children's Language," *British Journal of Psychology* 72 (1981): 217–22.
25. E. Clark, "Non-linguistic Strategies and the Acquisition of Word Meaning," *Cognition* 2 (1973): 161–82.
26. R. Grieve, R. Hoogenraad, and D. Murray, "On the Young Child's Use of Lexis and Syntax in Understanding Locative Instructions," *Cognition* 5 (1977): 235–50.

Critical Evaluation of Measurement Techniques

Many of the weaknesses and limitations of educational research can be attributed to the inadequacies of our measures. The tools and techniques of educational measurement available to us are often crude and of doubtful validity. A thorough check of all tests and measurement techniques reported in all studies reviewed would be a very time-consuming task, and it is not recommended for the student doing his first review of the literature. The student should make such a check, however, of the measures used in any studies that are of major importance in his review. Any study that has yielded findings that make an important contribution to the area of review or have an important bearing on the researcher's own design should be thoroughly checked. This review not only helps the student interpret relevant research but also helps him select measures for his own research. If standard measures are cited with which the student is not familiar, he should study a specimen set, consult the *Mental Measurements Yearbooks*, and check other sources of information (to be discussed in chapter 8). If the measure used is new or has been developed for the research being evaluated, the student should obtain a copy and weigh the measure carefully against his knowledge of test development techniques and the theoretical constructs upon which the measure is based. The findings of research that the student reads can only be evaluated after the measurement tools that produced these findings have been carefully appraised and the probable effects of flaws in these instruments have been considered.

Let us briefly summarize some of the questions that the student should ask when evaluating the measurement tools employed in research closely pertinent to his own topic.[27]

1. *What reliability data are available?* Reliability studies give us information on the degree to which a measure will yield similar results for the same subjects at different times or under different conditions. In other words, it gives us an estimate of consistency. Several procedures can be used to estimate reliability, and the type of reliability calculated and the reliability coefficient should both be checked. Since tests of very low reliability have large errors of measurement, they often obscure differences or relationships that would be revealed by the use of more reliable instruments. Thus, the student should consider carefully the possible effects of low reliability upon the reported results of studies he evaluates and should not reject a promising hypothesis for his own study because of negative findings based on unreliable measures.

2. *What validity evidence is available?* As discussed in chapter 8, there are four major types of validity. The validity evidence should be studied carefully

---

27. The procedures for evaluating tests are discussed in chapter 8.

because interpretation of the research results hinges on the validity of the measures upon which these results are based. The absence of extensive validity data in a new measure does not mean the measure lacks validity, but it definitely limits the interpretations that can be made. Many inexperienced research workers accept standardized educational measures at face value and assume that these measures are valid, although little evidence is put forth by the test publisher to support this assumption. In the case of measures of dubious validity it is generally safer to consider the results reported to be tentative at best.

3. *Is the measure appropriate for the sample?* In evaluating the research of others, you should remember that even a well-standardized and generally accepted measure will have little value if applied to an inappropriate sample. A typical mistake made by inexperienced researchers is to use a measure that is more appropriate for some subsamples of the research group than others, therefore biasing results in favor of the subsamples whose background gives them an advantage on the measure. Occasionally tests are employed that are either too easy or too difficult for the majority of the sample measured. For example, a study of achievement of children at different ability levels will have little meaning if the test used has too low a ceiling, thus limiting the level of achievement that a superior student can display.

4. *Are test norms appropriate?* Many educational research projects compare the performance of the research sample with normative data that have been provided with the measure. If normative data are to be used, the comparability between the research group and the test norm group should be checked. Some tests, although generally applicable to the sample tested, have single items that are invalid. Some of the older intelligence tests, for example, have drawings of such objects as automobiles, airplanes, and telephones that are so different in appearance from the form familiar to today's children that the test item so illustrated may have lost much of its validity. Such errors, although not immediately apparent to most adults, have a significant influence on test scores.

Subtle forms of measurement bias may also make significant differences in research findings. For example, the authors recently encountered a questionnaire being used in an educational follow-up study in which the respondent was to rate various aspects of a school attended using five quality levels. The quality levels provided were "excellent," "superior," "very good," "average," and "below average." It will be noted that, on this scale, average is not located in the middle of the alternate choices. When asked why the choices were arranged in this way, the research worker stated that he had observed in previous questionnaires that more responses occur above the average line of the scale, and he had, therefore, provided an extra classification on the above-average side. He was surprised to find that the ratings he had obtained in this follow-up study were somewhat higher than those obtained in previous studies of same school. When using the quality levels just mentioned, the mean response fell between the "superior" and "very good" categories as compared with a mean response between "average" and "good" in previous studies. This suggested a higher evaluation of the course of study being followed up. Actually, however, the errors of leniency and central tendency (see chapter 12) would lead most respondents to rate a course of study average or slightly above average if they had no strong feelings about it one way or the other. Because most people consider the average rating to be the one that falls in the middle, when the research worker changed the names of the categories, the respondents continued to check the middle category or the one adjacent to and higher than the middle. Thus, in terms of the mean position of the responses on a 5-point scale, no change occurred, but in terms of the adjectives employed, there was an apparent improvement in the respondents' evaluation of the school. Use of unbalanced response choices in which more opportunities are available for a favorable response than for an unfavorable response will tend to yield responses with a favorable bias. The danger of such biases is well known to experienced measurement specialists, and errors of the sort just described are more likely to be found in measures developed specifically for the research project by an inexperienced researcher. If the use of such measures is reported in research projects pertinent to the student's field of interest, he should request copies in order that he may study them for biases of the sort previously described.

Observer Bias

Human beings have a disturbing tendency to see what they want to see, hear what they want to hear, and remember what they want to remember. **Observer bias** has been recognized as a problem by workers in the physical sciences for centuries, and techniques to control such bias are routinely included in physical science experiments. Workers in the behavioral sciences not only have attempted to control observer errors, but also have studied these biases and found them to be much more subtle and complex than physical scientists had imagined.

J. Rostand tells a remarkable but true story that illustrates the dangers of observer bias, even in scientific areas such as physics that deal with phenomena that are much simpler, more concrete, and more adaptable to measurement than are the elusive substances of the behavioral sciences.[28] This example deals with the N ray, which was discovered by a distinguished French physicist, René Blondlot, while investigating X rays, which had been discovered a short time earlier by Röntgen. After discovering the N ray, Blondlot went on

28. Jean Rostand, *Error and Deception in Science* (New York: Basic Books, 1960).

to study its characteristics. He found the ray increased the brightness of any luminous object. A Nernst filament was found to be a rich source of N rays and produced a radiation so intense that Blondlot doubted that anyone with eyes could fail to see it. In fact, of the many persons who were permitted to observe these rays, Blondlot reports only three or four who failed to see them. As his experiments continued, Blondlot discovered that the sun was a source of N rays. He learned that N rays could be stored in certain substances such as quartz and later reemitted. Further experiments revealed that external stresses caused certain substances to emit N rays. Finally, Blondlot set up a series of careful experiments using three independent measures that resulted in measuring the wavelength of the N ray. The results of measurements using the three different approaches were highly consistent. By February 1904, photographs had been taken that showed the effect of N rays on an electric spark. Upon this discovery Bordier, lecturer at Lyons Medical School, rebuked the few doubters who had not been able to see the N ray by pointing out:

> Such observers have only themselves to blame; no doubt they used faulty techniques or else the source of radiation was impaired; in any case, the existence of N rays will never again be put in doubt, particularly now that their action has been recorded *photographically*, i.e., by a purely objective method. (p. 18)

Other researchers now began to report extensive findings from their experiments on the N ray. The experiments of one scientist revealed that sound vibrations gave rise to N rays; another found N rays emitted from a magnetic field, another from liquefied gases, and so on.

Charpentier, professor of biophysics at Nancy, discovered that N rays were liberated from the muscles and nerves of living animals and concluded that these rays might play a fundamental role in biology. Because N rays were emitted from nerves, studies of the anatomy of the nervous system became possible and were started. This technique, of course, had very important implications for medical science. For example, research workers soon discovered that changes in N radiation occurred as a consequence of certain diseases of the nervous system.

In 1904, less than two years after Blondlot had reported his original work, an imposing body of knowledge had been amassed concerning the N ray. Yet we hear nothing about N rays today. The fact is that *the N ray does not and never did exist*, and within a few short months after these later discoveries, the entire edifice erected by Blondlot and his colleagues had tumbled down.

Doubting voices had been raised from the very beginning of Blondlot's discovery and some specialist objections had never been silenced effectively. Still, no amount of doubting or criticism had been able to halt the triumphant progress of the new science. All the world had clearly observed a phenomenon that had never existed. Then, almost overnight, the hypnotic spell was broken.

The Nancy group and some of its faithful managed to put up some slight resistance, but the whole business was dropped and buried once for all. N-rays, N_1-rays, and physiological radiations would never again grace the pages of scientific journals, in which they had cut so marvellous a figure. . . .

The most astonishing facet of the episode is the extraordinarily great number of people who were taken in. These people were not pseudo-scientists, charlatans, dreamers, or mystifiers; far from it, they were true men of science, disinterested, honourable, used to laboratory procedure, people with level heads and sound common sense. This is borne out by their subsequent achievements as Professors, Consultants and Lecturers. Jean Becquerel, Gilbert Ballet, Andre Broca, Zimmern, Bordier—all of them have made their contribution to science.

No less extraordinary is the *degree of consistency, and of apparent logic that pervaded the whole of this collective delusion;* all the results were consistent, and agreed within fairly narrow limits. . . .

While we have no evidence that flattery or deception was at the roots of the discovery of N-rays, we may take it that the urge to make new discoveries, so powerful in all men of science, played a considerable role from the very start. Coupled with this urge were *preconceived ideas, and autosuggestion* together with the desire to break new ground.

The remarkable history of N-rays is full of morals both for the individual, and also for the social psychologist.[29]

Although observations are sometimes deliberately biased by the researcher with an ax to grind, the more serious danger is from biases of which the researcher is unaware, such as those that occurred in research on the N ray. These undeliberate and unconscious observer biases are often not detectable from the usual research report that appears in the professional journal. For example, an interviewer may unconsciously give the subject subtle signs of approval and disapproval of different responses that will tend to encourage the subject to give the approved answer whether it is true or not. Although the information available to the student is too limited for him to expect to detect many such biases, he should, nonetheless, search carefully for evidence of their existence, and weigh their possible effects when they are discovered.

The methods of descriptive research, especially interview and observation

29. Ibid., pp. 27–29.

studies, are perhaps most susceptible to observer bias. Let us review some of the main sources of such bias that the student should watch for in critically evaluating descriptive research:

1. Does the interview guide contain leading questions? Is it structured in such a way to give the subject clues as to the preferred answer?
2. Does the observer's or interviewer's method of recording behavior or responses permit undue emphasis upon behavior that is in accordance with observer biases or expectations? The use of tape recordings greatly reduces danger of this bias.
3. Do methods of recording behavior require that the observer or interviewer draw inferences about the meaning of the behavior he is observing? In general, the more inferences the observer must draw, the more the likelihood of bias. For example, an observer can usually record low-inference data such as the number of questions a teacher asks more accurately than high-inference data such as a rating of the cognitive level of each teacher question or a rating of the teacher's voice modulation used in asking each question.
4. Are questions asked that might threaten, embarrass, or annoy some respondents, thus leading them to give false or unsatisfactory replies?
5. Does the observer know the expected outcomes of the research? If the observer knows that the group he is observing has been exposed to treatment that is expected to bring about certain changes in behavior, he is more likely to see these changes than when observing a group that has not been exposed to the treatment. In a review of four studies of observer errors, Rosenthal reported that over 70 percent of the recording errors found in these studies were biased in the direction of the observers' hypotheses.[30] Recent experiments that deliberately manipulate observers' expectations further confirmed this kind of bias.[31]

EFFECTS RELATED TO THE RESEARCH SITUATION

The Hawthorne Effect

In experiments involving human subjects, a great many subtle influences can distort research results. If an individual is aware that he is participating in an experiment, for example, this knowledge may alter his performance and there-

---

30. See Rosenthal and Rosnow in Annotated References at the end of this chapter.
31. See Ennio Cipani and Vicki A. Waite, "Experimenter Bias Effects: A Direct Replication," *Perceptual and Motor Skills* 51 (1980): 129–30.

fore invalidate the experiment. A series of studies carried out at the Hawthorne Plant of the Western Electric Company first called attention to some of these factors.[32] In this study the illumination of three departments in which employees inspected small parts, assembled electrical relays, and wound coils was gradually increased. The production efficiency in all departments generally went up as the light intensity increased. It was found, however, that upon decreasing the light intensity in a later experiment, the efficiency of the group continued to increase slowly but steadily. Further experiments, with rest periods and varying the length of working days and weeks, were also accompanied by gradual increases in efficiency whether the change in working conditions was for the better or for the worse. It appears that the attention given the employees during the experiment was the major factor leading to these production gains. This phenomenon is referred to by psychologists as the **Hawthorne Effect.** The factory workers who carried out the same dull, repetitive task month after month were stimulated and motivated by the attention and concern for their well-being displayed by the research workers. A new element had been added to their dull existence—not illumination or the other variables that the researchers were studying, but the researchers themselves.

The term Hawthorne Effect has come to refer to any situation in which the experimental conditions are such that the mere fact that the subject is participating in an experiment or is receiving special attention tends to improve performance. Certainly many educational experiments report changes and improvements that are due primarily to the Hawthorne Effect. For example, research in which one group of teachers continues with the same teaching methods it has previously employed while another group is trained in a new method and receives considerable help and attention in implementing this method will usually result in changes in teacher performance or pupil achievement favorable to the new methods. Many school districts, in the process of trying out new methods, frequently set up a one-year experiment in which the new method is introduced to a limited number of pupils. The results of such experiments are almost certainly influenced by the Hawthorne Effect because teachers usually approach a new method with some enthusiasm; and the students, aware that they are being taught by a new and different method, are also likely to display more interest and motivation than usual. The influence of the Hawthorne Effect can be expected to decrease as the novelty of the new method wears off, and, therefore, studies extending over a period of two or three years can be relied upon somewhat more in evaluating the effectiveness of a new technique.

It is interesting that attempts to manipulate the Hawthorne Effect experi-

32. F. J. Roethlisberger and W. J. Dickson, *Management and the Worker* (Cambridge, Mass.: Harvard University Press, 1940).

mentally have failed to produce evidence of the effect.[33] However, there is much indirect evidence that the effect operates in some studies. The prudent researcher should take steps to reduce the novelty of experimental treatments and the awareness of participation in a research project that may contribute to this effect. Such precautions will improve the research design whether or not the Hawthorne Effect occurs.

The John Henry Effect

The legend of John Henry tells of a black railroad worker who pitted his strength and skill at driving steel railroad spikes againt a steam driver that was being tested experimentally as a possible replacement for the human steel drivers. The **John Henry Effect** refers to a situation often found in educational research in which a control group performs above its usual average when placed in competition with an experimental group that is using a new method or procedure that threatens to replace the control procedure. This phenomenon is probably quite common in educational studies in which a conventional teaching methodology is being compared with a new methodology. Teachers in the control group feel threatened by the new methodology and make a strong effort to prove that their way of teaching is as good as the new method.

This effect was named and described by Robert Heinich in 1970 while reviewing studies that compared televised instruction with regular classroom teaching. He found that the classroom teachers in the control group often made a "maximum" effort, and thus their students' performance matched the performance of students who viewed televised instruction.[34] Since Heinich's work, several studies have been conducted in which the John Henry Effect appears to have operated because unusual effort in the control group has been observed, and control subjects matched or exceeded the performance of experimental subjects. Gary Saretsky, who conducted much of the study of this phenomenon, concluded that the John Henry Effect is likely to occur when an innovation is introduced in such a manner as to be perceived as threatening to jobs, status, salary, or traditional work patterns.[35]

---

33. See Desmond L. Cook, *The Impact of the Hawthorne Effect in Experimental Designs in Educational Research* (Washington, D.C.: U.S. Office of Education, 1967). Also see Robert H. Bauernfeind and Carl J. Olson, "Is the Hawthorn Effect in Educational Experiments a Chimera?" *Phi Delta Kappan* 53 (1973): 271–73; and Patricia A. Rubeck, "Hawthorne Concept—Does It Affect Reading Progress?" *Reading Teacher* 28 (1975): 375–79.
34. Robert Heinich, *Technology and the Management of Instruction* (Washington, D.C.: Department of Audiovisual Instruction, 1970).
35. Gary Saretsky, "The John Henry Effect: Potential Confounder of Experimental vs. Control Group Approaches to the Evaluation of Educational Innovations" (paper presented at the annual meeting of the American Educational Research Association, Washington, D.C., 2 April 1975).

One of the authors of this text encountered this phenomenon in a study in which teachers who had been trained in verbal skills designed to improve pupil achievement were compared with teachers who had not received the training. In order to provide comparable pupil achievement data, a one-week curriculum unit was developed, and teachers in both experimental and control groups were asked to teach this unit. Observation indicated that not only were the control-group teachers devoting a great deal of time to their preparation to teach the unit, but they were also observed to be using many of the skills that had been taught to the experimental-group teachers. A questionnaire sent to both groups of teachers revealed that over half of the control-group teachers had obtained some of the training materials from the experimental group. At the outset of the study, the experimental-group teachers had been asked not to share any training materials with the control teachers. However, it is obviously difficult for teachers to refuse requests of their colleagues, since many of the experimental-group teachers did make the training materials available. The result, of course, was to reduce the apparent effects of the training, since the control-group teachers were obviously making a major effort to prove that they were as good as the experimental-group teachers and had learned many of the same skills that had been taught to the experimental group.

The John Henry Effect in educational studies probably reflects in part the competitive desire to prove that "I can do just as well as those people who are being trained." It is also probable that persons who know that they are members of a control group feel psychologically threatened by a situation in which they feel they are likely to come out second best.

Saretsky provides convincing evidence that the John Henry Effect resulted in a marked increase in the achievement in control-group classrooms when these classrooms were compared with classrooms in which performance contracting was employed.[36] He obtained data on performance of the control subjects for the two years prior to the experimental year. These data showed that during the experimental year control-group gains in mathematics as measured by standardized tests were much higher than in the two preceding years. Since performance contracting is very threatening to teachers, it seems obvious that the control teachers made a very strong effort during the year of the experiment.

It is fairly easy to confuse the John Henry Effect with the Hawthorne Effect. The two have somewhat opposite effects on an experiment, however, because the Hawthorne Effect reflects the impact of being part of an experiment upon the experimental group's performance, whereas the John Henry Effect reflects the impact upon the control group in experiments where the

36. Gary Saretsky, "The OEO P.C. Experiment and the John Henry Effect," *Phi Delta Kappan* 53 (1972): 579–81.

experimental group is perceived as competing with or threatening to surpass the control group.

The Pygmalion Effect

This effect takes its name from a controversial study by Robert Rosenthal and Lenore Jacobson, reported in *Pygmalion in the Classroom.*[37] These researchers demonstrated that teachers' expectations about their students' intelligence in some cases appeared to bring about changes in the students' intelligence test scores. Thus, the term **Pygmalion Effect** has come to refer to changes in the subject's behavior that are brought about by the experimenter's expectations. The effect has been replicated in some studies, but not in others. In any case, the possibility that this effect can occur should alert the researcher to the importance of *not* conveying *her expectations* to the subject.

Demand Characteristics

An important characteristic of human subjects when they are participants in an experiment is that they do not perceive their participation as an isolated event but instead try to relate it to past experience and the total context of the experimental situation. In other words, they are likely to be sensitive to all aspects of the research environment and to use cues present in that environment to come to conclusions as to what the experiment is attempting to achieve, what is expected of them as subjects in the experiment, and what the researcher hopes to find. M. T. Orne has used the term **demand characteristics** to describe all the cues available to the subject regarding the nature of the research.[38] These can include rumors about the research, the setting, instructions given to the research subject, the status and personality of the experimenter, subtle clues provided by the experimenter, and the experimental procedure itself.

Orne and his associates have carried out a number of studies designed to explore the effects of demand characteristics on the performance of subjects. In one of these studies, the demand characteristics were deliberately manipulated in order to measure their effects on the outcome of an experiment.[39] Both groups of subjects were told that the study was designed to determine the

37. Robert Rosenthal and Lenore Jacobson, *Pygmalion in the Classroom* (New York: Holt, Rinehart and Winston, 1968).
38. Martin T. Orne, "Demand Characteristics and the Concept of Quasi-Controls," in *Artifact in Behavioral Research*, ed. R. Rosenthal and R. L. Rosnow (New York: Academic Press, 1969).
39. Lawrence A. Gustafson and Martin T. Orne, "Effects of Perceived Role and Role Success on the Detection of Deception," *Journal of Applied Psychology* 49 (1965): 412–17.

effectiveness of the lie detector. However, one group was told that it was not possible to detect lying in the case of psychopathic personalities or habitual liars. The investigators hypothesized that this group would want to be detected in order to demonstrate that they were not psychopaths or habitual liars. Instructions for the other group stipulated that while it is extremely difficult to deceive the lie detector, this can be done by highly intelligent, emotionally stable, very mature persons. These instructions would create a desire on the part of the subjects to deceive the lie detector in order to appear highly intelligent, emotionally stable, and mature. The results show very large differences in the hypothesized direction between the number of persons whose lies were detected and not detected in the two groups. Since all other conditions of the experiment were identical for the two groups, this would clearly illustrate the tremendous power of demand characteristics to lead to markedly different behavior on the part of subjects.

Orne suggests three ways that the researcher can gain insight into the demand characteristics of an experiment. This information is necessary to estimate the possible effects of these cues on the performance of subjects or to determine how to restructure the research to eliminate research conditions that can distort results. The first of these is to interview subjects after the experiment in order to learn their perceptions of the experimental situation. A second procedure is to conduct preinquiry interviews with a group of subjects from the same population that will be employed in the experiment. In this case, the experimental procedures are explained to the preinquiry group in such a way as to provide them with the same information that would be available to the experimental subject. The preinquiry group, however, does not go through the experimental procedure. The participant is then asked to produce data of a type similar to what he would have produced if he had actually been subjected to the experimental treatment. If the data produced under these conditions are similar to the data obtained in the experiment, it shows that subjects in the actual experiment could have guessed what was expected of them. In a third procedure, subjects are asked to behave as if exposed to the experimental treatment, which they did not actually receive. In this case, a naive experimenter observes these "simulators," but he is unaware of the fact that they are simulating the experimental effects. Since the simulators are given no information about the experiment other than that which would be available to the actual research subjects, they must guess what the subjects might do in the experimental conditions. If their behavior is similar to that of the real subjects, it would indicate that the regular subjects could be responding to the demand characteristics rather than to the experimental treatment in the same manner as the simulators.

A number of behavioral scientists have recently studied demand characteristics, their theoretical foundation, and procedures that can be used to minimize their effect. Much of this work has been reviewed by Ralph Rosnow and D. J. Davis.[40] They concluded that in order for demand characteristics to affect research findings, two requirements must be met. First, the demand characteristics must be "received" by the subject, that is, he must be sensitive to or aware of the experimental conditions. Second, the subject must be motivated to respond to the demand characteristics. The most common response is probably to acquiesce, that is, to play the role of a "good subject." Some subjects may be counter-acquiescent, however, and may perform in a manner opposite to the way they perceive the investigator's expectations or desires. Of course, both types of response tend to distort the results of the research.

To reduce the subject's response to demand characteristics, Rosnow and Davis recommend that the researcher use procedures (1) to reduce the clarity of the demand characteristics, (2) to generate alternative demand characteristics that will not influence the research findings, and (3) to reduce the subject's motivation to respond to the demand characteristics. Specific procedures that can help achieve these three goals are summarized below.

Procedures for Reducing Artifact Influences in Laboratory Settings[41]

I. Receptivity Manipulations
  A. Minimize demand clarity
    1. Measure the dependent variable in a remote setting not obviously connected to the treatment setting.
    2. Measure the dependent variable removed in time from the treatment.
    3. Avoid pretesting by using posttest only or interchangeable groups designs.
    4. Use unobtrusive measures.
    5. Use "blind" procedures, i.e., keep the experimenter's knowledge of the research to a minimum.
    6. Standardize and restrict the experimenter's communication with the subjects. (Since the experimenter is the main channel for communicating demand characteristics, minimize his capacity to transmit such information.)
  B. Generate alternative demands
    1. Elicit false hypotheses about the purpose of the experiment. The false demand characteristics should be selected so that they will not interfere with possible research outcomes.

40. See Annotated References at the end of this chapter.
41. Adapted from Ralph L. Rosnow and D. J. Davis, "Demand Characteristics and the Psychological Experiment," *Et Cetera* 34 (1977): 301–13.

    2. Have the subjects play the role of experimenter's aide. This increases the probability that the subject will focus on the false demand characteristics as he plays his role as "experimenter."

II. Motivational Manipulations

    A. Give feedback of compliant behavior in a set of preexperimental trials.

    B. Maintain subject anonymity.

    C. Make the experimental setting and procedures low-keyed.

    D. Disclose the use of deception and enlist the subject's support.

    E. Use "bogus pipeline" to get the subject to monitor his behavior and reject demand-compliant responses. In the "bogus pipeline" the subject is told that a physiological monitoring device used in the experiment can detect when he is lying, thus motivating him to give honest responses rather than responses that acquiesce to demand characteristics.

    F. Use measures that require behavioral commitment as opposed to verbal report of commitment. For example, asking for a commitment to donate blood is more likely to elicit an honest response than merely asking for a verbal response indicating willingness to do so.

The effect of the cues available in the experimental situation upon the performance of subjects is probably a more important factor in psychological laboratory studies, such as Orne carried out, than in naturalistic field studies of the type frequently carried out in education. Furthermore, the college students who were the subjects in Orne's studies are probably much more perceptive of the demand characteristics of the experiment and more likely to respond to these cues than a child in an educational research project would. Nevertheless, in all likelihood changes in a subject's behavior related to the research situation occur to a degree in most studies in which the subject is aware of the fact that he has participated in an experiment. For example, Orne points out that in studies in which subjects see themselves as being evaluated, they will usually behave in such a way as to make themselves look good. This attempt to look good under research conditions is common in educational studies and is an important factor in both the Hawthorne Effect and the John Henry Effect.

PLACEBOS

A **placebo** is a chemically inert substance administered in the same manner as the drug or active substance under investigation. Placebos are employed in medical research and in educational and psychological studies in which the effects of various substances on human behavior are being tested. The purpose of the placebo is to make it impossible for subjects to determine whether or not they are receiving the active substance under study as this knowledge may have an effect upon their behavior. Many studies have demonstrated that if one group of subjects receives some sort of attention, such as the administration of a drug, while the control group receives no comparable attention, some of those receiving the drug will react in ways that cannot be explained by the chemical or medical effects of the drug. Although relatively little is known about the psychological factors causing such reactions, it seems likely that the human contact with the researcher and the subject's expectation that something will occur as a result of the substance received contribute significantly.

The results of drug studies that do not use placebos are always subject to doubt because the proportion of the effect that is attributable to psychological factors and the proportion that is caused by the drug cannot be determined. The placebo, in effect, acts as a control, permitting the psychological factors to operate. The physical or behavioral changes brought about by the active substance cannot operate in control-group subjects because the active substance is not present in the placebo.

In recent years the term *placebo* has been used in a broader sense to describe a control treatment that gives subjects the same amount and kind of attention as the experimental treatment but is unrelated to the dependent variable. For example, in a recent study aimed at reducing depression in children, the placebo treatment was of the same duration and in a similar format as the experimental treatments, but dealt with problems unrelated to depression.[42]

Even when placebos are used, it has been found that if the experimenter knows which subjects received the active substance and which subjects received the placebo, this knowledge can lead to observer bias. For example, the researcher unconsciously may give the subject subtle cues, such as watching for reactions more attentively in cases where subjects have received the active substance. Therefore, most studies aimed at evaluating the effects of drugs or other substances now employ what is called the "doubleblind" technique, in which neither the experimenter nor the subject knows when the active substance or when the placebo is being taken. Obviously, in order to achieve this degree of control, the placebo must be identical to the active drug in those characteristics that may be compared by the subject, such as appearance and taste.

42. L. Butler, S. Miezitis, R. Friedman, and E. Cole, "The Effect of Two School-Based Intervention Programs on Depressive Symptoms in Preadolescents," *American Educational Research Journal* 17 (1980): 111–19.

Although placebos play a useful role in helping to control psychological variables, many researchers fail to recognize that the control is still subject to error. If subjects know the active drug being used and its probable effect, those subjects who receive the placebo may react in the manner expected. For example, if subjects know that the active drug is a sleeping pill, they may exhibit a drowsy reaction to the placebo. The fact that these control subjects react like the subjects who received the drug would not negate the possibility of real drug effects. This error, of course, cannot occur if subjects do not know the expected effect of the drug being used.

Medical studies have demonstrated that there is considerable individual difference in reaction to placebos. Some individuals tend to react to placebos, while others do not. For example, some hospital patients will consistently report a reduction in pain following the administration of an inert substance, whereas others will not. Persons may show either a positive or negative reaction to the placebo. H. K. Beecher found that the incidence of relief reported in fifteen studies involving medical placebos ranged from 15 to 58 percent. However, he also found thirty-five different toxic effects that occurred after the administration of placebos.[43]

Persons who respond to placebos are referred to as "placebo reactors." There is some question as to whether this is an enduring trait or whether it varies with the situation; that is, a person may be a placebo reactor in one situation but not in another.[44] In small sampling studies, there is always a possibility that the control group will contain a larger number of placebo reactors than the experimental group. If this is the case, the results of the experiment may be negative, even though the active substance being tested has a definite effect upon the experimental subjects. Some studies have shown that if placebo reactors are screened out, significant differences sometimes emerge that would not show up otherwise.[45] As yet we know very little about the degree to which some persons are consistently placebo reactors, or whether such persons differ in personality or other respects from individuals who do not react to placebos. Some evidence suggests that these differences do exist, and until we know more about placebo reaction, differences in consistency can considerably distort research findings involving small samples.[46]

43. H. K. Beecher, "The Powerful Placebo," *American Medical Association Journal* 159 (1955): 1602–05.
44. Patricia J. Aletky and Albert S. Carlin, "Sex Differences and Placebo Effects: Motivation as an Intervening Variable," *Journal of Consulting and Clinical Psychology* 43, no. 2 (1975): 278.
45. H. K. Beecher, A. S. Keats, F. Mosteller, and L. Lasagna, "The Effectiveness of Oral Analgesics (Morphine, Codeine, Acetylsalicylic Acid) and the Problem of Placebo 'Reactors' and 'Nonreactors,'" *Journal of Pharmacology and Experimental Therapeutics* 109 (1953): 393–400.
46. L. Lasagna, J. Mosteller, J. M. von Felsinger, and H. K. Beecher, " A Study of the Placebo Response," *American Journal of Medicine* 16 (1954): 770–79.

Placebos in Educational Research

Few studies in educational research employ placebos to control psychological factors.[47] In educational research, however, psychological factors can differentially affect experimental and control groups in situations where no treatment is given the control group. Therefore, it is advisable to use a "placebo treatment" for control groups so that the experimental and control conditions are psychologically similar for all subjects. For example, if a new remedial mathematics program is being administered in experimental classrooms, the researcher could introduce a new music appreciation program of similar duration into control classrooms. The music program would have no effect on mathematics achievement, but would make the two treatments more similar because all classrooms are trying out a new program.

In evaluating educational research, the reviewer should be alert to studies that employ control groups that do not receive the treatment or recognition given to the experimental group. These studies are much more susceptible to the Hawthorne Effect and the John Henry Effect than those in which some sort of control treatment is employed.

EXPERIMENTER AND STATISTICAL CONTAMINATION

Contamination refers to any situation in which data that should be kept independent to satisfy the requirements for sound research have in some way become interrelated. Faulty research design often permits contamination to occur in educational studies. Contamination, in turn, tends to bias the results of the study. We discuss various ways in which contamination can weaken research design in later chapters. The major sources of contamination, as they affect interpretation of published research, are described below.

Experimenter Contamination

Experimenter contamination usually arises when the research worker has knowledge of the subject's performance on the independent variable, and this knowledge influences his observation of the behavior of the subject on the dependent variable. Let us suppose, for example, that we are doing a study of the relationship between the amount of conflict present in the home environment of the child (independent variable) and behavior in the classroom involv-

47. For a recent study that used placebos in educational research, see Carol K. Whalen et al., "A Social Ecology of Hyperactive Boys: Medication Effects in Structured Classroom Environments," *Journal of Applied Behavior Analysis* 12 (1979): 65–81.

ing direct and indirect aggression (dependent variable). If the observer collected data on conflicts in the home prior to carrying out his classroom observations, there would be a strong possibility that his knowledge of the child's home environment would influence his interpretation of the child's aggressive behavior in the classroom. In other words, if he had hypothesized that children coming from home environments involving conflicts would display more direct aggression in the classroom, he would tend to look for signs of direct aggression in these children and would be likely to see more direct aggression and interpret questionable behavior as direct aggression.

Experimenter contamination is not limited to studies in which the researcher uses observational techniques. Any situation that requires the research worker to obtain data (interviews, individual testing, etc.) on one variable that could influence his perception of another variable is subject to this form of contamination.

Statistical Contamination

Statistical contamination occurs when data that have in some way become related are treated as being independent in the statistical analysis. An example of statistical contamination was encountered by one of the authors in the work of one of his doctoral candidates. The student was carrying out a study of characteristics related to success of elementary school principals. The design called for the participation of each person to be evaluated in six role-playing situations. In each situation the subject was evaluated independently by two raters on a number of pertinent behaviors. These specific evaluations were combined in order to provide an overall evaluation of the individual as a principal. In carrying out the analysis, the student found a high correlation between observer ratings in the specific area of "human relations skills" and the overall evaluations of the individual's effectiveness. From this correlation he concluded that "human relations skills" constituted by far the most important factor in the effective performance of elementary school principals. He had failed to realize, however, that because the overall rating also included the rating of human relations skills, which was the most heavily weighted of the specific rating areas, he was in effect correlating human relations skills with itself to the extent that it was part of the overall rating. Such correlations are, of course, spurious and indicate statistical contamination.

CRITICAL EVALUATION OF STATISTICAL ANALYSES

As part of Wandt's study of the quality of educational research articles, which we discussed previously, a panel of experts was asked to identify shortcomings of articles that were rated "revise" or "reject." The two most frequently cited shortcomings were that the results of statistical analyses were not clearly presented and that incorrect statistical methods were used to analyze data. Gallagher's review of research in science education also cited inappropriate statistical treatment of data as a frequent error. Therefore, the student is advised to check carefully the appropriateness of statistical analyses presented in journal articles.

The first step in evaluating the statistical analyses used in a study is to see what information is reported. Many studies fail to report the minimum statistical information needed to evaluate the findings that have been reported. To illustrate, a survey of 33 randomly selected research articles by Alan Michalczyk and Lloyd Lewis found that 14 failed to report the standard deviation.[48] The mean and standard deviation of scores on each variable for each group of subjects involved in a study are essential to estimating the magnitude of treatment effects.

Other information that should be given in a research report includes the alpha level selected to reject the null hypothesis, the significance level of the obtained results, the sample size, and the specific statistical procedures employed.

If the researchers have reported this information, the next step is to check the results for possible errors. Many types of errors may be present in the statistical analysis of research data. As they acquire more training and experience with statistical tools, students become increasingly able to detect such mistakes. Often statistical errors occur simply because the researcher does not know how to use a particular statistical technique. For example, the researcher may use a t test to determine the statistical significance of a difference between mean scores, and in the process of doing the computations, she will compute the wrong degrees of freedom. Also the wrong statistical technique may be selected. The researcher may select a parametric statistical technique even though the distribution of scores is badly skewed; when this situation occurs, a nonparametric technique should be used. Another weakness of some statistical analyses is that they are carried out only for the total sample and not for subgroups as well. For example, the researcher may find a significant correlation between two variables in a sample of students. Assuming adequate sample size, the researcher should then determine whether the correlation also exists for selected subgroups, such as boys versus girls and students at different grade levels.

Errors frequently occur in the interpretation of statistical findings. Researchers often have a tendency to confuse the statistical significance of re-

48. Alan E. Michalczyk and Lloyd A. Lewis, "Significance Alone Is Not Enough," *Journal of Medical Education* 55 (1980): 834–38.

search results with their practical significance. An illustration of this point can be found in a study of readability of science materials.[49] In this generally well-designed study, the investigator determined the effect on student comprehension of rewriting a sixth-grade science textbook to a third-grade level of readability. The experimental group received the rewritten reading material, while the control group received the original text. On a test of comprehension of the reading passages, it was found that the experimental group scored significantly higher ($p<.05$) than the control group. There is no problem with the statistical analysis so far. However, on the basis of this finding, the investigator recommends that sixth-grade science textbooks be rewritten by publishers and by teachers during summer writing conferences. Is this recommendation, which entails a good deal of work for educators, warranted by the statistical findings? When we look at the data more closely, we find that the comprehension test administered to all students contained 129 items. The mean scores of the experimental and control groups on this test were 75.97 and 73.48, respectively. Thus there is a difference of only 2.5 items between the two groups on a test containing 129 items. The difference is statistically significant, but this can be attributed to the fact that a very large sample (417 students) was used. Even a very small difference between mean scores is likely to be statistically significant with this large a sample. In short, the research results achieve statistical significance, but they can hardly be said to have significance for educational practice. In critically evaluating research, the student should make a point of checking that the investigator has not "overinterpreted" the results of the statistical analyses.

MISTAKES SOMETIMES MADE IN CRITICALLY EVALUATING RESEARCH

1. Researcher gives equal weight to good and weak studies.
2. Fails to pull together evidence from all related studies in order to get an overall understanding of the state of knowledge.
3. Fails to weigh the possible effects of sampling bias in appraisal of the reported research results.
4. Overestimates the importance of research findings that are statistically significant but have no practical significance.
5. Does not detect important errors and then repeats these errors in his own research.

49. D. L. Williams, "Rewritten Science Materials and Reading Comprehension," *Journal of Educational Research* 61 (1968): 204–6.

6. Conducts her critical evaluation too late to apply what has been learned to her own research.
7. Overlooks situations that permit observer bias to occur.

ANNOTATED REFERENCES

Adair, J. G., and Spinner, B. "Subjects' Access to Cognitive Processes: Demand Characteristics and Verbal Report." *Journal for the Theory of Social Behaviour* 11 (1981): 31–52.

This excellent article analyzes the demand characteristics that seem to have operated in several studies. The behavior and verbal reports of research subjects are discussed in the context of demand characteristics theory. Perhaps most useful to the researcher is the authors' discussion of ways to improve the verity of self-report information gathered from research subjects. Among the strategies discussed are (1) the "funnel questionnaire," which begins with very general questions and gradually becomes more specific; (2) concurrent probing, in which subjects report on the strategy used; (3) "think aloud," in which each subject describes his thought processes as he goes through the problem at hand; and (4) videotape reconstruction, in which subjects are shown a replay of the experiment to help them recall their cognitions.

Cooper, Harris M. "Scientific Guidelines for Conducting Integrative Research Reviews." *Review of Educational Research* 52 (1982): 291–302.

The author conceptualizes the integrative research review as a form of scientific inquiry similar in many ways to the primary research process. Five stages in conducting an integrative research review are discussed: problem formulation, data collection, data evaluation, analysis and interpretation, and reporting. The functions, sources of variance, and potential threats to validity are described for each stage. The author has provided an excellent model for the scholar who wants to conduct an integrative review. This article is strongly recommended to students who want to develop a better understanding of the integrative review process.

Glass, Gene V; McGaw, Barry, and Smith, Mary L. *Meta-Analysis in Social Research.* Beverly Hills, Calif.: Sage Publications, 1981.

The authors describe the problems involved in reviewing and integrating research and explain in some detail how to use meta-analysis. Frequent examples, drawn from meta-analysis studies by the authors and others, are provided. In the final chapter, the four most frequent criticisms of meta-analysis are discussed.

Katzer, J.; Cook, K. H.; and Crouch, W. W. *Evaluating Information—A*

Guide for Users of Social Science Research. 2nd ed. Reading, Mass.: Addison-Wesley, 1982.

The purpose of this book is to teach students in the social sciences how to read and evaluate research information. The book avoids technical and procedural details and attempts to explain principles in nontechnical language. The evaluation process proposed by the authors is based on the "error model," which focuses on sources of errors, kinds of errors, and ways that researchers can control errors. A step-by-step evaluation guide is provided along with a list of questions the student should ask in evaluating a research article.

Millman, Jason, and Gowin, D. B. *Appraising Educational Research: A Case Study Approach.* Englewood Cliffs, N.J.: Prentice-Hall, 1974.

This book contains nine educational research articles covering a variety of educational topics and research procedures. Special notes and a detailed critique are provided for each article. The critiques were developed and modified on the basis of comments supplied by over 800 students and provide an excellent model for students who are studying the critical review process.

Persell, Caroline. *Quality, Careers and Training in Educational and Social Research.* Bayside, N.Y.: General Hall, 1976.

This book explores the dimensions of quality in educational research, reports on the evaluation of nearly 400 recent studies, and deals with specific flaws. Seven articles are included that give the reader insights into the range and nature of recent research in education. Information is also given on the amount of research being carried out in each of the broad areas of education.

Rosenthal, R. "Combining Results of Independent Studies." *Psychological Bulletin* 85, no. 1 (1978): 185–93.

This article describes nine procedures that can be used to combine the probabilities obtained from two or more independent studies to determine the overall significance of the combined results. Each method is described, and its use is illustrated. The advantages and limitations of each method are given, as are suggestions as to when each method is applicable.

Rosenthal, Robert, and Rosnow, Ralph L., eds. *Artifact in Behavioral Research.* New York: Academic Press, 1969.

All research is subject to error. Nevertheless, the complexity of human subjects and their interaction with human experimenters leads to an array of subtle and complex errors in the behavioral sciences. This book provides the best single source available on these errors. Included are chapters on topics such as suspiciousness of the experimenter's intent, pretest sensitization, demand characteristics, interpersonal expectations, and evaluation apprehension.

Rosenthal, R., and Rosnow, R. L. *The Volunteer Subject.* New York: John Wiley, 1975.

Since it is very difficult to obtain nonvolunteers for most research, it is important for behavioral scientists to understand volunteer subjects and use them effectively. This book builds upon the extensive research of the authors but also pulls together other important research on the volunteer subject. Topics covered include characteristics of the volunteer, suggestions for reducing volunteer bias, and implications for interpreting research findings. This is an essential source for the researcher who works with human subjects.

Rosnow, Ralph L., and Davis, D. J. "Demand Characteristics and the Psychological Experiment." *Et Cetera* 34 (1977): 301–13.

This is an excellent discussion of demand characteristics, factors that mediate these phenomena, procedures for reducing their influence on research results, and ways to detect their occurrence. Many useful references are provided.

Saretsky, Gary. "The John Henry Effect: Potential Confounder of Experimental vs. Control Group Approaches to the Evaluation of Educational Innovations." Paper presented at the annual meeting of the American Educational Research Association, Washington, D.C., 2 April 1975 (ED 106 309).

This paper, which is available on *RIE* microfiche, starts with a brief historical review of resistance to innovation. The author then reviews a number of factors that bias research, such as the halo effect, the placebo effect, and the Hawthorne Effect. He then discusses the John Henry Effect and describes several studies in which this effect seems to have occurred.

SELF-CHECK TEST

Circle the correct answer to each of the following questions. An answer key is provided on page 881.

1. Of the following, the factor that most often weakens educational research studies is
   a. deliberate distortion.
   b. sampling bias.
   c. inaccurate statistical analysis.
   d. inaccurate computer programming.
2. Loss of subjects during the course of a research project usually introduces bias because
   a. the resulting sample is too small.
   b. they are not lost on a random basis.
   c. descriptive statistics cannot be used on the resulting data.

      d. All of the above are correct.

3. If a research study cites standard measures concerning which the reader is unfamiliar, she should
    a. consult the *Mental Measurements Yearbooks.*
    b. disregard the study.
    c. try and interpret the study as carefully as possible.
    d. disregard the portion of the study related to the unknown standard measure.

4. Measurement tools are likely to invalidate the research findings if they are
    a. too easy or difficult for the majority of the research sample.
    b. administered only to a volunteer group of subjects.
    c. developed by the researcher.
    d. known to have high reliability.

5. Observer bias may be reduced by
    a. carefully structuring an interview guide.
    b. use of audiotape recordings.
    c. reducing the amount of inference required of the observer.
    d. All of the above are correct.

6. Technically, the chemically inert substance administered in the same manner as a drug under investigation is called a
    a. reactor.
    b. contaminator.
    c. placebo.
    d. catalyst.

7. Observer contamination arises when the research worker is
    a. influenced in his observation of an independent variable by knowledge of subjects' performance on a dependent variable.
    b. poorly instructed concerning his task.
    c. not thoroughly knowledgeable concerning the experiment.
    d. All of the above are correct.

8. Screening "placebo reactors" out of research studies has served to
    a. decrease observer bias.
    b. reveal significant differences not otherwise shown.
    c. eliminate deliberate bias.
    d. reduce statistical contamination.

9. A common error in statistical analysis is to select a parametric technique even though
    a. the sample size was very large.
    b. the sample included only volunteers.
    c. the distribution of scores was badly skewed.
    d. test scores were derived from observational data.

10. If a researcher finds a small difference in test scores between a large sample

of experimental subjects and a large sample of control subjects, it is likely that the difference will be
   a. statistically significant and have practical significance.
   b. not statistically significant, but have practical significance.
   c. statistically significant, but not have practical significance.
   d. of no consequence for determining the statistical or practical significance of the research findings.

APPLICATION PROBLEMS

The following problems are designed to give you practice in applying significant concepts and research procedures explained in chapter 6. Most of them do not have a single correct answer. For feedback, you can compare your answers with the sample answers on pages 887–88.

1. What sampling biases appear to be present in the following description of procedures used to select subjects? In order to determine the effects of a new discussion method on the achievement of college students, 156 psychology majors enrolled in an undergraduate course in educational psychology were selected to participate in the study. Each subject was assigned to one of four sections, each taught by a different instructor. Two sections were randomly designated as experimental and two as control. Since the course is required for graduation, the population consisted of sophomores, juniors, and seniors. Most of the subjects were commuters from the local community. Of the 75 students initially enrolled in the experimental course, 58 completed all course requirements. Totals for the control group were 81 and 78, respectively. Nine of the students in the treatment group who failed to complete did enough coursework to earn a passing grade, and the other eight dropped the course shortly after hearing the requirements. In the control group, three students dropped the course for administrative reasons.

2. Identify possible bias or contamination in the following hypothetical studies.
   a. In recent years a number of investigators have suggested that heredity plays an important role in determining individual differences in intelligence. The purpose of the research reported herein is to prove the invalidity of this racist belief once and for all. Underline indicators of bias, and state what type(s) of bias appear(s).
   b. An investigator hypothesizes that primary-grade female teachers who have young children of their own (ages 3-9) will display more warmth and understanding in the classroom than those who have no children. He selects 30 teachers who have young children and 30 who have no children. All are female and teach primary grades (i.e., K-3). He then observes each teacher

for two hours and rates the teacher on "warmth" and "understanding" using a 5-point scale for each trait. He then compares the mean scores of the two groups of teachers on "warmth" and "understanding" to test his hypothesis. What type(s) of bias or contamination appear(s) to be present?

3. Prior to the start of the school year, students who have preregistered will be randomly assigned to the four first-grade classrooms. Two of these classrooms will then be randomly assigned to treatment and two to control conditions. In the treatment classrooms each child will be given a multivitamin supplement in the 4-oz. serving of orange juice normally given to all children at 10:00 A.M. daily.
   a. Is this study subject to the Hawthorne Effect? If so, why?
   b. Is a placebo needed? If so, why?

4. An investigator carries out a correlational study designed to identify variables that relate to success in solving word problems in mathematics. He administers a word-problem test to 1000 high school seniors, all of whom have completed second-year algebra with passing grades. He obtains a correlation of .17 between word-problem test scores and a test in which the subjects are shown pictures of common objects (such as book, pencil, bell, knife, etc.) and their speed in naming the objects is measured. This correlation is statistically significant at the .01 level. Is the relationship of practical significance for predicting success in solving word problems? Explain your answer.

5. A professor of elementary education develops a special 10-week program of role playing and simulated teaching problems to train teachers to improve their explaining skills. She wants to evaluate the effectiveness of this program by determining whether teachers who are trained in these skills obtain better pupil achievement than teachers who are not. She explains the study at a district teachers' meeting and locates 40 teachers who are willing to participate. These teachers are randomly divided into two groups. Group A is given the training and group B is not. Six teachers drop out of group A at the end of the second week. At the end of the program, pupil achievement tests would be given in the classrooms of all 34 teachers who remain.
   a. Is sampling bias present in this study? Discuss.
   b. Could the Hawthorne Effect occur? Why?
   c. Could the John Henry Effect occur? Why?
   d. How could the study be changed to reduce these effects?

SUGGESTION SHEET

If your last name starts with letters from Dod to Fis, please complete the Suggestion Sheet at the end of the book while this chapter is still fresh in your mind.

Part III.

SAMPLING AND MEASUREMENT

One of our main goals in educational research is to obtain valid knowledge about some aspect of education and to apply that knowledge to a defined population. We almost never collect data from all individuals who make up our population, however. Instead, we select a sample of subjects from that population for study. The procedures we use in selecting our sample are very important because they determine the extent to which we can apply our findings to the population from which our sample was drawn.

Our measurement procedures in research are no less important than sampling procedures. All science uses measurement, and the progress of a given science is determined to a large extent by the accuracy of the instruments developed to measure its domain of phenomena. Since educational research is concerned with the human subject, by far the most complex organism on our planet, the problems of educational measurement are much more difficult than those of other sciences. Many of the measures currently available to the educational researcher are of questionable validity. The findings reached through use of such measures are therefore also of questionable validity. To improve this situation, researchers need to develop a thorough understanding of educational measurement principles and a knowledge of how to locate, evaluate, and interpret educational measures.

7.

POPULATIONS AND SAMPLES

OVERVIEW

Usually researchers cannot investigate the entire population of students or educators in whom they are interested. They must limit their investigation to a small sample. Among the most crucial decisions that confront researchers, then, is the selection of a sample of subjects who are representative of the population to which they wish to generalize research findings. Researchers often make errors in selecting their samples. Three major errors are discussed. You are then given procedures for using a variety of sampling techniques and their rationale. Since most educational research must be conducted with volunteer samples, the characteristics of volunteers are discussed along with suggestions for interpreting research data collected on such samples. Next, you are presented with a number of factors to be considered in determining how many subjects you should include in your research design. Since the educational researcher desires that the findings have as great an impact as possible on the field of education, it is imperative that serious consideration be given to the sampling procedure. Once a decision is made with respect to sampling, the degree of generalizability of the findings to students and educators other than those included in the actual project is likewise fixed.

OBJECTIVES

After studying this chapter, you should be able to:

1. Discuss three common errors in selecting samples.
2. Describe the procedure for generalizing from the accessible population to the target population.
3. Describe the procedure for selecting a simple random sample from a defined population.
4. Describe the procedure for selecting a stratified sample from a defined population.
5. Describe the procedure for selecting a cluster sample from a defined population.

6. Describe seven types of situations in educational research that require a fairly large sample.
7. Estimate the sample size needed for a particular research problem.
8. Give two reasons why volunteers are likely to constitute biased samples in research projects.
9. Distinguish between known characteristics of volunteer and nonvolunteer samples.

The usual purpose of educational research is to learn something about a large group of people by studying a much smaller group of people. The larger group we wish to learn about is called a **population,** whereas the smaller group we actually study is called a **sample.** In this chapter we will discuss how populations are defined and how samples are selected.

COMMON MISTAKES IN SAMPLING

A common mistake in educational research is to investigate persons from the appropriate population simply because they are available. For example, a researcher might select all subjects from one school because she happens to know the school principal and is sure that the principal will grant permission to do the study in that school. The problem with this strategy is that the research results cannot be applied with much confidence to other subjects who are members of the same population. Suppose that the researcher has selected all subjects from one school, and subsequently finds that subjects exposed to teaching method A learn significantly better than subjects exposed to teaching method B. A principal in another school can legitimately raise the question: "How do I know that teaching method A will be superior in my school?" Generalization from one school to another or from one sample of students to another is risky, unless the researcher has selected subjects by means of appropriate sampling techniques.

An even worse error is to select subjects who are not even in an appropriate population for the contemplated research, merely because they are easily available. For example, many studies on the effects of different types of psychological counseling or therapy are conducted using normal college students who have no need for counseling but who are drafted as subjects merely because they are students in a class in psychology. It is doubtful whether the responses of such students to counseling bear any relationship to responses of persons in the real target population, that is, persons who seek counseling because of serious emotional problems.

College sophomores, who are available but often inappropriate, have been the subjects for so much research in education and psychology that the use of sophomores in research projects finds its way into many of the jokes about research workers in these fields. Some studies suffer relatively little from using available subjects. For example, exploratory studies on the effects of drugs upon behavior may not be seriously weakened by the use of available subjects. Whenever the research worker wishes to generalize the results to specifically defined populations, however, the use of subjects merely because they are available is inappropriate.

Many educational field studies are biased because the research worker chooses experimental and control groups from different populations. For example, some early studies on the effectiveness of TV instruction used high school students receiving conventional instruction as a control group, but used adults who wanted to complete their high school education in home study as an experimental or TV-instruction group. The age, interests, motivation, and dropout rates for the two groups are very different, thus making the results of such studies meaningless.

Occasionally identification of a suitable sample is sufficiently time-consuming and expensive to warrant the use of shortcuts. Nevertheless, the possible effects of shortcuts should be carefully studied before they are used. Terman's famous study of "gifted children" provides an example of a sampling shortcut that seriously affected the research results.[1] In this study Terman wished to locate 1000 children with IQs over 140 on the Stanford-Binet Intelligence Scale. The Stanford-Binet test is expensive and time-consuming to administer. Therefore, rather than test many pupils who had little chance of obtaining a score of 140, Terman decided to ask teachers to suggest the names of students whom they considered superior. Only those students nominated by the teacher were tested. The difficulty with this procedure is that teachers tend to underestimate the intelligence of pupils who create disturbances and are not cooperative in the classroom. Thus Terman's sample does not include this type of individual, and as a result of this shortcut in selecting the original sample, all the findings of his important study must be qualified. Terman's results, instead of being applicable to gifted children in general, refer primarily to a particular type of gifted child.

The method of selecting a sample is critical to the whole research process. If research findings are not generalizable to some degree beyond the sample used in the study, then the research cannot provide us with new knowledge, cannot advance education as a science, and is largely a waste of time.

The sample should be selected by some process that permits us to assume that the sample is *representative* of the population from which it has been drawn on those variables that are relevant to the research we are planning to conduct.

1. Lewis M. Terman, ed., *Genetic Studies of Genius*, vol. 1, *Mental and Physical Traits of a Thousand Gifted Children* (Stanford, Calif.: Stanford University Press, 1926), p. 21.

By "representative" we do not mean identical. The only way we could be certain that the sample was identical to the population would be to take the entire population for our "sample." Instead, we define a sample as representative if we have drawn the sample in a manner that makes it probable that the sample is approximately the same as the population on the variables to be studied. The word "approximately" implies some degree of difference between the sample and the population. We can never be sure of the magnitude of this difference unless we have measured the entire population and compared the population and the sample. We do know, however, that the probable size of this difference is closely related to the size of the sample. The sample ideally should be large enough that the investigator can be confident, within a reasonable limit, that if he should draw a different sample of the same size and using the same procedures he would obtain approximately the same result in his research.

This difference between the characteristics of a sample and the characteristics of the population from which the sample was drawn is called *sampling error* and can be estimated for random samples. As indicated above, sampling error is a function of the size of the sample, with the error being largest when the sample is small. Research findings based on a sample of two or three subjects are apt to be highly unreliable.[2] If we were to study another sample of this size, it is quite likely that different findings would be obtained. It is important to select a sample of adequate size in order to produce research data that reliably approximate the data that would be obtained if the entire population were studied.

This chapter discusses sampling techniques that enable the researcher to select a sample that is representative of a larger population. We also discuss procedures that the researcher can use to determine the sample size needed for a given study. Although our discussion is concerned primarily with the selection of subjects for a research project, the student should note that the sampling techniques discussed here also pertain to the selection of events or objects for research. For example, sampling techniques would be used if the researcher wished to select a sample of class periods for systematic observation, or a sample of textbooks in order to do a content analysis.

DEFINING THE POPULATION

Sampling means selecting a given number of subjects from a defined population as representative of that population. One type of population distinguished by

---

2. Certain kinds of research can be conducted with very few cases or even a single case. This topic is discussed in chapter 16.

educational researchers is called the **target population.** By target population, also called **universe,** we mean all the members of a real or hypothetical set of people, events, or objects to which we wish to generalize the results of our research. The advantage of drawing a small sample from a large target population is that it saves the researcher the time and expense of studying the entire population. If the sampling is done properly, the researcher can reach conclusions about an entire target population that are likely to be correct within a small margin of error by studying a relatively small sample.

The first step in sampling is to define the target population. Typical populations from which educational research samples might be drawn include school superintendents in Utah; practice-teaching supervisors in state-supported teachers' colleges, bilingual children in the primary grades of the San Antonio city school district, pupils failing algebra in New York City schools, and seniors graduating from American public high schools in June 1983. These examples illustrate that the target population may represent a large group scattered over a wide geographical area or a small group concentrated in a single area.

It is seldom possible for a researcher to draw a representative sample from a target popuation such as all first-grade pupils in public schools in the United States. In order to obtain a representative sample of this broadly defined population, a complex method of selecting cases from different areas, different-sized communities, and different types of schools would have to be developed.

Obviously the selection of such a sample and collection of data from it would involve a tremendous amount of work and expense. Instead, the researcher must usually draw his sample from an **experimentally accessible population** such as all first-grade pupils in the San Francisco school district.[3] Even though the sample is selected from the accessible population, the researcher may want to know the degree to which the results can be generalized to the target population. This type of generalization requires two inferential leaps. First, the researcher must generalize the results from the sample she actually studied to the accessible population from which she selected the sample. Second, she must generalize from the accessible population to the target population. The leap from sample to accessible population presents no problem if a **random sample** of the accessible population was obtained, that is, a sample in which all members of the population had an equal chance of being selected. If the sample was not formed randomly, the researcher must gather data about the sample and the population on characteristics critical to the study. Often such data are available in school records, but some testing may also be neces-

3. See Glenn H. Bracht and Gene V Glass, "The External Validity of Experiments," *American Educational Research Journal* 5, no. 4 (November 1968): 437–74, for a more detailed discussion of this topic.

sary. It will rarely be possible to obtain all data that would be useful, but the researcher should obtain comparative information on as many critical variables as possible with the resources she has at her disposal. These data will demonstrate that the sample is either biased or unbiased. If unbiased, the researcher can safely generalize the results to the accessible population. If, however, the sample is biased, she must report the nature of the bias and discuss how this bias is likely to affect the results.

In order to make the second leap from the accessible population to the target population, the researcher must gather data to determine the degree of similarity between these two populations. It is possible to gather comparative data on a very large number of variables. However, if the investigator can demonstrate that the accessible population is closely comparable to the target population on a few variables that appear most relevant to the study, she has done much to establish **population validity.** That is, she has established that the accessible population is reasonably representative of the target population. For example, suppose a researcher wants to compare the achievement of first-grade pupils who are taught with two different reading programs. If she selects a random sample from the accessible population of first graders in the San Francisco schools but can demonstrate by comparing local test data with national test norms that San Francisco first graders are not significantly different from first graders nationwide on such important variables as reading readiness, verbal IQ, chronological age, and socioeconomic status, then she has established population validity. This means that she can generalize her results from the accessible to the target population with reasonable confidence. Often financial limitations or the nature of the research problem limit us to sampling the student population of a single school district. Studies based on this narrow accessible population are, of course, less generalizable than those based on broader populations, but may still have important implications for other educators if it can be demonstrated that this population is reasonably similar to the target population on a few critical variables.

It is beyond the scope of most research projects to identify all the members of a defined population. For example, the identification by name of all fifth-grade teachers in even a single state would be a major undertaking. Thus, researchers usually rely on published lists, called sampling frames, of various populations that are of interest to educators. Most researchers will be able to draw samples from accessible populations only at the state or district level. In these cases the state or district education office should be contacted to find out if they have a list of persons in the population in which the researcher is interested. State and district education departments usually maintain complete lists of information about schools, such as school addresses, grades, enrollment, and names of principals and teachers for administrative purposes. In certain instances the researcher may wish to consult a national association or national directory, even though the defined population is at the state or district level. For example, suppose one wished to survey a sample of educational researchers in a given state. One might obtain a national directory, such as the current membership directory of the American Educational Research Association, and mark all the educational researchers residing in that state. From this defined population, a sample of educational researchers can be selected. The *Guide to American Educational Directories*[4] is a helpful source for locating directory lists that can be used to define populations.

In using any published list to define a population, the student should check to determine whether it is complete and up to date. School enrollment and memberships of organizations are constantly changing, so frequent updating of population lists is necessary. Also it should be realized that membership in most organizations is voluntary. Thus a student who uses an organization directory to define a population faces the risk of selecting a biased sample, since joiners of organizations may differ in important respects from nonjoiners. Should this be the case, the student should probably define the accessible population as all members of a given organization rather than as all members of the profession or group which the organization serves.

Two studies have been done to evaluate the degree to which research articles meet criteria of population validity. J. E. Permut et al. used four criteria to evaluate a sample of 460 articles in the field of marketing research.[5] The criteria were:

1. A clear description of the *population* to which the results are to be generalized should be given.
2. The *sampling procedure* should be specified in enough detail so that another investigator would be able to replicate the procedure. This should include at a minimum *(a)* the type of sample (simple random, stratified, convenience, etc.), *(b)* sample size, and *(c)* geographical area. In most educational studies, other descriptive data, such as sex, age, grade level, and socioeconomic status, should also be included.
3. The *sampling frame*, that is, the lists, indexes, or other population records from which the sample was selected, should be identified.
4. The *completion rate*, which is the proportion of the sample that participated as intended in all of the research procedures, should be given.

Only 10 percent of the studies reviewed by the researchers met all four criteria. In a similar analysis of 297 studies in communication research, Dennis

4. Barry T. Klein, *Guide to American Educational Directories*, 5th ed. (Rye, N.Y.: Todd Publications 1980).
5. J. E. Permut, A. J. Michel, and M. Joseph, "The Researcher's Sample: A Review of the Choice of Respondents in Marketing Research," *Journal of Marketing Research* 13 (1976): 278–83.

Lowry also found that only 10 percent met these criteria.[6] Although other data may be needed to establish the population validity of a given study, the student should try, as a minimum, to include data that satisfy the four criteria stated above.

SAMPLING TECHNIQUES

As we have already mentioned, sampling involves the selection of a portion of a population as representative of the population. To help ensure that the sample is representative, the ideal solution, seldom achieved, is to select a random sample from the target population. A random sample is one in which each individual in the defined population has an *equal* chance of being included.

It should be noted that the use of sampling techniques can be quite complicated. This is particularly true when these techniques are used to draw a random sample from a national population. However, sampling from a national population usually occurs only in survey research, such as public opinion polls. Samples used in experimental, causal-comparative, or correlational research are generally drawn from a much more limited accessible population, such as all the elementary school teachers in a particular school district.

The main purpose for using random sampling techniques is that random samples yield research data that can be generalized to a larger population within margins of error that can be determined statistically. Random sampling is also preferred because it permits the researcher to apply inferential statistics to the data. Inferential statistics enable the researcher to make certain inferences about population values (e.g., mean, standard deviation, correlation coefficient) on the basis of obtained sample values. If a random sample has not been drawn from a defined population, however, the logic of inferential statistics is violated and the results of inferential statistics must be interpreted with much more caution. We discuss the relationship between sampling and inferential statistics later in this chapter and again in chapter 10.

Simple Random Sampling

The usual definition of a *simple random sample* is that it is a procedure in which all the individuals in the defined population have an *equal* and *independent* chance of being selected as a member of the sample. By "independent" is meant that the selection of one individual does not affect in any way the selection of any other individual. A more precise definition of a simple random sample is that

6. Dennis T. Lowry, "Population Validity of Communication Research: Sampling the Samples," *Journalism Quarterly* 56, no. 1 (1979): 62–68, 76.

it is a process of selection from a population that provides *every sample of a given size* an equal probability of being selected. This is technically correct, since in the process of selecting cases, the selection of each individual changes slightly the probability for the next case being selected. For example, suppose there are 1000 sixth-grade pupils in our accessible population, and we want to select a simple random sample of 100. When we select our first case, each pupil has one chance in 1000 of being selected. Once this pupil is selected, however, there are only 999 cases remaining so that each pupil has one chance in 999 of being selected as our second case. Thus, as each case is selected, the probability for being selected next changes slightly because the population from which we are selecting has become one case smaller. For all samples of any given size selected from this population, however, the overall probability (i.e., the sum of individual probabilities) would be the same.

Various techniques can be used to derive a simple random sample. Suppose the research director of a large city school system wishes to obtain a random sample of 100 pupils currently enrolled in the ninth grade from a population of 972 cases. First, he would obtain a copy of the district census for ninth-grade pupils and assign a number to each pupil. Then he might use a **table of random numbers** to draw a sample from the census list. (A table of random numbers can be found in Appendix C.) Generally these tables consist of long series of five-digit numbers generated randomly by a computer. Table 7.1 is a small portion of a typical table.

To use the random numbers table, the researcher randomly selects a row or column as a starting point, then selects all the numbers that follow in that row or column. If more numbers are needed, he proceeds to the next row or

TABLE 7.1

A Typical Table of Random Numbers

Row	Column 1	2	3	4	5	6	7	8	9	10
1	32388	52390	16815	69298	82732	38480	73817	32523	41961	44437
2	05300	22164	24369	54224	35983	19687	11052	91491	60383	19746
3	66523	44133	00697	35552	35970	19124	63318	29686	03387	59846
4	44167	64486	64758	75366	76554	31601	12614	33072	60332	92325
5	47914	02584	37680	20801	72152	39339	34806	08930	85001	87820
6	63445	17361	62825	39908	05607	91284	68833	25570	38818	46920
7	89917	15665	52872	73823	73144	88662	88970	74492	51805	99378
8	92648	45454	09552	88815	16553	51125	79375	97596	16296	66092
9	20979	04508	64535	31355	86064	29472	47689	05974	52468	16834
10	81959	65642	74240	56302	00033	67107	77510	70625	28725	34191

column until enough numbers have been selected to make up the desired sample size. In effect the researcher may start at any random point in the table and select numbers from a column or row or diagonally if he wishes.

Suppose, in our example, the researcher selects row 1 column 5 as his starting point in the above table and selects numbers vertically. Since there are 972 cases in our illustrative city school system, it is only necessary to use the last three digits of each five-digit number. If the table of random numbers reprinted here were used, the researcher would select the 732nd pupil on the census list, the 970th pupil, the 554th pupil, and so on. He would skip the number 983 since there are only 972 cases in his population. This procedure would be followed (with a much larger table of random numbers, of course) until a sample of 100 pupils had been selected.

If a small population is used, another method of selecting a simple random sample is sometimes followed. This method involves placing a slip of paper with the name or identification number of each individual in the population in a container, mixing the slips thoroughly, and then drawing the required number of names or numbers.

Simple random sampling is well illustrated by a study involving the collection of a national random sample of secondary school physics teachers.[7] The researchers responsible for this curriculum evaluation study wished to avoid using a nonrandom sample consisting largely of "volunteer" teachers. This procedure, typical of many curriculum evaluation studies, makes it difficult to generalize the findings of the curriculum evaluation to other groups of teachers, especially nonvolunteers, who might be required to teach the new curriculum. The researchers first purchased a list of the names and addresses of 16,911 physics teachers compiled by the National Science Teachers Association. They point out in their report that this is the most comprehensive population list of high school physics teachers available, although it is not complete; it was based on responses received from 81 percent of all secondary schools in the United States. Thus, their population was not "all high school physics teachers" but rather "all high school physics teachers on the 1966 NSTA list." Each teacher on the population list was assigned a number according to his ordinal position on the list. Then a table of random numbers was used to select a total of 136 teachers. These 136 teachers were sent letters inviting them to participate in the study, but it was only possible to contact 124 of them.

It turned out eventually that 72 of the original 136 teachers agreed to participate in the study according to the conditions specified. Another 46 teachers were unable to participate for various reasons. In order to determine whether their final sample was biased, the researchers decided to compare several char-

7. W. W. Welch, H. J. Walberg, and A. Ahlgren, "The Selection of a National Random Sample of Teachers for Experimental Curriculum Evaluation," *School Science and Mathematics* 69 (1969): 210–16.

acteristics of the 72 accepting teachers against those of the 46 nonacceptors. When this comparison was made, the researchers found that significantly more acceptors than nonacceptors worked in larger schools and taught the Physical Science Study Committee (PSSC) physics course. The researchers interpreted these differences as indicating that the accepting teachers were more likely to be those who taught in large schools where previous innovations had been accepted. Thus, although they attempted to obtain a truly "random" sample, their actual sample was somewhat biased in favor of teachers working in innovative schools, and consisted of volunteers since only half the teachers contacted chose to participate. Nevertheless, the researchers' final sample was probably more representative than the samples used in most curriculum studies, and it was possible to generalize the study's findings to a national population of physics teachers, with certain qualifications.

Incidentally, the study just described illustrates another problem that sometimes occurs with research samples. Of the 72 accepting teachers, 46 were assigned to the experimental group teaching the new physics curriculum, and the remaining 26 were assigned to the control group. During the course of the year-long evaluation study, 10 teachers were lost from the experimental group and 5 were lost from the control group for various reasons—death, quitting one's job, transfer to a new position, and so forth. Whenever a research project extends over a considerable period of time, there is likely to be attrition of subjects. Not only can attrition lead to bias in the research sample (since those who leave the study may differ in important ways from those who persist), but also the reduced sample size can make it more difficult to find statistically significant differences. Thus, if the research study makes considerable demands on subjects or lasts over a long period of time, it is advisable to include more subjects in the random sample than are needed in order to provide for possible attrition. It is also important to take any steps possible to keep attrition to a minimum.

The human relations procedures described in chapter 4 can do much to reduce attrition, as can the ten steps for increasing the rate of volunteering given later in this chapter. Some attrition may reflect careless or poorly planned techniques for gathering, processing, and analyzing research data. Loss of data often occurs because the subject is not contacted by the data gatherer or the subject does not provide all the information needed for analysis. Much attrition in school research is the result of student absences on testing days or incorrectly completed measures. Prompt checking of data, careful recordkeeping, and a systematic follow-up procedure can greatly reduce this problem.[8] Great care is required at all stages of data collection, processing, and analysis if attrition is to be reduced and valid data obtained.

8. See Gloria Marshall, "Methods for Minimizing Attrition in Field Studies" (paper presented at the annual meeting of the American Educational Research Association, San Francisco, 22 April 1976), for a discussion of attrition in longitudinal studies.

In summary, simple random sampling is a powerful technique for select-ing a sample that is representative of a larger population. Nevertheless, it is rarely possible to study a simple random sample that is perfect. Even if a sim-ple random sample is initially selected, some subjects probably will refuse to cooperate and others will be lost through attrition, leaving the researcher with a sample that is not truly random.

Systematic Sampling

As with simple random sampling, the technique of **systematic sampling** is used to obtain a sample from the defined population. This technique can be used if all members in the defined population have already been placed on a list in random order. Suppose the researcher wants to select a sample of 100 pupils from a census list of 1000 pupils. To use systematic sampling, the researcher first divides the population by the number needed for the sample (1000 ÷ 100 = 10). Then the researcher selects at random a number smaller than the num-ber arrived at by the division (in this example, a number smaller than 10). Then, starting with that number (e.g., 8), she selects every tenth name from a list of the population.

Systematic sampling is a slightly easier procedure to use than simple ran-dom sampling. It differs from simple random sampling in that each member of the population is not chosen independently. Once the first member has been selected, all the other members of the sample are automatically determined. Systematic sampling can be used instead of simple random sampling if one is certain that the population list is in random order. If there is any possibility of periodicity in the list (that is, if every nth person on the list shares a character-istic that is not shared by the entire population), then simple random sampling should be used instead.

Stratified Sampling

In many educational studies, it is desirable to select a sample in such a way that the research worker is assured that certain subgroups in the population will be represented in the sample in proportion to their numbers in the popu-lation itself. Such samples are usually referred to as **stratified samples.** Let us say, for example, that we wish to conduct a study to see if there are significant differences on Thematic Apperception Test aggression scores of pupils at dif-ferent ability levels selected from ability-grouped sixth-grade classrooms. Un-der this grouping system, pupils are classified into three levels on the basis of general intelligence and placed in classrooms accordingly. In this case, if we were to define the population as all sixth-grade pupils in the district being studied and select a random sample, our random sample may not include a sufficient number of cases from one of the three ability levels. In this research we must also consider the possibility that girls will react differently in terms of aggression scores than boys. In order to avoid a sample that does not include a sufficient number of pupils of each sex at each ability level, a stratified sample can be selected. All sixth-grade pupils in the district would be divided into one of the following six groups: superior boys, superior girls, average boys, average girls, slow boys, and slow girls. Subsamples would then be selected at random from each of the six groups.

The proportion of subjects randomly selected from each group usually is the same as the proportion of that group in the target population. Therefore, if slow girls made up 8 percent of the sixth-grade population, they should also make up 8 percent of the sample. If this procedure is not followed, any analysis based on the total sample (i.e., all six groups combined) will produce inaccurate information. Suppose, for example, that we randomly selected 100 pupils from each of our six groups. Any statistics, such as the mean, that we computed on these 600 pupils would not accurately reflect the population since the proportion of average pupils in the population is higher than the proportion of superior or slow pupils, and even within ability levels, the proportion of boys and girls is different.

The size of the sample is usually determined by the minimum number of cases we decide is acceptable in the smallest subgroup. If we decide that the smallest must contain 30 cases, then we select a total sample large enough so that the correct proportion of our smallest subgroup will equal 30. For example, if 8 percent of our sample must be slow girls and this subsample must be 30 cases, then our total sample would be 375 (i.e., $30 \div .08$).

Stratified samples are particularly appropriate in studies where the research problem requires comparisons between various subgroups. In summary, stratified sampling procedure assures the research worker that the sample will be representative of the population in terms of certain critical factors that have been used as a basis for stratification, and also assures him of adequate cases for subgroup analysis.

Cluster Sampling

In **cluster sampling** the unit of sampling is not the individual but rather a naturally occurring group of individuals. Cluster sampling is used when it is more feasible or convenient to select groups of individuals than it is to select individuals from a defined population. This situation occurs when it is either impractical or impossible to obtain a list of all members of the accessible population. Suppose, for example, that one's defined population consists of all residents over the age of eighteen in a particular city. Simple random sampling

or systematic sampling could be used if an up-to-date, complete census of all
the city's individuals and their ages were available. If not, then cluster sampling is advisable.

The city might be divided into areas containing 16 square blocks. Each
area would be listed and numbered, and the areas to be sampled would be
drawn at random. All individuals who meet the age requirement in each sample area would be studied, excepting those who cannot be reached or who are
uncooperative. Thus, the unit of sampling is a 16-square-block area rather than
the individual citizen.

Multistage cluster sampling is a variant of cluster sampling. Once the
square block areas have been randomly selected, the researcher can further
reduce the sample size by only studying a random sample in each square-block
area. For example, the researcher might list the addresses of all houses in the
area and then study the residents of ten randomly selected houses in each 16-
block area included in the sample. In essence, multistage cluster sampling consists of two or more cycles of listing and sampling. Several sampling stages or
cycles may be carried out in order to arrive at the subjects to be ultimately
included in the sample.

Cluster sampling is sometimes used in educational research with the
classroom as the unit of sampling. Suppose that one wishes to administer a
questionnaire to a random sample of 300 pupils in a population defined as all
sixth graders in four school districts. Let us say there are a total of 1250 sixth
graders in 50 classrooms, with an average of 25 pupils in each classroom. One
approach is to draw a simple random sample using a census list of all 1250
pupils. In cluster sampling, though, one would draw a random sample of 12
classrooms from a census list of all 50 classrooms.[9] Then one would administer
the questionnaire to every pupil in each of the 12 classrooms.

The main advantage of cluster sampling is that it saves time and money.
The use of this sampling technique enables one to confine questionnaire administration to 12 of the 50 classrooms. If simple random sampling were used,
one might have to arrange for access to all 50 classrooms, even though in some
of these classrooms the researcher might have selected only one student for
the sample. Disadvantages of cluster sampling are (1) that it is less accurate
than simple random sampling because in simple random sampling there is
only one *sampling error* while in multistage sampling there is a sampling error
at each stage, and (2) one cannot use the conventional formulas for computing
statistics on one's research data.[10] Also, the statistics are less sensitive to pop-

9. One would select 12 classrooms because there are an average of 25 pupils in each classroom
and the desired sample is 300 pupils.
10. For statistical formulas to be used with data obtained from a cluster sample, the student is
advised to consult Kish (1965). See Annotated References at the end of this chapter for complete bibliographic information.

ulation differences. Nevertheless, these disadvantages must be weighed against the considerable savings in time and money that can result from using cluster sampling.

Besides the sampling techniques described above, which are sufficient for most educational research, a variety of more sophisticated techniques are intended primarily for use in large-scale survey research. See the Annotated References section of this chapter for sources that deal with these procedures.

VOLUNTEER SAMPLES

Random sampling of broad populations is possible for survey research in which slight demands are made on the subjects. For example, most public opinion polls are able to obtain random samples since they typically ask only a few questions and take only a few minutes of the respondent's time. Demands on the subject are much greater in most educational research; consequently, even if the researcher selects a random sample, he can rarely get cooperation from all the subjects selected. (You will recall that when some subjects refuse to participate in a study, the remaining subjects no longer constitute a random sample because persons who agree to participate are likely to be different from those who do not.) For educational studies that employ other methods than survey, such as correlational or experimental research, the demands on the subject are usually much greater, and consequently it is virtually impossible to obtain the cooperation of all subjects selected by random sampling.

Furthermore, as you learned in chapter 4, legal and ethical constraints on the researcher require him to obtain informed consent from human subjects (or their parents in the case of minors) before involving them in a research project.

As a result of the aforementioned conditions, nearly all educational research must be conducted with volunteer subjects. We know that volunteer subjects are likely to be a biased sample of the target population since volunteers have been found in many studies to differ from nonvolunteers.

There is a considerable body of research on the characteristics of volunteers. Robert Rosenthal and Ralph Rosnow have conducted an excellent review of research in this area and have identified a number of characteristics that have been found to occur in studies of volunteer subjects.[11] Conclusions about distinguishing characteristics are listed at four levels of confidence depending on the accumulation of research evidence that supports each conclusion. Within each category the conclusions are listed in order starting with those having the strongest evidence supporting them.

11. See Rosenthal and Rosnow (1975) in Annotated References at the end of this chapter.

Conclusions Warranting Maximum Confidence
1. Volunteers tend to be better educated than nonvolunteers, especially when personal contact between investigator and respondent is not required.
2. Volunteers tend to have higher social-class status than nonvolunteers, especially when social class is defined by respondents' own status rather than by parental status.
3. Volunteers tend to be more intelligent than nonvolunteers when volunteering is for research in general but not when volunteering is for somewhat less typical types of research such as hypnosis, sensory isolation, sex research, small-group and personality research.
4. Volunteers tend to be higher in need for social approval than nonvolunteers.
5. Volunteers tend to be more sociable than nonvolunteers.

Conclusions Warranting Considerable Confidence
6. Volunteers tend to be more arousal-seeking than nonvolunteers, especially when volunteering is for studies of stress, sensory isolation, and hypnosis.
7. Volunteers tend to be more unconventional than nonvolunteers, especially when volunteering is for studies of sex behavior.
8. Females are more likely than males to volunteer for research in general, but less likely than males to volunteer for physically and emotionally stressful research (e.g., electric shock, high temperature, sensory deprivation, interviews about sex behavior).
9. Volunteers tend to be less authoritarian than nonvolunteers.
10. Jews are more likely to volunteer than Protestants, and Protestants are more likely to volunteer than Roman Catholics.
11. Volunteers tend to be less conforming than nonvolunteers when volunteering is for research in general but not when subjects are female and the task is relatively "clinical" (e.g., hypnosis, sleep, or counseling research).

Conclusions Warranting Some Confidence
12. Volunteers tend to be from smaller towns than nonvolunteers, especially when volunteering is for questionnaire studies.
13. Volunteers tend to be more interested in religion than nonvolunteers, especially when volunteering is for questionnaire studies.
14. Volunteers tend to be more altruistic than nonvolunteers.
15. Volunteers tend to be more self-disclosing than nonvolunteers.
16. Volunteers tend to be more maladjusted than nonvolunteers, especially when volunteering is for potentially unusual situations (e.g., drugs, hypnosis, high temperature, or vaguely described experiments) or for medical research employing clinical rather than psychometric definitions of psychopathology.

17. Volunteers tend to be younger than nonvolunteers, especially when volunteering is for laboratory research and especially if they are female.

Conclusions Warranting Minimum Confidence

18. Volunteers tend to be higher in need for achievement than nonvolunteers, especially among American samples.
19. Volunteers are more likely to be married than nonvolunteers, especially when volunteering is for studies requiring no personal contact between investigator and respondent.
20. Firstborns are more likely than laterborns to volunteer, especially when recruitment is personal and when the research requires group interaction and a low level of stress.
21. Volunteers tend to be more anxious than nonvolunteers, especially when volunteering is for standard, nonstressful tasks and especially if they are college students.
22. Volunteers tend to be more extraverted than nonvolunteers when interaction with others is required by the nature of the research.[12]

The degree to which these characteristics of volunteer samples affect research results depends on the specific nature of the investigation. For example, a study of the level of intelligence of successful workers in different occupations would probably yield spuriously high results if volunteer subjects were studied, since volunteers tend to be more intelligent than nonvolunteers. On the other hand, in a study concerned with the cooperative behavior of adults in work-group situations, the tendency for volunteers to be more intelligent may have no effect on the results, but the tendency for volunteers to be more sociable could have a significant effect. It is apparent that the use of volunteers in research greatly complicates the interpretation of research results and their generalizability to the target population, which includes many individuals who would not volunteer.

The work of Rosenthal and Rosnow provides the researcher with valuable information that should be considered carefully when planning a study in which volunteer subjects are to be used. The researcher can review the characteristics listed above and for each ask such questions as: How relevant is this characteristic to the dependent and independent variables to be employed in my study? If relevant, how would the difference between volunteers and nonvolunteers on this characteristic be likely to influence the research results? Are any data available on my target population for checking whether these characteristics are present among the volunteers I will employ as subjects? The first two questions often can be answered on the basis of knowledge about the

12. Ibid., pp. 195–96.

variables in his study that the researcher gains during a review of previous research. Graduate students can also get help on these questions by discussing them with members of their research committees and other faculty members who have worked in the student's area of interest.

With regard to the third question, Rosenthal and Rosnow suggest two methods, which they refer to as *exhaustive* and *nonexhaustive*. In the exhaustive approach, all potential subjects are compared on as many relevant variables as possible in which volunteers and nonvolunteers may differ. For example, suppose the investigator plans to ask for volunteers from a sophomore general psychology class to participate in a study of client responses to different interview techniques used in counseling, such as directive versus nondirective counseling. Among the characteristics identified by Rosenthal and Rosnow, differences between volunteers and nonvolunteers on such variables as need for social approval, conformity, and authoritarianism may lead to differences in the responses of volunteers and nonvolunteers in the planned research. The researcher could first measure all students on these variables by administering appropriate tests in the class, could then call for volunteers, and then compare the scores of volunteers and nonvolunteers to determine how the groups differ on these variables. When working with student samples the investigator may not need to administer measures on all relevant variables. Most schools and colleges routinely administer batteries of tests to all students; these data can be drawn upon for comparisons between volunteers and nonvolunteers.[13]

In the nonexhaustive method, data on nonvolunteers are not available, but data are available on subjects who differ in their willingness to volunteer. For example, the investigator can compare the scores of easy-to-recruit volunteers and hard-to-recruit volunteers on some critical variable such as intelligence and then extrapolate to obtain an estimate of the intelligence of nonvolunteers in the target population. Easy-to-recruit volunteers may be those who will volunteer repeatedly over a period of time, those who will volunteer without being offered an incentive such as pay, or those who respond more promptly to requests for volunteers (such as newspaper advertisements or letters).

These procedures for obtaining information about characteristics of a specific volunteer sample, when combined with the general characteristics of volunteers described by Rosenthal and Rosnow, are of great assistance to the researcher in interpreting findings and generalizing to nonvolunteer populations. In reviewing research on the volunteer subject, Rosenthal and Rosnow also identified ten situational variables that tend to increase or decrease the rates of volunteering. These findings form the basis for the following suggestions for increasing the rate of volunteering and thus reducing volunteer bias:

13. It may be necessary, however, for the researcher to obtain the student's permission to obtain data from these records. See chapter 4.

Suggestions for Improving Rate of Volunteering

1. Make the appeal for volunteers as interesting as possible, keeping in mind the nature of the target population.
2. Make the appeal for volunteers as nonthreatening as possible so that potential volunteers will not be "put off" by unwarranted fears of unfavorable evaluation.
3. Explicitly state the theoretical and practical importance of the research for which volunteering is requested.
4. Explicitly state in what way the target population is particularly relevant to the research being conducted and the responsibility of potential volunteers to participate in research that has potential for benefiting others.
5. When possible, potential volunteers should be offered not only pay for participation but small courtesy gifts simply for taking time to consider whether they will want to participate.
6. Have the request for volunteering made by a person of status as high as possible, and preferably by a woman.
7. When possible, avoid research tasks that may be psychologically or biologically stressful.
8. When possible, communicate the normative nature of the volunteering response (i.e., volunteering is the normal thing to do).
9. After a target population has been defined, an effort should be made to have someone known to that population make the appeal for volunteers. The request for volunteers itself may be more successful if a personalized appeal is made.
10. In situations where *volunteering* is regarded by the target population as normative, conditions of public commitment to volunteer may be more successful; where *nonvolunteering* is regarded as normative, conditions of private commitment may be more successful.[14]

Most of these suggestions will not only increase the rate of volunteering but will also reduce attrition in both volunteer and nonvolunteer samples. The graduate student should consider these suggestions very carefully since following them will reduce volunteer bias and also result in better research planning.

RANDOM ASSIGNMENT

In experimental studies it is usually impossible to obtain a random sample since the typical treatment makes considerable demands upon the subject's time. The researcher usually must work with volunteers unless she can incor-

14. Rosenthal and Rosnow (1975), p. 198. See Annotated References at the end of this chapter.

porate her treatments into the regular school program and thus avoid the requirement of obtaining "informed consent" (see chapter 4). However, even in situations where random sampling is impossible, it is often possible to use random assignment. In **random assignment,** the subjects who will participate in the experiment are assigned randomly to the different experimental treatments.

Let us suppose that an investigator wants to compare the effectiveness of two second-grade reading programs in a large city school system. She locates five schools that are willing to participate and obtains permission from 90 percent of the parents of first-grade pupils for their children to participate during Grade 2. She then randomly assigns 48 pupils in each school to two classrooms, one to use each reading program. This provides a total sample of 240 children, with 120 for each of the two treatments. This approach is far superior to identifying two intact classes in each school and randomly assigning *classes* rather than *individuals* to the two treatments. Random assignment does not assure that the sample is representative of the accessible population, but it does ensure that children who receive the different experimental treatments are reasonably comparable.

To use random assignment in experimental studies in the public schools it is usually necessary to make arrangements sufficiently in advance so that students can be randomly assigned to classes at the start of the school year. Once classes are established it is virtually impossible to move pupils from one class to another in order to satisfy the needs of your research.

Even when random assignment is employed, some degree of difference may be expected to occur between groups. For example, one group may contain subjects who are more intelligent, more highly motivated, or in other ways different from the subjects in other groups in the experiment. Such errors may be large in groups made up of few cases, but may be expected to decrease as the number of subjects increases. Let us say that we wish to compare the achievement of a group of ninth-grade pupils taught algebra using an inductive method with the achievement of another group taught algebra using a deductive method. We could randomly assign 50 pupils who wish to take algebra to two classes at the start of the term and assign algebra teachers of comparable experience to teach the classes. In this experiment chance differences between groups may be expected to be large because only one class of 25 pupils is involved in each group. If, among the 50 subjects, there were two very brilliant students, and if these two students were both assigned to the same group (as could easily occur in the random assignment process), the achievement of these students could be high enough to raise the mean achievement of their entire group by several points.

Two approaches can be utilized to reduce the likelihood of this kind of error. One is to employ larger groups. For example, if ten classes of 25 subjects were to be included in each group, instead of one class, the chances of the 20 brightest students all being assigned to groups being taught by the same method would be remote. The other approach is to check your groups for "outliers," that is, subjects who do not appear to fit into the groups, and eliminate these cases from your sample. The use of random assignment in experimental studies is discussed further in chapter 15.

SAMPLE SIZE

Important Considerations

A problem that must be faced in planning every research project is to determine the size of the sample necessary to attain the objectives of the planned research. The general rule is to use the largest sample possible. The rule is a good one because, although we generally study only samples, we are really interested in learning about the population from which they are drawn. The larger the sample, the more likely is its mean and standard deviation to be representative of the population mean and standard deviation. Sample size is also closely connected with statistical hypothesis testing. The larger the sample, the less likely is the researcher to obtain negative results or fail to reject the null hypothesis when it is actually false. (We discuss this relationship between sample size and hypothesis testing in more depth in chapter 10, when we consider the theory underlying statistical hypothesis testing.)

In most research projects, financial and time restrictions limit the number of subjects that can be studied. In correlational research it is generally desirable to have a minimum of 30 cases. In causal-comparative and experimental research, it is desirable to have a minimum of 15 cases in each group to be compared. For survey research Seymour Sudman (see Annotated References) suggests that there be at least 100 subjects in each major subgroup and 20 to 50 in each minor subgroup whose responses are to be analyzed. In deciding on sample size, several factors should be considered. As a rule, larger samples are necessary under the following conditions:

1. *When many uncontrolled variables are present.* In many research studies, it is impossible for the investigator to control some of the important variables that could have an effect upon the research findings. Under these conditions the research worker can have more confidence in the findings if he employs large samples. The large random sample, if attainable, is the best solution since it ensures to some extent that the uncontrolled variables will themselves be operating randomly for the different groups being studied and therefore will

not have a systematic effect upon the results. Teaching ability, for example, is a difficult variable to control but is important in many educational studies. If a study of teaching methods involves only two teachers, one using method A and one method B, teaching-ability differences may cause more change in achievement than method differences. On the other hand, if fifteen or more teachers are randomly assigned to each method, teaching-ability differences are more likely to "randomize out," thus permitting us to appraise method differences.

2. *When small effect sizes are anticipated.* In research projects in which only small differences on the dependent variable are expected among the various groups being studied, or in correlational studies where small relationships are expected, it is desirable to use large samples. For example, a teacher may have developed a set of visual aids to help in teaching certain mathematical concepts. Such aids usually cannot be expected to make a large difference in student achievement. In order to evaluate these aids, large samples of pupils using and not using the aids would have to be compared. If small samples were used, the larger standard errors of the sample statistics could obscure small but important differences.

3. *When groups must be broken into subgroups.* Many educational research projects not only involve general comparisons of the different treatment groups but also can contribute additional worthwhile knowledge if these major groups are divided into subgroups and further comparisons are made. Let us suppose that we are carrying out a study of the possible effects of an extracurricular program upon the attitudes of high school students toward school. Ten schools having no organized extracurricular programs could be selected, and in five of these schools such a program could be developed. A pretest of student attitudes could be administered before the extracurricular program was introduced, and after a period of one or two years, final measures could be administered to determine what changes had taken place in student attitudes toward school. Attitude changes occurring in the schools that had adopted an organized program could then be compared with the changes that occurred in the schools in which no extracurricular program had been present. After an overall analysis of these comparisons had been made, however, the research worker might wish to compare the effects of the extracurricular program upon different groups in order to develop further understanding of the data. For example, he may hypothesize that girls' attitudes would be changed more markedly than boys' attitudes by the introduction of such a program because girls value social activities more highly at the high school level. This would require dividing the groups by sex and making further comparisons. It may then occur to the researcher that students at different socioeconomic levels might respond differently to the extracurricular program. Perhaps such a program would lead to favorable attitude changes on the part of middle-class students and unfavorable changes on the part of lower-class students. Again it would be necessary

to subdivide the original sample on the basis of social class in order to conduct this further analysis.

Such analyses often provide worthwhile knowledge and interesting theoretical insights, but they can be carried out only if the original groups are large enough so that, after such divisions are made, the subgroups still have sufficient numbers of cases to permit a statistical analysis. In the preceding example, a group of 100 students might be adequate to make the overall comparisons of the effects of the extracurricular program. However, in dividing the 100 cases into groups on the basis of sex and socioeconomic status, it may be found that only 7 of the subjects can be classified as lower-class girls. This would indicate that 100 cases are not sufficient for subgroup analysis.

A mistake commonly made by inexperienced research workers is to select a sample that would be large enough for division into the anticipated subgroups only if the subgroups are equally represented in the sample. If there is an unequal representation, such as in the above example, the researcher may have an insufficient number of cases in some groups to carry out the statistical analysis planned. This problem usually can be avoided by stratified sampling. But even with stratified sampling, because the research worker cannot always predict all subgroups she may want to study, a large number of cases is also desirable.

4. *When high attrition is expected.* Perhaps the best basis for estimating attrition is to check the losses experienced in similar previous research. The duration of a study is a major factor in the amount of attrition to be expected. Robert Goodrich and Robert St. Pierre estimated that 20 percent attrition per year is a realistic level for planning.[15] Thus, attrition in longitudinal studies often exceeds 50 percent.[16] Attrition can be reduced by the following strategies:

a. Keep demands made upon the subject to the minimum necessary.
b. Fully inform subjects about your study, emphasizing its importance.
c. Before subjects start participating, obtain a strong commitment from them to complete their part in the research.
d. Make frequent contacts with subjects in order to maintain interest and rapport.

5. *When a high level of statistical significance, statistical power, or both are required.* The level of significance of a statistical test is closely related to sample size. Therefore, fewer subjects are needed to reject the null hypothesis at the

15. Robert L. Goodrich and Robert G. St. Pierre, *Opportunities for Studying Later Effects of Follow Through* (Cambridge, Mass: ABT Associates, 1979).
16. For a discussion of factors affecting sample size, see Robert G. St. Pierre, "Planning Longitudinal Field Studies: Considerations in Determining Sample Size," *Evaluation Review* 4, no. 3 (June 1980): 405–15.

.05 level than at the .01 level. In exploratory studies, many researchers employ an alpha (significance level) of .10 because such studies are often carried out with small samples.

Statistical power is the probability that a given statistical test will result in rejection of a false null hypothesis. Statistical power is enhanced by a large sample size.[17]

6. *When the population is highly heterogeneous on the variables being studied.* If every person in the population were exactly alike on the variable studied, a sample of one would be sufficient. As the population becomes more variable, however, larger samples must be used in order that persons having different amounts of the characteristic in question will be satisfactorily represented.

7. *When reliable measures of the dependent variable are not available.* The reliability of a measure refers to its capacity to yield similar scores on the same individual when tested under different conditions or at different times.[18] The reliability of measures used in educational research differs greatly. Measures of variables such as academic achievement, reading comprehension, typing speed, and visual acuity are usually much more reliable than measures of variables such as personality, honesty, or self-concept. Nevertheless, research in many important areas of education must be done with measures of low reliability or not done at all, simply because the science has not yet advanced to the point where more reliable measures have been developed.

Measures that are less reliable have a larger error of measurement. This topic is discussed further in a later chapter; here it is sufficient to know that for an achievement test with a reliability of .95 and a standard deviation of 10, there is about one chance in three that an individual's true score will differ by more than 2.2 points from the score he obtains when he takes the test. In contrast, if the reliability had only been .50, there is the same probability that his obtained score will differ from his true score by more than 7.1 points. You can see that a test with a reliability of .50 is a rather crude measure and, because of its large error of measurement, may not be sufficiently sensitive to detect small differences. In studies that must employ measures of low reliability, the investigator has little chance of detecting small differences if he uses a small sample. As sample size increases, his chance of detecting small differences or slight relationships improves.

Suppose we wanted to study the difference between the adult height of males born in Germany in 1944-46 and the heights of their brothers born in 1954-56 to determine possible effects of diet on growth. If we use a highly accurate measure of height we can detect a much smaller difference than if we use a crude measure, such as a yardstick. Also, if a difference exists, it would

17. For a discussion of statistical power, see Jacob Cohen, *Statistical Power Analysis for the Behavioral Sciences* (New York: Academic Press, 1977).
18. Reliability is discussed further in chapter 8.

be more likely to show up if we measure a sample of 1000 pairs of brothers than if we measure only 50 pairs.

Small Sample Studies

In many educational research projects, small samples are more appropriate than large samples. This is often true of studies in which role playing, depth interviews, projective measures, and other such time-consuming measurement techniques are employed. Such techniques cannot be used in large sample studies unless considerable financial support is available. However, a study that probes deeply into the characteristics of a small sample often provides more knowledge than a study that attacks the same problem by collecting only shallow information on a large sample. For example, a number of studies have attempted to discover the reasons why many superior college students drop out of college. Most of these studies have consisted of little more than classifying the one-sentence responses made by students on the dropout cards they complete for the registrar. Our knowledge of related studies in sociology and social psychology would lead us to doubt whether students give their true reasons for dropping out of college on such a card. Many students write down a convenient or socially acceptable reason regardless of their true reason for withdrawal. Other students are not fully aware of the true reasons why they are dropping out. The senior author once participated in a research project in which superior students dropping out of Utah State University were given a carefully planned in-depth interview. These interviews, carried out by a trained psychologist, revealed that the student's true reasons for dropping out of college were almost always different from the reasons stated on the registrar's dropout card. Although it involved fewer than fifty superior dropouts, this study produced insights into the reasons for withdrawal from college that probably could never be obtained by the shallower approach employed by other studies.[19]

In other studies very close matching of subjects on the critical variables concerned in the study is possible, and under these conditions, small sampling studies often yield the information sought more efficiently than large sampling studies. The classic study by H. H. Newman, F. N. Freeman, and K. J. Holzinger on the intelligence of identical twins is a good example of such a study:[20] Since identical twins have the same genes, they are ideal for studying the relative influence of heredity and environment upon various human characteristics. One phase of this study, although concerned with only nineteen pairs of separated identical twins, provided information on the relative influences of

19. This study was conducted by Luna R. Brite.
20. H. H. Newman, F. N. Freeman, and K. J. Holzinger, *Twins: A Study of Heredity and Environment* (Chicago: University of Chicago Press, 1937).

heredity and environment upon intelligence that would have been difficult to obtain with large samples of less closely matched subjects.

Estimating Needed Sample Size

Many graduate students carry out studies in which they employ small samples to study variables that are related to each other to a low degree. Their research is doomed to producing negative results because the small differences they are likely to obtain will not be statistically significant with a small sample.[21] In such cases, if the student had carefully thought through the chances of success before starting, she could have revised her plan so as to increase either the power of her treatment or her sample size and thus improve her chances of obtaining significant results.

A procedure such as described in the next few pages, although providing only a rough estimate of minimum sample size, should be followed by students when designing their research.

First, we will consider the procedure for estimating sample size when two groups are to be compared on the dependent variable in order to determine if they are significantly different. Experimental and causal-comparative studies are usually carried out to explore problems of this kind.

The first step is to study carefully related research that has used the same or a closely related dependent variable in order to determine the approximate amount of difference in this variable one might expect to find in one's own study.[22] For example, suppose the researcher is planning a study designed to measure the effect of a new classroom management program on the attitudes toward school of sixth-grade pupils in inner-city schools. He locates three similar studies, each of which used different classroom management programs. However, these programs were all fairly similar to the program he plans to use. Since each study used a different measure of attitude toward school (the dependent variable), he must first review the studies and determine the standard deviation reported for each measure. If different standard deviations are reported for the experimental and control groups, the average will be sufficiently accurate for the estimation to be made. Next he should record the difference between the mean scores of the experimental and control groups for each study. Then, for each study he should divide this difference by the standard deviation to determine the difference in standard deviation units. Finally, he must estimate the power of the treatments used in the three studies. Length of treatment is usually a good estimate of power but there are many other factors the researcher might consider, such as (1) Did all subjects regularly partic-

---

21. See chapter 11 for a further discussion of sample size.
22. This is usually called *Effect Size* and abbreviated ES.

ipate, or was participation irregular? (2) How well were treatments controlled; i.e., did the investigator have methods of ensuring that the subjects actually did what they were intended to do? (3) Did the treatment employ procedures that appear effective? For example, in most cases a treatment in which the subjects perform a task is more effective than a treatment where the subjects read about the task. There are of course many other factors that would give clues to the effectiveness of a specific treatment, and the researcher should try to make the best estimate he can. This estimate is then used by the researcher to estimate how effective his treatment is likely to be compared with those used in previous research. The data on standard deviation, difference, and treatment for our three hypothetical studies is given below:

	A	B	C	D
	Standard Deviation of Dependent Variable	Diff. between Means on Dependent Variable	Diff. in SD (*B/A*)	Length of Treatment
Study 1	16	6	.38	40 hrs. over 8 wks.
Study 2	12	5	.42	32 hrs. over 4 wks.
Study 3	19	5	.26	16 hrs. over 2 wks.

The researcher reasons that in his study the experimental groups of teachers will be trained 48 hours over 12 weeks and tested on the Jones School Inventory, which according to the test manual has a standard deviation of 14. Since his treatment appears to be more powerful than those used in studies 1, 2, or 3, he estimates that the difference between his experimental and control groups in mean scores on the Jones School Inventory will be about half of a standard deviation, or 7 points (i.e., .50 × 14). Thus, the following values should be substituted into the formula for estimating the number of cases (*N*) he will need for each group in the research.[23]

N = number of cases needed in each group to achieve a difference significant at the .01 level. (This is what you want to estimate.)

s = 14 (standard deviation)

t = 2.7 (*t*-test value needed for significance at .01 level with about 45 cases)

23. This formula assumes that the standard deviation for both groups will be the same and that the experimental and control groups will be of the same size. Since the formula only provides a rough estimate, these assumptions would usually be acceptable.

D = 7 (estimated difference between mean scores of experimental and control groups)

$$N = \frac{2s^2 \times t^2}{D^2}$$

$$N = \frac{(2 \times 14^2) \times 2.7^2}{7^2} = \frac{392 \times 7.29}{49} = 58.32$$

The formula indicates that the researcher will need 58 cases in each of the two groups.

A critical point in this estimate, of course, is estimating the size of D, the difference between means. It is advisable for the researcher to be conservative in this estimate. If he has no previous research upon which to base this estimate he should carry out a small-scale pilot study and use his results to estimate D. A pilot study is almost always a desirable step, for reasons explained in chapter 3.

If the researcher is planning a study involving more than two treatments, he can select the two treatments for which he expects the largest mean difference and carry out the above procedure for each pair of groups separately and then decide on his group size by considering all of the N values that he obtains.

Correlational Studies

If the researcher is planning a correlational study, the process of estimating the number of cases needed is much easier. He would again estimate the probable size of the correlation he is likely to obtain based on previous research plus (if possible) the results of a pilot study. Then, using table 7.2,[24] he can go down the r column until he comes to his estimated correlation and then read the number of cases he will require in the N column to be statistically significant.

Since both the described procedures provide only estimates, the .01 level of significance is used. Thus, even if the researcher is a bit optimistic in his expectations, he still has a good chance to obtain a difference that is significant at the .05 level, which is the alpha level selected by most graduate students.[25]

24. This table is based on Henry E. Garrett, *Statistics in Psychology and Education*, 6th ed. (New York: David McKay, 1966), table D, p. 461.
25. For other methods of estimating sample size, see Annotated References at the end of this chapter.

TABLE 7.2
Approximate Number of Cases Needed for a Correlation of a Given Level to Be Statistically Significant at the .01 Level

r	N
.80	7
.75	8
.70	9
.65	10
.60	11
.55	14
.50	16
.45	20
.40	25
.35	32
.30	47
.25	62
.20	100
.15	175

MISTAKES SOMETIMES MADE IN SAMPLING

1. Researcher fails to define the accessible and target populations and to provide evidence of their similarity.
2. Uses a sample too small to permit statistical analysis of interesting subgroups.
3. Fails to use the stratified sampling technique when needed to obtain adequate samples of subgroups.
4. When using volunteer subjects, fails to determine how they differ from non-volunteers and fails to consider these differences in interpreting the findings.
5. Changes the sampling procedure in order to make data collection more convenient for the schools involved.
6. Does not allow for attrition in selecting the sample size.
7. Selects a sample that is not appropriate for the research project.
8. Selects the experimental and control groups from different populations.

ANNOTATED REFERENCES

Babbie, Earl R. *The Practice of Social Research.* Belmont, Calif.: Wadsworth, 1979.

A good source for students who plan to conduct survey research. Contains a chapter on survey sampling procedures and a chapter that gives examples of four sample designs.

Kish, Leslie. *Survey Sampling.* New York: John Wiley, 1965.

In spite of its age, this book is still the basic reference on the use of sampling techniques in the social sciences. The discussion is fairly technical, but it is well worth consulting before the student attempts to use one of the sampling techniques presented in this chapter.

Rosenthal, Robert, and Rosnow, Ralph L. The *Volunteer Subject.* New York: John Wiley, 1975.

Since virtually all educational research must be conducted with volunteer subjects, this book should be required reading for serious students. It pulls together available research evidence on the characteristics of volunteer subjects and discusses the implications of this research for interpreting research findings in studies in which volunteers are used. The situational determinants of volunteering are also reviewed and suggestions are made for reducing volunteer bias.

Sudman, Seymour. *Applied Sampling.* New York: Academic Press, 1976.

This is an excellent source for the educational researcher who plans to carry out survey research. The chapters on small-scale sampling and sample size are especially valuable for the graduate student. The latter chapter explores the question of information versus cost and provides useful formulas for estimating optimum sample size.

The following references provide a variety of procedures for estimating sample size and also effect size, which may be defined either as the size of the correlation or the difference the researcher estimates will be the outcome of the research or as the size of the effect necessary to be of practical significance. Most of the procedures described are somewhat more sophisticated than the procedure described in this text.

Brewer, J. K. "Effect Size and Power: The Most Troublesome of the Hypothesis Testing Considerations." Paper presented at the annual meeting of the American Educational Research Association, New York, 6 April 1977.

Cohen, J. *Statistical Power Analysis for the Behavioral Sciences.* Rev. ed. New York: Academic Press, 1977.

Lynch, M. D., and Huntsburger, C. V. *Elements of Statistical Inference for Education and Psychology.* Boston: Allyn & Bacon, 1976.

SELF-CHECK TEST

Circle the correct answer to each of the following questions. An answer key is provided on page 881.

1. A common error in selecting a sample of research subjects is to
   a. select whatever persons are readily available.
   b. select a sample that is too large for the scope of the research problem.
   c. rely only on stratified sampling.
   d. use tables of random numbers which are not truly random.
2. All the members of a real or hypothetical set of persons, objects, or events are called the
   a. population.
   b. random sample.
   c. stratified sample.
   d. collection.
3. The first step in sampling is to
   a. define the population from which the sample is to be drawn.
   b. determine whether the sample is to be stratified.
   c. determine sample size.
   d. identify desired characteristics of the sample.
4. If the researcher defines his population in a narrow fashion, the research results will be
   a. useless.
   b. generalizable to a limited population.
   c. generalizable to a broad population.
   d. of no theoretical value.
5. A random sample
   a. is one in which each member of a population has an equal chance of being chosen.
   b. must be large in number.
   c. can be selected only by using a specially designed computer program.
   d. All of the above are correct.
6. The main reason for using random sampling techniques is to select a sample that will
   a. include the correct number of subjects.
   b. be stratified.
   c. yield generalizable research data.
   d. yield research findings that are statistically significant.
7. Systematic sampling may be used instead of simple random sampling if the
   a. population list is in random order.
   b. sample size is small.

      c. population is heterogeneous.

      d. expected differences are small.

8. In cluster sampling the unit of sampling is the

      a. individual.

      b. population.

      c. naturally occurring group of individuals.

      d. population after having been subgrouped on characteristics not related to the research.

9. Compared to simple random sampling, the main advantage of cluster sampling is the

      a. degree of randomness it achieves.

      b. accuracy of sampling it achieves.

      c. reliability of research findings to which it leads.

      d. saving in time and money.

10. Large samples must be used when

      a. few uncontrolled variables are present.

      b. small differences are anticipated.

      c. subgroup analysis is not going to be conducted.

      d. the population is highly homogeneous.

APPLICATION PROBLEMS

The following problems are designed to give you practice in applying significant concepts and research procedures explained in chapter 7. Most of them do not have a single correct answer. For feedback, you can compare your answers with the sample answers on pages 888–89.

1. An investigator plans to select a simple random sample of 100 subjects from the population of all fifth-grade pupils attending public schools in Utah. List the steps that she might take to obtain this sample.

2. An investigator wishes to analyze the verbal praise used by primary-grade teachers in a large-city school district. Since he wants an adequate sample of teachers of both sexes and at three different levels of experience, he decides to collect a stratified sample by selecting 20 teachers from each stratum. List the steps he would take in selecting this sample. He does not plan to combine his subgroups for analysis so proportional numbers are not necessary.

3. An investigator wishes to study oral reading performance of second-grade children in a large school district. A total of 3172 second-grade children are enrolled in 104 classrooms in the district. The investigator wishes to obtain a total group of 100 subjects using a two-stage cluster sampling technique. Describe the steps she would take in selecting her sample.

4. An investigator plans to study the effects of learning a problem-solving strategy upon the mathematics achievement of sixth-grade students. He will select a sample of students and randomly assign half of them to the experimental group and half to the control group. All subjects will be given a pretest of mathematics achievement. The experimental group will receive a one-hour lesson which teaches a problem-solving strategy that students can follow when trying to solve word problems in mathematics. The control group receives no special training. Since he expects the problem-solving training to work best with the brighter students, the investigator will divide both his groups in terms of IQ using the following categories: (a) below 90, (b) 90-110, (c) 111-130, (d) above 130. He administers a mathematics achievement posttest two months after treatment to all subjects. What are two reasons why a fairly large sample size is required for this project?

5. What are four procedures in the following research description that are likely to cause sampling bias?

   An investigator teaches three sections of Remedial English for freshman in a large state university. A colleague teaches three sections of regular Freshman English. The investigator has developed a 20-hour program to teach rules of spelling. She gives a spelling test in her sections and in her colleague's sections. Next she selects 63 students from her sections and 36 from her colleague's sections who score below 50 percent on the test. She describes her program to her sections and asks the 63 low scorers to take the program by attending special sessions one hour per day for four weeks. Fifty-one agree to do so. The 36 students in her colleague's sections are used as a control group and receive no special treatment. At the end of four weeks, 26 of her students have completed the spelling program while the remainder have missed from 1 to 18 of the special sessions. She administers a spelling posttest to the 26 treatment subjects and the 36 control subjects and compares their gains since the pretest.

SUGGESTION SHEET

If your last name starts with letters from Fit to Gor, please complete the Suggestion Sheet at the end of the book while this chapter is still fresh in your mind.

8.

SELECTION AND ADMINISTRATION OF TESTS IN EDUCATIONAL RESEARCH

OVERVIEW

Standardized tests are often used in educational research projects to measure factors such as school achievement, aptitude, self-concept, and attitudes. Most tests used in educational research are norm-referenced. In recent years, however, domain-referenced tests of achievement have gained much attention, so these are also discussed. Among the important characteristics of tests discussed in this chapter are validity, reliability, conditions of administration, normative data, and alternate forms. Four kinds of test validity are discussed: content validity, predictive validity, concurrent validity, and construct validity. Also, three methods for determining test reliability are presented and their relationship to standard error of measurement discussed. A discussion of factors to consider in selecting a test for a research project follows, such as the amount of testing time available, whether to use individual or group measures, and how to select between available measures. The chapter concludes with a presentation of guidelines on how to use tests in the context of an educational research project.

OBJECTIVES

After studying this chapter, you should be able to:

1. Describe the four distinguishing characteristics of a standardized test.
2. Describe four types of test validity and identify the type of test validity that should be determined for different research problems.
3. Describe three types of test reliability and identify the type of test reliability that should be determined for different research problems.
4. Interpret the standard error of measurement and describe how it relates to reliability.

5. Describe three problems that arise when the researcher shortens a standardized test.
6. Describe the main steps the researcher must take to develop a measure.
7. Describe item-analysis procedures related to difficulty index, item validity, and item reliability.
8. List five major criticisms that have been made of educational tests.
9. Describe three procedures for ensuring that standard conditions for test administration are met.
10. State at least one procedure for handling each of these testing problems: gaining subjects' cooperation; eliciting maximal performance; obtaining honest answers on personality measures; and giving test results to those who ask for them.
11. Give three reasons why generally it is not advisable to use school-collected test data in a research project.

TESTS IN EDUCATIONAL RESEARCH

In educational research we are usually concerned with one of three major goals. Descriptive research, which includes most surveys, is aimed at describing the characteristics of a population or an educational phenomenon. Correlational and causal-comparative research explores relationships between two or more variables. Experimental research is concerned with the effects of manipulated variables.

Measurement plays an important role in each of these types of educational research. Any procedure that produces objective and quantifiable information is a form of measurement. In education such procedures include interviewing, observation, and the administration of questionnaires and tests. In this chapter we focus on tests, since they are by far the most widely used procedure for collecting information in educational research. Tests come in a variety of types, such as written and oral, norm-referenced and domain-referenced, individual and group. A test can be broadly defined as any instrument for assessing individual differences along one or more given dimensions of behavior.

Most tests used in the behavioral sciences are **norm-referenced**. Briefly, this means that the test produces a score that tells us how the individual's performance compares with other individuals. The manuals for these tests provide the user with tables of norms based on the scores obtained by relevant groups of subjects who have been tested by the test developer. Interpretations based on relative performance are very useful for most of the characteristics we study in the behavioral sciences, such as anxiety, creativity, dogmatism, or racial attitudes.

For some kinds of performance, such as achievement, a measure that tells what the subject knows in absolute terms is often more useful than one that describes his performance in relative terms. For example, it is sometimes more useful to know that a student can read sample articles from a typical newspaper and be able to explain 90 percent of what he has read than to know that he reads better than 62 percent of a sample of other fifth-grade pupils.

In recent years, **domain-referenced tests,** which measure the learner's absolute level of performance in a precisely defined content area or "domain," have been used to an increasing degree to measure achievement-related performance. This chapter emphasizes standardized norm-referenced measures because these are used in the vast majority of educational research. But it also introduces you to domain-referenced tests because these are more useful for many studies involving achievement.

Educational researchers also may develop tests to meet the special needs of a research project. Test development is a difficult process that often requires more training than the typical graduate student in education has acquired. Often, however, graduate students can use measures developed by other researchers, which, although not published, may be carefully developed.

To a degree all the aforementioned measures are "standardized." A **standardized test** is one (1) that produces very similar results when different persons administer and score the measure following the instructions given and (2) for which normative data are present to describe how subjects from specified populations perform. Not only have standardized tests become a basic part of methodology in educational research, but also their practical applications have become increasingly important in society. Think, for example, of the many tests you have taken as you progressed through the American school system— intelligence tests, teacher-made and published measures of school achievement, the Scholastic Aptitude Test, and the Graduate Record Examination. If you sought guidance in deciding upon an academic major and career, you probably completed tests pertaining to vocational interests and personality.

CHARACTERISTICS OF STANDARDIZED TESTS

As mentioned above, standardized tests have a number of important social applications for the classification, selection, evaluation, and diagnosis of persons. Our discussion focuses only on their uses in educational research, however. We begin by considering some of the defining characteristics of a standardized test.

1. *Objectivity.* The **objectivity** of a standardized test depends on the degree to which it is uninfluenced or undistorted by the beliefs or biases of the

individual who administers it. Prescientific measures and the measures used in the less mature sciences tend to have relatively little objectivity. Two individuals may use the same measure and arrive at two different observations or scores. In fact, the development of a science may be traced in terms of the progress it has made in recognizing the possibility of personal errors in measurement and in ruling them out to a greater and greater degree.[1]

The degree of objectivity of standardized tests in education can usually be determined by analyzing whether the administration and scoring procedures permit bias to occur. In our later discussion of individually administered tests (particularly projective techniques such as the Rorschach Inkblot Technique and the Thematic Apperception Test), we show how the conditions of administration and scoring provide a number of opportunities for bias to occur. Not surprisingly, then, these techniques usually do not yield high estimates of interobserver reliability. In contrast, multiple-choice tests are generally considered much more objective since they are self-administered in large part, and all scorers can apply a scoring key and agree perfectly. In fact, these types of standardized tests are often called "objective tests."

2. *Conditions of administration.* It should be apparent that a test is of limited value if its developers do not specify all the directions to be given in administering the test. For example, a standardized test typically includes such information as how much time is allowed for the test, whether guessing is penalized, whether instructions can be repeated, and how student questions are to be answered. The directions may also include specification of how much personal interaction (e.g., establishing rapport) is allowed between the tester and the subjects. An important advantage of using standardized tests in your research project is that if you produce significant research findings, other researchers will be able to replicate and expand on your work because they can create the same conditions of administration by consulting the test manual.

3. *Normative data.* The process of collecting normative data on a test is an important part of the process of standardization. Generally a test developer will administer his test to a carefully defined sample (or several samples, usually varying in sex and age) and collect a set of raw scores. Individual scores are then related to the performance of the group as a whole by compiling a table of **test norms.** Often the raw scores are converted to **percentile ranks.** Given a particular raw score, the table of norms based on percentile ranks enables one to determine the percentage of individuals in the standardization group who received the same or a lower raw score. Table 8.1 is a typical table for converting raw scores to percentile ranks.

The table of norms is very helpful to the researcher because, usually, she

---

1. For further review of experimenter errors and their effects on behavioral sciences, see chapter 15.

TABLE 8.1

Norms Based on Percentile Ranks

Raw Score	Percentile Rank	Raw Score	Percentile Rank
48		34	44
47		33	40
46		32	36
45	99 +	31	30
44	96	30	22
43	93	29	18
42	90	28	15
41	87	27	11
40	81	26	7
39	76	25	4
38	71	24	3
37	65	23	1
36	56	22	1 −
35	49		

is interested in a subject's performance relative to the group rather than the subject's absolute performance. However, the researcher should observe several precautions in using tables of norms prepared by developers of standardized tests. First, the researcher should check to determine whether her sample is comparable to the standardization group on which the table of norms is based. Suppose that the researcher tests a sample of twelve-year-olds with an aptitude test standardized on a group of high school seniors. If she uses the table of norms for that group, she will seriously underestimate the average level of her group. Moreover, the test may be inappropriate for her sample and consequently will yield spurious scores.

Although percentile scores are useful because they are easily understood by the layman, they cannot be used for the computation of statistics. This is because percentile ranks are not linear transformations of raw scores.[2] Therefore, the researcher should convert percentile scores to standard scores for the purpose of statistical analysis. Many standardized tests in use today are provided with a table of norms based on standard scores. Essentially, **standard scores** are a set of transformed scores derived from the mean and standard deviation of the raw scores. The topic of standard scores is developed further in our discussion on analysis of research data in chapter 20.

2. This problem is discussed in most textbooks on statistics.

The student has probably noted that the degree of confidence that can be placed in a table of norms depends on the care with which standard conditions of administration and scoring have been specified by the test developer. For example, if the tests on which normative data are based are scored by two individuals, one of whom is biased to assign lower scores, the resulting table of norms will reflect this bias and therefore will present an inaccurate picture of the distribution of test scores within a given population.

4. *Reliability and validity.* In addition to the characteristics of objectivity, standard conditions of administration, and normative data, standardized tests can also be described in terms of their reliability and validity. These important test characteristics are discussed next.

WHEN IS A TEST VALID?

In selecting a standardized test for use in a research project, the student will want to make a thorough review of the evidence regarding the test's validity. A commonly used definition of validity is that it is the degree to which a test measures what it purports to measure. However, this general definition does not take into account the fact that there is more than one kind of test validity. The prospective test user should ask not "Is this test valid?" but "Is this test valid for the purposes to which I wish to put it?"

Without standards for validity, tests can be misused and may actually have deleterious effects on the person being tested. For example, an unscrupulous test developer might claim, without benefit of supporting evidence, that a particular test predicts vocational success. If the scores from this invalid test are taken at face value by high school counselors, the result could be that many students will be erroneously advised to avoid vocations for which they had aptitude or pursue vocations for which they were unsuited. In general, the dangers arising from the use of invalid tests in research are less serious than those that can occur by using such measures to make educational decisions in the schools.

Researchers sometimes use measures of low or unknown validity because no better measures are available. Most researchers are careful to point out such weaknesses and tend to be cautious in interpreting their results and drawing conclusions. Invalid tests can lead to erroneous research conclusions, which in turn can influence educational decisions. For this reason the American Psychological Association has published guidelines for determining test validity.[3] In

3. See *Standards for Education and Psychological Tests* (1974) in Annotated References at the end of this chapter.

this set of guidelines and in the field of educational measurement generally, four types of test validity are recognized— content, concurrent, predictive, and construct.[4] Since the typical graduate student is probably familiar with these terms, our discussion will emphasize their relevance to the design of a research project.

Content Validity

Content validity is the degree to which the sample of test items represents the content that the test is designed to measure. Content validity should not be confused with *face validity*, which refers to the evaluator's appraisal of what the content of the test measures. For example, if a test purports to measure reading achievement and if the items appear to deal with relevant content in this area, the test can be said to have face validity. In contrast to face validity, which is a subjective judgment that the test *appears* to cover relevant content, content validity is determined by systematically conducting a set of operations such as defining in precise terms the specific content universe to be sampled, specifying objectives, and describing how the content universe will be sampled to develop test items.

Content validity is important primarily in achievement testing and various tests of skills and proficiency, such as occupational skills tests. For example, a test of achievement in ninth-grade mathematics will have high content validity if the items covered on the test are representative, in type and proportion, of the content presented in the course. If test items cover topics not taught in the course, ignore certain important concepts, and unduly emphasize others as compared with their treatment in the course, the content validity will be lower. Unlike some types of validity, the degree of content validity is not expressed in numerical terms as a correlation coefficient (sometimes called a *validity coefficient*). Instead, content validity is appraised usually by an objective comparison of the test items with curriculum content.

Often the test manual will describe the techniques used to arrive at the test content. Thus, a researcher who is interested in selecting a measure of ninth-grade mathematics achievement that is appropriate for his particular sample should determine whether the test developer derived test items from the same textbook or one similar to that which was studied by his sample.

Content validity is particularly important in selecting tests to use in experiments involving the effect of training methods on achievement. Suppose, for example, you are interested in doing a research project to determine whether

4. Concurrent and predictive validity are sometimes grouped together and called *criterion-related* validity because they relate to the ability of a test to measure an individual's behavior on some other variable, called a *criterion*.

an inquiry method of teaching social studies concepts is superior to a noninquiry method. The research project may involve training two groups of sixth-grade teachers to use one or the other method for one school term. At the end of the semester, a test of social studies achievement would be administered to determine whether the two teaching methods lead to different amounts of learning. To make a proper comparison, the researcher should administer an achievement test that is representative of the content covered during the term; in other words, the test should have a high content validity, otherwise one cannot confidently draw conclusions from the study. If the hypothesis states that an inquiry approach leads to superior learning, but the specific content that was learned is not measured by the achievement test, the hypothesis has not been given a fair test.

In many studies, the objectives of the different treatments are not identical. In such cases, the investigator should check the content validity very carefully to be sure that the measure selected is equally valid for all treatments. Obviously, a measure that is more valid for treatment A than for treatment B will produce results that spuriously favor the former. This problem occurred in some of the first research projects comparing the "new" mathematics program with the traditional curriculum. These studies yielded nonmeaningful findings because the content validity of the achievement tests used to assess outcomes was not carefully considered. The usual finding was no difference between the two curricula. However, the content of most mathematics achievement tests about a decade ago emphasized computational skills. With the development of new achievement tests with more emphasis on test items sampling basic concepts, research studies began to show that both curricula led to similar achievement in computational skills but that students in the "new" math curriculum showed superior achievement in their understanding of mathematical concepts. If you are planning a project involving comparision of the effects of several treatments (e.g., different teaching methods) on achievement, then you should select a test whose content is similar to that used in the treatments.

Predictive Validity

Predictive validity is the degree to which the predictions made by a test are confirmed by the later behavior of the subjects. Much educational research is concerned with the prediction of success in various activities. The usual method of determining predictive validity is to administer the test, wait until the behavior that the test attempts to predict has occurred, and then correlate the occurrence of the behavior with the scores of the subjects on the test. Let us take an algebra aptitude test as an example. Suppose that such a test were designed to be administered near the end of the eighth grade to predict success in ninth-grade algebra. At the end of the ninth grade, the test scores would be correlated with a measure of algebra achievement, such as grades in the algebra class or an algebra achievement test. In this case the algebra grades or the achievement test scores would be called **criterion measures.** The correlation between the algebra aptitude test and the algebra achievement test provides us a measure of the predictive validity of the aptitude test, that is, the degree to which its prediction of the student's success in algebra was borne out by his later performance.

It is important to assess the predictive validity of a standardized test before deciding whether to use it in making practical decisions requiring forecasts, such as selecting students for college. Predictive validity is also important in many research projects. As an illustration, suppose that you are interested in planning a research project to identify variables that predict success among high school students in doing remedial tutoring with younger students. In deciding which tests to include in your test battery, you might well look for measures that have been shown to have predictive validity in similar situations. For example, you might find that the Strong Vocational Interest Blank is a good predictor of which high school students will choose to major in education at college. On the basis of this evidence, you might include this vocational interest inventory in your test battery in expectation that it would predict this new criterion, i.e., success in remedial tutoring.

The student who plans to assess the validity of a test in predicting a particular criterion should be familiar with the concepts of base rate and cross-validation. Base rate is the proportion of persons who meet the criterion out of the total number of persons in the population. To illustrate, suppose that a researcher's project involves the use of personality tests to predict students who will be arrested for delinquency during a particular school year. Suppose further that the incidence of delinquency is 5 percent of the particular student population in which the researcher is interested. Thus, in a sample of 100 students it is likely that 5 will become delinquent, and 95 will remain nondelinquent. One can see that with this base rate, one can predict delinquency correctly 95 percent of the time simply by predicting that everyone in the sample will be nondelinquent. Although a valid personality test might further increase the predictability of delinquency under these conditions, the practical value of the test will be slight. The implication of this example is that the student should only attempt to predict a criterion whose base rate of incidence is not exceptionally high or low.

In many prediction studies, a number of tests are used to predict a specific criterion. The reseacher can then develop a prediction equation (see chapter 14) based on some or all of these tests that will yield a higher validity coefficient than the correlation between any one test and the criterion. This prediction equation may be spuriously high, however, because it capitalizes on chance fluctuations in the data. Therefore, to determine the value of the prediction equation it is necessary to cross-validate by administering the same tests to a new sample drawn from the same population. Generally the validity coefficient obtained in the initial study will shrink somewhat for the new sample.

Concurrent Validity

A second type of criterion-related validity is called concurrent validity. The **concurrent validity** of a test is determined by relating the test scores of a group of subjects to a criterion measure administered at the same time or within a short interval of time. The distinction between concurrent and predictive validity depends on whether the criterion measure is administered at the same time as the standardized test (concurrent) or later, usually after a period of several months or more (predictive).

In designing a research project, the student will often be interested in locating a short, easily administered objective test that has high concurrent validity with a criterion which, although important, is more difficult to measure. For example, if the researcher is interested in measuring intelligence, it might be quite impractical to use the Wechsler Intelligence Scale for Children or the Stanford-Binet, each of which must be individually administered and requires one or more hours of testing time. Even though these tests have considerable standardization data and much evidence of predictive and construct validity, it is much more economical to administer one of several brief, objective, group tests of intelligence that have high concurrent validity when compared with the Stanford-Binet or the Wechsler scales.

Tests with high concurrent validity can often be used as a substitute for ratings of a particular personality characteristic. One of the authors planned a research project to determine whether anxious college students showed more preference for female role behaviors than less anxious students.[5] To identify contrasting groups of anxious and nonanxious students, it might have been necessary to have a large sample of students evaluated for clinical signs of anxiety by experienced clinical psychologists. However, the author was able to locate a quick, objective test, the Taylor Manifest Anxiety Scale, which has been demonstrated to have high concurrent validity with clinical ratings of anxiety in a college population. The author saved considerable time conducting the research project by substituting this quick, objective measure for a procedure that is time-consuming and subject to personal error. Nevertheless, if the test's concurrent validity had been established with groups other than stu-

---

5. Meredith D. Gall, "The Relationship Between Masculinity-Feminity and Manifest Anxiety," *Journal of Clinical Psychology* 25 (1969): 294–95.

dents, such as military personnel or psychiatric inpatients, then the author would have had no justification for substituting this test for clinical ratings or other measures of anxiety. When you are deciding which measures to use in a research project, you should seriously consider using a brief standardized test before resorting to measures that require complicated administration procedures.

In evaluation of a test's concurrent validity, it is important to assess the adequacy of the criterion (as is true in evaluation of a test's predictive validity). Occasionally a test will be validated against another test rather than against a meaningful real-life criterion. It is of little value to know that one test of anxiety, for example, correlates highly with a criterion test of anxiety, unless the criterion test itself has been demonstrated to have significant construct or predictive validity. If the criterion is valid, so presumably is the other test that correlates highly with it.

Construct Validity

Construct validity is the extent to which a particular test can be shown to measure a hypothetical construct. Psychological concepts—such as intelligence, anxiety, creativity—are considered hypothetical constructs because they are not directly observable but rather are inferred on the basis of their observable effects on behavior. In order to gather evidence on construct validity, the test developer often starts by setting up hypotheses about the characteristics of persons who obtain high scores on the measure as opposed to those who obtain low scores. Suppose, for example, that a test developer publishes a test that he claims is a measure of anxiety. How can one determine whether the test does in fact measure the construct of anxiety? One approach might be to determine whether the test differentiates between psychiatric and normal groups, since theorists have hypothesized that anxiety plays a substantial role in psychopathology. If the test does in fact differentiate the two groups, then we have some evidence that it measures the construct of anxiety.

A variety of procedures may be used to establish the construct validity of a test, yet many published tests have only a limited amount of evidence to indicate that they are indeed measuring the constructs that they purport to measure. Construct validity is a particularly important factor to consider in planning a research study that proposes to test a hypothesis. For example, suppose that one plans to test the hypothesis that creative children will be able to state more meanings of a word than noncreative children. To test this hypothesis, the researcher will need to ask herself whether her hypothesis presupposes a particular concept of creativity, for example, potential or actualized creativity, artistic or scientific creativity, creativity as process or creativity as product.

On occasion the student may plan a research project in which it is not important to consider construct validity. This is the case when the primary purpose of the research is to find predictors of a criterion on an empirical basis without resort to theory. Here the concern is to identify tests that have predictive validity for a particular purpose. The construct validity of the tests is not necessarily relevant. In fact, it is not uncommon for a researcher to determine a test's predictive validity in one study and then investigate the test's construct validity in later studies. As an illustration, in the field of psychological research, Frank Barron empirically developed a test scale that predicted response to psychotherapy.[6] Since the test predicted an important criterion, Barron conducted additional studies and found that the test appeared to have construct validity as a measure of ego strength, an important concept derived from psychoanalytic theory.

DETERMINING TEST RELIABILITY

Reliability, as applied to educational measurements, may be defined as the level of internal consistency or stability of the measuring device over time. There are several methods of estimating reliability, most of which call for computing a correlation coefficient between two sets of similar measurements. Suppose we wished to measure students' knowledge of physics. A physics achievement test consisting of one multiple-choice item would be highly unreliable. Some students may know quite a bit about physics, yet may not happen to know the answer to this particular test item; in contrast, some students whose achievement level in physics is low may happen to know or guess the correct answer. Also, if we had selected a different item, the results would probably have been much different. Thus, the one-item test is susceptible to many chance factors and therefore is not a "reliable" estimate of the students' level of achievement in physics.

Reliability is an extremely important characteristic of tests, and it must be considered carefully in selecting measures for research purposes. The level of reliability that the research worker should expect from a test is determined largely by the nature of the research in which he plans to use the measure. If the research project is such that the research worker can expect only small differences between his experimental and control groups on a variable measured by the test, it is necessary that a test of high reliability be used. Conversely, if large samples are to be used and if the mean test scores are expected to differ materially for the experimental and control groups, the research worker may select a measure of relatively low reliability and still be

6. Frank Barron, "An Ego-Strength Scale Which Predicts Response to Psychotherapy," *Journal of Consulting Psychology* 17 (1953): 327–33.

reasonably sure that the test will discriminate adequately. The reason a test of high reliability is required in the first situation and not the second is that when only small differences are likely to be found, a test of low reliability may be too crude to reveal these differences. For example, let us say we wished to measure the height of two samples of adult men, but had only a crude measuring device, such as the span.[7] Let us further suppose that the true mean difference in height between the groups is one-half inch. One is unlikely to detect this small a difference because the span is a fairly unreliable measure; a person may not extend his hand to the same length each time, and if more than one person does the measuring, their hands probably will not be of the same size. However, if the true mean difference in heights between the two groups of men is four inches, it is much more likely that the taller group will be accurately distinguished from the shorter group despite the unreliability of the span as a measuring device.

It is much easier to establish the reliability of a test than to establish its validity. Therefore, if no specific information on reliability is provided in the test manual, the research worker may safely assume that the reliability of the test is low. A helpful list of representative reliabilities of standardized tests has been prepared by G. C. Helmstadter[8] and is reproduced in table 8.2. It should be noted that the values of the reliabilities vary with the type of characteristic being measured.

A point that must be watched for in evaluating test reliability is that many

TABLE 8.2
Range and Median Values of Reliabilities Reported for Various Types of Measures

Type of Test	Number of Reliabilities	Value of Reported Reliabilities		
		Low	Median	High
Achievement Batteries	32	.66	.92	.98
Scholastic Ability	63	.56	.90	.97
Aptitude Batteries	22	.26	.88	.96
Objective Personality	35	.46	.85	.97
Interest Inventories	13	.42	.84	.93
Attitude Scales	18	.47	.79	.98

7. The distance from the tip of the thumb to the tip of the little finger when extended.
8. G. C. Helmstadter, *Principles of Psychological Measurement* (Englewood Cliffs, N.J.: Prentice-Hall, 1964), table 8, p. 85.

tests yield a number of subscores in addition to a total score. This is the case for some intelligence and achievement tests that provide subscores in order to give a profile of the student's performance in the various areas making up the test. However, reliability is often reported only for the total score. Therefore, the subscores must be used cautiously unless reliability data are available for them. When such data are not available, the research worker will have difficulty making an intelligent appraisal of the worth of the subscores. He may be sure that all or most of these subscores will have lower reliabilities than the total test reliability. The reliability coefficients of the subscores, however, may differ considerably, with some being as reliable as the total test and others being of such low reliability that they should not be used in the planned research.

The reliability of a standardized test is usually expressed as a coefficient. Reliability coefficients vary between values of .00 and 1.00, with 1.00 indicating perfect reliability, which is never attained in practice, and .00 indicating no reliability. The reliability coefficient reflects the extent to which a test is free of error variance. Error variance may be defined as the sum effect of the chance differences between persons that arise from factors associated with a particular measurement. These factors might include wording of the test, the person's mood on the day the test is administered, the ordering of the test items, or the content that is used. The more closely a reliability coefficient is to the value of 1.00, the more the test is free of error variance and is a measure of the true differences among persons in the dimension assessed by the test.

Reliabilty coefficients can be obtained by several different approaches, and each type has a somewhat different meaning. A description of the types in common use follows.

Coefficient of Equivalence

This method of calculating reliability may be used whenever two or more parallel forms of a test are available. This method is often called *alternate form reliability* and is computed by administering two parallel forms of the test to the same group of individuals and then correlating the scores obtained on the two forms in order to yield a reliability coefficient. The two forms of the test may be administered at a single sitting, or an interval may be scheduled between the two administrations. Some interval between the administration of the forms is usually desirable, especially if the alternate forms are nearly identical, as is the case with some achievement measures. This interval tends to reduce practice effects that may be an important factor if the two forms of the test are administered at the same sitting. Administering the two forms at different times also results in some differences in both the setting and in the state of mind of the individuals who are tested. Therefore, the reliability obtained is usually lower, but reflects better the testing situation that exists in most research projects. At the present time, the **coefficient of equivalence** is the most commonly used estimate of reliability for standardized tests. It is very widely used with standardized achievement and intelligence tests.

Coefficient of Stability

This form of reliability is useful when alternate forms of the test are not available or not possible to constuct. To calculate the **coefficient of stability,** sometimes called *test-retest reliability*, the measure is administered to a sample of individuals, and then after a delay the same measure is again administered to the same sample. Scores obtained from the two administrations are then correlated in order to determine the coefficient of stability. The most critical problem in calculating this form of reliability is to determine the correct delay between the two administrations of the measure. If the retest is administered too quickly after the initial test, students will recall their responses to many of the items, which will tend to produce a spuriously high reliability coefficient. On the other hand, if the retesting is delayed for too long a period, there is a good possibility that the student's ability to answer some items will change. For example, the student may pass through a period of development or learning and thus be better prepared to answer questions on the retest.

Coefficient of Internal Consistency

Several methods can be used to estimate the internal consistency of a test. Unlike other procedures for computing test reliability, internal consistency can be determined from a single administration of a single form of the test. The commonly used methods of computing internal consistency are the *split-half* or *subdivided test*, the Kuder-Richardson *method of rational equivalence*, and Cronbach's *Coefficient Alpha. Hoyt's Analysis of Variance Procedure* is less often used.

The most widely used method of estimating internal consistency is through the split-half correlation. To determine the **coefficient of internal consistency,** the test whose reliability is under investigation is administered to an appropriate sample. It is then split into two subtests, usually by placing all odd-numbered items in one subtest and all even-numbered items in another subtest.[9] The scores of the two subtests are then computed for each individual, and these two sets of scores are correlated. The correlation obtained, however, rep-

---

9. Other methods of splitting the test are sometimes used, such as a logical division of the test into two sets of comparable items.

resents the reliability coefficient of only half the test, and since reliability is related to the length of the test, a correction must be applied in order to obtain the reliability of the entire test. The Spearman-Brown prophecy formula is used to make this correction.[10]

The **method of rational equivalence,** which also provides an estimate of internal consistency, is the only widely used technique for calculating reliability that does not require the calculation of a correlation coefficient. This method gets at the internal consistency of the test through an analysis of the individual test items. It requires only a single administration of the test. A number of formulas have been developed to calculate reliability using this method. These are generally referred to as the Kuder-Richardson formulas, after the authors of an article in which these formulas were first discussed.[11] The formulas in this article are numbered, and the two most widely used are usually referred to as K-R 20 and K-R 21. Items must be scored dichotomously (that is, right or wrong) in order to use these formulas.

Formula 20 is considered by many specialists in educational and psychological measurement to be the most satisfactory method of determining reliability. This formula is being used to an increasing degree to determine the reliability of standardized tests.

Formula 21, a simplified approximation of formula 20, is of value primarily because it provides a very easy method of determining a reliability coefficient. The use of formula 21 requires so much less time than other methods for estimating test reliability that it is highly appropriate for use in teacher-made tests and short experimental tests being developed by a research worker. One desirable aspect of the Kuder-Richardson formulas is that they generally yield a lower reliability coefficient than would be obtained by using the other methods described. Thus they can be thought of as providing a minimum estimate of reliability of a test.

Cronbach's **Coefficient Alpha** (α) is a general form of the K-R 20 formula that can be used when items are not scored dichotomously. For example, some multiple-choice tests and essay tests include items that have several possible answers, each of which is given a different weight. In this case, Alpha is the appropriate method for computing reliability.[12]

Hoyt's Analysis of Variance Procedure is occasionally mentioned in the research literature. It is rarely used, however, since it produces exactly the same results as K-R 20 and is more difficult to compute.

10. See R. L. Thorndike and E. P. Hagen, *Measurement and Evaluation in Psychology and Education,* 4th ed. (New York: John Wiley, 1977), p. 80.
11. M. W. Richardson and G. F. Kuder, "The Calculation of Test Reliability Coefficients Based upon the Method of Rational Equivalence," *Journal of Educational Psychology* 30 (1939): 681–87.
12. See Lee J. Cronbach, "Coefficient Alpha and the Internal Structure of Tests," *Psychometrika* 16 (1951): 297–334.

A Comparison of the Methods of Estimating Reliability

Although the different methods of estimating reliability usually produce similar results, there are usually some differences because different methods take into account different sources of error. Reliability coefficients based on one administration of the test, or of different forms of the test at a single sitting, exclude two sources of error that are present in many research situations where single administration is not possible. First, individuals differ from day to day on many subtle variables such as mood, level of fatigue, and attitude toward the test. Second, in spite of the researcher's efforts to maintain standard conditions, when tests are given on different occasions many small variations are likely to occur in the testing situation. For example, the administrator may read the instructions more rapidly, a light may burn out in the test room, or the school band may march past the classroom window.

The coefficient of stability, in which subjects are administered the same test on two different occasions, fails to reflect a different source of error because of the fact that the subjects are exposed to the same items on both occasions. The items on a particular test constitute only a small sample of all items that could be written in the area the test covers. The specific items on a single test are likely to discriminate in favor of some students and against others. This error will show up if the split-half or parallel-form reliability is computed since the two sets of scores that are correlated are based on different samples of items. However when the test-retest method is used, this source of error is not taken into account.

Only when different forms of the test are administered with a time interval between are all three of these sources of error taken into account. Thus, this method provides a more conservative estimate of reliability and one that reflects the conditions that maintain in most educational research projects. Since reliability data are fairly easy to collect, many standardized tests report reliability coefficients obtained from several different methods. In this case, the researcher should consider which of the aforementioned sources of error will be present in her research and should use, if available, the reported estimates of reliability that take these sources into account.

Standard Error of Measurement

The various forms of reliability give an overall estimate of test consistency that is very useful in comparing different tests that the researcher may want to consider for use in a research project. However, for interpreting test scores, the standard error of measurement is a more useful tool.[13] An individual's test

13. Also called the *standard error of the obtained score.*

score is likely to contain a certain amount of measurement error. The **standard error of measurement** allows the researcher to estimate the range within which the individual's true score probably falls. For example, suppose the test manual for an algebra aptitude test reports that the alternate form reliability coefficient (r_{11}) is .85, for a norm group of 300 eighth-grade students, and the standard deviation of the test scores (s) is 14. To compute the standard error of measurement (s_m) we use the following formula:

$$s_m = s\sqrt{1 - r_{11}}$$

Substituting the given values into this equation we have

$$
\begin{aligned}
s_m &= 14\sqrt{1 - .85} \\
&= 14\sqrt{.15} \\
&= 14 \times .387 = 5.42
\end{aligned}
$$

Since s_m is normally distributed, we can estimate the probability that an error of a given size will occur. The relationship between errors and the normal probability curve is covered in elementary statistics textbooks and is discussed briefly in a later chapter. At this point it is sufficient for you to know that about two-thirds of all test scores will be within plus or minus one standard error of measurement of their true score and about 95 percent will be within ± two s_m. In the above example, if a student obtained a score of 86 on the algebra aptitude test, there would be 2 chances in 3 that his true score would be between 80.58 and 91.42 (i.e., 86 ± 5.42); and 95 chances in 100 that his true score would lie between 86 ± 2 × 5.42 (86 ± 10.84 or 75.16 and 96.84).

It is clear from the formula that the size of s_m is inversely related to the reliability coefficient; i.e., as the reliability becomes higher, the error becomes smaller. If the algebra aptitude test had had a reliability of .96, the s_m would have been 2.8; while if the reliability had been .57, the s_m would have been 9.18. Thus, you can see that tests of low reliability are subject to large errors. Under these conditions an individual's true score on the test may vary by a large number of score points from the score obtained.

Standard error of measurement helps us to understand that the scores we obtain on educational tests are only estimates and can be considerably different from the individual's "true score." With this in mind we can avoid the blind faith in test scores that many educators seem to have. We can see, for example, that there may be no real intelligence difference between two pupils who receive IQ scores of 97 and 102. Standard error of measurement can also be regarded as an index of a test's reliability. In fact, as we have seen, the standard error of measurement can be determined directly from the reliability coefficient and the standard deviation of the test scores. The standard error of measurement cannot be used to compare the reliability of different tests, however, although the reliability coefficient can be used for this purpose.

DOMAIN-REFERENCED TESTS

Most achievement tests used in the public schools evaluate the performance of the individual relative to the performance of a well-defined group that was tested in order to develop the test norms, that is, the norm group. Such tests are called **norm-referenced tests.** Their main goal is to differentiate clearly among students at different levels of achievement. For example, a norm-referenced test in arithmetic achievement will typically contain items on addition, subtraction, multiplication, and division, ranging from easy to very difficult problems involving each operation. Note that arithmetic is broadly defined and that the student's score on the test, although telling how well he compares with other students in overall arithmetic achievement, usually tells little about his specific strengths and weaknesses. For example, consider the test performance of three students: Student A does very well on addition and subtraction, average on multiplication, and zero on division; student B answers about one-third of the items correctly in all four operations; student C gets all subtraction and division problems correct, except those that require regrouping (i.e., borrowing), and misses all addition and multiplication problems that require adding 9 plus 7. These students differ greatly on their specific strengths and weaknesses, yet all could obtain exactly the same score on a norm-referenced test of arithmetic achievement.

A **domain-referenced test** is one that draws a random or stratified sample of items from a very precisely defined content area or domain for which the content limits are clearly specified, such as "all arithmetic problems involving the addition of three two-digit whole numbers." Note that this domain is much more narrow and precisely defined than is "arithmetic achievement" on a norm-referenced test. To obtain a broader estimate of the learner's arithmetic achievement, the investigator would have to define several domains and develop a test to measure the learner's mastery of each. Broadly defined domains lead to heterogeneous content and should be avoided since the resulting test is likely to show that the learner has mastered some aspects of the domain but not others. Such results are less clear and less appropriate for criterion-referenced interpretation than are results based on precise definition of narrow domains.

One major function of domain-referenced tests is to estimate the learner's "domain status," that is, precisely what is his level of performance and specific deficiencies in the domain covered by the test? Another function of such tests is to make criterion-referenced decisions. Once a domain has been defined and items developed, a performance criterion can be established, such as, "Given a sample of problems requiring the addition of three two-digit whole numbers, all students will reach or exceed the 90 percent accuracy level." Scores are then interpreted in reference to this criterion. Domain-referenced tests that are interpreted in terms of students reaching or not reaching an established criterion are called **criterion-referenced tests.**

Norm-Referenced Versus Domain-Referenced Achievement Measures

Whether the researcher decides to use norm-referenced or domain-referenced achievement measures depends on the specific questions she wants to explore. Norm-referenced achievement tests can be used to answer questions such as the following:

1. Where does John stand in reading achievement compared to other children in his first-grade class and compared to the national norm group of first-grade children reported in the test manual?
2. How does the overall arithmetic achievement in Ms. Smith's class compare with that in Ms. Jones's class?
3. How does the science achievement of fifth-grade pupils in the Salt Lake City school district compare with the national norms, or with pupils in the Jordan school district?

Domain-referenced tests can provide answers to some of the aforementioned questions, but are not as useful for comparing relative achievement in a broadly defined content area as are norm-referenced measures. Domain-referenced measures, however, since they deal with a much more specific content domain, are more useful in answering such questions as:

1. What is John's level of knowledge in the domain, e.g., what percentage of addition problems of a given type can we expect him to solve correctly?
2. What are his specific deficiencies in the domain? Domain-referenced tests are much more useful for diagnosis of specific learning difficulties than the typical norm-referenced achievement tests.
3. How is Cheryl progressing relative to her past performance? This question is usually important in self-pacing or individualized instructional programs.
4. What are the specific strengths and weaknesses of a given school program or curriculum; for example, what specific objectives are we achieving with

our new first-grade reading program and what objectives are not being attained? Needs assessments, which examine differences between desired and actual learning status of students in a given school or district, often ask questions of this sort.

5. What specific changes in pupil performance have occurred as a result of changing the curriculum?

In summary, when we want information about student achievement *relative to other students*, we should select norm-referenced measures. When we want to diagnose difficulties or find out what students have achieved *in absolute terms*, we should select domain-referenced measures.

Reliability

Reliability of a domain-referenced test is defined as the consistency of the test in making estimates of the examinee's level of mastery of the test's domain. The correlational methods most often used to determine the reliability of norm-referenced tests are not suitable for domain-referenced tests because the correlation coefficient is not appropriate for comparing sets of scores having little variability, as is the case in domain-referenced tests. Norm-referenced test items are selected to produce maximum variability since the purpose of such tests is to discriminate clearly among students at different achievement levels. In fact, items that nearly all students answer correctly are eliminated from norm-referenced tests. On the other hand, the selection of items for a domain-referenced test is concerned only with selecting items that fit into the domain as defined. Items that everyone answers correctly are not eliminated if they fit into the domain. Therefore, if the training program has been successful, students will vary little on a domain-referenced test because most students will answer most items correctly. In the addition example given earlier, the goal was to bring all students up to the 90 percent mastery criterion. You can see that if this goal is achieved, there will be relatively little variability in the total test scores. In contrast, norm-referenced test items generally are selected at or near the 50 percent difficulty level, which produces maximum variability in the total test scores.

There are procedures for determining reliability of criterion-referenced measures that roughly parallel the split-half, test-retest, and alternate form methods used with norm-referenced tests.

You will recall that the user's main concern in criterion-referenced measures is whether or not students have achieved the criterion established. Reliability estimates compare different forms of the measure on their agreement in placing students into two groups: those who reached the criterion, and those who did not. Reliability is usually reported in terms of percentage of agreement rather than as a correlation coefficient, as is the case with norm-referenced measures.[14]

Validity

Because domain-referenced measures are generally aimed at measuring achievement, evidence of content validity is important. Several procedures have been developed that are generally similar to methods used to establish content validity of norm-referenced achievement tests. For example, R. Hambleton and his associates have developed the following procedure:

1. Select two content specialists.
2. Give each specialist the domain definition (which is a very specific description of the content domain to be tested) and the test items.
3. Have each expert independently rate the relevance of each item to the domain definition using a 4-point scale ranging from "not relevant" to "very relevant."
4. These data are then entered into a table and used to compute a measure of interrater agreement and an index of content validity.[15]

FACTORS TO BE CONSIDERED IN TEST SELECTION

Adjusting to Available Testing Time

A dilemma faced by many graduate students in planning their research is administering satisfactory measures of the variables that are important to their problem within the testing time they can obtain from their subjects. It is desirable to use the most valid and reliable measures available, but when the testing time for these measures is added up, the total often exceeds the time available.

The amount of time available to test research subjects is almost always limited. Suppose the researcher is working with a public school sample, and a total of one hour is available for testing. The researcher may want to administer several measures; however, one of these measures requires an hour to com-

14. For specific procedures for computing the reliability of domain-referenced tests, see Victor R. Martuza, *Applying Norm-Referenced and Criterion-Referenced Measurement in Education* (Boston: Allyn & Bacon, 1977), chap. 17. Another useful source on this topic is Jason Millman, "Reliability and Validity of Criterion-Referenced Test Scores," in *New Directions for Testing and Measurement; Methodological Developments*, ed. R. Traub (San Francisco: Jossey-Bass, 1979).
15. A description of this procedure and others for determining content validity of domain-referenced measures may be found in Martuza's text, listed in Annotated References at the end of this chapter.

plete. If she reads the test manual and reviews the literature, the researcher might learn that a short form of the test, requiring perhaps half the time of the long form, is available. Or she might find another test that is somewhat less reliable but requires only half the administration time. This savings in time permits the researcher to administer one or more additional measures, which may make an important contribution to her research.

The reliability of a test is related to its length. The more items in a test, the better estimate we can make of the person's true score, which would be his score on a test of infinite length. Since the reliability coefficient indicates the extent to which a test reflects true score variance, it follows that a shorter test will usually be less reliable. However, since the test developer retains his best items in the short form, the loss in reliability is often slight. For example, a recent study of the Beck Depression Inventory found that the standard form (21 items) had a reliability of .85, while the short form (13 items) had a reliability of .83.[16]

Many standardized tests in areas such as achievement and intelligence have very high reliability coefficients, typically above .90, and some loss in reliability can be accepted when the measures are to be used for research purposes. When measures such as achievement tests are administered as part of the regular school testing program, the results are usually used for diagnosis or for counseling of *individual* students. In contrast, most educational research projects are concerned with comparing the performance of *groups* of students. Since group performance is more stable than individual performance, lower test reliabilities are acceptable for group research.

If there is no short form available for a test the researcher wants to use and if an acceptable shorter test cannot be located, the researcher who must shorten her testing time has one final option. She may be able to shorten the measure herself. She can estimate the reliability of a shortened version of the test using the general form of the Spearman-Brown Prophecy Formula.[17]

For example, suppose the researcher located an achievement measure with a reliability of .90 that required approximately three times as much administration time as she had available. Using the Spearman-Brown formula, she would find that if she reduced the length of the test to one-third its original length, the estimated reliability would drop to .75. This level of reliability is satisfactory for many research projects.[18]

16. William M. Reynolds and Jonathan W. Gould, "A Psychometric Investigation of the Standard and Short Form Beck Depression Inventory," *Journal of Consulting and Clinical Psychology* 49 (1981): 306–7.
17. This formula can be used to estimate the reliability of either a longer or shorter form of the same test. See Henry Garrett, *Statistics in Psychology and Education*, 6th ed. (New York: David McKay, 1966), pp. 342–43.
18. As the expected difference between the groups studied and the size of the groups increases, the researcher can afford to accept some reduction in test reliability.

Reducing the length of a standardized test, however, should be considered only after other alternatives have been exhausted, for the researcher must deal with three important problems if she decides to shorten a standardized test.

First, she must be sure that in the process of shortening the test, she does not bias its content and therefore seriously lower validity. If the test is in an area such as mathematics achievement, where each concept is covered by several test items, one can usually reduce the length without making significant changes in the range of content covered. For tests of this kind it is often sufficient, if you wish to reduce the length by half, to select every second item; or by two-thirds, to select every third item; and so on.[19]

For many tests, this simple approach will not be sufficient. In this case, the investigator should select at least three judges who are experts in the test area and have them analyze the items and identify pairs or groups of similar items. The desired number of items can then be drawn from these groups. This process will permit shortening the test without making serious changes in its character and coverage. It is, however, difficult to obtain the cooperation of qualified judges and establish an objective procedure they can follow in identifying comparable items.

The second problem the researcher must deal with if she chooses to shorten a standardized test is that of obtaining permission from the publisher. Since most such tests are copyrighted, the researcher cannot ethically or legally copy parts of the test without permission. Some publishers are sufficiently supportive of research to give their permission if they believe the research evidence will contribute to a better understanding of the test in question. Others will charge the researcher for permission to copy or will require that she purchase copies of the test in question. In some cases, if the test author or the publisher believes that shortening the test will seriously reduce validity, permission will be denied. In any event, you can see that obtaining permission can be a slow and frustrating process.

A third problem is that data on norms, validity, and reliability that have been gathered on the original test can be applied to the shortened version only with great caution, if at all. Thus the researcher must collect new normative data if needed in her study; must recompute the reliability; and should collect data from a sample of subjects who are administered in both the original test and her revision, with a time interval, in order to have some basis for establishing the degree of comparability of the two measures.

You can see that shortening a standardized test for use in a research proj-

19. For a simple procedure for developing a short form, see L. Biggers, "An A Priori Approach for Developing Short Forms of Tests and Inventories," *Journal of Experimental Education* 44 (1976): 8–10.

ect adds up to a considerable amount of extra work, which can be avoided if a satisfactory existing measure can be found.

Individually Administered Versus Group Tests

Both group tests and individually administered tests are available for measuring many intellectual and personality characteristics. A group test is one that has been constructed so that a sample of subjects can take the test all at one time; the test giver distributes the tests, reads directions, and may time it if it is a speed test. Such tests usually yield objective scores, of the yes-no, multiple-choice, or true-false type. By definition the individual test is one in which the tester measures one subject at a time. Most projective tests, such as the Rorschach Inkblot Technique, and some measures of intelligence, are of this type.

Individually administered measures should be selected only when they make an essential contribution to the research project. This is usually the case when the researcher is interested in studying *process* rather than *product*, that is, *how* children respond to certain test items rather than what their total score is. Most standardized tests represent a product approach to measurement. An achievement test in mathematics, for example, usually yields a single score or set of scores that sums up an individual's performance on the test. Of course, it is important to have a measure of the product of performance, but there are also situations in which it is important to know the process by which an individual earned a particular score on the test. Why did the individual miss particular items on an arithmetic test? Did he guess, or was he careless in his computations, or did he lack understanding of basic mathematical concepts, such as regrouping as used in subtraction problems (e.g., $38 - 19 = \Box$)? The test would need to be individually administered in order to assess these aspects of a subject's performance. Tests developed in a clinical setting, such as the Rorschach Inkblot Technique and the Thematic Apperception Test, often are individually administered so that the clinician can measure not only a subject's responses but can also learn why the subject gave a particular response. Thus, if you are interested in such topics as the problem-solving techniques of fifth graders and eighth graders, or identification of reading disorders in low-achieving students, you probably will need to use individually administered measures in your research.

The nature of the sample will also determine whether individually administered tests are necessary. Very young children, for example, usually cannot be tested as a group because their attention span is limited and they do not have the reading skills required by group tests. Other groups, such as the retarded or physically handicapped, may also need to be tested individually.

Delinquents and potentially recalcitrant groups may require individual testing if there is reason to believe that their performance on a group test will be unreliable.

Individually administered tests generally have a number of disadvantages for the graduate student. First, specialized training is often required to administer such tests. If he is unable to administer the test himself, the student probably will have to incur the expense of hiring experienced testers. This in itself presents a problem since it is well established that for most projective measures, the tester affects the results.[20] As we shall find later in this chapter, it is usually necessary to employ more than one tester to control for a possible tester effect. Second, these tests generally cannot be scored with the objectivity of group tests. Therefore, you may need more than one scorer in order to increase reliability. Third, scores yielded by many individually administered tests are not immediately interpretable, but require interpretation by a trained educational or clinical psychologist.

The fact that individually administered tests have a number of disadvantages compared to group tests does not mean that the student should rule out using them in his research project. Nevertheless, since they are difficult to use, they should be selected only when they make an essential contribution to the research.

Selecting between Measures of the Same Variable

Much of what has been presented in this chapter is designed to help the graduate student make decisions about measures he will use in his research project. It is not uncommon for a student to search for a measure of a particular variable, only to find that several measures are available. Which measure should the student select? The answer to this question is complex. Some alternative measures can be ruled out because they are unsuitable for one's sample of subjects. Perhaps others will be found deficient in test reliability and validity or will require too much time. Yet occasionally situations arise when the student has a number of seemingly appropriate measures from which to select.

To consider an example of such a situation, suppose that the student wishes to investigate the hypothesis that creative college students will do better than noncreative students in courses in which grades are based primarily on essay tests, but no difference in grades is expected between the two groups in college courses that rely primarily on multiple-choice exams for grading purposes. To test this hypothesis, the student will need to measure individual differences in creativity among college students. A review of the literature would

20. Joseph M. Masling, "The Influence of Situational and Interpersonal Variables in Projective Testing," *Psychological Bulletin* 57 (1960): 65–85.

indicate that creativity in college students has been measured by a number of tests, including the Remote Associates Test, the Barron-Welsh Figure Preference Test, and the Myers-Briggs Type Indicator. These tests all have favorable evidence regarding their reliability and validity. Which of these tests should the student select for his research project? If he has not already done so, the student should examine the rationale of his hypothesis very closely. Perhaps his rationale is that grades on essay tests reflect in part the ability to generate novel ideas about a given topic, whereas grades on multiple-choice tests emphasize the ability to assimilate facts. In this case the Remote Associates Test may be the best test to use because it measures the ability to generate remote associations to words. (Of course, if another test could be located that had been demonstrated to predict creativity in essay writing, this would be the test to use.) If, on the other hand, he cannot arrive at an exact definition of creativity, then perhaps the student should consider doing an empirical study rather than a hypothesis-testing study. In this case he might want to select several measures, including those mentioned here, to correlate with grades in the two types of courses.

To summarize, selecting between alternate measures of the same or ostensibly the same variable involves several considerations: suitability for one's sample of subjects, appropriateness in terms of testing conditions such as administration time, evidence regarding the tests' reliability and validity, and the way in which each test measures the variable with which one is concerned.

Is the Test Appropriate for Your Research?

The student will need to evaluate a test carefully before deciding on its appropriateness for her research sample. Some of the considerations involved in this evaluation have been discussed already under other headings.

It is important to check the reading level of the test, particularly if it will be used by elementary school children. Occasionally one finds a test that the manual describes as usable at a particular grade level but that includes many words not generally known by students at that level. Such a test would be invalid since the score would depend to some degree on vocabulary and reading ability rather than on ability in the characteristic the test purports to measure.

In selecting an aptitude or achievement test, the student should judge its appropriateness in terms of the general aptitude or achievement level of her research sample. Each test is designed to work most efficiently at a particular level. Some tests claim to be usable over a fairly wide age or grade range, but such measures are generally more accurate at the center of their range than at the extremes. If it is not appropriate for the level of subjects to be tested, a test will not discriminate; that is, it will fail to reflect differences that exist among the subjects. A test that is too easy discriminates poorly because most subjects will receive perfect or near-perfect scores. For example, if we administer a third-grade arithmetic test to ninth-grade pupils, all but the poorest ninth-grade pupils will obtain nearly perfect scores. It is impossible to determine from this test how much arithmetic a ninth-grade pupil knows. Average students, above-average students, and highly superior students will all receive about the same score on the test. The same, of course, is true of a test that is much too difficult or advanced for the subjects. In this case, all but a few superior students will receive very low scores.[21]

In many research projects, the test norms provided by the publisher are used in some phase of the research. If they are to be used, these norms must be based on subjects who are reasonably comparable to the research subjects. Also, the test's reliability and validity data should have been collected on samples comparable to the one that will be used in the research. The importance of this point is illustrated by a study using the California F-Scale, a measure of authoritarianism, to predict plant workers' performance.[22] The researchers noted that most of the construct-validity studies on the F-Scale were based on urban middle-class Americans. They predicted that this measure would not be valid for subjects born and reared in rural environments. To test this prediction, the researchers measured plant workers' productivity before and after an experimental treatment in which the workers were extensively interviewed and observed by so-called researchers. The hypothesis was that increases in productivity would be positively correlated with presence of authoritarian trends, as measured by the F-Scale, in urban but not in rural workers, since the so-called researchers would be perceived as authority figures toward whom authoritarian personalities would be likely to respond positively. As hypothesized, a statistically significant correlation of +.39 was found between the F-Scale and productivity increases for the workers born and reared in an urban environment. For the subsample *born and reared in a rural environment*, however, a nonsignificant correlation of +.04 was found.

This study makes the point that a test may be valid for one population but not for another. Therefore, the student should make certain that a particular test's validity data are appropriate for her sample of subjects before deciding to use it in her research project.[23]

21. To get a sense of how tests are designed to be appropriate for particular populations varying in ability, the student should read Lee J. Cronbach, *Essentials of Psychological Testing*, 3rd ed. (New York: Harper & Row, 1970).
22. Stephen M. Sales and Ned A. Rosen, "Subcultural Variations in the Validity of the California F-Scale," *Educational and Psychological Measurement* 27 (1967): 1107–14.
23. For more information on differential validity, see Cameron Fincher, "Differential Validity and Test Bias," *Personnel Psychology* 28, no. 4 (1975): 481–500.

DEVELOPING MEASURES

The development of new measures in the behavioral sciences is a complex and difficult process that should not be attempted by the graduate student until he has had training in educational and psychological measurement. The development process, although generally similar for all measures, differs in many specifics depending upon the kind of measure to be developed. For example, the process of developing a multiple-choice achievement test in American history is much different than that involved in developing an attitude scale designed to measure teacher attitudes toward handicapped children.

Steps in the Process

It is beyond the scope of this book to provide detailed information on the test development process. The following brief outline is designed to give the student some insight into the general process of test development. Additional steps are necessary for some types of measures. The Annotated Reference section lists sources that provide more detailed coverage on test construction.

1. *Define objectives.* Any test development effort should start with careful thought about the specific outcomes that the measure is to achieve. Construction of achievement tests requires careful description of the knowledge or skills that the test should measure. In attitude scale construction, a clear definition of the attitude to be measured and a statement on how the results of the measure will be used are needed.

2. *Define the target population.* The target population should be defined in detail since characteristics of the target population must be considered in many of the decisions that must be made on such questions as item type, reading level, test length, and type of directions.

3. *Review related measures.* Much can be learned by a careful study of tests that measure similar characteristics. An in-depth review of a few relevant measures will provide many ideas on methods for establishing validity, how different types of items can be applied, what levels of validity and reliability can be expected, and possible formats.

4. *Develop an item pool.* Before starting to write test items, the developer should make a number of decisions, such as: What types of items should be used? How long should the test be? How much emphasis should be given to each aspect of the characteristic or content area to be measured?

A great deal of information is available in the measurement literature on procedures for writing test items. The process of writing items is much more complex than generally thought, with many pitfalls. Thus, the next step in developing an item pool is to develop some skill in writing items. Several of the references given at the end of this chapter give information on item writing. Since many of the prototype items will be found unsatisfactory when the test is tried out, it is usually necessary to write at least twice as many items as will be needed on the final form of the test.

Many strategies are used by professional test developers to obtain items. For example, achievement tests for the public schools are sometimes developed by bringing a group of outstanding teachers to a central location and paying them to define the content area and to develop prototype items.

5. *Prepare a prototype.* The first form of the test puts into effect the earlier decisions on format, item type, etc. The test is usually somewhat longer than the final product since one can expect that many items will be discarded after tryout. The prototype test represents the developer's best judgment about what form the test should take.

6. *Evaluate the prototype.* Often the first step in evaluating the prototype is to obtain a critical review by three or more experts in test construction. This review usually identifies needed changes and raises many questions that can be answered only by a tryout of the test. The prototype is then field-tested with a sample from the target population. It is usually desirable to have a sample of 100 or more subjects in order to obtain good enough data for item analysis. However, when small or difficult-to-reach populations are involved, the researcher must often settle for smaller samples.

Item analysis. After the data are collected, an item analysis is conducted. The general purpose of the item analysis is to identify good and bad items. The specific analysis and interpretation depends upon the nature of the test. For example, in developing norm-referenced achievement tests the item analysis is usually concerned with the difficulty level of each item and its ability to discriminate between good and poor students.

The **difficulty index** is usually computed for cognitive measures such as aptitude and achievement tests. It is simply a tally for each item of the number of subjects who answered the item correctly, divided by the total number of subjects taking the test. For most norm-referenced achievement measures the ideal item difficulty level is .50, i.e., half the subjects respond correctly. An exception is when the test has been designed to discriminate among subjects at a given cutoff point. Suppose, for example, that a vocational school wanted to develop a driving aptitude test to select students to be trained in truck driving. If they wanted to select the top 25 percent of the applicants, this could be done more accurately using items with a difficulty index of .25. For measures in which the subject can obtain a certain number of correct answers by guessing, a correction may be made to the difficulty index.[24]

Item validity is the correlation between subjects' responses to a particular

24. See Guilford and Fruchter in Annotated References at the end of this chapter.

item and their scores on the criterion measure. The validity coefficient therefore tells the degree to which correct responses on the given item relate to the subjects' performance on the criterion measure. The usual procedure for determining item validity is:

1. Compute the score of each subject on the criterion measure.
2. Select the 27 percent of the subjects who obtain the highest criterion score and the 27 percent who obtain the lowest criterion score.
3. For each of these two groups, tally the proportion who answer the first item correctly.
4. Using the proportions, consult Appendix D to determine the item-validity coefficient.[25]
5. Repeat steps 3 and 4 for each item on the test.

Item reliability is the correlation between subjects' responses to a particular item and their total test score. To determine item reliability the same steps are followed as for item validity except that total score on the test being developed is used instead of the scores on the criterion measure. For example, suppose you have carried out steps 1-3, using total test score, and have determined that .86 of the upper 27 percent group answered item 1 correctly as opposed to .50 of the lower group. We read along the top of the table until we come to 86.[26] We then read down the left hand column until we come to 50. At the intersection of the 86 column and the 50 row we find .42. This is the item-reliability coefficient.[27]

The student should study the references given at the end of this chapter before attempting to interpret these coefficients. The main purposes of the item analysis are to select valid and reliable items of appropriate difficulty level and to identify items that need revision.

7. *Revise measure.* On the basis of the experience gained in the field test and the results of the item analysis, the prototype test is revised and preparations are made for a field test of the revised measure. This cycle of field test and revision may have to be repeated several times in order to develop an effective instrument.

8. *Collect data on test validity and reliability.* Some data on the validity and reliability of the test will be obtained during development. The main effort is usually delayed until the instrument is in final form, however, since data on

---

25. The coefficients in the table are normalized biserial correlations. Other types of correlation are more appropriate under some conditions. See J. P. Guilford and B. Fruchter in Annotated References.
26. Decimals have been omitted from this table.
27. Some authors recommend multiplying the validity or reliability coefficient by the item standard deviation or variance to obtain a validity or reliability index.

earlier forms cannot be applied to the final form because of the revisions that have taken place. The *Standards for Educational and Psychological Tests* published by the American Psychological Association (see Annotated References) can provide useful guidelines on the kinds of data that should be collected. Tests developed for use in a single research project rarely meet all these standards, but a review of the standards can still provide many helpful ideas—especially with regard to reliability and validity.

You can see from this brief outline that developing a new measure is difficult and time-consuming. It is a task that the graduate student should not undertake until he has had adequate training in educational measurement. The progress of any science is closely linked to the development of new and better measures of the phenomena that are its concern. The rigorous development and validation of a new measure, therefore, can be a significant contribution to knowledge. Such an effort is, in itself, often an acceptable problem for the thesis or dissertation.

USING TESTS IN RESEARCH

Establishing Standard Conditions

Part of the meaning of the term *standardized test*, as we noted earlier, is that the test developer has specified the same conditions (directions, materials, timing, etc.) for every person who will take the test. Without standard conditions of administration, tables of norms and studies reporting validity and reliability would be worthless to the user. Similarly, the student's research findings can make no scientific contribution if he does not ensure standard conditions of administration for the tests used in his project.

The importance of this aspect of research procedure can be illustrated by a study investigating tester effects on the Stanford-Binet Intelligence Scale.[28] Six female and seven male testers administered the Stanford-Binet to a sample of four-year-old minority-group children. It was found that the children tested by females earned a significantly higher mean IQ (89.61) than those tested by males (83.19). Thus, it appears that some of the variance in these children's IQ scores is attributable to the testers rather than to "true" individual differences in intelligence. In this sense, the IQ scores are unreliable. The purpose of establishing standard conditions of administration is to reduce error variance (such

---

28. Victor J. Cieutat, "Examiner Difference with the Stanford-Binet I.Q.," *Perceptual and Motor Skills* 20 (1965): 317–18.

as that attributable to tester characteristics) and at the same time increase true-score variance.

The problem of tester effects is a particular concern with individually administered tests because this situation provides the tester with ample opportunity to bring his personality into the testing relationship.[29] To control for tester effects, the student is advised to employ experienced testers. Second, it is advisable to employ more than one tester. The data collected by each tester can then be compared to determine whether the findings have been influenced by tester effects. For example, suppose one is interested in comparing the intelligence of 30 sixth-grade students nominated as showing signs of creativity with 30 students nominated as noncreative. Futher, suppose that four experienced examiners are employed to test the subjects. Each examiner will then test 15 randomly assigned students, half (7 or 8) in each group. Then, using analysis of variance (see chapter 15) the student can determine whether the testers affected the results. One may find that some testers obtained higher IQ scores than others, or that there is an interaction; that is, for some testers creative childen score higher on the Stanford-Binet. In summary, when the tester is a potential source of variance, it is important to employ more than one tester.

Standard conditions of administration are also extremely important for group tests. The test manual will usually provide specific directions for the tester to read to the group that he is testing. These directions should be read carefully before he enters the test session. Otherwise he may find himself in the situation of being unable to answer subjects' questions, even though the answers are contained in the test manual; or he may use a test procedure that he finds afterward to be nonpermissible.

Although tests vary widely in conditions of administration (e.g., speededness vs. nonspeededness, encouragement or discouragement of guessing), two sets of conditions remain constant across tests. First, subjects should be tested in a comfortable physical environment. An overcrowded classroom, poor lighting, and excessive outside noise may all contribute to error variance in subjects' scores. Second, the state of the person or persons being tested should be a paramount concern. Someone who is overly anxious or fatigued is not likely to turn in a representative performance on a standardized test. To minimize such effects on subjects' performance, the researcher should take care not to test subjects at unusual times (e.g., orientation week, examination week, end of the school year), and as a general rule should not administer more than one or two tests in a single session.

29. For a review of studies on experimenter effects, of which tester effects is one aspect, see Robert Rosenthal and Ralph L. Rosnow, *Artifact in Behavioral Research* (New York: Academic Press, 1969).

Motivating and Gaining Subjects' Cooperation

The subjects' cooperation is important if test results are to be meaningful. Before administering a test, the researcher needs to ask herself the questions: How can I enhance the amount of cooperation I will receive from my subjects? What might motivate students to turn in a maximal or typical performance on the measures I will administer?

Some answers to these questions have been given in the previous section. A comfortable physical environment and the consideration for subjects' mental and physical state are likely to increase the cooperation they will give. Another important consideration is that the tester be very familiar with the test directions. It can be very annoying for a subject to be tested by someone who fumbles with materials, who appears unsure of herself, or who makes obvious errors. Subjects are likely to feel that if the research were of any importance, the tester would be more conversant with test materials and directions. Feeling that the research lacks significance, subjects may take a haphazard approach to the testing; as a consequence their test scores will be unreliable.

An obvious way for the researcher to gain familiarity with a particular test outside of a formal research testing session is to "pretest" the measure. The researcher can enlist the cooperation of a few friends or subjects and practice the testing procedures on them. One of the authors had to train eight testers to administer a test individually as part of a research project. Since none of the testers was familiar with the test, they were asked to study the directions first and then asked to practice administering it to the author until their proficiency reached an acceptable level.

If she wants to increase the likelihood that she is sampling subjects' maximal performance (as on tests of aptitude or achievement), the researcher should attempt to make the testing a reinforcing event for the subject. In the case of elementary and high school students, she can often do this by gaining the cooperation of the students' teacher beforehand.[30] Students often have a strong need to please their teacher; thus, you might request the teacher to tell her students that the test is important and that they should try to do their best on it. College and graduate students are usually intrinsically motivated to do well on tests. To increase the cooperation of these groups, the authors have found that a good technique is to tell them that you will reveal the purpose of the research after the testing is finished. This technique appeals to subjects' sense of curiosity and serves as a reinforcer for them to cooperate in taking the tests. Another good technique is to make the testing appear important; the use of a stopwatch and reading directions from a manual are likely to make subjects feel that their performance is of significance to the tester.

---

30. Procedures for gaining the cooperation of school and other officials are discussed in chapter 3.

In administering tests of personality, questionnaires, and attitude scales, the tester is often faced with the problem of having subjects depict themselves in a typical, honest manner. Some items in these tests may ask subjects to give personal information that they may feel uncomfortable about revealing. The tester should make it clear before the testing session begins that under no circumstances will data collected on any individual be revealed to anyone. It is also helpful to remind subjects that test scores will be reported in group form only. To protect subjects' sense of privacy and anonymity further, it is recommended that the researcher assign code numbers to all subjects. If the researcher plans beforehand, she should be able to arrange the testing session so that subjects can write a code number on the test instead of their names.

The testing of preschool and primary-grade children will present special problems to the researcher. Trained testers should be employed to administer the research measures to these groups; otherwise the resulting test scores are likely to be quite unreliable. Test manuals will often contain special directions to be used when testing these age groups.

Older students will often ask whether it is appropriate to guess on a test of aptitude or achievement. Usually the test manual will contain directions that can be given to subjects on this matter. However, if a subject persists in asking questions about guessing after the directions have been read, or if no directions are contained in the test manual, the tester should not attempt to influence the subject. When this situation arises, the tester's response should be something like "Do what you think is best" or "Use your judgment."

Occasionally after a testing session is ended, one or two subjects will ask if they can have access to their test results. As a rule, the researcher should not provide subjects with this information. Most subjects will be satisfied if they are told that the tests were administered for a research project, and therefore they can be used only for this purpose. If some subjects persist in wanting to learn their test scores, the researcher can recommend that they go the school counselor or campus counseling center where they will be able to receive professional assistance.

Scheduling and Administering Tests in the Schools

If the student plans to administer tests in the schools as part of his research project, his success will depend on how carefully the scheduling of tests meets the conditions that prevail in most schools. First, do not schedule excessively long testing sessions. The nature of the test and the motivation of the students must be considered in setting up a testing session. It is doubtful whether children in the upper elementary grades should be tested more than ninety minutes in a single session and whether single sessions should extend beyond three hours for students at the secondary level. The ideal testing times for most students are probably about one-half of these time limits. If testing is to be scheduled for more than one school period, it is usually necessary and desirable to schedule breaks. These breaks may be scheduled between tests or even during a nontimed test. It is usually sufficient to permit the students to stand at their chairs, stretch, and talk for two or three minutes.

In setting up the schedule, the research worker should attempt to complete all testing within a reasonably short period. If the testing program is stretched out over a period of several weeks, as is sometimes the case when large samples must be tested, there is some danger that the testing situation will be somewhat different for those persons tested last as compared to those persons tested first. In the case of achievement measures, for example, students tested last will have had additional time in which to achieve, and may therefore earn higher scores than pupils tested early in the program. The research worker should avoid testing near holidays or too close to the end of the school year. The excitement attending the holiday can make a significant difference in the attitude of students concerning the testing. Testing during the last month of the school year often causes problems because students are less likely to be attentive to the test, and it may be difficult to arrange makeup tests prior to the end of the term. Also, because numerous special programs and extracurricular activities are scheduled at this time, many students will be absent from the testing.

Whenever possible, students should be tested in small groups. The regular classroom unit is probably the most desirable group to test because the students are in a familiar environment and the group is small enough so that the test administrator can maintain good control over the situation. Testing in large groups, on the other hand, makes it difficult for the administrator to answer questions or to collect materials, and a single giggle can result in the test situation degenerating into chaos and confusion.

Although he will often be unable to achieve an ideal testing situation, the research worker should attempt to set up the most favorable situation possible. If experimental and control groups are to be tested separately, as is often the case, he should also attempt to equalize as much as possible the situation faced by the two groups. For example it would be undesirable to test all experimental subjects in the morning and all control subjects in the afternoon because students are often less alert and less highly motivated during the afternoon session. It would be similarly undesirable to test all experimental subjects during the first week of the testing program and all control groups during the second week. To whatever extent such scheduling variables can be equalized between the experimental and control groups, this should be done.

During the scheduling session, the research worker should also come to an agreement with the school principal involving such questions as: What help will the schools provide for the testing program? How will makeup tests be scheduled and who will administer them? What role will the classroom teacher play in the testing program? How will disciplinary problems that occur during the testing period be handled? This latter question is especially important because a prompt and efficient means of handling disciplinary problems often makes the difference between maintaining or losing control of the testing situation. If the testing is to be carried out in the classroom, the research worker should also visit each teacher who will be involved and discuss the teacher's role during the testing. Under certain conditions it would be more desirable for the teacher not to be present during the testing session, while in others the teacher might assist as a proctor and be responsible for disciplinary problems. The role of the teacher must be decided on the basis of the needs of the specific study, but should always be fully understood prior to the start of the session.

If he has done a thorough job of pretesting and preparing for the testing program in which he will collect his research data, the research worker has little to do during the actual session except follow closely the procedure he has developed and tried. In the event that some unusual or some unforeseen situation arises during a testing period, the research worker should make careful notes of what occurred in order to determine later whether the occurrence has introduced factors or biases that will reduce the value of the data.

Using Test Data Collected by Schools

The student is often under pressure in carrying out research for the master's thesis to use test data already collected by the schools. This is generally not advisable for several reasons. First, the measures available are often not those that are most appropriate for the research project. Second, there will probably be some subjects whom the student wishes to include in her sample who will not have taken the test. Third, the research worker does not know the conditions under which the test was administered and, of course, had no control over these conditions. The student is therefore urged to select and administer the measures that seem most appropriate for her research whenever this is possible and to avoid using data not collected under her control.

The Social Significance of Testing

In the last fifty years the testing movement has had a major impact on American society. Each year literally millions of tests are administered for the purpose of making important decisions about individuals—Who shall be admitted to college and to what college? Who shall be selected to fill a particular job opening? Who needs to be hospitalized for mental illness? Therefore, the researcher planning to use standardized tests needs to realize some of the ethical issues that have arisen in connection with the testing movement.

The early 1960s witnessed a rash of books attacking tests.[31] Chief among their criticisms of testing were these:

1. *Invasion of privacy.* Some tests, particularly those dealing with personality, ask individuals to reveal information usually considered personal. The individual's right to privacy is generally considered to be a basic American value.

2. *Accessibility of test data.* Test scores are not usually made available to the individual tested, yet important decisions about him are often made on the basis of these scores. This situation gives testers a potentially large degree of power over an individual's destiny and may make the individual feel helpless and under the control of testers.

3. *Rigid use of test scores.* Critics complain that testers make no allowance for change in the individual or in the environment. Although an individual may earn low achievement scores during a particular school year, this does not mean necessarily that he will continue to be a low achiever. Also, the individual's environment is often a changing one, and therefore test predictors may only be valid for a short period of time and within a limited environmental setting.

4. *Types of talent selected by tests.* Tests generally sample only a few of the aptitudes and personality traits important for success in a given area. Thus, if aptitude tests alone are used to select individuals for college, this practice may discriminate against individuals who do not have high scores on the aptitudes measured by these tests but who do have a high level of creativity or artistic aptitude. A related criticism is that tests can perpetuate the status quo rather than encourage change. For example, if college admission is determined only by scholastic aptitude tests, only persons of high scholastic aptitude will complete college. These graduates, now in a position of power, may continue the use of the same tests to select students who are similar to themselves. This approach to test use may keep individuals out of college who might bring about productive changes in the college system.

5. *Unfairness to minority groups.* It has been claimed that some aptitude and intelligence tests are unfair to minority groups because they contain test items pertaining to experiences that these groups may not have enjoyed. Therefore, minority groups will earn undeservedly low scores on these tests

31. Among those authors who criticized the testing movement most severely were H. Black, *They Shall Not Pass* (New York: Morrow, 1963); Martin L. Gross, *The Brain Watchers* (New York: Random House, 1962); and B. Hoffman, *The Tyranny of Testing* (New York: Crowell-Collier, 1962).

and not be selected for schools and jobs that would help them improve their social and financial status. The degree to which widely used intelligence measures such as the Wechsler Intelligence Scale for Children (WISC) and the Stanford-Binet discriminate against minority-group children is not clear at this time. Two major court cases (*Larry P.* v. *Riles* and *P.A.S.E.* v. *Hannon*) have examined this issue. In the former case the court ruled in 1979 that these measures were culturally biased, whereas in the latter case the court ruled in 1980 that the same measures did not discriminate against black children.

Recent federal legislation has required that tests used to identify handicapped children be selected and administered so as not to discriminate racially or culturally. In response to this requirement, Mercer and Lewis devised a set of tests and procedures, the System of Multicultural Pluralistic Assessment (SOMPA), which is designed to provide a fairer way of assessing children from different ethnic and cultural backgounds.[32] Although professionals are not fully in agreement on the effectiveness of SOMPA, it appears to be a significant step toward achieving a comprehensive nondiscriminatory assessment.[33]

In summary, the claim that many tests are unfair to minority groups is probably valid. However, work is progressing to eliminate or greatly reduce this discrimination.[34]

6. *Low predictive validity.* A criticism often heard in recent years is that many tests simply do not do the job they were designed for. Aptitude tests such as the Scholastic Aptitude Test and the Graduate Record Examination are often criticized because of their low validity for predicting both educational and vocational success. It is true that many such measures, when used alone, do a poor job of prediction. Nevertheless, critics often overlook the fact that most prediction studies, such as prediction of success in college, are based upon several variables of which the aptitude test is only one. The validity of the entire battery of measures is often high enough to make reasonably accurate predictions of the future success of the applicant.[35]

Although they are primarily addressed to situations in which tests are used to make practical decisions affecting individuals' lives, these criticisms are sometimes applied to research projects involving testing. This is particularly

32. Jane Mercer, *"SOMPA": Technical Manual* (New York: Psychological Corporation, 1979).
33. For an extensive discussion of SOMPA, see *School Psychology Digest* 8 (1979). The entire issue is devoted to this topic.
34. See Laura Hines, "Nondiscriminatory Testing: The State of the Art," *Peabody Journal of Education* 58, no. 2 (1981): 119–24.
35. See Allan Naire et al., "The Reign of ETS," *Today's Education* 69 (1980): 58–64, for a discussion of most of the arguments against aptitude testing. Note, however, that this article presents only one side of the issue.

true when tests are administered in the public schools. In one unfortunate episode in Houston, Texas, the answer sheets to six sociometric and psychological measures that had been administered to some 5000 ninth-grade students were ordered burned by the school board. In this instance accounts indicated that parents objected to having their children respond to such items as: "I enjoy soaking in the bathtub." "Sometimes I tell dirty jokes when I would rather not." "Dad always seems too busy to pal around with me."[36]

In another episode, in spite of a thorough and well-planned public relations program, a similar problem arose. In this case the research program dealt with mental health and was being carried out by a foundation that was well established and had good rapport in the community. An extensive public relations program was carried out, including meetings and discussions with school boards, superintendents, administrative personnel, school nurses and teachers, religious leaders, PTA groups, the Lions Club, and other civic groups. The research worker's difficulty started because a local right-wing group was currently involved in a campaign opposing the "mental health movement."

> The man who spearheaded this opposition was also a member of the American Legion and later read a statement along the same lines at a P.T.A. panel on which members of the research team appeared. He accused us of implanting "Red" ideas in children's minds and said our "Guess-Who" technique was a way of "fingering" certain children (designating them at an early age so they would be marked for life for our own ulterior motives).[37]

The authors have had some experience with a similar protest movement, and when this experience is compared with the previously described situations, it appears that all three have a number of things in common. First, individual test items are generally attacked without reference to their context or psychological foundations. Second, such attacks are usually led by small extreme groups of one sort or another. In the authors' experience, the protest group was made up almost entirely of a close-knit group of health-food faddists. Another characteristic of all three of these situations is that although it was vigorous and noisy, the protesting group did not represent any significant parent group. In the Houston episode, tests were returned to a number of small school districts—the Spring Branch Board of Education decided to destroy the answer sheets only of pupils whose parents objected to the testing. Six weeks after that decision, only 11 parents out of the possible 750 requested that the answer sheets be destroyed. In the second episode discussed, a similar

36. Gwynn Nettler, "Test Burning in Texas," *American Psychologist* 14 (1959): 682–83.
37. Leonard D. Eron and Leopold O. Walder, "Test Burning II," *American Psychologist* 16 (May 1961): 239.

offer was made and only three parents, those who started the original protest, requested that their children's records be destroyed. In the authors' experience, approximately 5000 children were tested, and in spite of the considerable bedlam raised by the small protesting group, only one parent came forward to request that her child's test papers be destroyed.

In dealing with such problems, a number of points might be worth mentioning. First, remember that in many instances these protests are led by demagogues who are not truly concerned about the testing but wish to use it merely as a vehicle to gain publicity or gratify some personal need. Second, it is impossible to explain adequately to a lay group the function of many items used on psychological tests. It is doubtful whether the research worker should ever attempt to debate the merits of specific test items. Instead, he should explain how the test was developed and attempt to demonstrate that the test as a whole is valid and useful. Third, it is important to take all action that seems appropriate at the very outset of any such protest. If the research is well designed and the measures are justified, those parents who are truly concerned can generally be convinced of the value of the study, thus depriving the extreme group of their support. The researcher should work closely with the newspapers and do everything possible to acquaint them with his side of the question. Finally, it is wise to offer to withdraw children from the study if the parents examine the tests and make a written request that their children be withdrawn, even though they had earlier given permission to test their children.

It should be clear to the student by this point that the use of tests in a research project is not a matter to be taken lightly. She should be aware of the main criticisms of testing and realize that tests can be used to advance scientific knowledge, or can be abused by those who are unethical or who are poorly trained.

MISTAKES SOMETIMES MADE IN SELECTING AND ADMINISTERING TESTS

1. Researcher fails to evaluate measures thoroughly before selecting those to be used in his research.
2. Uses a table of norms that is inappropriate for his research sample.
3. Does not evaluate carefully the criteria that have been used to determine the validity of a particular test.
4. Does not consider the problem of base rate in determining a test's predictive validity.

5. In attempting to measure a particular construct, selects a test on the basis of its name rather than its demonstrated construct validity.
6. Uses a norm-referenced achievement test in a study where a domain-referenced test would be more appropriate.
7. Selects measures of such low reliability that true differences between research groups are hidden by the errors of measurement.
8. Fails to consider the human relations aspect of testing.
9. Attempts to develop his own measure without first gaining skills in test construction.
10. Does not attempt to control for possible tester effects, particularly when a test is administered individually.
11. Does not study the test manual carefully before administering a test.
12. Attempts to administer too many tests in a single testing session.

ANNOTATED REFERENCES

Test Development Standards and Item Writing

American Psychological Association. *Standards for Educational and Psychological Tests.* Washington, D.C.: American Psychological Association, 1974. These standards are reprinted in *Tests in Print II.* Highland Park, N.J.: Gryphon Press, 1974.

Brown, Frederick G. *Measuring Classroom Achievement.* New York: Holt, Rinehart and Winston, 1981.
This small book is especially useful for the teacher or researcher who finds it necessary to develop an achievement test. Guidelines for writing different kinds of test items are brief and clear. Also included are chapters on planning a test and analyzing test scores and items. The book takes a practical, how-to-do-it approach and provides many examples.

Gronlund, Norman E. *Constructing Achievement Tests.* 3rd ed. Englewood Cliffs, N.J.: Prentice-Hall, 1982.
This is a good basic text on achievement test construction. It is written in simple, easy-to-understand language and contains clear step-by-step guidelines on item development.

Hopkins, Kenneth D., and Stanley, Julian C. *Educational and Psychological Measurement and Evaluation, Sixth Edition.* Englewood Cliffs, N.J.: Prentice-Hall, 1981.

Thorndike, R. L., and Hagen, E. P. *Measurement and Evaluation in Psychology and Education*. New York: John Wiley, 1977.

These are good introductory texts on educational measurement. Both provide brief but useful guidelines on test development and item analysis and will be useful to the student who needs to develop a basic understanding of this field.

Roid, Gale H., and Haladyna, Tom M. *A Technology for Test-Item Writing*. New York: Academic Press, 1982.

This book deals with test-item writing for criterion-referenced tests. The initial section introduces the student to criterion-referenced testing and its relationship to instruction. The main body of the book provides practical guidance on item writing, which is supported by numerous examples, and describes the rationale and procedures for six prominent item-writing methods. The final section is concerned with methods for the review and analysis of test items. In addition to being an extremely practical guide to item writing, the book pulls together virtually all the recent research on this topic. This is probably the best source currently available in this area.

Test Statistics

Guilford, J. P., and Fruchter, Benjamin. *Fundamental Statistics in Psychology and Education*. 6th ed. New York: McGraw-Hill, 1977.

Provides an excellent coverage of the statistical aspects of validity, reliability, item analysis, and test norms. Chapters 17, 18, and 19 should be studied by students who plan to develop a measure.

Lemke, Elmer, and Wiersma, William. *Principles of Psychological Measurement*. Chicago: Rand McNally, 1976.

This is an introductory text in psychological measurement that will be useful to the student with no training in this area. Gives a brief review of test statistics including standard score conversions, validity, reliability, and item analysis.

Domain-Referenced Tests

The field of domain-referenced testing is expanding and changing rapidly. Thus, the student who wants the most recent information in this field should carry out a computer search of the ERIC data base. The ERIC Clearinghouse on Tests, Measurement, and Evaluation at Princeton, NJ 08540, and the Instructional Objectives Exchange, Box 24095, Los Angeles, CA 90024, are excellent sources of up-to-date information in this field. Since many measurement texts do not cover this topic, several references are given here.

Educational Testing Service. *Criterion-Referenced Measures, Grade 7 and Above.* Princeton, N.J.: Educational Testing Service, October 1978.

This is one of a large series of *Test Collection Bibliographies* published by the Test Collection Division of ETS. This bibliography lists and provides brief annotations on more than 160 criterion-referenced measures.

Klein, S. P., and Kosecoff, J. *Issues and Procedures in the Development of Criterion-Referenced Tests.* Princeton, N.J.: ERIC Clearinghouse on Tests, Measurement and Evaluation, September 1973 (ED 083 284).

Describes the basic procedures for development of criterion-referenced tests including item construction and selection, improving item quality, and content validity. Also reports the results of a survey of current efforts in criterion-referenced testing by test publishers. This section contains descriptions of some of the criterion-referenced tests available such as the Prescriptive Mathematics Inventory developed by the California Test Bureau.

Martuza, Victor R. *Applying Norm-Referenced and Criterion-Referenced Measurement in Education.* Boston: Allyn & Bacon, 1977.

Contains a good coverage of several areas discussed in this chapter including test construction, reliability, and validity of both norm-referenced and domain-referenced tests and item analysis. Chapters 16 and 17 are especially useful to the student who wants to learn more about domain-referenced tests.

Millman, Jason. "Criterion-Referenced Measurement." In *Evaluation in Education—Current Applications,* edited by W. J. Popham. Berkeley, Calif.: McCutchan, 1974.

The author describes domain-referenced tests, compares them with tests designed to yield norm-referenced intepretations, and discusses their appropriateness for different educational problems. He then describes procedures for developing domain-referenced tests including defining the item population, selecting test items, establishing a passing score, estimating a domain score, determining test length, and evaluating the resulting measure.

Popham, W. James. *Criterion-Referenced Measurement.* Englewood Cliffs, N.J.: Prentice-Hall, 1978.

This is a highly readable introduction to criterion-referenced test development and use by one of the leaders in the field. An excellent discussion of the deficiencies of norm-referenced tests is provided. The chapters related to the development of criterion-referenced measures, preparing specifications for criterion-referenced tests, and practical application of these measures in instruction and evaluation are especially useful.

Porter, D. E. *Criterion-Referenced Testing: A Bibliography*. Princeton, N.J.: ERIC Clearinghouse on Tests, Measurement and Evaluation, December 1975 (ED 117 195).

This comprehensive bibliography lists 299 references related to domain-referenced and criterion-referenced tests. In addition to the alphabetical listing of references by author, a detailed subject index is provided. Thus the reader can quickly locate articles on any aspect of the topic. For example, 30 references on behavioral objectives are listed, 22 on item analysis, 4 on reliability, and 3 on validity.

SELF-CHECK TEST

Circle the correct answer to each of the following questions. An answer key is provided on page 881.

1. The degree to which a measure is undistorted by the beliefs or prejudices of the individual using it reflects the —— of the measure.
   a. validity
   b. objectivity
   c. consistency
   d. reliability
2. A table of norms enables the researcher to
   a. determine the construct validity of a test at a glance.
   b. compare the relative reliabilities of two or more tests.
   c. determine whether a subject's score was drawn from a defined population.
   d. compare a subject's score with the scores of a defined sample.
3. The degree to which a test measures what it purports to measure reflects its
   a. objectivity.
   b. validity.
   c. stability.
   d. reliability.
4. If a sample of test items adequately represents the subject matter of a given curriculum, the test is said to have —— validity.
   a. construct
   b. predictive
   c. content
   d. concurrent
5. A test which yields scores that are found to be highly correlated with subjects' later behavior is said to have high —— validity.
   a. concurrent
   b. rational
   c. predictive

    d. content
6. The type of test validity that is assessed by comparing subjects' scores on a test with their scores on some other measure within a short time interval is called —— validity.
    a. correlational
    b. rational
    c. concurrent
    d. predictive
7. The degree to which a test measures a given hypothetical construct reflects its —— validity.
    a. content
    b. rational
    c. internal
    d. construct
8. If the researcher is most concerned with the content validity of a test, the best source of information would be
    a. *Psychological Abstracts.*
    b. the test itself.
    c. *Mental Measurements Yearbooks.*
    d. *Review of Educational Research.*
9. Which of the following was a criticism of testing often heard in the early 1960s?
    a. invasion of privacy
    b. low reliability of the test data
    c. inflexible use of test scores
    d. too broad sampling of talents
10. It is not advisable to use test data collected by the schools for research purposes because
    a. the measures are often inappropriate.
    b. it is too expensive.
    c. test conditions are too rigidly controlled.
    d. students have knowledge of the test prior to its administration.

APPLICATION PROBLEMS

The following problems are designed to give you practice in applying significant concepts and research procedures explained in chapter 8. Most of them do not have a single correct answer. For feedback, you can compare your answers with the sample answers on pages 889–890.

1. An investigator has developed a new technique to teach eighth-grade students the characteristics of positive and negative numbers. She wishes to evaluate her technique by using it to teach group A while using group B, which receives

conventional instruction on positive and negative numbers, as a control. She needs a mathematics achievement test to measure the posttraining performance of the two groups. She considers the XYZ Test of Mathematics Achievement. In checking the test manual, she finds that when this test was administered to a sample of eighth-grade students at the end of the academic year, the test scores correlated .72 with their end-of-year grades in mathematics. No other validity evidence was given in the test manual.

    a. What type of validity evidence was given in the test manual?

    b. What type of validity is most relevant to the proposed study? Why?

2. An investigator has developed an algebra aptitude test to be given to eighth-grade students to determine which ones are likely to succeed in ninth-grade algebra. To validate his test, he administers it to 100 randomly selected eighth-grade students, all of whom are then placed in ninth-grade algebra the following term. At the end of the term he computes a correlation coefficient between aptitude scores and the achievement scores, the latter taken from an algebra achievement test given at the completion of the course.

    a. What type of validity did the investigator study?

    b. What type of validity is most relevant for this test? Why?

3. To determine the reliability of a new high school science achievement test, the developer selects a random sample of 1000 high school students, administers both form A and form B of the test to all subjects, and computes a correlation coefficient of .92. What type of reliability did she obtain?

4. For each of the following situations indicate whether an individual measure or a group measure would be more appropriate and why.

    a. An investigator wishes to study the reading speed and reading comprehension of a random sample of 100 freshmen entering a large state university for the fall semester.

    b. An investigator wishes to study the ability of retarded children (ages 6 to 9) to describe the content of pictures shown to them.

5. State at least one procedure for handling each of these testing problems.

    a. A researcher is planning to administer several aptitude tests to groups of college students as part of a research project. What can he do to increase the likelihood that students will give their maximum performance?

    b. A researcher wants to administer a measure of sex attitudes to high school and college students. What can she do to increase the likelihood that students will give frank, honest responses?

SUGGESTION SHEET

If your name starts with letters from Gos to Hav, please complete the Suggestion Sheet at the end of the book while this chapter is still fresh in your mind.

9.

TYPES OF STANDARDIZED TESTS

OVERVIEW

It is important to become familiar with the great variety of tests that have been developed. With this familiarity, you will be much more likely to select the measures that are most appropriate for your research project. This chapter tells you how to locate information about tests and discusses ten important types of standardized tests. Since it would be a vast undertaking for you to review all available measures, this chapter contains information about using the *Mental Measurements Yearbooks* as well as major sources of information on unpublished measures. The *Yearbooks* contain descriptions and reviews of nearly all published tests in psychology and education and greatly simplify the task of test selection.

OBJECTIVES

After studying this chapter, you should be able to:

1. If given a research problem, locate an appropriate measure in the *Eighth Mental Measurements Yearbook* and state at least three reasons for selecting the measure.
2. Evaluate a standardized test on the combined basis of data supplied by the test publisher and information given in the *Mental Measurements Yearbooks*.
3. List six sources of information on standardized tests and describe the kind of information that may be obtained from each source.
4. Describe at least one advantage and one disadvantage of self-report personality measures.
5. List at least one widely used test of each of the following types: intelligence, aptitude, achievement, diagnostic, creativity, personality, projective, self-concept, attitude, and vocational interest.

HOW TO LOCATE INFORMATION ABOUT TESTS

Before selecting a particular test, a student should accumulate as much information as possible about it. It is not uncommon for a student to hastily decide upon a test in planning his research and then find himself plagued with difficulties in using the test and interpreting the findings. For example, suppose that one wishes to test the hypothesis that empathy is an important trait for success in school counseling. Two groups of counselors rated as successful and unsuccessful are formed, and a test of empathy is administered. Since a measure of empathy is crucial to testing the hypothesis, if the measure is found to be invalid by those who might evaluate the research—such as editors of educational journals and professional counselors—then the findings that result from such a study are immediately cast in doubt.

The student will want to know how to obtain information about tests for another reason. In reviewing the research done by others, the student cannot make sound judgments concerning the findings without having access to information about the tests used to measure the research variables. The following are widely used, accessible sources of information about tests.

The Test Manual

The **test manual** provides the student with much of the information that she needs to evaluate the standardized test. Among the questions that the manual usually helps to answer are the following:

What validity data are available? What types of validity have been studied? Is the evidence of validity sufficient for use in the planned research?

What reliability data are available? Is the measure sufficiently reliable to meet the needs of the planned research?

For what types of subjects is the test appropriate?

What conditions of administration are necessary to use the test?

Does the test require special training for interpretation?

Is a shorter form of the test available that will yield substantially the same results?

While test manuals can provide much useful information to the student interested in evaluating a particular standardized test, the student must be able to evaluate the test manual itself. For example, test manuals will occasionally omit evidence regarding validity or reliability that is unfavorable to the test and that might dissuade potential purchasers.[1]

1. *Standards for Educational and Psychological Tests* (see Annotated References at the end of this chapter) gives a good summary of information that should be included in test manuals.

Some standardized tests, particularly those that have been extensively researched, are likely to pass through several revisions. Therefore, the student should be certain that her test manual is appropriate for the test version that she is evaluating.

The Mental Measurements Yearbooks

A very important source of information on standardized tests are the **Mental Measurements Yearbooks.** Over the past thirty years, Oscar K. Buros has edited this series of very useful references to standard tests in psychology and education. The most recent of the series is *The Eighth Mental Measurements Yearbook*, published in 1978.[2] This is a complete new work that supplements the earlier editions. The current edition lists 1184 tests. There are 898 critical test reviews and 17,481 references on the construction, use, and limitations of the specific tests included in this edition. Another section of the *Yearbook* lists and reviews books and monographs on measurement and related fields. The current edition lists 576 books, and many of the more important ones have several reviews. This section is useful to the student who needs to locate information on a specific aspect of measurement. For example, a student who plans to develop his own instrument can find many useful sources. He will, however, have to look in other sources such as *Psychological Abstracts* or *Books in Print* to locate references published since 1977.

The *Mental Measurements Yearbooks* can be used to obtain information on specific tests that the student has located elsewhere or they can help the student locate tests that are available in a particular field. The *Yearbooks* are also very valuable tools for checking on tests that others have used in their research. In using this reference the student first refers to the Scanning Index. Here he will find the tests classified under a number of broad categories such as Achievement Batteries, Personality, Foreign Language, and Intelligence. Under each category he will find the pertinent tests available in his area of interest. Upon locating tests in the Scanning Index that interest him, he may note the number of the test and check each number in the Tests and Reviews section of the book. Under the test number, he will find a brief listing of practical information, such as the types of subjects who may be administered the test, the scores yielded by the test, administration time, cost, and publisher. Following these data he will usually find a number of references containing information about the test. For the more widely used tests, several hundred references may be available. A quick examination of these references will often reveal several that are of particular relevance to the student's research project. Reviews are available for many of the tests listed. These reviews are perhaps the most val-

2. See Annotated References at the end of this chapter.

uable feature of the *Mental Measurements Yearbooks* because they give the student an evaluation of the test by one or more authorities in the field. They are generally written by persons who have worked extensively in the field with which the test is concerned and are written specifically to provide test users with appraisal that can help them in evaluating the test. The reviews are generally critical and treat most of the essential elements important in test evaluation, thus providing the student with a sounder evaluation than he could make for himself.

ETS Test Collection

If a student fails to locate the measures she needs in the *Mental Measurement Yearbooks*, her next step should be to search the relevant parts of the Educational Testing Service (ETS) collection. This is the most extensive collection of tests and other measurement devices available, consisting of more than 11,000 instruments. ETS established this collection to assist researchers and others who need test information.[3] Students may obtain specific information by writing or telephoning ETS. In most cases, however, the best way for a student to use this collection is to purchase the **Test Collection Bibliography** that relates to her interests and then order microfiche copies of the most promising measures described in the *Bibliography*.[4]

At present, annotated ETS bibliographies are available in more than 200 areas. The description of each measure in the bibliographies includes title, author, publication date, target population, and publisher or source. Because many tests cited in educational research literature are not available commercially, ETS makes them available on microfiche. The microfiche may be purchased for individual measures or for sets of 50 to 100 measures. Many university libraries have purchased these sets, so the student should check with the reference librarian before purchasing microfiches.

Measures for Psychological Assessment

A great many measures are developed as part of research projects and are published or referred to in the professional journals. Tests of this sort are usually not available from regular test publishers and are not covered in the *Mental Measurements Yearbooks*. Locating such measures is a difficult task and as a result, many promising measures receive little use. As K. T. Chun and his associates have pointed out, there is need for a center or repository for social science measures so that all such measures would be available to the researcher

3. See Annotated References at the end of this chapter.
4. See Appendix F for a listing of available *Test Collection Bibliographies*.

without making an extensive literature search.[5] **Measures for Psychological Assessment** was developed as an initial step in the development of such a center.[6] This book contains information on all measures located in a search of 26 measurement-related journals in psychology and sociology for the 1960–70 period. Over 3000 measures are listed. The volume contains an author index, descriptor index, primary reference section, and applications section. The usual strategy for locating measures in a given area is as follows:

1. Check the Descriptor Index, which is a cross-referenced subject index. The terms describe the characteristics that the measures intend to assess, such as avoidance, coping, empathy, rigidity, and so on. After each descriptor term you will find one or more letter-number combinations. For example, after "Attitudes, study" you will find B-74, C-225, and W-51, indicating that there are three measures available in this area.
2. Look up each of these number-letter combinations in the Primary References section. Here you will find the bibliographic data for the first source that described the measure, the title of the measure, description of content, and a list of Applications numbers.
3. For measures that you want to consider further, look up the listed numbers in the Applications section. Each of these gives you a reference to an article in which the measure has been used and a set of terms that describe the types of information given in the article, such as: correlates with the measure, criterion used, normative data, and validity and reliability data.

Although *Measures for Psychological Assessment* is far from exhaustive, even for the ten years it covers, it is a valuable source for researchers who are seeking a measure of a given characteristic. Listing a measure in this source does not guarantee anything about the evidence available on its quality or level of standardization. In fact, most of the measures listed have little evidence of validity and have not been developed using the rigorous process described earlier in this text. Thus, the student must carry out his own critical evaluation of those measures that he is considering for use.

A Sourcebook for Mental Health Measures[7]

This reference contains descriptions of about 1100 instruments related to various aspects of mental health drawn mostly from sources dating from 1968 to

5. K. T. Chun, J. T. Barnowe, S. Cobb, and J. R. P. French, Jr. "Publication and Uses of Psychological Measures in the 1960's" (manuscript, Institute for Social Research, University of Michigan, 1974).
6. See Annotated References at the end of this chapter.
7. See Annotated References at the end of this chapter.

1972. The descriptions are organized alphabetically under 45 major topics such as Alcoholism, Cognitive Tests, Educational Adjustment, Juvenile Delinquency, and Personality. The measures were located by a variety of techniques and include tests available from regular test publishers, tests reported in professional journals, and tests used in unpublished studies such as those carried out under National Institute of Mental Health (NIMH) grants. To use this sourcebook you review the 45 subject areas listed in the Contents, select the areas most relevant to your research, and then read the descriptions of measures listed. Copies of most of the unpublished measures may be obtained by writing to the authors, whose addresses are given.

Evaluating Classroom Instruction—A Sourcebook of Instruments[8]

This reference gives a comprehensive coverage of instruments used in teacher behavior research from 1954 through 1975. In the selection of measures, the following criteria were employed:

1. Relate to a major area in teacher research
2. Apply to the classroom setting
3. Available to researchers from commercial publishers or public sources
4. Measure operationally defined constructs related to specific teacher or pupil variables
5. Used in classroom research

Measures are classified into nine categories according to who supplies information about whom. Categories include, for example, measures "about the teacher from the pupil" and measures "about the pupil from an observer." This classification system is very helpful to the researcher who is looking for a particular type of measure. For each measure, all the information normally used by a researcher in making a preliminary selection is given, such as a description of the measure, data on validity and reliability, data on administration and scoring, and so on. This is a very useful source for students who plan to conduct research related to the classroom.

Family Measurement Techniques[9]

This reference contains information on 813 instruments concerned with measuring characterisics of the family. Over half of these instruments emerged

8. See Annotated References at the end of this chapter.
9. See Annotated References at the end of this chapter.

from a search of relevant journals dating from 1965 to 1974. The measures are organized by general topic so that the reader can first scan the Table of Contents to see if his area of interest is covered. For example, such general topics as family planning, parent-child conflict, and sex roles are listed in the Contents. If the reader is interested in a more specific topic, such as "eroticism in family relations," the Subject Index should be checked.

The abstract provided for each test is quite complete and provides the information needed to decide whether a given measure is appropriate for the reader's use and should be checked further.

Tests and Measurements in Child Development— Handbooks I and II[10]

These handbooks cover over 1200 unpublished measures, that is, measures not published by regular test publishers or included in Buros's *Mental Measurements Yearbooks*. The authors searched 148 journals for the period 1956 through 1965 for *Handbook I* and 1966 through 1974 for *Handbook II* to locate measures that can be administered to subjects from birth to age eighteen. Measures are classified into eleven major categories, such as Cognitive, Personality and Emotional, Attitudes and Interests, and Self-Concept. The information normally needed by the researcher to identify measures that may meet his needs is provided.

Directory of Unpublished Experimental Mental Measures[11]

These volumes provide information on 1034 tests. The measures are listed alphabetically by 23 major topics, such as Achievement, Creativity, Motivation, and Values. Data provided for each measure include name, purpose, number of item, time required, format, reliability, validity, source, and related research. A Subject Index is also included and is helpful in locating tests that measure a specific variable. Coverage is limited since only tests mentioned in 42 journals during the years 1970 to 1972 are included.

The Test Developer

The best source of recent information on a test is often the test developer. Since there is a considerable lag between the completion of research and its publica-

10. See Annotated References at the end of this chapter.
11. See Annotated References at the end of this chapter.

tion, the developer will often have information on the test that has not been printed. Also, the developer is likely to know of other researchers who have recently used the measure. This approach is especially useful in getting the latest data on recently developed tests. There may be very little published data on validity and other important characteristics of such measures, but much unpublished data. Thus it is advisable to write the test developer requesting any information that has not appeared in print. If the student's letter explains the purposes for which she wants to use the test, it is likely that the test developer will be cooperative. One reason for this cooperation is that the test developer may be able to add the findings from the student's research project to those he has already collected.

The Test Itself

One of the most important sources of information about standardized tests is a copy of the test in which you are interested, particularly if you are concerned about content validity or the appropriateness of the test for your sample. For example, the test manual may claim that a particular test is appropriate for students in the fifth grade. Your examination of a copy of the test may reveal that the reading level is beyond that of the fifth graders whom you are planning to test. Or suppose that your research project entails the evaluation of two methods for teaching reading. In selecting a test of reading achievement to evaluate the effectiveness of the two methods, you may find that the test manual and the *Mental Measurement Yearbooks* do not provide information about the reading content covered by the test. To determine whether the reading content covered by the test is representative of that included in your training materials, your best source of information will probably be a copy of the test itself.

Other Sources

In addition to the sources of test information we have discussed above, other compilations are listed in Annotated References at the end of this chapter. The student should refer to these if his search of the aforementioned sources does not locate a suitable measure for his study.

If these additional sources also fail to turn up a suitable measure, the student can design and carry out a computer search of the most relevant data bases, using the procedures described in chapter 5. There is an ERIC clearinghouse for tests and measurements at the Educational Testing Service, Princeton, New Jersey, that feeds much information into the ERIC system. If the computer search fails, the student's final alternatives are to change his research topic or develop his own measure.

How to Obtain Copies of Tests

Once she has decided on the standardized test (or tests) to be used in her research project, the student will need to obtain a number of copies of each test. If the test is distributed through a test publisher, such as Science Research Associates or California Test Bureau, the student should purchase copies of the test through them. The publisher and purchase price of a particular test can be found in the most recent edition of Buros's *Mental Measurements Yearbook*. College counseling or testing centers often have catalogues issued by test publishers that give information about test purchase. Under no circumstances should a student obtain a single copy of a test and then duplicate the items in order to make mimeographed copies, since this would constitute a violation of copyright. Occasionally a test with all its items will appear initially in a professional publication. If this is the case and if the author makes no reference to copyright, the test can be duplicated, with the author's permission, for use in a research project. It is a good practice to write the test developer to inform him of your project and to request any information not in the published article pertaining to the test's validity, reliability, administration, and scoring.

The qualifications needed to administer, score, and interpret tests vary greatly from test to test. Some require little more than the ability to read and understand the manual; others require a substantial amount of special training and supervised practice. Standards of the American Psychological Association specify that the test manual should state any special qualifications required to administer and interpret the test. In order to ensure that tests are used by qualified personnel, test publishers have the ethical responsibility of checking a prospective purchaser's qualifications. The test publisher may require sponsorship by a psychologist or educator holding the doctorate if a graduate student plans to purchase certain tests, particularly measures of personality. The student's thesis chairman or committee members are likely candidates to serve as sponsors.

TYPES OF STANDARDIZED TESTS

It is important in planning a research project to be familiar with the wide variety of standardized tests that have been published. *The Eighth Mental Measurements Yearbook* lists over 1100 tests. An organization of these tests by type is provided in the *Yearbook*'s table of contents, which is reproduced in figure

VOLUME I

Figure 9.1   Table of Contents of the *Eighth Mental Measurements Yearbook.*

9.1.[12] Another helpful item from the *Yearbook* is table 9.1, which lists the number and percentage of tests in each of the major classifications. Reference to this table indicates that the largest number of published tests is found in the areas of personality, vocations, and intelligence.

In this chapter standardized tests are classified into ten main types. Because the number of tests is so many, we shall describe only a few examples

12. *Eighth Mental Measurements Yearbook* (Highland Park, N.J.: Gryphon Press, 1978), pp. ix–x (figure 9.1) and p. xxxiv (table 9.1).

VOLUME II

Figure 9.1—Continued.

of each type. These examples were selected because they are used frequently in educational research.

Intelligence Tests

Intelligence tests provide an estimate of general intellectual level by sampling a person's performance on a variety of tasks. These tasks may include word definition, mathematical problem solving, general knowledge, and short-term memory of digits. Most intelligence tests yield a single global score of perfor-

TABLE 9.1

Tests by Major Classifications

Classification	Number	Percentage
Personality	220	18.6
Vocations	207	17.5
Miscellaneous	164	13.8
Reading	110	9.3
Intelligence	77	6.5
Foreign Languages	73	6.2
Mathematics	64	5.4
Speech and Hearing	52	4.4
English	45	3.8
Science	44	3.7
Social Studies	42	3.5
Achievement Batteries	38	3.2
Fine Arts	18	1.5
Sensory-Motor	18	1.5
Multi-Aptitude	12	1.0
Total	1,184	99.9

mance on these tasks. This score is called the IQ (intelligence quotient). Some intelligence tests also yield subscores such as verbal IQ and nonverbal IQ; subscores may also be provided for specific intellectual functions, such as spatial relationships, verbal ability, numerical reasoning, and logical reasoning. However, a student who plans to use subscores in his research analysis should carefully check to determine whether they are supported by sufficient evidence of construct validity and reliability.

Intelligence tests are held in high regard by educational researchers and school personnel because of their success in predicting school achievement. In fact, they are often called scholastic aptitude tests because the majority of them measure those aspects of intelligence that appear to be required for success in school learning.

Measures of intelligence may take the form of group or individually administered tests. The group intelligence tests have the advantage of low cost, and these tests provide a measure of scholastic aptitude that is satisfactory for most research purposes. Perhaps the most serious weakness of the group intelligence test is its inability to identify pupils in the group who are ill, negative toward the test, or suffer from some handicap that will cause them to make spuriously low scores. The individual tests overcome this difficulty because the examiner can usually determine by the student's answers and general behavior whether extraneous factors that would tend to lower the student's score are entering the testing situation. Another disadvantage of the group test that can seriously distort research results in studies involving young children or children of below-average achievement is that most of these tests depend to a considerable degree on the student's ability to read, and students whose reading ability is low will generally receive a spuriously low score on the test.

The disadvantage of the individual test, of course, is its expense. A trained examiner requires about an hour to administer the usual individual intelligence test to a single pupil. The individual tests also require considerable training to score and take much longer to score than the group tests, most of which are machine scorable. In spite of these disadvantages, the research worker should use an individual intelligence test whenever his subjects are such that he has reason to doubt the accuracy of results obtained from group tests. It is better for the research worker to reduce the size of his sample to permit individual testing than to test a large sample with a group measure of questionable validity.

Of the individually administered measures of intelligence, the Stanford-Binet Intelligence Scale is perhaps the best known. It is more suitable for the testing of children than of late adolescents and adults. A primary reason for the usefulness of the Stanford-Binet in educational research and practice is the considerable amount of evidence that has been collected regarding its validity and reliability. In recent years, though, the Wechsler Scales have achieved increasing prominence in the field of testing. This is perhaps due to the fact that these scales yield a number of useful subscores in addition to an overall IQ score. The Wechsler Adult Intelligence Scale (WAIS) is suitable for the testing of late adolescents and adults. The Wechsler Intelligence Scale for Children (WISC) is a downward extension of the WAIS and is suitable for the testing of children between the ages of five and fifteen. The most recent test in this series is the Wechsler Preschool and Primary Scale of Itelligence (WPPSI), which was published in 1967. It was designed for the testing of children between the ages of four and six and a half. The Peabody Picture Vocabulary Test (PPVT) has been used extensively as a measure of intelligence in Project Headstart research studies. In administering the PPVT, the examiner says a word and then the child points to the one picture in a display of pictures that represents that word. The main advantages of the PPVT are that it can be administered quickly and can be used when individual testing is required but a trained examiner is not available.

A number of group tests of intelligence are available. Some of these are actually batteries of tests. The reason for developing a battery of tests is that a single group test can usually sample only a restricted range of difficulty in content. For example, a group test to assess the intellectual performance of fifth graders would be totally inadequate to assess high school seniors: the items would be so easy that the test would not discriminate differences in intellectual level for the latter group. Therefore, a series of tests comparable with regard to type of content are developed for various grade levels. As an illustration, the Cooperative School and College Ability Tests (SCAT) have forms available for grades 4-6, 7-9, 10-12, and 13-14. Since they are comparable in content and in unit of measure, these forms make it possible for the researcher to study intellectual development over many years in school and to compare the intellectual performance of children at different grade levels. Other widely used batteries of group tests are the California Test of Mental Maturity, the Lorge-Thorndike Intelligence Tests, the Analysis of Learning Potential, and the Otis-Lennon Mental Ability Test.

Culture-Fair Tests of Intelligence

As we pointed out previously, tests have been criticized because they may discriminate unfairly against minority groups within a culture.[13] Test developers have responded to this criticism by constructing tests that purport to be culture fair. By "culture fair" is meant that words and facts that are culturally linked have been eliminated from the test. Consequently, most of these tests do not require the individual to use language. Among the intelligence measures designed to eliminate or reduce cultural bias are the Goodenough-Harris Drawing Test, the Safran Culture Reduced Intelligence Test, and the Culture Fair Intelligence Test.

Although the culture-fair testing movement has been gaining increasing favor by educators, there is reason for some caution in accepting the concept of a culture-fair test. For example, there is a growing body of evidence that verbal tests may actually be more culture-fair than nonverbal tests. Also, some psychologists and educators have argued that it is meaningless to construct tests that eliminate differences between groups, if these are true differences. Instead, training such as that provided by Project Head Start should be used to eliminate these differences.

Aptitude Tests

Aptitude tests are aimed at predicting the student's later performance in a specific type of behavior. Tests are available to measure aptitudes for many specific school subjects such as foreign language, art, music, and mathematics.

13. Examples of books critical of intelligence testing are: Alan Gartner, Colin Greer, and Frank Riessman, eds., *The New Assault on Equality, I.Q. and Social Stratification* (New York: Harper & Row, 1974); and Benjamin Fine, *The Stranglehold of the I.Q.* (New York: Doubleday, 1975).

Examples of such tests are the Modern Language Aptitude Test, the Orleans-Hanna Algebra Prognosis Test, and the Metropolitan Readiness Tests. Aptitude tests to measure skills needed in various occupations are also available. These include tests of sensory capacities, mechanical aptitude, and aptitude for selling.

A major trend in educational testing has been the development of test batteries that measure a wide range of aptitudes that are related to vocational and scholastic success. For example, the General Aptitude Test Battery (GATB) developed by the U.S. Employment Service measures these aptitudes: intelligence; verbal, numerical, spatial, form perception; clerical perception; motor coordination; finger dexterity; and manual dexterity. The student's scores on these aptitudes yield a profile that can be compared with profiles of successful persons in various occupations in order to locate types of work for which the student has the aptitude required for success. The Differential Aptitude Tests (DAT) are another frequently used test battery for counseling and research with high school students and adults. Eight aptitudes are measured by the DAT: verbal reasoning, numerical ability, abstract reasoning, clerical speed and accuracy, mechanical reasoning, space relations, spelling, and language use. Validity studies have demonstrated the value of the DAT in predicting students' scholastic success and vocational choice. The SRA Primary Mental Abilities is another multiaptitude battery often used in the public schools. This battery is available at six levels ranging from kindergarten to Grade 12. Each battery provides scores on five to six factors, which vary slightly from level to level.

The usual evaluation procedures should be followed by the research worker in the selection of aptitude tests for research purposes. Predictive validity is especially important in aptitude tests because they are primarily concerned with prediction of future behavior. Aptitude tests are often used in educational research initially to equate groups that are to receive two different experimental treatments. For example, let us say we wish to compare the effectiveness of two methods of teaching ninth-grade algebra. If the students to be used in the experiment are initially different in terms of algebraic aptitude, the group with the higher aptitude might learn more regardless of the method. Therefore, in order to evaluate the effectiveness of the two methods, it would be desirable either to equate the two groups being studied by matching students on algebraic aptitude or to make statistical adjustments for initial differences found by the aptitude test. By using one of these methods, the researcher can be more confident that achievement differences measured at the end of the study are due to differences in method than if she had no knowledge of the initial aptitude of the two groups.

Aptitude tests also are used in research to identify students of a particular aptitude level for special study. For example, the research worker may wish to identify students who have very low aptitude for learning a foreign language in order to determine whether a method could be developed to teach foreign language effectively to students at this level.

Achievement Tests

Because learning is one of the major goals of education, measures of amount learned (i.e., achievement) are often used in educational research. Many standardized achievement tests are available to the research worker. Some are intended to measure the student's knowledge of specific facts, whereas others, especially the more recent tests, attempt also to measure the student's understanding and mastery of basic principles. Although achievement tests have been criticized on social grounds, they are probably the most valid, reliable, and useful measures available to the educational researcher.

Administration time for different achievement tests varies greatly; some test batteries take as little as fifty minutes, whereas others require two days of testing to administer the entire battery. Achievement test batteries also differ in subject-matter coverage. The Wide Range Achievement Test, for example, contains tests in the areas of reading, spelling, and arithmetic, and requires less than thirty minutes to administer. In contrast, the intermediate level of the Metropolitan Achievement Test contains tests of word-knowledge, reading, language, spelling, mathematics, science, and social studies. Testing time is approximately five hours spread over six sessions.

In selecting an achievement test or battery for your research project, you first should decide what areas of achievement to measure and then evaluate the tests that purport to measure achievement in these areas. You should also consider carefully the research questions you want to answer and decide whether norm-referenced or domain-referenced achievement tests are more appropriate. These two types of tests were discussed in chapter 8. Because there is usually limited time available for testing in the public schools, it is often necessary to administer single achievement tests rather than an entire test battery. As a rule you will administer only tests measuring achievement in the content areas specified in the research problem.

In addition to studying the evaluations available in the *Mental Measurements Yearbooks* and evaluating the test manual, you should administer the test to yourself (even if it is at the elementary school level) in order to check the instructions and gain an insight into the specific content covered. A major problem in developing achievement tests is to select content sufficiently common to the curriculums of most school systems so that the test will have a satisfactory level of content validity. It is much more difficult to achieve content validity in areas such as social studies than in areas such as arithmetic where the sequence and content is reasonably standard. A test may be very well constructed and receive good reviews in the *Mental Measurements Yearbooks* and still be inappropriate if it does not fit the content covered in the schools to be used in the research.

In selecting an achievement test or battery to be used in more than one school district, the problem of content validity is increasingly acute because tests may fit the curriculum of one district better than the other. In this case obtained differences in achievement may be due to differences in content validity rather than actual differences brought about by the research conditions. Very often, some of the newer achievement batteries which place more emphasis upon principles and less upon specific facts, are more appropriate for use in studies involving more than one district. Another aspect of content validity that you should check when examining the test is the degree to which the test is up-to-date. Some achievement tests that were excellent several years ago are considerably less valid today. A common weakness found in the older tests is that illustrations of devices that have changed in physical appearance, such as the airplane, the automobile, and the telephone, may be so outdated that many students in today's schools would not even recognize them.

Another factor to be considered in selecting achievement measures for research is the test battery already being used by the schools from which the research sample will be drawn. Nearly all school districts now administer achievement tests on a regular basis as part of their program of self-evaluation and improvement. It is generally undesirable to use the same battery for research that is being used for other purposes in the public schools unless a very close control of the testing situation is possible. Achievement testing is psychologically threatening to many teachers because they fear that unless their students do well on the tests, it will be a reflection on the teacher's ability. Thus, it is not uncommon, if teachers have copies of the test at their disposal, for them to give their pupils special preparation in areas and sometimes even on specific items covered by the test. If the research worker selects his own measures, there is much less likelihood of the teacher's being able to give this sort of special assistance to his pupils. Finally, the researcher must consider the **test ceiling** when selecting an achievement measure. If the test is too easy for some pupils, they will score close to the test ceiling or maximum score. As a result, the test cannot reflect gains made by such pupils and does not provide an accurate indication of their achievement level. This problem often occurs in studies that extend over several years. The measure chosen is appropriate at the start of the study, but has too low a ceiling to provide an accurate achievement measure at the end of the study.

When the research conditions call for measures of very specific knowledge, it is often necessary for the research worker to develop an achievement test for use in the research project. In this case a domain-referenced test is often more appropriate than a norm-referenced test because domain-referenced tests typically provide a more complete coverage of the content domain. The principal advantage of the locally developed achievement test is that it can be tailored to the precise content area with which the research worker is concerned. The disadvantages are the additional time required to construct such a test and the fact that most research workers cannot bring a locally developed test to the high technical level attained by standardized tests.[14]

Diagnostic Tests

Occasionally the aim of a research project will be to evaluate the effectiveness of a remedial program. In this situation the researcher may find it helpful to use one of the variety of diagnostic tests that are available to identify students in need of remediation.

Diagnostic tests are a form of achievement test. However, an achievement test typically yields a single score indicating the student's general level of achievement in a given subject. Some diagnostic tests in common use are the Stanford Diagnostic Reading Test, the Stanford Diagnostic Mathematics Test, and the Diagnostic Screening Test: Spelling. There are several advantages to administering diagnostic tests in research or remedial programs. First, students who share a specific deficiency in a subject can be identified; otherwise, students might be selected whose deficiencies vary widely, even though they earn the same score on a general achievement test. Second, the use of diagnostic tests is helpful in planning individualized remedial instruction, an approach advocated by many educators. A disadvantage of some diagnostic tests, however, is that the subscores have low reliabilities and are highly intercorrelated with one another. A researcher who can locate a suitable domain-referenced test should consider it since such measures are usually very useful for diagnosis.

Measures of Creativity

The identification and nurture of creative talent has become a major concern of educational researchers in the last two decades. Not surprisingly, many new measures of creativity have been developed during the same period of time. A

14. There have been many interesting developments in achievement measurement in recent years, such as the emergence of mastery testing and criterion referenced testing, the renewed emphasis on basic skills, and the increase of public involvement in testing. The student who wants to learn more about such developments is referred to W. B. Schrader, ed., *Measuring Achievement: Progress over a Decade* (San Francisco: Jossey-Bass, 1982).

primary reason for this upsurge of research in creativity is that educators have become increasingly interested in the role of nonintellectual factors, such as creativity and personality characteristics, in school achievement.[15]

Most measures of creativity are intended to assess the aptitudes and personality traits that contribute to creative achievement. They are not direct measures of creative achievement itself. One of the major contributors in this area is J. P. Guilford, who has constructed a number of tests measuring divergent thinking processes. Some of these tests are Word Fluency (the person writes words each containing a specified letter); Brick Uses (the person lists uses for a common brick); Expressional Fluency (the person composes 4-word sentences, given only the initial letters, e.g., H—— r—— t—— s——); Plot Titles (the person composes plot titles, which are rated for their cleverness). Another major research effort was directed by E. P. Torrance; one outcome of this work was the development of the Torrance Tests of Creative Thinking. Since they were developed within a school context, these tests are frequently used by educational researchers in projects involving students at all grade levels. There are also a great many experimental tests of creativity. *Measures for Psychological Assessment* lists 64 measures under "creativity" as well as additional measures under "imagination" and "originality," which are closely related constructs.

Self-Report Measures of Personality

Many measures of personality rely on self-report to assess individual differences in traits, needs, adjustment difficulties, and values. These measures are used frequently in educational research to describe the personality characteristics of different groups of concern to educators, such as underachievers, minority groups, exceptional children, and members of a particular profession. They are also used to identify certain personality types for use in studies concerned with interrelationships between personality characteristics and other variables, such as intelligence, school achievement, or popularity.

Some of these measures are referred to as "general inventories" because a single instrument is used to measure a variety of personality traits. The inventory seeks information about the individual's personality by asking him questions or requiring him to respond to statements. Since a number of variables are assessed at the same time, there are usually several hundred of these statements. Consequently, most subjects will require an hour or more to complete a general inventory. One of the principal advantages of the personality

---

15. It should be noted, however, that some measures of creative aptitude have been found to be highly correlated with traditional measures of scholastic aptitude.

inventory is its low cost and ease of administration and scoring. The questions or statements are almost always in objective form, such as yes-no or multiple choice, a format that permits them to be scored by computer or with a template.[16] However, a few of these measures require training in order to interpret particular variables. For example, the student would have no difficulty administering the Minnesota Multiphasic Personality Inventory (the MMPI), since it is virtually self-administering and can be objectively scored. But suppose the student found that one of her research groups scored significantly higher on the Pt scale (psychasthenia) than a comparison group. Unless she has had training in the MMPI or can consult with someone who has had this training, the student probably will be unable to interpret the significance of this finding.

One of the potentially serious disadvantages of personality inventories stems from the fact that they are based on self-report. Like most self-reporting devices, they are only accurate to the degree that the self-perceptions are accurate and to the degree that the person is willing to express them honestly. This problem has been, and continues to be, a matter of concern to many educational and psychological researchers.

Unless rapport is established with the subjects, some may respond in a random fashion or deliberately lie or distort their answers. If such spurious answer sheets are not detected and omitted from the data analysis, they can lead the researcher to invalid conclusions. Many inventories contain a "lie scale" or "carelessness" index that helps identify spurious answer sheets. These vary in effectiveness, but some detect over 80 percent of randomly answered response sheets. For example, O'Dell developed a "carelessness" index for the Sixteen Personality Factor Questionnaire that correctly selected 88 percent of randomly completed answer sheets.[17]

There is ample evidence that self-report measures are subject to faking. This is not surprising because the link between the item and the construct it attempts to measure is rather obvious for most self-report personality tests. Some test developers have tried to reduce faking by using more subtle items. However, a recent study casts doubt on the degree to which faking is reduced by this method.[18]

Another variable that leads to spurious responses is called *response set*. If self-report inventories are to be used effectively in practical applications and in research settings, it is important to investigate the extent to which subjects are responding to the content of each item and the extent to which their responses

16. A template or window key is placed over the test paper. Holes in the key focus the test scorer's attention on the correct answers. This speeds up the scoring process and reduces errors.
17. J. W. O'Dell, "Method for Detecting Random Answers on Personality Questionnaires," *Journal of Applied Psychology* 55 (1971): 380–83.
18. Ronald R. Holden and Douglas N. Jackson, "Subtlety, Information, and Faking Effects in Personality Assessment," *Journal of Clinical Psychology* 37 (1981): 379–86.

are determined by a general "set." Three types of "response sets" have been extensively researched: social desirability, or the set to present oneself in a favorable light; acquiescence, or the set to respond "true," no matter what the content of the inventory item may be; and the set to respond deviantly. If the researcher has good reasons to believe that her sample may be motivated to fake or give atypical answers, then a self-report inventory should not be used.

It was pointed out in the previous chapter that there has been an increasing frequency of attacks on tests as an invasion of privacy. This is particularly true of personality measures. Therefore, the student should carefully review the personality inventory she is considering to see if items are present that might cause public relations difficulties with parents or community groups. For example, administering an inventory that contained questions dealing with sexual conduct to junior high school students might cause serious repercussions in the community and make it impossible to complete the research. If such items are essential to the research objectives, very extensive public relations work must be carried out before and during the study.

We will now briefly describe self-report measures of personality that are used frequently in educational research.

General Inventories

Minnesota Multiphasic Personality Inventory (MMPI). This inventory was developed by determining which items out of a 550-item pool differentiated empirically between particular psychiatric groups and normal groups. In addition to the original scales (e.g., hypochondriasis, depression, schizophrenia), many other variables can be assessed, including response sets and scales of ego strength, anxiety, and repression-sensitization. The *Mental Measurements Yearbooks* list 5028 references on the MMPI, many of them relevant to educational research. The MMPI may be an appropriate instrument to use when the student is interested in measuring various aspects of personality adjustment in late adolescents and adults.

The California Psychological Inventory (CPI). Although the CPI draws heavily on the MMPI item pool, its aim is to measure traits thought to be relevant to interpersonal behavior and intellectual functioning. Whereas the MMPI was developed for use in psychiatric settings, the CPI is oriented primarily to the assessment of normal persons. Some of its 18 scales are dominance, sociability, responsibility, good impression, flexibility, intellectual efficiency, and achievement via independence. The CPI can be used with high school and adult populations. Nearly 1400 references related to this measure are listed in the *Mental Measurements Yearbooks*.

The Edwards Personal Preference Schedule (EPPS). This inventory measures 15 needs based on Murray's need system. One of the merits of the EPPS is that an attempt has been made to control for the response set of social desirability by having subjects decide between pairs of statements of equivalent social desirability. Some of the 15 scales are autonomy, dominance, intraception, and abasement. Norms on the EPPS are available for college students and adults.

The Sixteen Personality Factor Questionnaire (16 P.F.). This inventory is different from those already described in that its scales were developed by the method of factor analysis. Some of the personality dimensions measured by the scales are reserved versus outgoing, affected by feelings versus emotionally stable, practical versus imaginative, relaxed versus tense. Primarily used for research purposes, the 16 P.F. can be administered to subjects who are age sixteen or older.

Specific Inventories

In addition to the general personality inventories just described, a group of inventories measure a single personality variable or small set of related variables.

Rokeach Dogmatism Scale. Although designed to measure the variable of closed-mindedness, this scale is often used in educational and psychological research as a measure of general authoritarianism. A sample item is: "When it comes to differences of opinion in religion we must be careful not to compromise with those who believe differently from the way we do." (Agreement with this item is scored in the direction of closed-mindedness[19]).

Fundamental Interpersonal Relations Orientation-Behavior (FIRO-B). This brief inventory is based on William Schutz's theory of small-group behavior.[20] It measures the strength of the individual's expressed inclusion, control, and affection, and the extent to which he wants these behaviors from others. FIRO-B can be administered to persons of high school age and older.

Study of Values. This inventory attempts to determine the predominant value system of the person tested. The Study of Values yields six scores indicating the relative strengths of the dominant values that shape the individual's personality: theoretical, economic, aesthetic, social, political, and religious.

A researcher who is interested in a measure of only one personality characteristic should first check *The Eighth Mental Measurements Yearbook* to see if a published measure is available. If this fails, she should next check the general inventories to see if any of these measure the variable in which she is interested. If so, she can either administer the entire inventory or, using the scoring key, can extract the items that measure the variable and administer only these

---

19. This scale may be found in Milton Rokeach, *The Open and Closed Mind* (New York: Basic Books, 1960).
20. William C. Schulz, *FIRO: A Three-Dimensional Theory of Interpersonal Behavior* (New York: Holt, Rinehart & Winston, 1958).

items. She should obtain the publisher's permission before using the latter approach since these inventories usually are copyrighted. The test norms for the variable must be used with caution if she administers only part of the inventory since there is likely to be some difference in response when items measuring a single variable are taken out of the context of the entire inventory.

A researcher who cannot find a suitable measure of the variable in a general inventory should check her variable in the Descriptor Index of *Measures for Psychological Assessment*. Many of the measures in this volume purport to measure single personality constructs. For example, 42 measures of acquiescence, 105 measures of aggression, 4 measures of cynicism, and 16 measures of risk taking are included, plus many others.

Finally, a computer search of the specific personality construct, using the ERIC or *Psychological Abstracts* data base, may be carried out if all of the aforementioned strategies fail to produce a satisfactory measure.

Checklists

Some self-report measures of personality take the form of checklists. A collection of items is presented to the individual, and he is asked to check those items that are applicable to himself. A great many checklists have been used in educational research. Over 100 of them are listed in *Measures for Psychological Assessment*.

The Adjective Checklist (ACL). This measure consists of 300 adjectives, such as imaginative, stubborn, relaxed. The person checks as many of these adjectives as are self-descriptive. The ACL data can be used to compare groups on the frequencies with which they endorse particular adjectives. The ACL can also be scored on 24 scales that assess such personality variables as defensiveness, self-confidence, dominance, and need for change. The ACL is a useful research instrument, since it yields a considerable amount of information in a relatively short period of time (it can be completed in fifteen or twenty minutes). Also, the ACL can be used by a person to describe himself or to describe another person or group.

Mooney Problem Checklists. This measure contains a list of problems that a student may have. The student simply checks off those problems applicable to himself. This checklist may be administered to students in grades 7 and up.

Projective Techniques

The term *projective technique* was popularized by L. K. Frank.[21] It was his contention that the use of instruments such as the Rorschach Inkblot Technique,

21. L. K. Frank, "Projective Methods for the Study of Personality," *Journal of Psychology* 8 (1939): 349–413.

with its amorphous stimuli and freedom of response, would reveal the individual's inner thoughts, fantasies, and idiosyncratic structuring of reality. One of the purported advantages of projective techniques over self-report inventories is that they are less subject to faking.

The most widely used projective techniques are listed in table 9.2 along with the number of references given for each in *The Eighth Mental Measurements Yearbook*. You will note that over 4000 studies have been conducted on the Rorschach Test alone.

In spite of the popularity of projective tests we would recommend that they be used with caution in a research project because, as a rule, these measures require extensive training and experience to administer, score, and interpret. Should the student decide to employ the Rorschach or similar projective techniques in his project, he should employ fully qualified persons to administer, score, and interpret the results.

A recent development in the field of projective techniques is the construction of group-administered instruments to measure classic Rorschach variables. The most widely used of these instruments is the Holtzman Inkblot Technique (HIT), which, from a psychometric point of view, is far superior to the Rorschach. Unlike the Rorschach, where the subject may give as many or as few responses to each stimulus as he chooses, the number of responses that the subject can give to each Holtzman card is controlled. Most of the Holtzman scoring variables have satisfactory reliability. The disadvantages of the HIT are that training is needed to interpret the scoring variables and that some of these variables seem to reflect verbal productivity rather than basic personality characteristics.

TABLE 9.2
Widely Used Projective Techniques

Test Title	References in 8th MMYB
Bender-Gestalt Test	1018
Holtzman Inkblot Technique	356
Rorschach Test (several variations)	4940
Thematic Apperception Test	2005

Measures of Self-Concept

The *self* or *self-concept* may be defined as the set of cognitions and feelings that each of us has about ourself. Researchers may want to measure the self-concept for various reasons. For example, it is sometimes important to investigate the effect of various educational practices on students' self-concept, or one may want to investigate whether students' self-concept is a determinant of school performance.

Interest in self-concept has increased markedly in recent years, and the student now has many measures available for research in this area. A few measures that provide information on self-concept are listed in the Personality section of *The Eighth Mental Measurements Yearbook*. Since most self-concept measures are not available from regular test publishers, however, the sources for unpublished measures are more useful for locating these tests. For example, *Tests and Measurements in Child Development: Handbook II* lists 45 self-concept measures, and *Measures for Psychological Assessment* lists 113 measures in this area.

One of the most widely used measures in this area is the Tennessee Self-Concept Scale. The clinical and research form of this test yields 30 scores in such areas as self-criticism, physical self, personal self, and social self. Other widely used self-concept measures include: Piers-Harris Children's Self Concept Scale, Coopersmith Self-Esteem Inventory, and Self-Concept as a Learner Scale.

Attitude Scales

Scales are frequently developed to measure the individual's attitude toward a particular group, institution, or institutional practice. An attitude is usually thought of as having three components: an affective component, which consists of the individual's feelings about the attitude object; a cognitive component, which is the individual's beliefs or knowledge about the attitude object; and a behavioral component, which is the individual's predisposition to act toward the attitude object in a particular way.

A review of research on the effectiveness of attitude measures as predictors of behavior indicated that general attitude measures are not very accurate predictors of specific behavior.[22] However, recent work suggests that specific

22. For more information on this topic, the student should refer to M. Fishbein and I. Ajzen, *Belief, Attitude, Intention, and Behavior: An Introduction to Theory and Research* (Reading, Mass.: Addison-Wesley, 1975); and I. Ajzen and Martin Fishbein, "Attitude-Behavior Relations: A Theoretical Analysis and Review of Empirical Research," *Psychological Bulletin* 84 (1977): 888–918.

behavior can be predicted from measures of attitude toward the specific behavior.

Several different procedures have been used to develop measures of attitude. On a Thurstone-type scale, the individual expresses *agreement* or *disagreement* with a series of statements about the attitude object. On a Likert-type scale, the individual checks one of five possible responses to each statement: strongly agree, agree, undecided, disagree, strongly disagree. Sometimes the Semantic Differential is used to assess attitudes. The individual gives a quantitative rating of an attitude object on a variety of bipolar adjectives, such as fair-unfair, valuable-worthless, and good-bad. Guttman scaling, interviews, and open-ended questionnaires are examples of other methods used to measure attitudes.

Attitudes are often measured in educational research because of their possible predictive value. For example, a researcher may be interested in measuring students' attitude toward high school, since this variable might predict which students will be high school dropouts. An important study concerned with this use of attitude scales was done by Tittle and Hill.[23] They compared the effectiveness of various types of attitude scales (Likert, Guttman, Semantic Differential, Thurstone, Self-Rating) in predicting objective indices of voting behavior. The Likert scale was superior to all the other scale types; it yielded a mean correlation coefficient of .54 with the objective indices of voting behavior.

In reviewing the research literature, the student may come across an attitude scale that she can use in her project.[24] For example, in a previous chapter a research study was mentioned in which a scale to measure attitudes about American Indians had been developed by the researcher. A very large number of attitude scales are listed in *Measures for Psychological Assessment*, which purport to measure attitudes toward such things as authority, change, death, health, job, mental illness, and school.

Sometimes the student will wish to measure an attitude for which no scale is available. For example, one of the authors found it necessary to develop a scale to measure teachers' attitudes toward ability grouping. Satisfactory attitude scales can be developed by the research worker if she follows closely the procedures outlined in textbooks on this subject (see Annotated References). The Likert technique is usually the easiest method of developing scales needed in research projects.

Attitude scales are direct self-report measures and so have the usual disadvantages of this type of instrument. The primary disadvantage is that we can never be sure of the degree to which the subject's responses reflect his true attitudes. Under certain conditions, for example, when the individual's attitude

23. Charles R. Tittle and Richard J. Hill, "Attitude Measurement and Prediction of Behavior: An Evaluation of Conditions and Measurement Techniques," *Sociometry* 30 (1967): 199–213.
24. Also, Shaw and Wright (see Annotated References) have made a useful compilation of published attitude scales.

is in conflict with the social norm, he may go to considerable lengths to hide his true attitude. Less direct attitude measures are needed to overcome this difficulty, but to date few such measures have been developed.[25]

Measures of Vocational Interest

Vocational interest inventories have proved to be of considerable value to educational researchers. They are used to investigate how students come to develop specific vocational interests, and they also provide an indirect assessment of personality characteristics (e.g., an individual interested in banking is likely to have a different personality structure than an individual interested in art as a career).

Vocational interest inventories typically require the individual to express his interest in various types of people, sports, hobbies, books, and other aspects of daily life. One of the first of these measures to achieve wide use and acceptance was the Strong Vocational Interest Blank (SVIB). Strong conducted a long-range research program demonstrating that occupational groups could be reliably differentiated on the basis of measured interests, that the same characteristic patterns of interest are found in different samples of the same occupational groups, that interest patterns are very stable over time, and that individuals who entered occupations for which they had obtained high SVIB scores were more likely to remain in the occupation than were individuals who entered occupations for which they had scored low. The current version of the SVIB is known as the Strong-Campbell Interest Inventory (SCII).To date this measure can be scored on a total of 155 scales, including 23 basic interest and 124 occupational.

Since the SCII primarily measures interest in professional and business occupations, this instrument is probably not appropriate for the researcher investigating the interests of students who are not college-bound. Measures such as the Minnesota Vocational Interest Inventory, the Career Assessment Inventory, and the Career Guidance Inventory are more likely to be useful in such cases because for the most part they cover occupations such as building trades, baker, and truck driver, which do not require a college education.

The Kuder General Interest Survey was developed to measure the individual's interest in 10 broad vocational areas rather than specific occupations. These areas are outdoor, mechanical, computational, scientific, persuasive, artistic, literary, musical, social service, and clerical. It can be administered to students in grades 6 through 12.

---

25. For examples of "disguised" techniques to measure attitudes, see David Krech, Richard S. Crutchfield, and Egerton L. Ballachey, *Individual in Society: A Textbook of Social Psychology* (New York: McGraw-Hill, 1962), pp. 161–67. See also the discussion of unobtrusive measures in chapter 12.

The Kuder Occupational Interest Survey is also widely used in counseling and research. This measure can be administered to students in grades 11 to 16 and to adults. There are 162 scales, including 114 occupational and 48 college major.

Although the Strong and Kuder inventories are the most widely used measures of vocational interest, several others have been developed and are more appropriate for some research projects. The student should consult the *Mental Measurements Yearbooks* and other sources of test information before selecting a vocational interest measure for his research project.

MISTAKES SOMETIMES MADE IN USING STANDARDIZED TESTS

1. Researcher selects the first test he is able to find rather than systematically selecting the test most appropriate for the research problem.
2. Uses subscores from a test without checking their validity and reliability.
3. Does not check the content of an achievement test to determine whether it corresponds to the content covered in the schools that will be used in the research.
4. Selects a test instrument, such as the Minnesota Multiphasic Personality Inventory, that he is not qualified to administer and interpret.
5. Fails to check the content of a personality test to determine whether it is likely to cause public relations difficulties.

ANNOTATED REFERENCES

The following references contain test compilations, descriptions, reviews, or other data that can be useful to the researcher. The most important references are described in the chapter. Others are described below, while only bibliographical data are given for the rest. Students should also consult the list of *Test Collection Bibliographies*, published by Educational Testing Service, given in Appendix F.

General (includes tests in most of the major areas of measurement)

Buros, Oscar K., ed. *The Eighth Mental Measurements Yearbook.* Highland Park, N.J.: Gryphon Press, 1978.
The earlier *Yearbooks* are also useful.

Chun, K. T.; Cobb, S.; and French, J. R. P., Jr. *Measures for Psychological Assessment: A Guide to 3,000 Original Sources and Their Application.* Ann Arbor, Mich.: Institute for Social Research, University of Michigan, 1974.

Comrey, A. L.; Backer, T. E.; and Glaser, E. M. *A Sourcebook for Mental Health Measures.* Los Angeles: Human Interaction Research Institute, 1973.

Goldman, B. A., and Busch, J. C. *Directory of Unpublished Experimental Mental Measures.* vol. 2. New York: Human Sciences Press, 1978. See also Vol. 1, published in 1974.

Johnson, Orval G. *Tests and Measurements in Child Development: Handbook II.* San Franscisco: Jossey-Bass, 1976.
The earlier volume by O. G. Johnson and J. W. Bommarito entitled *Tests and Measurements in Child Development: Handbook I,* published in 1971, is also useful.

Mehrens, William A., and Lehmann, Irvin J. *Standardized Tests in Education.* 2nd ed. New York: Holt, Rinehart & Winston, 1975.

Rosen, P., ed. *Test Collection Bulletin.* Princeton, N.J.: Educational Testing Service.
This quarterly bulletin provides brief annotations for tests recently acquired by the Educational Testing Service Test Collection. The title, author, publisher, and year of publication are given along with a brief description of each measure. Tests are classified into categories such as achievement, aptitude and personality, interests, attitudes and opinions. New references related to measurement are also listed in each issue.

Routh, Donald K. *Bibliography on the Psychological Assessment of the Child.* Washington, D.C.: American Psychological Association, 1976.

Straus, Murray A., and Brown, Bruce W. *Family Measurement Techniques: Abstracts of Published Instruments, 1935–1974.* Minneapolis: University of Minnesota Press, 1978.

Attitudes

Aiken, Lewis R. "Attitude Measurement and Research." *New Directions for Testing and Measurement* 7 (1980): 1–24.
This article provides a brief but informative review of the current status of attitude measurement. The major approaches as well as several less well known techniques for measuring attitudes are described. Reliability and validity of attitude measures are discussed. Several theories of attitude development and change are briefly reviewed, and an extensive list of references is provided.

Fishbein, Martin, and Ajzen, I. *Belief, Attitude, Intention and Behavior—An Introduction to Theory and Research.* Reading, Mass.: Addison-Wesley, 1975.

This is an excellent source for the student who wants to develop a better understanding of attitudes. Theories of attitudes, attitude formation, and attitude change are discussed in some depth and are placed in the context of relevant research. Attitude measurement is also covered in a brief, systematic fashion.

Lemon, Nigel. *Attitudes and Their Measurement*, New York: Wiley, 1973.

This book covers the procedures employed in attitude measurement including interviewing, questionnaires, checklists, scales, the Q technique, semantic differential, and indirect methods. A brief coverage of related topics, such as the nature of attitudes and the prediction of behavior from attitude measures, is also included.

Robinson, John P., and Shaver, Phillip R. *Measures of Social Psychological Attitudes.* Rev. ed. Ann Arbor, Mich.: Institute for Social Research, University of Michigan, 1973.

Shaw, M. E., and Wright, J. M. *Scales for the Measurement of Attitudes.* New York: McGraw-Hill, 1967.

These two sources, although fairly old, contain many attitude measures that are still useful for research. Robinson and Shaver review 127 scales in the areas of self-esteem, locus of control, alienation, authoritarianism, values, attitudes toward people, religious attitudes, and other sociopolitical attitudes. The Shaw and Wright volume includes descriptions and evaluations of 176 attitude scales dealing mainly with social, political, and religious issues.

The Classroom Situation

Borich, Gary D., and Madden, Susan K. *Evaluating Classroom Instruction— A Sourcebook of Instruments.* Reading Mass.: Addison-Wesley, 1977.

Projective Techniques

Semeomoff, Boris. *Projective Techniques.* New York: John Wiley, 1976.

Provides a very thorough coverage of the Rorschach Test and the Thematic Apperception Test as well as derivatives of these two measures. Projective techniques such as the Family Relations Indicator, the Structured Doll Play Test, and Lowenfeld Mosaic Test, and many others are covered in sufficient detail so that a researcher can make a preliminary decision on whether a given measure meets his needs.

Self-Concept Measures

Rosen, P., ed. *Self-concept Measures: Head Start Test Collection.* Princeton, N.J.: Educational Testing Service, 1973 (ED 086 737).

Covers 44 self-concept measures published between 1963 and 1972 for use with children from preschool to Grade 3. See also *Measures of Self-concept, Grades 4–6* (ED 083 320) and *Self-concept Measures: Grades 7 and Above* (ED 083 319), by same editor and publisher.

Wylie, R. C. *The Self-Concept: A Review of Methodological Considerations and Measuring Instruments.* Vol. 1. Lincoln: University of Nebraska Press, 1974.

Social Measures

Guthrie, P. D. *Measure of Social Skills: An Annotated Bibilography.* Princeton, N.J.: Educational Testing service, 1971 (ED 056 085).

Covers measures for use with children from preschool level through the third grade.

Lake, Dale G.; Miles, Matthew B.; and Earle, R. B., Jr. *Measuring Human Behavior: Tools for the Assessment of Social Functioning.* New York: Teachers College Press, 1973.

Miller, Delbert C. *Handbook of Research Design and Social Measurement.* 4th ed. New York: Longman, 1983.

SELF-CHECK TEST

Circle the correct answer to each of the following questions. An answer key is provided on page 881.

1. Sampling performance on a variety of tasks that include word definition, mathematical problem solving, general knowledge, and short-term memory of digits is typical of —— tests.
   a. achievement
   b. special aptitude
   c. intelligence
   d. creativity
2. Intelligence tests are held in high regard by educational researchers and school personnel because of their
   a. standardized formats.
   b. success in predicting school achievement.

     c. generalized format.

     d. instructional efficiency.

3. The most serious weakness of group intelligence tests is

     a. their inability to identify students who are performing at lower than capacity.

     b. the difficulty of creating a table of norms for test scores.

     c. the administration of the tests in a confidential manner.

     d. the interpretation of test results.

4. Tests aimed at predicting the student's later performance on a specific type of skill are termed —— tests.

     a. projective

     b. achievement

     c. aptitude

     d. self-concept

5. In selecting an achievement test for a research project, the first step is to

     a. refer to the *Mental Measurements Yearbooks*.

     b. decide what it is that is to be measured.

     c. evaluate tests that are available.

     d. pretest the instruments with individuals like your sample but not part of the sample.

6. Tests which are similar to achievement tests but which yield more data concerning the individual are labeled —— tests.

     a. diagnostic

     b. personality

     c. inventory

     d. projective

7. A potentially serious disadvantage of personality inventories is that they are

     a. expensive.

     b. difficult to score.

     c. difficult to administer.

     d. based on self-report.

8. Social desirability and acquiescence are examples of

     a. self-concepts.

     b. projective techniques.

     c. response sets.

     d. Likert-type scales.

9. One purported advantage of projective techniques over self-report inventories is they are

     a. less subject to faking.

     b. easier to score.

     c. less difficult to administer.

     d. cheaper.

10. One disadvantage of attitude scales is that
    a. they usually have low test-retest reliability.
    b. they usually have low construct validity.
    c. subjects' responses may not reflect their true attitudes.
    d. they require highly trained raters to ensure accurate scoring.

APPLICATION PROBLEMS

The following problems are designed to give you practice in applying significant concepts and research procedures explained in chapter 9. Most of them do not have a single correct answer. For feedback, you can compare your answers with the sample answers on pages 890–891.

1. Locate tests 776–82 in *The Seventh Mental Measurements Yearbook*. These tests provide measures of study skills. Suppose you are a researcher who plans to conduct a series of investigations concerning the effect of study skills on school achievement. In the course of the investigations you will be assessing the study skills of students ranging from the fourth through the twelfth grade.
    a. Which of tests 776–82 would best suit your needs? Why?
    b. According to the reviewer of the test you selected above, what is the main factor you should consider in deciding whether the test is appropriate for a particular sample of students?
    c. Why would the Bristol Achievement Tests: Study Skills (Test 776) probably not be appropriate for your research project?
    d. Check the Study Skills measures in the *Eighth Mental Measurements Yearbook*. Would any of these measures be of possible use in your study? Which?
2. A researcher wishes to make a general personality assessment of the 100 high school seniors who will participate in his research project. Both the California Psychological Inventory (CPI) and the Holtzman Inkblot Technique (HIT) measure the type of variables in which he is interested.
    a. What is one advantage that the CPI, a self-report measure, probably has compared to the HIT?
    b. What is one probable disadvantage of the CPI compared to the HIT?
3. List at least one standardized test that it would be appropriate to administer in each of the following situations (select tests described in this chapter):
    a. A researcher has only about 30 minutes of group testing time, and she wants to determine possible differences between a sample of high test-anxious students and a sample of low test-anxious students on a variety of personality dimensions. What would be an appropriate test to administer to the students?
    b. A researcher wants to determine the effectiveness of providing diagnostic

information about students' arithmetic skills to teachers at the beginning of the school term. What would be an appropriate test to administer to the students?

c. A researcher needs to obtain a measure of intelligence or aptitude for his project. The test will be administered to a group of ethnic-minority children, and he knows the community is suspicious about testing. What would be an appropriate test to administer to the students in this situation?

d. A researcher wants to test the hypothesis that graduating college seniors who have had joint majors (e.g., English and history) have a wider range of vocational interests than students who have majored in a single subject. What would be an appropriate test to administer to this group?

4. A researcher is asked by school district personnel to collect data for a period of three years to determine whether its plans to improve third-grade reading skills are successful. The researcher decides to administer the same reading achievement test at the end of the school year for the following three years. As she examines various achievement tests for possible use in the study, what are two aspects of their content that she should judge carefully?

5. Suppose you plan to conduct a study in which 30 mentally handicapped 4-year-old children would be given a special program designed to improve their self-help skills. You decide to use a rating scale or checklist that has a test-retest reliability of at least .80. Using *Tests and Measurements in Child Development: Handbook II,* locate two measures that might be appropriate for this study.

SUGGESTION SHEET

If your last name starts with letters from Haw to Jaa, please complete the Suggestion Sheet at the end of the book while this chapter is still fresh in your mind.

Part IV.

RESEARCH DESIGN AND METHODOLOGY

As important as the sampling techniques employed and the measures selected is the research design the investigator uses to study a problem. Research design refers to the procedures used by the researcher to explore relationships between variables, to form subjects into groups, administer the measures, apply treatment conditions, and analyze the data. A large number of research designs for use in educational studies have evolved over the years. Most of these designs have been adapted from the physical and biological sciences, and they are not always adequate for the study of problems involving human behavior.

Different research designs are appropriate for the study of different educational problems. In addition, some designs are more rigorous and less subject to error than others. The problem of selecting the best design is not a simple one, however, since the more rigorous designs call for a level of control of the research situation that is often impossible to achieve in educational research. Also, as rigorous control of the research situation increases, the real-life situation in which the researcher wants to apply his findings becomes harder to achieve. Thus the selection of a research design usually involves a complex compromise involving what is most rigorous, what is most natural, and what is possible.

10.

INTRODUCTION TO STATISTICAL ANALYSIS AND RESEARCH DESIGN

OVERVIEW

The main purpose of this chapter is to introduce you to the statistical tools that educational researchers commonly use to analyze their data. Measures of central tendency and variability are descriptive statistics that are helpful in summarizing data collected on a single variable (e.g., gradepoint average). In contrast, correlational statistics are used to describe the relationship between two or more variables (e.g., between gradepoint average and attentiveness in class). Test statistics are a set of specialized tools for analyzing the extent to which a particular test is a good measuring instrument. Finally, inferential statistics are mathematical procedures for determining whether the scores collected from a sample of research subjects are representative of the scores that would have been obtained if the entire population had been observed. Following presentation of the major statistical tools, the importance of replication research as a check on the statistical findings of one study is stressed. The chapter concludes with a discussion of problems that sometimes occur in statistical analysis.

OBJECTIVES

After studying this chapter, you should be able to:

1. Describe how descriptive, causal-comparative, correlational, and experimental designs differ in their power to reveal causal relationships.
2. Distinguish between the various types of scores used in educational research.
3. Compare the relative advantages and disadvantages of the mean and median as measures of central tendency.
4. Interpret the meaning of the standard deviation in relation to the normal curve.

5. Distinguish between the various types of bivariate and multivariate correlational statistics.
6. Describe the statistical tools that can be used to analyze test validity, test reliability, and item characteristics.
7. Describe how a test of statistical significance is used to decide whether to reject or not to reject the null hypothesis.
8. Interpret the meaning of a given level of statistical significance (p).
9. Describe the factors involved in using statistical power analysis.
10. Explain how confidence limits and the various tests of statistical significance are used.
11. Distinguish between literal, operational, and constructive forms of research replication.
12. Interpret the practical significance of results using measures of effect size or correlation.
13. Interpret stem-and-leaf displays in exploratory data analysis.
14. Explain the problems in data analysis caused by missing data.
15. Distinguish between situations in which the individual score or the group mean is the preferred unit of statistical analysis.
16. Explain why multilevel analysis in educational research is sometimes desirable.

PRELIMINARY CONSIDERATIONS

Types of Research Design

Most research in education can be classified as one of two types—descriptive studies and those aimed at discovering causal relationships. **Descriptive studies** are primarily concerned with finding out "what is." Examples of questions that might be studied by means of a descriptive approach are: Do teachers hold favorable attitudes toward the "new" mathematics? What kinds of activities occur in sixth-grade art classes and how frequently do they occur? What have been the reactions of school administrators to innovations in teaching the social sciences? Have first-grade textbooks changed in readability over the last fifty years? Observational and survey methods are frequently used to collect descriptive data.

Although description is an important aspect of the scientific approach in education, most research studies are concerned primarily with discovering causal relationships. Typical causal problems investigated by educational researchers are: What factors *determine* choice of college major? What *causes* underachievement? Does this new instructional strategy *lead to* increased learning when compared with conventional instructional strategies?

We may distinguish between research designs in terms of their effectiveness in establishing causal links between two or more variables. The **causal-comparative method** is aimed at the discovery of possible causes for the phenomenon being studied by comparing subjects in whom a characteristic is present with similar subjects in whom it is absent or present to a lesser degree. However, this research design can only be used to explore causal relationships, not confirm them.

Suppose that one is interested in testing the hypothesis that anxiety impairs performance on timed aptitude tests. If a causal-comparative design were used, one might select contrasting groups of high- and low-anxious students, and then compare their performance on a timed aptitude test. Suppose we found that the high-anxious group did indeed have lower test scores on the average than the low-anxious group. Although this finding is consistent with the research hypothesis, an alternative causal hypothesis is possible, namely, that poor performance on timed aptitude tests (and perhaps other academic tests) is likely to cause anxiety. Thus, the research results do not tell us whether anxiety causes impaired performance or whether impaired performance causes anxiety.

A similar problem occurs in correlational designs. **Correlational studies** include all research projects in which an attempt is made to discover or clarify relationships through the use of correlation coefficients. Like the causal-comparative method, correlational studies tell the researcher the magnitude of the relationship between two variables A and B, but they cannot be used to determine whether A causes B, B causes A, or whether a third variable, X, causes both A and B.

The **experimental research** design is ideally suited to establish causal relationships if proper controls are used. The key feature of experimental research is that a treatment variable is manipulated. Taking the research problem just mentioned, one might first select a sample of students and divide them randomly into two groups. Then one would manipulate the independent variable, level of anxiety, by raising it in one of the two groups (e.g., one could tell them that they are about to be administered a test that will be used to determine scholarship awards or college selection). The other group, called the *control group*, would not receive this treatment. If the experimental group scored significantly lower on the test than the control group, one could safely infer that their impaired performance was the direct result of increased anxiety. It should be apparent that the experiment is the most powerful research design for testing theories about causal relationships.

In doing research for the master's or doctoral degree, the student will probably use one of these three research designs—causal-comparison, correlation, or experiment. Therefore, in this and chapters 13–16 we will discuss at length how to use each design properly. Analysis of the data is also part of one's research design; therefore we will discuss the statistical techniques most commonly used with each research design.

Types of Statistical Analysis

There are two main types of statistical techniques. As the name implies, **descriptive statistics** (also called *summary statistics*) are used to "describe" the data we have collected on a research sample. The mean, median, and standard deviation are the main descriptive statistics; they are used to indicate the average score and the variability of scores for the sample. The advantage of descriptive statistics is that they enable the researcher to use one or two numbers (e.g., the mean and standard deviation) to represent all the individual scores of subjects in the sample. The reduction of a mass of "raw data" to a few descriptive statistics greatly simplifies the task of data interpretation. However, you should be aware that descriptive statistics sometimes oversimplify the data. The mean, standard deviation, and related statistics can distort one's understanding of how individual students, teachers, and others performed in the study. We shall return to this problem later in the chapter.

Inferential statistics, the second type of statistical technique, are used to make inferences from sample statistics to the population parameters.[1] Inferential statistics are important in educational research because we typically study a sample or samples, yet we wish to reach conclusions about the larger populations from which they were drawn. In this chapter we discuss the rationale of inferential statistics and how they can be used to answer such questions as "If I find a difference of 5 IQ points between the mean of sample A and the mean of sample B, how likely is it that I would find the same difference if the entire populations A and B (from which the two samples were randomly drawn) were studied?"

A third type of statistical technique is called test statistics. As its name implies, **test statistics** are mathematical methods for describing and analyzing the psychometric properties of tests and other instruments.

This chapter presents the range of descriptive, inferential, and test statistics commonly used in educational research. Some of these statistical techniques are discussed in greater depth in other chapters.

---

1. Descriptive values such as the mean, median, and standard deviation are usually referred to as *statistics* if they are computed from the scores of a sample of subjects. The same values are referred to as *parameters* if they are computed from the scores of the entire population.

WHAT YOU SHOULD KNOW ABOUT STATISTICS

To analyze research results effectively, researchers need to have four kinds of information about statistical tools. They need to know: (1) what statistical tools are available; (2) under what conditions each tool is used; (3) what the statistical results mean; and (4) how the statistical calculations are made. Let us take a brief look at these types of information and see how they will be discussed in this and the next chapters.

What Statistical Tools Are Available?

One of the most serious weaknesses of research studies is to fail to make maximum use of the data collected. Obviously, the more statistical techniques with which you are familiar, the more varied are the analyses that you can apply to your research data. This capability is important, since most research data can be subjected to more than one type of statistical analysis. Each analysis sheds a different light on the research data.

As an example of this principle, researchers usually will calculate and analyze the mean of the posttraining achievement scores of students who have received different instructional methods. This analysis will reveal whether a group of students exposed to one instructional method learned more, on the average, than a group of students exposed to a different method. But the analysis should not stop there. The standard deviations of the groups' scores should be calculated to determine whether the instructional methods caused the students to become more similar to each other (i.e., more homogeneous) or more different from each other (i.e., more heterogeneous) in their performance. Other types of statistical analysis, to be discussed elsewhere, also can be applied to these data.

The calculations required to apply statistical techniques do not usually involve complex or difficult mathematics. They can be easily mastered by the graduate student for the treatment of his research data. Mastering the mathematics involved is much less important than knowing what tools exist and how to apply them to research problems.

Under What Conditions Are Statistical Tools Appropriate?

One characteristic of a sound research plan is that it specifies the statistical tools to be used in the data analysis. Statistical tools should be decided upon *before* data have been collected, because different tools may require that the data be collected in different forms. For example, analysis of variance or analysis of covariance may become annoyingly complicated and difficult to interpret if the various cells (i.e., the various comparison groups to which subjects are assigned) have different numbers of subjects.[2] In fact, some computer programs for performing these analyses will not work unless an equal number of subjects has been entered into each cell of the analysis. A researcher who has not met this requirement may need to resort to a less powerful statistical technique and perhaps compromise what otherwise was an elegant research design.

Researchers sometimes use a statistical tool that is inappropriate for their data. A common mistake, for example, is to use the incorrect formula to calculate the standard error of the difference between means. If the mean scores of the comparison groups are correlated, a special formula should be used. If the simpler formula for uncorrelated means is used instead (see chapter 13), it will be less sensitive to detecting true differences between the comparison groups. The researcher may report his results as not significant when he would have found them to be significant if the correct formula had been used.

Another common error occurs in the statistical analysis of three or more comparison groups. The researcher may determine whether the groups' mean scores are significantly different from each other by performing t tests on all possible pairs of means. For example, if there are four groups (A, B, C, D), the researcher would perform six t tests (A vs. B, A vs. C, A vs. D, B vs. C, B vs. D, C vs. D). This procedure is incorrect. The proper statistical tool is analysis of variance, which compares all groups to one another simultaneously. If the analysis of variance is statistically significant, special post hoc t tests may be used to detect significant differences between pairs of means. This procedure is described more fully in chapter 13.

Occasionally a statistical tool is used when the data to be analyzed do not meet the conditions required for the tool in question. For example, most tests of statistical significance are based on the assumption that the characteristics we have measured are normally distributed in the population. The assumption of normality is justified for most variables studied in educational research, but when not justified, nonparametric or "distribution free" methods should be used. These methods make no assumptions about the shape of the distribution. We discuss these topics further in later chapters.

What Do the Statistical Results Mean?

After appropriate statistical tools have been selected and applied, the next step is to interpret the research results. The task of interpretation is not always obvious or easy. Research results are sometimes misinterpreted even when the

---

2. Analysis of variance and analysis of covariance are discussed in chapter 13.

researcher has selected the correct statistical tool and has made the necessary calculations without error. For example, a common misinterpretation is to confuse statistical significance with practical significance. A survey reported by Dunnette provides a good illustration of this point.[3] Dunnette studied a random sample of the statistical analyses reported in four psychological journals having high publication standards. The results of *t* tests and analyses of variance were converted to correlation ratios (this statistic is described in chapter 14) so that the degree of relationship between the variables measured in each study could be determined. In nearly a third of the studies, Dunnette found that the correlation ratio failed to reach .30; in a sixth of the studies the correlation ratio failed to reach .25; and 5 percent of the studies yielded correlation ratios below .20. Although all these correlations indicated a statistically significant relationship between the variables measured, the relationships were so small as to be of little or no value for most practical applications.

There is a lesson to be learned from Dunnette's survey in interpreting your own research results and those obtained by others. You should consider not only the statistical significance but also the practical significance of findings based on the *t* test, *F* test, or other statistical test that was used.

How Are Calculations Made?

This question is concerned with the mathematical procedures involved in the use of statistical formulas. The mathematical procedures demand the majority of time in most statistics courses and are not within the scope of this book. Most statistical calculations are laborious but not difficult.[4] Therefore, in this book it is more useful for you to direct your attention to learning what statistical tools are available, when they are used, and what the results mean after they are used. With this knowledge you can make most of the statistical decisions that are necessary during your review of the research literature and the development of your own research plan.

TYPES OF SCORES

Measurements in educational research are usually expressed in one of five forms: the continuous score, the rank, the artificial dichotomy, the true dichotomy, and the category. It is important to recognize the differences between these scores, since the form in which the data are expressed usualy determines one's

---

3. Marvin D. Dunnette, "Fads, Fashions, and Folderol in Psychology," *American Psychologist* 21 (1966): 343–52.
4. See Annotated References at the end of this chapter for textbooks that present statistical computations and theory.

choice of a statistical tool. For example, if he had collected continuous scores on two groups, the researcher would probably analyze group differences by calculating mean scores and by computing a z or Student's t. However, if the measurements were in the form of categories, the reseacher would analyze group differences by a chi-square (χ^2) test in which relative frequencies of category occurrence are compared.

Before deciding on a method of statistical analysis, you should determine the form of your research data. The five types of scores are discussed in the next sections.

Continuous Scores

Continuous scores are values of a variable that has an indefinite number of points along its continuum. When we say a variable is in continuous form, it means that scores on the variable could theoretically occur at any point along a continuum. Intelligence tests, personality inventories, and most other standardized measures employed in educational research yield continuous scores. For example, in the measurement of IQ, it is possible theoretically for a person to obtain a score at any IQ point within the broad range of IQs possessed by human beings. This not only means it is possible for a person to obtain a score of 101 while another person obtains a score of 102, it also means that theoretically it would be possible to find a person who would perform slightly better than a person at 101 IQ and slightly lower than a person at 102 IQ. In practice, continuous scores are usually limited to whole numbers, but in theory, fractional scores must be possible for the variable to be considered continuous.

A student's performance on each item of a test is usually summed to yield a total **raw score,** which is a form of continuous score. Raw scores, in the absence of other information, are difficult to interpret. For example, what does it mean that a student achieved a raw score of 30 items correct on a 50-item test? This raw score can represent good, poor, or average performance depending upon how other students scored or upon our expectations of how a particular student should have scored.

Because raw scores are difficult to interpret, they often are converted to "derived" scores, also a form of continuous score. **Derived scores** aid interpretation by providing a quantitative measure of each student's performance relative to a comparison group. Age equivalents, grade equivalents, percentiles, and standard scores are examples of derived scores.

Age equivalents and **grade equivalents** are average scores on a particular test for people who are at the same age or grade level. In constructing a new test, the test developers may administer it to a large group of people (sometimes called the standardization sample), and then determine the average score obtained by persons at each age or grade level. These average scores are arranged into tables of age and grade norms. Suppose a researcher administers the test to a sample of beginning fifth graders (mean age of 11.3 years) and determines that they have a mean score of 56.7 on the test. Referring to the table of norms in the test manual, the researcher may find that in the standardization sample a score of 57 (56.7 would be rounded off to this number) was the average score earned by sixth graders and by students who were 12.7 years of age. The researcher could conclude, on the basis of these norms, that the students in his sample were of above-average ability.[5]

Another form of derived score is the **percentile.** Percentiles are obtained by computing the percentage of persons whose score falls below a given raw score. For example, if 50 percent of the sample obtain a raw score of 16 or below, then anyone obtaining a raw score of 16 would be at the fiftieth percentile. Manuals for published tests sometimes contain percentile equivalents for raw scores based on the standardization sample.

A **standard score** is a form of derived score that uses standard deviation units (described later in this chapter) to express an individual's performance relative to the group's performance. The Z score is a type of standard score frequently used in educational research. The first step in calculating a Z score is to subtract the mean score of the total group from a person's raw score $(X - \overline{X})$. The next step is to divide the result by the standard deviation of the group. For any distribution of raw scores, Z scores have a mean of zero and a standard deviation of 1.00. Also, Z scores are continuous and have equality of units. Thus, a person's relative standing on two or more tests can be compared by converting the raw scores to Z scores.

Because Z scores can yield negative numbers (e.g., a person who is one standard deviation below the group mean would earn a Z score of -1.00), researchers sometimes convert raw scores to standard scores yielding only positive numbers. For example, T scores have a mean of 50 and a standard deviation of 10. The Stanine scale, developed by the U.S. Air Force, has a mean of 5 and standard deviation of 2. The 1960 version of the Stanford-Binet scales yields standard scores having a mean of 100 and a standard deviation of 16.

If you have administered a test for which age, grade, or percentile equivalents are available, it is advisable to report both the raw scores obtained by your research sample *and* the equivalents. Age, grade, and percentile equivalents provide useful information about your research sample by showing how their performance compares to the standardization sample. Equivalents should not be used in data analyses involving descriptive or inferential statistics, however. The reason for not using equivalents in these analyses is that they have

---

5. This conclusion assumes that the research sample was drawn from the same population as the standardization sample.

unequal units. For example, if you refer to the normal curve on page 367, you will find that there is the same range of scores from the fifteenth percentile (actually the 15.87th percentile) to the fiftieth percentile as there is from the second percentile to the fifteenth percentile.[6] Thus, if the mean of a test is 50 and its standard deviation is 10, a person with a score of 50 and a person with a score of 40 would be about 35 percentiles different from each other. However, two other persons with the same raw score difference of 10, but having raw scores of 40 and 30, would only be about 13 percentiles different from each other.

Because of the inequality of age, grade, and percentile units when applied to most variables in educational research, either raw scores or standard scores should be used in data analyses involving descriptive or inferential statistics.

Rank Scores

Some types of educational data are available only as ranks, for example, a student's high school graduation rank. A **rank score** expresses the position of a person or object on a variable, relative to the positions held by other persons or objects. In some educational research it is easier to rank individuals than to assign quantitative scores to them. For example, ranking procedures are used very commonly in the evaluation of teachers. A researcher may ask principals or teacher supervisors to rank a given group of teachers in terms of their effectiveness. The **rank scores** may then be used to form subgroups of effective and ineffective teachers, or the scores may be correlated with another variable thought to be related to teacher effectiveness.

Dichotomies

The term **dichotomy** refers to a variable that has only two values. For example, pass-fail grades are a dichotomous variable because the students can earn only one of two scores: pass or fail. An **artificial dichotomy** results when individuals are placed into two categories on the basis of performance on a continuous variable. It is easy to see that the dichotomy of pass-fail grades is artificial because if we carefully tested the individuals who complete a given course of study, we would find that their test scores would make a continuous distribution ranging from those persons who learned a great deal to those persons who learned little or nothing. The point at which we divide this continuous variable into pass-fail groups is based upon an arbitrary cutting point or criterion. If we compare the person who barely passes and the person who barely fails, we

6. This presentation of the inequality of percentile units assumes that the raw scores are normally distributed.

find that these individuals are very similar and do not have any characteristic except their score on the test to indicate that one individual belongs in the failing group and the other individual in the passing group.

Occasionally in education we encounter groups that are different because of some distinct and recognizable trait. When individuals are divided into two groups on the basis of a true difference on the variable, the dichotomy is referred to as a **true dichotomy.** The true dichotomy differs from the artificial dichotomy in that it is not necessary to establish any arbitrary cutting point for dividing the cases into two groups. Members of each group have some distinct characteristic that makes it possible to differentiate them from members of the other group.

Sex is probably the true dichotomy most frequently used in educational research. Many studies are concerned with differences between males and females in learning patterns, verbal fluency, personality, and other measurable characteristics. In these studies one of the variables is usually of a continuous nature, such as scores on a verbal fluency test. The other variable is sex, which is a true dichotomy.

Categories

The term **category** is used to refer to values of a variable that can yield more than two discrete, noncontinuous scores. (If there were only two categories, the variable would be an artificial or true dichotomy.) For example, student participation in high school athletics could be recorded in such categories as: (1) earned letter in varsity sports, (2) participated but did not earn letter, (3) participated in intramural sports, (4) participated in physical education classes, or (5) did not participate in any athletics.

Some of the variables that we wish to measure in educational research can be expressed only in the form of categories. For example, in studies of eye-hand dominance individuals are usually classified into one of these categories: left-left, left-right, right-left, and right-right. These characteristics cannot be measured meaningfully in any of the other score forms without changing the nature of the variable being studied.

DESCRIPTIVE STATISTICS

Measures of Central Tendency

A **measure of central tendency** is a single numerical value that is used to describe the average of an entire sample of scores. For example, if one has the scores of one hundred pupils on a test of algebraic ability, it is hard to get even a crude picture of the group's performance by examining these individual scores. By calculating a measure of central tendency, though, one can obtain an easily interpreted description of the "typical" or "average" performance of the one hundred pupils.

The mean, median, and mode are measures of central tendency. The **mean** is calculated by dividing the sum of the scores by the number of scores. The **median** is the middle score in the distribution of scores; and the **mode** is the most frequently occurring score in the distribution.

The mean is generally considered the best measure of central tendency. Computing the mean is one of the initial steps in applying many of the more advanced statistical tools, such as standard deviation, analysis of variance, and correlation. One advantage of the mean over the median is that it is more stable. Thus, if we study several samples drawn from the same population, the mean scores are likely to be in closer agreement than the median scores.

When a distribution of scores is symmetrical, the mean and the median are located at the same point on the distribution. When the distribution has more extreme scores at one end than at the other—that is, when it is skewed—the mean will always be in the direction of the greater number of extreme scores. In this situation, the median will reflect more accurately the average performance of the sample, as can be seen in the following example:

Distribution A	Distribution B
8	27
6	6
5	5
5	5
4	4
3	3
3	3
3	3
1	1
Mean = 4.2	Mean = 6.3
Median = 4.0	Median = 4.0

The two distributions differ by a single score. In the first distribution, both the mean and the median accurately represent average performance. In the second distribution, however, only the median provides an accurate representation of average performance. Just one person earned a score as high as or higher than the mean (6.3), even though the mean, as a measure of central tendency, is intended to represent "average" performance. As we shall discuss later in the chapter, this person (the one whose score was 27) is called an "outlier."

When a distribution is highly skewed, as in distribution B, it is desirable to report both the mean and the median. One also can use special statistics (presented in most textbooks of statistical methods) to describe quantitatively the skewness and shape of the distribution of scores. Generally, though, it is sufficient to make a visual presentation of the distribution of scores, as in the example in the preceding paragraph.

Measures of central tendency are calculated for continuous scores and ranks. Categorical data, including dichotomies, are summarized by creating frequency distributions, as in the following example:

Category	Frequency	(%)
Students earning letter in varsity sports	21	(11)
Students participating, but not earning letter	37	(19)
Students participating in intramural sports	115	(61)
Students not participating in athletics	16	(8)
	189	

The most frequently occurring category is easily determined by inspecting the frequency distribution. Also, the frequency of individuals or events in each category as a percentage of the total is readily determined.

Measures of Variability

Variability is the amount of dispersion of scores about a central value, such as the mean. Measures of variability provide information regarding the extent of individual differences on a given measure, for example, an intelligence test. If all persons had the same score on an intelligence test, this dimension would hold little interest for educational researchers. However, the fact that there is usually variability about a mean score leads researchers to ask, "Why do some subjects earn low intelligence scores, while others earn high scores? What accounts for this variability?" or "This educational program leads to increased achievement for some students but not others; what factors might account for this variability in achievement outcomes?" It is this concern to understand variability, or individual differences, that forms the basis of much educational research. Thus, the measurement of variability plays a central role in research design and statistical analysis.

The **standard deviation** (usually abbreviated SD) is the measure of variability most often reported in research studies. Basically, the standard deviation is a measure of the extent to which scores in a distribution, on the average, deviate from their mean. Thus, one step in the calculation of the standard deviation is to subtract the mean from each score. The resulting deviation scores are then squared and entered into a formula to yield the standard deviation.

The standard deviation is popular as a measure of variability because it is stable, that is, repeated samples drawn from the same population are likely to have similar standard deviations. Also, in the analysis of research data, the standard deviation is an intermediate step that is computed as part of other statistical calculations. The standard error of measurement, product-moment correlation, and many other statistical tools are based partially on the standard deviation. The standard deviation also forms the basis for various types of standard scores, such as Z scores, T scores, and Stanine scores, described earlier in this chapter.

The standard deviation, like the mean, provides a way of describing the scores of a group on the basis of a single measure. The mean and standard deviation, taken together, usually give a good description of the nature of the group being studied. For example, if we know that a group of subjects has a mean score of 10 on a test, and a standard deviation of 2, we can infer that approximately 68 percent of the subjects earned scores between 8 and 12, and that approximately 95 percent of the subjects earned scores between 6 and 14.

It is possible to use the standard deviation to make the inference described above because of the relationship between the standard deviation and the normal curve. The **normal curve** (also known as the normal probability curve) is a frequency polygon—that is, the height of the curve at a given point indicates the proportion of cases at that point. An example of a normal curve is shown in figure 10.1. This curve shows that the majority of individuals measured are clustered close to the mean. As we move farther and farther from the mean, fewer cases occur. The curve for most measures of complex human characteristics and behavior has a shape similar to that shown in figure 10.1.

The baseline shown in figure 10.1 has been divided into a number of equal units. Each unit is one standard deviation in length. It can be shown mathematically that, if a distribution of scores forms a normal curve, each standard deviation above or below the mean will include a fixed percentage of the scores. (These percentages are shown as percentiles in figure 10.1.)

Suppose that in one set of normally distributed scores, the mean is 3.0 and the standard deviation is 1.5. In another set of normally distributed scores the mean is 25.0 and the standard deviation is 5.0. Even though the values of the mean and standard deviation of the two sets of scores vary, the properties of the normal curve can be used to infer the dispersion of scores. For example, figure 10.1 indicates that approximately 16 percent of the scores will be one standard deviation or more above the mean (i.e., at the 84th percentile or higher). In the first set of scores, approximately 16 percent of the scores will be 4.5 (3.0 + 1.5) or larger. In the second set of scores approximately 16 percent of the scores will be 30 (25.0 + 5.0) or larger.

The variance, rather than the standard deviation, is occasionally given in research reports. If the standard deviation is 4.0, the variance is 16.0. The **variance** is simply the square of the standard deviation. Another measure of vari-

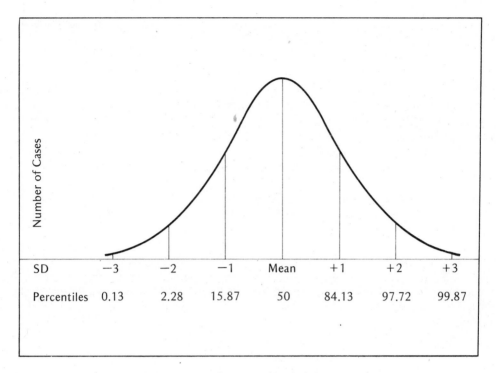

Figure 10.1   The normal probability curve.

ability that is sometimes reported is the **range.** This measure, as its name implies, is simply the lowest and highest scores in the distribution. It may be of interest to report the range, but the standard deviation also should be reported, since it provides important additional information about variability.

Occasionally continuous data are presented as a frequency distribution. A **frequency distribution** is a list of each score on a measure and the number of individuals who earned each score. For example, a frequency distribution would report the number of students who scored 30 on a test, the number of students who scored 31, the number of students who scored 32, and so forth. The frequency distribution can be inspected to determine the most frequently occurring score (i.e., the **mode**) and also the dispersion, or variability, of other scores around this central value.

Correlational Statistics

The descriptive statistics presented in the preceding sections involve the description of scores on a single variable. In some types of research, however, we are interested in describing the relationship between *two or more* variables. Correlational statistics are often used for this purpose.

The **bivariate correlation coefficient** is a statistic that enables the researcher to describe in mathematical terms the strength of relationship between two variables (e.g., student attentiveness in class and school achievement). There are many types of correlation coefficients. Selection of the appropriate coefficient depends upon the form of the scores (continuous, ranked, dichotomous, or categorical) that are to be related to each other.

Researchers are increasingly turning their attention to the use of **multivariate correlational methods.**[7] These methods allow the researcher to describe

TABLE 10.1
Table of Correlational Statistics

Bivariate Statistics	Purpose
Product-moment correlation Rank-difference correlation Kendall's *tau* Biserial correlation Widespread biserial correlation Point-biserial correlation Tetrachoric correlation *Phi* coefficient Contingency coefficient Correlation ratio	Used to describe the strength of relationship between two variables

Multvariate Statistics	Purpose
Multiple linear regression Discriminant function	Used to describe the strength of relationship between several independent variables and one dependent variable
Canonical correlation	Used to describe the strength of relationship between several independent variables and several dependent variables
Partial correlation Part correlation	Used to describe the strength of relationship between two variables after the influence of a third variable has been controlled
Factor analysis	Used to determine whether a set of variables can be reduced to a smaller number of factors

7. Bivariate correlational statistics, also called *zero-order correlations*, are a special case of multivariate methods, used when $N = $ two variables.

and explore the relationship between three or more variables. This capability is important, because the variables in which educational researchers are most interested (e.g., school achievement) usually are not affected by a single factor. Rather, they are affected by a complex of factors (e.g., home environment, personal characteristics, prior school experience), which themselves may influence each other in complex ways.

There are several multivariate correlational methods. **Multiple linear regression** is a statistical technique for exploring the strength of relationship between several independent variables (singly or in combination) and one dependent variable. **Canonical correlation** is similar to multiple linear regression, except that more than one dependent variable is included in the analysis. A **discriminant function** also is similar to multiple linear regression; it is used when the dependent variable is a dichotomous variable expressing group membership (e.g, college graduate vs. high school graduate). **Partial correlation** and **part correlation** are techniques used to describe the strength of relationship between two variables after the influence of one or more other variables on one (part) or both (partial) of the variables has been removed statistically. Finally, **factor analysis** is a statistical method for determining whether a set of variables can be reduced to a smaller number of factors. For example, if a researcher has administered achievement tests measuring thirty different variables to a group of subjects, factor analysis can be used to determine whether each variable measures a different type of achievement or whether two or more variables contribute to the measurement of the same type of achievement.

Correlational statistics and their use in correlational research are discussed more fully in chapter 14. A list of correlational statistics and their respective uses is presented in table 10.1.

Test Statistics

Statistics of various types can be used to describe and explore the psychometric properties of tests and other educational measures. Selection of the appropriate statistic depends upon the type of psychometric property being investigated. As indicated in chapter 6, psychometric properties of tests can be classified into three types: test validity, test reliability, and item characteristics.

Test validity is often investigated by calculating the correlation between subjects' test scores and their scores on a criterion measure. The resulting correlation coefficient (sometimes called a **validity coefficient**) indicates the magnitude of relationship between the two sets of scores. Any of the two-variable correlational statistics listed in table 10.1 can be used to calculate a validity coefficient; selection of the appropriate coefficient depends upon the form of the scores in the variables to be correlated. In the case of predictive validity, a special statistic—called the **standard error of estimate**—can be calculated to determine the margin of error to be expected in an individual's predicted score based on his or her score on the predictor measure.

The reliability of a test can be estimated by several methods, as discussed in chapter 8. Each method requires the calculation of a correlation coefficient. A different source, or sources, of error variance is controlled by each of the methods of reliability; split-half, test-retest, Kuder-Richardson, alpha. The selection of the appropriate reliability method also depends upon the form of the test scores (e.g., continuous, dichotomous).

Several types of statistics can be used to analyze characteristics of items in a test. The same statistics are also helpful in constructing and selecting items to be incorporated into a new test. These statistics are applied to each test item, one at a time. **Item validity** is determined by correlating subjects' scores on an individual item with their scores on a criterion measure. Since item scores are usually dichotomous (e.g., right-wrong, agree-disagree), biserial correlational statistics are often used to determine item validity. Another approach to determining item validity is to calculate the **index of discrimination,** which is based on an analysis of the proportion of persons in contrasting criterion groups who pass each item.

Item reliability is determined by correlating subjects' scores on an individual item with their total test score. Correlational statistics, especially biserial coefficients, are used to determine item reliability. (Item validity statistics use total test score on a *different* measure rather than total score on the test of which the item is a part.)

Finally, in test construction, it is important to calculate the **index of item difficulty,** which simply is the percentage of persons passing the particular test item.

A summary list of the test statistics presented above is included in table 10.2. Each of them is discussed in more detail in chapter 8.

STATISTICAL INFERENCE

The Null Hypothesis

It is rare in educational research to study every member of a specified population, for example, all sixth-grade students in the United States. Generally, measurements are made on a sample of subjects randomly drawn from a defined population. However, the research findings based on a random sample are of little value unless they can be used to make *inferences* about the defined population. For example, suppose that we are interested in testing the hypothesis that girls have greater verbal aptitude than boys. A measure of verbal aptitude is administered to random samples of 100 sixth-grade boys and 100 sixth-grade girls drawn from a defined population.

The first step in the statistical analysis is to calculate descriptive statistics. Means (M) and standard deviations (SD) would be calculated for the boys and girls separately. Suppose that we obtain the following results:

	N	M	SD
Boys	*100*	*80*	*4*
Girls	*100*	*85*	*5*

The mean verbal aptitude score for sixth-grade girls is five points higher than the mean score for sixth-grade boys. Thus we might conclude that girls at this grade level have greater verbal aptitude than boys. However, at this point the researcher must ask himself the following questions: "Is this a chance finding? Is it probable that if I studied a new random sample of sixth-grade boys and girls, no differences in verbal aptitude scores would be found? If I inferred that this is a 'true' difference between the entire population of sixth-grade boys and girls, how likely is it that my inference is false?"

Statisticians have developed a set of mathematical procedures that enable the researcher to answer these questions. The initial step in statistical inference

TABLE 10.2
Table of Test Statistics

Statistic	Purpose
Validity coefficient	Used to describe the strength of relationship between test scores and scores on a criterion measure
Standard error of estimate	Used to describe the margin of error to be expected in an individual's predicted score on a criterion measure based on his test score
Reliability coefficient	Used to describe the item consistency or stability of a test
Item-validity coefficient	Used to describe the strength of relationship between item scores and scores on a criterion measure
Index of discrimination	Used to describe the validity of a test in terms of the persons in contrasting groups who pass each item
Item-reliability coefficient	Used to describe the strength of relationship between an item score and total test score
Index of item difficulty	Used to describe the percentage of persons who correctly answer a particular test item

is to establish a null hypothesis. The **null hypothesis** states that *no* difference will be found between the descriptive statistics compared in one's research study.[8] In this example, the null hypothesis would be that the population of sixth-grade girls has the same mean verbal aptitude score as the population of sixth-grade boys. After stating the null hypothesis, the researcher carries out a test of statistical significance to determine whether the null hypothesis can be rejected (i.e., to determine whether there actually is a difference between the groups). As we shall find in the next section, this test enables us to make statements of the type: "If the null hypothesis is correct, we would find this large a difference between sample means only once in a hundred experiments. Since we have found this large a difference, it is quite probable that the null hypothesis is false. Therefore, we will reject the null hypothesis and conclude that the difference between sample means reflects a *true* difference between population means."

The Test of Statistical Significance

A **test of statistical significance** is done to determine whether the null hypothesis can be rejected. In the example we have been considering, suppose that the null hypothesis is correct, that is, the mean verbal aptitude scores for the populations of sixth-grade boys and sixth-grade girls are the same. Even if there was not a true difference between the two populations, we would probably find a difference if we measured a random sample from each population. In fact, if we selected many random samples of a given size, the differences between mean scores would approximate a normal curve. These difference scores would have a mean of zero and a standard deviation whose value depends on the population standard deviations. Assume that the standard deviation of difference scores in our example is 2. Thus, if we studied many samples of sixth-grade boys and girls, and each time subtracted the mean verbal aptitude score of the boys from that of the girls, about 68 percent of the time these difference scores would have a value between $+2$ and -2 (one SD above and below the mean). About 95 percent of the time the difference scores would have a value between $+4$ and -4.

In our example we have selected just one sample of sixth-grade boys and girls and have found a difference between the means of five points (85-80). How often would a difference score of this magnitude or larger be found between two populations whose means are the same? Since we do not know the population means or standard deviations that are necessary to answer this question, we must estimate them using the sample means and standard devia-

8. Null hypotheses are also discussed in chapter 3.

tions. These sample statistics are combined in such a way as to yield a z value (or Student's *t* if the samples are small).[9] The z value indicates how often a difference score of a given magnitude between samples of a given size would occur when there is no true population difference. For our sample of boys, N = 100, M = 80, SD = 4. For our sample of girls, N = 100, M = 85, SD = 5. These data yield a z value of 7.81. This large a z indicates that if there were no difference between the population means for sixth-grade boys and sixth-grade girls, we would obtain this large or a larger difference (five points or more) less than once in every thousand samples we studied. Since this is an extremely unlikely event, the researcher would reject the null hypothesis in favor of the alternative hypothesis, that is, there is a true population difference between sixth-grade boys and sixth-grade girls.

The z **distribution** (or **Student's** *t*) is used to determine a significance level. If the magnitude of z is 1.96 or larger, it indicates that the difference between means (or other statistics being compared) is significant at the .05 level, that is, there is one chance in 20 (.05) that this large or a larger difference would occur if there were in fact no difference between population means.[10] Generally, educational researchers will reject the null hypothesis if the z is significant at the .05 level. Occasionally, the more stringent .01 level is chosen, and in exploratory studies the .10 level may be used to reject the null hypothesis. The student should note that when the .10 level is chosen, there is one chance in ten that the researcher will reject the null hypothesis when, in fact, it is correct. If the significance level of .01 is chosen, however, there is only one chance in a hundred that this would occur. The rejection of the null hypothesis when it is correct is called a **Type I error.** Obviously, if we lower the significance level required to reject the null hypothesis, we reduce the likelihood of a Type I error. At the same time, we increase the likelihood of a **Type II error,** that is, the failure to reject the null hypothesis ("no difference") when there is, in fact, a difference.

The test of statistical significance, then, permits the researcher to measure the differences between two samples and to make an inference about the populations from which they were drawn. Given the finding that a random sample of sixth-grade boys earns a mean verbal aptitude score of 80 and girls a mean score of 85, the researcher would ask, "How likely is this difference of five points to be true of the total populations of sixth-grade boys and girls?" The test of statistical significance enables the researcher to answer the question in the following form: "Given sample means of 80 and 85, standard deviations of 4 and 5, respectively, and 100 subjects in each group, there is less than one

9. The z value is also called a critical ratio.
10. The problem of one-tailed versus two-tailed tests of statistical significance is discussed in chapter 13.

chance in a thousand that this large a difference would occur if the population means are equal; therefore, we conclude that the population means indeed differ."

Interpretation of Significance Tests

Statistical tests of significance are frequently misinterpreted both by inexperienced and experienced research workers. Because the test of significance plays such a large role in research design, we will consider its proper interpretation and common misinterpretations.

It is not uncommon for researchers to establish the level of significance (usually .10, .05, or .01) after the statistical analyses have been completed. A z or t will be computed, and the researcher will refer to a significance table to determine how "significant" it is. However, the logic of statistical inference dictates that the significance level be established *before* a z or t is computed. The researcher should make a decision at the outset of his study that if he finds a difference between his samples that exceeds a given significance level (for example, .05), the null hypothesis will be rejected. He cannot properly wait until after the statistical analysis to reject the null hypothesis at whatever significance level the z happens to reach.

As we have seen, the level of significance is expressed as a **probability value p.** The p value has been subject to a number of misinterpretations. Some researchers believe that the p value indicates the probability that the differences found between groups can be attributed to chance. For example, if one found that a mean difference of five IQ points between groups of subjects was significant at the .01 level, one might erroneously conclude that there is one chance in a hundred that this is a chance difference. The proper interpretation of such a finding is that the null hypothesis can be rejected (assuming that the .01 level of significance had been established beforehand), since the mean difference of five points exceeds the mean difference that we would find once in a hundred samples if the population mean difference was zero.

Another misinterpretation is that the level of significance indicates how likely it is that one's research hypothesis is correct.[11] For example, suppose that one had hypothesized that inquiry teaching will result in greater student achievement than expository teaching. If the difference between the mean achievement scores is found to be significant at the .01 level, one might conclude that the probability is 99 percent (1.00 - .99 = .01) that one's hypothesis is correct. However, the level of significance only helps to make a decision about rejecting the null hypothesis; it has only an indirect bearing on the confirmation of one's research hypothesis. For example, one may find a significant

11. The research hypothesis usually states that a difference between groups will be found, whereas the null hypothesis states that no difference will be found.

difference between two groups but not for the reason suggested by one's hypothesis. Similarly, one may find too small a difference between groups to reject the null hypothesis, but one's research hypothesis may still be correct. A Type II error may have occured, or the measures used to test the hypothesis may have been inadequate.

Still another misinterpretation of p values is to think that they indicate the probability of finding the same research results if the study were repeated. One might think, for example, that if a difference between the means of two groups is significant at the .05 level, a comparable difference will be found 95 times in every 100 repetitions of the study. However, even if the difference between means that we obtained in our study is a true population difference and is highly significant, we might still find considerable variations in the amount of difference from repetition to repetition of the study. In short, the level of significance cannot be used to predict the results of future studies (in which all conditions of the original study are replicated); it can only be used to make a decision about rejecting the null hypothesis.

Perhaps the most common and most serious misinterpretation of the test of significance is to confuse the level of significance (i.e., the p value) of the research results with the practical and theoretical significance of the research results. It should be realized that the level of significance is influenced to a considerable degree by the number of individuals tested in the research project. Thus, the larger the sample size, the smaller the difference needed to reach a given level of significance. For example, with a sample of 1000 subjects, a correlation coefficient of .08 is significant at the .01 level. Thus, the researcher would reject the null hypothesis (that the correlation coefficient for the population is .00) if he had established a p of .01 as the level of significance. This correlation, however, is extremely slight and would be of no practical value in working with the types of educational problems that we attempt to solve with correlational studies.[12] For example, if we studied 1000 subjects and found a correlation of .08 between school grades and a new aptitude test, the findings would be statistically significant, but they would be of very little use in helping to predict school grades from aptitude test scores.

As we have already observed, the test of significance is concerned with the inferences that we wish to make from sample statistics to population parameters. Thus, a test of significance is made when we wish to determine how probable it is that the differences we have found between our samples will also be found in the populations from which they were drawn. Therefore, to use the test of significance properly, one should use it only with samples randomly

---

12. Actually, in a negative sense a correlation this small might have practical or theoretical significance. It would indicate to researchers that future investigation of the relationship between the two variables under study would not be warranted (thus saving research time and money). Also, if only a small relationship were found when a large one had been predicted by one's theory, the finding might have the effect of leading one to revise the theory.

drawn from a specified population. However, researchers sometimes do not specify the population or do not use random sampling techniques, and thus the sample may not be representative. Also, on occasion they use the test of significance when the entire population has been studied. For example, suppose that a researcher defined all males and all females at a particular college as two populations. Then suppose he finds, as hypothesized, that the females have higher gradepoint averages than the males. In this situation it is meaningless to use a test of statistical significance. The difference between gradepoint averages is a *true* difference because the entire populations have been studied rather than samples drawn from their respective populations.

Criticism of statistical significance tests has become more pronounced in recent years.[13] One criticism is that educational researchers seldom work with samples randomly drawn from defined populations, even though random sampling is a requirement for using statistical significance tests. Another criticism is that the tests are often misinterpreted, as we indicated above. The p value is taken as a measure of the worth of a study rather than for what it really is: a basis for rejecting the null hypothesis. The third criticism is that the "power" of statistical significance tests in educational research tends to be low. (The concept of statistical power is discussed a bit later in the chapter.)

We believe that each of these criticisms is legitimate, yet they do not justify complete discontinuation of statistical significance testing. The tests are quite helpful under conditions of random sampling and high statistical power. Conversely, the tests should be used with caution or not at all under conditions of nonrandom sampling or low statistical power. Our recommendation is that researchers should be wary of accepting a difference or relationship as real on the basis of one study, no matter how statistically significant the results are. A significant p in a study is cause for optimism, but replications of the study should be done to get additional assurance that the observed result is real.[14] Also, other indices should be calculated in each study to set p values in proper perspective. We shall discuss these indices—effect size, measures of correlations, and confidence intervals—later in the chapter.

Types of Significance Tests

Thus far in our discussion of inferential statistics we have been concerned with how to determine whether the difference between two sample means reflects

13. S. Alan Cohen and Joan S. Hyman, "How Come So Many Hypotheses in Educational Research Are Supported? (A Modest Proposal)," *Educational Researcher* 8, no. 11 (1979): 12–16; R. P. Carver, "The Case Against Statistical Significance Testing," *Harvard Educational Review* 48 (1978): 378–99.
14. For a similar view stated by a distinguished statistician, see John W. Tukey, "Analyzing Data: Sanctification or Detective Work?" *American Psychologist* 24 (1969): 83–91.

population differences. A significance test based on the calculation of a t or z value is appropriate for this purpose. Other significance tests are available for answering other questions involving inference from sample statistics to population values (also called *population parameters*).

Occasionally a researcher is interested in determining whether a *single* sample mean correlation coefficient, or other statistic is significantly different from a specified population value. A critical ratio *(z)* or t value is calculated to determine whether this kind of inference is justified. A critical ratio or t value also can be calculated and used to determine whether the proportions (e.g., the percentage of "yes" answers to a questionnaire item) in two samples differ significantly from each other, whether two correlation coefficients differ significantly from each other, and whether two change scores differ significantly from each other.

Analysis of variance is an inferential technique with many applications. For example, it can be used to determine whether three or more sample means are significantly different from one another.[15] Analysis of variance results in an F value, which if statistically significant, tells the researcher that the means are likely to have been drawn from different populations. However, analysis of variance does not specify which of the three or more sample means differ significantly from one another. Special post hoc t tests are used for this purpose. Duncan's multiple-range test is an example of a post hoc t test.

Analysis of variance is used frequently in experimental research involving complex factorial designs. Depending upon the complexity of the factorial design, two or more F values can be generated from a single analysis of variance. The F values will tell whether sample means of the various factors represented in the experiment (e.g., treatments, sex of subjects, ability levels) differ significantly from one another, and whether the various factors interact significantly with one another.

The analysis of variance technique also can be used to test the statistical significance of an hypothesized trend. This application is called **trend analysis.** For example, the researcher may form five groups varying in perceptual ability (very low, low, average, high, very high), and hypothesize that students at each level will do better on a reading comprehension task than the students in the ability level just below it. Trend analysis can be used to test this hypothesis.

Still another application of analysis of variance is in the determination of whether two or more sample variances (the variance is the square of the standard deviation) differ significantly from each other.

15. Analysis of variance also can be used to determine whether two means differ significantly from each other. In this situation, analysis of variance will yield the same result as the calculation of a critical ratio or t value.

In certain situations, the researcher may wish to do an analysis of variance that controls for other differences that may exist in the samples being compared. **Analysis of covariance** can be used for this purpose if certain statistical assumptions are satisfied.

The tests of statistical significance presented above make certain assumptions about the form of the research data. If these assumptions are not satisfied, it may be more appropriate to use one of the **nonparametric tests of statistical significance.** The chi-square test is commonly used when the research data are in the form of categories or dichotomies rather than continuous scores or ranks. The Mann-Whitney U test, the Wilcoxon signed-rank test, and the Kruskal-Wallis test are nonparametric substitutes for the t test for uncorrelated means, the t test for correlated means, and one-way analysis of variance, respectively.

A summary list of tests of statistical significance is presented in table 10.3. These tests are discussed in more detail in chapters 13–16.

Statistical Power Analysis

Researchers rarely desire to prove the null hypothesis. They do not wish to demonstrate that there is no difference between groups, or no correlation between variables, or no difference between treatments. Instead, researchers usually conduct studies because they want to find differences and relationships. For example, a researcher is more likely to become interested in investigating a method of instruction because she believes it may be superior to conventional practice than because she believes it is no different than conventional practice.

Given researchers' interest in discovering differences and relationships, they will want to maximize the likelihood of rejecting the null hypothesis (which posits *no* difference or relationship). Fortunately, options are available to researchers for accomplishing this goal. **Statistical power analysis** is a procedure for studying the likelihood that a particular test of statistical significance will be sufficient to reject a null hypothesis. **Statistical power** is the probability that a particular test of statistical significance will lead to the rejection of the null hypothesis.

Statistical power analysis requires access to mathematical tables, but we can provide an overview of how the procedure works.[16] First, it is a fact that statistical power increases automatically with sample size. In other words, the larger the sample, the smaller the difference or relationship needed to reject the null hypothesis. For example, if a researcher obtains a correlation coefficient of .25 between two variables in a sample of 47 students, she cannot reject

16. Tables for statistical power analysis are in Jacob Cohen, *Statistical Power Analysis for the Behavioral Sciences.* Rev. ed. (New York: Academic Press, 1977).

Table 10.3

Table of Inferential Statistics

Tests of Statistical Significance (Parametric)	Purpose
t test Critical ratio (z)	Used to determine whether two means, proportions, or correlation coefficients differ significantly from each other; also used to determine whether a single mean, proportion, or correlation coefficient differs significantly from a specified population value
Analysis of variance	Used to determine whether mean scores on one or more factors differ significantly from each other, and whether the various factors interact significantly with each other; also used to determine whether sample variances differ significantly from each other
Analysis of covariance	Similar in use to analysis of variance, except that the influence of one or more independent variables on the dependent variable is controlled
Trend analysis	Used to test the statistical significance of an hypothesized trend
Duncan's multiple-range test Scheffé's test	Used, following a significant F ratio in analysis of variance, to test the statistical significance of differences between particular group means or combinations of group means
Confidence limits	Used to estimate a population value, based on what is known about a sample value

Nonparametric Tests	Purpose
Mann-Whitney U test	Used to determine whether two uncorrelated means differ significantly from each other
Wilcoxon signed rank test	Used to determine whether two correlated means differ significantly from each other
Kruskal-Wallis test	Used to determine whether three or more mean scores on a single factor differ significantly from each other
Chi-square test	Used to determine whether two frequency distributions differ significantly from each other

the null hypothesis at the .05 level of significance. If the researcher obtained the same coefficient (.25) but with a larger sample ($N = 62$), she would be able to reject the null hypothesis at the .05 level of significance.

The second determinant of statistical power is the level of significance (p) at which the null hypothesis is to be rejected. Statistical power can be increased by raising the level of significance. Thus, a test of statistical significance with p set at .10 is more powerful than the same test with p set at .05. ("More powerful" means that it is easier to reject the null hypothesis at the .10 level than at the .05 level.) In practice, p is usualy set at .05. However, some researchers feel that it is permissible to set p at .10 in exploratory studies to increase statistical power. A p of .10 increases the risk of Type I error, but it also might spotlight a potentially important difference or relationship that would have been overlooked had a lower p value been set.

The third determinant of statistical power is whether directionality is specified in the research hypothesis.[17] Directionality refers to the fact that observed differences and relationships can go in two directions. For example, in an experiment, treatment A can be better than treatment B (one direction), or treatment B can be better than treatment A (the other direction). However, a researcher might be able to argue, on the basis of theory or previous research findings, that treatment B cannot possibly be better than treatment A. If the researcher can reject this "direction" in advance of doing the experiment, she can increase statistical power by doing a one-tailed test of statistical significance.

The fourth determinant of statistical power is **effect size,** which is the magnitude of a difference or relationship in a sample or population.[18] To understand how effect size influences statistical power, you need to keep two facts in mind. First, it is a fact that the greater an observed difference or relationship, the lower is the level of significance (p) associated with it. For example, an r of .38 in a sample of 20 students is significant at the .10 level. In contrast, an r of .44 in the same size sample is significant at the .05 level. Thus, the null hypothesis can be rejected at the conventional significance level (.05) with an r of .44, but not with an r of .38.

Because the magnitude of r affects significance level, we need to ask what determines the magnitude of r. This leads us to the second fact: A researcher is more likely to obtain a large effect size in a sample when there is a large effect size in the population. Returning to our example, suppose the value of r is .65 in the population from which the sample of 20 students was drawn. It is likely, then, that samples drawn from this population will tend to yield similarly large values of r. Conversely, if the population value of r is small (for example, $r = .30$), samples drawn from this population will tend to yield similarly small values of r. In brief, if the population value of r is large, it will be easier to reject the null hypothesis than if the population value is small.

The effect size in a population is beyond the researcher's control. One

17. Research hypotheses are described in chapter 3. Directionality (one-tailed versus two-tailed) of statistical significance tests is described in chapters 13 and 14.
18. The concept of effect size is also discussed in chapter 6 (see section on meta-analysis). Later in this chapter, effect size is discussed as an index of practical significance.

researcher may decide to study an instructional method (A_1), which in the population is much more effective than another instructional method (B_1). Another researcher may decide to study method A supplemented by a technique (A_2), which in reality is just slightly better than method A without the technique (A_1). Both studies may be worth doing for different reasons. Yet, assuming that both researchers use the same sample size and significance level, the first researcher is more likely to reject his null hypothesis ($A_1 = B_1$) than the second researcher, even though his null hypothesis ($A_2 = A_1$) is also false.

What can the second researcher do to increase the power of his statistical significance test? He can establish a higher probability level for rejecting the null hypothesis, or he can increase sample size. Exercising both options will increase statistical power even more.

Statistical power analysis is used by researchers to understand how the four factors described above—sample size, significance level, directionality, and effect size—influence the ability of a statistical significance test to reject the null hypothesis.[19] By manipulating one or more of these factors, the researcher can increase the power of his statistical significance test. As we stated above, mathematical tables are available for the purpose of showing how changes in each factor increase or decrease statistical power.

SUPPLEMENTS TO SIGNIFICANCE TESTS

Tests of statistical significance should be supplemented by other procedures to explore further the statistical and practical significance of research data. Two of the procedures discussed here—calculation of confidence limits and replication studies—are concerned primarily with clarifying the statistical significance of research results. The other two procedures—calculation of effect sizes and measures of correlation—are intended to index the practical significance of research results.

Confidence Limits

Researchers sometimes calculate **confidence limits** (also called *confidence intervals*) in addition to testing for statistical significance. Confidence limits provide a method for estimating population values, based on what is known about sample value. For example, suppose that we know that the mean test score for

19. There are additional determinants of statistical power analysis, but we have described the main ones here.

a sample of subjects is 75. The sample mean and standard deviation can be used to estimate a range of values (the confidence limits) that are likely to include the true population mean. If our calculations reveal that the 95 percent confidence limits for the sample mean are 68 and 83, we can infer that there is a high likelihood that the true population mean lies between 68 and 83. Stated more precisely, we can infer that if we collected data on 100 research samples similar to the one we actually studied, only 5 of them would contain confidence limits that did not include the true population mean. In practice, we usually study a single research sample, but by calculating 95 percent confidence limits, we can be reasonably certain that ours is not in the 5 percent of sample means whose confidence limits do not contain the true population mean.[20]

A typical experiment will yield two posttreatment means—one for the experimental group and one for the control group. If the researcher calculates confidence limits for each mean, he will have an easily interpreted measure of whether the observed difference between two means indicates a true difference between the populations represented by the samples. Suppose the experimental group mean is 24 with 95 percent confidence limits of 20 and 28. The control group mean is 15 with 95 percent confidence limits of 12 and 18. Given these limits, one can conclude that the true mean of the experimental population is quite unlikely to be lower than 20, and the true mean of the control population is quite unlikely to be higher than 18. Thus, it appears that the experimental group "truly" outperformed the control group in this hypothetical study.

Now consider what happens under a different set of conditions. Suppose the experimental group mean remains the same (24), but the 95 percent confidence limits are 17 and 31. The control group mean also remains the same (15), but the 95 percent confidence limits are 7 and 23. Thus, the true mean for the experimental population is likely to be as low as 17, and the true mean for the control population is likely to be as high as 23. Thus, one cannot disregard the possibility that the two population means are the same, with a likely value between 17 and 23.

Confidence limits are a branch of inferential statistics in that they enable the researcher to make an inference from a sample statistic to a population value. Thus they are included in the summary list of inferential statistics in table 10.3. Tests of statistical significance also involve inference from sample statistics to a population value, but their purpose is to provide a basis for deciding to accept or reject a null hypothesis. In published research, tests of statistical significance are almost always reported. In addition, a few researchers will report the confidence limits for key statistics.

20. Sometimes the 99 percent confidence limits are calculated.

Replication of Research Results

Replication provides another method of determining whether observed effects are "true" effects. **Replication** is the process of repeating a research study with a different group of subjects using the same or similar methods. Results of a study are more "significant"—in the sense of inspiring confidence that they represent differences or relationships in the population—if a new study yields similar results, or if the present study repeats the findings of past research. Consider the case of mastery learning, the effectiveness of which has been demonstrated in many experiments.[21] Suppose a researcher decides to conduct a new experiment to determine whether mastery learning is superior to conventional instruction. As predicted, the experimental group that received instruction based on mastery learning principles earned a higher mean score on the posttest than the comparison group, but the difference was not statistically significant. The researcher is safe in concluding that this is most likely a true difference because it replicates a consistent set of previous findings.

In fact, it can be demonstrated that statistical significance is multiplicative across studies. Two or more studies using the same methodology can each yield nonsignificant results, but if the results of each study are in the same direction, the p values from the statistical significance tests can be multiplied. For example, if the p value in each of two studies is .20, their combined probability is .04 (.20 × .20). Thus, the null hypothesis (which would be the same in both studies) can be rejected at the .04 level of significance.

If possible, you should attempt to replicate your research project, particularly if your findings show promise of making a substantial contribution to knowledge about education. If you are able to replicate your findings, they are of much more "significance" to other educational researchers than a statistically significant but weak finding (e.g., a correlation of .20 significant at the .01 level) obtained in the original study. A replicated finding is strong evidence against the possibility that a Type I error (rejection of the null hypothesis when it is true) occurred in the original study.

Replication also provides other kinds of evidence, depending upon the type of replication study that is carried out. David Lykken distinguished three types of replication:

> *Literal replication* . . . would involve exact duplication of the first investigator's sampling procedure, experimental conditions, measuring techniques, and methods of analysis; asking the original investigator to simply run more subjects would perhaps be about as close as we could come

---

21. Benjamin S. Bloom, *Human Characteristics and School Learning* (New York: McGraw-Hill, 1976).

to attaining literal replication and even this, in psychological research, might often not be close enough.

In the case of *operational replication*, on the other hand, one strives to duplicate exactly just the sampling and experimental procedures given in the first author's report of his research. The purpose of operational replication is to test whether the investigator's "experimental recipe"— the conditions and procedures he considered salient enough to be listed in the "Methods" section of his report—will in other hands produce the results that he obtained.

In the quite different process of *constructive replication*, one deliberately avoids imitation of the first author's methods. To obtain an ideal constructive replication, one would provide a competent investigator with *nothing more than* a clear statement of the empirical "fact" which the first author would claim to have established, and then let the replicator formulate his own methods of sampling, measurement, and data analysis.[22]

Literal replication, which the student can carry out himself, can be used to evaluate whether a Type I error might have occurred in the original study. Operational replication is particularly important for experiments in which the researcher must determine the effectiveness of a procedure to improve learning. For example, suppose a researcher trained teachers in the use of the inquiry method and found that this method led to greater student achievement than conventional teaching methods. If other researchers can then use the first researcher's training procedures and materials and find similar achievement gains, we may conclude that the inquiry method is a superior instructional strategy. If operational replication does not support the original findings, then we would probably conclude that the effectiveness of the training procedure and materials is limited to the original researcher. Obviously, an educational procedure or product that holds up after an operational replication has more practical significance for the improvement of education than one that works only in the hands of the original researcher.

The third type of replication, constructive replication, increases the validity of theoretical studies in education. Suppose one hypothesizes that the presence of anxiety leads to a decrement in academic performance. To test this hypothesis, it is necessary to select or construct measures of anxiety and of academic performance. The hypothesis becomes increasingly credible when it is demonstrated that the relationship between the two variables holds up after several constructive replications in which different operational measures of the

22. David T. Lykken, "Statistical Significance of Psychological Research," *Psychological Bulletin* 70 (1968): 155–59.

same two variables are used each time. For example, if a given measure of anxiety predicts decrement in gradepoint average for each year of college, decrement in performance on a particular examination, and decrement in scores than if anxiety predicted only one of these performance variables.

Replication studies unfortunately are seldom done by educational researchers.[23] Yet is is an important strategy for determining the significance of results obtained in a particular study. As we indicated in chapter 3, the beginning researcher should seriously consider replicating and extending previous studies rather than try to investigate a previously unresearched problem.

Effect Size

If tests of statistical significance are inappropriate for making inferences about the practical significance of research results, what can be used in their place? The approach currently favored is to calculate an effect size (ES). We discussed effect size earlier in the chapter with respect to its use in statistical power analysis. Also, the calculation and interpretation of ES were discussed in chapter 6 as part of a method ("meta-analysis") for reviewing a set of research studies on a particular problem. Still another use of ES statistics is as an aid to interpret the results of a single study.

To understand this last-mentioned use of ES, suppose an experiment has been done comparing two methods of instruction. The mean score of the experimental group students on a posttest measure of academic achievement is 56, and the corresponding mean score of the control group is 47. The mean difference between the groups is 9 points. Is this difference large enough to have significance for the practice of education? Perhaps. Using the ES approach, the researcher would divide the mean difference (9 points) by the standard deviation of the control group on the posttest.[24] If the standard deviation happens to be 9, the ES will be 1.00 (9-point mean score difference divided by the standard deviation of 9).

An ES of 1.00 means that the average student in the experimental group scored at the 84th percentile of the control group distribution. This appears to be an impressive result. We must check, though, that the posttest measured an important outcome of learning. Also, the impressiveness of the result is dependent on the absolute difference in points between the 84th percentile and

23. James P. Shaver and Richard S. Norton, "Randomness and Replication in Ten Years of the *American Educational Research Journal,*" *Educational Researcher* 9, no. 1 (1980): 9–15.
24. Procedures for calculating ES when data do not conform to this example are in Gene V. Glass, Barry McGaw, and Mary Lee Smith, *Meta-Analysis in Social Research* (Beverly Hills, Calif.: Sage, 1981).

50th percentile of the control group distribution. In this case there is a 9-point difference between the two percentiles, which may be modestly substantial in a 70-item test.

The concept of ES is not new, but only recently has its use in educational research become popular. It is a helpful method for assessing the practical significance of relationships and group differences, as long as it is not applied unthinkingly. The meaning of ES is dependent on the measures used, the absolute difference between group means, the shape of the score distribution, the subjects in the sample, and possibly other factors. In sum, there is no simple answer to the problem of determining practical significance of research results. The ES is just an aid to interpretation, albeit an important aid.

Measures of Correlation

We discussed earlier in the chapter that correlational studies explore relationships between variables. As a general rule, the larger the relationship between two variables, the more likely is the relationship to be of practical significance. How does one know whether a relationship between variables is large? The correlation coefficient is used for this purpose: The larger the coefficient, the larger the relationship between the two or more variables being correlated. A coefficient of $+1.00$ or -1.00 indicates maximum relationship. A coefficient of 0.00 indicates a total absence of relationship. Thus, the magnitude of a correlation coefficient provides an index of the practical significance of an observed relationship between two or more variables.[25]

As with measures of effect size, correlation coefficients should be interpreted in context. The educational significance of the variables being measured, the distributions of scores on the measures, and characteristics of the sample each have an effect on how the magnitude of a correlation coefficient is to be interpreted. This issue is discussed further in chapter 14, which is about correlational research.

Some research data can be analyzed to yield either measures of relationship (correlation coefficients) or measures of effect size. This is especially true of data yielded by experiments. For example, experimental and control group means can be subjected to analysis of variance, from which *eta* (a measure of relationship) can be calculated. The same group means can be used to calculate the measure of effect size described above (difference between group means

---

25. The correlation coefficient *r* is sometimes squared (R^2) to yield a coefficient known as explained variance or common variance. Either statistic (*r* or R^2) can be used to interpret the practical significance of observed relationships.

divided by the standard deviation of the control group). Of the two procedures, effect size is probably more easily interpreted in considering the practical significance of research results.

PROBLEMS IN STATISTICAL ANALYSIS

The Need for Exploratory Data Analysis

A common problem in data analysis is to calculate the usual descriptive statistics (mean and standard deviation) before carefully examining the individual scores collected in the study. Some research data are "untouched by human hands" in the sense that they are entered onto computer cards by keypunchers; the cards then are entered into the computer, and a computer program generates the descriptive and inferential statistics specified by the researcher. Thus, the researcher is denied the opportunity to examine the "raw" data. As a result, the researcher may overlook important patterns and phenomena revealed by the individual scores.

Statistical techniques for examining patterns and phenomena in individual scores have been developed in recent years, most notably by the statistician John Tukey.[26] These techniques are not widely used, but they are worth studying because they have revealed new insights about the nature of data often collected in educational research. The techniques are known collectively as **exploratory data analysis,** which is a method for "discovering unforeseen or unexpected patterns in the data and consequently [for] gaining new insights and understanding of natural phenomena."[27]

Once the research data have been collected and quantified, exploratory data analysis can begin. An essential tool of exploratory data analysis is the **stem-and-leaf display,** which is a convenient method for displaying all of the individual scores on a particular measure. Table 10.4[28] presents a conventional display of individual scores provided by a computer program. The scores are from a group of learning disabled students who participated in an experimental reading curriculum. The problem with such a display is that it is difficult to "see" the data. Patterns and departures from the patterns are not easily detectable.

26. See Annotated References at the end of this chapter.
27. Gaea Leinhardt and Samuel Leinhardt, "Exploratory Data Analysis: New Tools for the Analysis of Empirical Data," in *Review of Research in Education* 8, ed. David C. Berliner (Washington, D.C.: American Educational Research Association, 1980), p. 86.
28. Ibid., p. 89.

TABLE 10.4
Example of Computer Printout of Raw Data

Sequential Location	CUR	School	Words	Silent	Overlap
1	0.00	1.00	2489.00	0.33	48.65
2	0.00	1.00	3755.00	0.80	94.59
3	0.00	1.00	3346.00	0.58	95.95
4	0.00	1.00	3057.00	1.27	44.59
5	0.00	1.00	7002.00	0.84	93.24
6	0.00	1.00	748.00	1.04	97.30
7	0.00	1.00	1462.00	0.36	54.05
8	0.00	1.00	9562.00	1.63	90.54
9	0.00	1.00	4434.00	0.44	91.89
10	0.00	1.00	4295.00	1.15	94.59
11	0.00	2.00	4426.00	0.82	86.49
12	0.00	2.00	1632.00	0.02	6.76
13	0.00	2.00	1626.00	0.92	54.05
14	0.00	2.00	2886.00	0.83	44.59
15	0.00	2.00	484.00	0.35	52.38
16	0.00	2.00	483.00	0.35	53.57
17	0.00	2.00	1867.00	0.25	83.43
18	0.00	2.00	1437.00	0.10	4.05
19	0.00	2.00	1162.00	0.35	6.76
20	0.00	2.00	1676.00	0.38	2.70
21	0.00	2.00	1218.00	0.44	6.76
22	0.00	3.00	0.00	0.52	87.84
23	0.00	3.00	0.00	0.32	81.08
24	0.00	3.00	4713.00	0.27	94.59
25	0.00	3.00	2823.00	0.23	89.19
26	0.00	3.00	1093.00	0.16	25.68
27	0.00	3.00	2560.00	0.17	22.97
28	0.00	3.00	3036.00	0.38	94.59
29	0.00	3.00	4423.00	0.75	98.65
30	0.00	3.00	5811.00	1.13	94.59
31	0.00	3.00	2948.00	0.19	71.62
32	1.00	4.00	198.00	0.48	100.00
33	1.00	4.00	198.00	0.66	97.30
34	1.00	4.00	293.00	0.42	82.43
35	1.00	4.00	293.00	0.25	87.84
36	1.00	4.00	198.00	0.77	85.14
37	1.00	4.00	253.00	0.69	100.00
38	1.00	4.00	253.00	0.64	100.00

TABLE 10.4—Continued

Sequential Location	CUR	School	Words	Silent	Overlap
39	1.00	4.00	32.00	0.13	64.86
40	1.00	5.00	20.00	0.35	39.19
41	1.00	5.00	999.00	0.62	58.11
42	1.00	5.00	20.00	0.11	52.38
43	1.00	5.00	67.00	0.16	18.92
44	1.00	5.00	20.00	0.35	5.41
45	1.00	5.00	0.00	0.06	39.29
46	1.00	5.00	0.00	0.09	42.86
47	1.00	5.00	67.00	0.48	32.43
48	1.00	5.00	419.00	0.17	24.32
49	1.00	6.00	88.00	0.27	20.27
50	1.00	6.00	212.00	0.44	52.70
51	1.00	6.00	88.00	0.32	10.81
52	1.00	6.00	212.00	0.69	44.59
53	1.00	6.00	212.00	0.49	39.19

NOTE: The first column is the student's identification (ID) code. The second column is the ID code for the curricular approach that each student received. The third column is the student's school ID code. The fourth column is number of words read by the students in a three-day period. The fifth column is a measure of silent reading time. The sixth column is a teacher prediction measure.

Now examine the same set of 53 scores summarized in a stem-and-leaf display in figure 10.2.[29] Each digit to the right of the vertical line represents a student's score. If you wish, you can transform each digit (technically a "leaf") by a few simple calculations into the individual's actual score.

One advantage of a stem-and-leaf display is that the researcher can easily see the shape of the distribution of scores. It is apparent in figure 10.2 that the scores do not form a normal distribution. Most of the scores are at the lower range of values, clustering around a value of approximately .30. Because the score distribution is skewed in this direction, the researcher should be alert to the possible need to use statistics that do not assume a normal curve distribution: for example, the median and range, and the various nonparametric statistics.

Another advantage of a stem-and-leaf display is that it provokes ques-

29. Ibid., p. 92.

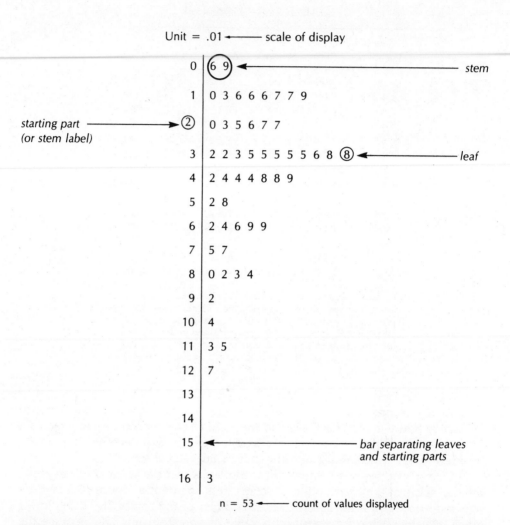

Figure 10.2 Example of a Stem-and-Leaf Display. Note that the display is of the data in column 5 of table 10.4. For example, the first score of column 5 (0.33) is represented in the fourth line of the stem-and-leaf display. Each leaf in the display can be converted to a regular score by placing the stem label to the left of it and then by multiplying by .01. For example, the bottom-most leaf is 3. Placing the stem label to the left of it yields the number 163. Multiplying this number by .01 results in a score of 1.63, which is the score of the eighth student in column 5.

tions about the data. For example, looking at figure 10.2, the researcher might speculate about the factors that caused most students to be at the lower end of the scale, while a minority of students scored at the upper end of the scale. The researcher might be able to formulate a hypothesis about these factors and test it using available data. Otherwise, the hypothesis might provide the basis for designing a new study.

The third advantage of exploratory data analysis is that it facilitates the detection of outliers. An **outlier** is a research subject whose scores differ remarkably from the general pattern established by other subjects in the sample. The student with a score of 1.63 in figure 10.2 is clearly an outlier. If you identify an outlier, you should check whether an error occurred in calculating the outlier's score. Some subjects show up as outliers simply because the researcher misplaced a decimal point or transposed the subject's score on another variable while preparing the data for computer analysis.

If the outlier's score is not attributable to a calculating error, you need to search elsewhere for an explanation. Perhaps the outlier was not exposed to the same conditions as the other subjects in the sample, as was the case in figure 10.2:

> In the actual research project from which these data were drawn, it was independently determined that the child on whom this outlier value was measured was, for administrative reasons, not under the control of the classroom teacher and was not, therefore, exposed to the same treatment as the other members of the class. He was ultimately removed from the study.[30]

The decision to eliminate one or more outliers from a research study is problematic. Even one or two outliers can distort the results yielded by conventional statistics, unless the sample is large. A researcher should not eliminate outliers just for this reason, though. Outliers should only be eliminated for good cause, as in the case of the student described above. If outliers are left in the sample, the researcher should consider analyzing the data using both parametric and nonparametric statistics. Comparison of the results yielded by these statistical tools will yield information about how much an outlier, or outliers, are distorting the data.

In the example above, there would be little argument about the decision to call the student with a score of 1.63 an outlier. But how about the student with a score of 1.27 in figure 10.2? Or the students with scores of 1.13 and 1.15? It is not clear that they should be considered outliers. Statistical techniques that yield quantitative decision rules for identifying outliers are avail-

30. Ibid., pp. 153–54.

able.[31] In reporting a study's findings, the researcher should note the occurrence of outliers and how they were handled in the data analysis.

Exploratory data analysis is a relatively new area of social science statistics. Computer programs for generating stem-and-leaf displays and other techniques of exploratory data analysis are not yet widely available. Therefore, you
may lack access to these computer programs and also may find that you do
not have sufficient time to generate stem-and-leaf displays by hand. Under
these conditions you can at least inspect the individual scores, in whatever
form they are available to you, for outliers and for gross departures from the
normal curve distribution.

Missing Data

Missing data are items of information that the researcher intended to collect as
part of the research design but that, for one reason or another, are not available
for the data analysis. Missing data may occur simply because the researcher
lost the data through her or someone else's carelessness. In large-scale research, tests may be administered to hundreds of students. Even though a
particular student was present for testing, his test can become lost in the process of handing it to the test administrator, in the process of returning it to the
central data collection center, in the process of keypunching, or in the process
of using the keypunched data card for computer analysis. Since the loss of data
complicates and may weaken the statistical analysis, caution should be exer-
cised to ensure that data are not lost through avoidable human error.

Missing data also can occur if a subject selected for the research sample
refuses to participate in all or part of the study. Even if a subject agrees to
participate, she may be unavailable at the time(s) that data are collected. The
likelihood of missing data becomes more probable as the number of data collection sessions increases, simply because there are more opportunities for subjects to become ill or called away by other commitments. Students tend to
come down with the flu or other illness at the same time. If a substantial number of students are absent from school or are unavailable for a scheduled data-
collection session, it probably is better to reschedule the session than to have
incomplete data for the statistical analysis. This is not a rigid rule, however; in
certain studies, the data may be uninterpretable unless they are collected at a
specific time. In this situation, the better compromise may be to collect data
from a partial sample, if the resulting data can be analyzed to yield interpretable findings.

Missing data are particularly challenging when several different tests have

31. Ibid.

been administered on several occasions to the same groups of subjects. Consider the following group of scores for two different tests administered at two intervals to an experimental and control group. Missing data are indicated by the symbol —.

	Test A				Test B			
	Exp. Group		Control Group		Exp. Group		Control Group	
Subject I.D.	Time 1	Time 2	Time 1	Time 2	Time 1	Time 2	Time 1	Time 2
001	5	7	4	5	—	37	38	40
002	4	—	4	4	42	63	—	51
003	8	12	—	7	53	71	45	43
004	—	17	15	—	36	63	55	55
005	6	—	4	3	15	17	38	50
006	10	13	8	10	52	—	63	64
007	3	5	5	7	49	45	—	36
008	7	5	5	5	38	—	50	48
009	—	10	10	—	47	65	36	40
010	12	17	9	—	50	54	47	51

The researcher had planned to perform a separate analysis of covariance for each test. Time 1 scores are the covariate, and the difference between experimental and control mean scores at time 2 is to be analyzed for statistical significance.

How should the missing data be handled? One solution is to eliminate incomplete cases, so that only subjects with time 1 and time 2 data are included in the statistical analysis. This solution would entail the loss of four experimental subjects and four control subjects in analyzing test A data, and the loss of three experimental subjects and two control subjects in analyzing test B data. However, note that different subjects would be eliminated across the two tests, such that the experimental and control groups would not have quite the same composition across the two samples. If the researcher wishes to include only those subjects who have complete data for both tests and both test sessions, even more data are lost. For example, the experimental group would include only three complete cases (003, 007, 010)! Another solution is to estimate the missing data by plugging the group mean into each cell or by using a regression analysis to estimate more precisely the missing values. The decision to use one solution or another involves complex considerations. In this type of situation, we recommend that you call upon the services of an expert statistician.

The best solution obviously is to avoid missing data. Extra effort to ensure that all data required by the research design are collected will save effort later in the statistical analysis phase of the study. Note, too, that beyond a certain point, missing data may hopelessly compromise the research design. In this situation, the only alternatives are to abandon or to repeat the study.

The Unit of Statistical Analysis

Educational researchers may study individuals as they learn in isolation, as they learn independently but within a group setting, or as they learn in a group. These distinctions are important to consider in deciding whether to use the individual learner or a group of learners as the unit of statistical analysis. The **unit of statistical analysis** is the sampling unit replicated within a research study. If the student is the sampling unit, then each student added to the sample can be considered a replication of the phenomena to be described, correlated, or experimentally manipulated.

The effect of the statistical unit on research results is illustrated by the following example. Suppose the relative effectiveness of two teaching methods, A and B, is to be compared by having them used in different classrooms. Ten sixth-grade classrooms, two from each of five schools, are selected for the experiment; one class in each school is randomly assigned to teaching method A and the other to teaching method B for a period of two months. Hypothetical posttest scores of individual students following the experimental period are shown in table 10.5. Elementary classrooms typically have 20–30 (or more) students, but to simplify the data presentation, the table shows classes containing between 5 and 8 students.

In this experiment the purpose of the statistical analysis is to determine whether the posttest scores of students who received teaching method A are significantly different from the posttest scores of students who received teaching method B. A critical ratio or t value can be calculated to test for statistical significance. The issue is, What is the unit of statistical analysis—the individual student or the classroom group? If the unit is the individual student, there are 32 students in teaching method A who can be compared with 34 students in teaching method B. If the class is used as the unit, there are only five class means for teaching method A to be compared with five class means for teaching method B.

Note, too, that the descriptive statistics vary as a function of the unit of analysis. The mean and standard deviation of scores in teaching method A are 23.6 and 5.42, respectively, when the student is the unit of analysis. In contrast, the mean and standard deviation of the group means (19.2, 24.2, 27.8, 20.2, 24.5) are 23.2 and 3.49, respectively, when the group is the unit of analysis.

Some researchers have recommended that the class mean should be used as the unit of analysis in the kind of experiment illustrated in table 10.5. Kenneth Hopkins demonstrated, however, that the individual student should be used as the unit of analysis in conducting tests of statistical significance.[32] He recommended doing a certain type of analysis of variance in which the classroom and experimental treatment are considered "factors" (the concept of factor is explained in chapter 16). In the experiment illustrated in table 10.5, the

TABLE 10.5
Posttest Scores of Students under Two Teaching Methods

Method A ($N = 32$)				
School 1 Class 1	School 2 Class 2	School 3 Class 3	School 4 Class 4	School 5 Class 5
18	25	28	17	22
22	18	27	19	24
27	29	29	23	30
15	30	30	18	15
9	19	24	24	27
24	$\bar{X} = 24.2$	26	$\bar{X} = 20.2$	21
$\bar{X} = 19.2$		31		29
		27		28
		$\bar{X} = 27.8$		$\bar{X} = 24.5$

Method B ($N = 34$)				
School 1 Class 6	School 2 Class 7	School 3 Class 8	School 4 Class 9	School 5 Class 10
25	16	19	22	21
22	25	21	20	29
18	18	28	24	18
18	23	16	19	14
20	15	15	18	22
22	9	21	21	$\bar{X} = 20.8$
$\bar{X} = 20.8$	22	14	15	
	$\bar{X} = 18.3$	12	17	
		$\bar{X} = 18.3$	$\bar{X} = 19.5$	

32. Kenneth D. Hopkins, "The Unit of Analysis: Group Means Versus Individual Observations," *American Educational Research Journal* 19 (1982): 5–18.

ten classes constitute one factor and the teaching methods A and B constitute another factor. Hopkins demonstrated the appropriate form of analysis of variance to be used for experimental designs of different levels of complexity.

This discussion of the unit of statistical analysis highlights the fact that education occurs at many levels: individual students (e.g., tutorial instruction), small groups within classrooms (e.g., reading groups), classrooms, schools, school districts, regions, states, and even nations. You need to decide which of these levels include the phenomena of interest to you. Leigh Burstein has recently made the argument that educational researchers should consider several levels at once in designing a study:

> Schooling activities occur within hierarchical organizations in which the sources of educational influence on students occur in the groups to which an individual belongs. These groups (learning group within classrooms, classrooms within schools, schools within districts, families within communities, schools within communities) influence the thoughts, behavior, and feelings of their members. This hierarchical structure gives rise to multilevel data.[33]

By "multilevel data" Burstein means data that can be analyzed at more than one level of schooling. For example, if a researcher collects data on three classrooms within a school, the data can be analyzed at two levels: classroom (each classroom has a score, or set of scores, associated with it) and school (the mean score of the three classrooms on a variable yields some data about the school as a whole).

There is no correct level(s) of schooling on which research should be focused. Instead, each researcher will need to develop a theory or explanation for the particular phenomena that interest her. The theory or explanation will serve as a guide for deciding the level or levels to be included in the data collection and analysis. For example, suppose a researcher is interested in the effects of teacher praise on students. The researcher might focus on the incidence of praise statements delivered to the class as a whole. In this case, the researcher would need to study a sample of classes and would use the class as the unit of analysis. Another possibility is for the researcher to focus on teacher praise given to individual students. In this case, the researcher might measure the number of praise statements directed by the teacher to each student in the classroom. The student then would be the unit of analysis, and the sample size would be the number of students in the classroom. If the researcher studied more than one classroom, each classroom could be considered an independent replication of the study.

33. Leigh Burstein, "Issues in the Aggregation of Data," in Berliner, ed., *Review of Research in Education*, p. 158.

Another example is provided by the case of educational researchers who are interested in studying the effects of school principals. Suppose the researcher hypothesizes that the principals' emphasis on teacher supervision influences the morale of teachers in the school. This hypothesis should be tested by using the school as the unit of analysis. The researcher needs to form a sample of school principals, one per school, and measure the principals' emphasis on teacher supervision and the overall morale of the teaching staff. Suppose, instead, the researcher is interested in whether principals vary in their supervision of individual teachers, and whether these variations are related to individual differences in teacher morale. The individual teacher is the unit of analysis in this situation.

It is important to note that both units of analysis (principal and teacher) can be studied if the data are collected appropriately. Suppose the researcher measures emphasis on teacher supervision in terms of number of supervisory visits with teachers during a school year. If the data are collected for each teacher, the researcher would know the number of supervisory visits per teacher and each teacher's morale. The researcher can also aggregate the data to obtain a measure of the principal's general emphasis on teacher supervision and an overall measure of teacher morale in this school. (Aggregation in this case is the process of obtaining the mean score of teachers on each variable—supervisory visits and morale.)

If the data are collected in this way, they can be subjected to multilevel analysis. For example, one can determine the relationship between supervisory visitation and teacher morale within schools and across schools. Also, one can determine whether there is more variability in principal supervision or teacher morale within schools or across schools.

Policy studies in education are concerned with even larger units of analysis than the ones described in the preceding examples. Researchers working on the National Assessment of Educational Progress aggregate student data to the state level so that they can study differences between states in the educational attainments of their students.[34] Researchers involved in the International Association for the Evaluation of Educational Achievement aggregate student data to the national level so that they can compare differences in education between nations of the world.[35]

The problem of deciding an appropriate unit or units of analysis is indeed complex. The most critical step is to think through the phenomena that you wish to study. Consider especially whether the subjects in the sample are act-

34. An overview of this research program is provided in Frank B. Womer and Wayne H. Martin, "The National Assessment of Educational Progress," *Studies in Educational Evaluation* 5 (1979): 27–37.
35. An overview of this research program is provided in Torsten Husen, "An International Research Venture in Retrospect: The IEA Surveys," *Comparative Education Review* 23 (1979): 371–85.

ing alone or whether their actions are affected by some larger group of which they are a member. Once you have developed a working theory of the phenomena, you are advised to consult an experienced statistician to help you select appropriate procedures for data collection and analysis. Multilevel analysis should be considered as an option.

MISTAKES SOMETIMES MADE BY RESEARCHERS

1. Selects a statistical tool that is not appropriate or correct for the proposed analysis.
2. Collects research data before deciding on a statistical tool for analyzing them.
3. Uses only one statistical procedure when several can be applied to the data. This mistake often leads to overlooking results that could make a significant contribution to the study.
4. Uses parametric statistics when the data fail grossly to meet the necessary assumptions.
5. Overstates the importance of small differences that are statistically significant.
6. Initiates statistical analyses before carefully examining the individual scores collected in the study.
7. Does not consider how to adjust statistical analyses based on missing data.
8. Uses the individual as the unit of statistical analysis when it is more appropriate to use the group mean as the unit.

ANNOTATED REFERENCES

Bruning, James L., and Kintz, B. L. *Computational Handbook of Statistics.* 2nd ed. Glenview, Ill.: Scott, Foresman, 1977.

This book provides easy-to-follow computational procedures for most of the statistical techniques presented in this chapter. It is an excellent resource for the practicing researcher.

Hays, William L. *Statistics for the Social Sciences.* 2nd ed. New York: Holt, Rinehart & Winston, 1973.

This book is for the student who wishes a deeper understanding of the theoretical and mathematical bases of statistics. It is a fine reference book, having a well-organized, comprehensive table of contents covering the major topics in statistics: sets, probability theory, descriptive statistics, hypothesis testing, chi-square, analysis of variance, correlation, and nonparametric statistics.

Kerlinger, Frederick N. *Foundations of Behavioral Research: Educational, Psychological, and Sociological Inquiry.* 2nd ed. New York: Holt, Rinehart & Winston, 1973.

This test will be useful to the student seeking a more extensive discussion of the topics in research design and statistical analysis covered here. The author's writing style is quite readable, and many examples are provided. Since the logic of research design and statistical analysis is fairly complicated, the student will profit by reading several sources including this one. The use of statistics in educational research is presented particularly well.

Morrison, Denton E., and Hendel, Ramon E., eds. *The Significance Test Controversy.* Chicago: Aldine, 1970.

This is a very useful reference for the researcher who wishes to gain deeper insight into the logic, uses, and limitations of tests of statistical significance. The chapters by Morrison and Henkel (no. 31) and Lykken (no. 27) are particularly recommended.

Tukey, John W. *Exploratory Data Analysis.* Reading, Mass.: Addison-Wesley, 1977.

This landmark book presents an alternative view of how educational research data should be analyzed. Conventional data analysis emphasizes summarizing the data in a few descriptive statistics and testing the null hypothesis. Tukey's procedures emphasize exploring the shape of score distributions and unusual phenomena within data.

SELF-CHECK TEST

Circle the correct answer to each of the following questions. An answer key is provided on page 881.

1. The type of research study ideally suited to establish causal relationships, assuming that the proper controls are used, is the
   a. observational study.
   b. experiment.
   c. descriptive study.
   d. causal-comparative study.
2. The division of individuals into two categories on the basis of performance on a continuous variable is called a(n)
   a. artificial dichotomy.
   b. ranking.
   c. true dichotomy.
   d. artificial ranking.

3. The amount of dispersion of scores about a central value can be measured
   by the
   a. mean.
   b. standard deviation.
   c. median.
   d. p value.
4. If a group of students has a mean score of 20 on a test and a standard deviation
   of 4, approximately two-thirds of the scores lie between _____ and _____.
   a. 16, 28
   b. 18, 22
   c. 16, 24
   d. 12, 28
5. The rejection of the null hypothesis when it is correct is called a Type _____
   error.
   a. Alpha
   b. Beta
   c. I
   d. II
6. The p value indicates
   a. whether the null hypothesis can be accepted or rejected.
   b. how likely it is that one's research hypothesis is correct.
   c. the probability that the results would be the same if the study were re-
      peated.
   d. All of the above are correct.
7. Confidence limits are useful because they
   a. yield the probability of making a Type I error.
   b. provide a more stable test of statistical significance than the F ratio.
   c. determine the presence of outliers in research data.
   d. enable inferences from sample statistics to population values.
8. In operational replication the researcher
   a. deliberately avoids imitation of the original researcher's procedures.
   b. attempts to duplicate exactly all of the original researcher's procedures.
   c. only attempts to duplicate the original researcher's sampling and experi-
      mental procedures.
   d. deliberately avoids the Type I errors made by the original researcher.
9. For any distribution of raw scores the mean and standard deviation of z scores
   are _____ and _____, respectively.
   a. 1, 0
   b. 0, 1
   c. 0, 0
   d. 1, 1
10. The use of the student as the unit of statistical analysis is most justified when
    a. the sample size is small enough to warrant the t test.

    b. the variation between group means is statistically significant.

    c. intact classrooms have been assigned to the experimental treatments.

    d. each student has received the treatment independently of every other student in the sample.

11. The experimental group has a mean and standard deviation of 10.8 and 2.6, respectively. The control group has a mean and standard deviation of 8.0 and 1.4, respectively. Effect size is

    a. 2.0.

    b. 2.6.

    c. 1.4.

    d. 1.2.

12. The power of a statistical significance test is affected by

    a. sample size.

    b. the p value used to reject the null hypothesis.

    c. estimated effect size.

    d. All of the above are correct.

13. Stem-and-leaf displays are useful for

    a. estimating missing data.

    b. detecting outliers.

    c. estimating effect size.

    d. computing Type I error.

APPLICATION PROBLEMS

The following problems are designed to give you practice in applying significant concepts and research procedures in chapter 10. For feedback, you can compare your answers with the sample answers on pages 891–92.

1. Indicate whether the mean or the median would be a more accurate measure of central tendency in the following situation, and state why.

    You are interested in the average gain that can be made by students taking a speed-reading course. A reading test was given to 250 students before and after taking the course. In looking over the scores, you notice that most students have gained 100–300 words per minute. However, there are about 40 students who have really made outstanding gains ranging from 600 to 1000 words per minute. Mean or median? Why?

2. For each of the following studies, identify the design and decide whether each could be used to establish a cause-and-effect relationship between intake of vitamin B and academic performance.

    a. The diets of 200 children are analyzed daily for 6 months for amount of vitamin B consumed. The relationship between amount of vitamin B in the diet and grades on a standard achievement test is then computed.

   b. One hundred children, all of whom have diets deficient in vitamin B, are randomly assigned to two groups. Both groups continue present diet but group B receives a vitamin B pill each day while group A receives a placebo. At the end of 6 months, achievement gains of the two groups are compared.
   c. Interviewers collect detailed data on the diets of 1000 schoolchildren. On the basis of these data, 100 children are selected who have a history of vitamin-B-deficient diets. Another 100 are selected who have a history of vitamin-B-rich diets. The academic achievement of the two groups is compared on a standard achievement test.
3. What type of score is each of the following?
   a. Students are divided into two groups: those who have blue eyes and those who have brown eyes.
   b. These two groups of students are then measured on the time required for their eyes to adjust to different amounts of light.
   c. Each subject is also classified as a heavy smoker (31 + cigarettes per day), moderate smoker (20–30 cpd), light smoker (1–19 cpd), or nonsmoker.
   d. Each subject is classified as either having normal vision (20–30 or better) or below-normal vision (poorer than 20–30).
4. A study is carried out to test the relative effectiveness of two sixth-grade mathematics programs. A group of 120 sixth-grade pupils is randomly assigned to 4 classrooms. Two classrooms use program A and two use program B. At the end of training all subjects are given a 200-item mathematics test (reliability .97) that closely follows the content covered in the two programs. The mean achievement score for students in program A is 108.7 items correct, as compared with 106.2 for program B. This difference is statistically significant at the .05 level. Is the difference of practical significance?
5. A researcher has completed a study in which an experimental group of 60 college students was formed into pairs and then required to ask each other questions in preparation for an examination. A control group of 60 students was requested to quiz themselves in preparation for the same examination. Students' scores on the examination formed the dependent variable. What is the appropriate unit of statistical analysis for determining whether the examination performance of the experimental group differed from that of the control group?

SUGGESTION SHEET

If your last name starts with letters from Jab to Kee, please complete the Suggestion Sheet at the end of the book while the chapter is still fresh in your mind.

11.

THE METHODS AND TOOLS OF SURVEY RESEARCH

OVERVIEW

This introduction to survey research is the first of several chapters concerned with different types of educational research. In subsequent chapters you will be considering observational, historical, causal-comparative, correlational, and experimental research. You begin your study of survey research by considering the various types of knowledge that can be generated by analysis of survey data. Often surveys are used simply to collect information, such as the percentage of respondents who hold or do not hold a certain opinion; however, surveys can also be used to explore relationships between different variables. The main focus of the chapter is on the questionnaire and the interview as specific tools of survey research. You will be presented with specific techniques for preparing questionnaires and interview guides. Also, you will learn techniques for using them effectively in your research projects. Finally, since questionnaries and interviews are both aimed at gathering similar kinds of data, their relative advantages and disadvantages are compared so that you will be able to select the technique that is most appropriate for your project.

OBJECTIVES

After studying this chapter, you should be able to:

1. If given survey data measuring different variables, determine whether the variables are related to each other in terms of time-bound or time-ordered association.
2. Compare cross-sectional and longitudinal surveys.
3. Define trend studies, cohort studies, and panel studies.
4. If given the objectives of a survey, write both closed-form and open-ended questionnaire items to measure them.
5. State five rules for constructing questionnaire items.
6. State eight rules related to questionnaire format.

7. Write a letter of transmittal for a questionnaire survey using the guidelines recommended.
8. Describe procedures for dealing with nonrespondents after the initial letter of transmittal and after follow-up techniques have been tried.
9. Decide when it is appropriate to use the interview technique rather than a questionnaire.
10. Describe three specific sources of error in interview studies that can be traced to predispositions of the respondent, the interviewer, and the interview procedures.
11. Give four rules for conducting interviews.
12. State the advantages and disadvantages of telephone interviewing.
13. If given the objectives of an interview study, develop an interview guide to gather data on these objectives.
14. State at least one advantage and one disadvantage of note taking and tape recording as data-collection methods in interviews.
15. State several procedures for facilitating effective communication between the interviewer and respondent.

INTRODUCTION

The Survey as a Form of Educational Research

Survey research is a distinctive research methodology that owes much of its recent development to the field of sociology. Considered as a method of systematic data collection, though, surveys have a long historical tradition. As far back as the time of the ancient Egyptians, population counts and surveys of crop production have been conducted for various purposes, including taxation. The contribution of twentieth-century sociologists such as Lazarsfeld, Hyman, and Stouffer was to link instruments of data collection (e.g., questionnaires and interviews) to a logic and to statistical procedures for analyzing these kinds of data.

The information collected by surveys can be of various types. The Gallup poll is probably the best-known survey used to sample public opinion. Market researchers employ surveys to evaluate product acceptance and use. Among the scientific disciplines, researchers in economics, anthropology, psychology, and public health make frequent use of surveys to collect information relevant to interests and problems in their fields.

Studies involving surveys account for a substantial proportion of the research done in the field of education. For example, Lazarsfeld and Sieber did a content analysis of educational research appearing in 40 journals in 1964 and found that about a third of them involved use of the survey method.[1] A wide range of educational problems can be investigated in survey research, as illustrated by this list of recent studies:

Brawley, Edward A. "Community College Programs for the Human Services: Results of a National Survey." *Journal of Education for Social Work* 17, no. 1 (1981): 81–87.

Anderson, Gregory R., and Farmer, Helen S. "High School Counselor Training Needs in Career Interest Assessment." *Measurement and Evaluation in Guidance* 14, no. 2 (1981): 77–83.

Bradtmueller, Weldon, and Egan, James. "Perception of the Principal's Role in Reading Instruction." *Journal of the Association for the Study of Perception* 16, no. 1 (1981): 19–26.

Tomlinson, Sally. "Multiracial Schooling: Parents' and Teachers' Views." *Education* 9, no. 1 (1981): 16–21.

Gleaton, Thomas J., Jr., and Smith, Sidney P. "Drug Use by Urban and Rural Adolescents." *Journal of Drug Education* 11, no. 1 (1981): 1–8.

Local school districts sometimes need to do surveys. The comprehensive **school survey** explores and evaluates many aspects of the school system, such as buildings, maintenance, administrative procedures, financial support and procedures, teaching staff, learning objectives, curriculum, and teaching methods. Such surveys are usually carried out by a team of visiting specialists from universities and other school systems. Another type of survey, the school census, is conducted so that administrators can predict the educational needs their schools will be called upon to meet in future years. Local surveys are also used for the purposes of internal evaluation and improvement.

The student who must perform a research project for completion of an advanced degree might well consider employing the survey approach to investigate a particular educational problem. However, the student should be aware that surveys involve considerably more than administering a questionnaire to describe "what is." It is unfortunate but true that many research workers in education hold surveys in low esteem because they believe that surveys are limited to description. In fact, though, survey research utilizes a variety of instruments and methods to study relationships, effects of treatments, longitudinal changes, and comparisons between groups. In this chapter we discuss the basic design in survey research, the cross-sectional survey, and methods for conducting it.

1. Paul F. Lazarsfeld and Sam D. Sieber, *Organizing Educational Research* (Englewood Cliffs, N.J.: Prentice-Hall, 1964).

Data-Collection Tools in Surveys

Data-collection tools are used in survey research to obtain *standardized* information from all subjects in the sample. If he wishes to determine his subjects' socioeconomic status, for example, the researcher must administer the same instrument to all subjects. He cannot determine the socioeconomic status of half the sample using one set of questions and then change his questions to collect the same information for the remaining sample. Also, the conditions of administration must be as similar as possible for each subject in the sample.

It is assumed that the information collected by survey instruments is quantifiable. In the case of multiple-choice questionnaire items, the information is quantified at the time it is collected. If open-ended questions are used, the "open-ended" information that is obtained must be codified so that it can be analyzed and reported quantitatively.

The questionnaire and individual interview are the most common instruments for data collection in survey research. Accordingly, detailed steps in constructing and administering questionnaires and interview schedules are presented in this chapter. However, the student should be aware of the other methods that can be used to collect survey information. The telephone interview is one such method, and it has important advantages that we will discuss later in this chapter.

Another technique for collecting survey information is to examine records. For example, students' files often contain much information of interest to the researcher: parents' ages, income, occupations, marital status, the student's school attendance, course grades, extracurricular activities. Examination of records has the advantage of being relatively complete and quick, since all the relevant information is usually stored in one location. Of course, the student should be sensitive to the issue of invasion of privacy if this technique is used. Clearance from all involved groups should be obtained before proceeding to examine records. Depending on the situation, these groups may include the research subjects, the subjects' parents, and the administrators who have compiled the records.

The Cross-Sectional Survey

In the **cross-sectional survey,** standardized information is collected from a sample drawn from a predetermined population. (If information is collected from the entire population, the survey is called a **census.**) As we discussed in chapter 7, the sampling techniques most commonly used in educational surveys are simple random, stratified, or cluster sampling. Another basic feature of the cross-sectional survey is that the information is collected at one point in time (although the actual time required to complete the survey may be one day to a month or more).

Survey data from a cross-sectional survey can be analyzed by a variety of methods. The particular method or methods that the researcher selects will depend on the types of inferences she wishes to make from her data.

Descriptions of Single Variables

The simplest use to which survey data can be put is a description of how the total sample has distributed itself on the response alternatives for a single questionnaire item. These are sometimes called the "marginal tabulations." For example, newspapers often report the result of public-opinion polls in terms of marginal tabulations; 50 percent of the sample were in favor of a particular governmental policy, 30 percent disagreed with it, and 20 percent were unsure or had no opinion.

Survey research in education often yields this type of normative description. As an illustration, we may consider a study by W. G. Trenfield that was designed to investigate the degree of interest of high school students in participating in adult civic activities.[2] A Likert-type scale of 30 items, each describing a different civic activity, was administered to a sample of 300 students randomly drawn from a population of approximately 4000 high school students in a Texas school district. Students were asked to describe their degree of interest in participating in each activity on a 5-point scale. In the data analysis, the mean score of the entire sample on each attitude item was determined. This form of data analysis provides an interesting description of students' civic interests. We find, for instance, that these students are most likely to express their civic interest by voting in national elections and by signing a petition to be presented to a public official. They are least likely to express interest in running for public office and in attending night classes to improve their ability as a citizen.

Descriptions of this type may provide important leads in identifying needed emphases and changes in school curricula. Also, we should note that since proper sampling procedures were employed, Trenfield was able to generalize his descriptive findings from the sample to the population from which they were drawn.

Exploring Relationships

In addition to their value for determining the distribution of a sample on a single variable, surveys can be used to explore relationships between two or

2. W. G. Trenfield, "An Analysis of the Relationships Between Selected Factors and the Civic Interests of High-School Students," *Journal of Educational Research* 58(1965): 460–62.

more variables. The student who is aware of the possibilities for investigating relationships in her survey data will make a more substantial research contribution than the student who limits her data analysis to single variable descriptions.

Questionnaire items may refer to past, present, or future phenomena. If she studies relationships between questionnaire items that refer to the same point in time, the researcher is engaging in what is known as **"time-bound association."** If the items can be temporally ordered relative to each other, then the data analysis is referred to as **"time-ordered association."**

For example, suppose we wanted to study the relationship between the school-related interests and vocational interests of high school seniors. A questionnaire dealing with these two areas of interest could be administered to a sample of high school seniors and the relationships could be determined by computing correlation coefficients. Since the interest scores in both areas would be measures of the student's interests at a single point in time, namely the time when the questionnaire was administered, the results would be a time-bound association. However, suppose a similar survey were carried out with a sample of high school graduates who were asked to report their current vocational interests and recall what their school-related interests *had been* during their senior year. This questionnaire would provide time-ordered data since the person's school-related interests were reported for a different time than their vocational interests even though all data were collected at a single point in time.

If survey data are time orderable, then hypotheses with cause and effect implications can be tested. A. Huettig and J. M. Newell used the survey method to study whether amount of training in modern mathematics would result in more positive attitudes toward this subject. A sample of 115 elementary school teachers was administered a questionnaire designed to collect information about their teaching experience and attitudes about modern mathematics. They responded to 31 Likert-type attitude statements, and the data were analyzed in terms of whether 60 percent or more of each subgroup had a positive or negative attitude on each item. The hypothesis was considered confirmed because it was found that teachers with more training in modern mathematics were likely to respond favorably to more attitude items than teachers with little or no training (see table 11.1).[3]

Although surveys of this type can identify *possible* cause-and-effect relationships, it would be erroneous to conclude from these tests alone that training in modern mathematics *results in*, *leads to*, or *causes* these more favorable

---

3. Tables 11.1 and 11.2 are from A. Huettig and J. M. Newell, "Attitudes Toward Introduction of Modern Mathematics Program by Teachers with Large and Small Number of Years' Experience," *Arithmetic Teacher* 13 (February 1966): 125–30. Reprinted by permission.

TABLE 11.1

Amount of Training in Modern Mathematics and Attitude toward Modern Mathematics

Amount of Training	Number of Positive Attitudes	Number of Negative Attitudes	Number of Neutral Attitudes
Two courses	22	3	6
One course	20	4	7
One-half course	16	8	7
One workshop	11	11	9
No training	9	18	4

attitudes. Only an experiment with appropriate controls can determine with a high degree of certainty that the relationship between these two variables is causal. In survey research, though, there is a strategy that can be used to strengthen one's confidence that two variables that are correlated with each other (such as amount of training and positiveness of attitudes toward modern mathematics) are also causally related. This strategy consists of attempting to find another variable that explains the relationship between the two original variables. If we cannot find a variable that explains away the relationship, then we can be more confident, though not certain, that the relationship is causal-temporal. This strategy could be applied to Huettig and Newell's study. As we have already discussed, these researchers found a substantial relationship between amount of training in modern mathematics and positiveness of attitude toward this subject. What antecedent variable might explain this relationship? One possibility is suggested by another data analysis, presented in table 11.2, in which Huettig and Newell found that amount of teaching experience bore a

TABLE 11.2

Teaching Experience and Attitude toward Modern Mathematics

Teaching Experience	Number of Positive Attitudes	Number of Negative Attitudes	Number of Neutral Attitudes
1–2 years	18	2	11
3–9 years	13	10	8
10–20 years	7	18	16
21–48 years	5	17	9

strong negative relationship to the frequency of favorable attitudes toward modern mathematics.

Perhaps, then, the variable of teaching experience would explain away the relationship between favorable attitudes and training in modern mathematics. Since Huettig and Newell did not do this data analysis, we will work with hypothetical data as shown in table 11.3.

We see from this table of hypothetical data that irrespective of training in modern math, inexperienced teachers are likely to have positive attitudes toward modern mathematics. Also irrespective of training in modern math, very experienced teachers are likely to have negative attitudes. Thus, in our hypothetical situation, teaching experience "explains away" the original relationship that was found between training and attitudes. Accordingly, we can reject the hypothesis that these two variables are causally related to each other.

Now let us suppose that the original relationship is maintained after the third variable is introduced. If this is the case, *replication* of the original relationship is said to have occurred. Replication is illustrated by the hypothetical data of table 11.4.

The data of the table 11.4 indicate that irrespective of teaching experience, training is related to attitudes toward modern mathematics. If replication occurs, then we have further support for the hypothesis that training and attitudes are causally related.[4]

TABLE 11.3

Amount of Training, Teaching Experience, and Attitude toward Modern Mathematics (Based on Hypothetical Data)[a]

Training	1–2 Years' Experience		21–48 Years' Experience	
	Positive Attitudes	Negative Attitudes	Positive Attitudes	Negative Attitudes
Two courses	18	5	5	20
No training	18	5	5	20

[a]To simplify matters, only two levels of training in mathematics are shown, although in the actual study, five levels of training were distinguished.

4. Of course, there is always the possibility that another "third" variable could be found which explains this relationship. Also, it is possible that a "third" variable only *partially* explains away the original relationship. For example, it might be that both teaching experience and training affect the positiveness of attitudes toward modern mathematics.

TABLE 11.4
Hypothetical Data Illustrating Replication

	1–2 Years' Experience		21–48 Years' Experience	
Training	Positive Attitudes	Negative Attitudes	Positive Attitudes	Negative Attitudes
Two courses	18	2	18	2
No training	5	17	5	17

It should be noted that replication has no bearing on the problem of *direction* of causality, that is we still have no way of knowing whether training in modern mathematics leads teachers to form more positive attitudes toward this subject (irrespective of their original attitudes) or whether teachers with positive attitudes toward modern mathematics seek out training in the subject. To answer these questions an experimental approach is necessary. The experimental design would involve measurement of attitudes before and after training of an experimental and control group.[5]

An investigator who uses cross-sectional survey data to explore time-ordered relationships must be aware of a serious source of error: respondents may not remember accurately information related to a previous time. Such errors are likely to become larger as the researcher delves farther into the past. Also, although factual information may be recalled accurately, the respondent's recollection of past attitudes or opinions may be distorted by present attitudes. For example, a teacher may be able to remember the number of black children she had in her class three years ago, but if her attitude toward black children has changed, she may not recall accurately her attitude of three years ago.

In summary, the value of survey research of the type carried out by Huettig and Newell is that while it cannot establish causal relationships with any degree of certainty, it can be used to explore a variety of relationships (e.g., between training and attitudes) in a relatively economical way. If important relationships are found, then questions about causality can be resolved by means of an experiment.

The Longitudinal Survey

In **longitudinal surveys,** data are collected at different points in time in order to study changes or explore time-ordered associations. This design is, of course,

5. This type of research design is discussed in chapters 15 and 16.

superior to the collection of time-ordered data in a cross-sectional survey because the data are not distorted by the faulty recollection of the respondents.
Three longitudinal designs are commonly employed in survey research: trend
studies, cohort studies, and panel studies. These differ mainly in terms of the
respondents, who are studied at different points in time.

In **trend studies** a given *general* population is sampled at each data collection point. The same individuals are not surveyed, but each sample represents
the same population. For example, if an investigator wanted to study trends in
the use of pocket calculators in the teaching of high school mathematics, he
would select a sample each year from the current membership directory of a
national mathematics teachers association. Each year he would send questionnaires to the sample selected and would compare responses from year to year.
Although the population of mathematics teachers would change from year to
year, and different mathematics teachers would be surveyed each year, if appropriate sampling procedures such as random sampling were used, the responses could be regarded as representative of the population of mathematics teachers from which the samples were drawn. The investigator would
then compare responses from year to year to determine what trends were
present.[6]

In **cohort studies** a *specific* population is followed over a period of time.
Trend studies sample general populations such as high school students or voters in school bond elections, which are constantly changing in terms of the
specific individuals who are members of the population. In cohort studies,
however, a specific population such as members of the 1978 graduating class
at Stanford University is sampled throughout the course of the survey. Suppose, for example, we wanted to study the yearly vocational progress of all
elementary school teachers who were granted California teaching certificates in
1977. We would list the names of all members of this population and at each
data collection point would randomly select a sample from this list. Thus, although the population would remain the same, different individuals would be
sampled each year to determine vocational progress.

In **panel studies** the investigator selects a sample at the outset of her
study and then at each subsequent data collection point she surveys the same
individuals. Since panel studies follow the same individuals over time, the researcher can note changes in specific individuals and can therefore explore
possible reasons why these individuals have changed. Such individual changes
cannot be explored in trend or cohort studies since different individuals make
up the sample at each data collection point.

Loss of subjects is a serious problem in panel studies, especially if the

6. The National Assessment of Educational Progress is an example of a major trend study. For a
description of this study, see Frank B. Womer and Wayne H. Martin, "The National Assessment
of Educational Progress," *Studies in Educational Evaluation* 5 (1979): 27–37.

study extends over a long period of time. For example, in one large-scale panel study that followed a national sample of twelfth-grade students into adulthood, a response rate of 61.9 percent was obtained for the one-year follow-up, 37.9 percent after 5 years and 27.9 percent after 11 years. This study used a variety of procedures, including an annual newsletter to keep track of subjects, and sent four mailings at each follow-up period.[7]

Not only does the number of subjects become smaller, but the remaining subjects may be a biased sample because those who drop out are likely to be different from those who continue to cooperate in the study. In the aforementioned example, respondents to the 11-year follow-up were as much as one-half of a standard deviation higher in general academic aptitude than nonrespondents, reflecting a very serious bias.

Many trend and cohort studies are carried out using earlier data collected by other researchers. For example, if a survey of the vocational interests of seniors in Chicago high schools had been carried out in 1968, another researcher could collect comparable data in 1978 and compare the two sets of data in a trend study. In some areas of education such as vocabulary, mastery of number facts, or attendance, a graduate student may be able to locate several studies that have collected comparable data at different points in time. Such data, when combined with current data collected by the student, can provide insights into an important educational trend. Recent investigations have used this approach to study the downward trend in achievement in the public schools.

In conducting replications of this type, the researcher should try to use the same questions and format as in the earlier surveys. There is some evidence and much practical experience to indicate that small changes in question wording can produce large effects on answers.[8]

The Delphi Technique

This technique, although it employs questionnaires, is much different from the typical questionnaire survey. It was developed by the RAND Corporation as a method of predicting future defense needs but it can be used whenever a consensus is needed from persons who are knowledgeable about a particular subject. For example, it can be used to identify problems, define needs, establish priorities, and identify and evaluate solutions.

The first step in a typical Delphi study is to prepare a set of questions or statements for evaluation. For example, in a study of educational goals, the

7. L. L. Wise, "The Fight Against Attrition in Longitudinal Research" (paper presented at the annual meeting of the American Educational Research Association, New York, 8 April 1977).
8. For more information on this topic, see Robin M. Hogarth, ed., *Question Framing and Response Consistency* (San Francisco: Jossey-Bass, 1982).

initial questionnaire may list the school's current goals, ask a sample of community leaders to indicate the importance of each goal on a 5-point scale, and add any goals not included in the questionnaire. An open-ended approach can also be used in the initial questionnaire in which each respondent would be asked to list goals that he or she considers important.

Based on responses to the initial questionnaire, a revised questionnaire is then circulated. If ratings or rankings were obtained on the initial questionnaire, the median score for each item is given in the second questionnaire. This questionnaire is then returned to the same respondents, who are asked to compare their original ratings with the median score and to revise their original evaluations as they see fit. This procedure is repeated for at least four rounds in an effort to obtain a well-thought-out consensus.

In effect, the Delphi technique uses mailed questionnaires to engage the respondents in an anonymous debate in order to arrive at consensus on issues or on predictions of future events. There are several variations to the technique. For example, the interquartile range for each item may be included to give the respondents an idea of the variability of the responses. Usually, persons taking extreme positions relative to the median response are asked to give reasons for their ratings, and these reasons are included in the next questionnaire to give respondents additional insight into the question or problem.

The Delphi technique has several advantages. Issues are clarified, and the final result is likely to reflect much more careful thought than would be obtained from a single questionnaire. Since each respondent is called upon to reexamine his position at least three times, the method tends to build consensus. This is very desirable in areas such as school needs surveys because it will make it much easier to implement the findings.[9]

Although the variability of responses tends to decrease from round to round, the mean responses tend to shift very little. Thus, a single mailing of the questionnaire probably produces as good descriptive data as the four mailings required in a Delphi study.

Perhaps the main disadvantage of the Delphi technique is that it requires a considerable amount of time (usually two months or more) to carry out. It also makes rather heavy demands on the respondents' time. If respondents are not strongly motivated, they may drop out or may fill out the questionnaires in a few minutes, giving little thought to their responses.[10] For example, in a study of professional standards sponsored by the Council for Exceptional Chil-

---

9. See Orlich in Annotated References at the end of this chapter for a brief description of this technique.
10. For recent examples of studies using the Delphi technique in educational research, see D. K. Dayton, "Future Trends in the Production of Instructional Materials: 1981–2001," *Educational Communication and Technology* 29, no. 4 (1981): 231–49; and S. J. M. Senter and R. W. Houston, "Perceptions of Teacher Educators, Futurists, and Laymen Concerning the Future of Teacher Education," *Journal of Teacher Education* 32, no. 5 (1981): 35–39.

dren, questionnnaires were sent to 2865 persons in the first round. By the end of the second round, only 358 respondents remained (12.5 percent), and this had shrunk to less than 4 percent after the third round.[11] Losses of this magnitude almost surely introduce serious sampling bias and raise questions about the value of the Delphi technique as a research tool.

STEPS IN CONDUCTING A QUESTIONNAIRE SURVEY

With careful planning and sound methodology, the questionnaire can be a very valuable research tool in education. The next few pages will introduce you to the major steps that must be taken to carry out a successful questionnaire survey. These include: (1) **defining objectives,** (2) **selecting a sample,** (3) **writing items,** (4) **constructing the questionnaire,** (5) **pretesting,** (6) **preparing a letter of transmittal,** and (7) **sending out your questionnaire and follow-ups.** Analysis of the results and preparing the research report are covered in later chapters.

Although this section can give you a basic grasp of the survey research process, it cannot give you the in-depth knowledge necessary to conduct high-quality surveys. The Annotated References at the end of this chapter include several excellent sources for the student who wants to develop a better understanding of survey research.

Defining the Questionnaire Objectives

The first step in carrying out a satisfactory questionnaire study is to list specific objectives to be achieved by the questionnaire. It is not uncommon for a graduate student to develop a questionnaire before he has a clear understanding of what he hopes to obtain from the results. Unless you are able to state specifically and in detail what information you need, what you will do with this information after you get it, and how each item on the questionnaire contributes to meeting your specific objectives, you have not thought through your problem sufficiently.

In preparing your objectives, you should keep in mind the methods of data analysis that you will apply to the returned questionnaires. Suppose that you are interested in surveying the extent of usage of ability grouping in the schools of your state. The first objective of your study might be to determine

11. J. J. Barnette, L. C. Danielson, and R. Algozzine, "Problems and Potential Solutions in the Use of Delphi Methodology Using Mailed Questionnaires on a National Scale" (paper presented at the annual meeting of the American Educational Research Association, San Francisco, 20 April 1976).

the percentage of schools in the state that are using some form of ability group-ing. Therefore, you should include items in the questionnaire that will elicit reliable information from each school regarding its use of ability-grouping sys-tems. Of course, the objectives of your study need not be limited to describing the current situation in the schools. You might consider surveying your sample on such questions as: how administrators of schools with ability grouping think their grouping practices can be improved, whether administrators of schools without ability grouping have previously tried to institute an ability-grouping system, and how the community has reacted to the idea of ability grouping in its schools.

In our discussion of the cross-sectional survey, we pointed out that survey data can be used to achieve objectives other than description of how the responses of the total sample are distributed on each questionnaire item. In a survey of ability-grouping practices, one objective may be to investigate differences between types of schools. For example, the survey data could be analyzed to determine whether urban schools are more or less likely than suburban or rural schools to have an ability-grouping system. The study of relationships between variables may also be an objective. As an illustration, one could investigate the relationship between the schools' achievement test norms and the presence or absence of an ability-grouping system. As we dis-cussed earlier in this chapter, it is possible to describe such relationships as instances of time-bound association, that is, no inference is made about a causal relationship between the two variables. However, the testing of causal hy-potheses can be an objective of your study if the data are time-orderable. For example, one may hypothesize that schools which send a large proportion of their students to college will be more likely to institute an ability-grouping system than schools in which the percentage of college-bound students is low. To test this hypothesis, data should be collected about presence or absence of an ability-grouping system in each school and the percentage of college-bound students in each school.[12]

To summarize, surveys can have a variety of objectives. These objectives need to be identified at the outset of the study, otherwise you will find it very difficult to make sound decisions regarding selection of a sample, construction of the questionnaire, and methods for analyzing the data.

Selecting a Sample

The most obvious consideration involved in selection of subjects for a question-naire study is to get people who will be able to supply the information you

---

12. If such a study were to be done, the percentage of college-bound students should be based on data collected by the schools *prior* to the institution of an ability-grouping system.

want. Very often the group that will have the data you want is immediately apparent. But in some cases, if you do not have a thorough knowledge of the situation involved, you may send your questionnaire to a group of persons who do not have the desired information. For example, a graduate student seeking data on school financial policies sent questionnaires to principals of a large number of elementary schools. Many of the questionnaires returned were incomplete, and few specific facts of the sort wanted were obtained. This study failed because the trend in recent years has been for the superintendent and his staff to handle most matters concerning school finance. Inasmuch as the principals who received the questionnaire had little specific knowledge concerning this topic, they were unable to supply the information requested on the questionnaire.

Salience of the questionnaire content to the respondents is not only necessary to obtain accurate information but also has a significant influence on the rate of response. A review of 181 surveys using questionnaires judged to be "salient," "possibly salient," or "nonsalient" to the respondents revealed that for the salient studies the return averaged 77 percent, as compared with 66 percent for those judged possibly salient and 42 percent for those judged nonsalient.[13]

Most questionnaire studies conducted in education are aimed at specific professional groups. Once you have established that the professional group selected actually has access to the information you wish to obtain, you can survey the entire group or you can select a sample from the population.[14] Many professional groups in education have special organizations or societies, and in some cases a random selection of names from the directory of organization members gives a satisfactory group. This type of action, however, must be used cautiously, as there may be a tendency for the more competent members of the professional group to belong to the organization, thus leading the researcher to select a biased sample.

State public school directories are more satisfactory for selection of subjects because they list all persons involved in public education in the state and are usually up to date. When the population is very large, such as all elementary school teachers in the United States, and no complete name list is available, it is usually necessary to use a multistage procedure to obtain a random sample. The first stage in obtaining a nationwide sample could be to select randomly a specified number of school districts. Since most districts print rosters of their teachers, the next step would be to request a copy of the rosters

13. See Heberlein and Baumgartner in Annotated References at the end of this chapter.
14. A variety of sampling procedures are employed in survey research. These are briefly described in chapter 7. For more detailed information on sampling for survey research, see Annotated References at the end of this chapter.

from districts selected in the first stage. A specified number of teachers could then be randomly selected by name from each roster.

As we have discussed previously, it is often desirable to obtain responses from several specific categories of persons within the professional group being sampled. For example, you may wish to compare responses dealing with use of pupil-centered instruction gathered from teachers with different amounts of professional experience. If this is your objective, then it is desirable to use stratified sampling in order to select subsamples of sufficient size from different levels of population.

If the data from different subsamples are to be combined at some stage of the analysis, the number of subjects selected from each subsample should be proportionate to the number of subjects from each subsample in the population. For example, suppose the population of elementary school teachers includes 78 percent women and 22 percent men; then, if we stratify by sex, the proportion of women and men in our sample should be 78 percent and 22 percent, respectively. We could also maintain the correct proportions in combining our data by selecting the same number of men and women in our sample but weighting the women's responses .78 and the men's responses .22. Finally, if the men's and women's responses were to be *compared* but *not combined*, it would not be necessary for the two subsamples to be proportionate.

Constructing Questionnaire Items

Many of the questionnaires that are received by principals, superintendents, and other educators appear to have been thrown together by the graduate student during the short break between lunch and her two o'clock class. This type of questionnaire has led many school administrators to develop negative attitudes about the questionnaire as a research approach. Some of the more harassed administrators deposit the questionnaires they receive in the wastebasket with little more than a quick glance. This attitude, of course, presents an obstacle that the graduate student planning to use this technique must and can overcome by the careful construction and administration of her questionnaire. Each item on your questionnaire must be developed to measure a specific aspect of one of your objectives or hypotheses. You should be able to explain in detail *why* you are asking the question and *how* you will analyze the responses.

In fact, it is a good idea to make up dummy tables that show how the item-by-item results of your questionnaire will be reported. These tables can contain information such as planned data breakdowns, response categories, and titles. In fact the dummy tables can be complete except for the results that you can quickly add after your analysis has been completed.

Questions may be of either the **closed form** in which the question permits only certain responses (such as a multiple-choice question), or the **open form** in which the subject makes any response he wishes in his own words (such as an essay question). Which form will be used is determined by the objective of the particular question. Little research on the relative merits of closed and open questions has been reported. What evidence is available suggests that the two formats produce very similar information.[15]

Generally, though, it is desirable to design the questions in closed form so that quantification and analysis of the results may be carried out efficiently. Let us suppose you wish to know the size of the teacher's home town so that you can compare teachers from different-sized towns in terms of interests and vocational goals. There are several ways that this question could be asked. Perhaps the poorest technique would be to ask, "What is your home town?" This question requires that you be able to read the person's reply and look it up in an atlas to determine the population. A technique that would be some-what better would be to ask, "What is the population of your home town?" In this case you could classify the responses into population categories such as those used by the U.S. Census Bureau. A still better means of obtaining this information would be to ask "What is the population of your home town? (Check one.)"

_____ rural, unincorporated
_____ incorporated, under 1000
_____ 1,000 to 2,500
_____ 2,500 to 5,000
_____ 5,000 to 10,000
_____ 10,000 to 50,000
_____ 50,000 to 250,000
_____ over 250,000

This latter technique would provide you with the information you want in immediately usable form, thus requiring less effort on your part, while requiring no more effort by your subjects.

Perhaps the best method of determining the multiple-choice categories to use in closed questions is to ask the question in essay form of a small number of respondents, and then use their answers to develop the categories for the multiple-choice item that will be included in the final form of the questionnaire. In multiple-choice areas where a certain number of unexpected responses might occur, an "other" choice can be used along with a space for

15. See Norman M. Bradburn, "Question-Wording Effects in Surveys," in *Question Framing and Response Consistency*, ed. Robin M. Hogarth (San Francisco: Jossey-Bass, 1982).

explanation. For example, suppose that you are interested in provisions made for gifted pupils in elementary schools. First, you could ask a small number of respondents the question "How are gifted pupils in your school identified and what provisions are made for them? Please be specific and indicate the extent to which each technique was employed during the past school year." Examination of the respondents' answers will probably suggest a limited number of categories which can be incorporated into multiple-choice items, for example:

1. Do you have a systematic program for identifying gifted children in your school?_____ _____ If yes, what means of identification do you use?   yes   no
_____   a. Group intelligence test
_____   b. Individual intelligence test
_____   c. Achievement battery
_____   d. Aptitude battery
_____   e. Teacher ratings
_____   f. Other (specify)_____
_____

2. What provisions were made for gifted pupils in your school during the past school year? (Check appropriate answers.)
_____   a. Acceleration (grade skipping)
_____   b. Ungraded program
_____   c. Ability grouping
_____   d. Enrichment
_____   e. Special classes
_____   f. Other (specify)_____
_____

Depending on the specific objectives of the questionnaire, other questions could be added concerned with such matters as the number of pupils at each grade level who skipped a grade, the number of pupils in special classes, the criteria for establishing ability-grouped sections, and others.

In constructing questionnaire items it is important to avoid whenever possible questions that may in some way be psychologically threatening to the person answering. For example, a questionnaire sent to school principals concerning the morale of teachers at their schools would be threatening to some principals because low morale suggests that the principal is failing in part of his job. When he receives a questionnaire containing threatening items, a person usually does not return it. If he does return it, little confidence can be placed in the accuracy of his reply because of his ego involvement in the situation.

Many of the rules for constructing questionnaire items are similar to rules for constructing items for objective tests that are found in most textbooks in educational measurement. Among these are the following:

1. Clarity is essential. If your results are to be valid an item must mean the same thing to all respondents. For example, terms like "several," "most," and "usually" have no precise meaning and should be avoided. In his study of respondents' interpretation of questionnaire items, William Belson obtained 28 different interpretations of the word "usually." Only 60 percent of the interpretations reflected the approximate intent of the investigator.[16]
2. Short items are preferable to long items because short items are easier to understand.
3. Negative items should be avoided since they are misread by many respondents; i.e., the negative word is overlooked, resulting in the respondent giving an answer that is opposite to his real opinion.
4. Avoid "double-barreled" items, which require the subject to respond to two separate ideas with a single answer. An item such as "Although labor unions are desirable in most fields, they have no place in the teaching profession," cannot be answered with the usual closed-question format (such as strongly agree, agree, no opinion, disagree, strongly disagree) by a person who disagrees with one part of the item and agrees with the other part.
5. Do not use technical terms, jargon, or "big words" that some respondents may not understand. Remember, clarity is especially important in questionnaires since the respondent is usually reached by mail and has no one available to explain unclear items.
6. When a general and a related specific question are to be asked together, it is preferable to ask the general question first. If the specific question is asked first, it tends to narrow the focus of the following general question and to change responses to the general question.[17]
7. Finally, it is very important that an effort be made to avoid biased or leading questions. If the subject is given hints as to the type of answer you would most prefer, there is some tendency to give you what you want. This tendency is especially strong when the letter of transmittal that accompanies the questionnaire has been signed by someone that the subject is eager to please.

Questionnaire Format

The questionnaire and cover letter are the main sources of information that the subject will refer to in deciding whether or not to complete your questionnaire.

16. See Belson in Annotated References at the end of this chapter.
17. See Howard Schuman and S. Presser, *Questions and Answers in Attitude Surveys: Experiments on Question Form, Wording, and Context* (New York: Academic Press, 1981).

The following rules of questionnaire format have been developed from experience and research in this field and should be considered carefully.[18]

1. Make the questionnaire attractive. This can often be achieved by using colored ink or colored paper, or by laying out the front page in an artistic manner.
2. Organize and lay out questions so the questionnaire is as easy to complete as possible.
3. Number the questionnaire items and pages.
4. Put name and address of person to whom form should be returned at beginning and end of questionnaire even if a self-addressed envelope is included.
5. Include brief, clear instructions, printed in bold type.
6. Use examples before any items that might be confusing or difficult to understand.
7. Organize the questionnaire in some logical sequence. For example, you may decide to group together related items or those that use the same response options.
8. Begin with a few interesting and nonthreatening items.
9. Do not put important items at end of a long questionnaire.
10. Avoid using the words "questionnaire" or "checklist" on your form. Many persons are prejudiced against these words.
11. Include enough information in the questionnaire so that items are meaningful to the respondent. Items that are interesting and clearly relevant to the study will increase response rate. Length also has a small effect on response rate, so the questionnaire should be as short as possible consistent with the objectives of the study. A regression analysis of response rates obtained in 98 questionnaire studies showed that, on average, each page added to a questionnaire reduced the number of responses by about .5 percent.[19]

Attitude Measurement in Questionnaires[20]

Most questionnaires deal with factual material, and in many cases each item is analyzed separately to provide a specific bit of information that contributes to the overall picture that you are attempting to obtain. Thus, it is possible to look upon the questionnaire as a collection of one-item tests. The use of a one-item test is quite satisfactory when one is seeking out a specific fact, such as

18. See Berdie and Anderson in Annotated References at the end of this chapter.
19. See Heberlein and Baumgartner in Annotated References at the end of this chapter.
20. A discussion of the attitude scale as a type of standardized test can be found in chapter 9.

teacher salary, number of baseball bats owned by the physical education department, or number of students failing algebra. When questions get into the area of attitude and opinion, however, the one-item test approach is extremely unreliable. A questionnaire dealing with attitudes must generally be constructed as an attitude scale and must use a number of items (usually at least ten) in order to obtain a reasonable picture of the attitude concerned.

The attitudes measured in a questionnaire can cover a wide range of topics. For example, earlier in this chapter we reviewed two survey studies in which attitudes toward modern mathematics and participation in civic activities were measured. The student who is planning to collect information about attitudes should first search the literature to determine whether a scale suitable for his purposes has already been constructed.[21] If a suitable scale is not available, it will be necessary to develop one. Likert scales are probably the most common types of attitude scales constructed. If the student develops an attitude scale for his survey project, it should be pretested in order to collect reliability and validity evidence. Also, the student should investigate in his pretest whether the sample of subjects has sufficient knowledge and understanding to express a meaningful opinion about a particular topic. For example, you might want to learn the attitudes of a sample of teachers or administrators toward some of the newer developments in education, such as criterion-referenced evaluation, performance-based teacher education, and mainstreaming. If a sizable proportion of the sample is not adequately familiar with these developments, the attitude responses will be of questionable value.

One method of dealing with subjects who are not familiar with a particular topic is to include a "no opinion" category as one of the response alternatives for each attitude item. The disadvantage of this method is that subjects with little or no information about a particular topic will often still express an opinion in order to conceal their ignorance or because they feel social or professional pressure to express an opinion. This point is illustrated by an interesting study dealing with interview surveys.[22] A total of 625 respondents in three Iowa urban communities were interviewed about their attitudes regarding nine persons (e.g., Barry Goldwater, John F. Kennedy) and seven organizations (e.g., CORE, John Birch Society). The respondents could express a favorable or unfavorable attitude on six Likert-type categories, or they could use a seventh category to express no knowledge of a particular person or organization. To determine whether respondents would express an attitude toward an organization about which they were uninformed, the interviewers asked for their opinion of a nonexistent organization called the League for Linear Programs.

---

21. See the Annotated References for chapter 9.
22. Irving L. Allen, "Detecting Respondents Who Fake and Confuse Information About Question Areas on Surveys," *Journal of Applied Psychology* 50, no. 6 (1966): 523–28.

To their surprise the interviewers found that 10 percent of the sample expressed a favorable or unfavorable attitude toward this organization about which it was impossible for them to have any knowledge! It was further found that this same 10 percent of the sample were also more likely to express attitudes toward the other organizations and persons rather than check the "don't know" category. They also were more likely to express favorable attitudes and to have less formal education than the rest of the sample.

The implication of these findings is that the respondents' knowledge and expertise is an important factor in interpreting attitude data. Therefore, the student planning a questionnaire survey involving attitude measurement should investigate his respondents' familiarity with each attitude object covered in the survey. One technique for doing this is to administer an information test to a small sample of respondents similar to those to be queried in the main survey, to determine whether they are capable of expressing an informed opinion about the persons, organizations, or educational practices mentioned in the attitude or opinion items.

Effect of Anonymity on Questionnaire Response

In most educational studies, the respondent is asked to identify himself. Anonymity is sometimes called for if data of a personal nature or data that may be threatening to the individual are requested. A questionnaire dealing with sexual behavior, for example, may receive more honest responses if the subject remains anonymous.

The anonymous questionnaire poses many research problems. Follow-ups are difficult and inefficient because nonresponding individuals cannot be identified. Furthermore, it is usually not possible to make some of the statistical breakdowns of the group that may be desirable. For example, in a study of teacher-principal relationships, it may be desirable to divide the respondents into men and women teachers, married and unmarried teachers, and teachers with different amounts of experience, and then compare the responses of these different groups. In the anonymous questionnaire, breakdowns of this sort that were not anticipated and provided for in the questionnaire cannot be made. Often the desirability of analyzing certain subgroups separately is not apparent until the data are collected.

The essential question that must be answered, however, is whether anonymity is necessary to get accurate replies. The research on this problem suggests that the need for assuring anonymity varies from one research situation to another and that it is influenced by such variables as respondent's age and sex and the content of the questionnaire. In a study of attitudes toward religion, Francis randomly assigned 300 ten- and eleven-year-old children to three groups.[23] All subjects were administered an attitude scale that included a lie detection scale. One group was instructed to write their names on the front page, another group was told to write their initials in the top right corner of the first page and then fold over the corner, while a third group was instructed specifically not to write their names. All subjects were told that their replies would be confidential and that no one at their school would read them. Differences between the groups on both the attitude scale and the lie scale were very small, none approaching significance.

Since attitude toward religion is a sensitive topic, this study suggests that anonymity is not as important as some researchers have suggested. Anonymity has been found to affect responses in other studies, however. Therefore the safest approach is to conduct a small-scale pilot study that closely duplicates the procedures to be used in the main study and to compare subject responses under anonymous versus identified conditions. The results can then be used to decide whether anonymity is necessary for the specific study to be conducted.

If a pilot study cannot be conducted, the factors to be considered in deciding whether identification is to be asked for are the importance of identification in the analysis of results, the level of maturity of the respondents, the degree to which questions involve answers that the respondent might be reluctant to give if he is identified, the probable effect of anonymity on the number of returns, and the procedures that can be used in the analysis of results.

Pretesting the Questionnaire

In addition to the preliminary check that you make of your questions in order to locate ambiguities, it is very desirable to carry out a thorough pretest of your questionnaire before using it in your study. For the pretest you should select a sample of individuals from a population similar to that from which you plan to draw your research subjects. For example, if you were concerned with mechanical aids used for teaching foreign languages in California high schools, you could pretest your questionnaire using a sample of foreign language teachers employed in another state. The pretest form of the questionnaire should provide space for the respondents to make comments about the questionnaire itself so they may indicate whether some questions seem ambiguous to them, whether provisions should be made for certain responses that are not included

---

23. Leslie Francis, "Anonymity and Attitude Scores Among Ten- and Eleven-Year-Old Children," *Journal of Experimental Education* 49 (1981): 44–76.

in the questionnaire, and other points that can lead to improving the instru-ment.

A useful pretesting strategy was proposed by William Belson. Respon-dents are asked to repeat their understanding of the meaning of the question in their own words. Questions can then be revised and retested until they are understood by all or most members of the pretest sample.[24] Except for changes required to collect pretest feedback, the techniques for administering the ques-tionnaire during the pretest should be essentially the same as planned for the main study. When there is some doubt as to which of two questions or two approaches might be most useful, both can be tried on portions of the pre-test sample. The number of cases in the pretest sample need not be large. If the subjects are taken from a well-defined professional group, such as school superintendents, as few as twenty cases will often be sufficient. For more heterogeneous groups, such as persons paying property taxes or parents with one or more children in elementary school, a larger pretest group is advis-able.

When the pretest results are in, first check the percentage of replies ob-tained. Educational studies generally can be expected to yield a higher per-centage of replies than questionnaires sent to random samples of the general population because the educational questionnaire usually aims at a reasonably homogeneous group, and this makes it possible to prepare an appeal to the group for cooperation, which is more likely to be successful. If, in checking the percentage of replies, you have received less than 75 percent of the pretest sample, it is probable that major changes will be needed in the questionnaire or in the procedures for administering it. The next step is to read the subjects' comments concerning the questionnaire. These comments often give specific information on how the questionnaire can be improved. Then, check the re-sponses item by item. If you find items that are often left blank or answered in ways that you did not predict, it is very likely that the item was misinter-preted by some of the subjects.

It is now possible to do a brief analysis of the pretest results. This will give you a chance to determine whether the methods you have planned to use for summarizing and quantifying the data will work satisfactorily. Also, the pretest results may suggest additional questions to you. For example, if sharp disagreement is found in the responses to a particular item of the question-naire, it may be desirable to construct additional items that will help you un-derstand the reasons for this disagreement.

After the preceding procedure has been completed and all improvements made in the pretest questionnaire, you are ready to administer your revised questionnaire to the sample you have selected.

24. William A. Belson, "Respondent Understanding of Survey Questions," *Polls* 3 (1968): 1–13.

Precontacting Your Sample

Contacting respondents before sending a questionnaire has been found in several studies to increase the response rate. The precontact can take the form of a letter, postcard, or telephone call. Evidence to date suggests that telephone contacts are the most effective.[25] Such contacts usually identify the investigators, discuss the purpose of the study, and request cooperation. Respondents return a self-addressed postcard indicating their willingness to cooperate. Such precontacts are effective probably because they alert the respondents to the imminent arrival of the questionnaire, thus reducing the chance that it will be thrown out as "junk mail." Precontacts may also put a more personal or human face on the research. Finally, having once agreed to cooperate, the respondent is under some psychological pressure to do so when the questionnaire arrives.

The Letter of Transmittal

The student's major problem in doing a questionnaire survey is to get a sufficient percentage of responses to use as a basis for drawing general conclusions. Perhaps the most important single factor in determining the percentage of responses you will obtain is the letter of transmittal used with your questionnaire. This letter must be brief but yet must convey certain information and impressions to the subjects if you are to obtain a satisfactory percentage of responses. First, it is essential that you give the subjects good reasons for completing your questionnaire and sending it back to you. A brief assurance of confidentiality should be included; it is especially important if any sensitive questions are to be asked. When highly sensitive or potentially threatening questions are included in your questionnaire, a specific description of how confidentiality will be maintained should be added.

Whenever possible, the purposes of the study should be explained briefly and in such a way as to make the subject feel that the study is significant and important. If your questionnaire is aimed at a group with specific professional ties, such as mathematics teachers, it is usually desirable to make some reference to the person's professional status and his feelings of affiliation with this group. In some cases a certain amount of subtle flattery is also useful in preparing the letter of transmittal. This is usually accomplished by stressing the importance of the subjects' professional group and the value of the information the group can supply. Research has shown that both altruistic and egoistic

25. See Linsky in Annotated References at the end of this chapter for a review of 12 studies on this topic.

appeals are effective in increasing response rate.[26] An offer to send the respondent a copy of the results is often effective. If made, however, such a promise should be honored; neglect of such matters is not ethical and will weaken future studies involving persons in your sample.

If possible, it is also desirable to associate your study with some professional institution or organization with which individuals in your sample might be expected to identify. For example, superintendents within a particular state might be expected to respond favorably to a letter signed by the state superintendent, the state or national president of a superintendents' association, or the dean of education at the state university. If your study is well designed and deals with a significant problem, it is usually possible to have someone sign your letter of transmittal who will represent a favorable authority symbol to the persons responding.

If your questionnaire is not aimed at a specific professional group, it is much more difficult to obtain responses because specific appeals cannot be made. Under these conditions you might slant your appeal along the lines that you might expect even the members of a widely diversified group to have common views, such as patriotism and a desire to improve the community. If your study is one where these general appeals are obviously inappropriate, the best approach is probably an appeal to the individual's sense of humor. For example, several years ago a national magazine wished to obtain information from its readers on the extent to which they used commercial flying in pursuing their sports activities. As the subscribers were a highly heterogeneous group having very little in common except subscription to this periodical and as the topic was not one where a general appeal could be expected to work, the magazine sent their very brief questionnaire along with a letter of transmittal on which was glued a dime. The letter of transmittal started out by asking the person to take a coffee break at the expense of the magazine and while drinking the coffee to check off answers on the attached postcard. This sort of approach is likely to get a good response because it amuses the subject while making very modest demands upon his time.

Another alternative that has proven effective is to include a small cash reward or a premium such as a ballpoint pen with your letter of transmittal. Several studies have explored the effect of enclosing a small cash reward with the questionnaire. Such rewards, usually ranging from a quarter to a dollar, have consistently increased the response rate, as have small gifts or premiums. Usually the reward should be given as a token of appreciation rather than as payment for the respondent's time. Since most studies dealing with cash rewards are over twenty years old, it may be that inflation has weakened the

26. For a brief review of literature on letters of transmittal and questionnaire design, see J. G. Odom, " Validation of Techniques Utilized to Maximize Survey Response Rates" (paper presented at the annual meeting of the American Educational Research Association, San Francisco, 8–12 April 1979). ED 169 966.

effect of small rewards.[27] A recent study that offered a reward of two dollars to complete a 25-page questionnaire got a quicker reply from persons offered the reward, but the eventual response rate was about the same.[28]

One of the items contained in the letter of transmittal is a request that the questionnaire be returned by a particular date. It is important to set this date so that the subject will have sufficient time to fill out and return the questionnaire without rushing or inconvenience, but on the other hand, will not be likely to put it aside to do later as is the tendency if too generous a time allowance is given. A satisfactory rule of thumb would be to calculate the probable mailing time and allow the individual an additional week or less to complete the questionnaire and return it. Included with the questionnaire and the letter of transmittal should be a stamped, self-addressed envelope so that the individual can respond with a minimum of inconvenience.

There is some evidence to indicate that the type of mailing also has an effect on the response rate. Special-delivery mailing has been found more effective than first-class mail, which in turn is more effective than third-class mail. The use of hand-stamped envelopes also has been found in several studies to produce more returns than postal-permit envelopes.

The neatness and composition of your questionnaire and accompanying material is an important factor in determining the number of replies. The more expensive methods of duplication are usually worth the extra cost. A letter of transmittal reproduced by the offset process on letterhead paper and signed with a different color ink will command more attention than one poorly dittoed on cheap paper. If a word processor is available, individually typed letters, differing only in the names and addresses of the recipients, can be produced at a low cost. These letters are superior to the best offset copies and have the added advantage that small changes can be made at a reasonable cost in each letter to make it more individualized. A sample letter is shown in figure 11.1.

The questionnaire should also be attractively composed with a moderate amount of white space and should be duplicated using offset or some other procedure that produces high-quality copies. A poorly reproduced questionnaire indicates to the respondent that the study is of little importance to you or anyone else in spite of your protestations to the contrary.

Follow-Up Techniques

A few days after the time limit that you have set in your letter of transmittal, it is usually desirable to send a follow-up letter along with another copy of the

27. See Linsky, and Heberlein and Baumgartner in Annotated References at the end of this chapter for reviews of studies offering cash rewards and premiums.
28. V. J. Shackelton and J. M. Wild, "Effects of Incentives and Personal Contact on Response Rate to a Mailed Questionnaire," *Psychological Reports* 50 (1982): 365–66.

questionnaire and another self-addressed envelope to individuals who have
not responded. Since your original letter of transmittal failed with the nonre-
spondent group there is no point in sending the same letter again. Instead, try
to change your approach and use a different basis for making your appeal for
cooperation. For example, if you used a personal appeal in your initial letter,
you may want to try a professional appeal in your first follow-up letter.

Letterhead paper———→   OKLABAMA STATE UNIVERSITY
                                Collegetown, Oklabama
                                M. A. Brown, President

                                                        College of Education
                    February 1, 1983   I. B. Smith, Dean

Typed with same   Mr. A. B. Jones
machine used in———→ Superintendent of Schools
cutting offset stencil   Mediumtown, Oklabama

Duplicated using offset   Dear Sir:
process to look like
individually typed ———→   The attached survey instrument concerned with proce-
letter   dures used in selecting elementary school principals is part of a
                               statewide study being carried on cooperatively by the State De-
Purpose of study   partment of Public Instruction and Oklabama State University.
                               This project is concerned specifically with determining the
                               present status of principal selection in our state. The results of
Importance of———→ this study will help to provide preliminary criteria to be used
study   for developing better selection procedures and for improving
                               the administrator training program at Oklabama University.

Importance of   We are particularly desirous of obtaining your responses
respondent   ———→ because your experience in principal selection will contribute
                               significantly toward solving some of the problems we face in
                               this important area of education. The enclosed instrument has
                               been tested with a sampling of school administrators, and we
                               have revised it in order to make it possible for us to obtain all
                               necessary data while requiring a minimum of your time. The
Reasonable but   average time required for administrators trying out the survey
specific time limit   instrument was 9.5 minutes.
                                   It will be appreciated if you will complete the enclosed
Special delivery   form prior to February 10th and return it in the stamped, spe-
further stresses   cial delivery envelope enclosed. Other phases of this research
importance   cannot be carried out until we complete analysis of the survey

                    Figure 11.1   Sample letter of transmittal.

Assurance of
confidentiality ————→

data. We would welcome any comments that you may have
concerning any aspect of principal selection not covered in the
instrument. Your responses will be held in strictest confidence.

Offer results ————————→
Thank ————————→
respondent

We will be pleased to send you a summary of the survey
results if you desire. Thank you for your cooperation.

Sincerely yours,

Print in different color to _____ ————→ *I. B. Smith*
appear personally signed

I. B. Smith, Dean

Signed by important educator _____
rather than graduate student ————————————————————→

Enc.

sjc

Figure 11.1—Continued.

The follow-up letter should generally assume the tone that you are sure
the individual wished to fill out the questionnaire, but perhaps because of an
error on your part or some oversight, it was overlooked. The follow-up letter
should then go on to point out again the importance of the study and value of
the individual's contribution to this important project, using different language
and emphasis from your original letter. Postcard reminders have also been
used, and in some cases they have been found as effective as letters. However,
in one carefully conducted experimental study the investigators found that a
form letter with another copy of the questionnaire obtained up to 7 percent
more responses than a postcard with the same message.[29]

As a rule, if careful attention is given to the design of the questionnaire,
the letter of transmittal, and follow-up letter, a sufficient percentage of subjects
will respond. In cases where a very high percentage of response is required, it
may be necessary to conduct further follow-ups using different approaches. A
second follow-up letter will generally bring in a few percent of the sample but
if a new approach is used, it might bring in the additional cases needed. On
some occasions as many as four follow-up letters are used. Figure 11.2 shows

---

29. Blaine R. Worthen and E. J. Brezezinski, "An Experimental Study of Techniques for Increasing
    Return Rate in Mail Surveys" (paper presented at the annual meeting of the American Edu-
    cational Research Association, New Orleans, February 1973).

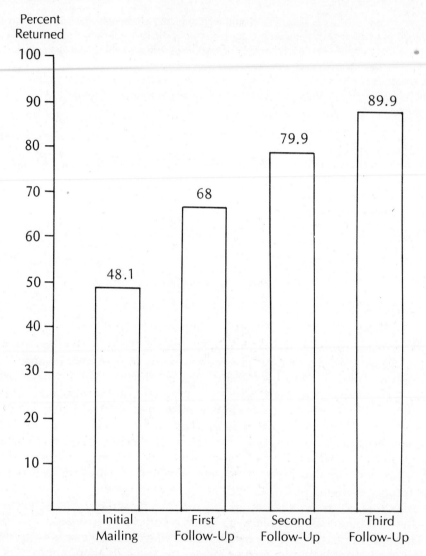

Figure 11.2   Response rates taken from studies recording response rates for initial mailing and different numbers of follow-ups.

the pattern of responses reported in a review of 98 experimental studies in this area. Although the reviewers point out that results varied considerably from study to study, these average percentages give a reasonable indication of what can be expected from different numbers of follow-ups. A few of the studies reviewed used four or more follow-ups, but this did not lead to a significant increase in returns over three follow-ups.[30]

Let us now examine a study that illustrates a variety of follow-up strategies.[31] The researcher was particularly interested in whether follow-up techniques would increase the percentage of college dropouts responding to a questionnaire. This questionnaire was mailed to all college men who had enrolled at a large state university a number of years prior to the study. Three waves of mail resulted in a 67 percent mail-back response. In the first wave, respondents were sent a questionnaire, a cover letter, and a stamped return envelope. The second wave of mail came twenty days later, when the nonrespondents were sent the same enclosures again except for a new cover letter. The third wave of mail resulted when a reminder card was sent out. At this point different follow-up techniques were used to encourage mail-backs by the 383 resistant nonrespondents. All nonrespondents whose phone number could be located were telephoned. Those who could not be reached by phone were sent a certified letter and new questionnaire.

The use of the telephone and certified mail as follow-up techniques resulted in an 82 percent mail-back return from the 383 resistant nonrespondents in this study. The total mail-back return was thereby raised to 94 percent of the original sample, which is an unusually high percentage for this type of survey. One further point is worth noting regarding respondents who had been college dropouts. Had follow-up techniques been discontinued after the first three waves of mail-back response, college dropouts would have comprised 23 percent of the respondents. After the telephone calls and certified mailings, college dropouts accounted for 31 percent of the total number of respondents. Since college dropouts possessed special characteristics of interest to the investigator, it was worth the additional follow-up time in order to get a more adequate representation of them.

In a more recent study, researchers sought to contact the parents of a sample of about 5000 male adults who had graduated from high school seven years earlier. The questionnaire, which was concerned with post-high-school education and employment, was very brief, fitting on a regular postal card. The initial mailing produced responses from 56.6 percent of those contacted. The first follow-up produced an additional 22.5 percent, the second follow-up 7.4 percent, and the third follow-up 5.5 percent, for a total response of 92 percent. A telephone interview after the third follow-up provided data on an additional 4 percent.[32] In contrast, a national study that employed a much longer

---

30. See Heberlein and Baumgartner in Annotated References at the end of this chapter.
31. Bruce K. Eckland, "Effects of Prodding to Increase Mail-Back Returns," *Journal of Applied Psychology* 49 (1965): 165–69.
32. See Sewell and Hauser in Annotated References at the end of this chapter.

questionnaire obtained a total response of only about 25 percent, even though a very extensive effort was made to reach the subjects.[33]

It is clear from the research we have discussed that although the number of follow-ups is a major factor in response rate, many other factors also influence it.[34]

What to Do about Nonrespondents

After the responses have been obtained, the research worker faces the problem of analyzing her results. The question that usually arises at this point is "How would the results have been changed if all subjects had returned the questionnaire?" If only a small percentage of your subjects failed to respond, this question is not critical. If more than 20 percent are missing, however, it is very likely that most of the findings of the study could have been altered considerably if the nonresponding group had returned the questionnaire and had answered in a markedly different manner than the responding group. This could be the case if the nonresponding group represents a biased sampling; that is, if those people who did not respond to the questionnaire are in some measurable way different from those who did respond. A common sampling bias of this type is that persons having a good program are more likely to respond than those having a poor program. For example, a questionnaire dealing with the physical education program at the elementary school level will get a higher percentage of responses from those schools having programs that the respondents believe to be above par. School administrators are often reluctant to admit the deficiencies of their schools and therefore fail to return questionnaires in which these deficiencies would be revealed.

Several studies have investigated whether personality and intellectual differences exist between respondents and nonrespondents.[35] The general finding of these studies is that respondents and nonrespondents do not differ on any significant personality dimensions. However, nonrespondents tend to have achieved less academic success than respondents.

If more than 20 percent of the questionnaires are not returned, it is desirable to check a portion of the nonresponding group even though this checking usually involves considerable effort. The ideal method of checking is to select a small number of cases randomly from the nonresponding group and then

---

33. Lauress L. Wise, "The Fight Against Attrition in Longitudinal Research" (paper presented at the annual meeting of the American Educational Research Association, New York City, 4–8 April 1977).

34. Students who plan to conduct a questionnaire survey should read the relevant Annotated References at the end of this chapter before developing their research plans.

35. See Robert Rosenthal and Ralph L. Rosnow, *The Volunteer Subject* (New York: John Wiley, 1975), for a review of these studies.

interview these subjects in order to obtain the necessary information. If the questionnaire has been sent over a wide geographical area, interviewing a random selection of nonresponding cases is usually not possible. Under these circumstances the students can get some insight into the nature of the nonresponding group by checking those persons who are within a reasonable distance. In most educational studies of the sort conducted by graduate students, 20 cases are adequate to check the nonresponding group. After data have been obtained from these cases, the responses of this group to each item are compared with the responses of those who replied initially to determine whether the nonresponding sample is biased. If this sample of nonresponding subjects answers the questions in about the same manner as the responding group, it is probably safe to assume that the responding group is an unbiased sample of those to whom you mailed the questionnaire. If this sample, however, is considerably different in their responses, these differences should be noted and their significance discussed in reporting the results of the responding sample. Also, serious consideration should be given to using some of the follow-up techniques discussed earlier in this chapter. Telegrams, telephone calls, and certified mailings can be effective devices for substantially increasing the percentage of responding subjects.

THE INTERVIEW AS A RESEARCH TOOL

The steps in conducting an interview study are essentially the same as those for conducting a study that uses the mailed questionnaire as the primary data collection tool. Therefore, only the main points of the previous section are repeated here.

The first step is to write a statement describing the general purpose of the research. In writing this statement, the student should be aware of the various research designs that can be used in the cross-sectional survey. These designs make it possible to describe the distribution of the sample's responses on a single variable, to make differentiated descriptions of selected groups (e.g., male vs. female, college-educated vs. non-college-educated), and to study time-bound and time-ordered relationships.

Next, a sample of respondents should be selected using appropriate survey sampling techniques. A serious weakness of interview studies done by graduate students is the usual necessity of using small samples. The research worker should remember that the dangers of a biased sample are particularly serious when only a small number of individuals can be included in the research. After a sample has been selected, it is advisable to obtain some commitment of cooperation from these individuals before the interviewing starts.

Every effort should be made to obtain the cooperation of all individuals initially selected. If some of the subjects selected refuse to cooperate this refusal will almost certainly lead to some biasing of the research results. The random selection of substitutes for these noncooperating individuals does not remove the possibility of this bias.

In the first part of this chapter, we described in detail the complexities involved in constructing a sound research questionnaire. The construction of an interview guide and the conduct of the interview are similarly complex. Therefore, these topics are given extensive treatment in the next sections.

Advantages and Disadvantages of the Interview

The interview as a research method in survey research is unique in that it involves the collection of data through direct verbal interaction between individuals. This direct interaction is the source of both the main advantages and disadvantages of the interview as a research technique. Perhaps its principal advantage is its adaptability. The well-trained interviewer can make full use of the responses of the subject to alter the interview situation. As contrasted with the questionnaire, which provides no immediate feedback, the interview permits the research worker to follow-up leads and thus obtain more data and greater clarity. The interview situation usually permits much greater depth than the other methods of collecting research data. A serious criticism of questionnaire studies is that they are often shallow, that is, they fail to dig deeply enough to provide a true picture of opinions and feelings. In contrast, the skilled interviewer, through the careful motivation of the subject and maintenance of rapport, can obtain information that the subject would probably not reveal under any other circumstances. The reason why such information may be difficult to obtain is that it usually concerns negative aspects of the self or negative feelings toward others. Respondents are not likely to reveal this type of information about themselves on a questionnaire and will only reveal it in an interview situation if they have been made to feel comfortable by a skillful interviewer.

The advantages of the interview over the mailed questionnaire in certain situations were shown in a study by Robert Jackson and J. W. M. Rothney.[36] These investigators conducted a follow-up study of 890 high school students, some of whom had received intensive counseling. The entire sample was sent a four-page mailed questionnaire five years after its high school graduation. A subsample of 50 cases was then drawn for a personal interview in which the same items that appeared on the questionnaire were asked. The information

36. Robert M. Jackson and J. W. M. Rothney, "A Comparative Study of the Mailed Questionnaire and the Interview in Follow-Up Studies," *Personnel and Guidance Journal* 39(1961): 569–71.

collected by means of the two techniques was then compared. It was found that a higher proportion of the sample completed each interview item than the corresponding questionnaire item. Also, 98 percent of the planned interviews were completed, compared with 83 percent of the mailed questionnaires. Two experienced counselors read and evaluated the questionnaire and interview data for evidence of personal problems. The mean number of problems yielded by the interview data was 8.82, whereas the corresponding figure for the questionnaire data was only 2.82. Thus it appears that under favorable conditions the interview tends to yield more complete data and also more data regarding negative aspects of the self.[37]

Another finding of this study was that respondents were fairly consistent when their interview and questionnaire responses to fact or yes-no items were compared. A study by W. Bruce Walsh[38] yielded a similar finding. This investigator compared the relative accuracy of the interview and questionnaire in collecting factual data from a college sample (e.g., gradepoint average, number of failed courses, quarter hours completed). The interview and questionnaire proved to be of comparable accuracy when the data collected by each method were compared with the records on file at the university. Since it is considerably less expensive than interviewing, the mailed questionnaire is usually used when factual, unambiguous information is to be collected. However, as the study by Jackson and Rothney indicates, the interview is likely to yield more complete information when open-ended questions pertaining to negative aspects of the self need to be asked.

Although it has a number of important advantages over other data-collection tools in certain situations, the interview does have definite limitations as a research tool. Because it is easier to ask questions than to administer tests or conduct observations, the interview is often misused to collect quantitative data that can be measured more accurately by other methods.[39] For example, college gradepoint averages obtained from the registrar are much more accurate than those obtained by asking students. Another important limitation of the interview stems from the nature of the process. The flexibility, adaptability, and human interaction that are unique strengths of the interview also allow subjectivity and possible bias that in some research situations are its greatest weakness. The interactions between the respondent and the interviewer are subject

---

37. These findings are generally supported by a more recent study; see J. Legacy and F. Bennett, "A Comparison of the Mailed Questionnaire and Personal Interview Methods of Data Collection for Curriculum Development in Vocational Education," *Journal of Vocational Education Research* 4, no 3 (1979): 27–39.

38. W. Bruce Walsh, "Validity of Self-Report: Another Look," *Journal of Counseling Psychology* 15 (1968): 180–86.

39. See Robert M. Guion and Andrew S. Imada, "Eyeball Measurement of Dexterity: Tests as Alternatives to Interviews," *Personnel Psychology* 34 (1981): 31–36, for an example of a misuse of the interview.

to bias from many sources. Eagerness of the respondent to please the interviewer, a vague antagonism that sometimes arises between interviewer and respondent, or the tendency of the interviewer to seek out answers that support his preconceived notions are but a few of the factors that may contribute to biasing of data obtained from the interview. These factors are called *response effects* by survey researchers.

Response Effect

Response effect is the tendency of the respondent to give inaccurate or incorrect responses, or more precisely is the difference between the answer given by the respondent and the true answer. For example, a respondent, if asked his annual income, may give an incorrect reply for any of a great many reasons. He may forget some sources of income such as stock dividends, he may be ashamed of or wish to hide some income such as money won gambling, he may want to impress the interviewer and therefore exaggerate his income, and so on.

C. H. Weiss discussed several potential sources of error present in the interview situation.[40] Three of these are basic and should be carefully considered by the researcher in planning his study, designing his interview guide, and selecting and training his interviewers. The first can be traced to *predispositions of the respondent*. A few examples of respondent predispositions that can lead to errors include:

1. He is suspicious of or hostile to the research.
2. He is indifferent or not motivated to cooperate.
3. He lacks the information the interviewer is seeking.
4. He wants to please the interviewer or be accepted by him.
5. He wants to present himself in favorable terms.

To reduce these sources of error, the researcher should carefully study his target population, try to identify predispositions that are likely to be present, and then design his study so as to eliminate or minimize their effect. For example, if he suspects his respondents are likely to be hostile (e.g., a juvenile delinquent sample), he should try to develop procedures to reduce this hostility and build satisfactory rapport.

40. For more detailed treatment of this topic, see C. H. Weiss, "Interviewing in Evaluation Research," in *Handbook of Evaluation Research*, vol. 1, ed. Elmer L. Struening and Marcia Guttentag (Beverly Hills, Calif.: Sage, 1975).

The second source of error relates to *predispositions of the interviewer* and includes:

1. She is uncomfortable with the people she is interviewing.
2. She is ill at ease in the environment in which she is working.
3. She allows her own opinions to influence what she hears and/or records.
4. She cannot establish rapport with the respondents.
5. She has stereotyped expectations of what people are like and what they will say.

Obviously, the researcher must select interviewers very carefully and train them thoroughly in order to avoid or eliminate such predispositions. Perhaps most important is the need to select interviewers who can relate to the respondents in a positive fashion. An interviewer who might do a fine job of interviewing successful teachers may be totally unsuited to interview unmarried pregnant teenagers.

There is, in fact, some evidence to indicate that matching interviewers and respondents on variables such as social class, race, age, and sex is likely to produce more valid responses.[41] Some researchers have also recommended selecting interviewers from the respondent target population, and there is some evidence to support this strategy.[42]

The third source of error relates to the *procedures used in conducting the study*. Examples of a few procedures that can lead to errors include:

1. The way the study is explained to the respondent.
2. The methods used for gaining the respondent's cooperation.
3. The length of the interview.
4. The place where the interview is held.
5. The presence of other people during the interview.

Careful planning and small scale tryouts are essential in developing procedures that will produce good cooperation and accurate responses. A good way to start is for the researcher to place himself in the role of the respondent and try to identify elements in the research situation that could be disturbing. Discussing the research procedures with a few subjects from the respondent

41. For examples of the kind of research that has explored these variables, see Anton J. Nederhof, "Impact of Interviewer's Sex on Volunteering by Females," *Perceptual and Motor Skills* 52 (1981): 25–26; and Herschel Shosteck, "Respondent Militancy as a Control Variable for Interviewer Effect," *Journal of Social Issues* 33, no 4 (1977): 36–45.
42. See Carol H. Weiss, "Research Organizations Interview the Poor," *Social Problems* 22, no 2 (1974): 246–58.

population, who will not be included in the sample, is also very useful in helping the researcher see his research from the respondent's point of view. Finally, a tryout of the interview with a few respondents with frequent probes of their perceptions and feelings is recommended.

Survey researchers have conducted considerable research to determine the conditions under which response effects are most likely to occur. Many variables related to the nature and structure of the interview situation, the characteristics of the interviewer, and the characteristics of the respondent have been explored. The most comprehensive review of research in this field is that of Seymour Sudman and Norman Bradburn.[43] They analyzed evidence of response effects for threatening and nonthreatening questions about respondent behavior and for attitudinal questions. Response effects were generally largest for threatening questions (i.e., questions about which many respondents are reluctant to talk). For example, in face-to-face interviews, 47 percent of persons identified as drunk drivers gave distorted responses to questions on this topic. Sudman and Bradburn identified three sources of response effects: characteristics of the interview format, characteristics of the interviewers, and characteristics of the respondents. Characteristics of the interview format were most important in influencing response to the three kinds of questions (threatening, nonthreatening, and attitudinal).

Threatening Questions

Norman Bradburn, Seymour Sudman, and their associates carried out an extensive series of experimental studies on response effects, built on the conceptual framework of their earlier research review.[44] This work focused on threatening questions, since it is with this type of question that response effects are most serious.

The design of the interview format was again found to be the most important factor in generating response effects. The following findings emerged from this research and should be carefully considered when planning an interview in which sensitive or threatening topics are to be covered:

1. There was no consistent advantage to using a particular method of data collecting. Results obtained from face-to-face interviews, telephone interviews, and self-administered questionnaires were generally similar, although each method was superior under certain specific conditions.
2. Open-ended questions using a long introduction to the topic and wording

---

43. See Annotated References at the end of this chapter.
44. See Annotated References at the end of this chapter.

familiar to the respondent obtained much higher levels of reporting and smaller response effects than short, closed-form, standard questions.

3. Asking questions about the behavior of friends in conjunction with questions about the respondents' own behavior increased responses.

4. The presence of third parties during an interview generally made little difference in responses obtained.

5. Assuring respondents of absolute confidentiality increased their willingness to answer threatening questions.

6. More detailed information and truthful introduction to questionnaires had no effect on overall response rates or responses to individual questions.

7. If a signed consent form is needed, it is preferable to ask for a signature *after* the interview is completed.

8. If an interviewer *expects* to have difficulties with the questions to be asked, he should not be employed in the study. Such interviewers in fact have more difficulties and obtain less accurate and complete responses.

This series of studies produced additional findings, which you are advised to examine if you plan to use interviews in your research project.

The Interview Guide

You must develop a guide to be used during the interview. This guide makes it possible to obtain the data required to meet the specific objectives of the study and to standardize the situation to some degree. The **interview guide** lists, in the desired sequence, the questions that are to be asked during the interview. The questions are usually asked exactly as they appear on the guide.

Whenever possible, the guide should be structured to require a minimum of writing by the interviewer. In trying out the preliminary form of the interview guide, the researcher will usually find that most answers to a given question can be placed in a few categories. Even though the actual responses in a given category differ in detail, they are all essentially the same answer and can therefore be classified together. If these typical response categories are listed under the item, the interviewer simply checks the category a respondent's answer fits into and writes down only the unusual answer that does not fit into a category.

If probes are likely to be needed, it is desirable to list acceptable probing questions so that all respondents will be exposed to the same interview situation. Interviewers must be given some latitude in dealing with unusual problems or responses. However, more comparable data will be obtained if the researcher anticipates such situations and provides the interviewers with standard ways of dealing with them. The form that the interview questions will take depends upon the level of structure of the interview, that is, the amount of direction and restriction imposed by the interview situation. An interview can be thought of as being highly structured, semistructured, or unstructured. Of course, within a single interview, the questions asked by the interviewer may vary along this entire continuum. Certain types of information, such as the limited specific facts or opinions collected in public-opinion polls, call for a highly **structured interview** situation. In these studies the interviewer usually asks each respondent a brief series of questions that can be answered either yes or no, or by selecting one of a set of alternate choices. The respondent's answers are not followed up to obtain greater depth, and the level of structure in this case is such that the data could be collected quite satisfactorily with a mailed questionnaire. The main advantage of the interview over the mailed questionnaire for this type of data collection is that the interviewer is likely to get responses from more of the persons in the sample selected and will get fewer "don't know" and unusable responses than would occur on a questionnaire. The disadvantage, of course, is the greater expense of collecting data.

Interviewers in educational research will generally include some highly structured questions in their interview guide, but they will aim primarily toward a semistructured level. At this level the interviewer first asks a series of structured questions and then probes more deeply, using open-ended questions in order to obtain more complete data. Suppose the interviewer is trying to understand the relationship between the student's high school experiences and his college achievement. First he may ask a sample of college students structured questions having to do with the size and location of their high schools, their grades, extracurricular activities, courses taken, and so forth. Then he may probe by asking open-ended questions, such as "How well do you think your high school experience prepared you for college?" and "If you could repeat your high school experience, would you want to do anything different on the basis of what you have learned in college so far?" After the respondent gives his initial reaction to these questions,, the interviewer can use the resulting information to probe deeper for additional insight into his central concern, namely, the relationship between high school experiences and college achievement. The **semistructured interview,** therefore, has the advantage of being reasonably objective while still permitting a more thorough understanding of the respondent's opinions and the reasons behind them than would be possible using the mailed questionnaire. The semistructured interview is generally most appropriate for interview studies in education. It provides a desirable combination of objectivity and depth and often permits gathering valuable data that could not be successfully obtained by any other approach.

The **unstructured interview** is best illustrated by the client-centered approaches used in clinical psychology and psychiatry. In this type of interview, the interviewer does not employ a detailed interview guide but has a general plan and usually asks questions or makes comments intended to lead the respondent toward giving data to meet the interviewer's objectives. Unstructured interviews are generally called for in situations where the type of information sought is difficult for the subject to express or is psychologically distressing to the individual. Because of the threatening nature of topics usually covered by unstructured interviews, this procedure must constantly adapt to the respondent and is highly subjective and time-consuming. The graduate student can very seldom employ the unstructured interview in his research because skillful use of this technique requires a great deal of training and experience.

In developing the interview guide and conducting interviews, the researcher should carefully observe a few common-sense rules:

1. Try out the guide in a few interviews in order to check vocabulary, language level, respondents' understanding of questions, and respondents' reactions to the interview. A pedantic or poorly phrased question can antagonize respondents and greatly reduce the validity of the data obtained. These first tryouts should be done by the researcher since she will gain a feel for the interview procedure that cannot be gained if someone else does this work.

   During the tryout, do some in-depth questioning to determine the respondent's understanding of questions that seek anything more than simple and obvious responses. In a recent study of subjects' understanding of survey questions, William Belson found that for the 29 questions he evaluated, on average only 29 percent of the respondents in his study interpreted the questions within permissible limits of the intended interpretation. These questions were designed to incorporate difficulties frequently found in survey questionnaires. The very high level of misinterpretation found by Belson illustrates the need to check respondents' interpretations *very* carefully during the tryout of your instrument.[45]

2. Interact with the respondent as an equal. Don't talk down to respondents, and don't try to court their favor.

3. If sensitive questions are to be asked, remind the respondent that answers will be held in strict confidence. If the respondent seems to hesitate, explain specifically the procedures that will be used to assure confidentiality.

4. Never hint, either by specific comment, tone of voice, or nonverbal cues such as shaking the head, to suggest a particular response. The interviewer must maintain a neutral stance on all questions to avoid biasing the responses.

45. See Belson in Annotated References at the end of this chapter.

Interviewer Training

Even for highly structured interviews, the interviewers must be trained if reliable and objective information is to be obtained. The amount of training needed increases as the depth of the interview increases and structure decreases.

The training usually is carried out in two phases. In the first phase the trainees study the interview guide and learn about the interview conditions, logistics, necessary controls and safeguards, variables being studied, and similar information. Before conducting any interviews, the interviewer should become so familiar with the interview guide (wording, format, recording procedures, and allowable probes) that he can conduct the interview in a conversational manner without hesitating, backtracking, or needing to reread or study the guide.[46] The researcher's expectations should not be discussed with the interviewers since this can bias the interviewers' perceptions.

In the second phase, research on interviewer training suggests that the trainees should conduct practice interviews and receive corrective feedback until their performance becomes standardized and reaches the desired level of objectivity and reliability.[47] Videotape recordings of practice interviews are very effective in providing models of the correct interview procedures and in giving corrective feedback. The tape can be replayed several times and trainees can locate procedural errors, suggest better procedures, and discuss alternative ways of dealing with problems that arise.

Recording the Interview

Note taking or tape recording are the usual methods for preserving the information collected in the interview. Before choosing one of these methods, the interviewer will need to consider carefully the advantages and disadvantages of each.

If note taking is employed, the interviewer should duplicate a supply of interview guides containing the questions to be asked during the interview and typical responses derived during the tryout of the guide listed under each question. Space should also be provided for the interviewer to add any necessary information or to write down answers that do not fit one of the usual response categories. As each question is answered by the respondent, the interviewer simply checks the appropriate response category and jots down any

---

46. See Henry S. Dwyer, *The Interview as a Measuring Device in Education*, TM Report 56 (Princeton, N.J.: Educational Testing Service, 1976), for a discussion of interviewing and a list of common-sense rules.
47. For a review of research related to interviewer training, see Mark D. Spool, "Training Programs for Observers of Behavior: A Review," *Personnel Psychology* 31 (1978): 853–88.

additional information as necessary. The interview guide should of course allow more space after open-ended questions than after closed-form questions, which can be answered in a few words. The chief advantage of the note-taking method is that it facilitates data analysis, since the information is readily accessible and much of it has already been classified into the appropriate response categories by the interviewer. Since the respondent's answers are recorded beside the appropriate questions on the interview guide, it is easy for the researcher to go through the guides, processing all the data for each question separately in a relatively short period of time.

One disadvantage of the note-taking method is that it may disrupt the effectiveness of the communication between interviewer and respondent. Whether this happens is to some extent dependent on the type of question being asked. When interviews include a large number of unstructured questions, involve extensive probing to get more depth, or produce answers that do not fit into a set of predeveloped categories, the note taking can require so much time that it is impossible to maintain rapport with the respondent.

When questions deal with simple factual information, the respondent expects her answers to be written down and may become annoyed or offended if they are not. On the other hand, if the respondent is asked to reveal sensitive or confidential information, taking notes may distract or upset her and prevent her from giving information she otherwise might have given. If confidential information is desired, the interviewer should carefully prepare the respondent. It is particularly important to stress the fact, before the formal interview begins, that the information provided by the respondent will be anonymous and reported only in group form (that is, combined with the data of other respondents). Another way to avoid the possibly disruptive effect of note taking is for the interviewer to consider delaying this procedure until after the interview is completed and the respondent has left the setting. However, the delay may lead the interviewer to forget important details, for instance, details that disagree with the interviewer's expectations. Of course, even if the note taking is done during the interview, the interviewer may unconsciously emphasize responses that agree with his expectations and fail to record responses that do not.

The use of tape recorders has several advantages in recording interview data for research. Most important perhaps is that it reduces the tendency of the interviewer to make an unconscious selection of data favoring his biases. The tape-recorded data can be played back more than once and can be studied much more thoroughly than would be the case if data were limited to notes taken during the interview. It is also possible to reanalyze the taped interview data to test hypotheses not set up in the original study. For example, interview data originally taped to study the interests of college freshmen could be reanalyzed to study their grammatical errors. Finally, it is possible with tape-recorded data for a person other than the interviewer to evaluate and classify the responses. This permits calculation of a reliability coefficient for the interview data. Reliability estimates can be made by comparing interviewer evaluations with evaluations of another research worker using the tape only, or by comparing initial interviewer evaluations with evaluations made by the same interviewer at a later date based on playback of the taped interview. In well-designed interview studies, these reliability coefficients may be as high as .90. The tape recorder also speeds up the interview process because there is no necessity for extensive note taking, although some minimal notes may be desirable. For example, some record of gestures might be appropriate in certain interview situations.

The principal disadvantage of the use of the tape recorder with the interview is that the presence of the tape recorder changes the interview situation to some degree. In interviews involving information of a highly personal nature, the respondent may be reluctant to express her feelings freely if she knows that her responses are being recorded. The interviewer should carefully explain the purpose of the recording and gain the confidence of the respondent, so as to minimize any undesirable effects of having the interview recorded. In interviews not aiming primarily at the collection of research data, it is seldom necessary to tape record the results. The opportunity to calculate reliability coefficients and the gain in objectivity provided by the taped record are very important factors, however, in research, and therefore the use of the tape recorder should be seriously considered for research interviews.

Telephone Interviewing

The use of the telephone in interview studies has greatly increased in recent years. As interviewers' salaries increase, the cost of long-distance telephone calls becomes competitive, and we can expect more interview studies to use this communication medium. Many universities now have WATS lines, which further reduce long-distance charges.

One major study used identical questionnaires to gather data from face-to-face interviews and telephone interviews and found that the latter cost about half as much.[48] In many educational surveys where members of the target population are spread over a large geographical area, such as all superintendents in the Rocky Mountain states, the cost advantage of telephone interviewing would be much greater. Although reduced cost is probably the greatest advantage of the telephone method, there are some other significant advantages.

48. See Graves and Kahn in Annotated References at the end of this chapter.

1. The researcher can select subjects from a much broader accessible population than would be the case if interviewers traveled to the location of each respondent.
2. Since all interviewers can work from a central location, monitoring of interviews and quality control is much easier for the researcher. Automatic data entry and computer-assisted interviewing are also possible when all interviewers telephone from a central location.
3. Occasionally in regular interview studies an interviewer does not actually carry out his assigned interviews but instead fakes the data. This is much less likely under the controlled conditions possible in telephone interviewing.
4. In telephone interviewing, when no one answers little cost is incurred, making frequent callbacks feasible.
5. Many groups, such as business people, school superintendents, and teachers, are easier to reach by telephone than by personal visits.
6. Telephone interviewing provides access to dangerous neighborhoods and to security buildings where interviewers are not admitted.

The relative advantages of telephone and face-to-face interviews have been studied by researchers. There is some evidence that telephone interviews can be used to collect sensitive data. One major study found that for nonthreatening questions, respondents' distortions were slightly higher for telephone interviews than for face-to-face interviews. For threatening questions, the reverse was true.[49] Although it would seem easier to establish rapport in a face-to-face interview, the physical presence of the interviewer may stimulate response distortion.

Obviously it is easier to hang up a phone than eject an interviewer from one's home or office. However, some investigators have been successful in completing a very high percentage of telephone interviews, even when dealing with sensitive topics. In one carefully controlled study by Graves and Kahn it was found that completed interviews were obtained from 74 percent of the sample in personal interviews and 70 percent in telephone interviews.[50] Since this study used the same questionnaire for the personal and telephone interviews it was possible to compare the distribution of responses for the two methods. It was found that the results were generally very similar over a wide range of topics and item formats.

The most serious problem with telephone interviewing is that some persons do not have telephones, thus eliminating them from the accessible population. For populations like the working poor, eliminating persons without

49. See Bradburn, Sudman, and associates in Annotated References at the end of this chapter.
50. See Graves and Kahn in Annotated References at the end of this chapter.

phones could seriously bias the sample. For most adult populations, however, the number of persons not having a telephone would be very small, and their omission from the accessible population would probably not introduce a significant bias.

Another consideration in planning a telephone survey is that many persons have unlisted numbers. If the study involves random samples of persons within a given geographical area, this problem can be overcome. Select four-digit numbers from a table of random numbers and add these to the exchange (i.e., the first 3 numbers); dial the numbers, and you will reach both listed and unlisted numbers.[51] Graves and Kahn report that random digit dialing reaches approximately 90 percent of all U.S. households, while an area probability sample, such as is used for personal interviews, provides access to about 95 percent of all dwellings.[52]

In summary, research has shown that telephone interviewing reaches nearly the same proportion of the target population, obtains nearly as high a percentage of returns, and produces comparable information at about one-half the cost of personal interviews.

Microcomputers in Telephone Interviewing[53]

Microcomputers are increasingly accepted as part of our everyday life. Small as the machines are, they can be a powerful tool in educational research. Microcomputers can be used to gather, analyze, and display research data.

Only a few years ago microcomputers cost tens of thousands of dollars, and so the use of these machines was relegated to special purposes. Recently the price of microcomputers has dropped drastically. At present, several excellent machines are available for below $500, and the lower limit is not yet in sight!

The microcomputer can be used to gather data in several ways. Three examples are: automated data gathering, where the subject sits at the computer solving a problem, carrying out a learning task, or playing a game; computer-assisted data gathering, where the microcomputer is used by the researcher to gather data; and computer-assisted interviewing.

In automated data gathering the subject interacts directly with the computer. While the subject is working on a problem at the computer, the subject's

---

51. See M. Hauck and M. Cox, "Locating a Sample by Random Digit Dialing," *Public Opinion Quarterly*, 38 (1974): 253–56.
52. See Graves and Kahn in Annotated References at the end of this chapter.
53. This section was prepared by Carl F. Berger, Mark Shermis, and Paul Stemmer, School of Education, University of Michigan. Dr. Berger and his associates have done a great deal of research and development on the use of microcomputers in educational research.

inputs, such as answers, opinions, and estimates, are not only recorded by the computer to guide the student's work on the problem, but the data are also stored for later analysis by the researcher. Data may include actual input of the keys pressed or knobs turned or buttons pressed plus the time taken for response. Such results can then be analyzed to infer that learning has or has not occurred. As an example, in a study of students' estimation skills, students may estimate the position of an object on a number line with only the numbers at each end of the line visible on the screen. Not only is each actual estimation recorded but the time taken to make each estimate is also recorded.

In computer-assisted data gathering, the researcher uses the computer as an observational device. We will discuss this use in chapter 12.

One of the most effective uses of the microcomputer is to assist in gathering information in telephone interviews. While computer-assisted telephone interviewing (CATI) may seem a trivial use of the computer, its use virtually eliminates two major sources of errors in interviews, namely, recording data in the wrong place on the form and asking the wrong questions. Most telephone interviews require the interviewer to jump to a different part of the form depending on the response of the person interviewed. For example, if the question is "Are you employed?" a response of yes might indicate that this response be recorded and that the interviewer turn three pages to a set of questions on mode of employment. If the interviewer fails to turn three pages, inappropriate or embarrassing questions may follow with the possible result of a badly shortened interview! Using a microcomputer, a program can be developed that not only records the subject's responses but also branches to the next question the interviewer should ask. Thus, as the interviewer types *yes* into the microcomputer, the response *yes* is recorded, and the computer is programmed to jump three pages in the computer program and display the first question on modes of employment. Not only does the researcher not have to worry about turning the pages but the interviewer does not even see the questions that are inappropriate. To the interviewer the next question that appears is the one needed. Response accuracy generally climbs with such computer-assisted interview techniques because the interviewer can concentrate on responses rather than worry about a wrong decision on what question to ask next.

Because of these and other advantages, an increasing number of researchers are turning to computer-assisted telephone interviewing. In using CATI, the interview guide or survey instrument is stored on a magnetic disk and questions are displayed individually for the interviewer in program-controlled sequences on a terminal. Responses to individual items are entered on the terminal keyboard. Specific applications of CATI vary, but precoded answers are generally recorded by alpha-numeric codes, while answers to open-ended questions, respondent qualifications, and interviewer notes are typed out in full. Also, respondent answers can be stored in data files, which are continuously updated as interviewing and coding proceed.

Nicholls,[54] and Groves, Berry, and Mathiowetz[55] highlight several advantages of CATI over standard telephone interviewing techniques.

1. Question branching is controlled by the system. This sophistication allows for the implementation of complex survey instruments and eliminates an important form of interviewer error.
2. CATI systems require the investigator to spell out clear and explicit procedures that were formerly unspecified.
3. "Wild codes" (codes that do not have any meaning) can be detected while the interview is in progress and resolved by questions directed by the computer to either the interviewer or the respondent.
4. Close supervision is possible by monitoring both the interview conversation and interview entries. There is also an opportunity to have an additional interviewer simultaneously code the interview. Comparison of the codes given by each interviewer for the same interview can then be made to look for inconsistencies and to estimate interrater reliability.
5. Since data entry and error checking are concurrent, the system can produce a fully cleaned (error free) data file ready for analysis shortly after the completion of field work.

In order to have a fully functioning CATI system, the computer needs to perform some or all of the following functions:

1. Random digit dialing (RDD)
2. Storage and retrieval of telephone lists
3. Automatic dialing
4. Presentation of questions
5. Code checking and storage of responses
6. Input and merging to a dataset
7. Interviewing management

Because of the complexities of tasks required by CATI, such systems were initially developed for use with large computers. With the advent of more sophisticated microcomputers with 16 bit memory, CATI systems are beginning

---

54. See W. Nicholls, "Computer Assisted Telephone Interviewing," *Computer Center Newsletter* 3, no. 1 (1980) (University of California at Berkeley).
55. See R. M. Groves, M. Berry, and N. Mathiowetz, "Some Impacts of Computer Assisted Telephone Interviewing on Survey Methods," in American Statistical Association, *Proceedings of the Section on Survey Research Methods, Houston, Texas, 11–14 August 1980* (Washington, D.C.: American Statistical Association, 1980), pp. 519–24.

to be developed for them, too. For example, Berger, Shermis, and Stemmer have demonstrated a microcomputer application to a statewide vocational education follow-up survey.[56]

Effective Communication in Interviews

Interview questions must be framed in language that ensures effective communication between the interviewer and the respondent. The respondent must fully understand the language in which the question is framed. In those educational research studies where the respondents are professional educators, the problem of phrasing questions in language common to both interviewer and respondent is not usually serious, but for studies involving interviews with lay people, the educational jargon we in the profession know and use can seriously block effective communication. For example, if a question such as "What is your opinion of homogeneous grouping in the public schools?" were asked, it is likely that many of the persons answering would not have a clear understanding of the term "homogeneous grouping." Often the respondent is reluctant to admit that she doesn't understand the meaning of the question. The fact that she has been asked the question implies that she should understand it, and rather than admit her ignorance, she may give an evasive or noncommital answer.[57] To avoid this difficulty, the interviewer should explain technical terms in plain language before asking for the respondent's opinion. Also, it is advisable to ask a few information questions about the topic first. If the respondent cannot answer the information questions, then the opinion item can be skipped since the respondent's answer will have little value or meaning.

Occasionally a graduate student is carried away by his enthusiasm for a research idea and asks for information that no one could reasonably be expected to have. An example of this was an interview study proposed recently by a graduate student that would ask college students to recall conversations the students had during their childhood with teachers or other adults that exerted a major influence on the moral values and educational and vocational goals of the students. The graduate student believed that there are certain critical moments in everyone's childhood when the words of a parent or teacher become a major factor in determining the future goals and behavior of the child. Such a theory may be valid, but the line of questioning planned by the graduate student called for a level of recall as well as a level of insight that few

56. See Carl F. Berger, Mark L. Shermis, and Paul Stemmer, "Data Gathering Using Microcomputers" (American Educational Research Association Training Session, New York, April 1982).
57. The student may recall our discussion of the study by Allen (p. 423), who found that 10 percent of a sample expressed an opinion about a bogus organization, the League for Linear Programs, rather than check the "don't know" category.

persons could be expected to possess. Another error frequently made in educational studies is to ask parents to comment on technical aspects of education about which they have little or no knowledge. For example, an interview study carried out to learn the parents' opinions of different methods of teaching reading could produce very little useful information. Many of the parents would probably have opinions concerning the teaching of reading, but for the most part these opinions would have little foundation except their limited personal experiences.

Effective communication between interviewer and respondent is facilitated if the respondent appreciates the purpose of each question that is asked. With the help of the interviewer, the respondent develops an idea of the purpose of the interview, and if he can see no connection between his perception of the purpose and a question that is asked, he is likely to react negatively. He may become suspicious of the interviewer and wonder whether the interview actually has some purpose other than the one he has been told. Inasmuch as he cannot be sure of what this hidden purpose is, his suspicions are aroused, and he is immediately placed on his guard. Under these circumstances his answers will be evasive and his attitude guarded or hostile. On the other hand, he may consider such a question as indicative of a lack of ability or poor planning on the part of the interviewer. In this case he is likely to feel that his participation is a waste of time. This loss of confidence in the interviewer is serious in that it is often followed by a refusal to cooperate. If the status of the respondent is higher than that of the interviewer, a special effort must be made to avoid questions that the respondent can interpret as wasting his time. The problem of questions that appear irrelevant arises often in studies involving psychological data, such as personality. Indirect questioning is often necessary in this area, and unless considerable groundwork is laid by the interviewer, resistance by the respondents will be encountered.

There are a number of other techniques that the skillful interviewer can use to promote effective communication with the respondent. Before the formal interview begins, she engages the respondent in a few minutes of small talk to help him relax and to establish rapport. The interviewer also assures the respondent that all his statements will be held in strictest confidence and be used for research purposes only. In some instances it may be desirable to use subtle social pressure to impress on the respondent the importance of the interview. For example, the interviewer might make a statement such as "I am doing this study in collaboration with Dr. —— at the state university in order to learn how men in your position feel about these issues." Once the interview has been initiated, other techniques may be helpful in maintaining respondent cooperation and participation. After the respondent has completed an answer, the interviewer can sometimes elicit additional information by pausing before asking the next question or by saying, "Tell me more about that." Of course, it is undesirable to contradict or appear to cross-examine the respondent, since he may become threatened and deceptive in answering further questions. If the respondent does appear to be threatened by a particular question, then the interviewer should change the subject; at a later point in the interview, it may be possible to raise the subject again in such a way that the respondent is not threatened. Finally, it is inadvisable to ask too many closed-form questions in succession or to change the subject of the interview too frequently. Otherwise a respondent may feel that the interview is not necessary and that the interviewer is not interested in obtaining his views in depth.

Leading Questions

A factor that often biases the results of interview studies is the use of leading questions by the interviewer. A leading question is any question that, because of the phrasing of the question, leads the respondent to consider one reply more desirable than another. Let us say, for example, that we were interviewing a random sampling of voters concerning their attitudes toward federal aid to education. After establishing whether the respondent was familiar with the issue of federal aid to education, a reasonable question might be, "What is your opinion of federal aid to education?" A question that might be classified as moderately leading would state, "Do you favor federal aid to education?" This question is a little easier for the respondent to answer in the affirmative than the negative. A more serious attempt to lead the respondent would result in a question such as "In view of the dangers of federal control, do you feel that federal aid to education is advisable?" Here the respondent is strongly motivated to give an unfavorable response to federal aid. Questions can be slanted even further by the use of emotionally toned words to which the individual is inclined to react for or against with little thought for the basic issue involved. Such a question might be, "Do you favor federal aid to education as a means of providing each child with an equal educational opportunity?" In this case the concept of "an equal opportunity for all" is likely to elicit favorable replies.

The Respondent's Frame of Reference

Each person is the product of an environment that is unique. Words recall different experiences and have different shades of meaning for each of us. Unless the interviewer establishes a common ground for communication—a common frame of reference—these differences can seriously interfere with the communication process. If the respondent's frame of reference is different from that of the interviewer, his replies are likely to be misinterpreted. For example, if a group of mothers was asked, "What do you think of the teacher your child has this year?" one might answer in terms of the teacher's personal appear-

ance, another may think of the teacher's willingness to help on a PTA committee, another may have never seen the teacher but may feel that her child is not
getting proper reading instruction, while another may have had a conference
with the teacher the day before about her child's misbehavior and think of
nothing but this meeting in making an evaluation. Thus, we can see that unless the interviewer and respondent are using the same frame of reference,
many difficulties can arise when obtaining interview data. In research perhaps
the most desirable solution to this problem is to specify the frame of reference
wanted by the interviewer. The preceding question could be placed in a specific frame of reference by asking, "What do you think of the way your child's
teacher handles parent-teacher conferences?"

Pretest of the Interview Procedures

Although the interview can provide us with valuable data, the research worker
must remember that it is a highly subjective technique. When this technique is
used in research, all possible controls and safeguards must be employed if we
expect to obtain reasonably objective and unbiased data. A careful pilot study
is the best insurance the research worker has against bias and flaws in design.
After the interview guide has been developed, a pilot study should be conducted to evaluate and improve the guide and the interview procedure and
help the interviewer develop experience in using the procedure before any
research data for the main study are collected. The number of subjects interviewed in the pilot study need not be large—10 to 20 are sufficient for most
educational studies. The interviewer can usually determine from the progress
of her last few pilot interviews whether more are needed to improve her procedures further. The subjects interviewed in the pilot study should be taken
from the same population as the main study sample whenever possible and
from a very similar population when research design does not permit drawing
from the main study population.

The pilot study should be carried out with specific objectives in mind.
The interviewer should determine from the pilot study whether the planned
procedures actually produce the data desired. The interviewer should be alert
to communication problems, evidence of inadequate motivation, and other clues
that suggest a rephrasing of questions or revision of procedure.

The pretest can also be used to identify threatening questions. Bradburn
and Sudman define a question as threatening when 20 percent of respondents
feel that most people would be very uneasy talking about the topic. This criterion can be employed by investigators in the pretest to identify such questions. Such items should then be omitted or revised if possible. However, if
these items are essential to the research, which is often the case, then the

techniques recommended by these authors can be employed to reduce response effects.[58]

Several methods of opening the interview should also be tried and perfected. Unwillingness of the respondent to cooperate generally indicates that the techniques that have been established are not sufficient for motivation and maintenance of rapport. The pilot study also gives the interviewer an opportunity to evaluate her methods of recording the interview data, to determine whether adequate information is being recorded, whether the recording method causes excessive breaks in the interview situation, and whether the mechanics of reporting can be improved.

During the pilot study, the research worker also should assess carefully the methods she has planned to use for quantifying and analyzing her interview data. If the pilot study results indicate that data obtained cannot be quantified or are not falling into the areas anticipated, the interview procedures must be revised until satisfactory quantification and analysis are possible.

Tape recording of pilot study interviews is especially important even if the tape recorder is not to be used during the regular interview procedure. By playing back the interview, the interviewer can gain many insights into her handling of the questions and will be made aware of problems that may have escaped her during the interview situation.

MISTAKES SOMETIMES MADE IN SURVEY RESEARCH

Survey research in general:

1. Researcher does not formulate clear, specific objectives for his research.
2. Relates data-gathering procedure to objectives in only a general way and thereby fails to get quantitative data specific to the problem.
3. Selects sample on the basis of convenience instead of attempting to obtain a random sample.
4. Analyzes survey data one variable at a time instead of analyzing relationships, longitudinal changes, and comparisons between groups.

Questionnaire studies:

5. Researcher uses a questionnaire to investigate problems that could be better studied with other research techniques.
6. Gives insufficient attention to the development of the questionnaire and fails to pretest it.

---

58. See Bradburn, Sudman, and associates in Annotated References at the end of this chapter.

7. Asks too many questions, thus making unreasonable demands on the respondent's time.
8. Overlooks details of format, grammar, printing, and so on that give the respondent an unfavorable first impression.
9. Fails to check a sample of nonresponding subjects for possible bias.

Interview studies:

10. Researcher does not adequately plan the interview or develop a detailed interview guide.
11. Does not conduct sufficient practice interviews to acquire needed skills.
12. Fails to establish safeguards against interviewer bias.
13. Does not make provisions for calculating the reliability of interview data.
14. Uses language in the interview that is not understood by the respondents.
15. Asks for information that the respondent cannot be expected to have.

ANNOTATED REFERENCES

Survey Research

Orlich, Donald C. *Designing Sensible Surveys.* Pleasantville, N.Y.: Redgrave, 1978.

This small book deals briefly with most aspects of survey research including interviews, questionnaires, construction of survey items, sampling, research designs, data processing, and writing the research report. It is a very practical guide, containing many examples. Highly recommended for students who plan to conduct a survey.

Selltiz, C.; Wrightsman, L. S.; and Cook, S. W. *Research Methods in Social Relations.* 3rd ed. New York: Holt, Rinehart & Winston, 1976.

Contains a chapter on questionnaires and interviews that includes an interesting discussion of different types of question content. Appendix B on questionnaire construction and interview procedure will also be useful to the student who plans to conduct research in this area.

Sudman, Seymour, and Bradburn, Norman M. *Response Effects in Surveys.* Chicago: Aldine, 1974.

This book pulls together virtually all the research on response effects. Many variables related to the interview process such as degree of structure, question length, and topic of the study are discussed. The effects of memory and the effects of interviewer and respondent characteristics on response to different kinds of questions are also reviewed. Comparisons are also made of the relative effectiveness of the questionnaire and the interview for gathering various kinds of survey data. A very thorough bibliography is included.

Warwick, Donald P., and Lininger, Charles A. *The Sample Survey: Theory and Practice.* New York: McGraw-Hill, 1975.

Gives a good coverage of survey planning and design. The chapter on questionnaire design provides detailed instructions and examples. There is also a thorough discussion of the survey interview.

Questionnaires

Belson, William A. *The Design and Understanding of Survey Questions.* Aldershot, England: Gower, 1981.

In this study 29 experimental questions designed to study respondent interpretations were imbedded in 4 questionnaires. The questions were administered to a total of 265 subjects in an initial interview. A second in-depth interview was then conducted with each respondent to determine how the experimental questions asked during the first interview had been understood. The researcher then very carefully analyzed the interpretations of each item. This study gives the reader many useful insights into the questioning process and is a valuable guide to the design of better questions.

Berdie, D. R., and Anderson, J. F. *Questionnaires: Design and Use.* Metuchen, N.J.: Scarecrow Press, 1974.

This short book is filled with useful information on designing and carrying out a questionnaire study. The sections on item construction and procedures to stimulate responses are especially valuable. The appendices contain four sample questionnaires, follow-up letters, and a case history of a questionnaire study. Finally, an extensive annotated bibliography is provided that includes most important references on questionnaires published over the past 30 years.

Heberlein, Thomas A., and Baumgartner, Robert. "Factors Affecting Response Rates to Mailed Questionnaires: A Quantitative Analysis of the Published Literature." *American Sociological Review* 43 (1978): 447–62.

Linsky, Arnold S. "Stimulating Responses to Mailed Questionnaires: A Review." *Public Opinion Quarterly* 39 (1975): 82–101.

These two reviews summarize a large amount of research information that can help a researcher maximize response rate on a questionnaire survey.

Linsky has written a conventional review of research literature from 1935 to the time of his article. For most of the major areas he presents data related to response rates in tabular form, which helps the reader see the overall patterns of research evidence. In contrast, Heberlein and Baumgartner used a procedure similar to Glass's meta-analysis to combine the results of 98 experiments concerned with response rates. Their multiple regression analysis is especially useful in revealing the effects of combining various strategies for increasing response rates. They have also developed an interesting model that can be used to predict the final response rate an investigator can expect to obtain, based on such variables as saliency, use of cash incentive, and number of follow-ups to be used. The student planning a questionnaire survey should give both articles careful attention.

Schuman, Howard, and Presser, S. *Questions and Answers in Attitude Surveys: Experiments on Question Form, Wording, and Context.* New York: Academic Press, 1981.

This book describes a series of experiments that manipulated a number of question-form variations to learn their effect on results obtained on survey questionnaires. Among the variations studied were: open vs. closed questions, encouragement vs. discouragement of "don't know" responses, variations in question order, and changes in the tone of wording. Their results indicate that even minor differences in wording can bring about major differences in responses. The context in which the question is asked also was found to have a substantial effect on answers received. These findings are especially important for researchers doing longitudinal surveys or replicating earlier studies, but should be studied by anyone doing survey research.

Sewell, W. H., and Hauser, R. M. *Education, Occupation, and Earnings.* New York: Academic Press, 1975.

A large-scale follow-up survey of about 5000 male high school seniors several years after graduation is reported in this book. The sections describing the research procedures provide a good model for this type of research.

Interviews

Bradburn, Norman M.; Sudman, Seymour; and Associates. *Improving Interview Method and Questionnaire Design.* San Francisco: Jossey-Bass, 1981.

This excellent book reports the results of a series of large-scale experimental studies carried out over a seven-year period by the National Opinion Research Center at the University of Chicago and the Survey Research Laboratory of the University of Illinois. These studies investigated the response effects related to threatening questions in survey research. Anyone planning to conduct survey research on sensitive topics will profit greatly from a careful study of this important work.

Graves, R. M., and Kahn R. L. *Surveys by Telephone: A National Comparison with Personal Interviews.* New York: Academic Press, 1979.

This book describes an excellent experimental study designed to compare the results of a personal interview survey (N = 1548) with two telephone surveys (Ns of 865 and 869), all conducted simultaneously. The questionnaires employed in the two modes were essentially identical. The researchers explored most of the important questions related to these two interview modes. This is the best research we have located on this topic, and the book is strongly recommended to anyone planning an interview study.

Gorden, Raymond L. *Interviewing Strategy, Techniques and Factors.* Rev. ed. Homewood, Ill.: Dorsey Press, 1975.

A detailed treatment of interviewing is presented, including such topics as locating and contacting respondents, selecting interviewers, taking notes, planning the interview, arranging topics, and dealing with resistance. The interview is also compared with other data-gathering procedures such as observation and use of questionnaires.

Stewart, Charles J., and Cash, William, B., Jr. *Interviewing: Principles and Practices.* Dubuque, Iowa: William C. Brown, 1974.

A readable coverage of the broad field of interviews. Includes sections on most of the major kinds of interviews including employment, appraisal, and counseling. The chapters on communication, questions, and informational interviewing provide a good introduction for the student who is interested in the interview process.

Survey Research Center. *Interviewer's Manual.* Rev. ed. Ann Arbor, Mich.: Institute for Social Research, University of Michigan, 1976.

This manual provides much useful information on the use of interviews in survey research. Specific instructions are given on such topics as making initial contact with the subject, asking questions, probing, and recording responses. Many examples are given.

Weiss, Carol H. "Interviewing in Evaluation Research." In *Handbook of Evaluation Research,* edited by Elmer L. Struening and Marcia Guttentag. Beverly Hills, Calif.: Sage, 1975.

Although focused on evaluation research, the information on interviewing given in this chapter would be very useful in planning any type of interview study. The author's presentation is readable, well-organized, and complete.

SELF-CHECK TEST

Circle the correct answer to each of the following questions. An answer key is provided on page 881.

1. The goal of the data-collection tools used in survey research is to
   a. obtain standardized information from all subjects in the sample.
   b. gather as much data as possible in the shortest period of time.
   c. collect only information that will prove to be significant.
   d. collect nonquantified data.

2. The most commonly used instruments for data collection in survey research are the
   a. questionnaire and standardized test.
   b. questionnaire and individual interview.
   c. individual interview and situational testing.
   d. standardized test and critical-incident technique.

3. The term "time-bound association" indicates that the variables being studied
   a. refer to future events.
   b. refer to psychological processes that will hold constant over time.
   c. are measured at the same point in time.
   d. correlate highly with each other.

4. The first step in conducting a questionnaire survey is to
   a. select the sample.
   b. define the population from which the sample is to be taken.
   c. list specific objectives to be achieved by questionnaire.
   d. construct questionnaire items.

5. The most basic consideration involved in selecting subjects for a questionnaire study is the
   a. size of sample.
   b. identification of a group that has the desired information.
   c. definition of method used for data collection.
   d. identification of data analysis techniques.

6. In writing a letter of transmittal to accompany a mailed questionnaire, the researcher is advised to
   a. avoid associating the research project with a professional institution.
   b. request that the questionnaire be returned by a certain date.
   c. avoid setting a time limit for return of the questionnaire.
   d. state that follow-up techniques will be used if the questionnaire is not returned by a certain date.

7. Compared with the mailed questionnaire, the principal advantages of the interview are

   a. low cost and high adaptability.
   b. adaptability and depth of information collected.
   c. objectivity and ease of administration.
   d. ease of administration and high reliability of information collected.
 8. The research interview has the following disadvantage(s):
   a. Considerable training is required to administer the interview.
   b. It is a time-consuming and expensive technique.
   c. It is subject to interviewer bias.
   d. All of the above are correct.
 9. The principal disadvantage of tape recording a research interview is
   a. its relatively high cost.
   b. the complexity of its operation.
   c. the change that it produces in the interview situation.
   d. the low validity of tape-recorded data compared to the validity of the note-taking technique.
10. It is good interview technique to
   a. ask leading questions.
   b. avoid engaging in small talk before starting the formal interview.
   c. cross-examine respondents if they seem deceptive.
   d. make sure that respondents appreciate the purpose of each question asked.

APPLICATION PROBLEMS

The following problems are designed to give you practice in applying significant concepts and research procedures explained in chapter 11. Most of them do not have a single correct answer. For feedback, you can compare your answers with the sample answers on pages 892–93.

1. Suppose that you are doing a survey to determine college seniors' plans for the year immediately following June commencement. Your first step is to write sample closed-form and open-ended items for pilot testing.
   a. Write a closed-form questionnaire item in multiple-choice format that you think will elicit the desired information. Include at least five choices in the item statement.
   b. Write an open-ended questionnaire item that you believe will also elicit the desired information.
2. The open classroom is a relatively new development in American education. A researcher decides to survey the attitudes of elementary school teachers toward this new approach to instruction. She develops an attitude scale for this purpose. A colleague advises that she should also give the teachers a short test to

determine what they know about the open classroom. Why might the colleague have made this recommendation?

3. A graduate student has designed a survey questionnaire that will serve as the main data-collection instrument of his dissertation. He plans to send the questionnaire to a random sample of textbook publishers throughout the United States. He prepares the following letter, which is to be sent to each publisher along with a copy of the questionnaire:

Dear Sir:

The enclosed questionnaire will take only a few minutes of your time to complete. The purpose of the questionnaire is to collect data for my doctoral dissertation in the Department of Education at the University of Ingleside. My field of specialization is curriculum development.

A prepaid addressed envelope is enclosed for return of the questionnaire. If you have any questions about the study, I will be happy to answer them. Thank you for your cooperation.

Sincerely,

ARTHUR JONES

What are three ways in which the content of this letter can be improved?

4. A researcher has received back 72 percent of the questionnaires that she sent to a sample of high school counselors. What are three methods the researcher can use to contact nonrespondents to request that they return their questionnaire?

5. A researcher wishes to survey a sample of parents in a school district to determine their satisfaction or dissatisfaction with particular schools. He has included the following questions in his interview guide:

1. How many children do you have?
2. What are their ages?
3. What school(s) do they attend?
4. How long have they attended the school(s):
5. What do you like best about the school(s) your children attend?
6. What do you like least?
7. What kinds of contact have you had with your children's teachers and other school staff?

a. Do these questions constitute a structured interview, semistructured interview, or an unstructured interview?
b. Why do you think the researcher organized the questions into the above sequence?

c. Which questions will most likely require probing by means of open-ended questions?

SUGGESTION SHEET

If your last name starts with letters from Kef to Lev, please complete the Suggestion Sheet at the end of the book while this chapter is still fresh in your mind.

12.

THE METHODS AND TOOLS OF OBSERVATIONAL RESEARCH

OVERVIEW

A variety of methods can be used to collect research data relating to human behavior. In the previous chapter you considered the methods and tools of survey research, principally the questionnaire and the interview. It was shown that one of the principal disadvantages of these techniques is that individuals tend to bias the information they offer about themselves. This problem can be overcome by using a set of techniques that can be grouped under the general heading of observational research methods. The purpose of chapter 12 is to give you information concerning the collection of observational data. It covers topics such as use of standard observational forms, use of audiotape and videotape recorders to collect data, training of observers, and procedures for reducing observer bias. Also discussed are the use of situational testing, observations by untrained groups, participant observation, ethnographic research, and the technique of content analysis.

OBJECTIVES

After studying this chapter, you should be able to:

1. If given a broad characteristic such as "friendliness," identify specific behaviors that might be indicative of this characteristic and prepare low-inference items for use in an observation schedule.
2. State at least one advantage and one disadvantage of using a standard observational schedule in a research project.
3. If given a particular observation schedule, establish a procedure for training observers in its use.
4. Describe four types of factors that reduce the reliability and validity of observational data.

5. Describe six precautions that the researcher should take to reduce observer bias, rating errors, and contamination.
6. Describe criteria that can be used to evaluate a study involving participant observation.
7. Define "nonreactive measure" and describe four errors that can occur when reactive measures are used in educational research.
8. Describe ethnographic research and discuss some of its advantages and disadvantages for educational studies.
9. If given a research variable, identify at least one nonreactive measure that could be used to assess it.
10. Identify appropriate situational tests for use in particular research projects.
11. Describe how anecdotal records, sociometry, supervisory ratings, and the critical-incident technique can be used in educational research.
12. Describe the steps a researcher takes in planning a content analysis.
13. If given a particular construct and a body of written material, develop appropriate content-analysis procedures for measuring this construct.

STEPS IN COLLECTING OBSERVATIONAL DATA

In preceding chapters we discussed standardized tests, survey questionnaires, and interviews as methods for collecting research data. These methods are similar in their reliance on self-report as the basic source of data. Although as a rule self-reports can be obtained easily and economically, people often bias the information they offer about themselves, and sometimes they cannot accurately recall events and aspects of their behavior in which the researcher is interested. The observational method, if used properly, overcomes these limitations of the self-report method. Sechrest, for example, has argued that social attitudes, such as prejudice, should be studied by means of naturalistic observations, since self-reports of these attitudes are often biased by the set to give a socially desirable response.[1] Prejudice has been studied naturalistically by observing the seating patterns of black and white students in college classes.[2] Even when bias is not present in self-report data, the observational method usually yields more accurate quantitative data than could be obtained by self-report. For example, many educators have noted that in class discussions teachers dominate the talk at the expense of student participation. But what are the actual percentages of teacher and student talk in these discussions? It is unlikely that teachers or students could provide accurate information on this

1. Lee Sechrest, "Naturalistic Methods in the Study of Social Attitudes" (paper presented at APA Annual Convention, 1966).
2. Donald T. Campbell, William H. Kruskal, and William P. Wallace, "Seating Aggregation as an Index of Attitude," *Sociometry* 29 (1966): 1–15.

question. However, an observational study in which an audiotape recorder or videotape recorder was used could yield precise quantitative data.

Although they overcome some limitations of self-report instruments, observational techniques have potential limitations of their own. It is not uncommon in observational studies to find the experimenter attempting to study complex behavior patterns but finding that the more straightforward behaviors, which can be objectively observed and recorded, are only slightly related to the complex behaviors he wishes to study. Thus, he is faced with the choice of getting objective data that is of little value because of its limited relationship to a complex behavior or getting data more closely related to the complex behavior he is studying but finding it of limited value because of its subjectivity. Obtaining data related to complex behavior that is objectively observable and yet pertinent to the problem requires careful planning.

Another problem that must be faced in conducting the observational study is to determine the degree to which the presence of the observer changes the situation being observed. In observations of classroom behavior, for example, a change in the behavior of both the teacher and class members usually occurs when an observer enters the room. Classrooms in laboratory schools are often provided with adjacent rooms fitted with one-way screens so that observations can be carried on without disturbing the situation. Occasionally studies are conducted in which the observer visits the classroom a number of times before recording any observational data so that the class will become accustomed to his presence and will react normally when the research data are actually collected. Very often the graduate student with limited control over the situations that he wishes to observe finds it difficult to solve this problem satisfactorily.

The time factor often makes observational research difficult for the graduate student. This method of gathering data is time consuming, and the student usually finds it difficult to make enough observations of a sufficiently large sampling of individuals to provide reliable data. To provide reasonably sound data and to permit reliability estimates, observational studies usually require that at least two independent observers evaluate the situation being observed. This again poses a problem for the graduate student, who must often rely entirely on his own resources for obtaining research data.

Defining Observational Variables

Developing observational measures for one's research project is difficult. This section presents some techniques for developing and simplifying observational measures. To illustrate these techniques, we will use as an example a research problem that requires observation of behavior. Suppose our research problem is to determine whether a particular type of workshop in modern mathematics affects what teachers do in their classrooms.

This broad statement of the problem suggests that some type of classroom observations cannot be specified until several decisions are made.

First, it is necessary to limit the number of observations that will be made. Because of the problem, observations will be limited to teachers' daily mathematics class, probably an hour or less. This still includes too broad a range of behavior. It would be quite unrealistic to expect an observer to record everything that transpires in a classroom for an hour. Even in a minute's time many different kinds of activities may occur. In order to determine what the observer should look for, it is useful to develop hypotheses or expectations about the effect of the workshop on classroom teaching. At this point one should be able to limit the focus of the observations considerably. Suppose that one's main hypothesis is that teachers who have had workshop training in modern mathematics will spend more time explaining new mathematical concepts than teachers without this training. If this is the case, the observation process is simplified considerably, since the observer need only focus on the teacher rather than on students and teacher simultaneously. However, the total length of observation may need to be increased beyond a single class period. Teachers with workshop training may spend as much time as teachers without training in explaining a new concept on the first day, but they may spend more days developing a complete explanation. To detect this difference, observations over a period of several days, perhaps a week, may be necessary.

The first step then is to narrow or focus one's observation by referring to one's hypotheses or expectations for the pertinent variables to be observed and recorded. The next step is to define a behavior unit and a time unit. This process may in turn result in a still more focused range of observation. For the present example, it would be necessary to decide what behavior or behaviors consitute an "explanation of a new mathematical concept." One may decide to define explanation as "all teacher statements that define some aspect of the new concept, that present examples of the concept, or that direct students to perform tasks pertaining to the concept." In this case one might decide to make the individual sentence the basic unit of observation, which would enable one to express research findings in the following form: "Teachers with workshop training uttered _____ sentences to explain the new mathematical concept compared with _____ sentences for teachers without this training."[3] Next, it is necessary to define a precise time unit based on the total length of the observation. In our example the time unit might reflect a week's period of instruction in mathematics class, or about four hours. Thus, research findings would now be stated in this form: "In four hours of observed mathematics instruction, teachers with workshop training uttered _____ sentences compared with _____ sentences for teachers without this training." Now, ratios can also

---

3. To simplify the process of recording, it might be desirable to just observe the time spent uttering such sentences. Thus, minutes and seconds become the basic unit of observation.

be expressed thus: "Ten explanatory sentences were uttered per hour of class time."

Three types of observational variables may be distinguished: descriptive, inferential, and evaluative. Descriptive variables have the advantage that they require little inference on the part of the observer. Researchers often refer to such variables as "low inference" variables. Consequently, they generally yield reliable data. For the present research example, it might be desirable to have observers record all utterances of certain key phrases as each teacher explains a mathematical concept, such as regrouping. (These phrases include "place value," "base ten," "expanded notation," "renaming.") This is a purely descriptive task, and thus there would be high agreement between observers recording the behavior of a given teacher. Other observational variables require the observer to make an inference before a variable can be scored. For example, observers may be asked to record the self-confidence with which a teacher explains a mathematical concept. Some teachers may speak with a good deal of confidence, while others may appear uncertain, confused, or anxious because their understanding of the topic is weak. Confidence, uncertainty, confusion, and anxiety are not behaviors but rather are inferences made from behavior. These are often referred to as "high inference variables." It is much harder to collect reliable data when observers are asked to make inferences from behavior.

Related to inferential variables are evaluative variables. These also require an inference from behavior on the part of the observer, but in addition, the observer must make an evaluative judgment. For example, the researcher may be interested in obtaining ratings of the quality of the teacher's explanation of a mathematical concept. Quality ratings are not behavior but rather are inferences made from behavior. Since it is difficult to make reliable observations of evaluative variables, the researcher should collect examples of behavior that define points along the continuum of excellent-to-poor explanations and use these in training the observers.

To ensure accurate recording, observers should be required to score only one behavior at a given point in time. For example, most observers would find it quite difficult to record certain aspects of the teacher's talk and at the same time record the percentage of children who appear to be paying attention to the teacher. Consequently, the reliability of both sets of observations would probably be low.

Recording Observational Information

New techniques for recording observational data are continually being developed. Most recording procedures, however, can be classified into four major categories: (1) duration recording, (2) frequency-count recording, (3) interval recording, and (4) continuous recording.

Duration Recording

In **duration recording** the observer simply uses some timing device, such as a stop watch, to measure the elapsed time during which the target behaviors occur. In many studies, the observer records time for a single behavior, such as the length of time a given student is out of his seat. However, if the researcher is interested in duration of time during which several behaviors are emitted by a single subject, these can be recorded by a single observer if they generally do not occur at the same time. For example, the observer could record the length of time a given pupil was on-task, off-task but not disruptive, mildly disruptive, or seriously disruptive. Duration recording can be used to observe the amount of time several pupils emit a single behavior if it is a behavior that not more than one pupil will emit at the same time. For example, the duration of pupil verbal responses to teacher questions can be recorded for several pupils if, as a rule, only one pupil responds at a time. Reliability of duration recordings can be estimated by computing a correlation coefficient for the sets of duration scores that two observers recorded for a group of subjects. For example, each of the two independent observers might record each pupil's seconds of verbal input during a one-hour classroom discussion; the researcher would enter the two sets of scores into the raw score formula for the Product-Moment correlation. The resulting correlation coefficient is the inter-observer reliability of the duration data. Either the time of the two observers for each specific incident or cumulative time can be compared. In the latter case, the shorter time is usually divided by the longer time in comparing the two observers. For example, if observer A reported 82 minutes of out-of-seat behavior while observer B reported 96 minutes, the estimate of *inter-observer agreement* would be 82/96 or .85. Inter-observer reliability and inter-observer agreement are not the same; and there are several ways that each may be computed. Therefore, the investigator should specify which he has computed and what method was used in the computation.[4]

Frequency-Count Recording

In **frequency-count recording** the observer records each time the target behavior or behaviors occur. Usually, a tally sheet or a counting device such as a wrist counter is used. If the target behavior occurs at very high frequency, an observer may be able to record only one behavior. However, observers can be

4. For more information, see Ted Frick and Melvyn I. Semmel, "Observer Agreement and Reliabilities of Classroom Observational Measures," *Review of Educational Research* 48 (1978): 157–84.

trained to tally several moderate to low-frequency behaviors. Frequency counts are most useful in recording behaviors of short duration and those where duration is not important. For example, one of the authors recently completed a study in which observers were trained to tally 13 teacher behaviors related to classroom management, such as goal-directed prompts, concurrent praise, and alerting cues. Since the behaviors were of short duration and were such that more than one could not occur at the same time, interobserver reliabilities were satisfactory, ranging from .71 to .96 for the 13 behaviors.[5]

Interval Recording

Interval recording involves observing the behavior of the **target subject** (i.e., the subject being observed) at a given interval. For example, in the Flanders Interaction Analysis System the observer checks the behavior of the target subject each three seconds and records which of ten specific behaviors he is emitting at each interval. All classroom behavior can be classified into one of the ten Flanders categories.[6] Length of interval varies with nature of the behaviors being observed but usually ranges between ten seconds and one minute. In the simplest systems, the observer tallies whether the subject is or is not emitting a single target behavior at each interval, e.g., a pupil is either on-task or not on-task. In more complex systems, such as Flanders's, all behavior is classified into a set of categories and the appropriate behavior is tallied at each interval. Such systems usually permit the researcher to study the sequence of behavior. Also, multiplying the frequency of a given behavior by the time interval gives an estimate of duration.

Continuous Observation

In **continuous observation** the observer records all the behavior of the target subject (or subjects) during each observation session. This method does not usually focus on a specific set of behaviors. Typically, the observer writes a **protocol,** which is a brief narrative in chronological order of everything that the subject does or everything that occurs in a given setting such as a classroom, a faculty meeting, a reading group, or an arithmetic lesson. This approach is often used in exploratory studies to help the researcher identify important behavior patterns that can subsequently be studied using one of the other methods of recording. Since it is virtually impossible to record everything, the observer must be very perceptive and must have a clear understanding of the kinds of behavior that are likely to be important when the protocols are analyzed. To analyze the protocols, the researcher reads them, sets up a

5. Walter R. Borg, "Changing Teacher and Pupil Performance with Protocols," *Journal of Experimental Education* 45, no. 3 (1977): 9–18.
6. Ned A. Flanders, *Analyzing Teaching Behavior* (Reading, Mass.: Addison-Wesley, 1970).

content analysis system that fits the data, and then rereads and classifies the observed behavior into the system she has developed. Continuous observation is also used in ethnographic research, which we discuss later in this chapter. Figure 12.1 is an example of a protocol made during a reading lesson in a second-grade classroom as part of a study of teacher behavior conducted at the Far West Laboratory for Educational Research and Development.[7]

Time Sampling

Time sampling involves selecting intervals out of the total time available for observation and then observing only during the selected periods. This procedure can be used in conjunction with any of the four recording techniques we have just described. The intervals may be selected either at random or on a fixed basis. Random selection provides representative data for behaviors that can occur at any point in the total observational period. For example, an investigator could randomly select a one-hour period each day in which the teacher's use of questions would be observed, since questioning behavior occurs throughout most of the school day. On the other hand, if the researcher was interested in the ways teachers greet their pupils, a fixed period, perhaps the first 15 minutes of the school day, would be selected for observation.

The Observation Form

Once the observational variables to be used in the research study are identified, it is necessary to develop a form on which they can be recorded. A paper-and-pencil observational form can accommodate a variety of scoring procedures. Perhaps the most common scoring procedure is to use a form that describes the behaviors to be observed in considerable detail so that the observer can check each behavior whenever it occurs. This form of scoring requires a minimum of effort on the part of the observer and can usually be developed so as to require the observer to make few inferences. The first item of the observation form presented in figure 12.2 is of this type. This scoring procedure is fairly easy for the observer to use, particularly if the categories are well defined and do not require a high level of inference.

Some studies require that the observer not only record the behavior as it occurs, but also evaluate it on a rating scale. Item 2 of the sample observation form is of this type. It is obvious that this scoring procedure requires a higher

---

7. William J. Tikunoff, David C. Berliner, and Ray C. Rist, *Special Study A: An Ethnographic Study of the Forty Classrooms of the Beginning Teacher Evaluation Study Known Sample Technical Report #75–10–5(A)* (San Francisco: Far West Laboratory for Educational Research and Development, 1975).

Protocol Number: 06
Name of Researcher: Gail
Date of Observation:
Subject of Observation: 2nd Grade Class, Open Class-
           1. room, with two team teacher and two other adults, this
           2. is a joint observation with Elizabeth. I will be
           3. observing two reading groups today, simultaneously,
           4. including 9 children. Out of the 9 children, 2 are
           5. girls, 7 are boys.
           6.
8:30 Noise level 2   7. At 8:30 the noise level is 2. The children have just been
           8. let into the classroom, taking their coats off and
           9. wandering around the room. Several boys are in the corner
         10. fighting, and some girls are sitting on the floor
         11. doing a puzzle. The teacher is walking back and forth
         12. in the back of the classroom not attending the children.
         13. The noise continues and the children are running
         14. around. There is much confusion in the room. The teachers
8:35   15. stand at the desk talking to one another. At 8:35,
         16. Mrs. Tyler leaves the room. The team teacher
         17. stays seated behind the classroom at her desk. At 8:40
         18. Mrs. Tyler comes back into the room. She walks to the
         19. desk at the far-left-hand side of the classroom,
         20. which is a round table, and sits on the edge. She says,
         21. "Blue Group, get your folders and go up in the front.
         22. Green Group, come here." Noise level drops to 1, and
         23. the children begin to follow her orders. She says,
         24. "Anybody lose a quarter." No one responds, and she
         25. repeats the question again with irritation in her voice.
         26. She says, "I know someone lost a quarter
         27. because it was found in the coat room. Look in your
         28. pockets and see." No one says anything. She now

Figure 12.1   Sample of a continuous observation protocol.

level of inference on the part of the observer. The observer must not only record the behavior, she must also evaluate it, and this is much more difficult to do objectively. If she uses a rating scale as part of her scoring procedure, the research worker should avoid the common mistake of attempting to obtain excessively precise discrimination from the observer. Most human behavior studied in educational research cannot be reliably rated on more than five levels. The 3-point rating scale, breaking the behavior observed into such categories as "above-average," "average," and "below average," is often as fine a

29. stands up and pulls a pile of workbooks from across the
30. table over to her. They are the _____ reading work-
31. books. She opens one of them on the top and says,
32. "Ah Daniel!" She says this with a loud sharp voice.
33. She continues, "Your work yesterday was not too bad
34. but you need some work. Evidently there are still some
35. words you don't understand." She thumbs through the rest
36. of his lesson. Danny is standing at the outside of
37. the circle around her, not listening to what she is saying.
38. Mrs. Tyler now stands and gives instructions to the Green
39. Group. She tells them to go through 8 through 13, reading
40. the two stories between those pages and to go over the
41. work in the workbooks that she is about to give back.
42. She tells them that they may sit any place but
43. not together and she says, "And I don't want any funny
44. business." She now opens the next workbook which is
45. Nicole's. She tells Nicole that she is having the
46. same problem that Danny is having without specifying
47. further. Nicole looks up at her with an expectant look
48. on her face. She then looks at a third book and says,
49. "Michelle you're having the same problem." She says
50. "Snatch means to grab. Beach, what does it mean?" Michelle
51. doesn't answer. She has her finger in her mouth and looks
52. anxious. The teacher closes the workbook and pushes it
53. to Michelle. Michelle takes it and walks away, with
54. Nicole. Teacher then opens the next workbook and says,
55. "Mike, I don't appreciate all these circles." She points

Figure 12.1—Continued.

discrimination as can be made with satisfactory reliability. Five-point rating scales, however, are often used in educational research and can be employed effectively in observing well-defined behavior. It is almost never advisable to attempt to obtain ratings for finer than a 5-point scale. Furthermore, the more inference the observer must use in making the rating, the fewer rating levels should be employed. An "Officer Effectiveness Report" that was employed by the U.S. Air Force provides the ultimate example of attempting fine discriminations in the evaluation of characteristics that, at best, can only be differen-

1. Check each question asked by the teacher into one of the following categories (observe for the first fifteen minutes of the class hour):

	Frequency	Total
a. Asks student to solve a problem at blackboard.	xxxx	4
b. Asks student to solve a problem at his seat.	xxxxxxx	7
c. Asks students if they have any questions or if they understand.	xx	2
d. Other.	xxxxx	5
	Grand Total	18

2. Each time the teacher asks a student to solve a problem, rate its level of difficulty on a 5-point scale.

	Frequency	Total
1. Difficult	xxx	3
2.	x	1
3. Average	xxxxx	5
4.	x	1
5. Easy	x	1
	Grand Total	11[a]

[a] The sum here should equal the sum of categories *a* and *b* in item 1.

Figure 12.2   Sample observation form.

tiated roughly. This instrument, for example, required the senior officer to make an evaluation on the individual's cooperativeness. Fifteen levels of cooperativeness were provided by the scale. It is doubtful whether a complex behavior requiring as high a level of inference as "cooperativeness" can be accurately discriminated at more than three levels by most observers.

Figure 12.2 illustrates the way the observers' recording task can be made more simple and accurate by providing a checklist. The first item of the sample observation form in figure 12.2 could have required the observer to write down each question that is asked by the teacher. Since teachers ask questions fairly frequently, the observer would need to do much writing; if the writing demand is excessive, the accuracy of the observer's report is likely to be affected adversely. The use of the four categories that appear in the sample observation form is preferable since the observer's task is simplified and the resulting data are in quantitative form.

After a prototype of the observation form has been developed, the researcher should try it out in a number of situations similar to those to be observed in the research and correct any weaknesses he discovers. A common weakness in prototype forms is that they require the observer to record more kinds of behavior or watch more subjects than can be done reliably. Although observers can be trained to record twenty or more different behaviors, a great deal of training is needed when the number of behaviors exceeds ten.

Similarly, the more subjects the observer must watch, the more difficult the task becomes and as a result the data obtained will be less accurate. In many studies better data will be obtained if the observer watches a random sample of subjects rather than all subjects in the observed situation. For example, in classroom observation the observer can obtain more reliable data on a random sample of six pupils than if called upon to observe every pupil in the class.

Another weakness found in prototype observation forms is that the behaviors to be observed are not defined in sufficient detail. These definitions are used by the observer to determine whether or not a given behavior occurred. They should be detailed and specific and give examples of the behavior taken from observations made by the researcher. They should also give examples of behaviors that are similar but should *not* be recorded so that the observer can compare these with situations that occur during observations. Usually an instruction sheet is attached to the observation form so that these detailed definitions and guidelines are always available to the observers. During observer training these instructions are refined further, as we will discuss later in this chapter.

Standard Observational Schedules

Instead of developing his own observational schedule for a research project, the researcher may prefer to use one of the many **standard observational schedules** that have been developed by educational researchers. In planning an observational study, you should consider the various advantages of using one of these schedules. First, as is true of standardized personality and aptitude tests, standard observational schedules have usually reached a stage of development where they are valid and reliable measuring instruments. Second, use of a standard schedule saves you the considerable amount of time that it takes to develop your own schedule. Third, since most of these standard schedules have been used in a number of research studies, it is possible to compare your findings with those obtained by other researchers using the same instrument. The obvious disadvantage of standard schedules is that they sometimes do not include all the variables that you are interested in measuring. However, in this case you can use just the part of the schedule that you need.

The standard observational schedules that have been developed vary in complexity, the type of behavior they record, and the settings in which they can be used. An exhaustive coverage of classroom forms is provided in *Mirrors for Behavior* and *Evaluating Classroom Instruction* (see Annotated References).

A good illustration of the research contribution that standard observational schedules can make is provided by Wayne Herman's study of how a six-week social studies unit was taught in classrooms of above-average, average, and below-average ability students.[8] Flanders's system of interaction analysis and Medley and Mitzel's OScAR (Observation Schedule and Record) were used to observe classroom interaction. Several interesting differences in teachers' instructional style were found between the three types of classrooms. Analysis of the observational data collected using the Flanders system (which classifies all classroom verbal behavior) showed that teachers of above-average students tend to use more indirect techniques[9] than teachers of average and below-average students. Also, teachers very infrequently criticize above-average and average students, but criticize below-average students to a moderate extent. Another finding was that above-average students tend to talk more than average and below-average students, who, in turn, do not differ from each other in talkativeness. The OScAR data provided somewhat different insights into classroom interaction. The reason is that this observational schedule classifies different behaviors (primarily classroom activities) from the Flanders system. Analysis of the OScAR data indicated that teachers of above-average students spend only half as much class time (7.7 percent) using illustrations[10] as teachers of average students (20.8 percent). Teachers of below-average students rely on illustrations most of all (41.5 percent of class time). Herman's interpretation of this finding is that "this progression should appear because as the intelligence level of the groups decreases there is more need for concrete instructional materials of a visual nature, such as maps, pictures, blackboard, and three-dimensional activities" (pp. 342–43). Further analysis of the OScAR data indicated that students of above-average ability spend more total class time (30.8 percent) in independent seatwork than do students of average (10.6 percent) or below-average (12.6 percent) ability. This finding suggests that above-average students are more independent and less in need of teacher direction.

It should be apparent from this summary of Herman's research project that use of standard observational schedules, such as the Flanders system and OScAR, can yield important insights into the nature of classroom interaction. Since classroom interaction is becoming a topic of increasing interest to educational researchers, the use of these observational schedules should become more prevalent in the future.

8. Wayne L. Herman, Jr., "An Analysis of the Activities and Verbal Behavior in Selected Fifth-Grade Social Studies Classes," *Journal of Educational Research* 60 (1967): 339–45.
9. Indirect techniques include accepting feelings, praising students, accepting student ideas, and asking questions.
10. Illustrations include maps, pictures, and blackboard activities.

Use of Audiotape and Videotape Records

In some situations it is impractical to collect observational data at the same time the critical behavior is occurring. If several of the behaviors to be rated occur at the same time or closely together, the observer's task can be complicated to the point that her observations lose validity. For example, the observer may be required to rate each teacher and student response on one or more dimensions. If teacher-student interaction occurs with high frequency, the observer is likely to be frustrated in her attempts to record all the necessary observational data. Also, we have already noted that observational ratings differ in the level of inference required of the observer. When ratings require a high level of inference, an observer will probably want an opportunity to study the behavior carefully before making a rating. However, in a live observational setting, there is no chance to have several "instant replays" of a critical event. Another situation in which it may be impractical to collect observational data at the time the behavior occurs is when the researcher wants to check on the reliability of observers' ratings. We have discussed elsewhere the desirability of reporting the interrater reliability of observational data, otherwise one has no way of knowing the extent to which observations reflect the biases and idiosyncrasies of a single observer. However, it is not always possible to have two or more observers present at the same time to observe the events on which ratings are to be made. A similar situation occurs when one wishes to have specially qualified observers rate samples of behavior. As an illustration, suppose that one wishes to describe and rate the techniques that children use in the process of drawing pictures. Art teachers are probably the best qualified to make observations, but they may not be free to observe at the time the children are working on their pictures.

It is obvious that all the situations just described present obstacles to the researcher's using the observational method. Audiotape and videotape recorders overcome these obstacles. When recorders are used, it is no longer necessary for observers to make ratings at the time particular events are occurring. These events may be recorded on audiotape or videotape so that they can be replayed several times for careful study or for several observers to rate at their convenience. Therefore, you should consider carefully the advantages of these recording techniques if you are planning to do an observational study. At the same time you should note certain disadvantages. Videotape recorders provide a fairly complete record of behavior, but they are not easy to obtain, and videotape is fairly expensive.[11] Audiotape recorders are much more accessible, but they are limited to recording verbal behavior; also, it is often hard to identify and differentiate among speakers when listening to audiotape. In certain

11. Many universities have audiovisual centers from which videotape recording equipment may be borrowed. Also, if the student's research is being carried out in the public schools, needed equipment may sometimes be borrowed from the schools involved.

situations technical competence is required in order to obtain satisfactory video/ audio recording. For example, it is usually necessary to have more than one microphone and to adjust the camera frequently so that a reasonably complete record of classroom behavior can be obtained.

If these disadvantages are overcome, it is highly desirable to record behavior so that it can be observed and rated at a later time. Sometimes it is not possible to obtain enough videotape or audiotape recorders to use in the main data-collection phase of one's study. However if they are available, one or two recorders can be used to collect samples of behavior to facilitate the development of an observation form and the training of observers. The recordings can be replayed as often as necessary, thus making it easier to develop observational categories and to test the reliability with which observers can use these categories in rating behavior.

Another possibility when a limited amount of videotape is available is to make typed transcripts of the videotaped records. Once the transcript has been made, the videotape can be erased and reused. This approach is especially useful when sophisticated analysis of language is required or when the observer is working with a complex category system or one requiring a high level of inference. Typed transcripts of videotape have been used in many of the Stanford University studies on microteaching and have yielded highly reliable data.[12]

Training Observers

After it has been developed and tried out on a small scale to correct its more serious deficiencies, the observation form should be employed to train the individuals who will conduct the observations required by the research. The first step in the training is to discuss the observation form with the observers, describing each item sufficiently to develop a thorough understanding of what is to be observed and how it is to be recorded. Usually brief and precise definitions of each behavior to be observed should be included on the form or on a separate instruction sheet. The trainee should become very familiar with the form and behavioral definitions before moving to the next level of training. It is usually desirable to test the trainee on this basic information to ensure his mastery.

The researcher should then make videotape recordings of situations similar to those to be observed in the study and replay these *before* the training sessions to fill out the observation form and to be sure that examples of the

12. These studies are described in Walter Borg, Marjorie Kelley, Philip Langer, and Meredith Gall, *The Minicourse: A Microteaching Approach to Teacher Education* (Beverly Hills, Calif.: Macmillan Educational Services, 1970).

behaviors to be observed are present. Then start the training session by showing 10-15 minutes of the videotape. Stop the recorder each time one of the behaviors to be scored occurs, call the trainees' attention to the behavior, and discuss specifically *why* this event fits the definition of the behavior in question. This process of relating actual examples of each behavior to the behavioral definitions helps give each trainee a clear understanding of what is to be observed.

The next step is to set up practice observations in which all observer trainees participate. The videotapes made earlier can be used in the practice observations. Show a brief segment of the videotape, instructing the trainees to record each behavior on the observation form as it occurs. Be sure that trainees are seated so that they cannot see each other's forms, since you wish to determine how accurately each trainee can *independently* record what he has seen. After the videotape has been played, the researcher should individually check each trainee to determine if he has correctly tallied the behaviors he has observed using the observation form completed earlier by the researcher as a criterion. If the observers disagree with each other or with the criterion, as is usually the case, replay the videotape, stopping at each behavior to explain how it should have been recorded, and why. During these discussions the observers' instruction sheet should be revised to include any clarifications that come about as a result of using the observation form. Usually, a few special rules will also be developed during this time to help the observers make decisions about how to record unusual behavior that was not foreseen when the observation form was developed. This process of practice and feedback should be repeated with different videotape segments until you reach the desired level of agreement among the observer trainees. For tallying highly specific descriptive behavior, such as counting the number of times the teacher smiles, the percentage of agreement between observers should be above 90 percent. When the observer must make inferences or evaluations about the behavior he observes, however, 70 to 80 percent agreement is usually considered satisfactory. To determine the level of agreement, check whether observers agreed or disagreed on each behavior that should have been recorded during the observation and divide the number of agreements by the total of agreements and disagreements. Start the training with short segments, but as the observers gain expertise use longer segments until the later phases of training are being conducted for periods that are the same length as the observations that will be conducted in the study.

After the observers have been trained by observing videotape recordings, it is desirable for them to practice further in the setting where they will actually carry out their observations, for example, regular classrooms. They should not, of course, practice in classrooms that will be used in the research, but in similar classrooms. If possible, videotape recordings of these practice sessions should

be made so that after the observation the recording can be replayed and discussed. Research on observer training has demonstrated that programs such
as those we have recommended result in accurate and reliable observational
data.[13]

Once the observers have been trained to the desired level of agreement
and accuracy, the observations should be started promptly since a delay will
result in some loss in observer skills. If the observations are to extend for more
than one week, a weekly refresher training session should be held for the observers. If this is not done the observational data will become less reliable since
the observers will gradually lose the common frame of reference they developed during training. This "observer drift" can be a major source of error in observational studies. If each observer interprets and records the same
behavior differently, it is obvious that no objective information will be produced.

During the training period, in addition to computing percent of agreement for each session, interrater reliability coefficients may be calculated after
every ten practice sessions in order to estimate the degree to which observers
are developing a common frame of reference. These correlations are usually
computed separately for each behavior across the ten sessions. All observers
are compared, pair by pair, to determine if certain observers consistently disagree with their colleagues or if certain behaviors cannot be reliably observed.
Interrater reliabilities should reach at least .70, and much higher reliabilities
can be obtained if training is adequate and observations are of specific behavior.

As the training progresses, it is likely that some observers will be found
who cannot develop a reliable frame of reference. Some persons seem to be
unable to interpret consistently the behavior they observe or in the same way
that it is interpreted by the rest of the group. After a reasonable training period, it is usually advisable to replace these persons with other observers.

Reducing Observer Effect

It is well documented that observers are sometimes not very objective in their
use of observational schedules. When this situation occurs, the research data
will reflect the biases and characteristics of the observer rather than the observational variables that one seeks to measure. It is also well documented that
the presence of the observer can affect the behavior of those being observed.
As a consequence, the research data may reflect atypical rather than naturally

13. See Mark D. Spool, "Training Programs for Observers of Behavior: A Review," *Personnel Psychology* 31 (1978): 853–88, for a review of research on this topic.

occurring behavior. The student planning an observational study should be aware of these unwanted observer effects and take steps to remove or reduce them. They include:

1. *The effect of the observer on the observed.* Unless she is concealed, the observer is likely to have an impact on the observed. For example, an observer entering a classroom for the first time probably will arouse the curiosity of the students and possibly the teacher. The resulting inattentiveness of the students to the teacher may not reflect their usual behavior and thus may provide non-representative observational data. To reduce this effect the observer should not record any observations for at least the first five or ten minutes that she is in the classroom. It may be necessary in some cases for the observer to make several visits to the classroom before students take her for granted and behave as if she were not present. It is also advisable for the teacher to prepare students beforehand for the observer's visit and to introduce the observer when she enters the classroom. This procedure is usually sufficient to satisfy student curiosity and to restore the normal classroom situation within a few minutes.

A more serious problem caused by the presence of the observer occurs when the person or persons being observed are influenced in their behavior by the observer's intentions. Suppose the purpose of an observational study is to record the number and length of dyadic interactions between teacher and student in art classes. If they learn that this is the purpose of the study, teachers will probably increase the frequency of their dyadic interactions, particularly if they are led to believe that this is desirable behavior. As a result, the research data based on recorded observations will be nonrepresentative of the teachers' actual classroom behavior and thus possess little or no validity. It is therefore advisable to meet with the teachers before observations are made. At this meeting the teachers should be informed candidly that they cannot be told the nature of the research project because this might affect their behavior. However, it is good procedure to also tell the teachers that after the observational data have been collected, they will be informed of the study's purpose. Occasionally while the study is in progress a teacher will attempt to learn the purpose of the research from the observer or to secure a copy of the observation form. The training of observers should include directions not to give this information to teachers while the study is in progress.

2. *Observer bias.* This type of bias refers to systematic errors that are traceable to characteristics of the observer or of the observational situation. In contrast to random errors, which are distributed around "true" scores or values, bias usually produces errors in a single direction, yielding scores that are consistently too high or too low. It is doubtful whether any observations we conduct are completely free from bias, and there is evidence to suggest that in

many studies that have a high potential for bias, the investigators do not take sufficient precautions to avoid it.[14]

In the observation process, the observer brings to bear all his past experience, and as this past experience will differ for each observer, it will lead to different perceptions of the situation, different emphases, and different interpretations. Biases, of course, have a much greater chance of operating when the observer is called upon to draw conclusions or make involved inferences from the behavior he has observed. Possible sources of bias should be looked for and eliminated if they are found. For example, it would be unwise to use an observer who was prejudiced against blacks in a study in which he would observe the creative ability of black children and white children in a nursery school. His bias would almost certainly lead him to see more creative behavior among white children and either ignore, misinterpret, or minimize the creative efforts of black children in this group. In addition to racial and ethnic biases, many other subject characteristics have been shown to bias the ratings of some observers. These include social class, physical attractiveness, and labels such as "emotionally disturbed" or "mentally retarded."[15]

The best method to control for the possible presence of observer bias is to check carefully for bias during training when comparative data are available on all observers, and to eliminate any observers whose data appear to be biased. A further safeguard is to assign two observers to each situation to be observed. Generally the combined records of two or more observers provide more reliable data than the record of a single observer. The extent of interobserver agreement can be determined by computing the appropriate statistic. Usually a measure of correlation or a percentage of agreement is obtained. (Correlational statistics are discussed in chapter 10.) When more than one observer is used, each should work independently. If observers work together, one usually influences the other, and the judgments of this observer are therefore given more weight since they are reflected in the ratings of his colleague. Also, when observers work together, each observer's ratings are contaminated by the judgments of the other observer, thus making reliability coefficients spuriously high. In many studies it is not possible to employ two observers for every observation. In this case enough observations are carried out with two observers to check interrater reliability and the rest are conducted with one observer.

3. *Rating errors*. In our discussion of standardized measures of personality, we noted that the validity of these measures is sometimes weakened by the presence of response sets. Some persons will give a socially desirable response to a personality item irrespective of the item's content. Thus, the per-

14. J. A. Salvia and C. J. Mersel, "Observer Bias: A Methodological Consideration in Special Education Research," *Journal of Special Education* 14 (1980): 261–70, reviewed 153 studies having a high potential for bias and found that only 22 percent reported adequate safeguards.
15. See ibid. for a brief review of research on this topic.

son's score on the test is more a reflection of his response set than whether he possesses the personality trait measured by the test. A similar situation is found sometimes with observational rating scales. As a result, several kinds of systematic errors are often found in observational data. Three common errors of this sort are called *error of leniency, error of central tendency,* and *halo effect.*

Some observers assign the same rating to the majority of research subjects even when there are obvious individual differences among them. For example, some observers have a tendency to rate most individuals at the high end of the scale. This tendency is called the **error of leniency.** In studies where the research worker has an opportunity to train his observers thoroughly and has complete control over the situation, the error of leniency is rarely a problem. In many observational studies, however, research workers have relied upon observers over whom they have little control. As an illustration, studies of teacher effectiveness often use the school principal as an observer. It is rarely possible in studies of this sort to train the observers sufficiently to rule out errors of leniency and other rating errors. Therefore, if at all possible the research worker should attempt to train impartial observers.

Another error common in observational ratings is the **error of central tendency.** This error is caused by the inclination of the individual to rate the person he has observed at the middle of the scale. This error is often made in cases where some of the behaviors to be rated have not occurred during the observation. The observer, feeling the need to register some sort of information on the form, rates the individual at the average, or center, of the rating scale.

Still another error frequently encountered is the so-called **halo effect.** This is the tendency for the observer to form an early impression of the person being observed and to permit this impression to influence his ratings on all behaviors involving the given individual. For example, if he forms an initially favorable impression of the person being observed, the observer will tend to rate the individual favorably in subsequent performance areas. An initially un favorable impression can lead to the opposite effect. All three errors—i.e., leniency, central tendency, and halo effect—are most likely to occur when the observer must draw inferences or evaluate abstract qualities rather than record specific behaviors. Thus, it is much easier for these errors to occur when the observer rates such characteristics as "cooperativeness," "integrity," and "interest in the job" than it is when he rates specific behavior such as "shakes hands with the visitor," "rises from his chair when the visitor enters the room," and "offers the visitor a chair."

4. *Contamination.* A frequent flaw in observational studies is contamination. While bias is usually the result of predispositions of the observer, **contamination** occurs when the observer's knowledge of one aspect of a study tends to corrupt by contact his perception of data recorded in another aspect of the study. The most common source of contamination is the influence of the ob-

server's knowledge concerning the performance of the subjects on one of the variables being studied on his observation of another variable. Let us say, for example, that we are doing a study of the human relations skills of successful elementary school principals. Unsuccessful and successful principals could be identified by a composite evaluation made by teachers, parents, and school superintendents. It may then be possible to observe the performance of the successful and unsuccessful principals in faculty meetings and evaluate them on certain human relations skills. If, however, the persons observing the faculty meetings are aware of which principals have been classified as successful and which as unsuccessful, this knowledge will almost certainly influence their perceptions of the principal's behavior.

Contamination is an especially serious problem in master's degree studies because one graduate student often collects all data involved in the study. If she is aware of the dangers of contamination, however, the student can usually avoid it. For example, if we are studying relationships between academic achievement and leadership in the classroom, observations of leadership behavior could be carried out before achievement data are gathered; or the achievement test could be administered, if necessary, but not scored until leadership ratings are completed. Either approach would make it impossible for the observer's perceptions of leadership behavior to be influenced by knowledge of the subject's achievement level.

Observer expectations are also a powerful source of contamination. Research has demonstrated that an observer's expectations can have a significant effect on how she interprets and records what she sees. For example, in a study by Anita Kolman, different observer groups were shown identical videotapes of nursery children at play and were asked to record instances of aggression.[16] One group of observers was told it was viewing middle-class children and to expect a large amount of aggression (MC); another group was told it was viewing lower-class children and to expect a high level of aggression (LC). The third group was told nothing about the children or what level of aggression to expect (CON). Significant differences were found among the three observer groups. The MC observers did see more aggression than the CON observers, which supports the researchers' hypothesis. However, the LC observers saw *less* aggression than the CON observers, a result that was counter to the hypothesis. Remember, all observers were looking at the same videotapes. One of the videotapes showed clear examples of aggression, while the other showed more ambiguous situations that required more observer judgment. More bias occurred when observers viewed the ambiguous situations as the researchers had hypothesized. Thus, both observer expectations and the

---

16. Anita Sue Kolman, "Definition of the Situation and Observer Bias" (paper presented at the annual meeting on the Midwest Sociological Society, April 1975). ED 118600.

ambiguity of the observed situation led to increased bias, but in the case of the LC group, the bias was not in the expected direction.

In an earlier study by Karlton Skindrud, although observers remembered the expectations conveyed by the researchers, these expectations had no effect upon their observations of a videotape of deviant child behavior in a family situation.[17] The author believed no observer contamination occurred because mature, well-trained observers were used. Observer bias or contamination are most likely to occur when observers are not adequately trained, when the observational task is difficult, when behavior to be observed is defined in global or ambiguous terms, and when observer drift from standard code definitions is not controlled.

Observer expectations can also distort results when some form of pre-post observations are to be made. If he knows the expected outcomes of the experimental treatment, the observer may watch more closely for these outcomes on the post-treatment observations. This effect can be avoided by having the observer score tape recordings or typed transcripts of the classroom situation. Under these conditions the investigator should wait until both pre- and post-treatment recordings have been made and then assign tapes or transcripts to observers in random order so that they do not know whether they are observing a pre-treatment or post-treatment recording. An even better method is the "doubleblind" technique in which all tapes or transcripts are number coded and neither the observers nor the person distributing them to the observers knows which tapes or transcripts were made at the beginning and which at the end of the study.

In summary, experience and research evidence indicate that the following precautions should be taken to minimize observer bias, rating errors, and contamination:

1. Make the observational task as objective as possible. Avoid requiring the observer to make evaluations, interpretations, or high-level inferences.
2. Give the observer as little information as possible about your hypotheses, research design, and expectations.
3. Do not reveal to the observer information about the characteristics of your subjects, such as social class, IQ, or composition of experimental and control groups, that he does not need to know.
4. Train observers to a high level of reliability and objectivity, and retrain as necessary to avoid observer drift.
5. Construct your observation form to minimize recording errors.[18]

17. Karlton D. Skindrud, *An Evaluation of Observer Bias in Experimental-Field Studies of Social Interaction* (Eugene, Ore.: Oregon Research Institute, 31 July 1972). ED 072105.
18. A review of recording errors in 21 studies by Robert Rosenthal, "How Often Are Our Numbers Wrong?" *American Psychologist* (1978) 1005–8, found an error rate of about 1 percent. Two-thirds of the errors found were in a direction favoring the researcher's hypothesis.

6. Check for bias when training observers, and eliminate those who submit biased observations.[19]

Computer-Assisted Observation[20]

The observation of behavior in educational and psychological research yields a wealth of valuable information. However, it is a complicated and labor-intensive process. The complexity of behavior and of observation methods leads to technical errors, such as miscoding, as well as problems in achieving and maintaining satisfactory interrater agreement.

Tools have been devised to alleviate some of the technical problems of research observation. For many years, computers and event-recording devices have been used in controlled laboratory studies of animals and in the study of human behavior.[21] More recently, microcomputers[22] and even handheld calculators have been used as tools in observational data collection.[23]

This section describes the use of a microcomputer in combination with the Behavioral Event Recording Package (BERP) as a data-collection and storage encoder for observational studies. BERP features a multichannel event-recording and data-storage device. Ten user-defined keys act as ten independent timing devices (stopwatches) while also recording event sequences.

Our experience indicates that this package can be extremely helpful and cost effective when used with videotape observation. To bring a microcomputer into a classroom might be too obtrusive in some instances. Under these conditions, a keyboard number pad adaptation (with a long ribbon cable) or a handheld calculator would seem to be a less obtrusive means of event recording. However, handheld calculators lack a clock for timed study, and the information must be later transferred to computer storage media.

The BERP package features real-time error prevention. Wild codes are simply not permitted. The direct storage of the data reduces the number of steps required, thereby decreasing the likelihood of error in the transfer pro-

19. An infomative review of observer bias is provided by A. E. Kazdin, "Artifact, Bias, and Complexity of Assessment: The ABC's of Reliability," *Journal of Applied Behavioral Analysis* 10 (1977): 141–50.
20. This section was written by Carl Berger, Mark Shermis, and Paul Stemmer, University of Michigan.
21. See J. G. Baker and G. Whitehead, "Technical Note: A Portable Recording Apparatus for Rating Behavior in Free-Operant Situations," *Journal of Applied Behavior Analysis*, no. 5 (1972): 191–92.
22. See R. A. Owings and C. H. Fiedler, "Measuring Reaction Time With Millisecond Accuracy Using the TRS-80 Microcomputer," *Behavior Research Methods and Instrumentation* 11 (1979): 589–91.
23. See Jeffrey L. Edleson, "An Inexpensive Instrument for Rapid Recording of In Vivo Observations," *Journal of Applied Behavior Analysis* 11, no. 4 (1978): 502.

cess. The ease of use of this system appears to show great promise in increasing interrater agreement. Previous research has shown that event-recording devices generally improve rater accuracy.

The number of keys allows for ten simultaneous behavior codings. This number was chosen so that the observer need only be trained so that each finger represents an event. An experienced user need not look away from the event being recorded.

The package can provide evidence of systematic errors, thus providing a means of observation training.[24] The program could be modified to make a total training package, or without modifications, the data may be used in training to provide the observer-trainees with feedback on Interval-by-Interval and Occurrence Agreement.

In the typical observational study the microcomputer can help with several of the necessary steps. During the observation itself, recording is much easier using the computer than entering data into a manual observation form. When one of the selected behaviors occurs, the observer presses the key that represents the behavior being observed. Pressing the key a second time records the cessation of that behavior. The microcomputer stores the sequence of behaviors as they occur and records the duration of each event. If a second behavior starts before the first is finished, the observer presses the key for the second behavior, and the microcomputer keeps track of both. The BERP permits recording data on ten different behavioral categories simultaneously and timing and recording the duration of each. Without the computer, it would be virtually impossible for the observer to record this amount of information. Since the task of the observer is greatly simplified when she is aided by the microcomputer, there is much less chance of the observer missing events or making coding errors. As the observational task becomes more demanding, the microcomputer's contribution becomes increasingly important since observer errors made during manual recording increase greatly as the demands of the situation approach the observer's capacity to respond.

Several of the steps usually required when conducting an observational study in which data are collected manually and analyzed by a large computer can be done in part or in total by the microcomputer. Steps that can be handled by the microcomputer include:

1. *Recording and timing* the events being observed and transcribing the data onto coding sheets.
2. *Transferring the data* from the coding sheets into computer storage, ready for data analysis.

---

24. See George C. Thornton and S. Zorich, "Training to Improve Observer Accuracy," *Journal of Applied Psychology* 65 (1980): 351–54.

3. *Cleaning up the data* by locating coding errors and detecting "wild codes," which are codes that have no meaning in the coding system being used.
4. *Aggregating and analyzing the data.*
5. *Interpreting the results of data analysis.* Microcomputers have the capacity to produce a variety of graphic data representations, which can greatly help the researcher in understanding his results. Often the cost of doing this activity on a large computer is prohibitive.

Microcomputers offer the promise of an efficient and cost-effective tool. We have found that the micro is most cost-effective when it is used to perform several types of information processing, such as word processing, telecommunication, networking to larger computers, data analysis, graphic representation, and data gathering and storage.

OTHER TYPES OF OBSERVATION

Case Study

The case study, in its simplest form, involves an investigator who makes a detailed examination of a single subject or group or phenomenon. Until recently, this approach was rejected by many educational researchers as unscientific, mainly because of its lack of research controls. However, the increased acceptance of qualitative research methods such as educational ethnography and the use of participant observers has revived the case-study approach. In fact, some researchers consider case study, participant observation, and ethnography as essentially synonymous.[25] Thus they are presented together in this chapter.

The case-study approach has had a long history in educational research and has also been used extensively in other areas of research, such as clinical psychology and the study of individual differences. For example, much of the work of Sigmund Freud and Jean Piaget employed case studies.

Most case studies are based on the premise that a case can be located that is typical of many other cases, that is, the case is viewed as an example of a class of events or a group of individuals. Once such a case has been located, it follows that in-depth observations of the single case can provide insights into the class of events from which the case has been drawn. Of course, there is no way of knowing how typical the selected case really is, and it is therefore rather

25. See Smith in Annotated References at the end of this chapter.

hazardous to draw any general conclusions from a single case study. The main justification for case studies is that they have the potential to generate rich subjective data that can aid in the development of theory and empirically testable hypotheses.[26]

A case study must involve the collection of very extensive data in order to produce an in-depth understanding of the entity being studied. Shallow case studies, which are still being done in education, have little chance of making any useful contribution to educational thinking. For example, a case study recently reported in the literature involved interviewing one teacher for less than ten hours and observing in the teacher's classroom for two class periods.

Several kinds of case studies can be found in the behavioral science literature. These include:

1. *Historical case studies of organizations.* These studies trace the development of an organization over time. Studies of experimental schools such as Summerhill are often of this kind.[27] This type of case study usually relies heavily upon interviews and documents.

2. *Observational case studies.* These studies usually focus on an organization, such as a school, or on some part of an organization, such as a classroom. A group of individuals who interact over a period of time is usually the focus of the study. Such studies are concerned with ongoing groups and generally use participant observation as the major data collecting tool.

3. *Oral histories.* These are first-person narratives that the researcher collects using extensive interviewing of a single individual. For example, a case study could be used to help understand an educational phenomenon like the one-room school or to trace the development of a program for handicapped children as seen by a teacher closely involved in this area over a period of 20 to 30 years.

4. *Situational analysis.* In this form of case study a particular event is studied from the viewpoint of all the major participants. For example, an act of student vandalism could be studied by interviewing the student involved, his parents, teachers, peers, the school principal, and the juvenile court judge. When all of these views are pulled together, they provide a depth that can contribute significantly to understanding the event being studied.[28]

5. *Clinical case study.* This approach is aimed at understanding a particular type of individual, such as a child with a specific learning disability. Such case studies usually employ clinical interviews and observations but may also in-

26. See Robert E. Stake, "The Case Study Method in Social Inquiry," *Educational Researcher* 7 (1978): 5–8, for an interesting philosophical article supporting the case-study method.

27. See A. S. Neill, *Summerhill* (New York: Hart, 1960).

28. See Bogdan and Biklen in Annotated References at the end of this chapter for a more detailed discussion of the aforementioned kinds of case studies.

volve testing and other forms of data collection. The usual goals are to better understand the individual and her disability and identify possible treatments. Teachers also conduct clinical case studies. For example, a case study might be conducted by a teacher to determine why a given child is having difficulty with reading.[29]

Participant Observation

The **participant observer,** by virtue of being actively involved in the situation she is observing, often gains insights and develops interpersonal relationships that are virtually impossible to achieve through any other method. The level of participation may be varied. In complete participation the individual becomes a full member of the group and her role as observer is concealed. Or her role may be somewhat open but she may function primarily as a participant, keeping her observational activities as unobtrusive as possible. This level is commonly used in studies of organizational behavior such as those often carried out by industrial psychologists. Or she may function primarily as an observer but may participate enough to gain rapport with the group and develop a better understanding of the group's functions and relationships. This level is typical of anthropological studies such as the work of Margaret Mead.

Complete participation, although sometimes the best way to collect accurate information, involves many problems. Perhaps most serious of these is the ethical problem of deception and the reaction that will occur if the deception is discovered. Another problem that must be considered when observing small groups is that the observer's participation may significantly modify the phenomenon she is studying. The participant observer may also become emotionally involved and lose objectivity, in which case the data collected will be of dubious value. The observer will also have difficulty recording her observations and must rely on memory or use hidden recording equipment. Finally, the complete participant cannot take advantage of many special situations that arise without risking detection. For example, contacts with persons who are rejected by the group may provide valuable information but must be limited in order to preserve the observer's own group status.

Although participant observation is not widely used in educational research, the method is well suited for the investigation of many educational problems. For example, studies of the organizational structure of school districts, teachers' unions, and other educational organizations and problems re-

---

29. For a recent example of a case study in education, see J. Raim and R. Adams, "The Case Study Approach to Understanding Learning Disabilities," *Journal of Learning Disabilities* 15 (1982): 116–18.

lated to effective group interaction such as in team-teaching situations or parent-teacher activities seem appropriate for this method.

Louis Smith developed the following criteria to judge the validity of a study in which participant observation is used:[30]

1. *Quality of direct on-site observation.* Smith noted that individuals, organizations, and groups often "mask" what is really going on from the researcher. Masking is much more difficult to do with participant observers than with other kinds of data collection, such as questionnaires.

2. *Freedom of access.* In doing participant observations in the school setting, broad access is essential. If the administrator succeeds in steering the observer to particular schools, teachers, or events, then biased data will probably be gathered. Similarly, free access to attend classes, meetings, and so forth unannounced and without prior arrangements is necessary to obtain a normal, unbiased picture of what is going on.

3. *Intensity of observation.* A great many hours of observation are needed when this method is used. As the amount of direct observation increases, the chances improve of obtaining a valid and credible picture of the phenomena being studied. As intensity increases, the data are likely to improve for a number of reasons. First, the likelihood of "faking" or "putting on an act" is decreased. Second, since schools operate over long, established cycles—the semester or year—it is necessary to observe the entire cycle in order to gain a complete picture.

4. *Qualitative and quantitative data.* Although traditionally ethnographic data have been almost entirely qualitative, there is a trend in educational ethnography to collect both qualitative and quantitative data. The use of recordings, such as videotape, permits both qualitative and quantitative analysis. Smith considers arguments about these two forms of data to be "pseudo-issues" and sees a gradual merging of the two views.

5. *Triangulation and multimethods.* This refers to the strategy of using several different kinds of data, such as tests, direct observation, interview, and content analysis, to explore a single problem or issue. Although educational ethnography is built primarily upon participant observation, this method should be supplemented by other data-collection procedures if possible.

6. *Sampling of data.* Since the participant observer cannot see everything that is relevant in the situation being studied, some procedure for getting a representative sample of the total data universe is necessary. The first step is to get a picture of the total territory that is relevant to the observer's goals. In a school this could include the principal, parents, teachers, students, and nonteaching staff in a variety of settings such as the classroom, faculty lounge, cafeteria, and playground. Then, with the total amount of observation time in

---

30. See Smith in Annotated References at the end of this chapter.

mind, the observer can develop a sampling plan that covers the entire territory to some degree.

7. *Unobtrusive measures.* The participant observer should be alert to unobtrusive cues that provide insights into the behavior being observed. Such cues can do much to provide the observer with a clearer picture of what is going on. For example, a teacher who is always late for appointments with the observer may be giving an important cue about his or her attitude, and this could be probed.

Ethnographic Research

This method was designed by anthropologists and is sometimes called the *anthropological field-study approach.* An *ethnography* can be defined as an in-depth analytical description of an *intact* cultural scene. Although anthropologists have usually used the participant observation method in their ethnographics in order to obtain an insider's viewpoint, educational researchers frequently conduct ethnographics with either participant or nonparticipant observers or both. The main characteristic of ethnographic research is that the observer uses continuous observation, trying to record virtually everything that occurs in the setting being studied. The specific procedure usually followed by the nonparticipant observer is to make lengthy handwritten notes that give a continuous account of the classroom activities and interactions (see figure 12.1). The participant observer usually makes an audio or video recording and analyzes it after the observation. Or he may make very brief notes during the observation and enlarge on these immediately after the observation. For most educational studies, such as those concerned with classroom interactions, educational researchers have generally used nonparticipant observation because a more complete and accurate record is obtained. Also, they have collected data over a much shorter period of time than is customary in anthropological field studies. Such deviations from the procedures developed by anthropologists have resulted in rather severe criticisms of educational researchers using ethnographic techniques.

Anthropologists employ ethnographic techniques within the context of a value system that is quite different from the values of most other behavioral scientists. The main elements of this value system are:

a. *Phenomenology:* which requires the researcher to develop the perspectives of the group he is studying, that is, to adopt the "insider's" viewpoint.
b. *Holism:* emphasis on attempting to perceive the big picture or the total situation rather than focusing upon a few elements within a complex situation as is usually done in educational research.

c. *Nonjudgmental orientation:* since judgments, hypotheses, or preconceptions may distort what the researcher sees, the emphasis is on recording the total situation in qualitative terms without superimposing one's own value system.

d. *Contextualization:* requires that all data be considered only in the context of the environment in which it was gathered.

Educational researchers have been accused of using ethnographic techniques without accepting or understanding the values that the enthnographers consider an essential part of this methodology.[31]

In most observational research, the researcher starts with a set of hypotheses and develops an observation form that is designed to collect specific information related to these hypotheses. In ethnographic research, researchers do not start with specific hypotheses. In fact they try to put aside specific expectations or preconceptions in order to avoid the danger that these will bias what they see in the observational situation. They are likely to start with a broad theoretical framework or with tentative working hypotheses that may provide some general guidelines to the observer about what behavior may be important. For example, an ethnographic study of elementary classrooms used the categories from an earlier study to focus the perceptions of the observers (see table 12.1).[32] Note that these questions focus the observer but contain no preconceived hypotheses.

Detailed notes are needed because the ethnographer believes that only through the study of a complete sociocultural system such as a school, a classroom, a PTA chapter, or a teachers' union can the system and the behavior of individuals in the system be understood. In other words, the ethnographer rejects the study of the individual outside of the context in which he functions. As the observational data accumulate, the researcher tries to develop hypotheses that help to explain or understand the phenomena observed.

Such hypotheses are therefore much more thoroughly *grounded* in the real world than are many of the hypotheses that emerge from armchair speculation in the behavioral sciences and are often referred to as *grounded theory* or *grounded hypotheses*. Thus, the ethnographic method tends to generate hypotheses that can then be tested using further observation or other methods such as correlational or experimental research.[33]

---

31. See David M. Fetterman, "Ethnography in Educational Research: The Dynamics of Diffusion," *Educational Researcher* 11, no 3 (1982): 17–22.
32. This table was taken from William Tikunoff et al. (see Annotated References at the end of this chapter). The table is based on Jules Henry, "The Cross Cultural Outline of Education," *Current Anthropology* 4 (1960): 269–305.
33. See George E. Overholt and William M. Stallings, "Ethnographic and Experimental Hypotheses in Educational Research," *Educational Researcher* 5, no. 8 (1976): 12–14.

TABLE 12.1

Major Categories in Henry's Cross-Cultural Outline of Education

I. On what does the educational process focus?

II. How is the information communicated (teaching methods)?

III. Who educates?

IV. How does the person being educated participate?

V. How does the educator participate? (What is his attitude?)

VI. Are some things taught to some and not to others?

VII. Discontinuities in the educational process.

VIII. What limits the quantity of information a child receives from a teacher?

IX. What forms of conduct control (discipline) are used?

X. What is the relation between the intent and the results of education?

XI. How long does the process of formal education last?

To summarize, the ethnographic method has a number of advantages and disadvantages. Among the advantages:

1. It provides a very complete picture of the environment being studied, and since these studies usually extend over several months, they give a longitudinal perspective not present in most educational research.
2. It is more likely than other research methods to lead to new insights and hypotheses.
3. The hypotheses or theories developed are grounded solidly in observational data gathered in a naturalistic setting.
4. Since the observer does not start with specific hypotheses, he is less likely than the conventional observer to overlook phenomena that do not fit his expectations.

Some of the disadvantages of the ethnographic method are:

1. A very alert and sophisticated observer who can write clearly and rapidly is needed. Even if persons with considerable training in sociology or social anthropology are employed, it is still necessary to train them further in observational techniques.
2. A great many hours of observation are needed to understand the environment being studied. Most ethnographic studies extend over several months and some over two or three years. This makes the original research very costly and also makes it very difficult for other scientists to replicate the research.

3. The observational records are very long and very difficult to quantify and interpret.
4. Since the observations are subjective and since checks of interrater reliability usually cannot be made, the observer's biases or preconceived ideas may seriously distort the findings.
5. It is virtually impossible to observe and write down everything that occurs in the classroom. Thus, the observer is constantly called upon to make instant decisions on what to write down and what to omit.
6. The observer often becomes an active participant in the environment she is studying. This can lead to role conflicts and emotional involvement, which can reduce the validity of the data being collected.[34]

Nonreactive Measures

All research requires some measurement. In educational research, paper-and-pencil tests are the dominant form of measurement, but methods such as interviews and questionnaires are also widely used. A major problem encountered in using such measures with human subjects is that the subjects are aware that they are being measured and often react in ways that tend to produce inaccurate or distorted information. In our discussion of demand characteristics (see chapter 6), we mentioned that the typical research subject uses cues from the research environment to come to conclusions about the purposes of the research and the expectations of the researcher. Since different subjects perceive and react to the research situation in different ways, a variety of errors may be introduced.

A main source of cues available to the subject are the measures employed in the research. Measures vary greatly in their degree of reactivity, that is, the degree to which the subject is aware of being measured and of the information the measure is attempting to obtain. The more reactive a measure is, the greater is the potential for distortion by the subject. For example, a self-esteem scale currently in use includes these items: "All in all, I am inclined to feel that I am a failure" and "I wish I could have more respect for myself."[35] Although many subjects will respond honestly, the purpose of the items is not difficult to discern; the *potential* for distortion is therefore large.

E. J. Webb and his associates identified several errors in subject re-

---

34. See Le Compte and Goltz in Annotated References at the end of this chapter for further information on ethnographic research.
35. John P. Robinson and Phillip R. Shaver, *Measures of Social Psychological Attitudes* (Ann Arbor: University of Michigan, Institute for Social Research, 1973), p. 83.

sponses that can occur as a result of using reactive measures.[36] Briefly these errors include:

1. *The guinea pig effect.* This effect occurs because of the subject's awareness of being tested. Although it does not necessarily follow that awareness leads to measurement errors or distortion, the probability of such errors increases as the subject's awareness of being measured increases.

2. *Role selection.* When the subject is selected for participation in research, he is forced into a role-defining decision, that is, "What kind of person should I be as I respond to these questions?" If the role selected by the person as research subject differs from his role in similar natural situations, then his responses will be invalid, even though the subject is not giving dishonest answers. For example, in a study of air force officers, one of the authors found considerable differences between their responses to situational test questions related to on-the-job activities and their actual behavior in similar real situations. Interviews revealed that in framing their situational test answers, most adopted the role of officers "who always follow air force regulations to the letter." In real situations most adopted the role of officers who ignored or "bent" the regulations when common sense so dictated.

3. *Change due to reactive measurement.* Another problem that occurs when using reactive measures is that the initial measure may bring about real changes in what is being measured. For example, a scale designed to measure racial attitudes may, by the use of direct statements, make the subject more sensitive to some of the illogical aspects of racial prejudice and consequently change his attitudes. Such change obviously introduces an error into the research procedures that can lead to invalid conclusions about the effect of the experimental treatment.

4. *Response sets.* Finally, subjects often develop response sets when answering questions on reactive measures. For example, a response set frequently adopted by subjects is the *acquiescence set*—the tendency to agree rather than disagree. Any such response pattern clearly introduces an error into the subject's responses.

These errors do not occur when nonreactive (or "unobtrusive") measures are used. *Nonreactive measures* are characterized by the fact that the data are collected in a natural setting, and the subjects are unaware that they are being measured. For example, suppose you are interested in studying how teachers individualize instruction. To measure this variable you might give the teacher a questionnaire, interview the teacher, or observe the teacher and record behavior that relates to individualization. Because individualization of instruction is generally regarded as desirable, the teacher may exaggerate her use of individualization in responding to a questionnaire or interview. When an observer

36. See Webb et al. in Annotated References at the end of this chapter.

is present, the teacher may "put on an act" and display behavior that is far from typical.

Although the researcher can take some steps to reduce the teacher's reaction, such as establishing rapport and giving the teacher assurances of confidentiality, the potential for reaction would remain. Another approach to this measurement problem would be to look for nonreactive measures of individualized instruction. One possibility would be simply to record the variety of textbooks and workbooks in use in each classroom. If she is individualizing instruction, a teacher should be using a wider variety of curriculum materials than a teacher who instructs her class as an undifferentiated group. Another unobtrusive measure would be the written work that students complete during a class period. In a classroom that has individualized instruction, students will be working on different assignments, whereas in a conventional classroom all students will be working on the same assignment. Therefore one can measure the extent of individualization in the classroom by counting the number of different assignments being worked on by students during a particular period of time.

Educational researchers have not exploited the uses of nonreactive measures to a significant degree, yet the classroom and other educational settings contain many artifacts which can be used to measure research variables.

One of the authors has worked with a number of nonreactive measures in school settings. In one project where the objective was to estimate student attitude toward school authority, the principal mentioned over the school public address system that there was a great deal of littering in the school halls and urged students to use wastebaskets. The weight of litter collected from halls the day before the announcement was compared with that collected the day after the announcement. A reduction was considered indicative of a favorable attitude toward the principal, while an increase suggested a negative attitude. Samples of such measures may be found in Appendix E.

Webb and his coworkers have collected many examples of unobtrusive measures used in research studies. Some of them are listed here to suggest their usefulness as a substitute for behavioral observations, interviews, or questionnaires:

> The floor tiles around the hatching-chick exhibit at Chicago's Museum of Science and Industry must be replaced every six weeks. Tiles in other parts of the museum need not be replaced for years. The selective erosion of tiles, indexed by the replacement rate, is a measure of the relative popularity of exhibits.
>
> The accretion rate is another measure. One investigator wanted to learn the level of whiskey consumption in a town which was officially "dry." He did so by counting empty bottles in ash cans.

The degree of fear induced by a ghost-story-telling session can be measured by noting the shrinking diameter of a circle of seated children.

Chinese jade dealers have used the pupil dilation of their customers as a measure of the client's interest in particular stones, and Darwin in 1872 noted this same variable as an index of fear.

Library withdrawals were used to demonstrate the effect of the introduction of television into a community. Fiction titles dropped, nonfiction titles were unaffected.

The role of rate of interaction in managerial recruitment is shown by the overrepresentation of baseball managers who were infielders or catchers (high-interaction positions) during their playing days.

Sir Francis Galton employed surveying hardware to estimate the bodily dimensions of African women whose language he did not speak.

The child's interest in Christmas was demonstrated by distortions in the size of Santa Claus drawings.

Racial attitudes in two colleges were compared by noting the degree of clustering of Negroes and whites in lecture halls.[37]

In addition to being effective substitutes for conventional educational measures, nonreactive measures are very useful as supplements to such measures. A serious threat to our ability to generalize research findings is the possibility that these findings are due, at least in part, to the unique characteristics of the instrument we used to measure the variables being studied.[38] If we use several different kinds of instruments to measure the same variables, and if similar results are obtained from these different instruments, then we can be much more confident that our results are valid. Nonreactive measures are especially useful when used in conjunction with conventional reactive measures because they usually employ much different measurement approaches.

Although nonreactive measures seem to have some important advantages as tools in educational research, they also have some limitations that must be considered. *Validity* is a problem for many nonreactive measures. As Webb and his colleagues point out, it is often difficult to determine just what is being measured. For example, the lost-letter technique (a nonreactive measure) has been used frequently to estimate attitudes related to sensitive topics such as political elections because a direct approach probably would not produce valid responses. In the lost-letter technique, large numbers of letters are addressed to organizations that reflect different attitudes on an issue. These letters are

37. Ibid.
38. The degree to which the results of an experiment can be generalized (that is, applied to other situations and samples) is called external validity. This concept is discussed in chapter 15.

then "lost," that is, dropped in various locations designed to sample the geographical area (such as a city) being studied.

The technique is based on the assumption that a person who finds a letter is more likely to mail it if the address represents a candidate or attitude that he supports. Thus the rate of returns for letters representing different attitudes should reflect the percentage of persons holding each attitude in the community under investigation. In several election studies, however, the proportion of letters returned failed to predict the election results, thus raising doubts about the validity of the technique.

It has been hypothesized that some addresses arouse more curiosity in the finder than others and that letters with these addresses are more likely to be opened and read than mailed. This hypothesis was supported in a recent study. Letters were addressed to Education Research Project, Marijuana Research Project, and Sex Research Project. Letters addressed to Education Research Project were most often returned. Letters addressed to Sex Research Project were least often returned, and of those that were returned, more had been opened.[39] Because curiosity and other variables may affect the return rate, the lost-letter technique cannot safely be asumed to provide a valid measure of attitudes.

Reliability is also a problem with many nonreactive measures; many of these measures are essentially similar to a one-item test or to one question from a questionnaire. Even for nonreactive measures for which reliability can be computed, the data are of limited use to other researchers because most such measures are designed to study a very specific attitude or question and are rarely used more than once. In contrast, conventional measures, such as achievement tests, personality inventories, and attitude scales, are used in many studies. Over a period of time a useful body of knowledge about the measure is developed.

Sensitivity. Many nonreactive measures deal with dichotomies such as mail vs. don't mail, support vs. oppose, or volunteer vs. nonvolunteer. Such data are much less sensitive than a Likert-type attitude scale that measures the individual's level of agreement along a continuum that typically includes 5 or 7 points.

The lack of sensitivity in nonreactive measures can be overcome somewhat by developing *sets* of nonreactive measures that attempt to measure different facets of the same question or attitude. This is not as easy as it may seem, however, and brings us to some of the practical limitations of nonreactive measures. First, a great deal of creativity is required to think of ways to

39. Lee Sechrest and J. B. Grove, "The Lost Letter Technique: The Role of Curiosity" (unpublished manuscript, Florida State University, 1980).

measure phenomena nonreactively. Second, if a set of nonreactive measures is used, much more time and effort are required than if a direct measure of the same variable was administered. Third, since nonreactive measures are generally unique to a single research project, no compilations (such as Buros's *Mental Measurements Yearbooks*) are available to the researcher who wants to use them.

CONTRIVED OBSERVATIONS

Naturalistic Contrived Situations

Two kinds of contrived observations are used in behavioral science research. In the first, which employs **naturalistic contrived situations,** the researcher intervenes in a natural situation in a manner than cannot be detected by the subject; thus the naturalness of the situation is preserved. In the second, *situational testing,* the situation is totally artificial, and the subject is aware of this fact. The main reason for manipulating the situation is to assure that the events of interest to the researcher will occur. In simple naturalistic observations many hours of observation might be required to record one two-minute event. For example, suppose the researcher wants to observe the responses of teachers to such behavior as cheating, fighting, or open defiance by pupils. Since these behaviors occur at a very low frequency in most classrooms, a great deal of observer time would be needed to gather data on a reasonable sample of such behavior. By using pupil confederates, contrived situations can be set up to collect the necessary data in a reasonably short time.

Another advantage of establishing contrived situations to be observed is that the level of intensity of the situation can be manipulated. For example, in a study of pupil cheating, opportunities to cheat involving several levels of risk can be set up. In fact, the classic studies of Hartshorne and May on pupil cheating employed just such situations.[40] Observing behavior at several specific and clearly defined levels of intensity, while fairly easy in contrived situations, is in many cases virtually impossible in natural situations.[41]

There are two serious limitations to observing in contrived situations. First, in many cases believable situations cannot be contrived without arousing the suspicion of the subjects. Second, difficult ethical problems may arise because

40. H. Hartshorne and M. A. May, *Studies in the Nature of Character*, vol. 1, *Studies in Deceit* (New York: Macmillan, 1928). These classic studies and others by the same authors made extensive use of contrived observation. The ingenuity of their work still sets a standard for this field.
41. For a recent example of a study using contrived observation, see Robert D. Foss and Carolyn B. Dempsey, "Blood Donation and the Foot-in-the-Door Technique: A Limiting Case," *Journal of Personality and Social Psychology* 37 (1979): 580–90.

of the deception involved. When one or both of these problems rule out the use of naturalistic contrived observation, a similar technique, situational testing, can be employed.

Situational Testing

Situational testing is another form of contrived observation in which the subjects are aware of the fact that they are playing a role. The research worker devises a situation and assigns appropriate roles to the subjects, who are asked to play these roles to the best of their ability. The situations are aimed at bringing out the specific types of behavior that the researcher is interested in observing. Originally developed by social psychologists to study leadership behavior and small-group interaction, situational testing has many applications for the educational researcher. For example, many studies have attempted to identify the factors related to successful teaching or successful administrative behavior through the use of personality inventories and other paper-and-pencil measures. The results of these studies have been disappointing, probably because it is difficult to break down the complex behavior patterns that teachers or principals display in their work, and study them piece by piece. Situational testing permits a study of the total behavior pattern and thus seems more likely to provide insight into the characteristics required for success in complex activities.

Like other forms of contrived observation, situational testing has advantages over the observation of behavior in natural settings. By setting up the situation, the research worker can control, to a greater degree than is usually possible in the naturalistic contrived situation, the behavior that is likely to occur. This permits her to focus the observation on behavior that appears to be critical in the area being studied. In order to observe such critical behavior in a natural situation, it may be necessary for the observer to be present for weeks or even months.

The artificial situation also permits much more careful training of the observers. Inasmuch as she has a good idea of the types of behavior that will occur, the research worker can develop observational rating forms that fit the situation specifically and can train her observers in the specific situations that they will later observe in the collection of research data. Because a number of subjects can be exposed to essentially the same situation (although each, of course, will respond differently), it is much easier to obtain comparable data on the behavior through this technique than through observation of behavior in natural situations or naturalistic contrived situations.

In situational tests the subjects are usually aware of the observer's presence, although in some cases the observer watches through a one-way mirror.

In naturalistic contrived situations, the observations in many cases are covert, and hidden recording devices are used to collect the data. Both approaches can produce satisfactory data, but generally it is easier to develop an effective observational procedure in situational testing because of the higher degree of control by the researcher.

The principal criticism of situational testing is that the situation itself is artificial and therefore may not give an accurate indication of how the individual would behave in a natural situation. In using role-playing situations in research, however, the authors have been impressed by the degree to which subjects appear to forget that they are involved in an artificial situation. Particularly in situations that lead to emotional interaction between the subject and actors, it appears that most subjects become deeply involved in the situation, and many seem to forget, at least for the moment, that the situation is an artificial one.

Perhaps the principal disadvantage of situational testing for the graduate student is the time required to develop and carry out a project using this technique. Small-scale situational studies, however, can be carried out by the graduate student. For example, parent-teacher conference situations could be developed and used in a study of teacher behavior. In research problems concerned with human relations, situational testing offers perhaps the best chance of producing meaningful data.

Several types of situational tests might be adapted to educational research. We will briefly discuss three of these: the leaderless-group discussion, team problem-solving activities, and individual role-playing situations.

Leaderless-Group Discussion

In a **leaderless-group discussion,** a group of subjects (usually six or eight) is given a problem by the research worker and asked to discuss this problem and arrive at possible solutions. Observers record the behavior of the different group members. The technique of the leaderless-group discussion is said to have been developed originally around 1925 to study leadership behavior in the German army.[42] More recently, this technique has been used to study decision making and interaction in various military groups, student groups, and executive-groups in business. Its value is that it provides a good simulation of important situations that occur in real life. For example, the behavior of school board members in a leaderless-group discussion working on a problem presented them by the researcher is probably quite similar to the behavior of these same individuals as they tackle the problems they confront in real-life school board meetings. Consequently, ratings of leadership, cooperation, and teamwork made

---

42. H. L. Ausbacher, "History of the Leaderless Group Discussion," *Psychological Bulletin* 48 (1951): 383–91.

on the basis of observations of leaderless group discussions have been found to have high predictive validity. In education this technique could be used to study such problems as decision making by school boards, leadership behavior among schoolchildren at different levels, and teacher interaction in faculty meetings.

Team Problem Solving

Team problem solving usually involves a situation where a team is presented with a problem that it is called upon to solve. These problems differ from the leaderless-group discussion in that in addition to discussing solutions, the team arrives at a solution and attempts to carry it out. Problems involving the escape of the team from a prison compound or getting the team across a difficult physical barrier have been used in research by military psychologists. Observers may be assigned to evaluate total team activities or to evaluate the behavior of individual members of the team. This technique has been used for the most part in the study of military leadership.[43] However, it could be applied to research in a number of educational areas, such as studies of player interaction in team sports, studies of group behavior in high school clubs, and studies of work groups in parent-teacher projects.

Individual Role Playing

The individual role-playing situation is a form of situational testing that is generally aimed at collecting research data in a situation where only one research subject is involved, usually in a key role. The situation may also involve actors who are trained to play other roles necessary to bring out the subject's behavior that is to be evaluated. The subject is usually given material that describes the situation in which he is to work and sometimes discusses the nature of the problem he will attempt to solve and the identity of other persons who will participate. He studies this material prior to the start of the situation, arrives at his solution or method of handling the problem, and then attempts to carry out this solution in the role-playing situation. In observing his behavior in the situation, it is possible to evaluate his decisions, but more important, it is also possible to evaluate his skill in carrying them out. For example, one of the authors participated in a study aimed at developing criteria for measuring the effectiveness of elementary school principals.[44] In this study each subject played the role of a principal in several different situations aimed at revealing different aspects of the behavior important in the elementary principal's position. Six

---

43. Ernest Tupes, Walter R. Borg, and A. Carp, "Performance in Role-Playing Situations as Related to Leadership and Performance Measures," *Sociometry* 21 (1958): 165–79.
44. Walter R. Borg and J. A. Silvester, "Playing the Principal's Role," *Elementary School Journal* 64 (1964): 324–31.

situations were developed. In each of these the person being tested took the part of the principal. Actors were trained to take other roles called for. In one of these situations, the person tested was given the following instructions:

Instructions to Principal

You are the principal of a large elementary school of about 1000 pupils, from kindergarten to sixth grade, in a city of about 30,000 population. The schools in the city are up-to-date, progressive, and have a high rating. The people in the community are proud of their schools and support them enthusiastically.

There is a Mr. Jones waiting to see you about getting his son registered in school. Mr. Jones is a successful businessman who is active in civic affairs, is well liked, and has a lot of influence in the community. He is proud of his children (two of them are already in school), and he is interested in giving them every opportunity to grow and develop.

It seems that, when he attempted to enroll his son in kindergarten, the son was turned down because he was five hours too young. Ms. Roberts was so busy enrolling new pupils that she did not have time to discuss the matter with Mr. Jones and just told him that his son did not come up to the age requirement. Mr. Jones was a little disturbed and has asked you for an appointment to discuss the matter. He will probably try to get you to make an exception for his child.

You have had problems before on the age requirements for enrollment, so take a few minutes to think it through. The superintendent is out of town for ten days, and a decision has to be made before he returns.

Main Points:

1. Mr. Jones is an important man in the community.
2. Entrance age requirements or some other entrance requirements are necessary.
3. You are proud of your school and its high rating.
4. You cannot afford to have the public unhappy about the school.
5. You have 15 minutes to spend with Mr. Jones, and you should make a decision within the time limit.

The actor trained to play the role of Mr. Jones had the following instructions:

Instructions to Actor

You are a successful businessman in a community of about 30,000 population. You are active in civic affairs and interested in the progress of the community. You are generally well liked and have considerable influence.

You are the father of three children and are very proud of your family and interested in their welfare. Two of your children are already in school and are well adjusted and doing very good work. You have your own set of cumulative records on each child that you keep up-to-date. These records are complete and show that your children are superior.

Your youngest boy, Edward, was just turned down when you tried to get him enrolled in the kindergarten because he was five hours too young. This disturbed you because the records you received from the private nursery school Edward has been attending show that his IQ is 136; he is well above the average in physical size and development; he is socially well adjusted; he is in excellent health; and is an active, alert, and happy boy.

You know he is ready for school and that he will make a good adjustment. You feel that it is in the child's best interest to start now, and if they will not take him into the public schools you will have to enroll him in a private school. You do not want this extra expense, and besides you are a taxpayer and have donated a lot of time and money for public welfare and feel that your children have a right to public education.

You think that the chronological age rule used to determine who is ready for school is old-fashioned and silly, and you know that your boy is more ready to enter kindergarten than 90 percent of the children being enrolled.

You did not like the way Ms. Roberts turned you down when you tried to get Edward enrolled because she did not take time to listen to the reason why you thought Edward was ready for school. So you decided to go to the principal about it. This bothers you because you are a busy man, and you do not like to waste time over something that seems so unreasonable and wrong.

You are not acquainted with the principal, Mr. Smith, but you are well acquainted with the superintendent of schools. You know the superintendent is a reasonable man and you tried to see him, but he is out of town for a few days, and this enrollment has to be taken care of now or it will be too late.

When you go to the principal's office, you present your problem and wait for his reaction.

There are several possible approaches the principal might follow:

1. He might dogmatically say no. If he does, threaten to make a public issue of it. You have rights as a taxpayer; your boy is superior, and so forth. Just do not take no for an answer. Do not hesitate to show your anger under those circumstances.
2. He may try to win you over without yielding—here again you should point out that your boy is better prepared for kindergarten than most of the children who were accepted because he has been in private nursery school and the test results show him to be superior.
3. He may refuse to yield but agree to study the policy and see how exceptions

could be made. But your boy is ready now and the policy could be studied and rules made for exceptions later.

4. He may accept Edward if it is kept quiet, as a special favor, and so on. You do not want any underhanded admission because the boy is qualified to go in the "front door," on his own merits, and so on.

5. He may accept Edward without qualifications. If he does, tell him that your neighbor has a boy who has been in the same nursery school that Edward attended. There is a complete set of records showing that this boy is superior also. He is only 15 days younger than Edward, and his parents would like to get him enrolled also.

Keep in mind that you are an important man, that the records show that Edward is superior, that his experience in the private nursery school gives him an added advantage, that you think the chronological age rule is no good, and that other superior children should also be allowed in.

Situations such as these seem to provide a better basis for evaluating some of the complex human-relations skills needed by a principal than any number of trait-oriented personality, aptitude, or interest measures.

A highly significant study using role-playing situations to study school administrator behavior was carried out at Columbia University.[45] In this study the subjects were introduced to a mythical school district through the study of handbooks, motion pictures, and participation in meetings, and then played the role of a principal attempting to solve administrative problems related to the school and district.

In a more recent study, students at different grade levels ranging from first grade through college played the role of teachers in evaluating student achievement. Important insights into the way that students perceive teachers emerged.[46]

Observations Made by Untrained Groups

Most of our discussion of observational studies to this point has been concerned with closely controlled scientific observation. In many educational studies, however, it is not possible to maintain this control over the observational situation. We now discuss techniques that provide less precise scientific data

45. John K. Hemphill, Daniel E. Griffiths, and Norman Fredericksen, *Administrative Performance and Personality: A Study of the Principal in a Simulated Elementary School* (New York: Teachers College Press, 1962).
46. See Oren Harari and Martin V. Covington, "Reactions to Achievement Behavior from a Teacher and Student Perspective: A Developmental Analysis," *American Educational Research Journal* 18 (1981): 15–28.

and are to some extent less direct, as they are based on the observations and recollections of special groups whom we cannot train thoroughly or control closely. This type of observation is much more likely to be subjective and biased. Nevertheless, in many instances the very subjectivity of the observations may be of value to the researcher. For example, the leadership ability of students could be determined by trained adult observers. However, nominations of leadership ability by a student's peers may be of more value in predicting a student's later standing in her peer group, even though these nominations are not based on objective observations.

The Anecdotal Record

One technique used quite commonly in education is the **anecdotal record.** Anecdotal records are generally based on teacher observations and involve descriptions of behavior that the teacher considers typical of the individual described. With some training teachers can provide anecdotal records of considerable value to the scientist. The anecdotal record should be an objective description of the child's behavior without interpretations by the observer. In preparing the instructions and forms for anecdotal records, the research worker should strive toward as great objectivity as possible. The most serious danger in anecdotal records is that the teacher will write these records while emotionally upset about the incident being described. For example, in compiling anecdotal records dealing with disciplinary problems and misbehavior, the teacher is much less likely to be objective than an observer who is not directly involved in the disciplinary situation.

Sociometric Techniques

Sociometric techniques are designed to measure the social structure of a group and to appraise the social status of each individual with respect to other members of his group. A number of different techniques can be used to collect these data. In the usual approach, each group member is asked to select persons in the group most preferred by him on the basis of a specific criterion. For example, he may be asked to indicate the three persons with whom he would most like to work on a committee assignment. In studies involving classroom groups, pupils are often asked to indicate persons with whom they would most like to do an assignment, near whom they would prefer to have their desks, and so on.[47] J. L. Moreno, in the earliest development of sociometric

---

47. For a recent example of a study using sociometric techniques to measure pupil peer relationships, see Thomas F. Tyne and William Geary, "Patterns of Acceptance-Rejection Among Male-Female Elementary School Students," *Child Study Journal* 10 (1980): 179–90.

measurement, used such methods as a means of rearranging groups of school-children so that they could study together more harmoniously.[48] Occasionally selections of least preferred individuals are also made. In another version of the sociometric technique, the individual is asked to identify persons whom he believes have chosen him. The choices that he believes were made can then be compared with actual choices in order to obtain an indication of his insight into his social position. Still another type of sociometric measure is the "guess who test." These measures contain descriptions of various social roles, and subjects are asked to indicate the group member who best fits each role. For example, the researcher might present a group of students with these descrip-tions:

"This student would make a good class president."

"This student would be the most fun at a party."

"This student is the smartest in my class."

"If I had difficulty with arithmetic, I would ask this student for help."

The instructions would direct each student to write down the names of one or two students who fit each description.

Sociometric techniques are often used to measure popularity among stu-dents in a classroom. Since popularity among one's peers is an important per-sonal attribute, many researchers have investigated factors that might be re-lated to popularity as measured by sociometric techniques. An interesting study of this type was carried out by J. W. McDavid and H. Harari.[49] They investi-gated whether people, like objects, tend to be judged favorably or unfavorably by their labels, that is, by their first name. Their sample consisted of 59 fourth and fifth graders who belonged to one of four youth groups at a community center. These students were asked to indicate on a 3-point scale how much they liked or disliked each of 49 different names (being all the first names of those children in the sample). Two social desirability ratings were completed for each name. One rating (SDI) was the mean of the ratings made by the members of the youth group to which a particular student belonged. The other rating (SDO) was the mean of the ratings made by nonmembers of the youth group; the purpose of this rating was to minimize the possibility that a student would rate a name in terms of an actual person whom he knew rather than as a label. Once these social desirability ratings of names had been obtained, the popularity status of each student was established by the sociometric technique of having students nominate others with whom they would like to play to-gether, and so on. The correlation between a student's popularity and the so-cial desirability of his or her name was high (r for SDI was .63, and r for SDO

48. J. L. Moreno, *Who Shall Survive?* (New York: Beacon, 1953).
49. John W. McDavid and Herbert Harari, "Stereotyping of Names and Popularity in Grade-School Children," *Child Development* 37 (1966): 453–59.

was .49), leading McDavid and Harari to conclude that "the child who bears a generally unpopular or unattractive name may be handicapped in his social interactions with his peers" (p. 458).

Supervisory Ratings

Ratings, such as those made of teachers by their principals or of principals by their superintendents, provide a commonly used method of gaining data concerning the behavior of subjects in educational research. Supervisory ratings, of course, are difficult to conduct on a scientific and tightly controlled basis. In some studies the supervisor makes special observations as part of the research plan, but as he has already formed an opinion of his subordinates prior to the time these observations are made, this opinion will inevitably have an effect upon his observational ratings even if he tries to be objective. Under these conditions we may be sure that observed behavior that agrees with the observer's bias is most likely to be noted and recorded. "Halo effect" also operates strongly in this type of evaluation. In many cases, however, the behavior of the individual as seen through the eyes of his supervisor, although different perhaps from the objective behavior of the individual, still has an important meaning in educational research. For example, a researcher may be interested in studying factors related to promotion or nonpromotion of teachers. Principals' ratings of the teacher's competence may be an important factor in predicting promotion and therefore should be obtained, even though in some instances these ratings may not be objective.

The Critical-Incident Technique

One form of observational rating that has been employed to a considerable degree in recent years is the **critical-incident technique** developed by John Flanagan.[50] This technique, as usually applied, involves studying the performance of one group of individuals (such as teachers) by asking another group of individuals (such as principals) to describe "critical incidents" that relate to the performance of the first group. In vocational studies, the informants are usually supervisors, but the method can be used whenever a group can be identified that has information about the performance of another group.

The researcher usually uses interviews to obtain from the supervisor descriptions of the subject's specific behavior patterns that are considered to be critical to the skills being studied. Some studies of military leadership ability, for example, have used the critical-incident technique. One of the authors once had the opportunity to read hundreds of the critical incidents collected by Flan-

---

50. John C. Flanagan, "The Critical-Incident Technique," *Psychological Bulletin* 51 (1954): 327–58.

agan in his research on military leadership. In reading these incidents, it was apparent that many of the incidents recorded would not be considered "critical" by a psychologist, because they were global evaluations and general comments about the subject's performance rather than specific incidents involving the subject. Perhaps the most serious problem encountered in using the critical-incident technique is to obtain incidents from the individuals interviewed that seem to be truly critical to the behavior or skills being studied. If incidents can be collected that are truly critical, that truly differentiate between successful and unsuccessful behavior, then this method can be a very useful research approach.

The critical-incident technique seems to be well suited to many educational problems, particularly those involving the qualifications of school administrators and teachers. In one such study, the researcher was interested in how educators viewed professionalism in the field of education.[51] Specifically, Leles was concerned with whether educators have the same notion of professional and nonprofessional behaviors as do other occupational groups. The critical-incident technique permitted collection of a large amount of data on this subject. Leles asked teachers, administrators, counselors, and others to recall an incident that involved nonprofessional conduct on the part of an educator. The use of the critical-incident technique was a simple yet effective alternative to training observers and having them carry out lengthy observations of professional and nonprofessional conduct in a variety of educational settings. To give an idea of the data that can be collected by this technique, some of Leles' reported incidents are presented in the following paragraphs:

> In coaching, we are often asked to do things for administrators. Once last year, a friend of mine who was a coach had to chauffeur women around to various schools. These women were very influential, and the administrators were afraid of them, so the coaches more or less became ambassadors of goodwill to them. We hated every minute of it.

> My principal took a master copy from my files (book report form), had copies made, and then presented them to our faculty meeting as his own idea. This was done without my knowledge or permission, although the form was original with me. Other teachers reported similar incidents with the same principal.

> A teacher who, while chairman of the Salary Committee, used classroom time to carry on duties related to that position. This was an elementary situation, and the children were put to work at busy work.

51. Sam Leles, "Using the Critical Incidents Technique to Develop a Theory of Educational Professionalism: An Exploratory Study," *Journal of Teacher Education* 19 (Spring 1968): 59–69.

This same teacher, who exercises a good deal of control over many of the personnel, voices long and loud protests over teachers associating with custodial help, etc. This, she says, is unprofessional.

Many teachers in my building have children standing in the halls because they are unable to cope with their behavior in the classroom. I believe that much of this stems from failure to provide for individual differences and the discipline in the classroom.

Several instrumental music teachers in the area are receiving 10 percent kickbacks from the musical instrument dealers who sell instruments to their students. Such awards (in confidence of course) are made in a direct cash handout or accumulated into something like a grand piano.

What seems to me to be unprofessional behavior is the discussion by teachers in the teachers' lounge. By this I mean discussing students in a derogatory manner.

Arriving late and leaving early. There have been examples of teachers who do not show up at the school at an appropriate time—time enough to enable students to talk with the teacher if necessary before classes—and they leave immediately after the last bell—again not permitting the students an opportunity to talk with the teacher.

English teacher approaches superintendent and board of education with regard to large classes and the lack of time to work with children on their writing of themes. She wanted more help or fewer students. Superintendent answered by accusing her in presence of board of education of not being able to handle classes. Some superintendents do not want problems to exist and will deny their existence. (pp. 67–68)

CONTENT ANALYSIS

Types of Studies Employing Content Analysis

"**Content analysis** is a research technique for the objective, systematic, and quantitative description of the manifest content of communication."[52] The raw material for the research worker using the content-analysis technique may be any form of communication, usually written materials, but other forms of com-

---

52. Bernard Berelson, *Content Analysis in Communication Research* (Glencoe, Ill.: Free Press, 1952), p. 18.

munication such as music, pictures, or gestures should not be excluded. Textbooks, high school compositions, novels, newspapers, magazine advertisements, and political speeches are but a few of the sources available. Content
analysis is often used in conjunction with observational studies. The researcher
tape records classroom verbal behavior, for example, and makes a typed transcript from the audiotape. The content of the transcript is then analyzed in
order to measure variables formulated by the researcher.

Most content analyses in education have been aimed at answering questions directly relating to the material analyzed. These analyses have generally
been concerned with fairly simple classifications or tabulations of specific information. Content analyses of pupil compositions, for example, can give us a
classification of grammatical and spelling errors as well as information on the
frequency of different types of errors. This information can be directly applied
to the revision of English courses or the development of remedial programs. A
content analysis of current textbooks in first-year algebra can tell us such things
as What topics are covered by all books? What emphasis is placed on each
topic? In what sequence are topics usually presented? What mathematical terms
are introduced? What system of symbols is most frequently used? Such textbook analyses are often carried out by test publishing companies that produce
standardized achievement tests in order that their tests can be constructed to
have high content validity. Among the important early content analyses carried
out in education were simple frequency counts of words in order to identify
those words most commonly used in the English language.[53] Such word lists
then formed the basis for determining the readability of textbooks and for the
development of elementary reading textbooks and spelling lists. However,
readability is a function of other factors besides frequency of word occurrence.
Therefore, later researchers attempted a more complex content analysis of textbook materials in developing readability formulas.[54] Other areas of education
that have been studied using content analysis include the analysis of propa-
ganda; the sociological effects of reading; the treatment of blacks in history
textbooks, the Soviet Union in American textbooks and nationalism in children's literature; television programs; the readability of books and newspapers; and the social ideas in McGuffey readers.[55] It may be seen from these
examples that content analysis can be a valuable tool for obtaining certain types
of information useful in identifying or solving educational problems.

Whereas most early studies employing content analysis relied on simple

53. Edward L. Thorndike, *A Teacher's Word Book of the Twenty Thousand Words Found Most Frequently
    and Widely in General Reading for Children and Young People* (rev. ed.; New York: Teachers Col-
    lege Press, 1932).
54. Irving Lorge, "Predicting Readability," *Teachers College Record* 45 (1944): 404–19; and Rudolf
    Flesch, *How to Test Readability* (New York: Harper & Row, 1951).
55. See Berelson, *Content Analysis*, pp. 199–200, for an extensive listing of research using content
    analysis.

frequency counts of objective variables (e.g., spelling errors), recent studies more often aim at using content analysis to gain insights into complex social and psychological variables. Such studies are much more difficult to carry out than the simple frequency studies and often depend on a high level of sophistication of the researcher in psychology, sociology, or other behavioral sciences.

For example, a recent study compared the kinds of words used by black children aged three, four, and five.[56] Such research can give us valuable insights into theoretical issues related to the development of affective and cognitive processes in young children. This study also employed a computer to conduct the content analysis and tried out wireless microphone-transmitters to gather samples of the children's language. The use of modern technology can remove most of the tedious and time-consuming operations that have been required by earlier content analyses and should permit researchers to work with larger samples and explore more complex relationships.

A recent trend in content analysis studies is to consider not only content frequencies but also the interrelationships among several content variables, or the relationship between content variables and other research variables. An illustration of this trend in content analysis is provided by Zahorik's study of the types of feedback statements that teachers use to inform students about the adequacy or correctness of their responses.[57] Teacher feedback includes statements such as "All right," "Fine," "Why did you say that?" and "Could anyone give us another point?" To study teacher feedback behavior, Zahorik tape recorded and transcribed discussion lessons of third-grade and sixth-grade teachers. The content of these discussions was then analyzed by means of an instrument developed for the study, which contained 25 categories for classifying teacher feedback. In the first part of the data analysis, Zahorik simply computed the frequencies with which different types of teacher feedback were given. Then, more sophisticated analyses of the content data were made. Teachers' use of different types of feedback was related to grade level of the classroom, purpose of the lesson (introduction-readiness discussions versus development discussions), teachers' use of questions, and quality of student answers. Such analyses can yield valuable insights into the nature of classroom interaction. One of the main findings of Zahorik's study, for example, was that teachers' verbal feedback tends to be rather limited in variety and depth: "Only a few types of feedback are used with regularity and these types may be less informational than others which are used infrequently" (p. 149). Such a finding might serve as the basis for improving teachers' instructional practices. Zahorik

56. James C. Montague, Jr., "A Preliminary Methodological Verbal Computer Content Analysis Study of Preschool Black Children," *Journal of Educational Research* 69 (1976): 236–40.
57. John A. Zahorik, "Classroom Feedback Behavior of Teachers," *Journal of Educational Research* 62, no. 4 (1968): 147–50.

raises the possibility that a wider variety of types of feedback, including types that seem to carry more information, would benefit learners. He suggests that teachers develop wide feedback repertoires, including more emphasis on elaborate types of praise, direct negatives such as simple reproof-denial, reasons or explanations as to why a comment had or lacked value, and clues or prompts regarding what to do next to improve a response. These types of feedback should improve the learning process, since they give learners a clearer idea of the worth of their responses.

Planning a Content-Analysis Study

Specifying Objectives

The first step in planning a content-analysis study is to establish specific objectives to be achieved or hypotheses to be tested. Content analyses usually aim at achieving one of the following kinds of objectives:

1. *Produce descriptive information.* For example, a content analysis of themes found in history textbooks used in Soviet schools provided descriptive information that gave us a better understanding of what the average Soviet citizen knows about history and how he might interpret current international situations.[58] Most content analysis in education is aimed at producing descriptive information.

2. *Cross-validate research findings.* Content analysis is a useful tool to check research findings obtained from studies using other methods, such as the interview. For example, the findings of a study of the written communication deficiencies of college freshmen based on interviews with English professors could be checked by conducting a content analysis of a sample of freshman compositions. We can place much more confidence in research evidence that holds up when the research is replicated using a different methodology. Since content analysis is nonreactive and often less costly than other methodologies, this approach is well suited for replication.[59]

3. *Test hypotheses.* Content analysis can be used to explore relationships and to test theories. For example, a recent study by Richard Brown used content analysis of newsmagazine coverage of the family-planning issue to test Lewin's theory of gatekeeping.[60]

58. Charles D. Cary, "Natural Themes in Soviet School History Textbooks," *Computers and the Humanities* 10 (1976): 313–23.
59. For an article that discusses the use of content analysis in conjunction with other research methodologies, see Joan E. Broderick, "A Method for Derivation of Areas for Assessment in Marital Relationships," *American Journal of Family Therapy* 9 (1981): 25–34.
60. See Richard M. Brown, "The Gatekeeper Reassessed: Return to Lewin," *Journalism Quarterly* 56 (1979): 595–601.

Locating Relevant Data

Once objectives have been spelled out, the next step in the content analysis is to locate data that are relevant to these objectives. Klaus Krippendorff observed that anything connected with the phenomenon that interests the researcher qualifies as data for content analysis.[61] In most content analysis studies in education, the relationship between the content to be studied and the researcher's objective is clear and direct. However, the investigator should be alert to subtle and indirect relationships that can provide information relevant to his hypotheses.

A recent study of changes in black identity and self-image provides an excellent example of the content analysis of indirect evidence.[62] The researchers hypothesized that the black power movement that started in the mid-1960s led to a positive change in black identity and self-perception. They reasoned that if such a change had taken place, a search of black publications would reveal a decrease in advertisements for hair straighteners and skin-bleaching cremes and an increase in advertisements offering Afro wigs or using models with Afro hairstyles. They then conducted a content analysis of 272 issues of *Ebony* magazine to determine the number and proportion of such advertisements for each year from 1949 to 1972. The results in fact demonstrated major changes, starting around 1966, in the numbers of advertisements of the selected types. For example, the annual mean number of ads for hair straighteners was 9.69 from 1961 to 1966 and 6.51 from 1967 to 1972. Similarly, a very sharp increase in ads featuring Afro hairstyles or wigs started in 1967. This study shows that content analysis can employ unobtrusive and indirect measures to draw inferences about attitudes and behavior. In many cases this indirect approach to sensitive issues probably produces more valid information than direct methods such as interview or questionnaire.

Gathering Contextual Evidence

Having selected the data he intends to analyze, the researcher must next establish an empirical link between the data selected and the inferences he plans to make from these data. In other words, he should create a rationale that the content-analysis data are really related to his objective or hypothesis. The usual ways of providing this contextual evidence include presenting a theory or model, reviewing previous research, or citing expert opinion that supports the relationship between the data and the objectives upon which the study is based.

For example, in the study of black identity just discussed, the authors cite

---

61. See Krippendorff in Annotated References at the end of this chapter.
62. See J. Spencer Condie and James W. Christiansen, "An Indirect Technique for the Measurement of Changes in Black Identity," *Phylon* 38 (1977): 46–54.

expert opinion and previous research to support their contention that the "natural look" is related to the quest for black identity. However, the investigators have still taken a rather large inferential leap in equating a change in advertising in *Ebony* magazine to a change in black identity. It is not difficult to think of alternate hypotheses that could explain the changes in the number of ads related to Afro hairstyles, hair straighteners, and skin-bleaching cremes. For example, (1) some of these products may have contained substances that led the Food and Drug Administration to ban their use; (2) the Afro style may be a fashion fad that has nothing to do with black identity, although it does result in more Afro ads and fewer hair-straightener ads; (3) *Ebony* may be read primarily by a certain group of blacks (e.g., middle class), and the results of the study may not reflect a general change in black identity.

We are not suggesting that any of these alternative hypotheses are correct. The point is that as the content-analysis data become less directly linked to the research objectives, it becomes a much more difficult task to demonstrate that these data really measure what the researcher thinks they measure. Thus, there are both advantages and disadvantages to the use of indirect data in content-analysis studies.

Developing a Data Sampling Plan

The next step in planning a content-analysis study is to develop a plan to obtain a representative sample of the universe of possible data that has been identified. Content analyses can be misleading or biased if the research worker does not use satisfactory methods for selecting the sample of content to be studied. In many content analyses, all content specifically pertinent to the research problem is studied. For example, an analysis concerned with the educational theories of a single author would usually be conducted by analyzing all the writing of the author in question. Content analyses dealing with topics that draw from a very large body of documentary materials, however, usually select material to be analyzed by some sampling technique. A study of trends in educatonal philosophy as reflected in newspaper editorials over the past fifty years would involve a very large volume of "raw material." In this case a sampling technique would be used to reduce the content to be analyzed to manageable size. One might, for example, limit one's selection to newspapers published every fifth year; thus only ten years of newspaper publishing need be considered rather than all fifty years. Next, one might use a table of random numbers. If the numbers 125, 5, 300 appeared, one would examine newspapers published on the 125th, 5th, and 300th day of the year. One could go through the table of random numbers until a specified number of editorials on educational philosophy had been selected for each year.

A problem that the researcher faces in many content-analysis studies is that all the data in his universe are not available. Of course, some data are unavailable for accidental or random reasons. These do not usually pose a problem for the researcher because in most cases he can randomly select another unit to replace the missing one without incurring any serious danger of bias. For example, a librarian may have misfiled an occasional issue of a daily newspaper.

In some cases, however, there are nonrandom reasons for the survival of certain kinds of data and the loss of other kinds. For example, in cleaning out his files, a psychiatrist may retain files of patients with whom he was successful and destroy files for those with whom he has failed because he hopes someday to incorporate his successful cases in a book. On the other hand, his colleague in the next office may do just the opposite because he has no plans to write a book and believes that his failures may eventually return for additional treatment. In either case, the data that remain are a biased sample of the universe. Such bias is referred to by Krippendorff as "self-sampling bias."[63] When the researcher suspects that self-sampling bias has occurred, she should make a special effort to obtain the missing data; if this fails, she should try to determine why the data are missing and how their absence may affect the representativeness of the sample.

Sampling data for a content-analysis study may employ any of the sampling procedures discussed in chapter 7. However, random sampling is generally the best procedure and is much easier to achieve in content analysis than in most other kinds of research.

Developing Coding Procedures

Once the content has been selected using appropriate sampling techniques, a coding or classification system needs to be developed for analyzing the content. When possible, it is desirable to use a coding system that has already been developed in previous research. First, this option saves the time needed to develop one's own system, which for most content-analysis studies is a difficult and time-consuming task. Also, the use of available content-analysis dictionaries or standard coding categories permits comparisons with other studies that have used the same system. Consequently, the research project is more likely to make a contribution to theory and knowledge in the field under investigation. A number of content-analysis dictionaries have been developed, and these should be carefully checked to see if one of them meets the researcher's needs. For example, the *Harvard III Psychosociological Dictionary* is frequently used in conjunction with content analysis in both psychology and sociology. This dictionary includes content categories in such areas as persons,

---

63. See Kryppendorff in Annotated References at the end of this chapter.

roles, cultural objects, cultural processes, psychological processes, and social-emotional actions.[64]

If the researcher cannot locate a content-analysis dictionary or classification system that fits his research, he will have to develop his own because it is necessary to define content categories that measure the variables indicated by the research objectives or hypotheses. For example, if one were interested in the frequency of positive and negative self-references in first and last counseling interviews, it would be necessary to develop a set of categories and rules for deciding what types of statements are to be scored. Objective categories such as specific words (e.g, all occurrences of the word "I") are relatively easy to develop and score. Content categories involving inference or evaluation on the part of the rater are more difficult to develop. Since content analysis usually depends on frequency counts, it is very important to control for the length of the communication. For example, one may find that clients of student counseling services make more negative self-references in the first interview than in the last interview. Before interpreting this finding, one must examine the length of interviews to make sure they are comparable. It may be that clients talk more in the first interview than in the last interview. Thus, the apparent change in frequency of negative self-references can be attributed to the change in clients' talkativeness.

After initial development of the content classification system, one should determine whether several raters can use it with a high degree of interrater reliability. If interrater reliability is low, it will be necessary to identify points of ambiguity in the content classifications system and to clarify them. Sometimes it is helpful to develop a set of scoring rules in order to increase the reliability with which the classification system can be used. This was the case in a study carried out by one of the authors.[65] It was hypothesized that creative persons would be more sensitive to aesthetic, dynamic, and affective properties of objects than noncreative persons. To test the hypothesis, the frequency with which creative persons used certain kinds of noun modifiers (adjectives, participles, predicate adjectives) in describing Rorschach inkblots was compared with the frequency of noun modifier use by noncreative persons.[66] In order to ensure that raters would reliably tally appropriate noun modifiers, it

64. For an example of a study that used this content analysis dictionary, see J. C. Montague, Jr., E. C. Hutchinson, and E. Matson, *Computerized Verbal Content Analysis of Institutionalized Versus Community Retarded Children* (Little Rock: University of Arkansas, 1973), ED 085949.

65. Meredith D. Gall, "An Investigation of Verbal Style in Creative and Noncreative Groups" (Ph.D. dissertation, University of California, Berkeley, 1968).

66. For example, in describing one of the Rorschach inkblots, a creative architect said, "It's *live* and *growing, soft* and *fragile* . . . could move in the wind." By contrast, a noncreative person might say, "Just looks like an inkblot . . . side things look like two animals."

was necessary to make up a set of rules for scoring noun modifiers to resolve the ambiguities which had become apparent in initial development of the classification system. The following lists the rules for scoring noun modifiers:

Rule 1: Noun modifiers usually immediately precede or follow a noun, or they immediately follow: is, are, looks, appears, seems.

Rule 2: Words immediately preceding or following nouns are almost always scored as a noun modifier if they end in -ed, -ing, -en, -y, -some, -like, -ful.

Rule 3: Do not score these adjectives or adjectives of the type: a, an, the, this, that, these, those, his, her, our, your, my, its, their, some, any, no, other.

Rule 4: Do not score adjectives having to do with number, such as first, second, one, two, few, many, each, both, every.

Rule 5: Do not score adjectives referring to location on the blot (e.g., "the *top* part of the blot looks like. . .") or on an object percept (e.g., "looks like the *top* part of a beetle") such as top, bottom, upper, lower, side, back, entire, whole.

Rule 6: Score such adjectives as "huge," "tremendous," "tiny," but do not score these specific words: big, large, small, little.

Rule 7: Do not score color words, such as white or black. The exceptions are combination colors, such as "blue-gray" (which is scored as one word) and words like "reddish."

Rule 8: Do not score adjectives that are an integral part of a noun phrase, such as praying mantis, United States. However, the adjective "high" in the phrase "high heels" is scored, since it refers to a particular style of shoes.

Rule 9: Only those noun modifiers that reflect one or more of the seven qualities previously stated are to be scored. This means that several types of adjectives are not scored, such as location (e.g., "marine life"), general class of human, animal, or inanimate (e.g., "human figures," "bearskin rug," "cloud formation," "anatomical shape"), critical-evaluative words (e.g., "obvious," "strange," "appropriate," "fantastic").

Rule 10: The noun modifiers that are not usually scored because of rule 9 are scored if they modify a quality noun (e.g., "a sense of *anatomical* form," "an *underwater* quality").

By the use of such rules, it is possible to achieve near-perfect agreement between raters in scoring Rorschach protocols for appropriate noun modifiers. Interrater reliability is very important in content analyses in which human coders are employed and should always be computed and reported.

Planning Analysis Procedures

The final step in planning a content analysis is to decide upon the specific analytical procedures to be used. As in most other research, statistical procedures are needed to summarize the data and aid in its interpretation.

By far the most common method of summarizing content-analysis data is through the use of absolute frequencies, such as the numbers of specific incidents found in the data, and relative frequencies, such as the proportion of particular events to total events. Descriptive statistics such as the mean, median, and standard deviation are also used to compare the occurrences of different events. In content analyses that explore relationships, simple cross tabulations or chi-square analysis are often used since these techniques are suited to the analysis of categorical data.[67]

The Computer in Content Analysis

In the past 20 years the computer has revolutionized content analysis. Many common operations, such as tallying word frequencies, are extremely dull and time-consuming when done by hand and can be carried out at great speed and accuracy and at small cost by computers. This permits the analysis of large sets of data that would be practically impossible using manual procedures. The technology is approaching the point where, using optical readers, it will soon be possible for the entire works of an author to be transferred from the printed page directly into the computer with virtually no human interface.

Perhaps the most serious problem to be overcome by the content analyst in using computers is the need to develop highly detailed computer programs to take the place of the coding instructions that would be used by human coders. While the human coder can interpret, draw inferences, and apply common sense to the making of coding decisions, the computer cannot do anything it is not programmed to do. Thus, developing a computer program to code content-analysis data requires the researcher to think through the process much more carefully than would be required if human coders were to be employed.

Fortunately, a number of computer programs have already been developed for use in content analysis. Perhaps the most widely used of these is the General Inquirer.[68] These programs (1) identify systematically instances of words

---

67. A variety of multivariate techniques, such as discriminant analysis and cluster analysis, are also used. See Peter R. Monge and Joseph N. Capella, eds., *Multivariate Techniques in Communication Research* (New York: Academic Press, 1980).

68. See P. J. Stone et al., *The General Inquirer: A Computer Approach to Content Analysis* (Cambridge, Mass.: M.I.T. Press, 1966). For a study using the General Inquirer, see E. Aries, "Sex Differences in Small Group Behavior" (paper presented at the conference on Sex Roles in American Society, Troy, New York, 1 May 1976), ED 136089.

and phrases specified by the researcher, (2) count occurrences, (3) print and graph tabulations, (4) perform statistical analyses, and (5) sort and regroup sentences according to whether they fit a particular category system.[69] For example, by punching spelling lists from different textbooks onto IBM cards, one can have them stored in the computer. Then by using appropriate retrieval routines, one could have the computer print out a variety of research data such as a set of words common to every spelling list, a set of words unique to each spelling list, a readability index computed for each spelling list, and even a classification of the words in each list by themes and types (e.g., sports, science, adjectives, number of syllables).

In closing we should like to note that the content-analysis technique is very well suited for small-scale educational research projects, and it is surprising that more students do not carry out content-analysis studies. It is usually much easier to obtain communications such as textbooks and newspapers than it is to obtain research subjects. There is less opportunity to bias the data collection process, since communications are usually "nonreactive." Also, communications can be analyzed directly, whereas one generally needs to collect data first from subjects by means of interview, standardized test, or observation before proceeding to the data analysis phase of the research project. In short, many graduate students may find that the content-analysis technique can provide a basis for their research project that is significant yet economical in terms of time and money. Although we have learned much about word frequency, spelling and grammatical errors, and textbook content, we know almost nothing about the more subtle effects of the different forms of educational communication upon the personality, goals, and values of our youth.

MISTAKES SOMETIMES MADE IN OBSERVATIONAL RESEARCH

1. Student does not sufficiently train her observers and thus obtains unreliable data.
2. Uses an observation form that requires too much from the observer.
3. Fails to take adequate precautions to avoid having the observer disturb or change the situation she is to observe.
4. Asks observers to make excessively precise discriminations among behaviors.
5. Does not use at least two observers in order to determine interrater reliability.

69. Stone et al., *The General Inquirer.*

6. Does not ensure that observers work independently of each other.
7. Allows contamination of data collection to occur.
8. Does not use random sampling techniques when appropriate.

ANNOTATED REFERENCES

Observation

Ahola, J. A., and Lusthaus, C. "The Development of the Participant Observer's Role in the Elementary and Secondary School." Paper presented at the annual meeting of the American Educational Research Association, Boston, April 1980.

This paper provides much practical information concerning a participant-observation study carried out by one of the authors. Such topics as gaining entree and acceptance in schools and classrooms, the development of the observer's role, and the impact of teacher and student behavior on the observer's role are discussed. The article gives the reader insights into this research methodology that are seldom provided in the typical research report.

Boehm, A. E., and Weinberg, R. A. *The Classroom Observer—A Guide for Developing Observation Skills.* New York: Teachers College Press, 1977.

This book provides a brief and practical introduction to classroom observation. Most of the major parts of an observational study are discussed including problem definition, behavioral categories, sampling behavior, and recording behavior.

Dunnette, Marvin D., ed. *Handbook of Industrial and Organizational Psychology.* Chicago: Rand McNally, 1976.

See the chapter on field research methods for a useful discussion of participant observation. This chapter also covers systematic observation, interviewing and questionnaires. This is also an excellent source for students who are planning studies in educational organization. Includes very extensive list of references.

Schatzman, Leonard, and Strauss, Anselm L. *Field Research.* Englewood Cliffs, N.J.: Prentice-Hall, 1973.

This book discusses field research from the viewpoint of the sociologist. It is a practical guide, dealing with such topics as entering the environment to be observed, getting organized, watching, listening, recording, and analyzing data. A useful source for the student who plans to use interviews or observations in research.

Selltiz, C.; Wrightsman, L. S.; and Cook, S. *Research Methods in Social Relations.* New York: Holt, Rinehart and Winston, 1976.

This book discusses the use of observation in several behavioral sciences and briefly describes several observational methods. The section on participant observation provides useful guidelines on making field notes.

Observational Instruments

Borich, G. D., and Madden, S. K. *Evaluating Classroom Instruction: A Sourcebook of Instruments.* Reading, Mass.: Addison-Wesley, 1977.

This book reviews a large number of instruments that can be used to evaluate teacher and pupil behavior. Many are observation forms. Most of the information that a researcher needs to select an instrument is provided.

Herbert, J., and Altridge, C. "A Guide for Developers and Users of Observation Systems and Manuals." *American Educational Research Journal* 12 (1975): 1–20.

The authors have developed 33 criteria that can be used to evaluate observation instruments. These criteria are useful to the researcher who wishes to select an instrument from those available as well as providing guidelines for the researcher who plans to develop his own instrument. Each criterion is discussed, and many examples are given.

Simon, Anita and Boyer, E. Gil. *Mirrors for Behavior III: An Anthology of Observation Instruments.* Wyncote, Pa.: Communications Materials Center, 1974.

The original anthology was published in 1967 in 6 volumes and covers 26 observation instruments. Volumes 7 through 14, published in 1970, cover 53 additional instruments. Two supplemental volumes to the 1970 edition covered an additional 12 observation systems. This 1974 anthology covers observation instruments selected from fields such as group dynamics, psychotherapy, medicine, industry, and anthropology, as well as providing an extensive coverage of instruments related to education. A total of 99 observation systems are covered which deal with a wide range of phenomena including cognitive and affective processes, nonverbal behaviors, and interactions with materials. Brief abstracts are provided on the 99 systems that help the reader locate instruments that may meet her needs. These are followed by a more detailed treatment of each system which briefly describes the system on eight dimensions and also defines the categories of behavior that are observed. Most of the systems are described in more detail in the earlier volumes. For example, the Flanders System of Interaction analysis, perhaps the most widely used system, is given 3 pages in the 1974 edition while the entire observer's manual (51 pages) is included in the 1967 edition.

Ethnographic Research

Bogdan, R. C., and Biklen, S. K. *Qualitative Research for Education: An Introduction to Theory and Methods.* Boston: Allyn and Bacon, 1982.

This book traces the foundations of qualitative research in education from the social research of the nineteenth century to present-day educational ethnography. The collection of qualitative data is discussed along with design of qualitative studies and data analysis. The chapter on fieldwork relations gives important and practical guidance to the researcher. The section dealing with common questions about qualitative research is especially useful for students trained in the quantitative-experimental tradition.

Dobbert, M. L. *Ethnographic Research: Theory and Application for Modern Schools and Societies.* New York: Praeger, 1982.

This is an excellent source for students who want to conduct ethnographic research in the schools. In the section on design, eight research techniques are described along with research examples. Detailed information on gathering and analyzing data and preparing the research report is also provided.

LeCompte, Margaret D., and Goetz, Judith P. "Problems of Reliability and Validity in Ethnographic Research." *Review of Educational Research* 52 (1982): 31–60.

The authors compare ethnographic research with experimental research and discuss differences between the two approaches. Internal and external reliability and validity are examined in some depth. This is an excellent source for students who want to develop a better understanding of ethnographic research.

Rist, Ray C. "Ethnographic Techniques and the Study of an Urban School." *Urban Education* 10, no. 1 (1975): 86–108.

Discusses the rationale for ethnographic research and explores some of its limitations. Includes a general description of a 2½-year study carried out by the author. Also describes in some detail the process of becoming accepted by the teachers, principal, and children in the school that was studied.

Smith, Louis M. "An Evolving Logic of Participant Observations, Educational Ethnography, and Other Case Studies." In *Review of Research in Education,* edited by Lee S. Shulman. vol. 6, Itasca, Ill.: F. E. Peacock, 1978.

This chapter weaves a great deal of useful information about the case-study approach into a narrative of the personal experiences of the author and his colleagues in this field. The author considers case study, participant observation, and ethnography as different names for the same process. Thus his discussion focuses primarily on the kind of case study in which ethnographic field-study methods are used. Students who are planning to conduct this kind of research should pay special attention to the criteria Smith has established.

Spindler, George, ed. *Doing the Ethnography of Schooling: Educational Anthropology in Action.* New York: Holt, Rinehart and Winston, 1982.

This text contains an excellent coverage of the theories and methods of ethnography as applied to the study of schooling. A number of original studies applying ethnographic methods to problems related to the school are reported. The final section of the book consists of a review of work on ethnographic methodology and its application to educational research.

Tikunoff, William J.; Berliner, David C.; and Rist, Ray C. *Special Study A: An Ethonographic Study of the 40 Classrooms of the Beginning Teacher Evaluation Study Known Sample BTES Technical Report 75-10-5.* San Francisco: Far West Laboratory for Educational Research and Development, 1975.

Discusses the problems involved in studying teaching with conventional educational research methods. Describes the ethnographic method and its advantages as well as problems that may arise in its use. Also describes in some detail procedures used to select and train observers. The information on observer training, data collection, and analysis should be studied carefully by students who are planning an ethnographic study.

Wilson, Stephen. "The Use of Ethnographic Techniques in Educational Research." *Review of Educational Research* 47 (1977): 245–65.

This is a well-documented article designed to introduce the educational researcher to the ethnographic approach. Provides a good discussion of the rationale underlying this method and briefly describes the research process. Two sets of questions are provided to give the educational researcher some basis for judging ethnographic research. These questions can also be used by students who are planning an ethnographic study to evaluate their own plans.

Nonreactive Measures

Sechrest, Lee, ed. *Unobtrusive Measurement Today.* San Francisco: Jossey-Bass, 1979.

This small book contains several interesting chapters concerned primarily with the use of unobtrusive (nonreactive) measures in a variety of research situations. The chapters on designing unobtrusive field experiments and on using nonverbal behaviors as unobtrusive measures are especially recommended.

Webb, E. J.; Campbell, D. T.; Schwartz, R. D.; Sechrest, L.; and Grove, J. B. *Nonreactive Measures in the Social Sciences.* Boston: Houghton Mifflin, 1981.

This is the second edition of the classic reference in this area. A variety of nonreactive measures including physical traces, archives, and observation are discussed. The chapters on the ethical problems and limitations of such measures, which were not included in the first edition, are especially useful to the investigator who is considering the use of nonreactive measures in a research project.

Content Analysis

Krippendorff, Klaus. *Content Analysis, An Introduction to Its Methodology*. Beverly Hills, Calif.: Sage, 1980.

This book systematically covers the major steps in planning and conducting a content analysis. Students planning a content-analysis study should first read the final chapter, "A Practical Guide," and then read other chapters as needed. The author's style is difficult and requires careful study and rereading.

SELF-CHECK TEST

Circle the correct answer to each of the following questions. An answer key is provided on page 881.

1. Observational methods of data collection are often useful when
    a. the researcher needs a data collection system that is more economical than self-reports.
    b. subjects are apt to bias self-reports.
    c. subjects can accurately recall events.
    d. the Hawthorne Effect is likely to occur.
2. A major disadvantage of observational research is that
    a. it is easily biased by the subject.
    b. no standardized observational instruments are available.
    c. the presence of the observer changes the situation.
    d. only the most simple behaviors can be observed.
3. The "halo effect" is most apt to occur when the observer is required to
    a. evaluate abstract qualities.
    b. record specific behaviors.
    c. record descriptive variables.
    d. operate from a concealed position.
4. Observer contamination means that a person observes the occurrence of a variable
    a. without prior training in observing that variable.

    b. without realizing the need to control for the error of central tendency.

    c. with prior knowledge of the statistical techniques to be used in analyzing the data.

    d. with knowledge of subjects' performance on other variables.

5. Asking individuals to assume certain roles in a setting devised by the researcher and then observing the individuals in these roles describes one kind of

    a. peer evaluation.

    b. critical-incident testing.

    c. situational testing.

    d. supervisory rating.

6. Collecting data on a group by asking each member to select persons in the group most preferred by him on the basis of a specific criterion describes the _____ technique.

    a. sociometric

    b. anecdotal

    c. critical-incident

    d. supervisory rating

7. The error most often noted in supervisory ratings is the

    a. error of central tendency.

    b. halo effect.

    c. conscious observer bias.

    d. placebo effect.

8. Research analysis of transcripts from audiotapes of classroom verbal behavior is called _____ analysis.

    a. content

    b. critical-incident

    c. sociometric

    d. anecdotal

9. A recent trend in content analysis research is to

    a. compare content frequencies.

    b. study the relationship between content variables and other research variables.

    c. compare the types of words most frequently used in the English language with those used in other languages.

    d. compute readability indices for school textbooks.

10. Selection of a sample of material for content analysis

    a. cannot be done, since the entire population of material must be studied in order to draw valid inferences.

    b. will determine the objectives of the research project.

    c. cannot be done by using a random sampling technique.

    d. should be done by using a random sampling technique.

APPLICATION PROBLEMS

The following problems are designed to give you practice in applying significant concepts and research procedures explained in chapter 12. Most of them do not have a single correct answer. For feedback, you can compare your answers with the sample answers on page 893.

1. a. Some educators believe that enthusiasm is an important characteristic of the good teacher. Nevertheless, enthusiasm is a "high-inference" variable. Name three observable teacher behaviors that you think are indicative of enthusiasm in classroom teaching.
   b. Suppose that one behavioral indication of teacher enthusiasm is use of facial expressions such as smiles, laughter, or raised eyebrows. Write an observation-schedule item that could be used for observing this behavior during a 20 minute class discussion.
2. A researcher plans to train five observers to use the Flanders Interaction Analysis system, which is a standard observational schedule. Her schedule of training includes the following steps to be carried out at a series of meetings with the observers.
   a. Explain the ten categories of the observation form.
   b. Explain how teacher or student behavior is coded on the observation form every three seconds.
   c. Have the observers score three videotapes of classroom interaction and compare their scoring of each tape with the researcher's criterion scoring.
   d. Provide the observers with their classroom observation assignments.
   What important step has been omitted from the researcher's training plan?
3. A researcher is interested in testing the theory that children learn by imitating the behavior of others. To test the theory, he asks one group of teachers to act exceptionally neat in their class for a period of weeks, for example, conspicuously taking time to arrange their desks neatly. He asks another group of teachers to act sloppy for a similar period of time. The researcher's prediction is that children who have "neat" teachers will be acting more neatly at the end of the experiment than children exposed to "sloppy" teachers. What is one unobtrusive measure of children's degree of neatness that could be used in this experiment?
4. Suppose that you wish to test the hypothesis that high school students' popularity with their peers is related to indices of mental health, such as freedom from anxiety and positive self-image. What are two methods involving untrained observers that could be used to measure peer popularity?
5. A researcher wants to determine whether the thought level of students' essays improves from the first to fourth year of college. She has available a collection of essays written by the same students over a four-year period of college atten-

dance. What are three aspects of essay writing style that could be analyzed to yield a measure of thought level? Why these particular aspects?

SUGGESTION SHEET

If your last name starts with letters from Lew to May, please complete the Suggestion Sheet at the end of the book while this chapter is still fresh in your mind.

13.

EXPLORING RELATIONSHIPS BETWEEN VARIABLES: THE CAUSAL-COMPARATIVE METHOD

OVERVIEW

The causal-comparative method is an accepted research technique for exploring causal relationships among variables that cannot be manipulated experimentally. The causal-comparative method involves comparing samples that are different on a critical variable but otherwise comparable. For example, juvenile delinquents have been compared with nondelinquents who are drawn from the same population in order to identify possible causes of delinquent behavior. The first part of the chapter discusses advantages and disadvantages of using this type of research design. Next, detailed techniques are given for conducting a causal-comparative study, particularly in the critical area of selecting appropriate comparison groups. The second half of the chapter deals with statistical techniques for analyzing the research data yielded by this method.

OBJECTIVES

After studying this chapter, you should be able to:

1. Explain the relationship between causal-comparative, correlational, and experimental research.
2. Describe three interpretations that can be made if a relationship between two variables, A and B, is discovered through causal-comparative research.
3. State plausible alternative hypotheses to challenge a research hypothesis in a causal-comparative design.
4. Form meaningful subgroups, given an initially defined sample of subjects to be used in causal-comparative research.

5. Define suitable comparison groups, given an initially defined group in which a particular characteristic is present.
6. Interpret the *t* value resulting from a *t* test for the difference between means, and describe situations in causal-comparative research in which it would be used.
7. Describe situations in causal-comparative research in which it is necessary to use the *t* test for correlated means rather than the *t* test for independent means.
8. Compare the interpretations of one-tailed tests versus two-tailed tests, and describe situations in which each would be used.
9. Interpret the *t* value resulting from a *t* test for a single mean and describe situations in causal-comparative research in which it would be used.
10. Interpret the *F* ratio resulting from an analysis of variance, and describe situations in causal-comparative research in which it would be used.
11. Interpret the *F* ratio resulting from an analysis of covariance, and describe situations in causal-comparative research in which it would be used.
12. Interpret the results of a multivariate analysis of variance.
13. Interpret the *F* ratio resulting from a test for differences between variances, and describe situations in causal-comparative research in which it would be used.
14. Describe situations in causal-comparative research in which it is necessary to use nonparametric tests of significance rather than parametric tests.
15. Interpret the results of a chi-square test, and describe situations in causal-comparative research in which it would be used.
16. Interpret the results of the Mann-Whitney *U* test, the Wilcoxon signed-rank test, and the Kruskal-Wallis test; describe situations in causal-comparative research in which the tests would be used.
17. Explain the extreme-groups procedure, and specify correlational techniques that can be used following a test of statistical significance.

INTRODUCTION

The Study of Relationships between Variables

The common thread that underlies most research in education is the intent to discover **relationships** between variables. Two variables are said to be related to each other if values of one variable are predictable from values of another variable. For example, many studies have found that scholastic aptitude and gradepoint average (GPA) are related to each other, meaning that if we know a student's score on a measure of scholastic aptitude, we can predict his GPA to a certain extent.

The study of relationships between educational variables is extremely important. Gains in knowledge about such relationships provide a basis for improving educational practice. For example, researchers have consistently found a positive relationship between teacher enthusiasm and student achievement. This means that higher levels of student achievement are more likely to occur when there is a high level of teacher enthusiasm in the classroom. This observed relationship suggests that education might be improved by training teachers to be more enthusiastic or by including enthusiasm as a criterion for selecting among applicants to teacher education programs. Before such major steps are taken, however, one would need to conduct experiments to determine that the relationship between teacher enthusiasm and student achievement is causal and replicable in different situations.

The causal-comparative method is one approach for exploring relationships between variables. In a sense, it is not a method at all, but rather a particular way of analyzing relational data. The correlational method, discussed in chapter 14, provides another approach for exploring relationships. Like causal-comparative research, the distinguishing characteristic of correlational studies is the way in which the relational data are analyzed. We will discuss the similarities between causal-comparative and correlational research again at the end of the chapter. Also we advise you to read this chapter and chapter 14 together so that you can see the connections between the two methods.

One other point deserves mention before you start your study of the causal-comparative method. This method was more widely used years ago than it is now. This is because the statistical techniques associated with the causal-comparative method were well known to researchers then. The *t* test and analysis of variance were the most common statistics for testing the null hypothesis. In recent years, however, the field of correlational statistics has developed rapidly. Researchers have discovered that correlational statistics, especially multiple regression, can do everything that the *t* test and analysis of variance can do and more. Correlational statistics are particularly useful for studying relationships between three or more variables. Because educational processes typically reflect complex interactions between numerous variables, it is no wonder that researchers now rely on correlational statistics.

Even though correlational research is increasingly popular, we recommend that you learn the causal-comparative method in depth. The statistics associated with the causal-comparative method (especially the *t* test and analysis of variance) are widely used in experimental research. Therefore, we will make repeated reference to these statistical techniques in our subsequent discussion of experimental designs (chapters 15 and 16). Also, some relational data are better understood by the *t* test, analysis of variance, or similar technique than by correlational statistics. For example, relationships involving dichotomous groups (e.g., boys versus girls) or categorical groups (e.g., elementary school administrators versus junior high school administrators versus middle school administrators) are more easily interpreted using the statistical tools presented in this chapter. Finally, you may find it easier to understand the logic of discovering relationships between variables if you study the causal-comparative method first. The correlational method is ultimately a more powerful approach, but for many beginning researchers it is not as easily understood as the causal-comparative method.

Advantages and Disadvantages of Causal-Comparative Studies

The **causal-comparative method** is aimed at the discovery of possible causes for a behavior pattern by comparing subjects in whom this pattern is present with similar subjects in whom it is absent or present to a lesser degree. This method is sometimes called **ex post facto research,** since causes are studied after they have presumably exerted their effect on another variable.

A classic example of the causal-comparative method is the research on juvenile delinquency by Sheldon and Eleanor Glueck.[1] They located subjects who were juvenile delinquents and compared their behavior with that of similar subjects who were not juvenile delinquents. Characteristics that were present more frequently among the delinquent subjects than among the nondelinquent subjects were examined as possible causes of juvenile delinquency.

The causal-comparative method is often used instead of the experimental method because many of the cause-and-effect relationships that we wish to study in education do not permit experimental manipulation. For example, an experiment to test the hypothesis that aggressiveness is a cause of juvenile delinquency would require, first, random selection of two groups of children. The environment of one of these groups would be manipulated to provoke aggressive behavior in them over a prolonged period of time. The environment of the other group (the control group) might be manipulated to minimize the occurrence of aggressive behavior. If the hypothesis is correct, a significantly greater percentage of children in the aggression-provocation group should become juvenile delinquents than children in the control group.

This type of research cannot be done because of ethical considerations. The hypothesis can be tested with a causal-comparative design, though. A group of juvenile delinquents and a group of nondelinquent youth would be selected, and their aggressiveness would be measured by standardized personality tests,

---

1. Sheldon Glueck and Eleanor Glueck, *Unraveling Juvenile Delinquency* (New York: Commonwealth Fund, 1950).

observational ratings, or other assessment techniques. If the hypothesis is correct, the delinquent group should have significantly higher scores on measures of aggressiveness than the group of nondelinquents.

Suppose that the scores are as predicted. Because a causal-comparative design was used, the researcher can conclude only that a *relationship* between these two variables exists. The researcher cannot infer that aggressiveness *causes* juvenile delinquency.

Interpretations of causal-comparative findings are limited because the researcher does not know whether a particular variable is a cause or result of the behavior pattern being studied. In the Gluecks' study of juvenile delinquency, they found that delinquent boys displayed more aggression than did nondelinquent boys. We do not know the aggression patterns that were present in both groups *before* any of the boys became delinquent. Thus, in attempting to interpret the findings, we are faced with the following questions: Do boys who are more aggressive more frequently become delinquents? Do boys become more aggressive in the process of becoming delinquent? Or does some third factor such as social frustration cause both the aggression and the delinquency?

A similar dilemma occurs in causal-comparative studies aimed at identifying possible effects of acceleration in school. These studies usually compare pupils who have been accelerated two more years with pupils who have not been accelerated. Both groups are matched for intelligence. The results usually show higher achievement for the pupils who have been accelerated, but these questions arise: Did the accelerated students achieve more because they were accelerated? Were they accelerated because they had developed patterns of high achievement before they were accelerated? Or does some third factor, such as high parental intelligence, cause both a pattern of high achievement and school acceleration, thus leading to a relationship between these latter two variables, even though they are not causally related? It usually is impossible to select the correct answer to such questions on the basis of causal-comparative data.

Despite problems of interpretation, the causal-comparative method is useful for identifying possible causes of observed variations in behavior patterns. These tentative causes can be verified in subsequent experimental studies. To illustrate, we can examine a study of ethnically mixed classrooms in the Southwest conducted by Gregg Jackson and Cecilia Cosca.[2] These researchers investigated whether teachers behave differentially toward Chicano and Anglo students in their classes. Their working theory was that the depressed school achievement of Chicano students relative to Anglo students might be caused by differences in the way that teachers interacted with them.

---

2. Gregg Jackson and Cecilia Cosca, "The Inequality of Educational Opportunity in the Southwest: An Observational Study of Ethnically Mixed Classrooms," *American Educational Research Journal* 11 (1974): 219–29. Table 13.1, on the next page, is reprinted from this article.

Classroom observers tallied the frequency with which teachers directed certain behaviors toward Anglo and Chicano students. The frequency statistics are shown in table 13.1. Of the twelve variables measured, *nine* were teacher behaviors. Had the researchers used the experimental method, they would have been able to manipulate *only one* or *two* of the behaviors in a single experiment.

Table 13.1 shows that the difference between Anglo and Chicano students on five of the teacher behaviors was statistically significant. These five behaviors may well warrant further investigation using the experimental method. In contrast, such behaviors as giving directions or criticizing are not promising

TABLE 13.1

Average Frequency of Coded Behaviors Associated with Average Individual Mexican American and Average Individual Anglo Students[a]

Teacher and Student Behaviors	Average Mexican American Student	Average Anglo Student	t Value
1. Teacher acceptance of students' feelings	.004	.008	1.73
2. Teacher praising or encouraging students	.137	.186	2.95[b]
3. Teacher acceptance or use of students' ideas	.156	.219	3.32[b]
4. Teacher questioning	.525	.636	2.41[b]
5. Teacher lecturing	.584	.710	1.87
6. Teacher giving of directions	.146	.141	.20
7. Teacher criticizing or justifying authority	.055	.052	.37
8. Student response speaking	.771	.948	1.99
9. Student initiated speaking	.796	1.034	1.66
10. Teacher giving of positive feedback	.296	.413	3.73[b]
11. All noncriticizing teacher talk	1.551	1.901	2.99[b]
12. All student speaking	1.567	1.982	2.45[b]

[a]The values in the first two columns represent the number of times during a ten-minute period that the average individual student of the indicated ethnicity was coded as involved in the specified interaction; coding was done at a fixed rate of 20 times per minute.

[b]t is statistically significant at .01 level for a one-tailed test with 428 degrees of freedom when equal to or greater than 2.326. The one-tailed test was used because prior to seeing the data the authors had hypothesized that all measures except the teacher's giving of directions and teacher criticizing would be greater for Anglos than for Mexican Americans.

variables for experimental studies involving Anglo and Chicano students since the two groups do not differ on them.

Behavior 10 in table 13.1 (teacher giving of positive feedback) might provide the focus for an experiment. The results indicate that Chicano students do not receive as much positive feedback from the teachers as do Anglo students. Using an experimental design, the researcher could train one group of teachers to give positive feedback to Chicano students at the same level as the positive feedback given to Anglo students. A control group of teachers would follow their normal instructional behavior. Measures of academic achievement, self-concept, and related variables would be administered to all students periodically. Suppose, as predicted, the academic gap between Anglo and Chicano students in the experimental group lessened over time relative to the Anglo and Chicano students in the control group. We could conclude with confidence that teachers' positive feedback has *an effect on* Chicano students. We cannot reach such a conclusion from the results presented in table 13.1. These results only permit us to conclude that there is a *relationship* between teacher behavior and student ethnicity.

To summarize, the major advantage of the causal-comparative method is that it enables researchers to investigate relationships between many variables in a single study. The major weakness of the method is that it does not reveal the causal connections underlying the observed relationships.

PLANNING A CAUSAL-COMPARATIVE STUDY

Statement of the Research Problem

The steps in a causal-comparative research project are illustrated by a recent study of test anxiety.[3] The researchers, Ralph Culler and Charles Holahan, investigated the relationship between three variables: test anxiety, gradepoint average (GPA), and study behavior.

The initial step in a causal-comparative study is to speculate about the causes of the phenomena that interest you. Your speculations can be based on previous research findings and theory, and on your own observations of the phenomena. In the study mentioned above, Culler and Holahan were interested in the possible causes of test anxiety in college students. They viewed test anxiety as an important phenomenon because other researchers had found that high test-anxious students tend to earn lower GPAs than low test-anxious

---

3. Ralph E. Culler and Charles J. Holahan, "Test Anxiety and Academic Performance: The Effects of Study-Related Behaviors," *Journal of Educational Psychology* 72 (1980): 16–20.

students. Culler and Holahan speculated that poor study habits might be a cause of test anxiety. It seems reasonable that students would be anxious in testing situations if they had not studied the test material adequately. In turn, adequacy of study would be a function of students' study habits. The researchers did a review of the literature and found several studies that supported this line of reasoning.

After possible causes of the phenomena have been identified, they should be incorporated into the statement of the research problem. As you will recall, the research problem is stated in the form of objectives or hypotheses. In the Culler and Holahan study, the main research problem was stated as an objective: ". . . to examine possible differences in a range of study-related behaviors between high and low test-anxious individuals."[4] We shall discuss the results relating to this objective in a later section of this chapter (see "The *t* Test for Differences between Means").

A secondary objective of the study was to replicate previous research findings: "Specifically, this study proposed *(a)* to replicate the findings from previous studies (Allen et al., 1972; Alpert & Haber, 1960; Carrier & Jewell, 1966; Desiderato & Koskinen, 1969) that test anxiety is associated with a significant decrement in GPA."[5] We shall discuss the results relating to this objective in the section on the chi-square test.

The researcher should attempt to state and test alternative hypotheses about other factors that might explain observed differences between two groups. We mentioned the possibility above that poor study habits might be one cause of the anxiety that some students experience in test situations. An alternative hypothesis is that *amount* of study rather than quality of study (as reflected by one's study habits) is the cause of test anxiety. It seems plausible that students who spend little time preparing for an exam will experience more test anxiety than students who prepare extensively for it. Culler and Holahan considered a number of alternative factors that might distinguish between high and low test-anxious students: study habits, amount of study reliance on "cramming," missed classes during the semester, and missed exams and tests that were made up at a later date.

The research results can confirm more than one alternative hypothesis. This is a common occurrence because complex behaviors such as test anxiety are often determined by a variety of factors. The magnitude of difference between the two groups on each measure can be examined to determine which factor, or set of factors, appears most likely to cause the phenomenon being studied.

The testing of plausible alternative hypotheses is called **strong inference.**[6]

4. Ibid., p. 17.
5. Ibid.
6. J. Platt, "Strong Inference," *Science* 146 (1964): 347–53.

Whenever possible, it should be used in causal-comparative research to formulate the variables on which the comparison groups are to be contrasted. Measures of these variables then can be selected on a rational basis, instead of relying on the "shotgun approach" in which a large number of measures are administered because they appear interesting or are available. Also, the use of alternative hypotheses provides a helpful reminder to the researcher that the findings of a causal-comparative study, no matter how well done, are subject to various causal interpretations.

Selecting a Defined Group

After the research problem has been stated, the next step in the causal-comparative method is to define the group that possesses the characteristic one wishes to study. Procedures used to define this group will determine the meaning and applicability of the results. Underachievers, for example, might be defined conceptually as pupils whose achievement is less than would be expected from their measured aptitude. An operational definition, however, must be much more precise. It must specify the measure of achievement to be used, the measure of aptitude to be used, and the degree of difference between them that is to be considered indicative of underachievement. One such definition might be: an underachiever is any pupil whose T score on the total Stanford Achievement Battery is five or more points lower than his T score on the California Test of Mental Maturity.[7] Obviously, a study using the aforementioned definition of an underachiever will yield different results from one defining the underachiever as any pupil whose grade-placement score on an achievement test is more than one year below his current grade placement. This latter definition, which is sometimes used, ignores the aptitude factor and will result in a sample that includes few pupils of high aptitude even if they are working well below their potential. Thus, studies that appear at first glance to be similar may really be different because of differences in procedures for defining the samples.

Another problem is whether the underachievers obtained by applying the operational definition are likely to be reasonably homogeneous in terms of factors causing underachievement. Can we identify types of underachievers that are underachieving for different reasons, or are the same causes likely to be operating for all underachievers? This is an important question for the researcher to ask. Suppose that the researcher's hypothesis is that a basic cause of high school underachievement is poor personal adjustment. Further suppose that, in actuality, un-

---

7. T scores are specified so that direct score comparisons may be made. See chapter 12 for a discussion of T scores.

derachievement in English is due to difficulties in personal adjustment, but that underachievement in mathematics is totally unrelated to this factor. If she fails to discriminate between English and mathematics underachievers in selecting her sample, the researcher will seriously weaken her chances of finding any support for her hypothesis. Having treated all underachievers as a homogeneous group, the researcher will probably find no difference between them and a comparison group (e.g., a normally achieving or overachieving group) on a measure of personal adjustment. Had she tested the hypothesis using only underachievers in English, however, the researcher would probably have found significant differences between English underachievers and an appropriate comparison group on a measure of personal adjustment.

Even in this instance it may be necessary to further define one's group. For example, it may be that there are sex differences in the factors leading to underachievement in English. We might find that problems in personal adjustment are a factor in underachievement for females but not for males. If this were the case, further data analysis would reveal differences between female underachievers in English and an appropriate comparison group of females, whereas no differences would be found for male underachievers in English.

It should be evident from the preceding discussion that the success of a causal-comparative study depends on the investigator's skill in selecting groups that are homogeneous with respect to certain critical variables. The essential skill is to ask oneself the question: Is this a homogeneous group or can further subgroups be defined? A few examples of subgrouping follow:

Initial Defined Group	*Further Subgrouping*
1. first-grade teachers	1. male vs. female teachers
2. juvenile delinquents	2. delinquents who commit crimes against property vs. delinquents who commit crimes against persons
3. mathematics instructors	3. instructors who have had training in new math vs. those who have not
4. school administrators	4. school superintendents vs. assistant school superintendents

In the study of test anxiety described above, Culler and Holahan selected a defined group of high test-anxious students. They described their selection procedure for the defined group (and for the comparison group, too) as follows:

Subjects in the study were first-semester freshmen enrolled in an introductory psychology course. At the beginning of the semester, 800 students were pretested on the Test Anxiety Scale (TAS; Sarason, Pederson, & Nyman, 1968). Freshmen scoring in the upper and lower 25th percentile were identified. To control for statistical regression and to avoid the selection of students who were generally anxious about beginning college, the upper and lower cutoffs were applied again to a second administration of the TAS during the last 2 weeks of the semester, and subjects who scored in the upper and lower 25th percentiles on both test administrations were selected for the study. This procedure resulted in a final sample of 65 high test-anxious and 31 low test-anxious subjects.

The researchers did not define subgroups from the initially defined group. Had they done so, a reasonable variable for forming subgroups would be students' sex. Other researchers have found that female students generally report more anxiety than male students. Also, females generally earn higher GPAs than males, at least through high school. It may be that different factors are responsible for high test anxiety in females and high test anxiety in males. Another grouping variable that comes to mind is students' college major. Perhaps high test anxiety in mathematics has a different set of causes than, for example, high test anxiety in English.

Often the review of the literature will provide ideas about the types of subgroups that need to be formed if one is to find significant differences. If you plan to study a characteristic not researched previously, common sense and reasoning based on psychological or educational theory can be used to form homogeneous subgroups.

Selecting Comparison Groups

Once the researcher has selected a homogeneous group having the characteristic he wishes to study, the next step is to select a group not having this characteristic in order to permit comparisons. The population from which the comparison sample is to be selected is usually defined to be similar to the characteristic-present group except for the variable being studied. In the Culler and Holahan study, the comparison group of low test-anxious students was drawn from the same pool of subjects as the high test-anxious students.

The comparison group may either be selected at random from the defined population, or it may be matched with the characteristic-present group on the basis of one or more variables. The process of matching "controls" certain variables by holding them constant. For example, the Gluecks matched their delinquent and nondelinquent boys for ethnic origin, IQ, and age, thus producing closely comparable groups with respect to these variables. The problem with the matching procedure is that, once groups have been matched so as to have similar scores on a factor, they cannot differ on that factor. Yet it is the detection of differences between two groups which suggests that a particular factor is a potential cause of an observed behavior pattern.

To illustrate, suppose that low scholastic ability is one cause of delinquent behavior. If a causal-comparative study is done in which delinquent and non-delinquent groups are equated on this factor by matching, it will be impossible for this factor to emerge as a possible cause of delinquent behavior. The design of the study has prevented true differences between the two groups in scholastic ability from being detected. Because of the disadvantages of matching, random selection is the preferred method for identifying a comparison sample from a defined population.

In the Culler and Holahan study, the researchers could have considered matching the groups on scholastic aptitude. This factor has been found to correlate substantially with college GPA. To remove scholastic aptitude as a possible cause of observed differences between high test-anxious and low test-anxious students, the researchers would match the groups on this factor. They would identify a high test-anxious student with a particular scholastic aptitude score and then match that student with a low test-anxious student having a similar aptitude score.

Generally, matching creates more problems than it solves. The influence of such factors as scholastic aptitude is usually better controlled by the use of analysis of covariance, a statistical technique described later in the chapter.

It is occasionally desirable to form multiple comparison groups. In the study that we have been describing, high test-anxious students were contrasted with one comparison group, that is, low test-anxious students. Had the researchers wanted, they could have formed a third comparison group: moderate test-anxious students, defined as students scoring in the middle 25 percent of the test anxiety score distribution (38th through 62nd percentiles).

Multiple comparison groups are good because they provide a rich set of data that can be analyzed for factors that explain the phenomenon being studied. The major problem in forming multiple comparison groups is obtaining a large enough sample. A suitable number of subjects may not be available, or the researcher may not have adequate resources to collect and analyze data from a large sample having multiple comparison groups.

The data that result from forming multiple comparison groups are often analyzed by a statistical technique called analysis of variance. This technique is discussed later in the chapter.

Data Collection

Biographical data are often collected in causal-comparative research when the purpose is to seek past causes for present behavior patterns. Knowledge of a student's family relationships, school behavior, and experiences during the time she was developing her current behavior patterns often tells us more than data on her *present* personality, attitudes, or behavior. The degree of emphasis placed upon the two types of data is determined by the nature of the study.

There are no limitations on the types of measuring instruments that can be used in causal-comparative studies. Standardized tests, questionnaires, interviews, and naturalistic observations are all useful for collecting data about causal factors. In the study of test anxiety we have been describing, the researchers used standardized scales, a reseacher-constructed questionnaire, and institutional data:

> The TAS is a 37-item reported by Sarason et al. (1968). The test items are statements relating to the experience of test-related anxiety and its physiological correlates. Subjects responded on a 4-point scale rather than the true-false format used by Sarason et al. Along with the second administration of the TAS during the last 2 weeks of the semester, subjects were asked to complete the 50-item Study Habits scale of the Survey of Study Habits and Attitudes (Brown & Holtzman, 1967). Subjects responded to statements about the nature and style of their study behavior on a 5-point scale (1 = rarely; 5 = almost always). In addition, subjects were asked to complete a questionnaire designed by the investigators to obtain information about a number of other study-related behaviors. These included the following:
>
> *Study hours.* Students were asked to estimate the number of hours spent studying per week for each course taken during the semester. The course by course estimates were totaled, yielding a measure of total weekly hours for each subject.
>
> *Cramming.* Students were asked to estimate the degree to which they crammed in preparation for tests and exams by responding on a 7-point scale to the item, "In preparing for an exam, do you generally" (1 = work uniformly through the semester; 7 = "cram" the night before the exam).
>
> *Classes missed.* Students were asked to estimate the total number of classes they missed during the semester for each course they were taking. The course by course estimates were totaled, yielding a total number of missed classes for each subject.
>
> *Late exams.* Students were asked to estimate the total number of exams or tests they missed and made up at a later date during the semester for each course they were taking. The course by course estimates were totaled, yielding a total number of late exams for each subject.
>
> Finally, the semester's GPA for each subject was obtained from the University's registrar at the completion of the semester.[8]

8. Culler and Holahan, "Test Anxiety and Academic Performance," p. 17.

Data Analysis

The first step in an analysis of causal-comparative data is to compute descriptive statistics for each comparison group in the study. These generally will include the group mean and standard deviation. Descriptive statistics for the test anxiety study are shown in table 13.2.

The next step usually is to do a test of statistical significance. The choice of a significance test depends on whether the researcher is interested in comparing groups with respect to mean score, variance, median, rank scores, or category frequencies. The student should be familiar with the various significance tests, which were introduced in chapter 10 and are presented more fully here. Also, the student should note that many of the same significance tests can be used in analyzing data from experimental designs, which are presented in chapter 15.

STATISTICAL ANALYSIS: THE *t* TEST

The *t* Test for Differences between Means

The basic rationale for testing the significance of the differences between two sample means was explained in chapter 10. (You may wish to reread the sections that describe the standard error of the mean, the null hypothesis, and the test of statistical significance.) In that chapter the following situation was presented: To test the hypothesis that girls have greater verbal aptitude than boys, a measure of verbal aptitude is administered to random samples of 100 sixth-grade boys and 100 sixth-grade girls. Suppose the following results are obtained:

	N	M	SD
Boys	100	80	4
Girls	100	85	5

We showed that the z distribution, which follows the normal curve distribution of differences between sample means, can be used to test the null hypothesis that there is no difference between population means. It is appropriate to use the z distribution when large samples are studied ($N = 30$ or larger). When small samples are studied ($N = 29$ or smaller), it is advisable to use the **t test** instead. Most statistics textbooks provide separate tables listing significance levels for the z and the t distributions.

The t test is probably the most commonly used statistical tool in causal-comparative studies. Many research problems require a great deal of time and money, and so it is not possible to include many subjects in the sample. For example, suppose one wishes to compare the performance of creative and non-creative adolescents on individually administered intelligence tests. If the researcher's resources are limited, it may only be possible to work with a total sample of 20 or 30 subjects in each group. If the researcher's criterion of creativity is very restrictive (e.g., the production of work that is of high artistic or scientific merit), the sample size may be smaller because of the difficulty in finding subjects who meet the criterion. In this situation the t test is the appropriate statistical tool to determine whether the sample means differ significantly from one another.

The t test makes three assumptions about the scores obtained in causal-comparative research. The first assumption is that scores form an interval or ratio scale of measurement. The second is that scores in the populations under study are normally distributed. The third is that score variances for the populations under study are equal.

In the example we just considered, the first assumption is probably satisfied because most measures of verbal aptitude are interval scales. The second and third assumptions require information about the populations represented by the samples of sixth-grade boys and sixth-grade girls. Researchers usually do not have this information, however. Therefore, they must infer this information (score distribution and score variance) from the sample statistics. In our example, visual inspection of the sample statistics suggests a normal curve distribution for both boys and girls because the standard deviation is small relative to the means. Also, visual inspection of the sample statistics indicates that the difference in score variances is not too disparate: variance for boys = 16; variance for girls = 25. (The variance is the square of the standard deviation.) The two variances can be compared by a test of statistical significance (see p. 557) to determine whether the difference observed in the samples reflects a population difference.

Statisticians have conducted research to determine what happens when the assumptions underlying the t test and other parametric statistics are violated. They have found that these tests provide accurate estimates of statistical significance even under conditions of substantial violation of the assumptions.[9] If you are concerned about score distributions in your data, you should consider doing both a t test and its nonparametric counterpart—either the Mann-Whitney U test or the Wilcoxon signed-rank test. If the two tests yield different

---

9. For an extended discussion of this problem, see C. A. Boneau, "The Effects of Violations of Assumptions Underlying the t Test," *Psychological Bulletin* 57 (1960): 49–64.

results because the data depart substantially from *t* test assumptions, you can just report the results of the nonparametric test.

The *t* tests for the study-related behaviors in the test anxiety research project are shown in table 13.2.[10] Statistically significant differences between high test-anxious and low test-anxious students were observed in study habits and in total study hours.

A researcher may wish to compare groups on many variables. Each comparison requires a separate *t* test. In the test-anxiety study, the groups were compared on five study-related variables requiring a total of five *t* tests. You should keep in mind that the risk of a Type I error increases with the number of *t* tests done. For example, suppose two groups are compared on 20 variables, resulting in 20 different *t* tests. It is almost certain that one of the comparisons will yield a significant *p* (assuming *p* is set at .05) even if there is no difference between the populations represented by the samples on any of the variables. To understand how this happens, think about coin-tossing. On any given toss of a coin, your probability of the coin turning up heads is .50. But the probability is much higher (.9) that you will turn up a head at least once if you toss the coin ten times.

To summarize, you can increase your chance of finding a significant difference between groups on some variable by comparing the groups on many variables. Unfortunately, you also increase the risk of committing a Type I

TABLE 13.2
Means, Standard Deviations, and *t*-Test Results for the Five Coping Variables

Variable	High Test Anxiety		Low Test Anxiety		
	M	*SD*	*M*	*SD*	*t*
Study habits	37.2	14.8	53.4	14.2	5.42*
Total study hours	21.7	12.7	14.1	7.0	−3.11*
Cramming	4.5	1.4	4.7	1.4	.57
Missing classes	10.5	7.7	10.7	11.1	.08
Late exams	.6	1.1	.3	.6	−1.52

*$p < .002$

10. Culler and Holahan, "Test Anxiety and Academic Performance," p. 18.

error. To avoid this problem, you can set the significance level low (e.g., $p =$ .01). The preferred option, though, is to use a statistical technique called multivariate analysis of variance, which is described later in the chapter.

The problem of multiple t tests is more serious when one is doing an exploratory study in which variables are included because they are interesting or because measures of them are easily available. Some of the group differences on these variables are likely to reflect chance effects. The more such variables, the more likely is one to be statistically significant. Multiple t tests are much less a problem if the direction of the group difference on each variable has been predicted in advance based on theory or previous research findings. Such research is less likely to include variables that do not reflect real differences between the populations represented by the sample groups.

Correlated and Uncorrelated Means

It is important to realize that there are two kinds of t tests for determining the significance of differences between sample means. The researcher's choice of one of these t tests depends on whether the scores of the two groups are correlated or independent. Suppose that the hypothesis to be tested is that juvenile delinquents earn lower academic achievement test scores than a nondelinquent control group. One method of testing this hypothesis is to select random samples of delinquent and nondelinquent students and to administer achievement tests to them. If this method is used, the difference between the mean scores for the two groups can be tested by the **t test for independent means.** In this example the samples are independent. There is no reason to expect that the two sets of achievement test scores are correlated with each other.

Another method of testing the hypothesis would be to first select a random sample of delinquent students. One then *matches* each delinquent student with a comparison student who shares certain pertinent characteristics (e.g., intelligence, social class, grade level), but who is not delinquent. Matching procedures are discussed in chapter 15.

As a result of matching, each delinquent student will have a counterpart in the comparison group who has approximately the same scores on the matching variables. It is likely that the achievement test scores for the two groups will be correlated with at least one of the matching variables, for example, intelligence. If this condition occurs, the difference between the mean scores for the two groups should be tested by the **t test for correlated means.** The advantage of this t test is that it results in a smaller standard error than the t test for independent means. Consequently, one's chances of detecting a significant difference between mean scores for samples of a given size are increased. To think of it another way, the *t* test for correlated means has more statistical power than the *t* test for uncorrelated means.

In the study of test anxiety, there is no reason to believe that the scores of high-anxious and low-anxious students are related to each other in any way. Although the researchers do not report which *t* test they used, one can assume that it was the *t* test for independent means.

One-Tailed vs. Two-Tailed Tests of Significance

The ends of a normal curve (i.e., where it approaches the baseline) are called the tails of the distribution. When we compare two means to determine whether they are significantly different, we are checking the degree of overlap between the tails of the standard error curves of these two means (see chapter 10 for a discussion of standard error curves). Notice that in figure 13.1(a) mean A is significantly higher than mean B because almost no overlap exists between the two error curves, whereas in figure 13.1(b) some overlap exists. There is a good chance that mean C would be higher than mean D in some repetitions of the research. For example, in some repetitions of the study, mean C may move to C-1 and mean D to D-1, reversing the relationship between C and D.

In research comparing two groups, group B may prove to be superior to group A, but we must not ignore the possibility that the reverse will be true. In figure 13.1(a) we are comparing the overlap between tail B-2 of error curve B and tail A-1 of error curve A to determine whether the means are significantly different. If mean B had been higher, however, we would compare the overlap between tail B-1 and tail A-2. A **two-tailed test of significance,** in which both tails of the error curve are considered, allows the researcher to determine the significance level of differences between two means in either direction, that is, A greater than B, or B greater than A.

In some studies, we can be almost positive that if a difference is observed, it will be in the hypothesized direction. In the case of the test-anxiety study, the researchers had reason to believe, based on previous research findings, that high test-anxious students would be skill deficient relative to low test-anxious students. Therefore, a one-tailed *t* test would be justified in testing the difference between groups on this variable. The other variables (e.g., cramming and missed classes) appear to have been included because of researcher interest. There is no *a priori* reason to think that high test-anxious students would score differently than low test-anxious students on these variables. Therefore, group differences on these variables should be tested using a two-tailed *t* test.

The main advantage of the **one-tailed test of significance** is that a smaller critical ratio (*t* or *z* value) is needed to be statistically significant. Inexperienced

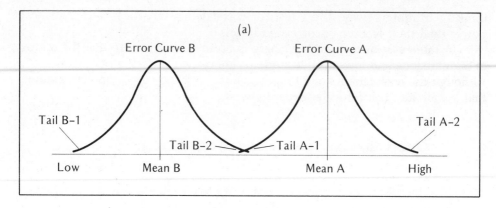

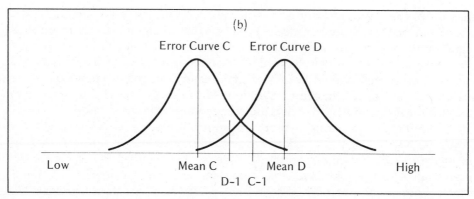

Figure 13.1   Error curves and statistical significance.

researchers often use the one-tailed test where it is not justified in order to make their results appear more significant. The student should avoid the one-tailed test unless she is quite certain that its use is justified in her study.

The *t* Test for a Single Mean

In most causal-comparative research, one is interested in comparing the mean scores of two samples to determine whether they are significantly different from each other. The *t* tests for independent means or for correlated means is used for this purpose. Occasionally, however, the researcher is interested in whether a sample mean differs significantly from a specified population mean. For example, suppose the researcher investigates a sample of twelfth-grade students who share a particular characteristic (such as being college bound). The researcher administers the Wechsler Adult Intelligence Scale to each student, and finds that the mean IQ score is 109. As part of the data analysis, the researcher may wish to determine whether this sample mean deviates significantly from the population mean. Assuming a population mean of 100, we may use the **t test for a single mean** to determine whether this difference (109 − 100) is statistically significant.

Generally, population means are not known in educational research. Some standardized tests provide norms based on very large samples, however. The means of these samples are usually close approximations of their respective population means. Also, population norms are available for some physical measures (e.g., height, weight, strength) that may be of interest to the educational researcher.

STATISTICAL ANALYSIS: ANALYSIS OF VARIANCE

Comparison of More than Two Means

As we have already indicated, causal-comparative research may involve the study of more than two groups. In a study by Vernon C. Hall, Ralph R. Turner, and Willian Russell, four groups were compared to determine whether they differed in performance on the Raven Coloured Progressive Matrices, which is a nonverbal measure of general cognitive functioning.[11] The four groups were: (1) urban lower-class black boys, (2) urban lower-class white boys, (3) rural lower-class white boys, and (4) suburban middle-class white boys. The researchers studied separate samples of these groups at two different grade levels, but here we will consider only the first-grade sample. The data are presented in table 13.3.

The data for the four groups could be analyzed by performing six *t* tests to compare: (1) urban blacks with urban whites, (2) urban blacks with rural whites, (3) urban blacks with middle-class whites, (4) urban whites with rural whites, (5) urban whites with middle-class whites, and (6) rural whites with middle-class whites. The total number of *t* tests increases dramatically with each additional comparison group. For example, if the number of groups is five, a total of ten comparisons can be made.

Instead of doing many *t* tests, researchers usually start by doing a simple analysis of variance. The purpose of **analysis of variance** in this situation is to

---

11. Vernon Hall, Ralph R. Turner, and William Russell, "Ability of Children from Four Subcultures and Two Grade Levels to Imitate and Comprehend Crucial Aspects of Standard English: A Test of the Different Language Explanation," *Journal of Educational Psychology* 64 (1973): 147–58.

TABLE 13.3

**Means and Standard Deviations
of Raven's Coloured
Progressive Matrices**

Group	M	SD
Urban black	13.4	4.1
Urban white	13.1	3.6
Rural white	13.7	4.2
Middle-class white	17.9	5.5

determine whether the groups differ significantly among themselves.[12] If the analysis of variance yields a nonsignificant F ratio (the ratio of between-groups variance to within-groups variance), the computation of t tests to compare pairs of means is not appropriate. An exception to this rule occurs when the researcher, in advance of data collection, hypothesizes that a specific pair of means differ significantly from each other.

In the study by Hall and his colleagues, the analysis of variance did indicate that the four groups differed significantly from one another. The F value was 4.3, which is statistically significant ($p<.05$).[13]

If the F ratio is statistically significant, the researcher can do t tests to determine which group means differ significantly from one another. However, the student should note that a special form of the t test is used following analysis of variance. The standard error of this t test is derived from the variances of all the groups rather than from the variances of the two specific groups being compared. Also, if the student has not planned to make specific comparisons *before* undertaking the research, then a *t* **test for multiple comparisons** should be used. There are several t tests for multiple comparisons, including Duncan's multiple-range test and the techniques developed by Newman-Keuls, Tukey, and Scheffé. These special t tests take into account the probability that the researcher will find a significant difference between mean scores simply because many comparisons are made on the same data.

In the study by Hall and his colleagues, the Scheffé method for making post hoc comparisons was used. The researchers found that the mean scores of the three lower-class groups each were significantly lower ($p<.05$) than the mean score of the middle-class group. The mean scores of the three lower-class groups did not differ significantly from each other.

12. In more technical terms, analysis of variance is used to determine whether the between-groups variance is significantly greater than the within-groups variance.
13. Tables of significant F values are given in most statistics texts.

Analysis of variance also allows the researcher to compare subgroups that vary on more than one factor. As an illustration, consider the research study by Philip Friedman on the frequency of child-initiated utterances directed to the teacher in a natural classroom setting.[14] One purpose of the research was to determine whether the frequency of child-initiated statements varied by grade level and by sex. Friedman's data relating to this problem are presented in table 13.4.

Each child represented in this table is a member of two subgroups: (1) each child is either male or female; and (2) each child is either a first grader, third grader, fifth grader, or seventh grader. A single analysis of variance enabled the researcher to make two types of comparison. First, the mean score of all boys was compared with the mean score of all girls. The child's grade level was irrelevant to this comparison; *all* boys were compared with *all* girls. The F value for this analysis was 1.93, which was not statistically significant ($p > .10$).[15] It appears that boys do not reliably initiate more statements in a classroom setting than do girls, even though the number of male-initiated statements was greater at three of the four grade levels.

The same analysis of variance yields a comparison of the mean scores of students at the four grade levels (grade 1 vs. grade 3 vs. grade 5 vs. grade 7) represented in the research. The child's sex was irrelevant to this comparison; *all* students at a given grade level were compared with *all* students at each of the other grade levels. A significant F value of 5.13 was obtained ($p < .01$) indicating that the four mean scores differed reliably from one another. At this point the researcher might do post hoc comparisons to determine which pairs of grade-level mean scores differed significantly.

The same analysis of variance yields still further information when subjects representing two or more factors (e.g., sex and grade level) are compared with each other. This information concerns whether the interaction between two or more factors is statistically significant. The concept of "interaction" is discussed in chapter 16 in the section on aptitude-treatment interaction.

The analysis of variance used to compare the mean scores on the Raven Coloured Progressive Matrices in table 13.3 is sometimes called a **one-way analysis of variance** because the subgroups differ on one factor, namely, socioethnic membership. The analysis of variance used to compare the mean scores in table 13.4 is sometimes called a **two-way analysis of variance** because the subgroups differ on two factors, namely sex and grade level. Three-way and

14. Philip Friedman, "Relationship of Teacher Reinforcement to Spontaneous Student Verbalization within the Classroom," *Journal of Educational Psychology* 65 (1973): 59–64.
15. You should note that the comparison of boys and girls involves two groups. Thus this comparison could be tested for statistical significance by a *t* test. Indeed, an analysis of variance for two groups is identical to a *t* test. The equivalence is shown mathemtaically by the equation $F = t^2$.

TABLE 13.4

Means and Standard Deviations of Pupil-Initiated Interchanges by Sex at Each of Four Grade Levels

Grade Level	Male $\overline{X}$	SD	Female $\overline{X}$	SD
1	7.61	3.77	7.39	4.01
3	10.67	4.21	11.28	5.26
5	14.28	5.90	11.50	3.95
7	9.61	3.94	8.83	3.83

even four-way analyses of variance can be done, depending upon the complexity of the data. For example, if each child in the Friedman study had been classified further as high achieving or low achieving, a three-way analysis of variance might be done. Each child would be represented on three factors: sex, grade level, and achievement level.

The number of levels represented in each factor is sometimes used to describe a particular analysis of variance design. One can say that a "2 x 4 factorial analysis of variance design" was used to compare the various mean scores shown in table 13.4, because there were two levels of one factor (male and female) and four levels of another factor (first, third, fifth, and seventh grades).

Further variations in analysis of variance designs are not described here because they involve complex statistical considerations. The student should consult an expert statistician to ensure that the correct analysis of variance design is selected for her research. We also suggest that you read the sections pertaining to analysis of variance in chapter 15. If employed properly, analysis of variance is a powerful technique. A single set of calculations allows the researcher to test the statistical significance of several comparisons and interactions among groups of subjects who vary on one or more factors.

Analysis of Covariance

In doing causal-comparative studies, researchers sometimes need to determine whether a difference between two groups on a particular variable can be explained by another difference that exists between the two groups. Suppose the researcher's hypothesis is that seventh-grade boys make more grammatical errors in writing class papers than seventh-grade girls. A sample of papers written by the two groups is scored for grammatical errors, and it is found by *t* test that the mean number of errors is significantly greater for the boys than for the girls.

At this point the researcher needs to ask the question, "Can this obtained difference be explained in terms of some other variable on which the groups might differ?" In other words, alternative hypotheses (see p. 538) need to be tested. The researcher might consider the length of the students' papers as a possible explanatory variable. Suppose it is found that the sample of boys wrote significantly longer papers than the sample of girls, thus increasing their opportunity to make grammatical errors. The researcher now needs to determine whether controlling for initial differences in writing productivity eliminates the obtained difference in mean number of grammatical errors.

The statistical technique of **analysis of covariance** is used to control for initial differences between groups.[16] The effect of analysis of covariance is to make the two groups equal with respect to one or more control variables. If a difference is still found between the two groups, one cannot use the control variable to explain the effect. In our example, suppose the researcher found that boys still made significantly more grammatical errors than girls after using analysis of covariance to control for initial differences in writing productivity. The researcher would be able to conclude that the sex difference in grammatical errors was not due to the fact that boys write longer papers.

Analysis of covariance is useful in causal-comparative studies because the researcher cannot always select comparison groups that are matched with respect to all relevant variables except the one that is the main concern of the researcher's investigation. Analysis of covariance provides a post hoc method of matching groups on such variables as age, aptitude, prior education, and socioeconomic class. The research data need to satisfy certain statistical assumptions before analysis of covariance can be applied, however.[17]

The assumptions, such as homogeneity of regression, can be checked empirically, but the computations are complex. The inexperienced researcher is advised to consult an expert statistician if he plans to use analysis of covariance.

Multivariate Analysis of Variance

Multivariate analysis of variance (usually abbreviated MANOVA) is a statistical technique for determining whether several groups differ on *more than one* de-

---

16. In the next chapter we shall find that similar statistical techniques (partial and part correlation) can be used to determine whether a correlation between two variables is the result of their mutual relationship to one or more other variables.

17. The assumptions are discussed in an article by Janet Elashoff (see Annotated References at the end of this chapter).

pendent variable. MANOVA is quite similar to the *t* test and to analysis of variance. The only noteworthy difference between the techniques is that the *t* test and analysis of variance can only determine whether several groups differ on one dependent variable. For example, in the study of test anxiety discussed above, five separate *t* tests were done to determine whether high and low test-anxious groups differed on any of the five dependent variables (see table 13.2). Instead, a single MANOVA could have been done to determine whether high and low test-anxious students differed on all these variables considered together.

Another example is provided by the data in table 13.4 from Friedman's study. These data could have been tested for statistical significance using MANOVA rather than analysis of variance if other dependent variables besides frequency of child-initiated utterances were available. For example, the researcher might have collected data on frequency of teacher-initiated questions directed to each child and frequency of teacher praise directed to each child. The MANOVA would determine whether the subgroups representing the two independent variables (sex and grade level) differed significantly from each other on the three dependent variables (child-initiated utterances, teacher questions, and teacher praise) considered together.

Each subject included in a MANOVA will have a score on two or more dependent variables. These scores are represented by a mathematical expression called a **vector**. Each subject in the study has a vector score. Also, a mean vector score can be calculated for a group of subjects. This mean vector score is called a **centroid**. The purpose of MANOVA is to determine whether there are statistically significant differences between the centroids of different groups.

The concept of representing several dependent variables by a single vector can be understood in a nontechnical way. Consider the case of two groups—high- and low-achieving students—who have been measured on two dependent variables: attitude toward their present school and attitude toward being engaged in further schooling. Each student's scores can be expressed in the form (6, 8), indicating that a student had a score of 6 on the first variable and a score of 8 on the second variable. The scores can also be represented on a graph. Each single point on the graph represents a student's scores on two variables. Suppose the graph points (comparable to "vector" scores) for high-achieving students tend to occupy a different space on the graph than the points for the low-achieving students. The purpose of MANOVA, in a sense, is to determine whether these two "spaces" differ significantly from each other.

Our example has been of two dependent variables represented on a two-dimensional graph. You might try imagining the case of three dependent variables and how each subject's vector of scores on them can be represented by a single point on a three-dimensional graph.

The first step in doing a MANOVA should be to test the assumption of the equality of group dispersions. If a nonsignificant F is obtained, one can conclude that the assumption is satisfied. (Researchers sometimes skip this step because MANOVA is robust, meaning that the assumption can be violated to an extent without violating the validity of the test.) The next step is to do a test of the statistical significance of the difference between group centroids. The most commonly used test for this purpose is **Wilks lambda** (λ). This test yields an F value, which can be looked up in an F ratio table to determine its level of statistical significance. If a significant MANOVA F is obtained, the researcher can then do an analysis of variance on each dependent variable to determine which of these variables are statistically significant and contributing to the overall MANOVA F. Although unlikely, it is possible to obtain a significant MANOVA F without finding a significant F in any of the analyses of variance.

A typical causal-comparative study will include a substantial number of dependent variables. Our preceding discussion should not be construed to mean that all of the variables must be tested for statistical significance by a single MANOVA. The researcher should group the variables into clusters (that is, vectors) that include educationally or psychologically related variables. Each cluster of variables can be analyzed by a separate MANOVA.

The use of MANOVA in causal-comparative research is illustrated in a study conducted by Patricia Elmore and Ellen Vasu.[18] One purpose of their study was to determine whether male and female students taking a statistics course differed from each other on a variety of characteristics. Sex differences were examined on a total of 29 variables, which were organized into the following clusters: spatial-visualization ability (5 variables); math attitudes (9 variables); mathematical background (3 variables); masculinity-feminity of interest pattern as measured by the MMPI (2 variables); masculinity-feminity of interest pattern as measured by the Attitude Toward Feminist Issues Scale (9 variables); and statistics course achievement (1 variable). Sex differences on each cluster of variables were tested for statistical significance using MANOVA.

Table 13.5 presents the MANOVAs that were done on the first two clusters.[19] The five measures of spatial-visualization ability were taken from the Kit of Factor-Referenced Cognitive Tests. The nine measures of math attitudes consisted of the subscales of the Fennema-Sherman Mathematics Attitudes Scales. The first set of six data columns presents descriptive statistics on the variables. The next set of four columns shows the MANOVA results. The first of these columns presents Wilks's test of statistical significance. Next one finds the F ratio associated with Wilks's lambda; the degrees of freedom (*df*) associated

18. Patricia B. Elmore and Ellen S. Vasu, "Relationship Between Selected Variables and Statistics Achievement: Building a Theoretical Model," *Journal of Educational Psychology* 72 (1980): 457–67.
19. Ibid., p. 460.

TABLE 13.5

Descriptive Statistics and Univariate/Multivariate Analyses of Variance for Measures of Spatial Visualization Ability and Mathematics Attitudes

Variables	Male			Female			MANOVA				ANOVA		
	M	SD	N	M	SD	N	Wilks's criterion	F	df	p	F	df	p
Spatial visualization ability													
Kit of Factor-Referenced Cognitive Tests							.8713	5.17	5,175	.0002			
Card rotations	104.41	28.92	98	91.73	25.25	83					9.59	1,179	.0023
Cube comparisons	25.83	6.92	98	23.01	7.59	83					6.78	1,179	.0100
Form board	120.71	39.93	98	102.93	38.79	83					9.03	1,179	.0030
Paper folding	10.60	4.22	98	11.04	3.55	83					.56	1,179	.4539
Surface development	36.85	15.58	98	33.52	15.65	83					2.07	1,179	.1519
Attitudes toward mathematics-related coursework													
Fennema-Sherman Mathematics Attitudes Scales							.8668	2.94	9,172	.0030			
Confidence in learning math	42.68	9.82	98	41.50	11.29	84					.57	1,180	.4504
Teacher	40.63	5.74	98	41.49	7.46	84					.76	1,180	.3840
Usefulness of math	46.48	6.73	98	47.31	7.15	84					.65	1,180	.4215
Mother	39.94	5.31	98	41.45	7.50	84					2.52		.1142
Attitude toward success in math	45.41	7.01	98	49.45	6.78	84					15.52	1,180	.0001
Effectance motivation in math	39.98	8.88	98	41.36	9.47	84					1.02	1,180	.3130
Math anxiety	39.22	9.90	98	37.36	11.77	84					1.35	1,180	.2465
Father	39.95	7.41	98	41.35	7.84	84					1.52	1,180	.2188
Math as a male domain	50.90	7.55	98	53.57	6.02	84					6.82	1,180	.0098

with the F ratio; and finally the p value for the F ratio. Both MANOVAs are statistically significant, meaning that male and female students differ reliably on the clusters of variables that measured spatial visualization ability and math attitudes.

Because the MANOVAs revealed a significant overall effect, it was appropriate for Elmore and Vasu to do an analysis of variance on each of the variables in the two vectors. The results of these analyses are shown in the last three columns of table 13.5. With respect to the first vector, males and females differed significantly on three of the variables: card rotations, cube comparisons, and form board. Only two of the variables in the second vector yielded significant differences (attitude toward success in math and math as a male domain), although most of the variables yielded differences in the same direction.

MANOVA is a useful statistical technique because it helps the researcher see the data in a multivariate perspective. Well-defined groups, such as those studied in causal-comparative research, are unlikely to differ from each other because of a single, superficial trait or ability. Rather, groups are likely to differ in some respect because of many interrelated differences in their personal background. MANOVA helps the researcher conceptualize and analyze the nature of these multiple influences.

The correlational counterpart of MANOVA is canonical analysis, which is described in the next chapter. Either technique can be used to analyze data that consist of one or more independent variables and two or more dependent variables. Although one does find instances of MANOVA in the literature, canonical analysis appears to be becoming the method of choice among educational researchers.

Tests for the Difference between Variances

The standard deviation and its square, the variance, are two statistics for describing the variability of scores obtained from a sample of subjects. The researcher might want to do a statistical test to determine whether the variances in scores for two samples differ significantly from each other, just as she might want to determine whether the mean scores differ significantly. There are two main reasons for doing this test. The first reason is that most of the commonly used statistical tests—including the t test for differences between means—assume that the variances of the two samples are approximately equal. If the score variances of two samples differ markedly, then one of the nonparametric tests discussed later in this chapter should be used.

The second reason for testing variance homogeneity between two samples is that the researcher's hypothesis may concern the variability of sample scores. For example, the researcher might hypothesize that college graduates are more like one another in scholastic aptitude than college dropouts. The rationale might be that all college graduates are apt to be fairly intelligent but that, for various reasons, both students of high and low aptitude may leave college before graduation. To test this hypothesis in a causal-comparative study, the researcher would administer a measure of scholastic aptitude to a sample of college graduates and a sample of college dropouts. Next the researcher would do a statistical test to determine whether college graduates have less variable scores on the aptitude measure than do the college dropouts.

The statistical tool used to test for significance of differences between variances is analysis of variance, which is the same tool used to test for differences between several means. The larger the F ratio the less likely is it that the variances of the populations from which the samples were drawn are equal. If the F ratio exceeds the significance level set by the researcher, she will reject the null hypothesis (stating equality of variances) and conclude that the obtained difference between the sample variances is a true one.

You should be aware that several statistical tests are available for comparing differences between variances. If the two sets of scores are obtained from independent samples, the **test for homogeneity of independent variances** is used. If the two sets of scores are obtained from repeated measures on a single sample or from two matched samples, then the **test for homogeneity of related variances** is used. Should the student wish to determine whether the variances of more than two sets of scores differ significantly from one another, the F **maximum test for homogeneity of variance** can be used.

STATISTICAL ANALYSIS: NONPARAMETRIC TESTS

Advantages and Disadvantages of Nonparametric Tests

The tests of statistical significance discussed in the two previous sections are known as **parametric statistics.** A parameter, you will recall, is a population score, whereas a statistic is a score for a sample randomly drawn from the population. Parametric statistics make certain assumptions about population parameters. One assumption is that the scores in the population are normally distributed about the mean; another assumption is that the population variances of the comparison groups in one's study are approximately equal. When large deviations from these assumptions are present in the research data, parametric statistics should not be used. Instead, one of the **nonparametric statistics** should be selected since, as their name implies, they do not make any assumptions about the shape or variance of population scores.

Parametric statistics assume that the scores being analyzed are derived from a measure that has equal intervals. The student will recall from our discussion in the previous chapter that most continuous scores meet this criterion. When scores are dichotomous or in the form of categories or ranks, one of the nonparametric statistics should be used for data analysis. In the next sections we shall discuss the common types of nonparametric statistics used to analyze data in the form of ranks, frequency counts, or dichotomies.

When research data meet the assumption of being interval scores but do not meet the assumptions of normal distribution and variance homogeneity, it is still advisable to use one of the parametric statistics presented earlier in the chapter. The main reasons for recommending the use of parametric statistics in these situations are that: (1) studies have shown that moderate departure from the theoretical assumptions has very little effect upon the value of the parametric technique;[20] (2) nonparametric statistics are generally less powerful, that is, they require larger samples in order to yield the same level of significance; and (3) for many of the problems encountered in educational research, suitable nonparametric tests are not available.

The Chi-Square Test

Chi-square (χ^2) is a nonparametric statistical test that is used when the research data are in the form of frequency counts. These frequency counts can be placed into two or more categories. Chi-square was used to investigate one of the objectives of the test-anxiety study by Culler and Holahan. This objective involved replicating previous research findings that high test anxiety is associated with a decrement in GPA.

The researchers formed two categories of GPA: 2.00 or higher, and 1.99 or lower. The reason for splitting GPA, a continuous variable, into two categories is that "a GPA of 2.00 (on a scale of 0–4) is generally considered a cutoff for success in college, since it is a requirement for graduation."[21] After forming the two categories, the researchers counted the number of high test-anxious and low test-anxious students who fell into each category. The frequency counts are shown in table 13.6.[22] Next, the frequency counts were converted to percentages. For example, 19 high test-anxious students had GPAs lower than 2.00. The total number of high test-anxious students is 65. Nineteen divided by 65 is 29 percent, as shown in table 13.6.

The percentages indicate clearly that high test-anxious students are much

20. Refer to the discussion earlier in the chapter on the effects of violating assumptions underlying the *t* test.
21. Culler and Holahan, "Test Anxiety and Academic Performance," p. 17.
22. Ibid., p. 18.

TABLE 13.6

Frequencies and Percentages for Above/Below 2.00 GPA by Test-Anxiety Group

GPA	High Test Anxiety		Low Test Anxiety	
	Frequency	%	Frequency	%
Less than 2.00	19	29	2	7
Above 2.00	46	71	29	93

NOTE: GPA = gradepoint average. $\chi^2(1)$ = 5.11, $p <$ .03.

more likely to have a failing GPA than low test-anxious students. The question now is whether the difference between groups is statistically significant. The null hypothesis to be tested is that there is no difference between the populations of high test-anxious and low test-anxious students in their distributions of passing and failing GPA scores. The chi-square statistic is used to test the null hypothesis. Applied to the data in table 13.6, chi-square is 5.11, which has a p value of .03. Since the null hypothesis is usually rejected at the .05 level, we can reject the particular null hypothesis that high and low test-anxious students have the same distribution of passing and failing GPA scores. (Note that p = .03 is less than p = .05, meaning that p = .03 exceeds the requirements for rejecting the null hypothesis at the .05 level.)

The student should be aware that there are several types of chi-square tests from which one can choose. A simple chi-square test can be done when the frequencies are in the form of a fourfold table, as illustrated in Table 13.6.

When the frequency data are grouped into more than four cells, a more complex chi-square test is done. The student also should be aware that when the expected frequency in any cell is less than five, a correction needs to be applied to the regular chi-square test. (The student can apply Yates' correction, or he can do a Fisher exact test.) In the process of doing a chi-square test, the student might also compute a **phi coefficient** (for a fourfold table) or a **contingency coefficient** (for more than four cells). These correlation coefficients provide an estimate of the magnitude of the relationhip between the variables in a chi-square table.[23]

The chi-square test is most often used when the categories into which frequencies fall are discrete rather than continuous. Let us suppose we want to determine whether large families contribute more or fewer than the expected proportion of children appearing before juvenile courts. The number of chil-

---

23. The phi coefficient and the contingency coefficient are discussed further in the next chapter.

dren is a discrete variable (because a family can have 3 or 4 children but not 3½). Appearance before juvenile court is similarly a situation that has either occurred or not occurred and is also discrete. Under these conditions, chi-square is the appropriate test of statistical significance.

Chi-square is equally useful when the traits or characteristics being considered are actually continuous variables that have been categorized. This was the case with the GPA scores used in the chi-square analysis shown in table 13.6. GPA is a continuous variable because GPAs can take on any value within a given range (in this study, between 0.00 and 4.00). The researchers were justified in transforming GPA into a categorical variable, though, because each category has personal and social significance: failure versus success in college coursework.

Other Nonparametric Tests

Of the nonparametric tests of significance, chi-square is probably the most frequently used by educational researchers in causal-comparative studies. Other nonparametric tests are sometimes used, particularly when the research data are in the form of rank-order scores or interval scores that grossly violate the parametric test assumptions of normality and homogeneity of variance.

The **Mann-Whitney *U* test** can be used to determine whether the distributions of scores of two independent samples differ significantly from each other. If *U* is statistically significant, it means that the "bulk" of scores in one population is higher than the bulk of scores in the other population. The two populations are represented by the two independent samples on which the *U* test is made.

The **Wilcoxon signed-rank test** is used to determine whether the distributions of scores in two samples differ significantly from each other when the scores of the samples are correlated (either through matching or because repeated measures are taken on the same sample). The Wilcoxon test is analogous to the *t* test for correlated means except that it makes no assumptions regarding the shape of the score distribution or homogeneity of variance between the two sets of scores. If more than two groups of subjects are to be compared, a nonparametric one-way analysis of variance (the **Kruskal-Wallis test**) can be used.

INTERPRETATION OF CAUSAL-COMPARATIVE FINDINGS

The process of interpreting causal-comparative findings can be illustrated using the test-anxiety study. The findings of interest to us are presented in table 13.2.

You will recall that high test-anxious and low test-anxious students differed significantly on two variables: study habits and total study hours. High test-anxious students devoted more time to study, and they had poorer study habits.

We can conclude from these results that there is a reliable relationship between test anxiety, study habits, and study time. Can we reach beyond this conclusion and infer that study habits and study time *cause* test anxiety? The results are consistent with this interpretation, but because this was a causal-comparative study, other interpretations must be considered. It may be that students with poor study habits feel they must compensate by devoting extra time to study. They would still feel anxious during tests, though, because they would realize that they inadequately processed the course material due to poor study habits. In this interpretation, poor study habits are a determinant both of study time and test anxiety; study time by itself is not a determinant of test anxiety. The results in table 13.2 are consistent with this interpretation.

At least three other interpretations of the results come to mind. Perhaps students who habitually feel anxious during tests decide to deal with their anxiety by studying more hours in preparation for tests. If this interpretation is correct, text anxiety is a determinant of study time, rather than study time being a determinant of test anxiety. The other two interpretations refer to factors not measured by the researchers. For example, it is plausible that students who have low scholastic aptitude will have poor study habits and will compensate by studying more. They will experience test anxiety because they are not able to perform well on tests due to low scholastic aptitude. In this interpretation, scholastic aptitude is a determinant of study habits, study time, and test anxiety.

Note further that all three variables were assessed by self-report measures. Students' answers on the measures might have reflected a certain response set rather than their actual behavior. For example, students with negative academic self-concept might be inclined to report high test anxiety, low study skill, and the need to spend much time on study. In this case, academic self-concept is the determinant of all the observed relationships.

All of the above interpretations, and others not mentioned, are consistent with the researchers' data. This is the basic problem of causal-comparative studies. They are good for revealing relationships between variables, but they offer little help in clarifying the causal patterns underlying these relationships.

Two procedures can be used to improve the interpretability of causal-comparative studies. First, as we discussed earlier in the chapter, alternative hypotheses should be formulated and tested whenever possible. For example, scholastic aptitude is a plausible determinant of the factors that were measured in the test-anxiety study. Students usually take a scholastic aptitude test for admission to college, and their test scores are recorded in college files. Had these scores been available to the researchers, they could have included them in the research design. For example, scholastic aptitude test scores could have been used as a covariate in an analysis of covariance. This analysis would determine whether the observed relationships are maintained after the influence of scholastic aptitude has been removed statistically. A similar analysis could have been done for academic self-concept, had this variable been measured.

The second procedure to improve interpretability is to examine the relationships between all the variables in the study using the techniques of path analysis. (Path analysis is discussed in the next chapter.) For example, one of the interpretations mentioned above is that students with poor study habits are likely to compensate by devoting more time to study. This interpretation could have been tested in the test-anxiety study by correlating the study habits measure and the study time measure.

The most powerful method for demonstrating the causal properties of causal-comparative findings is to do experiments. The presumed cause, or causes, of the outcome being studied would be manipulated. Given the findings presented in table 13.2, a researcher might consider manipulating study habits and/or study time. How might the experiment be done? One possibility is to select a sample of high test-anxious students. Half the students would receive training that has demonstrable success in improving their study skills. The other half would not receive the training. The total sample's level of test anxiety would be measured at subsequent points in time. If the test anxiety of the trained students decreased relative to the untrained students, we could conclude that study habits are in fact a determinant of test anxiety.

We wish to emphasize once again that both causal-comparative research and experiments have advantages. A single causal-comparative study can reveal the relationships among a substantial number of variables. Experiments then can verify the causal properties of the most promising relationships discovered.

THE CAUSAL-COMPARATIVE METHOD AND CORRELATION

We noted at the outset of the chapter that the causal-comparative method and the correlational method are similar in certain respects. Both methods are non-experimental in that they do not involve manipulation of a treatment variable. Also, in both methods the researcher studies the relationship between variable X (e.g., delinquency) and variable Y (e.g., school achievement). The major differences between the two methods are in the measurement of variable X and in the analysis of the resulting data.

Suppose variable X is juvenile delinquency. In the Gluecks' research, which was described at the beginning of this chapter, the variable of juvenile delinquency had two values—present (delinquent) and absent (nondelinquent). If the researcher wished, delinquency could be conceptualized as a continuous variable. For example, one might construct 25 items each of which described a different type of delinquent behavior. Students could be requested to check each item that reflected behaviors in which they had engaged recently. (Naturally, procedures to ensure protection of human rights would be followed in administering this scale.) Scores on the scale could vary from 0 to 25, resulting in 26 different values of the variable of juvenile delinquency. Students' scores on the 25-item scale could be correlated with their scores on another variable (e.g., academic achievement) to determine the strength of relationship between the two variables. This conceptualization of variables X and Y is an example of the correlational method.

The same variables can be investigated by the causal-comparative method. Students' scores on the 25-item scale can be used to form two or more groups, for example, high-delinquent students (scores of 13 or higher) and low-delinquent students (12 or lower). Sometimes the **extreme-groups method** is used.[24] In this approach, students at extreme ends of the distribution (e.g., students with scores of 20 or higher, and students with scores of 5 or lower) are used to form two contrasting groups. Students with scores between 6 and 19 are eliminated from further involvement in the research. The two or more groups then are compared in order to determine whether the difference between their mean scores on variable Y is statistically significant.

The extreme-groups approach is generally used when it is expensive or difficult to measure subjects on variable Y. This situation usually arises when variable Y requires extended observation or individual testing. Suppose that the researcher can include only 20 students in the sample. If he administers the 25-item scale described above to 20 students, he probably will include only a few students who are high or low in expressed delinquency. The range of delinquency resulting from this procedure may be too limited to reveal relationships with variable Y.

This problem can be avoided by administering the 25-item scale (which we will assume can be done quickly and inexpensively) to 100 students. This large sample almost certainly will contain many more students with high and low scores than the other procedure. The researcher then can select extreme groups from the large sample for more intensive study. If the final sample must be limited to 20 students, the extreme groups would include the 10 highest-scoring students and the 10 lowest-scoring students.

Irrespective of how the groups are formed in causal-comparative research, the resulting data usually are analyzed by the *t* test, analysis of vari-

---

24. For a technical discussion of the extreme groups approach and its relationship to the correlational method, see Edward F. Alf, Jr., and Norman M. Abrahams, "The Use of Extreme Groups in Assessing Relationships," *Psychometrika* 40 (1975): 563–72.

ance, analysis of covariance, or by one of the nonparametric tests. The appropriate inferential statistic enables the researcher to test the null hypothesis that there is no difference between the groups on variable Y. However, inferential statistics do not tell the researcher the magnitude of the relationship between variable X and variable Y. Thus, researchers sometimes first analyze causal-comparative data to determine whether observed differences are statistically significant. If a statistically significant difference is obtained, the researcher will compute one of the correlational statistics (presented in the next chapter) to determine the magnitude of relationship between the two variables. A bivariate statistic such as the product-moment correlation coefficient is usually computed following a *t* test. The correlation ratio (eta) is computed following analysis of variance. The phi coefficient or contingency coefficient can be computed as part of the process of doing a chi-square test.

MISTAKES SOMETIMES MADE IN DOING CAUSAL-COMPARATIVE RESEARCH

1. The researcher assumes the results of causal-comparative research are proof of a cause-and-effect relationship.
2. Does not form homogeneous groups to be compared. After the initial groups have been defined, does not form subgroups on the basis of age, sex, socio-economic status, or similar variables.
3. Uses the wrong sampling distributions when testing the statistical significance of data obtained from small samples.
4. Does not use the correct *t* test when comparing independent means or correlated means.
5. Does a one-tailed test of statistical significance when a two-tailed test should be done.
6. When comparing several means, does not do an analysis of variance prior to determining which group means differ significantly from each other.
7. Does not control for initial differences between groups that might explain the differences that are found.
8. Neglects to use a nonparametric test of significance when the data grossly violate the assumptions of parametric statistical tests.

ANNOTATED REFERENCES

Amick, Daniel J., and Crittenden, Kathleen S. "Analysis of Variance and Multivariate Analysis of Variance." In *Introductory Multivariate Analysis,* edited by Daniel J. Amick and Herbert J. Walberg. Berkeley, Calif.: McCutchan, 1975.

This book chapter describes the uses and mathematical bases for the following statistical techniques: one-way analysis of variance, tests for homogeneity of variance, factorial analysis of variance, and multivariate analysis of variance. Also, the authors show how these techniques relate to each other.

Bruning, James L., and Kintz, B. L. *Computational Handbook of Statistics.* 2nd ed. Glenview, Ill.: Scott, Foresman, 1977.

A step-by-step computational guide is given for these statistical tests frequently used in causal-comparative studies: *t* test for a difference between a sample mean and a population mean, *t* test for a difference between two independent means, *t* test for a difference between two correlated means; one-way analysis of variance; test for difference between variances of two independent samples, test for difference between variances of two related samples, test for differences among several independent variances; Duncan's multiple-range test; test for significance of difference between two proportions; Mann-Whitney *U* Test for independent samples; Wilcoxon signed-rank test for related samples; simple and complex chi-square tests, phi coefficient and contingency coefficient.

Campbell, Donald T., and Stanley, Julian C. "Experimental and Quasi-Experimental Designs for Research." In *Handbook of Research on Teaching*, edited by N. L. Gage. Chicago: Rand McNally, 1963.

This classic chapter, which is available as a separate reprint from the *Handbook*, is primarily about experimental design, although the concluding section discusses ex post facto research, including causal-comparative designs. The authors stress the problems involved in drawing causal inferences from ex post facto data.

Elashoff, Janet D. "Analysis of Covariance: A Delicate Instrument." *American Educational Research Journal* 6 (1969): 383–99.

In this classic article the author discusses the purpose of analysis of covariance and its advantages and limitations. The author also describes the assumptions about the data which must be satisfied if analysis of covariance is to be used correctly. Procedures for checking these assumptions in a set of data are given.

Siegel, Sidney. *Nonparametric Statistics for the Behavioral Sciences.* New York: McGraw-Hill, 1956.

Nonparametric techniques have a number of advantages that make them particularly well suited for certain data of the behavioral sciences. These techniques make no assumptions concerning the population distribution, are easy to compute, and are particularly useful with small samples such as are often used by the graduate student. This text presents nonparametric techniques in a form that can be understood by the average behavioral scientist who lacks advanced mathematical training. Siegel's emphasis is upon research application of these techniques, and he strengthens his presentation with many interesting examples taken from the behavioral sciences. Although some of the techniques presented such as chi-square and Spearman's *rho* are treated in most textbooks in educational and psychological statistics, many of the techniques covered in this text are not generally found in these sources.

SELF-CHECK TEST

Circle the correct answer to each of the following questions. An answer key is provided on page 881.

1. The main situation in which a researcher would use a causal-comparative design rather than an experimental design is when
   a. random sampling is not possible.
   b. experimental manipulation is not possible.
   c. use of standardized tests is not possible.
   d. young children are the subjects of the research.
2. One of the main limitations of causal-comparative research is that
   a. it is more expensive than other types of research.
   b. control groups cannot be studied.
   c. cause-and-effect generalizations cannot be drawn from the research data.
   d. null hypotheses cannot be tested.
3. In most statistical analyses of causal-comparative data, the first step is to compute
   a. correlations.
   b. means and standard deviations.
   c. ranges.
   d. variances.
4. If sample size is greater than appropriate for the *t* test, the appropriate statistical tool is the
   a. *F* test.
   b. analysis of covariance.
   c. correlation coefficient.
   d. *z* distribution.
5. One of the assumptions that the *t* test makes about scores obtained in causal-comparative research is that
   a. score variances for the populations under study are equal.
   b. means of the scores are equal.
   c. population means do not differ.
   d. score variances for the populations under study are not equal.

6. If a researcher matches subjects between groups, the appropriate *t* test is the *t* test for
   a. independent means.
   b. equal variances.
   c. correlated means.
   d. unequal means.
7. If a researcher conducting causal-comparative research is almost certain that any detected change will be in the hypothesized direction, it is appropriate to use the
   a. two-tailed *t* test.
   b. analysis of covariance.
   c. one-tailed *t* test.
   d. correlation coefficient.
8. A post hoc method of matching groups on certain variables is the
   a. analysis of covariance.
   b. multiple regression equation.
   c. *t* test for correlated means.
   d. *t* test for independent means.
9. Multivariate analysis of variance is used to detect statistically significant group differences in
   a. vectors of independent variables.
   b. vectors of dependent variables.
   c. correlations between dependent variables.
   d. correlations between independent and dependent variables.
10. The most important characteristic of nonparametric statistics is that they
   a. make no assumption about the variance of the population scores.
   b. demand that scores in the population be normally distributed about the mean.
   c. require equal population variances.
   d. can be used only with the interval scale of measurement.
11. The purpose of computing a correlational statistic following a *t* test or analysis of variance is
   a. to determine whether the sample variances are equal.
   b. to determine the magnitude of the relationship between the variables.
   c. to determine the directionality of the observed differences.
   d. All of the above are correct.

APPLICATION PROBLEMS

The following problems are designed to give you practice in applying significant concepts and research procedures explained in chapter 13. Most of them do not have a single correct answer. For feedback, you can compare your answers with the sample answers on page 894.

1. Define a suitable comparison group for each of the following defined groups.
   a. High school mathematics teachers with high scores on authoritarianism.
   b. Bilingual first-grade children of Mexican ancestry.
   c. Fourth-grade Pueblo Indian boys who have attended school only on the reservation.
2. An investigator studies the difference in achievement of third-grade children who learned to read using the "phonetic" method and those who learned to read using the "look-say" method. Children in the two groups were matched within three *T*-score points on scholastic aptitude. What type of *t* test should the investigator use to analyze the results? Why?
3. You hypothesize that low-achieving children who receive special tutoring will make significantly greater achievement gains than those who spend an equal amount of time in the regular classroom. Would this hypothesis be tested with a one-tailed or two-tailed test of significance? Why?
4. An investigator is interested in learning whether attendance at an authoritarian high school might tend to produce authoritarian students. He locates two high schools that are located in very similar neighborhoods serving similar racial and socioeconomic groups. School A employs a rigid authoritarian structure, and both teachers and administrators have high-average scores on a measure of authoritarianism. School B employs a democratic administrative structure with major student involvement in running the school. Both teachers and administrators in School B have low-average scores on a test of authoritarianism.
   a. In a pilot study the investigator randomly selects 25 students from each school and administers a 40-item scale of authoritarianism to them. What statistical technique should be used to analyze these data?
   b. Each high school had 12 extracurricular activities that were classified by a group of independent judges as either high, average, or low in terms of authoritarian structure and activities. The investigator wishes to compare the proportion of students in each school who had joined each of the three types of organizations. What statistical technique should be used to make this comparison?
   c. In checking school records, the investigator finds that most seniors in the two high schools had been administered a California *F* scale (a measure of authoritarianism) during their last year of junior high school. He decides to administer a different but similar authoritarianism measure to seniors who had taken the earlier test, and then see how the senior-level authoritarianism scores differed between students in the two schools when their earlier scores were taken into consideration. What statistical technique should be used?

SUGGESTION SHEET

If your last name starts with letters from May to Mor, please complete the Suggestion Sheet at the end of the book while this chapter is still fresh in your mind.

14.

EXPLORING RELATIONSHIPS BETWEEN VARIABLES: THE CORRELATIONAL METHOD

OVERVIEW

This chapter describes how the correlational method is used in prediction studies and in studies that explore relationships between two or more variables. In prediction studies the researcher determines the extent to which subjects' scores on a predictor variable (e.g., aptitude test scores) predict their scores on a criterion variable (e.g., school grades). In relationship studies the researcher's objective is to discover possible cause-and-effect patterns among several variables. A variety of correlational statistics are available to estimate the magnitude of relationship between variables. Selection of a particular correlational statistic depends upon the variables to be included in the analysis. Recent correlational studies are characterized by researchers' interest in including a large number of variables in the formulation of the research problem. The multivariate technique of multiple regression is rapidly becoming one of the most widely used methods for analyzing research data in education.

OBJECTIVES

After studying this chapter, you should be able to:

1. Draw appropriate inferences from research data presented in the form of correlation coefficients.
2. State at least one advantage and one limitation of the correlational method.
3. Describe the procedures involved in conducting a relationship study, including selection of the problem, selection of subjects, data collection, and data analysis.
4. Describe three uses for prediction studies.
5. Describe the procedures involved in conducting a prediction study, including

selection of the problem, selection of subjects, data collection, and data analysis.

6. Describe research situations in which the different types of bivariate correlational statistics are used.
7. Plot a scattergram and explain its use in correlational research.
8. Describe research situations in which correction for attenuation, correction for restriction in range, and partial correlation are used.
9. Describe research situations in which multiple regression, discriminant analysis, canonical correlation, path analysis, and factor analysis are used.
10. Describe the phenomenon of shrinkage in prediction research and how it can be handled.
11. Interpret the results of a multiple regression analysis, factor analysis, path analysis, and correlation matrix.
12. Formulate subgroups and moderator variables for use in correlational research.
13. Explain the use of Taylor-Russell tables in group prediction.
14. Interpret the meaning of correlation coefficients that differ in magnitude and statistical significance.

THE NATURE OF CORRELATION

Correlational studies include all those research projects in which an attempt is made to discover or clarify relationships through the use of correlation coefficients. Since an understanding of correlation coefficients is essential to what follows, we will briefly discuss their meaning in nonmathematical terms.

Individual differences are of prime importance to the researcher. If everyone had the same school achievement, for example, there would be little interest in studying the determinants of school achievement, in predicting school achievement, or in measuring school achievement. Yet people do *vary* with respect to this attribute, and the researcher is interested in understanding this variability. Why do scores on a particular test of school achievement vary from 40 to 100? Or to state it another way, what factors are related to these variations in scores? The correlation coefficient is a statistic that was designed to help researchers answer such questions.

To understand how the correlation coefficient helps us in this situation, consider an achievement test on which a group of students earned scores varying from 40 to 100. How would we know if students' scores on some other measure, such as an intelligence test or personality inventory, are related to their scores on the achievement test? Suppose that students who earned a score of 40 on the achievement test had an IQ of 85 on an intelligence test; those with an achievement score of 41 had an IQ of 86; and so on through the range of scores, so that students with an achievement score of 100 had IQs of 145. If this were the case, we could say that there is a perfect relationship, or correlation, between the two variables.

Suppose, by contrast, that for any given achievement score there are students with widely varying IQs. For example, suppose students with scores of 40 on the achievement test had IQs ranging from 85 to 145. Then we would conclude that there is little relationship, or correlation, between the two variables. Another possibility is a negative relationship between achievement test scores and IQ, which would occur if students with progressively higher achievement scores earned progressively lower IQ scores.

The purpose of the **correlation coefficient** is to express in mathematical terms the degree of relationship between any two variables. If the relationship is perfectly positive (for each increment in one variable there is a corresponding increment in the other), the correlation coefficient will be 1.00. If the relationship is perfectly negative, it will be -1.00. If there is no relationship, the coefficient will be zero. If two variables are somewhat related, the coefficients will have a value between zero and 1.00 (if the relationship is positive) or between zero and -1.00 (if negative). Thus, the correlation coefficient is a precise way of stating the extent to which one variable is related to another. To express the idea another way, the correlation coefficient tells us how effectively persons' scores on one variable (e.g., an intelligence test) can be used to predict their scores on another test (e.g., an achievement test).

Several types of correlation coefficients are presented in this chapter. Different coefficients are necessary because certain variables (e.g., most measures of intelligence) are in the form of interval scales or ratio scales, whereas other variables are in the form of rank orderings (e.g., ranking of teachers in terms of their effectiveness) or dichotomies (e.g., true-false data). Also, the relationship between two variables is not always linear, as we shall find in our discussion of the correlation ratio.

The basic design in correlational research is very simple, involving nothing more than collecting data on two or more variables on the same group of subjects and computing a correlation coefficient. We might, for example, select a group of college freshmen and attempt to predict their first-year grades (variable 1) on the basis of their overall Scholastic Aptitude Test scores (variable 2). Many valuable studies in education have done little more than follow this simple design. Recent studies have employed more sophisticated correlational techniques in order to obtain a clearer picture of the relationships being studied.

As is the case with most research, the quality of correlational studies is determined not by the complexity of the design or the sophistication of the correlational techniques used, but by the depth of the rationale and theoretical constructs that guide the research design. In the past, many correlational studies in education have involved little more than locating available scores on a group of pupils and then correlating these scores in hopes that some meaningful relationship would emerge.

This approach might produce usable bits of information, but the chances of gaining significant knowledge are far less than if the researcher uses theory and the results of previous research to select variables to be correlated with one another.

Correlation and Causality

The correlational approach to analyzing relationships between variables has the same limitations with respect to causal inference as the causal-comparative approach discussed in the preceding chapter. For example, if one found a positive correlation between years of education and level of interest in cultural activities, one might infer that each year of formal schooling is likely to *cause, determine,* or *result in* greater interest in cultural activities. Two other causal inferences are equally plausible. Level of interest in cultural activities may determine how much education a student will seek for himself. Also, some third variable may determine both amount of education and level of interest in cultural activities, thus creating a relationship between these two variables. Parents' education is a possible third variable. Parents who are college graduates may encourage their children to stay in school longer and to develop more cultural interests than parents with less formal education. If this is true, then the observed relationship between education and cultural interests is not a cause-and-effect relationship in either direction but rather the result of their common determination by a third variable.

A correlational relationship between two variables is occasionally due to an "artifact." For example, if one correlates two scales from the same personality inventory, a significant relationship between the scales may be found because both scales contain some of the same items, not because the personality dimensions that they measure are causally related. In this situation a statistical technique can be used to correct the correlation coefficient for covariation due to overlapping test items.[1] Also, when raters are used to collect data, relationships between variables may be found because the same rater scores both variables. This is particularly likely when there is rater bias due to halo effect (see chapter 12). One may find, for example, interrelations between several "good" traits if raters form an initial positive or negative impression of a person. If the impression is positive, they will probably score the person high on all the traits;

1 This statistical technique is described in W. Grant Dahlstrom and G. S. Welsh, *An MMPI Handbook: A Guide to Use in Clinical Practice and Research* (Minneapolis: University of Minnesota Press, 1960), p. 83.

if the impression is negative, they probably will assign him low scores. Any relationship found between the traits would be due to this artifact rather than to a cause-and-effect pattern.

In summary, correlation coefficients cannot be used to determine cause-and-effect relationships, although they may be used to explore or predict relationships between two variables A and B. A correlation between A and B can mean that A is a determinant of B, that B is a determinant of A, that a third variable X determines both A and B, or that the relationship between A and B is due to an artifact. Only an experiment can provide a definitive conclusion about cause-and-effect. Correlation coefficients are best used to measure the *degree* of relationship between two variables and to explore *possible* causal factors that can later be tested in an experimental design.

In recent years a statistical technique known as path analysis has become popular for testing cause-and-effect hypotheses using correlational data. This technique requires the measurement of three or more variables and the formulation of a theory that makes explicit their causal relationship to each other. We shall discuss path analysis later in the chapter.

Advantages and Uses of the Correlational Method

The correlational method of analyzing research data is very useful in studying problems in education and in other behavioral sciences. Its principal advantage is that it permits one to analyze the relationships among a large number of variables in a single study. In the behavioral sciences we are frequently confronted with situations in which several variables are contributing causes of a particular pattern of behavior. The correlational method allows the researcher to analyze how several variables, either singly or in combination, might affect a particular pattern of behavior. The usual experimental technique, in contrast, permits the manipulation of only a single variable.

Another advantage of the correlational method is that it provides information concerning the degree of relationship between the variables being studied. As discussed in the previous chapter, this is an advantage over the causal-comparative method. For example, causal-comparative studies of teaching ability generally start with the identification of a group of good and a group of poor teachers. Comparisons are then made between the two groups on a number of dependent variables in order to identify possible causes for differences in teaching ability. It is obvious that such a dichotomy is artificial because, within both of these groups of teachers, some will certainly be better than others. These differences in degree are ignored when using the causal-comparative method. In reality, what we have in this population is not two groups of teachers of distinctly different ability, but a single group ranging in degree of teaching ability from very poor to very good. The correlation coefficient provides a measure of degree of relationship over the entire range of teaching ability or within certain ranges.

The correlational method is used for two major purposes: (1) to explore relationships between variables and (2) to predict scores on a variable from subjects' scores on other variables. In relationship research the variables may be measured at the same point in time or at different points in time. In prediction research the variables used for prediction must be measured prior to the variable to be predicted.

The design of relationship research and prediction research is presented in the next two sections of this chapter. The remainder of the chapter describes the types of correlational statistics that can be used to analyze relational or predictive data. Most of the statistics can be used in either type of research. A few statistical techniques have been developed specifically for prediction research, and these are so noted. In subsequent chapters on the experimental method (chapters 15 and 16) you will find that the same correlational statistics can also be used to analyze data from experiments.

PLANNING A RELATIONSHIP STUDY

The Basic Research Design

Relationship studies are concerned primarily with gaining a better understanding of complex behavior patterns (e.g., school achievement) by studying the relationships betweeen these patterns and variables to which they are hypothesized to be causally related (e.g., intelligence). This research design is especially useful for exploratory studies in areas where little or no previous research has been done. To understand the steps involved in conducting a relationship study, we will consider a study by Henriette Lahaderne on the correlates of children's attention in class.[2]

The Problem

The first step in planning a relationship study is to identify specific variables that appear to be important determinants of the complex characteristic or behavior pattern being studied. Past research and a knowledge of pertinent theory usually gives the researcher the insight he needs to identify such variables. In

---

2. Henriette M. Lahaderne, "Attitudinal and Intellectual Correlates of Attention: A Study of Four Sixth-Grade Classrooms," *Journal of Educational Psychology* 59 (1968): 320–24.

Lahaderne's study the behavior pattern was children's attention in class. Attention is an important behavior since, as the researcher notes, teachers often evaluate students and their teaching on the basis of the child's apparent involvement in classroom activities. Therefore, it seems worthwhile to identify the factors that are related to attention to increase our understanding of this behavior pattern. In this study it was possible to locate previous research findings which suggested that classroom attention is related to intelligence, school achievement, and attitude toward school.

Selection of Subjects

The next step in a relationship study is to select subjects who can be measured on the variables with which the research is concerned. As we pointed out in our discussion of causal-comparative studies, it is very important to select a group of subjects who are reasonably homogeneous. Otherwise, relationships between variables may be obscured by the presence of subjects who differ widely from each other. In Lahaderne's study, only sixth-grade pupils were selected. Furthermore, correlation coefficients were computed separately for boys and girls since, as we shall find later, relationships between variables may be obscured by treating the two sexes as a homogeneous group.

Data Collection

Data for relationship studies can be collected by various methods, including standardized tests, questionnaires, interviews, or observational techniques. The only requirement is that the data must be in quantified form. In Lahaderne's study several measurement techniques were used. The state of students' attention was measured by an observation schedule. Each student was observed on many occasions over a period of several months. On each occasion the observer checked the student's state of attention in one of four categories: attentive, inattentive, uncertain whether the student was attentive or inattentive, student's attention nonobservable. Attitude toward school was measured by two questionnaires, and standardized tests were used to assess students' achievement and intelligence.

Data Analysis

In a simple relationship study, the data are analyzed by correlating: (1) measures thought to be related to a complex behavior pattern with (2) a measure of the behavior pattern itself. In Lahaderne's study the measures of attitude toward school, school achievement, and intelligence were each correlated with the measure of attention. These correlations are presented in tables 14.1, 14.2,

TABLE 14.1
Correlations between Attention and Students' Attitudes

| | Attitudes | | | |
| | Student Opinion Poll II | | Michigan Student Questionnaire | |
Attention	Boys[a]	Girls[b]	Boys[c]	Girls[d]
Attentive	.12	−.13	.02	−.09
Inattentive	−.07	.10	.00	.03
Uncertain	−.08	.10	−.02	.11
Nonobservable	−.16	.19	−.09	.22

[a]$N = 62.$
[b]$N = 63.$
[c]$N = 61.$
[d]$N = 63.$

and 14.3.[3] The correlation coefficients in table 14.1 reveal a lack of relationship between students' attention and their attitude toward school. Thus, knowing whether a student has a positive or negative attitude toward school tells us very little about how attentive he is likely to be in class (at least for the sample of students observed in this research project). The results for achievement and intelligence, which are presented in tables 14.2 and 14.3, respectively, reveal a different set of findings. The pattern of positive and negative correlations for each variable indicates that the brighter the student and the more he has achieved in school, the more likely he is to be attentive in class. One should note, too, that the relationship of attention to achievement and intelligence is generally greater for boys than for girls. This finding suggests that girls are likely to be attentive irrespective of ability, whereas boys' degree of attentiveness is dependent on this factor.

The Shotgun Approach

As we have already noted, one advantage of the correlational method is that it permits the researcher to study the relationship between several variables simultaneously. However, this potential advantage can become a weakness if the researcher administers a very large number of measures to a sample of

3. Ibid.

subjects in the hope that some of these measures will turn out to be related to the complex behavior pattern being studied. In the **shotgun approach,** measures are included even though the researcher can think of no theoretical basis or common-sense rationale to justify their inclusion.

It is not uncommon in correlational studies for the researcher to correlate

TABLE 14.2
Correlations between Attention and Measures of Achievement

	Achievement							
	Scott-Foresman		Stanford					
	Reading		Reading		Arithmetic		Language	
Attention	Boys[a]	Girls[b]	Boys[c]	Girls[d]	Boys[c]	Girls[d]	Boys[c]	Girls[d]
Attentive	.51**	.49**	.46**	.39**	.53**	.39**	.48**	.37**
Inattentive	−.47**	−.53**	−.42**	−.44**	−.52**	−.39**	−.47**	−.38**
Uncertain	−.28*	−.33**	−.37**	−.24	−.36**	−.37**	−.34**	−.31**
Nonobservable	−.23	.07	−.08	.05	−.06	.17	−.03	.11

[a]$N = 61$.
[b]$N = 63$.
[c]$N = 56$.
[d]$N = 55$.
*$p < .05$.
**$p < .01$.

TABLE 14.3
Correlations between Attention and IQ

	IQ	
Attention	Boys[a]	Girls[b]
Attentive	.48**	.44**
Inattentive	−.35**	−.46**
Uncertain	−.49**	−.33**
Nonobservable	−.20	.07

[a]$N = 61$.
[b]$N = 63$.
**$p < .01$.

20 or more variables with a criterion measure. Sometimes there are several criterion measures, and if they are each related to all the other variables the number of correlation coefficients can become quite large. Some computer programs enable the researcher to correlate up to 120 variables with one another simultaneously. A total of 7200 different correlation coefficients would result from such a data analysis. Although the shotgun approach of correlating this many variables with one another sometimes yields significant relationships, it should be avoided by the research worker. Because of the large number of measures that must be administered, this approach is costly and inefficient. Finding tests that correlate with a given criterion is not enough because these tests may correlate for entirely irrelevant reasons, and, upon repeating the study, many of these correlations will disappear. The only situation in which this approach may be justified is when a quick research solution is required without regard to cost in an area where previous work is insufficient to form the basis for a more theory-based approach.

Limitations of the Relationship Study

We have already discussed the fact that correlations obtained in a relationship study cannot establish cause-and-effect relationships between the variables correlated. Also, many researchers have criticized relationship studies because they attempt to break down complex behavior into simpler components. Although this atomistic approach is appropriate for many research areas in education and psychology, there is some question as to whether a complex characteristic, such as artistic ability, can be meaningful if broken into its elements. It is not uncommon to find people who seem to possess all or most of the specific skills that appear related to artistic ability and yet are unable to produce creative art work. On the other hand, many of the recognized masters in the graphic arts have been notably deficient in some specific skill related to their media and yet have produced masterpieces.

Another problem involving the use of the correlational technique to identify variables related to complex skills or abilities is that success in many of the complex activities that interest us can probably be attained in a number of different ways. For example, a study attempting to relate success of high school principals to specific independent variables might fail because of the lack of any set of characteristics common to all successful principals. In one group of administrators, for example, forcefulness might be significantly correlated with success, while in another group of administrators, who employ different administrative techniques, this characteristic might be negatively correlated with success. We know so little about certain behavior patterns, and many of these patterns are so highly complex, that only the most careful interpretation of correlational data can provide us with an understanding of the phenomenon being studied.

PLANNING A PREDICTION STUDY

Types of Prediction Studies

Educational researchers carry out many prediction studies, usually with the aim of identifying variables that forecast academic and vocational success. The scope of prediction studies can be illustrated by the titles of these journal reports:

Arlin, Patricia K. "Piagetian Tasks as Predictors of Reading and Math Readiness in Grades K-1." *Journal of Educational Psychology* 73 (1981): 712–21.

Markman, Howard J. "Prediction of Marital Distress: A Five-Year Follow-Up." *Journal of Consulting and Clinical Psychology* 49 (1981): 760–62.

Munroe, Barbara H. "Dropouts from Higher Education: Path Analysis of a National Sample." *American Educational Research Journal* 18 (1981): 133–41.

Watkins, David, and Astilla, Estela. "Field Independence as a Predictor of Filipino University Engineering Grades." *Educational and Psychological Measurement* 41 (1981): 893–95.

Prediction studies provide the researcher with three types of information: the extent to which a criterion behavior pattern can be predicted; data for theory building about possible determinants of the criterion behavior pattern; and evidence regarding the predictive validity of the test or tests that are correlated with the criterion.

Prediction studies can be differentiated in terms of which of these types of information the researcher is most interested in obtaining. In some studies the emphasis is on a particular criterion behavior (e.g., first-year college grades), and one or more personality and aptitude tests are used to predict this criterion. Those tests that are good predictors are then applied to practical problems, such as selection of students for college admission. In other studies a similar research design is followed, but the researcher is primarily concerned with the theoretical significance of her findings. Finally, researchers may carry out prediction studies for the purpose of test development. The emphasis is on writing test items and determining the test's predictive validity for one or more criteria. The particular criterion predicted is of secondary importance.

Prediction research has made a major contribution to educational practice. Many prediction studies have been aimed at short-term prediction of the student's performance in a specific course of study, and others have been aimed at long-term prediction of general academic success. The findings of these studies have greatly aided school personnel in choosing students most likely to succeed in a particular academic environment or course of study. Also, prediction studies provide the scientific basis for the counselor's efforts to help students plan their academic future. The counselor can administer and interpret to the students his results on vocational interest tests that have proved highly effective in predicting a person's future occupation.

Prediction research can also be done to reduce the cost of training new personnel for today's complex vocational skills. For example, a selection system such as that employed by the U.S. Air Force for pilot training can save vast sums of money because it eliminates a certain number of persons who would fail during the training program. Such training is extremely costly, and the cost of training the unsuccessful candidate up to the point of failure must be added to the per capita cost of training successful candidates. A selection program that will reduce the number of failures is of great value. Prediction research is done to determine which criteria to incorporate in the selection process.

The Basic Research Design

Prediction studies are similar to relationship studies in that both involve computing correlations between a complex behavior pattern (the criterion) and variables thought to be related to the criterion. However, in prediction studies the other variables (sometimes called *predictor variables*) are measured some time before the criterion behavior occurs. In contrast, in relationship studies the criterion behavior and other variables need not be measured in a particular order; they are usually measured at the same point in time. Also, prediction studies tend to be more concerned with maximizing the correlation between the predictor variables and the criterion. As we shall see later in the chapter, correlations sometimes can be increased by use of multiple correlation and moderator variables.

The Problem

As we have already observed, researchers can carry out prediction studies for different purposes. They may be interested in testing the predictive validity of a particular test, in predicting a behavior criterion for use in an applied situation, or in predicting a behavior criterion to test a theoretical hypthesis. An example of the first type of research is Holtzman and Brown's study of a paper-

and-pencil measure called the Survey of Study Habits and Attitudes (SSHA).[4] The main purpose of the study was to determine the validity of the SSHA for predicting the gradepoint average of junior high and high school students. The researchers already had some reason to believe that the SSHA would predict this criterion, since the college version of the test, developed earlier, correlated significantly with college grades (r ranged from .27 to .66 for several samples).

Another important aspect of prediction studies is the proper definition of one's criterion behavior pattern. It is likely that many studies have failed to find predictive relationships because a poor criterion was specified. For example, gradepoint average is sometimes used as a criterion, as in Holtzman and Brown's study. However, a gradepoint average usually includes a person's grades in several subjects, such as mathematics and literature. Since it is likely that different aptitudes, skills, and interests are required for success in each subject, grades for each subject probably should be predicted separately in order to obtain maximum correlations between the predictor variables and the criterion gradepoint score. For example, study habits may be a critical determinant of success in mathematics, but not in literature. If the correlation is computed between a measure such as the SSHA and the combined gradepoint average for both academic subjects, the predictive relationship between study habits and grades in mathematics is obscured.

Selection of Subjects

As we have discussed with respect to other research designs, it is important to draw subjects from the specific population most pertinent to your study. Because Holtzman and Brown wanted to determine the predictive validity of the SSHA separately for junior high and high school students, they formed separate groups of students for each grade level from the seventh through the twelfth grades. The correlational data for each grade level were analyzed separately. The researchers could have made their groups still more specific by forming separate subgroups of male and female students at each grade level.

Data Collection

Standardized tests, questionnaires, interviews, or observational techniques can be used to measure predictor variables and the criterion behavior pattern in a prediction study. Of course, the predictor variables must be measured a period of time before the criterion occurs. Otherwise, one cannot claim that a particular test has "predicted" the criterion. In Holtzman and Brown's study, the

---

4. Wayne H. Holtzman and William F. Brown, "Evaluating the Study Habits and Attitudes of High School Students," *Journal of Educational Psychology* 59 (1968): 404–9.

SSHA was administered at the beginning of the fall semester in grades 7 through 12 of various schools. Students' scores on scholastic aptitude tests administered by each school system were also obtained. At the end of the fall semester, students' gradepoint averages were computed and used as the criterion behavior.

Prediction of events or behaviors that will occur in the near future is generally easier and more accurate than prediction of events or behaviors that will occur in the more distant future. This is because in short-term prediction, more of the determinants of the behavior being predicted are likely to be present. Furthermore, short-term prediction allows less time for important predictor variables to change or for the individual new determinants to emerge. For example, if we wish to predict the probable success of individuals in management positions, we would probably start with variables that have been found in previous research to be related to later success in management positions. This type of test battery might include such factors as verbal intelligence, social attitudes, emotional maturity, and so on. However, certain variables important to success could not possibly be measured because they are not present at the time the prediction must be made. For example, the individual's ability to work well with superiors in the management hierarchy—a likely determinant of management success—cannot be measured because the superiors are unknown at the time of prediction.

Data Analysis

The basic form of data analysis in a prediction study consists of correlating each predictor variable with the criterion. In the study we have been describing, the SSHA and scholastic aptitude test scores (the predictor variables) were each correlated with students' gradepoint average. The correlations are shown in table 14.4 in columns 3 and 5.[5] Both predictor variables yield rather high correlations; both would be considered useful in counseling and in selecting students who have academic promise.

In prediction studies multiple regression is often used to determine whether two or more of the predictor variables in the study can be combined to predict the criterion better than any one predictor variable does alone. The correlation coefficients in column 6 of table 14.4 indicate that the SSHA and the Scholastic Aptitude Test can be combined by a multiple regression equation to yield a better prediction of gradepoint average than either test alone. The **multiple regression equation** uses the subject's scores on two or more tests to predict his performance on the criterion measure. For the total sample (see bottom row of table 14.4), the combined tests acount for 45 percent of the variance in the

5. Ibid.

TABLE 14.4

Mean Correlation of Survey of Study Habits and Attitudes (SSHA), Form H; Scholastic Aptitude (SA); and Gradepoint Average (GPA) Together with Multiple (R) and Partial (r) Correlations of Scores with Gradepoint Average

Grade	N	SSHA (1) with GPA (3)	SSHA (1) with SA Test (2)	SA Test (2) with GPA (3)	$R_{3.12}$	$r_{31.2}$	SSHA Total M	Study Orientation Score SD
7	1684	.55	.32	.61	.72	.47	106.5	33.1
8	1628	.52	.29	.59	.69	.45	107.0	32.8
9	2005	.49	.29	.52	.63	.41	101.6	31.5
10	2064	.49	.29	.62	.70	.41	97.9	31.6
11	1840	.47	.24	.57	.67	.42	97.7	30.9
12	1667	.46	.20	.53	.66	.43	102.9	30.3
Total	10,888	.49	.27	.57	.67	.43		

NOTE—Mean correlations were obtained by converting each r into its Fisher's z function, weighting by the appropriate number of cases, averaging the values, then reconverting. Multiple and partial coefficients were derived from the weighted averages.

criterion (.67 squared), as compared with the 24 percent accounted for by the SSHA (.49 squared) or the 32 percent accounted for by the Scholastic Aptitude Test (.57 squared).

In addition to multiple regression, moderator analysis is sometimes used to maximize the correlation between variables. Although this technique was not used intentionally in the Holtzman and Brown study, we can see that the SSHA and the Scholastic Aptitude Test predict the criterion differentially for various subgroups, that is, grade levels, within the entire sample of students. For example, in grade 7 the SSHA accounts for 30 percent of the variance in students' gradepoint average, whereas in the twelfth grade the amount of explained variance drops to 21 percent. The purpose of **moderator analysis** is to identify a subgroup for whom the correlation between a criterion and a predictor variable is significantly greater than the correlation for the total sample from which the subgroup was formed. We shall discuss moderator analysis again later in the chapter.

BIVARIATE CORRELATIONAL STATISTICS

In this section we discuss ten correlational techniques that can be used to analyze the degree of relationship between two variables. Because two variables are involved, these techniques are sometimes called *bivariate* correlational statistics. The form of the variables to be correlated and the nature of the relationship determine which technique is used. Variables in relationship studies are usually expressed in one of five forms: continuous score, rank, artificial dichotomy, true dichotomy, and category.[6] Table 14.5 lists the ten correlational techniques and the conditions under which they are used.

Product-Moment Correlation, *r*

The **product-moment coefficient** *r* is used when both variables that we wish to correlate are expressed as continuous scores. For example, if we administer an intelligence test such as the California Test of Mental Maturity and an achievement test such as the Stanford Achievement Test to the same group of individuals, we will have two sets of continuous scores, each individual having a score on each of the two tests. Because most educational measures yield continuous scores, this is the most frequently used correlational technique. The product-moment correlation has a smaller standard error than the other bivariate techniques and is generally preferred when its use is possible. A product-moment *r* can be calculated for any two variables, no matter how they have been measured.

Correlation of Rank Scores

Rank-Difference Correlation, *rho*

The **rank-difference correlation** *rho* is a special form of the product-moment correlation. The rank-difference correlation is used to correlate two variables when one or both of these variables are available only in rank form. For example, studies correlating various measures of intelligence with graduation standing in high school would generally employ the rank-difference correlation because the individual's graduation standing is expressed as a rank. To use this correlational technique, however, both variables must be expressed as a rank, so in this case the scores of the subjects on the other variable (intelligence test), which is available in the form of a continuous score, would have to be converted to ranks before the correlation could be calculated. Converting continuous scores to rank scores involves the simple procedure of listing the continuous scores in order of magnitude and then assigning ranks.

---

6. These five types of scores are described in chapter 10.

TABLE 14.5

Bivariate Correlational Techniques for Different Forms of Variables

Technique	Symbol	Variable 1	Variable 2	Remarks
Product-moment correlation	r	Continuous	Continuous	The most stable technique, i.e., smallest standard error
Rank-difference correlation (rho)	ρ	Ranks	Ranks	Often used instead of product-moment when number of cases is under 30
Kendall's *tau*	τ	Ranks	Ranks	Preferable to *rho* for numbers under 10
Biserial correlation	r_{bis}	Artificial dichotomy	Continuous	Sometimes exceeds 1—has a larger standard error than *r*—commonly used in item analysis
Widespread biserial correlation	r_{wbis}	Widespread artificial dichotomy	Continuous	Used when you are especially interested in persons at the extremes on the dichotomized variable
Point-biserial correlation	r_{pbis}	True dichotomy	Continuous	Yields a lower correlation than r_{bis}
Tetrachoric correlation	r^t	Artificial dichotomy	Artificial dichotomy	Used when both variables can be split at critical points
Phi coefficient	ϕ	True dichotomy	True dichotomy	Used in calculating inter-item correlations
Contingency coefficient	C	2 or more categories	2 or more categories	Comparable to r_t under certain conditions—closely related to chi-square
Correlation ratio, *eta*	η	Continuous	Continuous	Used to detect nonlinear relationships

Kendall's *tau,* τ

Tau is another form of rank correlation that has some theoretical advantage over the better known Spearman's *rho*. Like *rho*, *tau* is used to correlate two sets of ranks. Data not in rank form can be converted to ranks if it is desired to use *tau*. Its principal advantage is that it has a more normal sampling distribution than *rho* for samples under ten. It is more difficult to calculate than *rho* and yields lower correlation coefficients when computed from the same data. As *rho* very closely approximates the Pearson *r* calculated from the same data, it is less likely than *tau* to be misinterpreted by the educator.

Correlation of Dichotomous Scores

The Biserial Correlation, r_{bis}

The **biserial correlation** r_{bis} is used when one of the variables is in the form of continuous scores and the other variable is in the form of an artificial dichotomy. For example, if we wish to determine the relationship between success and failure in algebra and scores on an algebra aptitude test, we would use the biserial correlation. In this case the aptitude test yields continuous scores, while the record of each subject as having passed or failed algebra takes the form of an artificial dichotomy. As a rule, the correlation coefficients obtained using the biserial technique are somewhat higher than those obtained on the same data using the product-moment technique.

Although the theoretical limits of any correlation are +1 to −1, it is mathematically possible to obtain biserial correlations greater than one if the variables are not normally distributed. This fact should be kept in mind by the research worker when employing the biserial technique. If she is unaware of this characteristic of the biserial and obtains a correlation greater than one, she will spend a great deal of time looking for an error that does not exist. In addition to yielding higher correlations, the biserial technique is somewhat less precise than the product-moment correlation and has a larger standard error reflecting this lesser degree of accuracy. Therefore, if we wished to conduct a study relating success in school to IQ, it would be better to employ a continuous variable as a measure of school success, such as gradepoint average, rather than use the pass-fail dichotomy. With this approach we would have two continuous variables and could use the product-moment correlation. In many instances, however, information cannot be obtained in continuous form for one of the variables. Under these circumstances the research worker should not hesitate to use the biserial correlation.

The Widespread Biserial Correlation, r_{wbis}

There are many instances in educational research where it is desirable to correlate scores on a continuous variable, such as intelligence, with extreme scores on some other characteristic. Let us say, for example, that we wished to determine whether teaching success was correlated with certain personality traits.

The measurement of teaching success is a difficult task for which satisfactory measures are not easily obtained. Evaluations of teaching ability are usually based on a composite evaluation made by two or more raters. In making ratings raters usually find it easier to pick out the extremes (i.e., the better and poorer teachers in the group) than to discriminate among teachers who are within the average range of teaching ability. For example, if five raters were used to evaluate a hundred teachers, we would find that the raters would agree much more closely in their identification of the ten best teachers and the ten poorest teachers than they would agree on the relative ability of teachers close to the average. This situation occurs in many studies where ratings are used as a basis for evaluation.

When only those individuals whose scores are at the two extreme ends on a dichotomized variable are used, the extreme groups constitute a widespread dichotomy. The **widespread biserial correlation** is used to correlate a continuous score with a widespread dichotomy. The cutoff points for identifying extreme cases are defined in such a way that the two extreme groups have an equal number of cases.

The Point Biserial Correlation, r_{pbis}

The **point biserial correlation** r_{pbis} is used when one of the variables we wish to correlate is in the form of a continuous score and the other variable is in the form of a true dichotomy. This type of correlation is used in studies relating sex to different continuous variables, such as intelligence, verbal fluency, reading ability, and achievement. In such studies sex provides the true dichotomy, and the other measure provides the continuous variable.

As a rule the point biserial coefficient will be somewhat lower than if the same data were analyzed using the biserial correlation. However, it has several advantages over biserial correlation. It does not yield correlations greater than 1.0. Its standard error is easier to calculate, and its statistical significance can be determined using the product-moment r significance tables, which are found in most elementary statistics texts.

The Tetrachoric Correlation, r_t

Occasionally we encounter a situation in educational research where both variables that we wish to correlate are in the form of artificial dichotomies. Under these conditions the **tetrachoric correlation statistic** is used. Use of this coefficient requires the assumption that the variables underlying the dichotomies in the tetrachoric correlation analysis are continuous and normally distributed. Also, the tetrachoric coefficient is considerably less stable than the product-moment coefficient. Thus, this type of correlation should not be used unless the research problem clearly warrants it. The standard error of the tetrachoric correlation coefficient is also quite difficult to compute, which means that considerable effort is required to determine whether the observed correlation coefficient is significant. The tetrachoric correlation statistic is most stable when a large number of cases is used and when the dichotomies divide the sample into approximately equal groups.

The *Phi* Coefficient, φ

The *phi* coefficient is used to correlate two variables that are both true dichotomies. Because we deal with relatively few true dichotomies in education, *phi* coefficients are seldom calculated in educational research. The main use of this technique is to determine the correlation between two items on a test during item analysis. Each subject's response to each item can be classified as either correct or incorrect, thus giving us two true dichotomies.

The Contingency Coefficient, C

The **contingency coefficient** C is used when the variables to be correlated are in the form of categories. Although C can be used when the variables are divided into dichotomies, the *phi* coefficient or tetrachoric correlation is preferable under these conditions. When either or both variables are classified into more than two categories, however, φ or r_t cannot be applied; instead, the contingency coefficient is used to measure the degree of relationship.

C is closely related to the chi-square statistic (see chapter 13) and is computed using a contingency table. If chi-square has been computed, C can easily be derived from chi-square. Conversely, chi-square can be computed from C; this is usually done because chi-square provides the easiest method of determining the statistical significance of C. The contingency coefficient yields correlations closely comparable to the product-moment r if each variable is split into at least five categories and if the sample is large. C should not be used unless the data are available only in categories or unless converting the scores to categories presents the data in a more logical or understandable form.

Scattergrams and the Correlation Ratio, η

We have observed that the magnitude of the relationship between two variables can be represented by a correlation coefficient. The magnitude of the relationship can also be pictorially represented by making a **scattergram**. All that is required is to draw an X axis and a Y axis representing the score ranges of the two variables involved. The two scores of each individual in one's sample can then be represented by a single point (i.e., coordinate) on the graph.

Figure 14.1 presents several scattergrams. The first scattergram shows a perfect correlation, indicated by the straight line, since each unit of increment in the X-axis variable is accompanied by a unit of increment in the Y-axis variable. The correlation is 1.00, because if we know a person's score on one variable, we can predict perfectly his score on the other. The second scattergram indicates a fairly high degree of positive correlation between the two variables. If we know a person's score on the X-axis variable, we cannot predict his score on the Y-axis variable perfectly, but the score given by the straight line ("the line of best fit") will yield a fairly accurate prediction. If the line that described the relationship between two variables slanted down from left to right (instead of down from right to left, as in the second scattergram), the correlation coef-

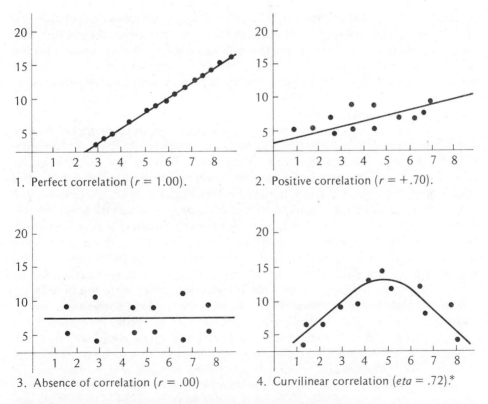

1. Perfect correlation ($r = 1.00$).

2. Positive correlation ($r = +.70$).

3. Absence of correlation ($r = .00$)

4. Curvilinear correlation ($eta = .72$).*

*The product–moment correlation for the same data would be about $+.29$.

Figure 14.1   Examples of scattergrams.

ficient would be negative. The third scattergram is a graphic representation of a complete lack of relationship between two variables. Knowing a person's score on the X-axis variable is of no value at all in predicting his score on the Y-axis variable.

The line of best fit (the straight line in scattergrams 1, 2, and 3 of figure 14.1) can be calculated using the equation

$$Y = bX + a$$

where Y is the variable being predicted, b is the slope of the line (sometimes called "regression weight"), X is the predictor variable, and a is the point where the line intersects with the Y axis. You will see an elaboration of this basic equation when we discuss multiple regression later in the chapter.

Using a scattergram to represent graphically the relationship between the variables involved in a correlational study is particularly helpful in detecting nonlinear relationships. The correlation techniques described previously assume that the relationship is linear, in other words, that a straight line best describes the relationship between the two variables. However, sometimes the relationship is nonlinear, as in the fourth scattergram of figure 14.1. In this example a curved line rather than a straight line best describes the relationship between the two variables and therefore leads to better predictions from scores on the X axis to scores on the Y axis.

Sometimes nonlinear relationships are discovered in correlational studies only after scattergrams have been plotted, but occasionally they are hypothesized to describe the relationship between two variables. For example, some researchers have hypothesized a curvilinear relationship between anxiety and intellectual performance. The rationale for this hypothesis is that persons low in anxiety will not be motivated to do well on a performance task and thus will earn low scores. Persons with a moderate amount of anxiety will be motivated by their anxiety to perform well, and since their anxiety is moderate, it will not disrupt their performance. Therefore, they should earn higher scores than the nonanxious group. By the same reasoning, highly anxious persons should be even more motivated to perform well. If high motivation were the only factor operating, highly anxious persons should earn the highest scores, and the relationship between anxiety and performance would be linear. However, it has been hypothesized that highly anxious persons, though well-motivated, are disrupted by their anxiety and thus will earn low performance scores. Consequently, the hypothesized relationship between anxiety and performance is curvilinear with high- and low-anxiety groups hypothesized to have low performance scores, and the middle-anxiety group hypothesized to have high performance scores.

If the scattergrams for one's research data indicate that the relationship between two variables is markedly nonlinear, then one should compute the **correlation ratio** *(eta)*. The advantage of the correlation ratio is that it provides a more accurate index of the relationship between two variables than other correlational statistics when the relationship is markedly nonlinear. Other types of correlation coefficients will generally underestimate the degree of relationship when nonlinearity exists. Researchers sometimes perform a special statistical test to determine whether the *eta* statistic yields a coefficient that is of significantly greater magnitude than the coefficient yielded by a linear correlation statistic.

The disadvantage of the *eta* coefficient is that it is relatively difficult to compute, but this disadvantage has been virtually eliminated by the advent of computer programs designed to compute *etas* and scattergrams with little researcher effort needed.

In addition to revealing nonlinear relationships, scattergrams are useful for detecting outliers in research data. (The phenomenon of outliers was discussed in chapter 10.) The points in each of the scattergrams in figure 14.1 are generally clustered near each other. If one of the points was quite far away from the other points in the scattergram, the researcher would have reason to suspect that the subject represented by that point was an outlier.

ADJUSTMENTS TO THE CORRELATION COEFFICIENT

Correction for Attenuation

When we correlate scores on two measures, the obtained correlation coefficient is lower than the true correlation to the extent that the measures are not perfectly reliable. This lowering of the correlation coefficient due to unreliability of the measures is called attenuation. **Correction for attenuation** provides an estimate of what the correlation between the variables would be if the measures had perfect reliability. In prediction studies correction for attenuation is not usually applied because we must make predictions on the basis of the measures we have, and the reliability of these measures, even if low, must be accepted as a limitation.

This correction is sometimes used, however, in exploratory studies. In these studies crude measures of low reliability are often used, thus lowering the obtained correlation coefficient. The correction for attenuation helps the researcher determine what the relationship between two variables might be if perfect measures of the variables were available. Because correction for attenuation is only an estimate, it sometimes yields corrected correlations above one. These are spurious and are usually dropped to .99 in research reports. Finally, one should remember that a correlation corrected for attenuation tells us "what might be" rather than "what is."

Correction for Restriction in Range

Correction for restriction in range is applied to correlation coefficients when the researcher knows that the range of scores for a sample is restricted on one of the variables being correlated. Restriction in range leads to a lowering of the correlation coefficient. To illustrate this phenomenon, let us suppose one wishes to study the correlation between scholastic aptitude and achievement in college students and the only sample that is accessible consists of students who are generally very high in scholastic aptitude. In other words, there is restriction in range of measured aptitude. If one knows the variability of aptitude scores in this "restricted" sample and the variability of aptitude scores in the population to which one wishes to generalize, it is possible to apply the correction for restriction in range to the obtained correlation coefficient. The corrected coefficient will provide a good estimate of the degree of relationship between scholastic aptitude and achievement in the larger population of college students. Use of the correction requires the assumption that the two variables are related to each other linearly throughout their entire range. If the relationship for the total range of scores is curvilinear, the correction for restriction in range is not applicable.

Partial Correlation

Partial correlation is sometimes employed in relationship and prediction studies. This method is useful when we wish to rule out the influence of one or more variables upon the criterion behavior pattern in order to clarify the role of other variables. The usefulness of partial correlation is illustrated by Lahaderne's study of classroom attention. If you refer back to table 14.2, you will find that attention is related to achievement. This means that students who pay attention in class are likely to have a higher level of school achievement than their nonattentive peers. But the findings also indicate that students who pay attention in class tend to be more intelligent than their nonattentive peers. Thus one can argue that the attentive students achieve more, not because of their attentiveness, but simply because they are more intelligent.

To determine whether this argument has merit, we can use the statistical technique of partial correlation. In this instance partial correlation serves the purpose of removing the influence of intelligence both on school achievement and on attention.[7] In Lahaderne's study the partial coefficient between achievement and attention for boys, with IQ held constant, was .31 using the Scott-Foresman Reading Test as the measure of achievement, and .26 using the Stanford Arithmetic Achievement Test. These coefficients are considerably less than the coefficients obtained when intelligence is not held constant (the coefficients are .51 and .53, respectively). Thus it appears that attentive male students have a higher level of school achievement primarily because they are more intelligent than their nonattentive peers. The statistically significant partial coefficients suggest that attention does play a minor role, however, independent of intelligence, in school achievement. The situation is somewhat different for girls. Partial coefficients between achievement and attention for girls, with intelligence held constant, indicate that attentive female students have a higher level of achievement than their nonattentive peers almost entirely because they are brighter.

In using partial coefficients, the researcher must keep in mind the difficulties associated with making causal assumptions based upon the correlational method. In the preceding example, we assumed that it was necessary to hold intelligence constant since intelligence may *determine* both how well the student attends in the classroom and how well he does on measures of school achievement. But one can also assume another causal chain, namely, that the capacity to attend to intellectual tasks *determines* how well the student performs both on intelligence tests and on measures of school achievement. If the latter is the case, then it is meaningless to hold intelligence constant by using partial correlation.

Use of the partial correlation rests on the assumption that the factor held constant has a causal influence on the other two variables. Faced with this situation of two plausible causal linkages between attention, school achievement, and intelligence, Lahaderne reported the partial coefficients (in which intelligence was held constant to remove its causal influence) but also raised "the question of whether it is proper to search for the effect of attention independent of IQ. Maybe the ability to attend is an integral part of intelligent performance and contributes as much to a child's performance on an IQ test as to achievement in school."[8]

Partial correlation is closely related to the method of path analysis. Therefore, we will refer to partial correlation again when we discuss path analysis later in the chapter.

---

7. If a researcher was interested in removing the influence of intelligence from one of the factors (e.g., the influence of intelligence on attention), then the statistical method of part correlation would be used instead of partial correlation.
8. Lahaderne, "Attitudinal and Intellectual Correlates of Attention," p. 323.

MULTIVARIATE CORRELATIONAL STATISTICS

The correlation techniques presented above are intended to help the researcher measure the degree of relationship between two variables. Most of the research problems we study in the field of education, though, involve three or more variables. The multivariate techniques presented in the following sections allow the researcher to measure and study the degree of relationship between various combinations of three or more variables. You should study these techniques in depth. They are used to analyze correlational data, but they are also used increasingly to analyze data from experiments. We shall discuss this latter use of multivariate techniques in chapters 15 and 16. Furthermore, they can be used in place of or as a supplement to the statistical techniques, especially analysis of variance and related methods, that have been used traditionally in causal-comparative research (see chapter 13).

Multiple Regression

Multiple regression has become one of the most widely used statistical techniques in educational research. Its popularity stems from its considerable versatility and information yield about relationships between variables. Multiple regression can be used to analyze data from causal-comparative, correlational, or experimental research. It can handle interval, ordinal, or categorical data. Also, multiple regression provides estimates both of the magnitude and statistical significance of relationships between variables. We can define **multiple regression** as a multivariate technique for determining the correlation between a criterion variable and some combination of two or more predictor variables.

The use of multiple regression is illustrated in a prediction study conducted by Lorrie Shepard.[9] Our explanation of multiple regression is not limited to prediction research, however. It applies as well to any type of research in which multiple regression is used to analyze relationships between variables.

One purpose of Shepard's study was to determine the predictive validity of the California Entry Level Test (ELT). This test has been administered for years to every first-grade student in California. It is used as a baseline measure of prereading skills at the start of first grade. The names of the ELT subtests indicate the variables they are designed to measure: Immediate Recall, Letter Recognition, Auditory Discrimination, Visual Discrimination, and Language

9. Lorrie Shepard, "Construct and Predictive Validity of the California Entry Level Test," *Educational and Psychological Measurement* 39 (1979): 867–77.

Development. The total of the subtest scores was used in the analyses reported here.

In addition to ELT scores, Shepard had available data relating to other background characteristics of the students. One characteristic was Socioeconomic Status (SES). High scores on this variable indicate high SES. Another characteristic was whether the student's family received support from the Aid to Families with Dependent Children Program (AFDC). The third background variable was whether the student was bilingual.

One purpose of Shepard's study was to determine how well the four measures (ELT, SES, AFDC, and bilingualism) predicted students' reading achievement in 1974–75 (second grade) and again in 1975–76 (third grade). The California Reading Test was administered in May 1975 and May 1976 as the criterion measure of reading achievement.

Students' scores on each of the predictor and criterion variables were aggregated to the school level for some of the multiple regression analyses. For example, the ELT scores of students in a particular school were summed and divided by the school sample size to yield a mean ELT score for that school. Mean scores for ELT, SES, reading achievement, and percentage of AFDC and bilingual students per school were available for several thousand elementary schools.[10] Thus the multiple regression was based on a very large sample size.

A typical multiple regression analysis generated by a computer program will generate several statistics and equations. Only a few of these may appear in the published report. Others can be calculated if appropriate statistics are provided by the author. We can explain this point further by examining the multiple regression results presented in table 14.6.[11]

The first column of the table lists the variables in the multiple regression analysis. Note that two multiple regression analyses were done. In the first analysis, the criterion variable of reading achievement (second-grade level) was predicted from three variables—ELT, SES, and percent AFDC. A separate multiple regression analysis was done for the third-grade level of reading achievement, which was predicted from four variables—ELT, percent AFDC, SES, and percent of bilingual students in the school.

Skip for a moment to the third column of table 14.6. This column presents the product-moment correlation coefficient between each predictor variable and the pertinent criterion variable. For example, the coefficient at the top ($r = .76$) is the correlation between ELT and Grade 2 reading achievement. The fourth coefficient from the top ($r = .77$) is the correlation between ELT and Grade 3

10. The exact number of schools is not given in the published report. Our estimate is based on the author's statement that a similar multiple regression analysis with data aggregated to the school district level included 900 school districts.

11. Table 14.6 adapted from Shepard, "Construct and Predictive Validity," p. 875.

TABLE 14.6

Weighted Regression Analysis for the Reading Test: Second and Third Grades at School Level, 1975–76

Variable	Beta	Correlation Coefficient (r)	Stepwise Multiple Correlation (R)	Stepwise R^2	R^2 Increment
Grade 2 Reading					
Entry Level Test (ELT)	.41	.76	.76	.58	
Socioeconomic Index (SES)	.27	.75	.81	.66	.08
Percent AFDC	−.19	−.65	.82	.67	.01
Grade 3 Reading					
Entry Level Test (ELT)	.36	.77	.77	.59	
Percent AFDC	−.25	−.67	.81	.65	.06
Socioeconomic Index (SES)	.21	.74	.82	.67	.02
Percent Bilingual	−.13	−.59	.83	.68	.01

reading achievement. It appears that each background variable is a good predictor of reading achievement.

We are now ready to consider the multiple regression analysis of the data. We will concentrate on the analysis of the Grade 2 reading achievement data (rows 1–4 of table 14.6). You can extend the analysis to the Grade 3 data (rows 5–8) on your own. The first step in multiple regression is usually to compute the correlation between the best predictor and the criterion variable. This procedure yields a multiple correlation coefficient (R), which is shown in column 4. Since ELT is the best predictor (r = .76), it is the first predictor entered into the multiple regression. Note that the correlation coefficient (r = .76) is the same as the multiple correlation coefficient (R = .76).

Unless you specify otherwise, the computer program will start the multiple regression analysis with the most powerful predictor of the criterion variable. There are situations, however, in which the researcher will want to enter a less powerful predictor first. For example, if the predictor variables can be ordered chronologically, the researcher may wish to start the multiple regression analysis by entering the "earliest" predictor first. Another situation occurs when one of the predictors is well established in the field of education and another predictor is novel. For example, IQ as a predictor of school achievement is well established. Suppose the researcher has developed a new measure of scholastic aptitude and is testing its predictive validity relative to an IQ measure. It makes sense to enter IQ scores first in the multiple regression—irrespective of their correlation with the criterion—and then to see how well the new measure improves upon the prediction.

Suppose the researcher has not specified the order in which the predictor variables are to be entered into the multiple regression analysis. In this case, after selecting the best predictor, the computer program will search for the next best predictor of the criterion variable. This second predictor is not chosen on the basis of its product-moment correlation (r) with the criterion. Rather, the second predictor is chosen on the basis of how well it improves upon the prediction achieved by the first variable.

What qualities should a variable have to be a good second predictor? First, it should correlate as little as possible with the first predictor variable. If it correlates with the first variable entered in the multiple regression analysis, there is the possibility that it will predict the same variance in the criterion variable as the first variable. For example, suppose an IQ test and a scholastic aptitude test are used to predict fifth-grade reading achievement. The two predictor variables are likely to correlate highly with each other because they measure the same underlying factor. If IQ scores are entered in the multiple regression first, the scholastic aptitude test is unlikely to improve upon the prediction since it mostly represents the same factor as the IQ test. The situation is comparable to using the same IQ scores a second time to improve upon the prediction achieved by using them the first time.

The second quality of a good second predictor is obvious: It should correlate as highly as possible with the criterion variable. In short, a good second predictor is one that correlates as highly as possible with the criterion.

Table 14.6 indicates that SES was the second variable entered in the multiple regression analysis. The two predictor variables together yield a multiple correlation coefficient of .81. This is a small improvement upon the prediction achieved by just using ELT as a predictor ($R = .76$). At this point you may ask why SES improves the prediction relatively little, given that SES on its own correlates .75 with the criterion. The reason for this phenomenon was discussed just above. Students' scores on the Entry Level Test and their socioeconomic status are undoubtedly highly correlated. Because of this overlap,[12] SES does not have a chance to improve upon the prediction made by ELT, which was entered in the multiple regression analysis first.

To pursue this point a bit further, note that in the multiple regression analysis for Grade 3 reading achievement, percent AFDC was the second variable entered. Yet percent AFDC by itself has a lower correlation with the criterion ($-.67$) than does SES ($r = .74$).[13] In all likelihood, though, it overlaps

12. The technical term for this overlap, or shared variance between two variables, is collinearity.
13. The sign of a correlation coefficient is irrelevant to its usefulness in predicting a criterion. One can make just as good a prediction with a negative coefficient as with a positive coefficient of the same magnitude.

less with ELT than does SES in predicting Grade 3 reading achievement; hence, it is entered second in the multiple regression analysis.

The third predictor entered in the multiple regression analysis is determined by whether it improves upon the prediction made by the first two predictors. We can see in table 14.6 that percent AFDC improves the multiple correlation coefficient very slightly to .82. The computer program usually will keep adding predictor variables until there are none left. Each new predictor will usually contribute less to R than the preceding predictor, however, in which case there are rapidly diminishing returns for adding new predictors. This principle probably explains why there are four predictors for Grade 3 reading achievement in table 14.6, whereas there are just three predictors for Grade 2 reading achievement. You will note that the fourth predictor, percent bilingual, improves R slightly from .82 to .83. The same predictor may not have contributed sufficiently to the prediction of Grade 2 reading achievement to make even this much difference in R. Therefore, it was omitted from the presentation of results.

At this point we can consider further the meaning of R. The **multiple correlation coefficient** *(R)* is a measure of the magnitude of relationship between a criterion variable and a predictor variable or some combination of predictor variables. The value of R will vary depending on which predictor variables have been entered in the multiple regression analysis and the order in which they have been entered. The value of .82 for the Grade 2 data represents the best prediction one can make of Grade 2 reading scores from students' scores on ELT, SES, and percent AFDC. The value of R can range from 0.00 to 1.00; negative values are not possible. The larger the R, the better the prediction.

If R is squared, it will yield a statistic known as the **coefficient of determination** *(R²)*. Column 4 of table 14.6 shows the R^2 coefficients corresponding to the Rs in column 3. For example, the topmost R^2 coefficient is .58, which is the square of the corresponding R coefficient (.76). R^2 expresses the amount of variance in the criterion variable that is predictable from a predictor variable or combination of predictor variables.

The fifth column of table 14.6 presents the R^2 increments for the multiple regression analyis. The **R^2 increment** is a statistic that expresses the additional variance in the criterion variable that can be explained by adding a new predictor variable to the multiple regression analysis. For example, the addition of SES to the analysis explains 8 percent more of the variance in the criterion variable (.66 − .58 = .08) than can be explained by ELT alone. Adding percent AFDC to the analysis results in an R^2 increment of just 1 percent, meaning that it predicts 1 percent more of the variance than can be predicted by ELT and SES in combination.

Two tests of statistical significance are commonly done in multiple regression analysis. One test is done to determine whether the obtained value of R is significantly different than 0. The other test is done to determine whether the R^2 increment is statistically significant. The R^2 increment test is done to determine whether the R^2 for a new predictor added to the multiple regression analysis is significantly different than the R^2 for the analysis without the predictor. For example, one could test whether the R^2 of .67 obtained by adding percent AFDC to the multiple regression analysis is significantly different from the R^2 of .66 obtained without using percent AFDC as a predictor.

The mathematical basis for multiple regression is an equation that links the predictor variable(s) to the criterion variable. Suppose that Grade 2 reading achievement = Y, ELT = X_1, SES = X_2, and percent AFDC = X_3. Using "c" to stand for a constant term, the multiple regression equation can be stated as:

$$Y = b_1X_1 + b_2X_2 + b_3X_3 + c.$$

Note that Y is italicized to indicate that the Y scores are being predicted from X_1, X_2, and X_3. The predicted values of Y will deviate from students' actual Y scores because X_1, X_2, and X_3 are not perfect predictors. Note, too, that this equation is similar to the straight-line equation for bivariate correlation ($Y = bX + a$).

Each b value in the multiple regression equation is a **regression weight,** which can vary from -1.00 to $+1.00$. A separate regression weight (sometimes called a b weight) is calculated for each predictor variable. When each student's scores on the predictor variables are multiplied by their respective regression weights and then summed, the result is the best possible prediction of the student's score on the criterion variable.

Sometimes b weights are converted to beta (B) weights. **Beta weights** are the regression weights in a multiple regression equation in which all of the variables in the equation are in standard score form. Some researchers prefer beta weights because they form an absolute scale. For example, a beta weight of $+.40$ is of greater magnitude than a beta weight of $+.30$ irrespective of the predictor variable with which it is associated. In contrast, the magnitude of a b weight is dependent upon the scale form of the predictor measure with which it is associated. Beta weights can be converted to b weights, and vice versa, using the formula $b = B\left(\dfrac{S_y}{S_x}\right)$, where S_y and S_x are the standard deviations of the Y and X variables, respectively.

If you look at table 14.6, you will see that the researcher decided to present beta weights, rather than b weights, for each of the predictor variables. With this information, we can construct the multiple regression equation as follows:

$$\hat{Y} = .41X_1 + .27X_2 - .19X_3$$

where each of the variables is in standard score form. In other words, we can predict a school's mean reading achievement score quite well if we multiply its mean ELT score by .41, its mean SES score by .27, and its percent AFDC by $-.19$, and then sum the results. (Note that these "scores" are all in standard score form since beta weights are used.)

In the multiple regression equation just presented, the beta weight for X_1 $(+.41)$ is greater than for X_2 (.27), which in turn is greater than that for X_3 $(-.19)$. These declining beta weights correspond to the order in which the predictor variables were entered into the equation. If a fourth predictor were entered, it would have a value less than $+$ or $-.19$. The magnitude of a predictor variable's beta weight should not be confused with its importance, however. A predictor variable can be theoretically significant and highly correlated with the criterion, yet have a low beta weight. The beta weight is arbitrary to an extent, since it depends on the predictor variable's correlation with the other predictors. If the researcher has chosen to enter the predictors in a prespecified order, the beta weights will be dependent on that factor, too.

There are several variations of multiple regression analysis: stepup (also called "forward"), stepdown (also called "backward"), and stepwise. Each variation uses a different procedure for selecting a subset of predictor variables that yields the best prediction of a criterion variable. The heading for column 4 of table 14.6 indicates that Shepard used a stepwise multiple regression procedure.

Multiple regression analysis is sometimes misused by researchers. One common problem is to confuse prediction with explanation. The procedures are relatively straightforward if the researcher's purpose is to optimize prediction of a criterion variable. In contrast, the researcher should be very careful if he has a theory that attributes causal significance to the predictor variables. In this situation the researcher should not confuse the causal significance of a predictor variable with its regression weight or R^2 increment in a multiple regression equation. If you wish to test a causal theory using multivariate correlational data, you are advised to consider path analysis (discussed later in the chapter) rather than multiple regression.

Another caution is to retain a reasonable balance between sample size and number of predictor variables. In the extreme case where sample size equals number of predictors, R will equal 1.00 (perfect prediction), even if none of the predictors is correlated with the criterion. The multiple regression equation resulting from this analysis will almost certainly yield very poor predictions for a new sample of subjects. A rough rule of thumb is to increase sample size by at least 15 subjects for each variable that will be included in the multiple regression. Using this rule, a researcher would select a sample of at least 45 subjects for a multiple regression analysis involving three predictor variables.

Discriminant Analysis

Discriminant analysis is similar to multiple regression in that both statistical techniques involve two or more predictor variables and a single criterion variable. Discriminant analysis is limited to the special case in which the criterion is a person's group membership. Examples of group membership are male versus female; high-achieving student versus low-achieving student; engineer versus physicist versus doctor. The discriminant-analysis equation uses a person's scores on the predictor variables in an attempt to predict the group of which the person is a member. Discriminant analysis, then, is useful whenever the criterion variable is in the form of categories reflecting discrete groups. If the criterion variable is in the form of a continuous variable (e.g., most achievement test scores), multiple regression would be used instead of discriminant analysis.

Discriminant analysis was used in a study of engineers by Bryan Clemens, James Linden, and Bruce Shertzer.[14] The purpose of the study was to discover differences in vocational interests between engineers classified into three groups: (1) freshman engineering students at Purdue University in 1935, (2) the same engineers in 1966, and (3) freshman engineering students at Purdue University in 1966. Each of the three groups had been administered the Strong Vocational Interest Blank (SVIB), a measure of vocational interest described in chapter 9. The engineers' scores on 50 scales from the SVIB were used as the predictor variables in the discriminant analysis equation. The equation was created using part of the sample and then cross-validated on the remaining subjects. In the cross validation each engineer's SVIB scores were entered into the discriminant analysis equation in an attempt to predict whether the engineer was a member of the 1935 testing group, the 1966 retesting group, or the 1966 freshman testing group. Table 14.7 indicates that the discriminant analysis equation was quite accurate in assigning engineers to their respective group memberships. The success of the discriminant analysis led the researchers to conclude that each of the three engineering groups had different patterns of occupational interests.

14. Bryan Clemens, James Linden, and Bruce Shertzer, "Engineers' Interest Patterns: Then and Now," *Educational and Psychological Measurement* 30 (1970): 675–85.

TABLE 14.7

**Frequencies of Successes[a] and Failures in
Classifying Cross-Validation Groups**

Membership Predicted	1935 FR	Membership Actual 1966 RT	1966 FR
1935 FR	92	7	13
1966 RT	9	93	14
1966 FR	13	15	78
Total	114	115	105

FR = Freshmen, RT = Retesting.
[a]Chi-square = 311.98, significant beyond .01 level.

If you read the preceding chapter on causal-comparative design, you may be aware of an alternative method for analyzing these data, namely, one-way analysis of variance. First, the researcher would compute the mean score of each of the three groups on a particular SVIB scale. Then the differences between the three mean scores would be compared by one-way analysis of variance. If the resulting F value is statistically significant, post hoc comparisons (see p. 550) can be done to determine which of the three means differ significantly from one another. Because Clemens and his colleagues used 50 scales from the SVIB, 50 analyses of variance and possibly many post hoc comparisons would be required. This is a very large number of statistical analyses; it would require considerable effort to perform, report, and interpret all of them. In contrast, the discriminant technique provides a concise method for combining all the data into one statistical analysis.

Although discriminant analysis is elegant in its conciseness, it requires complex computations and a sophisticated knowledge of the mathematical basis of statistics to interpret the results. For this reason, the beginning researcher planning to use this technique is advised to work alongside an expert statistician. The researcher also may wish to supplement the discriminant analysis by using laborious but simpler statistical methods, such as analysis of variance.

Canonical Correlation

Canonical correlation is a multivariate correlational technique in which a combination of several predictor variables is used to predict a combination of several criterion variables. This technique is similar to multivariate analysis of variance (described in the previous chapter), which has a dependent variable that is a composite of two or more variables. Canonical correlation is also similar to multiple regression, which involves the combination of several predictor variables to predict a criterion. In multiple regression, however, there is a single criterion variable to be predicted. In canonical correlation, two or more variables form the criterion.

Suppose that the researcher has access to students' scores on a set of predictor variables such as scholastic aptitude, family socioeconomic status, high school gradepoint average, vocational interests, and extraversion-introversion. Also available are students' scores on criterion variables measured later in life, such as years of postsecondary education, annual salary, levels of physical and mental health, and contributions to the community. One method for understanding the relationships between the predictor variables and criterion variables is to correlate each predictor variable with each criterion variable using the bivariate correlational techniques (e.g., the product-moment correlation coefficient) described earlier in this chapter. Another approach is to ask the question, What *set* of predictor variables best predicts what *set* of criterion variables? The method used to answer this question is canonical correlation.

A research project by Herbert Walberg illustrates the use of canonical correlation.[15] The purpose of the research was to study the effects of classroom social climate, student biographical characteristics, personality, and intelligence on student learning in high school physics classes. A large number of variables was included in the data analysis: 14 scales measuring classroom social environment; 7 personality scales; 20 biographical items; a measure of ability; and 6 achievement measures (3 cognitive and 3 noncognitive) related to physics curriculum. This mass of data was first analyzed simply by correlating each predictor variable with each achievement variable. Canonical correlations then were computed in order to describe relationships more concisely.

Two significant canonical correlations emerged from this analysis. (These correlations yield variates, which are similar to the "factors" in factor analysis, described later in this chapter.) The first canonical correlation indicated that classes which gained the most on cognitive criteria of physics learning tended to have nonauthoritarian students who have high IQs and high grades and who see their classes as difficult. The second canonical correlation indicated that classes which gained the most on noncognitive criteria of physics learning tended to have students who win more prizes in science contests, spend more time in nonschool study, like school, and who do not think there is much apathy or friction in their classes.

The mathematical basis for canonical correlation is quite complex, as are

---

15. Herbert J. Walberg, "Predicting Class Learning: An Approach to the Class as a Social System," *American Educational Research Journal* (1969): 529–42.

the computational procedures and interpretation of the results. Yet canonical correlation appears with increasing frequency in the research literature, as researchers become interested in including more variables in their projects. Canonical correlation can be used in practical prediction, although this application seems limited because the purpose of practical prediction usually is to select persons who are likely to do well on a single important criterion. Canonical correlation is most often used when the researcher plans to undertake an exploratory relationship study to determine how a large number of variables measured at the same or different points in time relate to one another.

Path Analysis

Path analysis is a method for testing the validity of a theory about causal relationships between three or more variables that have been studied using a correlational research design. Path analysis is similar to the other multivariate methods described above—multiple regression, discriminant analysis, canonical correlation, and factor analysis—in that its concern is with the relationships between *three* or more variables. The primary difference between path analysis and the other multivariate methods is in its purpose. Path analysis is used solely to test theories about hypothesized causal links between variables. In contrast, the other multivariate methods are used primarily to maximize the correlation between various combinations of variables. Occasionally they are used to examine hypotheses about causal relationships between variables, but they are much less powerful than path analysis for this purpose.

Path analysis has a complicated rationale and set of statistical procedures associated with it. Despite its difficulty, you are advised to become familiar with path analysis for several reasons. First, knowledge about the method of path analysis should deepen your understanding of the limitations and uses of correlational research design. Second, path analysis provides a better basis for examining causal relationships in correlational data than other methods, even though some of the other methods are simpler to apply.

To illustrate path analysis, we will consider a study by Edwin Bridges and Maureen Hallinan on teacher absenteeism in school districts.[16] These researchers were interested in identifying factors that explain why some teachers more often do not show up for work than other teachers. The basic theory guiding their search for explanatory variables is that teacher absenteeism is sometimes used to achieve temporary relief from an unrewarding work context.

Teacher absenteeism was measured in this study by counting the number of one-day absence episodes occurring on Mondays and Fridays over an entire

16. Edwin M. Bridges and Maureen T. Hallinan, "Subunit Size, Work System Interdependence, and Employee Absenteeism," *Educational Administration Quarterly* 14 (1978): 24–42.

school year. For the primary analysis, the following variables were also measured:

   1. Work system interdependence. Measured by having teachers rate the extent to which they interact with others in various school activities.
   2. Group cohesion. Measured by having teachers complete a scale of how well they like their co-workers.
   3. Communication. Measured by having teachers estimate the frequency with which they talk to other teachers about certain topics.
   4. Subunit size. Measured by the number of full-time teachers spending their entire workday in the school.

With the exception of subunit size, all the variables were measured for each teacher in a participating school and then averaged to yield a single score for that score. Thus, the unit of analysis was the school. A total of 57 K-6 elementary schools participated in the study.

Table 14.8 presents the correlation matrix of all the variables mentioned above.[17] How are we to interpret these results? Since the purpose of the study was to identify possible causes of teacher absenteeism, we can examine how well each of the other variables predict it. Three of the four variables are statistically significant predictors of teacher absenteeism: subunit size ($r = .35$), work system interdependence ($r = -.24$), and group cohesion ($r = -.32$). However, just because these variables predict teacher absenteeism does not mean they "cause" the absenteeism. Also, a very real problem is created by the fact

TABLE 14.8

Correlation Matrix for Variables in Teacher Absenteeism Study

	Work System Interdependence	Communication	Group Cohesion	Absenteeism
Subunit size	.00	.24*	−.14	.35*
Work system interdependence		.51*	.34*	−.24*
Communication			.28*	.10
Group cohesion				−.32*
Absenteeism (MF total)				

*p<.05.

17. Table 14.8 is adapted from Edwin M. Bridges and Maureen T. Hallinan, "Subunit Size, Work System Interdependence, and Employee Absenteeism," *Educational Administration Quarterly*, Vol. 14, No. 1 (Winter 1978), pp. 24-42, © University Council for Educational Administration, with permission of Sage Publications, Inc.

that the predictor variables correlate with each other. For example, work system interdependence and group cohesion both predict teacher absenteeism, and they also correlate with each other ($r = .34$). Does group cohesion affect absenteeism independently of work system interdependence? Does work system interdependence affect absenteeism independently of group cohesion? And what about the fact that the variable of communication correlates significantly with both work system interdependence ($r = .51$) and group cohesion ($r = .28$)? Partial correlation, which was described earlier in the chapter, might be used to illuminate some of the relationships stated in these questions. Path analysis, however, is a much more powerful method for disentangling the varied connections between variables suggested by the correlation matrix.

Path analysis consists of three basic steps. The first step is to formulate a theory that links the variables of interest. In the case of Bridges and Hallinan's study, two theories were formulated. The first theory linked size of the work unit to teacher absenteeism by positing the following causal connections: "Large size increases the difficulties of maintaining communications among employees; lower levels of communications reduce group cohesiveness; low group cohesiveness leads to higher rates of employee absenteeism."[18] The second theory linked work system interdependence (the extent to which an organization's primary mission is planned and carried out collaboratively by employees) to teacher absenteeism. The theory posited that higher degrees of interdependence in school work systems will increase the rate of interaction (communication) among teachers; increased interaction will be reinforcing to teachers and thus group cohesion will increase over time; and increased group cohesion will lead to reduced teacher absenteeism.

After a theory has been formulated, the next step in path analysis is to select or develop measures of the variables (sometimes called "theoretical constructs" in this context) that are specified by the theory. This step is important because the path analysis will yield invalid results if the measures are not valid representations of the variables. It may be desirable to identify more than one measure for each variable. Alternate measures of important educational variables are often available.[19]

The third step in path analysis is to compute the statistics that show the strength of relationship between each of the pairs of variables that are causally linked in the theory. Finally, the researcher must interpret the statistics to determine whether they support or disconfirm the theory.

We can illustrate the procedures of path analysis by considering again Bridges and Hallinan's study of teacher absenteeism. You will recall that their

---

18. Ibid., p. 25.
19. The use of alternate measures of variables in path analysis is discussed in a paper by David Rogosa (see Annotated References at the end of this chapter).

basic theory was that teachers resort to absenteeism because they are trying to achieve temporary relief from an unrewarding work context. In the more articulated form of the theory, subunit size and work system interdependence were linked to teacher absenteeism through their effects on communication and group cohesion. These connections are shown in figure 14.2.[20] This type of figure is the standard way of representing path analysis variables. Note that each variable in the theory is represented in the figure. Also note the use of arrows in the figure. Each straight arrow indicates a hypothesized causal relationship in the direction of the arrow; for example, size of subunit influences communication, communication influences group cohesion, and so on.

Several other features of the path analysis in figure 14.2 should be observed at this time. Note that all the straight arrows point in one direction. For example, communication is hypothesized to influence group cohesion, but group cohesion is not hypothesized to influence communication. When a path analysis is ordered in this way, it is said to be based on a recursive model. A **recursive model** is one which only considers unidirectional causal relationships. If variable A is hypothesized to influence variable B, one cannot also hypothesize that variable B influences variable A. A **nonrecursive model** should be used if one wishes to test hypotheses involving reciprocal causation between pairs of variables.

Two of the arrows in figure 14.2 are curved and double-headed. This type of arrow linking two variables indicates that the researcher has not hypothesized how the variables might be causally related to each other. Figure 14.2

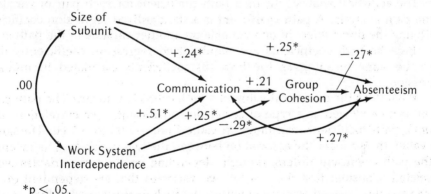

*p < .05.

Figure 14.2 Path analysis of the effects of subunit size and work system interdependence on teacher absenteeism.

20. Reprinted from Edwin M. Bridges and Maureen T. Hallinan, "Subunit Size, Work System Interdependence, and Employee Absenteeism," *Educational Administration Quarterly*, Vol. 14, No. 1 (Winter 1978), pp. 24-42, © University Council for Educational Administration, with permission of Sage Publications, Inc.

indicates that in designing their path analysis, Bridges and Hallinan did not hypothesize how subunit size and work system interdependence might be causally related, nor how communication and absenteeism might be causally related. To clarify, a curved arrow in a path analysis indicates the lack of a hypothesis about causality. A straight arrow indicates the presence of a hypothesis about causality: The hypothesis can predict no correlation, a positive correlation, or a negative correlation between the two variables.

Two types of variable are commonly distinguished in path analysis. **Exogenous variables** are variables that lack hypothesized causes in the path analysis model. Subunit size and work system interdependence are exogenous variables because no variables are hypothesized to influence them. **Endogenous variables** are variables that have at least one hypothesized cause in the path analysis model. For example, group cohesion is an endogenous variable because it is hypothesized to be influenced by communication.

The next step in path analysis is to measure each of the variables specified in the model. You will recall that we described above how each of the variables in figure 14.2 was measured by the researchers.

At this point in the path analysis, the exogenous and endogenous variables have been identified and measured; and the causal links specified by the researchers' theory have been identified by arrows. The next step is to perform a statistical analysis to determine the strength of association between each set of variables. The mathematical basis of the statistical procedures is complex. Basically the procedures are a form of multiple regression.

The statistical analysis yields a path coefficient for each pair of variables in the path analysis. A **path coefficient** is a standardized regression coefficient indicating the direct effect of one variable on another variable in the path analysis. Because path coefficients are standardized regression coefficients, they have the same meaning as the beta (B) coefficients calculated in multiple regression.

What does the numerical value of a path coefficient mean? The path coefficient can be viewed as a type of correlation coefficient. Like correlation coefficients, path coefficients can range in value from -1.00 to $+1.00$. The larger the value, the stronger the association between the two variables. The meaning of the path coefficient differs, though, depending on the two variables being correlated. Consider first the case of two variables that are dependent on no other variables (viewed as causes) within the path analysis model. Size of subunit and work unit interdependence in figure 14.2 are two such variables. Neither variable is caused by any other variable within the model. In this case the path coefficient is equal to the product-moment correlation (r) for the two variables. If you refer to table 14.8 and figure 14.2, you will see that the path coefficient and correlation coefficient for subunit size and work unit interdependence are exactly the same $(p = r = .00)$.

The path coefficient also equals the product-moment coefficient when one variable (A) is viewed as dependent on a single cause (variable B) within the path analysis model. For example, in the following figure variable A is viewed as the single cause of variable B, and therefore the path coefficient (P_{ab}) is equal to the product-moment correlation coefficient for these variables.

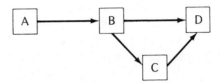

Still another situation where p equals r is the case of a variable that is dependent on more than one cause within the path analysis, but the causes are viewed as independent of each other.

Now we can consider the case of path coefficients that do not satisfy the requirements described above. In fact, none of the path coefficients in figure 14.2—except the path coefficient for subunit size and work system interdependence—satisfies the requirements. These path coefficients are similar, but not identical, to partial correlation coefficients in that they represent the strength of association between two variables with the effect of other pertinent variables partialed out. For example, the path coefficient between subunit size and absenteeism in figure 14.2 is .25, which represents their strength of association with communication and group cohesion partialed out.

You will note that the path coefficient (.25) is somewhat less than the product-moment r for the same variables ($r = .35$, as shown in table 14.8). This result means that subunit size has some direct effect on teacher absenteeism, but that part of its effect is indirect. The "indirect" effect means that part of the effect of subunit size on teacher absenteeism is due to its effect on communication. The total indirect effect of a variable is equal to the r between it and the dependent variable minus the corresponding path coefficient. For the effect of subunit size on teacher absenteeism, the direct effect is .25 and the indirect effect is .10 (.35 − .25). This analysis indicates that the direct effect of subunit size upon teacher absenteeism (.25) is substantially more potent than its indirect effects (.10).

The final step in path analysis is to determine whether the results support one's theory. In the case of the research study we have been considering, Bridges and Hallinan concluded that their theory was not supported since the effects of subunit size and work system interdependence on teacher absenteeism are not entirely mediated by communication and group cohesion.[21]

In summary, the major advantage of path analysis is that it enables the researcher to test causal theories using correlational data. Other multivariate techniques, such as multiple regression and canonical correlation, are not well suited for this purpose. Rather, these techniques are best used to maximize the prediction of one or more criterion variables from a set of predictor variables.

If you plan to do a path analysis, you should study this method carefully and consult an expert statistician if necessary. The calculation of path coefficients and testing them for statistical significance are difficult procedures. The data need to satisfy certain assumptions, and the results of the path analysis can be misleading if the variables are not well measured, if important causal variables are left out of the theoretical model, or if the sample size is insufficient for the number of variables being considered.

Of these problems, underspecification of the causal model is probably the most serious. Thomas Cook and Donald Campbell provide an example of how underspecification can distort the interpretation of path results.[22] They note that students who have attended a Head Start program (HS) are likely to have lower first-grade achievement scores (Ach) than students who have not attended such a program. Thus, if HS → Ach specifies a complete causal model, the path coefficient will be negative ($B = -.19$), as shown in figure 14.3a.[23] We would conclude that Head Start has a harmful effect on student learning.

The problem with this causal model is that it omits an important cause of first-grade achievement. We can call this causal variable Educational Advantage (EA), which is usually measured by some index of socioeconomic status. Students from high socioeconomic status homes usually perform better in school, and so the correlation between EA and Ach is positive (.49) in figure 14.3b. Students with high EA are also less likely to attend a Head Start program; hence, the negative correlation between EA and HS ($-.70$).

Now examine the path analysis in 14.3c based on the correlation coefficients of figure 14.3b. You will note that the path coefficient for the HS → Ach link is positive ($B = .3$), whereas in figure 14.3a the path coefficient is negative. This example thus provides a demonstration of how a path coefficient can change signs depending on how completely the model is specified. Underspecified models should be avoided because they can lead to serious errors of causal inferences.

21. Bridges and Hallinan's results have been simplified for our purposes. Additional data analyses related to their theory can be found in their journal report.
22. Thomas D. Cook and Donald T. Campbell, *Quasi-Experimentation: Design and Analysis Issues for Field Settings* (Chicago: Rand McNally, 1979).
23. Figure 14.3 adapted from ibid., p. 306.

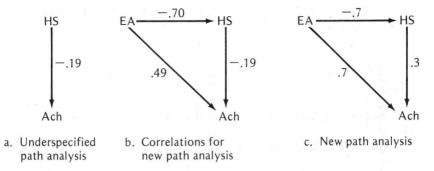

a. Underspecified   b. Correlations for   c. New path analysis
   path analysis   new path analysis

Figure 14.3   Underspecified and better-specified path analyses.

The Correlation Matrix and Factor Analysis

Factor analysis is one of the most frequently used techniques in multivariate research. Researchers often measure a large number of variables in a single research project. Data analysis and interpretation become quite unwieldy in this situation. Factor analysis is helpful to the researcher because it provides an empirical basis for reducing the many variables to a few factors. The factors then become manageable data for analysis and interpretation.

Factor analysis performs the function of data reduction by grouping variables that are moderately or highly correlated with one another. The first step in a factor analysis is to compute a correlation matrix. This procedure can be illustrated by considering the data from a study of patterns of college grades across different curriculum areas by Lyle Schoenfeldt and Donald Brush.[24] For each college graduate in the sample, a separate gradepoint average (GPA) was computed for his/her grades in each of the following twelve areas: fine arts, languages, humanities, biological sciences, physical sciences, social sciences, agriculture, business, education, home economics, speech/journalism, and physical education/ROTC. The researchers also collected each graduate's high school GPA and high school Scholastic Aptitude (SAT) verbal and math scores.

As shown in table 14.9, a **correlation matrix** is constructed by listing all the variables on both the horizontal and vertical columns.[25] Since the Schoenfeldt and Brush study included 15 variables, there are 15 rows and 15 columns, each corresponding to a particular variable; for example, Biological Sciences

24. Lyle F. Schoenfeldt and Donald H. Brush, "Patterns of College Grades Across Curricular Areas: Some Implications for GPA as a Criterion," *American Educational Research Journal* 12 (1975): 313–21.
25. Table 14.9 adapted from ibid.

TABLE 14.9

Intercorrelations of GPAs in 12 Curricular Areas, High School GPA, and SATs

Variable	1	2	3	4	5	6	7	8	9	10	11	12	13	14	15
1. Fine Arts		.38	.47	.41	.36	.44	.39	.32	.40	.35	.29	.27	.34	.25	.17
2. Language			.50	.43	.49	.49	.19	.35	.32	.36	.29	.27	.44	.22	.21
3. Humanities				.59	.52	.69	.44	.50	.44	.53	.47	.34	.47	.43	.26
4. Biological Sciences					.51	.63	.56	.48	.37	.45	.34	.34	.41	.30	.28
5. Physical Sciences						.55	.45	.46	.41	.37	.32	.33	.43	.18	.31
6. Social Sciences							.39	.59	.47	.58	.44	.39	.45	.40	.28
7. Agriculture								.22	.66	.31	.44	.38	.38	.19	.17
8. Business									.31	.23	.35	.28	.36	.23	.23
9. Education										.46	.36	.21	.37	.15	.14
10. Home Economics											.36	.27	.34	.34	.20
11. Speech/Journalism												.22	.33	.23	.13
12. Physical Educ/ROTC													.31	.06	.09
13. High School Grade Point														.20	.17
14. SAT—Verbal															.41
15. SAT—Math															

GPA is represented by row 4 and column 4. The correlation between any two variables is given at the point where the row and column corresponding to the variables cross. For example, the correlation between Humanities GPA and Education GPA is .44, which is located at the intersect of row 3 and column 9. Note that only half the matrix is needed to show all the possible intercorrelations.

After preparing a correlation matrix, the researchers did a factor analysis to determine whether the 15 variables could be described by a smaller number of factors. The factors identified as a result of the analysis are presented in table 14.10.[26]

The mathematical basis for factor analysis is beyond the scope of this book. Basically, it involves a search for clusters of variables that are all correlated with each other. The first cluster that is identified is called the first factor;

TABLE 14.10
Loadings of GPAs in 12 Curricular Areas, High School GPA, and SATs

	Factor		
Variable	I General Academic Achievement	II Grades Independent of Achievement and Aptitude	III Tested Aptitude
1. Fine Arts	.42	.33	.20
2. Language	.63	.10	.16
3. Humanities	.64	.32	.39
4. Biological Sciences	.56	.39	.27
5. Physical Sciences	.62	.31	.13
6. Social Sciences	.73	.27	.36
7. Agriculture	.18	.92	.09
8. Business	.60	.12	.19
9. Education	.33	.63	.10
10. Home Economics	.43	.30	.33
11. Speech/Journalism	.36	.36	.19
12. Physical Educ/ROTC	.41	.27	−.01
13. High School Grade Point	.52	.29	.12
14. SAT—Verbal	.11	.08	.84
15. SAT—Math	.20	.07	.42

26. Table 14.10 from ibid.

it represents the variables that are most intercorrelated with each other. The factor is represented as a score, which is generated for each subject in the sample. Thus it is possible to compute a correlation coefficient between students' factor score and their score on a particular variable that was entered into the factor analysis. These coefficients are presented under the heading Factor I in table 14.10. The individual coefficients are sometimes called the **loading** of each variable on the factor.

Inspection of the Factor I loadings indicates that all the variables, with the exception of Agriculture GPA and the two SAT scores, correlate moderately or highly with the factor. The researchers chose to label the factor General Academic Achievement to reflect the fact that there is a general positive relationship between students' performance in different curriculum areas. If you refer back to the correlation matrix, you will see that Agriculture GPA and the two SAT scores generally correlate lower with other variables than the other variables correlate with each other.

After the first primary factor has been identified, additional factors can be generated, depending upon on how many other clusters of interrelated variables exist. The second factor in table 14.10 has high loadings on Agriculture GPA ($r = .92$) and Education GPA ($r = .63$). This result suggests that achievement in agriculture and education have something in common that is not shared or is shared only moderately by other curriculum areas. The third factor shown in table 14.10 is called Tested Aptitude because the two SAT variables correlate highly with it, but not the GPA variables.

These three factors represent much of the information contained in the larger correlation matrix. Each factor can be treated as a variable, and each student can be given a score on it, called a **factor score**. The factor scores can be used in subsequent statistical analyses. For example, a t test might be done to determine whether male and female students differ significantly on the first factor.

Factor analysis is a valuable tool in educational research, but it needs to be used carefully. A frequent caution given to the novice researcher is "Garbage in, garbage out," meaning that the factors generated by a factor analysis are only as interpretable as the variables entered into the correlation matrix. For example, the researcher should carefully consider the number and types of variables that are to be entered into the factor analysis. Factor analysis is most appropriate when the researcher has good reason to explore the interrelationships and commonalities among a particular set of variables. Even when a factor analysis is done for good reason, as in the Schoenfeldt and Brush study, the factors may be more or less interpretable. For example, in table 14.10 it appears to us that Factors I and III are more interpretable than Factor II.

A final caution is that several variations of factor analysis are available. The beginning researcher should consult an expert statistician for assistance in planning a factor analysis for a particular set of data.

Differential Analysis

Subgroup Analysis in Relationship Studies

In discussing causal-comparative research, we stressed the importance of forming well-defined groups as a basis for studying possible causal factors. The same principle also applies to relationship studies. The formation of homogeneous subgroups may uncover relationships that are obscured when correlations are computed for the total sample. The importance of this point was impressed on the authors in a study of the relationship between personality and teaching behavior.[27] This study was part of a larger study to investigate gains in teachers' use of classroom skills as a result of an inservice teacher education program called a Minicourse (see chapter 18). Before the sample of 16 male and 32 female elementary school teachers took the Minicourse, they were administered two personality measures—the Edwards Personal Preference Schedule and the Rokeach Dogmatism Scale. In addition each teacher taught a 20-minute lesson that was videotaped and later scored on several indices of teaching behavior.

The relationship of the personality scales to two measures of teacher behavior (percentage of teacher talk in a class discussion and frequency with which a teacher asks a question and then answers it himself) is presented in table 14.11. First examine the correlations for the entire sample of 48 teachers. Percentage of teacher talk is related to only three of the personality variables at the .10 level of statistical significance, and frequency of answering one's own questions is significantly correlated with but one personality variable. The correlation coefficients are of quite low magnitude.

However, it should be noted that the total sample includes both male and female teachers. The authors thus decided that it might be worthwhile to compute the correlation coefficients separately for both groups of teachers. This data analysis is also presented in table 14.11. Many sizable correlation coefficients at a high level of statistical significance are found for male teachers. Our interpretation of these results is that a male teacher's tendency to talk a lot in class and to answer his own questions reflects a general personality disposition to be assertive, inflexible, and not interpersonally responsive. In contrast, the data for female teachers yield few significant relationships between teacher personality and personality variables. These results suggest that female teachers' classroom behavior is more reflective of specific classroom conditions than of general personality dispositions. This research study illustrates the importance of forming subgroups for data analysis when exploring relationships be-

27. Meredith D. Gall, Walter R. Borg, Philip Langer, and Marjorie L. Kelley, "The Relationship Between Personality and Teaching Behavior Before and After Inservice Microteaching Training" (paper presented at the annual meeting of the California Educational Research Association, Los Angeles, March 1969).

tween variables. Had the data not been analyzed separately by sex, the authors might have reached the erroneous conclusion that there is little relationship between the personality variables and teacher behaviors measured in the study.

Two other points should be made about the data analysis presented in table 14.11. First, it is important to take into account the number of correlation coefficients that were computed in order to properly interpret their statistical significance. Thirty-four coefficients were computed for the total sample. By chance alone three of these coefficients should reach statistical significance at the .10 level. The results indicate that three of the coefficients were significant at the .10 level and one at the .05 level. Thus, one should be wary about concluding that there is a relationship between the personality variable of defer-ence and percentage of teacher talk (for the total sample), since this is likely to

TABLE 14.11

Relationships between Personality Variables and Teacher Behavior

EPPS[a] Scales	Percentage Teacher Talk			Answering Own Question		
	Total Sample N = 48	Males N = 16	Females N = 32	Total Sample N = 48	Males N = 16	Females N = 32
Achievement	.40	.65***	.29	.30**	.74***	.11
Deference	−.25*	−.46*	−.14	−.05	−.18	.04
Order	.12	.14	.11	.16	−.35	.07
Exhibition	.10	.36	−.02	.00	.16	−.09
Autonomy	.09	.70***	−.27	−.15	.15	−.31*
Affiliation	−.21	−.68***	.10	−.10	−.47*	.16
Intraception	−.21	−.13	−.30*	.11	.21	.15
Succorance	.01	−.08	.05	−.14	−.44*	.04
Dominance	−.10	−.33	.06	−.07	.06	−.19
Abasement	.25*	.19	.27	.08	.04	.11
Nurturance	.03	−.47*	.32*	−.08	−.56**	.18
Change	−.16	−.16	−.19	.00	.10	−.01
Endurance	−.02	.04	−.04	.13	−.10	.19
Heterosexuality	−.19	.17	−.36**	−.07	.12	−.22
Aggression	.08	.53**	−.11	.03	.13	.04
Consistency	.25*	.54**	.15	.12	.68***	−.01
Rokeach Dogmatism	−.01	.51**	−.20	.08	.12	.05

[a]Edwards Personal Preference Schedule.
  *$p < .10$.
 **$p < .05$.
***$p < .01$.

be a chance finding. However, it is quite clear that the number of statistically significant correlation coefficients for male teachers far exceeds the number that would be expected by chance alone. For example, 5 of the coefficients are significant at the .01 level, whereas the operation of chance would dictate that less than one of the 34 computed coefficients should be significant at this level.

The second point regards the interpretation of the difference between two correlation coefficients. For example, we find that the correlation between need for achievement and percentage of teacher talk for male teachers ($r = .65$) is significantly different from zero, but the corresponding coefficient for female teachers ($r = .29$) is not significantly different. But is the difference between the correlation coefficients for male and female teachers statistically significant, that is, can the difference be accounted for by the operation of chance? The student should be aware that there is a statistical test available for answering this question.[28]

A useful strategy for identifying variables for differential analysis is to ask yourself what characteristics or relationships, other than the one you have hypothesized, could have contributed to the correlation you have obtained. Then select subjects from your sample that have the characteristic and recompute the correlation for the two subgroups, that is, those having and those not having the characteristic in question. If the resulting correlations are about the same, you may conclude that the characteristic in question has not contributed to your initial correlation, but if these two correlations are significantly different, you have gained a new insight into the relationship you are studying.

Moderator Variables in Prediction Studies

Sometimes a test is more effective in predicting the behavior of certain subgroups than in predicting the behavior of other subgroups. In this situation we can use differential prediction, which is a form of differential analysis. For example, it has been found that aptitude test scores generally predict school grades better for females than for males.[29] In this instance sex is designated a **moderator variable** because it moderates the predictive validity of a test. Sex, education, and socioeconomic status are frequently used as moderator variables. Also, one test is sometimes used as a moderator variable to improve the predictive validity of another test. In a study by Lawrence Malnig, the Taylor Manifest Anxiety Scale (TMAS) was used as a moderator variable to improve the correlation between scores on the School and College Aptitude Test (SCAT) and

28. See Bruning and Kintz in Annotated References at the end of this chapter. Their handbook includes computational procedures for a test of the statistical significance of the difference between two correlation coefficients.
29. See H. G. Seashore, "Women Are More Predictable Than Men," *Journal of Counseling Psychology* 9 (1962): 261–70.

college grades.[30] TMAS scores of a total sample of 210 students were used to form subgroups of high-, intermediate-, and low-anxious students. Then separate correlations between SCAT scores and school grades were computed for each anxiety subgroup. The findings, shown in table 14.12, indicate that anxiety is an effective moderator variable.[31] It is possible to make much better predictions with the SCAT for students low in anxiety than for students intermediate or high in anxiety. The total SCAT score explains 44 percent of the variance in grades for low-anxious students, 20 percent for intermediate-anxious students, and only 3 percent for high-anxious students. These results suggest an interesting problem for further investigation: If aptitude does not have predictive validity for high-anxious students, then what other variables might predict school achievement within this subgroup?

To identify possible moderator variables, the student should undertake a careful analysis of how various factors interact in determining academic or occupational success. An example of this kind of analysis occurred in a study by air force psychologists to determine whether success in pilot training could be predicted from the cadet's interest in aviation. The psychologists developed a test containing many items of general information about aviation. It was hypothesized that an individual interested in aviation would have gained the information needed to answer the questions, while persons not interested would not have this information. The test was tried on a sample of aviation cadets and found to correlate moderately with the later success in pilot training. It was then hypothesized that the test would be a more satisfactory predictor for

TABLE 14.12

Correlations between Grades and SCAT Scores
(V = Verbal, Q = Quantitative, T = Total)

Group	N	V Score and Grades	Q Score and Grades	T Score and Grades
Total population	210	.377**	.266**	.334**
High anxiety	42	.252	−.034	.158
Middle anxiety	42	.279	.407**	.447**
Low anxiety	42	.577**	.507**	.644**

**Significant at .01 level.

30. Lawrence R. Malnig, "Anxiety and Academic Prediction," *Journal of Counseling Psychology* 11 (1964): 72–75.
31. Ibid.

individuals with low interest in reading than individuals with high interest in reading. This hypothesis was based upon the premise that the individual who did a great deal of reading might have gained much of the information on the test without having a strong interest in aviation. On the other hand, individuals who had little interest in reading would almost surely not have the information on the test unless they had a strong interest in aviation. Further research proved this hypothesis to be correct.

Statistical Factors in Prediction Research

Group Prediction

The goal of many prediction studies is to develop measures with sufficient predictive validity to be used in practical selection programs in education or industry. The effectiveness of a measure for selection purposes, however, is not determined solely by its predictive validity. Two other factors influence effectiveness in practical selection problems. The first is the selection ratio. This is the proportion of the available candidates that must be selected. A predictive measure gives better results when only the few candidates scoring highest need be chosen than when all but the few who score lowest must be chosen. In other words, the smaller the proportion of candidates that must be chosen, the more of those chosen will be successful.

The other factor influencing the effectiveness of a predictive measure is the proportion of candidates who would be successful if no selection were applied. In most vocational applications, this is the proportion of employees hired for the given activity, prior to the selection system, whose work was satisfactory. In educational selection it would be the number of students who succeeded in the given course of study prior to the use of selective admission. This number provides a baseline. If the baseline figure is high, the predictive measure will need to have very high validity in order to improve on the success of "natural" selection. If the baseline figure is low, the predictive measure can have low predictive validity yet manage to improve on "natural" selection.

The **Taylor-Russell Tables** were developed to combine the three factors of predictive validity, selection ratio, and proportion successful without selection.[32] If these three factors are known, the researcher can predict the proportion of the candidates selected who will be successful if the predictive measure is used.

---

32. H. C. Taylor and J. T. Russell, "The Relationships of Validity Coefficients to the Practical Effectiveness of Tests in Selection: Discussion and Tables," *Journal of Applied Psychology* 23 (1939): 565–78.

Shrinkage

In using correlations for prediction, the usual procedure is to select a test or battery of tests that we believe will predict the behavior with which we are concerned. These tests are then tried out on a sample in order to determine their predictive validity, that is, the degree to which they will predict the behavior that we wish them to predict. The correlation between the prediction made by the test and the later behavior of the individual provides an estimate of the predictive validity of the test. This correlation, however, will almost certainly become smaller if we repeat the experiment with a new sample.

The tendency for predictive validities to decrease when the research is repeated is referred to as **shrinkage.** More shrinkage is likely to occur when the original sample includes a small number of subjects and when the number of predictor variables is large.

Shrinkage is due primarily to the fact that when we initially validate our measures, some of them will yield significant correlations by chance. In other words, characteristics unique to the group of subjects we have tested tend to yield a maximum predictive validity for some of our predictive measures. In fact, it can be demonstrated mathematically that if the researcher keeps adding predictor variables to the multiple regression equation, she eventually will be able to predict each person's score on the criterion variable perfectly. Upon repetition of the study, however, these same chance predictive relationships are not likely to be present, and thus the correlation initially obtained becomes smaller or disappears. As it is not possible to carry out predictions on the basis of correlations that only apply to one sample of subjects, it is always advisable to conduct a cross validation of predictor variables before using them in practical prediction situations. Thus, after preliminary validation of the battery, the predictive validity of each prediction instrument should be cross-checked using another sample, and those correlations that have dropped to the level that makes them impractical for inclusion in the regression equation should be eliminated.

INTERPRETATION OF CORRELATION COEFFICIENTS

Statistical and Practical Significance of Correlational Data

Beginning researchers often have a difficult time interpreting the correlation coefficient after computing it. In fact, a correlation coefficient is a mathematical way of expressing the degree of relationship between two or more variables. To state it another way, the coefficient expresses the degree to which the variables covary. A coefficient of .50 does not mean that the two measures have

50 percent of their variance in common. Rather, the square of the correlation gives this "common variance." Two tests that are correlated .50 have $(.50)^2$ or 25 percent of their variance in common. As a statement of prediction, a correlation of .50 means that the variance in one variable predicts 25 percent of the variance in the other variable.

Statistical significance of a correlation coefficient usually expresses whether the obtained coefficient is different from zero at a given level of confidence. If the coefficient is not significantly different from zero, the null hypothesis of no difference cannot be rejected. If the coefficient is statistically significant, we can conclude that the relationship between the variables is nonzero. You should keep in mind, though, that the population coefficient may be greater or less than the obtained correlation coefficient. If you wish, you can calculate confidence limits to estimate the range of coefficients within which the population coefficient is likely to fall. (Confidence limits are discussed in chapter 10.)

Most statistics texts include a table from which the statistical significance of a product-moment correlation can be determined directly. The level of statistical significance of a correlation coefficient is determined in large part by the number of cases upon which the correlation is based. For example, with 22 cases, a product-moment coefficient of .54 is needed to be significant at the 1 percent level. If 100 cases are available, however, a correlation of .25 is significant at the 1 percent level, and with 1000 cases a correlation of only .08 is significant at the 1 percent level.

Statistical significance is also dependent on whether a one-tailed or two-tailed test is performed. In a two-tailed test the researcher determines whether the obtained coefficient (ignoring its sign) is at either tail of the normal curve of positive and negative coefficients that could occur by chance in samples drawn by chance from a population in which $r = .00$. In a one-tailed test, only coefficients on one side of the normal curve distribution are considered.

Relationship studies are aimed primarily at gaining a better understanding of the complex skills or behavior patterns being studied, and therefore low correlation coefficients are as meaningful as high coefficients. Prediction studies are concerned with forecasting certain kinds of future behavior and therefore require higher correlation coefficients than those usually found in relationship studies. In prediction studies statistical significance is of little consequence because correlations usually must exceed this point to be of practical value. In other words, practical significance is more important than statistical significance.

Interpreting Magnitude of Correlation Coefficients

The following rules provide a rough basis for interpreting correlation coefficient obtained in relationship and prediction research. These rules are, of course, only a general guide, but will be appropriate for most types of educational research.

Correlation coefficients ranging from .20 to .35 show a slight relationship between the variables, although this relationship may be statistically significant. A correlation of .20 indicates that only 4 percent of the variance in the two measures that have been correlated is common to both. Correlations in this range may have meaning in exploratory research where relationships are being investigated using crude measures. Correlations at this level, however, are of little value in practical prediction situations.

With correlations around .50, crude group prediction may be achieved. As a correlation of .50 between a test and the performance predicted only indicates 25 percent common variance, it is obvious that predictions based on a correlation this low can be expected to be frequently in error. Correlations within this range, however, are useful when combined with other correlations in a multiple regression equation. Combining several correlations in this range can in some cases yield individual predictions that are correct within an acceptable margin of error. Correlations at this level used singly are of little or no use for individual prediction because they yield only a few more correct predictions than could be accomplished by guessing or by using some chance selection procedure. The exception is when a very favorable selection ratio is present.

Correlation coefficients ranging from .65 to .85 make possible group predictions that are accurate enough for most purposes. As we move toward the top of this range, group predictions can be made very accurately, usually predicting the proportion of successful candidates in selection problems within a very small margin of error. Near the top of this correlation range individual predictions can be made that are considerably more accurate than would occur if no such selection procedure were used.

Correlation coefficients over .85 indicate a very close relationship between the two variables correlated. A correlation of .85 indicates that the measure, or combination of measures, used for prediction has about 72 percent variance in common with the performance being predicted. Prediction studies in education very rarely yield correlations this high. When obtained at this level, however, correlations are very useful for either individual or group prediction.

MISTAKES SOMETIMES MADE IN DOING CORRELATIONAL RESEARCH

1. Researcher assumes correlational findings to be proof of cause-and-effect relationships.
2. Relies on the "shotgun" approach rather than theory and previous research findings in selecting variables for correlational studies.

3. Fails to develop satisfactory criterion measures for use in prediction or relationship studies.
4. Uses simple correlational techniques in situations where adjustments such as partial correlation are needed to obtain a clear picture of the way the variables are operating.
5. Uses the incorrect bivariate correlation coefficient; for example, uses the biserial correlation when the widespread biserial correlation is called for.
6. In studies incorporating many variables, limits analyses to use of bivariate correlational statistics without using multivariate statistics to clarify relationships between variables.
7. Does not use multiple regression to maximize correlations in prediction studies.
8. Fails to specify an important causal variable in planning a path analysis.
9. Does not carry out a cross-validation study in order to determine shrinkage of multiple regression coefficients obtained in the original prediction study.
10. Confuses practical significance with statistical significance in interpreting magnitude of correlation coefficients.

ANNOTATED REFERENCES

Amick, Daniel J., and Walberg, Herbert J., eds. *Introductory Multivariate Analysis.* Berkeley, Calif.: McCutchan, 1975.

This collection of contributed writings presents good expositions of the following multivariate correlational techniques: multiple regression, path analysis, canonical correlation, factor analysis, and discriminant analysis. Each chapter describes the mathematical basis for the technique, research applications, and misuses to be avoided.

Bruning, James L., and Kintz, B. L. *Computational Handbook of Statistics.* 2nd ed. Glenview, Ill.: Scott, Foresman, 1977.

This book provides easy-to-follow computational procedures for these correlational techniques: product-moment correlation, Spearman rank-order correlation, Kendall rank-order correlation, point biserial correlation, the correlation ratio, *phi* coefficient, contingency coefficient, partial correlation, multiple regression, and the test for difference between independent/dependent correlations.

Cook, Thomas D., and Campbell, Donald T. *Quasi-Experimentation: Design and Analysis Issues for Field Settings.* Chicago: Rand McNally, 1979.

Chapter 7 of this book contains a discussion of sophisticated statistical techniques for making causal inferences from correlational data. A critical review of path analysis procedures is included.

Jackson, Douglas N., and Messick, Samuel, eds. *Problems in Human Assessment*. New York: McGraw-Hill, 1967.

Many of the articles reprinted in this book will be of assistance to the student planning a prediction or selection study. Among them are: Robert L. Thorndike, "The Analysis and Selection of Test Items," pp. 201–16; J. P. Guilford, "Some Lessons from Aviation Psychology," pp. 335–45; David R. Saunders, "Moderator Variables in Prediction," pp. 362–67; Edward E. Cureton, "Validity, Reliability, and Baloney," pp. 372–73.

Pedhazur, Elazar J. *Multiple Regression in Behavioral Research: Explanation and Prediction*. 2nd ed. New York: Holt, Rinehart and Winston, 1982.

The author provides an in-depth discussion, with many research examples, of the multivariate correlational techniques presented in this chapter. The presentation is mathematically sophisticated yet readable.

Rogosa, David. "Causal Models in Longitudinal Research: Rationale, Formulation, and Interpretation." In *Longitudinal Research in the Study of Behavior and Development*, edited by John R. Nesselroade and Paul B. Baltes. New York: Academic Press, 1979. Pp. 263–302.

This chapter presents a critique of path analysis and an alternative formulation, called causal modeling, which uses correlational data to test causal hypotheses. The author provides a substantial number of examples of causal modeling in longitudinal research.

SELF-CHECK TEST

Circle the correct answer to each of the following questions. An answer key is provided on page 881.

1. A perfect negative correlation is described by a correlation coefficient of
   a. 0.00.
   b. +1.00.
   c. −1.00.
   d. −.50.
2. A principal advantage of the correlation method is that it allows
   a. establishment of cause-and-effect relationships.
   b. simultaneous study of relationships between a great number of variables.
   c. many types of experimental designs to be used.
   d. for adjustment in pretreatment measures.
3. In contrast to relationship studies, prediction studies are more concerned with
   a. reducing restriction in range.
   b. maximizing the correction for attenuation.

    c. maximizing the correlation of each variable with a criterion.

    d. criterion measures.

4. A correlational technique appropriate when both variables are expressed as continuous scores is the

    a. product-moment correlation.

    b. rank-difference correlation.

    c. biserial correlation.

    d. *phi* coefficient.

5. Spearman's *rho* and Kendall's *tau* are both used to correlate two sets of

    a. continuous scores.

    b. true dichotomies.

    c. artificial dichotomies.

    d. ranked scores.

6. The scattergram is useful for

    a. deciding whether to compute a partial coefficient.

    b. deciding whether to do a factor analysis.

    c. correcting for restriction in range.

    d. studying nonlinear relationships between variables.

7. The lowering of a correlation coefficient between two sets of scores due to lack of reliability of the measures is called

    a. attenuation.

    b. restriction in range.

    c. regression.

    d. correlation ratio.

8. The process used to rule out the influence of one or more variables upon the criterion behavior pattern is called

    a. regression.

    b. partial correlation.

    c. correction for attenuation.

    d. analysis of variance.

9. The process of determining the correlation between the criterion behavior and a combination of predictor measures is called

    a. simple correlation.

    b. multiple regression.

    c. differential analysis.

    d. moderator analysis.

10. The purpose of canonical correlation is to determine the magnitude of the relationship between

    a. a set of predictor variables and a set of criterion variables.

    b. a set of predictor variables and a person's group membership.

    c. two or more factor scores.

    d. two or more discriminant functions.

11. A systematic representation of the correlations between all variables measured in a study is called a
    a. scattergram.
    b. correlation ratio.
    c. plot.
    d. correlation matrix.
12. The most useful correlational technique for testing causal hypotheses is
    a. factor analysis.
    b. path analysis.
    c. discriminant analysis.
    d. moderator analysis.
13. In factor analysis the term *factor* refers to
    a. product-moment correlations.
    b. test scores.
    c. mathematical constructs.
    d. regression equations.
14. Shrinkage occurs because, at the time of initial validation, some statistically significant correlations were
    a. not discovered.
    b. underestimated.
    c. obtained by chance.
    d. present due to measurement bias.
15. If a set of tests predicts a criterion variable better for males than for females, sex is said to be a
    a. predictor variable.
    b. regression element.
    c. moderator variable.
    d. group predictor.

APPLICATION PROBLEMS

The following problems are designed to give you practice in applying significant concepts and research procedures explained in chapter 14. Most do not have a single correct answer. For feedback, compare your answers with the sample answers on pages 894–95.

1. A researcher intercorrelates a number of measures she has collected on a sample of college seniors. She finds a correlation of +.65 between (1) the amount of time a student has been employed during his or her college years and (2) a paper-and-pencil measure of the student's personal maturity. On the basis of this finding, would you be justified in concluding that:

a. The college should institute a work-study program in order to increase the maturity level of its students? Explain your answer.

b. It is probable that the *longer* a student has worked during college, the *higher* will be his score on the personal maturity measure? Explain your answer.

c. More mature students are better able to obtain jobs while in college than their less mature peers? Explain your answer.

2. A researcher decides to investigate possible determinants of interest in science among elementary school children. First he develops and validates a measure of this variable. Then he locates tests that measure as many variables as possible in as short a time as possible to correlate with his interest test. He figures that he will increase the likelihood of discovering significant relationships if he maximizes the number of variables included in his correlational design. What is wrong with the researcher's reasoning?

3. A researcher has collected a large amount of data on a sample of college students: scores on the Stanford-Binet Intelligence Scale, scores on the Wechsler Adult Intelligence Scale, scores on the Scholastic Aptitude Test, high school class rank, scores on a test anxiety scale, and whether or not they successfully completed the first year of college (pass-fail and gradepoint average). The following are statistical analyses to be made of these data:

a. Correlation of scores on the Stanford-Binet Intelligence Scale with scores on the Wechsler scale. What statistical technique should be used, and why?

b. The researcher finds that test anxiety correlates significantly with the criterion variable of gradepoint average in the first year of college. The Scholastic Aptitude Test (SAT) also correlates significantly with test anxiety and the criterion. What statistical technique should be used to determine the correlation between test anxiety and college gradepoint average after the influence of SAT on both variables has been removed?

c. Correlation of Scholastic Aptitude Test scores with the dichotomous variable of pass-fail in the first year of college. What statistical technique should be used, and why?

d. Determine whether all of the measures used in this study, when intercorrelated with each other, measure a common factor. What statistical technique should be used, and why?

e. Determine whether the relationship between scores on the test anxiety scale and high school class rank is nonlinear. What statistical technique should be used, and why?

4. A researcher administered a battery of 20 different tests to a group of entering medical students. She also collected their gradepoint average at the end of their first year of medical school. What statistical technique should be used to maximize the usefulness of the 20 tests as predictors of the gradepoint average, and why?

5. In the table that follows, the criterion variable is gradepoint average. What are the moderator variables? What are the predictor variables?

Group	N	Verbal Aptitude and GPA*	Quantitative Aptitude and GPA*	Creative Aptitude and GPA*
High self-esteem	35	.65	.60	.35
Middle self-esteem	35	.34	.45	.10
Low self-esteem	35	.27	.10	−.27

*GPA = gradepoint average.

SUGGESTION SHEET

If your last name starts with letters from Mos to Osb, please complete the Suggestion Sheet at the end of the book while this chapter is still fresh in your mind.

15.

EXPERIMENTAL DESIGNS: PART 1

OVERVIEW

The experiment is a powerful research method. Unlike the correlational and causal-comparative methods, it can be used to establish cause-and-effect relationships between two or more variables. Experiments are not easy to conduct, however. This chapter describes the major problems that arise in conducting experimental research, and methods for solving them. Commonly used experimental designs are introduced here, with additional designs presented in the next chapter.

OBJECTIVES

After studying this chapter, you should be able to:

1. Critically evaluate possible threats to the internal validity of an experiment.
2. Critically evaluate possible threats to the external validity of an experiment.
3. Describe procedures for increasing the representativeness of experimental designs.
4. Explain how experimenter bias can affect the outcome of an experiment, and state procedures for reducing experimenter bias.
5. Explain why it is not usually possible to assign students randomly within a classroom to different experimental treatments.
6. Create commonly used experimental designs, including specifications for random assignment, formation of experimental and control groups, and use of pretests and posttests.
7. State threats to the internal and external validity of commonly used experimental designs.
8. Specify statistical techniques used to analyze data yielded by experiments.

The experiment is the ultimate form of research design, providing the most rigorous test of causal hypotheses that is available to the scientist. Although correlational and causal-comparative designs can uncover relationships between variables, the experiment is needed to determine whether the relationship is one of cause-and-effect.

An example of the correlational-experimental loop in research was described by Barak Rosenshine and Norma Furst.[1] They reviewed a set of studies concerning teaching, which were done over a period of several years at Canterbury University, New Zealand. In a correlational study the researchers found a significant correlation ($r = .54$) between level of student learning and the extent to which a teacher followed a student's answer by redirecting the question to another student for comment. In other words, teachers who made extensive use of redirection generally had better-achieving classes than teachers who made little use of this technique.

This research finding would appear to justify training teachers in the redirection technique in the expectation that this would improve their classroom performance. Later experiments did not confirm the correlational findings, however. Rosenshine and Furst report that the Canterbury researchers conducted experiments in which they manipulated teachers' use of redirection. No differences in student learning were found between redirection-present and redirection-absent conditions. Thus correlational studies demonstrated a relationship between two variables, but experiments indicated that the relationship was not one of cause-and-effect. It is possible that a third variable created the relationship, or perhaps student performance affected teachers' use of redirection, which is the reverse of the causal pattern that the researchers hypothesized.[2]

Many experiments carried out by educational researchers are concerned with testing the effect of new educational materials and practices on students' learning. Thus the results of educational experiments may have a direct impact on the adoption of new curriculum materials and teaching methods in the schools. The scope of present-day experimentation in education is illustrated by the titles of these journal articles:

Linda Skon, David W. Johnson, and Roger T. Johnson, "Cooperative Peer Interaction Versus Individual Competition and Individualistic Efforts: Effects on the Acquisition of Cognitive Reasoning Strategies," *Journal of Educational Psychology* 73 (1981): 83–92.

1. Barak Rosenshine and Norma Furst, "The Use of Direct Observation to Study Teaching," in *Second Handbook of Research on Teaching*, ed. R. M. W. Travers (Chicago: Rand McNally, 1973), pp. 122–83.
2. See chapter 14 for a discussion of causal inference in correlational research.

M. L. Land. "Teacher Clarity and Cognitive Level of Questions: Effects on Learning," *Journal of Experimental Education* 49 (1980): 48–51.

Francis W. Beck, Jimmy D. Lindsey, and Greg H. Frith, "Effects of Self-Contained Special Class Placement on Intellectual Functioning of Learning Disabled Students," *Journal of Learning Disabilities* 14 (1981): 280–82.

Michael Pressley, Jennifer Samuel, Marsha M. Hershey, Sue Ellen L. Bishop, and Dale Dickinson, "Use of a Mnemonic Technique to Teach Young Children Foreign Language Vocabulary," *Contemporary Educational Psychology* 6 (1981): 110–16.

Howard Ebmeier and Thomas L. Good, "The Effects of Instructing Teachers about Good Teaching on the Mathematics Achievement of Fourth Grade Students," *American Educational Research Journal* 16 (1979): 1–16.

Most experiments in education employ some form of the classic single-variable design. **Single-variable experiments** involve the manipulation of a single treatment variable followed by observing the effects of this manipulation on one or more dependent variables. The variable to be manipulated will be referred to in this chapter as the **experimental treatment.** (It is sometimes also called the *independent variable, experimental variable,* or *treatment variable*). The variable that is measured to determine the effects of the experimental treatment is usually referred to as the *posttest, dependent variable,* or *criterion variable.* In this chapter we will use the term **posttest** to describe this measure. Occasionally, a variable is measured before administering the experimental treatment; it is called the **pretest.**

To understand how these terms are used, consider an experiment to determine the effect of a new reading program on students' reading achievement. The *experimental treatment* would be the introduction of the new reading program into students' daily schedule of learning activities. The *pretest* would be the measurement of students' reading achievement before the new reading program had been introduced into the curriculum. The *posttest* would be the measurement of students' reading achievement after the introduction of the new program.

The key problem in experimentation is establishing suitable control so that any change in the posttest can be attributed only to the experimental treatment that was manipulated by the researcher. As we shall find in the next sections, many extraneous variables need to be controlled in order to allow an unequivocal interpretation of experimental data. Also, there is no single correct approach to designing and carrying out experiments. Rather, different experimental designs can be used depending upon the variables that the researcher wishes to "control," that is, rule out as possible causes of changes on the posttest.

INTERNAL AND EXTERNAL VALIDITY OF EXPERIMENTS

Holding Variables Constant

As we just stated, the most difficult task in applying experimental methods to educational problems is holding all variables in the educational situation constant except the administration of the experimental treatment. The classic single-variable experiment was first developed in the physical sciences, where it has been most fruitful in the production of knowledge. This is because physical matter is very adaptable to the rigorous requirements of the experimental laboratory. It is doubtful whether the rigorous control of the physical science laboratory can ever be achieved in the behavioral sciences, where human subjects are the object of experimentation.

Donald Campbell and Julian Stanley wrote a classic paper distinguishing between experimental designs in terms of their internal validity.[3] The **internal validity** of an experiment is the extent to which extraneous variables have been controlled by the researcher. If extraneous variables are not controlled in the experiment, we cannot know whether observed changes in the experimental group are due to the experimental treatment or to an extraneous variable.

To demonstrate the importance of controlling for extraneous variables, we will consider a simple research problem amenable to experimental analysis. Suppose a researcher wishes to evaluate the effectiveness of a newly developed program in remedial reading. At the beginning of the school year, he selects 100 students for participation in the program; all these students meet the requirement of scoring at least two grades below age norm on a standard test of reading achievement. After participation in the remedial program for a school year, the students are once again given a reading achievement test. Suppose the researcher finds that a large, statistically significant gain (as determined by *t* test for correlated means) in reading achievement has occurred.

Can the researcher conclude that the achievement gain was caused by the experimental treatment, that is, the remedial reading program? The answer is no. The researcher cannot safely infer cause-and-effect unless extraneous variables have been adequately controlled. **Extraneous variables** refer to aspects of the situation that occur while the experimental treatment is in progress; these aspects are irrelevant to the treatment, but because they occur concomitantly with the treatment, they can become confounded with it. Campbell and Stan-

---

3. Donald T. Campbell and Julian C. Stanley, "Experimental and Quasi-Experimental Designs for Research on Teaching," in *Handbook of Research on Teaching*, ed. N. L. Gage (Chicago: Rand McNally, 1963).

ley identified eight types of extraneous variables, some of which are pertinent to the experiments that we have been considering. They are as follows:

1. *History*. Experimental treatments extend over a period of time, providing opportunity for other events to occur besides the experimental treatment. The students in our example participated in the remedial program over the period of a school year. It is conceivable that other factors, such as the students' regular instruction from teachers, could have accounted for all or part of their achievement gain.

2. *Maturation*. While the experimental treatment is in progress, biological or psychological processes within the student are likely to occur. They may become older, stronger, more cognitively complex, more self-confident, or more discouraged. During the year of the remedial program the students were developing physically, socially, and intellectually. Possibly maturation in one of these areas, rather than the remedial program, enabled the students to overcome their reading deficiency.

3. *Testing*. In most educational experiments a pretest is administered, followed by the experimental treatment and then a posttest. If the two tests are similar, students may show an improvement simply as an effect of their experience with the pretest, that is, they have become "test-wise." In the case of our research example, it is unlikely that this extraneous variable is operating because of the long period of time between pre- and posttesting.

4. *Instrumentation*. A learning gain may be observed from pretest to posttest because the nature of the measuring instrument has changed. Suppose that in our research example the students had been administered a different, easier posttest of reading achievement compared to the pretest. The gain in achievement could be attributed to the testing instruments rather than to the effect of the experimental treatment. In experiments involving observational measurements, instrumentation effects can be a special problem: observers who assess teachers or students before and after an experimental treatment may be disposed to give more favorable ratings the second time simply because they "expect" a change to have occurred.

5. *Statistical regression*. Whenever a test-retest procedure is used to assess change as an effect of the experimental treatment, the possibility exists that **statistical regression** can account for observed gains in learning. We will not present the mathematical basis for statistical regression here, but simply describe its effects on test scores.[4] In our research example, a group of students was selected who fell below the 15th percentile on a test of reading achievement. If the same students are tested again on a similar test (i.e., one that is correlated with the first test), they will earn a higher mean score because of

---

4. A discussion of statistical regression can be found in ibid., pp. 180–82. Also, see p. 721 in the next chapter.

statistical regression, with or without an intervening experimental treatment. Furthermore, if another group of students was selected who earned very high scores on the first test, for example, above the 85th percentile, these students would earn a lower mean score when retested on a similar measure, again as a result of statistical regression. The researcher should be alert to the confounding effects of statistical regression whenever students have been selected for their extreme scores on a test and are retested later on a measure that is correlated with the first test. Upon retesting, regression always tends to move the subject's score toward the mean. The probable regression can be estimated and considered in the results.

6. *Differential selection.* In experimental designs in which a control group is used, the effect of the treatment can sometimes be confounded because of differential selection of students for the experimental and control groups. Suppose that in our research example students need to meet the requirements of falling below the 15th percentile in reading achievement and of *volunteering* to participate in the program. Further suppose that the achievement gains of this group are compared with a control group of students that has equivalent reading deficiencies but that did not volunteer for the program. If the experimental group shows greater achievement gains that the control group, the effect could be attributed to "volunteer spirit" rather than to the experimental treatment itself. To avoid this confounding effect, the experimenter needs to select experimental and control groups that do not differ except for exposure to the experimental treatment. The best way to accomplish this condition is to assign subjects *randomly* to the two groups.

7. *Experimental mortality* (sometimes referred to as *attrition*). This extraneous variable might be operative in our research example if there were a systematic bias in the type of students who dropped from the remedial program during the school year. For example, some students might leave the program because they perceived they were not making any achievement gains. If the researcher measures only the achievement gains of those students who completed the program, the effectiveness of the experimental treatment will be exaggerated. To avoid this error, it is first necessary to measure the achievement gains of all students who entered the remedial program irrespective of whether they completed it or not; then their achievement gain should be compared to that of a suitable control group. Procedures have been developed for analyzing research data to determine whether systematic bias in loss of subjects from experimental and control groups has occurred.[5]

8. *Selection-maturation interaction.* This extraneous variable is similar to differential selection (see number 6), except that maturation is the specific con-

5. Stephen G. Jurs and Gene V. Glass, "The Effect of Experimental Mortality on the Internal and External Validity of the Randomized Comparative Experiment," *Journal of Experimental Education* 40 (1971): 62–66.

founding variable. Suppose that first-grade students from a single school district are selected into the remedial program previously described. The control group is drawn from the population of first-grade students in another school district. Because of differential admissions policy the average age of the control group is six months older than that of the experimental group. Now suppose the research results show that the experimental group makes significantly greater achievement gains than the control group. How should we explain these results? Do they indicate that the experimental treatment is effective, or do they show that reading gains in younger students are more influenced by maturational factors than in slightly older students? Because of differential assignment of students varying in maturation to the experimental and control groups, it is not clear which of these alternative explanations is correct.

At this point we propose to extend Campbell and Stanley's list by adding two more extraneous variables that can threaten the internal validity of an experiment.

9. *The John Henry effect.* We previously discussed the John Henry effect in chapter 6. This effect refers to a situation in which control group subjects perform beyond their usual level because they perceive that they are in competition with the experimental group. If this phenomenon occurs, the observed difference, or lack of difference, between the experimental treatment and control groups on the posttest can be attributed to the control group's unusual motivation rather than to treatment effects.

10. *Experimental treatment diffusion.* If the treatment condition is perceived as very desirable relative to the control condition, members of the control group may seek access to the treatment condition. Experimental treatment diffusion is especially likely if the experimental and control subjects are in close proximity to each other. For example, some teachers in a school building (the treatment group) may be assigned to use an innovative, attractive curriculum, whereas other teachers in the same school (the control group) may be assigned to continue using the regular curriculum. As the experiment progresses, some of the control group teachers may discuss the new curriculum with treatment group teachers, even if instructed not to do so. They may even borrow some of the materials and activities to use in their classsrooms. Thus, over time the treatment "diffuses" to the control group.

If experimental treatment diffusion occurs, effect of the treatment on the posttest will be clouded. To avoid this problem, the researcher should try to arrange conditions so that contact between the experimental and control groups is minimized. Also, he can directly tell members of each group not to speak with each other about the experiment while it is in progress. After the experiment is completed, the researcher is advised to interview some or all of the sample to determine whether experimental treatment diffusion in any form occurred.

We have seen now how ten different kinds of extraneous variables can threaten the internal validity of an experiment. It is necessary for the researcher to select an appropriate experimental design that controls these factors. With good experimental control, any observed changes can be attributed with a high degree of confidence to the experimental treatment rather than to extraneous variables.

Generalizability of Findings

As we learned in the previous section, the educational researcher faces many potential threats to the internal validity of his experiment. A variety of controls are needed so that the effect of the experimental treatment is not confounded by extraneous variables. However, the educational researcher is faced with the dilemma that, as more rigorous controls are applied to the experiment, less carryover can be expected between the experiment and related field situations. In other words, the behavioral sciences are constantly faced with the choice of obtaining rigorous laboratory control at the cost of realism or of maintaining realistic experimental situations at the cost of losing scientific rigor in the process. Most educational studies aim at a compromise between these goals. They attempt to attain sufficient rigor to make the results scientifically acceptable while maintaining sufficient realism to make the results reasonably transferable to educational situations in the field.

Campbell and Stanley identified four general factors that affect the generalizability of findings from experiments—what they call the experiment's external validity.[6] **External validity** is the extent to which the findings of an experiment can be applied to particular settings. It is possible for the findings of an educational experiment to be externally valid for one setting, less externally valid for a different setting, and not externally valid at all for some other setting.

Glenn Bracht and Gene Glass subsequently differentiated Campbell and Stanley's four general factors into more specific sources of external validity.[7] The following section is a description of Bracht and Glass's list of factors that affect the generalizability of findings from experiments.

6. The four general factors are: the reactive effect of testing; the interaction of the experimental treatment with particular student characteristics, measuring instruments, and the time of the study; the possible artificiality of the experimental treatment and the students' knowledge that they are involved in an experiment; and multiple-treatment interference. The meaning of these factors will become clear as you read the following discussion of Bracht and Glass's list of external invalidity sources.
7. Glenn H. Bracht and Gene V. Glass, "The External Validity of Experiments," *American Educational Research Journal* 5 (1968): 437–74.

Population Validity

Population validity concerns the extent to which the results of an experiment can be generalized from the specific sample that was studied to a larger group of subjects. Bracht and Glass distinguish two types of population validity.

The first type is *the extent to which one can generalize from the experimental sample to a defined population.* To illustrate, suppose a researcher is concerned with determining whether a programmed instructional format leads to greater achievement gains than conventional textbook presentation of curriculum materials. The researcher performs the experiment on a sample of 125 high school students randomly selected from a particular school district. The experiment demonstrates that programmed instruction leads to greater achievement gains. Although the researcher might wish to generalize the findings to the population of "all" students, strictly speaking he can generalize only to the population from which the sample was drawn—namely, high school students in the particular school district. Bracht and Glass call this limited group the **experimentally accessible population,** defined as the population from which the sample is drawn. The accessible population is usually "local," normally within driving distance of the experimenter's office or laboratory. Assuming that the sample described above has been randomly selected, one can validly generalize the research findings from the 125 participating students to the experimentally accessible population (i.e., all high school students in the school district).

Often the researcher or the reader of a research report wishes to generalize from the experimentally accessible population to a still larger group (e.g., all high school students in the United States). This larger group of subjects is called the **target population.** Generalizing research findings from the experimentally accessible population to a target population is risky. One must compare the two populations to determine whether they are similar in critical respects. For example, if the experiment was done in a school district composed almost entirely of middle-class suburban families, generalization of the research findings to all U.S. high school students may be invalid.

The second type of population validity is *the extent to which personological variables interact with treatment effects.* In the experiment described above the researcher does not know whether instructional format interacts with student characteristics. That is, although programmed instruction was found to be superior to conventional textbook presentation for high school students, quite different results might be obtained with students at other grade levels. Students' ability, sex, extroversion-introversion, anxiety level, and level of independence are examples of other personological variables that may affect the generalizability of findings from experiments. The systematic study of these interactions is called aptitude-treatment interaction research. This topic is discussed in the next chapter.

Ecological Validity

Ecological validity concerns the extent to which the results of an experiment can be generalized from the set of environmental conditions created by the researcher to other environmental conditions. If the treatment effects can be obtained only under a limited set of conditions or only by the original researcher, the experimental findings are said to have low ecological validity. Bracht and Glass identified ten factors that affect the ecological validity of an experiment. They are as follows:

1. *Explicit description of the experimental treatment.* It is important for the researcher to describe the experimental treatment in sufficient detail so that other researchers can reproduce it. Suppose a researcher finds that the discussion method is more effective than the lecture method in promoting higher cognitive learning, but the researcher's description of the discussion method is so vague and incomplete that it is impossible for other researchers to know whether they are using the method in the same way. In this case the experimental findings have virtually no generalizability to other settings.

2. *Multiple-treatment interference.* Occasionally a researcher will use an experimental design in which each subject is exposed to more than one experimental treatment. Suppose that each subject in the experiment receives three different treatments: A, B, and C. Treatment A is found to produce significantly greater learning gains than treatments B and C. Because of the experimental design that was used, the researcher cannot safely generalize her finding to a situation in which treatment A is administered *alone*. It is possible that the effectiveness of treatment A depends on the coadministration of the other two treatments. Whenever it appears that multiple-treatment interference will affect the generalizability of one's findings, the researcher should choose an experimental design in which only one treatment is assigned to each subject.

3. *Hawthorne Effect.* In chapter 6 we discussed how the Hawthorne Effect and the placebo effect often occur when researchers perform experiments to determine the effectiveness of innovative educational practices. Researchers often give participating teachers and students special attention; this factor, not the experimental treatment itself, may cause a change in their behavior. Should the Hawthorne Effect or the placebo effect occur, the external validity of the experiment is jeopardized because the findings may not generalize to a situation in which researchers or similar personnel are not present.

4. *Novelty and disruption effects.* A novel experimental treatment may be effective simply because it is different from the instruction that subjects normally receive. If this is true, the results of the experiment have low generalizability because the treatment's effectiveness is likely to erode as the novelty wears off. The reverse problem occurs with experimental treatments that disrupt the normal routine. This type of experimental treatment may be ineffec-

tive when tried out initially. With continued use, subjects may assimilate the treatment into their routine and find that it is effective. Thus, the findings of the initial tryout are not generalizable to a condition of continued use.

5. *Experimenter effect.* An experimental treatment may be effective or ineffective because of the particular experimenter (teacher) who administers it. The treatment effects, then, cannot be generalized to conditions in which a different person is the experimenter (teacher). The various ways in which experimenters can influence and bias the administration of a treatment are discussed on pp. 645–648.

6. *Pretest sensitization.* In some instances the pretest may act as part of the experimental treatment and thus affect one's research results. If the experiment is repeated without the pretest, different research results will probably be obtained. Let us consider a hypothetical experiment in which this reactive effect could occur. Suppose a researcher is interested in the effect of point of view in a film on students' attitudes. For example, the researcher might develop a film in which the narrator takes a strongly slanted, positive view of controversial decisions made by a contemporary politician. To assess the effect of the film, the researcher might administer pretest and posttest of students' attitudes toward the politician.

Suppose there is a significant positive shift in students' attitudes, which the researcher attributes to the experimental treatment, that is, the film. Can the researcher generalize this finding and assert that the film will have the same effect when used in other situations? The generalization is not warranted unless the researcher can demonstrate that the pretest has no effect on the experimental treatment. The possibility exists that the pretest activates students' awareness of their attitudes toward this politician and sensitizes them to the narrator's attitude. It may be that this sensitization, induced by the pretest, is the factor that interacts with the film to produce the attitude shift. By contrast, if they are shown the film alone, students might be most sensitized to learning the facts presented in the film. Thus, they might show little or no attitude shift because they did not have a set to attend to the narrator's point of view.

Bracht and Glass's review of the literature on pretest sensitization indicated that it is most likely to occur when the pretest is a self-report measure of personality or attitude. A more recent review of the research on pretest sensitization effects was conducted by Victor Willson and Richard Putnam.[8] They located 32 studies of this phenomenon and did a meta-analysis (see chapter 6) to determine the average effect size across studies. Willson and Putnam found a substantial effect of pretests on posttest performance. In other words, an experimental group that receives a pretest is likely to perform at a higher level

8. Victor L. Willson and Richard R. Putnam, "A Meta-Analysis of Pretest Sensitization Effects in Experimental Design," *American Educational Research Journal* 19 (1982): 249–58.

on the posttest than a corresponding experimental group that does not receive a pretest. This effect occurs even when the posttest is different than the pretest. In fact, the meta-analysis revealed that the pretest effect was stronger when pretest and posttest were different. Furthermore, administration of a pretest was usually found to have a positive effect irrespective of the outcome being measured—cognitive, attitudinal, or personality.

7. *Posttest sensitization.* This source of ecological invalidity is similar to pretest sensitization. The possibility exists that the results of an experiment are dependent upon the administration of a posttest. This can happen if the posttest is a learning experience in its own right. For example, the posttest may cause certain ideas presented during the treatment phase to "fall into place" for some of the participating students. When the experiment is repeated without a posttest, the treatment may be of diminished effectiveness. Although posttest sensitization is plausible, it has not been studied as an experimental phenomenon to the extent of its counterpart, pretest sensitization.

8. *Interaction of history and treatment effects.* In a strict sense one cannot generalize beyond the time period in which the experiment was done. An experiment evaluating an innovative educational method might be done at a time when teachers are particularly disenchanted with a corresponding conventional method. They might be exceptionally motivated to demonstrate the superiority of the new method. At a later time, a researcher might repeat the experiment and find no difference because teachers no longer see the method as "innovative."

9. *Measurement of the dependent variable.* The generalizability of the experiment may be limited by the particular pretest and posttest designed to measure achievement gains or other outcome variable. Suppose the superiority of a programmed instruction format over a regular textbook-oriented format was demonstrated using multiple-choice tests. Since programmed instruction is well adapted to the multiple-choice format, the results could be due to this similarity between programmed content and multiple-choice questions. Thus the experiment does not permit the researcher to generalize the findings to other measuring instruments. For example, no difference between instructional formats might be found if essay-type pretests and posttests were administered.

10. *Interaction of time of measurement and treatment effects.* Administration of a posttest at two or more different points in time may result in different findings about treatment effects. The usual practice is to administer the posttest immediately after subjects have completed the experimental treatment. Conclusions about treatment effectiveness are based on the results of this posttest administration. Nevertheless, it is advisable to administer the same or a parallel posttest several weeks or months later to measure retention of learning. Bracht and Glass cite several examples in the research literature in which treat-

ment effects change from posttest to delayed posttest; the effects may be enhanced, remain the same, or diminish over time.[9]

In designing an experiment, the researcher should carefully consider the "real-life" educational setting to which she wishes to generalize the results of the experiment. Then the researcher should review the design of the experiment using the ten factors described above to determine the extent of discrepancy, if any, between the experimental conditions and the "real-life" educational setting. If a discrepancy cannot be minimized, it should at least be noted in the research report as a limit on the generalizability of the research findings.

Representative Design

In recent years some educational researchers, most notably Richard Snow,[10] have criticized conventional experimental design for its artificiality and lack of generalizability. Building upon the earlier work of Egon Brunswick, Snow used the label "systematic design" to characterize the usual form of experimentation. In systematic design a few treatment variables and pretest-posttest measures are administered. All other variables are either controlled or ignored. Most of the experiments reported in education research journals are based on systematic design principles.

The problem with systematic design is that it often produces artificial learning situations and unnatural behavior in the learner. Snow advocates the use of representative design to combat these problems and also to increase the generalizability of findings from experiments. **Representative design** is a process for planning experiments so that they reflect accurately: (1) real-life environments in which learning occurs, and (2) the natural characteristics of learners.

The need for representative design is based on a number of assumptions about the environment and the human learner. One assumption is that the characteristics of the natural environment are complex and interrelated. The researcher cannot simply choose to vary one environmental characteristic and hold others constant; as one characteristic changes, so do others. Educational researchers need to study the learning environment as an ecology in the same way that biologists study the ecology of the natural environment.

Another assumption of representative design is that humans are active processors of information; they do not react passively to experimental treatments. Therefore, the active nature of human learners needs to be considered in designing experiments. A related assumption is that human learners, if al-

9. Bracht and Glass, "Validity of Experiments," p. 466.
10. Richard E. Snow, "Representative and Quasi-Representative Designs for Research on Teaching," *Review of Educational Research* 44 (1974): 265–91.

lowed, will adjust and adapt to their environment. Systematic experiments are artificial in that they constrain the range of behavior that might be exhibited if the learner is allowed to act naturally. Finally, representative design assumes that, because the behaving organism is complex, any experimental intervention is likely to affect the learner in complex ways. An instructional method may be designed only to increase students' knowledge of a specific subject, but the effect may generalize students' attitudes and also may affect their knowledge of other subjects. Furthermore, the instructional intervention might be designed primarily to affect short-term performance, but the effects may "radiate" out to affect long-term performance as well.

Snow believes that educational researchers should design experiments to reflect this view of the environment and the learner. That is, experiments should become more *representative* of the natural environment and of human subjects as active learners. Snow notes that true representative designs are very difficult to achieve in education, but he suggests compromises that will make experiments more representative. The following are some of his recommendations:

1. When appropriate, conduct the research in an actual school setting or other environment to which you wish to generalize your findings.

2. Incorporate several environmental variations into the design of the experiment. For example, if the purpose is to evaluate a new instructional method, it is advisable to have not just one teacher but rather a sample of teachers use it. Also, the experimenter might vary the educational setting. For example, an instructional method could be tested in a sample of inner-city schools, suburban schools, and rural schools.

These planned variations are most meaningful if the researcher can conceptualize relevant dimensions of the educational ecology. Suppose the researcher is interested in the possible effects of inserting questions into instructional materials. What are "instructional materials" in this context? Are they the first textbook that the researcher happens to pick off a shelf, or the textbook that the sample of subjects happens to be studying? A more systematic approach is to conceptualize relevant dimensions of instructional materials: readability of prose (difficult, average, easy), modality (film, audiotape, print), subject area (math, social studies, language arts), and so forth. Then the researcher can select instructional materials that sample one or more of these dimensions.

3. Observe what students are actually doing during the experiment. These observations may prove helpful to the researcher in interpreting the results of the experiment. For example, the experimenter may observe that the subjects were not attentive to a particular treatment or were distracted by other events. If the research data later indicate that the treatment was not effective, the observations would be helpful in interpreting this result and in planning future research.

4. A related technique to the one preceding is to observe the social context in which the experiment is being conducted. Certain events that occur in schools or in other educational settings may affect the experimental treatments. If these events are observed and recorded, the research findings should be more interpretable.

5. Prepare students for the experiment. Snow claims that the typical practice is for researchers to give students simple instructions and perhaps a few minutes' training prior to the start of an experiment. More extensive preparation may be necessary to ensure a smooth transition from students' current mental set to the one required by the experimental task.

6. Incorporate a control treatment that allows students to use their customary approaches to learning. Suppose an experiment is designed in which students are formed into dyads and trained to ask questions of each other about curriculum materials. An appropriate control treatment might be to form some students into dyads and allow them to use any procedures they wish to review the same materials. The control groups form a naturalistic baseline against which the behavior and learning of the experimental group can be evaluated. This use of control groups is analogous to animal research in which the behavior of animals in captivity is studied by comparing it with their behavior "in the wild."

The ideas about representative design expressed here are not yet widely known and used. Yet, aware or not, educational researchers do make decisions about representation of the natural environment and the natural behavior of learners each time they design an experiment. Effective use of the procedures described here should increase the generalizability of findings from experiments to the real world of educational practice.

Experimenter Bias

Robert Rosenthal's studies of experimenter bias effects have made a significant contribution to experimental methodology.[11] It is likely that researchers will have expectancies about the outcomes of their experiments, and Rosenthal has demonstrated that these expectancies are sometimes transmitted to subjects in such a way that their behavior is affected. This phenomenon is known as the **experimenter bias effect.** It should be noted that the phenomenon occurs outside the awareness of the experimenter. The experimenter bias effect does not refer to situations in which an experimenter, with full awareness of his actions and intentions, manipulates subjects' behavior or falsifies data in order to yield an "expected" finding.

11. Robert Rosenthal, *Experimenter Effects in Behavioral Research* (New York: Appleton-Century-Crofts, 1966).

Rosenthal and his associates have carried out many experiments on the experimenter bias effect, and we shall describe one of them here.[12] A group of undergraduates was instructed in procedures for running albino rats through a simple T maze and for training the rats to solve a discrimination learning problem. The student experimenters were told that, as a result of generations of inbreeding, some rats they would train were "maze-bright" while others were "maze-dull." They were then given instructions regarding expected findings:

> Those of you who are assigned the Maze-Bright rats should find your animals on the average showing some evidence of learning during the first day of running. Thereafter performance should rapidly increase.
> Those of you who are assigned the Maze-Dull rats should find on the average very little evidence of learning in your rats. (p. 159)

In fact, though, a homogeneous group of albino rats (not varying on the dimension of maze brightness-dullness) was randomly assigned to the experimenters for training. Nevertheless, Rosenthal and Fode found that rats trained by experimenters who thought their rats were maze-bright earned significantly higher learning scores than rats trained by experimenters with the opposite expectancy. The differential learning gains were the result of an experimenter bias effect rather than genetic differences between groups of rats.

The implication of this finding for educational experiments is obvious. An educational researcher might do an experiment to determine whether a technique or product he has developed is superior to conventional practice. If the researcher has a strong expectancy that his innovation is superior to conventional practice, his experiment might yield this finding. In this case the finding is attributable to an experimenter bias effect rather than to the innovation per se. Should impartial researchers carry out further experiments to evaluate the innovation, they are not likely to replicate the original finding since the experimenter bias effect is no longer operating.

The method of transmission of the experimenter's expectancy to the subject is not clearly understood, although Rosenthal and others have conducted studies directed at this problem.[13] Yet the experimenter bias effect does appear to be a real threat to the internal validity of experiments. The researcher should

12. Robert Rosenthal and K. L. Fode, "The Effect of Experimenter Bias on the Performance of the Albino Rat," *Behavioral Science* 8 (1963): 183–89.
13. Robert Rosenthal and Lenore Jackson have also reported an experimental study of how teachers' expectancies affect their students' behavior in *Pygmalion in the Classroom* (New York: Holt, Rinehart and Winston, 1968). Although Rosenthal's experimental procedure has provoked some controversy, his book has stimulated much interest and concern regarding whether teachers' expectancies about their students' potential (based on knowledge of their IQ scores) can actually affect student achievement.

take steps to avoid the operation of this effect in designing and carrying out an experiment. One effective technique is to train naive experimenters to work with students or teachers participating in the study. Whenever possible the researcher himself should not work directly with the subjects. Also, the researcher should avoid suggesting to his experimenters, directly or indirectly, that one experimental treatment is better than another.

To some degree the tools used to measure the dependent variables can be selected so as to reduce the chance of experimenter bias. For example, if the rats in the Rosenthal and Fode experiment had been trained in mazes having sensitized pathways so their progress was measured and recorded automatically, there would have been much less chance of observer bias influencing the results. Observer expectations are most likely to influence research results when scores on the dependent variable rely upon subjective judgment by the observer, or when the investigator can make inputs (often subconsciously) into the experimental treatment itself.

Theodore Barber has extended the work of Rosenthal by identifying additional sources of investigator and experimenter bias.[14] The investigator is the person who designs the experiment and interprets the data. The experimenter is the person who administers the experimental treatments and collects the data. The investigator and experimenter often are one and the same person, but it is not necessary that this be so.

One type of bias identified by Barber occurs when the experimenter fails to follow the exact procedures specified by the investigator for administering the treatments. Barber cites several studies which demonstrate empirically that this type of bias occurs. An experiment conducted by one of the authors also found this effect.[15] A group of teachers was trained to conduct several different instructional treatments. In treatment 1 they were trained to use certain questioning techniques; they were told to withhold these techniques completely in treatments 2 and 3. The teachers' verbal behavior was tape-recorded to check on their adherence to the treatment requirements. Analysis of the tape recordings indicated that the teachers used the techniques several times per instructional session in treatments 2 and 3, in spite of their good intentions not to do so. When shown the data, the teachers admitted that the techniques just "slipped out," or they expressed surprise that the behavior had occurred.

---

14. Theodore Barber, "Pitfalls in Research: Nine Investigator and Experimenter Effects," in *Second Handbook of Research on Teaching*, ed. R. M. W. Travers (Chicago: Rand McNally, 1973), pp. 382–404.

15. Meredith D. Gall, "The Importance of Context Variables in Research on Teaching Skills," *Journal of Teacher Education* 28 (1977): 43–48. For further discussion of treatment fidelity, see also W. W. Charters, Jr. and J. E. Jones, "On the Risk of Appraising Non-Events in Program Evaluation," *Educational Researcher* 2 (1973): 5–7; Gene Hall and Susan F. Loucks, "A Developmental Model for Determining Whether the Treatment Is Actually Implemented," *American Educational Research Journal* 14 (1977): 263–76.

This type of bias was labeled the "experimenter failure to follow the protocol effect" by Barber. Other researchers refer to the phenomenon using the term "treatment fidelity." **Treatment fidelity** is the extent to which the treatment conditions, as implemented, conform to the researcher's specifications for the treatment.

Researchers should try to maximize treatment fidelity, and if possible, to assess it. To accomplish these goals, the investigator first needs to write precise specifications for the experimental treatment. Then the investigator must carefully train the experimenters to follow these specifications. Finally, during the actual experiment the investigator should collect data on the experimenter's behavior to determine the congruence between behavior and treatment specifications. Data on experimenter behavior can be collected by a variety of observational techniques (see chapter 12).

Strong Versus Weak Experimental Treatments

One of the major problems of experimental research is producing a treatment that is strong enough to have an effect on the dependent variable. For example, a researcher may do an experiment to determine whether a particular teaching method affects student achievement. The experimental design might require a group of teachers to use the method for a period of one week, with student achievement measured at the beginning and end of this time period. Also, there might be a control group of teachers that use a conventional teaching method for the same period; the achievement of their students would be measured in the same way as that of the experimental students. Suppose no differences are found between the experimental and control groups. Should the researcher conclude that the experimental teaching method does not produce greater achievement gains? If he did, others might raise the criticism that he used a "weak" treatment. That is, one might argue that the experimental teaching method would have produced greater achievement gains than the control method had it been used over a longer time period, perhaps an entire school year.

Of course, as the researcher increases the strength of the treatment, the experiment is likely to increase in complexity, time, and cost. Thus, many educational problems amenable to an experimental approach cannot be tackled by student researchers. They require a well-funded and well-staffed organization in order to be investigated properly. Before doing an experiment the student should determine whether he has the resources necessary to design a treatment that can reasonably be expected to have an effect on student achievement or other dependent variables.

EXPERIMENTAL DESIGNS AND STATISTICAL ANALYSIS TECHNIQUES

This section discusses types of experimental designs in educational research that incorporate random assignment of subjects to treatments. Experimental designs that do not involve random assignment are presented in the next chapter.

Table 15.1 provides a schematic presentation of single-group designs and control-group designs with random assignment. Some designs are more complex than others. They vary in use of control groups and administration of a pretest. The table shows that some experimental designs are much more likely than others to possess high internal and external validity. As we shall find, however, all have application in educational research. The selection of a particular design will depend upon the type of problem the experimenter is attempting to solve and the conditions under which he must work.

In presenting each experimental design, we shall briefly discuss the statistical procedures used to analyze the data yielded by the design. The *t* test, analysis of variance, and analysis of covariance are widely used in experimental research. Multiple regression techniques are becoming increasingly popular, too, particularly as educational experiments become more complex. All these techniques were introduced in chapters 13 and 14, in the context of analyzing data from nonexperimental research.

The experimental designs presented here often involve the measurement of change, which poses difficult methodological problems. We shall discuss this topic at some length in chapter 16. We suggest that you also review chapter 10, which provides an overview of statistical analysis and its relation to research design.

Random Selection and Random Assignment

We have previously discussed randomization in terms of selecting a sample of persons to participate in one's study (see chapter 7). Briefly stated, **randomization** means that each person in a defined population has an equal chance of being selected to take part in the study. When doing an experiment, the researcher needs to consider another type of randomization, namely, random assignment of persons to experimental treatments. **Random assignment** means that each sampling unit (e.g., student, class, school district) has an equal chance of being in each treatment in the experiment. Random assignment is not relevant to single-group designs (designs 1 and 2 in table 15.1) because they incorporate only a single treatment.

TABLE 15.1

Experimental Designs and Their Sources of Invalidity

Design	Sources of Invalidity	
	Internal	External
Single-group designs		
1. One-shot case study X O	History, maturation, selection, mortality	Interaction of selection and X
2. One-group pretest-posttest design O X O	History, maturation, testing, instrumentation, interaction of selection and other factors	Interaction of testing and X; interaction of selection and X
3. Time-series design O O O O X O O O O	History	Interaction of testing and X
Control-group designs with random assignment		

4. Pretest-posttest control-group design
  R O X O
  R O   O
	None	Interaction of testing and X

5. Posttest-only control-group design
  R   X O
  R   O
	Mortality	None

6. Solomon four-group design
  R O X O
  R O   O
  R   X O
  R   O
	None	None

This table was adapted from tables 1, 2, and 3 in the Campbell and Stanley report. Please note that only definite weaknesses in various experimental designs have been indicated here. In Campbell and Stanley's tables, some invalidating factors have been shown as possible sources of concern in certain designs, but they are not shown here.

  Key: R = Random assignment
      X = Experimental treatment
      O = Observation, either a pretest or posttest of the dependent variable

   In designing an experiment, you should make every effort to incorporate random assignment in your experimental design. Random assignment is the best technique available for assuring initial equivalence between different treatment groups. To illustrate this point, consider the case of a researcher who wishes to compare the effectiveness of two worksheet formats. She has available a sample of 50 students for the experiment, and wishes to form them into two treatment groups. Treatment group 1 will use one of the worksheet formats. Treatment group 2 will use the other format.

   If the names of the students are on a list in alphabetical order, the researcher might simply divide the list in half, and assign each half of the list to a treatment group. This method of assigning students to treatments seems innocuous, but it has the potential for creating nonequivalent treatment groups. For example, if several students have last names associated with a particular ethnic group (e.g., names beginning with Mc or Mac), they will most likely all be in the same treatment group. If there are several siblings on the list, they too will most likely be in the same treatment group. Should such conditions occur, the two treatment groups will not be equivalent on these dimensions.

   Random assignment uses the operation of chance to determine which students are selected for each treatment group. The procedure described above does not use chance. Students were selected for treatment groups by their position on a list; and their position on the list was determined by their last name (which is hardly determined by chance).

   How is random assignment of students to treatment groups accomplished? The procedures are basically the same as for drawing a random sample from a defined population (see chapter 7). One good procedure is to use a table of random numbers. In the example we have been considering, the students on the list can be numbered from 1 to 50; it does not matter that the names are in alphabetical order. Next consult a table of random numbers, such as the one in Appendix C. Identify an arbitrary starting point, let's say, the top of the fourth column on page 905 (number = 81292). Since 50 students must be assigned, we will need to use two of the columns of each number. Let's use the first two columns. The first ten numbers selected by this procedure are: 81, 25, 38, 78, 99, 37, 34, 68, 50, 17. The numbers 81-78-99-68 are of no use to us. The first usable number, 25, identifies the 25th student on the list, who is assigned, let's say, to treatment group 1. The 38th student on the list is assigned to treatment group 2, the 37th student is assigned to treatment group 1; the 34th student is assigned to treatment group 2; and so on. The researcher would keep using the table of random numbers until all 50 students had been assigned—by chance—to one treatment group or the other.

   It is important to realize that random assignment does not *ensure* initially equivalent treatment groups. Siblings and students whose last names begin with Mc or Mac may still wind up in the same treatment group. Or the groups may be nonequivalent on some other dimension; for example, one group may have a larger number of girls or bright students. Random assignment is not a perfect method for assuring treatment group equivalence, but it is the best method available.

Random assignment, then, is instrumental in bringing about treatment group equivalence. In turn, treatment group equivalence is essential to the internal validity of an experiment. To the extent that threats to the internal validity of the experiment are present, they should affect each treatment group to an equal extent if the groups are initially equivalent. Therefore, differences between the groups on the posttest can be attributed, with a high degree of confidence, to the treatment rather than to extraneous factors.

Random assignment can be easily achieved in brief experiments that occur under laboratory conditions. The situation is much different in field experiments conducted in schools, students' homes, or elsewhere. It may be difficult to obtain the cooperation or to establish the conditions necessary for random assignment. Furthermore, even if initially equivalent groups are formed through random assignment, the equivalence may break down as the experiment proceeds. Thomas Cook and Donald Campbell have identified a number of specific obstacles to forming and maintaining equivalent treatment groups in field experiments.[16] We turn now to a discussion of some of these obstacles, and how they might be avoided or overcome.

1. *Withholding the treatment from the control group.* If one treatment is perceived as more desirable than the other, the researcher may encounter strong resistance to the use of random assignment. For example, suppose an experiment is planned to test the effects of introducing a mini-computer in elementary school classrooms. The researcher wishes to randomly assign ten classrooms to receive a mini-computer (the treatment group), and another ten classrooms (the control group) to continue functioning without a mini-computer for the duration of the experiment.

Upon hearing about the proposed experiment, elementary school principals and teachers in the district may desire to have the mini-computers in their classrooms. They may well view the mini-computer as innovative and exciting—a real "plus" for their school and classroom. Principals and teachers may solicit parent support and lobby central office administrators to be in the favored group that receives the mini-computer. They are likely to express resistance to being in the low-prestige control group. In short, they will fight against the use of random assignment to allocate what is perceived as a scarce and valuable resource—mini-computers.

---

16. Thomas D. Cook and Donald T. Campbell, *Quasi-Experimentation: Design and Analysis Issues for Field Settings* (Chicago: Rand McNally, 1979). Some of their obstacles to treatment group equivalence are not listed here because they are discussed elsewhere in this chapter.

The best solution to this problem—perhaps the only solution—is to tell participants that the control group will receive the treatment after the experiment is concluded. In the example above, the 20 teachers and their principals could be told that 10 of the teachers will receive a mini-computer the first year, and the other 10 teachers will receive a mini-computer the second year.

We have found that educators are usually amenable to this solution. The second author recently chaired two dissertation committees involving an innovative enthusiasm-training program for intern teachers. Directors responsible for the training would not permit the program to be used unless all interns received it. They were quite satisfied with the researchers' offer to provide the program in two phases.

The major difficulty with this solution obviously is that it creates additional work for the researcher. The length of the experiment is effectively doubled. However, the researcher can save a great deal of effort by not collecting data during the administration of the treatment to the control group. On the other hand, if the researcher does collect the additional data, he will have an "internal" replication of the experiment. The first treatment group can be compared with the control group; and the control group can be compared with itself (before and after receiving the treatment).

The option of administering the treatment to the control group may not appeal to the researcher concerned about time. If the research is being done for a master's thesis or doctoral dissertation, the student's graduation may be delayed appreciably. The other options are even less appealing, however. The researcher may not get permission to do the experiment at all because the treatment is withheld from the control group. Or the researcher may resort to nonrandom assignment of subjects to treatment groups, in which case the experimental results will be difficult or impossible to interpret.

One other option might be feasible in certain situations. Suppose the researcher anticipates that some subjects will refuse to participate in the experiment because they do not want to be in a no-treatment control group or for some other reason. In this case he can contact potential subjects and ask them if they would be willing to participate in the experiment irrespective of whether they are assigned to the treatment group or control group. Persons willing to abide by this condition would form the sample, which then would be randomly assigned to the treatment conditions. The advantage of this procedure is that the researcher does not have to administer the treatment to the control group subsequent to the main experiment; and it is unlikely that subjects will refuse to participate after randomization has occurred because they found that they were assigned to the control group. The major disadvantage of this procedure is that the experiment is conducted on a volunteer sample, hence limiting severely the external validity of the research results.

2. *Faulty randomization procedures.* A defect in the researcher's random as-

signment procedure may result in nonequivalent treatment groups. Cook and Campbell cite the famous case of the 1969 military draft lottery. Each day of the year was put on a slip of a paper, and the slips were put in an urn. The order in which the slips were drawn out of the urn determined the order in which draft-age males would be drafted into the military service. For example, if February 12 was drawn first, men with that birth date would be drafted first. Evidently the urn was not shaken well because the slips of days put into it last (those of December, November, October) remained near the top and were drawn out first. The solution to the problem is obvious.

Another problem that can occur with randomization procedures is that participants in the experiment may not believe the researcher's statement that random assignment to treatment groups occurred. This problem may be more likely to occur if the researcher is well known to the participants, and if they have reason to believe that the researcher is positively or negatively biased toward some of the participants. To avoid this problem, it is always advisable to have a credible witness observe the random assignment process. For example, if teachers in a school district are to be assigned to treatment groups, the researcher might ask a teachers union or association representative to observe the randomization process.

As we indicated earlier, random assignment does not ensure equivalent treatment groups. Suppose the researcher notices that randomly constituted groups are obviously not equivalent based on available data about the sample—one group may have a disproportionate number of males, students from a particular grade level, students with high scholastic aptitude scores, and so on. If nonequivalence occurs at the time of random assignment, the researcher has two alternatives. First, the researcher can start again with the total sample and redo the random assignment procedures; for example, he can pick a new starting point in a table of random numbers and reassign each subject to a treatment group. Hopefully, a second—or even third—attempt at randomization will result in treatment group equivalence on known dimensions.

The second alternative is to stratify the total sample on the factor or factors for which equivalence is desired. (Stratification procedures are discussed in chapter 7.) After the total sample has been stratified, subjects can be randomly assigned within strata to treatment groups. This procedure insures treatment group equivalence on the stratified factors.

3. *Small sample size.* The probability that random assignment will produce initially equivalent treatment groups increases as sample size in each group increases. For example, it is much more likely that two equivalent groups will result if 100 subjects are randomly assigned to two treatment groups ($N = 50$ per group) than if they are assigned to four treatment groups ($N = 25$ per group).

There are several solutions to the problem of a small sample that is to be randomly assigned to two or more treatment groups. One obvious solution is to attempt to increase sample size. The additional expenditure of resources is well worth it if the result is equivalent treatment groups, and consequently, more interpretable research results. Another solution is to use matching procedures, which are discussed later in the chapter.

The third solution is to consider whether one or more treatment groups can be eliminated. Suppose, for example, that the researcher is interested in testing the relative effectiveness of four training variations for an unusual learning disorder. The researcher can only locate a sample of 16 students having the disorder. If the students are randomly assigned to the four treatments, there will only be four students per treatment group. Even if there are real differences between treatments, statistical power (see chapter 10) will probably be so low that the null hypothesis of no difference between treatments will not be rejected. In this situation the researcher should consider comparing just the two most theoretically interesting or most promising treatments, in which case there will be eight students per treatment group.

4. *Intact groups.* Although not mentioned specifically by Cook and Campbell, intact groups in education pose a difficult obstacle to using random assignment procedures. An **intact group** is a set of individuals who must be treated as members of an administrative defined group rather than as individual persons. For example, most school classes are intact groups. The intact group is usually defined in terms of a particular grade level, teacher, and classroom (e.g., the fourth-grade class taught by Ms. Jones in Room 16).

Suppose that a researcher wishes to do an experiment in which the individual student is the appropriate sampling unit. The researcher has available a sample of 50 fourth-grade students—25 from a classroom in school A and another 25 from a classroom in school B. Random assignment requires that each student be assigned, by chance, to the experimental or control group. School administrators and teachers, however, may require the researcher to deal with students, not as individuals, but as members of an intact group. Thus, all students in a classroom must be given the same treatment in order to preserve the "intact" nature of the classroom group.

Given this situation, the researcher might opt to institute one treatment condition per classroom. Students in the fourth-grade class of school A could be assigned to the treatment condition (a new instructional method designed to improve learning) and students in the fourth-grade class of school B could be assigned to the no-treatment control condition. The integrity of the public school structure is thus preserved.

Several problems arise with this procedure, though, because students have not been randomly assigned to the treatment conditions. Consider, for instance, what would happen if students in school A came from predominantly upper-middle-class families and students in school B came from lower-class families. Since scholastic achievement is correlated with social class, it is likely that students in school A will have higher posttest achievement scores than students in school B, with or without the instructional treatment. Thus we cannot conclude on the basis of the findings that the instructional treatment is superior to conventional instruction. An equally plausible interpretation is that the differential achievement gain results from initial differences in the treatment groups.

The preceding illustrations typify the thorny problems encountered by the researcher doing a field or laboratory experiment in which random assignment to experimental treatments is not possible because the subjects are members of intact groups. Nonetheless, it is possible to design an experiment in which the limitations of nonrandom assignment are partially or wholly overcome. Experimental designs of this type have been designated "quasi experiments" by Campbell and Stanley to distinguish them from "true" experiments, that is, experiments having random assignment. In the next chapter we discuss procedures for developing equivalence between intact groups receiving different experimental treatments.

SINGLE-GROUP DESIGNS

The One-Shot Case Study

The **one-shot case study design** hardly qualifies as an experimental design. In this design an experimental treatment is administered, and then a posttest is administered to measure the effects of the treatment. As table 15.1 shows, this design has poor internal validity. Suppose one selects a group of students, gives them remedial instruction (the experimental treatment), and then administers a measure of achievement (the posttest). How can one determine the influence of the treatment on the posttest? Unfortunately, there is no way of making this determination. The students' scores on the posttest could be accounted for by their regular school instruction or by maturation, as well as by the treatment. Also, the fact that students were tested only once makes it impossible to measure change in their performance. Without a measure of change, it is impossible even to determine whether the students' achievement improved over time, regardless of whether this change was due to the treatment or to some other variable. In short, the one-shot case study, although relatively simple to carry out, yields meaningless findings. If she is limited to studying a single group of subjects, the investigator should administer at the very least both a pretest and a posttest. This is the design that we shall discuss next.

One-Group Pretest-Posttest Design

The **one-group pretest-posttest design** involves three steps. The first step is the administration of a pretest measuring the dependent variable. The second step is the application of the experimental treatment (independent variable) to the subjects, and the final step is the administration of a posttest measuring the dependent variable again. Differences due to application of the experimental treatment are then determined by comparing the pretest and posttest scores.

The one-group pretest-posttest design was used in an experiment conducted by Eleanor Semel and Elisabeth Wiig.[17] The purpose of their experiment was to determine whether a new training program—based on an auditory processing model—would improve the language skills of learning-disabled children. The sample consisted of 45 elementary school students who were diagnosed as learning disabled in language because they scored two or more grades below age-grade expectation in two or more academic areas, one of them being reading.

All children in the sample received the training program, which was provided 30 minutes daily for 15 weeks. One might reasonably expect that the children, though language disabled, might make some language gains over this long a time period even without special instruction. Realizing this, the researchers made a generous estimate of gains that might be expected due to regular instruction (i.e., history), maturation, and so on; then they judged the effectiveness of the training program by whether it exceeded this estimate. Semel and Wiig explained their reasoning and procedures as follows:

> . . . standardized and age referenced tests were used as pre- and post-training measures. In fact, then, the standardization samples were considered to be acceptable as a substitute for a control group. A rigid criterion of performance gains (+ 6 months) was set for the magnitude of gains which could be considered educationally significant. In reality, children with language-learning disabilities would not be expected to gain language skills at the rate expected for children with normal language development.[18]

The same battery of language proficiency tests was administered before and after the training program. The performance of the students on the pretest and posttest measures is shown in table 15.2.[19] Mean raw score gains

17. Eleanor M. Semel and Elisabeth H. Wiig, "Semel Auditory Processing Program: Training Effects Among Children with Language-Learning Disabilities," *Journal of Learning Disabilities* **4** (1981): 192–96.
18. Ibid., pp. 195–96.
19. Table 15.2 was constructed from data presented in ibid., pp. 194–95.

TABLE 15.2

Pretest and Posttest Results for Students Receiving a Language Training Program

	Pretest $\overline{X}$	Posttest $\overline{X}$	Age-Level Gain (in months)	% of Ss with Gains > 6 mos.
1. ITPA Grammatic Closure	17.51	23.09	15.48	75.57% $X^2 = 11.76**$
2. DTLA: Auditory Attention Span for Unrelated Words	32.67	37.68	15.73	68.92% $X^2 = 6.42*$
3. DTLA: Auditory Attention Span for Related Syllables	30.89	39.29	10.13	51.13% $X^2 = .02$
4. DTLA: Verbal Opposites	19.44	23.64	7.27	37.79% $X^2 = 2.68$
5. DTLA: Verbal Absurdities	.96	5.36	22.00	71.13% $X^2 = 8.02**$
6. Carrow Elicited Language Inventory	36.12	40.00	30.37[a]	76% $X^2 = 8.76**$

[a]This score is the mean percentile gain using the percentile norms for this measure.
*$p < .05$.
**$p < .01$.

were observed on each of the measures (see columns 1 and 2). To determine whether the gains were educationally and statistically significant, the researchers first converted students' raw scores on each measure to an age-level equivalent.[20] The pretest age-level equivalent then was subtracted from the posttest age-level equivalent to yield an age-level gain score. The mean age-level gain on each measure for the total sample is shown in column 3 of table 15.2.

Next the researchers determined the percentage of students whose age-level gain on a particular measure was more than six months. These percentages are shown in the last column of the table. For example, 75 percent of the students made age-level gains of more than six months on the ITPA Grammatic Closure Test. The researchers tested whether these percentages were significantly different from a "chance" figure of 50 percent. The chi-square test revealed that more students made gains of 6+ months than could be expected if this was a chance event.

20. See page 360.

The researchers used the one-group pretest-posttest design in this experiment because the school system in which it was conducted did not permit differential services for its students. The absence of a control group was not a serious threat to the internal validity of the experiment, though, because the researchers had a good idea of pretest-posttest gains due to extraneous factors. The gains of the experimental group could be evaluated against estimated gains under normal, nonexperimental conditions.

The researchers' results, shown in table 15.2, indicate that the new training program was quite effective. However, even though the rationale for their experimental design appears sound, replications of the experiment would be desirable to increase educators' confidence in the effectiveness of the training program. For example, it would be desirable to test the program in a school district that would permit use of a pretest-posttest control group design.

The one-group pretest-posttest design is especially appropriate when the researcher is attempting to change a behavior pattern or internal process that is very stable. For example, attitudes are quite stable in most individuals by adulthood and are unlikely to change unless some significant effort is made. The one-group design is also justified when the behavior pattern or characteristic is out of the ordinary or recalcitrant to change. For example, if I participate in an experimental program to learn how to speak Ukrainian (an out-of-the-ordinary behavior), it is unlikely that extraneous factors could be involved to account for the change. Similarly, if an experimenter trains a cat to say a few human words, one would hardly dismiss the results as due to extraneous factors.

In summary, the one-group pretest-posttest control group design is most justified when extraneous factors can be estimated with a high degree of certainty or can be safely assumed to be nonexistent.

Statistical Analysis

The data in the Semel and Wiig study were analyzed by comparing whether an observed measure of pre-post gains (6+ months of age-level gain) differed significantly from a chance distribution of gain—a 50-50 split. The more usual procedure for analyzing data from a one-group pretest-posttest design is to do a *t* test for correlated means. This test determines whether the difference between the pretest and the posttest mean is statistically significant. The *t* test for correlated means—rather than the *t* test for independent means—is used because the same subjects take both the pretest and posttest.

If the scores on either the pretest or posttest show marked deviation from the normal distribution, a nonparametric statistic should be used. Most likely the researcher would select the Wilcoxon signed-rank test.

Time-Series Design

In the **time-series design** a single group of subjects is measured at periodic intervals. The experimental treatment is administered between two of these time intervals. The effect of the experimental treatment, if any, is indicated by a discrepancy in the measurements before and after its appearance. The time-series design is useful when it is not feasible to form a control group and when subjects can be measured periodically with the same instrument. It is particularly appropriate for field research where the experimental treatment is a naturally occurring event, such as a change in school administrative policy or in teaching method. For example, a researcher might count the mean attendance of college students at six consecutive lectures in several different courses. Suppose the mean attendance at the first three lectures is 100, 115, 104 (out of the mean total enrollment of 175 students). Between the third and fourth classes, all enrolled students are informed that the professor will conduct a question-and-answer session instead of giving a lecture. The attendance at the fourth class session subsequently increases to a mean of 160 students. For the fifth and sixth class sessions the professor again gives lectures, and the attendance falls back to a mean of 112 and 107 students, respectively. These hypothetical results suggest quite strongly that the use of a question-and-answer session leads to increased student attendance.

If one refers to figure 15.1, it can be seen that the time-series design is similar to the one-group pretest-posttest design. Both designs involve the study of a single group, and both designs involve a measurement before and after the experimental treatment. The use of *additional* measurements preceding and following the experimental treatment makes the time-series design more powerful than the other design. These additional measurements enable the researcher to rule out maturation and testing effects as sources of influence on shifts from pretest to posttest.

To understand how maturation effects are controlled in a time-series design, consider the example given above. Suppose that the researcher had only counted attendance at the third class (the pretest) and the fourth class (the posttest), this being the occasion of the question-and-answer session. The shift from a mean attendance of 104 students to 160 students could be attributed to the experimental treatment. However, one could argue that the study was carried out early in the school term, during the first four class sessions, and an increase in attendance is part of the natural "maturation" of a class as the term gets under way.

The time-series design provides a basis for testing this argument. If maturation explains the shift in attendance from 104 to 160 students, we would expect additional increases in attendance, or at least maintenance of the 160-student level, over successive class sessions. The time-series data, however,

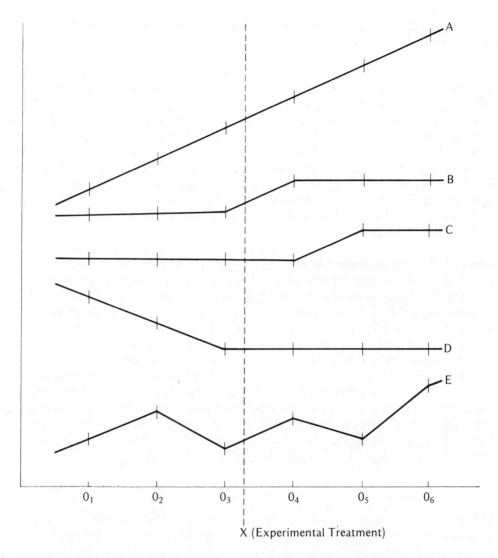

X (Experimental Treatment)

Note: Each horizontal line refers to a different experiment but using the same treatment and measurement.

Figure 15.1. Possible outcomes of a time-series design.

reveal a dramatic drop in attendance after the treatment ceased. Thus, the maturation argument can be rejected with confidence.

The shift in mean attendance from 104 students to 160 students can also be attributed to a testing effect rather than to a treatment effect. One can argue that the presence of a researcher counting class attendance (even if unobtrusive) sensitized students to think that the professor planned to stress attendance in evaluating their performance in the course; as a result, nonattendees decided that they had better start coming to class. If this argument is correct, we would expect class attendance to remain high so long as the reseacher continues to be present. Yet class attendance dropped following withdrawal of the treatment, despite the continued presence of the researcher. Thus, the time-series data allow us to reject the testing-effect hypothesis.

Although the time-series design is quite useful when circumstances preclude a control-group experiment, you should be aware of its sources of internal validity, especially history. Even if a shift in the measurements is found as expected, it could be attributed to another event occurring at the same time as the experimental treatment (the effect of history). In the example just given, suppose that students were told during the third class session that they would be given a test following the fourth class session. As you will recall, students were also told in the third class session that the next session would be question-and-answer, which constitutes the experimental treatment.

The imminence of the test rather than the use of a question-and-answer teaching approach could account for the dramatic increase in class attendance. Thus, in using a time-series design, the researcher should attempt to introduce the experimental treatment at a time when no other event could be reasonably expected to affect subjects' performance. It is also helpful to keep note of extraneous events that might also account for any obtained shifts in the measures.

Statistical Analysis

Unlike other experimental designs we have discussed, the time-series design does not yield data that are amenable to straightforward statistical analysis. Figure 15.1 presents some possible outcomes of a time-series design. Let us suppose that the measuring instrument (O) is an attitude scale assessing favorableness of attitudes toward teaching. This scale is administered to a sample of preservice teachers at one-month intervals on six occasions. Between the third and fourth months, the teachers are given a series of lectures designed to encourage positive attitudes toward the teaching profession.

One approach to data analysis would be to use the t test to determine the significance level of the difference between mean attitude scores at O_3 and O_4. We find in figure 15.1 that times series A, B, and E yield the same size shift from O_3 to O_4. Even if this shift is statistically significant in each time series, we should not conclude that the experimental treatment caused the shift in attendance in time series A and E. For example, although there is a shift in attitude from O_3 to O_4 in time series A, there are similar shifts at other intervals when the experimental treatment was not administered. The shift is plausibly explained as part of a general trend of increasing favorableness toward teaching by preservice teachers, rather than due to the experimental lectures. In the case of time series E, the shift from O_3 to O_4 cannot be attributed to the experimental treatment in view of the generally erratic pattern that emerges over the six occasions on which teachers' attitudes were measured.

The ineffectiveness of using a simple *t* test to evaluate time-series data can be demonstrated further by examing time series C and D. In time series C there is no immediate effect of the experimental treatment (O_4-O_3), but there does appear to be a delayed effect a month later (O_5-O_4). Of course, the delayed effect interpretation is tenable only if it has been hypothesized in advance of data collection. Otherwise the "delayed effect" could be attributed to one of many events that occurred between O_4 and O_5. In the case of time series D, there is also no shift from O_3 to O_4. The experimental treatment does seem to have an effect here, however. Whereas teachers' favorableness of attitude had been declining over a period of months, the lectures appear to have had the effect of at least halting the downward trend. Of course, this interpretation must be evaluated in view of the possibility that teachers' attitudes had reached their lower limit on the scale by O_3, and further decline was not measurable.

The proper analysis of time-series data depends on the particular pattern of findings obtained. Generally analysis of variance or a special type of correlation, called *trend analysis*, is used to determine the statistical significance of time-series data. The student planning to use time-series data should be prepared to consult an expert in research methodology and an advanced statistics textbook.[21]

CONTROL-GROUP DESIGNS WITH RANDOM ASSIGNMENT

We discuss in this section two of the experimental designs shown in table 15.1: the pretest-posttest control-group design (no. 4); and the posttest-only

---

21. Three references on time-series analysis are: Gene V Glass, "Estimating the Effects of Intervention Into a non-Stationary Time-Series," *American Educational Research Journal* 9 (1972): 463–77; John M. Gottman and Gene V Glass, "Analysis of Interrupted Time-Series Experiments," in *Single Subject Research: Strategies for Evaluating Change*, ed. Thomas R. Kratochwill (New York: Academic Press, 1978); Richard McCleary, Richard A. Hay, Jr., Errol E. Meidinger, and David McDowall, *Applied Time Series Analysis for the Social Sciences* (Beverly Hills, Calif.: Sage, 1980).

control-group design (no. 5). We also present two variations on these designs: the pretest-posttest control-group design with matching; and the multiple-treatment group design.

The Solomon four-group design is shown in table 15.1, but we will defer our discussion of it until the next chapter. This is because the Solomon four-group design is an example of a factorial design. Therefore, to understand how this design works, you need to understand the logic of factorial design—a topic covered in chapter 16.

Pretest-Posttest Control-Group Design

Nearly any study that can be conducted using a single-group design can be carried out more satisfactorily using one of the control-group designs, which we will now discuss. The essential difference between the single-group design and the control-group design is that the latter employs at least two groups of subjects, one of which is called the *control group* and is included primarily to make it possible to measure the effect of extraneous factors upon the posttest. The experiences of the experimental and control groups are generally kept as identical as possible with the exception that the experimental group is exposed to the experimental treatment. If extraneous variables have brought about changes between the pretest and posttest, these will be reflected in the scores of the control group. Thus, only the posttest change of the experimental group that is over and above the change that occurred in the control group can be attributed to the experimental treatment. If properly carried out, this experimental design effectively controls for the eight threats to internal validity identified by Campbell and Stanley: history, maturation, testing, instrumentation, regression, selection, mortality, and interaction effects.[22] However, table 15.1 indicates that the external validity of this design may be affected by an interaction of the pretest with the experimental treatment, that is, the experimental treatment may produce significant effects, only because a pretest was administered. When it is tried on a group that has not been pretested, the treatment does not work. If he thinks that his experimental treatment is affected by pretesting, then the researcher should use the posttest-only control-group design or the Solomon four-group design.

The essential features of the **pretest-posttest control-group design** are: formation of an experimental treatment group and a control treatment group, and administration of a pretest and posttest to each group. It is one of the most commonly used experimental designs by educational researchers. The following steps are involved: (1) random assignment of subjects to experimen-

22. Campbell and Stanley, "Designs for Research in Teaching."

tal and control groups, (2) administration of a pretest to both groups, (3) administration of the treatment to the experimental group but not to the control group, and (4) administration of a posttest to both groups. It is important to realize that the experimental and control groups must be treated as nearly alike as possible except for the treatment variable. For example, both groups must be given the same pretests and posttests and be tested at the same time.

It should be noted that these steps apply to a special case of the pretest-posttest control-group design. This is the case where the control group receives no treatment from the experimenter except a pretest and a posttest. In certain situations the experimenter may want to administer an alternative experimental treatment to the control group. Suppose, for example, a researcher wishes to determine the effect of a film about race relations on student attitudes toward minority groups. To determine the film's effectiveness, the researcher might have the experimental group view it while the control group goes about their regular school work. If the researcher was interested instead in the relative effectiveness of the film as compared to a discussion group (in which students meet as a group to discuss their attitudes about race relations), a different experimental design would be used. The experimental group would view the film while the control group would hold a discussion. Thus, both groups receive a treatment, and within the same time interval.

In this hypothetical experiment the discussion group is not a classic "control" for extraneous factors. Because the discussion treatment is an educational intervention in its own right, one might properly call it a "comparison" treatment. In fact, if the researcher is equally interested in both treatments, he might call both of them "experimental treatments." Extraneous factors should operate equally in both treatments under normal conditions. Therefore, the difference between the two treatment groups on the posttest can be attributed to the effect of the film treatment over and above the effects produced by extraneous factors and by the discussion method.

The pretest-posttest control-group design is illustrated in a recent study of initial reading instruction conducted by Betty Reifman, Ernest Pascarella, and Anna Larson.[23] The purpose of their experiment was to test the effectiveness of a variant on the language-experience approach to teaching beginning reading. In the language-experience approach the child tells a story or makes some other oral communication, the teacher writes what the child has dictated, and the child then tries to read the written version of his oral communication.

The sample consisted of 19 first-grade students in a middle- to upper-middle-class school in a suburban district. The students were randomly assigned to the experimental ($N = 10$) and control ($N = 9$) treatments. Both

23. Betty Reifman, Ernest T. Pascarella, and Anna Larson, "Effects of Word-Bank Instruction on Sight Word Acquisition: An Experimental Note," *Journal of Educational Research* 74: (1981): 175–78.

treatment groups received the language-experience approach described above for 12 weeks. The experimental group in addition received supplemental instruction in vocabulary and word-analysis skills. The words chosen for this supplemental instruction were drawn from the children's dictated stories.

The dependent variable in this study was the ability to read sight words, as measured by recognition of words on a subset of the Dolch Sight Word List. The subset consisted of 178 words commonly found in preprimer through second-grade curriculum. Students' scores could vary between 0 and 178, depending upon the number of words correctly identified. The Dolch List was administered to experimental and control-group students before and after the experimental treatment period.

Statistical Analysis

The pretest-posttest control-group design typically yields four mean scores. These mean scores for the language experience study are shown in table 15.3.[24] There are two pretest means and two posttest means associated with the experimental and control-groups' performance on the Dolch List. The standard deviation for each score distribution is also shown. You will note that there is some discrepancy between the experimental and control groups on the pretest, even though a random assignment procedure was used. This result illustrates the principle that random assignment does not ensure initial equivalence between groups. Random assignment only ensures absence of systematic bias in group composition.

Campbell and Stanley observed that researchers often use the wrong statistical procedure to analyze such data. The incorrect procedure is to do a t test on the pretest and posttest means of the experimental group (90.40 vs. 165.10) and another t test on the corresponding means of the control group (111.78 vs.

TABLE 15.3
Pre- and Posttest Statistics for Dolch List Scores

Group	Pretest		Posttest		Adjusted Posttest
	M	SD	M	SD	M
Experimental (N = 10)	90.40	50.07	165.10	20.67	169.58
Control (N = 9)	111.78	60.57	148.78	40.29	143.35

24. Ibid., p. 177.

148.78). If the t value for the experimental group is statistically significant, but the t value for the control group is not, the researcher would conclude—wrongly—that the experimental treatment was superior to the control treatment. This method of statistical analysis is wrong because it occasionally yields statistically significant differences that do not really exist between the experimental and control groups; in other words, it has a tendency to produce Type I errors.

The preferred statistical method is analysis of covariance in which the posttest means are compared using the pretest scores as a covariate. If the assumptions underlying analysis of covariance cannot be satisfied, the researcher might consider an analysis of variance of the posttest means. (Since there are two posttest means, one for the experimental group and one for the control group, this is equivalent to doing a t test). Another approach is to do a two-way analysis of a variance; this statistical technique is discussed in the next chapter, in the section on factorial designs.

Reifman and her associates tested the statistical significance of the results using analysis of covariance. The analysis of covariance summary is shown in table 15.4.[25] The first row of the table shows the relationship between pretest Dolch List scores and posttest Dolch List scores. Since $R^2 = .51$, the correlation coefficient for these variables is .71. The next row shows the statistical significance of the difference between the posttest means after the effect of the pretest was removed statistically. These "adjusted" posttest means are shown in the last column of table 15.4. Note that the posttest mean for the experimental group has been adjusted upward, whereas the posttest mean for the control group has been adjusted downward. In this way the pretest "inequity" between the groups is compensated. The significant F value (10.95) indicates that

TABLE 15.4

Analysis of Covariance of Dolch List Scores

Source	R^2	Degrees of Freedom	F
Pretest Dolch List scores (A)	.51	1	32.34**
Experimental treatment (B)	.17	1	10.95**
A × B	.08	1	5.43*
Residual	.24	15	

*$p < .05$.
**$p < .01$.

25. Adapted from ibid.

the null hypothesis of no difference between posttest means can be rejected.

The third row indicates a significant interaction between the pretest and the treatments. The concept of interaction effects will be discussed in chapter 16. Here it is sufficient to note that the significant interaction occurred because there was a larger difference between the experimental and control treatments for students with low pretest scores than for students with high pretest scores.

The first column of table 15.4 shows the R^2 value for each of the variables incorporated in the experimental design. These values were calculated from a multiple regression of the data. As we indicated above, the R^2 value of .51 shows the effect of pretest scores on posttest scores. The experimental treatment accounts for another 17 percent of the variance in posttest scores; and the A × B interaction accounts for an additional 8 percent. These three factors together predict 76 percent of the posttest variance. The residual value of .24 is simply the remaining unexplained variance in the posttest.

Table 15.4 illustrates nicely the close relationship between analysis of covariance techniques and multiple regression. In fact, the analysis of covariance F values were calculated from a multiple regression analysis. The treatment factor was entered into the multiple regression by creating what is known as a dummy variable. Each student receives a score on this variable: a score of 1 if the student was in the experimental group; 0 if the student was in the control group.

Pretest-Posttest Control-Group Design with Matching

A variation on the pretest-posttest control-group design is the use of the matching technique to obtain additional precision in the statistical analysis of the data. **Matching** in such designs refers to the selection of subjects for experimental and control groups in such a manner that they are closely comparable on a pretest that measures the dependent variable or variables correlated with the dependent variable. The main purpose of matching is to reduce initial differences between the experimental and control groups on the dependent variable or a related variable.

Matching is most useful in studies where small samples are to be used and when large differences between an experimental and control group on the dependent variable are not likely to occur. Under these conditions the small differences that do occur are more likely to be detected if sampling errors are reduced by the use of matching. The more closely the matching variable correlates with the dependent variable, the more effective the matching will be in reducing these errors. Thus it is necessary, if matching is to be employed, to have available a matching variable that correlates highly with the dependent variable. For example, in studies concerned with achievement gains that occur under different conditions of learning, alternate forms of the same achievement test can usually be used for the initial matching and for posttesting. Inasmuch as these alternate forms usually correlate highly, standard error is reduced considerably by the matching technique. This increase in precision is reflected, for example, in the standard error of the difference between means formula used for correlated means versus the formula used for uncorrelated means. The formula for the standard error of the difference between uncorrelated means is $\sigma_D = \sqrt{\sigma^2_{m1} + \sigma^2_{m2}}$, whereas the formula for the standard error of the difference between correlated means for matched groups is $\sigma_D = \sqrt{\sigma^2_{m1} + \sigma^2_{m2} - 2r_{12}\sigma_{m1}\sigma_{m2}}$. The two formulas are identical except for the last factor in the matched-group formula and, as this factor is subtracted, it always reduces the standard error (the size of the reduction increasing as the size of the correlation increases).

Steps

The usual steps in carrying out a study using the pretest-posttest control-group design with matching are as follows:

1. Administer measures of the dependent variable or of a variable closely correlated with the dependent variable to the research subjects.
2. Assign subjects to matched pairs on the basis of their scores on the measures described in step 1.
3. Randomly assign one member of each pair to the experimental group and the other member to the control group.
4. Expose the experimental group to the experimental treatment and if appropriate administer a placebo or alternative treatment to the control group.
5. Administer measures of the dependent variables to the experimental and control groups.
6. Compare the performance of the experimental and control group on the posttest(s) using tests of statistical significance.

A method of matching that many statisticians favor is to place all subjects in rank order on the basis of their scores on the matching variable. After subjects have been placed in rank order, the first two subjects are selected (regardless of the difference in their scores on the matching variable) and by random means, such as flipping a coin, one subject is assigned to the experimental group and the other to the control group. The next two subjects on the rank list are then selected, and again one is randomly assigned to the experimental group and the other to the control group. This procedure is continued until all subjects have been assigned.

Edelwina Rivera and Michael Omizo used this matching procedure in an experiment that evaluated a method for increasing attention and reducing impulsivity among hyperactive children.[26] Their procedure for matching and randomly assigning students to treatments was as follows:

> The sample consisted of 36 male hyperactive children between the ages of seven and eleven years (M = 9.5). . . .
>
> Subjects were identified through teachers' ratings on Conners' Behavior Rating Scale, Abbreviated Form . . . which has been reported to be the most extensively used teacher rating scale in existing research identifying and diagnosing hyperactive children. . . . Subjects were matched by ranking them on their behavior rating scores. Starting from the highest score, two subjects were taken at a time and randomly assigned to one of two groups by flipping a coin. After the groupings had been established, the two groups were randomly assigned to either experimental (N = 18) or control (N = 18) condition again by flipping a coin.[27]

The teacher ratings were not used as a posttest measure. However, the ratings correlated significantly (r = .43, p < .01) with pretest electromyogram (EMG) scores, which form a measure of muscular relaxation-tension, and which were readministered as a posttest. Because of this matching procedure, the pretest EMG means of the experimental and control groups were almost identical.

An alternative approach to matching is to stratify the sample on a pertinent variable and then to randomly assign subjects to treatment groups by stratum. The advantage of stratified random assignment is that the researcher can test whether treatment effects on a posttest measure vary from one stratum (i.e., subgroup) to another. Because of this advantage, stratified random assignment has been used with increasing frequency in recent years. We shall discuss this procedure in more detail in the section on factorial designs in chapter 16.

Posttest-Only Control-Group Design

This design is similar to the pretest-posttest control-group designs except that pretests of the dependent variable are not administered to the experimental and control groups. The steps involved in the **posttest-only control-group design** are as follows: (1) randomly assign subjects to the experimental and control groups, (2) administer the treatment to the experimental group but not to the control group, and (3) administer the posttest to both groups.

26. Edelwina Rivera and Michael M. Omizo, "The Effects of Relaxation and Biofeedback on Attention to Task and Impulsivity Among Male Hyperactive Children," *Exceptional Child* 27 (1980): 41–51.
27. Ibid., p. 43.

This design is recommended when it is not possible to locate a suitable pretest or when there is a possibility that the pretest has an effect on the experimental treatment. In choosing this experimental design, the researcher should consider three possible disadvantages of not administering a pretest of the dependent variable. First, random assignment may not be fully successful in eliminating initial differences between the experimental and the control groups. If initial differences still exist, then any differences found on the posttest can be attributed to them rather than to the effect of the experimental treatment. When random assignment fails to control for initial differences, then the researcher needs pretest scores to use as a covariate in analysis of covariance; thus the initial differences are controlled statistically. In the posttest-only control-group design, however, pretest scores on the dependent variable are not available and therefore cannot be used to control for initial differences. Since random assignment is most effective in equating groups when large numbers of subjects are involved, the posttest-only control-group design is best employed when the researcher has a large pool of subjects available for study.

The second disadvantage of not administering a pretest is that the researcher does not have an initial status measure to form subgroups to determine whether the experimental treatment has a different effect on subjects at different levels of the measure. The third disadvantage of not administering a pretest occurs when there is differential attrition during the course of the experiment. For example, if subjects in the control and the experimental group drop out of the experiment before it is over, then one can argue that any differences on the posttest are due to differential dropout characteristics of the two groups, rather than due to the effect of the experimental treatment. The administration of a pretest of the dependent variable makes it possible to examine the validity of the differential attrition hypothesis. Thus, the posttest-only control-group design should not be used when it seems likely that there will be considerable attrition of subjects during the course of the study.

Statistical Analysis

The data yielded by this experimental design can be analyzed simply by doing a *t* test comparison of the mean posttest scores of the experimental and the control group. If more than two groups have been studied, then the mean posttest scores can be analyzed using analysis of variance. If the scores depart radically from the normal distribution, then a nonparametric test should be done.

Multiple-Treatment Design

The multiple-treatment **Single-Factor** design is a simple extension of the control-group designs we have considered. The pretest-posttest control-group design, the pretest-posttest control-group design with matching, and the post-test-only control-group each involve random assignment of a sample to *two* groups. Each of these designs can be extended to include cases where a sample is randomly assigned to *three* or more groups. We call such extensions **multiple-treatment single-factor designs.**

An example of such a design is found in an experiment on class size conducted by Stan Shapson and his colleagues.[28] The purpose of the experiment was to determine the effects of different class sizes on student achievement, classroom process, and other variables. The random assignment procedures were described as follows:

> In the first year of the study, teachers and students in the fourth grade were randomly assigned to classes of four sizes: 16, 23, 30, or 37. The student assignments were stratified by sex and by ratings of academic performance. For the second year, the same teachers and students were similarly assigned to Grade 5 classes, with the constraints that students not be in a class size of 16 or 37 for both years of the study and that teachers who taught classes of the two larger sizes receive classes of the two smaller sizes (and vice versa). The actual size of each participating class was closely monitored during the study to ensure that enrollment did not vary by more than ± 3 from the assigned class size.[29]

Note that a two-group experiment would have severely restricted the usefulness of the study. For example, if class sizes of 16 and 37 had been evaluated, one would learn nothing about the effects of intermediate class sizes. If class sizes of 16 and 23 had been evaluated, we would not learn about the effects of "testing the limits" by forming much larger classes ($N = 37$). And so on. The formation of four treatment groups allows an interesting continuum of class sizes to be investigated. Also note that the researchers were unable to maintain perfect treatment fidelity (see p. 648), which constitutes a slight threat to the internal validity of the experiment. A nice feature of the random assignment procedure in this study is that both teachers and students were randomly assigned to treatment groups in the first year. Thus, both teachers and students had an equal chance of being in any of the treatment groups.

Achievement measures were administered to students each year of the study. Four subscales of the Canadian Tests of Basic Skills were administered: vocabulary, reading comprehension, mathematics-concepts, and mathematics-problem solving. Also, art samples and writing samples were collected under standard conditions and were scored on rating scales.

---

28. Stan M. Shapson, Edgar N. Wright, Gary Eason, and John Fitzgerald, "An Experimental Study of the Effects of Class Size," *American Educational Research Journal* 17 (1980): 141–52.

29. Ibid., p. 142.

Statistical Analysis

The results of the data analysis for the class size study are shown in table 15.5.[30] The class mean was used as the unit of statistical analysis. The headings of the table indicated that there were 15 or 16 classes in each treatment group.

The first row of results for each dependent variable shows the mean score of each treatment group on that variable. For example, the mean rating on the art sample for the classes having 16 students was 6.47. These mean scores are "unadjusted" in that they are based on the actual scores of students in the sample. If one wishes to determine whether the unadjusted treatment-group means were significantly different from each other, one would do an analysis of variance. If a significant F ratio resulted, one would do a t test for multiple

TABLE 15.5

Effects of Class Size on Student Achievement

	Class Size				
Variable	16 (N = 16)	23 (N = 16)	30 (N = 15)	37 (N = 15)	F ratio
Art (maximum = 10)					
Unadjusted mean	6.47	6.30	6.49	6.58	
Residual mean	−0.07	0.01	−0.11	0.18	1.29
Composition (maximum = 5)					
Unadjusted mean	4.56	4.40	4.51	4.46	
Residual mean	0.14	0.02	−0.06	−0.11	0.88
Vocabulary					
Unadjusted mean	43.16	43.58	42.42	42.84	
Residual mean	−0.00	0.04	0.03	−0.07	0.71
Reading					
Unadjusted mean	44.08	44.47	44.05	44.28	
Residual mean	−0.00	−0.04	0.02	0.02	0.16
Mathematics-concepts					
Unadjusted mean	47.41	45.60	43.03	44.69	
Residual mean	0.15	0.00	−0.09	−0.07	4.11*
Mathematics-problem solving					
Unadjusted mean	51.17	49.33	48.20	48.82	
Residual mean	0.14	0.04	−0.09	−0.10	2.57

*$p < .05$.

30. Adapted from ibid., p. 147.

comparisons to determine which pair, or pairs, of group means differed significantly.

You will note that the second row of research results for each dependent variable consists of "residual mean scores." These scores were formed because, to a certain extent, students' performance on the achievement tests were a function of their grade level and teacher, as well as a function of their treatment-group assignment. The variance in achievement test scores attributable to grade level and teacher was removed statistically using multiple regression. The remaining standardized mean scores are called residual mean scores. This procedure is similar to analysis of covariance in which achievement scores are the dependent variable, and grade level and teacher assignment are covariates.

As table 15.5 indicates, an analysis of variance was done on the residual mean scores for each achievement variable. Only one of these analyses (mathematics-concepts) resulted in a significant F ratio (4.11). This means that the researchers can reject the null hypothesis that the residual mean scores of the treatment groups are chance fluctuations in a single population. Instead, the researchers conclude that at least one of the treatment groups is drawn from a population having a different residual mean score than the other treatment groups.

A t test for multiple comparisons was used to determine which pairs of treatment-group residual mean scores were significantly different from each other. This analysis revealed two significant results. Students in classes of size 16 had significantly higher mathematics-concepts scores than their peers in classes of size 30 ($t = 3.16$, $p < .005$) and their peers in classes of size 37 ($t = 2.87$, $p < .01$). Note that the treatment-group scores for the variable mathematics-problem solving formed the same pattern of differences although the results were not statistically significant. It appears that reducing class size has a positive impact on students' mathematics achievement.

As we indicated above, the researchers removed the effects of grade level by using multiple regression. Another approach would have been to consider the Grade 4 year and Grade 5 year as two separate experiments, and to analyze the data for each year separately. In this approach each experiment would be a replication of the other. Thus, we would have some indication of the generalizability of class size effects across different instructional conditions.

MISTAKES SOMETIMES MADE IN CONDUCTING EXPERIMENTS

1. Researcher selects an experimental design that is inappropriate for the research problem.

2. Does not consider confounding variables such as history, maturation, statistical regression, and differential loss of subjects, which might have brought about changes attributed to the experimental treatment.
3. Generalizes the research findings to other situations and populations not warranted by the experimental design and sampling procedures.
4. Does not take steps to reduce the possibility of experimenter bias.
5. Designs an experimental treatment that is too weak to have an effect on the dependent variable.
6. Confuses the concept of random selection of subjects with the concept of random assignment of subjects to different experimental conditions.
7. When using a control-group design, matches the subjects on variables that do not correlate sufficiently with the dependent variable.
8. Uses the posttest-only control-group design with a small sample of subjects.

ANNOTATED REFERENCES

Dayton, C. Mitchell. *The Design of Educational Experiments.* New York: McGraw-Hill, 1970.

This text provides a comprehensive survey of experimental designs. One of its helpful features is the use of examples from the research literature in education to illustrate each type of design. There is a separate chapter on the application of analysis of covariance to different experimental designs.

Keppel, Geoffrey. *Design and Analysis: A Researcher's Handbook.* Englewood Cliffs, N.J.: Prentice-Hall, 1973.

This is a more advanced text on experimental design than Dayton's. A background in statistical analysis is necessary to follow the discussion of the various experimental designs. For the student who can appreciate it, this text provides a good in-depth perspective on the nature of experimentation in the behavioral sciences.

Richey, Harold W. "Avoidable Failures of Experimental Procedure." *Journal of Experimental Education* 45 (1976): 10–13.

The author provides much down-to-earth advice about conducting experiments in this article. The advice is based on a personal experience in which an experiment failed. Most of the reasons given for the failure are described in other sources, but the author's presentation is especially convincing. Recommendations to other investigators are given, including the suggestion that an investigator imagine himself (herself) a subject in the experiment and then intuit how he would react to each experimental procedure.

Rosenthal, Robert, and Rosnow, Ralph L., eds. *Artifact in Behavioral Research*. New York: Academic Press, 1969.
This collection of papers is organized around the theme of biases and errors that can distort the results of experimental research. The topics include the subject's awareness of and compliance with the experimenter's intent, the nature of the volunteer subject, pretest sensitization, the effects of researchers' expectancies about the outcomes of their experiments, and subject apprehension about being evaluated in an experiment.

SELF-CHECK TEST

Circle the correct answer to each of the following questions. An answer key is provided on page 881.

1. A posttest in an experiment is sometimes called the
   a. dependent variable.
   b. experimental treatment.
   c. experimental variable.
   d. treatment variable.
2. An experiment in which the extraneous variables are controlled is said to be
   a. internally reliable.
   b. internally valid.
   c. externally valid.
   d. externally reliable.
3. If students' scores tend to move toward the mean upon retesting, _____ is said to have occurred.
   a. experimental mortality
   b. statistical regression
   c. maturation
   d. reactive effect of pretesting
4. If a pretest functions as part of the experimental treatment, the _____ of the experiment would be weakened.
   a. internal validity
   b. internal reliability
   c. external validity
   d. external reliability
5. Representative design of experiments assumes that
   a. the learning environment is a complex, interrelated ecology.
   b. the human learner is an active processor of information.
   c. the intended effects of an experimental intervention may radiate out to affect other aspects of performance.
   d. All of the above are correct.

6. Researchers often give participating teachers and students special attention that, though not part of the experimental treatment, may cause change. This phenomenon has been called the
   a. Hawthorne Effect.
   b. placebo effect.
   c. effect of multiple-treatment interference.
   d. reactive effect of experimentation.
7. A useful technique to minimize the effects of experimenter bias upon the outcome of an experiment is to
   a. train naive experimenters to collect the data from subjects.
   b. use objective measuring instruments.
   c. avoid suggesting to the experimenters that one experimental treatment is better than another.
   d. All of the above are correct.

For questions 8–10, use the following key:
   R = random assignment
   X = experimental treatment
   O = observation (pretest or posttest)

8. O X O describes the
   a. one group pretest-posttest design.
   b. one-shot case study.
   c. pretest-posttest control-group design.
   d. posttest-only control-group design.
9. R O X O describes the
      O   O
   a. posttest-only control-group design.
   b. Solomon two-group design.
   c. counterbalanced design.
   d. pretest-posttest control-group design.
10. R   X O is a useful design if
         O
    a. it is thought the pretest will have an effect on the experimental treatment.
    b. no matching group is available.
    c. no control group is available.
    d. a large sample is available.

APPLICATION PROBLEMS

The following problems do not have a single correct answer. For feedback, you can compare your answers with the sample answers on pages 895–96.

1. A researcher is planning an experiment to test the effectiveness of the discussion method at the high school level. One teacher has agreed to use the discussion

method in her class several times a week for a semester. Another teacher has agreed to teach the same content, but without using the discussion method. The researcher will collect the following data: student scores on an achievement test and on a scale measuring attitudes toward the instruction. What are three recommendations that you can offer to improve the representativeness of this experimental design?

2. A researcher has developed a new training program for teachers, which he firmly believes will bring about observable changes in their classroom behavior. To test its effectiveness, he plans to conduct an experiment in which he observes and compares teacher behavior before and after training.

   a. What type of methodological flaw has been introduced into the study at this point?

   b. What is an alternative procedure that might eliminate this flaw?

3. A researcher wants to test the effectiveness of providing high school students with a note-taking outline of each chapter they are assigned to read in a history class. She has permission to conduct the experiment with two history classes, each containing 30 students. She randomly forms two groups within each class. The experimental group receives a note-taking outline each time they are assigned a chapter; the control group receives the same assignment, but not a note-taking outline. On the basis of this information, what flaw has the researcher introduced into the experimental design?

4. A researcher is planning to test the effectiveness of a new reading program. A sample of 40 teachers distributed evenly among five schools in one school district has volunteered to use the program for a semester. Using only this sample, the researcher wishes to form two equivalent groups, one of which will participate in the special program while the other receives its regular program. State two methods by which equivalence can be achieved through random assignment.

5. A researcher carried out an experiment in mathematics instruction involving a pretest-posttest control-group design. The mean achievement scores for the experimental group were 35 on the pretest and 65 on the posttest. The mean scores for the control group were 45 on the pretest and 55 on the posttest. What statistical technique would most likely be used to analyze these data, and why?

SUGGESTION SHEET

If your last name starts with letters from Osc to Pri, please complete the Suggestion Sheet at the end of the book while the chapter is still fresh in your mind.

16.

EXPERIMENTAL DESIGNS: PART 2

OVERVIEW

This chapter applies principles of experimentation discussed in chapter 15 (especially internal and external validity) to additional experimental designs. One set of designs, called *quasi-experimental,* is used when random assignment of subjects to experimental and control groups is not possible. Another set of designs, called *factorial* experiments, involves simultaneous manipulation of two or more treatment variables. An important recent trend in educational research has been the *single-subject* experiment, which is discussed at some length here. The chapter concludes with a consideration of problems involved in measuring change. This is an important topic because experiments in educational research are often done to determine the effect of a training procedure on student gain in achievement or other change in performance.

OBJECTIVES

After studying this chapter, you should be able to:

1. Describe three procedures to lessen initial group differences that occur because of nonrandom assignment of students to experimental and control treatments.
2. Describe the methods and statistical procedures used in the following quasi-experimental designs: static-group comparison, nonequivalent control-group, time-series, and counterbalanced.
3. State threats to the internal and external validity of quasi-experimental designs.
4. Classify the independent variables that appear in factorial research designs into five types.
5. Explain the purpose, design, and statistical analysis of aptitude-treatment interaction experiments.
6. Compare the nature and uses of single-subject and multisubject experimental designs.

7. Create several variations of A-B-A and multiple-baseline designs in single-subject research, and describe statistical techniques for analyzing the data yielded by these designs.
8. State several threats to the internal and external validity of single-subject experiments.
9. Describe problems in using gain scores to measure change, and state two statistical techniques for solving them.

QUASI-EXPERIMENTAL DESIGNS

As we have already discussed, random assignment of subjects to the experimental and control groups is a very important feature of experimental design. Nonetheless, random assignment of subjects to the experimental and control groups is sometimes not possible, particularly in field studies. Such experiments have been termed **quasi-experiments** by Campbell and Stanley[1] to indicate that random assignment of subjects to treatment groups was not accomplished. Quasi-experiments, if carefully designed, can yield useful knowledge. However, the researcher should be aware of the special problems that may arise when subjects are not assigned randomly to groups, and should take steps to solve them.

Static-Group Comparison Design

The **static-group comparison design** is a type of experiment in which two treatment groups are administered a posttest but not a pretest; and subjects are not randomly assigned to the treatment groups. This design is identical to the posttest-only control-group design discussed in chapter 15, except for the absence of random assignment.

The steps involved in the static-group comparison design are as follows: (1) one group of subjects is administered the experimental treatment and is then posttested, and (2) another group of subjects is given the posttest only. These steps are represented in the following diagram:

$$\underline{\quad\underline{X}\quad\underline{O}\quad}$$
$$O$$

---

1. Donald T. Campbell and Julian C. Stanley, "Experimental and Quasi-Experimental Designs for Research on Teaching," in *Handbook of Research on Teaching*, ed. N. L. Gage (Chicago: Rand McNally, 1963).

where X represents the experimental treatment, O represents measurement of the dependent variable after the treatment phase has ended, and the broken line indicates that the experimental and control groups are not formed randomly.

The main source of internal invalidity affecting this design is that posttest differences between groups can be attributed to characteristics of the groups as well as to the experimental treatment. For example, suppose teachers in one school are given the experimental treatment and posttest, and teachers in another school are given only the posttest. If differences on the posttest are found, it can be argued that they are due to differences between teachers in the two schools rather than to the effect of the experimental treatment. In this situation where random assignment cannot be used, it is preferable to use the nonequivalent control-group design discussed next. This design is similar to the static-group comparison design except that both groups are given a pretest. The pretest results can be used to determine whether the two groups are equivalent even though they have not been formed by random assignment.

Another possible source of internal invalidity in this design is differential mortality. To illustrate this problem Campbell and Stanley discuss a hypothetical experiment comparing first-year and fourth-year college women.[2] This experiment can be considered a static-group comparison since the fourth-year women have received the experimental treatment (i.e., a college education) but not the first-year women, and the two groups have not been formed randomly. Now suppose it were found that the first-year women received significantly higher ratings of beauty than fourth-year women. Would we conclude from these results that college education has a "debeautifying" effect on women? The finding can be explained more plausibly in terms of differential mortality. Although the first-year women are an intact group, many fourth-year women have dropped out of college during the course of the treatment. We could argue, then, that the differences between groups are caused by the more beautiful women leaving college to be married, or for other reasons. Thus the findings are explained more plausibly in terms of mortality in the experimental group rather than in terms of effects of the experimental treatment.

The static-group comparison design is a relatively weak experimental design. The researcher planning to use it should consider carefully the feasibility of administering a pretest to the subjects. If this simple addition can be made to the experiment, the researcher has created in effect a nonequivalent control-group design, which is discussed below. The nonequivalent control-group design enables the researcher to make stronger inferences concerning the effect of the experimental treatment on the posttest.

2. Ibid., pp. 182–83.

Statistical Analysis

The data yielded by this quasi-experimental design can be analyzed simply by doing a t test comparison of the posttest mean scores. If the scores deviate considerably from the normal distribution, then a nonparametric test (most probably the Mann-Whitney U Test) would be used instead.

Nonequivalent Control-Group Design

Probably the most widely used quasi-experimental design in educational research is the nonequivalent control-group design. This design is represented by the following diagram:

$$\frac{\underline{O} \quad \underline{X} \quad \underline{O}}{O \qquad O}$$

where X represents the experimental treatment, O represents pretest or posttest measurement of the dependent variable, and the broken line indicates that the experimental and control groups are not formed randomly. Thus, the distinguishing features of the **nonequivalent control-group design** are: administration of a pretest and posttest to both treatment groups, and nonrandom assignment of subjects to the groups.

The nonequivalent control-group design was used in an experiment on social studies instruction conducted by Charles Curtis and James Shaver.[3] The purpose of the experiment was to test the effectiveness of a new social studies curriculum designed to improve the self-esteem of slow learners at the secondary school level. The experiment was conducted in four schools, each of which had two special classes for slow learners and nonachievers.[4]

It was not possible to randomly assign students to the experimental treatment (the new social studies curriculum) and to the control treatment (the school's regular social studies curriculum). Rather, all students in a particular class had to receive one treatment or the other. Because random assignment was not possible, the experiment is classified as employing a nonequivalent control-group design.

The dependent variable in the experiment was student self-esteem. The researchers believed that the new curriculum, which involved out-of-classroom

---

3. Charles K. Curtis and James P. Shaver, "Improving Slow Learners' Self-Esteem in Secondary Social Studies Classes," *Journal of Educational Research* 74 (1981): 217–21.
4. A replication experiment, using a single-group design, was conducted at the same time as the nonequivalent control-group experiment. The replication study is not discussed here, but a report of it is presented in ibid.

study of contemporary community problems, would motivate, challenge, and reward students for personal accomplishment. They hypothesized that ". . . students' awareness of their growth in interest and knowledge, coupled with an understanding of the amount and difficulty of the work involved, along with positive reactions from persons interviewed and parental interests in the topic, would have a positive influence on student self-esteem."[5] The control classes used a conventional textbook approach to study such topics as Canadian urbanization, Canadian history, and the European economy. There was no reason to believe that such learning experiences would have an effect on students' self-esteem. The Self-Esteem Inventory (SEI), a measure of self-esteem, was administered as a pretest and posttest to both the experimental and control classes. The experiment extended over a period of five months.

Statistical Analysis

The main threat to the internal validity of nonequivalent control-group experiments is the possibility that group differences on the posttest are due to preexisting group differences rather than to a treatment effect. Analysis of covariance (first discussed in chapter 13) is frequently used to handle this problem.[6] Analysis of covariance reduces the effects of initial group differences statistically by making compensating adjustments to the posttest means of the two groups.

Curtis and Shaver had available two pieces of information about the students before the experiment began: their IQ scores and their pretest scores on the SEI. The means and standard deviations of the two groups on these two measures are shown in table 16.1.[7] SEI pretest scores of the two groups are similar, but there is a substantial difference in IQ scores. The experimental and control groups were equated on these two measures by using them as covariates in an analysis of covariance. First, though, the major assumptions underlying analysis of covariance (homogeneity of group variances and homogeneity of regression) were checked. If the assumptions had not been satisfied, the researchers could have done an analysis of variance on the posttest scores. In effect, the researchers would ignore the covariate data in determining the statistical significance of the difference between posttest means.

The analysis of covariance revealed a significant F value for the treatment effect ($F = 4.81$, $p < .05$). This result indicates that the posttest means of the experimental and control groups were significantly different from each other,

5. Ibid., p. 219.
6. Other statistical procedures for analyzing nonequivalent control-group data are discussed in David A. Kenny, "A Quasi-Experimental Approach to Assessing Treatment Effects in a Nonequivalent Control Group Design," *Psychological Bulletin* 82 (1975): 345–62.
7. Adapted from table 1 in Curtis and Shaver, "Improving Slow Learners' Self-Esteem," p. 221.

TABLE 16.1

Descriptive Statistics for Self-Esteem and IQ Scores for Experimental and Control Groups

Variable	Experimental Group (N = 64)		Control Group (N = 66)	
	M	SD	M	SD
IQ	96.74	11.63	105.66	10.93
SEI Pretest	57.20	16.12	58.88	15.01
SEI Posttest	62.46	13.91	56.09	16.41
Adjusted SEI Posttest	62.03		56.53	

after taking into account preexisting differences in IQ and self-esteem. The analysis of covariance also provides an estimate of what the posttest means would have been if the two groups were equal on the preexperiment covariates. These estimates (called "adjusted posttest means") are shown in the last row of table 16.1.

You should keep in mind that analysis of covariance is an imperfect statistical technique for equating experimental groups prior to the treatment period. Only the variables that are measured can be used as covariates. The groups may differ on other variables, but if these variables have not been measured, they cannot be entered into the analysis of covariance. Furthermore, analysis of covariance will distort the adjustment of the posttest means unless a variety of assumptions concerning the data are satisfied.

Another approach to analyzing data from a nonequivalent control-group experiment is to enter all of the measured variables as predictors in a multiple regression analysis, with posttest scores as the criterion variable. Pretest variables would be entered first into the multiple regression. Then the researcher would determine whether the treatment variable significantly improves the prediction. (You will recall from chapter 14 that the statistical significance of the R^2 increment is tested.) The advantage of multiple regression is that it does not make as stringent assumptions as does analysis of covariance.

In the preceding discussion we presented the case of a nonequivalent control-group design with two groups: a treatment group and a no-treatment control group. This design is easily expanded to include these variations: experiments in which the control group receives a contrasting treatment rather than a no-treatment condition, and experiments having more than two groups. These variations are considered nonequivalent control-group designs as long as there is absence of random assignment and each group is administered a pretest and posttest.

FACTORIAL DESIGNS

The classic single-factor experiment aims at holding all elements of the experimental situation constant except the treatment variations. In most educational situations, however, the experimental treatment cannot realistically be considered in isolation from other factors. For example, using the classic single-factor design, a researcher might test the effectiveness of a new reading program (the experimental treatment) by administering it to a large sample of third-, fourth-, and fifth-grade classrooms. If the mean achievement gain is significantly greater for this sample than for a sample receiving a conventional program (the control group), the researcher would conclude that the reading program is effective. Further statistical analysis might reveal that the reading program leads to greatly superior achievement gains in the third grade, but not in the fourth or fifth grades. Thus we cannot consider the effect of the reading program independently of the effect of grade level; the two factors *interact*.

Single-factor designs and statistical techniques used to analyze them (primarily the *t* test or simple analysis of variance) do not permit the researcher to investigate interaction effects. It is necessary to use a factorial design for this purpose. **Factorial designs** are a type of experiment in which the researcher determines the effect of two or more independent variables (i.e., factors)—each by itself and also in interaction with each other—on a dependent variable. The effect of each independent variable on the dependent variable is called a **main effect**. The effect of the interaction of two or more independent variables on the dependent variable is called an **interaction effect**.

The simplest type of factorial experiment involves a 2 × 2 design. The expression "2 × 2" means that two variations of one factor (A_1 and A_2) and two variations of another factor (B_1 and B_2) are manipulated at the same time. This factorial design requires the formation of four treatment groups, with each group receiving a different combination of the two factors: A_1B_1, A_1B_2, A_2B_1, and A_2B_2. Subjects should be randomly assigned to the four treatment groups. If random assignment procedures are not used, the design is a quasi-experiment. The data resulting from a factorial quasi-experiment are very difficult to interpret because main effects and interaction effects must be disentangled from possible selection effects due to initial differences between subjects in the various treatment groups.

Jay Gottlieb conducted a 2 × 2 factorial experiment to determine factors that affect regular students' attitudes toward retarded children.[8] One factor that was manipulated in the experiment was labeling a child as mentally retarded. An assumption of mainstreaming programs is that the attitudes of reg-

---

8. Jay Gottlieb, "Attitudes Toward Retarded Children: Effects of Labeling and Behavioral Aggressiveness," *Journal of Educational Psychology* 67 (1975): 581–85.

ular students toward mentally retarded students are more positive when the latter are "delabeled" and educated in regular classes. Some educators, however, believe that regular students are likely to be more tolerant, and hence more positive, toward mentally retarded students if they know, through explicit labeling, that these children are mentally retarded.

Another factor that may affect students' attitudes toward their peers is the peers' actual behavior. Students may form negative attitudes toward socially aggressive children and positive attitudes toward children who exhibit socially appropriate behavior. Also, labeling may interact with the demonstration of aggressive behavior. For example, labeling a child as mentally retarded may affect students' degree of tolerance for their peers' aggressive behavior.

The factor of aggressiveness was manipulated by producing two videotapes. In one videotape, a twelve-year-old boy was seen engaged in socially appropriate behavior, modeling clay while seated quietly behind his desk at school. In the other videotape, the same boy displayed aggressive behavior by throwing the clay on the floor, stomping on it, and banging it with his fist. Forty-eight third-grade children were randomly assigned to view one videotape or the other. Additionally, a random half of the children in each treatment group were told that the boy in the videotape was mentally retarded and in a special class for retarded children. The other half of the children were told that the boy was a fifth-grade student.

The 2 × 2 design can be depicted as follows:

	Nonaggressive Videotape	Aggressive Videotape
Labeled Retarded	$N = 12$	$N = 12$
Labeled Normal	$N = 12$	$N = 12$

After viewing the videotape, each subject completed two measures of his or her attitude toward the boy in the videotape. One measure was a modification of the Cunningham Social Distance Scale. The other measure was a rating scale using adjective pairs. High scores on either scale indicate a positive attitude.

Table 16.2 presents the descriptive statistics for the four treatment groups on the rating scales.[9] Differences between treatment-group means were first tested for statistical significance by multivariate analysis of variance (MANOVA). You will recall from chapter 13 that MANOVA is used to test for treatment group differences on two or more dependent variables considered simul-

---

9. Table 16.2 adapted from table 1 in ibid., p. 583.

taneously. As shown in table 16.3, both main effects and the interaction effect were statistically significant.

Gottlieb clarified the meaning of the MANOVA results by doing a separate 2 × 2 analysis of variance (ANOVA) on each dependent variable. Consider the ANOVA results for the rating scale. The significant main effect for the labeling factor ($F = 10.44$) means that students who were told the boy in the videotape was a fifth-grade student had a reliably more positive attitude

TABLE 16.2

Mean Effects of Labeling and Aggressive Behavior on Student Attitudes

	Nonaggressive Videotape	Aggressive Videotape
Labeled retarded	41.50	34.42
Labeled normal	43.17	41.42

(a) Rating scale

	Nonaggressive Videotape	Aggressive Videotape
Labeled retarded	5.58	4.00
Labeled normal	5.58	5.00

(b) Social distance scale

TABLE 16.3

Multivariate and Univariate Analysis of Variance on Student Attitude Measures

	MANOVA		ANOVA Rating Scale		ANOVA Social Distance	
	F	P	F	P	F	P
Labeling effect (L)	8.32	.003	10.44	.004	3.56	.07
Behavior effect (B)	16.71	.001	10.85	.004	16.73	.001
L × B effect	4.57	.05	3.96	.06	3.56	.07

toward him (M = 42.29) than did students who were told that the boy was mentally retarded (M = 37.96). Note that in this main effect analysis the aggressive behavior factor is ignored; all students in the retarded label condition (N = 24) are compared with all students in the regular label condition (N = 24).

The main effect for the boy's behavior was also statistically significant (F = 10.85), meaning that students who viewed the nonaggressive boy had a reliably more positive attitude toward him (M = 42.33) than did students who viewed the aggressive boy (M = 37.92).

The nearly significant F ratio for the interaction effect complicates the interpretation of the result.[10] The presence of an interaction effect means that the effect of labeling variations on students' attitudes is dependent upon the labeled child's actual behavior. If you reexamine the data in table 16.2a, the nature of the interaction effect should be readily apparent. The mean scores on the rating scale for three of the treatment groups are quite similar and positive. Students were negative only toward the boy who was aggressive and was labeled as retarded. If a child is labeled normal, the aggressiveness of his behavior does not affect students' attitude toward him. If a child is labeled retarded, however, the aggressiveness of his behavior does affect students' attitude toward him. In brief, one factor (labeling) *interacts* with another factor (behavior) to affect attitude. This particular interaction effect is so clear and strong that the separate main effects of labeling and behavior have little educational or psychological significance on their own.

We recommend at this point that you reexamine the treatment-group means in table 16.2b to determine the interaction effects for the social distance scale.

Three-factor experiments. Two factors were manipulated in the experiment described above. Researchers sometimes investigate more complex problems by manipulating three or even four factors within the same experiment. Such experiments are efficient in that once resources have been expended for the basic experiment (travel, development and reproduction of measures, data processing, etc.), additional factors usually can be added to the design at little extra cost. The problem with three- and four-factor experiments, though, is that the interaction effect may overwhelm the researcher. For example, a three-factor experiment (factors A, B, C) will yield three two-way interaction effects (A × B, B × C, A × C) and a three-way interaction effect (A × B × C). Should any of these interaction effects prove statistically significant, they may be difficult to interpret unless the researcher has hypothesized their existence.

An example of a three-factor experiment is the study of individual and

---

10. Even though the p value for the interaction effect (.06) is above the conventional cutoff point (.05) for statistical significance, the difference is so slight that the null hypothesis can be rejected without undue risk of a Type I error. The rejection of the null hypothesis is further warranted by the fact that the MANOVA interaction effect was significant.

group problem solving conducted by George Rotter and Stephen Portugal.[11] The purpose of their experiment was to test the hypothesis that a combination of individual and group brainstorming would be more effective than either individual or group brainstorming alone. Brainstorming is a problem-solving technique in which an individual or group tries to think of as many problem solutions as possible without regard to their correctness or quality.

To test the hypothesis, three different variables (individual vs. group brainstorming, type of problem, and sex of subject) were manipulated. First, four experimental treatments (called *conditions* by the authors) were devised: individual brainstorming (I), group brainstorming (G), I followed by G (I-G), and G followed by I (G-I). Thirty-two students were assigned to each treatment and asked to produce as many solutions as possible to a given problem. This design made it possible to determine whether treatments I-G and G-I were more effective than I or G. Rotter and Portugal were also interested in determining whether the effectiveness of the treatments depends on the type of problem being solved. Therefore, they manipulated this variable by having half the subjects within each treatment ($N = 16$) solve a tourist problem (T) and the other half solve an educational problem (E). The researchers also wished to study the effect of a third variable, sex of subject. Thus, within each treatment × problem combination, half the subjects were male ($N = 8$) and half were female. The factorial design can be depicted in the following form:

	I		G		I-G		G-I	
	T	E	T	E	T	E	T	E
Male students	8	8	8	8	8	8	8	8
Female students	8	8	8	8	8	8	8	8
						Total $N = 128$		

The preceding table illustrates how three different variables can be manipulated in a single experiment. This particular factorial design is designated a 4 × 2 × 2 experiment because four levels of one variable (treatments I, G, I-G, G-I), two levels of a second variable (problems T and E), and two levels of a third variable (male and female students) are manipulated.

Table 16.4 presents the results of an analysis of variance of the problem-solving data from Rotter and Portugal's study. Table 16.5 presents the group means on which the analysis of variance was based.[12]

Looking at Conditions (A) first, we find that there is a statistically signif-

---

11. George S. Rotter and Stephen M. Portugal, "Group and Individual Effects in Problem-Solving," *Journal of Applied Psychology* 53 (1969): 338–41.
12. Tables 16.4 and 16.5 are from ibid., pp. 339 and 340.

TABLE 16.4
Factorial Analysis of Variance of Number of Ideas

Source	df	MS	F
Conditions (A)	3	585.875	5.02*
Problems (B)	1	50.000	
Sex (C)	1	990.125	8.49*
A × B	3	390.917	3.35*
B × C	1	13.500	
A × C	3	53.208	
A × B × C	3	186.417	1.60
Error	16	116.688	

*$p < .05$.

icant F ratio. The F ratio is similar in meaning to the t ratio; it indicates that there is a significant difference between the treatment means. Since there were four treatment means (I, G, I-G, G-I), it is necessary to next do t tests to determine which pairs of treatment means differ. It was found that the two mixed treatments (I-G and G-I) produced more solutions (52.6 and 54.5, respectively) than the group problem-solving condition (42.9).[13] Contrary to the researchers' expectations, individual problem solving (I) produced significantly more problem solutions (63.8) than did the two mixed conditions (52.6 and 54.5). The F

TABLE 16.5
Mean Production of Ideas under Condition, Sex, and Problem Type

Condition	Tourist Problem			Education Problem		
	Male	Female	X̄	Male	Female	X̄
I	78.0	52.0	65.0	61.5	63.5	62.5
G	37.0	34.0	35.5	58.0	42.5	50.2
I-G	52.0	40.5	46.2	71.0	47.0	59.0
G-I	66.5	57.5	62.0	48.0	46.0	47.0

13. These means were derived by averaging the mean scores for the two problems presented in table 16.5. For example, the mean for the group problem-solving condition (42.9) was derived by calculating the mean of the two problem means (35.5 and 50.2).

ratio for the problems was not statistically significant, meaning that one problem did not elicit more solutions than the other (Tourist Problem $M = 52.2$; Education Problem $M = 54.7$). The significant F ratio for sex can be traced to the fact that males produced more problem solutions than did females (male $= 59.0$; female $= 47.9$).

Finally, there is a significant interaction between the problems and the brainstorming conditions. The meaning of this *interaction effect* can be clarified by referring to the mean scores of students in each treatment group shown in table 16.3. It can be seen that the G-I condition was more effective than the I-G condition (62.0 vs. 46.2 ideas) when solving the tourist problem. The reverse is true for the education problem: the G-I condition is less effective than the I-G condition (47.0 vs. 59.0 ideas). Thus we cannot conclude that one of these mixed conditions is more effective than the other without considering the type of problem to be solved. In other words, there is a condition by problem interaction.

The three-way interaction (A × B × C) shown in table 16.4 was not statistically significant. Three-way interactions are difficult to interpret, though, and so statistically significant interactions of this type are often ignored by researchers. Basically a three-way interaction means that the effect of a two-way interaction on the dependent variable varies according to the levels of the third factor. For example, we discussed above the significant two-way interaction involving brainstorming conditions (I-G and G-I) and problems. Suppose it was found that this two-way interaction occurs in male subjects, but not in female subjects. This would constitute a three-way interaction because the interaction between two factors (brainstorming conditions and problems) is contingent upon a third factor (sex of the problem solver). Three-way interactions are most meaningful when they have been hypothesized in advance of doing the experiment and when they have been replicated across experiments.

The differences between treatment group means in this experiment, and in the 2 × 2 experiment by Gottlieb, were tested for statistical significance by analysis of variance. Multiple regression is now often used to accomplish the same purpose. We shall present an example of this use of multiple regression when we discuss aptitude-treatment experiments later in the chapter.

Solomon Four-Group Design

The Solomon four-group design is a special case of a factorial design. The **Solomon four-group design** is used to achieve three purposes: (1) to assess the effect of the experimental treatment relative to the control treatment; (2) to assess the effect of a pretest; and (3) to assess the interaction between pretest and treatment conditions.

You will recall from the preceding chapter that pretest sensitization is a possible threat to the ecological validity of an experiment. Different experimental results might occur if a pretest is administered to the experimental and control groups than if a pretest is not administered. The pretest might have an effect on student achievement or attitudes because it provides an opportunity to *practice* or think about the content incorporated in the pretest. Also, the pretest might have a special effect on the experimental group students because it *sensitizes* them to study specific content incorporated in the experimental treatment. The pretest would not have this effect on the control group because, by definition, they are not exposed to the experimental treatment content.

A systematic investigation of pretest effects can be made by using the Solomon four-group design. Two factors—pretest and treatment—are varied in this design, as shown in this diagram:

> Group 1. R O X O
> Group 2. R O   O
> Group 3. R   X O
> Group 4. R   O
>   *Key:* R = random assignment
>   X = experimental treatment
>   O = observation, either a pretest or posttest

If the pretest provides a practice effect, this should result in higher posttest performance by groups receiving the pretest (1 and 2), than by groups not receiving the pretest (3 and 4). If the pretest sensitizes the experimental group to study specific content, this should result in a pretest-treatment interaction. Specifically, there should be a greater difference on the posttest between groups 1 and 3 than between groups 2 and 4. This is because a sensitization effect means that the pretest facilitates the learning of the experimental group but not of the control group.

The Solomon four-group design is well-illustrated in an experiment conducted by Wayne Welch and Herbert Walberg.[14] The purpose of the experiment was to determine the possible effect of pretests in curriculum evaluation. The experimental treatment was an innovative curriculum program called Harvard Project Physics. The control treatment consisted of the regular physics curriculum taught in secondary schools at the time of the experiment. The sample consisted of 57 high school physics classes, which were randomly assigned to the experimental curriculum ($N = 36$) and to the regular physics

---

14. Wayne W. Welch and Herbert J. Walberg, "Pretest and Sensitization Effects in Curriculum Evaluation," *American Educational Research Journal* 7 (1970): 605–14.

TABLE 16.6

Descriptive Statistics for Solomon Four-Group Experiment

Group	Condition	N	Physics Achievement		Understanding Science		Process Knowledge		Physics Interest		Physical Science Interest		Physics Activities	
			Mean	SD	Mean	SD	Mean	SD	Mean	SD	Mean	SD	Mean	SD
	Experimental													
1	Pretested	330	24.4	6.2	35.6	8.3	108.9	11.6	4.91	1.55	2.42	.44	2.69	.75
2	Not Pretested	350	24.1	6.2	35.4	8.0	107.8	10.8	4.91	1.64	2.38	.47	2.64	.72
	Control													
3	Pretested	180	23.6	7.3	35.0	8.0	108.2	10.8	4.60	1.71	2.28	.48	2.59	.87
4	Not Pretested	180	22.6	6.7	34.1	8.6	106.6	10.8	4.75	1.78	2.35	.50	2.64	.86

Note: Ns vary slightly among tests.

curriculum (N = 21). A total of six pretests and six posttests were administered to measure these variables:

1. Physics achievement
2. General understanding of science
3. Knowledge of scientific processes
4. Interest in physics
5. Interest in physical science
6. Participation in extracurricular physics activities

All students took the posttests, but only a random half of the experimental and control group students took the pretests. This procedure resulted in the four groups needed for the Solomon four-group design: experimental group-pretest present, experimental group-pretest absent, control group-pretest present, and control group-pretest absent.

Statistical Analysis

The first step in analyzing data from a Solomon four-group experiment is to compute descriptive statistics for each of the groups. Table 16.6 shows the mean and standard deviation of each group's scores on the six posttests.[15]
    The next step is to determine whether the posttest scores are affected by the factors being studied: pretest, curriculum, and pretest-curriculum interaction. Analysis of variance is commonly used for this purpose. (Multiple regression can also be used to determine the effects of these factors.) Table 16.7 shows the results of the analysis of variance.[16] The effect of treatment (first row of results) is statistically significant for three of the posttests: Students in the experimental physics curriculum had reliably higher scores than control group students on the physics achievement test, the measure of physics interest, and the measure of interest in physical science.
    The effect of the pretest (second row of table 16.7) was not statistically significant for any of the posttests. If you look back to table 16.6, you can see that this result makes sense. The differences between the mean posttest scores of groups 1 and 2 and of groups 3 and 4 are slight. Also, none of the interaction effects (third row) are statistically significant. This result means that the effect of the pretests on the posttests is not reliably different for the experimental and control groups. According to Welch and Walberg, these results suggest that ". . . pretest and sensitization effects are not serious problems when the treatment occurs in a normal classroom situation over the academic year and

15. Table 16.6 is from ibid., p. 611.
16. Table 16.7 is from ibid., p. 612.

TABLE 16.7

Analysis of Variance for Solomon Four-Group Experiment

		Cognitive						Affective					
		Physics Achievement		Understanding Science		Process Knowledge		Physics Interest		Physical Science Interest		Physics Activities	
Effect	df	MS	F	MS	F	MS	F	MS	F	MS	F	MS	F
Treatment	1	4330.21	7.08**	4408.84	3.38	23788.01	2.02	115.39	4.43*	38.28	6.56**	1.97	<1
Pretest	1	1013.74	1.66	1136.25	<1	43973.66	3.74	7.08	<1	0.15	<1	0.15	<1
Interaction	1	401.40	<1	687.99	<1	956.26	<1	11.12	<1	18.08	3.10	12.40	1.62
Within		611.30		1304.02		11772.21		26.06		5.83		7.67	
N		1033		1052		1060		1055		1050		1049	

*p < .05
**p < .01

when test taking is part of the daily routine. In designing curriculum evaluation studies under these circumstances, one might be inclined to dismiss elaborate allowances for detecting sensitization effects."[17]

    The Solomon four-group design is a powerful experimental design. Its
main drawback is that it requires a rather large sample and much researcher
effort. The effort is justified if there is a high probability that pretesting will
have an effect on the experimental treatment and if the researcher wishes to
measure this effect. Otherwise, the pretest-posttest control-group design or the
posttest-only control-group design would be the designs of choice because they
are more efficient.

Types of Treatment Variables

In discussing Rotter and Portugal's study, we stated that three variables were
manipulated. Strictly speaking, only the type of brainstorming group and
problem was "manipulated." One cannot manipulate the sex of the subject; it
is a given of the situation (i.e., the experimenter cannot manipulate subjects to
make them male or female). Campbell and Stanley[18] have provided a useful
classification of the types of independent variables that might appear in an
educational experiment along this dimension of manipulability:

1. Manipulated variables, such as teaching method, assignable at will by the
   experimenter
2. Potentially manipulable aspects, such as school subject studied, that the experimenter might assign in some random way to the pupils he is using, but
   rarely does
3. Relatively fixed aspects of the environment, such as community or school
   or socioeconomic level, not under the direct control of the experimenter but
   serving as explicit bases for stratification in the experiment
4. "Organismic" characteristics of pupils, such as age, height, weight, and sex
5. Response characteristics of pupils, such as scores on various tests.

As Campbell and Stanley point out, the experimenter's primary interest is usually in the class 1 variable. Variables in classes 3, 4, and 5 are used to group
subjects in order to determine how generalizable the effects of manipulated
variables are. For example, the researcher's primary independent variable may
be a new teaching method. She might also group students by intelligence level
(a class 5 variable, since intelligence is usually determined by a test score) in

17. Ibid., p. 613.
18. Campbell and Stanley, "Designs for Research on Teaching," p. 200.

order to determine whether the teaching method is effective for students of all intelligence levels or just for students of a particular intelligence level. This type of research is discussed in the section immediately following.

Aptitude-Treatment Interaction Research

Different students have different learning styles and aptitudes. Therefore, a single instructional method or program may not be suitable for all students. Improvement in education may result from efforts to match instructional methods and programs with students who are best able to learn from them. In recent years a line of educational experimentation has been developed to explore effective "matches" between learner characteristics and different instructional methods. This line of experimentation is sometimes called aptitude-treatment interaction (ATI) research.[19] The purpose of **ATI research** is to determine whether the effects of different instructional methods are influenced by the cognitive or personality characteristics of the learner.

ATI research does not assume that one instructional method is better than another; nor is it assumed that students with certain characteristics are better learners than others. Instead, ATI research proceeds under the assumption that the two factors (method and learner characteristics) may interact in ways that have educational significance. Interactions are revealed by designing factorial experiments similar to the studies by Rotter and Portugal and by Gottlieb described above.

There are usually two independent variables in the factorial design. The first independent variable may be teaching method, school subject, type of school, or similar instructional variable. These variables correspond to the first three types of independent variables in Campbell and Stanley's classification (see above): manipulated variables, potentially manipulated variables, or relatively fixed environmental variables. The other independent variable is a student characteristic such as an aptitude, personality dimension, level of academic achievement, or learning style. The initial focus of ATI research was on aptitudes, hence the designation "aptitude-treatment interaction." More recently the label "attribute-treatment interaction" has been used to indicate that a wide range of learner characteristics—not just aptitude—may interact with instructional methods.[20] Attribute variables correspond to the last two types of independent variables in Campbell and Stanley's classification: "organismic" characteristics of students and response characteristics of students.

19. Surveys of ATI research have been done by Cronbach and Snow and by Berliner and Cahen (see Annotated References at the end of this chapter).
20. Sigmund Tobias, "Achievement Treatment Interactions." *Review of Educational Research* 46 (1976): 61–74.

An example of ATI research is the study on calculus instruction conducted by Ernest Pascarella.[21] The experiment compared two methods of college instruction: a personalized system of instruction (PSI) and conventional instruction consisting of lectures and problem-solving sessions. PSI is a form of individualized instruction that incorporates (1) individual student pacing, (2) mastery of material prior to proceeding to the next unit, (3) use of student tutors, (4) use of study guides, and (5) use of lectures to motivate and stimulate rather than to impart information. Pascarella criticized past studies on PSI for making simple global comparisons of PSI and conventional instruction. He hypothesized that ". . . PSI may be most effective for a subgroup of students at certain levels of a particular trait, while conventional methods may be more appropriate for another subgroup of students at different levels of the same trait. For still another subgroup, achievement may be unaffected by instructional treatment."[22]

College students in this research project were assigned to receive a semester of calculus instruction by PSI or by conventional methods. Before beginning the course, each student completed personality and achievement measures.[23] One of these was the Mathematics Placement Examination (MPE), a measure of mathematics aptitude and achievement. Students were classified as low, middle, or high in level of prior mathematics preparation depending upon their MPE score. Pascarella hypothesized that PSI instruction would be of most benefit to students at the lowest levels of prior mathematics preparation. Students in both instructional groups (PSI and conventional) received the same end-of-semester examination. The score on this examination provided the student achievement measure.

The independent variables of the experiment were organized into a 2 × 3 factorial design. There were two levels of instruction (PSI and conventional) and three levels of prior mathematics preparation. The results of the analysis of variance of the treatment groups' performance on the final examination are shown in table 16.8.[24] The significant F ratios for the two independent variables indicate that students in PSI and conventional instruction differed significantly from each other on the final examination; and that students who vary in level of prior mathematics preparation differed significantly from one another on the same examination. The interaction between the two independent variables also was statistically significant.

21. Ernest T. Pascarella, "Interaction of Motivation, Mathematics Preparation, and Instructional Method in a PSI and Conventionally Taught Calculus Course," *AV Communication Review* 25 (1977): 25–41.
22. Ibid., p. 26.
23. Selected measures and results of Pascarella's study are presented above. The student should read the published report (see note 21) for additional details.
24. Table 16.8 is adapted from Pascarella, "Interaction of Motivation," p. 34.

These findings are depicted graphically in figure 16.1.[25] First, we observe that each of the PSI groups outperformed each of the conventional instruction groups. It is also clear that the superiority of PSI is greater for some types of students than for others. This reflects the significant interaction effect shown in table 16.8. Students low in prior mathematics preparation did much better under PSI than under conventional instruction. Students high in mathematics preparation did just about as well under both methods.

Assuming these findings are replicated in other research studies, they may have prescriptive value for educators. If one is teaching students who have a weak background in mathematics, it may be important to design a learning environment that incorporates elements found in PSI. If one is teaching students who have a good background in mathematics, design of the learning

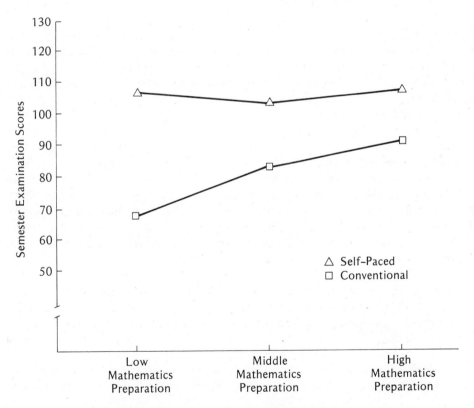

Figure 16.1   Mathematics preparation × instructional method interaction.

25. Figure 16.1 is from ibid., p. 35.

TABLE 16.8

Analysis of Variance of Final Examination Scores

Source	df	MS	F
Mathematics Preparation (A)	2	1830.20	8.13*
Instructional Method (B)	1	8732.74	38.78*
A × B	2	1783.47	7.92*

*$p < .001$.

environment may not be so critical; conventional and individualized instruction may be of about equal effectiveness.

The data from this ATI experiment, and the other factorial experiments described above, were analyzed by the statistical technique of analysis of variance. It is also possible to analyze the data using multiple regression. This statistical technique was used in an ATI experiment conducted by Robert Reiser.[26] The experiment compared three variations of PSI (Personalized System of Instruction). In one treatment students were rewarded by adding points to their test scores if they mastered unit tests by suggested deadlines; another treatment penalized students by subtracting test score points if they failed to master unit tests by suggested deadlines; in the control treatment suggested deadlines were presented, but they were not linked to rewards or penalties.

Locus of control, measured by the Internal-External Locus of Control Scale (I-E scale), was the student attribute variable examined in the experiment. High scores on the scale indicate an external locus of control, meaning that a person believes rewards and penalties are under the control of others. Low scores indicate internality, meaning that a person believes rewards and penalties are contingent upon his own actions. Reiser hypothesized that "internal" students would do better than "external" students on the posttest irrespective of the PSI treatment variation to which they were assigned. He also hypothesized that "external" students would do better in the reward and penalty treatments because these contingencies would prompt them to pass the unit tests on time; they would do less well in the control treatment because there were no external contingencies to motivate their behavior.

Sixty undergraduate students were randomly assigned to the three treatments, each of which was a variation of a PSI course on speech communica-

26. Robert A. Reiser, "Interaction Between Locus of Control and Three Pacing Procedures in a Personalized System of Instruction Course," *Educational Communications and Technology Journal* 28 (1980): 194–202.

tion. At the end of the course all students took a 60-item final examination, which comprised the dependent variable for the experiment. Reiser used four predictor variables in the multiple regression analysis: students' gradepoint average (GPA—used here as a general measure of academic ability), their I-E scale score, their treatment-group assignment,[27] and a variable that represents the interaction between I-E scores and treatment group. Final examination scores formed the criterion variable.

Results of the multiple regression analysis are summarized in table 16.9.[28] You can see that GPA predicted 14 percent of the variance in the final examination scores. I-E scores and treatment together accounted for another 5 percent of the variance. The ATI effect accounted for 17 percent of the variance, which is quite substantial. (It is unusual to find ATI effects accounting for more than 5 percent of the variance in the dependent variable.) The "residual" figure is simply the amount of variance in the final examination scores left unexplained by the predictor variables.

The multiple regression analysis shown in table 16.9 tells us that there is a statistically significant ATI effect, but it does not reveal the nature of the interaction. The researcher can "see" the interaction by first constructing a separate regression equation for each treatment group. The equations are then used to plot a regression line for each treatment group on the same graph. The graph for the data in Reiser's experiment is shown in figure 16.2.[29] The horizontal line (the abscissa) represents the I-E scale, and the vertical line (the ordinate) represents the exam scores.

TABLE 16.9

**Summary of Multiple Regression Analysis
in Locus of Control × PSI Treatment
Experiment**

Source	R^2 Increment	F	P
GPA	.14	11.20	.01
I-E Score (A) Treatment (B)	.05	1.44	N.S.
A × B	.17	6.80	.01
Residual	.64		

N.S. = not significant.

27. Treatments can be assigned artificial scores, using a procedure known as dummy-coding, so that they can be used as a predictor variable in a multiple regression analysis.
28. Table 16.9 adapted from Reiser, "Interaction Between Locus of Control," p. 197.
29. Figure 16.2 is from ibid., p. 198.

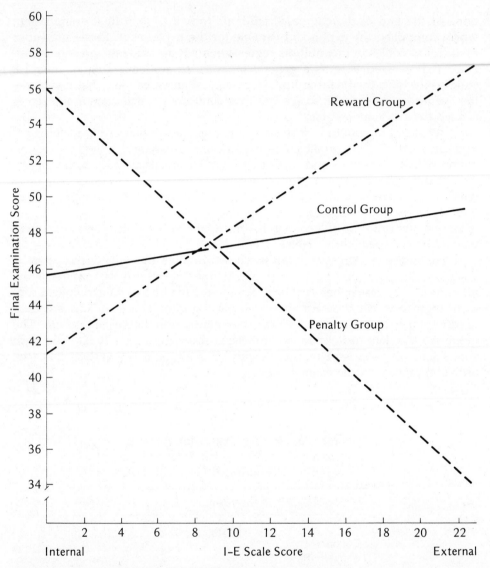

Figure 16.2 Relationship between final examination performance and scores on the I-E Scale.

The results shown in figure 16.2 did not support Reiser's hypotheses. "Internal" students outperformed "external" students in the penalty treatment, but not in the other two treatments. "External" students did better in the reward treatment than in the control treatment; however, they did worse in the penalty treatment than in the control treatment. Although the hypotheses were not confirmed, the observed ATI effects are quite interesting in their own right.

Counterbalanced Experiments

All the experimental designs considered in chapter 15 and in this chapter share one feature in common. Each subject is assigned to just one treatment condition. In a 2 × 2 factorial experiment, for example, there are four treatment conditions. Each subject is assigned to just one of these conditions. Some research problems, however, can be investigated by assigning each subject to more than one treatment condition. The advantage of assigning subjects to several treatments is that the experiment can be done with fewer subjects. Thus, subject recruitment is easier, and financial expenses of conducting the experiment may be reduced. Another advantage is that the statistical analysis of the data is more sensitive because each subject is "matched" with himself across treatments.

If subjects participate in more than one treatment, the effect of a treatment can become confounded with its order of administration relative to the other treatments. The influence of order of treatment administration on a dependent variable is called an **order effect.** For example, an order effect can occur if subjects become fatigued by participating in several treatments. They may do less well on the posttest associated with the last-administered treatment, not because this treatment is less effective, but because they were fatigued from responding to the demands of the previously administered treatments. Order effects can also occur due to the subject's opportunity to practice during each treatment. In many educational experiments the treatments represent different instructional methods. If a subject is assigned to several such treatments, he may do better on the posttest associated with the last-administered treatment than on the other posttests. The reason for the improved performance may be because the subject had the opportunity to practice the skills measured by the posttest during earlier-administered treatments, rather than because the last-administered treatment is superior.

Counterbalanced designs are used to avoid the problems of interpretation due to order effects. In a **counterbalanced experiment,** each subject is administered several treatments, but the order of administering the treatments is varied across subjects to eliminate the possible confounding of order effects with treatment effects. An example of counterbalancing is a recent experiment on reading conducted by Philip DiStefano, Michael Noe, and Sheila Valencia.[30] These researchers were interested in the effects of purpose for reading and text difficulty on reading rate. The basic design involved the manipulation of two factors (a 2 × 2 factorial experiment).[31] One factor was text difficulty. Two text passages of approximately 1400 words each were used to represent this factor. One passage had a readability level of eighth grade, and the other had a readability level of eleventh grade. The other factor was purpose for reading. Half the subjects were asked to read each passage for the purpose of gaining an *overview* of it. The other half of the subjects read each passage for the purpose of gaining *detailed* knowledge of its content.

This type of 2 × 2 design would normally require the formation of four treatment groups, shown in the following diagram:

	Overview	Detail
8th-Grade Level	Group A	Group B
11th-Grade Level	Group C	Group D

The researchers only needed to form two treatment groups, though, because each subject participated in two of the treatment variations. Half of the subjects were randomly assigned to read the eighth-grade passage for detail and then to read the eleventh-grade passage for overview. The other half of the subjects first read the eleventh-grade passage for overview and then the eighth-grade passage for detail. This design can be represented as follows:

Group A: 8—Detail   11—Overview
Group B: 11—Detail   8—Overview

You will note that the order of administering the easy (8th-grade level) and difficult (11th-grade level) passages was counterbalanced: group A read the easy passage first, whereas group B read it second. You will also note that the purpose-for-reading factor was not counterbalanced; both groups read for detail in the first-administered treatment. DiStefano and his colleagues explained that this factor was not counterbalanced because previous researchers had found that the purpose-for-reading treatments are not susceptible to order effects.

Analysis of variance is generally used to examine the data resulting from

30. Philip DiStefano, Michael Noe, and Sheila Valencia, "Measurement of the Effects of Purpose and Passage Difficulty on Reading Flexibility," *Journal of Educational Psychology* 73 (1981): 602–6.
31. The experiment included additional elements (a grade-level factor and a practice test) not discussed here.

a counterbalanced experiment. In the experiment described above, statistically significant differences were found for the main effects of purpose-for-reading ($F = 262.43$, $p < .001$) and for passage difficulty ($F = 13.24$, $p < .001$). The interactive effect of these two factors was also significant ($F = 13.24$, $p < .001$). When specific comparisons were done, it was found that students read the easy and difficult passages at the same rate when they were concentrating on detail. Students read the easy passage much faster than the difficult passage, however, when their purpose was to get an overview.

We conclude this discussion of counterbalancing by noting that it can be used in situations other than the assignment of subjects to more than one treatment. In an experiment conducted by the second author and his colleagues,[32] each teacher-experimenter was assigned to teach four different treatments. (Each student participated in a single treatment, so there was no need to counterbalance treatments with respect to students.) To avoid the possibility of an order effect, each experimenter taught the four treatments in a different order. Thus the treatments were counterbalanced with respect to the order in which the experimenter taught them.

Another situation that may require counterbalancing is order of testing. Suppose two posttests are to be administered to each subject in an experiment. If there is a possibility that the order in which the posttests are given will affect subjects' scores, this factor can be counterbalanced. A random half of the subjects in each treatment group can take posttest A followed by posttest B. The other half of the subjects can take posttest B followed by posttest A.

Variation in Factorial Designs

The design and analysis of factorial experiments is a complicated matter. There are many factorial designs to select from, depending upon: the number of independent variables, the nature of the independent variables, whether subjects receive repeated measures of the same variable, whether there are unequal numbers of subjects in each treatment group, the scale and distribution properties of scores on the dependent variables, and the need for a covariate to compensate for initial differences between treatment groups. It is useless to develop a sound research hypothesis and to carefully execute the experiment unless the proper factorial design has been chosen. The student who is planning a factorial experiment is advised to consult a reference textbook on experimental design (see Annotated References) and to consult an expert in the area of factorial design and statistical analysis.

32. Meredith D. Gall, Beatrice A. Ward, David C. Berliner, Leonard S. Cahen, Philip H. Winne, Janet D. Elashoff, and George C. Stanton, "Effects of Questioning Techniques and Recitation on Student Learning," *American Educational Research Journal* 15 (1978): 175–99.

Single-Subject Designs

As its label implies, the distinguishing feature of a **single-subject experiment** is the fact that the sample of subjects is one. If two or more subjects are treated as one group, this also is considered a single-subject experiment.

The single-subject experiment is particularly well suited to research on behavior modification. The field of behavior modification seeks to change the behavior of individuals by applying experimentally validated techniques such as social and token reinforcement, fading, desensitization, and discrimination training.[33] As an educational strategy, behavior modification is used extensively in classroom management, skill development, and training of the handicapped. It also is employed widely in counseling, psychotherapy, institutional caretaking, and in drug research. Many single-subject experiments of interest to educators appear in the *Journal of Applied Behavior Analysis,* but this type of experiment appears increasingly in other journals as well.

Single-subject experiments should not be equated with the case-study method of investigation. Both focus on the single individual, yet they differ in degree of experimental control. As we discuss later, single-subject designs use several procedures to achieve experimental control: reliability checks on the experimenter's observations of the subject's behavior, frequent observations of the behaviors targeted for change, description of the treatment in sufficient detail to permit replication, and replication of treatment effects within the experiment. In contrast, case studies usually are limited to impressionistic descriptions of a student or group problem and how the author intervened to solve the problem. Quantitative data and replication attempts are not usually reported.

Some researchers think that the single-subject experiment is a watered-down, easier version of one of the multisubject designs[34] presented earlier in this chapter and in chapter 15. This is not true. Experimenters who work with single-subject designs are equally as concerned with problems of internal validity and external validity as multisubject experimenters. Most single-subject designs are rigorous, time-consuming, and may involve as much data collection as a multisubject control-group design.

A study by Hill Walker and Nancy Buckley illustrates the use of the single-subject experiment.[35] The purpose of their experiment was to modify the

33. There are many publications on the educational uses of behavior modification techniques, including Albert Bandura, *Principles of Behavior Modification* (New York: Holt, Rinehart, & Winston, 1969).
34. We use the term *multisubject* experiment to refer to the experimental designs presented earlier in this chapter and in chapter 15. These designs are also called *between subject* or *group* experiments.
35. Hill M. Walker and Nancy K. Buckley, "The Use of Positive Reinforcement in Conditioning Attending Behavior," *Journal of Applied Behavior Analysis* 1 (1968): 245–50. Figure 16.3, on page 708, is reprinted from this article.

classroom attending behavior of Philip, a nine-year-old boy in the fourth grade. Philip was referred for treatment because of such deviant classroom behaviors as provoking other children, not completing tasks, talking out of turn, and being easily distracted from academic tasks. An experimental treatment was devised to increase Philip's attending behavior and to decrease his distractive behavior. A series of 40-minute treatment sessions were conducted in a special room where extraneous stimuli were reduced to a minimum. Each session was divided into three 10-minute study sessions.

Philip was observed for a period of time to determine his baseline rate of attending to academic tasks. Then the experimental treatment was initiated: Philip was told that he would earn a point for each time interval that he worked on a task with no distractions. The time intervals began at 30 seconds and gradually were lengthened to 10 minutes. When Philip had accumulated enough points, he was allowed to exchange them for a toy model. The reinforcement contingency (i.e., awarding of a point dependent upon correct behavior) was withdrawn after he had completed three 10-minute study periods in succession without distraction. The act of withdrawing the treatment sometimes is called **extinction** by behavioral researchers.

Observational data on Philip's attending behavior were carefully recorded during the three phases of the experiment—baseline, treatment, and extinction. Attending behavior included looking at the assigned page, working problems, and recording answers. Nonattending behaviors included looking away from the text, bringing an extraneous object into his field of vision, and doodling or making other unnecessary marks. Interobserver reliability was checked on several occasions; reliability remained at .90 or above throughout the experiment.

Figure 16.3 presents the results of the experiment in graph form. Each point on the graph has two coordinates: the abscissa (horizontal line) indicating the number of the treatment session during which the observation was made; and the ordinate (vertical line), which indicates the percentage of time that the student was attending during the session. The vertical broken lines separate the three phases of the experiment.

The graph clearly shows that the student had a low initial rate of attending (mean of baseline observations = 33 percent). Introduction of the treatment, which consisted of a reinforcement contingency, led to a high rate of attending (mean of treatment observations = 93 percent). When the reinforcement contingency was withdrawn, the rate of attending declined dramatically (mean of extinction observations = 44 percent). In the next phase of the experiment, which we will not discuss here, a similar reinforcement contingency was used successfully by Philip's regular teacher to increase his attending rate.

The major conclusion of this study is that a particular cause (use of reinforcement contingency) had a particular effect (increase in attending rate). The

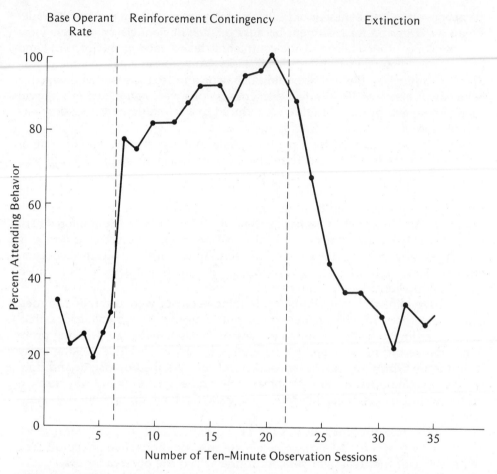

Figure 16.3   Percentage of attending behavior in successive time samples during the individual conditioning program.

use of baseline and extinction observations provided control to increase the internal validity of the experiment. Walker and Buckley note: "Upon withdrawal of reinforcement contingency, the behavior returned to pretreatment levels, thus indicating that the alteration in behavior was due to the manipulated, experimental variable rather than to the influence of an unknown or chance variable."

Baseline-treatment-extinction is one of many single-subject designs. In the following sections we describe general features of single-subject design, steps to follow in using some of the more common designs, and statistical techniques for analyzing single-subject data. We conclude by discussing factors to consider in choosing between multisubject and single-subject designs.

General Design Considerations

Single-subject experiments should be designed to have high internal validity. As is true of multisubject designs, the internal validity of a single-subject design is a function of the researcher's ability to rule out factors other than the treatment variable as possible causes of changes in the dependent variable. In multisubject experiments, internal validity is achieved primarily by random assignment of subjects to the experimental treatment and a control condition. Since $N = 1$ in single-subject research, random assignment and control groups are not possible. Internal validity is achieved by other design techniques, which are described below. These techniques are not exclusive to single-subject designs, but they are especially important to them.

   Reliable observation. Single subject designs typically require many observations of behavior. If the observations are unreliable, they will obscure treatment effects. Certain precautions and procedures should be followed in making observations, including careful training of observers, operational definition of the behaviors to be observed, periodic checks of observer reliability, and control of observer bias. When appropriate, the researcher should consider measurement of behavioral products (e.g., number of problems solved in a school assignment) as a substitute for observation of behavior. These procedures are discussed in chapter 10 and in works on single-subject design (see Annotated References, especially Hersen and Barlow).

   The simplest procedure is to target one behavior for observation throughout the experiment. It is possible to monitor additional behaviors, but as each new behavior is added to the research design, observational procedures become increasingly complicated.

   Repeated measurement. In the typical multisubject design, data are collected at two points in time: before (pretest) and after (posttest) the experimental treatment. Single-subject designs require many more measurements, since the behavior of individuals varies even within short time intervals. Consider the fact that the Walker and Buckley experiment presented above had three phases: baseline, treatment, and withdrawal of treatment. If the student's attending behavior were measured only once in each phase, it would be impossible to interpret whether variations in rate of attending were a function of the treatment variable or of other naturally occurring events. The use of frequent measurements provides a clearer, more reliable description of how the student's behavior naturally varied and how it varied in response to the treatment condition. Furthermore, statistical significance tests of single-subject data are more powerful if many measurements of the dependent variable are available.

Because of the need for repeated measurements in single-subject design, it is important to standardize the measurement procedure. Preferably each measurement occasion would involve the same observers, the same instructions to the subject, and the same environmental conditions. Otherwise, treatment effects are likely to be contaminated with measurement effects.

Description of experimental conditions. The researcher should provide a precise description of each experimental condition that is important for replication. Some single-subject designs require reintroduction of the baseline and the treatment variable. For example, the baseline condition appeared twice in the Walker and Buckley experiment. If the conditions involving the baseline or the treatment variable are not specified precisely, they will be difficult to replicate within the experiment. As a consequence, the internal validity of the experiment is threatened. Furthermore, imprecise specification makes it difficult for other researchers to replicate the treatment and baseline conditions, thus threatening the external validity of the experiment.

Baseline and treatment stability. The baseline in single-subject designs is the natural frequency of the target behavior before the experimental variable has been introduced. If the baseline frequency of occurrence did not vary at all during the period of observation, it would be easy to assess the effect of the treatment variable. Yet most behaviors vary. If the variation is too great, the researcher will have difficulty in separating treatment effects from naturally occurring changes in the subject's behavior.

One may use a standard for determining when a baseline has stabilized, for example, no more than 5 percent range of variation from the mean over a period of ten observations. There are occasions, though, when this type of standard is inappropriate. An example of this is a researcher who plans to use an experimental intervention with a subject whose behavior is systematically worsening or improving. If the subject's behavior is systematically improving during the baseline period, the researcher is faced with a difficult problem. If the subject continues to improve during the treatment phase, one could easily argue that the continued improvement was due to some condition that existed during the baseline period rather than to a treatment effect. In this situation the researcher should consider withholding the treatment variable until baseline improvement has peaked and then stabilized.

The same need for stability applies to the treatment phase of a single-subject design. Suppose a researcher has planned four treatment sessions. No effects appear after the first three sessions, but improvement is apparent after the fourth session. Should the researcher discontinue treatment, as planned? It is probably advisable in this situation to continue treatment until a stable, interpretable pattern of treatment effects has emerged.

Length of baseline and treatment phases. As a general rule, there should be approximately the same length of time and number of measurements in each phase of a single-subject design. Otherwise, the imbalance complicates the statistical analysis and interpretation of treatment effects. There are occasions, though, when the rule of equal phases conflicts with the need to maintain baseline or treatment conditions until a stable pattern of measurements has emerged. The researcher may also need to maintain baseline or treatment conditions longer than intended because of institutional or ethical factors. One way to overcome this problem is to do several pilot studies to investigate baseline and treatment parameters. These parameters can be used to design a more rigorous experiment in which baseline and treatment conditions are equalized in duration and number of measurements.

A-B-A Designs

A-B-A designs are single-subject experiments in which *A* stands for the baseline condition and *B* stands for the treatment. A-B-A designs are similar to the time-series designs described earlier in this chapter, except for the fact that the latter are multisubject experiments.

A-B Design

The **A-B design** is the simplest of the single-subject designs. The researcher begins by selecting a subject for the experiment, one or more target behaviors, measures of the target behaviors, and experimental treatment. Then the target behavior is measured repeatedly during the baseline period (A). Finally, the experimental treatment (B) is administered, while the target behavior continues to be measured.

The A-B time-series design is low in internal validity.[36] If the B measurements are reliably different from the A measurements (see the section on statistical analysis on p. 716), one may reasonably conclude that a change occurred from the baseline phase to the treatment phase. It is difficult to attribute the change to a treatment effect, however, since other factors cannot be ruled out, these factors might be other events occurring during the treatment phase or the effects of testing during the baseline period. The A-B design should be used only when no suitable alternative is available or when the researcher intends it as a pilot study to be followed by more rigorous designs.

---

36. The uses and internal validity problems of the A-B design are discussed in D. T. Campbell, "Reforms as Experiments," *American Psychologist* 24 (1969): 409–29.

A-B-A Design

Walker and Buckley's experiment on attending behavior in a young boy exemplifies the **A-B-A design.** The first phase was a baseline condition (A) in which the student's natural rate of attending was observed. The second phase was a treatment condition (B) in which a reinforcement contingency was established. In the third phase the treatment condition was removed, resulting in a return to baseline conditions (A). The A-B-A design follows the same steps as the A-B design, except that a second baseline condition is added. The second baseline typically involves **withdrawal** of the treatment, as in the Walker and Buckley experiment. It is also possible to bring about **reversal** of the treatment in the second baseline condition. For example, in the Walker and Buckley experiment, the researchers might have reinforced the student for "not attending" behavior in the second baseline condition.

The A-B-A design has good internal validity. If the target behavior changes as expected in each phase of the experiment, one can conclude that the changes were due to the effect of the treatment variable. One difficulty with this design is that the experiment ends on a negative note, since the treatment (presumably positive in nature) is withdrawn or reversed. This condition may be ethically unacceptable to the researcher and to others involved in the experiment.

Another limitation of this design, and of all baseline designs, is that the observed treatment effect is dependent upon the particular baseline conditions included in the experiment. Assuming a reliable A-B change is found, one can conclude only that the effect will occur reliably for that particular baseline. Therefore, it is important to describe the baseline conditions precisely. This restriction is similar to the pretest limitation in multisubject designs that include a pretest (see discussion of internal validity in previous chapter). Reliable treatment effects found in such designs cannot be presumed to be independent of the particular pretest that was used to discover the effects.

A-B-A-B Design

This design overcomes the ethical issue that may arise with the A-B-A experiment. In the **A-B-A-B design,** the experiment ends with reintroduction of the treatment variable. Furthermore, this design provides two within-subject replications of the treatment variable. In using this design, the researcher needs to plan for four phases: initial period of baseline observation, initial introduction of the treatment variable, withdrawal or reversal of the treatment variable (second baseline), and reintroduction of the treatment variable. If the measurements of the target behavior vary as expected, the researcher has a convincing demonstration of the effects of the treatment variable.

Gary Woodward, Duane Ollendick, and Kimberly Butcher used an

A-B-A-B design to test the effectiveness of a technique for controlling disruptive classroom behaviors.[37] The "single subject" in this experiment was a second-grade classroom consisting of 14 boys and 14 girls. You will recall that if two or more subjects are treated as one group, this is considered a single-subject experiment.

The technique was a clock-light wing device placed in the classroom so that it was easily visible to all students. The light remained on whenever the children were engaged in instructionally relevant behavior. If the light remained on for a specified period of time, the whole class received a predetermined reward. The light was switched off whenever a target misbehavior by a student occurred. Talking without permission, leaving one's seat, and pushing or shoving were among the six target misbehaviors. The researcher predicted that the clock-light wing device and related procedures would reduce the incidence of student misbehavior. An A-B-A-B design was used to test the prediction.

Table 16.10 shows the mean number of student misbehaviors per school day over each phase of the experiment.[38] Introduction of the treatment resulted in a dramatic decrease in the frequency of student misbehavior. Following withdrawal of the clock-light wing device, student misbehavior increased slightly. In the final treatment phase, the device was reintroduced but without class rewards for absence of misbehavior. Even with this change in the treatment, student misbehavior decreased again. The fact that the dependent variable (student misbehavior) changed as predicted in each phase of the A-B-A-B design is compelling evidence that the results were due to a treatment effect rather than to extraneous factors.

TABLE 16.10

Number of Student Misbehaviors
During Baseline and Treatment Periods

Experimental Phase	M	SD
Baseline (days 1–9)	28.22	14.25
Treatment (days 10–22)	2.54	2.99
Baseline (days 23–27)	3.40	3.58
Treatment (days 28–32)	2.10	1.70

37. Gary L. Woodward, Duane G. Ollendick, and Kimberly J. Butcher, "A Rapid, Effective Technique for Controlling Disruptive Classroom Behaviors," *Journal of Educational Research* 74 (1981): 397–99.
38. Table 16.10 adapted from ibid., p. 398.

Other A-B-A Designs

The preceding discussion presented the basic A-B-A designs. There are several other A-B-A designs, including several for investigating interaction effects involving treatments. These designs are discussed in surveys of single-subject research (see Annotated References).

Multiple-Baseline Designs

As described above, time-series designs (A-B-A) use the natural occurrence of the target behavior as a control condition for assessing treatment effects. In contrast, **multiple-baseline designs** are experiments in which conditions other than the naturally occurring target behavior are used as controls for assessing treatment effects.

Multiple-baseline designs are used when reinstatement of baseline conditions in an A-B-A type design is not possible. This problem may occur if the researcher is unable to withdraw or reverse the treatment for ethical reasons. Also, it may not be possible to demonstrate a treatment effect using an A-B-A design. That is, the target behavior may not return to the pretreatment baseline rate after the treatment is withdrawn or reversed. If this occurs, the researcher cannot conclude that the treatment had an effect, even though the target behavior changed reliably from the initial baseline phase to the treatment phase. As an alternative, the researcher can use a multiple-baseline design to investigate the treatment.

In one of the more commonly used multiple-baseline designs, several target behaviors in the same subject serve as controls for assessing treatment effects. This method was used in a single-subject experiment reported by R. Vance Hall and his associates.[39] The subject of the experiment was Lisa, a ten-year-old girl. Her mother, who was enrolled in a course on behavior management, acted as the experimenter. The purpose of the experiment was to increase the amount of time that Lisa spent on clarinet practice, a Campfire Girl project, and reading. Each of the target behaviors was defined operationally, and a classmate of the mother provided a reliability check on the observational procedures.

Figure 16.4 illustrates the design and results of the experiment. Before the initial baseline period, Lisa was told that she was to spend 30 minutes four evenings a week on each of the three target activities. Then baseline observations were made for a week (these observations are the first four data points in figure 16.4). The mean baselines for time spent on clarinet practice, the

39. R. Vance Hall, Connie Cristler, Sharon S. Cranston, and Bonnie Tucker, "Teachers and Parents as Researchers Using Multiple Baseline Designs," *Journal of Applied Behavior Analysis* 3 (1970): 247–55. Figure 16.4, on the next page, is reprinted from this article.

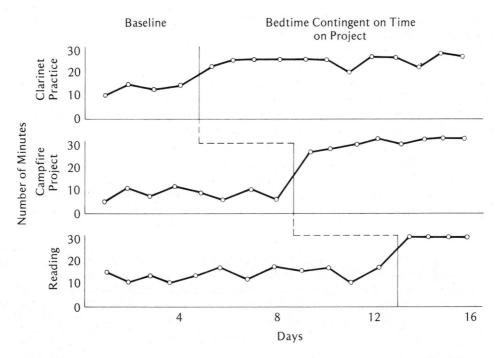

Figure 16.4   Time record. A record of time spent in clarinet practice, Campfire honors project work, and reading for book reports by a ten-year-old girl.

Campfire Girl project, and reading were 13.5 minutes, 3.5 minutes, and 11 minutes, respectively.

During the second week a treatment condition was imposed on the first target behavior—clarinet practice. The treatment condition was to require Lisa to go to bed one minute earlier for each minute less than 30 minutes that she spent practicing the clarinet. Second-week observations, shown in figure 16.4, indicate that the treatment was effective. The mean length of clarinet practice increased to 29 minutes, whereas the time lengths of the other two target behaviors were virtually unchanged. During the third week bedtime was made contingent both on length of clarinet practice and on the Campfire Girl project. Bedtime was made one minute earlier for each minute less than 30 minutes spent on clarinet practice and each minute less than 30 minutes spent on the Campfire Girl project. The data presented in figure 16.4 indicate that these target behaviors increased as expected, whereas the control behavior remained virtually unchanged. In the final week of the experiment the treatment was applied to all three target behaviors, again with the expected outcomes.

Note that in Hall's multiple-baseline design the treatment condition, once instituted, was never withdrawn or reversed. Instead, the condition was applied to different target behaviors at different points in the experiment. Since the measurements of the target behaviors varied as expected, one can reasonably conclude that the treatment condition was the cause of the changes in the child's performance.

The basic steps of the multiple-baseline design are to select a subject, an experimental treatment, and two or more operationally defined target behaviors together with reliable procedures for observing them. The research also needs to decide the order in which the target behaviors are to shift from the baseline condition to the treatment condition. Although two target behaviors are the minimum, at least three or four behaviors are recommended in order to provide several replications of the treatment effect.

An important assumption of the multiple-baseline design is that the target behaviors are independent of one another. Independence is demonstrated by a change in the target behavior to which the treatment is being applied while other target behaviors maintain a stable baseline rate. If other behaviors change reliably from baseline, the multiple-baseline design is invalid. In effect, the experiment becomes an A-B design with multiple target behaviors. The problem of nonindependence is analogous to a multisubject control-group design in which the control group somehow receives the same treatment as the experimental group. Contamination has occurred, and so the control-group data no longer are a meaningful contrast for assessing changes in the experimental group.

The multiple-baseline design, like other experimental designs, can be used to make causal inferences. It is generally considered weaker than A-B-A designs, however, because the effects of withdrawal or reversal of the treatment condition are not demonstrated.

Other Multiple-Baseline Designs

A variety of multiple-baseline designs have been developed to solve different research problems. Some of these designs involve use of multiple subjects or multiple stimulus settings to provide baseline control. The design discussed above used multiple target behaviors to provide baseline control. These designs are discussed in more detail elsewhere (see Annotated References).

Statistical Analysis of Single-Subject Data

Many researchers rely exclusively on raw data and a few descriptive statistics for interpreting the results of single-subject experiments. Figures 16.3 and 16.4 are typical graphic representations of single-subject data. The abscissa (horizontal line) represents units of time, and the ordinate (vertical line) represents units of the target behavior. Each data point is plotted separately on the graph, and the data points may be connected by lines. Vertical broken lines are used to indicate the transition from one phase to another (e.g., from baseline to treatment).

Several features of the graphical data plot should be noted by the researcher. Within each phase the data points for measures of the target behavior should be analyzed for mean level and presence and direction of slope. Adjacent phases should be compared with respect to change in mean level, change in slope, and change in level between the last data point for one phase and the first data point for the next phase.

Researchers are not entirely agreed on the need for inferential statistics to interpret single-subject data. Some argue that the large magnitude of change often obtained in single-subject research and within-subject replication of treatment effects in many single-subject designs (e.g., A-B-A-B) make it unnecessary to use inferential statistics. Others argue that inferential statistics are helpful for reaching conclusions about single-subject treatment effects, especially if the baseline or treatment data points are highly variable.

Several inferential statistics are available for determining whether variations in measurements between phases represent "true" differences or chance fluctuations. Suppose the researcher has used an A-B-A-B design with ten measurements for each phase. The mean of the twenty A (baseline) measurements can be compared with the mean of the twenty B (treatment) measurements. A simple t test can be done to determine whether the two means differ significantly from each other.[40] If the difference is statistically significant, one can conclude that a reliable treatment effect exists.

Another type of inferential statistics that can be used is time-series analysis. The purpose of **time-series analysis** is to detect reliable changes in slope and level between phases of the experiment. Time-series analysis is particularly well suited to single-subject experimentation. The computations are complex, however, and many data points are necessary to yield interpretable results.

External Validity

One of the major criticisms directed at single-subject designs is that they have low external validity: the findings cannot be generalized beyond the single subject used in the experiment. The same critics are likely to look with favor on the traditional multisubject experiment, in which the findings can be generalized from the sample to the population from which it was drawn. However, many multisubject experiments do not involve random selection of the sample from a defined population. Rather, the particular sample is chosen because it

---

40. Some statisticians claim that the t test and analysis of variance are inappropriate because single-subject data are not likely to satisfy some of the assumptions underlying use of these tests (see Hersen and Barlow in Annotated References).

is readily accessible and the results are generalized through logical inference to a larger population having similar characteristics. Also, researchers such as Richard Snow (see chapter 15) have questioned the generalizability of some multisubject experiments because they do not accurately reflect the natural environment. In balance, it appears that both single-subject and multisubject experiments can be criticized on similar grounds for lack of external validity. The real issue is how to increase the external validity of each type of experiment, rather than rejecting one type in favor of the other.

The most satisfactory method for increasing the external validity of single-subject experiments is to conduct replication studies. Replication can involve variation in investigators, settings, and subjects. The investigators, settings, and subjects can be the same or similar to those of the original experiment, or they can vary along specified dimensions. For example, the subject of the original experiment might be a fifth-grade male student. The replication experiment might involve another fifth-grade male student, or it might involve an individual who is representative of a different population (e.g., a twelfth-grade female student). Essential to any replication experiment is a careful description of baseline and treatment conditions, subject characteristics, and measurement procedures. This description provides a basis for determining the degree of generalizability from one experiment to another.

Choosing between Multisubject and Single-Subject Designs

Single-subject designs place the focus of investigation on the individual. The multisubject designs presented earlier in this chapter and in chapter 15 tend to subordinate the individual to the population of which he or she is a member. In planning your own experiments, you will need to choose between one or the other type of design.

One important basis for choosing between these types of design is whether you are more concerned with how populations and samples function, or how the individual learner functions. Both levels of inquiry are legitimate and complementary. Generalizations about education derived from research on samples or populations eventually need to be applied to the individual learner. Sometimes this is difficult to do. For example, learning curves based on averaging the performance of many students may not represent the performance of any individual student in the group. On the other hand, conclusions from single-subject research need to be replicated continually in order to determine their generalizability to populations of individuals.

Another important basis for choosing between multisubject and single-subject designs is the methodological requirements of the research problem. Single-subject designs ideally require many measurements of the dependent variable over time, but many dependent variables are not easily measured on this basis. Behavior change appears to lend itself well to repeated observational measurements. Cognitive and affective learning outcomes require more complex measurement procedures, and it is difficult to administer the same procedure repeatedly.

Many, if not most, teaching and curriculum methods are designed for groups of students rather than for the individual student. In research on group-administered methods, then, multisubject designs probably yield more useful data than single-subject designs. On the other hand, research on methods of individualized instruction probably should make more use of single-subject designs than is currently found in the literature.

It has been suggested that exploration of new educational techniques should begin with single-subject designs. This strategy enables the researcher to make intensive observations over a reasonably long period of time, to "play with" treatment variations, and to formulate hypotheses. Insights derived from single-subject data then can be tested for generalizability in a multisubject design.

OTHER EXPERIMENTAL DESIGNS

In chapter 15 and in this chapter we have presented the main designs used in experimental research. Our presentation is by no means exhaustive. There are many factorial designs that we have not considered here. Also, Campbell and Stanley discuss additional experimental designs that have application to some educational research problems.[41] These designs are essentially variations on designs presented in this chapter. For example, the equivalent-time-samples design uses a single group of subjects who are measured repeatedly; sometimes the experimental treatment is presented before the measurement, and other times it is not. In an experiment using this design, a researcher compared the effect of 56 days of music on industrial production interspersed with 51 days of no music.[42] Essentially, this design is the same as the time-series design except for the repeated introduction of the experimental treatment.

At this point it should be apparent to you that a wide range of experimental designs can be used in educational research. In selecting a design, you should consider its internal and external validity carefully. The main objective is to select a design that will give the clearest picture of the effect of the experimental treatment, unconfounded by the effect of such variables as history, maturation, and so forth. Another important objective is to select a design that

41. Campbell and Stanley, "Designs for Research on Teaching."
42. W. A. Kerr, "Experiments on the Effect of Music on Factory Production," *Applied Psychology Monographs*, no. 5 (1945).

will yield results that can be generalized to other situations in which one is interested. This is not an easy task. Therefore, the researcher should consider a range of experimental designs before selecting one to use in her research project.

MEASUREMENT OF CHANGE

All experiments are attempts to determine the effect of an independent variable on a dependent variable. In educational research the independent variable is often a new educational practice or product, and the dependent variable is a measure of student achievement, attitude, or personality. If it has an effect, the independent variable should be reflected as a *change* in students' scores on the measure that was administered before (the pretest) and after (the posttest) the experimental treatment. Thus, an important aspect of experimental design is the measure of change from pretest to posttest scores.

To measure change one might think it sufficient to subtract a student's pretest score from his posttest score. For example, if the student's initial score on a measurement of achievement was 50, and his score rose to 65 after the administration of the experimental treatment, the change score—also called the *gain*—would be 15. However, it is very important for the researcher to realize that there are serious difficulties regarding the legitimacy of change scores as psychometric variables.

These difficulties can be illustrated by considering a study of achievement gains from the beginning to the end of the freshman year of college conducted by Paul Dressel and Lewis Mayhew.[43] Table 16.11 lists gains made by students in nine colleges on various tests of achievement.[44] The gain scores are presented separately for subgroups formed on the basis of their pretest scores on each test. It is evident that there is a strong inverse relationship between pretest score and achievement gain. For example, on the test Critical Thinking in Social Science, the students whose scores were lowest at the beginning of the year made considerably larger gains (6.89 points) than the students whose scores were initially highest (an average gain of 2.26 points).

How are we to interpret such data? Do they mean that students with low initial achievement are likely to learn more (as measured by their change scores) than students with initially high achievement? Although this interpretation is conceivably correct, it is much more likely that the inverse relationship be-

43. Paul L. Dressel and Lewis B. Mayhew, *General Education: Explorations in Evaluation* (Washington: American Council on Education, 1954).
44. Table 16.11, reporting Dressel and Mayhew's results, is fom Paul B. Diederich, "Pitfalls in the Measurement of Gains in Achievement," *School Review* 64 (1956): table 1, p. 60.

TABLE 16.11

**Average Gains of Students on Posttests, Classified
according to Pretest Standing**

Test	Low Group	Low Middle Group	Middle Group	High Middle Group	High Group
Critical thinking in social science	6.89	5.48	3.68	4.20	2.26
Science reasoning and understanding	6.26	5.16	2.93	2.04	0.31
Humanities participation inventory	18.00	5.05	4.94	1.39	−2.07
Analysis of reading and writing	5.33	2.89	1.81	1.22	0.25
Critical thinking	6.68	4.65	3.47	2.60	1.59
Inventory of beliefs	9.09	5.31	4.65	3.32	1.01
Problems in human relations	3.19	1.67	1.31	1.51	−0.36

tween pretest scores and achievement gain scores is due to the peculiar psychometric attributes of change scores.

The first psychometric attribute to consider is ceiling effect. The concept of **ceiling effect** means that the range of difficulty of the test items is limited. Therefore, the test does not measure the entire range of achievement possible on the dimension being measured. For example, if a student answers 90 items correctly on a 100-item pretest, it is only possible for the student to improve his score by 10 points on the posttest. In contrast, a student with a score of 40 on the pretest can make a potential gain of 60 points. Thus, the ceiling effect places an artificial restriction on the distribution of gain scores across levels of initial ability.

It is possible that the tests used in Dressel and Mayhew's study were subject to a ceiling effect. Students in the high-middle and high groups may have scored near the ceiling of the pretest. Thus, they could earn only a minimal gain score when they took the posttest.

The interpretation of gain scores is also confounded by the phenomenon of **regression toward the mean.** The regression effect means that students who earn a high score on the pretest will earn a somewhat lower score on the posttest, whereas students with a low pretest score will earn a somewhat higher score on the posttest.[45] The regression effect occurs because of errors of mea-

---

45. The student may recall that the regression effect was discussed earlier in this chapter as a threat to the internal validity of an experiment. It is possible to get significant achievement gains in an initially low achievement group of students because of the regression effect, even if the experimental treatment has no effect.

surement in the pretest and posttest and because the tests are correlated with each other.

To explain the regression effect in nonstatistical terms, suppose that a student earns a very high score on a multiple-choice achievement test. This is probably not his "true" score. At least one determinant of his high score was probably the operation of chance factors. For example, he may have made lucky guesses on some of the multiple-choice items of which he was unsure; or the test by chance may have included a high proportion of items that he knew. Now it is unlikely that the student will have the same good luck when he next takes a parallel form of the test (equivalent to a posttest in an experiment). Thus, he will probably earn a somewhat lower score. The reverse situation applies to the initially low scorer. This student has probably earned his low score in part because of exceptionally bad luck. Because of the laws of probability, it is likely that his luck will improve when the posttest is administered. Thus, he will earn a somewhat higher score. We can see now that gain scores are distorted in part because of the regression effect. In table 16.11 the students with initially low achievement have regression working for them to produce a larger gain score, whereas the students with initially high achievement have regression working against them.

A third problem with gain scores is that they assume equal intervals at all points of the test. For example, on a 100-item test, a gain in score from 90 to 95 is assumed to be equivalent to a gain in score from 40 to 45. This assumption is almost never valid for educational measures. In fact, it is probably much harder to make a gain of 5 points when one's initial score is 90 (because of ceiling and regression effects) than when one's initial score is 40. If the test measures knowledge of word definitions, for example, a student whose initial score is 45 can perhaps earn 5 points by learning the meaning of easy, frequently used words, whereas the student with the initially high score may have to learn the meanings of difficult, rarely used words to improve his score.

The usual inequality of intervals in test scores is complicated by another problem. With the exception of factorially pure tests, a given score on a test may reflect different levels of ability for different students. For example, a mathematics achievement test may include a variety of subtests in addition, subtraction, mathematical reasoning problems, algebra, and so on. Two students may earn the same score on the test, yet this score may reflect a different pattern of strengths and weaknesses. (For example, one student may be weak in subtraction but strong in reasoning problems, whereas another student may be strong in subtraction but weak in reasoning problems.) After a period of time, the two students may earn the same gain score because they overcame their respective deficiencies. Thus the gain score for the first student reflects improvement in subtraction, whereas the gain score for the second student reflects improvement in mathematical reasoning. Because the gain scores are not equivalent in meaning, it is questionable whether they can be compared statistically.

The fifth difficulty with change scores is that they are not reliable. The higher the correlation between pretest and posttest scores, the lower the reliability of the change score. Also, the reliability of the change score is affected by the degree of unreliability of the pretest and posttest themselves.

Many factors adversely affect the meaning and reliability of change scores, yet some measure of change is necessary if the researcher is to compare the effects of different experimental treatments. Although the limitations of change scores cannot be overcome entirely, statistical procedures are available for overcoming some of the limitations.[46] First, we may consider the situation in which the researcher is interested in the change scores of individual students. For example, the researcher may want to know why, in table 16.11, some freshman college students showed more gain in Critical Thinking in Social Science (abbreviated here CTSS) than other students. The researcher may hypothesize that the gain scores will be correlated with the students' high school gradepoint average (GPA). To test this hypothesis, the researcher should not simply correlate GPA with the CTSS gain scores. Since there is a negative correlation between students' initial score on CTSS and their gain score (most likely due to regression and ceiling effects), any obtained correlation of GPA with gain scores can be interpreted two ways: the correlation may mean that GPA is related to students' college learning potential, or may mean that GPA is only related to students' initial achievement score. It is necessary, therefore, to use **partial correlation**.[47] In partial correlation GPA is correlated with change scores adjusted statistically so that initial score is held constant.

The other situation in which change scores are used is the analysis of mean change. Suppose a researcher administers an achievement pretest to two groups—one group is to receive an experimental treatment and the other is to serve as a control group. If they have been randomly assigned to the two groups, subjects should have equivalent means on their pretest scores. If this is the case, then the researcher can use *t* tests to determine the statistical significance of the mean change scores.

Occasionally the mean pretest scores will differ significantly by chance even when subjects have been assigned randomly to treatment groups. Also, pretest means may differ when quasi-experimental designs are used. To adjust for initial differences in pretest means, analysis of covariance should be used.

46. Other recommendations on the measurement of change are presented in a paper by Cronbach and Furby (see Annotated References).
47. The technique of partial correlation is discussed in chapter 13. The particular form of partial correlation to be used with change scores is discussed in Carl Bereiter, "Some Persisting Dilemmas in the Measurement of Change," in *Problems in Measuring Change*, ed. C. W. Harris (Madison: University of Wisconsin Press, 1963).

Analysis of covariance is a statistical technique that permits the researcher to attribute mean change scores to the effect of the experimental treatment rather than to differences in initial scores. For example, analysis of covariance could be applied to the data of table 16.11. By using this statistical technique, we could compare the mean achievement gain scores of each of the five subgroups *as if* they had all earned the same mean achievement score at the beginning of the freshman year. As we discussed in chapter 13, the data need to be examined to determine whether they satisfy certain assumptions underlying analysis of covariance.

Still another approach for determining the statistical significance of pretest-posttest change in experiments is **analysis of variance for repeated measures.** In this form of analysis of variance the occasions on which the measure of the dependent variable is administered (pretest and posttest) are considered one factor; the experimental and control treatments are the other factor.

The *F* ratios for the two factors (sometimes called main effects) are not of interest in this analysis of variance. For example, it is not meaningful to compare the mean of all the pretest scores with the mean of all the posttest scores, ignoring whether the scores are from experimental or control students. Of interest instead is the *interaction* between time of measurement and treatment; that is, we are interested in whether the difference between the pretest and posttest means of the experimental group is significantly greater or less than the difference for the control group.

This type of statistical analysis is illustrated in a study conducted by Norbert Johnson, Jerome Johnson, and Coy Yates.[48] The purpose of their experiment was to evaluate the effectiveness of a particular counseling program (the Vocational Exploration Group) in improving the career maturity of students. Sixty eighth- and ninth-grade students were randomly assigned to the counseling program or a no-treatment control group. The Career Maturity Inventory (CMI) was administered to all students as a pretest, posttest (immediately following conclusion of the experimental program) and as a follow-up posttest (six months following the program). The CMI, which consists of seven scales, measures maturity of attitudes and competencies necessary for making realistic career decisions.

Table 16.12 presents the pretest, posttest, and follow-up means on the CMI for the experimental and control groups.[49] It is apparent that the pretest-posttest difference on each scale is greater for the experimental group than for the control group. For example, the pretest-posttest difference on the Attitude

48. Norbert Johnson, Jerome Johnson, and Coy Yates, "A Six-Month Follow-Up on the Effects of the Vocational Exploration Group on Career Maturity," *Journal of Counseling Psychology* 28 (1981): 70–71.
49. Table 16.12 adapted from ibid., p. 71.

TABLE 16.12

Pretest, Posttest, and Follow-Up Mean Differences on the Career Maturity Inventory (CMI)

CMI Scale	Pretest		Posttest		Follow-Up		Pre-Post Difference	Pre-Follow-up Difference
	Exp. M	Control M	Exp. M	Control M	Exp. M	Control M	F	F
Attitude	34.3	34.3	38.1	35.1	38.0	34.7	4.15*	4.57*
Competence scale								
Knowing yourself	9.3	9.6	12.1	10.3	10.4	10.4	N.S.	N.S.
Knowing about jobs	10.1	10.6	15.8	11.3	13.4	11.2	16.13**	12.92**
Choosing a job	11.3	11.6	13.9	12.2	11.9	12.2	N.S.	N.S.
Looking ahead	10.6	11.6	13.1	12.2	12.7	11.8	N.S.	N.S.
What should they do?	9.9	10.1	11.4	10.8	11.4	10.8	N.S.	N.S.

NOTE: N.S. = not significant.
*$p < .05$.
**$p < .001$.

Scale is greater for the experimental group (3.8) than for the control group (0.8).

The statistical significance of these differences is determined by doing a two-way (Treatment Group × Time of Testing) analysis of variance. A statistically significant F ratio for the interaction effect indicates that the pretest-posttest difference for one group is reliably greater or less than the pretest-posttest difference for the other group. The last two columns of table 16.12 present these F ratios for the pre-post difference and pre-follow-up difference on each CMI scale. Significant F ratios were obtained for the Attitude scale and the Knowing Yourself Competence scale. A series of t tests for multiple comparisons (see chapter 13) revealed significant gains on these scales for the experimental group, but no change for the control group.

MISTAKES SOMETIMES MADE IN CONDUCTING EXPERIMENTS

1. Researcher does not consider confounding variables such as selection of subjects, history, regression, and loss of subjects, which might have brought about changes attributed to the treatment in quasi-experimental and single-subject designs.
2. Does not use a factorial design when possible in order to study the effects of several independent variables at once on the dependent variable.
3. In conducting single-subject research, does not check on reliability of measurement procedures.
4. In conducting single-subject research, does not collect enough data to yield a stable baseline or treatment effect.
5. Attempts to use a counterbalanced design even though each treatment tends to alter performance on subsequent treatments.
6. In analyzing experimental data, attempts to work with simple change scores when it might be more appropriate to use partial correlation or analysis of covariance.

ANNOTATED REFERENCES

In addition to the following sources, you may wish to review Annotated References in chapter 14; some of them are pertinent to topics discussed in this chapter.

Berliner, David C., and Cahen, Leonard S. "Trait-Treatment Interaction and Learning." In *Review of Research in Education,* vol. 1, edited by F. N. Kerlinger. Itasca, Ill.: F. E. Peacock, 1973.

This paper covers many of the same topics as the Cronbach and Snow text (see below), but in briefer form. It is a useful introduction to aptitude-treatment interaction as a focus for educational research.

Birnbrauer, Jay S.; Peterson, Christa R.; and Solnick, Jay V. "Design and Interpretation of Studies of Single Subjects." *American Journal of Mental Deficiency* 79 (1974): 191–203.

This article provides a good brief review of single-subject methodology. The authors describe procedures for using a variety of single-subject designs and problems of internal validity and external validity associated with each design.

Cook, Thomas D., and Campbell, Donald T. *Quasi-Experimentation: Design and Analysis Issues for Field Settings.* Chicago: Rand McNally, 1979.

This entire book is worth careful study. Chapter 3 discusses the quasi-experimental designs presented here and also includes several more sophisticated designs that may yield interpretable data even though random assignment was not used. Chapter 4 discusses possible problems in using analysis of variance or analysis of covariance to detect treatment effects in quasi-experiments.

Cronbach, Lee J., and Furby, Lita. "How Should We Measure 'Change'— Or Should We?" *Psychological Bulletin* 74 (1970): 68–80.

This classic paper makes recommendations for estimating change in various research contexts, including the following: change in a dependent variable as a result of experimental intervention, measurement of growth or learning rate, identification of deviant developmental patterns, and use of change scores as personality and cognitive constructs (e.g., overachievement or discrepancy between perceived actual self and perceived ideal self). The authors generally advocate multiple-regression estimates of change rather than the calculation of simple gain scores.

Cronbach, Lee J., and Snow, Richard E. *Aptitudes and Instructional Methods.* New York: Irvington, 1977.

This is a book-length survey of the field of aptitude-treatment research. The authors review findings and methodological problems of previous research, and they make recommendations for future work in this field.

Hersen, Michael, and Barlow, David H. *Single Case Experimental Designs.* New York: Pergamon Press, 1976.

The authors provide a comprehensive discussion of the methodology of single-subject experiments. Examples of single-subject studies in education, counseling, psychiatry, and medicine are used to illustrate design techniques. There are several chapters on A-B-A and multiple baseline designs, and a chapter on statistical techniques for analyzing single-subject data.

Kratochwill, Thomas R., ed. *Single Subject Research: Strategies for Evaluating Change*. New York: Academic Press, 1978.

The papers in this volume deal primarily with the statistical analysis of single-subject and time-series experiments. Substantial discussion is devoted to the relative merits of visual inspection and formal statistical analysis in reaching conclusions about treatment effects in such experiments.

Linn, Robert L., and Slinde, Jeffrey A. "The Determination of the Significance of Change Between Pre- and Posttesting Periods." *Review of Educational Research* 47 (1977): 121–50.

This article reviews research on the psychometric properties of individual and group gain scores. Like Cronbach and Furby (see Annotated References above), the authors do not recommend using gain scores either in research or in the practice of education. Instead, they advocate the use of a regression approach in which pretest scores are used as predictors of posttest scores.

SELF-CHECK TEST

Circle the correct answer to each of the following questions. An answer key is provided on page 881.

1. The distinguishing characteristic of the nonequivalent control-group design is that
   a. the control group does not receive a posttest.
   b. subjects are not randomly assigned to the experimental and control groups.
   c. repeated measures are made on the experimental group but not on the control group.
   d. the experimental treatment has external validity, but the control treatment does not.
2. The difference between treatment group means in a nonequivalent control-group design is usually tested for statistical significance by
   a. a *t* test on the posttest means.
   b. the *t* distribution for the correlation between pretest and posttest scores.
   c. analysis of covariance on the posttest means.
   d. separate *t* tests of the pre-post difference for the experimental group and for the control group.
3. Factorial designs are used in order to
   a. control for the effects of nonrandom assignment to treatments.

    b. collect data that can be entered into a factor analysis.

    c. control for statistical regression.

    d. test for the interaction of several variables in the same experiment.

4. A 2 × 2 × 2 × 2 factorial design means that the experiment includes
    a. 2 dependent variables.
    b. 4 dependent variables.
    c. 2 independent variables.
    d. 4 independent variables.

5. Which of the following variables is most experimentally manipulable?
    a. student ability
    b. student age
    c. socioeconomic level of community in which a school is located
    d. teaching method

6. The effect of a pretest on the dependent variable in an experiment is best investigated using a
    a. Solomon four-group design.
    b. counterbalanced design.
    c. aptitude-treatment interaction design.
    d. A-B-A design.

7. Research on aptitude-treatment interaction seeks to discover whether
    a. students with certain characteristics are better learners than others.
    b. certain instructional methods are better than others.
    c. certain students learn better under one instructional method than under another instructional method.
    d. the interactions between students of differing ability are ordinal or disordinal.

8. Counterbalanced experiments are particularly susceptible to
    a. regression effects.
    b. order effects.
    c. maturation effects.
    d. ATI effects.

9. Within-subject replication of the treatment variable is provided by
    a. the A-B design.
    b. the A-B-A design.
    c. the A-B-A-B design.
    d. All of the above are correct.

10. Multiple-baseline designs are used instead of A-B-A type designs when
    a. only one subject is available for the experiment.
    b. reinstatement of baseline conditions is not possible.
    c. reinstatement of treatment conditions is not possible.
    d. All of the above are correct.

11. Data of single-subject experiments are often analyzed to determine

   a. change in mean performance level from one phase of the experiment to another.
   b. change in performance level between the last data point for one phase and the first data point for the next phase.
   c. change in slope from one phase of the experiment to another.
   d. All of the above are correct.
12. The higher the correlation between pretest and posttest scores, the
   a. lower the reliability of the change score.
   b. higher the reliability of the change score.
   c. more difficult will be prediction of posttest scores based on pretest scores.
   d. lower the validity of the posttest.
13. When doing an analysis of variance for repeated measures, the researcher is most interested in
   a. the main effect for treatment.
   b. the main effect for testing occasion.
   c. the interaction between treatment and time of testing.
   d. the interaction between treatment and multiple baselines.

APPLICATION PROBLEMS

The following problems are designed to give you practice in applying significant concepts and research procedures explained in chapter 16. Most of them do not have a single correct answer. For feedback, you can compare your answers with the sample answers on pages 896–97.

1. A school district has made available 12 elementary school classes for an experiment to determine which of two comprehensive reading programs is superior. Of the 12 classes, 4 are first grade, 6 are second grade, and 2 are third grade. The district administrators have imposed the requirement that students within classrooms cannot be randomly assigned to treatments. Under these conditions, what are two procedures that the researcher can use to help ensure equivalence of the two treatments (reading program A and reading program B)? If the two treatments are found to differ on the pretest, how can these differences be controlled statistically?
2. A researcher plans to test the effectiveness of self-paced instruction vs. conventional instruction for male and female students of varying levels of ability. There are a total of 150 students: 60 boys and 90 girls. Within each of these groups (boys and girls), there are an equal number of high-, middle-, and low-ability students. Make a chart that illustrates the experimental design for this research project, and show the number of students in each experimental group. Also, list each interaction effect that can be analyzed.

3. The purpose of an experiment was to decrease the frequency with which a college professor said "uh" and "you know" during lectures. The treatment consisted of a small signal at the rear of the room which the experimenter flashed each time that the professor uttered one of the verbal behaviors targeted for extinction. An A-B-A design was used to assess the treatment effect. The results indicated a high baseline frequency of the behaviors, followed by a dramatic decrease in frequency when the treatment was instituted. The behaviors did not increase again when the treatment was withdrawn. Since reinstatement of baseline conditions is required in an A-B-A design, describe an alternative single-subject design that can be used to demonstrate a treatment effect.

4. A new program has been developed to increase students' speed and accuracy in doing simple arithmetic computations. You have been asked by the school district's curriculum specialist to evaluate its effectiveness. One of the first decisions you must make is whether to use a multisubject or single-subject experimental design. What are several questions you might ask the curriculum specialist about the program and about the purpose of the experiment that will help to determine the more appropriate type of experimental design to be used?

5. A researcher conducted an experiment in which he administered an arithmetic test before and after students had participated in a new individualized curriculum. Parallel forms of the tests were used as pretest and posttest, and the range of possible scores was 0-100 on each. In analyzing data from the experiment, the researcher found that students in the lowest quartile of the pretest ($\overline{X}$ = 15.5) made a good gain (posttest $\overline{X}$ = 37.6), whereas students in the highest quartile ($\overline{X}$ = 83.7) declined slightly ($\overline{X}$ = 80.1). From these differences in gain scores, he concluded that the new curriculum is more effective for students of low ability than for students of high ability. What are two other interpretations that could be made of the differences in gain scores?

SUGGESTION SHEET

If your last name starts with letters from Pro to Rur, please complete the Suggestion Sheet at the end of the book while this chapter is still fresh in your mind.

17.

EVALUATION RESEARCH

OVERVIEW

Evaluation research has become an integral component of policy analysis, program management, and the political decision-making process in education. The chapter discusses this and other trends in educational evaluation. Thirty criteria for judging the professional quality of an evaluation study are described. The major models of evaluations are presented. Much of the chapter concerns procedures for analyzing program characteristics and for conducting various types of evaluation research.

OBJECTIVES

After studying this chapter, you should be able to:

1. Describe several recent trends in educational evaluation.
2. Compare the purposes of educational evaluation and educational research.
3. Describe the major criteria and uses of the *Standards for Evaluations of Educational Programs, Projects, and Materials.*
4. Analyze an educational program in terms of its goals, resources, procedures, and management.
5. Explain the difference betwen individual assessment and objectives-based evaluation.
6. Explain the difference between responsive evaluation models and objectives-based evaluation models.
7. Describe the purpose and major features of the CIPP evaluation model.
8. Describe the procedures used in needs assessment.
9. Compare the procedures used in formative and summative evaluations.
10. Describe the procedures used in a responsive evaluation study.

THE NATURE AND PURPOSE OF EDUCATIONAL EVALUATION

Educational evaluation is the process of making judgments about the merit, value, or worth of educational programs, projects, materials, and techniques. This type of inquiry in education and other human service fields has grown remarkably in the last decade or so. Federal expenditures for evaluation were over 243 million dollars in 1977[1] and approximately 300 million dollars in 1979.[2] Financial support for program evaluation has increased greatly at state and local government levels, too. For example, a substantial number of school districts have established departments of evaluation as part of their central administration. Many educational researchers have moved into the field of evaluation because of the widespread demand for their services.

Why has educational evaluation attracted so much interest from government? The main reason is that public administrators have come to view evaluation as an important tool in policy analysis, in the political decision-making process, and in program management. With respect to policy analysis, evaluation research yields important data about the costs, benefits, and problems of various program alternatives. Policy analysts can use these data to prepare position papers, which are then reviewed by persons with decision-making authority. The growth in this type of evaluation research is demonstrated by the fact that in 1979 the American Educational Research Association initiated a new journal called *Educational Evaluation and Policy Analysis.*

With respect to the political process, evaluation findings are used increasingly by politicians to create advocacy for particular legislation and budget appropriations. In fact, opponents of the legislation are then pressed to sponsor their own evaluations that hopefully will yield findings favoring their cause. We need only think of the data cited by proponents and opponents of nuclear power and of military build-up to realize that evaluation has become closely intertwined with the political process. (Adversary evaluation, discussed later in the chapter, formalizes this use of evaluation.)

Finally, evaluation research is becoming an increasingly important tool of program management. For example, cost-benefit evaluations (also called "efficiency evaluations") are done to determine whether programs are producing benefits that justify their costs. Another use of evaluations is to hold managers accountable for producing results. Evaluations are done, too, to generate data

1. Executive Office of the President, *Resources for Program Evaluation: Fiscal Year 1977* (Washington, D.C.: U.S. Office of Management and Budget, 1977).
2. W. H. Shapley and D. I. Phillips, *Research and Development in Federal Budget: Fiscal Year 1979, R&D, Industry, and the Economy* (Washington, D.C.: American Association for the Advancement of Science, 1978).

that will help managers make sound decisions relating to program design, personnel, and budget.

Trends in Educational Evaluation

We have already noted the trend toward connecting educational evaluation directly to policy analysis and political decision-making. A related trend is for evaluation—or the lack of it—to become part of the public's concern about the "failures" of the educational system. For example, an investigative report appeared recently in a California newspaper under the title, "Remedial Summer School Plan: No One Knows If It Works."[3] The article stated that

> California's multimillion-dollar summer program [$15.4 million in 1981] to raise the academic proficiency of lagging students is running unchecked, with few educators able to determine whether the effort is paying off. . . .
>
> Few school officials have been able to determine whether students are actually learning and retaining what they are taught, and the number of students who take the summer courses, only to fail again, is a mystery. . . .
>
> "There ought to be some kind of reporting to determine how well those summer school programs are doing, some kind of indication of whether the whole program is worthwhile, in the interest of the children in the district," said State Schools Superintendent Wilson Riles.

Such criticisms and demands for accountability are serving as a strong impetus to including an evaluation component in any new publicly-funded program in education.

Another trend in educational evaluation is to place more value on doing longterm evaluations of continuing programs than on doing a single, decisive study. Many evaluators share the view of Robert Boruch and Paul Wortman that ". . . evaluative research does include several distinct activities, with short-term, decision-oriented projects and longer term efforts to estimate program effects among them" (p. 312).[4] Major studies such as the evaluations of equality of educational opportunity (sometimes called the Coleman Report),[5] Head-

3. Charles C. Hardy, "Remedial Summer School Plan: No One Knows If It Works," *San Francisco Examiner* (August 8, 1982): B1 and B5.

4. Robert F. Boruch and Paul M. Wortman, "Implications of Educational Evaluation for Evaluation Policy," in *Review of Research in Education 7*, ed. David C. Berliner (Washington, D.C.: American Educational Research Association, 1979), pp. 309–61.

5. James S. Coleman and others, *Equality of Educational Opportunity* (Washington, D.C.: Government Printing Office, 1966).

start,[6] Follow Through,[7] and public vs. private schools[8] have seldom produced indisputable findings or clear directions for decision making. Each of the studies just mentioned has been the subject of much debate and data re-analysis.[9]

Some evaluators see this type of extended dialogue and continued investigation as a strength rather than weakness of evaluation research. Even if policy questions are not answered decisively, at least the issues and areas of ignorance become more clearly understood. This approach to evaluation places much more emphasis and value on formative strategies of evaluation than on summative strategies. The distinction between formative and summative evaluation is discussed later in the chapter.

A major trend in current educational evaluation is a broadened view of program phenomena that should be evaluated. Early models of evaluation emphasized a program's *objectives*. The critical question to be answered by evaluation research was how well the objectives of a program were achieved in practice. This approach is still widely used, but contemporary evaluators emphasize investigation of the *issues, concerns,* and *decisions* that surround a program. They not only evaluate how well objectives have been achieved, but also whether the objectives are worth achieving, and who thinks so.

Educational evaluators today tend to be much more realistic about how their findings will be used. No longer do they naively believe that their findings will lead to direct action. Experience has shown that programs with good evaluations are sometimes cancelled and programs found to be ineffective are continued. This experience has led to the definition of a more humble, yet still powerful role for evaluation. Lee Cronbach and his associates described this new role for evaluation in the following terms:

> Excellence ought to be judged against how evaluation *could* serve a society. A society is an arrangement for making lives more satisfactory. Evaluations can improve the welfare of citizens only by contributing to the political process that shapes social actions. An evaluation pays off to the extent that it offers ideas pertinent to pending actions and people think more clearly as a result. To enlighten, it must do more than amass good data. Timely communications—generally not "final" ones—should dis-

6. Sheldon H. White, "The National Impact Study of Head Start," in *Disadvantaged Child: Compensatory Education, a National Debate,* ed. Jerome Hellmuth (New York: Bruner-Mazel, 1970).
7. Linda B. Stebbins and others, "An Evaluation of Follow Through," in *Evaluation Studies Review Annual, Volume 3,* ed. Thomas D. Cook and others (Beverly Hills, Calif.: Sage, 1978), pp. 571–610.
8. James S. Coleman, Thomas Hoffer, and Sally Kilgore, *High School Achievement: Public, Catholic, and Private Schools Compared* (New York: Basic Books, 1982).
9. For example, see: Ernest R. House, Gene V. Glass, Leslie D. McLean, and Decker F. Walker, "No Simple Answer: Critique of the Follow Through Evaluation," in *Evaluation Studies Review Annual, Volume 3,* ed. Thomas D. Cook and others (Beverly Hills, Calif.: Sage, 1978), pp. 611–640.

tribute information to the persons rightfully concerned, and those hearers should take the information into their thinking. To speak broadly, an evaluation ought *to inform and improve the operations of the social system.*[10]

This view of evaluation is incorporated in some of the criteria and models of evaluation discussed later in the chapter.

Another trend in educational evaluation is the increasing awareness that evaluation activities can be both beneficial and harmful. Gene Glass described this problem as a paradox.[11] On the one hand, persons involved in a program appear to do best when they feel that they are valued unconditionally and do not have an evaluator watching over their shoulder. On the other hand, Glass observed, "it appears that people move truer and more certainly toward excellence to the extent that they clarify their purposes, measure the impact of their action, judge it, and move on—in a few words, evaluate their progress."[12] The perils of evaluation involve not only people, but the program itself. A program may be good, but a poor evaluation can misjudge it and contribute to its downfall. A program may have the potential to be good, but a negative evaluation while it is under development can lead administrators to withdraw funding. Furthermore, evaluation activities use up resources that could be allocated to support good program development.

The beneficial and harmful effects of evaluation are difficult to reconcile. Some evaluators recommend that the evaluator should weigh all possible consequences of a planned evaluation activity. The potential benefits should outweigh the potential harm before making a decision to proceed with the evaluation.[13]

How do these trends in educational evaluation affect the student who is planning to do evaluation research as a thesis or dissertation? The trends reflect issues and problems that the student should take into account in planning her project. For example, the student should analyze whether each aspect of her research design has the potential to harm the entity that she plans to evaluate. Also, the student needs to think very clearly about how the results of her evaluation research might be used by administrators and policy makers.

Some theses and dissertations involve doing research on the evaluation process itself.[14] A question of current concern is the extent to which and the

---

10. Lee J. Cronbach and Associates, *Toward Reform of Program Evaluation* (San Francisco: Jossey-Bass, 1981).
11. Gene V. Glass, "A Paradox About Excellence of Schools and the People in Them," *Educational Researcher* 4 (1975): 9–13.
12. Ibid., p. 12.
13. See p. 301 of Egon G. Guba and Yvonna S. Lincoln, *Effective Evaluation* (San Francisco: Jossey-Bass, 1981).
14. For example, Diane L. Reinhard, "Methodology for Input Evaluation Utilizing Advocate and Design Teams" (Ph.D. dissertation, Ohio State University, 1973).

manner in which evaluation findings are utilized by decision-makers.[15] Another important question is whether an evaluation is more useful when conducted at "arms-length" from the program or when the evaluator is an integral member of the program staff.

Educational Evaluation and Educational Research

Is evaluation research the same as educational research? This question is frequently raised. For example, you may wonder whether an educational researcher is qualified to fill a position involving program evaluation duties; or whether the graduate preparation required to train an educational researcher is different from that required to train an educational evaluator.

We take the position, which is generally accepted, that there is a great degree of overlap between educational research and educational evaluation. In practice, evaluators make considerable use of the controlled research designs, measurement tools, and statistical analyses that constitute the methodology of educational research. Yet there are important differences between the two fields in purpose. We describe three of them here.

First, evaluation research is usually intitiated by someone's need for a *decision* to be made concerning policy, management, or political strategy. The purpose of the research is to collect data that will facilitate decision making. In contrast, educational research is usually initiated by a *hypothesis* about the relationship between two or more variables. The research is conducted in order to reach a conclusion about the hypothesis—to accept or reject it. Of course, the findings of educational research can be used to guide decision making; and evaluation data may be relevant to the testing of a research hypothesis. The critical difference between the two fields is in the emphasis that is placed on making practical decisions versus accepting, rejecting, or formulating a hypothesis.

The second difference between educational research and educational evaluation is in the extent to which findings can be generalized. Evaluation is often done for a limited purpose. Decision makers may be interested in how well their program works, and thus they commission a site-specific evaluation study to collect data relevant to their special concerns. In contrast, researchers are more likely to be interested in discovering widely applicable principles explaining relationships between variables. Researchers may use a particular set of curriculum materials or group of teachers to test a hypothesis, but they typically view these as samples of larger populations of materials or groups to

15. An example of such a study is Marvin C. Alkin, Richard Daillak, and Peter White, *Using Evaluations: Does Evaluation Make a Difference?* (Beverly Hills, Calif.: Sage, 1979).

which the research findings will be generalized. Again, the difference is not pure: some evaluation research is designed to yield generalizable results, and some basic research has extremely limited generalizability.

The third difference concerns judgments of value. Evaluators design their studies to yield data concerning the worth, merit, or value of educational phenomena. Their findings tend to be stated in such phrases as "This reading program is better than the other program because" or "The respondent group of teachers preferred this mode of inservice training because." Researchers, though, design their studies to discover the truth about educational phenomena. Their findings tend to be couched in such terms as "It appears that variable X is a determinant of variable Y" or "A moderate relationship between variables X, Y, and Z was observed." Educators may make value judgments and decisions based on research findings, but this is a secondary use of the findings. The primary use is to contribute to our basic understanding of educational phenomena.

As we stated, educational evaluation draws extensively on methodology used by educational researchers, despite differences in purpose. In many respects this book can serve as a primer on evaluation even though it was intended primarily as a survey of research methods. The latter part of this chapter contains examples of evaluation studies that illustrate research methods described elsewhere in the book. First, though, is a discussion of criteria of good evaluations, types of educational phenomena that are frequently evaluated, and models of evaluation.

JUDGING THE QUALITY OF EVALUATION RESEARCH

The publication of *Standards for Evaluations of Educational Programs, Projects, and Materials* in 1981 marked an important advance in evaluation research.[16] The standards were developed by the Joint Committee on Standards for Educational Evaluation. The Joint Committeee, under the direction of Daniel Stufflebeam, represented may important organizations in education: American Association of School Administrators, American Educational Research Association, American Federation of Teachers, American Personnel and Guidance Association, American Psychological Association, Association for Supervision and Curriculum Development, Council for American Private Education, Education Commission of the States, National Association of Elementary School Principals, National Council on Measurement in Education, National Education As-

16. Joint Committee on Standards for Educational Evaluation, *Standards for Evaluations of Educational Programs, Projects, and Materials* (New York: McGraw-Hill, 1981).

sociation, and National School Boards Association. Several hundred educators nationwide were involved in developing and field-testing the standards.

The standards were created by the Joint Committee for use in judging the quality of educational evaluations, just as the *Standards for Educational and Psychological Tests* (see chapter 8) were developed for judging the quality of tests. A total of 30 standards are described in the Joint Committee's book-length report.

The standards were developed for several reasons. First, there was a growing awareness that the technical quality of some evaluation studies was poor and that some studies were insensitive to the entity being evaluated. Another realization was that the process of evaluation could be corrupted by persons with ulterior motives. As we noted in the introduction, educational evaluation usually involves political considerations. Evaluators and clients can bend the evaluation process to produce results that reflect their biases or self-interests. Third, the Joint Committee felt that a published set of standards could help to improve the professionalism of educational evaluation. Also, the Joint Committee found that no adequate standards were available at the time they began their work.

The Joint Committee came to an agreement that a good evaluation study satisfies four important criteria: utility, feasibility, propriety, and accuracy. An evaluation has **utility** if it is informative, timely, and useful to the affected persons. **Feasibility** means, first, that the evaluation design is appropriate to the setting in which the study is to be conducted, and second, that the design is cost-effective. An evaluation has **propriety** if the rights of persons affected by the evaluation are protected. The ethical procedures for educational research described in chapter 4 are pertinent to this standard. Finally, **accuracy** refers to the extent to which an evaluation study has produced valid, reliable, and comprehesive information about the entity being evaluated.

Each criterion for judging an educational evaluation was operationalized in terms of specific standards. The following is a brief description of the 30 standards. Each standard is listed below the criterion to which it most closely relates.

Utility

1. *Audience identification.* All of the audiences affected by the evaluation should be identified.
2. *Evaluator credibility.* The evaluator should be competent and trustworthy.
3. *Information scope and selection.* The questions to be answered by the evaluation should be pertinent and responsive to the affected audiences.
4. *Valuational interpretation.* The bases for interpreting the results and for making value judgments should be clearly described.

5. *Report clarity.* The affected audiences should find it easy to understand the evaluators' reports.
6. *Report dissemination.* Evaluation reports should be disseminated to all clients and right-to-know audiences.
7. *Report timeliness.* The evaluation findings should be reported in a timely manner.
8. *Evaluation impact.* The evaluation should be conducted so as to encourage appropriate action by the affected audiences.

Feasibility

9. *Practical procedures.* The evaluation procedures should be practical and minimally disruptive to participants.
10. *Political viability.* The evaluators should obtain the cooperation of affected interest groups and should keep any group from subverting the evaluation process.
11. *Cost effectiveness.* The benefits produced by the evaluation should justify the resources expended on it.

Propriety

12. *Formal obligation.* Obligations of all involved parties should be agreed to in writing.
13. *Conflict of interest.* Conflicts that arise in the evaluation process should be treated openly and honestly.
14. *Full and frank disclosure.* Evaluation reports should be direct and honest.
15. *Public's right to know.* The public's right to know about the evaluation should be assured whenever legally or ethically permissible.
16. *Rights of human subjects.* The rights and welfare of persons involved in the evaluation should be protected.
17. *Human interactions.* Evaluators should respect the worth and dignity of persons involved in the study.
18. *Balanced reporting.* The strengths and weaknesses of the entity being evaluated should be reported completely and fairly.
19. *Fiscal responsibility.* Expenditure of resources for the evaluation should be prudent and ethically responsible.

Accuracy

20. *Object identification.* All pertinent aspects of the entity being evaluated should be described.

21. *Context analysis.* All pertinent aspects of the conditions that surround the entity being evaluated should be described.
22. *Described purposes and procedures.* A careful record of the evaluation purposes and procedures should be kept.
23. *Defensible information sources.* Sources of data should be described in sufficient detail that their adequacy can be judged.
24. *Valid measurement.* A range of validated measures should be used in the data collection process.
25. *Reliable measurement.* The measures should have adequate reliability for their intended uses.
26. *Systematic data control.* Human error in data collection should be minimized.
27. *Analysis of quantitative information.* Analysis of quantitative data in an evaluation study should be accurate and thorough, and should yield clear interpretations.
28. *Analysis of qualitative information.* Analysis of qualitative data in an evaluation study should be accurate and thorough, and should yield clear interpretations.
29. *Justified conclusions.* The conclusions of an evaluation must be based on sound logic and appropriate data analyses.
30. *Objective reporting.* Evaluation reports should be thorough and free of biases of pressure groups.

Helpful case studies that illustrate each standard are presented in the Joint Committee's report.[17] The evaluation models and procedures described in this chapter reflect many of the standards.

Application of the 30 standards is not always straightforward. For example, the evaluators' efforts to produce an accurate evaluation (standards 20–30) may conflict with their desire to issue timely reports (standard 7). Also, some of the persons involved in the evaluation may be more committed to achieving the standards than are other persons. If it appears that important standards have been compromised, the Joint Committee recommends that the evaluators should consider dropping the project.

The importance of individual standards will vary depending upon the situation. For example, the public's right to know (standard 15) may not be an important consideration in a privately funded, inhouse evaluation of a product under development. However, the use of valid, reliable measures (standards 24 and 25) may be quite important to the developers whose product is being evaluated. You should keep in mind, too, that the standards were specifically intended for judging evaluations of programs (educational activities that provide services on a continuing basis), projects (activities that are funded for a defined period of time), and materials (physical items such as books, films,

17. Ibid.

tapes, and other instructional products). The standards were not intended for judging evaluations of institutions, professional personnel, or students.

The standards should be useful to anyone who commissions an evaluation study, or to anyone who will be involved in the study. Also, the standards should be very useful if you are planning to do evaluation research for your thesis or dissertation project. You can use the standards to judge the soundness of your evaluation design and to judge previous evaluations in your area of interest.

PROGRAM DELINEATION AND ANALYSIS

The "Objects" of Evaluation

It is the rare federally funded program that does not have an evaluation component attached to it. Evaluation research is also becoming increasingly prevalent as a subject for master's and doctoral dissertations in education. When in doubt, find an educational program and evaluate it!

The following list suggests the range of educational phenomena that have been the object of evaluation research:

1. Instructional methods (e.g., lectures, inquiry teaching, linguistic approach to reading instruction, manipulatives in mathematics instruction)
2. Curriculum materials (e.g., textbooks, slidetapes, multimedia packages)
3. Programs (e.g., Head Start, language arts programs, teacher education programs, after-school programs)
4. Organizations (e.g., kindergartens, alternative schools, resource centers)
5. Educators (e.g., inservice teachers, teacher aides, school principals, volunteer tutors)
6. Students (e.g., elementary students, college students, gifted students, students with behavior problems)

Hereafter we will use "program" as a generic label to refer to the objects of educational evaluation.

One of the first tasks that confronts the evaluator is to delineate carefully the salient characteristics of the program. For example, if a set of curriculum materials is to be evaluated, the researcher should include, at a minimum, the following kinds of information about it: author, publisher, publication date, list of materials, purchase cost, maintenance and replacement costs, and reports of previous evaluation studies. Careful program delineation is important even in local evaluation research. **Program delineation** is the process of analyzing and describing the significant characteristics of an educational program. It is not uncommon for persons working in a program to know only those aspects that affect them directly. Unless all program components are delineated, an important component may be overlooked in the evaluation process.

Following program delineation, the evaluator needs to analyze the program to determine which of its aspects or components are to be included in the evaluation study. Aspects and components can be grouped into the following categories: goals, resources, procedures, and management. These categories are useful for designing an evaluation irrespective of the evaluation model that is used.

Goals, Resources, Procedures, and Management

Program Goals

Judgments about the merit of program goals are central to most evaluation studies. If a program does not have goals, or does not have worthwhile goals, it is hard to imagine how it can be worthwhile in any other respect. A **goal** is the purpose, effect, or end-point that the program developer is attempting to achieve.

Some programs have carefully specified goals. In other programs the evaluator must infer the goals that the developer has in mind. Once the program goals have been identified, the evaluator's major task may be to determine the extent to which the program achieves the goals in practice. In formative evaluation, the evaluator's task may be to help the developers determine what the goals of the program should be.

Michael Scriven has argued that evaluators should not know the program goals in advance.[18] Instead, the evaluators should conduct research to discover the actual effects of the program in operation. The actual effects may differ markedly from the program developers' stated goals. An evaluator who knows the goals in advance may become co-opted by them and overlook other effects of the program, especially adverse side effects. Scriven's strategy for evaluation has come to be known as **goal-free evaluation.** Although the strategy has merit, there are many situations in which an evaluator is employed to collect evaluative data about specific program goals. In these situations the evaluator is required to attend to certain goals; yet it is advisable to remain alert to the pos-

18. Michael Scriven, "Goal-Free Evaluation," in *School Evaluation: The Politics and Process*, ed. Ernest R. House (Berkeley, Calif.: McCutchan, 1973).

sibility that the program may have actual effects, both beneficial and adverse, that are quite different from those intended by the program developers.

Program goals can be stated at different levels of specificity. The goal is usually the longer-term, general outcome of the program. The short-term, more specific outcomes of the program usually are called **objectives.** For example, the broad goal of a training program developed by one of the authors was "to help high school teachers and students develop skill in discussing controversial issues effectively." Each of the four lessons of the training program had a more specific objective. For example, the objective of the fourth lesson was "to help high school teachers and students develop skill in evaluating the effectiveness of their issues discussions." This objective was further analyzed into more specific objectives, for example, "to develop teachers' skill in concluding a discussion by asking selected students to give a brief review of what happened in the discussion" and "to develop students' skill in telling the discussion group their current opinion and how the discussion affected it."

Program objectives are sometimes stated in behavioral terms, meaning that the program outcomes are stated as behaviors that anyone, including evaluators, can observe in a program participant.[19] This type of objective, commonly called a **behavioral objective,** usually has three components: statement of the program objective as an observable, behavioral outcome; criteria for successful performance of the behavior; and the situational context in which the behavior is to be performed. "Given a set of twenty single-digit multiplication problems, the learner will be able to solve them by writing the correct answer beneath each problem in less than three minutes with no more than two errors" is an example of a behavioral objective.

Behavioral objectives are frowned upon by some educators, but one of their advantages for evaluators is that they simplify the task of developing suitable instruments (especially domain-referenced instruments[20]) to measure the learner's attainment of the objective. Indeed, a major reason why clearly stated goals and objectives are important in evaluation is that they make it possible for the evaluator to select or develop appropriate outcome measures. For example, an evaluator may be requested to collect rigorous data about the extent to which outcomes of a program have been achieved. This task necessitates the selection or development of instruments that measure the outcomes. If the program has vague goals, or none at all, the task of instrumentation is difficult and may prove to be impossible. The evaluator is then vulnerable to the criticism that her findings are invalid because inappropriate measures were used.

19. Procedures for writing behavioral objectives are explained in many sources. The classic work is Robert F. Mager, *Preparing Instructional Objectives*, 2nd ed. (Belmont, Calif.: Fearon-Pitman, 1975).
20. Domain-referenced measurement is discussed in chapter 8.

There are important exceptions to the principle of tying instrumentation closely to program goals and objectives. In goal-free evaluation, discussed above, the researcher has the task of discovering and measuring the actual effects of the program. As a consequence, the measures may have little relation to the program developer's intended goals. Also, there are occasions when an evaluator includes a particular outcome measure simply out of curiosity. Many important discoveries in medicine have been made because a medical researcher explored whether a particular drug, intended or known to cure one disease, had curative effects on another disease. An example in education of this phenomenon is the evaluations that have been done on DISTAR, an academic program intended to develop the cognitive skills of low-income disadvantaged children. Although the evaluation research has focused on measurement of these cognitive skills, self-concept instruments have been routinely administered as well. The evaluation findings indicate that DISTAR affects students' cognitive growth and also has a positive effect on their self-esteem.[21]

Resources and Procedures

Resources and procedures are the means used by developers to achieve program goals. Many evaluation studies are focused exclusively on goal identification and goal attainment, but program resources and procedures are also a legitimate focus for evaluation.

Resources are the personnel, equipment, space, and other cost items needed to implement program procedures. Decision makers may want to know the answers to such questions as, Are our present resources sufficient to operate the program as intended by its developers? Is the program too expensive? Are there "hidden" costs in the program? Will the program take away resources needed by other programs? Each of these questions requires the evaluator to focus on program resources.

An important type of evaluation research concerns the relation between the resources required by the program and the outcomes achieved by the program. Studies that investigate this relationship sometimes are called **cost-benefit research** or input-output research. The needed resources are the costs/inputs, and the outcomes are the benefits/outputs. "Which of these two reading programs is a better buy?" and "Are the financial rewards of a college education still sufficient to offset its costs?" are examples of questions that call for cost-benefit research methodology. This type of evaluation research has been done primarily by economists, although there have been some applications within the field of educational research.[22]

---

21. Stebbins and others, op. cit.
22. This type of evaluation research is discussed in Mark S. Thompson, *Benefit-Cost Analysis for Program Evaluation* (Beverly Hills, Calif.: Sage, 1980).

Procedures are the techniques, strategies, and other processes used in conjunction with resources to achieve program goals. Some evaluation research is concerned primarily or exclusively with procedure. Examples of evaluation questions that concern program procedures are: How long did teachers need to use the materials before students mastered the content? How well did the audiovisual equipment hold up over the school year? Did teachers have difficulty in using the inquiry approach to science teaching? To what extent did teachers actually use the inquiry approach? Answers to these questions usually require close and repeated observation of the program while it is in operation.

Evaluation of program resources and procedures is especially helpful for understanding the observed effects of the program. Suppose a program is observed to have negligible effects on student achievement. Decision makers may choose to discontinue the program because the evaluation was negative. Yet it may be that the program was ineffective because needed materials did not arrive on time, or because teachers experienced many interruptions that reduced the total time allotted to program implementation. If the evaluator had collected data on these resource and procedural problems, the decision makers might have chosen an alternative course of action (e.g., to remove the "bugs" from the program and try it again). Indeed, collection of data on both resources/procedures and program-goal attainment is very important in any type of formative evaluation. Decisions about the program revision can be made more effectively if developers know both how well the current version of the program is working *and* why.

Program Management

Most programs have a **management system** to monitor resources and procedures so that they are used effectively to achieve program goals. We usually think of management only in relation to large-scale programs such as a system of secondary education or curriculum coordination in a school district. Yet many curriculum materials contain built-in management procedures to monitor the student's instructional progress. One may also think of self-management (e.g., a teacher monitoring his classroom teaching in order to improve on-the-job performance).

Evaluation research may be focused on management systems as they relate to resource utilization and program procedures. Or the evaluation may be concerned with the impact of the management system on program-goal attainment. Decision makers may need answers to such questions as: Is the management system insuring the effective use of program resources? Is the management system as efficient as it can be? Are the management procedures being used as intended by the program developers? Each of these questions requires the evaluator to design research that delineates the management system and examines its workings.

EVALUATION MODELS

Evaluation research in education has proceeded at two levels. At one level evaluators have conducted many evaluation studies of specific educational phenomena. At the other level evaluators have spent much effort trying to understand evaluation itself. What is evaluation? What purposes should an evaluation serve? What is the proper relationship between evaluator and client? Should evaluators limit themselves to description or should they also make judgments and recommendations? Evaluators take different positions about these and related questions. Some evaluators have developed their positions into formal models of the evaluation process.

This section reviews the major formal models of educational evaluation. The models do not tell one explicitly how to conduct evaluation research. Rather they address questions of purpose and role and methodological orientation. Evaluators working within different models may use the same research techniques but for quite different purposes. If you are planning to do evaluation research, you should study the various models to determine which one best suits your educational philosophy and the philosophy of the clients whose program you will evaluate.

Evaluation of the Individual

Evaluation research can be traced back to at least the early 1900s when the testing movement began. Binet's intelligence test was published in 1904, and group ability testing began during World War I. Evaluation primarily involved the assessment of individual differences in intelligence and school achievement. This model of evaluation is still widely followed in American education. Also, evaluation of teachers, administrators, and other school personnel has become a matter of increasing interest to researchers and administrators.[23] Like assessment of students, personnel evaluation focuses on measurement of individual differences, and judgments are made by comparing the individual with a set of norms or a criterion.

Evaluation of Performance Relative to Objectives

Ralph Tyler's work on curriculum evaluation in the 1940's brought about a major change in educational evaluation.[24] Tyler's view was that curriculum should

---

23. For example, see Jason Millman, ed., *Handbook of Teacher Evaluation* (Beverly Hills, Calif.: Sage, 1981).
24. Ralph W. Tyler, *Basic Principles of Curriculum and Instruction: Syllabus for Education 360* (Chicago: University of Chicago Press, 1949).

be organized around explicit objectives and that the success of the curriculum should be judged on the basis of how well students achieve the objectives. The Tyler model marked a shift from evaluating individual students to evaluating the curriculum. Also, the Tyler model implied that students might perform poorly not because of lack of innate ability, but because of weaknesses in the curriculum.

Some later developments in evaluation reflect Tyler's emphasis on evaluation of objectives. We mentioned goal-free evaluation and the behavioral objectives movement in the preceding section. Formative and summative evaluation, to be discussed later, also are organized primarily around the assessment of objectives. Other evaluation models not discussed in this chapter—Provus's discrepancy model,[25] Popham's instructional objectives model,[26] and Stake's countenance model[27]—are designed to evaluate programs, curriculum, materials, and personnel in terms of explicit objectives. The Tyler model and its subsequent refinements continue to be a major force in educational evaluation.

Evaluation to Assist Decision-Making

The objectives-based models described above tend to focus on arms-length evaluations of completed programs. As evaluators began to work more closely with programs under development, they became interested in how they might contribute to this process. Evaluators saw that critical *decisions* needed to be made at each stage of program development. Also, they realized that they could collect evaluative data which would be useful to program developers in making these decisions. The CIPP model was formulated by Daniel Stufflebeam and his colleagues to show how evaluation could contribute to the decision-making process in program development.[28] CIPP is an acronym for four types of educational evaluation included in the model: context evaluation, input evaluation, process evaluation, and product evaluation. Each type of evaluation is tied to a different set of decisions that must be made in the planning and operation of a program.

Context evaluation involves analysis of problems and needs in a specific educational setting. A **need** is defined as a discrepancy between an existing condition and a desired condition. For example, if a teacher-pupil ratio of 1 to

25. Malcolm Provus, *Discrepancy Evaluation* (Berkeley, Calif.: McCutchan, 1971).
26. W. James Popham, *Educational Evaluation* (Englewood Cliffs, N.J.: Prentice-Hall, 1975).
27. Robert E. Stake, "The Countenance of Educational Evaluation," *Teachers College Record* 68 (1967): 523–40.
28. The CIPP Model is described in Daniel L. Stufflebeam et al., *Educational Evaluation and Decision Making* (Itasca, Ill.: F. E. Peacock, 1971).

25 is the existing condition in a school system, and if there is consensus that 1 to 20 would be a desirable ratio, we can say that a need exists. Once needs have been identified, the next step in context evaluation is to delineate program objectives that will alleviate the needs, that is, reduce the discrepancy between actual and desired conditions.

Input evaluation concerns judgments about the resources and strategies needed to accomplish program goals and objectives. Information collected during this stage of evaluation should help decision makers choose the best possible resources and strategies within certain constraints. The input evaluator may deal with such issues as whether certain resources are too expensive or unavailable, whether a particular strategy is likely to be effective in achieving program goals, whether certain strategies are legally or morally acceptable, and how best to utilize personnel as resources. Input evaluation requires the evaluator to have a wide range of knowledge about possible resources and strategies, as well as knowledge about research on their effectiveness in achieving different types of program outcomes.

Process evaluation involves the collection of evaluative data once the program has been designed and put into operation. A process evaluator might be called upon to design a data collection system for monitoring the day-to-day operation of a program. For example, the evaluator might keep attendance records on an inservice teacher-training program based on voluntary participation. If attendance data reveal deviations from what was anticipated, the program's decision makers can take action based on their appraisal of the data. Without such a recordkeeping system, the program might deteriorate, perhaps irreversibly, before the decision makers become aware of what is happening. Another function of process evaluation is to keep records of program events over a period of time. These records may prove useful at a later time in detecting strengths and weaknesses of the program that account for its observed outcomes.

The fourth element of the CIPP model is **product evaluation.** The task of product evaluation is to determine the extent to which the goals of the program have been achieved. Measures of the goals are developed and administered. The resulting data can be used by program administrators to make decisions about continuing the program and modifying it.

Developers of the CIPP model stress the desirability of close collaboration between evaluators and program decision makers. Each of the types of evaluation described above requires that three broad tasks be performed: delineating the kinds of information needed for decision making, obtaining the information, and synthesizing the information so that it is maximally useful in making decisions. The first and third steps (delineation and synthesis) should be done as a collaborative effort between evaluator and decision maker. Obtaining information is a technical activity and should be delegated primarily to the evaluator.

Evaluation to Identify Issues and Concerns

The evaluation models described above are very useful, but they do not satisfactorily address a number of important problems of evaluation. The objectives-based models, for example, take a program's objectives or observed effects as givens. The models do not question whether the objectives are worthwhile or whether there is consensus among interested parties on the objectives. What point is there in conducting a rigorous evaluation of students' achievement of trivial objectives or of objectives that are not valued by significant constituencies?

The politics of evaluation is another matter that is not addressed by traditional evaluation models. Various groups have a stake in the outcome of an evaluation study, and may try to influence the evaluation process accordingly. Should the evaluator resist these political influences or incorporate them into the design of the evaluation study? Another problem is that under certain conditions evaluations may do more harm than good. As we stated above, people generally do not like being evaluated, and the evaluation process may hamper the very performance that is being assessed. How can the evaluator work with the client so that the evaluation produces the most benefit and least harm?

Traditional objectives-based models also have come under increasing criticism because of their reliance on positivistic methods of inquiry. The experimental-control group design with random assignment was viewed as the most desirable method, even though it was rarely achievable in practice. Some evaluators became more interested in using subjective methods of inquiry such as naturalistic observation and ethnography. (Positivistic versus subjective methods of inquiry are discussed in chapter 1.)

These problems and limitations of traditional evaluation led to the development of several new evaluation models. One of these models is **responsive evaluation,** which is described in detail later in the chapter. The focus of responsive evaluation is the concerns and issues of stakeholding audiences. A **stakeholding audience** is a group of persons who are involved in or affected by the entity being evaluated. A **concern** is any matter about which a stakeholder feels threatened or any claim that they want to substantiate. An **issue** is any point of contention among the stakeholders. Concerns and issues provide a much wider focus for evaluation than the behavioral objectives of traditional evaluation. Responsive evaluation relies extensively on methods of subjective inquiry to gain insight into concerns, issues, and related matters.

Major differences between traditional and responsive evaluation models are summarized in table 17.1.[29] You can see that choice of an evaluation model

---

29. Table 17.1 from Egon G. Guba and Yvonna S. Lincoln, *Effective Evaluation* (San Francisco: Jossey-Bass, 1981), p. 28.

TABLE 17.1

Comparison of Objectives-Based and Responsive Evaluation Modes

Comparison Item	Type of Evaluation	
	Preordinate	Responsive
Orientation	Formal.	Informal.
Value perspective	Singular; consensual.	Pluralistic; possibility of conflict.
Basis for evaluation design (organizer)	Program intents, objectives, goals, hypotheses; evaluator preconceptions such as performance, mastery, ability, aptitude, measurable outcomes; the instrumental values of education.	Audience concerns and issues; program activities; reactions, motivations, or problems of persons in and around the evaluand.
Design completed when?	At beginning of evaluation.	Never—continuously evolving.
Evaluator role	Stimulator of subjects with a view to testing critical performance.	Stimulated by subjects and activities.
Methods	Objective; "taking readings," for example, testing.	Subjective, for example, observations and interviews; negotiations and interactions.
Communication	Formal; reports; typically one stage.	Informal; portrayals; often two stage.
Feedback	At discrete intervals; often only once, at end.	Informal; continuously evolving as needed by audiences.
Form of feedback	Written report, identifying variables and depicting the relationships among them; symbolic interpretation.	Narrative-type depiction, often oral (if that is what the audience prefers), modeling what the program is like, providing vicarious experience, "holistic" communication.
Paradigm	Experimental psychology.	Anthropology, journalism, poetry.

751

is important because the models lead the evaluator to emphasize certain phenomena and to select particular methods of inquiry. We would not argue that
one type of evaluation model is better than another. Each type is useful depending upon the purpose to be served by the evaluation.

Adversary Evaluation

Adversary evaluation is a model of evaluation that is related in certain respects
to responsive evaluation, described above. This model was derived from procedures used in jury trials and administrative hearings in the field of law.[30]
The distinguishing features of adversary evaluation are its use of a wide array
of data; its reliance on human testimony; and, most importantly, the fact that
it is "adversarial," meaning that both positive and negative judgments about
the program are encouraged. Adversary evaluation is more structured and limited than the responsive evaluation model described later.

Adversary evaluation has four major stages. The first stage is to generate
a broad range of issues. To do this, the evaluation team surveys various groups
involved in the program (users, managers, funding agencies, etc.) to determine
what they believe are relevant issues. Examples of such isues are: "Should this
program be terminated, so that the alternative program can be instituted?"
"Should funding for this program be increased by at least fifty percent?" "Are
students making the learning gains that we expect them to make?"

The second stage involves reducing the list of issues to a manageable
number. One method of doing this is to have a group of respondents list the
issues in order of importance. The third stage is to form two opposing evaluation teams (the adversaries) and provide them an opportunity to prepare arguments in favor of or in opposition to the program on each issue. As part of
this process, the teams can interview potential witnesses, study existing evaluation reports, and collect new data. The final stage is to conduct prehearing
sessions and a formal hearing. In the formal hearing the adversarial teams
present their arguments and evidence before the program's decision makers.

A large-scale adversarial evaluation of a teacher education program at Indiana University was conducted by Robert Wolf and his associates.[31] A decision maker who witnessed the process made the following comment: "The
process illuminated decision alternatives and consequences that could not be
anticipated prior to the hearing. The hearing generated new decision points,
alternatives, and potential ramifications."[32] This statement illustrates the fact

30. Robert L. Wolf, "Trial by Jury: A New Evaluation Method," *Phi Delta Kappan* 57 (1975): 185–87.
31. Ibid.
32. Ibid., p. 187.

that the end-goal of the adversarial model, indeed, of any evaluation model, is to facilitate educational decision making.

Although adversarial evaluation is very "human" in its tolerance for opposing views about programs and its respect for a wide array of data sources, it does have problems.[33] Adversarial evaluation is expensive and time-consuming. Also, its results can be biased if one of the evaluation teams is more skilled in argumentation than the other. Adversarial evaluation is intriguing, however. Elements of the model perhaps can be simplified and adapted for use in evaluation research that has limited resources.

TYPES OF EVALUATION RESEARCH

Needs Assessment

A **need** is usually defined as a discrepancy between an existing set of conditions and a desired set of conditions. For example, suppose an educator makes the assertion, "We need to place more emphasis on science education in our elementary school curriculum." The educator is saying in effect that there is a discrepancy between the existing curriculum and a desired curriculum. Note, too, that this statement of need reflects a **judgment** about the present merit of the curriculum. For this reason professional evaluators are interested in the determination of need states in education.

Educational needs can be assessed systematically using research methodology. This type of evaluation research is important because assessment of needs provides the foundation for developing new programs and for making changes in existing programs. The substantial resource expenditures typically required for program development will be wasted if they are based on a faulty needs assessment.

Jamil Effarah conducted a needs assessment as a dissertation project.[34] He collected information about the extent to which electronic data processing (EDP) *is* and *should* be taught as a curriculum topic in high school business education programs. The information was intended to be of use to state education agencies, curriculum developers, and other groups charged with the responsibility of making decisions about EDP instruction. The study addressed many evaluation issues; we shall consider only a few of them here.

---

33. W. James Popham and Dale Carlson, "Deep Dark Deficits of the Adversary Evaluation Model," *Educational Researcher* 6 (1977): 3–6. See also Paul Thurston, "Revitalizing Adversary Evaluation: Deep Dark Deficits or Muddled Mistaken Musings," *Educational Researcher* 7, no. 7 (1978): 3–8.
34. Jamil E. Effarah, "The Impact of Electronic Data Processing on Business Education in the Secondary Schools of Oregon" (Ph.D. dissertation, University of Oregon, 1977).

The research was designed as a questionnaire survey (see chapter 11) to collect information from high school business education teachers about the current status of EDP instruction in their program, and to collect their opinions about the desired status of EDP instruction. The *Oregon Business Teachers Directory* was used to define the population of secondary business education programs to be surveyed. Using the directory, Effarah selected a stratified random sample of ten small programs (one or two teachers) and ten large programs (five or more teachers). All teachers in each of the selected programs were requested to complete a questionnaire.

The questionnaire was contructed to collect data about a variety of issues related to decision making about EDP instruction: the relative importance of certain EDP instructional objectives, training for careers in EDP, and integration of EDP instruction into the business education program. For one part of the questionnaire, Effarah conducted a review of literature to identify the range of EDP instructional objectives that have been considered by educators. These objectives were synthesized into a new list and included in the questionnaire. The teachers were asked to rate each objective on a 6-point scale (0 = not at all; 5 = extensively) with respect to current and desired status; teachers also were asked for their opinion on how it should be integrated into coursework. A sample item from the questionnaire is shown in table 17.2.[35]

The primary data analysis was to compare ratings of current and desired status for each objective. Ratings for small programs and large programs also were compared. The results of these analyses are shown in table 17.3.[36] The major finding is that EDP instruction should be given more emphasis in high school business education programs, according to teachers surveyed in the study. This finding is based on the observed discrepancy between the "current" and "should" rating for all the objectives. An additional finding is that large programs currently place more emphasis on EDP instruction than do small programs; also, teachers in large programs desire more emphasis on EDP instruction than do teachers of small programs. These differences between large and small programs may reflect the fact that teachers in large programs have more actual and potential personnel, equipment, and other resources with which to conduct EDP instruction.

Effarah used the results of this discrepancy analysis to make recommendations to various decision-making groups. For example:

1. . . . . The author recommends that the schools training secondary business teachers should develop a "Computers in Business Education" course and require it of all preservice business teachers. The course should cover the

---

35. Ibid.
36. Ibid.

major objectives deemed important by business educators (especially objectives 12, 14, 15, 2, 11, and 4), which are not in the typical introductory programming course. (p. 150)
2. The business education teacher [should] work with other business teachers in the school to develop a comprehensive school plan for EDP instruction. (p. 152)

TABLE 17.2

Excerpt from Questionnaire on Electronic Data Processing

This questionnaire deals with instructional objectives related to electronic data processing (EDP). In this questionnaire EDP is defined as the handling of information by means of a machine (that is, the computer) using electronic circuitry at electronic speed, and as the use of electromechanical equipment for similar purposes. Please rate the extent to which these objectives are *currently* taught in your school's business education program. Also rate the extent to which these objectives *should* be taught in your school's business education program.

Please circle the appropriate number on the scale from 0 to 5 as follows:

0 = Not at all
1 = Giving basic information about such an objective for one or more class periods of instruction dealing with related topics
5 = Extensive and in-depth efforts on the part of business teachers during a semester program of instruction or more.

The undefined points 2, 3, and 4 represent intermediate levels between basic ("1") and extensive, in-depth ("5") instruction.

If you do not understand an objective sufficiently to rate it, leave blank the scales relating to it. However, please make an effort to rate every objective.

Objective 1

Student will develop an understanding of the history of electronic data processing, including recent trends.

Is now taught in the business education program in my school.	0 1 2 3 4 5
Should be taught in the business education program in my school.	0 1 2 3 4 5

_____ In a course devoted exclusively to this objective?
_____ As part of a course in electronic data processing?
_____ As part of a course in another business subject, such as office procedures, accounting. Specify the subject: _____
_____ As part of a course in a department other than business education. Specify the department: _____

TABLE 17.3

Extent to Which EDP Instructional Objectives Are Currently Taught and Should Be Taught

EDP Instructional Objectives	Small Programs (N = 10)		Large Programs (N = 10)	
	Current	Should	Current	Should
	$\overline{X}$(SD)	$\overline{X}$(SD)	$\overline{X}$(SD)	$\overline{X}$(SD)
1. Understanding the history of EDP	0.33(0.48)	2.00(0.97)	2.14(1.70)	3.28(1.29)
2. Understanding changes in business resulting from growth of computer technology	1.00(1.08)	2.44(125)	2.28(1.50)	3.38(1.29)
3. Understanding the basic concept of EDP functions	0.61(0.85)	2.28(1.07)	2.10(1.70)	3.21(1.32)
4. Skills in data representation, coding, and data entry	0.67(1.03)	2.44(1.15)	2.12(1.81)	3.14(1.35)
5. Understanding the operation of different unit record equipment	0.50(0.79)	2.00(1.49)	1.81(1.68)	2.81(1.57)
6. Skill in using computer for running canned programs	0.0(0.0)	1.28(1.27)	1.07(1.49)	2.21(1.46)
7. Knowledge about basic hardware components and concepts of EDP	0.22(0.55)	1.50(1.29)	1.75(1.73)	2.79(1.53)
8. Understanding measuring and data collection devices as related to EDP	0.06(0.24)	1.00(1.03)	1.12(1.54)	1.12(1.54)
9. Knowledge about software and operating systems	0.11(0.32)	1.06(0.94)	1.10(1.25)	2.32(1.32)
10. Skill in using a high-level language at an introductory level	0.22(0.94)	1.56(1.38)	1.53(1.75)	2.72(1.51)
11. Understanding the role of EDP in solving problems	0.33(0.77)	2.22(1.31)	1.95(1.77)	3.25(1.40)
12. Understanding the effects of EDP in our daily life	0.94(1.21)	2.83(1.69)	2.05(1.62)	3.40(1.27)
13. Understanding EDP applications in business systems and operations	1.00(1.14)	2.78(1.39)	2.40(1.58)	3.54(1.12)
14. Understanding existing jobs and opportunities in EDP	0.94(0.87)	2.72(1.56)	2.30(1.46)	3.56(1.20)
15. Understanding the educational requirements for EDP job-entry level positions	0.72(1.07)	2.39(1.42)	2.03(1.53)	3.54(1.50)

3. The Oregon Business Education Council, [which] is the statewide advisory council to the Oregon State Specialists in business and office education and in marketing and distributive education. . . should exchange information and initiate a change in high school graduation requirements to include a course in data processing for business majors. (pp. 154, 156)

These recommendations illustrate how a needs assessment can improve the decision-making process by providing a discrepancy analysis of current and desired conditions in education.

This example suggests that needs assessment research is relatively uncomplicated and clear. Further analysis, however, suggests that needs assessment is problematic. For example, the definition of *need* at the beginning of this section is ambiguous in certain respects. What is a *desired* set of conditions? J. Roth identified five types of desired states: ideals, norms, minimums, desires (wants), and expectations.[37] A need is a discrepancy between an actual state and any one of these five desired states. The goal of a college degree for all citizens (ideal desired state) is certainly a different kind of need than the goal of basic skill in reading for all children (a minimum desired state). Many needs assessments do not make clear how urgent or optional are the desired states that are being determined. For example, do the "should" data in table 17.3 reflect preferences (wants) or feelings about minimum necessary conditions for the curriculum?

Another problem with the needs assessment process is that the values underlying needs are often left unarticulated. It is helpful to determine quantitatively whether certain groups view elements of education (e.g., small class size, compulsory school prayer, computer-assisted instruction) as needs. These quantitative expressions of need just scratch the surface, though. Personal values and standards are important determinants of needs, and they should be assessed to round out one's understanding of needs among the groups being studied.

You should also be aware that needs assessment data are usually reported as group trends. There may be important individual differences in stated needs that should be explored. For example, the data in Table 17.3 reveal substantial standard deviations for some of the "should" statements. If these variations are not examined and understood, one may assume a consensus exists and proceed to act accordingly. Program development can fall apart, though, as conflicts among participants eventually surface.

The problems identified above can be handled by supplementing quantitative methods (of the type used in Effarah's study) with case study method-

---

37. J. Roth, "Needs and the Needs Assessment Process," *Evaluation News* 5 (1977): 15–17.

ology. Naturalistic observation, ethnography, and personal interview can fill in the description of need states given by quantitative analyses.

Formative and Summative Evaluation

Michael Scriven made what has come to be considered an important distinction concerning the purpose of educational evaluation.[38] He observed that evaluation serves two different functions. The function of **formative evaluation** is to collect data about educational programs while they are still being developed. The evaluative data can be used by developers to "form" and modify the program. In some instances the evaluation findings may lead to a decision to abort further development so that resources are not wasted on a program that ultimately has little chance of being effective. The preliminary field test and main field test of the research and development cycle described in chapter 18 exemplify the formative role of evaluation.

The summative function of evaluation occurs after the program has been fully developed. **Summative evaluation** is conducted to determine how worthwhile the final program is, especially in comparison with other competing programs. Summative data are useful to educators who must make purchase or adoption decisions concerning new products, programs, or procedures.

The distinction between formative and summative evaluation applies not only to education but to many other fields as well. Industry frequently uses techniques of formative evaluation to guide the development of new products. The results of each evaluation provide data to help engineers and others improve the design or functioning of the product. The same formative data may also help managers decide how much and what kinds of resources to commit to further development of the product. When the completed product reaches the marketplace, other groups are likely to conduct summative evaluations. Each potential purchaser will evaluate the product against personal criteria and perhaps against other products that are commercially available. Summative evaluations of high rigor are conducted by such groups as Consumers Union, the publisher of *Consumer Reports*. Ralph Nader and his associates have become widely known because of their summative evaluations of certain products and programs.

The distinction between the formative and summative function of evaluation is important because it affects the process by which evaluation is carried out. Formative evaluation is often done by an "in-house" evaluator, whose job it is to help the team of developers. In fact, during the program development process, some members of the team may perform a dual function, being both

38. Michael Scriven, "The Methodology of Evaluation," in *Curriculum Evaluation*, ed. Robert E. Stake (Chicago: Rand McNally, 1967).

developers and evaluators. Summative evaluation, though is usually done by an external evaluator. This person probably should not be associated with the development team, in order to avoid being biased or co-opted by them. The summative evaluator is more likely to be responsive to the needs and requirements of educational decision makers, potential users of the program, and the agency that has funded the development of the program.

Formative and summative evaluation often differ in instrumentation, research control, and generalizability. Formative data tend to be collected through observation, questionnaire, and interview. Research control and generalizability are not major concerns. (These features of formative evaluation also characterize the preliminary field test phase in research and development; see chapter 18.) In contrast, summative data tend to be collected with standardized instruments having validity and reliability. Research control and generalizability of results are built into the design of the summative evaluation study.

The distinctions between formative and summative evaluation described above are not universally applied. One occasionally finds an example of formative evaluation that is rigorous and extensive. One also may find summative evaluation studies that approach the casualness of a consumer who gives a product no more than a quick looking over before making a purchase decision.

An Example of Summative Evaluation

As we stated above, summative evaluations are done on completed programs. The results of summative evaluations can be very useful to educators who must make adoption decisions concerning particular programs. The following example of summative evaluation concerns the effectiveness of a new moral education curriculum.[39]

The curriculum materials, published by Guidance Associates, are intended to develop the moral reasoning ability of primary-grade children. The materials are based on a cognitive-developmental approach, which posits that moral reasoning develops under two conditions: first, the child must experience a situation that causes a moral conflict about the proper course of action; and second, the child is exposed to moral reasoning slightly more evolved than his own. The materials consist of sound filmstrips that incorporate these conditions and that are appropriate for primary-grade children. The filmstrips present moral dilemmas involving truth telling, sharing and taking turns, promise keeping, property rights, and rules.

A pre-post control-group experiment (see chapter 15) was designed to test the effectiveness of the curriculum. Six second-grade classes were randomly assigned to three treatment conditions. Of the two classes assigned to each

39. Robert L. Selman and Marcus Lieberman, "Moral Education in the Primary Grades: An Evaluation of a Developmental Curriculum," *Journal of Educational Psychology* 67 (1976): 712–16.

treatment, one contained both middle- and working-class students, and the other middle-class students only. Students in the first treatment observed the filmstrips and participated in discussions led by teachers who were expert in the cognitive-developmental approach to moral reasoning. Students in the second treatment also observed the filmstrips and participated in discussions; but in this case the discussions were led by teachers without training in moral reasoning development. The third treatment was a control condition in which teachers and students went about their regular schedule, without exposure to the filmstrips or discussions on moral reasoning.

A measure of moral reasoning was administered to the students on three occasions: before the intructional program (pretest); in the winter immediately after the program (posttest); and at the end of the school year to determine long-term effects (delayed posttest). The measure was based on students' verbal responses to standard moral dilemmas; the responses were probed to determine level of moral reasoning. A score of 100 indicates simple awareness of moral intentions that may underlie a course of action. A score of 200 indicates ability to consider how one person might judge another person's moral intentions.

The moral-concept scores for the various treatment groups are presented in table 17.4.[40] Analysis of covariance was used to test the statistical significance of observed differences. The results of this analysis indicated that the two treatment conditions significantly outperformed the control condition both on the posttest and on the post-posttest. The mean scores of the expert-led and untrained-teacher-led groups were not significantly different from each other. An interesting result in table 17.4 is that students in the treatment conditions continued to gain from posttest to post-posttest, even though the curriculum terminated prior to the posttest. Selman and Lieberman suggest that the continued growth is due to the fact that "the four teachers whose classes defined the experimental group continued to use the methods of small group discussion to resolve interpersonal and moral conflicts which arose in the classroom throughout the school year."

Of what use are the evaluation findings for decision makers? The findings may help educators who are interested in promoting the development of moral reasoning as a school outcome. The promising results of this study may encourage them to try out the curriculum program in their own school district. They may also decide to conduct their own evaluation, since a small range of schools and student characteristics were represented in the original experimental design. Furthermore, Selman and Lieberman note that "the biggest gains occurred not in an expert-led class but in the class of the lay teacher who showed the greatest interest in the program, its techniques, and the underlying process."[41] This finding suggests that it may be desirable for decision makers

40. Ibid.

TABLE 17.4

Pretest, Posttest, and Post-posttest Mean and Standard Deviations of Moral Concept Scores

Social Class of Students	Expert-Led Group		Informed Lay-Led Group		Control Group	
	M	SD	M	SD	M	SD
Mixed middle and working class						
Pretest	109.1	9.08	116.7	21.58	103.6	26.73
Posttest	125.0	15.80	125.0	24.97	110.7	13.36
Post-posttest	163.6	28.19	147.2	26.33	117.9	18.91
Middle class						
Pretest	112.5	20.03	122.9	24.94	116.7	21.60
Posttest	137.5	16.67	135.4	14.77	122.2	19.55
Post-posttest	156.2	28.75	189.6	32.75	130.6	20.82

to recruit interested teachers to try out the curriculum program, at least initially, rather than require all teachers to adopt the program.

Curriculum materials like those evaluated by Selman and Lieberman are a worthwhile focus for summative evaluation. New curriculum materials continually appear in the marketplace. Some years ago a survey by Educational Products Information Exchange revealed that more than half a million different curriculum materials are available in this country.[42] These include textbooks, pamphlets, audiotapes, slide-tapes, films, and other media formats. Only a small percentage of these materials have ever been evaluated for effectiveness.

Experiments are the most common type of research design used to evaluate the outcomes of curriculum materials and programs. Therefore, the student planning to do a curriculum evaluation is advised to read chapters 15 and 16 carefully and to consult other sources on experimental design.

An Example of Formative Evaluation

The following example illustrates the use of formative evaluation in the development of a teacher training program called the Minicourse. The format of minicourses is described in chapter 18.

41. Ibid.
42. Educational Products Information Exchange, *Report on a National Study of the Nature and Quality of Instructional Materials Most Used by Teachers and Learners* (New York: EPIE, 1976, Report No. 76).

Discussing Controversial Issues (DCI) is one of the minicourses that was developed at the Far West Laboratory for Educational Research and Development and that has been published as a completed product.[43] While DCI was under development, it was subjected to several formative evaluations. One of these was the main field test (see chapter 18). A total of 43 high school teachers volunteered to participate in the field test by undertaking training in the minicourse. Another 19 high school teachers participated in a no-training control condition.

The goal of DCI is to improve the discussion skills of both teachers and students in dealing with curriculum-related, school-related, and social issues. Since DCI is directed at two distinct groups (teachers and students), it was necessary to design the formative evaluation to include both of them. Also, it was necessary to collect several types of data in order to address the developers' various concerns about the program's effectiveness.

One aspect of the formative evaluation was to conduct an experiment to determine whether the trained teachers and students made greater gains in use of the discussion skills than did the control group.[44] The experimental design was similar to the one used in the evaluation of the moral-development curriculum, described earlier. The experimental and control groups were asked to conduct videotaped discussions before and after the training period. The videotapes were scored for occurrences of the minicourse's discussion skills.

Analysis of the videotapes indicated that DCI resulted in improvement in the use of discussion techniques by the majority of experimental classes. There were problems, however:

> Some of the behaviors exhibited substantial shifts in the desired direction, while others were of too low a magnitude to be of practical value when considered individually. . . . As utilized in the main field test, DCI did not accomplish its specific objectives with . . . opportunity and compensatory classes in urban schools.[45]

These results suggested the need for substantial revision in the training program. The lack of change in some behaviors indicated that more intensive training over a longer period of time was necessary. Nevertheless other data indicated that most teachers would be unwilling to devote more time to this type of training. Thus the developers decided to retain the same number of training hours as before; they also decided to include a list of additional training activ-

43. Meredith D. Gall, Rita Weathersby, Rachel Ann Elder, Morris K. Lai, and Barbara Dunning, *Discussing Controversial Issues* (Bloomington, Ind.: Agency for Instructional Television, 1976).

44. Morris K. Lai, Meredith D. Gall, Rachel Ann Elder, and Rita Weathersby, "Main Field Test Report of Discussing Controversial Issues" (San Francisco: Far West Laboratory for Educational Research and Development, 1972, Report A72–12).

45. Ibid., p. 46.

ities in the Teachers Handbook for those teachers who might wish to develop a higher level of discussion skill in themselves and in their students. The low motivation and performance levels that were observed in some urban schools were dealt with by revising DCI to include more film models of urban school discussions. Although the developers did not feel this solution was fully satisfactory, there were insufficient resources to consider other, potentially more effective alternatives.

Additional data for formative evaluation were obtained through a series of questionnaires, interviews, and classroom observations. These instruments were used during and at the end of the training program with the experimental classes. (Since the control groups did not take DCI, they lacked an experience base for making recommendations to the developers.) The instruments focused both on strengths and weaknesses of the program—on what participants liked or disliked, on procedures that ran smoothly and on procedures that were difficult or inefficient. Also, participants were asked directly for their ideas on how the program could be improved. These data proved very helpful to the developers in revising the program to increase its effectiveness. Some of the revisions that were based on the formative evaluation data are as follows:

1. Students complained that the Student Handbook was boring and difficult. In response, the developers completely rewrote the Student Handbook making extensive use of cartoons and other visuals. The reading level was lowered, and humor was added. The writing style became more direct and informal.
2. Both teachers and students had difficulty with the discussion skill of asking about value bases underlying a person's opinion on an issue. Since the program already had so much content, the developers decided to respond to the criticism by dropping this skill from the revised version.
3. Teachers complained about the rigidity of the four-week schedule used in the main field test of DCI. Consequently, the revised version was made self-pacing.
4. Teachers stated that they had difficulty in integrating the program with their regular course content. In response, the developers prepared a set of sample lesson plans to show teachers how they can use course-related issues as a vehicle for discussion skill training, and how homework assignments can relate both to course content and in-class discussions.

Many other revisions in DCI were made as a result of the formative evaluation. Without these evaluation data, the developers would have had only their own intuition to rely on in revising the program. Indeed, they might have seen no need for revision and would have attempted to distribute the materials as is.

The student planning to do a formative evaluation needs to identify a program that is in the process of being developed. The student should consult with the developers to determine the critical attributes of the program that need to be evaluated for possible revision. In designing instruments for formative evaluation, one should not hesitate to include questions that ask program participants directly for their recommendations about needed program revisions. The student is also advised to read chapter 18 carefully and to consult other sources on educational research and development and on formative evaluation.

Responsive Evaluation

As we stated above, the distinguishing characteristic of responsive evaluation is its focus on the concerns and issues of the persons who have a stake in the evaluation. Egon Guba and Yvonna Lincoln identified four major phases that occur in an evaluation of this type.[46]

The first major phase involves initiating and organizing the evaluation. Guba and Lincoln recommend that the evaluator and client negotiate an evaluation contract that specifies such matters as: identification of the entity to be evaluated, the purpose of the evaluation, rights of access to records, and guarantees of confidentiality and anonymity. It is particularly important to identify the stakeholders in the evaluation. A **stakeholder** is anyone who is involved in or affected by the entity being evaluated. Each stakeholder has the right to have his or her concerns and issues reflected in the evaluation process. It is also important to identify political factors that can affect the evaluation process. Guba and Lincoln cited the example of an evaluator who was asked to evaluate the effectiveness of paraprofessional teacher aides in improving student learning. It became apparent to the evaluator, though, that the position of teacher aide also served important political purposes: it provided linkages between school and community, and it provided jobs for community members. Thus, there was much pressure on the evaluator by school officials to show teacher aides in a positive light.

The second phase of a responsive evaluation is to identify the concerns, issues, and values of the stakeholders. These factors are usually identified by a series of interviews and questionnaires administered to all or a sample of stakeholders. Guba and Lincoln cited the example of a responsive evaluation of the governance structure in a particular school system. The special focus of the evaluation was whether the governance structure was open to inputs from various stakeholding audiences in establishing school policy. Stakeholders included the school board, school administrators, teachers, students, parents, the city's mayoral staff, and influential members of the community.

Interviews with the stakeholders revealed several serious concerns, such

46. Guba and Lincoln, op. cit.

as citizen lockout in decision making (for example, the school board cut out elementary art despite parental opposition) and arrogation of power by a small elite (for example, school staff felt that they had little say in school affairs). Several issues were also identified: whether school policy formulation should be centralized or decentralized; whether policy should be formulated by professionals or by lay groups; and whether the school board should be elected or appointed. These issues and concerns express the underlying values of the stakeholders. For example, some of the stakeholders were found to value a high quality curriculum, a rational decision-making process, equality of representation in decision-making, and accountability.

The third phase of a responsive evaluation is to gather information that pertains to the concerns, issues, and values identified by the stakeholders. The evaluator also should collect descriptive information about the entity being evaluated and about standards that will be used in making judgments concerning the entity. Information in responsive evaluations can be gathered by a variety of methods: naturalistic observation, interview, questionnaire, standardized tests. Consider the example of evaluating a school system's governance structure. A concern of some stakeholders was that the school board cut out elementary art despite parental opposition. The evaluator could reconstruct this occurrence to determine what kind of evidence there is to substantiate this concern. The evaluator also needs to work extensively with the various stakeholders to gain a deeper understanding of the issues, values, and standards involving the entity that is being evaluated.

The final phase of a responsive evaluation is to prepare reports of results and recommendations. The case study format is used frequently in such reports, but when appropriate, a traditional research reporting format (see chapter 21) can be used. A responsive evaluation report will contain extensive descriptions of the concerns and issues identified by the stakeholders. Guba and Lincoln also recommend that the evaluator—in negotiation with the stakeholders—make judgments and recommendations based on the gathered information.

Unlike the other types of evaluation research described above, responsive evaluators do not specify a research design at the outset of their work. Instead, responsive evaluators use **emergent designs,** meaning that the design of the research changes as the evaluator gains new insights into the concerns and issues of the stakeholders. For example, Guba and Lincoln compared sampling techniques in emergent and traditional research design: "Sampling is almost never representative or random but purposive, intended to exploit competing views and fresh perspectives as fully as possible. Sampling stops when information becomes redundant rather than when subjects are representatively sampled."[47]

47. Ibid., p. 276.

We have described responsive evaluation here because it represents an important development in educational evaluation. However, we caution the student who is thinking about doing a responsive evaluation as a thesis or dissertation. Responsive evaluations are usually quite complex and are best done by a team of evaluators rather than by an individual working alone. Members of a team can act as a check on each other and ensure that a comprehensive picture of the entity being evaluated is formed. Also, the responsive evaluator should be conversant with a variety of research designs ranging from formal experiments to ethnographic inquiry. The reason for this requirement is that emergent design requires the selection of different research methodologies depending upon the phenomena being investigated at a particular point in the evaluation. The graduate student is unlikely to have this range of expertise. A responsive evaluation project can be considered if the student will be working as a member of an experienced team. In this situation the student might select one set of concerns or issues as a focus for the thesis or dissertation.

MISTAKES SOMETIMES MADE IN DOING EVALUATION RESEARCH

1. Evaluator ignores some standards relating to utility, feasibility, propriety, and accuracy in designing an evaluation study.
2. Fails to delineate all aspects of the program that is being evaluated.
3. Does not use measures that are directly linked to program goals.
4. Ignores possible side-effects not included in the formal statement of program goals.
5. Does not relate evaluation findings to decisions that need to be made about the program.
6. Does not consider alternative models of evaluation in designing a study.
7. Does not consider using both qualitative and quantitative instruments in designing a formative or summative evaluation.

ANNOTATED REFERENCES

Berk, Ronald A., ed. *Educational Evaluation Methodology: The State of the Art.* Baltimore: Johns Hopkins University Press, 1981.

The chapters in this book were written by noted researchers specializing in educational evaluation. The book presents procedures for dealing with such aspects of evaluation as measurement of program effects, evaluation design, data analysis, and communication of evaluation results.

Cook, Thomas D., and Reichardt, Charles S., ed. *Qualitative and Quantitative Methods in Evaluation Research.* Beverly Hills, Calif.: Sage, 1979.

This book of contributed chapters would be especially useful for the researcher planning a responsive evaluation study or a quantitative study that will include collection of qualitative data. Several examples of studies that used qualitative methodology are presented.

Eisner, Elliot W. *The Educational Imagination: On the Design and Evaluation of School Programs.* New York: Macmillan, 1979.

This is an original conception of curriculum and evaluation by a prominent art educator. Eisner develops the notion of educational evaluator as connoisseur and critic. His views are closely related to his advocacy of an artistic, subjective approach to research (see chapter 1 of this book).

Freeman, Howard E., and Solomon, Marian A., eds. *Evaluation Studies Review Annual,* vol. 6. Beverly Hills, Calif.: Sage, 1981.

Each volume in this annual publication includes 30 or so chapters on evaluation. Some of the chapters deal with problems of evaluation methodology and utilization. Other chapters are reports of evaluation studies in such fields as education, law and public safety, health, the environment, and social services. Volume 6, for example, includes evaluation studies of the 4-H program, Public Law 94–142 (mainstreaming), income maintenance programs, psychotherapy, motorcycle helmet laws, and offshore nuclear power plants.

House, Ernest R. "Assumptions Underlying Evaluation Models." *Educational Researcher* 7, no. 3 (1978): 4–12.

This article compares and contrasts the evaluation models presented in this chapter. The author uses underlying theoretical assumptions of the models as a basis for comparison.

Morris, Lynn; Fitz-Gibbon, Carol; and Henerson, Marlene. *Program Evaluation Kit.* Beverly Hills, Calif.: Sage, 1978.

This "kit" consists of eight small books, each of which covers a different aspect of objectives-based evaluation. The books provide step-by-step procedures for dealing with such problems as program goal identification, research design, measurement, data analysis, and report preparation. The first volume in the kit provides an overview of program evaluation, including both formative and summative types of evaluation.

Walker, Decker F., and Schaffarzick, Jon. "Comparing Curricula." *Review of Educational Research* 44 (1974): 83–111.

The authors review evaluation studies in which innovative curricula are compared with traditional curricula. The findings of their review demonstrate the importance of curriculum content in determining learning outcomes and

RESEARCH DESIGN AND METHODOLOGY

the need to include a variety of achievement measures to reflect the distinctive objectives of the curricula being compared.

SELF-CHECK TEST

Circle the correct answer to each of the following questions. An answer key is provided on page 881.

1. Educational evaluation can be used to assist
    a. program management.
    b. policy analysis.
    c. political decision-making.
    d. all of the above.
2. Educational evaluation and educational research
    a. have the same purpose, but use different methodologies.
    b. have the same purpose, but are conducted in different settings.
    c. have different purposes, but use the same methodologies.
    d. use the same methodologies, but differ in degree of experimental control.
3. The propriety standard in educational evaluation means that
    a. the evaluation design is appropriate to the settings in which the study will be conducted.
    b. the rights of persons affected by the evaluation are protected.
    c. reports are submitted to stakeholders in a timely manner.
    d. the criterion tests used in the evaluation are content-valid.
4. In evaluating a program, it is important to delineate
    a. goals.
    b. resources.
    c. the management system.
    d. all of the above.
5. A basic principle of goal-free evaluation is that
    a. the evaluator should not know in advance the program goals.
    b. the evaluator should not know in advance the decisions that need to be made about the program.
    c. the evaluation design should not have goals.
    d. the evaluation should be organized around behavioral objectives rather than goals.
6. Objectives-based evaluation is used primarily to
    a. determine how well a program is achieving its objectives.
    b. compare the performance of an individual student with group norms.
    c. identify concerns of stakeholding audiences.
    d. help evaluators identify their objectives for doing an evaluation study.

7. In the CIPP model, close collaboration between evaluators and program decision makers
   a. is strongly encouraged throughout the evaluation process.
   b. is strongly discouraged throughout the evaluation process.
   c. is strongly discouraged once the goals of the evaluation research have been settled.
   d. is encouraged only for the purpose of summative evaluation.
8. Adversary evaluation is characterized by
   a. use of various data sources.
   b. reliance on human testimony.
   c. encouragement of positive and negative judgments about a program.
   d. all of the above.
9. In evaluation research, a discrepancy between an existing condition and a desired condition is called a
   a. standard.
   b. need.
   c. cost-benefit.
   d. input-output.
10. The major difference between formative and summative evaluation is that
    a. formative evaluation relies on basic research methodology, whereas summative evaluation relies on applied research methodology.
    b. formative evaluation is more time-consuming than summative evaluation.
    c. formative evaluation is more likely to be carried out in field settings than is summative evaluation.
    d. formative and summative evaluation are conducted at different stages of product development.
11. An emergent design in research is one that is specified
    a. by the stakeholding audiences.
    b. by the contractor.
    c. during the course of the evaluation process.
    d. after concerns have been identified, but before issues are identified.

APPLICATION PROBLEMS

The following problems do not have a single correct answer. For feedback, you can compare your answers with the sample answers on pages 897–98.

1. The manager of a new program is preparing an annual budget. She needs to decide how much money, if any, should be spent on program evaluation. She realizes that the less spent on evaluation, the more that is available for program operations. What arguments can you present in favor of allocating a fair amount of the budget for program evaluation?

2. A curriculum developer plans to pilot test a set of self-instructional materials designed to improve the writing skills of college freshman. List five questions that a developer might want to have answered about the materials' effectiveness.
3. You are asked by an elementary school principal to conduct an evaluation of the school. When you, as evaluator, ask the principal what it is about the school that he wishes to have evaluated, he responds, "I don't know. What do you usually evaluate?" How might you respond to this question?
4. A program has one stated goal—to train high school nonswimmers to swim freestyle two lengths of an Olympic-size pool. You are a "goal-free" evaluator who is called in to evaluate the program's success. How would you approach the task of evaluation?
5. You are conducting a responsive evaluation of the summer remedial program described on page 734. What audiences are likely to have a stake in the evaluation? What concerns might be expressed by each of these audiences?

SUGGESTION SHEET

If your last name starts with letters from Rus to Sme, please complete the Suggestion Sheet at the end of the book while this chapter is still fresh in your mind.

18.

EDUCATIONAL RESEARCH AND DEVELOPMENT[1]

OVERVIEW

This chapter describes a strategy for developing educational products of proven effectiveness. This strategy is called *research and development* (R & D). It consists of a cycle in which a version of the product is developed, field-tested, and revised on the basis of field-test data. Although product development sometimes occurs in basic and applied research studies, their primary goal is to discover new knowledge. In contrast, the goal of R & D is to take this research knowledge and incorporate it into a product that can be used in the schools. In a sense, the purpose of R & D is to bridge the gap that frequently exists betwen educational research and educational practice. The various steps of the R & D cycle are described in this chapter as well as some of the problems and issues that confront developers as they design a new product.

OBJECTIVES

After studying this chapter, you should be able to:

1. State two deficiencies of basic and applied research as strategies for developing educational products.
2. Describe the ten steps of the R & D cycle.
3. State four criteria that can be used to select an educational product to be developed.
4. Defend the importance of stating behavioral objectives in educational R & D.
5. Describe why it is important to field-test a product in a setting similar to that in which it will be used when fully developed.
6. Explain the function of the main field test in the R & D cycle.

---

1. Based on material from *The Minicourse: A Microteaching Approach to Teacher Education* by Walter R. Borg, Marjorie L. Kelley, Philip Langer, and Meredith Gall (New York: Macmillan, 1970).

7. Give arguments for and against refinement of educational materials during the initial stages of development.
8. Describe two opportunities for a graduate student to do an R & D project.

WHAT IS EDUCATIONAL RESEARCH AND DEVELOPMENT?

Educational research and development (sometimes called *research-based development*) appears to be the most promising strategy we now have for improving education. Because research and development is relatively new in education, we will define the term and show how it differs from educational research, which in the past was considered by many to be the best method for improving our schools.

Educational research and development (R & D) is a process used to develop and validate educational products.[2] The steps of this process are usually referred to as the **R & D cycle,** which consists of studying research findings pertinent to the product to be developed, developing the product based on these findings, field testing it in the setting where it will be used eventually, and revising it to correct the deficiencies found in the field-testing stage. In more rigorous programs of R & D, this cycle is repeated until the field-test data indicate that the product meets its behaviorally defined objectives.

In contrast, the goal of educational research is not to develop products, but rather to discover new knowledge (through basic research) or to answer specific questions about practical problems (through applied research). Of course, many applied research projects involve development of educational products. For example, in a project concerned with comparing the effectiveness of two methods for teaching reading, the researcher may develop materials that incorporate each method because suitable materials are not available. Typically, however, these materials are developed and refined only to the point where they can be used to test the investigator's hypotheses. For this reason it is very rare for applied educational research to yield products that are ready for operational use in the schools.

Although they have many important contributions to make to education, basic and applied research are generally poor methodologies for developing new products that can be used in the schools. In applied research particularly, the researcher often finds himself comparing poorly designed, unproven, or incomplete products to determine which is less inadequate. This methodology

2. Our use of the term "product" includes not only material objects, such as textbooks, instructional films, and so forth, but is also intended to refer to established procedures and processes, such as a method of teaching or a method for organizing instruction.

generally produces negative or inconclusive results, and at best brings about improvement in education at a slow rate. Even when they are obtained, positive findings are usually significant only in a statistical sense and have no practical significance for the regular classroom. Another deficiency of many basic and applied research studies is that the situations they study are too removed from the typical classroom to have much direct effect upon educational practice. It is true, of course, that basic and applied research produce the findings that are eventually used to improve educational practice. However, the gap between these findings and educational practice is often so great that many scholars have devoted a lifetime to worthwhile basic and applied research problems without improving the schools one whit.

Educators and researchers have been seeking a way to bridge the gap between research and practice for many years. This is precisely the contribution of educational R & D. It takes the findings generated by basic and applied research and uses them to build tested products that are ready for operational use in the schools. We should emphasize here, though, that educational R & D is not a substitute for basic or applied research. All three research strategies—basic, applied, and R & D—are required to bring about educational change. In fact, R & D increases the potential impact of basic and applied research findings upon school practice by translating them into usable educational products.

The field of educational evaluation is closely related to educational research and development. Evaluation techniques play a major role in R & D, although evaluation is also used for other purposes in education. The student is advised to reread chapter 17 after completing this chapter.

Educational R & D is sometimes equated with curriculum development. This is a mistaken notion. Curriculum development does not necessarily involve the use of R & D methodology. For example, curriculum development is often guided by a curriculum philosophy or academic discipline rather than by the findings of empirical research. Also, the development of curriculum guides and materials does not usually involve a field-test-revise cycle. Studies by the Educational Products Information Exchange revealed that less than 1 percent of the half million or so curriculum materials sold by the publishing industry have ever been field-tested with students and revised prior to publication.[3] Increasingly, though, curriculum developers use elements of educational R & D methodology in their work. As more of these elements are used, curriculum development approximates educational R & D.

R & D methodology does bear a close relationship to the field of instructional technology. **Instructional technology** can be defined as the use of re-

---

3. "How to Tell Whether Your Schools Are Being Gypped," *American School Board Journal* 162 (1975): 38–40.

search-validated techniques to bring about prespecified learning outcomes. The field of instructional technology used to be concerned primarily with audiovisual hardware and materials, but in recent years it has been heavily influenced by educational R & D and by advances in instructional psychology. The R & D worker of the 1960s and '70s is today's instructional technologist.

If you plan to do an R & D thesis or dissertation, we advise you to study instructional technology to determine whether some of its methods are appropriate to your project. The design of an R & D product does not need to be based on trial and error; there are many validated methods of instructional technology. These methods cover various aspects of R & D design: front-end analysis (needs assessment, systems analysis, task analysis, analysis of skill hierarchies, etc.); typologies of learning outcomes; match of instructional techniques to learning outcomes; match of learner characteristics to instructional methods; meta-cognitive processes in learning; individualized instruction (Keller Plan, auto-tutorial instruction, mastery learning, etc.); and domain-referenced assessment. These methods and others are descibed in several textbooks mentioned in the Annotated References at the end of this chapter. Also, it is useful to become acquainted with professional organizations of instructional technologists and their publications: National Society for Performance and Instruction (*NSPI Journal, Human Performance Quarterly*), Association for Educational Communications and Technology (*Instructional Innovator, Educational Communications and Technology Journal*), and American Society for Training and Development (*Training*).

THE R & D CYCLE

In the remainder of this chapter we shall discuss each of the major steps in the R & D cycle. The specific R & D cycle that will be presented was developed by the staff of the Teacher Education Program at the Far West Laboratory for Educational Research and Development, with which the authors were formerly affiliated. The Far West Laboratory is one of 10 regional laboratories funded by the U.S. Office of Education to bring about educational improvement through R & D.[4] The Teacher Education Program develops products called minicourses, which are designed to improve teachers' use of specific classroom skills.

Since we will be using the development of our first minicourse to illustrate the R & D cycle, we will briefly describe here the characteristics of this product. Each minicourse involves about 15 hours of teacher training in either the preservice or inservice setting. During this time, the teacher being trained

4. For more information about the regional laboratories, see chapter 2.

is introduced to a number of specific clasroom skills. These skills are first described and illustrated in an instructional film. The trainee then sees the skills demonstrated in a "model film," that is, a film of a brief classroom situation conducted by a model teacher. Then the trainee plans a short lesson in which he attempts to apply the skills that have been presented, teaches the lesson to a small group of pupils, and records the lesson on videotape. Immediately after the lesson, the trainee views the videotape, focusing his attention on the specific skills he is attempting to learn.

This lesson is called a *microteach lesson* because the regular classroom situation is scaled down in time and number of pupils. Having seen and evaluated the videotape recording of his lesson, the teacher then replans the same lesson and reteaches it the following day to another small group of pupils. This lesson is also recorded on videotape, and he again views and evaluates his performance immediately after the lesson is completed. The teacher then proceeds to the next sequence of instructional lesson, model lesson, microteach, and reteach.

The major steps in the R & D cycle used to develop minicourses are as follows:

1. Research and information collecting—Includes review of literature, classroom observations, and preparation of report of state of the art.
2. Planning—Includes defining skills, stating objectives determining course sequence, and small scale feasibility testing.
3. Develop preliminary form of product—Includes preparation of instructional materials, handbooks, and evaluation devices.
4. Preliminary field testing—Conducted in from 1 to 3 schools, using 6 to 12 subjects. Interview, observational and questionnaire data collected and analyzed.
5. Main product revision—Revision of product as suggested by the preliminary field-test results.
6. Main field testing—Conducted in 5 to 15 schools with 30 to 100 subjects. Quantitative data on subjects' precourse and postcourse performance are collected. Results are evaluated with respect to course objectives and are compared with control group data, when appropriate.
7. Operational product revision—Revision of product as suggested by main field-test results.
8. Operational field testing—Conducted in 10 to 30 schools involving 40 to 200 subjects. Interview, observational and questionnaire data collected and analyzed.
9. Final product revision—Revision of product as suggested by operational field-test results.
10. Dissemination and implementation—Report on product at professional

meetings and in journals. Work with publisher who assumes commercial distribution. Monitor distribution to provide quality control.

This sequence of ten steps, if followed properly, yields an educational product based on research, which is fully ready for operational use in the schools. Although each of the ten steps wil be discussed in detail, we should point out here that most of these steps are also included in many educational research projects. This is particularly true of step 6, main field testing, in which quantitative data are collected to determine whether the product meets its performance objectives. This part of the R & D cycle is essentially the same as an evaluation research project (see chapter 17).

Product Selection

Before the educational R & D process can be applied, it is necessary to describe as specifically as possible the educational product that is to be developed. This description should include: (1) an overall narrative description of the proposed product, (2) a tentative outline of what the product will include and how it will be used, and most important, (3) a specific statement of the objectives of the product. In the case of a course of study such as the minicourse, the objectives should state the specific performance levels to be achieved by teachers completing the course, that is, the number of times they will demonstrate each skill within a given time period.

In most cases the nature of the product will change substantially during the development process. This does not mean that the initial planning should be taken lightly. This planning provides the foundation upon which later revisions are built. Without careful planning at the start, the likelihood of building a good product is much reduced.

Since very few well-developed products are available in education, the developer has an almost unlimited range of possible products that he can develop. However, there are a number of criteria that he can apply in selecting an area to work in. The criteria for product selection used at the Far West Laboratory include the following:

1. Does the proposed product meet an important educational need?
2. Is the state of the art sufficiently advanced so that there is a reasonable probability that a successful product can be built?
3. Are personnel available who have the skills, knowledge, and experience necessary to build this product?
4. Can the product be developed within a reasonable time?

It was apparent to the staff of the Teacher Education Program that there was a pressing need to develop effective products for inservice teacher education. School districts generally provide very little inservice education, and what is available is generally poor. Conventional teacher education programs have four serious weaknesses: (1) the teacher is told what to do most of the time, rather than being given the opportunity to practice good teaching techniques; (2) most training programs provide teachers with vague generalities, such as "individualize your instruction," but fail to train them in specific, behaviorally defined classroom skills; (3) student teachers lack effective models to emulate; and (4) conventional training programs provide little or no feedback to the teacher on his classroom performance. The minicourse was designed to overcome these weaknesses of existing teacher training programs.

Literature Review

Once the nature of the educational product has been tentatively identified, a literature review is undertaken to collect research findings and other information pertinent to the planned development. As in basic or applied research, one purpose of the literature review is to determine the state of knowledge in the area of concern. In R & D projects, the researcher must also be concerned with how this knowledge can be applied to the product he wishes to develop.

A preliminary review of the literature on teaching methods suggested that questioning techniques in classroom discussions would be a good choice for our first minicourse. The title eventually given to Minicourse 1 was "Effective Questioning—Elementary Level." Since Minicourse 1 was the first product developed by the Teacher Education Program, it was necessary to conduct two literature reviews. The purpose of the first review was to locate research that could be used to develop a basic instructional model for training teachers. Research in four areas was studied: microteaching, learning from films, feedback in learning, and modeling in learning. Through this review we were able to identify several instructional techniques that improve learning. For example, it was found that providing the teacher with videotape feedback on her teaching performance is an effective technique for developing new classroom skills. Another effective technique is to provide a model of the skills to be learned. Interestingly, research findings indicate that the presence of a supervisor is not necessary to bring about teacher improvement when modeling and videotape feedback are provided.[5] In fact, Bruce Tuckman and W. F. Oliver[6] found that

5. M. E. Orme, "The Effects of Modeling and Feedback Variables on the Acquisition of a Complex Teaching Strategy" (Ph.D. dissertation, Stanford University, 1966),
6. Bruce W. Tuckman and W. F. Oliver, "Effectiveness of Feedback to Teachers as a Function of Source," *Journal of Educational Psychology*, August 1968, 297–301.

supervisor feedback led to a change in teachers' rated behavior over a three-month interval in the direction *opposite* that recommended by the supervisor. Yet many educators believe that the supervisor is a necessary element in training teachers. This example demonstrates that opinion and prevailing practice are often poor guides for developing educational products that work as they are intended to.

Our second literature review was concerned with questioning and discussion skills. We found that research in this area extended back to Stevens's 1912 study of high school classrooms.[7] Stevens found that two-thirds of teachers' questions required students to recall facts rather than to think about facts. Furthermore, teachers talked two-thirds of the discussion time, thus allowing students to participate only one-third of the time. Similar findings have been obtained in more recent studies.[8] It appears that even though they have known about the prevalence of such undesirable teaching practices for a long time, educators have not succeeded in bringing about needed improvements in teachers' classroom skills. We decided that major goals of Minicourse 1 would be to reduce teacher talk and correspondingly to increase student talk, and to increase the percentage of teachers' thought questions.

In the next phase of the literature review, it was necessary to identify specific techniques that teachers could use to accomplish these goals. Although a few research studies were pertinent, it was also necessary for us to give considerable attention to the opinions and experience of practitioners. For example, Groisser advocates several teaching strategies which were included in Minicourse 1, but he presents no evidence on their effectiveness.[9] Since our later field experience with Minicourse 1 indicated that most of the strategies bring about improved class discussion, they were included in the final form of the course.

Interviews and direct field observations have also been useful supplements to the research literature in providing us with a foundation of knowledge upon which to develop a given educational product. For example, in Minicourse 5, which is concerned with mathematics tutoring skills, we could find no research findings regarding what occurs between pupil and teacher in the typical tutoring sequence. In order to partially fill this gap, the laboratory sent

7. R. Stevens, "The Question as a Measure of Efficiency in Instruction," *Teachers College Contributions to Education* 48 (1912).
8. Arno A. Bellack, Herbert M. Kliebard, Ronald T. Hyman, and Frank L. Smith, Jr., *The Language of the Classroom* (New York: Teachers College Press, 1966); Ned Flanders, "Teacher Influence in the Classroom," in *Interaction Analysis: Theory, Research, and Application*, ed. Edmund Amidon and John B. Hough (Reading, Mass.: Addison-Wesley, 1967), pp. 103–18; W. D. Floyd, "An Analysis of the Oral Questioning Activity in Selected Colorado Primary Classrooms" (Ph.D. dissertation, Colorado State College, 1960).
9. P. Groisser, *How to Use the Fine Art of Questioning* (New York: Teachers Practical Press, 1964).

observers into a number of classrooms to study tutoring interactions between teachers and pupils. We learned from these observations that the usual tutoring contact between the teacher and the individual pupil was brief, averaging only 15 seconds. The content of these tutoring contacts suggested that the teacher typically gave the pupil an answer or pointed out his error and then moved on. Efforts to guide the pupil toward the identification of his errors or to develop understanding of mathematical concepts and problem-solving procedures were rare. Although they were not collected in a tightly controlled research setting, these data did provide us with basic information about the nature of mathematics tutoring in the intermediate grades and suggested to us that teachers could profit from learning a tutoring sequence in which the pupil is guided toward discovery of his errors and understanding of mathematical concepts and problem-solving procedures.

In developing an educational product using the R & D approach, the researcher will often have certain questions that cannot be answered by referring to pertinent research. Thus the researcher will find it helpful to carry out one or more small-scale studies prior to developing the product. Also, as we point out in the next sections, the R & D cycle permits several opportunities to collect research data and to revise the product. These phases of the R & D cycle can be used to answer pressing research questions involved in the construction and use of the product.

Planning

Once she has completed her review of the literature and collected other pertinent information, the developer proceeds to the planning step of the R & D cycle.

Perhaps the most important aspect of planning a research-based educational product is the statement of the specific objectives to be achieved by the product. A frequent criticism of existing educational practices is that no objectives or criteria are available to judge their effectiveness. New curriculum programs are often recommended for their content, format, educational philosophy, and acceptance by teachers and students. Yet what is missing is a statement of the program's objectives in terms of student outcomes. For example, an objective of a social studies program might be stated as, "At least 75 percent of the students who complete the program will earn a score of 90 or better on a test measuring various map skills." Such student-based objectives enable educators to determine in quantitative terms whether the program "works." Objectives also provide the best basis for developing an instructional program, since the program can be field tested and revised until it meets its objectives.

Precise specification of educational outcomes—or **behavioral objectives,** as they are also called—requires considerable skill on the part of the developer.[10] In some ways developing a behavioral objective for an educational product is similar to developing a good criterion in a research study.

During the planning phase, behavioral objectives are usually stated somewhat loosely. For example, in the initial planning of Minicourse 1, one of our objectives stated that after the course most teachers would increase their use of thought questions in a discussion situation. We did not have sufficient knowledge in the planning phase, though, to specify the percentage of thought questions that we would expect teachers to ask in order for the course to be considered effective. As we proceeded through the R & D cycle and accumulated research data, we were able to refine the statement of the behavioral objective so that it took the following form: "Given a 20-minute discussion lesson, at least half of all questions asked by teachers will be classified as thought questions. This criterion will be met by at least 75 percent of teachers who complete Minicourse 1."

Another important element of the planning phase is estimation of the money, manpower, and time required to develop the product. Generally ample resources are needed to carry out a single R & D project. Our experience has been that the cost of developing a single minicourse, which provides about 15 hours of instruction, is in excess of $100,000. A major curriculum project will cost several million dollars. Manpower needs are considerable, too. The development of a minicourse requires an average of 104 man-weeks of professional work, 50 man-weeks of clerical work, and 50 man-weeks of production work. In contrast, most research projects involve small sums of money, often less than a thousand dollars, and the efforts of a single investigator with perhaps a few part-time graduate assistants.

In R & D work, unless careful planning is done, the investigators may find that their resources have run out before the product has been fully developed. Planning is necessary in order to anticipate needed materials, professional help, and field-test sites. Consideration of field-test sites is particularly important when testing is done in the schools, which generally are receptive to testing only at certain times of the year. For example, if the product is ready for testing in June, one may have to wait until September or October unless the product can be tested during a summer school session. Also, school administrators generally require a few months' prior notice before agreeing to have their schools serve as a test site.

Although the R & D specialist must devote a considerable amount of

10. A good source of information about behavioral objectives is Norman E. Gronlund, *Stating Objectives for Classroom Instruction,* 2nd ed. (New York: Macmillan, 1978).

time to initial planning, the planning function is never really ended. As work progresses he is likely to discover several areas in which initial planning was insufficient or in error. Replanning must then be done. Nonetheless, it is wise to devote major effort to building a sound initial plan. A good plan can help the developer avoid much wasted work during later phases of the R & D cycle.

Development of the Preliminary Form of the Product

After the initial planning has been completed, the next major step in the R & D cycle is to build a preliminary form of the educational product that can be field tested. In the case of Minicourse 1, this involved a wide range of tasks. Scripts describing the specific skills that teachers are to learn were written for each instructional sequence. The scripts were then produced on videotape and edited to include clips showing the skills being used in classroom situations. Prospective model teachers were located, observed, and trained to conduct model lessons designed to further illustrate the minicourse skills. The model lessons were then recorded on videotape and edited. A teacher handbook designed to supplement the videotaped instructional lessons was drafted, revised, and printed. A set of forms for the teacher to use in self-evaluation of his micro-teach and reteach lessons was developed and printed. Questionnaires and interview guides to be used in the preliminary field test were developed, and laboratory staff members were trained in their use. An important principle that should be observed in developing the preliminary form of an educational product is to structure the product so as to permit obtaining as much feedback as possible from the field test. Thus, the preliminary form should include many more procedures for evaluation than will be included in the final product.

The reader who has attempted a major educational R & D effort will realize that these steps, stated so simply, are far from simple to carry out. The developer must expect many false starts and setbacks in developing a new educational product. Because the actual procedures involved in product development vary greatly depending upon the nature of the product, there is little specific guidance that can be given in this phase of the R & D cycle. One point that applies to most R & D work in education, however, is that the developer should strive from the outset to develop products that are fully ready for use in the schools. Partially developed products force the local practitioner to make additions and changes in order to use the product. Since few schools are equipped to make such adjustments, a partially developed product cannot be used effectively and is often badly misused.

Preliminary Field Test and Product Revision

The purpose of the **preliminary field test** is to obtain an initial qualitative evaluation of the new educational product. For the minicourse this evaluation is based primarily upon the feedback of a small group of teachers who take the course and the observations of laboratory personnel who coordinate the field test. As a rule, from four to eight teachers have been sufficient for the preliminary field test, since the emphasis of this evaluation is upon qualitative appraisal of course content rather than quantitative appraisal of course outcomes.

In all phases of the R & D cycle involving product evaluation, it is important to establish field sites similar to those in which the product will be used when it is fully developed. If a different type of field site is used, the investigator faces the problem of generalizing findings obtained in one setting to another. For example, Minicourse 1 was designed to be used by elementary school teachers during their regular school day. Therefore, the preliminary field test was carried out with six teachers from two elementary schools. Instead of this procedure, we might have invited the teachers and some of their students to our laboratory to take the course, perhaps on a speeded-up basis. The major problem with this procedure is that we might have obtained a very unrealistic impression of the course. Elements of the course that raise no problem in a laboratory setting might create havoc when used in the schools, causing an adverse effect on the course outcomes.

Throughout the preliminary field test of Minicourse 1, two field representatives from the laboratory worked closely with the six teachers in order to obtain as much teacher feedback and observational data as possible. Each teacher was interviewed individually three times during the field test. These interviews focused upon specific problems and course deficiencies as well as suggestions for improvement. At the end of the course, each teacher completed a questionnaire regarding the course and participated in a group discussion with laboratory personnel. In addition to these formal contacts, each teacher had informal contacts with one of the laboratory representatives each day.

The need to obtain extensive feedback from teachers during the preliminary field test can create a problem. Obtaining the necessary feedback results in the teacher's receiving a great deal of attention from the investigators. This attention can produce a Hawthorne Effect, which will lead the developer to overestimate the effectiveness of his product.[11] Thus, the developer must strive toward a delicate balance in which feedback is obtained without giving the participating teachers an undue amount of attention.

Observing the participating teachers near the end of the preliminary field test of Minicourse 1 revealed that the teachers were generally unable to use

11. The Hawthorne Effect is discussed in chapter 6.

the course skills effectively either in their regular classrooms or in their micro-teach lessons. Thus, from the standpoint of bringing about specific changes in the classroom behavior of these teachers, the preliminary form of the course was a failure. End-of-course interviews and questionnaires obtained from these teachers, however, indicated that they perceived the course as being very effective and as providing them with a great deal of help in improving their teaching. These responses suggest that teachers as a group are not highly critical and are likely to be charitable in their evaluation of new educational practices.

More generally, we have found that global ratings are of little value in evaluating specific educational objectives. Furthermore, they can be detrimental to educational development since they might mislead the investigator into believing that an educational product meets its objectives and is ready for use when actually it is not. In the case of the minicourse, favorable testimonials are perhaps in part a result of the extremely poor quality of most previous inservice teacher education programs which teachers use as a standard of comparison. Nevertheless, our experience has made clear the danger of making user judgment the basis for measuring the success of an educational product. Educational products should have objectives that are couched in terms of terminal behaviors and should be evaluated on the basis of their success in bringing about these terminal behaviors. Although we put little trust in global teacher evaluations, we rely heavily in the preliminary field test upon specific teacher feedback in helping to develop and improve our educational products. We obtained many specific criticisms and suggestions during the preliminary field test of Minicourse 1 that led directly to changes and improvements in the course structure. In fact, throughout the development cycle, our main source of information for revising a minicourse is the classroom teachers who participate in the field tests.

After the preliminary field test of Minicourse 1, all data were compiled and analyzed. The development team used these results to replan the course and then went on to make the revisions called for.

Main Field Test and Product Revision

The purpose of the **main field test** in the minicourse R & D cycle is to determine whether the educational product under development meets its performance objectives. Generally an experimental design is used to answer this question. In the case of Minicourse 1, a single-group pre-post design (see chapter 15) was used to determine whether teachers would significantly increase their use of discussion skills. About 50 teachers participated in the experiment. Shortly before the course began, each teacher was asked to conduct a 20-minute discussion in her regular classroom, and this discussion was videotaped. After the course was completed, each teacher again conducted a 20-minute videotaped discussion.

Each videotape was viewed by trained raters who made quantitative observations of teachers' use of the skills and behavior patterns presented in the minicourse. Since each videotape was coded and given to raters in random order, the raters did not know which were pretapes and which were posttapes. Table 18.1 presents the major findings of this experiment to determine the effectiveness of Minicourse 1. Most of the changes in teacher and student behavior brought about by Minicourse 1 are not only statistically significant, but are also significant in their implications for educational practice. Although a control group was not used in the main field test, subsequent studies have indicated that teachers who take the course make substantially larger gains than teachers who either do not have the course or who receive some form of minimal treatment.

In addition to the primary purpose of the main field test, which is to determine the success of the new product in meeting its objectives, the secondary purpose is to collect information that can be used to improve the course in its next revision. Therefore, questionnaire and interview data should be obtained from all participants in the main field test.

If the main field test findings indicate that the new product falls substantially short of meeting its objectives, it is necessary to revise the product and conduct another main field test. This cycle of field testing and revision would continue until the product meets the minimum performance objectives set for it. In practice the product would probably be abandoned if substantial progress were not made in the second main field test.

Operational Field Test and Final Product Revision

The purpose of the **operational field test** is to determine whether an educational product is fully ready for use in the schools without the presence of the developer or his staff. In order to be fully ready for operational use, the package must be complete and thoroughly tested in every respect. In the case of the minicourse, all materials needed to coordinate the course are normally tried out during the preliminary and main field tests. Since these field tests are conducted by laboratory personnel, however, a satisfactory test of how well the total course package works "on its own" cannot be obtained. The operational field test is set up and coordinated by regular school personnel and should closely approximate regular operational use. Feedback from both the coordinators and the teachers taking the course are collected by means of questionnaires which are mailed in to the laboratory. The main use of these data is to

TABLE 18.1

Main Field-Test Results from Minicourse 1

Behavior Compared	Pretape Mean (N = 48)	Posttape Mean (N = 48)	t	Significance Level
Increase considered desirable				
1. Number of times teacher used redirection.	26.69	40.92	4.98	.001
2. Number of times teacher used prompting.	4.10	7.17	3.28	.001
3. Number of times teacher used further clarification.	4.17	6.73	3.01	.005
4. Number of times teacher used refocusing.	0.10	0.02	0.00	NS[a]
5. Length of pupil responses in words (based on 5-minute samples of pre- and post-tapes).	5.63	11.78	5.91	.001
6. Length of teacher's pause after question (based on 5-minute sample of pre- and post-tapes).	1.93	2.32	1.90	.05
7. Proportion of total questions that call for higher cognitive pupil responses.	37.30	52.00	2.94	.005
Decrease considered desirable				
8. Number of times teacher repeated his own questions.	13.68	4.68	7.26	.001
9. Number of times teacher repeated pupil answers.	30.68	4.36	11.47	.001
10. Number of times teacher answered his own questions.	4.62	0.72	6.88	.001
11. Number of one-word pupil responses (based on 5-minute samples of pre- and post-tapes).	5.82	2.57	3.61[b]	.001
12. Frequency of punitive teacher reactions to incorrect pupil answers.	0.12	0.10	0.00	NS
13. Proportion of discussion time taken by teacher talk.	51.64	27.75	8.95	.001

[a]Not significant.
[b]Means would have been about four times larger if entire tape had been analyzed; t test would have been higher.

determine whether the course package is complete. Interviewers focus on parts of the course that fail to do their job or on materials that are needed in order to make the operation of the course easier or more effective. Precourse and postcourse videotapes are not obtained during the operational field test.

After the operational field test is complete and the data have been analyzed, a final revision of the total course package is carried out. In the case of the minicourse program, the laboratory makes a final revision of all scripts and printed materials and turns these over to a commercial publisher for final production. The course is then sold or rented to schools for operational use in their inservice training programs.[12] During operational use of the course, the publisher supplies course coordinators with evaluation questionnaires and interview forms so that the laboratory can maintain a continuous appraisal of the course's effectiveness and can identify new problems that arise in its operational use. The final step, however, is essentially a quality control procedure and would not be regarded as further field testing of the course.

Dissemination and Implementation

The R & D cycle is often a time-consuming and expensive process. The way to justify the costs is by demonstrating effective dissemination of the resulting product to its intended audience. **Dissemination** refers to the process of helping potential users become aware of R & D products. Also, it is necessary to demonstrate that the R & D product is implemented according to the developers' specifications so that it produces the intended effects. **Implementation** refers to the process of helping the adopter of an R & D product to use it in the way intended by the developers.

Despite the importance of R & D dissemination and implementation, these processes were seldom studied until the mid-1970s. The concern of educational R & D personnel prior to this time was on the conceptualization and development of large-scale curriculum products using the R & D cycle of develop-test-revise. Little funding was available for monitoring these products after they had been developed. Priorities shifted dramatically in the mid-1970s, though. Many educators stopped using the term "research and development," preferring instead to talk about "research, development, and dissemination" (R, D, & D). **Research, development, and dissemination** refers to the research-based development of products that meet behaviorally defined objectives and dissemination and implementation criteria.

The ratio of 1:10:10 is sometimes used in industry to estimate funding requirements for R, D, & D. For example, suppose it requires $1 million to do

12. Minicourse 1 is marketed commercially by the Macmillan Company.

the basic research for a new product. It will then require $10 million to develop the product through the operational field test revision. Ten times that amount ($100 million) will be required to manufacture and disseminate the product.

Educators are not accustomed to think about the large sums of money implied by the 1:10:10 ratio for the dissemination of R & D products. Commercial educational publishers do expend large sums of money for production facilities, inventory storage and shipping departments, branch offices, advertising, sales forces, and inservice trainers. Even today, though, these facilities and personnel are largely nonexistent in the federal and state educational systems. For example, when the first minicourses completed their development cycle in the early 1970s, there were no official plans either at the Far West Laboratory or at the U.S. Office of Education for their dissemination. A dissemination plan was developed piecemeal with a commercial publisher. This plan was based largely on the publisher's established distribution procedures rather than on a rational analysis of the dissemination and implementation requirements for the particular product.

A dissemination and implementation capability for R & D products is slowly developing in this country. For example, the **National Diffusion Network (NDN)** was established by the U.S. Office of Education to disseminate successful R & D products.[13] This dissemination agency links successful products with school systems that might benefit from them. An R & D product is not automatically accepted for dissemination by NDN. It first must be judged exemplary by a group called the Joint Dissemination Review Panel (JDRP). This panel accepts R & D products for dissemination by NDN if educationally significant effects have been demonstrated and if the effects have been replicated across several school sites. One of the services provided by NDN is catalogs of approved projects and newsletters about NDN activities.[14] The NDN also provides technical assistance to school systems that are interested in adopting and implementing an approved project. NDN facilitators assigned to each state are available for this purpose.

Another national dissemination and implementation capability is the **Research and Development Exchange (RDx)**. The RDx disseminates information about innovative R & D products to local educators. It also collects and forwards information about local needs to researchers and policy makers. There

13. The address of the National Diffusion Network is U.S. Department of Education, 1832 M Street NW, Suite 802, Washington, DC 20036.
14. The catalogs (called *Educational Programs That Work*) and newsletters *(ED Newsletter* and *NDN Reporter)* are available from Order Department, Far West Laboratory for Educational Research and Development, 1855 Folsom Street, San Francisco, CA 94103. Current R & D projects being carried out by regional educational laboratories and centers are described in the periodical *Educational R & D Report* published by the Council for Educational Development and Research, 1518 K Street NW, Washington, DC 20005.

are 8 regional exchanges, which work with the 50 state departments of education. The names, addresses, and states served by the exchanges are:

AEL Regional Exchange. Appalachia Educational Laboratory, P.O. Box 1348, Charleston, WV 23525. Serves: Alabama, Florida, Georgia, Kentucky, North Carolina, Tennessee, Virginia, and West Virginia.

Midwest Regional Exchange. CEMREL, 3120 59th Street, St. Louis, MO 63139. Serves: Illinois, Indiana, Iowa, Michigan, Minnesota, Missouri, Ohio, and Wisconsin.

McREL Regional Exchange. McREL, 4709 Belleview Avenue, Kansas City, MO 64112. Serves: Colorado, Kansas, Nebraska, North Dakota, South Dakota, and Wyoming.

Northeast Regional Exchange. 101 Mill Road, Chelmsford, MA 01824. Serves: Connecticut, Maine, Massachusetts, New Hampshire, New York, Rhode Island, and Vermont.

Northwest Regional Exchange. NWREL, 300 S.W. Sixth Avenue, Portland, OR 97204. Serves: Alaska, Hawaii, Idaho, Montana, Oregon, and Washington.

RBS Regional Exchange. Research for Better Schools, 444 N. Third Street, Philadelphia, PA 19123. Serves: Delaware, Maryland, New Jersey, and Pennsylvania.

SEDL Regional Exhange. Southwest Educational Development Laboratory, 211 E. Seventh Street, Austin, TX 78701. Serves: Arkansas, Louisiana, Mississippi, New Mexico, Oklahoma, and Texas.

Western Regional Exchange. SWREL, 4665 Lampson Avenue, Los Alamitos, CA 90720. Serves: Arizona, California, Nevada, and Utah.

The student planning an R & D dissertation might choose to focus on the dissemination and implementation phases of the R & D process. For example, the student might develop and test methods for improving the dissemination and implementation of a particular R & D product. Another possibility is to do research on the dissemination and implementation process. This type of research focuses on such questions as: How do educators come to learn about new R & D products? Why are some R & D products better implemented than others? Why do some teachers implement a curriculum or instructional strategies to a greater extent than other teachers?[15]

15. Research relating to these questions is reviewed in Michael Fullan and Allan Pomfret, "Research on Curriculum and Instruction Implementation," *Review of Educational Research* 47 (1977): 355–97. A recent example of implementation research is: Georgea G. Mohlman, Theodore Coladarci, and N. L. Gage, "Comprehension and Attitude as Predictors of Implementation of Teacher Training," *Journal of Teacher Education* 33 (1982): 31–36.

PROBLEMS AND ISSUES IN EDUCATIONAL R & D

Since there was virtually no guidance available on the educational R & D process when the Far West Laboratory started its programs in 1966, it was necessary for us to develop our procedures as we went along. In so doing we uncovered several problems and issues that are basic to the R & D approach. Since these issues are likely to be faced by other investigators who do educational research and development, we will describe some of them.

Learning Versus Polish

The first problem concerns how far the educational developer should go in building the preliminary form of a product involving an expensive component, such as instructional films or tapes. The development of the preliminary form of Minicourse 1 presented us with an interesting dilemma. On the one hand, it was desirable to spend as little money as possible on initial development, since the feedback obtained from the preliminary field test would almost surely call for extensive revision. On the other hand, a poorly developed set of materials might produce poor results even though the ideas underlying the development were sound. The most defensible resolution of this dilemma is to put most of the initial development effort into a simple product that makes maximum use of learning principles, that is, a theoretically sound product. Little or no effort should be devoted to such activities as correcting minor errors in narration, building attractive charts where crude ones would serve the purpose, or reshooting motion picture footage because of poor camera work. In summary, our strategy calls for giving the essentials our best effort and doing everything else as cheaply and quickly as possible. In effect, this approach amounts to a logical application and extension of findings of M. A. May and A. A. Lumsdaine and other researchers who have studied the learning outcomes of audiovisual media.[16] These studies generally show that variations in technical quality of visual materials have little effect on learning outcomes.

Our experience indicates that the educational developer will not find this an easy road to follow. Media specialists on the development team, such as artists, actors, and television production personnel, may apply great pressure to improve the nonessential aspects of the product. If these pressures are not

16. M. A. May and A. A. Lumsdaine, eds., *Learning from Films* (New Haven: Yale University Press, 1958).

controlled by the educational developer, he will see an increasing proportion of his resources going into unnecessary polish.

A more subtle reason for resisting efforts to apply polish during the development cycle is that if the developer yields to this pressure, he may well create a monster he is unable to destroy. It is very difficult to scrap a polished product even if field-test data indicate that it is not achieving its objectives. First, the developer has spent a great deal of money which he does not want to admit has been wasted. Second, the product looks good and he knows that most consumers of educational products are not very concerned with hard evidence on effectiveness. Finally, even though an educational product fails to achieve its objectives, it is easy to rationalize that it is probably better, or surely no worse, than the competing materials currently in use.

Realism Versus Pertinence

The second question of development strategy concerns the extent to which educational developers should work with "real" teachers in "real" classrooms who are teaching "real" lessons. Our work with model lessons in the minicourse instructional model brought us face to face with this problem. Since the use of model teachers seems to offer a great deal of promise as a method of helping other teachers develop effective classroom skills, our experience in developing model lessons during Minicourse 1 seems well worth reviewing.

Initially, we were devoted to the idea that our model lessons would have to be as realistic as possible. We felt that if we could set up videotape equipment and record the teacher and his pupils without their awareness of what was happening, we would be approaching the ideal model lesson. In practice we found that this idea was often incompatible with the purposes for which model lessons were to be used in the minicourse. In the minicourse model lessons have two main functions. The first is to provide clear-cut examples of the desired skills within the context of a lesson. The second is to give the learner who is taking the minicourse practice in identifying these skills and discriminating among the skills that are being studied. In our initial efforts to develop model lessons, we started by selecting teachers who were reported to have outstanding teaching skills by principals and supervisory personnel. We then worked individually with each teacher, describing the skills that were to be displayed in the model lesson and discussing in general terms methods for fitting these skills into a lesson and modeling them effectively. We then brought videotape recording equipment into the classroom, and teachers conducted the lessons that they had planned.

The typical outcome of these early efforts was a very long model lesson that contained very few examples of the skills that we wished the teacher to model. For example, one of our first model lessons ran for a full hour. During this time the specific skills that the teacher was to model were demonstrated less than five minutes. Though providing a realistic picture of typical classroom teaching, this model was extremely inefficient in terms of the objectives we had set up for the model lesson. Furthermore, if this realistic lesson had been edited to reduce the amount of time that the viewer was required to watch irrelevant behavior, the lesson would have become highly unrealistic, since large segments would have been removed. It became increasingly apparent that if the model lesson were to provide numerous examples of the skills to be learned and contain a minimum of nonpertinent teaching behavior, it would be necessary to plan the model lesson very thoroughly with the model teacher. Thus, although the model lessons for Minicourse 1 were not scripted (the teacher and pupils went through the lesson using their own words), they presented a less natural situation than one finds in the typical classroom. In developing other minicourses, we have found it necessary on occasion to prepare complete scripts so that the model lessons would provide enough clear-cut examples of the skills to be learned within a reasonable period of time. As we have increased our sophistication in working with teachers during the planning and recording of model lessons, their length has gradually been reduced while the number of examples of the skills being modeled has increased.

The idea of creating a less realistic classroom situation in order to gain clarity and save time is a difficult one for many educators to accept. In Minicourse 5, which trains the teacher to use a specific strategy to tutor pupils in mathematics, we found it necessary for teachers to work from a complete script in order to provide a clear illustration of the tutoring strategy. The question then came up: Should we use teachers or actors to play the teaching role in the model lessons? As a compromise we used teachers in two model lessons and actors in the other two. In the main field test of this course we asked the participating teachers whether actors should be used. (These teachers did not know the identity of the model teachers.) Of the 27 responding, 18 said that only actual school teachers should be used. Nevertheless, in rating the model lessons, the two done by actors were consistently rated higher than those done by teachers. These findings clearly question the necessity of using "real" teachers in "real" classrooms, teaching "real" lessons for the purpose of teacher training.

Other Lessons

Our experience in developing Minicourse 1 also taught us other lessons about educational research and development. First, we learned that the rule so often stated by researchers—if anything can possibly go wrong in a research project, it will—seems to be equally true of research and development. For example, during the preliminary development of Minicourse 1 in 1966, portable video-tape equipment was still at a rather primitive level of development. Since we were building a product that relied very heavily upon the use of this equipment for presenting instructional and model lessons and providing feedback during the microteach and reteach sessions, the limitations in the equipment were very important. It was necessary, therefore, for us to put a major effort into developing procedures that would reduce the degree to which our plans could be disrupted by deficiencies or failures in the videotape recording equipment.

Finally, we began to see that developing an educational product was a far more difficult and time-consuming task than we had anticipated. Major development work in education requires a large and competent professional staff and significant long-term financial support. Our experience to date indicates that a large amount of money and labor is required to carry a minicourse through the entire development cycle. Yet we frequently encounter local school administrators who want to develop their own minicourses. There are probably very few school districts that have the resources to attempt a development task of this magnitude. It appears at this time that major educational development programs should be left to organizations such as the regional laboratories and research and development centers, which have the personnel, equipment, and financial support for such work

AN EXAMPLE OF SMALL-SCALE R & D

We have already discussed the considerable resources required to carry out even a single educational R & D project. It is highly unlikely that a graduate student will be able to find the financial and manpower support to complete a major R & D project. In fact, educational R & D is beyond the abilities of most school districts. It is being realized increasingly that most educational R & D efforts are economical only when a new product is developed at one place and then distributed nationally.

If you plan to do an R & D project for a thesis or dissertation, you should keep these cautions in mind. It is best to undertake a small-scale project that involves a limited amount of original instructional design. Also, unless you have substantial financial resources, you will need to avoid expensive instructional media such as 16-mm film and synchronized slidetape. Another way to scale down the project is to limit development to just a few steps of the R & D cycle.

An example of an R & D dissertation is the project undertaken by Dan

Isaacson.[17] The purpose of the project was to develop a self-instructional course on the use of the microcomputer as a classroom tool. The course was intended for K-12 preservice teachers and inservice teachers.

Each chapter in the dissertation described a step of the R & D process used to develop the course, which was titled *Discover the Microcomputer*. Chapter 2 reported on a review of the literature. This review focused on such topics as the current status of microcomputer technology and availability, major projects on educational uses of the microcomputer, and the current status of training teachers to use microcomputers in the classroom. One of Isaacson's conclusions pertinent to his R & D project was that "although training in the use of instructional media has been a recognized need by most teacher education institutions for a long time . . . the literature seems strangely silent regarding recognition by schools of education of the need to expose every pre-service teacher and every in-service teacher to the computer, not as a specialty skill to prepare to teach *about* computers, but as an instructional media tool to prepare to teach *using* computers" (p. 25).

The next chapter described the process of choosing objectives and instructional design parameters for the product. Eight product objectives were finally selected based on a literature review and analysis of the context in which the product would be used. Sample objectives were:

1. The learner shall correctly operate a microcomputer, using courseware from the courseware library supplied with the course materials. (The library included computer materials for drill-and-practice, games, simulations, computer-managed instruction, etc.)
2. The learner shall be able to alter data lines in a courseware program so as to make the program better suit a current lesson or other specific instructional situation.
3. The learner shall be able to evaluate courseware using the Courseware Review and Rating form developed for use with this product.

An example of an instructional design parameter was the choice of available computer courseware to which teachers would be exposed. Isaacson decided to have teachers experience high-quality and low-quality courseware so that they would develop evaluation skills.

Chapter 4 of the dissertation described the development of the preliminary version of the product. The major development effort was the self-instructional text that guides the teacher through a variety of microcomputer experiences. The design of the text and related materials was guided by the product objectives.

17. Dan Isaacson, "Discovering the Microcomputer as an Instructional Media Tool in Teaching: A Laboratory for Elementary and Secondary Educators" (Ph.D. dissertation, University of Oregon, 1980).

The next chapter described the product's preliminary field test, in which 33 preservice and inservice teachers participated. Isaacson used the following device as one way to obtain user feedback for revising course materials:

> In the text for the course, the written material was printed only on two-thirds of the page width. . . . The remaining third was left for notes and comments on the material. Students handed in these notes and comments which pointed out spelling and grammar errors, and unclear sentences and paragraphs. Corrections and clarifications to the text were based primarily on this feedback. (p. 63)

Feedback from participants was also obtained by meeting with participants as a group and by questionnaires.

Chapter 6 presented revisions of the product based on the preliminary field test. A major revision was to reduce the number of computer programs in the product's courseware library. Some programs were eliminated because they would not run on the computer or because they were of too poor quality. Changes were also made in the text, for example:

> Additions were necessary in Chapter 1 to remind learners of the difference between the letter 'o' and the number '0' (zero), of the time it takes to load a cassette (2 to 3 minutes when beginners expect an immediate load), and how to stop a program if one tires of it before it ends normally. (p. 72)

The revised product was tested again with a small sample of preservice teachers, and then was incorporated into the regular program of the institution at which it was developed. A commercial publisher for the product was being sought at the time the dissertation was completed.

The student planning to do an R & D project should give careful consideration to the time required. The dissertation described above took well over a year for completion of product development through the preliminary field-test phase. A research project for the master's thesis or doctoral dissertation can usually be completed in much less time. The additional time required for an R & D project is worthwhile, though, if the student is interested in making a contribution that will lead to an immediate tangible improvement in educational practice.

ANNOTATED REFERENCES

Bain, Helen P., and Groseclose, J. Ronald. "The Dissemination Dilemma and a Plan for Uniting Disseminators and Practitioners." *Phi Delta Kappan* 61 (1979): 101–103.

The authors describe the current status of national and local efforts to improve the dissemination of educational research knowledge and R & D products. The National Diffusion Network, Research and Development Exchange, and NEA networks are featured.

Baker, Eva L. "The Technology of Instructional Development." In *Second Handbook of Research on Teaching*, edited by R. M. W. Travers. Chicago: Rand McNally, 1973.

This chapter provides a comprehensive overview of the literature on educational research and development. The author includes many examples of R & D in education and other fields, variations in R & D techniques, and issues that face the research-based product developer.

Briggs, Leslie J., and Wager, Walter W. *Handbook of Procedures for the Design of Instruction.* 2nd ed. Englewood Cliffs, N.J.: Educational Technology Publications, 1981.

The authors describe a variety of instructional technology topics, such as: determining needs, goals, and priorities; determining resources and constraints; writing objectives; organizing units of instruction; selecting media; and conducting evaluations.

Gagné, Robert M., and Briggs, Leslie J. *Principles of Instructional Design.* 2nd ed. New York: Holt, Rinehart & Winston, 1979.

This book describes effective instructional techniques that can be incorporated in the design of educational products. The authors stress the importance of analyzing learning outcomes (e.g., verbal information, intellectual skills, attitudes, motor skills), since each type of learning outcome requires the use of different instructional techniques.

Gall, Meredith D. *Handbook for Evaluating and Selecting Curriculum Materials.* Boston: Allyn and Bacon, 1981.

One way to understand the development of effective educational products is to consider the process from the perspective of consumers. This book describes research on curriculum materials selection, textbook adoption policies, and 39 criteria for analyzing and evaluating materials.

Schutz, Richard E. "Learning about the Costs and Instruction about the Benefits of Research and Development in Education." *Educational Researcher* 8 (1979): 3–7.

This article provides a capsule history of the work of one educational R & D laboratory since the mid-1960s. Schutz focuses on the contributions that R & D has made, and can make, to school improvement.

SELF-CHECK TEST

Circle the correct answer to each of the following questions. An answer key is provided on page 881.

1. The basic goal of educational R & D is to
    a. discover new knowledge through action research.
    b. develop research-based products.
    c. test educational materials.
    d. improve existing educational products.
2. The first major step of the R & D cycle involves
    a. doing a review of the literature.
    b. making classroom observations.
    c. preparing a report on the state of the art.
    d. All of the above are correct.
3. In the R & D cycle the general aim of the literature review is
    a. focused on product evaluation.
    b. focused on R & D strategies.
    c. the same as in basic and applied research.
    d. narrower than in basic or applied research.
4. The most important aspect of planning in the R & D cycle is
    a. defining skills.
    b. determining course sequence.
    c. feasibility testing.
    d. stating product objectives.
5. Developing behavioral objectives for an educational product is similar in some ways to developing a
    a. proposal for a research study.
    b. good criterion for a research study.
    c. product for assessment of learning.
    d. All of the above are correct.
6. When initial planning has been completed, the next logical step in the R & D cycle is to
    a. do a literature review.
    b. conduct preliminary field testing.
    c. construct a preliminary form of the product.
    d. prepare a report on the state of the art.

7. In conducting product evaluation, the developer should use field-test sites that
   a. have been randomly selected.
   b. are similar to the sites in which the completed product will be used.
   c. approximate an experimental laboratory setting in terms of control over extraneous variables.
   d. provide the most difficult test of the product's effectiveness.
8. The need during preliminary testing for extensive feedback from the learner may create the problem of
   a. observer bias.
   b. observer contamination.
   c. the Hawthorne Effect.
   d. the placebo effect.
9. The primary purpose of the main field test in the R & D cycle is to determine whether
   a. sampling is accurate.
   b. observer bias is minimal.
   c. the criterion measures are valid.
   d. the product meets its objectives.
10. According to Borg and Gall, the answer to the "learning versus polish" question is to
    a. give essentials best effort, and do everything else as cheaply and quickly as possible.
    b. follow carefully the suggestions of team media specialists.
    c. produce a polished product for initial testing.
    d. produce a polished product only for the main test.

APPLICATION PROBLEMS

The following problems are intended to give you practice in applying significant concepts and research procedures explained in chapter 18. Most do not have a single correct answer. For feedback, compare your answers with the sample answers on pages 898–99.

1. Suppose you are asked to develop a brief training program to help students overcome fifteen common spelling errors involving homonyms (e.g., "principal" and "principle"). As part of the development of the program, you are asked to collect evidence that it is effective. Make up a brief plan with specific steps that you would take to accomplish this objective.
2. An educational R & D specialist has a choice of four products he can develop. Product A probably would be very popular and well received by school personnel. Product B probably would qualify for additional funds so that audiovisual

aids could be developed. Product C has well-defined behavioral objectives. Product D is supported by a base of research knowledge concerning learners' achievement of the product's objectives. Given this information, which product has the best chance of successfully completing an R & D cycle? Why?

3. An R & D specialist is developing a new set of curriculum materials. Since it is very complicated to test a preliminary version of the materials in a regular classroom, she arranges to take students from class and have them use the materials in a special classroom at a school site set aside for this purpose. What is one risk that she takes by following this strategy?

4. A group of developers conducted a main field test of some new audiovisual aids. They found that the materials achieved three behavioral objectives quite satisfactorily, but not the other two objectives. However, the developers feel they acquired insight from the field test concerning why the materials failed to achieve these objectives. Given this information, what is a reasonable course of action for the developers to follow next?

5. An R & D specialist has a certain amount of development money to work on a new approach to teaching introductory statistics. He wants to use attractive printed media; a series of pamphlets instead of a single book; ample use of illustrations; typeface in several colors. For his preliminary field test, however, he is intending to try out cheap Xerox copies of the text. A colleague points out that this cheap version may produce poor results, even though his approach is basically sound. What is one argument that he can use in defense of a cheap printed version?

SUGGESTION SHEET

If your last name starts with letters from Smf to Stu, please complete the Suggestion Sheet at the end of the book while this chapter is still fresh in your mind.

19.

TECHNIQUES OF HISTORICAL RESEARCH

OVERVIEW

Historical reseach in education is important for several reasons. The findings of historical research enable educators to learn from past discoveries and mistakes; to identify needs for educational reform; and, to a certain extent, to predict future trends. This chapter presents the major steps and techniques in historical research: (1) identifying a problem or topic, (2) searching for and recording relevant sources of historical evidence, (3) evaluating the evidence for authenticity and validity, and (4) synthesizing historical facts into meaningful chronological and thematic patterns. The chapter emphasizes the various interpretive processes that the historian uses in a research project.

OBJECTIVES

After studying this chapter, you should be able to:

1. Describe the major differences between contemporary and nineteenth-century historical research.
2. State several uses of historical research.
3. List the major steps involved in doing a historical research project.
4. Describe five types of historical research in education.
5. Distinguish between documents, quantitative records, spoken sources of information, and relics.
6. Distinguish between primary and secondary sources of historical information.
7. State several procedures and considerations involved in recording information from historical sources.
8. Explain the various features of a document which are examined in the process of external criticism.
9. Distinguish between subjectivity and bias in reporting an event.
10. Explain the statement "History means interpretation."

11. Describe how the use of concepts affects historical interpretation.
12. Explain the interpretive problems and processes involved in making causal inferences or generalizations from historical evidence.
13. Discuss factors involved in organizing the historical research dissertation.

INTRODUCTION

Historical research involves the systematic search for documents and other sources that contain facts relating to the historian's questions about the past. By studying the past, the educational historian hopes to achieve better understanding of present institutions, practices, and problems in education. The distinguished British historian Edward Carr, in response to the question, What is history? stated, ". . . it is a continuous process of interaction between the historian and his facts, an unending dialogue between the present and the past."[1]

Contemporary historians of education are increasingly aware of the role that interpretation plays in their work. Historical research necessarily deals with events that have occurred *prior* to the historian's decision to study them. Unless the event has been recorded in some manner—for example, by a journalist, court reporter, diarist, or photographer—the event is inaccessible to the historian. The recording of the event (a "historical source") involves an interpretative act by the journalist or other recorder because his biases, values, and interests will cause him to attend to some details and omit others. Thus, historical sources are cloaked in interpretation before the historian touches them. The historian adds another layer of interpretation in the way that he chooses to emphasize or ignore facts about the past and in the way that he fits them into categories and patterns.

The contemporary emphasis on interpretation in historical research contrasts with the popular nineteenth-century view that "history consists of the compilation of a maximum number of irrefutable and objective facts."[2] Consequently, nineteenth-century histories often consisted of multivolume compilations of details about rather limited topics. In contrast, contemporary histories tend to be shorter and to subordinate historical facts to the interpretative framework within which they are given meaning and significance.

That historical research involves interpretation does not mean that it is less objective than other types of educational research. There is an interpretive

1. Edward H. Carr, *What Is History?* (New York: Random House, 1967), p. 35.
2. Ibid., p. 14.

element in all types of research; the researcher's bias can affect the results as much in a laboratory experiment as in historical inquiry.[3]

Historical research in education differs from other types of educational research in that the historian *discovers* data through a search of historical sources such as diaries, official documents, and relics. In other types of educational research, the researcher *creates* data by making observations and administering tests in order to describe present events and present performance. In the discussion that follows, the terms "historian" and "historical researcher" are used interchangeably.

The Subject Matter of Historical Research

The subject matter of historical research in education is as broad as the field of education. Arthur Moehlman and his colleagues at the University of Texas have developed a set of categories for classifying the various types of historical research that appear in the literature.[4] Their classification scheme, in adapted form, is presented here:

1. General educational history
2. History of educational legislation, which includes such topics as taxation, bonds, school land boards and districts, equalization programs, curriculum, state-supported schools and universities, and court cases
3. Historical biographies of major contributors to education
4. History of major branches of education, which includes such topics as school goals, school accreditation and attendance laws, community education, school organization and administration, school finance, school enrollment, school personnel, school plant, instructional methods and materials, and school curriculum
5. Institutional history of education, which includes such topics as kindergarten, elementary school, secondary school, colleges and universities, correspondence education, vocational schools, armed forces schools, mass media, research organizations, and foundations
6. Cultural history of education, which includes such topics as ethnology, anthropology, sociology, and technology
7. History of educational planning and policy
8. Historical critiques of education

3. Experimenter bias is discussed in chapter 15.
4. Adapted from A. H. Moehlman et al., *A Guide to Computer-Assisted Research in American Education* (Austin: University of Texas, 1969), pp. 76, 83–94.

9. Comparative history of international education
10. History of contemporary problems in education.

The Uses of History

Histories of education are useful for several reasons. Sol Cohen, an educational historian, made this statement about the liberating function of history: "To Freud, neurosis is the failure to escape the past, the burden of one's history. What is repressed returns distorted and is eternally reenacted. The psychotherapist's task is to help the patient reconstruct the past. In this respect the historian's goal resembles that of the therapist—to liberate us from the burden of the past by helping us to understand it."[5]

As an example of this liberating function, consider what might happen if educational researchers did not do reviews of the literature in their areas of interest. Researchers might "discover" what was already known to past researchers; they might test hypotheses that previously had been shown to be unproductive; and they would reinvent research methodology or continue to make the same methodological errors as their predecessors. Indeed, without continually updated historical reviews of the research literature, progress would be impossible.

The same liberating function of history applies to educational practice. For example, the educator who is ignorant of past bond issues in her school district might campaign for a new bond issue, making unjustified historical assumptions and overlooking effective techniques used by her predecessors.

Historical research in education sometimes serves the function of social reform. This use of history characterizes the work of recent revisionist historians of education. These historians have attempted to sensitize educators to unjust or misguided practices in the past that, perhaps unwittingly, have persisted into the present and require reform. Because the past provides a detached perspective, it may be easier for educators to detect and achieve an understanding of misguided practices than if their perspective were limited to the immediate present.

To a certain extent, historical research can assist the educator in predicting future trends. If we know how an educator or group of educators has acted in the past, we can predict how they will act in the future. The educator whose past actions have been motivated by a desire for liberal reform is likely to be similarly motivated in the future. As in other types of educational research (see chapter 13), however, prediction is rarely perfect. For example, new social, political, or economic conditions may arise that create fundamental changes in

5. Sol Cohen, "The History of the History of American Education, 1900–1976: The Uses of the Past," *Harvard Educational Review* 46 (1976): 298–330.

the conditions under which educators work. These new conditions may well invalidate predictions based on past performance. Indeed, historical research can help prevent poor decisions by demonstrating that two situations (one in the past and one in the present), which appear similar on the surface, are in fact different in important ways.

Historians of education traditionally have influenced practice through the training of educators. For example, preservice teachers are usually required to take a course in the history of education. In recent years historians have become more involved in educational policy making. A notable example is Patricia Graham, a historian who was director of the National Institute of Education from 1977 to 1979.[6]

Some educational researchers think that historical methodology is irrelevant to their work. In their view, empirical research belongs to the sciences, whereas history belongs to the humanities. In fact, empirical research and history have much in common. Any competent researcher is a historian. This is because research involves reviewing the literature to determine what investigations and theoretical work have already been done on a particular problem. The search for relevant documents (journal articles, technical reports, unpublished manuscripts, etc.) and the interpretation of their significance are tasks that characterize the work of empirical researchers and historians alike. The study of historical methodology should help you become a better researcher, whether or not you choose to do a study that is essentially historical.

Steps in Doing Historical Research

The essential steps involved in doing a historical research project are as follows: define the problems or questions to be investigated, search for sources of historical facts, summarize and evaluate the historical sources, and present the pertinent facts within an interpretive framework. Each of these steps is discussed in this chapter.

The search for historical facts and the interpretation of these facts are not necessarily discrete, sequential phases of a historical research project. Edward Carr has provided the following description of how a historian engages in research:

> Laymen . . . sometimes ask me how the historian goes to work when he writes history. The commonest assumption appears to be that the historian divides his work into two sharply distinguishable phases or periods. First, he spends a long preliminary period reading his sources and filling

6. Patricia Graham described her experiences as director of NIE in "Historians as Policy Makers," *Educational Researcher* 9, no. 11 (1980): 21–24.

his notebooks with facts; then, when this is over, he puts away his sources, takes out his notebooks, and writes his book from beginning to end. This is to me an unconvincing and unplausible picture. For myself, as soon as I have got going on a few of what I take to be the capital sources, the itch becomes too strong and I begin to write—not necessarily at the beginning, but somewhere, anywhere. Thereafter, reading and writing go on simultaneously. The writing is added to, subtracted from, re-shaped, cancelled, as I go on reading. The reading is guided and directed and made fruitful by the writing: the more I write, the more I know what I am looking for, the better I understand the significance and relevance of what I find.[7]

Researchers who use other methodologies (e.g., controlled experimentation) often interpose similar processes. As a first step, a researcher may formulate a few tentative hypotheses and plan a research design for testing them. After reviewing the literature and conducting pilot studies, he may decide to make further changes in the hypotheses and research design. Even after the formal experiment has been conducted and all the data collected, the researcher may formulate new hypotheses that he never intended at the outset, but which can be tested by the available data.

This analysis of the historical research process does not imply that the researcher can follow any sequence he desires. A structured sequence of steps is needed to guide the project. Variations within this sequence will occur, depending upon idiosyncrasies in the search for historical facts and in the shifting interpretations of the historian as he attempts to understand the facts.

DEFINING A PROBLEM OR TOPIC FOR HISTORICAL RESEARCH

As with other types of educational research, the first step in planning a historical research project is to define the problems or topics to be investigated. A review of problems and topics studied by other educational historians is often useful for initiating this process.

Mark Beach analyzed the problems and topics that prompt historical inquiry into five types.[8] Current social issues are the most popular source of historical problems in education. For example, loyalty oaths in educational institutions, urban education, proposals for radical reform in education, and in-

---

7. Carr, *What Is History?* pp. 32–33.
8. Mark Beach, "History of Education," *Review of Educational Research* 39 (1969): 561–76.

telligence testing are examples of social issues that have provided a focus for recent historical research projects.

Histories of specific individuals (i.e., biographies), histories of specific educational institutions, and histories of educational movements form a second type of historical inquiry. These studies are often motivated by "the simple desire to acquire knowledge about previously unexamined phenomena."[9] Even when a history of an educator, institution, or movement exists, the researcher needs to determine whether it adequately explores the events in which he is interested. In fact, gaps in knowledge of the past often provide the basis for a historical study. Bernard Bailyn, an educational historian, offered the following rationale for this type of research:

> The motivation here is to learn something new and to present this new information; but the precise issues are not defined. There are no specific questions and no hypothetical answers. Thus the motivation for writing a narrative of a battle may be simply to discover what happened in it; to find out how it was that the victors won it. Or, again, one decides to do research and write about Wilson's Administration because we are ignorant of it, and any thorough, clear narrative of it will be valuable because it fills an important gap, an evident vacuum.[10]

The third type of historical inquiry in education involves an attempt to interpret ideas or events that previously had seemed unrelated. For example, a researcher may find that histories of textbook publishing have been written and that separate, unrelated histories of school curriculum also have been written. In the process of reviewing these separate histories, the researcher may detect relationships and raise questions that did not concern either of the historians. These perceived relationships and questions may provide the basis for an original historical inquiry. A fourth, related type of historical inquiry occurs when the researcher attempts to synthesize old data or to merge it with new historical facts that she or others have discovered.

The fifth type of historical inquiry involves reinterpretation of past events that have been studied by other historians. These reinterpretations are sometimes called **revisionist history,** in that they are attempts to revise existing histories within the framework of new (and sometimes politically radical) interpretive frameworks.

As in any type of research, the beginning researcher planning a dissertation or thesis should review the literature and talk with experienced researchers before attempting to define a set of problems or topics for historical inquiry.

9. Ibid., p. 562.
10. Bernard Bailyn, "The Problems of the Working Historian," in *The Craft of American History*, ed. A. S. Eisenstadt (New York: AHM Publishing, 1969), pp. 202–3.

Sometimes the student will find through her review of the literature that other historians have formulated important problems and questions for investigation. For example, H. Warren Button has recently described the need for historical research on the functions and contributions of our own field—educational research.[11] Among Button's interests are the investigation of how quantitative analysis came into education and what types of educational research have been funded over the years and why.

An important guideline in identifying a problem or topic for historical research is to check that the sources needed for the investigation are available. It would be unwise to select a problem that required use of documents in a language that the researcher does not know, or documents that might be difficult to obtain access to (e.g., classified records in government archives).

SEARCHING FOR HISTORICAL SOURCES

Types of Historical Sources

Virtually any object or written record that one can imagine is a potential source of information about the past. We will distinguish four types of historical sources here: documents, quantitative records, oral records, and relics.

The most commonly used type of historical source is written or printed materials (sometimes called **documents**). These materials can take varied forms: diaries, memoirs, legal records, court testimony, newspapers, periodicals, business records, notebooks, yearbooks, diplomas, committee reports, memos, institutional files, tests. Documents can be classified in several ways: handwritten (i.e., in manuscript form) or printed, published or unpublished, prepared for public or private use. Another distinction is whether the document was prepared intentionally as a historical record or whether it was unpremeditated. Some documents, such as memoirs and yearbooks, are written primarily to serve as a record of the past. Other documents, such as memos and teacher-prepared tests, are intended to serve an immediate purpose, with no thought that at a later time they might be used as a historical record. The distinction between **intentional documents** and **unpremeditated documents** may be important to consider when evaluating the source for authenticity and genuineness (see later section on historical evaluation).

Quantitative records can be considered as a separate type of historical source or as a subtype of document. Census records, school budgets, school

---

11. H. Warren Button, "Creating More Usable Pasts: History in the Study of Education," *Educational Researcher* 8, no. 5 (1979): 3–9.

attendance records, test scores, and similar compilations of numerical data provide a valuable source of facts for the historical researcher. Historians are making increasing use of computers to analyze the large amounts of numerical data that are available for answering certain historical questions.

Another important type of historical source is the spoken word. Ballads, tales, sagas, and other forms of the oral tradition have been used to convey a record of events for posterity. Also, historians can conduct oral interviews of persons who have witnessed and participated in events of potential historical significance. The interviews are recorded on audiotape and may be transcribed to form a written record. This branch of historical research, known as **oral history,** currently is quite active. For example, the oral history program at Columbia University, initiated in the 1940s, includes records of interviews with more than 2700 people who supplied more than 14,000 hours of recollections.[12] The Oral History Association is an organization of historians interested in this type of research.[13]

Relics are the fourth type of historical source. **Relics** include any object whose physical or visual properties provide information about the past. School buildings, school furniture, architectural plans for school physical plants, textbook drawings, and instructional devices are examples of objects that can be used as relics in the study of past practices in education. Some objects can be classified as both documents and relics, depending on how they are used in a historical research project. For example, in a study of printing methods used in the production of textbooks, the textbooks would be classified as a relic. This is because one of their physical properties is being examined. On the other hand, in a study of the viewpoints concerning some phase of American history presented by textbooks of different periods, the textbook would be used as a document. The reason for classifying the textbooks as documents is that the verbal communications contained in them are the focus of the historical research.

Another basis for classifying historical sources is whether they are "primary" or "secondary." The distinction between primary and secondary sources is the same as in other types of educational research (see chapter 5). In historical research, **primary sources** are defined as those documents in which the individual describing the event was present when it occurred. **Secondary sources** are documents in which the individual describing the event was not present but obtained his description from someone else, who may or may not have directly observed the event. Thus, reports of historical research generally are classified as secondary sources because the historian rarely is a direct wit-

12. Charles W. Crawford, "Oral History—the State of the Profession," *Oral History Review*, 1974, pp. 1–9.
13. Oral History Association, University of Vermont, Burlington, Vermont. The association has several publications, including the *Oral History Review*, published annually

ness to the past events described in the reports. Instead, the report usually is based on the historian's interpretation of other primary and secondary sources.

A Tentative Search Plan

The historian's search for facts relating to his problem or topic should be systematic. To a certain extent, the historian needs to know what he is looking for even before the search begins. Otherwise, he is likely to search aimlessly and to overlook important sources of relevant facts. Philip C. Brooks suggests the following approach for initiating a search for historical sources:

> Resourcefulness and imagination are essential in the preliminary exploration as well as in the later actual study. One can suppose that certain kinds of sources would exist if he thinks carefully about his subject, the persons involved, the government or institutions concerned, and the kinds of records that would naturally grow out of the events that he will be studying. He should ask himself who would have produced the useful documents in the transaction he is concerned with. What would be the expected flow of events? What kinds of records would have been created? What would be the life history of the documents, from their creation through current use, filing, temporary storage, and eventual retention in a repository where he can consult them? What kinds of materials would one expect to be kept rather than discarded?[14]

The search for historical facts in primary and secondary sources cannot be entirely determined in advance, however. A tentative search plan should be created and revised as one's interpretive framework develops. Changes in one's plan will occur as a particular primary or secondary source reveals pertinent sources whose existence the historian had not anticipated.

Preliminary Sources

The first step in a search plan is to identify and consult relevant preliminary sources of historical information. A number of published aids for identifying the secondary source literature in history are available. These are called *preliminary sources*. An important requirement for using these aids effectively is to list

14. Philip C. Brooks, *Research in Archives: The Use of Unpublished Primary Sources:* (Chicago: University of Chicago Press, 1969), pp. 19–20.

key descriptors for one's problem or topic. Procedures for identifying descriptors are presented in chapter 5.

Published Bibliographies

Published bibliographies are a useful starting point for the researcher in constructing her own bibliography. Bibliographies can be initiated by consulting "bibliographies of bibliographies," which include the following references:

Sheehy, Eugene P. *Guide to Reference Books.* 9th ed. Chicago: American Library Association, 1976.

Walford, A. J., ed. *Guide to Reference Material.* Chicago: American Library Association, vol. 1 (4th ed.), 1980; vol. 2 (3rd ed.), 1975; vol. 3 (3rd ed.), 1977.

Bibliographic Index. A Cumulative Bibliography of Bibliographies. New York: H. W. Wilson, 1938–.

A number of other general bibliographic aids, such as *Education Index,* publications of the Educational Resources Information Center (ERIC), and indexes to periodicals and dissertations are described in chapter 5. The library catalog also can serve as a general bibliographic aid.

There are several compilations of bibliographies in history. One of them is *Historian's Handbook* by Helen J. Poulton and Marguerite S. Howland (Norman: University of Oklahoma Press, 1977), which includes bibliographies among other research aids. An especially helpful reference for the educational historian is *A Bibliography of American Educational History* by Francesco Cordasco and William Brickman (New York: AMS Press, 1975). This is a comprehensive annotated bibliography of references. Part 1 lists general reference works on American education. Part 2 is organized under the following headings: elementary education and curriculum; secondary education and curriculum; vocational education; education in the individual states; higher education; school books; the teaching profession; church, state, and education; the federal government and education; the education of women; biographies; foreign influences on American education; and contemporary issues in American education. Part 3 lists references dealing with specific historical periods in American education.

The journal *History of Education Quarterly* occasionally includes specialized bibliographies intended for the educational historian.

Reference Works

Since historical research is often concerned with persons who played a critical role in past events, biographical directories are a useful aid. The *Biography Index,* published by H. W. Wilson (New York), lists biographical material that has appeared in journals and in books; it is updated quarterly. There are many collections of brief biographies, including these:

Dictionary of American Biography. 10 vols. Edited by American Council of Learned Societies. New York: Scribner, 1927–80.

Dictionary of National Biography. 7 Supplements. New York: Oxford University Press, 1882–1971.

Who's Who in America. Editions 1–41. Chicago: Marquis Who's Who.

Encyclopedias are another useful source of biographical information.

Historical researchers also need to know about places, events, and things. An atlas can be consulted to determine the location of an unfamiliar place. Many atlases are available, including: William R. Shepherd, *Shepherd's Historical Atlas,* 9th rev. ed. (New York: Barnes & Noble, 1976). *Webster's New Geographical Dictionary,* rev. ed. (Springfield, Mass.: G. & C. Merriam, 1977) is another useful reference for identifying locations. Specialized chronologies, dictionaries of terms, and dictionaries of quotations have been prepared to help the historical researcher determine dates of past events, the meaning of words no longer in common use, and the origin of sayings.

Secondary Sources

The search of preliminary sources will result in a tentative bibliography of secondary sources, usually published histories relating to one's problem or topic. These histories will include the historian's interpretations and conclusions, historical information, references to other secondary sources, and references to primary sources, which provide the ultimate basis for the historian's "facts." An important issue to the historical researcher is whether he should use another historian's facts without personally checking the primary sources from which they were derived. The historical researcher needs to exercise judgment in this matter, considering such factors as the other historian's reputation, likelihood of bias, and accessibility of the primary source documents. If the historical researcher chooses to use the other historian's facts without further check, he should footnote the other historian's work as the source for the historical facts used in his own work.

Primary Sources

Primary sources of historical information (e.g., diaries, manuscripts, school records) are often contained in institutional repositories or archives. This is especially true of primary sources relating to historical events in which the principal witnesses are deceased or otherwise inaccessible. For histories of events that have occurred in the recent past, the historical researcher may contact witnesses on an individual basis in order to study documents in their possession or to interview them.

There are many repositories of primary sources relating to American history. *A Guide to Manuscripts and Archives in the United States,* edited by Philip M. Hamer (National Historical Publications Commission, 1961), describes the holdings of 1300 repositories. Another guide to historical repositories is the *National Union Catalog of Manuscript Collections,* 2 vols. (Hamden, Conn.: Shoestring Press, 1964). Most of these repositories contain handwritten or printed documents. In recent years some oral history repositories have been instituted.

Repositories are maintained by many institutions and groups: federal, state, and local governments, religious institutions, professional societies, business firms, and newspapers. Because of the many repositories that potentially can be consulted, it is important for the historical researcher to delimit her problem or topic so that the task of searching for primary sources is a manageable one.

Repositories vary in the ease of access of their primary sources. The holdings of official archives are often well-indexed, and archivists may be available to assist the historical researcher in her work. In other situations the researcher will be on her own, assuming that she has been able to obtain permission to examine the institution's or agency's records. It is likely that the researcher will need to search through files for certain primary source materials. Before the task can be undertaken, the researcher first should learn the filing system that was used. Records also may be stored on microfilm or microfiche, in which case the researcher may need to acquire specialized information retrieval skills.

If the researcher is interested in quantitative data, she almost certainly will need to enlist the aid of a staff member in interpreting them. A researcher who is interested in recent quantitative data, for example, may be confronted with printouts generated from computer programs prepared specifically for the institution's needs.

This brief description of procedures for searching for primary sources suggests how time-consuming it is. The task is more manageable, though, if the research problem has been carefully delimited and if a search plan has been constructed. Although any search for primary sources of information is time-consuming, the researcher may well achieve satisfaction in knowing that she is dealing with the ultimate "stuff" from which history is made.

RECORDING INFORMATION FROM HISTORICAL SOURCES

In examining a particular primary or secondary source, the historical researcher may not know what information will be useful to him at a later time. Quite possibly the interpretive phase of a study will involve searching for new facts that the historian had not viewed as relevant earlier in the study. The problem of deciding what information to abstract from a historical source becomes critical when the source is not easily accessible. The researcher may need to travel to repositories where historical sources are stored. Unlike libraries, repositories usually do not allow their materials to leave the premises. Thus, the researcher will need to decide, then and there, what information he should record for later use.

Before deciding what information to record, the researcher needs to deal with two preliminary issues. The first issue is whether the materials—especially primary sources—will be made accessible to him. Institutional records are often available for study, but this does not mean that someone can automatically examine them. The researcher should anticipate making a formal request for permission to study documents relating to his topic. Some documents may be totally inaccessible or accessible for study only under certain conditions.

The other issue facing the researcher concerns the types of material that can be copied and reproduced in his dissertation. An institution may allow the researcher to examine documents but not to quote directly from them; or the institution may allow only certain portions to be copied. Occasionally the researcher may wish to reproduce a series of documents that can be considered as "literary property," for example, a series of essays or speeches that could be published for profit. In this situation, the researcher needs to take care that he does not infringe on someone's actual or potential copyright. Under the doctrine of "fair use," however, the researcher can copy and quote a "reasonable" part (short passages) of a primary or secondary source without concern for copyright infringement.

Note Taking and Photocopying

One procedure for recording information from historical sources is to make written or typed notes. Reports of empirical research usually can be outlined on a single note card (see chapter 5), but historical sources are best reviewed by placing only one item of information on each card. The difference in procedure is necessary because many small bits of information relating to the historian's research questions may be obtained from one important document, such as an autobiography or a diary. Each card may be coded to indicate the question or topic to which the note relates. If all notes from the document were copied on a single card, the process of rearranging the information would be quite difficult.

Many historical researchers now simply photocopy documents that are of interest to them. Modern technology has made photocopying quick and relatively inexpensive. Some repositories even have facilities that enable the researcher to record documents on microfilm. Although photocopies do not necessarily eliminate the need for note taking, they often reduce the amount required. The purpose of the notes should be to provide brief reminders to the researcher of information presented in detail in the source document which is readily accessible through the photocopy.

Photocopies do have a few limitations. It may not be possible to photocopy old historical documents because the exposure to the photocopy process may damage them. Some documents, especially newspaper clippings, may not photocopy well. If one wishes to reproduce oversize documents, maps, and charts, special photographic techniques may be necessary.

Summarizing Quantitative Data

The historical researcher who has collected large amounts of quantitative data pertaining to past events faces a different kind of problem in recording and summarizing her information. For example, she will need to consider the possible advantages of entering the data onto keypunch cards for later computer analysis.

Before quantitative data are recorded in any form, the researcher needs to think carefully about the kinds of data that are necessary to her investigation. Data recording and analysis is time-consuming; it also may be expensive, depending upon the amount of data. The researcher needs to define variables carefully (e.g., income, socioeconomic status, voting record on particular issues) and appropriate measures of them. Also, the researcher needs to define in advance the sample or population on which data are to be recorded. In other words, one should not just record whatever data one happens to come across. For example, if the historical researcher is interested in changes in teachers' salaries over time, she will need to specify the population of teachers in which she is interested and sampling techniques to be used, if any. The researcher also will need to determine whether she wishes to define subgroups of teachers, for example, males versus females, elementary teachers versus secondary teachers.

Once the relevant data have been "discovered" through a search of quantitative historical records, the researcher likely will need to apply descriptive statistics. If the data are based on a sample from a defined population, the researcher also may wish to determine the statistical significance of obtained results.

Quantitative analysis of historical data has emerged as a topic of considerable interest to historians in the last decade. The reason for this trend is that historical conclusions based on large amounts of carefully selected quantitative data are likely to be more representative of the past than conclusions based on a few case studies. Also, quantitative analysis makes it possible to study the "average" citizen rather than the few "great" men and women who have dominated traditional historical research. H. Warren Button, a noted educational historian, has commented on this approach to historical research:

> A part of the advantage of quantification in social and educational history is that it allows historians to follow a recent interest, an interest in the history of the common man—no depreciation intended—"history from the bottom up"—grassroots history. Records for history in this vein are likely to be thin and fragmentary; for coherence it is necessary to mine every source. For instance, for a quantitative study of Buxton, a black antebellum haven in Ontario, it is necessary to assemble data from perhaps fifteen thousand entries in the census manuscripts of 1861, 1871, and 1881; from town auditors' accounts, and church records.[15] The research necessity for compilation and statistical treatment, by unfortunate paradox, produces history almost without personalities, even without names. Still, this new history has and will produce new understandings and will counterweight our longstanding concern for "the better sort."[16]

The historian who plans to conduct a quantitative investigation will need to be conversant with the range of research methodology—sampling techniques, variable definition and measurement, research design, data reduction, and statistical analysis. Therefore, students should refer to other sections of this book and to specialized works on quantitative history (see Annotated References at the end of the chapter) before planning this type of study.

EVALUATION OF HISTORICAL SOURCES

The historical researcher needs to adopt a critical attitude toward documents, quantitative data, and relics found in his search for historical facts. A historical source may be genuine, or it may be forged. A document may have been written by someone other than the person whose name appears as author. The historical source may refer to events that did not occur or that occurred differently from the description given by a witness. The researcher, then, should question the genuineness and credibility of each historical source used in his study. If this critical process reveals any doubts about the source, they should be noted in the research report.

One can never be completely certain about the genuineness and accuracy

15. Beverly H. Nenno, dissertation in progress, State University of New York at Buffalo.
16. Button, "Creating More Usable Pasts," p. 4.

of historical sources. There is always a possibility that a source has been forged or that the information in it was intentionally falsified. All that the researcher can do is to generate and test hypotheses that question each source critically; for example, one can ask, "Was this document really written by the person designated as the author?" As these hypotheses are shown to be untenable, the researcher increases the probability—although never to the point of absolute certainty—that the sources are genuine and credible. Some historical sources may prove to be of mixed value, credible in some respects and highly biased in other respects.

The evaluation of historical sources is usually referred to as **historical criticism.** Historical criticism is generally divided into two major categories: external criticism, which is the evaluation of the nature of the source; and internal criticism, which is the evaluation of the information contained in the source. The following discussion of external and internal criticism is directed toward evaluation of documents, although the principles also apply to the evaluation of historical quantitative data and relics.

As one primer of historical research methods indicates, historical criticism is a complex, sophisticated process:

> It relies on attention to detail, on common-sense reasoning, on a developed "feel" for history and chronology, on familiarity with human behavior, and on ever enlarging stores of information. Many a " catch question" current among schoolboys calls forth these powers in rudimentary form— for instance the tale about the beautiful Greek coin just discovered and bearing the date "500 B.C." Here a second's historical reflection and reasoning is enough for verification: the "fact" is readily rejected.[17]

The ultimate value of a historical investigation is determined in large part by the researcher's ability to evaluate the worth and meaning of an historical source once he has located it.

External Criticism

In **external criticism** the researcher raises a number of questions about the nature of the historical source: Is it genuine? Is it the original copy? Who wrote it? Where? When? Under what conditions? Many factors must be considered in answering these questions. We can suggest only a few of them here.

Some historical sources have been shown to be **forgeries,** that is, fabrications claimed to be genuine. The student of educational history is less likely to encounter forged and spurious documents than would be the historical re-

17. Jacques Barzun and Henry F. Graff, *The Modern Researcher*, 3rd ed. (New York: Harcourt Brace Jovanovich, 1977), p. 91.

search worker studying some political or religious movement, where stronger motivations usually exist for creating forgeries.

The existence of **variant sources** may prove to be a problem in determining whether one has the original copy of a primary source. For example, in going through the files of an educational institution, the researcher may discover copies of internal memoranda that relate to her topic. But perhaps the file copy was not distributed in exactly that form to its intended receiver or receivers. Sometimes the writer of a memo adds a personal note or qualification to one of the receivers. Thus, the researcher may find a slightly different version of the memo in the receiver's files than was placed in the sender's file. In this situation, both versions of the memo may be considered original primary sources and both may reveal relevant, but different, information about a past event.

Variant sources present a special challenge in working with documents predating the introduction of the typewriter (circa 1880). Copies of these documents, called manuscripts, were written in longhand, often resulting in small errors. In working with old manuscripts, the researcher should make an effort to determine whether they are the only version or whether copies were made; if copies are known to exist, the researcher can be on the alert for them.

Authorship of a document is usually listed on the document itself. This is not always a reliable indicator. Some publications, especially recorded speeches, may be ghostwritten; and occasionally an author will use a pseudonym to conceal his or her real identity. Barzun and Graff cite the example of a historian who spent thirty-five years in an attempt to identify the author of a series of unsigned installments that appeared in a periodical at the time of the Civil War.[18] If a document has multiple authors, it may be impossible to determine who wrote the parts of it that are of particular relevance to one's study.

The place of origin of a document is often apparent from where it is stored, or from indications in the document itself. The date when it was written may be indicated on the document. Sometimes it can be ascertained from statements in the document or from its location in a set of records or files. Dates indicated on the document should be viewed critically, since people often make innocent, but misleading, errors. For example, at the start of a new year it is not uncommon for someone to enter the previous year, which throws the true date off by a year.

Finally, knowledge of the conditions under which a document was prepared is most helpful in determining its nature and usefulness to the problem under investigation. If you are studying documents from a particular institution, it is very helpful to learn everything that you can about the institution's

18. Ibid., p. 107.

table of organization and operating procedures. This knowledge will help you understand the purpose of certain documents and for whom they were intended. Furthermore, having this knowledge in the early stages of the study will help you limit your search to certain kinds of documents in the institution.

Internal Criticism

Internal criticism involves evaluating the accuracy and worth of the statements contained in a historical document. In examining the statements, the researcher needs to ask himself such critical questions as, Is it probable that people would act in the way described by the writer? Is it physically possible for events to have occurred this quickly? Do the budget figures mentioned by the writer seem reasonable? In making these judgments, the researcher needs to be careful not to reject a statement just because the event it describes appears improbable. Most of us can recall several highly improbable events that have occurred in our own lives.

Although internal criticism can be directed at the statements themselves, it also is necessary to evaluate the person who wrote them. For example, it is important to know whether the writer was a competent observer of the events to which he refers. Was he present at the events? Was he an expert on the matters discussed? Was he considered an accurate, truthful observer? Many studies in psychology have demonstrated that eyewitnesses can be extremely unreliable, especially if they are emotionally aroused or under stress at the time of the event. Even under conditions where no emotional involvement occurs, some individuals are a great deal more competent as observers than others.

Even if witnesses are competent and truthful, they may still record different accounts of the events that transpired. One has only to read accounts of an event (e.g., a school board meeting) in different newspapers to determine how widely witnesses can vary in their perceptions. This does not mean necessarily that one witness is correct and the others are wrong. Nor is the converse necessarily true: that because the majority of witnesses agree in their accounts, they are right and the witness with a different perception is wrong.

The beginning historical researcher, subjected to differing accounts of an event, may conclude that there is no "objective" reality, only the subjective impressions of witnesses and historians. This conclusion may lead to the skeptical view that there is no "objective" historical truth and that all accounts and impressions are equally valid. This need not be so. The researcher must consider that, though persons' accounts may be subjective, there is still an objective reality to be discovered. As the historian Edward Carr noted: "It does not follow that, because a mountain appears to take on different shapes from different angles of vision, it has objectively either no shape at all or an infinity of shapes."[19] The task of the historical researcher is to combine one or more witnesses' accounts, admittedly subjective, and to interpret them (admittedly, also a subjective process) in an attempt to discover what actually happened.[20]

Although all accounts of historical events are subjective, they are not all necessarily biased or prejudiced. A **bias** or prejudice is a set to perceive events in such a way that certain types of facts are habitually overlooked, distorted, or falsified. The person who has an ax to grind or who has strong motives for wanting a particular version of a described event to be accepted can usually be expected to produce biased information. For example, a school superintendent, when writing an account of a school board meeting in which a dispute occurred between himself and members of the school board, will tend to present his side of the argument in the most favorable light, may subconsciously alter his position to agree with facts that have become apparent since the meeting, and may forget or deliberately omit statements of his opponents that have been found to have merit since the meeting occurred. Historians must often delve to a considerable degree into the race, political party, religious group, and social status of the observer in an effort to appraise the likelihood of prejudice or biases. The use of emotionally charged or intemperate language, whether of a favorable or unfavorable nature, suggests bias and should be watched for.

People often exaggerate ther own roles in important affairs. The exaggeration may not be deliberate but merely reflects the occurrences from the point of view of the individual concerned. Much material that is basically untruthful can be traced to the tendency of many individuals to elaborate or color their description of events in order to make a more interesting story or call more attention to their role in the events being described. Sometimes, on the other hand, the social or political position of the individual is such as to require him to make conventional statements rather than honest ones. For example, a school superintendent faced with internal difficulties with principals or other members of his organization might, upon being questioned, give the usual answers, indicating the high morale and level of agreement of his staff, because he may feel that airing the internal difficulties of the school district can serve no useful purpose. People in public life frequently make conventional statements concerning political opponents or in eulogizing other individuals. These statements may have little or no bearing upon their true feelings.

If the researcher finds a discrepancy between a person's public or private statements, this does not mean necessarily that they are of no value as histor-

---

19. Carr, *What Is History?* pp. 30–31.
20. The distinction between "objective" and "subjective" is a concern in all types of educational research. A distinction originally made by philosophers, it reflects certain assumptions about the nature of science. Further discussion can be found in Barzun and Graff, *The Modern Researcher*, pp. 140–48.

ical evidence. Rather, the discrepancy itself is evidence concerning the person involved in making the statement and about the social environment in which he or she functioned.

INTERPRETATION IN HISTORICAL RESEARCH

The Historian as Interpreter

In discussing internal criticism, we noted that witnesses to an event will report different impressions based on their competence, biases, and relationship to the event. The historian is in a similar situation:

> The facts are really not at all like fish on the fishmonger's slab. They are like fish swimming about in a vast and sometimes inaccessible ocean; and what the historian catches will depend partly on chance, but mainly on what part of the ocean he chooses to fish in and what tackle he chooses to use—these two factors being, of course, determined by the kind of fish he wants to catch. By and large, the historian will get the kind of facts he wants. History means interpretation.[21]

If you choose to do historical research, you will need to become aware of your biases, values, and interests as they release to the historical problem or topic that you selected. Biases, values, and personal interests allow you to "see" certain aspects of past events, but not others. As you become aware of your own interpretive framework, you also will have increased sensitivity to interpretive biases of other historians who conducted research on the same or similar topics.

Because "history means interpretation," historians are constantly rewriting the past, as their interests and concerns change. The last decade of historical research in education has seen the emergence of a **revisionist** (also called "reconstructionist") group of researchers who are viewing American educational history from a new interpretative framework:

> [Reconstructionist] Historians of education are questioning stereotyped notions of the words *reform* and *progressive* and are thinking in terms of the *irony* of school reform. Historians of education are now ready to examine the public schools as instruments of social control. Historians of

21. Carr, *What Is History?*, p. 26.

education are now disclosing phenomena long hidden by official pieties: the maltreatment of immigrants and ethnic groups, the discriminatory treatment of women and minority groups, the connections between schools and politics and between education and social stratification.[22]

In contrast, earlier historians tended to look for evidence in the past of how American education contributed to the improvement of our society and of students' lives. Recent historians, it appears, have a "radical" bias in their interpretation of the past, whereas older historians had a "liberal reform" bias. Joel Spring's study of intelligence testing, described in a later section of the chapter, is an example of revisionist history.

Another bias of educational historians was exposed by Bernard Bailyn in a landmark historical study published in 1960.[23] In his book Bailyn observed that historians of American education had interpreted education predominantly as a process of formal schooling. He urged historians to overcome this bias so that they could view education "not only as formal pedagogy but as the entire process by which a culture transmits itself across the generations" (p. 14). Partly as a result of Bailyn's influence, educational historians have enlarged their perspective to conduct research on many nonschool influences that affect the learning and socialization of citizens.

Presentism is another form of bias that the educational historian needs to avoid. Presentism is the tendency to interpret past events using concepts and perspectives that originated in more recent times. For example, there has been much interest recently in educational "accountability." The historical researcher who is interested in this problem may look for evidence of how earlier educators viewed their responsibility to be accountable to the public and to the students whom they served. The historian may find information in primary sources that, to her, reflects concern for accountability. Yet, this may not have been at all how earlier educators viewed their sense of responsibility to the community. They may have used concepts similar in name to "accountability" but having quite different meanings. Therefore, the historian needs to discover how the various concepts were used in their own time and settings, rather than attaching present meaning to them.

The preceding analysis might suggest that historical research is more subjective and therefore less "scientific" than other types of educational research. This is not true; other types of educational research are equally interpretive, but perhaps in a less obvious manner. To give just one example, the researcher who conducts an experiment to evaluate the effects of a new educational pro-

22. Cohen, "History of American Education," p. 329.
23. Bernard Bailyn, *Education in the Forming of American Society: Need and Opportunities for Study.* Chapel Hill: University of North Carolina Press, 1970 (reprint of 1960 ed.).

gram usually will measure a limited number of outcomes (e.g., achievement on a paper-and-pencil test, attitudes expressed on a set of semantic differential scales). The choice of outcome instruments reflects the researcher's interpretation of the effects that are worth measuring. Many other outcomes could be measured and, indeed, might have been measured if another researcher had conducted the experiment. Furthermore, a researcher with a bias in favor of the new program might select instruments, purposely or unwittingly, that are sensitive only to positive effects of the program. Another researcher, with a different bias, might select instruments sensitive only to negative effects. Interpretation also centers on the conclusions that the researcher draws from the data analyses. One researcher may interpret the data as indicating that the program "works"; another researcher may draw more tentative, cautionary conclusions.

David Tyack's study of compulsory education illustrates well the role of interpretation in historical research.[24] As Tyack observes, the rise of compulsory education is a remarkable part of American educational history:

> . . . I see two major phases in the history of compulsory school attendance in the United States. During the first, which lasted from [the] mid-nineteenth century to about 1890, Americans built a broad base of elementary schooling which attracted ever-growing numbers of children. Most states passed compulsory attendance legislation during these years, but generally these laws were unenforced and probably unenforceable. The notion of compulsion appears to have aroused ideological dispute at this time, but few persons paid serious attention to the organizational apparatus necessary to compel students into classrooms. Therefore, this phase might be called the *symbolic* stage. The second phase, beginning shortly before the turn of the twentieth century, might be called the *bureaucratic* stage. During this era of American education, school systems grew in size and complexity, new techniques of bureaucratic control emerged, ideological conflict over compulsion diminished, strong laws were passed, and school officials developed sophisticated techniques to bring truants into schools. By the 1920s and 1930s increasing numbers of states were requiring youth to attend high school, and by the 1950s secondary school attendance had become so customary that school-leavers were routinely seen as dropouts.[25]

The question arises, Why did schooling in the United States gradually become compulsory under force of law? Tyack examined five interpretations to

24. David B. Tyack, "Ways of Seeing: An Essay on the History of Compulsory Schooling," *Harvard Educational Review* 46 (1976): 55–89.
25. Ibid. p. 60.

see how well each answered this question. For example, the ethnocultural interpretation argues that compulsory education came about because of the belief that it would inculcate a single "correct" standard of behavior, especially among the nineteenth-century immigrants from Southern and Eastern Europe who were provoking much concern among certain religious and ethnic groups already established in this country. Another interpretation, drawn from the economic theory of human capital, states that compulsory schooling grew out of a belief that education would improve the productivity and predictability of the work force. In the words of the noted educator Horace Mann, education is "the most prolific parent of material riches."[26]

Each of the five interpretations explains some of the historical evidence, leaves other evidence unexplained, and suggests new lines of research. In Tyack's view, alternative interpretations help the historian "to gain a more complex and accurate perception of the past and a greater awareness of the ambiguous relationship between outcome and intent—both of the actors in history and of the historians who attempt to recreate their lives."[27] In planning your own historical study, you are advised to delineate the phenomena you wish to study and at least two interpretive frameworks for explaining the phenomena. Even if you choose to operate primarily within one interpretive framework, the other framework will provide a basis for assessing the worth of your research procedures and thinking.

Use of Concepts to Interpret Historical Information

Concepts are indispensable for organizing the phenomena that occurred in the past. **Concepts** group together those persons, events, or objects that share a common set of attributes. For example, without a concept such as "progressive education," a great many historical phenomena would remain separate from each other; they could not be formed into a meaningful pattern. Concepts, however, also place limits on the historical researcher's interpretation of the past. For example, a researcher who is doing a historical study of teachers may assume that the defining attribute of this concept is "holds a state certificate acknowledging completion of a college-level teacher education program." This definition of "teacher" will cause the researcher to study certain persons in a certain historical period but not others, such as teacher aides, school volunteers, and certain resource personnel. This may be the researcher's intent, but he should be aware of the assumptions that underlie his use of key concepts and what these

26. David B. Tyack, "Ways of Seeing: An Essay on the History of Compulsory Schooling," *Harvard Educational Review* 46 (1976): p. 79.
27. Ibid., p. 89.

concepts imply will be included as relevant or irrelevant phenomena for study.

Recent historical research has made much use of concepts from other social science disciplines. Concepts from sociology (e.g., role, bureaucracy, institution), anthropology (e.g., culture, transmission of culture), and psychology (e.g., motive, attitude, personality development) are used to describe and interpret past phenomena. Again, these concepts may be useful tools, but the historical researcher needs to be aware of how these concepts are defined in the social science discipline from which they originate to ensure that they are used appropriately in his study.

Causal Inference in Historical Research

An essential task of historical research consists of investigating the causes of past events. As one historian said, "The study of history is a study of causes."[28] What were the forces and events that gave rise to the intelligence-testing movement? Why did American educators adopt so readily the British open-classroom approach? How did the role of the principal originate in this country? These are the types of "causal" questions that guide historical inquiry.

Causal inference in historical research is the process of reaching the conclusion that one set of events brought about, directly or indirectly, a subsequent set of events. The historian cannot "prove" that one event in the past caused another, but she can be aware of, and make explicit, the assumptions that underlie the act of ascribing causality to sequences of historical events. An assumption that some historians make is that humans act similarly across cultures and across time. Thus, they may use a currently accepted causal pattern to explain an apparently similar pattern in the past. For example, a historian might find an instance in nineteenth-century American education when college students stopped attending classes and started attacking the school's administration; this event was preceded in time by administrative rulings abridging students' rights and privileges. The historian might infer—perhaps correctly—that the rulings led to the student revolt, reasoning that this was the apparent chain of events in the student revolts of the 1960s. Other historians, however, believe that historical events are unique; that is, history does not repeat itself. Occurrences at one point in history cannot be used to help explain occurrences at another point in historical time.

In making causal inferences, the historian should be aware of her assumptions about the causative factors sometimes invoked to explain the course of history. Historians have emphasized various types of causes in their at-

28. Carr, *What Is History?* p. 113.

tempts to explain past events. They have attributed significant historical occurrences to the actions of certain key persons (the "great man" view of history), the operation of powerful ideologies, advances in science and technology, economic factors, geographical factors, sociological factors, and psychological factors. Some historians take an eclectic view and explain historical events in terms of a combination of all these views.

It appears that the more we know about the antecedents of a historical event, the more likely we are to discover possible causes of the event. In the example stated above, the historian could make a plausible inference that the school's administrative rulings were a factor in causing the student revolt. But was it *the* cause? Suppose the researcher also discovered that other events were occurring simultaneously that might upset students, e.g., the imminence of war, revolts of the citizenry against government tax increases, or a rapidly increasing enrollment that strained the college's facilities. All these circumstances are potential causes, and there may be others that the historian did not yet discover. Therefore, the historical researcher would have difficulty in justifying the attribution of a historical event to a single cause. It is more defensible to identify an antecedent event as *a* cause. Also, the historian, by her choice of language, can convey her interpretation of the certainty of the causal link ("it is highly likely that" or "it is possible that") and strength of the causal link ("it was a major influence" or "it was but one of many events that influenced").

Generalizing from Historical Evidence

As in other types of educational research, the historical researcher cannot study the entire population of persons, settings, events, or objects in which he is interested. Instead, the historical researcher usually studies only a small sample of the phenomena that interest him. Furthermore, the sample is determined by the remains (e.g., documents and relics) of the past. These remains may not be at all representative. For example, a historical researcher may study the diaries, correspondence, and other written records of teachers in the 1800s in order to develop an understanding of teaching conditions then. The researcher is limited to documents that remain from this period. Therefore, he needs to bear in mind that teachers who were interested in making a written description of their work may not have been typical of teachers in general. One way to determine generalizability is to look for consistency across teachers in different circumstances. For example, did teachers who wrote about their work for publication describe similar conditions as did teachers who wrote about their work in private diaries and correspondence?

Another problem of **generalizability in historical research** occurs in interpretation of historical evidence relating to a single individual. The researcher may come across a document in which the individual being studied takes a stand on a particular educational issue of the time. It is difficult to generalize from this one document that the individual consistently held the same opinion across time.

As in any research, the historical researcher's findings are strengthened by increasing the sample of data on which they are based. The researcher is advised to search for as many primary and secondary sources relating to the topic as possible. Where the evidence is limited, the researcher should limit the generalizability of his interpretations accordingly.

The branch of historical research known as *quantitative history* is improving the researcher's ability to study representative samples of the phenomena in which he is interested. The computer has made possible the analysis of data about large groups of people represented in census reports, school records, and similar documents.

WRITING THE HISTORICAL RESEARCH DISSERTATION

The organization of the historical research dissertation does not usually follow the chapter outline of other types of educational research dissertations.[29] Reports of historical research have no standard format. The particular problem or topic investigated determines how the presentation of findings will be organized.

One obvious method of organization is to present the historical facts in chronological order. Thus, each chapter of the dissertation might cover a discrete period of time in the life of an individual, institution, or educational movement. The other obvious method of organization is to present the historical facts according to topic or theme. For example, if the purpose of the study was to examine how different school districts came to establish a kindergarten program, the dissertation might have a separate chapter for each school district included in the study.

Sometimes, neither method of organization is satisfactory. Suppose the researcher's purpose is to describe the development of a particular university. The researcher may organize the dissertation chonologically, with each chapter devoted to different periods of time. This approach, though, may obscure certain themes that have continuity across time periods (e.g., the development of the university's relationship to the government as a prime research contractor, the development of its graduate school, and the development of its undergraduate curriculum). Thematic continuity could be achieved by having a separate chapter for each aspect of the university's development, but then one would lose a sense of the institution's unity and overall state of development at par-

---

29. See chapter 21 for guidelines on organizing the typical dissertation or thesis.

ticular points in time. Also, it would be difficult for the researcher to show how the various areas of the university's development influenced and related to each other.

A possible solution to this problem is to combine the chronological and thematic approach. Each chapter might cover a discrete time period, but the internal organization of the chapters might be thematic. Ultimately, the decision to use a particular organizational pattern depends upon the questions that the historical researcher has chosen to ask.

The major part of the dissertation probably will consist of the chapters in which the researcher's findings are presented. In addition, the researcher may wish to have a separate chapter that reviews other historians' interpretation of the same or a similar topic. The methodology used in the research may be presented in a separate chapter, especially if the historical sources posed unusual problems of external or internal criticism. The researcher's interpretation, and reflections on the interpretive process, are sometimes presented in a separate chapter.

Choice of words must be considered carefully in writing the dissertation, since they reflect the researcher's interpretive framework. We have noted above, for example, how the use of certain words can convey differences in probability and degree of causal relationships between past events. Adjectives have particular interpretive significance. Suppose that the researcher decides to describe a particular institution as a "major" university. The use of this adjective is interpretive, but does it reflect the researcher's own awe of the institution or does it reflect the expert judgment of other educators? The researcher needs to think carefully about why she has chosen to use this particular word in describing the topic of her research. This is not to suggest that the use of words having affective or value connotations should be avoided. Without the presence of such words, the historical research dissertation would be exceedingly boring; and it would fail in its responsibility to reconstruct the past so that it becomes alive for the reader.

EXAMPLES OF HISTORICAL RESEARCH IN EDUCATION

Origins of the Intelligence-Testing Movement

Joel H. Spring has conducted historical research on the development of intelligence tests during World War I.[30] He attempted to re-create the intellectual

---

30. Joel H. Spring, "Psychologists and the War: The Meaning of Intelligence in the Alpha and Beta Tests," *History of Education Quarterly* 12 (1972): 3–15.

climate of this time by examining the writings and public statements of psychologists who played a prominent role in the development of the Alpha and Beta tests, which were used to classify recruits in the U.S. Army. Spring also examined the tests themselves to determine what they measured and whether this was consistent with what the psychologists said they were measuring.

Spring found evidence that the psychologists who developed the Alpha and Beta tests were guided by a social-efficiency view of human intelligence. For example, Spring refers to a public lecture of H. H. Goddard, one of the army test developers, in which he stated that a good social organization "is not so much a question of the absolute numbers of persons of high and low intelligence as it is whether each grade of intelligence is assigned a part, in the whole organization, that is within its capacity."[31] Spring demonstrated how this conception of intelligence was extended to army intelligence testing: "The purpose of the Alpha and Beta tests was first to weed out the intellectually unfit and then to classify the rest on the basis of native intelligence. Native intelligence in this context meant the ability to function within the army."[32] Social efficiency was accomplished by assigning each recruit to his appropriate role in the army's organizational structure.

Spring cited one research study on Alpha and Beta test validation in which soldiers' test scores were correlated with officers' ratings of their "practical soldier value." The correlations were high (.50 to .70). Spring also found parallels between the intelligence-test instructions (e.g., "I am going to give you some commands to see how well you can carry them out") and army routine, which requires soldiers to follow orders and to work within an organization characterized by rigid discipline and a high degree of bureaucratic structure.

As part of his research, Spring traced the impact of army intelligence tests on school testing programs. He found that after the end of World War I, the government flooded the market with unused Alpha and Beta test booklets, many of which were purchased by colleges for their testing programs. Also, some of the psychologists who had worked on the army's test, such as L. M. Terman and H. H. Goddard, turned their attention to developing testing programs for the public schools. Spring noted that contemporary tests of intelligence are often validated by correlating them with earlier measures, which bear the influence of a social-efficiency conception of intelligence. His major interpretive conclusion is that "the measurement of intelligence is at all times based on a conception of the good society and the good man. . . . Unwittingly, today's test constructors and users are only perpetuating the beehive concept of society and intelligence."[33]

This study is valuable because it gives educators new data and insights

31. Ibid., p. 3.
32. Ibid., p. 8.
33. Ibid., p. 14.

for critically examining the assumptions underlying current practices. Although the popular conception of intelligence tests is they measure the ability to learn, Spring's historical analysis suggests that they measure the ability to function within a certain type of organizational structure. If this is true, we are compelled to examine whether it is right to engage in this type of intelligence assessment.

Critical evaluation of Spring's research is also necessary. For example, one should ask whether he surveyed a representative sample of psychologists of the World War I era, and a representative sample of their writings. It may be true that the social-efficiency view of intelligence influenced the army's testing program, but other psychologists may have had different views that also exerted an influence on intelligence testing then and now.

Antecedents of Village High Schools in Alaska

A doctoral dissertation by Margo Zuelow provides an example of how historical research can form one part of a larger study.[34] The major purpose of her study was to examine the recent development of self-contained village high schools in isolated areas of Alaska. The study was in three parts: a formative evaluation (see chapter 17) of a school district that had instituted these schools, a review of the literature to determine techniques that other societies have developed for delivering instruction to geographically isolated areas, and research on historical antecedents of the new village high schools.

The search for primary sources relating to Alaskan secondary education required two trips to Alaska, according to the author. One trip was to the Alaska State Department of Education and the Historical Library in Juneau; the other was to the Center for Northern Education Research in Fairbanks. Among the documents examined were: the minutes of the State Department of Education; the reports of the Alaska commissioner of education; the annual reports of the U.S. secretary of the interior; the *Alaska Teacher*, which is the journal of the National Education Association affiliate in Alaska; and clippings from major Alaskan newspapers on education issues.

Zuelow noted that early Alaskan documents usually were based on personal observation. For example, the early reports of the Alaska commissioner of education were typed by the commissioner and were in the form of a travel narrative describing his inspection trips to all the schools in the territory. As

34. Margo C. Zuelow, "An Historical Perspective for, and Evaluation of, Changes in Secondary Education Programs for Rural Alaskans in One Regional Education Attendance Area" (Ph.D. dissertation, University of Oregon, 1977).

the Alaskan agencies concerned with education grew, the reports generally
were written by department heads, who described the work and observations
of their subordinates. Zuelow found that different reports often conflicted on
the specific date that an event occurred, although they usually agreed on the
month.

Zuelow chose a chronological format to present the historical antecedents
of current Alaskan secondary education policy. Her two major chronological
divisions and stages within each are:

1. Pre-Statehood (–1959)
   a. Alaska's First Settlers (–1741)
   b. Russian Discovery (1741–85)
   c. Russian Control of Education (1785–1867)
   d. United States Governmental Neglect (1867–99)
   e. United States Governmental Schools (1884–99)
   f. Introduction of Reindeer (1890–1959)
   g. Territorial Schools for Non-Native Children (1890–1959)
   h. Schools outside Incorporated Towns (1901–59)
2. Statehood and the Alaska Constitution (1959–76)
   a. State Responsibility Recognized (1959–64)
   b. Johnson-O'Malley Act Reorganized (1965–76)

These stages and divisions reflect Zuelow's interpretation of patterns of events
and influences on Alaskan education policy. Note that the stages are not necessarily discrete phases, but sometimes overlap each other (e.g., 1d and 1e).

Zuelow identified several themes that characterize the development of
Alaskan secondary education. Probably the most significant is the issue of local
control of education by Native Alaskans. She found that "up until the 1960's,
Alaska Natives were not consulted on legislative action which would affect the
education of their children."[35] A critical event occurred in April 1969, when
Native Alaskan spokesmen had an opportunity to present their views before a
hearing of the Special Indian Subcommittee of the U.S. Senate. The spokesmen
strongly criticized the boarding schools, which at that time provided much of
the secondary education for rural Native Alaskan students. The boarding schools
required the students to live away from their home communities, with adverse
consequences. The spokesmen advocated the development of local village high
schools and greater involvement of the Native Alaskan community in school
matters.

Zuelow's historical analysis provides a valuable perspective for examining

35. Ibid., p. 74.

recent developments in Alaskan education. The formation of small village high schools, which may serve as few as five students, can be questioned from the standpoint of economic efficiency and educational quality. Yet history suggests other factors, such as local control and appropriateness of curriculum, that need to be considered in judging these schools. It may be that the village high school provides benefits that offset the high costs and other apparent disadvantages. Also, Zuelow's historical analysis identified solutions that did not work in the past, especially the notion of the regional boarding school. Although the past is by no means a certain guide to the future, it is useful in suggesting caution. Any future proposal for a regional boarding school (or other change) should cause one to ask whether conditions have changed sufficiently to augur success despite failures in the past.

MISTAKES SOMETIMES MADE IN HISTORICAL RESEARCH

1. The researcher selects a problem or topic for which historical sources are inaccessible or nonexistent.
2. Makes excessive use of secondary historical sources.
3. Fails to subject historical sources to external and internal criticism.
4. Is unaware of personal values, biases, and interests that influence selection and interpretation of historical sources.
5. Uses concepts from other disciplines inappropriately to explain past events.
6. Makes unwarranted causal inferences or refers to a particular factor as *the* cause rather than *a* cause.
7. Generalizes to a larger set of people, places, or institutions than is justified by the available historical information.
8. Lists facts without synthesizing them into meaningful chronological and thematic patterns.

ANNOTATED REFERENCES

Barzun, Jacques, and Graff, Henry F. *The Modern Researcher*. 3rd ed. New York: Harcourt, Brace Jovanovich, 1977.

This classic textbook provides a comprehensive survey of the historian's work. Techniques of fact finding, historical criticism, and interpretation are presented. In addition, there is an extensive section on procedures for writing the historical report.

Brooks, Philip C. *Research in Archives: The Use of Unpublished Primary Sources.* Chicago: University of Chicago Press, 1969.

This is a short, unusually well written reference work. Its major purpose is to describe techniques for working with primary historical sources. In addition, it provides an insightful look at contemporary methodology involved in doing a historical research project.

Carr, Edward Hallett. *What Is History?* New York: Random House, 1967.

This set of published lectures has become a classic reference on the nature of historical investigation. The problem of causal inference in historical research, the nature of historical facts, the historian's role as interpreter, and the uses of history are among the topics covered by this eminent historian. This book is "must" reading for the student who wishes an in-depth understanding of what history is.

Cutler, William W. "Oral History: Its Nature and Uses for Educational History." *History of Education Quarterly* (1971):184–94.

This article provides an overview of oral history as a method of recording past events. The author describes its uses, its accomplishments to date, procedures for making oral recordings, and specific applications to the study of educational history.

Dollar, Charles M., and Jensen, Richard J. *Historian's Guide to Statistics: Quantitative Analysis and Historical Research.* Huntington, N.Y.: Krieger, 1974 (reprint of 1971 ed.).

This textbook is intended to serve as a general introduction to the methods of quantitative historical research. The authors present step-by-step procedures for using statistical techniques and the computer to analyze historical data. An extensive annotated bibliography of books and articles on quantitative history is included.

Fischer, David H. *Historians' Fallacies: Toward a Logic of Historical Thought.* New York: Harper & Row, 1970.

The author provides an insightful analysis of historical research methodology by exposing the many errors of reasoning that historians can and do commit. The book contains a wealth of actual examples grouped under three main headings: errors of inquiry, errors of explanation, and errors of argument.

Gottschalk, Louis. *Understanding History: A Primer of Historical Method.* New York: Alfred A. Knopf, 1969.

This textbook, as its title suggests, contains many useful techniques for doing historical research. The author discusses in depth many of the topics mentioned in this chapter: defining a problem, searching for sources, note-taking methods, external and internal criticism, causal inference, and historical writing.

Graff, Harvey J. "'The New Math': Quantification in the 'New' History, and the History of Education." *Urban Education* 11(1977): 403–40.

The author discusses how recent historical research has been influenced by the use of quantification, which he defines as "a reliance and a recognition of the peculiar value of standard and comparable numerical data for the examination of a wide range of important questions." The essay also contains a brief review of quantitative historical studies of literacy, school attendance, higher education, the family, the economics of education, and the role of elite groups in municipal educational reform.

Sloan, Douglas. "Historiography and the History of Education." In *Review of Research in Education*, vol. 1, Fred N. Kerlinger, ed. Itasca, Ill.: F. E. Peacock, 1973.

This literature review provides a useful survey of recent research in educational history. The focus of the review is on the identification of the major themes and problems that concern contemporary historians of education and how they differ from previous views of the historian's mission.

Winks, Robin W., ed. *The Historian as Detective: Essays on Evidence*. New York: Harper & Row, 1979.

This is an enjoyable collection of readings about how historians track down factual evidence. The readings, especially the ones about the Kennedy assassination (by John Kaplan) and manuscript hunting (by Richard D. Altick), demonstrate the fragile quality of historical "facts" and the creative processes required to discover them.

SELF-CHECK TEST

Circle the correct answer to each of the following questions. An answer key is provided on page 881.

1. In historical research the wide range of written and printed materials recorded for the purpose of transmitting information is called
   a. relics.
   b. documents.
   c. primary sources.
   d. preliminary sources.
2. In historical research the physical objects related to the period being studied are called

   a. documents.
   b. primary documents.
   c. secondary sources.
   d. relics.
3. In other forms of research the review of the literature is considered a preliminary step to gathering data. In historical research the review of the literature is usually .
   a. omitted.
   b. the step providing the research data.
   c. the step conducted after the data-gathering phase.
   d. not of great importance.
4. The type of evaluation aimed at determining whether the evidence being evaluated is authentic is termed
   a. internal criticism.
   b. external criticism.
   c. external validation.
   d. historical criticism.
5. Internal criticism of a document
   a. is usually more difficult than external criticism.
   b. is directed at evaluating the writer.
   c. is assisted by other accounts of the same events.
   d. All of the above are correct.
6. Presentism is defined as
   a. the belief that the present is more important than the historical past.
   b. the use of contemporary concepts to interpret past events.
   c. the belief that the present cannot be understood by study of past events.
   d. the set of assumptions underlying contemporary revisionist history.
7. Causal inference in historical research is a process in which the historian
   a. proves that one historical event determined another event.
   b. uses internal criticism to establish causal links between documents written at different points in time.
   c. uses interpretation to ascribe causality to a sequence of historical events.
   d. demonstrates the unique nature of each historical event.
8. Reports of historical research
   a. are organized chronologically.
   b. are organized thematically.
   c. can be organized chronologically or thematically.
   d. are organized no differently from reports of experimental research.
9. One of Bernard Bailyn's contributions to historical research in education was
   a. to originate the "liberal reform" framework for reinterpreting historical events in education.
   b. to originate a new theory of causal inference in historical research.

c. to bring "accountability" to historical research in education.
d. to include nonschool influences on learning as a legitimate topic for historical research in education.
10. Quantitative analysis of historical data is intended primarily to facilitate
a. external criticism.
b. internal criticism.
c. study of large samples of populations.
d. study of secondary sources.

APPLICATION PROBLEMS

The following problems are designed to give you practice in applying significant concepts and research procedures explained in chapter 19. Most do not have a single correct answer. For feedback, compare your answers with the sample answers on pages 899–900.

1. A historian is planning to do research on the origins of intelligence testing in this country. List three preliminary sources he might consult, and three possible repositories of historical data relating to intelligence testing.
2. Suppose you were doing a historical study concerned with allocation of funds to teacher salaries, books, other instructional materials, plant maintenance and operation, and administrative costs in three rural elementary schools during the period from 1900 to 1930. Your main sources for this study are the account books for each school, in which the principals listed by date each expenditure as it occurred and entered a brief description. In studying these sources, how would you prepare note cards for use in your research?
3. Suppose you are doing a historical study on the teaching of pseudo sciences in U.S. public schools during the period 1870–99. You find the following article in the April 15, 1891, issue of the *Sonoma Farmer,* a rural weekly published in California:

Wonders of the Science of Phrenology

Local citizens attending the County Fair this week are being amazed by Professor Horatio Horton, a leading practitioner of the science of Phrenology. Professor Horton can make infallible analyses of the character and personality of any man or woman by feeling the bumps on the individual's head. Most persons overheard by your reporter agreed that the Professor's analyses of people out of the audience were uncanny.

After the performance your reporter interviewed the Professor in his dressing room and learned that he is a leader in the movement to teach Phrenology in the public schools. The Professor himself has taught the science to thousands of students in colleges and high schools throughout most of the civilized nations of the world. Phrenology is now a required subject in the secondary schools of France, Italy and several other European countries. Students in these countries usually devote a year to the study of this valuable science.

The Professor strongly recommends that local citizens apply pressure to county officials to bring about inclusion of Phrenology in the local curriculum. He is available to give teachers a short course in the science and has also written several books and pamphlets that would be useful to students.

Your reporter feels that adequate training in Phrenology should be provided in our schools as soon as possible. After all, your children are entitled to a modern education.

3. List four reasons why the accuracy of the information might be questioned.

4. A historian is planning to do research on how early-nineteenth-century school officials and psychologists influenced each other with respect to advocacy of intelligence testing. (a) What concepts does the historian need to define in doing this research? Why? (b) What are several factors that will affect the generalizability of his findings?

SUGGESTION SHEET

If your last name starts with letters from Stv to Tuc please complete the Suggestion Sheet at the end of the book while this chapter is still fresh in your mind.

Part V.

DATA PROCESSING AND REPORTING

Many researchers do not think through their data-processing procedures until the data have been collected. This lack of planning can add considerably to the time and cost of a research project. During the planning of your research project, you should carefully examine your procedures, to identify ways that data can be collected and processed efficiently.

Early in this book we pointed out that most advances in science come about as a result of many researchers making small contributions that eventually add up to significant new knowledge. The reporting of your research is therefore very important; unless it is reported, your contribution to the field will be lost. Research is a waste of time unless the findings are made available to other researchers and practitioners.

Thus it is your responsibility to prepare a scholarly report of your research and try to make your work available to others through reporting at a professional meeting or publishing in a journal.

20.

PROCESSING RESEARCH DATA

OVERVIEW

A substantial amount of data is often collected even in small research projects. Processing of the data can be very time-consuming and susceptible to error unless efficient procedures are used. This chapter starts by describing how to summarize the raw data collected by use of standard tests, unstructured tests, or other instruments. Once the raw data have been put into summary form, the next step is to analyze them using statistical techniques. Guidelines are given for determining situations in which it is appropriate to use computer processing or a desk calculator for statistical analyses. Also, the basic principles of computer data analysis are described. The chapter concludes with a section on procedures for storing research data so that they are readily accessible for later reference.

OBJECTIVES

After studying this chapter you should be able to:

1. Describe procedures for handscoring or machine-scoring standard tests.
2. Describe procedures for scoring unstructured or self-developed measures.
3. Prepare hand-data cards, computer recording forms, or mark-sense cards to summarize data collected in a research project.
4. Prepare an I.D. code that includes a unique identifier and subgroup codes.
5. Describe the input-output process involved in using a computer.
6. State at least four types of statistical analysis usually done by computer.
7. Explain how to check data analyses done by desk calculator or computer for accuracy.
8. Describe at least two desirable procedures to use in storing research data.

After the research data have been collected, the next phase is to convert them to a form that permits easy statistical analysis. Tests must be scored, and scores sometimes need to be converted to standard form. Qualitative data collected by interview or observation must be coded. All data must be recorded in such a way that the analysis can be carried out rapidly and with minimum chance of error.

An important point to remember in processing data is that a systematic, well-planned procedure is necessary in order to avoid errors and to get the most out of the research data.

SCORING OF TESTS AND OTHER MEASURES

Steps in Scoring Standard Tests

The first step in scoring standard tests is to restudy the test manual and the test in order to be completely familiar with the test content and scoring procedure. Keys are provided with standard tests, and the key should be checked carefully against the test items to be sure that it is correct. Often the handscoring keys supplied with standard tests are less convenient to use than a window key that the research worker can prepare for himself.

A **window key** is a sheet of stiff paper approximately the same size as the test sheet on which the student records his answers. Small holes ("windows") that overlay the correct choice for each test item are cut in the sheet of stiff paper. The scorer then can place the window key over each student's test sheet and quickly count the number of correct test items by checking each "window" to determine whether a pencil mark has been placed there. The scorer should check whether the student marked more than one choice for a particular test item. The test manual may specify scoring rules for dealing with multiple responses to an item. Otherwise the researcher will need to develop his own rules.

After keys have been prepared, a definite scoring routine should be set up. In some tests scoring may be done more quickly by scoring the first page of all tests before turning to the second page. On other tests it is more feasible to score each test in its entirety before going to the next. The student can usually arrive at a satisfactory scoring routine by examining the test and answer sheet. When the researcher is faced with a lengthy test-scoring job, it is usually advisable to work for periods of one or two hours rather than attempt to complete the entire job at one sitting. After an hour or two, most people become tired and bored, which leads to mistakes. If periods of study or recreation are alternated with periods of test scoring and other clerical work, the researcher will find the work less fatiguing and will make fewer errors.

After all the copies of a test have been scored, the researcher should select every tenth copy for rescoring. When rescoring, he should tally each error indicating its size and direction and, if possible, the item on which the error was made. After completing the rescoring of 10 percent of the tests, the researcher should examine the error distribution and decide whether sufficient errors have been found to necessitate rescoring all copies of the test. A few small errors are usually found, and these have relatively little effect upon the research results.

After all the copies of a given test have been scored and checked, the tests should be packaged and labeled, giving the date of testing, the subjects tested, and other pertinent information that may be needed later to identify the data. The importance of this step cannot be overemphasized. The researcher may forget these details between the time of scoring and the time when the data are analyzed and the dissertation is written. Hours can be wasted in tracking down details at a later time, whereas only a few minutes are needed to record details at the time that the tests are administered and scored.

Machine Scoring of Standard Tests

Many colleges and universities have test-scoring machines and can supply test-scoring services at a low cost. The scoring machine automatically records the person's response to each test item and assigns a total score. The machine saves a great deal of time and should be used to score standard tests whenever the researcher's budget permits. Some universities will permit the student to score his own tests on the machine during off-hours. If this is permitted, the student should do so because it provides him with valuable experience. Many test-scoring machines are also equipped with a graphic item counter that permits item analysis of the test with very little extra work. Item analysis is usually called for if the student has developed his own measure or if he is using a measure for which item data (e.g., internal reliability and percentage of students responding correctly to each item) are not available.

If an IBM test-scoring machine is used, the first step is to check carefully all answer sheets to see that electrographic pencil marks are heavy and to erase random pencil marks that might cause the machine to give an incorrect score. The IBM key should be checked, too, before scoring the test on the machine. Test-scoring machines can make errors, so it is advisable to hand-score 10 percent of the tests and analyze the errors. Errors can be made by the person reading the score from the machine, or they may be due to internal difficulties with the machine.

Scoring Unstructured or Self-Developed Measures

A research worker may find it necessary to develop her own measures for a particular study. For example, she may use a projective technique such as the Rorschach Inkblot Test or the Thematic Apperception Test to measure the variables in which she is interested. Under these circumstances the procedures for scoring the variables should be fully developed during a pilot study or a tryout of the measurement tools.

The pilot study should include subjects similar to those who will be used in the main study. During this phase of the project, the research worker can make any changes in scoring rules that seem appropriate, and she may also make changes in the measure itself. After a scoring procedure has been developed, it usually is necessary to administer the measure to another pilot group in order to collect data for item analysis. A measure should not be administered to the main research sample until the researcher is fully satisfied with the scoring procedure and has completed the item analysis.

Once the scoring of the measure for the main research sample has been started, the scoring procedure must remain the same. Occasionally the researcher will do an inadequate job of developing scoring procedures. Then, during the scoring of the research data, he discovers changes that should be made. At this point, however, changes cannot be made because some subjects would be scored on one basis and others on another basis. The alternative of rescoring all subjects on the new basis is also questionable unless the measure is highly objective, because the previous scoring may affect the researcher's perception of the subjects' responses.

The greatest difficulties in developing scoring methods occur for measures that are unstructured, such as interview data, observational rating forms, and responses to projective tests. If one of these techniques is used, the measure should be scored independently by two or more raters. This will reduce the likelihood that the biases of a single observer will unduly influence the results, and it also permits the determination of interrater reliability. This topic is discussed further in chapter 12.

It is extremely important to keep detailed records of the scoring procedure used with self-developed tests or with any test for which the usual scoring procedure is not followed. This information should be included in the research report so that anyone reading it can understand the scoring procedure in evaluating the results or replicating the study. The research worker, in developing a scoring system for such measures, should write down her procedure as a series of definite steps to be followed. She should also establish scoring rules and definitions that will help her score the same responses in the same manner on all her tests. An example of this process is given in chapter 12 in the section on content analysis. During the actual scoring of the measures, the researcher should refer back to her written scoring procedures frequently, or there may be a tendency to drift away from them.

RECORDING DATA FOR STATISTICAL ANALYSIS

Hand Data Cards

After all the measures have been scored, the data should be entered on a form that lends itself to the planned statistical analysis. The **hand data card** is generally the most efficient method of recording the research data in studies involving relatively few cases or when calculations will be done by hand or on a desk calculator.

As a rule, a separate hand data card is prepared for each subject in the study. The hand data card contains all information concerning the subject. A sample hand data card with a key describing each entry is shown in figure 20.1. The research worker can usually have the format mimeographed on 3-by-5-inch or 4-by-6-inch note cards at relatively little expense. He then writes in

I.D.	_____	Ach 9/81	_____
Sex	_____	Ach 5/82	_____
D.B.	_____	CEFT	_____
School	_____		_____
Group	_____		_____
F.O.	_____		_____
IQ	_____		_____

Figure 20.1 Sample hand data card and key.

I.D.	Pupil's identification number
Sex	1 = boy; 2 = girl
D.B.	Date of birth: first two digits give month, second two give year (Example: 0273 = February 1973)
School	1 = Harrison; 2 = Washington; 3 = Horace Mann
Group	1 = Experimental; 2 = Control
F.O.	Level of Father's Occupation using Warner scale
IQ	Wechsler Intelligence Scale for Children, total IQ score
Ach 9/81	Comprehensive Test of Basic Skills, level 1, form S, total score
Ach 5/82	Comprehensive Test of Basic Skills, level 1, form T, total score
CEFT	Children's Embedded Figures Test, total score
—	Other blanks may be used to record additional data

the pupil's name or identification number and copies the research data from the various tests, biographical forms, school records, and other sources. When he is finished, each card contains all the information collected about one individual in the study.

Hand data cards simplify analysis in studies where the subjects are to be divided into a number of subgroups for different analytical approaches. With hand data cards, the cards for a given subgroup can quickly be pulled from the deck and data taken directly from them. These cards can then be returned to the deck for analysis of other subgroups or analysis of the overall sample.

The hand data card is too small to permit a complete description of each entry. Therefore, a key sheet describing exactly what is contained in each entry of the card is ncessary. The researcher should use a hand data card large enough to permit a few extra blanks in case he generates additional variables in the course of the study.

Test scores may often be recorded directly from the test answer sheet to the hand data card. Much of the material collected in educational research, however, must be coded to make it readily adaptable to analysis procedures. Descriptive data, such as sex, social class, homeroom teacher, and school attended, are much easier to record if code numbers are assigned. For example, the key for figure 20.2 contains a number code (1, 2, 3) to represent the three schools in the study.

Computer Recording Forms and IBM Cards

Research data that are to be analyzed by computer usually are recorded on **computer recording forms.** These forms can be obtained at business stationery stores or at computer centers. They may be bound in packets of 50 or 100 sheets. On each sheet is a grid containing 80 columns and a number of rows. The data for a particular subject are put on one row of a sheet; data from two or more subjects are never put on the same row. Each column contains scores of subjects on a particular single-digit variable. If the variable scores involve two or more digits, a corresponding number of columns is used to record the data. Scores from two or more different variables are never recorded in the same column.

A partial computer recording form is shown in figure 20.2. Each row gives the data for one, and only one, subject in the sample. Each column gives the data corresponding to one, and only one, variable. Every column and row is used, resulting in no blank spaces between variables or between subjects. If there are not enough rows on a sheet to record data of everyone in the sample, additional sheets are used.

Additional sheets can also be used if there are not enough columns on a sheet to record all the variables. However, this procedure violates the rule that

Figure 20.2 Computer recording form.

Columns	Description
1–3	Student's identification number
4	Sex (1 = boy; 2 = girl)
5–6	Grade in school
7–8	Reading Achievement Score
9–10	Math Achievement Score
11–13	Scholastic Aptitude Test Verbal Score
14–16	Scholastic Aptitude Test Quantitative Score
17–26	Item scores, Attitude toward Reading Scale
27–36	Item scores, Attitude toward Mathematics Scale
37–46	Item scores, Attitude toward Computers Scale
80	Grid identification number

each column gives the data corresponding to one, and only one, variable. For example, column 19 on one sheet cannot be used for variable X, while column 19 on another sheet is used for variable Y. This problem is avoided by considering each sheet to be a separate grid. Each grid is numbered, usually in column 80. For example, column 19 of grid 1 could be reserved for variable X, and column 19 of grid 2 could be reserved for variable Y.

Grid designations are necessary only when the researcher has so many variables that they cannot fit in the 80 columns of a computer recording form. A large number of subjects does not generate the need for grid designations, though. Each row represents a separate subject. It does not matter whether a particular row is on one sheet or another.

The design of the computer recording form makes better sense when one realizes that the data on the form will be punched on an IBM card. An **IBM card** is a stiff piece of paper having 80 columns. Each IBM card can be used to record the data on one, and only one, row of a computer recording sheet. If all the variables can be included on a single recording sheet, then each IBM card will correspond to a particular subject in the sample. If the variables are recorded on two or more computer recording sheets, then each subject will require two or more IBM cards. The last column of a computer recording sheet and IBM card are often used to identify the particular grid from which the data came. In figure 20.2 column 80 indicates that this was the third grid needed to record scores of the variables included in the study.

Errors can be made in transferring data from a hand data card or other format to the computer recording form. Therefore, the data on the recording form should be doublechecked for accuracy. Errors can also occur in punching data on IBM cards from the computer recording form. A special machine, called a **keypunch,** is used to do the punching. Once the cards have been punched, they can be run through the machine again to verify their accuracy. The keypunch operator repeats all the punching operations, except that the cards are not actually punched. The machine jams when there is a discrepancy between the numeral already punched on a particular column of the card and the numeral that the operator has punched in the verification process. The operator checks to determine whether the error occurred in the original punching or in the verification process.

The range of scores for a particular variable may vary in number of digits. Suppose the scores on a test range from 0 to 147. Three columns of the computer recording form, and of the IBM card, must be allotted for this variable. A student with a score of 0 would receive an entry of 000 on the recording form; a student with a score of 47 would receive an entry of 047; and a student with a score of 136 would receive an entry of 136. The number of columns needed for a particular variable is determined by the largest value of the variable in the data collected.

If data on a hand data card are to be transferred directly to IBM cards, the column numbers are given on the hand data card instead of, or in addition to, the abbreviated identification. For example, in figure 20.1, instead of "I.D.," the first entry could be identified as columns 1–3. This would indicate to the keypunch operator that the 3-digit entry in this column would be punched in the first three columns of the IBM card. Instead of "sex," the next entry could be identified as column 4; only one digit would be required to record this information. "Date of birth" would be identified as columns 5–8 since up to four digits may be required to record the month and year.

An advantage of IBM cards is that they are easily reproduced. Although it happens infrequently, it is possible for the computer center to misplace IBM cards. This means that all the cards must be repunched, a costly procedure. Therefore, the student is advised to make a duplicate set of all IBM cards that are submitted to the computer center for analysis. Most computer centers have a duplicating machine that can reproduce a large deck of IBM cards in a few minutes. These few minutes of precaution can save many hours of repeat keypunching should the cards be misplaced. Another machine that is available at most computer centers prints out on a sheet all the data contained on one's IBM cards. This is a helpful method to check for errors in keypunching. Also, there is a machine that automatically counts and sorts IBM cards.

IBM cards are not restricted to recording numerical data. Data in the form of alphabetic characters can be recorded as well. Suppose one wishes to do a computer analysis of textbook passages. The passages can be punched directly onto an IBM card; each card will record a combination of words, punctuation, and spaces between words totaling 80 columns. The computer can be programmed to do a variety of analyses, including computation of word frequencies, average sentence length, and readability levels.

Instead of using IBM cards, the researcher can record data on **computer tape.** Another option is to punch the data on IBM cards, and then to have the contents of the cards transferred to computer tape. The advantage of tape is that it is much less bulky than IBM cards when the amount of data is large. Also, the tape can be kept at the computer center, whereas decks of IBM cards usually cannot. This advantage means that the researcher does not need to carry his data to the computer center each time he wishes to do a statistical analysis. Computer tape technology is fairly sophisticated, however, and should be used only by someone who is expert or who has access to expert assistance.

Data Grids

In describing the use of computer recording forms, we introduced the concept of **data grids.** (A data grid sometimes is called a *data matrix*.) It is important to understand how research data, especially in large amounts, can be managed by constructing grids. The basic elements of a grid are its rows and columns. Each row records the data for a particular person in the research sample. Each column, or set of columns, records the scores of the research sample on a particular variable.

Sometimes research data need to be transferred from one grid to another. Suppose that the researcher has administered five 10-item attitude scales to a sample of 30 students. Each item consists of 7 response options, so that students can earn scores from 1 to 7. The initial statistical analysis is to investigate the item properties of each of the five scales. Thus, each item is entered as a discrete variable in a separate column of the grid. Since there are five scales, each with 10 items, the grid will have 50 columns for variable data. There also are 3 additional columns for an I.D. code and a grid I.D. number in column 80, making a total of 54 columns. Since there are 20 students in the sample, the grid will have 20 rows. The grid is now ready for computer analyses on the scales' item properties.

After the item analyses are completed, the researcher may want to do additional analyses using students' total score on each of the five scales. A new grid needs to be constructed for this analysis. As we stated above, each scale has 10 items, with scores ranging from 1 to 7. Thus, students' total scale score can range from 10 to 70. Each scale score, then, will require two columns of a grid. Since there are five scales plus a 3-digit I.D. code and a 1-digit grid I.D., a total of 14 columns are needed in the new grid. Since there are still 20 students in the sample, the new grid will have 20 rows. The new grid can be generated by hand or by computer processing.

The use of data grids makes it possible to easily transform data from one set of variables to another, as in the example above. Data grids also make it easy to check back and forth between grids, since rows always represent individual subjects in the sample and columns always represent discrete variables. Data grids are particularly well suited for managing large amounts of research data. Hand data cards are appropriate for small amounts.

Sometimes the inexperienced researcher will use neither data grids nor hand data cards, but instead will record all the data for a particular variable on a separate sheet of paper. If there are 10 variables, there will be 10 sheets of paper. This technique of data management should be avoided. It creates difficulties in organizing the data for computer processing and in doing statistical analyses, especially analyses that involve relationships between variables.

I.D. Codes

Subjects in a research sample usually are assigned an **I.D. code** (identification code) for two purposes. The first purpose, as explained in chapter 4, is to protect the subject's privacy. The researcher makes a list of each person's name accompanied by an I.D. code. Access to the list is restricted and is used only when necessary for research purposes. The subjects are identified by their I.D. code in all data analyses. The second reason for using an I.D. code is that is easier to identify a subject by a numerical code on an IBM card than by the subject's actual name, which is an alphabetic code.

Each subject in the research sample must be given a unique number as part of the I.D. code. This is easily accomplished by giving the first person in the list of subjects an I.D. code of 01, the second person an I.D. code of 02, and so on. This unique identifier should have as many digits as there are in the number that represents the size of the total sample. If there are 250 students in the sample, then the first student on the list would be assigned an I.D. code of 001, the second student an I.D. code of 002, and so on.

Sometimes the researcher will want to extend the I.D. code in order to identify the subjects further as members of particular subgroups. For example, the first three digits of an I.D. code could be used as the unique identifier; the fourth digit could be used to identify the subject as male (0) or female (1); and the fifth digit could be used to identify whether the subject attended a public school (1), a private school (2), or a denominational school (3). A subject with an I.D. code of 09512 would be a female attending a private school who is identified on the researcher's master list as subject number 95. Extended codes of this type are useful whenever the researcher plans to do subgroup analyses and when the research data for each subject in the sample extends over several computer recording forms or other data grids.

Research variables also can be identified by an I.D. code. Computer programs generally require that each variable be labeled by a discrete number or by a brief descriptor. For example, the variable "reading achievement" might be identified by the numerical code 01 or by the descriptor READACH. In the computer printout that presents the results of the statistical analyses, the I.D. code is used as a label to identify the results pertaining to a particular variable.

USE OF THE COMPUTER AND CALCULATOR IN DATA PROCESSING

The Computer as a Data Processing Tool

If the research data are to be analyzed by computer, the researcher will need to select or develop appropriate computer programs. A **computer program** is an explicit series of instructions to the computer, which directs it to perform each set of operations in a particular statistical analysis. Each statistical technique (e.g., a *t* test, product-moment correlation, or analysis of variance) requires a separate program. If the researcher is using a common statistical technique, a program is probably available at the computer center or other university facility.

The computer programs most commonly used in educational research are contained in **SPSS,** which is an acronym for "Statistical Package for the Social Sciences." SPSS is a comprehensive, integrated collection of procedures for statistical analysis and data management. The collection includes virtually every statistical procedure mentioned in this book, from simple descriptive statistics to multivariate statistics. Also, SPSS is available in two formats. In the batch format, the researcher prepares all the directions for SPSS analysis, using control cards, before submitting the data to the computer. In the interactive format, the researcher interacts with the computer through each step of the statistical analysis. The researcher can submit a request and get an immediate response. Thus, he can make data analysis decisions as he goes along. By contrast, the batch format requires the researcher to make all of his data analysis decisions at one time. Manuals for using SPSS are described in the Annotated References.

If a suitable computer program cannot be found in SPSS, a literature search may help you locate the one you need. Sometimes, though, a prepared program cannot be located. This usually occurs when the data analysis involves special transformations of the data (e.g., summing a particular set of scores to yield a total score or converting a set of scores to percentiles). In this situation the researcher can write her own program if she has had the necessary training. Otherwise it may be necessary to consult a professional computer programmer who can write a program that will carry out the desired statistical analysis. If the amount of data is not large, it may be most efficient to do the analysis by hand.

If an established computer program is used to perform the statistical analyses, the student should learn the requirements of the program *before* punching the IBM cards and submitting them to the computer center. Some programs require that the cards be punched in a certain format; for example, the program may require that only the first 72 columns on the card (an IBM card has a total of 80 columns) be used. If the student ignores this requirement, the computer will not be able to use the program to perform the statistical analysis. Also, programs usually have certain limits on the number of subjects and variables that can be analyzed. If the student's data exceed these limits, the program cannot be used.

Once the computer program has been selected or developed, it is a relatively simple matter to complete the statistical analysis. The usual procedure is to bring one's deck of IBM cards to the computer center for processing. The deck contains the keypunched data cards plus control cards. The **control cards** are standard IBM cards that contain such information as number of subjects, number of variables, and card format. (Card format refers to the number of variables on each data card, the number of data cards per subject, and the number of columns that each variable occupies.) Generally, for established computer programs there is a handbook that describes how these control cards are to be punched. It is especially important to determine how the program requires missing data to be handled. The control cards also will indicate that a particular program located at the computer center is to be used. If the researcher has written her own computer program, the program will be key-punched on IBM cards and submitted along with the data cards and other control cards.

Once the data have been submitted as "input" to the computer center, the researcher need only wait for the "output." The **computer output** contains the results of the statistical analyses printed on special computer paper. It is advisable not to write notes on the output; some of the printed results may be photo-reduced and included directly in the dissertation or research report. This procedure saves the tedious and sometimes error-ridden task of typing large amounts of statistical information.

Usually the computer output can be interpreted without difficulty. When this is not the case, the researcher will need to consult a professional computer programmer or a handbook that describes how the program's output is to be interpreted.

The time interval between input and output can vary from a few minutes to several days, depending on the complexity of the statistical analysis, the computer center's workload, and computer malfunctions. It can be very frustrating to wait several days for one's output, only to find that the computer analysis did not work because of an error in the control cards or data cards. Therefore, it pays to check the deck of punched cards carefully before submitting it for computer analysis.

The procedure described above requires the researcher or assistant to travel to and from the computer center. More sophisticated procedures, involving the use of off-site computer terminals and computer tape, eliminate the need to visit a central computing facility. The researcher should determine the most practical and efficient procedures for using the computer center where her data analyses will be done.

An important recent development in data processing is the appearance of the desk computer. These computers, which are not much larger than the traditional desk calculator, sometimes come equipped with standard statistical programs. Many of them are programmable. Another new development is the handheld computer. These machines are usually much more limited in their data analysis applications than desk computers or the large computers used in a typical university computing facility.

Choosing between Data Processing Tools

The use of electronic data processing machines saves a great deal of time and effort in studies involving large numbers of cases or complex analysis procedures. As a rule, the bigger the research job the more is gained by use of electronic data processing. A student can calculate a product-moment correlation involving 100 pairs of scores in about an hour by hand. If he has a desk calculator, this time can be cut to 20 or 30 minutes. Some of the most recent electronic computers can calculate hundreds of product-moment correlations per minute. In fact, high-speed computers can carry out up to 15 million operations per minute. Even though the charge for using such computers is about $300 an hour, the student may be able to carry out all his statistical analyses in only a few minutes' time. At the rate of about $5 per minute, the cost of using a computer is quite reasonable. This figure, however, does not include the expense involved in setting up the computer program and putting the material in a form the computer can use. Program libraries and exchanges have been set up so that much statistical work can be done at little programming cost.

Small studies, or studies involving relatively simple analysis, can often be done most efficiently using a desk calculator or desk computer. This is true because the cost of programming small studies involving a few subjects is the same as programming the same operations for a great many cases. Inasmuch as programming costs are high, the use of large computers for small studies is often inefficient. A study, for example, involving a number of breakdowns of the research groups into small subsamples followed by comparisons of the mean scores of these subsamples with the t test, is often easier and cheaper to do with a desk calculator than with an electronic data processing system because of the small number of cases involved and the large amount of programming required to obtain the necessary information by machine.

In deciding whether to use the computer or desk calculator for statistical analyses, the student needs to consider a variety of factors: the number of cases, the number of variables, the complexity of statistical analysis, the number of analyses to be done, and the availability of a suitable computer program and consultant who is familiar with the program. Let us consider a situation that might arise in a research project. A researcher has investigated whether differences in vocational interests and personality traits exist between those high school students who plan to go to junior college (JC) and those who plan to attend a regular four-year college (RC). Vocational interest and personality inventories, yielding a total of 15 variables, are administered to 30 JC students and 30 RC students. A t test is used to determine whether the two groups differ on any of the variables. If the researcher plans to use the t test on only a few of the variables, the desk calculator or desk computer would probably be the best method to do the analysis. If the researcher plans to analyze all 15 variables and a computer program is available, the computer would be the method of choice. If the researcher plans subgroup comparisons (e.g., male students vs. female students) after the main analysis is completed, a computer is even more desirable, because once the IBM cards are punched and the initial *t* tests completed, it is usually a simple matter of punching a few new control cards (to give new instructions to the computer) in order to conduct further statistical analyses of the same data.

Since many factors are involved in data analysis, the student should consult a person knowledgeable about computer applications in the behavioral sciences before making the decision to use a computer program. Nevertheless, we can say here that there are at least two types of statistical analyses that are almost always best done by means of a computer program. These are the various types of multivariate correlation, such as factor analysis and multiple regression, and some types of item analysis (used to select items for new tests). Both types of analysis involve hundreds of complex computations, even when the number of cases and variables is not large. Also, the student is advised to consider seriously the use of a computer program when a complex analysis of variance or covariance must be done.

A great many universities have electronic computers and offer courses in their use. Often, if he can prepare his own program for the computer and can operate the computer, the student is permitted to use the equipment without charge. The student who plans a career in educational research should get such training, if available, at his university, even if electronic equipment is not called for in his graduate research project. At present virtually all analysis of major educational research is being done with electronic equipment.

There is some doubt whether it is advisable for the student to turn his data over to the processing center of his university if he is not able to participate actively in the data processing. The student who processes his own research data on a desk calculator has a much better insight into what his data indicate—a better "feel" for the data. This insight often leads to discoveries that would be lost if the data were analyzed by electronic equipment under the supervision of a statistician who may know little about the nature of the data he is processing. However, the value of electronic data processing for studies involving large numbers of correlations or a complex analysis procedure cannot be overestimated. This method of data processing has opened the door to many research problems that never could have been attacked at all using other methods. The aforementioned precautions are given mainly to help you become aware that electronic equipment does not provide a panacea. Each research task should be evaluated carefully to determine what form of data processing is the most efficient for that task.

Checking Data Analyses for Accuracy

Whatever data processing machine is used, the results should be checked to ensure accuracy. When using the desk calculator, a series of checks at different points in the calculation are usually made. Some desk calculators now provide a printed tape record of operations that is valuable in checking procedure. Most, however, do not have this feature, and the student must write down the results obtained at key points in her analysis in order to simplify checking. If such checks are not practical, it is advisable to make all calculations twice. Rechecking a major analysis procedure in toto is a frustrating procedure. There are many places where an error may be made, and the graduate student who is not highly skilled in the use of a desk calculator may make a different error on each repetition, thus never obtaining a satisfactory check of her results. Checking the work of an electronic computer is usually much more difficult because the student has no data on intermediate steps. She can usually check the program by working out one example on a desk calculator. For example, if the computer has calculated a large number of correlations, she may work one of the correlations on a desk calculator to check the computer program. Generally, if the correct data are entered and the program is correct, the answer given by the computer will be correct.

STORING RESEARCH DATA

After you have completed all the planned data analyses, you should file the raw data, the hand data cards or computer recording forms, and hand computations and computer printouts. All materials should be labeled in such a way that you can easily locate items for later checking. It is particularly important to retain the raw data, which are the test answer sheets, observation forms, recordings of interviews, and other research material as initially received from subjects. For example, you may wish to refer back to the raw data to check a particular score that seems doubtful. Also, retaining the raw data makes it possible to use the data in future research. It is not uncommon to hit upon an idea for reanalyzing one's data after the original study has been completed. The reanalysis may yield new and interesting information that would be lost if the raw data had been destroyed at the end of the original analysis. If any research findings are challenged, the raw data provide the only fully satisfactory source for rechecking them.

The process of checking will be greatly simplified if you record the steps neatly and systematically, and label each step for future reference. The time consumed in keeping systematic records is a good investment. It is much less than the time that would be required to decipher unlabeled raw data or to redo lost calculations.

MISTAKES SOMETIMES MADE IN PROCESSING DATA

1. Researcher fails to set up a systematic routine for scoring and recording data.
2. Does not record details and variations in scoring procedures and is then unable to remember what was done when called upon to describe these procedures.
3. Does not check scoring for errors.
4. Changes scoring procedure when in the process of scoring research data.
5. Does not label data so that they can be located easily and accurately.
6. Uses the computer to analyze data when it might be more efficient to use a desk calculator, particularly when only a few statistical analyses are needed.

ANNOTATED REFERENCES

Arbib, Michael A. *Computers and the Cybernetic Society*. New York: Academic Press, 1977.

The author presents a comprehensive overview of electronic data processing. The book describes what computers are, how they work, and their various applications in education and other fields. It is written at a level that can be understood without special training in mathematics or electronic data processing.

Bruning, James L., and Kintz, B. L. *Computational Handbook of Statistics*. 2nd ed. Glenview, Ill.: Scott, Foresman, 1977.

The appendix to this book contains FORTRAN IV computer programs for the commonly used statistical techniques. The programs are coordinated with computational examples presented earlier in the book.

Nie, Norman H., and others. *Statistical Package for the Social Sciences Primer*. 2nd ed. New York: McGraw-Hill, 1975.

The Statistical Package for the Social Sciences (commonly known as SPSS) is probably the most widely used set of computer programs designed for statistical analysis. SPSS programs are available at most university computing centers. This primer orients the reader to the use of computers and to SPSS programs for simple descriptive and inferential statistics. Recent additions to the SPSS collection of statistical programs are described in *SPSS Update*, edited by Norman H. Nie and C. Hadlai Hull (a continuing series of manuals published by McGraw-Hill). Finally, there is *SPSS-11*, a manual describing the version of SPSS developed for the DEC PDP-11 minicomputer. The manual was edited by Norman H. Nie and C. Hadlai Hull (New York: McGraw-Hill, 1980).

Nie, Norman H.; Hull, C. Hadlai; Franklin, Mark N.; Jenkins, Jean G.; Sours, Keith J.; Norusis, Marija J.; and Beadle, ViAnn. *SCSS: A User's Guide to the SCSS Conversational System.* New York: McGraw-Hill, 1980.

This manual provides a detailed description of the interactive version of SPSS. A briefer description of this SPSS version can be found in *SCSS Short Guide: An Introduction to the SCSS Conversational System* by Keith J. Sours (New York: McGraw-Hill, 1982).

Many computer programs are described in educational and psychological journals. *Educational and Psychological Measurement* regularly includes reports of this type. For example, the Spring 1982 issue describes computer programs for calculating several types of correlation coefficient and for scoring several published measures.

SELF-CHECK TEST

Circle the correct answer to each of the following questions. An answer key is provided on page 881.

1. The first step in scoring standardized tests used in research is to
   a. restudy the test manual and the test.
   b. check the *Mental Measurements Yearbooks* concerning the test.
   c. check for interrater reliability.
   d. prepare an answer key.
2. The first step in using a test scoring machine is to
   a. run all answer sheets through the machine and check for scoring errors.
   b. check all answer sheets, darkening pencil marks if needed, and erasing random pencil marks.
   c. prepare the IBM control cards.
   d. select an appropriate computer-scoring program.
3. In order to calculate interrater reliability, it is necessary to
   a. convert scores into a form suitable for machine scoring.
   b. first measure test reliability and validity.
   c. have the test scored by two or more independent raters.
   d. use a computer program because of the complexity of the task.

4. The procedures and rules for scoring unstructured measures should be recorded in detail in order to
   a. make them available to other researchers.
   b. be able to state them precisely in the research report.
   c. control the actual scoring of the measures with greater accuracy.
   d. All of the above are correct.
5. One advantage of a hand data card over a summary sheet is that hand data cards
   a. can be entered directly into the computer.
   b. are easier to use in doing subgroup analyses.
   c. permit quicker recording of the data.
   d. All of the above are correct.
6. The standard IBM punch card contains _____ for entering numerical data.
   a. 80 columns
   b. 10 columns
   c. 20 rows
   d. 10 rows
7. An explicit series of instructions entered into a computer for the purpose of solving a problem is called a(n)
   a. program.
   b. input deck.
   c. control card.
   d. mathematical formulation.
8. Cards which contain such information as number of subjects, number of variables, and computer program to be used are called _____ cards.
   a. sequence
   b. program
   c. control
   d. data
9. Given a set of data, which one of the following statistical analyses would a researcher most prefer to do using a computer program rather than a desk calculator?
   a. *t* test
   b. analysis of variance
   c. factor analysis
   d. correlation coefficient

APPLICATION PROBLEMS

The following problems are designed to give you practice in applying significant concepts and research procedures explained in chapter 20. Most of them do not have a single correct answer. For feedback, you can compare your answers with the sample answers on page 900.

1. Suppose you are handed one hundred answer sheets for the *California Psychological Inventory*, a test not familiar to you. Your task is to score the answer sheets for the standard scales of this inventory. What would be the recommended first step in performing this task?

2. A researcher has administered a projective test to a sample of 50 students. She has available a detailed set of instructions for scoring a particular variable measured by this test. In previous studies, the interrater reliability for scoring this variable was approximately .75. Given this information, how should the researcher go about scoring the variable in her study?

3. The following is a partially completed hand data card for a subject who participated in a research study:

I.D. 06	Social Class upper middle class
Sex male	Pretest Score 37
School Westhaven Junior High	Posttest Score 55

What procedure would you recommend for simplifying the information on this card to facilitate later data analysis?

4. The first step in preparing data for the computer is for the researcher to decide how he wishes to enter the data on IBM cards. After punching the data on IBM cards, the researcher should try to locate an existing computer program which will perform the statistical analyses he wishes to have done. What is wrong with the procedures described in this statement?

5. Which *three* of the following statistical analyses would most preferably be carried out on a computer rather than on a desk calculator?
   a. Twenty correlation coefficients
   b. Three *t*-tests
   c. One factor analysis
   d. An item analysis of a fifty-item test
   e. Four means and standard deviations
Assume that the number of subjects is the same for all analyses.

SUGGESTION SHEET

If your last name starts with letters from Tud to Wex, please complete the Suggestion Sheet at the end of the book while this chapter is still fresh on your mind.

21.

PREPARING THE RESEARCH REPORT

OVERVIEW

This chapter presents guidelines for preparing a thesis or dissertation, a journal article, or a professional paper. The section on writing a dissertation presents an outline of main headings and the type of content that is usually included under each heading. Making a detailed outline of the dissertation prior to writing it contributes greatly to achieving a well-organized, complete presentation of a doctoral or master's research project. The section on preparing a journal article emphasizes the need for brevity and careful selection of a journal to which to submit the research article. The chapter concludes with suggestions for preparing a paper to be read at a professional meeting.

OBJECTIVES

After studying this chapter, you should be able to:

1. Describe the content and purpose of each section of a dissertation.
2. Write dissertation titles that are descriptive yet brief.
3. State the criteria considered most important by editors in evaluating manuscripts for journal publication.
4. Describe the procedures for submitting a research article to a professional journal.
5. Describe the procedures for submitting a research paper to be read at a professional meeting.

The purpose of this chapter is to give you a general guide for preparing the thesis, dissertation, or research article. The emphasis will be upon general principles of organization and presentation. Errors and weaknesses commonly found in theses and dissertations will be discussed. No attempt will be made to present detailed information on format. Most colleges and universities have established rules on style and format that must be followed closely; for this reason, specific information on format in a book of this type is of little value to the student.

THE THESIS OR DISSERTATION

In carrying out your review of the literature, you will observe that all research articles are organized in essentially the same manner. Theses and dissertations follow this same organizational pattern, but because they are less restricted in length, some topics are covered more thoroughly than in the published research article. Figure 21.1 is an outline giving the usual organization of the thesis or dissertation. Some variations in this outline will be found in the requirements of different universities.

Students often wait until all data have been collected and all analysis has been completed before starting to write their thesis or dissertation. It is more efficient, though, for the student to prepare some portions of the research report much earlier. It seems to be an almost inevitable feature of research that the student encounters some periods when she is extremely busy and some periods when she must sit and wait. These lulls in the research routine can be used profitably by the student to prepare drafts of the first chapters of her report.

Most students find that the easiest way to prepare a well-organized research report is to outline carefully each section before starting to write it. This outline may start merely as a listing of all major points that you wish to discuss in the section. These major points can then be placed in what appears to be the most logical order, and finally the topics to be discussed under each subheading can be added to the outline. A well-thought-out set of subheadings helps the reader a great deal in understanding the organization of the report and the nature of the research project.

If you have followed good procedure in planning and carrying out the study, you will have many guides for organizing the report. For example, the research proposal, which is prepared early in the research sequence, will contain a detailed statement of the problem and hypotheses that can be filled out quickly to become part of the introductory chapter of the thesis or dissertation.

Stylistic Considerations

When you are ready to start writing the thesis, you should obtain specific information concerning the format required at your university. This information usually can be obtained from the research committee chairman or from the

Preliminary Materials

1. Title page
2. Preface and Acknowledgments
3. Table of contents
4. List of tables
5. List of figures

Body of the Paper

Chapter 1.   Introduction
 a. General statement of the problem
 b. Statement of the hypotheses, objectives, or questions
 c. Definition of terms

Chapter 2.   Review of the Literature
 a. Review of previous research
 b. Pertinent opinion
 c. Summary of the state of the art

Chapter 3.   Method
 a. Description of subjects
 b. Research design and procedures
 c. Description of measures employed

Chapter 4.   Findings
 a. Overview of statistical procedures
 b. Description of findings pertinent to each hypothesis, objective, or question
 c. Other findings

Chapter 5.   Summary and Discussion
 a. Summary of research problem, method, and findings
 b. Conclusions
 c. Implications

Reference Materials

1. Bibliography
2. Appendix

Figure 21.1.   Organization of the thesis or dissertation.

dean of the graduate school. Some universities prepare a style manual for graduate students; others refer the student to one or more of the published style manuals. It is often helpful to ask the committee chairman to refer you to two or three outstanding theses or dissertations in education recently completed at your institution. An examination of these reports, along with the prescribed style manual, will give you most of the information that you need to meet the style and format requirements. A study of the organization, method of presentation, and language used in these reports will also give you some idea of the sort of thesis or dissertation that your chairman considers superior. As your own report will probably be subjected to the same criteria used by the chairman to evaluate previous reports, this information can be very helpful to you.

Questions of style not addressed by your university's style manual can usually be answered by referring to the *Publication Manual of the American Psychological Association* (see Annotated References). You should be particularly careful to use nonsexist language in your thesis or dissertation. For example, it is considered sexist to write: "Subjects were 16 boys and 16 girls. Each child was to place a car on his board so that two cars and boards looked alike." A nonsexist alternative would be: "Each child was to place a car on his or her board so that two cars and boards looked alike." Similarly, it is considered sexist to state: "The use of experiments in education presupposes the mechanistic nature of man." A nonsexist alternative would be: "The use of experiments in education presupposes the mechanistic nature of the human being." Accepted guidelines for nonsexist technical writing have been prepared by the American Psychological Association.[1]

A common problem in writing a thesis, dissertation, or other research report is figuring the proper tense to use. The general rule is to use the past tense to describe events that occurred at a point in time prior to the writing of the report. For example, one might write: "Sixty students were selected from a local school district . . ."; "Harber (1968) found in her study that . . ."; "The Stanford Achievement Test was developed to measure . . ."; "A *t* test was done. . . ." Each of these statements refers to an event or activity that occurred prior to the writing of the report.

The present tense is used to refer to assertions that continue to be true at the time the report is written. For example, one might say: "Research has shown consistently that inserted questions in text facilitate retention of the text content." The research has already occurred; hence the past tense ("has shown") is used. We can presume that the relationship between inserted questions and

---

1. American Psychological Association, "Guidelines for Nonsexist Language in APA Journals," *Educational Researcher* 7, no. 3 (1978): 15–17.

retention continues to be true beyond the observations made by the researchers; hence the present tense ("facilitate" is used). Similarly, one might state that, "the Stanford Achievement Test measures various aspects of academic performance" because this feature of the test continues to be true at the time the report is written. Also, one would state that, "table 2 shows that" because the table continues to perform a function. The table did not show a phenomenon just at one point in time. By the same logic, one would state that "this *t* value is statistically significant" because statistical significance continues to be true or not true of observed statistical tests.

Preliminary Materials

Preparing the preliminary materials (title page, preface, table of contents, list of tables, and list of figures) is essentially a matter of following the format at your college or university. In selecting a title, you should attempt to be brief while giving a specific description of what the study is about. Let us say, for example, that a student has done an experiment comparing the achievement gains of sixth-grade pupils who completed a course in American history through closed-circuit television with the achievement gains of a matched group of sixth-grade pupils who completed the same course through regular classroom instruction. An appropriate title might be "An Experiment Comparing Regular and Televised Instruction in Sixth-Grade American History." This title is reasonably brief and yet gives the reader some clue about the purpose of the study. Another title might be "A Study Comparing the Achievement of Sixth-Grade Students Instructed in American History through Closed-Circuit Television and Regular Classroom Procedure." This title tells what the study is about, but it is too long. It also starts out with "A Study," which is superfluous. A third title for the study might be "Teaching With Television." This title fails in that it does not tell what the study has done but merely identifies the broad area of the research. In doing your review of the literature, you will find such brief titles exasperating. The titles tell so little that it is necessary to check each article even though the majority of them will have nothing to do with the area of your review. Many reference books such as *Education Index* list only the title of research reports, and a general title that does not give the reader an idea of what the study has done is misleading and often is not indexed properly.

In preparing the table of contents and the headings for tables and figures, you should keep in mind that such materials should follow parallel grammatical construction. In other words, chapter titles, headings, and titles of tables and figures should be prepared so that they are consistent and comparable in their wording and grammatical construction.

The Introductory Chapter

The introductory chapter usually starts with a general statement of the problem. This statement should help the reader develop an appreciation for the problem, its place in education, and its theoretical and practical importance. The next section in this chapter is usually a specific statement of the objectives or hypotheses of the study. These may usually be taken directly from the research plan that the student developed prior to data collection. The third section of the introductory chapter is sometimes devoted to definition of terms. This section is very important because educational terms such as "underachiever," "gifted child," "core curriculum," and many others are defined differently by different educators. A specific definition of the term in this research project is necessary, therefore, so that the reader will fully understand the meaning and significance of the results. The terms need not be defined in a separate section. Some researchers prefer to define each term the first time that it appears in the text of the report.

The student can often prepare a good rough draft of the introductory chapter early in the conduct of the study. Most writers find that if they prepare a rough draft and then set it aside for a week or two before revising it, they will see weaknesses that would not have been apparent if immediate revision had been attempted. Also, new points or different approaches often occur to the writer during the intervening weeks. If you wait until all the data have been collected and analyzed before drafting any of the report, you may not have sufficient time to lay each section aside for this period of germination. Another advantage of drafting the early chapters of the report while carrying out the research is that a less demanding schedule of writing can be followed. Many people find it difficult to write steadily for any period of time. It is much easier for them to write a few pages and then put the work aside and do something else. Such a procedure is often not possible if you wait too long to start preparing the report.

Review of the Literature

The chapter reviewing the literature is meant to give the readers an understanding of previous relevant contributions to the problem so that they can better understand why the present research project was undertaken.

The first step in preparing this chapter is to make a rough outline. The coding system applied to the note cards during the review of the literature (see chapter 5) is often useful for this purpose. After a rough outline has been prepared covering the major topics of the review, you should read all the note cards and sort them into the topics contained in the outline. You must then decide upon the order in which these topics will be presented. After ordering the topics, you should review the cards dealing with the first topic until you are thoroughly familiar with their contents. Usually in the process of rereading the cards, you will get some additional ideas on how the topic should be presented. You can also organize the cards for the given topic into the order that you will present them and can decide which studies in this area are to be emphasized.

Often you will find two or three studies on each topic that, being more pertinent and carefully done, can serve as the foundation of your review. You may find several other studies that have been done in essentially the same manner and have produced similar findings. In this case it is recommended that you pick out the best studies and describe them in some detail. The other studies are often summarized by saying, "findings of the above studies have been largely supported by a number of other studies that have employed essentially the same approach." These supporting studies may then be referred to in a footnote or referenced using whatever system you have adopted for the thesis. This procedure has the advantage of presenting the pertinent findings and letting the reader know what other studies support these findings without laboriously discussing each study in detail.

You should repeat the aforementioned procedure for each of the topics to be covered in the review of the literature. The review of the topics can then be combined into a rough draft of the chapter that is well organized and that gives the reader a brief, yet reasonably complete, picture of the status of research in the area reviewed. The journal *Review of Educational Research* can be referred to for examples of good critical reviews of the literature.

A more difficult task in preparing the review of the literature is to organize all the findings under the various topics into a unified picture of the state of knowledge in the area reviewed. The process of combining and interpreting the literature is much more difficult than merely reviewing what has been done. In doing the review, you should have gained some insights into the field that are not apparent to a person who has not carried out a thorough review. These insights should be shared with your reader because they can make a significant contribution to his understanding of the field. This final section of the review is by far the most difficult to write, because it requires that you have a thorough understanding of the research you have read.

A well-organized review of the literature followed by an insightful interpretation is not only of great value to the reader, but its preparation greatly helps the research worker to develop his own understanding of the field. If the graduate student's schedule permits, a rough draft of the review of literature chapter should be prepared immediately after completing the review and prior to the start of data collection. At this time the material is fresh in the student's mind, and the insights gained by preparing the rough draft may well lead to new ideas and improvements in the research design.

The student is cautioned against an article-by-article presentation in the review of the literature. Many students do little more than prepare an abstract of each article they wish to discuss, and then they string these abstracts together without any attempt at continuity or logical organization. Such a review is excessively long and fails in its purpose of giving the reader an understanding of the field. Another pitfall the student should avoid in preparing his review of literature is that of presenting each study in essentially the same way. It is not uncommon, for example, to find reviews of literature in which the student treats each article in a separate paragraph and starts each paragraph with the name of the researcher who has written the described report. Often the student using this approach also devotes the same amount of space to each study he reports, without regard to its importance or pertinence to the topic. Such a stereotyped coverage of the literature, even if well organized, is boring and tiresome to read.

Another error commonly made in preparing the review of the literature is excessive use of quotations. Generally a research report can be made more interesting if quotations are used only when the material quoted is especially well written and can be inserted without spoiling the continuity of the presentation. Nothing is more tiresome or difficult to follow than a review of the literature that is merely an accumulation of quotations, each linked to the next with a sentence or two by the person preparing the review. Inasmuch as each quotation comes from a different context and has a different style, this technique invariably results in a review that is disjointed, poorly organized, and difficult to read.

Research Procedures

The chapter on research procedures has separate sections describing the sample, the research design, and the measures used. It usually starts with a detailed description of the sample. This description is needed by the reader to determine the degree to which the research sample is representative of the population and is comparable to other samples to which she may wish to apply the research results. The specific information given in describing the sample varies with the nature of the study, but often includes such information as the age range of the subjects, proportions of each sex if both males and females are used, IQ distribution, scores of the experimental and control groups on variables where comparability is important, urban-rural nature of subjects, education of parents, and so forth.

The population from which the sample was drawn should be defined, and the method of selecting the sample should be described in detail. If random sampling was employed, a detailed description of the procedure for selecting cases should be given. If a matching system was used, the matching criteria, rationale for selecting these criteria, the number of cases lost because of inability to obtain a satisfactory matching, and the possible effect of the loss should be discussed in detail. In matching studies some evidence of the comparability of matched groups, that is, an indication of the success of the matching, also should be given. If stratified sampling was used, the criteria for identifying cases at each of the strata or levels should be described, and the method for selecting the cases from those available in each level should also be described. If the study involves comparison of two large groups that are later broken into subgroups, the criteria for establishing the subgroups should be discussed.

In most educational studies, it is desirable to describe in considerable detail the schools or other settings from which the sample was drawn. This might include descriptions of the curriculum, the socioeconomic groups served by the school, the experience of teachers participating in the study, the performance of the school or district on standardized achievement measures, and the distinctive characteristics of the school and the geographical area.

In the next section of this chapter, the writer should describe the research procedures. This section usually starts with identification of the type of research design that has been employed, such as descriptive questionnaire study, causal-comparative design, correlational design, or experimental design. The writer then should discuss how this basic design was applied in the study, providing enough detail that another research worker reading the report could set up an identical study. The description of the research procedures usually reviews the steps taken to collect the data, including any occurrences that may have influenced the results, such as changes in the schedule for administering tests, disturbances during the testing situation, or unexpected subject reactions. This section should also include a discussion of any steps taken to establish controls or reduce errors in the study, such as administering measures to all groups simultaneously or at the same time of day, attempts to equate teacher ability, standardization of the testing situations for different groups, procedures employed to obtain makeups on students absent in the initial testing, methods of avoiding contamination, or controls employed to reduce observer bias. If the researcher has become aware of any flaws in carrying out the study that might have affected the results, these should be discussed so that the reader may consider them in his appraisal of the research findings and so that future research workers may avoid the same mistakes. For example, if measures or techniques are employed that are found to be impractical or inappropriate for the sample, these should be discussed even though the research worker may have discarded the results obtained from them.

The next section of this chapter should include a description of all measures used to collect data in the research project. If well-known standard measures such as the California Psychological Inventory, the Wide Range Achievement Test, or the WISC are used, this description can be quite brief. With well-known measures of this sort, it is usually sufficient to provide a description of the types of scores obtained, the variables measured by these scores, evidence of reliability and validity, and the relationship of each measure to the research hypotheses or objectives.

If new or little-known measures are used, or if measures have been developed especially for the research project, a much more detailed description is required. This should include a description of the types of items used in the measure, reliability data, evidence of validity, findings of other studies in which the measure has been used, and any other material necessary to give the reader a thorough understanding of the measure. If a measure has been developed for the study, a detailed description of how the measure was developed and standardized should be provided. Sometimes a separate chapter in the thesis or dissertation is devoted to the development of the measure, unless the measure is of a routine nature, such as a biographical data sheet. Measures are normally administered either to test one of the hypotheses of the study or to obtain data that can be used to select or describe the sample. In either case the writer should explain why the measure was selected and the specific purpose that it served in the research.

A description of scoring procedures is necessary when using new or locally developed measures or when the scoring procedures of a standard measure have been changed to meet the needs of the study. This description should be sufficiently detailed so that another researcher can use the scoring system if he so wishes. In most cases the scoring procedure, keys, a copy of the measure, item-analysis results, and other standardization data on new measures are included in the appendix of the report.

Research Findings

The next chapter in the thesis or dissertation is concerned with the research findings. If a single analytic technique such as the *t* test has been employed, this technique and the reasons for using it are usually discussed at the beginning of the chapter on findings. If, on the other hand, the research is such that different techniques have been employed for testing different hypotheses, the reasons for using each technique are usually included with the findings obtained from the use of the technique.

Perhaps the best method of obtaining clarity in the discussion of the findings is to organize this section of the report around the research hypotheses or objectives. After a brief introduction, the writer repeats the first hypothesis as it appears in chapter 1 and then presents all findings pertinent to this hypothesis. This same technique is then repeated for each hypothesis immediately before reading the pertinent results.

The writer should be careful to use the appropriate language in describing each result and the hypothesis that it tests. A research result (defined here as the result of a statistical significance test applied to a correlation coefficient, difference between mean scores, and so forth) does not *prove* or *disprove* a particular hypothesis. Since the test of statistical significance is based on the null hypothesis (see chapter 10), the writer can only say that his research results *support* or *do not support* a particular hypothesis. James Raths has pointed out that many journal publications contain this error of terminology.[2] Although the use of the term "support" rather than "prove" may seem like a small point, Raths argues that it alerts readers to the limitations of the null hypothesis method and increases the likelihood that readers will draw the proper conclusions from the research results.

An approach that many investigators use in preparing the results chapter is to first put the results in tabular form. Then they study the tables carefully, noting the most important results. Next, using the tables as a basis for organizing the chapter, they prepare the text. Tables and figures are useful in describing the research results and in showing trends that have emerged from the analysis. A table or figure can present the overall picture of the data more clearly and more economically than would be possible if each specific fact was discussed in the text. By using tables and figures, the writer is relieved of presenting a tedious recitation of all the research results. Instead, he can emphasize those results that seem to be most important or noteworthy. Students who are inexperienced in writing research reports often make the mistake of preparing a table and then discussing every entry in the table whether significant or not. This approach results in a boring report and defeats the purpose of using tables and figures.

Each table or figure should contain all the information necessary for the reader to interpret it. This information usually includes the type of statistics used, a descriptive label for each variable, sample size for each analysis, probability levels (if inferential statistics are used), and footnotes (if necessary). The student is advised to study tables and figures in such journals as *Journal of Educational Psychology* and *American Educational Research Journal* and to follow their format.

A researcher will occasionally confuse tables and graphs. Any presentation of numerical information or prose in column form is called a table. The usual table in a research report consists of a column of variables followed by

2. James Raths, "The Inductive Process: Implications for Research Reporting," *Educational Leadership* 24 (1967): 357 ff.

other columns of descriptive or inferential statistics relating to the variables. A listing of sample sites or participants would also be called a table.

The typical figure in a research report consists of information in pictorial form. Histograms, charts, pie graphs, scattergrams, and time-series plots are common examples of figures. Reproductions of prose from another source in a special format are also labelled as figures. Two such examples in this book are the letter to a research participant (figure 4.1) and the sample page from *Psychological Abstracts* (figure 5.2).

Supplemental analyses should also appear in this chapter, in a section following the planned analyses. Often the findings obtained from the analysis originally planned by the student will suggest other analytic procedures to the student that will either provide additional data concerning his hypotheses or will yield interesting information not related to his initial hypotheses. In either case the further analysis should be done. Sometimes research workers may be surprised to find that the most important results of their research are unrelated to their original hypotheses.

Summary and Discussion

The last chapter usually includes: a brief summary of the problem, methodology, and results; an interpretation of the findings in the context of previous research; limitations of the study; and implications of the findings. The summary should be as brief as possible consistent with a clear presentation of all important information concerning the problem, method, and findings.

The most important task in writing this chapter is to identify and interpret the major findings. The writer should discuss possible reasons why the results occurred, fit them into the findings of previous research, suggest field applications, and make theoretical interpretations. Because the person doing the study has usually developed a deeper insight into his research problem than will be the case for most of the persons reading the study, his interpretations usually have greater depth than any that most readers would make for themselves. A great deal of thought and careful study is required in interpreting research results. One of the most common weaknesses found in the writing of graduate students is that their reports present important and interesting findings but fail to provide a thoughtful interpretation of these findings.

The chapter should include a discussion of the study's methodological limitations. The researcher should note flaws and problems that occurred in sampling procedures, instrumentation, data collection, and data analysis. Some of the problems may have been inherent in the research design. Others may have occurred during the execution of the study. If an ex post facto design (i.e., causal-comparison or correlation) was used, it is advisable to remind the reader about the limitations of this design with respect to causal inference. The researcher should also entertain alternative explanations of the observed results. For example, a hypothesis might be disconfirmed (i.e., the null hypothesis is not rejected) when the researcher had strong reason for thinking it to be true. In this situation the researcher should consider possible methodological flaws in the study that might account for the negative finding.

It is often desirable to add a section on implications. In this section the writer can present interpretations, speculations, and ideas that would be out of place in the section on conclusions. Possible applications of the findings to the public schools or other field situations may also be discussed.

Reference Materials

The usual reference materials in a thesis or dissertation include the bibliography and appendix. The bibliography must list all references that have been referred to in footnotes or otherwise cited in the study and may also include pertinent references not cited.[3] The format of the bibliography should be decided upon when the student starts reviewing the literature so that the data on the bibliography cards are recorded in the correct format. If this has been done, compiling the bibliography is a very simple matter because it merely requires selecting the bibliography cards that have been cited, placing them in alphabetical order, and copying the bibliographic data onto a sheet. If the bibliography cards have been carelessly compiled, the student will find it necessary to spend a considerable amount of time checking each card and making the changes necessary to get the reference in the accepted format.

The most common fault found in the bibliographies of theses and dissertations is inconsistent format. The method of referencing a particular type of source should be consistent down to the last comma. Common errors include failure to use the same punctuation marks in different bibliographic entries, the use of the author's first name in some entries and initials only in other entries, the abbreviation of some journal titles while not abbreviating others, and the use of different abbreviations for the same journal title. Each bit of information in a bibliographic citation offers the opportunity to make a mistake, so many mistakes can be made in a bibliography unless the student exercises a great deal of care.

Most theses and dissertations require one or more appendices for presenting items that may be of interest to some readers but are not sufficiently pertinent to be included in the body of the report. Materials commonly placed in the appendix include: (1) tables that are very long or that contain material

3. Some universities require that the bibliography be limited to references actually cited in the study.

not essential to understanding the study; (2) locally developed research aids, such as forms and instruction sheets; (3) copies of the data-gathering instruments used in the study; (4) item-analysis data and other materials pertinent to measures; (5) scoring protocols and procedures; and (6) lengthy quotations that may be of interest to some readers, particularly if the source containing the quotations is not readily available.

PREPARING A JOURNAL ARTICLE

The graduate student has much to gain by preparing one or more research articles based on the thesis or dissertation immediately after completing it. At this time all phases of the research are fresh in her mind, and she can prepare the article for publication much more easily than if she puts aside this task and does it later. Most persons who employ holders of graduate degrees in education are interested in their publications. If the graduate student is able to list one or two publications, she will have an advantage in obtaining a position.

The first step in preparing a research article is to decide what journal is most likely to publish work in your area. Journals that are likely to accept your article can easily be identified by checking the bibliography of your thesis or dissertation to determine which journals have published articles pertinent to your research topic. You usually can identify one or two journals that have published most of the articles closely related to your research, and these are the ones most likely to accept your article.

A factor that should be considered in selecting a journal to which the research article will be submitted is the publication lag. If you plan to seek a position in which research publication is especially important, such as an assistant professorship at a university, it may be to your advantage to submit the article to a journal that provides for early publication. Most journals in education have publication lags ranging from six months to two years. Some journals, however, will publish an article with almost no lag if the author pays an early publication fee.

Another factor to consider in selecting a journal is its reputation. Some education journals are more widely read and are more influential than other journals. Terrence Luce and Dale Johnson conducted a survey to determine how members of the American Educational Research Association would rank a sample of 74 education and education-related journals.[4] Approximately 700 members ranked ten of these journals as those "in which you would most like

4. Terrence S. Luce and Dale M. Johnson, "Ratings of Educational and Psychological Journals," *Educational Researcher* 7, no. 10 (1978): 8–10.

to be published and/or those in which you expect to find material important to you as an educator." The ten highest-ranked journals and their ranks are as follows:

1. *American Educational Research Journal*
2. *Review of Educational Research*
3. *Harvard Educational Review*
4. *Phi Delta Kappan*
5. *Journal of Educational Research*
6. *Educational Researcher*
7. *Journal of Educational Psychology*
8. *Educational and Psychological Measurement*
9. *Journal of Educational Measurement*
10. *American Psychologist*

Most of these journals will publish reports based on thesis or dissertation studies if the research is well-done and important.

Once you have decided upon the journal in which you wish to publish, you should examine several recent issues in order to determine the format and usual length of articles accepted. Although it follows the same format as the thesis or dissertation, the research article is much shorter. Brevity is essential in articles for publication in professional journals because the available space is very limited and the editor usually wishes to include as many studies as possible.

The general statement of the problem is usually shortened to a paragraph and is often omitted completely—the article then starting with a statement of the specific hypotheses. The review of the literature is also shortened a great deal, with brief reference made only to those studies that are very closely related to the research being reported. The section on procedures is also shortened to some extent, usually giving only a brief description of the design, sample, and measures used. If, however, some of the procedures or measures employed are new or unusual, they should be covered in some detail. The section on findings makes up a considerably larger proportion of the research article than of the thesis or dissertation. This section is shortened less when revised for publication.

Tables are used extensively because they can present the findings in briefer form. Only the most important findings are discussed at any length in the text. The summary and discussion of the results should be presented briefly. The bibliography must only include the sources cited in the text of the article.

In some cases a thesis or dissertation deals with a subject that can be logically divided into more than one article, and such division usually makes it possible to prepare shorter articles that have a better chance of being accepted for publication. For example, if a researcher had investigated character-istics of successful and unsuccessful business school students, she may have collected some data dealing with personality characteristics and other data con-cerning vocational aptitudes, interests, and intelligence. In this case, if suffi-cient important findings were obtained, it may be advisable to prepare two articles for publication—one dealing with personality characteristics of success-ful and unsuccessful business students and the other comparing vocational aptitudes, interests, and intelligence of the two groups.

After preparing a satisfactory draft of a research article, the researcher should have a copy typed (double-spaced) in the format of the journal to which she plans to submit her article. Some journals provide publication manuals that will be of considerable help to you in preparing an article in acceptable format. If you have decided to submit your article to one of the journals published by the American Psychological Association, you should purchase a copy of the APA publication manual (see Annotated References at the end of this chapter). Usually, however, an article meeting the format requirements of the journal can be prepared without a publication manual if you carefully follow the for-mat of articles published in a recent issue of the journal. You should be partic-ularly careful to convert the bibliography to the accepted format for the journal you have selected. The manuscript as submitted to the journal should be thor-oughly checked at least two or three times to be certain that no further changes are needed and no errors are present.

After the final manuscript has been prepared, the author may check a recent issue of the journal to find out where the manuscript should be sent. A brief covering letter should be written, and stamps should be included for the return of the manuscript if it is not accepted for publication. Most journals require two or three copies of the manuscript so that copies can be sent to different persons on the editorial board. After the editor receives the manu-script, a postcard is usually sent to the author acknowledging receipt, and the manuscript is sent to members of the editorial board who are most familiar with the topic covered by the article. There is usually a considerable lag before the author is informed whether the article is accepted, and after receiving this information, it may be a year or more before receiving the galley proofs. The galley proofs of an article are set up in type as it will appear in the journal. It is necessary that the author check the galley proofs very carefully and correct any errors discovered.

If the student's manuscript is rejected by the first journal to which it has been submitted, this rejection will usually be accompanied by a statement of the reasons for the rejection. This article, however, may be revised and sub-mitted to another journal. The fact that it has been rejected by one journal does not necessarily mean that it is unsuitable for publication. Many factors operate in the evaluation of an article, such as editorial policy, a particularly heavy backlog of accepted articles, or personal biases of editorial board members, any of which can result in an article's being rejected even though it has merit.

Thomas Frantz did a study of the criteria used by journal editors to evaluate manuscripts, and his findings may be helpful to the student who plans to submit a research report for journal publication.[5] Frantz asked members of the editorial boards of six journals (*Personnel and Guidance Journal, Journal of Counseling Psychology, Journal of Educational Psychology, Journal of College Student Personnel, School Counselor,* and *Journal of Educational Research*) to rank a list of criteria commonly used in evaluating manuscripts to determine whether they should be accepted by the journal. The average rank of each criterion is shown in table 21.1. It can be seen that the most important criterion is the research report's contribution to scientific knowledge. The student is advised, therefore, to briefly state in the introduction of the report how her research builds upon or goes beyond existing educational theory and previous research findings. The second most important criterion is the design of the study. Journal editors are concerned about the researcher's choice of subjects, design of treatments, selection of test measures, and control of possible confounding effects.

It is interesting that the editors' third highest ranked criterion was the

TABLE 21.1

Summary of 14 Criteria for Evaluation of Manuscripts Ranked in Importance by 55 Members of the Editorial Boards of Six Journals

Criteria	Mean Rank	SD
1. Contribution to knowledge	1.8	1.2
2. Design of study	3.5	2.1
3. Objectivity in reporting results	4.7	2.3
4. Topic selection	5.5	2.9
5. Writing style and readability	5.7	2.7
6. Practical implications	6.4	3.3
7. Statistical analyses	6.5	2.5
8. Theoretical model	7.0	2.7
9. Review of literature	7.2	2.3
10. Clarity of tabular material	8.1	2.3
11. Length	10.2	1.6
12. Punctuation	11.5	1.9
13. Reputation of author	12.6	1.9
14. Institutional affiliation	13.5	0.9

5. Thomas T. Frantz, "Criteria for Publishable Manuscripts," *Personnel and Guidance Journal* 47 (1968): 384–86.

researcher's objectivity in reporting findings. Before submitting an article for publication, you should have a colleague read it critically to ensure that the article deals primarily with the research data (rather than the researcher's subjective impressions), and that undue importance is not attributed to the findings, particularly if the absolute size of the correlation coefficients, mean score differences, and so forth is not large. Although ranked fifth in importance, writing style and readability were cited by more editors than any other criterion in their criticisms of manuscripts submitted to them. Experienced researchers usually write several drafts of an article (four or five drafts are not uncommon) and ask their colleagues to criticize the readability of each draft. New researchers would do well to follow the same practice. The new researcher should also be somewhat assured to learn that the journal editors assigned the reputation and institutional affiliation of the author the lowest ranks of the 14 criteria. In fact, some journal editors make it a practice to omit the name and affiliation of the author before submitting a manuscript for editorial review.

PREPARING A PAPER FOR A PROFESSIONAL MEETING

Graduate students are advised to prepare a paper based on their thesis or dissertation for presentation at a professional meeting. This is usually done prior to journal publication (see previous section) because most professional associations will not accept a paper if it has appeared in print or if it has been presented at another professional meeting. Presentation of a paper is desirable for two reasons: you can list it on your vita as a professional accomplishment; and it helps you become better known to your professional colleagues.

Educational associations such as AERA (American Educational Research Association) and ASCD (Association for Supervision and Curriculum Development) announce a "call for papers" many months in advance of their annual meeting. The call for papers will appear in one of the association's publications, which are sent to all members. Its purpose is to invite members to submit proposals for papers to be delivered at the meeting. The call for papers states who can submit a proposal (nonmembers usually must be sponsored by a member), format for writing the proposal, and directions for submitting the proposal to the association's proposal review committee. The length of the proposal varies with the association. A short abstract of the proposed paper may be all that is required; occasionally the complete paper must be submitted for review.

After the proposal has been reviewed for its merit and appropriateness, you will receive notification of the committee's decision. If the proposal is accepted, you usually are obligated to attend the meeting in order to deliver the paper in person. Therefore, it is inadvisable to submit a paper proposal unless you are reasonably certain that you will be able to attend the meeting.

It is likely that your paper, if accepted, will be grouped with papers on similar topics to form a symposium or paper-reading session. The time allotted to each participant is often too short to permit the actual reading of the paper; besides, doing so is likely to bore the audience. Instead, you probably will be asked to distribute copies of the paper to the audience. In your talk you will stress the highlights of your research. Many associations will make overhead projectors, or other devices, available for use in your presentation.

Some associations automatically submit copies of papers presented at their meetings to ERIC (see chapter 5) in order to promote wider distribution of the paper. If the association does not do this, you can, on your own initiative, submit a copy of the paper to the appropriate ERIC clearinghouse.

MISTAKES SOMETIMES MADE IN PREPARING RESEARCH REPORTS

1. Researcher fails to prepare draft version of information that must later be included in the thesis or dissertation while it is still fresh in his memory.
2. Organizes the review of the literature chronologically instead of arranging research articles into related topics.
3. Treats each study in the review of literature in mechanical fashion, devoting about the same amount of space to each regardless of pertinence or importance.
4. Uses too many quotations and selects quotations that do not make their point as well as the researcher could make it using her own words.
5. Provides an inadequate description of the research sample, instrumentation, and data analysis techniques.
6. Confounds presentation of the findings with interpretation and implications of the findings.
7. Fails to discuss methodological limitations of the study.

ANNOTATED REFERENCES

American Psychological Association. *Publication Manual of the American Psychological Association.* 2nd ed. Washington, D.C.: American Psychological Association, 1974.

This manual contains detailed instructions for preparing articles for the journals published by the American Psychological Association. Much of the material presented is equally appropriate as a guide to publishing in other professional journals in the behavioral sciences. Copies may be ordered by writing: Publication Sales, American Psychological Association, 1200 Seventeenth St., NW, Washington, D.C. 20036.

Etzold, Thomas H. "Writing for Publication: The Art of the Article." *Phi Delta Kappan* 57 (1976): 614–15.
The author provides a useful guide to writing articles for professional education journals. Most of the suggestions are more appropriate for preparing opinion articles than for research articles. Importance of orderly procedure and of a good outline is stressed.

Marquis. *Directory of Publishing Opportunities in Journals and Periodicals*. 4th ed. Chicago: Marquis Academic Media, 1979.
This reference volume provides pertinent information about approximately 3500 publications, including more than 200 publications specifically in the field of education. Style and length requirements, payment procedures, and time needed for an acceptance decision are among the information provided for each publication.

Mullins, Carolyn J. *A Guide to Writing and Publishing in the Social and Behavorial Sciences*. New York: Wiley-Interscience, 1977.
The author presents procedures for preparing both journal articles and professional books. She discusses such practical matters as working with journal editors, writing a book prospectus, choosing an appropriate publisher, and negotiating a book contract.

Van Til, William. *Writing for Professional Publication*. Boston: Allyn and Bacon, 1981.
Van Til, a widely published author in the field of education, provides many tips for getting your research report or article published. Among the topics covered in this book are how to get published for the first time, how to ensure that your manuscript is in publishable shape, and how to deal with editors.

SELF-CHECK TEST

Circle the correct answer to each of the following questions. An answer key is provided on page 881.

1. In a thesis the review of literature should conclude with a
   a. definition of terms.

     b. summary of the state of the art.

     c. description of measures to be employed.

     d. bibliography.

2. In a thesis the description of a well-known standardized test should probably
     a. be highly detailed.
     b. be rather brief.
     c. include findings of other studies using the same measure.
     d. include detailed data concerning construct validity.

3. In a thesis the description of new or little-known measures should include
     a. reliability data.
     b. validity (especially construct) data.
     c. findings of other studies including the measure.
     d. All of the above are correct.

4. The best method of obtaining clarity in reporting research findings is to organize the discussion
     a. according to the order in which the data were analyzed.
     b. according to the order in which the data were collected.
     c. by presenting the most statistically significant findings first.
     d. according to the hypotheses which guided the research.

5. If the researcher obtains positive results with respect to a hypothesis, he can state that the results _____ the hypothesis.
     a. verify
     b. prove
     c. confirm
     d. support

6. The appendix is the appropriate place in the thesis to include
     a. copies of data-gathering instruments used in the study.
     b. sampling techniques used to select subjects.
     c. the results of tests of null hypotheses.
     d. the review of literature.

7. The method section of a dissertation usually contains
     a. the literature review and hypotheses.
     b. the research design, subjects, and measures.
     c. the definition of terms, literature review, and data analysis procedures.
     d. the research design and literature review.

8. The first step in preparing a research article is to
     a. determine the journal most likely to publish it.
     b. give it a title.
     c. develop an outline of its content.
     d. write the introduction.

9. After identifying a journal to which his article can be submitted, the researcher should
     a. examine recent issues of the journal.

   b. contact the journal editor.
   c. select two alternative publication sources.
   d. set the date for publication.
10. According to the study by Frantz, journal editors report that the most important criterion used in evaluating a manuscript is
   a. its contribution to scientific knowledge.
   b. the soundness of the research design.
   c. the author's objectivity in reporting findings.
   d. the accuracy of the statistical analyses.

APPLICATION PROBLEMS

The following problems are designed to give you practice in applying significant concepts and research procedures explained in chapter 21. Most of them do not have a single correct answer. For feedback, you can compare your answers with the sample answers on page 900.

1. Prepare an outline of the major headings and subheadings of a dissertation.
2. Rewrite the following dissertation titles so that they are brief yet descriptive:
   a. "A Study Investigating the Relationship between Selected Personality Factors in First-, Second-, and Third-Grade Children and Their Attitudes Toward School at Various Intervals in the School Year."
   b. "A Preliminary Investigation into the Effects of Participation in a High School Counseling Program on Student Perceptions of Various Aspects of College."

SUGGESTION SHEET

If your last name starts with letters from Wey to Zzz, please complete the Suggestion Sheet at the end of the book while this chapter is still fresh in your mind.

SELF-CHECK TEST ANSWERS

Chapter 1

1*c*, 2*d*, 3*a*, 4*b*, 5*b*, 6*d*, 7*a*, 8*b*, 9*c*, 10*c*.

Chapter 3

1*b*, 2*c*, 3*b*, 4*c*, 5*d*, 6*b*, 7*a*, 8*c*, 9*b*, 10*d*.

Chapter 4

1*c*, 2*c*, 3*d*, 4*c*, 5*b*, 6*b*, 7*c*, 8*c*, 9*d*, 10*a*.

Chapter 5

1*a*, 2*b*, 3*b*, 4*a*, 5*a*, 6*d*, 7*b*, 8*a*, 9*c*, 10*c*.

Chapter 6

1*b*, 2*b*, 3*a*, 4*a*, 5*d*, 6*c*, 7*a*, 8*b*, 9*c*, 10*c*.

Chapter 7

1*a*, 2*a*, 3*a*, 4*b*, 5*a*, 6*c*, 7*a*, 8*c*, 9*d*, 10*b*.

Chapter 8

1*b*, 2*d*, 3*b*, 4*c*, 5*c*, 6*c*, 7*d*, 8*b*, 9*a* or *c*, 10*a*.

Chapter 9

1*c*, 2*b*, 3*a*, 4*c*, 5*b*, 6*a*, 7*d*, 8*c*, 9*a*, 10*c*.

Chapter 10

1*b*, 2*a*, 3*b*, 4*c*, 5*c*, 6*a*, 7*d*, 8*c*, 9*b*, 10*d*, 11*a*, 12*d*, 13*b*.

Chapter 11

1*a*, 2*b*, 3*c*, 4*c*, 5*b*, 6*b*, 7*b*, 8*d*, 9*c*, 10*d*.

Chapter 12

1*b*, 2*c*, 3*a*, 4*d*, 5*c*, 6*a*, 7*b*, 8*a*, 9*b*, 10*d*.

Chapter 13

1*b*, 2*c*, 3*b*, 4*d*, 5*a*, 6*c*, 7*c*, 8*a*, 9*b*, 10*a*, 11*b*.

Chapter 14

1*c*, 2*b*, 3*c*, 4*a*, 5*d*, 6*d*, 7*a*, 8*b*, 9*b*, 10*a*, 11*d*, 12*b*, 13*c*, 14*c*, 15*c*.

Chapter 15

1*a*, 2*b*, 3*b*, 4*c*, 5*d*, 6*a*, 7*d*, 8*a*, 9*d*, 10*a*.

Chapter 16

1*b*, 2*c*, 3*d*, 4*d*, 5*d*, 6*a*, 7*c*, 8*b*, 9*c*, 10*b*, 11*d*, 12*a*, 13*c*.

Chapter 17

1*d*, 2*c*, 3*b*, 4*d*, 5*a*, 6*a*, 7*a*, 8*d*, 9*b*, 10*d*, 11*c*.

Chapter 18

1*b*, 2*d*, 3*b*, 4*d*, 5*b*, 6*c*, 7*b*, 8*c*, 9*d*, 10*a*.

Chapter 19

1*b*, 2*d*, 3*b*, 4*b*, 5*d*, 6*b*, 7*c*, 8*c*, 9*d*, 10*c*.

Chapter 20

1*a*, 2*b*, 3*c*, 4*d*, 5*b*, 6*a*, 7*a*, 8*c*, 9*c*.

Chapter 21

1*b*, 2*b*, 3*d*, 4*d*, 5*d*, 6*a*, 7*b*, 8*a*, 9*a*, 10*a*.

SAMPLE ANSWERS FOR APPLICATION PROBLEMS

Chapter 1

1. The proposal could be defended by identifying types of research that could be done with the funds. For example:

   a. Basic research to discover the process that students use in studying. Determine whether high-achieving and low-achieving students use different processes.
   b. Applied research to determine study methods that are effective in improving student achievement.
   c. Systematic R & D to develop validated study-skill programs.
   d. Evaluation studies to determine whether study-skill programs are being implemented properly and whether they are producing the desired results.

   A more general defense is that money alone does not produce results. There are many examples of government-funded programs that were well-intended but proved ineffective. Research may mean less money for highly visible programs in the short run, but it may produce more effective impact on practice in the long run.

2. See table 1.3 on page 27 for ten differences between scientific (positivistic) and artistic (case study) approaches to research.

Chapter 3

1. Areas of interest and problems:

   a. Evaluation of teaching effectiveness
      (1) Development of classroom observation systems
      (2) Studies of the relationship between particular teaching techniques and student outcomes

   b. Teacher supervision
      (1) Characteristics of effective supervisors
      (2) Studies of typical interaction patterns between supervisors and teachers

   c. Creativity
      (1) Development of techniques for increasing creativity
      (2) School achievement of creative children

Sample null hypothesis, problem a(2):
   Mathematics teachers who use specific feedback during math lessons and comparable

teachers who use general feedback do not obtain different levels of pupil gain in mathematics achievement.

Sample directional hypothesis:
Mathematics teachers who use specific feedback during math lessons obtain higher pupil achievement gains than comparable teacher who use general feedback.

Sample objective:
The objective of this study is to determine whether there is a difference in pupil mathematics achievement for mathematics teachers who use specific feedback as compared with those who use general feedback.

2. Topics usually covered in a research plan:

    a. Introduction, including purpose of study and literature review
    b. Hypotheses or objectives
    c. Measures
    d. Subjects
    e. Research design
    f. Data analysis
    g. Chronological list of procedures

3. Advantages of a detailed research plan:

    a. A written plan is easily given to experts for their advice.
    b. A researcher may forget to carry out important steps of a project if she does not put them in writing beforehand.

4. Research hypothesis evaluation:

The researcher appears to have a definite reason for testing the hypothesis. This is good. Second, the hypothesis appears testable; however, the researcher should identify the specific self-concept measures on which no change is expected. Third, the hypothesis could be shortened by omitting the rationale, "since we believe . . . in the ability-grouped class." A better statement of the hypothesis might be, "Low-ability children placed in an ability-grouped class will show no significant change on self-concept measures (specify) over a certain time period." The hypothesis, and the study itself, could also be improved if the researcher made a prediction about self-concept changes of low-ability students who are not placed in ability-grouped classes.

5. Arguments favoring a pilot study:

    a. The pilot study may help her develop new hypotheses to be tested.
    b. It may help her discover problems that were not mentioned in the report of the previous study.
    c. It may help her discover new procedures that are more effective than those tested in the previous study.
    d. It provides a test of the modifications that she has added to the previous study.

Chapter 4

1. Each individual's consent will be obtained prior to the start of the project. The test data will be kept confidential; names of subjects will be removed from the tests as soon as possible. When the research design permits, tests will be anonymous.

2. No. School people usually will want specific information about details of the research project that will affect them. For example, they will want to know who is to be involved, whether the tests are controversial, how the individual's right to privacy is to be protected, and whether the results will reflect unfavorably on the school district.

3. In this study the investigator should take steps that would assure desensitization of subjects. These steps could include:

   a. Plan a procedure and conduct a small-scale pilot study to be sure you have developed an adequate procedure for desensitizing your subjects. If not, do not conduct study until such a procedure is developed. The procedure should probably include steps such as the following:
   b. Point out that most people tell a great many small lies in situations in which they believe there is no chance to be caught.
   c. Provide evidence to support the above statement, if available. This could include data from previous research as well as the research in question.
   d. Check on whether all subjects have accepted your arguments. If not, carry out individual conferences and if necessary counseling with subjects who are still troubled.

4. Incorrect scores on this test could lead students to develop incorrect self-perceptions and aspirations. Therefore, the investigator should carry out a program to dehoax students at the end of the study. Steps in this program could include the following:

   a. Describe the purpose of the study and explain why the deception was necessary.
   b. Hold individual conferences with subjects, show them their test papers pointing out their correct score and discussing how this score was changed.
   c. Give students a questionnaire to determine if they are dehoaxed; i.e., do they believe your explanation and accept their actual score on the test?
   d. Offer to give students another algebra aptitude test so they can be sure of their actual performance.

5. Ethical and legal steps that should be taken by the researcher.

   a. Inform parents of the purposes of the study and obtain parental permission for subjects to participate.
   b. Describe the specific school records you will need and obtain parental permission to use the records.
   c. Inform participants of the essential features of the research and answer questions they raise.

d. Be sure that the study is structured so as to remove any serious negative effects such as resentment and more negative attitudes among control-group subjects. For example, such resentment could probably be removed by giving control-group subjects a "large" gift at the end of the study.

e. Explain the study to all subjects at the end of the research.

f. Set up procedures to ensure confidentiality of all data related to the study.

Chapter 5

1. A primary source is one in which the writer was a witness to what is being reported. In educational research literature this usually means the writer is reporting on personal investigations. Most articles appearing in journals such as the *Journal of Educational Psychology, Journal of Experimental Education,* and the *Journal of Educational Research* are primary source references.

   On the other hand, a secondary-source author is reporting on events that he did not himself witness. In educational research literature, secondary sources discuss investigations done by other researchers. Textbooks contain secondary source information for the most part. The review of literature you prepare for your graduate research project will also be a secondary source since you will be reviewing the work of other investigators.

2. a. Praise, Positive Reinforcement, Reinforcement, Verbal Reinforcement, Social Reinforcement, Sharing (Social Behavior), Prosocial Behavior.

   b. Positive Reinforcement, Reinforcement, Social Reinforcement, Rewards.

   c. Barton, Edward J. "Developing Sharing: An Analysis of Modeling and Other Behavioral Techniques." *Behavior Modification,* 1981 (July) Vol. 5 (3), 386–398. (Several other articles peripheral to this topic may also be found in 1982 Psychological Abstracts; see for example abstracts 1090 and 7530.)

3. To complete this problem you should have carried out the following steps:

   a. Selected two preliminary sources in the faculty member's area, searched the author indexes, and made up bibliography cards.

   b. Searched *Social Science Citation Index* for the name of the faculty member. Put a tally mark on each bibliography card for each time the article was cited. If the selected faculty member was in psychology, you should also have checked *Science Citation Index.*

   c. Selected bibliography card with most tally marks, located article, read and made up note card following procedures described in chapter 5.

4. a. The following data should be included on your bibliography card. The sample is in *Psychological Abstracts* format:

   Richey, Harold W. (Univ. of Missouri) Avoidable failures of experimental procedure. *Journal of Experimental Education,* 1976 (Win), Vol. 45 (2), 10–13.

b. This article was selected because it contains some very useful information for the student in educational research. If you plan to conduct an experimental study, keep your note card and review these causes of failure when designing your study. This is not a research article so it is recommended that a sentence outline format be used. Your 5-by-8 note card should have the bibliographic data at the top and should include the following information:

(1) Common reasons for failures of experimental procedures:

   (a) Experimental task is too demanding for ordinary levels of subject motivation.
   (b) Procedures are intellectually too demanding or too unfamiliar for subjects.
   (c) Study imposes requirements that are repugnant or annoying to subjects.
   (d) Study involves inherently funny situations that subjects may not take seriously.
   (e) Study ask subjects to respond in ways that make them look inadequate.
   (f) Experimental manipulation is overly contrived or unbelievable.
   (g) Impact of manipulation too weak to offset established behavior patterns.
   (h) Experimental confederates not convincing actors.
   (j) Study takes insufficient notice of special needs or circumstances of subjects which may affect responses.

(2) Suggestions for avoiding these errors:

   (a) Investigator should serve as own prepilot subject.
   (b) Run pilot study with subjects and conditions as similar as possible to main study.
   (c) During pilot study, check in as many ways as possible the adequacy of the experimental manipulation.
   (d) Discuss your plans with other researchers and seek critical feedback.
   (e) Consider what possible flaws could result in negative findings and correct them before doing the research.
   (f) Do a thorough job of planning; it pays off in better research.

5. Locate descriptors in the *Thesaurus of ERIC Descriptors:*

a. Teacher behavior	k. Teaching programs
b. Teacher influence	l. Teaching skills
c. Teacher characteristics	m. Teaching styles
d. Teacher influence	n. Teaching techniques
e. Teacher evaluation	o. Achievement
f. Teaching	p. Academic achievement
g. Effective teaching	q. Knowledge level
h. Teaching methods	r. Achievement gains
i. Classroom techniques	s. Achievement ratings
j. Teaching procedures	t. Performance

Search Plan:

> (1 or 2 or 3 or 4 or 5 or 6 or 7 or 8 or 9 or 10 or 11 or 12 or 13 or 14) and (15 or 16 or 17 or 18 or 19 or 20)

Note the use of a high number of *or* connections used to obtain high coverage. It is doubtful whether any two researchers would plan a search such as this in exactly the same way. If you have employed a high number of relevant descriptors in a similar *and, or* configuration, your search plan may be regarded as correct. You should have included many of the same descriptors given above, but you could have omitted some and added others and still have a satisfactory search plan. If you included only the two descriptors "teaching techniques" and "achievement," you would obtain an inadequate search.

Chapter 6

1. a. Subjects were lost from both treatment and control groups. However, treatment-group losses were greater and probably consisted of students with low motivation.
   b. If the researcher is interested in generalizing the findings to all U.S. college students, the sample is probably nonrepresentative, since it was drawn from one commuter college.
   c. Students were not randomly assigned to the sections (at least, the description makes no mention of this procedure), although sections were randomly assigned to treatments.

2. a. Underlined phrase should be "prove the invalidity of this racist belief once and for all." This statement suggests that the investigator is emotionally involved with his topic, that is, he has an ax to grind. This indicates a biased viewpoint and suggests that deliberate bias might have occurred.
   b. The investigator uses a high-inference global rating of "warmth" and "understanding." Such ratings are highly susceptible to observer bias. More objective ratings would occur if these general traits were defined in terms of specific teacher behaviors. For example, "warmth" could be defined in terms of the number of times the teacher smiled, the number of times she touched children, etc. The design also permits observer contamination, since the investigator both selects and observes the teachers. Thus, he knows which teachers have small children, and this knowledge could influence his rating of the teacher.

3. a. Since orange juice is given daily as part of the normal school routine, no Hawthorne Effect is likely to take place.
   b. If children are unaware that a supplement is being added to their orange juice, no placebo is necessary. If children in the treatment group are aware that a supplement is added, then a placebo (perceived by the children as the same supple-

ment) should be added for the control group. Nevertheless, in a study of this nature it is usually not necessary for children to know that they are receiving a supplement, although parental approval is required.

4. The correlation of .17 is not of practical significance for prediction. A correlation of .17 indicates that the two variables only have 2.89 percent ($.17^2$) common variance. This amount of common variance is too low to have any practical significance in prediction.

5. a. Both groups are volunteers. However, the most serious problem is sampling bias that occurs because of the loss of teachers from group A. These teachers probably differ in motivation (and perhaps other characteristics) from the 14 who completed the training. For example, the dropouts could be more effective teachers who decided they don't need the training or weaker teachers who are afraid of the achievement comparisons. Thus, group A is likely to differ from group B in ways that could bias the results.
   b. Yes, it is a new and nonconventional program. The Hawthorne Effect is likely to occur. There is no control-group program.
   c. Yes. The control teachers are likely to feel threatened because they will be compared with the experimental group on pupil achievement.
   d. (1) Set up reward and motivational systems to reduce dropouts. Also try to get a firm commitment at outset from all participating teachers.
      (2) Introduce a control treatment that deals with some other aspect of teaching that would not affect achievement.
      (3) Set up procedures that would reduce the anxieties of the control teachers such as assuring complete confidentiality of the results obtained by individual teachers.

Chapter 7

1. a. Obtain the names of all elementary school principals and the addresses of their schools from the state education directory.
   b. Contact each principal by mail and request a roster of fifth-grade pupils enrolled in his schools.
   c. Order the rosters randomly, and assign a number to each name.
   d. Using a table of random numbers, select 100 subjects.

2. a. Obtain the names, sex, and years of experience of all primary-grade teachers in the district.
   b. Divide the population into male and female.
   c. Set up several experience classifications. This could be done by making a frequency distribution of years of experience and then selecting cutoff points so as to provide three categories of about equal numbers of teachers. Or a division

could be made on some logical basis without regard to numbers of teachers. An example of a logical division could be:
   First-year teachers
   Teachers who have 1 to 5 years of experience
   Teachers who have 6 or more years of experience
   d. Divide each sex into subgroups based upon whatever experience categories you have established.
   e. Check number of teachers in each subcategory to be sure each contains more than 20. (If not, categories should be changed.)
   f. Randomly select 20 teachers from each subcategory (male first-year teachers, female first-year teachers, male teachers with 1–5 years of experience, and so on), using a table of random numbers or by drawing names from a container of name slips.

3. a. Identify the 104 second-grade classrooms and assign each a number.
   b. Randomly select 10 classrooms using a table of random numbers or by drawing numbers from a container.
   c. Obtain the names of all students in the selected classrooms. Randomly select 10 subjects from each classroom to give a total of 100 subjects.

4. a. *Small differences anticipated.* Since the treatment lasts only one hour and is concerned only with word problems, the investigator might well expect the treatment to bring about only a small difference in mathematics achievement.
   b. *Groups must be broken into subgroups.* The investigator has broken his sample into subgroups based on IQ. This requires an increase in sample size. Since only about 2–3 percent of his subjects are likely to have IQ scores above 130, he must further increase sample size to get enough subjects in this category.

5. a. Investigator used volunteers for treatment group.
   b. Treatment group suffered large loss of subjects. Subjects who finished the program were probably highly motivated. No control-group subjects were lost since they were not called on to do anything.
   c. Subjects were used because they were available, i.e., not drawn randomly from any defined population.
   d. Subjects not drawn from same subject pool. That is, the experimental group was drawn from the remedial course, whereas the control group was drawn from the regular course. Since subjects were drawn from different populations, they probably differed in ways relevant to the study, such as overall mastery of English.

Chapter 8

1. a. Concurrent validity since test scores and grades were obtained at same time.
   b. Content validity since the training was concerned with a limited content area.

Most regular achievement tests would be inappropriate because they deal mainly with content not covered in the new instructional technique. What is needed is a measure that deals only with positive and negative numbers. This can be determined only by comparing the test content with the training content.

2. a. Predictive validity was studied.
    b. Predictive validity is most relevant because the aptitude test will be used to predict students' future performance in algebra.

3. Coefficient of equivalence; this is also known as alternate-form reliability.

4. a. Group measure. It is easier, cheaper, and adequate for investigating these variables with college freshmen.
    b. Individual measure. These children will be too limited in writing skill to express their responses in writing. Thus, each child must be shown the pictures individually and his responses recorded by the examiner.

5. a. Make the testing appear important. Tell the students you will tell them the purpose of the research after the testing is completed.
    b. Before administering the measure, tell students that the individuals' responses will not be revealed to anyone and that results will be reported in group form only. It is also recommended that subjects not be obliged to write their names on the measure; if later identification is needed, code numbers can be used.

Chapter 9

1. a. Comprehensive Tests of Basic Skills: Study Skills (Test 778). This is the only one of the tests that covers the whole range of grades to be investigated.
    b. You should compare the readability level of the test (each level of the Comprehensive Tests has a different readability level) with the reading level of the students.
    c. The Bristol Achievement Tests were developed and standardized in England and Wales. Therefore, the test content might not be appropriate for American students. Also, this test covers ages 8–14 only; thus it is not appropriate for high school students.
    d. The only measure in the *8th MMYB* that could be used is the Test of Library/Study Skills (Test 821); none of the others cover the necessary grade range. There is, however, very little information given on the test in the *8th MMYB*, so it would be necessary to check it very carefully in other sources before deciding to use in a research project. It would also be desirable to obtain the ETS Test Collection Bibliography on Study Skills since there are so few appropriate measures in the *Mental Measurements Yearbooks*.

2. a. Low cost and ease of administration.

b. Susceptibility for faking and response sets such as social desirability and acquiescence.

3. a. Adjective Check List.
   b. Stanford Diagnostic Mathematics Test.
   c. Culture-Fair Intelligence Test; Goodenough-Harris Drawing Test; Safran Culture Reduced Intelligence Test.
   d. Strong/Campbell Interest Inventory.

4. a. The degree of similarity between the content of the achievement test and the content of the district's third-grade reading curriculum.
   b. The extent to which the content of the achievement test is up to date and reflects the students' culture.
   c. Is the test appropriate for testing fourth-, fifth-, and sixth-grade pupils? Is the test ceiling high enough?

5. The *Fairview Development Scale* and the *Fairview Self-Help Scale* provide self-help scores, fit the appropriate age range, and have satisfactory reliability. The *Self-Help Skill Assessment Checklist* could be used if reliability data could be obtained. The author of this measure might have obtained reliability data since *Tests and Measurements in Child Development Handbook II* was published. The researcher would probably contact the author and perhaps even conduct his own reliability study if the measure appeared to meet his needs.

Chapter 10

1. The median would be more accurate than the mean, because it would not be affected as much by the 40 extreme scores.

2. a. Correlational study. No cause-and-effect relationship can be established.
   b. Experimental study. Results will indicate whether cause-and-effect relationship is present.
   c. Causal-comparative study. No cause-and-effect relationship can be established.

3. a. True dichotomy.
   b. Continuous variable.
   c. Category score.
   d. Artificial dichotomy.

4. No. Although statistically significant, a mean difference of only 2.5 items on a 200-item test is of virtually no practical significance. In deciding which program to use in a school system, factors other than the small achievement difference would probably be more important.

5. The researcher should use each pair of students in the experimental group as the unit of analysis, because the learning of each student probably was affected by his or her partner. The scores of each pair would be averaged to yield a mean score. Since there are 60 experimental group students, there will be 30 mean scores in the statistical analysis. The unit of analysis for the control group should be the individual, because each student engaged in the learning activity independently of the other students. Thus, there will be 60 control group scores in the statistical analysis.

Chapter 11

1. a. What are your current plans for the year following your graduation in June? Check appropriate answers and indicate period of time during which you anticipate doing the activity.

   _____ 1. Obtain paid employment.
   _____ 2. Attend graduate school.
   _____ 3. Travel.
   _____ 4. Join the Peace Corps or other volunteer service.
   _____ 5. Join the armed forces.
   _____ 6. Other (specify). _____

   b. What are your current plans for the year following graduation in June? Please state all significant activities that you expect to undertake.

   _____
   _____
   _____
   _____

2. Some teachers might express an attitude toward open education on the basis of inadequate information. The short test enables the researcher to determine whether this possibility exists in actuality. If so, the test also provides a method of eliminating these teachers from the sample.

3. a. Describe the purpose of the study.
   b. Describe the importance of the study.
   c. Request that the questionnaire be returned by a specified date.
   d. Appeal to the respondent's pofessional authority in his field or sense of professionalism.
   e. Offer to provide a summary of the study's findings.

4. a. Send a follow-up letter with another copy of the questionnaire and a self-addressed envelope. The letter could be sent by certified mail.
   b. Telephone the nonrespondents, requesting them to return the questionnaire.
   c. Send a telegram to the nonrespondents, requesting them to return the questionnaire.

5. a. Semistructured interview.
   b. In a semistructured interview, it is advisable to begin with structured questions requiring factual answers.
   c. These are followed by questions that will probably require further probing. 5, 6, 7.

Chapter 12

1. a (1) Animated vs. unchanging facial expression (e.g., presence of smiles, raised eyebrows).
   (2) Inflected vs. monotone speech.
   (3) Movement about the classroom vs. stationary position.
   (4) Verbal statement reflecting personal interest in and appreciation of the subject being taught (e.g., "This was one of the most exciting discoveries of late nineteenth-century physics").
   (5) Presence of arm gestures.

   b. Observe the teacher's face during a 20-minute class discussion. Count the frequency of occurrence of these facial expressions:

   Frequency

   Smiling ————————————————————————————
   Laughter ———————————————————————————
   Raised eyebrow ——————————————————————
   Other animated expression ————————————————

2. The research did not include plans to calculate interrater reliability coefficients to determine the degree to which observers are developing a common frame of reference.

3. a. The neatness with which objects are organized in the children's desks.
   b. The amount of litter on the floor at the end of the school day.
   c. The neatness of the children's paperwork.
   d. If there is a cloak room, the neatness with which the children's clothes are arranged in it.
   e. The alignment of desks in an orderly pattern at the end of the school day.

4. a. Sociometry.
   b. Ratings made by the students' teachers.

5. a. Frequency of use of low-frequency words.
   b. Frequency of words denoting abstract concepts, e.g., "nationalism," "logic," "symbolism."
   c. Frequency of connectives such as "if," "but," "therefore," "whereas."
   d. Average length of sentences.
   e. Frequency of cited evidence in support of a position.

Chapter 13

1. a. High school teachers of comparable age, sex, and experience who have average or low scores in authoritarianism.
   b. Monolingual first-grade children of Mexican ancestry (i) who speak English only and (ii) who speak Spanish only.
   c. Fourth-grade Pueblo Indian boys who have attended school off the reservation.

2. The *t* test for correlated means would be most appropriate since children were matched for scholastic aptitude, which in turn is probably correlated with the dependent variable, achievement.

3. A one-tailed test would be appropriate, since there is already some evidence that special tutoring increases achievement. Thus, if a difference is found, it will probably favor the group that received the special tutoring.

4. a. A *t* test for uncorrelated means would be used to compare the authoritarianism scores of the two samples.
   b. A chi-square contingency table would be used. The table would be set up as follows:

Number of Students Belonging to Clubs Rated:

	High	Average	Low
School A			
School B			

   c. Analysis of covariance should be used, since it permits adjusting the senior level scores for differences found in the junior high school scores.

Chapter 14

1. a. No. This conclusion assumes that there is a causal connection between working while in college and degree of personal maturity. Causal inferences cannot be made with a high degree of assurance from correlational data.
   b. Yes. The correlation of +.65 means that the two variables are positively related,

that is, an increment in amount of employment is likely to be associated with an increment in personal maturity score.

  c. No. As in (a) above, this conclusion makes a causal assumption that is not warranted on the basis of the correlational data obtained in this study.

2. Increasing the number of variables will not necessarily increase the likelihood of finding significant relationships. Also, some of the variables may correlate significantly with the criterion variable for irrelevant reasons; these relationships will probably disappear when the study is repeated. A better strategy is to include measures which theory and previous research suggest are related to the criterion variable, that is, interest in science.

3. a. Product-moment correlation coefficient, because both scales yield continuous scores.
  b. Partial correlation. This is a statistical technique that is used to determine the degree of relationship between two variables after the effect of a third variable on both has been removed.
  c. Biserial correlation, because the Scholastic Aptitude Test yields continuous scores and the pass-fail criterion is an artificial dichotomy.
  d. Factor analysis, because this technique determines the extent to which all the measures entered into a correlation matrix represent the same basic behavior pattern or characteristic.
  e. Plot a scattergram to represent graphically the relationship between the two variables. If the relationship appears to be nonlinear, compute the correlation ratio *eta*. There are statistical tests that can be used to determine if the regression lines depart significantly from linearity.

4. Multiple regression, because this statistical technique yields a prediction that is more accurate than could be obtained by correlating any single test with the criterion variable, that is, gradepoint average.

5. a. High self-esteem, middle self-esteem, low self-esteem.
  b. Verbal aptitude, quantitative aptitude, creative aptitude.

Chapter 15

1. a. Recruit a sample of teachers to be in each experimental treatment. The courses represented in each treatment (e.g., English, history) also might be varied.
  b. Plan for observation of in-class activities during the experimental period.
  c. Incorporate an experimental treatment that allows teachers to us their regular instructional methods. These methods may or may not include discussion.

2. a. Since the researcher developed the training program, he probably has a bias that it is effective. This bias can influence his observations of teacher behavior. Even if teachers have not improved after training, the bias may lead him to record observations that show favorable changes.

b. The researcher could train persons other than himself to make the observations. Preferably these persons would not know the purpose of the experiment in order to eliminate the influence of their own biases on the observations. Another method of reducing the possibility of experimenter bias is to make videotapes of teacher behavior before and after training. The videotapes could be scored later by observers in random order so that they do not know which are pretapes and which are posttapes.

3. It will be very difficult to ensure that none of the students in the control group will try to obtain the note-taking outline (which is the experimental treatment) from a classmate who is in the experimental group. If some of the control-group students obtain the outline, the experiment is no longer a pure comparison between two types of experimental treatment.

4. One method is to assign teachers randomly to an experimental and control treatment. Another method is to assign students randomly in each classroom to the experimental and control treatments.

5. Analysis of covariance. The posttest scores of the two groups cannot be compared directly because the groups did not start at the same pretest level (35 vs. 45). The analysis of covariance technique is used to equate their pretest scores statistically.

Chapter 16

1. One procedure is to assign classes randomly to treatments. Preliminary matching by grade level can be done to ensure equivalence of treatment groups. For example, two first-grade classes can be randomly assigned to one treatment, and the other two classes can be assigned to a second treatment. Thus, each treatment will have the same number of classes at each grade level. Analysis of covariance can be used to control for initial differences between groups.

2.

Ability	Conventional Instruction		Traditional Instruction	
	Boys	Girls	Boys	Girls
High	10	15	10	15
Middle	10	15	10	15
Low	10	15	10	15

Interaction effects: A × B
                A × C
                B × C
                A × B × C
Where A = treatment
      B = sex of student
      C = ability level of student

3. A multiple-baseline design can be used. The researcher might elect several target behaviors for experimental manipulation. These would include the verbal mannerisms (i.e., "uh" and "you know") and several other behaviors such as frequency of eye contact with the audience, movement away from the podium, and eliciting student questions. One behavior at a time would be targeted for experimental manipulation. If each behavior changed as expected, the researcher can conclude that the treatment was responsible for the decrease in frequency of the verbal mannerisms.

4. a. Is the curriculum specialist more interested in the learning of individual students or in the learning of students as a group? (Single-subject designs focus on the individual learner; multisubject designs focus on group trends.)
   b. Is it possible to give students many tests of the computational skills? (Single-subject designs require frequent measurement of the same variable.)
   c. Is it possible to meet the requirements of an A-B-A design (e.g., reinstating baseline conditions after withdrawal of the treatment) or of a multiple-baseline design (e.g., changing one computational skill at a time) in the classes that will participate in the experiment?

5. a. Regression toward the mean could have occurred.
   b. Students in the highest quartile may have made a substantial gain but it was not reflected in the posttest due to a ceiling effect; that is, the posttest may not have measured the entire range of possible achievement for the particular variables of concern.

Chapter 17

1. You can point out that the manager will need to make decisions continuously about the program (e.g., whether to reallocate resources, change timelines, redesign operating procedures). Evaluation can provide data that will improve these decisions. Also, the manager is probably accountable to others (e.g., a funding agency, clients) for program results. Evaluation can provide quantitative data about program results so that the manager does not need to rely exclusively on his or others' subjective impressions.

2. a. To what extent do the materials achieve the objective of improving writing skills?
   b. In what ways are the materials easy or difficult to understand?

c. Do the materials require more time than is available?

d. What are college instructors' judgments about the worth of the materials, and what are their recommendations for improving them?

e. What are college students' judgments about the worth of the materials, and what are their recommendations for improving them?

3. You might point out that the school is composed of several programs (e.g., a college preparation program, a school lunch program, an athletic program). Each program can be evaluated with respect to one or more aspects—goals, resources, procedures, and management. The principal needs to decide which program(s) and which aspect(s) of the program should be evaluated.

4. Either you would not ask what the program's goal is, or you would disregard it in designing the evaluation. Instead, you will look for the program's actual effects. These effects might include the extent to which the students swim after the program is completed; fear of swimming, even though the students achieve proficiency; other students' expressions of acceptance, avoidance, or ridicule of nonswimmers entered into the program; changes in the pool's regular schedule as a result of the new program.

5. Students. They might have these concerns:

a. They aren't learning anything.

b. They are made to feel like they are "dummies."

Parents. Their concerns might be:

a. Remediation should take place during the regular school year.

b. The summer program is keeping their children from getting summer jobs.

c. Educators are using the program as a means of earning extra pay.

Legislators. They might be concerned that:

a. The public will view the summer program as an indictment of the regular school year program.

b. The appropriated funds might be insufficient to really get the job done.

c. Parents of gifted students will want a special summer program to provide enrichment courses, at great expense to the public.

Chapter 18

1. Compare your steps with those described on pages 775–776.

2. Product D. A product may be popular (product A), well-funded (product B), with well-defined objectives (product C), but these qualifications do not necessarily mean it will work. However, pertinent research knowledge can guide the developer in designing and evaluating the product so that it will yield significant results.

3. The R & D specialist may overlook problems that would be exposed if she tested the materials in a regular classroom.

4. The developers could revise the materials on the basis of their insights and then submit them to another main field test. An alternative would be to revise the materials, but first conduct a preliminary field test before another main field test.

5. By not using expensive media, he will have more development money to use in revising the materials. If quality of media is a matter of concern, he can produce a small part of the materials in high-quality format to test its effect.

Chapter 19

1. Possible preliminary sources are:

   a. Eugene P. Sheehy, *Guide to Reference Books* 9th ed.
   b. *Bibliographic Index.*
   c. *Education Index.*
   d. *A Bibliography of American Educational History.*

   Possible repositories are:

   a. Publishers of tests, especially the publisher of the Stanford-Binet Intelligence Scale.
   b. Libraries that have collections of papers of prominent psychologists and educators involved in the intelligence testing movement.
   c. Professional organizations in education and psychology that were in existence at the time that the intelligence-testing movement began.

2. A separate note card would be made for each entry relevant to the study. The note card would identify the source and give the date, amount, and classification of the entry (teacher salary, books, etc.), plus anything about the entry that was worthy of special note (such as payment of a teacher in goods rather than money). Once all note cards were completed, they could be sorted in different ways to answer specific questions such as: How similar were the spending patterns of the different principals? What trends occurred in expenditures for educational materials from 1900 to 1930?

   If you used the note-card procedure usually employed for abstracting research articles, you would have only one card for each account book, and these cards would each contain such a large amount of material as to be of little use.

3. a. The reporter had not himself witnessed the teaching of phrenology referred to by the professor.
   b. The professor had an interest in making phrenology appear important.
   c. The professor may be distorting his role in the account.
   d. The professor's entire story could be a fabrication designed to get publicity for his act.

4. a. "School official," "psychologist," "intelligence test," and "early nineteenth century" need to be defined, since these concepts identify the range of phenomena to be included in the historical search.

   b. The number of years in the early nineteenth century for which historical sources are sought; the range of psychologists and school officials whose views are studied; the geographical locales (e.g., entire United States, individual states, European countries) for which historical sources are sought.

Chapter 20

1. Obtain a copy of the test manual in order to familiarize yourself with the test content and scoring procedure.

2. Since the test variable cannot be scored with high reliability, she should train at least two independent individuals to score it. These scorers should be trained using the detailed set of instructions until they reach an acceptable level of interrater reliability. Then they should score each test independently.

3. Use code numbers instead of writing a description. For example, 1 = male, 2 = female. Similarly, the subject's school and social class can be identified by a code number.

4. The researcher should select the computer program *first*, then punch the data. Otherwise he may find that the program requires the data to be entered on IBM cards in a format different than the one he has chosen.

5. a. Twenty correlation coefficients.
   c. One-factor analysis.
   d. An item analysis of a 50-item test.

Chapter 21

1. Compare your outline with the one presented on page 861.

2. a. "The Relationship Between Personality and Attitudes Toward School in Primary-Grade Children."
   b. "Effect of a High School Counseling Program on Student Perceptions of College."

Appendix A.

ERIC NETWORK COMPONENTS

There are currently 16 ERIC Clearinghouses, each responsible for a major area of the field of education. Clearinghouses acquire, select, catalog, abstract, and index the documents announced in *Resources in Education (RIE)*. They also prepare interpretive summaries and annotated bibliographies dealing with high-interest topics and based on the documents analyzed for *RIE*; these information analysis products are also announced in *Resources in Education*.

ERIC Clearinghouses:

ADULT, CAREER, AND VOCATIONAL EDUCATION (CE)

Ohio State University
1960 Kenny Rd.
Columbus, Ohio 43210
Telephone: (614) 486-3655

COUNSELING AND PERSONNEL SERVICES (CG)

University of Michigan
School of Education Building,
Room 2108
East University & South University Sts.
Ann Arbor, Michigan 48109
Telephone: (313) 764-9492

EDUCATIONAL MANAGEMENT (EA)

University of Oregon
Eugene, Oregon 97403
Telephone: (503) 686-5043

ELEMENTARY AND EARLY CHILDHOOD EDUCATION (PS)

805 West Pennsylvania Avenue
Urbana, Illinois 61801
Telephone: (217) 333-1386

HANDICAPPED AND GIFTED CHILDREN (EC)

Council for Exceptional Children
1920 Association Drive
Reston, Virginia 22091
Telephone: (703) 620-3660

HIGHER EDUCATION (HE)

George Washington University
One Dupont Circle, N.W., Suite 630
Washington, D. C. 20036
Telephone: (202) 296-2597

INFORMATION RESOURCES (IR)

Syracuse University
School of Education
Syracuse, New York 13210
Telephone: (315) 423-3640

JUNIOR COLLEGES (JC)

University of California at Los Angeles
Powell Library, Room 96
405 Hilgard Ave.
Los Angeles, California 90024
Telephone: (213) 825-3931

EDUCATIONAL RESOURCES INFORMATION CENTER

(Central ERIC)
National Institute of Education
Washington, D.C. 20208
Telephone: (202) 254-7934

ERIC PROCESSING & REFERENCE FACILITY

4833 Rugby Avenue, Suite 301
Bethesda, Maryland 20814
Telephone: (301) 656-9723

LANGUAGES AND LINGUISTICS (FL)

Center for Applied Linguistics
3520 Prospect Street, N.W.
Washington, D.C. 20007
Telephone: (202) 298-9292

READING AND COMMUNICATION SKILLS (CS)

National Council of Teachers of English
1111 Kenyon Road
Urbana, Illinois 61801
Telephone: (217) 328-3870

RURAL EDUCATION AND SMALL SCHOOLS (RC)

New Mexico State University
Box 3 AP
Las Cruces, New Mexico 88003
Telephone (505) 646-2623

SCIENCE, MATHEMATICS, AND ENVIRONMENTAL EDUCATION (SE)

Ohio State University
1200 Chambers Road, Third Floor
Columbus, Ohio 43212
Telephone: (614) 422-6717

SOCIAL STUDIES/SOCIAL SCIENCE EDUCATION (SO)

Social Science Education Consortium, Inc.
855 Broadway
Boulder, Colorado 80302
Telephone: (303) 492-8434

TEACHER EDUCATION (SP)

American Association of Colleges for Teacher Education
One Dupont Circle, N.W., Suite 610
Washington, D.C. 20036
Telephone: (202) 293-2450

TESTS, MEASUREMENT, AND EVALUATION (TM)

Educational Testing Service
Princeton, New Jersey 08541
Telephone: (609) 921-9000

URBAN EDUCATION (UD)

Teachers College
Columbia University
Box 40
New York, New York 10027
Telephone: (212) 687-3437

ERIC DOCUMENT REPRODUCTION SERVICE

P.O. Box 190
Arlington, Virginia 22210
Telephone: (703) 841-1212

The ORYX PRESS

2214 North Central Avenue at Encanto
Phoenix, Arizona 85004
Telephone: (602) 254-6156

Appendix B.

RESEARCH ARTICLE EVALUATION

A. Introduction

1. Does investigator report on relevant literature?
   a. Review covers three or more sources published within 5 years that appear to be important and relevant.
   b. Review covers only one or two recent and important sources.
   c. No important sources are cited.
2. Is a statement of the problem given? Is it clear?
3. Is a justification given, i.e., why is this research important or worth doing?
4. Is the problem related to theory? Discuss.
5. Is there evidence of bias in the investigator's language? If yes, give examples:

B. Objectives or Hypotheses

1. What form is used to state hypotheses?
2. Evaluate the hypotheses using the criteria given in chapter 3 of Borg and Gall. If objectives are stated, are they clear and specific? Do they describe outcomes rather than procedures?

C. Sample

1. Is the sample appropriate for the study? Discuss.
2. Is the sample large enough?
3. Do the sampling procedures result in possible biases in the sample? If so, describe possible sources of bias.

D. Measures

1. Is evidence of validity and reliability given? If so, describe the data reported, and evaluate.
2. Are there any specific weaknesses in the measures or the measurement procedures?

E. Treatments

1. What type of research design is used?
2. Are the treatments described in sufficient detail? If not, what specific information is omitted?

3. Are there weaknesses in the treatments that could affect the results? If so, describe weaknesses and discuss how results could have been affected.

F. Results and Conclusions

1. Are appropriate statistical tools used? Comment.
2. Are results reported in clear, understandable terms? If not, give example.
3. Does investigator relate his results to his hypotheses or objectives?
4. Does investigator overconclude, i.e., are her conclusions supported by her results? If not, comment.

G. Overview

1. What are the main strengths of this research?
2. What are the most serious deficiencies of this research?
3. In what way and to what extent are these deficiencies likely to have affected the research findings?

Appendix C.

TABLE OF RANDOM NUMBERS

23795	97005	43923	81292	39907	67758	10202	24311	92262	94571
57096	70158	36006	25106	92601	54650	27591	66340	81852	85246
52750	69765	42110	38252	80201	21099	70577	98650	32570	70616
90591	58216	04931	78274	10943	27273	28333	26528	05363	70678
20809	23068	84638	99566	41598	25664	02400	86856	15690	21895
57292	76721	75277	37751	79009	75957	22333	80932	63678	98611
02266	97120	05055	34236	42475	80604	02227	74799	01606	84330
61795	15534	45465	68798	02943	90934	63729	64185	67378	68604
18021	45643	82756	50833	16365	87969	78079	76533	91675	22641
52404	24573	72667	17693	04332	43579	24459	88992	88875	22902
53104	80180	30612	24735	63414	67892	37053	68277	82713	08798
78245	43321	64458	95647	57757	82849	15238	80647	00195	91936
96198	06398	76790	63703	85749	07026	46901	62065	04240	55270
64823	65665	43284	84972	92214	97669	62556	62765	96414	61991
65083	67708	58513	18046	88476	13211	11675	03250	03976	61793
30047	05312	47866	90067	41508	44709	70493	08790	93571	01781
27052	80915	10914	62544	01245	59280	95348	12568	98058	34935
84438	29174	15154	97010	53558	58741	53713	05690	67826	68041
09083	21005	15203	76311	39195	62019	29929	58151	94437	43455
96548	06390	56577	99863	58951	08673	26284	11180	96169	71823
68927	37828	17069	73928	26582	08496	19678	85603	80533	29303
07519	29067	53047	49285	05174	86393	19820	73942	18184	76756
15246	16092	88491	46453	01504	61322	55766	05181	89467	54054
97306	47296	94565	29597	34592	67680	33930	77474	13161	68380
72590	71948	34123	04318	55899	96852	90471	84147	73053	73654
89228	75728	32272	24197	71581	14731	42090	12581	27281	29504
35188	64410	86923	25630	91336	05930	16148	69690	64229	50576
79344	21677	43388	36013	37128	48252	36783	30953	41674	30600
92450	37916	46903	53061	38117	65493	06579	21503	56726	81829
42567	05694	82727	39689	77779	53564	49126	32864	93794	46365

Table of Random Numbers—Continued

88541	53575	41679	00275	42844	21185	56205	22097	15512	93679
48490	44531	58369	05146	29999	49853	70192	45752	01891	89879
48498	60958	77913	74738	27821	56080	46295	83244	07909	79598
66570	93573	73521	99191	90791	94440	83853	07269	45272	64172
14134	59770	58818	47782	14536	08728	26317	70618	62286	86600
02628	51111	71749	88386	80882	64862	44220	26333	71612	17538
34303	51306	14555	54950	32979	94909	73544	25237	68846	36997
36555	60193	58493	94436	17809	10573	44606	08827	86732	03596
96123	33332	79671	39903	58640	31862	34378	61853	85252	57568
74657	55345	98139	21947	12934	43220	79446	50791	82101	39841
16357	98838	04651	13592	79790	11164	06929	96812	48725	26200
39257	41070	52928	62728	18733	89729	45718	71281	20705	79362
85385	09094	57205	36910	49021	67081	46062	60302	75730	87285
42990	06851	87583	09817	30589	15822	16152	29534	83027	09408
20095	74511	13101	99675	64987	90859	09421	28141	00471	81498
85634	29225	61789	50214	40938	89135	92887	96677	21520	17625
86485	43039	06163	11600	12947	98321	65895	16677	14185	33029
17387	35584	21532	93242	02735	40710	67210	80906	34297	72084
47896	15137	02461	91770	15902	18042	06513	70892	68573	87932
84184	56437	29770	82718	34059	51473	18661	86916	96651	94597
30544	26847	34801	92192	62034	80502	81955	90455	48695	50967
57943	23208	97061	85407	36072	86131	34986	75316	32620	18339
24378	18075	30285	68126	28612	04809	90668	31212	53287	75156
07562	26987	33492	95717	52625	71019	73339	25848	17942	60477
04290	81873	16024	63178	67665	48912	07004	40560	93696	68208
35047	90224	94622	97187	21471	14521	62568	49439	30594	58235
14302	22399	46015	60528	04465	61708	19844	84106	86489	43088
35326	67950	86153	24999	04348	48990	16602	88466	55509	62742
55637	84138	05740	13206	76209	01011	98869	48213	19290	06185
88114	37944	74658	30615	86141	81485	39630	42042	56132	09058
08393	03099	20248	55960	55318	10078	67927	08282	64522	95902
05617	10105	74931	09584	51870	27165	05194	03762	97149	32865
46085	21887	66245	69041	09346	27206	92883	86026	51453	06910
09019	34355	98391	66641	34424	13823	33256	53010	90047	34647
22398	54887	29195	60132	97777	87900	34890	30510	33341	10944
58588	63524	01478	08462	25803	38837	21958	47809	86052	50529
70258	37280	02450	04668	44812	17163	29204	97396	53437	63681
81321	82945	18083	23736	10014	80676	60415	77122	09602	25499
04686	92158	47128	86932	06775	50713	74466	18569	71250	19115
04391	01898	45790	82710	56848	66167	41540	93622	59639	49386

12894	53767	68758	64614	22875	18221	07808	00270	08686	07785
63217	63546	32102	13928	62441	21844	97625	14146	55840	58707
97703	41682	69641	87876	48778	19165	47177	11837	64577	23292
98539	19670	23783	44554	84825	42986	78079	94383	22338	78442
63597	40735	54417	90536	73859	72462	53993	79332	75583	52779
38517	84270	50087	72740	50600	47352	72497	06823	32505	26791
48604	54578	50541	85598	64948	74747	56505	28597	21571	31350
57455	76026	58884	24939	52421	92135	10189	26563	35104	83107
59673	16955	05138	90140	12025	09015	27187	80682	34332	47894
76965	33580	63541	89825	66164	72315	33482	08281	94365	74500
14360	14144	85161	25472	24570	55298	76043	39105	19844	30345
97013	89823	37948	61157	41459	36370	28550	69530	54504	19993
77340	44427	88820	37504	91115	18138	55880	73067	96291	42137
81614	71577	67147	16496	09674	01166	92134	30464	32758	32617
56664	66094	22935	09396	19055	51817	25412	43499	32673	78425
26898	99502	71809	56125	59522	71932	01420	48187	04168	69516
41654	14153	63170	43854	66892	83658	31487	89733	96068	10647
57764	49562	26137	77068	02133	25312	83798	75131	16163	87866
71945	47769	42025	25824	16825	58159	02778	43604	29476	41023
83584	52050	30789	10836	34717	43809	03376	15216	11433	60356
75441	75429	53040	87861	61959	00313	43971	14943	36697	44871
43182	96919	35016	60367	64910	48288	41834	98977	93610	77952
51798	42888	68819	40101	49411	75175	31774	47688	95759	47900
34747	35088	75466	81577	26417	11784	02602	99474	91981	69855
57556	10196	95300	44530	78200	51578	92014	29247	08203	58119
07418	64410	62954	18034	50763	02451	59299	14454	18751	50819
19150	38401	75128	59161	49054	20858	30631	97256	67871	97608
37927	16126	53019	63467	09774	46307	52037	97127	15291	14392
10780	04029	59044	01725	52129	81525	50568	77550	49856	08063
78016	62918	31163	46180	58803	71302	58383	77846	02395	77173

Appendix D.

NORMALIZED BISERIAL CORRELATION TABLE

Normalized biserial coefficients* of correlation as determined from proportions of correct responses in upper and lower 27 percent of the group

(Lower)	|	02	06	10	14	18	22	26	30	34	38	42	46	50	54	58	62	66	70	74	78	82	86	90	94	98	|	(Lower)
Proportion of Correct Responses in the Upper 27 Percent**																												
02		00	19	30	37	43	48	51	55	58	61	63	66	68	70	72	73	75	77	79	80	82	84	86	88	91		02
06			00	11	19	26	31	36	40	44	47	50	53	56	59	61	64	66	68	71	73	76	78	81	84	88		06
10				00	08	15	21	26	30	34	38	41	45	48	51	54	57	60	63	65	68	71	74	77	81	86		10
14					00	07	12	18	22	27	31	34	38	42	45	48	51	54	57	60	63	67	70	74	78	84		14
18						00	06	11	16	20	25	28	32	36	39	43	47	49	53	56	60	63	67	71	76	82		18
22							00	06	10	15	19	23	27	31	34	38	42	45	49	52	56	60	63	68	73	80		22
26								00	05	09	14	18	22	26	30	33	37	41	44	48	52	56	60	65	71	79		26
30									00	04	09	13	17	21	25	29	33	37	40	44	49	53	57	63	68	77		30
34										00	04	09	13	17	21	25	29	33	37	41	45	49	54	60	66	75		34
38											00	04	08	13	16	20	25	29	33	37	42	47	51	57	64	73		38
42												00	04	08	12	16	20	25	29	33	38	43	48	54	61	72		42
46													00	04	08	12	16	21	25	30	34	39	45	51	59	70		46
50														00	04	08	13	17	21	26	31	36	42	48	56	68		50
54															00	04	08	13	17	22	27	32	38	45	53	66		54
58																00	04	09	13	18	23	28	34	41	50	63		58
62																	00	04	09	14	19	25	31	38	47	61		62
66																		00	04	09	15	20	27	34	44	58		66
70																			00	05	10	16	22	30	40	55		70
74																				00	06	11	19	26	36	51		74
78																					00	06	12	21	31	48		78
82																						00	07	15	26	43		82
86																							00	08	19	37		86
90																								00	11	30		90
94																									00	19		94
98																										00		98
		02	06	10	14	18	22	26	30	34	38	42	46	50	54	58	62	66	70	74	78	82	86	90	94	98		

(Row labels at left: Proportion of Correct Responses in the Lower 27 Percent)

Source. This table is abridged from J. C. Flanagan's table of normalized biserial coefficients originally prepared for the Cooperative Test Service. It is included here with the generous permission of Dr. Flanagan.

*Decimal points are omitted.

**If the proportion of correct responses in the lower 27 percent exceeds that in the upper, enter the table with the lower 27 percent proportion at the top and attach a negative sign to the coefficient.

Appendix E.

EXAMPLES OF UNOBTRUSIVE MEASURES

The following behavioral situations were designed as unobtrusive measures of student attitudes toward various aspects of school experience.[1]

Category 1: Student Willingness to Support Nonacademic School Projects
Behavioral Situation 1: Student body activities
Procedure: A record will be kept of the number of students who purchase student body cards. If this situation is used, a similar sales campaign should be followed each year so that results will be reasonably comparable from year to year.
Scoring: The score to be applied to the total behavior attitude measure will be the number of students purchasing student body cards divided by the total number of students enrolled at the school. A high score indicates favorable attitude.

Category 2: Student Perception of the Importance of Education and His Identification with the School's Academic Goals
Behavioral Situation 2: Educational Television
Procedure: If the school is within range of an educational television channel, the principal will obtain program notes for the month of March and will select two programs offered between 5 and 7 P.M. and two programs offered between the hours of 7 and 10 P.M. that appear to be of good quality and of general interest to high school students. An announcement of each program will be made the day before the program is to be shown and also the day of the program. On the first school day following the program, students of all classes will be given a very brief test and asked to indicate whether they saw the program and, if so, to answer five multiple-choice questions concerning the program.
Scoring: The score on this measure will be the number of pupils indicating they watched the program who also answered at least three of the five objective questions correctly divided by the total number of pupils in attendance on the day the program was televised. High score is favorable.

Category 3: Student Respect for School Authority and School Property
Behavioral Situaton 3: Promptness in returning library books

---

1. The situations were taken from Walter R. Borg, *Behavioral Situations to Be Used in Measuring Over-All Student Attitudes* (for the Western States Small Schools Project) (Salt Lake City: Utah State Department of Public Instruction, 1962).

Procedure: During the period of February 1 to February 15 inclusive, a special record will be kept of all books checked out by students. As these books are returned, the librarian will indicate whether books have been returned on time or are late.

Scoring: The score will be the number of books returned on time divided by the total number of books checked out.

Category 4: Overall Attitudes toward Teachers and School

Behavioral Situation 4: Truancy data

Procedure: Truancy will be defined as any absence of a pupil from school, for which no excuse is given or for which an inadequate or unsatisfactory excuse is given. The school will maintain truancy data during all school days in the month of April. Students returning from absences will be questioned concerning their reasons for being absent. Unless the student has a written excuse from his parent which the school considers genuine, his excuse should be checked with the parent by telephone. After necessary information has been obtained, the number of days and fractions of days truant should be recorded in the proper classification on the record sheet.

Scoring: The score on this item to be applied to the total attitude measure will be the number of days truant divided by the number of pupils in the school.

Appendix F.

TEST COLLECTION BIBLIOGRAPHIES[1]

Achievement

Achievement Batteries, Preschool-Gr. 3
Achievement Batteries, Gr. 4–6
Achievement Batteries, Gr. 7 and Above
Achievement Tests, College Level
Algebra Tests
American Government
American History
Art Achievement Tests
Art Education
Basic Skills Competency Tests
Biology Achievement
Chemistry—College Level
Chemistry—Gr. 7–12
Composition and Writing Skills
Consumer Competency
Criterion-Referenced Measures, Preschool-Gr. 3
Criterion-Referenced Measures, Gr. 4–6
Criterion-Referenced Measures, Gr. 7 and Above
Economics, Gr. 9 and Above
Environmental Education
French—Foreign Language
Geography
Geometry
German—Foreign Language
Health and Physical Education
Hebrew—Foreign Language
History
Home Economics
Industrial Arts—Gr. 7–12
Italian—Foreign Language
Language Development

Language Skills—Preschool-Gr. 3
Language Skills—Gr. 4–6
Language Skills—Gr. 7 and Above
Library Skills
Literature
Mathematics—Preschool-Gr. 3
Mathematics—Gr. 4–6
Mathematics—Gr. 7 and Above
Mathematics—College Level
Mathematics—Diagnostic, Preschool-Gr. 3
Mathematics—Diagnostic, Gr. 4–6
Mathematics—Diagnostic, Gr. 7 and Above
Metric System
Music Performance
Music—Theory and Appreciation
Oral Reading and Listening Skills
Physics and Physical Science
Psychology
Reading—Preschool-Gr. 3
Reading—Gr. 4–6
Reading—Gr. 7 and Above
Reading—Diagnostic, Preschool-Gr. 6
Reading—Diagnostic, Gr. 7 and Above
Reading Readiness
Russian—Foreign Language
School Readiness
Science—Kindergarten-Gr. 6
Science—Gr. 7 and Above
Sex Education
Social Studies—Kindergarten-Gr. 6
Social Studies—Gr. 7 and Above

1. These bibliographies may be purchased from *Test Collection*, Educational Testing Service, Princeton NJ 08541. Price in early 1983 is $3 each.

Spanish—Foreign Language
Speech Abilities
Spelling—Kindergarten-Gr. 6
Spelling—Gr. 7 and Above
Study Skills
Vocabulary, Preschool-Gr. 3
Vocabulary, Gr. 4–6
Vocabulary, Gr. 7 and Above

Aptitude

Artistic Aptitude
Cognitive Style and Information
  Processing
Concept Formation and Acquisition
Creativity and Divergent Thinking
Curiosity
General Aptitude, Adults
General Aptitude, Kindergarten-Gr. 6
Intelligence—Group Administered,
  Preschool-Gr. 3
Intelligence—Group Administered, Gr.
  4–6
Intelligence—Group Administered, Gr.
  7 and Above
Intelligence—Individually Administered,
  Preschool-Gr. 3
Intelligence—Individually Administered,
  Gr. 4–6
Intelligence—Individually Administered,
  Gr. 7 and Above
Mathematical Aptitude, Gr. 1–3
Mathematical Aptitude, Gr. 4–12
Mathematical Aptitude, College Level
Memory
Musical Aptitude
Non-Verbal Aptitude
Reasoning, Logical Thinking, Problem
  Solving
Scholastic Aptitude and Mental Ability
Spatial-Perceptual Relations
Verbal Aptitude, Gr. 7–12

Attitudes and Interests

Academic Interest
Children's Attitude Toward Parents
Curriculum, Attitudes Toward
Educational Techniques, Attitudes
  Toward
Occupational Attitudes and Job
  Satisfaction
Racial Attitudes
Religious Attitudes
School and School Adjustment,
  Attitudes Toward, Preschool-Gr. 3
School and School Adjustment,
  Attitudes Toward, Gr. 4–6
School and School Adjustment,
  Attitudes Toward, Gr. 7 and Above
Sex Roles and Attitudes Toward Women
Social Attitudes
Values
Vocational Interests

Personality

Aggression and Hostility
Alienation
Anxiety
Ascendance-Submission
Depression
Independence-Dependence
Introversion/Extroversion
Leadership
Locus of Control
Masculinity-Femininity
Motivation and Need Achievement
Personality—General
Personality Adjustment, Kindergarten–
  Gr. 3
Personality Adjustment, Gr. 4–6
Personality Adjustment, Gr. 7 and
  Above
Projective Measures
Psychosexual Development

Responsibility/Perseverance
Self-Concept, Preschool-Gr. 3
Self-Concept, Gr. 4–6
Self-Concept, Gr. 7 and Above
Stress
Task Orientation

Sensory-Motor

Auditory Skills
Motor Skills
Sensory-Motor Abilities
Vision and Visual Perception, Preschool-Gr. 3

Special Populations

Adult Basic Education
American Indians
Blind and Visually Handicapped
Brain-Damaged
Bright Children and Adults
Deaf and Hearing Impaired
Disadvantaged Preschool Child
Educationally Disadvantaged Adults
Educationally Disadvantaged Children
Emotionally Disturbed, Identification
English as a Second Language
Gifted and Talented Students,
    Identification and Evaluation
Juvenile Delinquents
Learning Disabilities, Identification of,
    Preschool-Gr. 3
Learning Disabilities, Identification of,
    Gr. 4 and Above
Mentally Retarded
Physically Handicapped
Spanish Speakers, Preschool-Gr. 3
Spanish Speakers, Gr. 4–6
Spanish Speakers, Gr. 7 and Above

Vocational Measures for the
    Handicapped

Vocational/Occupational

Business Skills
Clerical Aptitude and Achievement
Data Processing
Employment Interviews
Engineering Aptitude and Achievement
Mechanical Aptitude and Knowledge
Nurses
Occupational Knowledge, Skilled Trades
Professional Occupations
Salespersons—Selection and Evaluation
Supervisory, Management
Teacher Assessment
Trucking Personnel, Drivers, Diesel
    Mechanics
Vocational Aptitude
Vocational Choice—Perception-
    Development
Vocational Rating and Selection Forms

Miscellaneous

Behavior Rating Scales, Preschool-Gr. 3
Behavior Rating Scales, Gr. 4–6
Behavior Rating Scales, Gr. 7 and Above
Biographical Inventories
Child Rearing Practices and Related
    Attitudes
Classroom Interaction
Counseling Aids
Courtship and Marriage
Culture-Fair and Culture-Relevent Tests
Curriculum and Program Evaluation
Decision-Making Process
Developmental Scales for Preschool
    Children
Drugs—Knowledge and Abuse
Educational Record and Report Forms

Environments
Family Interaction and Related Attitudes
Group Behavior and Influence
Human Sexuality
Infant Development
Item Pools
Manual Dexterity

Moral Development
Piagetian Measures
Social Perception and Judgment
Social Skills, Birth-9
Social Skills, Gr. 4 and Above
Systematic Observation Techniques
Teaching Style

NAME INDEX

SUBJECT INDEX

Instructions: The purpose of this suggestion sheet is to get student feedback that can be used to improve the next edition of this book. We have asked for your comments on only one chapter in order to minimize the time needed for you to respond. All comments and suggestions will be greatly appreciated.

Items 1–4: The first four questions are aimed at learning more about the students who use this book. Please circle appropriate alternatives.

Item 5: Be sure to indicate the chapter you are evaluating.

Items 6–9: These are the most important questions. Please be as specific as possible.

When you complete the suggestion sheet, cut along the dashed line, then fold as indicated on the back of this sheet, tape closed, and mail. Thanks very much for your help.

Walter Borg and Meredith Gall

SUGGESTION SHEET

1. Degree you are seeking (circle one): **BA, BS, MA, MS, MEd, EdD, PhD,** **other:** _____.
   (specify)
2. Graduate major (circle one): **elem educ, sec educ, spec educ, bus educ, educ** **psych, psych, soc, other:** _____.
   (specify)
3. Have you taken elementary statistics? (circle): **yes, no;** educational measurement? **yes, no;** computer science? **yes, no;** psychometrics? **yes, no;** second course in statistics? **yes, no.**
4. Does your degree program require a thesis or a dissertation? (circle): **yes, no;** a non-research paper? **yes, no;** no paper? **yes, no.**
5. Chapter commented on _____.
6. What specific ideas, definitions, descriptions, or examples in this chapter are not clear? (Please give page number and brief description.)

   _____

   _____

7. Should the book include more information on any of the sections in this chapter? (Please give page number and subheading.)

   _____

   _____

8. What sections should be shortened or omitted? (Give page number and subheading.)

   _____

   _____

9. Other comments _____

   _____

   _____

   _____

   _____

SEE REVERSE SIDE FOR MAILING INSTRUCTIONS.

9 8 7 6 5

CUT ALONG DASHED LINES, FOLD, TAPE, AND MAIL.

BUSINESS REPLY MAIL
FIRST CLASS   PERMIT NO. 9401   NEW YORK, N.Y.

POSTAGE WILL BE PAID BY ADDRESSEE

LONGMAN INC.
95 Church Street
White Plains, New York 10601
Attn: Education Editor